# STRUCTURED PRODUCTS & HYBRID SECURITIES

# STRUCTURED PRODUCTS & HYBRID SECURITIES
Satyajit Das

John Wiley & Sons (Asia) Pte Ltd
Singapore  New York  Chichester  Brisbane  Toronto  Weinheim

*Other Wiley Editorial Offices*

John Wiley & Sons, Inc., 605 Third Avenue, New York, NY 10158-0012, USA
John Wiley & Sons Ltd, Baffins Lane, Chichester, West Sussex PO19 1UD, England
John Wiley & Sons (Canada) Ltd, 22 Worcester Road, Rexdale, Ontario M9W 1L1, Canada
John Wiley & Sons Australia Ltd, 33 Park Road (PO Box 1226), Milton, Queensland 4064, Australia
Wiley-VCH, Pappelallee 3, 69469 Weinheim, Germany

*Library of Congress Cataloging-in-Publication Data*
Das, Satyajit.
    Structured products and hybrid securities / Satyajit Das.
       p. cm. – (Wiley frontiers in finance)
    Rev. ed. of: Structured notes and derivative embedded securities. 1996.
    Includes bibliographical references and index.
    ISBN 0-471-84775-5 (cased : alk. paper)
      1. Structured notes (Securities) 2. Derivative securities 3. Fixed-income securities.
I. Das, Satyajit. Structured notes and derivative embedded securities. II. Title. III. Series.

HG4651.5 .D37 2000
332.63'2–dc21                                                                                          00-043851

Typeset in 10 points, Times by Linographic Services Pte Ltd
Printed in Singapore by Saik Wah Press Pte Ltd
10   9 8 7 6 5 4 3 2 1

*This book is dedicated to
my partner Jade Novakovic
and my parents Sukumar and Aparna Das*

# Table of Contents

## Chapter 16: Pricing and Valuation of Structured Note Transactions    899

## Chapter 17: Taxation & Accounting for Structured Notes      931

# Chapter 18: The Market for Structured Notes   955

# Index   999

# Preface

## 1. Introduction

The concept of structured notes, the combination of a fixed income security with derivative elements, is perceived as a relatively recent innovation in financial markets. In reality, the format has been in existence for a considerable time. Structures such as callable notes and equity-linked securities, for example convertibles and debt with equity warrants, are the precursors to the structured note products that are commonplace today.

The distinguishing feature of modern structured notes is the different role played by the derivative element. In traditional configurations, such as the callable bond or equity convertible, the call option is utilized to make the security more attractive to investors as part of the overall investment package and the issuer *assumes the derivative risk*. In contrast, in modern structured notes, the derivative element being incorporated is highly engineered and is specifically utilized to allow the creation and transfer of the risk embodied in the derivative component. This may entail, for example, an investor creating the derivative element that is then securitized through the security structure with the issuer transferring the derivative element to a derivative market maker who in turn reallocates the risk element to ultimate users of that particular instrument. In this way, modern structured notes are utilized as a complex basis for transference of risk through an often long chain of transactions.

The modern demand for structured note products is driven primarily by the following factors:

- Regulatory arbitrage.
- Customization.
- Credit enhancement.

The most significant factor is the capacity to use these instruments to engineer highly customized risk-reward profiles for investors seeking exposure to market price movements.

The structured note market enjoyed a period of explosive growth in the early 1990s. The growth was driven by a combination of low absolute interest rates, a steep yield curve (in a number of currencies) and low credit spreads. The growth was accompanied, not unpredictably, by excesses, particularly in the area of excessive leverage (effectively the incorporation of derivatives exceeding the face value of the underlying fixed income transaction) and a lack of understanding of and controls on the risks of such transactions. The well-publicized problems of Orange County and others were a direct result of these factors.

The fall in volumes that followed the emergence of these problems prompted market observers to forecast the demise of the market in structured note products. In reality, this reflects a profound misunderstanding of the role of structured notes in financial markets. In fact, the need for credit risk enhancement for investors, such as mutual funds in entering into derivative transactions for longer terms, alone would ensure the survival of the market. When added to the continued demand for separation of market risk from issuer risk and the requirement to monetize expectations regarding the evolution of market parameters, the existence of structured notes is well vouchsafed. Indeed, the gradual recovery in structured note activity through the late 1990s bears testimony to this thesis.

## 2.  Background and Objectives of Book

*Structured Products & Hybrid Securities — Second Edition* is the successor to *Structured Notes & Derivative Embedded Securities*, which was first published in 1996. The major changes in the market since the publication of the first edition have necessitated this revised edition.

*Structured Products & Hybrid Securities* is designed to bring together all aspects of these instruments within a cohesive and integrated framework. The text covers all aspects of structured notes including:

• The structuring and design of the instruments themselves.
• The pricing, valuation and trading/hedging of these instruments.
• The rationale for individual structures, including the nature of the risks assumed and the applications of the instruments.

The coverage extends to structured notes entailing exposures to all asset classes. Structured notes featuring linkages to debt/interest rates, currencies, commodities and equity are all considered. In addition, the text covers structured notes with embedded exotic options, the important emerging area of credit-linked or credit derivative-linked transaction structures, insurance-(catastrophe)-linked structures and inflation-linked bonds. The focus is completely global with coverage of transactions in both developed and emerging markets.

The approach taken is a practical rather than theoretical one designed to examine structured notes from the different perspectives of the investor, the issuer, and the dealers/traders in these securities. The emphasis is on actual transactions that are stripped down to analyze and illustrate the dynamics of individual structures, and to understand the types of products available.

The book has as its target audience investors, issuers, commercial and investment bankers, and dealers in structured notes seeking either an understanding of the market or a reference work on the market that can serve as a source of information on transaction structures, and so on. The book will also appeal to regulators, analysts, accountants, lawyers and consultants active in advising financial market participants involved in or contemplating involvement in these products as well academics and students interested in this component of capital markets.

The text is structured either to be read through from start to finish or, for the more experienced user of these products, to be used as a reference source where individual sections are read as required.

## 3. Structure of Book

The book is structured as follows:

- Chapter 1 sets out the concept of structured notes with special emphasis on the rationale for such transactions, particularly their use in regulatory arbitrage, credit enhancement, return customization and the creation of liquid tradeable derivative positions. The chapter also covers the use of special purpose repackaging vehicles to create or re-profile structured notes.
- Chapters 2 to 6 (inclusive) focus on interest rate-linked structured note products.
- Chapters 2 and 3 analyze callable notes/bonds. Chapter 2 examines traditional callable structures including the concept, application and valuation issues involved. Chapter 3 extends the coverage to more recent innovations, in particular, the step-up and multi-step callable and puttable structures that have provided an important area of growth in recent times. A major focus is the inter-relationship between the callable bond products and the market for options on swaps/swaptions.
- Chapter 4 examines notes with specifically engineered exposures to interest rates/debt prices including the growing market for bond index-linked products.
- Chapter 5 focuses on the market for Constant Maturity Treasury (CMT) linked structures and its counterpart outside the US market, the Constant Maturity Swap (CMS) products that have emerged.
- Chapter 6 analyzes the index amortization notes entailing linkage of liquidity risk (through prepayment) to defined financial market indexes. Coverage of index amortization structures linked to noninterest variables, particularly currencies, is also examined.

- Chapter 7 covers currency-linked note structures including dual currency and specific currency-linked coupon or redemption value products.
- Chapter 8 focuses on commodity-linked note structures with a particular focus on their use by commodity producers and users as a mechanism for fund-raising as well as risk management.
- Chapters 9 to 11 (inclusive) provide integrated coverage of equity-linked note structure encompassing securities with engineered links to both individual equity stocks as well as equity indexes.
- Chapter 9 analyzes traditional convertible and debt with equity warrant transaction including consideration of the transaction rationale from the viewpoint of both issuer and investor as well as pricing, structuring, and trading considerations.
- Chapter 10 focuses on extensions and innovations in convertible and exchangeable structures including: converting preferred stock; zero-coupon or discount convertibles (including LYONs); step-up or step-down convertible; mandatory convertible structures; structured equity option embedded structures such PERCs, DECs, YES, ACEs, PRIDES, STRYPES, and so on; exchangeable bonds; going public warrants and bonds; synthetic equity conversion structures; puttable convertibles; and, exotic option-embedded convertibles and warrant transactions, such as those completed by Roche and Bennetton.
- Chapter 11 examines modern *equity index*-linked note structures including the large market in capital guaranteed equity-linked structures targeted at retail investors and capital guaranteed funds.
- Chapter 12 covers credit derivatives-embedded notes (including structures linked to loan assets, credit spreads, and pure default risks), repackaged and synthetic credit-linked securities and synthetic CLOs/securitization structures.
- Chapter 13 (in contrast to the previous chapter that has an individual asset class emphasis) focuses on the combination of structured notes and exotic optionality (path-dependent structures (average rate, look-back, ladder etc. options), limit-dependent structures (barrier options), multi-factor structures (basket options, exchange options, quanto options including index differential products), and payoff modified options (digital and power options).
- Chapter 14 examines inflation-linked bonds.
- Chapter 15 covers various types of insurance-linked securities (in particular those linked to catastrophe insurance).
- Chapter 16 examines the dynamics of pricing of structured notes both in the primary and secondary markets using examples to illustrate the trading approaches to these instruments.
- Chapter 17 covers the accounting and tax treatment of structured note transactions in a number of key jurisdictions.

- Chapter 18 focuses on the market for structured notes, including the evolution of the product and the key characteristics of the major participants and the nature and pattern of their activities.
- Chapters 19 and 20 outline the accounting and tax aspects of structured products in a number of key jurisdictions.

Each chapter includes selected references designed to allow readers to expand their knowledge of these instruments as required.

The second edition of *Structured Products & Hybrid Securities* has been completely rewritten. Extensive new material has been added to all sections to both update existing areas of coverage as well as add several new chapters covering areas of current interest.

## 4. Acknowledgments

I would like to thank PricewaterhouseCoopers and the individual authors within the firm for contributing the chapter on accounting and taxation of structured note transactions. In particular, I would like to thank John Masters and Bill Testa for coordinating the project.

I would like to thank Euromoney Publications for publishing the first edition of this book.

I would like to thank the publishers of this edition — John Wiley (Nick Wallwork) — for agreeing to publish the second edition of the book. I would like to thank Gael Lee and Katherine Krummert who edited the book.

I would like to thank my parents Sukumar and Aparna Das for their continued support and encouragement in my work. In particular, I would like to thank my friend and partner Jade Novakovic. Without her support, help, patience and encouragement this book, like so many others before it, would never have been completed. This book is dedicated to these three people.

**Satyajit Das**
September 2000

# About the Author

Satyajit Das is an international specialist in the area of financial derivatives, risk management, and capital markets. He presents seminars on financial derivatives/ risk management and capital markets in Europe, North America, Asia and Australia. He acts as a consultant to financial institutions and corporations on derivatives and financial products, risk management, and capital markets issues.

Between 1988 and 1994, Mr. Das was the Treasurer of the TNT Group, an Australian based international transport and logistics company with responsibility for the Global Treasury function, including liquidity management, corporate finance, capital markets, and financial risk management. He was also involved in the financial restructuring of the TNT Group in the early 1990s. During 1994, Mr. Das acted as a consultant to the TNT Group in the areas of financial strategy and policy, capital allocation/ management and strategic risk management.

Between 1977 and 1987, he worked in banking with the Commonwealth Bank of Australia, Citicorp Investment Bank and Merrill Lynch Capital Markets specialising in fund raising for Australian and New Zealand borrowers in domestic and international capital markets and risk management, involving the use of derivative products.

In 1987, Mr. Das was a Visiting Fellow at the Centre for Studies in Money, Banking and Finance, Macquarie University.

Mr. Das is the author of *Swap Financing* (1989, IFR Publishing Limited/ The Law Book Company Limited), *Swaps and Financial Derivatives: The Global Reference to Products, Pricing, Applications and Markets* (1994, IFR Publishing Limited/The Law Book Company Limited/Irwin Professional Publishing), *Exotic Options* (1996, IFR Publishing/ The Law Book Company) and *Structured Notes and Derivative Embedded Securities* (1996, Euromoney Publications). He is also the major contributor and editor of *The Global Swaps Market* (1991, IFR Publishing Limited), *Financial Derivatives & Risk Management: A Guide to the Mathematics* (1997, Law Book Company/ Irwin Professional Publishing/ MacMillan Publishing), *Credit Derivatives* (1998, John Wiley & Sons) and *Credit Derivatives & Credit Linked Notes- Second Edition* (2000, John Wiley & Sons). He has published on financial derivatives, corporate finance, treasury and risk management issues in professional and applied finance journals (including: *Risk, Journal of International Securities Markets, Capital Market Strategies, Euromoney Corporate Finance, IFR Financial Products, Futures & OTC World* and *Financial Derivatives & Risk Management*).

Mr. Das holds Bachelors' degrees in Commerce (Accounting, Finance and Systems) and Law from the University of New South Wales and a Masters degree in Business Administration from the Australian Graduate School of Management.

# About the Contributors

Richard D. Clarke – is a tax partner in PricewaterhouseCoopers' Banking & Capital Markets Group and a qualified chartered accountant. Since the mid-1980s his experience has concentrated on financially based transactions working with both the users and the creators of structured products. He is the author of a leading text on the UK taxation of loan relationships and has both written and spoken on a variety of other related topics.

Richard S. Collier – is a tax partner in PricewaterhouseCoopers' Banking & Capital Markets Group and a qualified barrister and chartered accountant. Richard writes and lectures extensively on taxation and is a member of Council of the Institute for Fiscal Studies. Richard has specialized in capital markets and banking tax issues for over ten years and he is the Tax & Legal Services' global leader of the firm's capital markets tax practice. He has been particularly closely involved in the tax changes to the securities markets including the manufactured dividend, stocklending and gilt repo tax rules. Richard has extensive experience of the investment-banking sector and has serviced clients and carried out a vast range of related assignments.

Antony Eldridge – is an UK Assurance and Business Advisory Services partner, based in Tokyo and specializing in investment and wholesale banking. During his time in London, Tokyo and tours of duty in New York and Zurich, he has served many of the leading names in international banking, providing audit, accounting, advisory and due diligence services. He is a qualified chartered accountant and has a first class honors degree in Business Administration from the University of Bath, England.

Regina Fikkers – is a Financial Reporting director of PricewaterhouseCoopers based in Sydney. She specializes in advising on the practical applications of Australian and International accounting standards, in particular financial instrument standards, and in training on the implementation of new standards. She was principal author of the firm's IAS Illustrative Bank Financial Statements and has contributed to numerous other publications on financial reporting.

Sachihiko Fujimoto – is a tax partner in the Tokyo office of PricewaterhouseCoopers and is in charge of the Japanese financial services industry tax practice. Mr. Fujimoto is a member of the Japanese Institute of Certified Public Accountants and the Japanese Licensed Tax Accountant

Association. He graduated from the Kyoto University, Law Faculty and received a Master of International Management from the American Graduate School of International Management. Mr. Fujimoto has authored several articles for various tax publications and co-authored *Accounting and Taxation of Derivatives* (1996). He spent 10 years with a Japanese bank, 4 of which were spent in London. He joined PricewaterhouseCoopers (formerly Chuo Coopers & Lybrand International Tax office) in 1990.

Viva Hammer – is a Principal Consultant in the Financial Services Industry group at PricewaterhouseCoopers New York. Prior to joining the financial services practice, Ms Hammer specialized in US International tax, and was involved with designing and implementing global tax planning for multinational corporate clients. She has a Bachelor of Economics, and a first class honors degree in Law, both from the University of Sydney, Australia.

Ian Hammond – is the Assurance & Business Advisory Services practice leader of PricewaterhouseCoopers Australia Financial Services Industry Group. He is based in Sydney. Ian is currently an Australian representative on the International Accounting Standards Board and was a member of the Australian Accounting Standard Board 1992-1999. He has specialist experience in financial reporting aspects of treasury and capital markets.

Martin B. Kelly – is a partner in the Assurance and Business Advisory Services, Banking Practice of PricewaterhouseCoopers LLP. He specializes in providing auditing, accounting, and business advisory services to financial institutions, particularly money center and wholesale banks. Mr. Kelly has a bachelor of Commerce in Finance and Accounting (University of New South Wales, Sydney Australia) and a Graduate Diploma in Applied Finance (Securities Institute of Australia). Mr. Kelly is a chartered accountant and licensed as a CPA in the State of Delaware.

Georg Klusak – is a lawyer based in Frankfurt. After having worked for Deutsche Bank, he joined Coopers & Lybrand and is now heading the Capital Markets and the Investment Management Groups of PricewaterhouseCoopers in Germany.

Nabi Niang – is a manager in the Assurance and Business Advisory Services, Banking Practice of PricewaterhouseCoopers LLP. Before assuming his current position in 1996 in New York, he worked three years in France on the audit of large banking institutions. He has provided assistance to several firms' banking clients on accounting issues related to various financial instruments. Mr. Niang holds a master degree in audit and finance from the University of Paris IX, and a graduate diploma in finance from the London School of Economics. He is licensed as a CPA in the State of Delaware.

Grahame Roach – is a Senior Taxation Manager in the financial services group at PricewaterhouseCoopers, Sydney. He has 14 years experience in providing taxation services to a broad range of clients, including those in the banking and funds management industry. His professional qualifications include a Masters in Taxation and a Graduate Diploma in Applied Finance and Investment.

Arnaud Serres – is an Audit Manager in the specialist Banking and Capital Markets Group in PricewaterhouseCoopers, Tokyo, on assignment from the Paris office. He has provided a wide range of audit and business advisory services to several international banks with particular experience on capital markets and structured finance activities. Prior to join PricewaterhouseCoopers, Arnaud was Internal Auditor within Societe Generale's Capital Markets Division. He has a Master of Science in Capital Markets from Nice-Sophia Antipolis Business School.

Hisashi Shirahata – is a Director of the Financial Services Industry Practice of PricewaterhouseCoopers in Tokyo. He has 15 years of experience including 8 years spent with the Bank of Tokyo-Mitsubishi Ltd. Over that time Hisashi has gained extensive commercial experience in corporate planning including management accounting, unification of accounting systems post merger, budget and cost accounting and systems development. He is a qualified CPA in Japan and has a Master of Business Administration from Boston University.

Kenneth Shives – is a tax manager in the Tokyo office of PricewaterhouseCoopers and is a member of the financial services industry practice. Mr. Shives is a member of the American Institute of Certified Public Accountants and the New York State Society of Certified Public Accountants. He graduated from the University of Washington with a bachelor degree in accounting and information systems and a graduate degree in accounting and taxation. Mr. Shives is a regular speaker at industry tax conferences on a variety of inbound and outbound tax issues faced by both foreign and domestic financial institutions. He has spent the majority of his career in the New York banking tax practice and is currently working in the Tokyo office to service financial services industry clients doing business in Japan.

Bill Testa – is a Tax Partner in the specialist Financial Services Tax Group in PricewaterhouseCoopers, Sydney. He has 15 years experience in providing taxation services to the banking financial services industry with particular experience advising on the income tax issues for derivatives and other complex financial transactions, as well as structured finance, leasing, funds management, offshore banking and cross border financing transactions. He is an Economics/ Law graduate from Sydney University and a qualified chartered accountant.

Ian D. Wright – is an Assurance & Business Advisory Services partner. He has 15 years experience as an audit partner on financial services companies covering banks, insurance companies, mutual funds and hedge funds, and the last five years as a technical partner specializing in UK and International Accounting Standards. He has the responsibility within PricewaterhouseCoopers for supervising the application of IAS to Financial Services Entities. Ian has a degree in Engineering from Exeter University and is a Chartered Accountant.

# 1
# Introduction

## 1. Introduction

Structured notes have emerged as an important instrument in financial markets. The combination of a fixed income security (typically, a fixed rate bond) and a derivative contract (a forward or option) to create a financial product has become a standard mechanism for enabling investors to broaden the range of investment opportunities to monetize their market expectations.

This chapter looks at the structure, rationale and design of structured notes. The concept of structured notes is first outlined. The rationale for structured notes is then analyzed. The credit implications of these types of arrangements and pricing implications of structured note products are considered. Structural aspects of derivative securities are examined using collared floating rate note (FRN) issues as an example. The concept of synthetic or repackaged structured notes is also examined as an important alternative to direct issuance of structured notes by highly rated issuers.

## 2. Concept of Structured Notes

The concept of a structured note is a security that combines the features of a fixed income instrument with the characteristics of a derivative transaction (in effect, the return profile of a forward or option on a selected class of asset). These types of instruments are often referred to as structured notes or as derivative-embedded securities.

Structured notes represent a special class of fixed income instruments. The principal appeal of structured notes is the capacity of these instruments to generate highly customized exposures for investors consistent with their nominated investment objectives.

While structured notes have proliferated in recent times, there is a long history of fixed income securities with embedded derivative elements. The most common types of *traditional* derivative securities have included fixed income bonds with call options allowing the issuer to retire the security before its scheduled maturity or equity convertible securities that embodied call options on the equity of the issuer.

The distinguishing feature of modern structured notes is the different role played by the derivative element. In traditional configurations such as the callable bond or convertible, the call option is utilized to make the security more attractive to investors as part of the overall investment package. In contrast, in modern structured notes, the derivative element being incorporated is highly engineered and is specifically utilized to allow the creation and transfer of the risk embodied in the derivative component. This may entail, for example, an investor creating the derivative element that is then securitized through the security structure with the issuer transferring the derivative element to a derivative market-maker who in turn reallocates the risk element to ultimate users of that particular instrument. In this way, modern structured notes are utilized as a complex basis for transference of risk through an often long chain of transactions.

# 3.  Creation of Structured Notes

As noted above, a structured note is usually defined as a conventional fixed income debt security combined with a derivative transaction. The derivative element is generally incorporated into the normal fixed income security structure by linking either the redemption value and/or the value of coupons payable to movements in the price of a specified asset. Typically, linkages to financial market variables such as interest rates, currencies, equity (market indexes or individual stocks), and commodities (both indexes and individual stocks) are utilized. The derivative element usually incorporated is either a symmetric position, such as a forward contract, or an asymmetric position, such as an option or a combination of options. Increasingly, nonstandard hybrid and exotic option structures as well as newer asset classes (credit, insurance risk and inflation risk) are also incorporated in structured note structures.

The combination of the base security and the derivative component is designed to produce the required sensitivity to the asset price movement sought. The *derivative element* is the mechanism by which the essential exposure to the market price component is created.

The essential elements of a structured note transaction include:

- **Identification of the investor requirements** — the investor requirements will entail, generally, identification of a number of distinct elements. This will encompass identifying the exposure sought to be introduced into the investment portfolio within a traditional investment management framework. This will include identifying the specific economic outlook and the specific asset price expectations sought to be captured. Risk-reward parameters as well as asset-liability/portfolio considerations will be considered.

- **Structuring of the instrument** — when the underlying exposure sought to be created has been identified, then the issue of the most effective means through which the exposure can be captured is considered. Where the exposure sought is either customized or where for regulatory, credit or other reasons the exposure cannot be created directly, the structured note represents an important alternative *mechanism* for creating the desired exposure. The structured note format will also offer, under certain circumstances, the potential opportunities to create the desired exposure in a format that is more efficient or incurs lower transaction costs. The process will by its intrinsic nature be iterative. The structured note may be either designed to investor specification or may be offered unsolicited to the investor with the latter forcing the investor to examine its investment strategy in the process of evaluating the *specific security.*
- **Execution of the transaction** (including arranging the issuer and undertaking the hedging of all relevant exposures and risks) — the structured note itself will be designed by an investment bank or securities/derivative dealer, based on the investor specifications or requirements. The principal components will be a fixed or floating rate security and the derivative elements that are engineered into the security structure.
- **Secondary market in the note** — the secondary market component entails the sale and purchase of the structured note prior to maturity. The liquidity of structured notes is generally lower than that of comparable conventional securities. The secondary market for these instruments is discussed in detail in Chapters 16 and 17.

The process of designing a structured note transaction requires further consideration. As noted above, an investment bank or securities/derivative dealer designs the structured note, based on the investor's specification or requirement. The principal components will be the following:

- A fixed or floating rate security.
- One or more derivative elements that are engineered into the security structure.

The derivative elements will be, in general, relatively standard instruments available in the market. This will encompass either exchange traded or more typically over-the-counter (OTC) instruments on the relevant asset class.

The principal design elements will include:

- The nominated credit risk and issuer.
- The exposure embedded and in particular the level of risk entailed.

Structured note issuers are, usually, of high credit quality. The vast majority of issuers are rated AA or better. The minimum credit rating will generally be A although issues by lower rated issuers have been undertaken in limited circumstances. The use of high credit quality issuers is directly linked to the investor requirement for credit enhancement and the separation of credit risk from market risk. Structured notes are viewed as a mechanism for taking market risk.[1]

As an alternative to arranging a highly rated issuer to undertake the issue of the structured note, the note may be created using a repackaging vehicle. The design of such structured notes is considered in greater detail below.

The creation of the desired market risk exposure requires the linkage or indexation of either the coupon or redemption value (in effect, the principal) to the nominated asset price or index. The critical issue in this context is the value placed at risk and the conditions under which the value is at risk of loss. The risk components are determined by the investor, in practice, and will encompass:

- Coupon (in part or full) at risk.
- Principal (in part or full) at risk.
- The type of instrument (forward or option).
- (In the case of optionality) whether the option is purchased or written.
- The degree of leverage (if any) sought to be introduced.

In general, the dynamics of structuring will entail the following process. The investor seeking lower risk will seek to risk only coupon. In contrast, the higher risk investor may risk coupon and/or part or all of principal. The latter may also seek to enhance the risk through incorporating leverage.

Where a forward is embedded the element linked (coupon or principal) will change in value in a linear and symmetric manner, both rising and falling in accordance with the movement in the asset price index. Where optionality is entailed, the structure reflects where the option is purchased or written. Where purchased, the option premium payment must be funded requiring a reduction in either the coupon or principal. Where written, the option premium will allow payment of a higher economic return most often in the form of a higher coupon. The payout under the option, if required where the option expires in the money, is made by reducing the coupon paid or the principal amount redeemed.

The issue of leverage relates to the *face value amount* of derivative contracts embedded in the structured note. The structured product concept does not limit the level of derivative components embedded. This allows the degree of derivative exposure (the mechanism by which the exposure to the required asset price movement is engineered) to be varied to both *increase or decrease* the sensitivity of the instrument's value to movements in the underlying asset price movements.

As will be evident, the investor requirement will shape the design and structure of the note. The universe of structured note investors and their

---

[1]  Issuer selection is discussed in detail in Chapter 17.

objectives in participating in this market is discussed in detail in Chapter 17. The execution of the transaction entails the following steps:

* The desired issuer is identified and approached to issue the security.
* The security is issued.
* Simultaneous to the agreement of the security terms among issuer, investor(s), and the investment bank, the investment bank executes all the required hedge transactions to insulate the issuer from any exposure to the embedded derivative element.
* The transaction is settled.

The execution of the hedge is central to the completion of a transaction for two reasons. It is essential to the pricing of the transaction.[2] It is also essential to allow the issuer to participate in the transaction. Issuers are typically participating on the basis of a guaranteed and known funding cost. Therefore, insulation from any exposure to the market risk elements embodied in the note is central to the transaction. In order to eliminate this exposure, the issuer enters into a separate derivative contract with the investment bank or dealer.

## 4. Example of a Structured Note Transaction

**Exhibit 1.1** sets out an example of the collared FRN transactions which emerged originally to take advantage of the relatively steep slope of the US$ interest rate yield curve in the period 1992 to 1993.[3]

---

**Exhibit 1.1**
**Example of Structured Note Transaction —**
**Collared Floating Rate Notes (FRNs)**

| | |
|---|---|
| Issuer | J.P. Morgan |
| Amount | US$200 million of Subordinated FRNs |
| Maturity | 10 years (due August 19 2002) |
| Spread | 3-month LIBID flat |
| Fixed Reoffer Price | 99.85 |
| Minimum Interest | 5% |
| Maximum Interest | 10% |
| Amortization | Bullet |
| Call Option | None |

---

[2]  See detailed discussion of pricing mechanics in Chapter 16.
[3]  A more detailed discussion of collared FRN structures is set out in Chapter 4.

| Denominations | US$5,000, US$100,000 |
|---|---|
| Commissions | 0.50% (management and underwriting 0.25%; selling 0.25%) |

*Source: International Financing Review*, Issue 940 56 (August 1, 1992).

The basic economics of the collared FRN is driven by the fact that it combines a standard FRN structure with a US$ LIBOR interest rate cap and floor. The investor effectively through the structure sold a cap and purchased a floor, which equates to, effectively, a sold interest rate collar on US$ LIBOR. **Exhibit 1.2** sets out the structure in terms of the individual components.

**Exhibit 1.2**
**Collared Floating Rate Notes — Transaction Components**

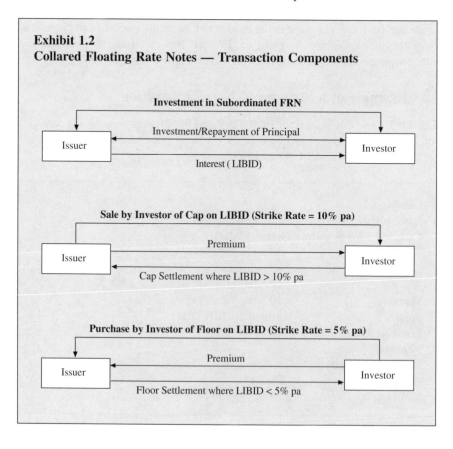

A number of key structural elements of this transaction should be noted:

- The issuer of the securities was typically a highly rated entity (usually AA rated or better).
- The issuer in these transactions, as a general rule, did not position or absorb the risk of the derivative elements created through the FRN structure. The issuer, in fact, typically onsold the derivative elements or, in turn, hedged its exposure to the derivative elements through the derivative market itself. Its primary motivation was the margin that it could make between the derivative element captured through the sale of the security and the price for which the derivative element could be hedged, repackaged or onsold in capital markets generally. The overall result for the issuer is its overall cost of funds that is attractive based on the margin earned between the purchase and onsale of the derivative element acting as a subsidy on its overall borrowing cost.
- The maturity of the structured note in the case of collared FRNs was quite long — (up to) 10/12 years. This contrasts with the more common structured note structures that usually entail shorter maturities (typically one to three years) although longer transactions are not unknown.
- Key elements in the cash flow structuring of the security are central to the efficacy of the arrangement. In the case of the collared FRN, the transaction entails the investor purchasing a package consisting of: a normal FRN, selling a cap on US$ LIBOR at the maximum rate (say, 10% per annum), and purchasing a US$ LIBOR interest rate floor at the minimum interest rate level (say, 5% per annum). The structure entails the investor both purchasing and selling option elements.

The discussion regarding the structural elements of the structured notes is related to the collared FRN example identified. In practice, almost all structured note transactions must, of necessity, embody similar structural features.

## 5. Rationale for Structured Notes

### 5.1 Overview

There are a number possible explanations for the use of such structures:

- **Regulatory arbitrage** — whereby investors and, less frequently, issuers utilize derivative-embedded structures to circumvent barriers to trading in the relevant derivatives directly.
- **Customization** — utilizing such structures to monetize positions/ expectations in a particular manner.
- **Credit enhancement** — utilizing such structures to provide credit enhancement to facilitate participation in the derivative market.

• **Denomination arbitrage** — allow derivative transactions to be undertaken in denominations that might otherwise not be feasible.

A number of other advantages that may be relevant in such structures include accounting or taxation, ease of administration and tradeability/liquidity of the instrument.

## 5.2 Regulatory Arbitrage

There is evidence that structured notes are utilized to circumvent regulations that would otherwise prevent an investor or, alternatively, an issuer from undertaking the underlying derivative transaction itself.

There is nothing sinister about the use of structured notes to circumvent barriers to dealing in derivatives themselves. In fact, arguably the capacity to utilize derivatives for this purpose is a necessary means by which issuers and investors who would otherwise be prevented from managing their financial risks to the fullest extent possible undertake required risk management actions. This is particularly true of investors who may be constrained by constituent documents created in an era before the availability of derivative instruments to manage risks. Such constituent documents may be difficult and cumbersome to change. In a sense, the use of structured notes, predicated on the fact that the investors are allowed to purchase or sell securities as part of their normal functions, is a means of overcoming the transaction costs of affecting the necessary change in the constituent documents of the relevant entity.

It is difficult to get direct evidence of the regulatory arbitrage element that motivates structured notes. Anecdotal evidence suggests that this is significant. In addition, the identity of major buyer groups, namely Japanese, European and Asian investors, suggests that this is a significant motivation for such transactions.

A significant factor in the design and sale of structured notes is the importance of transforming a derivative transaction into a security (for legal purposes) and a listed instrument (on a stock exchange). This is designed to overcome the investment constraints on investors who are only empowered to purchase *listed securities*. This prohibition limits the capacity of these investors to utilize over-the-counter derivative products. This limitation can be overcome through the use of structured note transactions.

A related issue is the legal restriction under gambling legislation still in operation in a number of jurisdictions that prevents the entry into derivative transactions by institutional and retail investors. The use of structured note formats can be designed to overcome these difficulties.

The impact of creating listed securities as a mechanism for facilitating entry into derivative transactions is most relevant in Europe, although it is a factor in other markets as well.

## 5.3    Customization

Customization entails the creation of specifically designed risk exposures for investors as well as enabling the monetization of asset price expectations. Structured notes are customized to fit the unique requirements of particular investors thereby facilitating the creation of risk-return trade-offs that would not be readily available to investors directly. This enables investors to capture higher returns on their investments provided their expectations about asset prices are realized.[4]

Central to this process of customization is the ability to access markets that would otherwise be difficult for investors to access directly. This difficulty of access may arise from two sources:

• The asset is synthetic, such as equity market or commodity indexes and consequently not tradeable directly.
• Transaction costs of participation are high, such as commodity markets and foreign equity investments.

In addition, the use of structured notes may allow creation of particular risk return payoffs that are difficult or expensive (in the sense of transaction costs) to create in the market for physical assets.

This allows structured notes to be utilized, frequently, to monetize positions and/or expectations regarding capital market variables. The advantage of structured notes, in this regard, is that they allow capture of value in a particular way that is of interest to the investor or issuer. The major elements of this monetizing aspect include:

• These transactions allow value to be captured by essentially allowing, say, an investor's expectation regarding particular values of financial assets to be embedded in the derivative. For example, a collared FRN or a reverse or inverse FRN structure[5] can be characterized as monetizing an investor view that forward rates currently implied by a yield curve are significantly above the actual rates that will prevail in the future.
• Monetizing positions or expectations within the structured note format may allow a degree of liquidity/tradeability that cannot be achieved in another manner. For example, in the case of a collared FRN, the investor can effectively trade a series of options, indirectly embodying views on forward interest rates in combination by purchasing and then selling the FRN itself.

---

[4]    For an interesting analysis or example of the process of creating/designing a structured note, see Dabansens, Frederic. "Relative Risk" (April 1997) *AsiaRisk* 30-32; Dare, Laurence "How the Investor Can Enhance Yield" (1996) *Corporate Finance Risk Management & Derivatives Yearbook* 34-36.
[5]    Inverse FRN structures are discussed in detail in Chapter 4.

The FRN eliminates the need to enter into a complex series of transactions that may require the availability of credit facilities in the form of counterparty risk lines. The liquidity or tradeability potential (at least, in theory) is an important incentive to utilize structured notes to monetize such positions and expectations.

- Utilizing structured notes in this manner allows interesting combinations of positions to be created. An example of this concept is evident in the case of reverse FRNs where in essence the security combines a fixed bond with an interest rate swap in which the investor receives fixed and pays floating rates. Under this combined structure, the investor has several sources of value including:
  1. The realized short-term money market rate relative to those embodied in the current yield curve.
  2. The movement in term rates will determine the value of the underlying bond and the embedded interest rate swap.

This particular combination of expectation/views may in practice allow value to be created from combinations of positions in a unique way. Importantly, creating such instruments in a package that is, potentially, both tradeable and liquid may enhance the value of the transaction.

## 5.4 Credit Enhancement

A key element of structured notes is that the mechanics facilitate a shift of all performance obligations onto the issuer (who as noted above is highly rated and considered to be relatively free of credit or default risk). Consider the example in **Exhibit 1.1**. This is most relevant in the case of option created by the investor (in this case, the cap sold by the investor to the issuer). This would normally entail performance obligations on the investor to make cash payments where US$ LIBOR exceeded the cap level. However, the structure obviates this requirement by effectively requiring the issuer to effectively assume the credit risk of the option writer (from whom the issuer purchases the cap to onsell). This also means that the ultimate buyer of the cap has as its counterparty for credit risk purposes the issuer.

However, the issuer assumes minimal risk on the derivative transaction because of the structure. From a mechanical perspective, in the case of the collared FRN, this is achieved by two separate mechanisms:

- The sale of the cap by the investor to the issuer is fully cash collateralized by the face value of the FRN itself. The investor invests this amount with the issuer through the purchase of the FRN.
- There is also no performance obligation on the investor. The issuer only pays interest *up* to the maximum interest rate to the investor. Any payment that

relates to the inherent value of the cap (reflecting the difference between US$ LIBOR and the maximum rate where LIBOR is above the maximum rate) is made to the ultimate purchaser of the cap.

In this manner, the performance obligations under the derivative element shift to the issuer allowing the issuer's credit risk to be substituted for that of the investor. In the reverse case, where the investor purchases an option, in the case of the collared FRN the floor purchased by the investor, the performance obligation is, from the outset, with the issuer.

The elements identified are all present in the transactions described in **Exhibit 1.1**. The importance of the cash flow structuring to shift the performance obligation onto the issuer is illustrated by the second transaction described in **Exhibit 1.3** — a World Bank transaction that entails a securitization of the collared FRN.

---

**Exhibit 1.3**

**Example of Structured Note — capped FRN with Floor Warrants**

*Capped FRN*

| | |
|---|---|
| Issuer | World Bank |
| Amount | US$200 million of FRNs |
| Maturity | 10 years (due April 28 2003) |
| Coupon | 6-month LIBOR plus 0.25% payable semi-annually on April 28 and October 28. |
| Maximum interest | 7-1/4% as from the beginning of the 5th interest period. |
| First Interest Determination Date | April 26 |
| Issue Price | 100% |
| Amortisation | Bullet |
| Call Option | None |
| Denominations | DM10,000 and DM250,000 (global note) |
| Commissions | 0.20% (management & underwriting combined 0.10%, selling 0.10%) |

*Floor Certificates*

| | |
|---|---|
| Issuer | World Bank |
| Number | 20,000 certificates |
| Exercise | Each certificate entitles the holder to payment on April 28 and October 28 corresponding to the |

| | |
|---|---|
| | positive difference between 7% pa and six-month LIBOR. Each certificate relates to DM10,000. |
| Issue Price | DM695 per certificate |
| Expiration | April 28 2003 |
| Selling concession | 0.25% |

*Source: International Financing Review,* Issue 970 72 (March 13, 1993).

In this transaction, the issue of FRNs is combined with a maximum interest rate (the capped FRN). The FRN is issued in conjunction with the issue by the borrower of floor certificates that are detachable. The economic benefit of such an arrangement is that the floor certificates, effectively the minimum interest rate element of the transaction, are allowed to be traded freely by the investor quite separately from the capped FRN itself.

From a cash flow structuring viewpoint, the two option elements—the cap *written by the investor* and the floor *purchased by the investor*—are treated differently. The floor element, where the performance obligation is on the issuer as the grantor of the option, can be freely securitized. In contrast, the cap element, where the performance obligation is on the investor as the grantor of the cap cannot be structured as a tradeable security as this would prevent the transfer of the performance obligation from the investor to the issuer.

As noted above, the cash flow structuring entailed in a structured note allows the investor, typically, to transfer the credit exposure of the transaction to the issuer. This effectively allows the investor to utilize the credit quality of the issuer in derivative transactions. This is particularly important in the case of investors dealing in small amounts of derivatives or investors whose structure, such as a mutual or pooled fund, may make it difficult for such entities to have access to the required credit arrangements to participate in derivative transactions more generally.

The case of mutual funds (or unit trust structures) is particularly important. The increasing amount of investment funds channeled through these investment vehicles reflects the major benefits provided through the process of aggregation covering economics of scale and scope, as well as the capability to allow diversification of smaller investor portfolios.

The counterparty credit risk of the mutual fund structure is problematic. As the arrangement entails no capital or guarantee from a creditworthy party, the credit assessment must focus on the capacity of the fund itself to meet its contractual obligations. This is dependent on the liquidity of the fund and the continued retention of investment funds at a sufficient level to meet the relevant obligations. This risk is, in reality, a difficult one to assess, particularly over long periods. This inherently limits the participation of mutual funds in derivative transactions. Structured notes play a central role in overcoming this limitation.

## 5.5    Retail Denomination

A related issue is what may be termed the denomination arbitrage feature. The use of structured notes allows investors, in particular, to participate in the derivatives market in denominations that are significantly lower than that which might be achieved through direct participation. In the case of the capped FRN transactions, which are not atypical, the low denominations of the FRNs themselves would allow investors to purchase and sell derivative elements for relatively modest amounts (say, $5,000 and above).[6] In this manner, structured notes allow retail participation in the derivatives market within a wholesale and institutional market structure.

The capacity of retail investors to utilize derivatives through structured notes also has a value arbitrage element. The structured note market through its structure entails wholesale prices for derivatives. This facilitates retail investor access to derivative products at prices that are significantly better than prices at which these products would be available to them without the availability of structured notes.

## 5.6    Other Considerations

Other factors that may enhance the demand for structured notes include accounting or taxation factors, ease of administration, the ability to rate the structure and tradeability/liquidity of the instrument.

The accounting and taxation benefits of embedding derivatives in a structured note format *should* not necessarily provide any significant advantages. In practice, there may be major advantages as the structured note may not be bifurcated into components and treated separately for accounting and tax purposes.

For accounting purposes, the structured note will generally be treated as a security and either held at book value (where it is a term or hold to maturity asset) or marked to market based on the market value *of the structured note*. The secondary market value of the structured note will be based on market prices or dealer quotes. The prices will encompass the market value of the derivative components but indirectly in the price of the security.

A major accounting advantage may be in the treatment of option premiums. Premiums paid can be amortised over the life of the note (as embodied in the note cash flows) in contrast to being recognized immediately as is required under

---

[6]    In reality, the typical investment is significantly higher being in the region of US$50,000 and higher.

certain circumstances for particular categories of investors in specific jurisdictions. Premiums received can be recognized gradually (as also embodied in the note cash flows) rather than have to be recognized upon receipt or deferred until the option expires. The nature of the income may also be altered where the option premium is built into the interest or other cash flows of the security.

A major advantage in this regard is for mutual funds that are able to avoid the complexity of option accounting, the premium being captured by the note cash flows. This allows the avoidance of complex issues for these investors regarding maintaining equality among the fund investors at different points in time as well as distribution of earnings.

The taxation advantages are similar to those identified in the context of accounting, with the major benefit being in the area of option premium treatment.

The ease of administration derives from the fact that in essence the structured notes can be settled, processed and administered as essentially a fixed interest security, albeit with customized cash flows. This is an additional advantage over outright derivative transactions for investors who are not appropriately equipped, in an operational and administrative sense, to handle derivative trades.

The incorporation of the derivative into a note format enables the instrument to be rated. This might be an important factor for investors restricted to investments rated by major rating agencies.[7]

The liquidity and tradeability aspect of the structured note as an instrument has been noted above. The major advantage in this regard is the capacity to reduce exposure to the market risk and the derivative component through the sale of the note. The sale also eliminates any counterparty credit risk. This contrasts with derivative transactions where eliminating the exposure would require the investor to either cancel the transaction with the existing counterparty or enter into an offsetting transaction with an alternative counterparty. The second alternative requires the commitment of additional credit lines and continued usage of the credit capacity utilized in the original transaction.

## 6.   Pricing Implications

The structural elements of and rationale for structured notes have direct implications on the pricing of such transactions. These implications exist at two levels:

- Value capture issues.
- The apportionment of value as between various parties involved in the transactions.

---

[7]   For a discussion of the process of rating, a structured note, see Efrat, Issac, Gluck, Jeremy, and Powar, David "Moody's Refines Its Approach to Rating Structured Notes," Moody's Investor Service Global Credit Research, New York, July 3, 1997.

Given the nature of the transactions, the investor who is seeking to purchase or sell the derivative element incorporated in the security structure, particularly if that investor has no alternative means of participating in the derivative market, is likely to have a relatively lower price sensitivity. In addition, it is probable that the investor will be prepared to pay a premium for the structure where it allows investors to monetize its particular position/expectation in a desirable manner. The investor will be also required to pay an additional premium for the credit enhancement elements of the transaction, as well as the implicit denomination reduction process that allows more widespread participation.

Against this background, investors, typically, will pay as in the case of the collared FRN a higher price for the structured note than the individual component values based on theoretical values under normal market trading conditions.

Value in this context for the overall transaction will be driven by several elements:

- The investor's desired position and the value that the investor accords to the structure.
- The issuer's target cost of funds and the value it places on its credit-enhancement role in the transaction.
- The return objectives of the intermediary arranging the overall package.

Predictably, there is significant competition among investors, issuers and intermediaries that creates a volatile market for such structures. Moreover, the value exchange equation is dynamic and would alter depending on changes in any of the various variables identified.[8]

# 7. Structured Notes Created Through Repackaging Vehicles

The form of structured notes described to date relies upon a highly rated issuer to undertake the issue of structured notes. However, increasingly, structured notes are created through special purpose repackaging vehicles.

Repackaged structured notes are a special class of structured notes. They involve using a special purpose issuance vehicle or asset repackaging structure to repackage the risk of securities to create structured notes. The repackaging vehicle purchases securities in the secondary market and then reprofiles the cash flows of the underlying securities by entering into derivatives transactions with a dealer. The repackaged cash flows are then bundled up as a security and placed with investors. Structurally, repackaged notes are based on asset swap technology.

The motivations underlying repackaged notes and repackaging vehicles are

---

[8]  For a detailed discussion of pricing and value dynamics see Chapter 16.

similar to that underlying the market for credit-linked notes generally. These include:

* Investor demand for investments and risk that is not directly available in the market.
* Relative value considerations under which the exposure can be created at a more attractive value than through structured notes.
* Regulatory and market considerations that favor indirect assumption of the exposure relative to direct investment or entry into a derivative transaction.

However, the demand for repackaged structured notes over *traditional structured notes* is predicated upon the following additional factors:

* The absence of any requirement to compensate the issuer for issuing the structured note (effectively the sub-LIBOR margin requirement).
* Relative value considerations whereby the repackaging structure provides the inherent opportunity to allow purchase of undervalued securities in the secondary market to collateralize the structure reducing the cost.
* Greater flexibility to structure investments, consistent with investor requirements, without the restriction of needing to satisfy the requirements of the note issuer.[9]
* Enhanced freedom to select the credit and issuer profile of the underlying securities that allows both customization of issuer risk and diversifies the universe of issuers of structured notes.

These factors (in particular, the first two factors) have greatly contributed to the development of repackaged notes generally. Repackaged structured notes complement and compete with standard structured notes. The market also operates parallel to the asset swap market.

## 8.   Repackaging Vehicles

### 8.1   History

The concept of repackaging vehicles evolved out of the asset swap market.[10] The term "asset swap" is a generic term covering repackaging of the cash flows of any security into a required cash flow configuration for an investor. Traditional asset swaps focused on repackaging the interest rate and/or currency risk profile of a security for placement with an investor.

---

[9]   This is relevant despite the fact that the issuer is perfectly insulated from the impact of the embedded derivative and is fully hedged back into LIBOR-based funding at an attractive cost.

[10]  For a detailed discussion of asset swaps, see Das, Satyajit (1994) *Swaps & Financial Derivatives*; LBC Information Services, Sydney; McGraw-Hill, Chicago at Chapter 18.

Asset swaps were predicated on the reverse of the liability arbitrage and focused on creating synthetic assets for investors. The dominant drivers of this market were: the opportunity to create securities not directly available in the market; generate returns in excess of those available from conventional securities of similar characteristics; and repackaging illiquid assets.

Traditional asset swaps were a combination of the purchase of a security and entry by the investor into a derivative transaction to transform the security's interest rate or currency characteristics. This was problematic for a number of reasons including:

- The inability of a number of investors to transact derivatives.
- The credit risk inherent in the derivative transaction.
- The lack of liquidity of the package and the difficulty in trading the synthetic asset except by unbundling it into its components that could be expensive.
- The administrative complexity of marking to market (both the security and the derivative), and the complexity of accounting for and establishing the taxation treatment of the transaction.

These problems led investment banks to create the concept of securitized asset swaps. Securitized asset swaps were the effective precursors of the repackaging vehicle.

## 8.2  Securitized Asset Swaps

Until September 1985, asset swaps had been traditionally undertaken as private transactions, being structured primarily as investor-manufactured swaps. In September 1985, the concept of the public or securitized asset swap was introduced with two transactions, one led by Hill Samuel and the other by Merrill Lynch Capital Markets. An analysis of the Merrill Lynch transaction provides an insight into the mechanics of the securitized asset swap. This structure is set out in **Exhibit 1.4**.

---

**Exhibit 1.4**
**Marketable Eurodollar Collateralized Securities Limited (MECS)**
**Securitized Asset Swap Structure**

Towards the end of September 1985, the UK raised US$2.5 billion through the issuance of 7-year FRNs, due October 1992. The notes were originally priced at 99.70% of face value, net of fees, with a coupon of 3-month US$ LIBID and were noncallable for three years from the time of issuance. Following the launch of this issue, the sales force of Merrill Lynch noted that there was considerable interest from its investors in fixed

rate UK government US$ denominated debt. In particular, the sales force
had reported a coupon of approximately 9.375% pa for a 3-year maturity
as acceptable to these investors. However, no fixed rate UK government
debt denominated in US$ was available. Consequently, the Merrill Lynch
swap and Eurobond syndicate desk set about designing, at that time, the
largest ever securitized asset swap.

The structure of the transaction was as follows:

1. Merrill Lynch bought US$100 million of UK FRNs.
2. The US$100 million of UK 1992 FRNs were then sold into a special-
   purpose vehicle known as Marketable Eurodollar Collateralized
   Securities Limited (MECS).
3. Simultaneously, Merrill Lynch arranged a swap with Prudential Global
   Funding Corporation (rated AAA) between MECS and the swap
   counterparty under which MECS made payments of US$ LIBID every
   three months in return for Prudential making payments equivalent to
   9.375% pa to MECS. This effectively converted the floating rate US$
   cash flow that MECS trust earned from the UK FRNs into a fixed rate
   US$ flow.
4. Merrill Lynch then arranged a Eurodollar bond issue in the name of
   MECS with a coupon of 9.375% pa and a final maturity of October
   1988. The bonds issued by MECS were collateralized with the assets of
   the trust that was a holding of US$100 million of UK FRNs and also
   the contingent liability reflecting the interest rate swap with Prudential.
   Essentially, the package constituted a high-quality (AAA) credit risk.

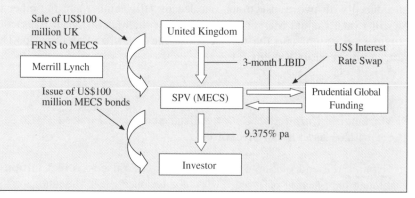

The end result of the repackaging was the creation of a conventional fixed
interest security for the investor. The investor, through the mechanism of the
securitized asset swap structure, avoided any need to either purchase the

underlying securities or enter into the derivative transaction. The structure met investor requirements in terms of:

• Credit quality.
• Interest rate and currency requirements.
• Capacity to have the security listed, rated and cleared, and settled through existing clearing systems.
• Liquidity and ability to be traded.

The basic structure described continues to be the basis of the design of all repackaging vehicles.

## 8.3 Structured Note Repackaging Vehicles

The use of the structure described gradually gained in popularity as a means for repackaging secondary markets assets.[11] An important step in the evolution of the repackaging markets was the development of a secondary market in structured notes.[12]

The impetus to secondary market trading in structured notes derived from the market distress period of 1994/1995. Prior to that, secondary market interest had been spasmodic. The activity that had occurred had been related to investors exiting structured investments with the dealer purchasing the note, engineering the reversal of the derivative component(s), and distributing the security as a higher yielding fixed or floating note security to conventional investors in asset swap products. The latter continues to be the basic mechanism for providing any required secondary market liquidity and establishing benchmark secondary market bid prices for these notes.

However, with the market conditions that prevailed in late 1994 and early 1995, the volume of structured notes that began to appear for sale increased dramatically as investors exited their investments.[13] The market conditions

---

[11] For a detailed discussion of the evolution of the market see Das, Satyajit (1994) *Swaps & Financial Derivatives*; LBC Information Services, Sydney; McGraw-Hill, Chicago at 594-598; see also Das, Satyajit *Swap Financing*; LBC Information Services, Sydney; IFR Publishing, London at 336-345.

[12] See Chapter 17.

[13] The most notable transaction during this period was the sale of the very large portfolio of structured notes held by Orange County. See Irving, Richard "County in Crisis." (March 1995) *Risk* 27-32; "Earthquake in Southern California" *International Financing Review* Issue (December 3, 1994) 1059 102; "Salomon to Clock Orange County's Work." *International Financing Review* (December 10, 1994) Issue 1060 82; "Orange County Begins Sale of Portfolio" *International Financing Review* Issue (December 17, 1994) 1061 86; "Banks Suck Up Orange Juice" *International Financing Review* Issue (December 24, 1994) 1062 60.

resulted in dealers rapidly repositioning their secondary market trading in these instruments to allow them to be repackaged. As noted above, the major buyers of the structured notes were asset-swap buyers prepared to purchase structured notes that had been asset swapped to reverse engineer the market risk component. The asset swap was used to create, typically, an FRN priced off LIBOR targeted to banks and, to a lesser extent, a fixed rate bond priced off US Treasuries targeted to the fixed income investor.

The development of the secondary market in structured notes saw the introduction of a number of structured note repackaging vehicles. These vehicles were modeled on the securitized asset swap vehicles identified above. Such vehicles include Merrill Lynch's STEERS (Structured Enhanced Return Trusts), Salomon Brothers' TIERS (Trust Investment Enhanced Return Securities), as well as similar vehicles operated by other investment banks.[14]

The central concept of these trust-based structures is their ability to create trust receipts that represent either repackaged structured notes or structured notes specifically created through repackaging that are sold to investors.[15] The trust receipts are rated by one or more of the major rating agencies and the trust receipt is tradeable to facilitate liquidity. In essence, it is the conversion of asset swaps into public and tradeable securities.

The process of utilizing a trust vehicle is set out in **Exhibit 1.5**. The diagram illustrates the creation of a trust receipt by reprofiling the risk of a structured note. The transaction entails the following steps:

- Purchase of a security in, generally, secondary markets.
- The lodgement of this security in the trust vehicle.
- The entry by the trust into a series of derivative transactions with a counterparty to engineer the required cash flow/risk profile. This can entail either reverse engineering a structured note to remove the derivative element to allow the security to be placed as a fixed income bond. Alternatively, a conventional fixed or floating rate security can be combined with the relevant derivative components to create a structured note.
- The trust then issues trust certificates or notes representing the restructured cash flows of the security (combining the security and the derivative transactions) to the investor in return for payment of the face value.
- The trust collects all cash flows (principal, interest, and derivative settlements from the relevant counterparties) and passes them through to the investor over the life of the transaction.

---

[14] For example, see Klotz, Rick, Dominguez, Nestor, Roy, Sumit, Schwartz, Mike, and Shaffran, Alan (March 30, 1995) *Trust Investment Enhanced Return Securities (TIERS$^{SM}$)*; Salomon Brothers US Derivatives Research.

[15] In non-US jurisdictions, as discussed below, a special purpose vehicle is used. The vehicle issues bonds instead of trust receipts.

The credit rating of this trust arrangement is the rating of the bond plus the derivative transactions. The typical counterparty to the derivative transaction is an AAA or AA entity. The issuer selects the credit quality of the underlying security. The resulting transaction can be, at the option of the investor, issued as a rated or unrated security.

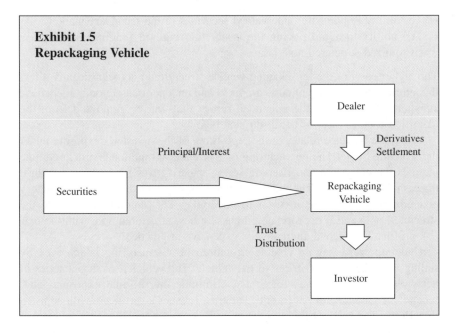

**Exhibit 1.5**
**Repackaging Vehicle**

The original purpose of these repackaging vehicles was to reengineer large volumes of structured notes that investors wanted to sell into conventional fixed income (primarily, floating or fixed rate straight bonds) for replacement with investors. However, the capacity of these structures to create structured notes as distinct from reverse engineering them into conventional securities came to be recognised. This lead to the emergence of the modern structure of repackaging vehicles that operates currently both in the primary and secondary markets.

### 8.4 Primary Market Repackaging Vehicles

The use of these special purpose repackaging vehicles in both the creation of *new* structured notes (the primary market) and in repackaging existing structured notes (the secondary market) was predicated on the advantages of the structure. The major advantages of the repackaging vehicle structures include:

- Relative value considerations.
- Restructuring risk exposure.

- Credit selection.
- Liquidity.
- Flexibility.

These structures can provide significantly higher returns to the investors. The sources of this enhanced return derives from a number of sources:

- The ability to purchase undervalued securities in the secondary market.
- The ability to avoid paying the issuer the required funding margin on a customized structured note issue.

The higher costs of the repackaging vehicle structure do not significantly affect the return as the majority of costs are fixed and on a per transaction basis may be substantially less than the enhanced return that can be generated from the identified sources (see further discussion below).

A major advantage relates to the reprofiling of the investor's exposure under the structured note. The restructuring of risk under a traditional structured note requires the entry into an offsetting series of derivatives transactions to adjust the cash flow and risks. The required transactions may be difficult for regulatory or credit reasons for the investor to undertake. The alternative is to sell the structured note and if appropriate purchase a new structured note with the *new* risk profile. The second alternative is expensive in practice.

Under the repackaging vehicle structure, the restructuring is achieved by selling back the trust certificate to the vehicle. The vehicle executes a series of derivative trades designed to, firstly, eliminate the original exposure, and, secondly, create the desired profile. The trust reissues a certificate with adjusted cash flows. The cost or benefit of the reprofiling is captured by either payment at the time of the restructuring or over the life of the transaction. The flexibility and cost economies of this flexibility are considerable.

As the repackaging vehicle enables the use of *any available security*, it allows significant expansion in credit selection processes that are no longer constrained by the issuer universe prepared to undertake the issue of the required structured note.

Secondary market liquidity should be comparable to that for traditional structured notes. In practice, secondary market liquidity is enhanced by the repackaging vehicle structure as the receipts or notes are tradeable. The underlying process of gaining liquidity is, at worst, unaltered and, at best, improved.

In overall terms, the structure significantly enhances the potential of both repackaging of structured notes by effectively allowing securitized and tradeable asset swaps and the creation of new structured notes as an alternative to new issues of such products. In fact, the repackaging vehicles currently operate in competition to the primary issuer market in these types of transactions.

# 9. Structure and Design

## 9.1 Generic Structure

The basic design of the repackaging vehicles is largely standardized. It follows the structure set out above in **Exhibit 1.5**.

The basic repackaging vehicle used is either a trust structure (favored in the US) or a single purpose special company. The vehicles are associated with but not owned by dealers or investment banks. The critical issue in this regard is to ensure that the vehicle is bankruptcy remote to the sponsoring entity (that is, the default or bankruptcy of the sponsor does not result in the default or bankruptcy of the special vehicle).

The steps in creating a structured note utilizing a repackaging vehicle take the following (fairly standardized) steps:

- The investor requirements are determined in terms of credit risk, risk profile and exposure required.
- The investment bank purchases the required collateral in the secondary market.
- The investment bank sells the collateral for value into the repackaging vehicle. The repackaging vehicle generates the liquidity needed to purchase the collateral from the issue of the structured note to the investor.
- The repackaging vehicle enters into derivative transactions with the investment bank to:
  1. Convert a structured security into a conventional fixed or floating rate bond by hedging out the derivative elements through the derivative transaction; *or*
  2. Convert a conventional security into a structured note with a defined risk profile by embedding the required exposure into the transaction through the derivative transaction. The derivative transaction is secured over the assets of the repackaging vehicle, the collateral securities.
- The repackaging vehicle issues either notes (in the case of a company) or trust receipts (in the case of a trust) to the investor in return for value (this cash is used to purchase the collateral securities and if necessary finance any payment required under the derivative contract).
- The repackaging vehicle collects the cash flows from the underlying collateral, as well as the settlements under the derivative contracts. The net cash flow is paid to the investor over the term of the transaction and at maturity. The structured note is cleared and settled through normal accepted mechanics.
- In the event of default under either the collateral securities or the derivative contract, the investor in the notes is fully exposed to the risk of loss and receives any payment received by the repackaging vehicle.

- The structured notes issued by the vehicle can, if required, be rated by a rating agency. The rating is dependent upon both the collateral and the credit risk of the derivative counterparty.

In effect, the repackaging vehicle acts as a conduit to allow the investor to access the underlying security and overlay the specific risk exposure required through the derivative contract. The repackaging vehicle funds itself through the issue of the structured notes. The risk and return profile of the structured note is attributable to the underlying collateral and the derivative contract.

Repackaging vehicles active in the market include the vehicles mentioned above, as well as other vehicles such as vehicles associated with J.P. Morgan (CRAVE — Custom Repackaged Asset Vehicle Trust) and Barclays (ALTS-Asset Linked Trust Securities).

### 9.2 Types of Vehicles

The types of vehicles used are:

- **Single purpose standalone issuers** — where a separate entity is established *for each issue* of structured notes.
- **Multiple issuance structures** — where a broad flexible structure is in place that allows the same entity to undertake different issues of structured notes.

The selection between these types of vehicles is dictated by the desire to maximize administrative flexibility and speed of execution and minimize the costs of establishing the repackaging vehicles.

Multiple issuance structures have grown in popularity. Their popularity derives from:

- The lower cost of such structures reflecting the capacity to amortize the set-up and ongoing costs over a larger volume of issues.
- The speed of execution as the structure is *permanently in place* enabling transactions to be completed in a relatively short time scale.
- The benefits of administration of fewer vehicles.
- The opportunity for individual investment banks to brand their repackaging products. The brand awareness has significant benefits in terms of achieving the status of an established issuer facilitating ready acceptance by investors.

Two types of multiple issuance vehicles are commonly used:

- Program issuers.
- Multiple issuer or "umbrella" programs.

Program issuers are designed as single legal entities that issue multiple series of structured notes. Each notes is specifically secured over the specific assets and derivatives used to create the note. This is achieved by limiting the recourse of the investor (as creditor) to specific assets and derivative transactions through a nonrecourse agreement. Each series of notes is isolated from other assets and contract held by or entered into by the issuer through this nonrecourse mechanism—often referred to as a "firewall."

**Exhibit 1.6** sets out the structure.

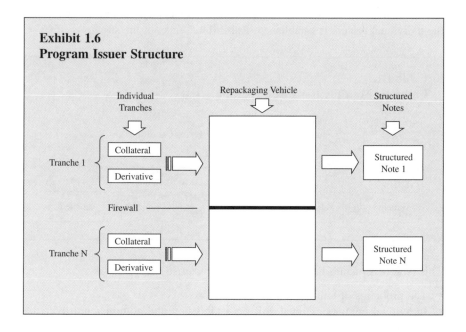

**Exhibit 1.6**
**Program Issuer Structure**

The program issuer format is especially attractive because of its low cost, lower administrative requirements, and speed and flexibility in use. However, the critical issue is in relation to the effective segregation of assets. This is important both from a legal and ratings perspective, as well as from the point of view of investors.

In the event that assets underlying one issue were in default and the required separation had not been achieved, the investors could potentially seek recourse to *all assets and contracts of the vehicle*. This phenomenon (referred to as *"tainting"*) would have far-reaching effects. The issuer itself could be in default compromising all issues, not just the one in default. This may lead to litigation against the issuer and could prevent the operation of the vehicle.

This means that the program issuance format is not used in all jurisdictions. It is only utilized in jurisdictions where an appropriate level of legal comfort with the firewalls can be established. In practice, two other provisions are generally also utilized to manage this risk:

- Program issuance structures are not utilized where the underlying assets being securitized vary significantly in terms of credit quality from one issue of structured notes to another.
- The structure incorporates substitution rights enabling assets to be removed from the structure in order to protect the rating of the vehicle.[16]

The alternative is the multiple issuers or umbrella structure where a separate vehicle is used for each issue, but a Master documentary framework governing the individual issuers is established. **Exhibit 1.7** sets out the structure:

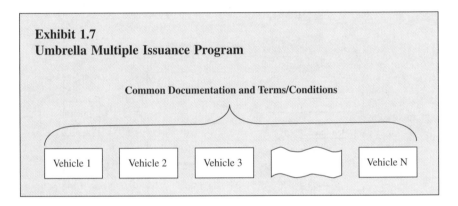

**Exhibit 1.7**
**Umbrella Multiple Issuance Program**

**Common Documentation and Terms/Conditions**

Vehicle 1    Vehicle 2    Vehicle 3              Vehicle N

This type of structure has the following characteristics:

- The problems of tainting are avoided.
- Individual companies must still be established and administered over the transaction term.
- The process is facilitated by the common master documentation with speed being increased by advance creation of a number of issuance vehicles.
- The cost is higher and the threshold size of the transaction and/or its profitability must be larger to support the higher cost.

The multiple issuer structure is generally favored where the underlying assets are of higher risk or the underlying assets are of significantly different credit risk.

The vehicles are generally based in favorable tax and regulatory environments such as Holland, The Netherlands Antilles, Jersey, or Cayman Islands. The major factors driving selection as between the jurisdictions includes:

---

[16] Following the emerging market collapse in 1997-98, this provision was used to, for example, remove Korean assets from some vehicles. This reflected the sharp deterioration in Korea's credit rating during this period.

- Tax regimes, including tax treaties in place with key investor jurisdictions.
- Legal framework, particularly in terms of contract law, segregation, and bankruptcy remoteness.
- A benign regulatory framework.
- Political stability.
- Cost factors.
- Availability of services such as legal firms, accounting firms, and management companies.
- Physical location, in terms of distance from major financial centers.
- Time zones that allow trading overlap with normal trading hours in key trading jurisdictions.

The vehicles are generally rated by the major rating agencies.[17] The rating is based on the individual issue and key factors driving ratings include:

- The credit quality of the collateral.
- The credit quality of the derivatives counterparty.
- The market risks, such as currency, interest rate risk, and term to maturity.
- The structure of the transaction including legal risks and taxation risks.

## 10. Repackaged Structured Notes

The concept of repackaged structured notes is based firmly on the asset swap/asset repackaging principles outlined above. The rationale is to deliberately create market risk exposure to selected risks and price movement using a derivative contract.

In general, there are two types of repackaged structured note transactions:

- **Reduction in market risk** (secondary market trades) — these are generally structured notes that are purchased in the secondary market from existing investors and then repackaged using derivatives to reduce or eliminate the embedded market risk exposure. The repackaged security (a high-quality fixed or floating rate bond) is then placed with a new investor (typically, a bank or institutional investor). The major objective is to provide secondary market liquidity for the original holder. The new investor can usually achieve a higher return on a relative value basis for the underlying credit (even after adjusting for the structural complexity).
- **Introduction of market risk** (primary market trades) — these are generally *new* structured notes created in response to investor specifications. The arranger purchases high-quality assets in the secondary market and enters into the required derivatives transactions to create the risk profile sought by the investor. The synthetic structured note is then placed with the investor.

---

[17] See Chapter 17.

The two structures are now an essential component of the market for structured notes. Primary market repackaging transactions now compete with traditional issuer-based structured notes. The essential rationale for these structures remains identical to that of structured notes in general. The benefits of regulatory arbitrage, risk customization, credit enhancement, and denomination arbitrage remain available to investors irrespective of the structure utilized.

## 11.  Summary

The structured note has emerged as a specific class of fixed interest security that occupies an important role in investment strategies of investors. The market structure currently encompasses two types of activities. Issues of structured notes by traditional high-quality issuers who effectively hedge their derivative exposure use the transaction as a mechanism to raise lower cost funding. Parallel to this process, the use of repackaging techniques to synthesize structured notes has emerged. These structures combine a fixed income asset (usually purchased in the secondary market) with a derivative transaction and use a special repackaging vehicle to issue the structured note to the ultimate investor. These structures allow access to markets or instruments otherwise inaccessible, create customized investment profiles, facilitate the participation of organizations whose participation would be constrained for credit reasons, as well as providing benefits in terms of accounting/tax treatment, liquidity, and administration. These factors make structured notes an important element in modern capital markets.

### Selected Bibliography

Crabbe, Leland E. and Argilagos, Joseph D. "Anatomy of the Structured Note Market." *Journal of Applied Corporate Finance* (Fall 1994): 85-98.

Cunningham, Michael M. "Selected Analysis of Recently Issued Index-Linked and Option Embedded Securities." Unpublished research paper presented to course on Swap Financing, Centre for Studies in Money, Banking and Finance, Macquarie University (1987).

Das, Satyajit. "Swaps and Financial Derivatives." LBC Information Services, Sydney; McGraw-Hill, Chicago (1994).

Das, Satyajit. "Derivative Embedded Securities — Structural Aspects" in Konishi, Atsuo and Dattatreya, Ravi E. (editors) *The Handbook of Derivative Instruments*. Probus Publications, Chicago (1996), Chapter 32: 681-693.

Klotz, Rick and Pilarinu, Efi "Understanding The Structured Note Process" Salomon Brothers US Derivative Research, Fixed Income Derivatives, New York (December 22 1994).

Koh, Kenny. "Option or Forward Swap Related Financing Structures." Unpublished research paper presented to course on Swap Financing, Centre for Studies in Money, Banking and Finance, Macquarie University, 1986.

Peng, Scott and Dattatreya, Ravi. *The Structured Note Market.* Probus Publications, Chicago, 1994.

# 2
# Callable Bonds (1): Concept, Valuation, and Applications

## 1.  Concept

A callable security can be defined as a debt security where the issuer has the right but not the obligation to repay the face value of the security at a pre-agreed value prior to the final original maturity of the security.

Callable bonds are an example of structured notes. They are among the most common and traditional of types of structured note transactions. A large universe of publicly traded, as well as privately placed transactions—covering fixed rate bonds, as well as equity linked securities such as convertibles and preference shares/preferred stocks—incorporate call provisions.

The concept has evolved over time and been extended to a variety of transactions where debt option features are embedded in securities. These variations include debt warrants, step-up/multi-step callable bonds and puttable bonds.

This chapter examines callable bonds and variations thereof as a special class of structured note transactions. The characteristics of callable bonds are first considered; the valuation of callable securities is discussed; the applications of callable bonds for both issuers and investors is then examined; and the use of options on swaps to monetize callable bonds is then analyzed. Variations on callable structures, particularly detachable debt warrants, step-up/multi-step callable bonds and puttable bonds and the market for callable securities are considered in Chapter 3.

## 2.  Callable Bonds — Characteristics

The terms and structure of a typical callable bond is set out in **Exhibit 2.1**. The example is of a bond with an original final maturity of ten years that is callable on each annual coupon date after five years; that is, the bond is *call protected* for a period of five years (often referred to as the noncall period). The call is exercisable at a premium to the face value of the bonds. The initial call premium is 3% of face value declining at the rate of 1% pa. Callable bonds where the call provision does not require payment of a premium upon repayment are also commonly utilized. The call provision in this case provides for the issuer to repay the bond in full at face value, at its sole choice, on the relevant dates.

---

**Exhibit 2.1**
**Structure of a Callable Bond Issue**

Issuer            ABC Corporation
Amount            US$100 million
Term              10 years (maturing September 15, 2012)
Coupon            8.50% pa (payable annually)
Call Provision    Callable, subject to 30 days, notice, as follows:

| Call Date | Call Price |
|-----------|------------|
| 5 years (September 15, 2007) | 103% of face value |
| 6 years (September 15, 2008) | 102% of face value |
| 7 years (September 15, 2009) | 101% of face value |
| 8 years (September 15, 2010) | 100% of face value |
| 9 years (September 15, 2011) | 100% of face value |

---

The transaction, in substance, can be characterized as the combination of a fixed interest security with an option on the price of the security. This characterization can be expressed as follows:

Callable bond = "Straight" (or noncallable) bond + Option

The option element can (utilizing put-call parity) be characterized in one of two ways:

- A call option on the price of the bond (having a maturity identical to that of the final maturity of the bond) with a strike price equal to the call price with an expiry date equal to the call dates sold by the investor to the issuer; or
- A put option on the price of the bond (having a maturity equivalent to the period *from the date on which the call is exercisable to the next call date or the final maturity of the bond*) with a strike price equivalent to the call price with an expiry date equal to the call dates sold by the investor to the issuer.

In the first case, the call option allows the issuer to repay the bond before its original scheduled maturity as of the call dates at the prescribed call prices. In the second case, the issuer would effectively issue a bond with a maturity equivalent to *the first call date* (five years in the above example) with the option, granted to the issuer by the investor, to issue additional debt with a maturity equivalent to the period between the call date and the next call date, or the final maturity of the original bond. Issues in terms of the put option would have a coupon equivalent to that on the original bond and would be issued at a price equivalent to the call price.[1]

The different forms of characterization (which impact upon the potential securitization or monetization of these embedded options through options on swaps) does not effect the fundamental economics of the option feature. In both cases, the option possesses economic value. This value derives from the fact that if interest rates decrease, then the issuer can refinance itself for the period between the call date and the original maturity of the bond at a lower effective cost than the coupon on the original bond adjusted for the call premium (if any).

Several features of the debt option embedded in the security should be noted:

- The underlying asset (the debt security) has a variable life (which will at the very least differ from that of the term of the original bond). This dictates that the value of the debt option will be a factor of the shape of the yield curve.
- The call option in the above example, in common with typical structures, has multiple exercise dates—in effect, it is a Bermudan-style option that is exercisable on specific dates prior to the final maturity of the option.
- The premium for the option sold by the investor is incorporated in the bond by way of a higher coupon (relative to a comparable noncallable transaction).

In summary, the callable bond may be characterized as a classical option "buy-write" transaction whereby the investor purchases a fixed maturity bond and sells an option on *that bond* to the issuer. The unique element of the transaction is the incorporation of the optionality into the terms of the bond itself.

## 3.   Callable Bonds — Price Behavior

The structure of the callable bond dictates its economic characteristics that can be analyzed in terms of traditional measures of fixed income securities such as price behavior, duration, and convexity. Each of these features is considered in turn.

The price behavior of a callable bond relative to an identical noncallable bond is dominated by the potential for early repayment of the callable bond where interest rates fall (the price of the bond rises). This possible shortening in the life of the callable bond means that as interest rates fall the callable bond

---

[1]   This is an application of put-call parity in relation to the underlying bond.

will begin to trade at a price lower than that of the comparable noncallable bond reflecting the possibility of early exercise. Economically, the accretion in value of the bond, resulting from the impact of discounting the bond cash flows at a lower interest rate, is offset by the increasing value of the option sold.

This characteristic dominates the trading price behavior of callable bonds. Where the interest rate structure is at a level well above that of the bond coupon (the option has low value), the bond trades below par. In this circumstance, the callable bond should in fact outperform a comparable noncallable issue reflecting the higher coupon on the callable bond. A fall in interest rates will generally cause an appreciation both in the value of the callable and corresponding noncallable bond. The increase in bond values as between the two bonds will be similar. In the case where the market interest rates are below the coupons on the bonds, the price behavior of the two securities will diverge. The callable bond will underperform its noncallable counterpart as the increasing value of the call starts to dominate price changes of the callable as the likelihood of a call increases. **Exhibits 2.2** and **2.3** set out the price characteristics of a callable and a noncallable bond.

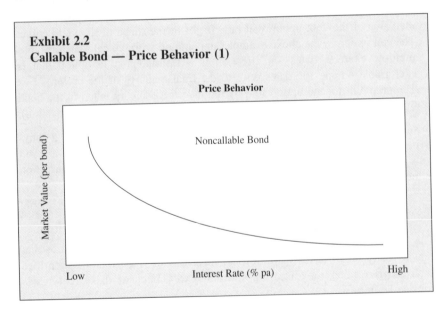

**Exhibit 2.2**
**Callable Bond — Price Behavior (1)**

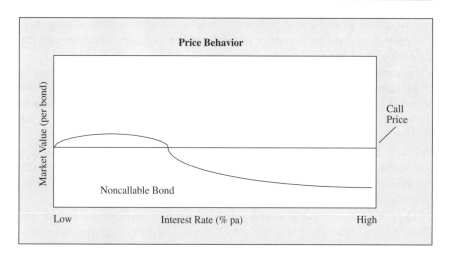

**Exhibit 2.3**
**Callable Bond — Price Behavior (2)**

The following table compares the performance of a noncallable and callable bond. The relative performance is calculated on the basis of the callable bond trading on a yield-to-worst basis. The yield curve is assumed to remain flat between years 5 and 10.

| Change in Rates (bps pa) | Price (%) of 8% pa Coupon 10-year Bullet Noncallable Bond | Price (%) of 8% pa Coupon 10-year Bullet Bond Callable After 5 Years at Par |
|---|---|---|
| −300 | 123.17 | 112.99 |
| −200 | 114.72 | 108.42 |
| −100 | 107.02 | 104.10 |
| 0 | 100.00 | 100.00 |
| +100 | 93.58 | 93.58 |
| +200 | 87.71 | 87.71 |
| +300 | 82.33 | 82.33 |

*Source:* CSFB as quoted in Stillit, Daniel. "Biting The Bullet." *Corporate Finance* (September 1988) 61-65 at 62.

Fixed income investors traditionally utilize the concept of duration to measure the life of the series of fixed cash flows embodied in a bond. Duration, in this context, serves as a means of measuring the interest rate sensitivity of a security. The concept of duration is capable of being applied to callable bonds to provide a measure of the price behavior of such securities.[2]

However, the application of duration approaches to callable securities is problematic because the measure typically can only be calculated where the bonds, cash flows are known with certainty. The uncertain maturity, which is interest rate related, in the case of a callable bond creates a number of difficulties. The central problem is that the embedded call option decreases, as observed above, the sensitivity of the price of a callable bond relative to that of a noncallable bond. Consequently, the estimation of the degree of sensitivity of the callable bond price to the embedded option is central to the determination of its duration characteristics.

The duration characteristics of a callable bond are most difficult to estimate where there is uncertainty as to the risk of exercise of the call option (effectively when the option is trading at-the-money). This reflects the fact that where the interest rates are very high (low) relative to the bond coupon, the lack of (high) probability of early repayment dictates that the callable bond exhibits duration characteristics similar to a noncallable bond (bond with a maturity coinciding with the call date).

Where the risk of exercise of the call feature is difficult to establish, a call-adjusted duration (bond duration adjusted for the impact of the call option) is utilized. This approach, in effect, uses option pricing methodology to establish the amount by which the price sensitivity of the bond is reduced by the presence of the embedded call. The duration of a callable bond is calculated as follows.[3]

- The duration of any security can be estimated utilizing the following relationship that is predicated upon the basis that it measures the price sensitivity of the security with respect to interest rates:

    $$D = -\Delta P/P \times (1 + y/2)/\Delta y$$

    Where:

    D   =   Duration
    $\Delta P$  =   Change in price of the bond for a small change in interest rates
    P   =   Current price of the bond
    y   =   Current bond equivalent interest rate

---

[2]   For a discussion on duration see Chapter 16. For a discussion on duration of a callable bond see Latainer, Gary D. and Jacob, David P. (October 1985) "Modern Techniques for Analyzing Value and Performance of Callable Bonds"; Morgan Stanley Fixed Income Analytical Research, New York at 7-10.

[3]   See Latainer, Gary D. and Jacob, David P. (October 1985) "Modern Techniques for Analyzing Value and Performance of Callable Bonds"; Morgan Stanley Fixed Income Analytical Research, New York at 8.

- In the case of a callable bond, this formula is utilized with the following input adjustments:

  y  =  Bond equivalent yield on underlying *noncallable* bond
  P  =  Price of the callable bond using an option pricing model
- The duration of a callable bond will, utilizing this approach, typically need to be solved numerically reflecting the absence of a closed form solution to the problem of pricing debt options.

Using this approach, consider the call-adjusted duration of the following security:

| | |
|---|---|
| Maturity | 27 years |
| Coupon | 12% pa |
| Call Provision | After 2 years at 109.60 |

Where the yield on the underlying bond is 11% pa and assuming an annualized yield volatility of 12%, the call-adjusted duration is approximately 6.6 years. If the yield falls to 9% pa, then the callable bond's duration falls to 4.4 years. This contrasts with a duration of a noncallable bond with the above characteristics of around nine years and a duration of a bond with a maturity equal to the call date of around 1.8 years.[4]

The duration behavior of a callable bond utilizing this concept of call-adjusted duration can be summarized as follows:

- The duration of a callable bond is most affected by the call feature where the call option has a high value as it reduces the price appreciation of a callable bond relative to a comparable noncallable bond.
- For bonds generally duration falls (increases) as interest rates increase (decrease). However, in the case of callable bonds, the sold call option has the effect of *decreasing* duration as rates fall reflecting the likelihood of early repayment (effectively, the reduction in the number of cash flows that will only extend to the call date).
- The more dominant the call value, the more likely it is that a callable bond's duration falls (increases) as rates decrease (increase). However, for a given change in rates, the duration change for a callable bond will in general terms be lower than that for an equivalent noncallable bond.
- The duration of a callable bond is sensitive to the passage of time. As the call protection period diminishes, the uncertainty regarding the remaining cash flows of the bond increases. The value of the call feature increases and impacts on duration to a greater degree.

---

[4] See Latainer, Gary D. and Jacob, David P. (October 1985) "Modern Techniques for Analyzing Value and Performance of Callable Bonds"; Morgan Stanley Fixed Income Analytical Research, New York at 7, 8.

An additional measure of the price risk of a fixed interest security is convexity—in effect, the price sensitivity of a bond for a given change in yields. Bonds generally have positive convexity characteristics reflecting the fact that a fall in yields will result in an increasing level of price appreciation. However, callable bonds, under defined circumstances, are characterized by negative convexity. This is a restatement of a callable bond's unfavorable duration behavior. This characteristic is most marked in long remaining term to maturity securities with little remaining call protection. These bonds are characterized by high negative convexity reflecting the uncertainty associated with these bonds' cash flows.

## 4.   Valuation of Callable Bonds

The valuation of callable securities is predicated on the decomposition of the security into its components:

Price of a callable bond = Price of comparable noncallable bond + Price of the call option

Utilizing this approach, the callable bond value is calculated as the combination of a purchase of or long position in a noncallable bond and a sold or short position in a call option where the purchaser has granted this option to the issuer. The premium receipt for the sale of the option is embedded in the higher yield of the callable bond.

This relationship can be used to derive the value placed on the embedded call. For example, given the price of comparable callable and noncallable bonds, the difference in value should equate, in an arbitrage-free world, to the price of the call option.

An important point to note regarding the valuation of the debt option component of a callable bond is that it is essentially an option on the *forward* price of the underlying bond *as at the call date*. Consequently, the value of the bond is driven by the changes in forward interest rates.

The fair value of the call option component can be valued utilizing conventional option pricing techniques. The factors impacting on the value of the option are consistent with those affecting other options. However, the specific characteristics of these debt options mean that a number of other factors are particularly relevant to their valuation:

- The payout on the asset (effectively, the bond coupon) must be adjusted for in one of two possible ways:
  1. The coupon is treated as a continuous return on the asset and used to adjust the carry cost or risk-free discount rate.
  2. The present value of the coupon is deducted from the value of the bond, which is then treated purely as a zero-coupon bond.

  – The structure of the underlying bond and the optionality embedded on
   that security dictate that the option value is a function of:
1. A term structure of interest rates, which consistent with the declining
   remaining life of the bond, dictates the accretion in the value of the bond
   that determines in turn the value of the debt option.
2. A term structure of volatility that is related to the declining maturity
   profile of the underlying asset that as the bond becomes shorter, the
   effective volatility, will decline towards zero.

The above issues are present in the pricing of debt options generally. A more
detailed discussion of the problems associated with the valuation of debt options
is set out in **Appendix A** to this text.[5]

In practice, a common means of determining the value of the embedded call
option is to establish the range of values that the bond underlying the option can
assume at maturity. Once the distribution is determined, the expected value of
the option at expiration or, in the case of a callable bond that has an inherent
series of mutually exclusive exercise dates reflecting its Bermudan
characteristic,[6] can be established and discounted back to the time of valuation.

The key issues in this valuation approach[7] are:

• The treatment of uncertain interest rates inclusive of term structure changes
  in determining the potential distribution of bond values.
• The incorporation of particular distributional assumptions in the pricing
  approach. Classical option pricing models assume a distribution of the changes
  in the underlying asset prices at maturity that is log normal. Given that bond
  prices are determined by complex movements in interest rates, the bond prices
  that would arise from the distribution of interest rates is unlikely to be log
  normal even if changes in the interest rates were log normal in distribution.
• Pricing consistency within the model must be maintained. The distribution of
  future bond prices based on an assumed interest rate process must ensure that
  the overall interest rate structure is consistent; for example, the distribution
  does not generate *negative* forward interest rates. Similarly, the model must be
  constrained to ensure that logical valuation relationships are maintained. For
  example, working within a yield curve of returns, the failure of put-call parity
  is possible leading to a fundamental inconsistency within the pricing logic.

---

[5]  See Kish, Richard J. and Livingston, Miles, "Estimating the Value of Call Options
   on Corporate Bonds" (1993) (Fall) 6 (no. 3) *Journal of Applied Corporate Finance*
   91-94.

[6]  A Bermudan option is one that is capable of being exercised at the option of the
   purchaser on a number of specified dates prior to the expiry of the option.

[7]  See Bookstaber, Richard, Hanley, William C., and Noris, Peter D. (December 1994)
   "Are Options on Debt Issues Undervalued?"; Morgan Stanley Fixed Income
   Analytical Research, New York at 4-16, 32.

An additional factor that influences the value of callable bonds is the possibility of early exercise of the call option. In the case of some bonds, exercise is only feasible on the specified call date. However, where exercise is feasible at any time before the expiration of the call option (the Bermudan structure incorporates this feature in part as the call is exercisable on specific dates before maturity), the risk of early exercise is relevant to the value of the option.

The key determinants of early exercise are:

- The tendency of the bond price volatility to decline as the life of the underlying bond declines (reflecting the tendency of the bond price towards par at maturity).
- The ability to lower the interest rate on the borrowing from the rate equivalent to the bond coupon upon exercise.

The latter aspect can be seen from the following example. Assume a bond with a coupon of 10% pa that is currently callable at any time but has a further five years to final maturity. Where interest rates fall to, say, 8% pa, early exercise would generate value equal to the 2% pa difference between the bond coupon and the current interest rate establishing a value of early exercise equal to the present value of these savings. For a callable bond, a sharp decrease in interest rates will generally favor early exercise as the intrinsic value of the option begins to dominate the remaining time value of the option.

# 5.    Applications of Callable Bonds

The utilization of callable bonds by both issuers and investors is based on the performance characteristics and value dynamics of these types of instruments. The applications of callable bonds can be classified into two distinct categories:

- Inclusion of callable securities in liability and asset portfolios as, primarily, a means of managing interest rate risk in these portfolios.
- Monetization of the value of the embedded call option through the innovative use of options on swaps structures.

In this section, the first class of application (which can be regarded as the traditional use of callable bonds) is examined. In the following section, the second class of application is analyzed.

## 5.1   Issuer Applications[8]

The incorporation of call provisions in a fixed interest bond provides, basically, the issuer with the valuable option to retire the debt and refinance the borrowing

---

[8]    See Kraus, Alan "An Analysis of Call Provisions and the Corporate Refunding Decision" (Spring 1983) *Midland Journal of Corporate Finance* vol. 1 no. 1 46-60.

at lower interest rates. The refunding would have the impact of reducing the interest cost of the issuer.

There are in essence two separate questions regarding the inclusion of a call option in a bond: firstly, the rationale for the issuer including a call option within the bond issue; and, secondly, the optimal refunding strategy for callable bonds.

Financial economists have questioned the advantage of incorporating a call feature. Financial economists argue that given a fair value of the call any *expected* gains to the issuer from refinancing the bond at a lower interest rate represents a corresponding loss to the investor. The higher return demanded by the investor in a callable bond relative to equivalent noncallable securities should offset any expected gain from the potential exercise of the call. The same argument can be restated as: if the call option is fairly valued then the incorporation of the call feature will offer advantages to the issuer that will be *exactly offset* by the premium charged.

An additional element to this argument is that the yield curve, including the implied forward interest rates, already embodies market expectations about future interest rates that should reduce the advantage conferred by incorporation of the call feature.

Against this background the incorporation of a call provision can only be justified economically on the basis of the superior knowledge or forecasting ability of the issuer in respect of future interest rates. This argument is unsustainable on the following basis:

• There is no compelling basis for accepting that issuers can systematically outperform investors in predicting the path of future interest rates.
• Even if the issuer did possess such superior knowledge then over time investors would interpret the incorporation of call features as signalling issuer expectations that rates were likely to fall below current expected and implied levels. The investors would increase the premium for the call option to levels that would negate any economic benefit of the call provision.

Consequently, it is difficult to attribute the incorporation of call features in bond issues *solely* to the interest rate expectations of the issuer.

Financial economists have identified at least three different possible reasons for issuers to issue callable bonds:[9]

• To enable the issuer to prepay debt to eliminate any restriction on the activities of the firm.
• To provide possible tax advantages.
• To reduce interest rate sensitivity of a bond's value to changes in interest rates to manage the equity value of the firm.

---

[9] See Kraus, Alan "An Analysis of Call Provisions and the Corporate Refunding Decision" (Spring 1983) *Midland Journal of Corporate Finance* vol. 1 no. 1 46-60.

The call provision allows the issuer to retire debt where the terms and conditions (particularly, the covenants associated with the issue) are restrictive to the company. Bondholders, in general terms, impose covenants on issuers imposing restrictions on the operating flexibility of the issuer.

These restrictions may cover maintenance provisions (requiring compliance with financial ratios such as leverage restrictions, fixed charge coverage, minimum capital levels, and so on), as well as negative provisions (preventing the issuer from undertaking certain investments, sale of business, corporate restructures, and so on). The inclusion of these covenants is usual to protect bondholders who are typically not otherwise, in the absence of ownership rights or representation, able to control the activities of the issuer. The nature of the restrictions is related to the credit standing of the issuer with issuers with lower credit standing being required to place more onerous restrictions on its activities. The provision of covenants facilitates both issuer access to capital, as well as effecting a reduction in the issuer's cost of debt funds.

Under certain circumstances, these restrictions may be of a magnitude that the cost to the issuer in terms of forgone business opportunities is greater than the savings on debt cost that are achieved through the provision of the covenants. The callable structure in these situations would provide an upper limit on the retirement cost of the bonds. It does not place the issuer in a position of having to seek to repurchase its bonds, which is of necessity purely voluntary for the investor as an alternative means of repaying the debt.

This flexibility to utilize the call to undertake otherwise restricted activities may provide a rationale for the incorporation of call features in funding transactions. In essence, the call, for the cost of the call premium, allows the issuer to preserve it's operating flexibility.

The call provision may also benefit issuers where there is a tax rate asymmetry whereby the marginal tax rate of the issuer is *higher* than that of the investor. This reflects the fact that the higher interest cost is deductible to the issuer at a higher rate than it is taxable in the hands of the investor thereby enhancing the present value of the debt tax shield for the company.

The call feature also may act as a mechanism to protect issuers from exposure to interest rate risk. The call provision decreases the interest rate sensitivity of a bond to movements in interest rates. Changes in bond prices equate to the risk for the investor. There is a relationship between changes in interest rates and economic activity and therefore the operating cash flows of a company. Changes in bond prices translate into changes in the market value leverage of the firm and the relative risk of the equity securities of a company. The incorporation of a call feature under these circumstances through a reduction in the sensitivity of bond prices benefits equity investors by lowering the risk to these capital providers that may in turn lower the company's required return on equity capital.

As is evident from the above discussion, the case for inclusion of call provisions in a bond issue is complex.

Where a bond is callable, the issuer must determine the optimal refinancing strategy that maximizes the value of the embedded option. As noted above, the key issue in this regard is the problem of early exercise that eliminates the remaining time value of the option.

The optimal refunding strategy has been the subject of considerable debate.[10] The basic strategy for calling a bond can be summarized as follows:[11]

- If there are no new issue costs associated with the refinancing issue, then the bond should be called if it trades above its call price.
- If new issue expenses are present and are significant, then the call should be exercised where interest rates decline sufficiently such that the bond has traded above the call price and then returned to the call price.

This optimal call strategy is dictated by the fact that the benefit to shareholders from calling the bond is a function of the repurchase of the coupon and principal at less than its market value and the difference is greater than the refinancing costs. This is reflected in the actual trading behavior of callable bonds that trade close to the call price when the market anticipates that the security will be repaid. Callable bonds often trade at a level above the call price even where the interest rates have fallen below the bond coupon reflecting investor consideration of issue expenses that will defer refunding.

The determination of the optimal refunding policy requires the issuer to estimate the critical interest rate at which exercise of the call is optimal. Alternatively, the issuer can rely solely on market pricing of the callable bonds or for any given level of interest rates compare the cash flow savings in present value terms against the cost of refunding. The latter strategy is not an optimal approach although, in practice, it is easier to implement.

## 5.2 Investor Applications

Investor applications of callable bonds focus upon two categories of applications:

---

[10] See Kraus, Alan "An Analysis of Call Provisions and the Corporate Refunding Decision" (Spring 1983) *Midland Journal of Corporate Finance* vol. 1 no. 1 46-60; Finnerty, John D. (1984*) An Illustrated Guide to Bond Refunding Analysis*; The Financial Analysts Research Foundation, Charlotteville, Virginia; Finnerty, John D., Kalotay, Andrew J., and Farrell Jnr, Francis X. (1988) *The Financial Manager's Guide to Evaluating Bond Refunding Opportunities*; Ballinger Publishing Company, Cambridge Massachusetts.

[11] See Kraus, Alan "An Analysis of Call Provisions and the Corporate Refunding Decision." (Spring 1983) *Midland Journal of Corporate Finance* vol. 1 no. 1 46-60.

- Yield enhancement.
- Asset liability matching.

The utilization of callable bonds to achieve yield enhancement is based on the capture of premium from the sale of the call option. The intrinsic strategy is that of covered call writing—the underlying security in this instance being the fixed interest bond in which the option is embedded with the issuer purchasing the bond from the investor as part of the sale of the security. Consistent with the strategy the investor trades off the potential appreciation of the bond above the call price against the premium received, which is inherent in the higher yield to maturity of the callable instrument.

The strategy of using callable bonds for portfolio return enhancement can be operated on a number of levels of varying degrees of analytical sophistication:

- **Naive strategies** — investing in callable securities and using the yield to call as the relevant return metric to generate higher nominal returns either relative to a benchmark or in absolute terms.
- **Structured risk return strategies** — entailing the use of covered call writes to generate premium income within specified risk reward criteria.
- **Value based strategies** — designed to value callable securities in terms of the underlying components and seek to sell expensive securities and purchase cheaper securities (based on the component values) arbitraging between the universe of comparable callable and noncallable securities.

The asset liability matching application of callable bonds is more complex. Traditionally, asset liability managers seek to match the relevant portfolios in terms of a nominated measure of interest rate risk. This measure is, typically, duration. This practice, referred to as portfolio immunization, is commonly utilized by a wide variety of portfolio managers including asset liability managers in financial institutions (responsible for the management of the overall interest rate risk of the institution's balance sheet), insurance company asset managers (seeking to match the interest rate characteristics of investment products that have cash flow characteristics which are defined and dependent on interest rates) and asset managers (seeking to manage fixed income portfolios within defined interest rate risk frameworks).[12]

The process of asset liability matching, to be practiced efficiently, requires matching of *not only duration but also convexity*. The major role of callable

---

[12] For a discussion of asset liability based applications of callable bonds see Latainer, Gary D. and Jacob, David P. (October 1985) *Modern Techniques For Analysing Value and Performance of Callable Bonds*; Morgan Stanley Fixed Income Analytical Research, New York at 20-23; Bookstaber, Richard, Hanley, William C., and Noris, Peter D. (December 1984) *Are Options on Debt Issues Undervalued?*; Morgan Stanley Fixed Income Analytical Research, New York at 17-24

bonds in the context of such an immunized portfolio structure is in assisting in achieving this convexity match.[13]

The duration and negative convexity feature of callable bonds is characterized by an underperformance in bond price performance in a falling rate environment. This can act as a hedge against the rest of the fixed interest portfolio. This second order portfolio matching—effectively selecting portfolio assets where the duration is not only matched but where duration changes with interest rate changes in a manner consistent with the corresponding changes in liability duration—should result in greater efficiency in portfolio management.

The utility of callable bonds in portfolio composition to achieve a nominated asset liability management target is further enhanced where the inclusion of callable bonds based on value analysis allows the desired portfolio to be created on a more cost-effective basis. This allows portfolio managers to increase returns on existing security holdings by selling or purchasing callable versus noncallable bonds based on the component analysis techniques previously identified. The increased universe of securities will tend on the whole to increase the capability to add value to the portfolio over time even where the callable bonds are not significantly cheaper than equivalent noncallable.

# 6. Monetization of Options Embedded in Callable Bonds

The traditional applications of callable securities have been increasingly supplanted by the issue of callable bonds where the issuer monetizes the embedded call option with the objective of using the value captured from the on sale of the option to lower its borrowing cost.

In this section, this particular type of transaction is considered. The potential use of options on swaps in combination with callable bonds is first examined. The role of these transactions in capital market arbitrage is then considered. The final section looks at utilizing value differences between the various participants concerning the value of the embedded options that can be used by investors to synthetically create callable securities. A brief overview of options on swaps[14] and their valuation are set out in **Appendix B** and **C** to this chapter.

## 6.1 Utilizing Options on Swaps with Callable Bonds

Options on swaps have been utilized with callable bond structures, primarily, in two situations:

---

[13] This characteristic is comparable to the price performance and characteristics of mortgage-backed securities and index-amortizing structures.

[14] Options on swaps are referred to as swaptions. The terms are used interchangeably in the text.

- To monetize the implicit call options on the underlying debt security (liability applications).[15]
- In conjunction with asset swaps where the underlying fixed rate security has an uncertain life as a result of call options embedded in the original issue terms (asset applications).

### *6.1.1  Liability Applications*

The first type of transaction represents attempts to securitize the value of options embedded in debt securities. An example of a transaction involving a puttable swap[16] is set out in **Exhibit 2.4**.

---

**Exhibit 2.4**
**Utilizing Swaps to Monetize the Embedded Option in Callable Bonds (1)**

*Terms of Bond*

| | |
|---|---|
| Issue Date | November 15, 2001 |
| Maturity | November 15, 2008 |
| Coupon | 10.00% pa |
| Call Provisions | At par on November 15, 2006 and November 15, 2007 |
| Issue Price | 100 |

*Terms of Puttable Swap*

| | |
|---|---|
| Maturity | November 15, 2008 |
| Fixed Rate | 10.00% pa |
| Floating Rate | LIBOR minus 25 bps |
| Put Provisions | At par on November 15, 2006 and November 15, 2007 |
| Swap Premium | 1.25% pa flat |

The combined transaction results in the following cash flows for years 1 to 5 (and years 6 and 7 if the bond is not called) of the transaction:

---

[15] For example see Buchmiller, Jack, "Stripping Options from Callable Debt" (1993) (February) *Corporate Finance*, Euromoney Publications 11-13.

[16] A puttable swap is a combination of an interest rate swap (where the counterparty pays fixed rate and receives floating rate) and the purchase of a receiver option on an interest rate swap (where the counterparty has the right to receive fixed rates (equal to the fixed rate on the original swap) and pay floating rate). Exercise of the receiver swaption has the effect of cancelling the original swap.

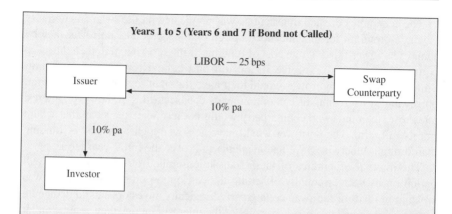

The all-in cost of funds to the borrower, after the proceeds of the up-front premium are factored in, is LIBOR minus 51bps (assuming a discount rate of 10.25% pa).

If the swap is canceled under the put on the swap, the borrower calls the underlying bond, which means it achieves lower cost funding but for a shorter period:

Six Years:          LIBOR minus 54bps
Five Years:         LIBOR minus 58bps[17]

The basic structure entails a borrower issuing, say, 5-, 7- or 10-year debt securities that are noncallable for three or five years. After the expiry of the call protection period, the borrower could redeem the issue usually at par or with the payment of a premium. The borrowers, in these cases, utilised these fixed rate issues as a basis for creating a synthetic floating rate borrowing. Consequently, the borrower would inevitably enter into a simultaneous swap wherein it received fixed rates and paid floating rates. The interest rate swaps, however, had an additional feature whereby the swap counterparty, paying fixed rates, had the right to terminate the swap at a future date, coinciding with the call date of the underlying bond. For example, in the situation described above, the 7-year issue might be swapped with the counterparty who agreed to pay fixed rates for seven years and receive floating rate but with the added right to cancel the swap after five or six years.

---

[17] In order to ensure that the full amount of the premium is received the typical structure of the swap would be for the issuer to pay LIBOR minus 58 bps for the first five years and LIBOR minus 25 bps for the last two years. In effect, the premium for the option on swap is amortized in full over the noncall period of the bond and swap.

The economics of such transactions was predicated on the swap counterparty paying a premium for the embedded option on the swap. The borrower thereby achieved a lower floating rate cost of funding. If interest rates fell, then the swap counterparty would exercise its option and cancel the swap agreement. Simultaneously, the borrower would then have the right to terminate the overall borrowing by exercising its call option on its debt securities. If, however, interest rates rose, then the swap counterparty would not terminate the swap that would run its full term. The borrower would have achieved a cheaper cost of funding than it might otherwise have had available to it over the full 7-year term.

The internal economics of these transactions relied on the borrower's call option on its debt essentially offsetting the call option on the swap that it was creating in favor of the swap counterparty. Logically, investors should demand a higher yield on callable bonds because of the interest rate risk they assume and it would be expected that this increase in yield would offset any premium received from the swap counterparty for the cancellation rights. However, as discussed in greater detail below, the fact was that the amount investors charged, by way of higher yields on the securities, for providing the borrower with a call option was substantially below what the swap counterparties were willing to pay for the right to cancel the swap. Consequently, the opportunity existed to securitize the call option on the debt securities via the puttable swap to effectively allow the borrower to achieve a lower all-in cost of funding (see discussion on relative option values above).

The counterparties for these swaps were borrowers seeking to hedge interest rate risk but also seeking some capacity to benefit from a favorable rate movement. However, some counterparties entered into such puttable swaps merely to buy the underlying call option on interest rates implicit in the puttable swap.

For example, in November 1987, Salomon Brothers, in a difficult market, brought approximately US$1.85 billion of fixed-rate debt involving puttable swaps to market. While the rationale for these transactions was not made public, observers speculated that the transactions were driven by an internal need by Salomon Brothers to purchase call options on US Treasuries. Under one theory, the US investment bank was using the options to hedge positions in its proprietary option book whereby it had previously sold treasury bond options or interest rate options positions. Under an alternative theory, Salomon Brothers was using the puttable swaps to hedge prepayment of mortgage-backed securities, either in its own portfolio, or a portfolio that it had sold to a client.

### 6.1.2  Asset Swaps Involving Callable Bonds

Options on swaps have also been utilized in asset swapped transactions where the underlying asset is a callable bond. The puttable swap allows investors to enter into transactions whereby a fixed-rate bond, which is callable, is swapped into a floating rate basis. If the bond is called, then the investor can terminate the original swap by cancelling or putting the swap to the provider of the puttable swap option. This allows the investor to terminate the swap at the time the underlying fixed rate security is called away.[18]

Such asset-based puttable swap transactions were extremely important in the development of this particular type of swap structure. Asset swaps where synthetic floating rate assets at attractive spreads relative to LIBOR are created have been an important component of the growth of the swap market. However, there has been a limited universe of noncallable fixed-rate bonds. As a result many of the bonds used in asset-based swaps have embedded call options.

When interest rates fall sharply, the assets are called away with investors being left with interest rate swap positions with high fixed coupons. In the lower interest rate environment, similar quality, high-yielding replacement assets are not available and the swaps are expensive to reverse, creating losses for investors. Puttable swaps are structured as a means of mitigating these losses resulting from early redemption in asset swap transactions.

In addition, this type of structure can be utilized to swap assets that have uncertain lives. This can be particularly important in structuring asset swaps against mortgage and receivable backed securities.

An example of an asset-based puttable swap is set out in **Exhibit 2.5**.

---

**Exhibit 2.5**
**Utilizing Options on Swaps to Asset Swap Callable Bonds**

Assume the following bond is available in the secondary market:

*Terms of Bond*

| | |
|---|---|
| Issue Date | July 1, 2006 |
| Maturity | July 1, 2016 (10 years) |
| Coupon | 7.00% pa annual |
| Call Provisions | Callable at the option of the issuer commencing July 1, 2011 (five years) and annually thereafter on each coupon date. |
| | Initially callable at a price of 101 decreasing by 0.50 each year and thereby callable at par as at July 1, 2013 and each coupon date thereafter. |
| Bond Price | Issued at par |

---

[18] See Stavis, Robert M. and Haghani, Victor J. (1987) "Puttable Swaps Tools for Managing Callable Assets;" Salomon Brothers Inc., New York.

An investor purchases the bond and enters into the following swap to convert the fixed rate returns from the bond into floating rate payments priced off LIBOR. To effect this, the investor transacts the following swap:

### Terms of Swap

| | |
|---|---|
| Final Maturity | July 1, 2016 |
| Fixed Coupon | Investor pays 7.00% pa annual matching the bond coupon. |
| Floating Coupon | Investor receives LIBOR + 48 bps |
| Swap Termination | The investor has the right to terminate the swap commencing July 1, 2011 and each anniversary of the swap. As at each termination date, the investor pays the following fee to the swap counterparty: |

| Date | Fee (%) |
|---|---|
| July 1, 2011 | 1.00 |
| July 1, 2012 | 0.50 |
| July 1, 2013 to final maturity | 0.00 |

The swap essentially combines a conventional interest rate swap where the investor pays fixed rate and receives floating rate with a receiver option on a swap purchased by the investor to receive fixed rates (at 7.00% pa) and pay floating (at LIBOR plus 48 bps). The swaption is a Bermudan-style exercise[19] whereby the investor can exercise the option on any July 1, commencing at July 1, 2011 (triggering a 5-year interest rate swap) and July 1, 2015 (triggering a 1- year interest rate swap).

There are no initial cash flows under this swap. The only initial cash flow is the investment by the investor in the underlying bonds.

The investor's cash flow on each interest payment date will be as follows:

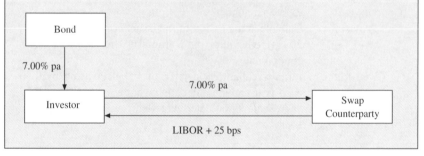

---

[19] A Bermudan option is a hybrid option, somewhat between an European and American option, allowing the purchaser to exercise the option on one or more pre-agreed days prior to maturity.

If the bond is called, the investor is paid 101.00% by the issuer (assumes call on July 1, 2011), but passes 1.00% to the swap counterparty for the right to trigger the swaption effectively and cancel the original 10-year interest rate swap. This effectively gives the investor back its initial investment of 100.

The pricing of the overall transaction will incorporate several elements:

- The interest rate swap rate as of the date of entry
- The pricing of the swaption purchased by the investor
- The call premium that may be received in the event of exercise of the swaption. In effect, this can be treated as an adjustment to the effective strike rate on the swaption.

If the bond was not purchased in the primary market and was trading at a premium or discount the initial cash payment of receipt may also be incorporated in the swap pricing.[20]

## 6.2   Capital Market Valuation of Debt Options

Central to the use of options on swaps for monetizing the embedded call options within bond issues is the relative valuation of options in the fixed interest and swap markets. Transactions entailing the securitization of embedded options in debt instruments rely on the capacity to securitize relatively lower priced options implicit within fixed interest instruments that are then sold, through the means of the option on the swap, at a higher price in a different market segment. This apparent anomalous pricing of such options and the sources of relative value of such transactions merits comment.

---

[20] For a discussion of the structuring of off-par interest rate swaps associated with asset swaps, see Das, Satyajit (1994) *Swaps and Financial Derivatives*; LBC Information Services, Sydney; McGraw-Hill, Chicago at Chapter 18.

Existence of this discrepancy of pricing suggests that implied volatility in the fixed interest market for corporate securities is lower than that in the swap market itself. Research on fixed interest markets indicates that the implied volatility of fixed interest markets, particularly corporate securities, may be lower than historical realized volatility for a number of reasons:[21]

- Investors focus on security yields rather than on their total return thereby systematically undervaluing the call option implicit in a callable bond.
- Investors often evaluate securities on the basis of their yield to worst or cash flow yield, implicitly assuming that interest rate volatility is zero.
- Investors have a different information set regarding the probability of corporate bond calls than that which is incorporated in the market model that provides an estimate of an option's value from the investor's point of view by assuming that any call will be exercised with perfect economic efficiency. This additional information about individual issuer's behaviour may reduce the value of the option being reflected in the lower implied volatility.

Research on yield curve relationships between the swap and corporate market, primarily undertaken in the US$ swap market, tends to indicate that swap spreads track A or AA corporate spreads, although the relationship is not exact.[22]

The difference in implied volatility between the corporate bond market and the swap market may be explainable, at least in certain circumstances, by the shape of the yield curve and the implied forward rate structure in the swap curve relative to the corporate bond market curve. For example, if the 3-year swap rate seven years forward is lower than the corresponding forward corporate rate, then the swap option will, utilizing option theory, be worth more than the embedded call, even if their implied volatility is equal.

Anecdotal evidence, during various periods in which swap market activity focused on options on swaps, indicates that such activity coincides with differences in the shape of the swap yield curve relative to the corporate bond yield curve. For example, in various periods, the swap curve was inverted while the corporate bond curve was not inverted. This implies that when forward rates are lower in the swap market (generally, when the swap curve is inverted relative to the corporate curve), options to receive fixed in the swap market will be worth more than call options in the corporate market. Conversely, when

---

[21]  William M. Boyce, Webster Hughes, Peter S. A. Niculescu, and Michael Waldman, (January 1988) "The Implied Volatility of Fixed-Income Markets"; Salomon Bros Inc. Research Department, New York.

[22]  See Das, Satyajit (1994) *Swaps and Financial Derivatives*; LBC Information Services, Sydney; McGraw-Hill, Chicago at Chapter 23; see also Evans, Ellen and Parente, Gioia M. (September 1987) "What Drives Interest Rate Spreads"; Salomon Brothers Inc. Bond Market Research, New York.

forward rates are higher in the swap market, options to pay fixed in the swap market will be worth more than put options in the corporate market. This discrepancy between the shape of the swap and corporate bond yield curves facilitates the type of capital market arbitrage described.

The second factor relates to an embedded quality spread differential within the corporate market. The swap market typically operates on the following pattern:

- Low-quality issuers issue floating rate debt and swap into fixed-rate debt utilizing an interest rate swap.
- High-quality issuers issue fixed-rate debt that is then swapped through an interest rate swap into floating-rate debt.

This pattern implies that, for the investor, the swap market is an attractive source of high-quality fixed-rate assets through the purchase of highly rated floating rate assets that can then be swapped into fixed rate. Conversely, it is an attractive source of low-quality floating rate assets created primarily through asset swaps entailing purchase of lower quality fixed-rate bonds that are then swapped into floating rate bases. Given that synthetic callable and puttable securities can be created through the combination of 1ctf11 physical noncallable or nonputtable securities combined with options on swaps (described in detail below), the synthetic component (that is, the part that relies on the underlying swap) that can be created will, by definition, be as follows:

- Where the synthetic component is floating rate, the asset is more likely to be attractive when the underlying corporate security is low quality.
- When the synthetic part is fixed rate, the asset is likely to be attractive when the underlying corporate security is high quality. This embedded quality spread differential again implies underpricing of volatility in the corporate bond market, particularly for issuers of high quality.[23]

Additional factors that may dictate the differences in relative value include yield curve differences between the swap and corporate market, and relative value of synthetic securities created utilizing options on swaps embeds a quality spread differential *within the corporate market*.

For example, in the case of monetizing the embedded call option described in **Exhibit 2.4**, the issuer through the transaction assumes an implicit maturity uncertainty. The funding in that case was for between five and seven years depending on the future path on interest rates. Implicit in that funding uncertainty is a credit *spread* position for the issuer. The current transaction is undertaken at a certain rate against an underlying benchmark (LIBOR).

---

[23] See Johnson, Cal (July 1989) "Options on Interest Rate Swaps: New Tools for Asset and Liability Management"; Salomon Brothers, New York at 5-6.

However, the forward spread implied for the issuer based on the implied forwards in the bond rate curve and the swap curve indicates a widening in the spread. In monetizing the call, in the event the call is exercised, the issuer will benefit from the on sale of the call only to the extent that its funding spread does not increase beyond that implied in the current yield curve structure.

### 6.3 Asset Management — The Creation of Synthetic Callable Bonds

In an interesting example of reverse financial engineering, the development of a substantial and liquid market in options on swaps has allowed both investors and borrowers to synthetically create callable/puttable structures consistent with their own interest rate expectations and portfolio requirements. In particular, disparities in pricing as observed above, between the fixed interest and swap markets, has allowed the creation of these synthetic callable and puttable structures at values superior to those obtainable directly from the fixed interest market.

Asset managers can create synthetic callable or puttable bonds by using a number of alternative combinations of physical securities and options on swaps.

For example, an asset manager can create a synthetic callable bond investment in at least three ways:

- Purchase a long-term straight bond and sell a receiver option on a swap.
- Purchase a floating rate note, enter into a swap under which it receives fixed/pays floating and sells an option to cancel the swap.
- Purchase a short-term bond and sell a payer option on a swap.

**Exhibit 2.6** details creating a synthetic callable bond utilizing each of these methods.

---

**Exhibit 26**
**Creation of Synthetic Callable Bonds Utilizing Options on Swaps**

Assume Investor A (A) wishes to create a synthetic callable bond to match its portfolio requirements.

Assume the following market conditions exist:

- 5-year AA corporate bonds with a one-time par call at three years are trading at 7.60% pa.
- 5-year AA corporate noncallable bonds are trading at 7.50% pa.
- An option on a 2-year swap to receive 7.50% pa against payments of US$ LIBOR exercisable in three years' time is valued at 180 bps premium payable immediately.

A can create a synthetic callable bond as follows:

### Alternative 1

A enters into the following transactions:

- Purchases 5-year noncallable bonds.
- Sells a receiver option on the swap whereby the counterparty can require A to pay 7.50% pa and receive US$ LIBOR for years 4 and 5 (if interest rates decrease).

The diagram below sets out the position:

**Years 1 to 3 (Years 4 and 5 if Option on Swap Unexercised)**

**Years 4 to 5 (if Option on Swap Exercised)**

If interest rates rise, then the option on the swap is unexercised and A continues to receive the fixed coupon of 7.50% pa. If interest rates fall, then the option on the swap is exercised and A earns a floating rate of interest (at prevailing money market rates) on its investment. The return characteristics are identical to those under an actual callable bond.

The effective return to A incorporating the premium received is:

Over three years:    8.19% pa
Over five years:    7.95% pa

### Alternative 2

A enters into the following transactions:

- Purchases a 5-year floating rate asset yielding US$ LIBOR.
- Enters into two swaps transactions:
    1. 5-year swap under which it receives 7.50% pa.
    2. Sells a receiver option on a swap as in *Alternative 1*.

(Steps 1 and 2 can be combined in a cancellable swap whereby A's swap counterparty can cancel the swap under which it pays fixed (presumably, if interest rates fall) after three years.)

The diagram below sets out the position:

**Years 1 to 3 (Years 4 to 5 if Option on Swap Unexercised)**

**Years 4 to 5 (if Option on Swap Exercised)**

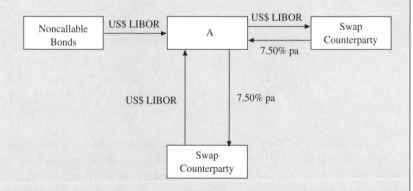

The result for A is identical to that in *Alternative 1*.

### Alternative 3

A enters into the following transactions:

- Purchases a 3-year noncallable AA corporate bond that yields 7.50% pa (for convenience, a flat yield curve is assumed).
- Sells a payer option on a swap whereby the counterparty can at its option pay 7.50% pa and receive US$ LIBOR for years 4 and 5 (if interest rates increase).

The diagram below sets out the position:

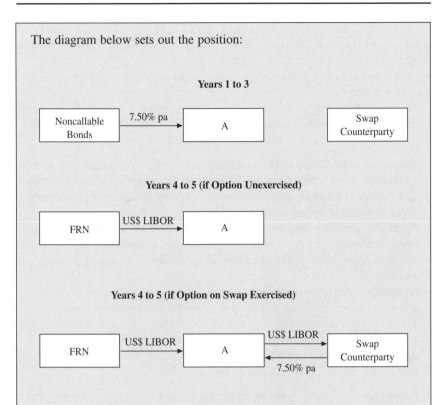

**Years 1 to 3**

| Noncallable Bonds | 7.50% pa → | A | | Swap Counterparty |

**Years 4 to 5 (if Option Unexercised)**

| FRN | US$ LIBOR → | A |

**Years 4 to 5 (if Option on Swap Exercised)**

| FRN | US$ LIBOR → | A | US$ LIBOR → / ← 7.50% pa | Swap Counterparty |

The return to A under various interest rate scenarios is identical to those in *Alternatives 1* and 2.

For convenience, the above examples assume flat yield curves and the returns from the different strategies are identical. In practice, considerable scope exists to extract additional value from one or other of the alternatives based on:

• The slope of the swap and/or corporate bond yield curves.
• The structure of forward rates implicit in the two yield curves.
• Different implied volatility and anomalies in the pricing of options on swaps.
• Capacity to enhance return by earning above US$ LIBOR return on floating rate investments.

*Source:* The above discussion draws on Johnson, Cal (July 1989) "Options on Interest Rate Swaps: New Tools for Asset and Liability Management"; Salomon Brothers, New York.

As is evident, the synthetic structures can be created utilizing a variety of combination strategies that are, by definition, economically equivalent. The availability of these alternative structures, however, allows the creation of the most efficient structure to take advantage of relative value considerations at any given point in time.

In a manner analogous to that of the investor, liability managers can create synthetic debt structures at attractive value levels to manage liability portfolios. For example, borrowers can create the following security structures:

- **Synthetic noncallable debt** — through issue of callable debt that is then converted into a synthetic noncallable issue by neutralizing the embedded call by entering into an option on a swap whereby it sells the right to receive fixed (a receiver option on a swap).[24]
- **Synthetic puttable bonds** — entailing the issue of a conventional bond combined with the sale of a receiver option on a swap whereby an issuer receives fixed, exercisable when the debt matures effectively extending the maturity of the debt.[25]
- **Synthetic portfolio shortening** — by selling payer options on swap, whereby the issuer has the right to pay fixed, thereby converting callable debt to fixed rate debt effectively maturing at the call date. Through this transaction, the issuer has purchased a call (embedded in the callable debt) and sold a put (the option on the swap is a put on the market), which effectively equates to a forward repurchase of the debt.

A major feature of these types of strategies is the capacity to tailor the strike price level (effectively the fixed rate under the swap), as well as other aspects of the transaction to specifically attune the synthetic liability structure to its specific requirements.

## 7.  Synthetic Callable (Ratchet) Bonds

As already noted, the key driver of callable bonds is that the issuer has the right to call the bond and refinance where interest rates decline. The traditional structure of a callable bond results in the issuer incurring refunding costs. In recent years, a new structure has evolved that seeks to synthetically replicate the performance of a callable bond but reduce transaction costs associated with the exercise of the call. The structure may also enhance the execution of the call option. This structure is known as the ratchet bond.[26] The Tennessee Valley

---

[24] This is essentially the logic of the monetization of the call option discussed above (see **Exhibit 4**).

[25] See discussion of synthetic puttable debt structures in Chapter 3.

[26] For a discussion of ratchet bonds see Kalotay, Andrew and Abreo, Andrew "Ratchet Bonds" (Spring 1999) *Journal of Applied Finance* 40-47.

Authority in an issue known as PARRS introduced the structure.
The basic structure of the ratchet bond is as follows:

- The issuer issued the bond normally (say, US$500 million for 10 years with a one-time call after 5 years).
- The coupon of the bond is fixed for the term of the bond (say 6.75% pa determined as the 10-year Treasury plus 100 bps).
- At the call date (5 years after issue), the coupon on the bond may be adjusted in accordance with a pre-agreed formula. This adjustment is based on an agreed credit spread over a benchmark Treasury bond[27] (in this case, 100 bps over the 5-year Treasury bond as at the call date). If the new rate (Treasury bond plus spread) is greater than the coupon (6.75% pa), then the coupon on the bond remains unchanged. If the new rate is lower than 6.75% pa, then the coupon is reset to the new rate.

The structure results in the coupon declining if interest rates fall but remaining constant if interest rates increase. The structure replicates the effective performance of a callable bond but without requiring retirement of the original bond. From the perspective of the investor, the ratchet bond behaves like the callable bond and assumes that the investor reinvests the maturing proceeds in a new bond for the remainder of the term of the original investment. The premium for the embedded call option is used to enhance the coupon of the bond as with other more conventional callable structures.

## 8.  Summary

Callable bonds represent one of the most traditional forms of option-embedded securities. In essence, such securities combine a traditional fixed income security with a call option written by the investor in favor of the issuer. The callable bond has particular price performance, duration and convexity characteristics that make such securities useful to both investors and issuers in terms of traditional asset and liability portfolio management. In recent times, the call feature has been effectively monetized or securitized through the use of options on swaps transactions that seek to capture the value differences between the pricing of these debt options as between the fixed income and derivative markets.

---

[27] The Treasury rate used is usually a Constant Maturity Treasury (CMT) rate.

# Appendix A

# Pricing Debt Options

## 1.    Distinctive Features of Debt Options

The basic mathematical option pricing models, such as Black and Scholes, were originally developed in the context of equity options.[28] The basic model requires significant amendments where it is used to value options on other instruments, such as futures contracts, currencies, and also debt instruments.[29]

The pricing of options on interest rates and debt instruments are particularly complex and several distinctive features of debt instruments must be incorporated into the pricing of debt options. The key features that require incorporation in the pricing mechanism include:

1. The underlying security in the case of debt instruments usually involves payouts in the form of interest during the life of the option.
2. The rate of interest cannot be assumed to be constant. Interest rate changes drive price changes in the underlying asset. Most interest rate security values do not depend on a single random variable but on a number of random interest rates (depending on the remaining time to maturity of the underlying security that may be variable).
3. Debt instruments, typically, have a defined maturity and their limited and declining life represents special problems in option pricing. This is in contrast to other assets, such as equities, currencies, and commodities that do not have fixed lives (they are perpetual in nature).
4. Volatility of the underlying debt instrument cannot be assumed to be constant.

---

[28] For an overview of option pricing see Das, Satyajit "Option Pricing" in Das, Satyajit (1997) *Risk Management & Financial Derivatives: A Guide to The Mathematics*; LBC Information Services, Sydney; McGraw-Hill, Chicago; MacMillan Publishing, England at Chapter 5. See also Hull, John (1997) *Options, Futures, and Other Securities — Third Edition*; Prentice Hall, Englewood Cliffs, NJ; Hull, John (1993) *Introduction to Futures and Options Markets – Second Edition*; Prentice Hall, Englewood Cliffs, NJ; Cox, John C. and Rubinstein, Mark (1985) *Option Markets*; Prentice Hall, Englewood Cliffs, NJ; (1992) *From Black-Scholes to Black Holes*; Publications, London; Dyer, Lawrence J. and Jacob, David P., "A Practitioner's Guide To Fixed-Income Option Models" (1989) (Spring) *Journal of International Securities Markets* 23-48.

[29] In this context it is important to note that there is no distinction drawn between the actual Black-Scholes model itself and discrete time implementation of the approach such as the binomial type of models [See Cox, John C., Ross, Stephen C; and Rubinstein, Mark "Option Pricing: A Simplified Approach" (1979) (September) 7 *Journal of Financial Economics* 229-263].

Of these four features, all but the first feature create considerable complexity in the pricing of options on debt instruments.

The impact of intermediate cash flows on the underlying debt instrument will depend on whether the underlying asset for the debt option is a cash market debt security or a futures contract on the relevant instrument. Where the option is on a futures contract on the relevant debt instrument, the underlying debt instrument is typically a hypothetical security with known characteristics. There are no coupon interest payments over the life of the option.

Where the option is on a physical security, there may be coupon payment over the life of the option. The assumption made by models such as Black-Scholes is that there are no intermediate cash payouts. However, this can be relaxed using a modification of the formula that allows for payments that are proportional to the price of the underlying security (that is effectively as a continuously compounded rate of return on the asset).[30]

However, the normal type of adjustment utilized may not be appropriate in the case of debt options. Where the option is on an underlying security that bears a coupon, the accrued interest is continuously added to the full price of the bond representing a continuous payout to the holder of the debt security. As the coupons are fixed in dollar amounts not proportional to the price of the underlying debt security, this type of proposed modification would be inappropriate. An alternative approach to this adjustment would be to deduct the present value of coupons on the underlying bond over the life of the option from the capital value of the security. The underlying asset price is then set at the *ex-coupon price of the bond* with the asset assumed to pay *no* income.

## 2. Types of Debt Options

The problems created by the distinctive features of options on debt instruments are best analyzed in the context of fixed deliverable versus variable deliverable options.

In practice, options on debt instrument take one of two forms:[31]

---

[30] See Merton, Robert C. "Theory of Rational Option Pricing" (Spring 1973) *Bell Journal of Economics and Management Science* 4 141-183.

[31] It is important to distinguish between two classes of options on debt instruments: options on the cash market debt instrument (that is, the actual physical debt security) and futures on the relevant debt instrument. In practice, both types of options co-exist and are available. This is despite the fact that in any market, a cash market, a futures market and one options market (either on the cash market instrument or the futures contract) would usually be sufficient to fulfil all risk transfer possibilities. The option on the cash market and the option on the futures market will, generally, serve similar functions.

- **Fixed deliverable option** — whereby the underlying debt instrument is a debt security *with specified maturity characteristics*. For example, a 6-month call option on a 90-day Eurodollar futures contract is a fixed deliverable option. The maturity of the underlying debt instrument is always a fixed 90 days commencing from the expiry date of the option.
- **Variable deliverable option** — whereby the underlying debt instrument is a *specified existing debt issue* with time dependent maturity characteristics. For example, a 3-year call option on the 5.50% August 15, 2012 US Treasury bond is a variable deliverable option. This option requires delivery of that specific security or the option payoff is a function of the price of this specific security. The maturity of the underlying security obviously varies depending on the date of exercise of the option. For example, as at expiry of the option, the remaining maturity of the underlying security will have reduced by three years.

Variable deliverable options create complex pricing issues. This reflects the fact that actual physical debt securities are affected by the passage of time. This is unlike other cash market assets that have infinite lives or futures contracts that are not based on a particular, wasting debt security (futures contracts have particular characteristics that are specified and constant). This has several implications:

- The underlying debt instrument itself has a shorter tenor or period to maturity as the option itself approaches expiration.
- At maturity, the value of the interest rate security converges to a known constant value (par or face value) and the volatility of the security approaches zero.

The distinctive features of debt options derive from these two characteristics of options on physical debt securities.

As noted above, the basic option pricing models assume that only one interest rate (the risk-free rate) is relevant. However, at any given point in time, a variety of risk-free interest rates for different maturities are observable. Each of these interest rates and, consequently, the shape of the yield curve as a whole is subject to change over time.

A major difficulty in relation to the pricing of debt options relates to the fact that the price of the underlying asset (the debt security) itself is a function of interest rates. Moreover, it is unlikely depending on the type of option, that it is a function of the risk-free interest rate utilized to present value the exercise price of the option. An additional complication arises from the fact that where the option is a variable deliverable option (as defined above) the exact interest rate required to value the underlying debt instrument itself is subject to change with the passage of time. These difficulties mean that the value of options on debt instruments or interest rates do not depend on a single random interest rate variable but may depend on a *number* of different random interest rates.

The effect of changes in interest rates and the time to expiration are particularly complex. For options on assets, such as shares, as the risk-free rate increases, the value of the call option increases as the present value of the exercise price in the event of exercise declines. In effect, if the call option and the security itself are regarded as different ways for an investor to capture any gain on the security price, as rates rise the increased cost of carry on the underlying security will make the call more attractive leading to an increase in its value.

However, in the case of debt options, it is unreasonable to assume (as is usually done in the case of equity options) that the price of the underlying debt security is independent of the level of interest rates. Significant movements in the price of the asset will occur as a result of changes in interest rates and, in general, any cost of carry consideration would be minor relative to the change in the value of the underlying security. For example, it would be reasonable to assume that rate increases will usually have a negative impact on the price of call options on debt instruments as a rise in interest rates will most likely cause a fall in the price of the underlying instrument or futures contract.

The assumption of constant variance or volatility of the price underlying debt instrument is also flawed. This results from two factors:

- Volatility of debt securities (in the case of a variable delivery option) is likely to tend to zero. This reflects the fact that at maturity, the value of the debt instrument itself must converge to a known value (the par value of the security). An additional factor in this regard is that the price volatility of a security is itself a complicated function of the actual volatility of interest rates of varying maturity and the time to maturity of the security itself. The different pattern of evolution of volatility for a debt instrument relative to other financial assets (with no fixed maturity) is set out in **Exhibit 2.7**.
- The stochastic process followed by interest rates appears to have a mean reversion quality; that is, there is an inbuilt drift that pulls them back to some long-run average level.

**Exhibit 2.7**
**Volatility Evolution – Bonds vs Stock/Other Financial Assets**

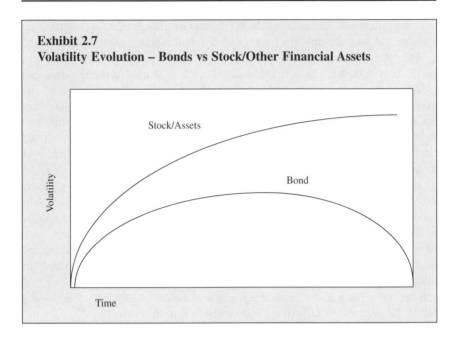

Consequently, the volatility of debt instruments will generally be a function of the assumed stochastic process of interest rate movements, assumptions about the shape and future movement of interest rates across the whole yield curve and the remaining life of the security at a given point in time. This dictates that constant variance cannot be assumed and it is probable that the volatility, itself, may also be stochastic variable.

The complexity of these interactions can be illustrated with reference to the effect of changes in time to expiration on such options. For options on assets with unlimited lives, an option with a longer time expiration will, generally, be worth more than a comparable option with a short term to expiry. This is on the basis that it has all the attributes of the shorter dated option plus more benefits for the holder; that is, there is greater probability that the option can be profitably exercised. This property need not necessarily hold for debt options, particularly variable deliverable options. Depending on the relative magnitude of the time value and the intrinsic value, it is conceivable that under certain circumstances, an option with a longer time to expiration may be worth less than one with a shorter term. This would reflect the fact that securities usually begin to trade closer to par as the instrument approaches maturity. The greater price stability may distort the value of the option.

# 3. Approaches to Pricing Debt and Interest Rate Options

In practice, the pricing of debt and interest rate options falls into two categories:

- **Options on instruments where the underlying asset is a standardized debt instrument** (with a fixed maturity, for example, options on futures and forwards on debt) — these options can be valued with Black-Scholes type models, in particular, the Black option pricing model.[32] This is because some of the problems identified can be minimized.[33]
- **Options on instruments where the underlying asset is nonstandard** (with variable maturity, for example, options on physical bonds) — these are more problematic and usually entail the use of term structure or yield curve models.

# 4. Pricing Debt Options Using Black-Scholes Approaches

As noted above, where the underlying asset has a fixed maturity, then Black-Scholes model approaches may be applied. This type of approach is commonly used with pricing futures on debt instruments, caps, floors, and options on swaps/swaptions. In the case of options on swaps, Bermudan-style swaptions pose problems of pricing similar to those affecting options on physical debt instruments. This is because the swap may be exercised on a number of dates but the final maturity of the underlying swap is fixed at the time of entry. This causes the actual maturity of the underlying swap to alter with time in a manner analogous to that for an option on a physical bond.

In certain circumstances, Black-Scholes approaches are also used to price options on physical bonds. These are predicated on either ignoring some of the distinctive characteristics of options on physical debt instruments or seeking to adjust the basic framework in one of a number of ways.

The original model for pricing debt options within a Black-Scholes framework is based on continuous time bond price dynamics.[34] The model examined the problem of pricing an option on equities where the interest rate is stochastic rather than deterministic as in the standard Black and Scholes framework. This model does not explicitly indicate how specific properties of bonds, namely a fixed maturity and a known maturity value, are guaranteed.

---

[32] See Black, Fischer, "The Pricing of Commodity Contracts'" (1976) (March) 3 *Journal of Financial Economics* 167-179.

[33] Please note options on standardized debt instruments can also be priced using term structure models.

[34] See Merton, Robert C. "Theory of Rational Option Pricing" (Spring 1973) *Bell Journal of Economics and Management Science* 4 141-183.

Subsequent models seek to overcome these deficiencies by seeking to model the bond price dynamics in a more complex way.[35]

In practice, this approach to pricing is applied only where the term of the option is short relative to the term of the underlying bond into which the option is capable of exercise. This reflects the fact that the key problems (the change in volatility and the need for a complete term structure of rates) are less relevant.

Using this approach to valuation allows the use of an adapted version of Black-Scholes. The basic adaptation is to ensure that the income on the asset is incorporated in the pricing analysis. A variation on this approach is to treat the option as being on the *forward price* of the underlying bond. This allows the valuation to be done using Black's option on a forward pricing model. The use of this model requires the volatility used to be the volatility of the *forward price* of the underlying bond.

# 5.  Pricing Debt Options Using Term Structure Models

## 5.1   Overview

The major identified problems with pricing options on interest rates or debt instruments are most evident in pricing options on physical debt instruments, particularly medium- to long-term bonds. A variety of approaches have emerged towards pricing these types of options. A brief overview of some of these pricing approaches is summarized below.[36]

---

[35]  For example, see: Ball, Clifford A. and Torous, Walter N. "Bond Price Dynamics and Options" (December 1983) *Journal of Financial and Quantitative Analysis* 18 517-531; Brennan, M.J. and Schwartz, E.S. "An Equilibrium Model Of Bond Pricing and a Test of Market Efficiency" (September 1982) *Journal of Financial and Quantitative Analysis* vol. 17 no. 3 301-29; Schaefer, S.M. and Schwartz, E.S. "Time Dependent Variance and the Pricing of Options" (December 1987) *Journal of Finance* 42 1113-28. For example, the Schaefer-Schwartz model utilizes a process whereby the bond price volatility is related to bond's duration as the basic model for the bond price dynamics.

[36]  A detailed treatment of these pricing approaches requires an understanding of mathematical techniques that are beyond the scope of this book. For readers interested in examining the details of the various approaches, see Rebanato, Riccardo (1998) *Interest Rate Option Models — Second Edition*; John Wiley, New York; Hull, John (1997) *Options, Futures, and Other Derivatives — Third Edition*; Prentice Hall, Upper Saddle River NJ; Chiarella, Carl, "A Survey of Models for the Pricing of Interest Rate Derivative Securities" Course presented by the School of Finance and Economics, University of Technology, Sydney, Australia (June 3-4, 1992) 985; Rowlands, Tim "Interest rate Option Pricing Models" in Das, Satyajit (1997) *Risk Management & Financial Derivatives: A Guide to The Mathematics*; LBC Information Services, Sydney; McGraw-Hill, Chicago; MacMillan Publishing, England at Chapter 6.

## 5.2   Concept

Interest rate term structure models are based on modelling interest rate term structure movements. These pricing approaches seek to overcome clear deficiencies in the simpler models whereby there is no model of the term structure of interest rates or the change in volatility with a reduction in the maturity of the underlying bond in the option pricing model. A further rationale of these models is to allow *all derivatives* on debt instruments to be priced within a consistent uniform framework.[37]

The models themselves entail three distinct components:

- **Choice of yield curve process** — these models require the specification of a dynamic process to generate the term structure of interest rates and the instantaneous volatility to allow the derivation of the option price.
- **Model calibration** — the model inputs must generally be calibrated to actual market interest rates, prices, and volatility.
- **Numerical implementation** — most of these models do not yield close form solutions for the option value. Accordingly, numerical procedures must be employed to solve for the price of the option.

The main difficulty with these approaches is the requirement to estimate certain model inputs from the market. The estimation of these parameters required to solve these pricing formulas is difficult. This problem is complicated by the fact that option prices appear to be sensitive to changes in this parameter.

## 5.3   Yield Curve Process

Central to the process underlying an interest rate term structure model is the specification of a yield curve process. This process generally involves specification of two elements:

- **Short-term interest rate** — this short-term rate (r) is modeled and utilized in conjunction with individual risk preferences to specify current term structure and the projected term structure.
- **Mean reversion** — the model will generally incorporate mean reversion effects. This means that the model of drift of r is specified to have average drift with volatility superimposed upon drift. The drift tendency is to pull interest rates to some long-term average level. Mean reversion is responsible

---

[37]   For a review of the different families of models see Smithson, Charles "Wonderful Life" (October 1991) *Risk* 37-44; Smithson, Charles "Extended Family (1) (October 1995) 19-21; Smithson, Charles "Extended Family (2)" (November 1995) 52-53; Smithson, Charles "Extended Family" (December 1997) 158-163; Smithson, Charles "Extended Family" (September 1998) 14-18.

for decline in forward rate volatility as maturity of the underlying instrument decreases. **Exhibit 2.8** sets out a model of the mean reversion effect.

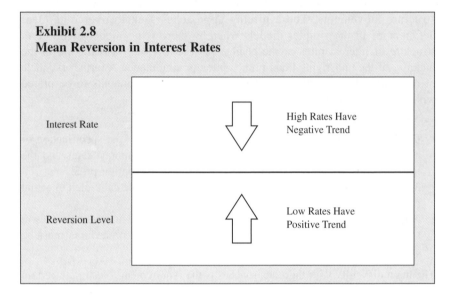

**Exhibit 2.8**
**Mean Reversion in Interest Rates**

Interest Rate

High Rates Have
Negative Trend

Reversion Level

Low Rates Have
Positive Trend

Typical yield curve processes used are set out in **Exhibit 2.9**.

**Exhibit 2.9**
**Yield Curve Process**

**1.  Simple Yield Curve Process Model**

A standard Black-Scholes-type relative diffusion process would be as follows:

$$dr/r = m.dt + \sigma.dw$$

Where:

dr  =  the change in the short-term interest rate
r    =  spot interest rate
m   =  deterministic drift function per unit of time
dt   =  unit of time
$\sigma$    =  volatility of process per unit of time
dw  =  standard normal random number generator

## 2. Mean Reverting Yield Curve Process Model

A typical mean reverting process would be as follows:[38]

$dr = a.(b - r) .dt + \sigma.dz$

Where:

| | | |
|---|---|---|
| dr | = | the change in the short-term interest rate |
| a | = | the parameter (greater than 0) that describes the speed at which r reverts to a long-term average value |
| b | = | the long-trem value of r |
| r | = | the short-term interest rate |
| dt | = | a short-time interval |
| σ | = | the volatility of r |
| dz | = | a random variable chosen from a normal distribution with mean 0 and variance dt |

In a mean reverting process, the model incorporates mean reversion with the r being pulled to level b at rate a. Superimposed upon this is overall drift is a normally distributed stochastic term (s.dz) that creates volatility in rates and prices.

## 5.4    Equilibrium Models

Within the basic approach outlined, equilibrium models assume certain economic variables and model the process for the short-term risk-free rate. The variables utilized are flexible and may include:

- **One state variable** — r depends only on r and time.
- **Two state variable** — r depends on r and one other uncertain variable.
- **Mean reversion** — r has an average drift or expected change towards some long-term average level.

The model uses the process specified to generate the relevant interest rates and creates a complete term structure of interest rates and volatility over time enabling the value of the option to be derived.

Equilibrium models are useful for understanding potential relationships. However, equilibrium models suffer from a significant disadvantage. The model

---

[38] The model specified is the Vasicek model; see Vasichek, O.A. "An Equilibrium Characterization of the Term Structure" (1977) *Journal of Financial Economics* 5 177-88.

does not automatically fit the current term structure. This is because the initial term structure is a model *output* rather than an input. This results in unsatisfactory pricing results as the projected yield curve may diverge significantly from the actual current yield curve.

## 5.5    No Arbitrage Models

The concept underlying no arbitrage models is that the initial current term structure is assumed and specified. The model defines how term structure evolves. This avoids the problem of equilibrium models.

Arbitrage models typically require the selection of an interest rate process and then model the evolution of interest rates over time. The evolution over time must satisfy a specified no arbitrage condition. This condition is that there should be no self-financing strategy that generates a risk-free gain (analogous to the risk-neutral valuation methodology that underlies option valuation generally). The probability description of interest rates is usually specified to conform to the arbitrage-free condition and also the current term structure of rates.

There are complex choices between no arbitrage models and the wide variety of models that have emerged.[39] The major advantage of no arbitrage models is that the model fits an initial yield curve. It also allows freedom to choose volatility in any way desired. The problem is that this approach generally yields a non-Markov model that can only be implemented using Monte Carlo simulation or nonrecombining trees.

## 5.6    Model Calibration

The no arbitrage approach requires a process of model calibration. A basic requirement of both equilibrium and no arbitrage models is the need to estimate

---

[39] For examples of different models, Rebanato, Riccardo (1998) *Interest Rate Option Models — Second Edition*; John Wiley, New York; Hull, John (1997*) Options, Futures, and Other Derivatives — Third Edition*; Prentice Hall, Upper Saddle River NJ; Heath, D., Jarrow, R., and Morton, A. "Contingent Claim Valuation With A Random Evolution Of Interest Rates" (1991) *Review of Futures Markets* 54-76; Heath, D., Jarrow, R., and Morton, A. "Bond Pricing And The Term Structure Of Interest Rates: A New Methodology For Contingent Claims Valuation" (1992) 60 (no. 1) *Econometrica* 77-105; Ho, T. S. Y., and Lee, S. B. "Term Structure Movements And Pricing Interest Rate Contingent Claims" (1986) 41 (no. 5) *Journal of Finance* 1011-29; Black, Fisher, Derman, E., and Toy, W., "A One Factor Model of Interest Rates And Its Application To Treasury Bond Options" (1990) 46 (no. 1*) Financial Analysts Journal* 33-39; Brace, A., Gatarek, D., and Musiela, M. (1997) The Market Model Of Interest Rate Dynamics; Preprint 95-2, Department of Statistics, University of New South Wales.

the required variables from market data. In the case of no arbitrage models the model parameters are constrained to fit:

- **Initial term structure** — that is, the current interest rates.
- **Market option prices** — that is, the implied volatility of traded market instruments.

The Black-Scholes model is central to the process of calibration. This is because any arbitrage-free yield curve model must recover a Black-Scholes price for plain vanilla instruments.

The overall process is depicted in **Exhibit 2.10**.

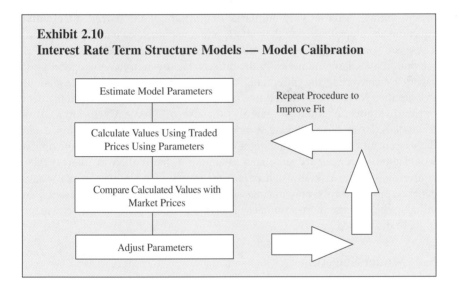

**Exhibit 2.10**
**Interest Rate Term Structure Models — Model Calibration**

Estimate Model Parameters

Calculate Values Using Traded Prices Using Parameters

Compare Calculated Values with Market Prices

Adjust Parameters

Repeat Procedure to Improve Fit

## 5.7  Numerical Solution Issues

The model of the interest rates generates forward term structures of interest rates and volatility. These rates and volatility must be then used to generate the distribution of prices of the underlying debt instrument to enable the option value to be derived. Most of these pricing models require numerical solution.

The process of numerical implementation entails several steps including:

- Tree construction.
- Numerical solution.

The basic intuition underlying tree construction is the construction of a discrete time representation of the stochastic process and the sequence of bond prices. It is conceptually similar to the binomial approach to option pricing. The difference between an asset tree and interest rate tree is that discounting in interest rate tree is done using different rates at each node and the volatility does not necessarily remain constant. The tree construction process may include a variety of techniques including trinomial trees. The tree may also include nonstandard branching, changing the length of the tree step.

The process of numerical solution will typically focus on backward induction techniques, solving partial differential equations using finite difference schemes and analytic solutions or Monte Carlo processes.

For example, in the case of discrete time models the option is evaluated by starting at expiration and working backwards through the lattice or price tree of bond prices or interest rates utilizing a procedure referred to as dynamic programming. Alternatively, numerical solutions of the partial differential equations developed utilizing the various pricing approaches must be computed. These are sometimes undertaken utilizing finite difference methods that value the option by solving numerically the differential equation that the option must satisfy by converting the differential equation into a set of different equations that are then solved using an iterative process.[40] A final approach to pricing debt options should be noted — namely, the use of Monte Carlo simulation techniques. Using this technique, a model of interest rates can be developed and the movement of the term structure of interest rates during the life of the option would then be repeatedly simulated assuming a distribution of interest rates conforming to the risk-adjusted parameter levels. The simulation run would generate payoffs for the option that would then be discounted to the present time utilizing the average short-term rates. The value of the option would be average of these discounted payoffs.

## 6.  Model Selection

The wide range of models available currently and the unsettled nature or the debate on pricing interest rate options forces the practitioner to confront the awkward question of which model to utilize.

In practice, the following trends are evident:

• Options on futures, particularly where the underlying debt instrument is a short-term interest rate or security or the time to expiration is relatively short, particularly, in relation to the life of the underlying debt instrument, are priced using the Black model.
• The pricing of caps and floors is generally undertaken utilizing the Black model.

---

[40]  See Paul Wilmott, Jeff Dewynne, and Sam Howison (1993) *Option Pricing: Mathematical Models and Computation*; Oxford Financial Press: Oxford, England.

- Options on swaps or swaptions are priced utilizing the Black model, particularly where the time to exercise it relatively short especially, in relation to the life of the swap. However, interest rate term structure approaches are increasingly being utilized for certain types of structures, particularly Bermudan options.
- Options on bonds are priced using Black's model where the time to expiry is short relative to the life of the underlying bond. For longer dated bond options, interest rate term structure models are utilized.
- Other debt options, particularly long-term options, such as those embedded in callable and puttable bonds, asset/mortgage-backed securities, and so on are priced utilizing interest term structure models.

The statement of practice should not be regarded as comprehensive but rather indicative of market practitioners' approaches. The approach to pricing in practice reflects a variety of factors including:

- None of the option pricing models described is perfect *for all situations*.
- Users will typically employ models that are easy to implement and that are not expensive to build or cumbersome to use. For example, interest rate term structure models require estimation of parameters (the mean reversion rate and the long-term average interest rate level). These parameters may in practice be difficult to verify. In addition, term structure models will generally require numerical solution. This requires significant amounts of computer resources and can take time to produce results (albeit, the increasing availability of very fast computers at ever decreasing costs is increasingly a factor).

These models form the basis of pricing and risk management systems within financial institutions, which are active in trading and hedging these instruments. This dictates that the need to actively manage the risk exposure of positions in a rapidly changing market means the risk managers are willing to sacrifice some theoretical niceties in favour of speed and direct relevance of the information generated by the model.

In fundamental terms, the pricing of these instruments utilizing often complex mathematics must be taken in the context of market realities. In particular, the underlying market for debt instruments does not fully reflect the assumptions of perfect liquidity, no transaction costs and perfect information made in the pricing models themselves. Given these failures of the real market to conform to the theoretical constructions underlying option pricing models, no model can be used risklessly to arbitrage mispricing. In addition, there are difficulties in evaluating the performance of individual models using rigorous empirical approaches. The difficulty in model selection necessarily makes the mathematical techniques merely indications of relative value of options on particular instruments.

A major advantage of Black and Scholes (and Black's variation thereto)[41] is their capacity to compress four observable variables into one other variable, volatility, which can then be interpreted in the pricing, trading, and hedging of these instruments. The enduring quality of the Black-Scholes model continues to be its ease of use, despite its theoretical shortcomings under certain conditions.

# Appendix B

# Options on Swaps

## 1.   Options on Swaps

Options on swaps (or swaptions) entail an option on the fixed rate component of a swap transaction. A variety of structures, known variously as swaptions, callable, puttable, collapsible, or extendible swaps, are available. While sometimes regarded as distinct and different types of transactions by market participants, the above structures are very similar. Each structure effectively represents an option to either enter into or provide the swap at a known price over a specified period. In essence, options on swaps combine the features of interest rate options with swap transactions.

It should be noted that the terminology associated with options on swaps is far from standardized. There are significant differences in usage as between jurisdictions. For example, as discussed in greater detail below, in the US a puttable swap would imply an option whereby the holder, a payer of fixed rates under a swap, would have the right to terminate a swap. In contrast, a callable swap would imply the right of the holder to enter into a swap as a payer of fixed rates. In some other jurisdictions terminology is exactly opposite with a callable swap giving the right to terminate the swap arrangement.

## 2.   Terminology

An option on a swap provides the purchaser or holder of the option with the right, but not the obligation, to enter into a swap where it pays fixed rates against receipt of a floating rate index as at a future date. The reverse type of transaction where the holder of the option on the swap will, if the option is exercised, receive the fixed rate is also feasible.

An option on a swap usually entails an option on the fixed rate component of a swap. It is designed to give the holder the benefit of the strike rate (that is, the

---

[41]   This refers to both the closed form and the binomial implementation of these models.

*fixed* rate specified in the agreement) if the market rates are worse, with the flexibility to deal at the market rates if they are better.

The terminology associated with options on swaps (much of it consistent with general option terminology) is as follows:

- **Receiver options on swaps** — whereby the purchaser or holder has the right to receive fixed rates under the swap.
- **Payer options on swaps** — whereby the purchaser or the holder has the right to pay fixed rates under the swap.
- **American style** — a swap option that can be exercised on any business day within the swap option exercise period.
- **European style** — a swap option that can be exercised only on the expiry date.
- **Exercise or strike price** — the specified fixed rate at which the buyer has the right to enter into the swap.
- **Expiry date** — the last date on which the swap option can be exercised and the effective date (if exercised) the fixed and floating components of the swap begin to accrue.
- **Premium** — the consideration paid by the buyer for the swap option.

The basic structure of a receiver and payer swaption is set out in **Exhibit 2.11** below:

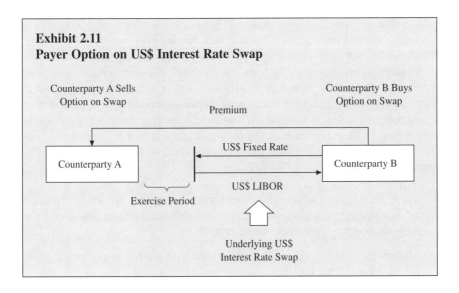

**Exhibit 2.11**
**Payer Option on US$ Interest Rate Swap**

Counterparty A Sells
Option on Swap

Counterparty B Buys
Option on Swap

Premium

US$ Fixed Rate

Counterparty A

Counterparty B

Exercise Period

US$ LIBOR

Underlying US$
Interest Rate Swap

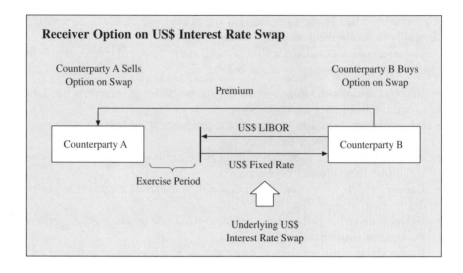

## 3.    Characteristics of Options on Swaps

Options on swaps primarily offer protection against interest rate uncertainty in a manner analogous to conventional debt options. The user of options on swaps is able to limit its downside risk in switching from fixed to floating interest rates or vice versa, without limiting potential benefits associated with unforeseen *favorable* interest rate movements. In return for this opportunity, the purchaser of an option on a swap pays a fee; that is, the option on swap premium.

An important aspect of options on swaps is that for certain classes of borrower, where they would ultimately be users of swaps, the emergence of options on swaps provides them with greater flexibility and certainty in managing their assets or liabilities. This can be seen from the fact that before the emergence of these instruments, the only management tool for asymmetric risk management available to customers were exchange traded options, usually on government bond rates or, to a lesser extent, OTC markets in options on government bond rates.

There are a number of specific characteristics of options on swaps that make these instruments particularly useful for asset or liability managers seeking to manage interest rate exposures. These include:

- **Maturity** — options on swaps are available with periods to expiration of (up to) 10 years, which is significantly longer than the maturity of options available on futures exchanges and other OTC options.
- **Options on term interest rates** — in contrast to caps and floors that are long dated options on short-term rates, options on swaps represent options on

intermediate- and long-term rates adding an extra dimension to interest rate risk management for asset and liability managers.

- **Spread component** — options and swaps provide an option on the all-in fixed cost of funds for borrowers (or return for investors) as they incorporate a credit spread component (the swap spread). This allows borrowers or investors who traditionally use swaps to manage their portfolios to avoid exposure to changing spreads between swap rates and underlying government bond rates.
- **Flexibility** — options and swaps, like other OTC products, are extremely flexible with the user being able to specify exercise dates, amounts, specific strike rates and other structural aspects without the constraint of standardized exchange options and administrative procedures such as deposits and margins.
- **Markets** — increasingly, options on swaps are available in a wide range of currencies facilitating their use. The market for options on swaps is also increasingly liquid, particularly in major currencies that further facilitates their utilization.

## 4. Types of Options on Swaps — Fundamental Equivalences

As noted above, the various swap structures, referred to variously as callable, puttable, collapsible, extendible, and so on swaps are ultimately versions of options on swaps. Most importantly, they are essentially equivalent transactions. The structuring, pricing, trading, and hedging of these various types of instruments are based on the fundamental equivalence of these transactions and the capacity to decompose them into either the receiver or payer options on swaps.

The structural features of the more common types of options on swaps that are available are summarized below:[42]

- **Callable swap** — under this structure, the fixed-rate payer is allowed to enter into swaps (under the terms of which it pays a fixed rate and receives a floating rate) at its option up to a maximum amount at a known cost up until the end of the expiry of the option. A callable swap is identical to a payer option on a swap. The reverse structure is also possible allowing the purchaser or holder of the option to, upon exercise, require the counterparty to pay fixed rate under the swap.

---

[42] The various structures described above are, by no means, a comprehensive listing of variations available. In addition, definitions of the various structures are not universal and variations in usage persist between jurisdictions and markets and even sectors within markets.

- **Puttable swap** — under this structure, a fixed-rate payer has the option to terminate the swap at some agreed future date without penalty. Analytically a puttable swap is identical to entry into an interest rate swap under which the holder pays a fixed rate and receives a floating rate combined with the purchase of a receiver option on a swap whereby the purchaser has the right to receive fixed rates and pay floating rates. The expiry date of the receiver option on a swap coincides with the date on which the fixed-rate payer wishes to have the choice of terminating the interest rate swap. Upon exercise of the receiver option on a swap, the fixed rate and floating rate flows under the original interest rate swap and the swap entered into as a result of exercise of the receiver option on a swap, match and offset each other, thereby effectively terminating the original transaction.

- **Extendible swap** — this represents a variation on the callable swap structure. Under the terms of an extendible swap, the fixed rate payer or receiver has the option to require the counterparty to continue the swap (upon existing terms) for a fixed period beyond the term of the original swap. Analytically, an extendible swap can be unbundled as follows:
  1. A payer extendible swap is equivalent to a conventional interest rate swap, under which the party pays fixed rates and receives floating rates, combined with the purchase of a payer option on a swap, where the expiry date of the option coincides with the maturity of the interest rate swap.
  2. A receiver extendible swap is identical to the payer extendible swap except that holder receives fixed rates under the original interest rate swap and purchases a receiver option on a swap.

- **Cancellable/collapsible swap** — under this structure, a fixed-rate payer provides the swap counterparty with the right to terminate the transaction. Effectively, the fixed-rate payer in an interest rate swap for a specified term, sells a receiver option on a swap (whereby it receives fixed rates and pays floating rates) on an underlying swap that commences sometime during the life of the original interest rate swap and matures as of the maturity of the original interest rate swap.

- **Contingent swap** — this structure is identical to a receiver option on a swap. This type of structure is utilized both with interest rate swaps and currency swaps and linked to contingent assets and liabilities such as call options on debt instruments in the form of warrants or options.

It should be noted that the party entering into structures such as the callable, puttable, extendible, and so on, structures usually compensates the provider of the option on the swap, for the additional flexibility and option element, either by payment of an upfront premium or, more typically, by an adjustment built into the swap rate (reflecting the amortization of the option premium at a nominated funding cost).

## Appendix C

## Pricing of Options on Swaps

### 1. Pricing/Premium Characteristics

Options on swaps represent combinations of the primary features of swaps and options on interest rates. Consequently, the pricing of options on swaps is based on traditional option pricing theories. In essence, an option on a swap is the purchase or sale of an option on the fixed rate component of the swap. The pricing of options on swaps reflects the underlying option embodied within the swap structure.

The primary determinants of the price or premiums payable on options on swaps include:

- The strike fixed rate.
- The forward swap rate.
- The maturity of the underlying swap.
- Exercise payments (if any).
- Time outstanding until exercise.
- The volatility of the forward swap rate.

The level of effective fixed rates on the swap is one of the key determinants of the value of the option on the swap. For example, the higher the effective fixed coupon (fixed rate minus any spread relative to the variable index) under the swap, the greater the value of being able to put the swap back to the counterparty and, conversely, the lower the value of being able to enter into the swap. Consequently, if all other parameters are held constant, the higher the fixed rate payable under the swap, the more valuable (less valuable) is the option to, at some future date, terminate (enter into) the swap for a fixed exercise fee.

However, the net effect on the total cost to a borrower or investor is more complex. For example, in the case of a puttable swap, while the value of the put option rises as the effective fixed rate on the swap is increased, the premium generated up-front by a higher effective coupon on the underlying swap increases at a faster rate. Consequently, although an increase in the fixed rate raises the cost of the put option, the net effect on the package may be a decrease in the up-front fee paid by the purchaser of the puttable swap.

The greater the exercise payment that must be paid to exercise the option, the lower is the value of the option on the swap. In essence, a large positive exercise payment can be equated to an increasingly out-of-the-money option with the consequent impact on the value of the option on the swap.

Generally, the longer the time to final maturity of the underlying swap as at the exercise date of the option on the swap, the more valuable the option on that swap will be. This reflects the increased price sensitivity of the swap with the longer maturity.

The impact of outstanding time until exercise in the case of options on swaps can be complex. For example, if the time to expiration of a European swap option is extended, holding the maturity of the swap constant, a variety of factors begin to influence its value. While the increasing period to expiration of the option increases the premium, the fact that the underlying swap is aging over the life of the option may, in fact, lower the value of the put option. In the limiting case, where the expiration date of the option equals the maturity date of the swap, the option will, in theory, have no value.

## 2.   Pricing Options on Swaps — Approach

The basic pricing methodology is derived from the underlying option element of option on swaps and utilizes basic option pricing techniques.

The pricing of swaptions is undertaken in a number of discrete steps:

- **Calculate forward swap rates** — this requires calculation of forward swap rates implicit in the swap yield curve. This is because the underlying asset of the swaption is effectively a forward swap.
- **Calculate the swaption price** — this requires the specification of the various inputs (necessary to determine option prices) and incorporating these into the selected option pricing model and calculating the price.

Assume the following option on a swap:

- **Structure** — A $1 \times 4$ payer option on a swap whereby the buyer has the right to enter into a swap to pay a fixed rate at 6.25% pa for three years. The option is European exercise and can only be exercised at the end of one year.
- **Swap rates** – the 1-year swap rate is 5.875% pa and the 4-year swap rate is 6.10% pa.
- **Volatility** – the volatility of the 3-year swap rate one year forward is assumed to be 5% (in price terms).

To calculate the price of the option, the parameters are reconfigured as input for the option pricing model and the price determined.

| Face Value | 100 |
|---|---|

**Dates**

| Transaction Date | 1-Oct-2001 |
|---|---|
| Exercise Date | 1-Oct-2002 |
| Final Maturity Date | 1-Oct-2005 |

**Swap Rates**

| | |
|---|---|
| To Exercise Date | 5.88% |
| To Maturity | 6.10% |
| Implied Forward Rate | 6.18% |
| Strike Rate | 6.25% |
| Risk Free Rate | 5.63% |
| Volatility | 5.00% |
| Type Of Option (European = 0; American = 1) | 0 |

| Premium | Payer | Receiver |
|---|---|---|
| Premium (%) | 1.79% | 1.98% |
| Premium ($/Million) | $ 17,933 | $ 19,847 |

These tables summarize the swaption premiums (% flat) for a range of strike prices (volatility held constant) and volatility (strike price held constant):

| Strike Rate (% pa) | Payer Option on Swap Premium (%) | Receiver Option on Swap Premium (%) |
|---|---|---|
| 7.25 | 0.85 | 3.59 |
| 6.75 | 1.26 | 2.72 |
| 6.25 | 1.79 | 1.98 |
| 5.75 | 2.47 | 1.38 |
| 5.25 | 3.28 | 0.91 |

| Volatility (% pa) | Payer Option on Swap Premium (%) | Receiver Option on Swap Premium (%) |
|---|---|---|
| 7.00 | 2.55 | 2.74 |
| 6.00 | 2.17 | 2.36 |
| 5.00 | 1.79 | 1.98 |
| 4.00 | 1.42 | 1.61 |
| 3.00 | 1.04 | 1.23 |

## 3.   Swaption Model Choice

The option on a swap premium calculations above are derived utilizing the Modified Black-Scholes Option Pricing Model. The Modified Black-Scholes formula relaxes some of the assumptions applicable to the original Black-Scholes formula. However, the following restrictive assumptions remain:

- The prices are for European options *only*. The option is not exercised before the expiration date.
- The underlying asset prices are log-normally distributed.
- The short-term interest rate is fixed over the life of the option.
- Volatility is known and constant over the life of the option.

In the case of an option on a swap, the major breakdowns in the assumptions are that the underlying asset price may not be log-normally distributed and the fact that interest rates are fixed over the life of the option. A number of alternative approaches (interest rate term structure models) that seek to address these problems are available.[43] The term structure model approaches to valuation of options on swaps are particularly important where the structure incorporates a Bermudan exercise feature. For example, where the option can be exercised on a number of dates but the maturity of the underlying swap is fixed. This means the actual term of the underlying swap is variable creating a number of valuation problems.[44]

The option model choice problem is compounded where the underlying option on a swap is American rather than European. This is primarily because of the possibility of early exercise. For example, with a call option on interest rates, there is always a possibility of early exercise if the holding costs are below the short-term rate assumed. The solution for the American-style exercise option on a swap can be derived in a number of ways:

- **Modified Black-Scholes** — this is the same as the Modified Black-Scholes European Option Pricing Formula except that the Black-Scholes American Formula checks to see if the value it is returning is below the intrinsic value of the option. Where the Black-Scholes European Option value is below the intrinsic price of the option, then the Modified Black-Scholes American Formula returns the intrinsic value of the option. That is:

  Black-Scholes American option value =
  Maximum (Black-Scholes European value, intrinsic value)

- **Quadratic approximation** — under this approach, it is assumed that an American option is equal to a European option plus a separate early exercise option. The quadratic approximation method determines the early exercise option value and then adds it to the value calculated by the Modified Black-Scholes European Formula. The early exercise option value is determined by an iterative process.

---

[43] For those interested in examining these approaches, refer to Appendix A.

[44] These problems are identical to the problem of pricing variable deliverable debt options generally.

- **Binomial model** — this uses a discrete time binomial process to create a tree of price outcomes to derive the value of the option. Within the tree, early exercise possibilities are identified and the tree modified to enable the American option to be priced.

In practice, the binomial model is generally used to value American-style exercise options on swaps.

# 4.   Volatility Estimation

Volatility estimation for an option on a swap is usually undertaken using one of the following methods:

- Implied volatility (determined from market premiums for options on swaps).
- Historical volatility.

In the case of historical volatility, it is theoretically necessary to get the volatility of the appropriate forward swap prices. In practice, the volatility of spot swap rates for the relevant maturity (in the above examples, the 2- and 3-year swap rates) is utilized.

A variety of alternative approaches are utilized in practice including:

- The volatility of government securities for the relevant maturity with an added element for swap spread volatility.
- The volatility of interest rate futures contracts (particularly where the underlying swap is of a relatively short maturity — less than two/three years — reflecting the use of interest rate futures to hedge the position).

# 5.   Pricing Options on Swaps in Practice

In practice, the pricing of options on swaps is subject to a number of constraints:
- The higher the degree of liquidity in the market, the closer the premium to theoretical option on a swap values.
- The depth and trading levels in the specific option on the swap market and the availability of a good two-way transaction flow that facilitates the assumption and hedging of exposures.
- The availability of hedging instruments and their cost and the efficiency of the hedge that can be achieved.

Option on swap markets vary significantly between currencies. However, a number of general trends are apparent. Shorter option on swaps (that is, those with periods to expiry of less than one/two years) tend to be priced close to their theoretical values. This reflects the following factors:

- The opportunity for arbitrage to force the prices to theoretical levels.
- Liquidity of the market that facilitates position clearing.
- The availability of a wide variety of hedging instruments including:
  1. Options on traded interest rate futures contracts.
  2. The capacity to generate forward/forward positions in interest rate swap portfolios.
  3. Availability of option and forward markets in government securities in the relevant currencies.

Option on swaps with longer maturities (that is, with periods to expiry in excess of, say, three years) are more problematic. This reflects the difficulty of hedging the options on swap positions. Consequently, these types of option on swaps tend to be driven by capital market arbitrage and, in particular, the stripping of options from capital market instruments, such as callable bonds.

# 3
# Callable Bonds (2): Extensions, Variations, and Markets

## 1.   Callable Bonds — Structural Variations

The concept of embedding a debt option within the format of a traditional fixed interest security has gradually been extended to encompass a broad variety of formats. In this chapter, three major variations, the puttable bond, detachable debt warrants and multi-step callable structures, are examined. A discussion of the market for callable securities concludes this chapter.

The structural variations considered have common characteristics with the callable bonds examined in detail in Chapter 1. In particular, the value dynamics and pricing behavior of the instruments have similarities. The major impetus to innovation derives from the desire to either overcome one or other deficiency of the traditional format of instrument or the opportunity to generate added value, in a specific market setting, by adjusting the structural features.

## 2   Puttable Bonds

### 2.1   Concept

A puttable bond entails a fixed income security where *the investor* has the right to terminate the investment by selling back the security to the issuer. The bond can usually be put to the investor at a pre-agreed price (typically, par or in some cases at a premium) on one or more predetermined dates prior to maturity of the security.

A typical transaction entails the borrower issuing a fixed interest security for a maturity of say five to 10 years with the investor having the right to terminate the transaction and put the bonds to the issuer prior to maturity, say, at the end of three years. In return for receiving the right to put the bonds to the issuer, the investors accept a lower return on the investment. Conversely, the issuer receives the benefit embodied in the lower borrowing cost, representing the option premium received from the sale of the put on its bonds, in return for accepting the interest rate and liquidity (maturity contraction) risk of the structure.

It is useful to differentiate the key features of a puttable bond with those of a callable bond:

- The callable bond combines a bond with a call option sold by the investor to the issuer. In contrast, the puttable structure consists of a bond combined with a put option sold by the issuer to the investor.[1]
- The coupon on the puttable bond is lower than that of a comparable non-callable bond reflecting the benefit of the option premium sold by the issuer to the investor. In contrast, the coupon on the callable bond will typically be higher than a comparable noncallable bond reflecting the purchase of the option by the issuer from the investor.
- The maturity extension risk is different as between the two structures. In the case of a callable bond, a fall in interest rates will under rational exercise conditions lead to the exercise of the call resulting in maturity contraction. In the case of a puttable bond, a fall in interest rates will lead to an unexercised expiry of the embedded option resulting in maturity extension.

## 2.2   Economics, Price Characteristics, and Valuation

In economic terms, the investor is purchasing a combination of a fixed interest security (with the final maturity of the bond) and a call option on interest rates or a put on the price of the bond. The option acquired by the investor has an expiry date coinciding with the put date or dates and has a strike price equivalent to the pre-agreed put value of the bond. The option premium is built into the coupon of the security.

As with a callable bond, the structure can be decomposed in a variety of ways. For example, using option on swaps/swaptions, a puttable bond can be restated, from the perspective of the investor, as:

Puttable bond  =  Nonputtable bond (final maturity equal to maturity of puttable bond)

+ Purchased payer option on swap

(strike equal to bond coupon, swap maturity equal to difference between put date and final maturity date and exercise date equal to put date)

---

[1]   Using put-call parity, the puttable can be stated also as a bond with a maturity equal to the put date combined with a call option on debt with coupon equal to that on the original bond and with a maturity equal to the original final maturity of the bond. The issuer sells the call option to the investor.

or

Puttable bond = Nonputtable bond (final maturity equal to put date)

+ Purchases receiver swaption

(strike equal to bond coupon, swap maturity equal to difference between put date and final maturity date and exercise date equal to put date)

The valuation of the embedded option can be undertaken using the analytical basis utilized with callable bonds.

The embedded option features, as in the case of callable bonds, impact upon the price characteristics and behavior of the puttable bond. The major price characteristics of the puttable bond include:

- The positive protection afforded by the put option against increases in interest rates dominates the price behavior. The likelihood of maturity contraction reflecting the exercise of the put option where interest rates increase reduces the price risk of the security without, given the asymmetric nature of the instrument payoff, reducing its sensitivity to price appreciation from decreasing interest rates.
- The puttable bond has favorable duration characteristics with the security life and number of cash flows increasing (decreasing) with decreases (increases) in interest rates.
- The puttable bonds have high positive convexity where interest rates fall, reflecting the extension of the life of the security. Conversely, puttable securities have negative convexity where interest rates increase. This is because the price does not fall for a rise in interest rates reflecting the dominant influence of the embedded put option that dictates a shortening life of the security and a payout of the agreed put price where rates increase.

The valuation of puttable bonds is complicated, in practice, by the fact that pricing is a function of two factors:

- The valuation of the fixed interest cash flows and the embedded debt option.
- The implicit credit or default risk option.

The valuation approach described above focuses on the first factor. The implicit credit or default risk option manifests itself in a number of ways. For example, to the extent that changes in credit risk of the issuer affect the spread relative to the benchmark risk-free security, value changes of the bond will be reflected in the altered valuation of the fixed interest cash flows and the embedded debt option.

A second and potentially more complex impact of changes in the default or credit risk occurs where the risk of default increases to the level where the risk of issuer default and the potential loss upon default dominates any value change on the first factor. For example, interest rates may have fallen dictating abandonment of the put in order to capture the price gains on the investment. However, deterioration in the credit quality of the issuer dictates exercise of the put in order to safeguard return of principal. Economically, under these circumstances, the present value of the capital received upon exercise of the put adjusted for the amount received under the bond if maturity is extended (effectively the recovery rate) times the probability of default is greater than the present value gains of the fixed interest security as a result of the fall in interest rates.

As discussed below, the incorporation of put options in longer term securities as a mechanism for mitigating the credit risk of the transaction necessarily requires increased consideration of this second factor in valuation. However, the difficulty in estimating the parameters required to value the default option is problematic.[2]

It should be noted that the implicit credit option applies equally to callable and puttable bond transactions. Research undertaken by Moody's Investor Services indicates that the value of the implicit credit spread option is significantly less than that of the interest rate option. This is particularly the case where the issuer's credit rating is high. However, the credit option becomes increasingly relevant as the issuer's credit rating declines.[3]

## 2.3 Applications

Puttable bonds have developed in response to a number of factors:

- The demand for fixed interest instruments that have defensive characteristics but significant positive convexity to allow the capture of maximum price benefit in a favorable interest rate environment.
- The need for credit enhancement in longer maturity debt and/or equity-linked transactions.

As in the case of callable bonds, the ability, under certain circumstances to arbitrage relative valuation of options as between the fixed income investors and the options on swaps market is also an important factor.

Investors have sought this type of security structure as a means of seeking protection from increases in interest rates. If rates increased, then investors would be able to protect the capital value of their investment by terminating the

---

[2]   The emerging market in credit derivatives shows considerable promise in allowing improved pricing of this aspect of value.

[3]   See Pimbley, Joseph M. and Curry, Daniel A. (July 1995) "Market Risk of the Step-Up Callable Structured Note"; Moody's Investor Services, New York.

borrowing transaction at the put date and reinvesting in higher yielding securities. In particular, the high positive convexity of this structure can be used to hedge the negative convexity arising from the prepayment risk in portfolios of mortgage securities. As interest rates decline, prepayment and refinancing of mortgages creates a general shortening in the term of mortgage securities. Holding puttable bonds that lengthen in maturity as interest rates decline allows investors to use these securities to hedge the characteristics of portfolios of mortgage securities.

The second application relates to the utility of the put feature in acting as a form of credit enhancement. It is typically used in both conventional debt and equity-linked transactions and takes the following form.

The issuer undertakes an issue of debt with a final maturity of, say, ten (10) years. The issue is puttable to the issuer after, say, five (5) years or every year commencing at year 5. The embedded put provides interest rate protection for the investor but in addition allows termination of the transaction prior to maturity where the investor's perception of the issuer's credit worthiness deteriorates. The put is usually unconditional and, consequently, there is no precondition to its exercise. This facilitates exercise irrespective of reason for exercise.

There are several aspects of this type of transaction that merit comment. Such features have been used, particularly, in relation to long-dated transactions (20 to 30 years in initial maturity) for lower rated borrowers within the investment grade category, usually A/BBB range. The put in such cases has been at year 7 to year 12.

The incorporation of the put feature in equity-linked transactions, usually convertibles, is designed to achieve a wider range of different objectives:

- Credit enhancement in a manner akin to that in debt noted above.
- Protection for the investor against failure of the equity price to show anticipated appreciation (remembering that the convertible coupon is reduced by the amortized premium on the equity option sold). The put on an equity convertible is designed, against this background, to convert the convertible into a debt instrument returning an interest rate comparable to the return on an equivalent non-equity-linked security. In practice, the return on exercise of the put may be equivalent to, at least, the return on a risk-free security of the relevant maturity (for example, the Treasury yield for the maturity to put at the time of issue). This requires, in the case of a convertible, the put to be exercisable at a premium to par value of the bond. This reflects the fact that the coupon on the convertible is lower than that of equivalent debt for the same maturity.[4]

---

[4] Refer to discussion in Chapter 10.

Issuers of puttable securities must be willing to absorb the liquidity and interest rate risks resulting from the potential shorter life of the security (if interest rates rose). The issuers of puttable bonds fall into two categories:

- Direct issuers who do not hedge out the embedded option preferring to generate cheaper coupon funding and accepting the maturity and liquidity risk. This risk is often assumed in the context of issuers who might find it difficult to access debt funding for the term achieved using the put structure.
- Arbitrage issuers who hedge out the embedded optionality through an offsetting derivative transaction. These issuers use this security structure as a basis for generating lower cost floating rate funding by swapping the issue proceeds into a floating rate basis. This entails the use of extendible swaps. The issuer enters into a swap where it receives fixed rates and pays floating rates for a maturity coinciding with the put date on the security. Simultaneously, the issuer purchases a receiver option on a swap to receive fixed rates (at the same rate) under a swap that commences at the put date and extends to the final maturity of the puttable security. In the event that interest rates fell and the put option was not exercised, the issuer exercises its option under the extendible swap or the receiver option on the swap to continue to maintain its status as a floating rate borrower. The lower coupon on the puttable bond allows the issuer to cover the cost of the purchase of the extendibile option or the receiver option on the swap. Typically the issuer's all-in cost of funding is below direct access to the term funding. This pricing advantage is driven by disparities in valuation of the embedded option as between the debt investor and debt derivatives markets.

In the absence of issuers prepared to undertake issues of puttable debt, an investor can create synthetic asset structures involving puttable bonds. For example, an investor can create a synthetic puttable bond by either:

- Purchasing a long-term conventional bond and purchasing a payer option on a swap whereby it pays fixed and receives floating; or
- Purchasing a short-term bond and purchasing a receiver option on a swap whereby it receives fixed and pays floating.

The reverse process is also feasible to arbitrage bond values. For example, **Exhibit 3.1** sets out an example of creating a synthetic conventional bond from a puttable bond.[5]

---

[5]    The example draws on Johnson, Cal (July 1989) "Options on Interest Rate Swaps: New Tools for Asset and Liability Management"; Salomon Brothers, New York.

**Exhibit 3.1**
**Utilizing Options on Swaps to Create a Synthetic Nonputtable Bond**

Assume Investor A (A) has purchased a 10-year AA corporate bond that is puttable to the issuer at year 5. The puttable bond yields 7.00% pa (versus the comparable yield on conventional 10-year nonputtable 10-year AA corporate bond of 7.50% pa).

In order to synthetically create a nonputtable security, A simultaneously sells a payer option on a swap transaction whereby the counterparty can pay 7.50% pa in return for receiving US$ LIBOR (if rates increase).

The diagram below sets out the position:

**Years 1 to 5 (Year 6 to 10 if Option Unexercised)**

**Years 6 to 10 (if Option Exercised)**

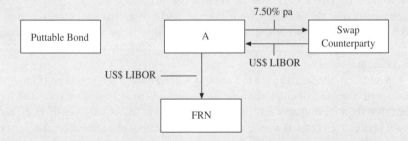

If interest rates fall, then A does not put the bonds at year 5, the option on the swap is unexercised and A receives the coupon of 7.00% pa for the full 10 years. If interest rates rise, then A puts the bond to the issuer at par, the proceeds are reinvested in a floating rate asset yielding US$ LIBOR and the option is exercised converting the floating rate investment into a fixed rate investment yielding 7.50% pa.

The effective return to A (incorporating an option premium of 4.00% flat) is:

- If option unexercised: 7.58% pa
- If option exercised:    7.79% pa

## 2.4    Puttable Bond — Structural Variations

### 2.4.1    Serial Puttable Bonds

One development in the puttable bond structure has been the serial put bond. The structure first emerged around 1996-97 in the US domestic debt market.[6]

The basic structure is a long-dated bond (40 years) that is puttable at year 1 or 2 *and every year thereafter*. Issuers of serial puttable bonds were motivated by the high value paid by investors for the embedded debt options that enabled the issuers to achieve funding rates often below US Treasury yield for comparable maturities.

The issues were driven by the environment of low nominal interest rates that were moreover decreasing. In this environment, there was strong demand for debt portfolio managers with large mortgage portfolios to purchase puttable bonds to hedge the prepayment risk of these investments. If interest rates fell, then the appreciation in values of the embedded option within the puttable bond would offset the decline in value of their mortgage investments. For these investors, the puttable structures represented a lower cost mechanism for purchasing volatility. This was predicated on the pricing of these debt options embedded in these issues being lower than in the debt derivatives market.

For the issuers, the low nominal cost of funds was the major driver of issuance. The issuer has to accept the prepayment risk. The issuers who undertook these issues were prepared to assume this risk on the basis that these types of issues did not constitute a significant part of their overall liability portfolios and hence did not expose them to significant liquidity or refinancing risk.

In addition, the structure of the serial put bonds was such that even if interest rates rose then the likelihood of an immediate put was low. This reflected the fact that the investor may not put the bond back to the issuer even if rates had risen because the options may increase in value further at a later date; that is, the future puts retain significant embedded value. The combined value of these series of puts were at a level where in a typical structure interest rates would need to increase by around 100-150 bps in the first few years of the term of the bond before it became economically desirable to exercise the put. This exercise behavior dictated that the issuer obtained very attractive rates for 1- or 2-year funding, but also was likely to retain this funding in an environment where interest rates were rising but not significantly.

---

[6]    See Salmon, Felix "Market Openings And Reopenings" (February 1998) *Corporate Finance* 32-37.

## 2.4.2 Synthetic Puttable Bonds

The synthetic puttable bond structure developed in response to issuers seeking to issue puttable bonds but concerned about the value for the embedded debt options being paid by investors relative to the value of these options in the derivatives market (specifically the market for options on swaps). The structure that evolved entailed the issue of a puttable bond that was repackaged by the underwriter in a way that sought to extract a higher value for the embedded options.[7] This market evolved in the US debt markets over 1997 and 1998.[8]

The basic structure of the synthetic puttable bond is set out in **Exhibit 3.2**.

---

**Exhibit 3.2**
**Synthetic Puttable Bond**

The structure entails the issuer undertaking an issue of a puttable bond, say a 10-year issue with a 5-year put. The bond issue is placed within a special purpose trust vehicle, arranged by the underwriter.

The trust undertakes two separate transactions:

• The trust issues a 5-year bond.
• The trust simultaneously arranges to sell the put option on the bond to the underwriter.

The 5-year bond is issued at par. The premium received for the put from the underwriter is 2.00%. The total cash flow paid to the issuer is 102% of face value of the issue.

The put option is onsold or hedged in either the bond derivatives or option on swaps/swaption portfolio of the underwriter. This derivative transaction (effectively the sale of the embedded option into the derivatives market) generates the premium that is paid through to the issuer.

---

[7] The structure appears to have been originated by UBS as the Pass Through Asset Trust Securities (PATS); variants have since emerged including Morgan Stanley's Reset Put Securities (REPs); Merrill Lynch's Mandatory Par Put Remarketed Securities (MOPPRS); CS First Boston's Term Enhanced ReMarketable Securities (TERMS).

[8] See Salmon, Felix "Market Openings And Reopenings" (February 1998) *Corporate Finance* 32-37; Rutter, James "Cross Capital Market Boundaries" (July 1998) *Euromoney* 140-142.

The transaction operates as follows:

- For the first five years, the issuer makes payments to the trust that are passed through directly to the bond investors.
- At the end of five years, the operation of the transaction is contingent on interest rates. The constant to the operation is the need to repay the investor *in the 5-year bond* the maturing principal.
- If interest rates have increased, then the underwriter exercises its right to put the bond back to the issuer through the trust. The cash received is used to fund the redemption of the 5-year issue.
- If interest rates have decreased, then the underwriter does not exercise its put. Instead, the underwriter undertakes a new issue of *5-year* securities by the trust (effectively, a sale of the original 10-year security that has five years remaining maturity). The bonds that are sold are an issue of high coupon bonds (reflecting the original coupon of the bonds that is now above the current market yield level). The sale of these bonds generates an amount in excess of par of the bonds. An amount equal to 100% of face value is used to redeem the original 5-year securities issued by the trust. The remaining value is dealt with as set out below.
- The embedded option that is stripped from the security and purchased from the trust by the underwriter and onsold or hedged settles as follows:
  - If rates rise, then the option expires out-of-the-money and no settlement is required.
  - If rates fall, then the option is exercised and the value of the option (in cash terms) is generated from the amount above par gained from the sale of *the second 5-year bond* by the trust. The sale as noted above is of a high coupon bond that generates a payment above par of which only par is required to retire the first 5-year issue.
- For the remaining 5-year life of the transaction, the issuer pays interest coupons and finally the principal redemption as normal to the trust that is used to service the second 5-year issue normally.

The structure is set out in the diagram below:

*Initial Position*

*Coupon Payments*

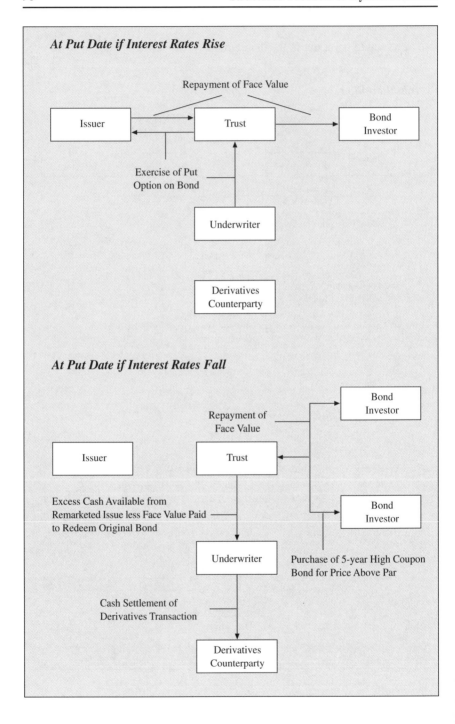

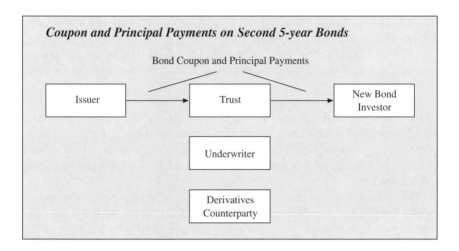

*Coupon and Principal Payments on Second 5-year Bonds*

The dynamics of the structure are as follows:

- From the viewpoint of the issuer, the transaction operates as a traditional directly issued puttable bond would operate in a liquidity/cash flow sense. The only major difference is that after five years if interest rates fall, the underwriter will undertake an issue of 5-year securities *of the issuer* indirectly through the trust without the direct participation of the issuer.
- From the viewpoint of the investor in the bonds (effectively, up to two separate 5-year bond issues), the transaction represents the traditional purchase of a bond. However, investors have generally received higher yields on the straight bonds issued as a direct result of a repackaging of a synthetic puttable security.[9] This has reflected a combination of factors:
  - The fact that the issuer is a trust entity not the direct issuer.
  - The securities issued because of the utilization of a trust-issuing entity are not SEC registered but are issued as a Rule 144a offering that usually requires a premium.
  - A premium for illiquidity of the trust offering that is considered unlikely to have the same liquidity as conventional securities of the same issuer.
  - The off-market high-coupon structure of the second 5-year bond.

In practice, the additional value that can be extracted from the sale of the embedded option into the derivatives market has more than allowed the

---

[9] For example, an issue for GMAC was undertaken at a 5 bps premium to standard GMAC bond and subsequently widened to 12 bps in secondary market trading; see Salmon, Felix "Market Openings and Reopenings" (February 1998) *Corporate Finance* 32-37 at 36.

transaction to generate both additional returns for the investors and a lower cost for the issuer overcoming the issues identified.

The evolution of the product has served to highlight some of the complexity and risks in such repackaging and has lead to a number of variations in the basic structure.

A risk inherent in the structure is the risk of changes in the credit spread of the issuer. The risk assumed by the underwriter and the ultimate purchaser of the embedded option entails both general interest rates risk (US Treasury yields rising) and specific interest rate risk (the issuer's credit spread increasing). The difficulty in hedging the second risk lead to the structure having to be amended.

The revised structure entailed the underwriter inserting a provision where by the coupon on the remarketed issue if rates fell could be different from that on the original bond. The underwriter if it sought to extend the life of the bond (if interest rates fell) would set the coupon on the second 5-year issue at the 5-year US Treasury rate at the time of original issue plus the issuer's credit spread plus the issuer's credit spread *at the time of remarketing* (that is, in five years).

This structure is designed to shift the credit spread risk to the issuer. This created additional problems:

- The exact cost of the issue to the issuer is uncertain as it is contingent on the future credit spread at the time of the remarketing.
- The credit spread applied might be high at the time the put decision is made. Given that the underwriter must remarket the bonds to generate liquidity to retire the original debt issue, there is little flexibility in undertaking the issue even in difficult market conditions. Moreover, the issuer may have little or no control over that process as the second issue is outside its control (at least, technically).

In a further series of developments, the product has evolved to accommodate the following variations:

- The trust structure has been discarded with the original longer dated bond being placed with the investor in combination with a *mandatory call* held by the underwriter. The bond is purchased back from the original investor at par as at the put date and then either put back to the issuer (if rates have risen) or remarketed (if rates have fallen).
- To increase flexibility, some issues have introduced a remarketing window that allows some timing discretion as to the date of remarketing the securities. This is designed to attempt to reduce the risk of the credit spread being reset in adverse market conditions.

To date, the substantial cost savings available to issuers have outweighed the risks of the market. These savings as noted above derive primarily from the extraction of higher values available for these options from the derivatives market as compared to the direct debt markets.

An additional driver for these structures has been the derivatives accounting directives of the US Federal Accounting Standards Board (FASB). These regulations require all derivative transactions to be marked to market. This discourages issuers from entering into the derivative transactions (in the form of an option on a swap/swaption) in the OTC market. However, the derivative in embedded form avoids the mark-to-market requirement under the current structure of the accounting framework.

The importance of this structure can be seen from the fact that in 1998 (in the period to June) 95% of puttable issuance totalling US$11.5 billion was synthetic (as distinct from direct cash). This is an increase from 1997 when only some 28% of puttable issuance totalling US$13.6 billion was in synthetic form.[10]

## 3. Debt Warrants

### 3.1 Concept

The second variation on the embedded debt option theme relates to the detachability of the embedded option. In the case of both callable and puttable bonds, the option embedded is nondetachable. Trading in the option requires the option purchaser to purchase or sell the underlying bond. The concept of facilitating the "stripping" out of the debt option and allowing the separate trading of the debt option underlies the concept of debt warrants.

Debt warrants are effectively call options on the debt of the issuer sold by the issuer to the warrant purchaser. The warrants are created in exchange for the receipt of an explicit or implicit premium (that is, the premium may be built into a lower than market cost on a related issue of debt).

From the borrower's viewpoint, the sale of warrants produces cash that reduces the cost of the borrower's total funding program. Exercise of the warrants requires the issuer to undertake issues of additional debt on terms that are pre-agreed creating additional debt funding for the issuer. The economic feature of the debt options entails the debt to be issued, under rationale exercise rules, at an effective return to the investor that exceeds the current market yields for comparable debt at the time of issue.

The difference between the callable and puttable bond structures considered above and debt warrant transactions should be noted. Debt warrants are sold by the *issuer*. In this regard, such transactions replicate puttable bonds rather than callable bonds. Conceptually, debt warrant transactions can be used to replicate

---

[10] Statistics from Credit Suisse First Boston, as quoted in Rutter, James "Cross Capital Market Boundaries" (July 1998) *Euromoney* 140-142 at 142.

puttable bonds by combining a bond issue with a maturity coinciding with the proposed put date and an issue of debt warrants exercisable on the maturity date of the bond on terms identical to that bond with a final maturity equal to the planned final maturity of the transaction. The relationship between debt warrants and callable bonds derive from the fact that the call option purchased by the issuer from the investor in a callable bond transaction can be securitized and on-sold through the issue of debt warrants.

## 3.2   Pricing and Valuation

The pricing of debt warrants is analogous to pricing of normal interest rate options. However, the following aspects of valuation of these instruments should be noted:

- As the option is not embedded within a bond, the cost of the warrant represents the purchased option premium. The lower absolute commitment of funds allows greater leverage (in the case of a buyer with low risk on a dollar amount committed basis). This feature, as discussed in detail below, may make this structure attractive to certain investors.
- The detachability of the warrants could influence valuation. The detachability allows liquidity and trading that in conjunction with the ability to optimise option value may attract a separate group of option-oriented investor.
- Warrants can more easily be structured as American-style exercise instruments due to the avoidance of a mechanical restriction derived from embedding feature in the bond. The possibility of early exercise may enhance debt value although the tendency of the bonds to move towards par as maturity approaches will affect the period of maximum option value making early exercise less likely.

## 3.3   Structural Examples

The types of debt warrant transactions can be categorized into two categories:

- Standalone issues of debt warrants.
- Fixed rate bonds with attached warrants.

The first class of transaction can be further subdivided into two separate types of transactions. The first entails debt warrants issued on *existing* securities. This type of transaction involves the creation, distribution, and trading of options on debt securities by investors or dealers. These transactions are packaged as either warrant issues or over-the-counter or exchange-traded option transactions.

The second class entails issues of debt warrant by *issuers* that are exercisable into new debt to be created and issued by the issuer. This type of transaction necessarily entails the receipt of cash from the new issue of debt. Fixed-rate bonds with attached warrants entail, generally, the second type of warrant identified. In this chapter, the focus is on this type of structure.[11]

Increasingly, in most transactions involving the issuance of debt options and warrants, the underlying funding has been swapped with the option element being stripped off and sold and the interest rate or currency basis of the funding altered. As discussed in detail below, the specific swap structure used can vary significantly depending on the overall structure of the debt warrant package.

### 3.3.1  Standalone Debt Warrant Issues

Standalone debt warrant issues entail the issue of call options on debt by the issuer. The holders of the warrants acquire the right to purchase fixed-rate bonds of the issuer on predetermined terms. Upon exercise, the issuer receives cash representing the sale proceeds of the fixed-rate bond. The issuer also receives the premium from the sale of the warrant that lowers the funding cost of the borrower.

The initial debt warrant transactions emerged in an environment of falling interest rates in the 1980s that prompted demand from investors for such instruments in order to allow them to increase their exposure to the anticipated decline in interest in a manner that was leveraged but low risk. The demand for this type of warrant was not matched by issuer interest. This reflected the fact that issuers were unwilling to issue warrants that obligated them to issue debt at above-market rates as rates fell. This demand-supply imbalance was resolved by the use of issuers who were insulated from the risk of falling interest rates through the swaption market.

The earliest examples of these structures emerged where a number of floating rate borrowers seeking to hedge interest rate risk entered into transactions requiring them to enter into additional amounts of a swap, under which they paid fixed rates in return for paying floating rates, during a specified period of sometimes up to five years. In effect, these borrowers had sold the right to pay fixed rates as rates declined in return for accepting a lower fixed cost on the swap (the swap fixed rate adjusted for the premium received on the call option sold). The transaction can be characterized as the sale by the fixed-rate payer of a receiver swaption.

One of the first such swaps allowed the counterparty to call additional amounts of the swap when fixed rates fell in the future. These swaps were created to allow issuers to undertake warrant issues or bond issues with attached warrants for additional bonds. If the warrants were exercised, additional amounts of the swap could be called to convert the fixed-rate funds into floating

---

[11] For a discussion of the evolution of this market, see Eilon, Amir "Debt Warrant Instruments" in (1987) *Warrants and Options*; IFR Publishing Limited, London 9-46.

rate debt. The counterparty, which was effectively providing a call option, received a premium for providing the option in return for absorbing the risk that rates might fall and the warrants would be exercised. The callable swap served to guarantee the borrower's spread below LIBOR on the additional funds raised.

The market for standalone debt warrants evolved to encompass two specific categories of transactions. The first entailed the issue of standalone warrants, usually by a high-quality issuer hedging its own exposure through the entry into a contingent swap (effectively, the purchase of a receiver option on a swap), capturing the value difference between the warrant premium and the cost of the option on the swap. The second structure entailed the issue of debt warrants by banks/financial institutions where the issuing institution hedged its own exposure by either repurchasing the option, replicating the option dynamically and/or repackaging existing options.

The first type of structure entailed a receiver option on a swap designed to hedge the contingent liability. The contingent liability was in the form of a call option on debt instruments (such as warrants exercisable into fixed-rate bonds) issued either in conjunction with a host bond or on a naked or stand alone basis. The call option embedded in the debt instrument could also take the form of an option to extend an existing issue.

There were two types of transactions:

- Contingent interest rate swap.
- Contingent currency swap.

The contingent interest rate swap entails purely an interest rate option. A contingent currency swap may entail either a purely interest rate option, or alternatively a combined interest rate and currency option.

The option on swap structure designed to hedge a naked debt warrant issue illustrates the mechanics of this type of transaction. In this example, a contingent swap (effectively, a receiver option on a swap) is tied to debt warrants exercisable at interest rates below current market levels.

When the warrants are issued, the two parties enter into a contingent swap agreement and the fixed-rate payer receives an up-front fee from the issuer of the warrants. The swap becomes effective if and when the warrants are exercised and is identical to a traditional interest rate or currency swap. If interest rate levels rise or remain constant, it is likely that the warrants will expire unexercised and the contingent swap provider will keep the premium. If, however, interest rates fall, the warrants are likely to be exercised and the two parties will enter into the swap as the contingent swap is triggered.

For the seller of the receiver option on the swap, the structure generates significant savings compared to a standard swap. This savings is generated from two sources:

- The fixed interest rate on a contingent swap is generally substantially below the current market level.
- The fixed-rate payer received an up-front premium that, if the warrants expire unexercised, will be retained as income, or, if the warrants are exercised, will lower the all-in cost of the swap.

The issuer of the warrants, meantime, is insulated from the fixed-rate level on the swap. If the warrants are exercised it immediately translates its fixed-rate funding into floating rate funds, usually at a predetermined margin under a floating rate index, which compares favorably to its alternative cost of floating rate funds. An example of a naked warrants issue and accompanying contingent swap is set out in **Exhibit 3.3**.

---

**Exhibit 3.3**
**Naked Warrants Issue and Contingent Swap Structure**

Institution A (A) issues warrants exercisable into A$ bonds on the following terms:

*Back Bonds*

| | |
|---|---|
| Amount | A$50 million |
| Term | 5 years |
| Coupon | 14.00% pa payable annually |

*Warrants*

| | |
|---|---|
| Number of Warrants | 50,000 (based on assumed exchange rate) each exercisable into A$1,000 bonds on above terms. |
| Assumed Exchange Rate | US$0.70/A$1.00 (see discussion below). |
| Warrant Price | See discussion below. |
| Expiry Date | The warrants will expire, unless exercised approximately one year after issue (that is, February 2007). The warrant can be exercised at any point in time before expiry. |

Institution B (B) provides a contingent currency swap (sells a receiver option on a swap) on the following terms:

| | |
|---|---|
| Amount | A$50 million |
| Term | 5 years |
| B to Pay A | 14.00% pa payable annually |
| B to Receive from A | 6-month LIBOR |

---

| Up-front Fee | See discussion below. |
| Commencement Date | The swap can be triggered at any time within one year after issue; that is, by February 2007 at the option of A. |

The rationale for the transaction is as follows:

- Issuer (A) is indifferent as, if warrants are exercised, it triggers contingent swap to achieve a margin under LIBOR.
- Purchaser of warrant gets a highly leveraged A$ interest rate play (possibly a currency play if the exchange rate is fixed (see discussion below)).
- Contingent swap provider (B) benefits from:
  - Receiving the theoretical value of the option (appropriate for a bank/financial institution that will seek to offset or hedge its exposure).
  - Gets attractively priced funding if the contingent swap is called upon (appropriate for a liability manager with funding targets that are currently unachievable in the market).

Where B is a liability manager, one possible analysis of its position is as follows:

- B can obtain funding at say 14.70% pa (payable semi-annually) (15.24% pa (payable annually)) for six years (the A$ bond rate).
- B can obtain funding for one year (the swap option period) at 17.00% pa (payable semi-annually).
- Consequently, if B can obtain funding at less than 14.24% pa (payable semi-annually) (14.75% pa (payable annually)) in one year from now, it can effect a cost saving.

The pricing dynamics of the transaction are as follows. Assume:

- A requires LIBOR minus 25bps.
- B requires 13.75% pa (payable annually) (13.25% pa (payable semi-annually) if warrants and contingent swaps are triggered to undertake the transaction.

Given these assumptions, it is possible to structure the transaction:

- B requires 25 bps under 14.00% pa (25 bps on A$50 million = A$ 125,000 pa discounted back at 15.24% pa (payable annually) (the bond rate)) equates to A$416,649 (US$291,654 at the assumed exchange rate). However, the swap may not be exercised for up to a maximum of one year; that is, B gets investment earning at 15.24% pa (payable annually) for this period, therefore allowing the up-front payment to be reduced (present valued at 15.24% pa) to A$361,549 (US$253,084). Therefore, depending on the assumption of the timing of the warrant and swap exercise, B would need between US$253,084 to US$291,654 to achieve 13.75% pa (payable annually).

- A requires 25 bps under LIBOR (25 bps on US$35 million (A$50 million @ US$0.70/A$1.00) = US$87,500 discounted back at 10.00% pa (payable annually) equates to US$331,694). Depending on the assumption of the timing of the warrant and swap exercise (see above discussion) A would need between US$301,540 and US$331,694 to achieve 25 bps spread under LIBOR.

- Given the size of the up-front payment to A and B the warrants would have to be sold for at least:

  [(US$253,084 +US $301,540)/50,000]  =  US$11.09
  [(US$291,654 + US$331,694)/50,000]  =  US$12.47

  Any price over and above that amount would be profit for the investment bank structuring and executing the transaction.

B may, in fact, require a considerably higher payment to enter into the contingent swap if it analyzes the transaction in terms of option theory to price the implicit interest rate option it is creating.

Assume that the warrants are sold for US$24.00 per warrant (net of fees, commissions, and expenses). This will result in a net inflow of US$1,200,000 (50,000 warrants @ US$24.00 each). The warrant proceeds received are utilized as follows:

- A is paid US$331,694 for acting as the issuer of the warrants.
- B is paid US$291,654 for entering into the contingent swap.
- The surplus of US$576,652 is retained by the investment bank.

The position for all participants in this transaction under different interest rate scenarios, is as follows:

| Scenario (Bond Rates % pa) | Warrant Purchaser | Warrant Issuer | Contingent Swap (Swaption) Provider |
|---|---|---|---|
| Above 14 | Not Exercised | Payment Retained | Retain premium |
| Below 14 | Exercised | Financing at LIBOR minus 25 bps pa | Fixed-rate funding at around 13.75% pa (assumes US$ funding at LIBOR flat) |

For the contingent swap provider, the opportunity loss (funding at 13.75% pa where market rates are lower) may not be relevant. For example, it may have an ongoing need for substantial fixed rate funding or is running an asset liability gap, such as a bank with high-yielding fixed-rate loans on its books that may be happy to take on the liability at an appropriate rate in any case. In the case of a professional derivatives counterparty, the position will be hedged and the value charged for the contingent swap will be the theoretical option premium that is the fair value of the option.

As a variation, the A$/US$ exchange rate on exercise of the warrant can be fixed at or near the spot rate on the date of launch or settlement.

This has the following effects:

- The purchaser of the warrants has a currency option as well as an interest rate option; that is, if the A$ appreciates irrespective of interest rate movements, the warrant may have value. The purchaser gives up the opportunity of paying less US$ to buy the bond if the A$ depreciates, but the decline in A$ is reflected in the lower US$ value of the underlying bond.
- The issuer is indifferent because it knows the maximum cost of US$ funding it is obtaining, if the exchange rate is not fixed.
- If the A$ appreciates, then it gets less US$ and achieves a higher margin under LIBOR.
- If the A$ depreciates, then it gets more US$ and achieves a lower margin under LIBOR.

The contingent swap provider is in this case granting a foreign exchange option on the A$/US$ rate. Consequently, it has an exposure to an appreciation in the A$ where it would suffer a loss as it would receive less A$ or conversely it would have to borrow more US$ to support the currency swap if it was to be triggered.

Where the underlying debt warrants are exercisable into foreign currency bonds and say the US$ amount required to buy the relevant bonds is fixed at the outset, the warrants entail both a specific interest rate and currency option that is usually covered by the contingent currency swap.

In late 1985, a currency option swap was created by Credit Commercial de France (CCF). CCF structured such a swap by issuing a US$ floating rate note for the first counterparty with attached warrants into an European Currency Units (ECU) issue. A contingent swap was then written with a second counterparty that wished to borrow ECU. If the warrants are exercised, then the contingent swap is invoked and the second counterparty pays the fixed-rate coupons on the ECU bonds. The first counterparty then pays US$ LIBOR to cover the second counterparty's interbank funding cost. The investors purchased the warrants for a premium that reflected their estimation of the potential currency and interest rate option value. Since the ECU bond warrant premium is shared by both counterparties, the first party effectively raises dollars at a sub-LIBOR rate while the second counterparty raises fixed-rate ECU at a borrowing cost well below current market levels, assuming that the warrants are exercised.

Contingent currency swaps involving DM were also pioneered by CCF with an issue of 250,000 warrants to buy a 6.375% DM bond attached to a US$250 million floating rate note issue. If the warrants are exercised, a swap is automatically triggered whereby a counterparty agrees, in return for an option premium, to assume the fixed DM liability on CCF's behalf and receive US$ coupon payments. CCF has thus hedged its currency exposure into US$ should the warrants be exercised. Similar deals were undertaken by Swedbank and PKBanken.

One innovative application entailing the use of debt warrants evolved in early 1986 when a marked decline in US$ interest rates resulted in a corresponding increase in the value of call options on existing fixed-rate bonds. This application was also relevant through the 1990s as interest rates around the world declined. In all cases, the call option on existing debt could not be exercised until some time in the future. This delay in the exercise of the call meant that its value was uncertain as an increase in interest rates between the present and the time the call was capable of being exercised would erode or eliminate the value of the option.

In this environment, two particular types of transactions evolved:

• Transactions that entailed ordinary callable fixed rate bonds.
• Transactions involving callable fixed-rate bonds that had been swapped to generate sub-LIBOR floating rate funds.

In the first case, the issuers entered into a forward swap coinciding with the call option on the outstanding securities. The issuers intended calling the bond as at the call date and simultaneously refinancing with new floating rate funds that, by virtue of the forward swap, would generate fixed rate funds at the current lower interest rates.

The second type of transaction was more complex. The borrowers had uncrystallized value from two sources: the value of the call and the value in the original interest rate swap written at rate levels above current market rates. In this environment, the borrower could call the original bond leaving it with an above-market rate swap (effectively, an in-the-money interest rate swap).

The value of the swap was realized by entering into a forward swap. The borrower made payments to the forward swap counterparty corresponding to its fixed-rate receipts from the original swap counterparty in return for receiving floating rate LIBOR payments that it passed onto the original swap counterparty.

The forward swap simply reversed the original swap between the call and final maturity of the original fixed-rate issue. This reversal left the borrower with a profit representing the movements in interest rates between the time the two swaps were entered into.

The value of the reversal was capable of being crystallized in a number of ways:

*   As a periodic flow being the difference between the two swap rates.
*   As an up-front payment representing the present value of the future cash flows.

In one case, the difference was taken as a subsidy on a new issue and swap dramatically reducing the cost of funds to the borrower. In that case, the borrower chose to effectively prefund its call by issuing debt, swapped into floating rate funds, with a maturity coinciding with that on the original issue. The value of the forward reversal of the original swap was applied to the new issue. This prefunding of the call resulted in the borrower having additional cash for the period until the call on the original issue that was consistent with its financing requirements. A number of these types of transactions, including a much publicised one for SEK, were concluded.

Forward swap structures compete with deferred call debt warrant issues as a means of crystallizing the current value in a call option not capable of being exercised until some time in the future.

Under the deferred call debt warrant structure, a borrower with a callable high coupon bond securitizes the call option by issuing debt warrants. The warrants are exercisable, on the call date, into the borrower's debt on terms coinciding closely with the original callable issue. If interest rates fall the warrants are exercised. The borrower simultaneously calls the original issue being left with funding on largely identical terms but with a lower effective cost as a result of the premium received from the issue of warrants. If interest rates increase the warrants will expire unexercised, with the borrower using the premium received to lower its all-in borrowing cost.

The forward swap structure and the debt warrant were effectively different financial engineering techniques designed to achieve similar economic objectives. The choice between the techniques is usually a purely mathematical decision based on the market conditions and the resulting economics of the debt warrant and forward swap transactions.

Key market factors include:

*   The shape of the swap yield curve that affects the pricing dynamics of the forward swaps.
*   The value characteristics of the debt warrant will be dependent upon:
    –   The warrant exercise period (that is, the period until call).

- The life of the back bonds underlying the warrants.
- The exercise period for the warrant (that is, if the warrant is a "window" warrant designed to avoid doubling up of outstanding debt).

The attitude of the borrower is also critical. In particular, the issuer's attitude to doubling up debt until call and so on is important in determining the choice between the two techniques.

### 3.3.2 Debt Warrant and Host Bond Packages

The second structural class of transactions involving debt warrants entails the issue of bonds (referred to as the host bond or debt) simultaneously with the issue of debt warrants into bonds issued by the issuer. The terms of the bonds to be issued under the terms of the warrants were, typically, similar or identical to that of the host bonds (referred to as the back bonds). The majority of these structures were arbitrage driven seeking to capture value discrepancies as between the market for debt warrants and the option on swaps market.

The transactions entailed utilizing one of two alternative arrangements:

- Where the total package has an uncertain level of proceeds over its life and/ or an uncertain maturity.
- Debt warrant packages where the amount of debt remains relatively constant and the cost to the issuer does *not* change when and if the warrants are exercised.

For example, time periods characterized by expectations of falling rates have resulted in issues entailing the offering of fixed rate bonds with attached warrants that allowed the holder of the warrant the right to further purchase fixed-rate bonds of the issuer at a predetermined coupon. The warrants that had lives of anywhere between one and seven years allowed the cost of the initial fixed-rate debt to be reduced by the proceeds of the warrants. This resulted in a saving in yield of between 50 and 100 bps pa relative to a conventional issue. The issuer was simultaneously exposed to issuing further debt at a coupon cost equal to that of the fixed-rate bonds into which the warrants can be exercised, which is generally 25 to 50 bps pa lower than the host coupon bond. Given that there are no issuance costs or fees on issuance of the warrant bonds, the cost of the warrant bond could be 70 to 100 bps pa below the issuer's current fixed-rate cost.

The overall yield savings (anywhere up to 100 bps compared to a conventional fixed-rate offering) was achieved at the expense of not being able to determine in advance how many of the warrants that create additional debt will be exercised, or indeed when they will be exercised. The issuer therefore had a known cost of debt, but an uncertain amount of debt over the life of the transaction. For fixed-rate issuers with absolute interest rate targets, the uncertainty regarding the amount of debt was not problematic. However, certain issuers were only attracted to a warrant issue on the basis of the underlying issue being swapped into floating rate US$.

If the borrower could insulate against the cost of the prospective issuance of additional fixed-rate debt as a result of the warrants being exercised, by being able to swap it into floating rate, then both parties could be accommodated simultaneously. The borrower no longer has an exposure to fixed interest rates, only to the uncertain amount of debt that might be outstanding at any time.

The perfectly matched interest rate swap allowed the issuer to swap the host issue immediately into floating rate US$. The swap provided for the swap notional principal to be increased at any time to accommodate further amounts of fixed debt created by the exercise of warrants (in effect, the purchase of a receiver option on the swap by the issuer). This structure allowed the issuer to substantially shift the exposure of warrant exercise to the swap counterparty.

The cost of the option on the swap could, however, outweigh most or even all of the advantages gained by issuing warrants. Consequently, the structure of warrant swaps increasingly began to trade off the quantum of the spread below LIBOR and warrant exercise risk. Typical warrant swap structures designed to provide cost savings and limit risk would feature a 7-year host bond issue callable at par at any time after four years with attached warrants into a 4-year bond with a life of three years. This structure was predicated on the assumption that warrants are not usually exercised until near to their expiry date and at their expiry date the host issue can be called. This capacity to call the host bond, allows the issuer to have a degree of control over the amount of debt outstanding, enabling it to keep the total volume of paper on issue constant. The issue is combined with a standard 7-year swap to convert the fixed rate into floating with the value of the warrants being used to subsidize the cost of the swap. This structure evolved into the harmless debt warrant structure.

Pioneered by the Kingdom of Denmark, debt and warrant issue packages were created to ensure that the amount of the debt outstanding remained relatively constant and the cost of the issue did not change significantly if the warrants were exercised. The host bond was made callable at any time should warrants be exercised to ensure that the amount of debt outstanding remains constant enabling a standard interest rate swap to be executed. This alternative entailed a higher cost of the host issue in terms of both coupon (approximately 0.125% pa) and call premium (approximately 1.00%). However, depending on the value of the attached warrants, the floating rate cost obtainable with this structure can be considerably better than a standard fixed rate issue without warrants. Under this structure, a conventional interest rate or (if applicable) currency swap could be utilized as the security issue's cash flows resemble a straight bond issue.

This structure essentially gave borrowers access to cheap funds designed in most cases to be swapped into floating rate at extremely competitive levels with extremely limited exposure to the implicit call option. This is illustrated in **Exhibit 3.4** with the example of an issue for Westpac Banking Corporation.

---

**Exhibit 3.4**
**Westpac "Harmless" Debt Warrant Issue and Swap**

The Westpac issue was on the following terms:
- US$100 million 10-year (maturing 1996) 10.00% pa coupon issued at 100 with 2.00% fees. The issue was callable after five years at 101.50 declining by 0.50% pa to par.
- 200,000 warrants @ US$50 each. Each two warrants are exercisable after five years into one 11.25% noncallable bond due 1996 at par (that is, US$100 per bond). During the first five years, the warrants pay 10.00% interest, and, if not exercised, they are each redeemable at US$50 in 1996.

The table below shows the cash flow (US$ million) to Westpac if the warrants are, or are not, exercised. It is assumed that the host bonds will be called if the warrants are exercised in years 6 to 10; the warrants will automatically be redeemed at maturity if they are not exercised.

| | | Year Warrants Are Exercised (Assumed Warrants Exercised at Year-end) | | | | | |
|---|---|---|---|---|---|---|---|
| Year | Not Exercised | 5 | 6 | 7 | 8 | 9 | 10 |
| 0 | 108.875 | 108.875 | 108.875 | 108.875 | 108.875 | 108.875 | 108.875 |
| 1 | −11.000 | −11.000 | −11.000 | −11.000 | −11.000 | −11.000 | −11.000 |
| 2 | −11.000 | −11.000 | −11.000 | −11.000 | −11.000 | −11.000 | −11.000 |
| 3 | −11.000 | −11.000 | −11.000 | −11.000 | −11.000 | −11.000 | −11.000 |
| 4 | −11.000 | −11.000 | −11.000 | −11.000 | −11.000 | −11.000 | −11.000 |
| 5 | −11.000 | −12.500 | −11.000 | −11.000 | −11.000 | −11.000 | −11.000 |
| 6 | −10.000 | −11.250 | −11.000 | −10.000 | −10.000 | −10.000 | −10.000 |
| 7 | −10.000 | −11.250 | −11.250 | −10.500 | −10.000 | −10.000 | −10.000 |
| 8 | −10.000 | −11.250 | −11.250 | −11.250 | −10.000 | −10.000 | −10.000 |
| 9 | −10.000 | −11.250 | −11.250 | −11.250 | −11.250 | −10.000 | −10.000 |
| 10 | −120.00 | −111.250 | −111.250 | −111.250 | −111.250 | −111.250 | −111.250 |

All in cost to Westpac as margin (bps pa) relative to US Treasuries:

| Year | Not Exercised | 5 | 6 | 7 | 8 | 9 | 10 |
|------|---------------|---|---|---|---|---|----|
|      | 43            | 43 | 27 | 13 | 0 | -8 | -8 |

*Note:* Assumes host bonds are called from the end of year 5. In the no-exercise case, warrants are redeemed at US$50.

From the table, it is apparent that the issue is structured such that the issuer is guaranteed a maximum rate, which can only decrease if the warrants are exercised. Through this structure Westpac paid a maximum of 9.82% pa (9.59% pa semi-annual or US Treasury bond plus 43 bps) a savings of approximately 20-25 bps pa on its normal cost of funds.

The issue was swapped into, at least initially, floating rate US$ LIBOR using a conventional US$ interest swap that would have been structured to accommodate the unusual cash flow pattern.

## 4.   Step-up/Multi-step Callable Bonds

### 4.1   Concept

While puttable bond structures and debt warrant structures have a lengthy history, the concept of step-up and multi-step callable bonds derives from recent history. These structures evolved in a period of low nominal interest rates and a very steep positive yield curve.

The dynamic driving this particular innovation was the fact that within a callable bond framework the value of the option component is related to the relativity of the bond coupon and the forward rate implied by the current yield curve. In the environment identified that prevailed through much of the 1990s, the high implied forward rates meant that the option embedded in a callable bond was, inevitably, substantially out-of-the money contributing to the low premium value for the option. This in turn made the additional yield available on a callable bond, relative to a noncallable bond, less attractive. This compensation for the sale of the call option was particularly small in relation to the perceived risk of exercise of the call that reflected an anticipation that the rate structure would stay relatively static and that forward rates were *overestimating* the rise in actual interest rates.

Against this background, two types of callable structures emerged in order to increase the value of the embedded option and enhance the attractiveness of the bond:

- Step-up callable notes.
- Multi-step callable notes.

The step-up callable structure (also referred to as a single step callable) entails a callable bond with a two-tier coupon—a lower coupon that prevails until the call date (usually, only a single call date is utilized) with an increase in the coupon applicable if the bond is not called. The increase in the coupon gives rise to the term "step-up." The typical structure of a step-up call involves a yield to call that is significantly higher than that on a comparable noncall bond with a maturity equivalent to the call date. The stepped-up coupon was usually set at or higher than the implied forward interest rate.[12]

An example of the terms of a typical step-up callable note is set out in **Exhibit 3.5**. In this case, the step-up callable returns around 64 bps above the 5-year Treasury at the time of issue and around 36 bps above the 5-year financing cost for the issuer. The step-up coupon is 8.25% pa, which is 156 bps over the equivalent 10-year Treasury.

---

**Exhibit 3.5**
**Example of Step-Up Callable Note**

| | | |
|---|---|---|
| Issuer | AAA/Aaa-rated issuer | |
| Amount | US$100 million | |
| Maturity | 10 years | |
| Issue Price | 100 | |
| Coupon | Year | Coupon (% pa semi-annually) |
| | 1 to 5 | 6.75 (64 bps above 5-year Treasury) |
| | 5 to 10 | 8.25 (156 bps above 10-year Treasury) |
| Call Options | Callable at the option of issuer as at year 5 | |

---

The multi-step callable structure is similar in concept to the step-up callable structure. The major difference was as follows:
- The multi-step callable entails the issuer having the right to call the bond on a sequence of successive dates, usually coinciding with the coupon payment dates, until maturity (effectively, a Bermudan option).
- The initial coupon to the first call date is set at a level that is higher than the comparable noncallable return to the call date. The coupon then increases *as at each call date*. The step-ups in the interest rate on the multi-step callable note generally follow the shape of the implied forward yield curve.

---

[12] See Chen, Shiuan and Macirowski, Tom (May 1994) "Step-uUp Callable Agency Notes"; Goldman Sachs Fixed Income Research, New York.

A multi-step callable note typically has a higher nominal spread than the traditional callable issue of the same maturity or an equivalent step-up callable note.

An example of the terms of a typical multi-step callable note is set out in **Exhibit 3.6**. The transaction described is a 5-year noncall one year. The coupon for the first year is set at an attractive spread over the 1-year Treasury rate and, if the note is not called, the coupon rises. A longer dated multi-step callable note is set out in **Exhibit 3.7**.

---

**Exhibit 3.6**
**Example of Multi-step Callable Note — 1**

| Issuer | AAA/Aaa-rated issuer | |
|---|---|---|
| Amount | US$100 million | |
| Maturity | 7 years | |
| Issue Price | 100 | |
| Coupon | Year | Coupon (% pa semi-annually) |
| | 1 | 4.75(67 bps above 1-year Treasury) |
| | 2 | 5.00 (31 bps above 2-year Treasury) |
| | 3 | 5.50 (22 bps above 3-year Treasury) |
| | 4 | 6.00 (21 bps above 4-year Treasury) |
| | 5 | 6.50 (34 bps above 5-year Treasury) |
| | 6 | 6.75 (42 bps above 6-year Treasury) |
| | 7 | 7.00 (41 bps above 7-year Treasury) |
| Call Options | Callable at the option of the issuer on each semi-annual coupon date commencing on the second coupon date (after one year). | |

---

**Exhibit 3.7**
**Example of Multi-step Callable Note — 2**

| Issuer | AAA/Aaa-rated issuer | |
|---|---|---|
| Amount | US$100 million | |
| Maturity Date | 10 years | |
| Issue Price | 100 | |
| Coupon | Year | Coupon (% pa semi-annually) |
| | 1 | 5.50 |
| | 2 | 5.75 |
| | 3-10 | Previous Coupon Plus 0.30% pa |
| Call Options | Callable at the option of the issuer on each semi-annual coupon date commencing on the second coupon date (after one year). | |

## 4.2    Economics, Price Characteristics, and Valuation

The fundamental economics of both the step-up callable and multi-step callable structures derive from the objective of extracting additional value from the embedded debt options. This additional value is created from two separate sources:

- The adjustment in the coupon, as at the call dates, has the effect of placing the call option at-the-money or closer to the money.
- In the case of the multi-step callable note structure, the option is structured as a Bermudan exercise option allowing for exercise at various dates up until final maturity that serves to further enhance the value of the option.

The value impact of this structure is evident from the examples set out above. In practice, a major determinant of value is the valuation of the embedded option as calculated by the option on swaps market that is utilized by the issuer to strip out the debt option and sell it out to lower its borrowing cost.

Development of an appropriate measure of the price characteristics of this type of security focuses on multiple metrics including:

- Duration and price convexity.
- Option-adjusted spread (OAS).
- Extension risk.

In practice, the concept of extension risk is perhaps the most important mechanism for analyzing these types of instruments.

The measurement of duration and price convexity of step-up callable and multi-step callable notes is problematic because of the uncertainty of the cash flows that are interest rate contingent. However, assuming nonexercise of the call allows estimation of the duration characteristics of such securities.

The duration characteristics of the step-up callable note may be illustrated with a simple example. The analysis compares the effective duration of two securities—a 10-year noncall note, and a 10-year note callable after five years. The duration of the noncall note declines with increasing rates reflecting the positive price convexity. The duration of the callable bond approaches that of the noncallable bonds for large movements in rates from present levels. The callable bond exhibits negative convexity characteristics for rate structure movement with duration increasing with yield reflecting the increasing likelihood of exercise or nonexercise of the calls. The step-up callable demonstrates a lower duration reflecting the higher probability that it will be called prior to maturity. Multi-step-up callables will generally have duration that is even shorter than for step-up callable structures.

An alternative means of estimating the duration characteristics is to measure the option-adjusted duration. The option-adjusted duration of the multi-step up callable will tend to be lower than that of a noncall bond and a normal callable structure. This reflects the high probability that the note will be repaid prior to maturity and is consistent with the fact that the bond has a maturity closer to the earlier call dates than the final maturity.

The concept of option-adjusted spread (OAS) calculates the effective spread of a callable bond to the underlying Treasury rate by adjusting the nominal spread by subtracting the cost of the option that is calculated within an arbitrage-free framework by generating future scenarios of interest rates. In theory, in an efficient market, the OAS of the callable note should equal the return on an equivalent noncallable security.

In practice, the concept of extension risk dominates the analysis of these types of callable notes. This reflects in part the behavior of issuers who normally set the front coupon at a higher level relative to their cost of borrowing for the shorter maturity and determine the step-up rate with reference to implied forward rates. Investors, in contrast, view these type of callable bonds as *short-term investments (to the call date) with extension risk*. This derives from the fact that unless interest rates rise at the rate implied by the forward curve, the rise in coupon on the callable as at the call date dictates that it will be prepaid. This will leave the investor with a short-term investment at an enhanced yield. Consequently, the central pricing characteristic is the trade-off between the spread of the initial coupon to comparable investments against the risk on extension of maturity.

The central factor determining extension risk is the likelihood of exercise of the call option. The three factors that will generally dictate callability are:

• Absolute level of interest rate.
• Yield curve shape.
• Volatility of interest rates.

The impact of changes in the absolute level of interest rates on call exercise relates primarily to how much rates will have to rise for the issuer not to exercise the call. The breakeven condition is the market rate for the term from call date to maturity relative to the yield to maturity of the bond if not called. The call will rationally be exercised only if the market rate exceeds the callable bond's yield to maturity.

For example, in the case set out in **Exhibit 3.7**, the yield to maturity after one year for the remaining 9-year term is 6.82% pa. If the market rate for nine years for the issuer is below this level, then the issuer would prepay the issue and refinance. If the yield curve stays static between the time of entry into the transaction and the call date in one year's time, and assuming parallel yield curve shifts, then the rate structure will have to rise by approximately 25 to 30 bps for the bond not to be called. **Exhibit 3.8** shows the expected final maturity of the bond assuming certain changes in interest rates.

**Exhibit 3.8**
**Multi-step Callable Note — Extension Risk**

The extension risk profile for a multi-step callable (on the terms set out in **Exhibit 3.6**) for a parallel and instantaneous yield curve shift is summarized below:

| Yield Curve Shift (bps) | Yield (% pa) | Average Life (Years) |
|---|---|---|
| −150 | 4.75 | 1 |
| −100 | 4.75 | 1 |
| −50 | 4.75 | 1 |
| 0 | 4.75 | 1 |
| +50 | 4.75 | 1 |
| +100 | 5.00 | 2 |
| +150 | 5.50 | 3 |

The extension risk of the multi-step-up callable note in practice is expressed as the amount interest rates will have to increase to economically dictate extension of note maturity.

The analysis highlights that the callability of the transaction is a function of how accurately the forward rates implied by the yield curve capture the actual increase of rates. To the extent that the forward rates are higher than the actual rates that prevail, the bonds are likely to be called.

The change in the shape of the yield curve will affect extension through its effect on the implied forward rate and therefore on the value of the embedded call. For example, in an upward-sloping yield curve, the forward rates will lie above the par curve. In addition, the rising yield curve will dictate that the forward rates will anticipate a flattening of the yield curve (generated by the fact that the short forward rates, say, one year, implied will be above the forward rates applicable for longer maturities. If the implied one-year forwards are realized, the call would not be exercised. A flattening of the yield curve would increase the value of the embedded options thereby requiring a higher nominal yield to create the same bond, making it more likely that the bond would not be called. For example, in the example detailed in **Exhibit 3.6**, in a curve-flattening scenario, the spread between short and long rates would have to decrease substantially before exercise of the call becomes uneconomical. In a curve-steepening scenario, the spread would have to increase equally significantly for the call not to be exercised. In general terms, in the conditions identified, a flattening (steepening) in the yield curve increases (decreases) the expected final maturity of a multi-step callable.

The impact of changes in volatility is manifested through the direct impact on option values. An increase (decrease) in volatility levels will create a corresponding increase (decrease) in the value of the embedded debt option. Increases in volatility will therefore make it more expensive to purchase the option with the result that the call will not be exercised. This is, of course, only relevant to the multi-exercise structure of the Bermudan call embedded in the multi-step callable transaction.

In practice, under conditions of stable interest rates, the multi-step callable structures have exhibited short duration with well-defined average lives and limited extension risk. The volatility of future values of callable and step-up callable structures has been found to be significantly less than that of a corresponding noncallable note.[13]

### 4.3    Applications

The applications of step-up/multi-step callable bonds is substantially investor-driven. The major issuer interest has been arbitrage driven.

The bulk of issuance has been by high credit quality issuers (in the US, it has been concentrated among federal government agencies) who have undertaken issues that have been simultaneously swapped into attractively priced floating rate funding. The value basis of such transactions has been the premium paid by the derivatives market for the Bermudan-style, step-up strike payer swaption relative to the return demanded by investors to take on the extension risk of these callable bonds.

There has been a limited volume of unswapped issuance, particularly by US mortgage financing institutions that have used the embedded call as a mechanism for hedging the prepayment risk on their mortgage loans.

Investor demand for these structures has been strong, reflecting the underlying investment and price characteristics of this security. The strongly positive slope of the yield curve in many currencies and the relatively low nominal rates of interest return has created an environment where investors have aggressively sought enhanced returns. The expectation that interest rates would not increase *at the rate* implied by the forward rate curve that could be monetized by the step-up callable format has been used aggressively to enhance fixed-income portfolio yields.

Step-up callable notes compete with a variety of other types of investments which provide similar return enhancement possibilities. These include:

---

[13]  See Pimbley, Joseph M. and Curry, Daniel A. (July 1995) "Market Risk of the Step-Up Callable Structured Note;" Moody's Investor Services, New York.

- Mortgage-backed securities (MBS).
- Index amortization rate (IAR) transactions[14]

In general, the single and multi-step-up callable notes have compared favorably with the competing options, particularly MBS transactions. The major consideration in this regard appears to have been the relative stability of the average lives and lower extension risk, as well as more predictable prepayment behavior of these structures. These characteristics have proven particularly suitable for investors seeking a final repayment of principal and easily quantified prepayment risk.

A significant part of the demand for step-up structures emerged from retail investors, particularly in the US domestic market. This demand was both directly for these securities and indirectly through retail financial institutions. In the latter case, the retail financial institutions purchased these notes as investments while simultaneously issuing retail deposit facilities, including CDs or deposit accounts that replicated the return profile of the step-up callable instrument.

## 4.4   Variations and Extensions

The development of the market for step-up callable structures has been reflected in the richer variety of structures that have become available. The major variations and product extensions include:

- Extending the credit range of issuers.
- Greater variety of maturity structures.
- Defined call structures.
- Zero-coupon callable bonds.
- Expansion of concept into other currencies.

The initial market for these structures was focused almost exclusively on the US agency market that was the largest single issuer group for these securities. As the market has developed, high-quality corporate issuers have entered the market as issuers of multi-step callable notes.

The range of maturities has also broadened with investors being able to choose from very short notes with a 6-month final maturity (with almost no call protection—3-6 months) to 20-year final maturities (with one to five years' call protection). The major trend in this regard has been a consistent shortening of maturities during the period 1994-95. Two examples of such short-dated structures—a 3-year noncall six-month and a 1-year monthly callable note—are detailed in **Exhibit 3.9** and **3.10**.

---

[14]   See Chapter 6.

**Exhibit 3.9**
**Example of Short-term Multi-step Callable Note (1) — 3 Year/**
**6-month Noncall**

| Issuer | AAA/Aaa-rated issuer | |
|---|---|---|
| Amount | US$100 million | |
| Maturity | 3 years | |
| Issue Price | 100 | |
| Coupon | Months | Coupon (% pa semi-annually) |
| | 0-6 | 5.50 (57 bps above 6-month Treasury) |
| | 7-12 | 5.75 (44 bps above 12-month Treasury) |
| | 13-18 | 6.00 (38 bps above 18-month Treasury) |
| | 19-24 | 6.25 (39 bps above 24-month Treasury) |
| | 25-36 | 6.50 (44 bps above 36-month Treasury) |
| Call Options | Callable at the option of the issuer on each semi-annual coupon date commencing on the first coupon date (after six months). | |

The extension risk of the multi-step-up callable note expressed as the amount interest rates will have to increase to economically dictate extension of note maturity is summarized below:

| Maturity (Months) | Maximum Rate Rise Up To Call Date (bps) |
|---|---|
| 6 | 27 |
| 12 | 89 |

---

**Exhibit 3.10**
**Example of Short-term Multi-step Callable Note (1) — 1 Year/**
**Monthly Call**

| Issuer | AAA/Aaa-rated issuer |
|---|---|
| Amount | US$100 million |
| Maturity | 1 year |
| Issue Price | 100 |
| Coupon | 6.10% pa payable monthly |
| Call Options | Callable on each monthly date in whole only. |

The yield advantage of the 1-year monthly call note over the 1-year Treasury was typically around 90 to 100 bps pa reflecting investor requirements. The extension risk of the multi-step-up callable note expressed as the amount interest rates will have to increase to economically dictate extension of note maturity was usually around 5-10 bps per month or around 25 bps per quarter usually reflecting investor expectations about the course of US monetary policy.

The index or defined callable structure (referred to hereinafter as defined callable notes) represents an interesting extension of the callable concept. In a defined callable note the fixed interest instrument is combined with a call option on a nominated index, typically 3- or 6-month LIBOR. If LIBOR is below the strike level, the issuer must call the note. If LIBOR is above the strike level, then the call cannot be exercised and the note maturity is extended. Both single-step and multi-step call structures are feasible within the defined callable framework. An example of a defined callable note is set out in **Exhibit 3.11**.

**Exhibit 3.11**
**Example of Index or Defined Callable Note**

| | |
|---|---|
| Issuer | AAA/Aaa-rated issuer |
| Amount | US$100 million |
| Maturity | 3 years |
| Issue Price | 100 |
| Coupon | 6.00% pa |
| Call Options | Callable at the option of the issuer after one year except if the Index is above the Index Strike Level |
| Index | 6-month LIBOR |
| Index Strike Level | 6.625% pa (200 bps over spot 6-month LIBOR) |

In typical cases, the note structure allowed the investor around 200 bps of protection against rising interest rates as the market rates must rise by, at least, this amount before these notes extend. In the event, the forward rates overestimate the rate of increase of the nominated index, the notes are unlikely to extend and provide investors with a high-yielding investment to the call date. These structures offered investors a return pick-up in the region of between 70 to 90 bps pa over the equivalent yield for a similar security.

The major advantage of defined call instruments is the fact that the call decision is based solely on the level of the agreed market index. The call is also mandatory, providing the call condition is satisfied. This is, in contrast, to the call decision in the case of a traditional callable bond that will be dependent on changes in the *issuer's* funding cost (which will incorporate changes in the issuer's credit spread) and/or changes in the shape of the yield curve. Consequently, the use of the defined call structure is designed to create certainty in the exercise of the call.

A more recent innovation (in the mid-1990s) has been the callable zero-coupon bond. The typical structure entails the investor purchasing a zero-coupon bond with a long maturity (usually 30 years). The bond is callable annually usually after a call protection period of around five years. The structure developed originally in Germany. The major investors were insurance companies seeking higher yielding securities. During the 1990s, as interest rates fell, these investors found it increasingly difficult to generate the returns often guaranteed to insurance policy-holders. This problem was exacerbated as high-yielding bonds (with coupon of 8 and 9% pa) matured. The callable zero-coupon bond proved valuable in this environment.

The rationale behind this structure was the steep German yield curve and the characteristics of the zero-coupon bond itself. The structure effectively uses a Bermudan option on a swap to enhance the return to the investor. The reinvestment of interest creates considerable leverage through the call structure. This is because the embedded option is also on the reinvested interest component. This means that the option premium is larger relative to the amount invested in the bonds.

An additional motivation underlying the structure was the ability to utilize the callable zero-coupon bonds to match asset returns to liabilities. The callable zero-coupon bonds provided the investor with a higher than market return. If the bonds were called and rates did not rise significantly, then the investor would receive a high short-term return and would face reinvestment risk. If the bonds were not called and rates increased rapidly, then the investor is guaranteed the above-market return over the life of the bonds. It is only where rates fall sharply exposing the investor to lower returns on the funds to be reinvested that the investors are in a disadvantageous position.

The concept of step-up callable bonds has been extended into a number of other currencies—most notably, Japanese yen, DM, other European currencies and Canadian dollars (C$). Examples of DM and C$ multi-step callable structures are set out in **Exhibit 3.12** and **3.13**.

**Exhibit 3.12**
**Example of DM Multi-step Callable Note**

Issuer           AAA/Aaa-rated issuer
Amount           DM100 million
Maturity Date    10 years
Issue Price      100
Coupon           Year        Coupon (% pa payable annually)
                 1-3         6.50
                 4-10        7.75
Call Options     Callable at the option of the issuer on each annual
                 coupon date commencing from the third coupon date.

The yield advantage of the note is as follows:

| Maturity (Year) | Step-up Yield (% pa) | Spread to German Swap Rate (bp) |
|---|---|---|
| 3 | 6.50 | 52 |
| 5 | 6.95 | 51 |
| 7 | 7.14 | 34 |
| 10 | 7.28 | 32 |

The extension risk of the multi-step-up callable note expressed as the amount interest rates will have to increase (assuming a parallel shift in DM interest rates) to economically dictate extension of note maturity is summarized below:

| Maturity (Years) | Maximum Rate Rise to Call Date (bps) |
|---|---|
| 3 | +25/35 |
| 5 | +75/85 |

**Exhibit 3.13**
**Example of C$ Multi-step Callable Note**

| Issuer | AA-rated issuer |
| --- | --- |
| Amount | C$100 million |
| Maturity Date | 5 years |
| Issue Price | 100 |

| Coupon | Year | Coupon (% PA payable annually) |
| --- | --- | --- |
| | 1 | 7.00 |
| | 2 | 7.75 |
| | 3 | 8.00 |
| | 4 | 8.25 |
| | 5 | 8.50 |

| Call Options | Callable at the option of the issuer on each annual coupon date commencing from the third coupon date. |
| --- | --- |

The yield advantage of this type of note required by investors was between 65 and 85 bps over the equivalent yield for a noncallable security.

The extension risk of the multi-step-up callable note expressed as the amount interest rates will have to increase (assuming a parallel shift in C$ interest rates) to economically dictate extension of note maturity in a typical transaction was around 50 to 75 bps in the first year with a gradual step-up to anywhere between 200 and 300 bps as at the final call date depending on the shape of the yield curve at the time of issue.

The motivation for conducting these transactions in other currencies is similar to that of operating in US$. The steep upward-sloping nature of the yield curve and the desire of investors to monetize expectations regarding the future path of actual rates creates an environment where the additional return available is attractive relative to the extension risk assumed.

An additional factor, at least for foreign currency fixed income investors, is the currency risk element of these investments. A major attraction of these structures has been the potential for appreciation as result of further strengthening in these currencies.

## 5.  Market for Callable Bonds

The market for callable bonds is extremely complex with the major market dynamics driven by:

• The market sectors:

- In currency terms, US$ versus other currencies.
- In market terms, US domestic versus international markets; in particular, the European markets.
- The market prior to and after the introduction and use of options on swaps to monetize and trade the embedded debt options in callable notes.

Callable bond issues have been, traditionally, a more significant part of the US domestic capital market than international markets and the bulk of callable bond issuance has been in US$. While there has been activity in other currencies, the activity is both more sporadic/opportunistic and lower in absolute volume terms.

The difference between the market sectors appears based on a variety of factors including:

- The fixed income investor in the US is predominantly institutional. In contrast, the corresponding investor base in European and Japanese markets has a stronger retail element.
- US investors tend on the whole to be among the most quantitative in their approach to fixed income portfolio management. In addition, US fixed interest investors are, often, benchmarked against indexes and are required to run interest rate immunized portfolios. In contrast, other markets, particularly retail investment, are less quantitative in investment approach and are also total rate of return investors.

The difference in investor base and investment approach manifests itself in relation to investment in callable securities in a number of ways. Institutional investors, such as those in the US, view callable notes in a relative value framework and use these instruments for the following purposes:

- To arbitrage between securities on a "rich/cheap" basis incorporating the option features of callable bonds to look for investment value.
- To adjust the return and price convexity profile of a portfolio against identified liability funding constraints.
- To sell optionality and trade volatility of interest rates as a means for generating yield enhancement, effectively assuming extension risk in return for premium income generation.
- Implementation of strategies to extract value from the yield curve.

In contrast, other investors, including retail investors and other European investors, seek to maximize fixed interest returns through a combination of leverage to anticipated interest rate movements through trading in options and investment timing.

The former approach favors both traditional and more recent callable bond approaches as means for incorporating debt options within fixed income portfolios. The latter approach does not favor the use of callable securities but favors the use of debt options in the form of debt warrants. These instruments combine low dollar value commitment (particularly where the option is structured out-of-the-money), low and known risk (the premium) for the buyer and the high leverage of returns to a favorable movement in the underlying. These instruments are particularly suitable for the type of investment approach identified.

This dichotomy in market structure results in a thriving market for callable notes of a wide variety of structures in the US domestic markets in US$. In contrast, other markets generally favor debt warrants. The advent of debt warrants as a means for securitization of the embedded debt option in bonds, interestingly, was substantively a European market phenomenon that is consistent with this hypothesis.

In recent times, the demand for debt options packaged as warrants has continued to thrive with concentrated periods of activity in particular currencies reflecting changing investor expectations on rate movements. Increasingly, this demand is met not by genuine debt issuers, issuing debt warrants exercisable into new debt of the issuer but rather, by either a financial institution or high-quality issuer, issuing debt warrants either on a standalone basis or embedded in a structured note. The underlying interest rate option exposure is hedged in the derivatives markets by dynamic replication of the option or the repackaging of existing options.

The above analysis is not designed to suggest that there is *no* activity in callable bonds in currencies other US$ or in markets other than the US market. It is, however, intended to convey the broad pattern of activity. Issuance of callable securities, when it occurs in these other currencies and markets, is in response to specific demand that is usually driven by particular market conditions. Such conditions have in recent times included investor demand for yield enhancement in a positive yield curve environment that has allowed investors to generate value through the sale of options embedded in callable bonds. These opportunities have existed from time to time in a variety of currencies.

The other major dynamic of the market for callable securities has been the gradual development of the market for options on swaps in the relevant currencies. The availability of options on swaps has fundamentally altered the nature of the market in two separate ways:

- The capacity to allow issuers to undertake callable issue without exposure to the embedded option.
- The ability to value, securitize and trade the underlying debt option through the option on swap market.

Traditionally, the market for callable securities suffered from problems of supply/demand imbalance reflecting periods where the market consensus on interest rates created either excess demand for or excess supply of callable securities. The fact that options on swaps can be used to repackage the embedded debt option and resell it into a different market has allowed more consistent use of these structures. It allows the introduction of opportunistic arbitrage borowers who use the callable issue as a means for capturing the value difference as between the fixed income and swaption markets in terms of lower borrowing cost. These issuers basically trade off maturity uncertainty or liquidity risk on their underlying funding in return for an improvement in their cost of borrowing.

The second benefit relates to the ability to accurately value the embedded debt option. The availability of a market for options on swaps facilitates the decomposition of the callable bond into a fixed interest security and a receiver or payer option on an interest rate swap as a means for accurately valuing the transaction. It also facilitates, as noted above, the capacity to recreate callable bonds and their variations by a process of reverse engineering using noncallable bonds and options on swaps. This creates naturally a deeper and more liquid market for callable securities.[15]

It is evident that the opportunities for securitizing options implicitly in debt issues is not available continuously. For example, within the deepest and most liquid options on swaps market in US$, the opportunities for this type of transaction occur relatively spasmodically. This is not to suggest that no options on swaps entailing securitization of debt options were undertaken outside these periods, however, there was a significant concentration of activity during these periods.

A possible explanation is the existence of market factors that were conducive to this type of arbitrage activity. The various phases of activity were also significantly different in terms of market sector and type of transaction undertaken.

For example, the period in the second half of 1987 was focused on the US domestic bond market and involved 5-year/3-year noncall issues and 3-year/2-year noncall structures. The issuers were generally banks and financial institutions, both US and foreign, which were issuing deposit notes.

This contrasts with other periods of activity that have been focused on the European markets with the issues being targeted to investors (primarily, Japanese institutions) that were seeking to generate higher running coupon yields than that achievable through conventional transactions. For example, the activity in late 1989 through early 1990 was focused on investors interested in high-running yield and willing to trade off yield for maturity. These investors were primarily Japanese regional banks and leasing companies. These

---

[15] See Bookstaber, Richard, Hanley, William C., and Noris, Peter D. (December 1994) "Are Options on Debt Issues Undervalued?;" Morgan Stanley Fixed Income Analytical Research, New York; Latainer, Gary D. and Jacob, David P. (October 1985) "Modern Techniques For Analyzing Value and Performance of Callable Bonds"; Morgan Stanley Fixed Income Analytical Research, New York.

transactions took the form of Eurobonds with final maturity of 10 years, with a call at three years.

As the arbitrage opportunities in the conventional debt option-stripping market were reduced through the systematic arbitrage process involving the use of options on swaps, a variety of other security structures evolved.

Through 1990, a number of fixed floating notes were issued. The typical structure entailed an issue with a floating rate coupon (priced relative to US$ LIBOR) for years 1 to 3 and then a fixed coupon for the remaining life of the transaction (typically, seven to 10 years). Such transactions were linked to the purchase by the issuer of receiver options on swaps designed to swap the fixed-rate coupon commencing in year 3 through to maturity into a floating-rate basis. In 1991-92, a number of US federal agencies undertook step-up callable issues in the US domestic market that ultimately evolved into the multi-step callable structure.

As noted above, callable notes/swaptions are also available in a number of other currencies. However, the level of activity in other currencies, with minor exceptions, is more sporadic, less systematic and linked to particular market conditions that prevail from time to time. The pattern of activity in options on swaps in the DM swap market are illustrative of the pattern of activity generally outside the US$ swap market.

The German option on swap market has been driven historically by the German Federal Government and its appetite for fundraising. In the early 1990s, for example, in an attempt to keep coupons below 9% pa, German issuers offered investors in Schuldscheindarlehen (often referred to as Schuldscheine) the ability to put these bonds back after one, two and three years. Investors purchasing the Schuldscheine typically strip the put option and sell it to the option on swaps market. The government's role as essential suppliers of long-term options on government securities, through this put option, effectively facilitated the development of the D-mark option on swaps market.

In summary, the market for callable bonds is, to a large degree, a market that focuses on the US$ and the US market. However, the basic technology is readily available and adaptable to other currency markets and is increasingly being applied to those markets.

## 6. Summary

Callable bonds represent one of the most traditional forms of structured note transaction consisting of an embedded debt option within a traditional fixed income instrument. The structure has developed, in response to market conditions, a rich and complex variety of variations and extensions that are largely concerned with improving the value captured through the embedded option and/or the adjustment of the investment characteristics to particular interest rate environments.

# 4
# Interest Rate-linked Notes

## 1.   Introduction

Interest rate-linked notes are a class of structured notes that link the value of coupon payments or principal repayments to an identified interest rate or the prices of a specific debt security.[1]

Interest rate-linked notes are similar to the callable bond structures detailed in Chapters 2 and 3. The major differences, which underlie the differences between traditional and more modern structured notes, relate to the specific incorporation of exposure to defined indexes to create a desired risk-reward profile for the investor.

There are two classes of interest rate-linked note structures:

- **Interest rate forward-embedded structures** — including inverse/reverse FRNs, superfloater notes, arrears reset/delayed LIBOR set structures and bond price or interest-linked structures.
- **Interest rate option-embedded structures** — including capped and collared FRNs.

An emerging area of relevance is bond index-linked derivatives, including bond index-linked notes.

---

[1]   For examples of interest rate-linked notes, see Koh, Kenny (1986) Option or Forward Swap-Related Financing Structures; unpublished research paper presented to course on Swap Financing, Centre for Studies in Money, Banking and Finance, Macquarie University; Cunningham, Michael M. (1987) Selected Analysis Of Recently Issued Index-Linked And Option Embedded Securities; unpublished research paper presented to course on Swap Financing, Centre for Studies in Money, Banking and Finance, Macquarie University; Das, Satyajit "Option Swaps: Securitising Options Embedded in Securities Issues" *Journal of International Securities Markets* (Summer 1988) 117-138; Das, Satyajit (1994) *Swaps and Financial Derivatives*; LBC Information Services, Sydney; McGraw-Hill, Chicago at Chapter 15.

In this chapter, the structures identified are analyzed in terms of their structural features, value dynamics for investors, pricing, and trading/hedging. Interest rate-linked notes that embed exotic options within the structure are also increasingly common. These structures are discussed in Chapter 13. Constant Maturity Treasury (CMT) notes are a special class of interest rate-linked securities and are covered in Chapter 5.

## 2.   Inverse Floating-rate Notes

### 2.1   Evolution

Inverse FRNs (also known as reverse or bull FRNs)[2] are fixed income structured notes that were popular among investors in the period 1985-1986 and again through the 1990s. The major attraction of the instrument is the higher returns generated in an environment of declining interest rates and/or steeply positively sloped yield curves.

In early 1986, during a period of sustained decreases in interest rates, investors seeking the benefit from expected declines in short-term interest rates sought an instrument whose yield increased as interest rates fell. The inverse FRN was created in response to this demand. The concept of inverse FRNs enjoyed a significant resurgence in the 1990s—a period characterized by a fall in global interest rates and the advent of sharply upward-sloping yield curves in a number of major currencies.

### 2.2   Structure[3]

#### 2.2.1   Key Terms

The inverse FRN carries a floating interest coupon (reset usually 3- or 6-monthly) that is calculated as a fixed rate (say, 17.25% pa) less a floating money market interest rate (say, 3- or 6-month US$ LIBOR). As LIBOR decreases, the return payable under the note increases commensurately. The return on the inverse FRN cannot be negative if floored at 0% pa. **Exhibit 4.1** sets out the terms of an inverse FRN.

---

[2]   The term inverse FRN is used throughout.

[3]   See Fisher, Mark "At Issue The Interest Rate"(February 1993) *Corporate Finance* 29-33; Powell, Amy "Structured Derivatives Boost Returns" in (1994*) Corporate Finance Risk Management & Derivatives Yearbook* 61-63.

---

**Exhibit 4.1**
**Inverse FRN Issue**

| | |
|---|---|
| Amount | US$100 million |
| Term | 5 years |
| Interest Payment | 17.25% less six months' US$ LIBOR flat. Interest is payable semi-annually (calculated on bond basis). |
| Minimum interest | 0% pa At no time will there be negative interest for the investor; that is, if US$ 6-month LIBOR reaches 17.25% pa or above, the investor will not be required to make any payment to the issuer |

---

The inverse FRN can be unbundled into three separate components (see **Exhibit 4.2**):

- A fixed-rate bond (yielding, say, 8.50% pa, in the example set out in **Exhibit 4.1**).
- An interest swap where the investor receives fixed rates and pays floating rate (say, receiving 8.75% pa versus payment of 6-month LIBOR, in the example set out in **Exhibit 4.1**).
- An interest rate cap on the floating-rate index purchased by the investor from the issuer (with a strike of 17.25% pa, in the example set out in **Exhibit 4.1**).

In effect, the inverse FRN is a fixed interest bond with an embedded interest rate swap and an interest rate cap.

**Exhibit 4.2**
**Decomposition of Inverse FRN**

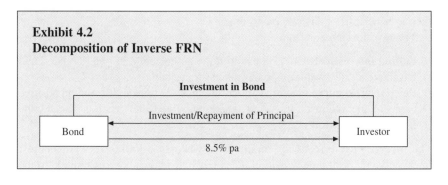

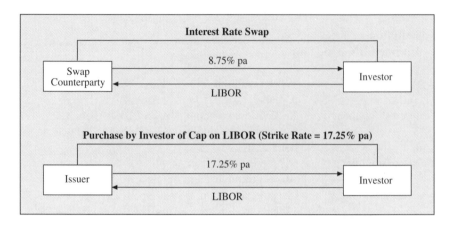

## 2.2.2 Investor Perspective

The major investors in inverse FRN structures were money market or traditional FRN investors.

From the perspective of the investor, the inverse FRN provides increased returns where interest rates fall or where the yield curve is upward sloping. The return behavior of the inverse FRN is exactly the opposite of a conventional FRN. This, in part, explains the type of investor in these instruments. In the yield curve environment identified, the traditional mechanisms for capturing value would entail in the physical market extension of the term/duration of fixed interest investments in the portfolio or in the derivative market purchasing forward the securities or receiving fixed/paying floating under an interest rate swap. The transactions would benefit from the continuation of a strongly upward-sloping yield curve or declines in interest rates. The inverse FRN provides similar exposure for the investor. The structure enables investors unable or unwilling to extend maturity or enter into derivative transactions to seek to benefit from this rate environment.

The investor benefits from:

- **Falling interest rates** — as a result of the appreciation of both the bond and the interest rate swap component of the transaction.
- **Positive yield curve** — which allows the investor to benefit from the positive carry in the interest rate swap where the fixed-rate receipts exceed the floating-rate outflows.

The inverse FRN effectively entails the investor purchasing forward interest rates on the relevant money market index (LIBOR in the above example). To the extent that the current implied forward rate curve *overestimates* the actual rise in interest rates over the term of the security, the investor will obtain a benefit from the inverse FRN investment.

**Exhibit 4.3** sets out an analysis of the financial performance of the inverse FRN described in **Exhibit 4.1**. The return to the investor is analyzed under a range of interest rate scenarios entailing progressive increases or decreases in the 6-month LIBOR rate.

**Exhibit 4.3**
**Inverse FRN — Return Analysis**

| | |
|---|---|
| Term (years) | 5 |
| Fixed Coupon | 17.25% |
| Floating Coupon | LIBOR |
| Current LIBOR | 7.25% |
| Swap Rate | 8.75% |

| Projected Cash Flows Case | | | | |
|---|---|---|---|---|

| Progressive Change in LIBOR (per semi-annual period) | −0.50% | −0.25% | 0.00% | 0.25% | 0.50% |
|---|---|---|---|---|---|

| | | | | | |
|---|---|---|---|---|---|
| Yield | 12.01% | 11.01% | 10.00% | 8.97% | 7.91% |
| Spread to Swap | 3.26% | 2.26% | 1.25% | 0.22% | −0.84% |

| Period (Semi-annual) | LIBOR | LIBOR | LIBOR | LIBOR | LIBOR |
|---|---|---|---|---|---|
| 0 | | | | | |
| 1 | 7.25% | 7.25% | 7.25% | 7.25% | 7.25% |
| 2 | 6.75% | 7.00% | 7.25% | 7.50% | 7.75% |
| 3 | 6.25% | 6.75% | 7.25% | 7.75% | 8.25% |
| 4 | 5.75% | 6.50% | 7.25% | 8.00% | 8.75% |
| 5 | 5.25% | 6.25% | 7.25% | 8.25% | 9.25% |
| 6 | 4.75% | 6.00% | 7.25% | 8.50% | 9.75% |
| 7 | 4.25% | 5.75% | 7.25% | 8.75% | 10.25% |
| 8 | 3.75% | 5.50% | 7.25% | 9.00% | 10.75% |
| 9 | 3.25% | 5.25% | 7.25% | 9.25% | 11.25% |
| 10 | 2.75% | 5.00% | 7.25% | 9.50% | 11.75% |

The analysis indicates that the inverse FRN returns a yield above the swap rate prevailing at the commencement of the transaction under a range of circumstances. If 6-month LIBOR increases at a rate exceeding 30 bps per semi-annual period, then the return on the inverse FRN underperforms the swap rate at the commencement of the transaction.

### 2.2.3  Issuer Perspective

Inverse FRNs hold little attraction for issuers who would be disadvantaged if short-term interest rates fell. Therefore, in most cases, the issuers are totally insulated from the embedded interest rate linkages in the structure. The derivative structure designed to protect the issuer from increases in its effective cost of funds is set out in **Exhibit 4.4**. Under this structure, the issuer undertook conventional interest rate swaps for *double* the amount of the FRN issue to create a synthetic floating rate liability. In the event that the issuer sought to create a fixed-rate liability it would have entered into an interest rate swap for an amount equal to the face value of the inverse FRN itself.

---

**Exhibit 4.4**
**Hedging an Inverse FRN**

The inverse FRN issue is hedged utilizing a derivative structure whereby the Issuer receives from swap counterparty under a conventional US$ interest rate swap:

| | |
|---|---|
| Notional Principal Amount | US$200 million |
| Term | 5 years |
| Issuer Pays Swap Counterparty | LIBOR-0.125% pa |
| Issuer Receives from Swap Counterparty | 8.625% pa payable semi-annually |

The total transaction can be depicted as follows:

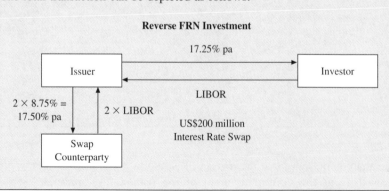

**Reverse FRN Investment**

---

The net effect of the transaction is to generate LIBOR less 25bps on a principal borrowing of US$100 million for the issuer.

Importantly, this result is achieved so long as LIBOR is less than 17.25% pa; that is, the basic fixed interest coupon on the FRN issue. Where LIBOR exceeds 17.25% pa S/A, the sub-LIBOR margin to the issuer would be eroded. This exposure is hedged by the issuer purchasing a cap with a strike price of 17.25% pa on US$ 6-month LIBOR from the swap counterparty.

## 2.2.4  Leverage

The inverse FRN structure has inherent leverage in that it creates an exposure to interest rate movements on *double* the face value of the instrument. This reflects the fact that the structure has, at least, two sources of exposure to interest rates—namely, the fixed-rate bond and the interest rate swap.

However, if required, the degree of leverage can be increased by combining the fixed-rate bond with an increased face value amount of interest rate swaps. In **Exhibit 4.5** an example of adding leverage is set out. In this case, the example discussed in **Exhibit 4.1** is leveraged by a factor of four times.

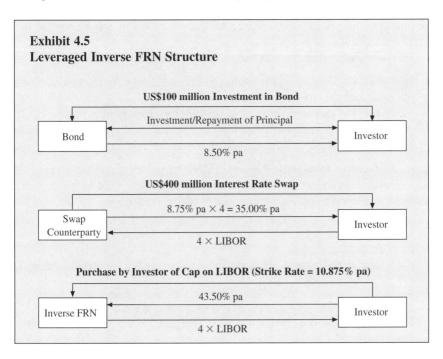

**Exhibit 4.5**
**Leveraged Inverse FRN Structure**

US$100 million Investment in Bond

Investment/Repayment of Principal

Bond — Investor

8.50% pa

US$400 million Interest Rate Swap

8.75% pa × 4 = 35.00% pa

Swap Counterparty — Investor

4 × LIBOR

Purchase by Investor of Cap on LIBOR (Strike Rate = 10.875% pa)

43.50% pa

Inverse FRN — Investor

4 × LIBOR

As is evident, the inverse FRN coupon is restated as:

Fixed-rate bond coupon + 4 times (Fixed-rate swap receipts – floating
rate swap payments)
= 8.50 + 4 × (8.75 – LIBOR)
= 43.50 – 4 × LIBOR

The strike level of the cap embedded must also be adjusted to 10.875%pa.

The adjustment to the cap reflects the fact that the inverse FRN coupon is constrained from becoming negative. The cap level is adjusted down to the level at which the coupon would become negative. The fall in the cap level also highlights the role played by the coupon on the fixed interest bond that effectively is available to offset a negative cash flow on the interest rate swaps. However, as the leverage of the structure is increased, the cash flow shortfall for a given movement up in rates is higher requiring a lowering of the cap level.[4]

## 2.3   Pricing/Valuation

The pricing and valuation of the inverse FRN flows from its structural components.[5] As is evident from the hedging structure set out in **Exhibit 4.4**, the value of the inverse FRN is the sum of the value of the fixed-rate bond, the interest rate swap and the interest rate cap. The only additional pricing parameter required is the target floating rate cost required by the issuer. The components are priced in accordance with normal pricing approaches for the individual instruments.

The sources of value shifts in an inverse FRN should be noted:

• Movements in *term* interest rates that will create changes in the value of both the bond and the interest rate swap.
• Movements in short-term rates that, through the changes in the shape of the yield curve when combined with term rate movements, will dictate changes in value in both the interest rate swap and in the cap.

Secondary market valuations of inverse FRNs, inevitably, entail the reversal of the embedded derivative elements and a repackaging as a fixed or floating rate security. **Exhibit 4.6** sets out an example of such a repackaging.

---

[4]   For a more recent example of a leveraged structure see "Reverse Thrust" (June 5, 1997) *Financial Products* Issue 67 8-9.
[5]   See Smith, Donald J. "The Pricing Of Bull And Bear Floating Rate Notes: An Application of Financial Engineering" (Winter 1988) *Financial Management* 72-81; Jones, Morven and Perry, Simon "How To Hedge A Reverse Floater" (September 1990) *Corporate Finance* 47-48.

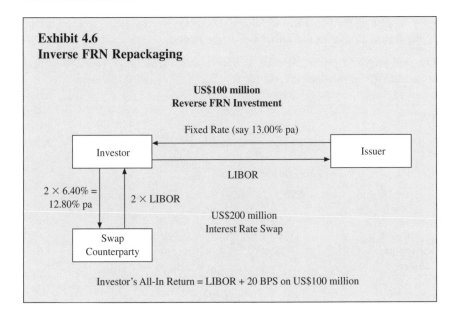

Exhibit 4.6
Inverse FRN Repackaging

US$100 million
Reverse FRN Investment

Fixed Rate (say 13.00% pa)

Investor                                                    Issuer

LIBOR

2 × 6.40% =
12.80% pa          2 × LIBOR

2 × LIBOR          US$200 million
                   Interest Rate Swap

Swap
Counterparty

Investor's All-In Return = LIBOR + 20 BPS on US$100 million

## 2.4   Product Variations

There are a number of variations on the basic structure of an inverse FRN.[6]
These structural variations reflect attempts to capture value from this format in
different market conditions. Two such variations are:

• Variations on the basic inverse FRN structures such as deferred inverse
  FRNs, step-up FRNs, and minimum coupon inverse FRNs.
• The superfloater (or bear) FRN.

Exhibit 4.7 details an example of a DM Inverse FRN issue. These issues were
undertaken in the early 1990s, particularly in Germany. The driving force behind
this type of structure was the negative slope of the yield curve and the
expectation of falling short-term money market rates.

The structure combines a fixed interest bond with a *forward* interest rate
swap and a deferred interest rate cap. The major benefits of this structure for the
investor includes:

• The capacity to enjoy higher interest rates in the early part of the transaction
  based on the prevailing yield curve.

---

[6]  See "Reverse Floaters – Riding High" (February 17, 1993) *IFR Swaps Weekly* Issue
6 6-7.

- A capture of the benefit from falling short-term interest rates over the life of the transaction after the initial fixed-rate period.

The hedging and pricing of this structure was identical in concept to that applicable to the standard inverse FRN.

---

**Exhibit 4.7**
**Deferred Inverse FRN Issue — Example 1**

*Terms of Deferred Inverse FRN Issue*

Issuer A undertakes a deferred inverse floater denominated in DM on the following terms:

| | |
|---|---|
| Amount | DM100 million |
| Maturity | 10 years |
| Interest | Years 1-3 fixed at 9.00% pa |
| | Years 4-10 floating calculated as 16.00% minus 6-month DM LIBOR |
| Minimum Coupon | The coupon cannot be negative. |

*Investor Perspective*

The investors in this instrument will benefit in years 4-10 if DM LIBOR falls. For example, the return to the investor at varying DM LIBOR levels is set out below:

| DM LIBOR (% pa) | Investor Return (% pa) |
|:---:|:---:|
| 9.00 | 7.00 |
| 8.50 | 7.50 |
| 8.00 | 8.00 |
| 7.50 | 8.50 |
| 7.00 | 9.00 |
| 6.50 | 9.50 |
| 6.00 | 10.00 |
| 5.50 | 10.50 |
| 5.00 | 11.00 |

*Hedging Structure*

The issuer is indifferent to whether rates rise or fall as it hedges itself against the inverse characteristics of the structure by entering into the following swaps:

- A forward DM interest swap for 7-years commencing three years forward whereby A receives fixed DM at 8.85% pa and pays 6-month DM LIBOR.
- A also purchases a deferred 7-year cap commencing in three years at a strike price at 16.00% pa for a premium of 25bps.

The cap is designed to protect A from the contingency that DM LIBOR rises above 16.00% pa as the coupon cannot be negative. If DM LIBOR rises above 16.00% pa, the investor receives no interest on the bond. A must pay DM LIBOR under the terms of the forward interest rate swap. A's payment under the swap is effectively hedged by the cap that generates the shortfall where DM LIBOR is above 16.00% pa.

The issue and accompanying swap structure is set out below:

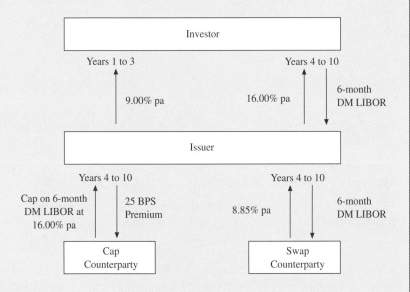

The all-in cost to the issue of the transaction is 7.86% pa (before any issue fees or the cost of the cap). Assuming issue fees of 1.25% and a cap premium of 25 bps, the all-in cost of the transaction to A is approximately 8.09% pa.

In the event that A wishes to generate floating-rate funding, A would enter into a 10-year DM interest rate where it receives DM fixed at 8.75% pa and pays 6-month DM LIBOR.

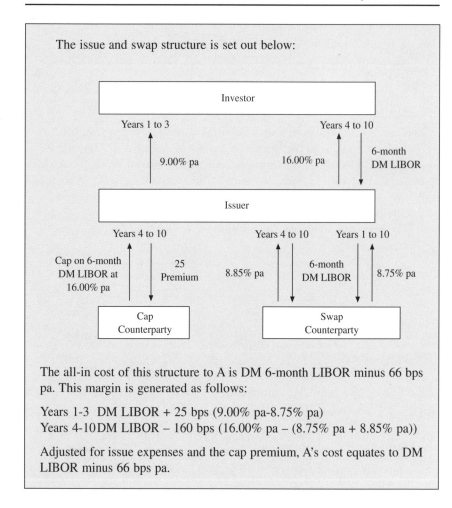

The issue and swap structure is set out below:

The all-in cost of this structure to A is DM 6-month LIBOR minus 66 bps pa. This margin is generated as follows:

Years 1-3  DM LIBOR + 25 bps (9.00% pa-8.75% pa)
Years 4-10 DM LIBOR – 160 bps (16.00% pa – (8.75% pa + 8.85% pa))

Adjusted for issue expenses and the cap premium, A's cost equates to DM LIBOR minus 66 bps pa.

In recent times a number of deferred inverse FRN structures have been issued in a number of European currencies. **Exhibit 4.8** on page 141 sets some examples of these structures. The minimum coupon on the second structure (as described in detail below) is created by adjusting the strike level of the embedded cap.

A variation on the inverse FRN is the incorporation of a step-up pattern in the coupons. **Exhibit 4.9** on page 141 sets out the terms of such an issue. **Exhibit 4.10** on page 142 sets out an example of this structure in yen. The structure basically embeds a series of forward swaps and deferred interest rate caps in the issue designed to maximize the value capture from the yield curve. The second structure in yen entails several additional structural features, including the variable amount of forward swaps embedded and the call options (effectively sold receiver swaptions) embedded in the structure.

**Exhibit 4.8**
**Deferred Inverse FRN Issue — Example 2**

*Structure 1*

| | |
|---|---|
| Issuer | A-rated issuer |
| Amount | Lira 20,000 million |
| Term | (approximately) 9 years |
| Coupon | Year | Interest rate (% pa) |

| Year | Interest rate (% pa) |
|---|---|
| 1-2 | 3-month lira LIBOR + 0.125 |
| 3-9 | 21% — 6-month lira LIBOR |

Coupon calculated semi-annually

| | |
|---|---|
| Minimum Coupon | 0% pa |

*Structure 2*

| | |
|---|---|
| Issuer | AAA rated issuer |
| Amount | Portuguese escudos 10,000 million |
| Term | 10 years |
| Coupon | Year | Interest rate (% pa) |

| Year | Interest rate (% pa) |
|---|---|
| 1-4 | 6.50 |
| 4-10 | 13% — 12-month Escudo LIBOR |

Coupon calculated annually

| | |
|---|---|
| Minimum Coupon | 4.00% pa |

**Exhibit 4.9**
**Step-up Inverse FRN — Example**

| | |
|---|---|
| Amount | US$100 million |
| Term | 3 years |
| Coupon | Year | Interest rate (% pa) |

| Year | Interest rate (% pa) |
|---|---|
| 1 | 10% — 3-month LIBOR |
| 2 | 11% — 3-month LIBOR |
| 3 | 12% — 3-month LIBOR |

Coupon calculated quarterly on bond basis.

| | |
|---|---|
| Minimum Coupon | 0% pa |

**Exhibit 4.10**
**Step-up Inverse FRN**

Issuer               AA-rated issuer
Amount               ¥5,000 million
Term                 5 years
Coupon               Year     Interest rate (% pa)
                     1        2.00
                     2        2.70% — (0.8 × 6-month ¥ LIBOR)
                     3        2.90% — (0.6 × 6-month ¥ LIBOR)
                     4        3.10% — (0.4 × 6-month ¥ LIBOR)
                     5        3.30% — (0.2 × 6-month ¥ LIBOR)
                     Coupon calculated semi-annually
Minimum Coupon       0% pa
Call Option          The note is callable at par after one year and every
                     year thereafter.

An example of an inverse FRN with a guaranteed minimum coupon is set out in
**Exhibit 4.11**. This transaction, undertaken in 1995, was designed to take
advantage of expected monetary policy easing in DM. The issue was a DM-
denominated inverse FRN whose coupon is linked to the 6-month DM LIBOR
rate. The typical coupon was 11.50% minus 6-month DM LIBOR. The only
unusual feature of these issues was the guaranteed minimum coupon of 4.50%
pa. The minimum coupon was generated by embedding a cap on 6-month DM
LIBOR at 7.50% pa in the issue. The issue return profile is also set out in
**Exhibit 4.11**.

**Exhibit 4.11**
**DM LIBOR FRN**

Issuer               AAA-rated financial institution
Amount               DM 100 million
Issue Price          100%
Maturity             5 year
Coupon               11.50% — 6-month DM LIBOR
                     Payable semi-annually on actual/360 day count basis
Minimum Coupon       3.50%

The return profile of the transaction is set out in the table below:

| Change in 6-month DM LIBOR (per semi-annual period) (bps) | Final 6-month DM LIBOR (%) | Inverse FRN Yield (%) | Approximate Spread to 5-year DM Swap Rate (bps) |
|---|---|---|---|
| –40 | 1.65 | 7.92 | 152 |
| –20 | 3.45 | 7.09 | 69 |
| 0 | 5.25 | 6.25 | –15 |
| +20 | 7.05 | 5.39 | –101 |
| +40 | 8.85 | 4.52 | –188 |

The superfloater FRN was designed to provide investors with an enhanced return in an environment of rising interest rates. **Exhibit 4.12** sets out the terms of a typical transaction. **Exhibit 4.13** sets out the hedging structure of such an issue.

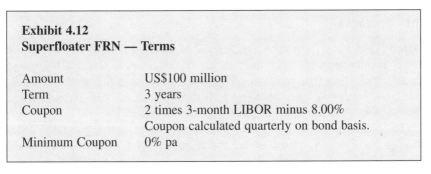

**Exhibit 4.12**
**Superfloater FRN — Terms**

| | |
|---|---|
| Amount | US$100 million |
| Term | 3 years |
| Coupon | 2 times 3-month LIBOR minus 8.00% |
| | Coupon calculated quarterly on bond basis. |
| Minimum Coupon | 0% pa |

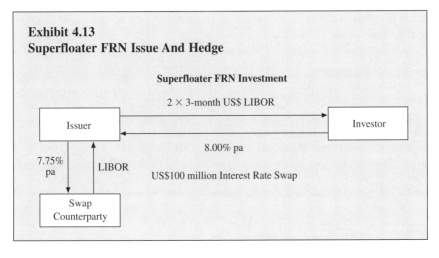

**Exhibit 4.13**
**Superfloater FRN Issue And Hedge**

The basic concept was an FRN that carried a coupon of two times LIBOR minus a fixed rate that was designed to appeal to investors concerned about future increases in short-term interest rates. The structure effectively combines the purchase of a LIBOR FRN by the investor with an interest rate swap where the investor pays fixed and receives floating rates. To eliminate the possibility of negative interest rates, the investor must also purchase a floor on the floating rate index (**Exhibit 4.10** shows a floor on US$ LIBOR at a strike of 4% pa).

Under this structure, as in the inverse FRN, the issuer is insulated from any interest rate risk as a result of fluctuations of interest rates achieving floating rate funding related to LIBOR at an all-in cost below its normal floating-rate funding cost.

The inverse FRN concept has also been adapted to mortgage-backed securities markets. Inverse floating rate Collaterallized Mortgage Obligations (CMO) issues have been undertaken in the US market.[7]

# 3. Arrears Reset/Delayed LIBOR Set Notes

### 3.1 Evolution

Arrears reset notes (also known as delayed or deferred set LIBOR FRNs)[8] are fixed income notes that were popular among investors in the mid-1980s and again in the 1990s. The product concept was introduced in September 1987 and has enjoyed periodic use coinciding with steeply positive-sloping yield curves. Transactions have been completed in a number of currencies.

The major attraction of the instrument is the higher returns generated under steeply positive yield curves where the progressively higher implied forward rates overestimate *the path or rate of increase* in actual short-term money market interest rates. Arrears reset notes, like a number of other structures incorporating derivative instruments, are available to take advantage of changes in the *shape* of the yield curve.

---

[7]    For a discussion of this market segment see Borg, Bella, Lancaster, Brian, and Tang, Jane "Inverse Floating-rate CMOs" in Fabozzi, Frank J. (1992) *The Handbook of Mortgage-backed Securities — Third Edition*; Probus Publishing, Chicago at Chapter 21; Winchell, Michael L. and Levine, Michael "Understanding Inverse Floater Pricing" in Fabozzi, Frank J. (1992) *The Handbook of Mortgage-backed Securities — Third Edition*; Probus Publishing, Chicago at Chapter 22.

[8]    See Das, Satyajit "Arrears Reappears" (December 14, 1994) *IFR Swaps Weekly* Issue 8 14-16; Marposon, Gregory E. "Arrears Reset Swaps" in Das, Satyajit (editor) (1991) *The Global Swaps Market*; IFR Publishing, London; Falloon, William "Curves And The Fuller Figure" (May 1992) *Risk* vol. 5 no. 5 19-25; Harpe, Michael and Simpson, Justin "The Interest Cost Lessons Of 1993" in (1994) *Corporate Finance Risk Management & Derivatives Yearbook* 7-11.

## 3.2    Structure

### 3.2.1    Arrears Reset Product Building Blocks

The key building block of the arrears reset product is the arrears reset interest rate swap. The structure of an arrears reset interest rate swap is as follows:

• The counterparty receives or pays a fixed rate normally.
• The counterparty pays or receives floating-rate payments based on a floating rate index set *two days before the payment date* whereas, in a normal swap, the floating rate is set *three or six months and two days prior to the payment date*.

The fixed rate in an arrears reset swap is, typically, higher than that in an interest rate swap. This higher fixed rate reflects the actual floating rate (say, LIBOR) rates payable in an arrears reset swap. Given an interest rate swap represents a portfolio of forward interest rates, in an arrears reset swap the fact that the forwards payable entails *different* forwards will result in a different fixed rate.

As discussed below in the context of pricing, in an arrears reset swap, the only rate payable that is different from that in a conventional swap is the last LIBOR set. This is *not* paid in a normal swap where the current spot LIBOR is paid. In a positive yield curve environment, the *implied* LIBOR for the last period is higher than the spot LIBOR dictating that a receiver of floating rates will require a higher rate to be paid on the fixed-rate side.

Arrears reset swap structures can be designed as a fixed rate against floating rate (calculated in arrears) transactions or unbundled into a floating-to-floating swap structure. Under this floating-to-floating structure (referred to as an arrears reset basis swap), one floating rate leg is set in arrears, while the other is calculated normally. **Exhibit 4.14** sets out the equivalence of a fixed against floating rate in arrears transaction and the second type of floating-to-floating structure.

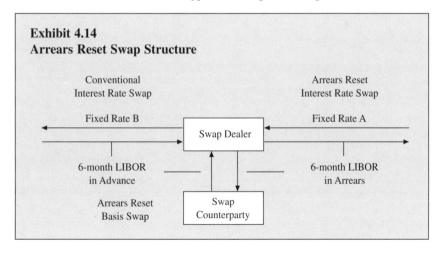

**Exhibit 4.14**
**Arrears Reset Swap Structure**

Fixed Rate A will be higher than Fixed Rate B with the difference being built into the floating-rate-to-floating-rate swap. For example, the swap dealer may receive 6-month LIBOR in arrears less a margin while paying 6-month LIBOR flat or receive 6-month LIBOR in arrears flat while paying 6-month LIBOR plus a margin

### 3.2.2   Arrears Reset Note Structures

The arrears reset note structures usually combine a conventional LIBOR-based FRN with an arrears reset swap. Two examples of these structures are set out in **Exhibit 4.15** and **4.16.**

---

**Exhibit 4.15**
**Arrears Reset Note Structure (1)**

*Terms*

| | |
|---|---|
| Amount | US$100 million |
| Term | 3 years |
| Coupon | 3- or 6-month LIBOR in arrears minus [margin] |
| | LIBOR in arrears is calculated and reset two business days prior to payment |

*Structural Decomposition*

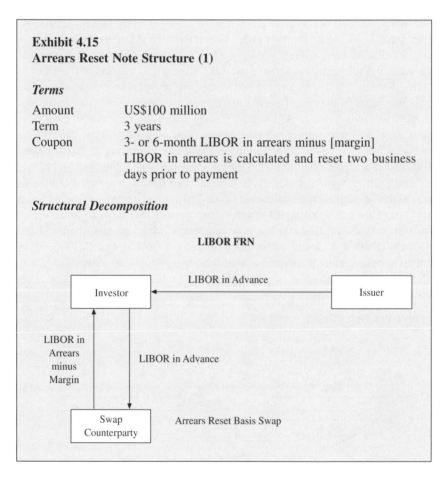

**Exhibit 4.16**
**Arrears Reset Note Structure (2)**

*Terms*

Amount                US$100 million
Term                  3 years

*First Format*
Coupon                3- or 6-month LIBOR plus [Spread].
Spread                (3- or 6-month LIBOR in advance minus 3- or
                      6-month LIBOR in arrears) plus [margin]
                      LIBOR in arrears is calculated and reset two
                      business days prior to payment.

*Alternative Format*
Coupon                [(2 times 3- or 6-month LIBOR in advance) minus
                      3- or 6-month LIBOR in arrears] plus [margin]
                      LIBOR in arrears is calculated and reset two
                      business days prior to payment

*Structural Decomposition*

**LIBOR FRN**

The first structure pays LIBOR in arrears *minus* a margin. The investor will receive incremental returns under this structure where interest *rise* by an amount *greater* than the margin over the interest rate period. In the second structure, the investor will earn incremental returns where the interest rates *increase by less than* the margin over the relevant interest rate period. In each case, the comparable benchmark is a standard LIBOR-based FRN with LIBOR set in advance.

Under both structures, the investor is trading the implied forward rates in the yield curve. The arrears reset structure is designed specifically to create value from a positively sloped yield curve where implied forward rates lie successively higher above the current yield curve. The higher implied forward rates are only an unbiased estimate of actual future interest rates. The actual spot rate at the relevant future date may differ from that implied by the forward rate curve. The structures identified allow the investor to generate value irrespective of whether the forward rates are expected to underestimate (Structure 1) or overestimate (Structure 2) actual interest rates.

The use of arrears reset structures to trade forward expectations of the short-term interest rates is similar to inverse FRN structures. The major distinguishing feature is that the inverse FRN is designed to allow investors to buy the complete series (or strip) of interest rate forwards. In contrast, the arrears reset products allow the capture of value from *a single forward* rate.

The issuer of the note has no exposure to the arrears reset feature. The exposure is hedged by entering into an arrears reset swap to convert its exposure to conventional floating rate funding at an attractive cost.[9]

### 3.3   Pricing/Valuation

As noted above, the pricing of an arrears reset structure revolves around extracting the value embedded in a strongly positively shaped yield curve in forward/forward interest rates that are above prevailing spot rates. **Exhibit 4.17** sets out the detailed mechanics of pricing and valuing an arrears reset swap and by implication arrears reset notes.

---

**Exhibit 4.17**
**Pricing and Trading Arrears Reset Structures**

*Pricing Approach*

The fixed rate in an arrears reset swap is, typically, higher than that in an interest rate swap. This higher fixed rate reflects the actual floating rate (say LIBOR) rates payable in an arrears reset swap. Given an interest rate swap represents a portfolio of forward interest rates, in an arrears reset

---

[9]   For other variations, see Pilarinu, Efi and Klotz, Rick (July 7, 1994) "Yield Enhancement Strategies For LIBOR Floaters In A Steep Yield Curve"; Salomon Brothers US Derivatives Research Fixed Income Derivatives; New York.

swap the fact that the forwards payable entails *different* forwards will result in a different fixed rate. Using arrears reset structures, counterparties would receive fixed rates under the swap against payment of floating rates receiving the benefit of the higher implied forward rates in the form of a higher fixed-rate flow under the swaps.

In an arrears reset swap, the only rate payable that is different from that in a conventional swap is the last LIBOR set. This is *not* paid in a normal swap where the current spot LIBOR is paid. In a positive yield curve environment, the *implied* LIBOR for the last period is higher than the spot LIBOR dictating that a receiver of floating rates will require a higher rate to be paid on the fixed-rate side.

This can be seen in the table below, which sets out the cash flows of an arrears reset structure and a corresponding convention interest rate swap.

| Time Period (t) | Year | Cash Flows | | | | Net Cash Flow |
|---|---|---|---|---|---|---|
| | | Arrears Reset Swap | | Conventional Swap | | |
| | | Fixed | Floating | Fixed | Floating | |
| 1 | 0.5 | F | $L(t1)$ | F | $L(t0)$ | $L(t0)-L(t1)$ |
| 2 | 1.0 | F | $L(t2)$ | F | $L(t1)$ | $L(t1)-L(t2)$ |
| 3 | 1.5 | F | $L(t3)$ | F | $L(t2)$ | $L(t2)-L(t3)$ |
| 4 | 2.0 | F | $L(t4)$ | F | $L(t3)$ | $L(t3)-L(t4)$ |

F = Fixed rate payable under swap
$L(t)$ = US$ 6-month LIBOR at time t

The net cash flows of an Arrears Reset Structure:

$$LIBOR\ (t4) - LIBOR\ (t0)$$

Therefore, if US$ 6-month LIBOR (as at time t4) is greater (less) than spot US$ 6-month LIBOR, then a floating rate receiver under an Arrears Reset Structure gains (losses). The approximate size of the gain or cost is:

$$[LIBOR\ (t4) - LIBOR\ (t0)] \times Notional\ amount \times (Number\ of\ days/360)$$

*Example*

Assume the yield curve set out below exists. The rates set out are the current yield curve rates, as well as implied 6-month LIBOR forwards derived from the yield curve.

| Years | Days (to Maturity) | Current Rates (% pa) | Forward Rates (% pa) |
|-------|-------------------|---------------------|---------------------|
| 0.00  | 0                 |                     |                     |
| 0.50  | 182               | 3.00                | 3.498%              |
| 1.00  | 366               | 3.25                | 3.765%              |
| 1.50  | 547               | 3.42                | 3.738%              |
| 2.00  | 731               | 3.50                | 5.787%              |
| 2.50  | 912               | 3.95                |                     |

The rate structure is set out in the graph below.

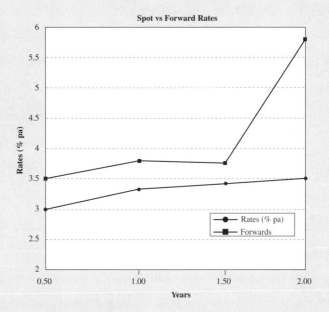

Based on the above yield, the benefit of the arrears reset structure can be estimated as follows:

$$(5.787\% \text{ pa} - 3.00\% \text{ pa}) \times 182/360 = 1.409\%$$

This gain can be amortized over the 2-year swap (at the swap rate) and built into the fixed-rate side of the swap whereby the fixed-rate payer increases the rate paid.

The approximation of the arrears reset structure benefit is only accurate where the yield curve is flat and all zero-coupon rates are the same. In practice, the exact adjustment is based on using the theoretical forward rates to generate the actual arrears reset structure cash flows (relative to cash flows under a conventional swap) that are then discounted using the zero rates. The table below sets out this analysis for the above swap.

| No. of Days (per Period) | No. of Days (Cumulative) | Six-month Forward | LIBOR Cash Flows under | | Net Cash Flows | Discount Rate | Discounted Cash Flows |
|---|---|---|---|---|---|---|---|
| | | | Normal Swap | Arrears Reset Swap | | | |
| | | 3.000% | | | | | |
| 182 | 182 | 3.498% | 1.517 | 1.768 | 0.252 | 3.0000% | 0.248 |
| 184 | 366 | 3.765% | 1.788 | 1.924 | 0.136 | 3.2500% | 0.132 |
| 181 | 547 | 3.738% | 1.893 | 1.879 | -0.013 | 3.4200% | -0.013 |
| 184 | 731 | 5.787% | 1.911 | 2.958 | 1.047 | 3.5000% | 0.978 |
| | | Total | 7.108 | 8.530 | 1.422 | | 1.345 |

The benefit derived from the arrears reset structure (on a net present value basis) is 1.345% or 70 bps pa (amortized over two years).

*Hedging*

For a swap counterparty, the exposure into an arrears reset structure transaction can be hedged as follows:

• The change in the PV of the cash flows of the arrears reset structure for a 1bp movement in interest rates is measured.
• To offset the arrears reset structure swap risk, the counterparty maintains a hedge (utilizing a portfolio of physical securities and/or derivatives (FRAs/futures)) to offset the NPV change in the arrears reset structure transaction.
• This hedge portfolio is adjusted periodically to align it with changes in the net value of the arrears reset structure.

Alternatively, the swap counterparty can structure hedges utilizing either FRAs, short-term interest rate futures (if available) or deferred start swaps to seek to structure offsetting cash flows to immunize the arrears reset structure.

In arrears reset structures, especially with long terms to maturity, it is necessary to incorporate a convexity adjustment.[10] One possible methodology for making the convexity adjustment is set out in **Exhibit 4.18.**[11]

---

**Exhibit 4.18
Convexity Adjustment**[12]

Where interest rate derivatives incorporate an *unnatural* time lag, a convexity adjustment is required. A *natural* time lag is defined as where the payoff on a derivative depends on the N period rate; the rate is observed at one point in time and is paid at a subsequent time exactly N periods later. Where the time lag is *natural*, the structure can be valued using the assumption that the expected future interest rate is equivalent to the forward rate. Where the time lag is *unnatural*, that is, a transaction such as an arrears reset swap, the expected future interest rate should be calculated as the forward rate adjusted for convexity.

One form of convexity adjustment is that proposed by Brotherton-Ratcliffe and Iben.[13] They show that the convexity adjustment that must be made to the forward rate (F) is:

$$-0.5 \ F^2 \ \sigma^2 \ T \ [P''(F)/P'(F)]$$

---

[10] The importance of the convexity adjustment is highlighted by an incident in mid-1995. At that time, several derivative dealers (J.P. Morgan and Goldman Sachs were reported to be among their number) arbitraged the valuation of other dealers on arrears reset swaps (1-year LIBOR in arrears in swaps of between five and 10 years in maturity). The dealers noticed that these swaps were valued *without the convexity adjustment*. The difference that was supposed to be worth around 8-10 bps arose from the long maturities of these transactions that accentuated the value of the convexity effect. See "Swap Model Arbitrage" (July 29, 1995) *International Financing Review* Issue 1092 at 101; Rombach, Ed "Zen and the Art of Trading the Convexity Bias" (December 1995) *Financial Derivatives and Risk Management* 17-22 at 20, 21.

[11] For other approaches see Coleman, Thomas S. "Convexity Adjustment For Constant Maturity Swaps And LIBOR-in-Arrears Swaps" (Winter 1995) *Derivatives Quarterly* 19-27; Li, Anlong "LIBOR-In-Arrears" (Spring 1996) *The Journal of Derivatives* 44-48.

[12] For a detailed discussion of the convexity adjustment see Hull, John (1997) *Futures, Options and Other Derivatives*; Prentice Hall, Upper Saddle River, NJ at 406-411.

[13] See Brotherton-Ratcliffe, R. and Iben, B. "Yield Curve Applications of Swap Products" in Schwartz, R. and Smith, C (editors) (1993) *Advanced Strategies in Financial Risk Management*; New York Institute of Finance, New York at Chapter 15.

Where:

| | | |
|---|---|---|
| F | = | forward rate |
| $\sigma$ | = | volatility |
| T | = | time to maturity of the forward |
| P'(F) | = | first derivative of the price of bond (P) with respect to yield (Y) |
| P''(F) | = | second derivative of the price of bond (P) with respect to yield (Y) |

This means that the adjusted forward rate should be:

$$F - 0.5 \ F^2 \ \sigma^2 \ T \ [P''(F)/P'(F)]$$

The application of this adjustment can be illustrated with an example. Assume the following:

$$F \ = \ 6\% \ \text{pa}$$
$$Y \ = \ 6\% \ \text{pa}$$
$$\sigma \ = \ 15\% \ \text{pa}$$

Assume that the instrument provides a payoff in three years' time linked to the 1-year rate. The value of the instrument is given by:

$$P(Y) = 1/(1 + Y)$$

The first and second derivatives are given by:

$$P'(F) = -1/(1 + Y)^2 = -1/(1 + 0.06)^2 = -0.89$$
$$P''(F) = 2/(1 + Y)^3 = 2/(1 + 0.06)^3 = 1.68$$

The convexity adjustment is given by:

$$-0.5 \times 0.06^2 \times 0.15^2 \times 3 \times (1.6792/-0.89) = 0.0002 \ \text{or 2 bps}$$

This means that a forward rate of 6.02% pa (rather than 6.00% pa) should be used in the valuation.

Changes in the shape of the yield curve shape will often provide counterparties with additional trading opportunities with arrears reset transactions.

The value of an arrears reset swap derives from two sources:

- The actual term swap (unadjusted for the arrears reset benefit).
- The arrears reset benefit, itself, which depends on the shape of the yield curve and, specifically, the difference between the final implied floating interest rate (as embodied in the forward yield curve) and current floating rate.

Consequently, counterparties can, depending on the pattern of interest rate movements, expect to derive value from one or both sources.

For example, assume a transaction where a counterparty has received fixed rates and is paying 6-month LIBOR in arrears. The transaction was entered into when the yield curve was strongly positively shaped, a flattening in the yield curve combined with a decrease in fixed term interest rates will provide a series of value-creation opportunities. Aside from the value implied by the move in the fixed term rate, the flattening will result in the arrears reset benefit being diminished. The arrears reset benefit may go to zero where the yield curve is perfectly flat to a cost where the yield curve inverts. As a consequence, the counterparty who has transacted in an arrears reset, in the structure outlined, could, in a flattening yield curve environment, reverse the 6-month LIBOR in the arrears leg of the transaction and substitute it for a normal 6-month LIBOR in advance floating rate. This could be done at a reduced or no cost (potentially a benefit) if the yield curve shape changes in its favor.

The arrears reset structure can be structured to take advantage of a variety of yield curve movements that are dependent purely on the changing term structure of interest rates and changes in the implied forward yield curve.

## 3.4   Variations

A number of variations on the basic concept of an arrears reset structure have evolved. Some transactions now embody option or asymmetric elements. Typical of this structure is what is sometimes called the "choice of LIBOR swap". Under this structure, the swap dealer pays fixed rate and has the right to receive 3- or 6-month LIBOR set at the beginning of the period or at the end of the period, whichever is higher. Under this structure, the fixed rate paid is higher than that payable under a normal structure. This additional yield pickup reflects two factors: the shape of the yield curve (identical to the format of the arrears reset described above), as well as the volatility of rates. The volatility relevant in this case is the volatility of the actual shape of the yield curve.

Another variation entails what is sometimes referred to as a "velocity" cap. Under this structure, a counterparty would pay a subsidized fixed rate and receive a floating rate that varied as a function of the change in LIBOR over a given interest period. The floating rate payment would vary according to a formula such as the following:

$$\text{LIBOR} - \max. \left[ (\text{LIBOR change} - x\%), 0 \right]$$

These types of structures represent different allocations of risk and reward relative to the changes in the yield curve shape. For example, the velocity cap structure protects the payer of fixed rates unless LIBOR rises by more than the specified percentage.

These variations are easily embedded into arrears reset notes for investors seeking to create these types of exposures.

# 4.  Interest Rate-linked Notes

## 4.1  Overview

The concept of embodying interest rates derivatives in capital market transactions also extends to transactions where the implicit interest rate derivative is engineered through a variable redemption amount. The movements in the value of the derivative component are reflected in the changes in the value of the principal repayment.

There are a variety of structures available including:

• Bull-bear structures
• Bond price or interest-linked notes
• Swap rate-linked notes

In each of these, the issuer avoids exposure to the underlying price fluctuations of the security through entry into a derivative transaction with a swap dealer that offsets the exposure to the value shifts of the bond itself.

For the investor, the linkage to a nominated interest rate provides full price exposure to fluctuations in that rate in a format sought. Importantly, the ability to engineer specific linkages allows the separation of liquidity risk (related to the *maturity*) of the security and the area of the yield curve to which *price* exposure is sought (related to the linkage). This significantly expands the range of investment strategies that can be implemented. The ability to create desired levels of leverage is also important in expanding the range of investment alternatives.

## 4.2  Bull-bear Structures

The concept of embodying interest rate derivatives in securities in the form of bull-bear bonds was originally introduced for Japanese investors in relation to Japanese interest rates. The concept has since been utilized in a variety of markets.

These types of transactions, basically, took the following forms:

• Bull-bear structures, involving the creation of offsetting tranches designed to appeal to bullish and bearish investors that produced a known maximum cost of funds to the issuer.
• High coupon yen issues where the redemption formula was calculated with reference to future Japan Government Bond (JGB) futures prices to engineer an implicit forward interest rate position into the security.

**Exhibit 4.19** sets out an example of a yen bull-bear JGB-linked bond. **Exhibit 4.20** sets out an example of a yen JGB-linked bond issue and swap. These structures were specifically designed for particular institutional investors seeking to create synthetic interest rate derivative exposures to manage asset positions within their investment portfolios.

---

**Exhibit 4.19**
**Yen Bull-bear JGB-linked Note**

In February 1988, Societe Generale issued ¥10 billion of 5-year bonds underwritten by Nikko Securities with the redemption value linked to the Tokyo Stock Exchange (TSE) Japanese Government Bond (JGB) December 1992 futures price.

The bonds carried a coupon of 7% pa, compared to 5-year JGB yield of approximately 4.40/4.50% pa. The issue consisted of two tranches: a ¥5 billion bear tranche and a ¥5 billion bull tranche. The redemption value of the bonds were indexed to the December 1992 JGB futures price as follows:

Bear Tranche: R   = 195.45% of principal minus TSE JGB December 1992 futures price

Bull Tranche: R   = TSE JGB December 1992 futures price minus 20.55%

where

       R   = redemption amount
TSE JGB   = Tokyo Stock Exchange Japanese Government Bond

The payouts on the security were subject to certain constraints:

Minimum price   = zero
Maximum price   = 17.90%

The offsetting nature of the two tranches and the counter-balancing changes in the value of the tranches ensures that Societe Generale is immunized from the risk of the JGB-linked redemption feature of the bond.

For example, assume the TSE JGB December 1992 price = 125%:

Bear Tranche:       R   = (195.45% − 125%) of ¥5 billion = 70.45% of ¥5 billion = ¥3,522,500,000

Bull Tranche:       R   = (125% − 20.55%) of ¥5 billion = 104.45% of ¥5 billion = ¥5,222,500,000

---

Total redemption payout = ¥3,522,500,000 + ¥5,222,500,000 equals
¥8,745,000,000

Assume TSE JGB December 1992 price = 75%:

Bear Tranche: R = (195.45% − 75%) of ¥5 billion = 120.45%
of ¥5 billion = ¥6,022,500,000

Bull Tranche: R = (75%-20.55%) of ¥5 billion = 54.45% of
¥5 billion = ¥2,722,500,000

Total redemption payout = ¥6,022,500,000 + ¥2,722,500,000 equals
¥8,745,000,000.

The structure results in identical payouts for the issuer.

The structure results in the issuer repaying less than par on the bonds. If Societe Generale borrows ¥10 billion and is only required to repay ¥8,745,000,000 it has an effective book profit of ¥1,255,000,000. At the risk-free 5-year JGB rate of 4.4%, this profit of ¥1,255,000 equates to an annual annuity of ¥229,862,335 each year for five years.

Incorporating the annuity of ¥229,862,335 benefit, the net funding cost of the issue equals ¥470,137,665 or 4.0% pa. This rate is 30 bps above the comparable ¥ risk-free rate, but is well below the coupons offered on conventional Euro-Yen issues raised at this time that were 4.90-5.00% pa allowing Societe Generale to swap into attractive floating US$ funding at a substantial margin below LIBOR.

*Source:* This example draws on Cunningham, Michael M. "Selected Analysis of Recently Issued Index-Linked and Option Embedded Securities"; unpublished research paper presented to course on Swap Financing, Centre for Studies in Money, Banking and Finance, Macquarie University, 1987.

**Exhibit 4.20
Yen JGB-linked Note**

In January 1988, Societe Generale undertook an issue, through Mitsui Finance International, of ¥7 billion 5-year bonds.

The issue's redemption value was linked to the value of TSE December 1990 JGB futures price. The issue carried a 7% pa coupon that was significantly above the equivalent 5-year JGB rate that was 4.40/ 4.50% pa or equivalent Euro-Yen yields that were in the range of 4.875/ 5.00% pa for comparable issues.

The redemption value of the bond was calculated in accordance with the following formula:

R = 193.60% minus opening TSE JGB December 1990 futures price

The redemption payment is calculated on the JGB futures index two years hence but not payable for a further three years. This allows both the issuer and investor to know in advance the payout profile of the debt.

The issue was targeted specifically at Japanese institutional investors as the issue is designed as a hedge for holders of Japanese bonds should rates increase markedly. This is reflected in the structure whereby as the JGB futures price falls (that is, the interest rates increase) the redemption payout increases, presumably compensating the investor for losses on its physical JGB portfolio. This redemption structure effectively embeds a forward position in the December 1990 JGB futures contract.

The issuer (investor) benefits from a general decrease (increase) in Japanese interest rate structures and a commensurate rise in the index price two years hence. While the investor would have had to accept the symmetric nature of the exposure, Societe Generale would have sought to insulate itself from the risk of the implicit JGB futures position through a derivative transaction with Mitsui.

Mitsui can hedge and securitize the inherent forward position in two ways:

- It could take a long forward JGB futures December 1990 position two years hence. By arranging this hedge, Mitsui could expect to receive ¥420m (6% of ¥7 billion) as payment for its services. Therefore a fall in the JGB December 1990 futures price in two years' time will work against Societe Generale on the redemption repayment. However, this impact will be offset by the short position it has been allocated by Mitsui (who matched out the position by establishing a corresponding long position for a counterparty).
- Mitsui could also strip and securitize the embedded option position. Mitsui could sell an at-the-money 2-year call on the JGB December 1990 futures contract. Mitsui could expect to receive ¥455 million (6.5% of ¥7 billion) for this position, considering the lack of "long-term" option hedging tools for Japanese institutions at the time the transaction was undertaken.

The funds received were ¥875 million (¥420 million for the forward position plus ¥455 million for the option), which equals ¥1,085,201,902 after five years using the risk-free rate of 4.40% pa that equates to a yearly annuity of ¥198,762,584.

This annuity, when offset against Societe Generale's annual interest cost of ¥490 million, results in an annual effective coupon cost of

¥291,237,416 equivalent to a nominal borrowing cost of 4.16% pa, 24
bps below the risk-free rate. Based on yen swap rates of approximately
4.60/4.80% pa, Societe Generale would have been able to obtain funding
at a substantial margin under LIBOR through a ¥/US$ currency swap.

*Source:* This example draws on Cunningham, Michael M. "Selected Analysis of
Recently Issued Index-Linked and Option Embedded Securities" unpublished
research paper presented to a course on Swap Financing, Centre for Studies in
Money, Banking and Finance, Macquarie University, 1987

## 4.3 Interest-linked Notes

The concept was introduced in two issues launched in April 1987 by Nomura
International for GMAC and Mitsui and Co. (USA).[14] The basic concept has
been extended to other structures, including dividing the issue into two tranches
with one tranche providing the upside potential and the other the downside
potential to better attune the structure to individual investor's interest rate
expectations.

The basic transaction entails the issue of debt securities bearing a higher
than market coupon. However, the redemption amount, that is, the amount
repaid to the investor at maturity, is linked to price fluctuations (and by
implication yield movements) on an identified debt instrument.

In a typical transaction, the coupon was set at, say, 10.00% pa
(approximately 200 to 250bps above the market yield) for three years. The
redemption of the bond was linked to a formula as follows:

- If the benchmark 30-year US Treasury bond at the end of three years
  (the maturity of the debt instrument) is at a breakeven yield (say 7.10% pa)
  the bonds are redeemed at par (100).
- If the yield is above (below) the breakeven yield, the amount received by the
  investor will be less (greater) than par.
- In any case, the redemption amount cannot be less than zero.

Implicit in the variable redemption formula inherent in this particular structure is
a long 3-year forward position on the 30-year US Treasury bond. The position
can also be restated using put call parity as (European) options with a maturity
of three years, the investor granting a put option on the 30-year bond with a
strike yield of 7.10% pa and simultaneously purchasing a call option with an
identical strike yield (effectively, a forward purchase of the 30-year Treasury
bond in three years).

---

[14] The GMAC issue was subsequently withdrawn due to problems with tax regulations.

The forward position is hedged with offsetting derivative transactions effectively insulating the issuer from the risk of variations in the redemption amount. The swap usually generates funding at an attractive margin relative to a floating rate index such as LIBOR.

The economic logic underlying the transaction would appear to be as follows: the investor (in the example) would usually be writing a put that was substantially in-the-money (by about 40 bps) and buying an out-of-the-money call (by the same margin). The swap provider would sell the put on the 30-year bond at a higher premium than the outlay needed to purchase the call with the difference being used to subsidize the issuer's cost. An alternative manner of expressing the same point is that the forward contract is entered into at an *off-market rate*.

The derivative could be simulated as an equivalent forward position by holding an appropriate amount of 30-year bonds purchased at market price (the yield would be approximately 7.50% pa) for the three years and liquidating them at market rates at the end of that period. The variable redemption structure would lock in the 40 bps profit on the bonds that could be used to subsidize the swap. The fact that the structure can be simulated through a long forward position with the underlying securities merely reflects the fact that a transaction that involves the simultaneous purchase of a put option and the granting of a call option is equivalent to a short forward position in the relevant security.

Where the issuer does not wish to alter the currency or interest rate basis of the borrowing, the transaction need *not* technically be a swap, but merely a series of option trades or forward transactions. This is basically a consequence of the fact that buying put options and selling call options at the same strike price is economically identical to paying fixed rates under a swap.

The detailed underlying transaction logic for such transactions is illustrated utilizing a transaction for Quatrain, a vehicle guaranteed by the South Australian Financing Authority, set out in **Exhibit 4.21.**

---

**Exhibit 4.21**
**Bond-linked Notes — Example 1**

Quatrain Co., through Nomura International, undertook a 3-year, 10.00% US$100 million issue of Treasury-indexed bonds on May 15, 1986. Redemption value is linked to the 9.25% of 2016 series of US Treasury bonds via the following formula:

$$R = US\$100,000,000 \times (MIP - 26.491782)/100$$

Where:

R = redemption value in US$
MIP = market index price of the 9.25% of 2016 US Treasury bond at maturity of the issue

This exposure to 30-year Treasuries is hedged by Quatrain with Nomura via a series of derivative transactions.

Nomura can hedge its exposure equivalent to taking on a short forward treasury position as follows:

- Purchase of a 30-year Treasury bond that is then funded and held for three years.
- Enter into a simultaneous forward commitment to buy US$100 million 9.25% 2016 bonds in three years' time.

Assume Nomura purchases the underlying treasury and funds it for three years at a rate not higher than the yield on the 30-year bond. Nomura can buy the 30-year Treasuries at the current market yield of 7.65% pa and lock in a corresponding 3-year funding cost, probably through a repurchase agreement, at or less than 7.65% pa.

The profit dynamics of the hedge are set out below.

Assume:

- 30-year US Treasury bond yield is 7.65% pa
- 3-year US Treasury bond yield is 7.50% pa.

Nomura's net profit position from the purchase that is offset by the short forward position (bond price of 118% equivalent to a yield of 7.65% pa) is:

$$
\begin{aligned}
\text{Profits} &= \text{US\$100,000,000} \times (\text{MIP} - 118\ )/100 + \text{US\$100,000,000} \times \\
&\quad (126.491782 - \text{MIP}\ )/100 \\
&= \text{US\$100,000,000} \times (\ 8.491782\ )/100 \\
&= \text{US\$8,491,782 at maturity}
\end{aligned}
$$

Where:

MIP = MIP at maturity.

Nomura's US$8,491,782 gain is equivalent to a US$2,628,526 annuity for three years at an interest rate of 7.50% pa. This annuity of US$2,628,526 can be used to reduce the Treasury-indexed bond's interest cost from US$10 million (that is, 10.00% of US$100 million) to US$7,371,474 (US$10,000,000 – US$2,628,526). The effective interest cost is 7.37% pa

(US$7,371,474/US$100,000,000); that is, below the equivalent 3-year treasury rate. In reality, the annuity stream will only be used to reduce the effective cost to a level at which the issuer's sub-LIBOR target is satisfied with the surplus representing Nomura's profit from the transaction.

The accompanying US$ interest rate swap will entail Quatrain receiving the fixed rate equivalent of US$10 million or 10.00% pa and paying LIBOR minus the agreed margin. Notice the off-market rates necessitated a premium swap structure.

The structure described is fairly generic and has been adopted in a large number of transactions in a variety of currencies. The above structures place principal at risk of loss with the derivative being linked to the transaction principal. This is achieved by embedding a (off-market) forward on the relevant bond within the structure (as in the structure described above). Alternatively, this structure entails the investor selling embedded options to enhance return. **Exhibit 4.22** sets out an example of this structure in yen where the investor is effectively writing an out of the money put on the bond.

In recent times, the bond price-linked structures employed have been more conservative in nature with the principal of the structure being protected. This is achieved by using some part or all of the interest coupon (and in some cases a part of the principal of the transaction) to purchase an option on the relevant bond. The payoff of this option is then engineered into the structure. **Exhibit 4.23** sets out an example of a bond linked to the 30-year US Treasury bond with principal protection. These structures have been utilized in a wide variety of markets. Structures where the coupon is linked to the underlying bond have also been utilized. **Exhibit 4.24** on page 165 sets out a structure where the note coupon is linked to yen bond futures.

More recently, German investors have invested in DM structured notes linked to US Treasury bond yields.[15] These types of issues were undertaken by German banks (primarily private banks and Landesbanks) in Schuldscheine format. The issues had a final maturity of between 30 and 40 years. The return on these bonds was a initial coupon of say 8% pa. After this initial period the note offered returns linked to the yield on 10-year US Treasury bonds. The bond was callable annually at a yield of around 8.00% pa. The notes offered returns of over 6.00% pa. This was significantly in excess of the yield on German bonds of comparable maturity. The structure was popular with

---

[15]  See "German Investors Lap-up Structured Diversification" (September 12, 1998) *International Financing Review* Issue 1250 72.

investors because it offered German investors the opportunity to create exposure to US Treasury yields with no currency rates.

The structures were feasible because the relative shapes of the DM and US yield curves that reduced the cost of currency protection (through the embedded quanto option). However, the structures were difficult to hedge for traders. This is because the note represented a complex mixture of currency risk and interest rate risk (to a constant maturity US Treasury bond).[16]

---

**Exhibit 4.22**
**Bond-linked Note — Example 2**

| | |
|---|---|
| Issuer | AA-rated issuer |
| Amount | ¥10 billion |
| Maturity | 1 year |
| Issue Price | 100.00 |
| Coupon | 1.00% pa |
| Redemption Value | Redemption amount is based on the following formula: |
| | • If JGB Number 1999 is trading at or above par at the Value Date, then 100.00. |
| | • If JGB Number 1999 is trading below par at the Value Date, then redemption is by way of physical delivery of the securities. |
| Maximum Redemption | 100.00 |
| Minimum Redemption | 0.00 |
| Value Date | 5 business days before maturity |

---

**Exhibit 4.23**
**Principal-protected Bond-linked Note — Example 1**

The following 1-year note entails an embedded exposure to the 30-year US Treasury bond. The note is structured to ensure that the investor's principal investment is fully protected against loss at all times.

The terms of the issue are as follows:

---

[16] The structure effectively combines a constant maturity swaption and a quanto option.

| Issuer | AAA/AA-rated |
|---|---|
| Amount | (up to) US$50 million |
| Maturity | 1 year from commencement |
| Issue Price | 100% |
| Interest Rate | 0% pa |
| Redemption Value | 100% of amount plus redemption payment payable at maturity |
| Redemption Payment | Amount $\times$ Leverage factor $\times$ $[Y_{0-} Y_m]$ where Leverage factor = 17 times $Y_0$ = yield on Reference bond at commencement of transaction (5.50% pa) $Y_m$ = Yield on reference bond at maturity |
| Reference Bond | The on-the-run 30-year US Treasury bond at the time of issue |
| Minimum Redemption | 100% payable at maturity |

The Note is designed to allow the investor to monetize expectations of a decline in interest rates on the 30-year US Treasury bond over the next 1-year period. The note provides the investor with a capital protected investment where in return for forgoing the interest coupon the investor has the ability to generate a highly leveraged exposure (17-18 times)[17] to the actual decline in the 30-year US Treasury bond yield.

The payoff profile of the Note is set out in the table below. The payoff profile is calculated using a 30-year yield of 5.50% pa at commencement of the transaction and a leverage factor of 17.

---

[17] Please note the leverage factor relates substantially to the fact that a 1 bps movement in yield resulting in a large price change in the *price* of the bond. The leverage factor therefore refers to the modified duration or PVBP of the underlying 30-year Treasury bond. Assuming a 30-year term and a coupon and yield to maturity of 5.50% pa, the modified duration of the bond is around 14.6. This means that a leverage factor of 17 translates into *true leverage* of around 1.16 x. This means that per US$100 of the bond approx. US$116 of options on the 30-year bond are embedded in the note.

| Yield on 30-year US Treasury Bond | Principal Redemption at Maturity | Redemption Payment | Total Redemption Amount at Maturity | One-year Yield to Maturity |
|---|---|---|---|---|
| 4.50% | 100 | 17.00 | 117.00 | 17.00% |
| 4.60% | 100 | 15.30 | 115.30 | 15.30% |
| 4.70% | 100 | 13.60 | 113.60 | 13.60% |
| 4.80% | 100 | 11.90 | 111.90 | 11.90% |
| 4.90% | 100 | 10.20 | 110.20 | 10.20% |
| 5.00% | 100 | 8.50 | 108.50 | 8.50% |
| 5.10% | 100 | 6.80 | 106.80 | 6.80% |
| 5.20% | 100 | 5.10 | 105.10 | 5.10% |
| 5.30% | 100 | 3.40 | 103.40 | 3.40% |
| 5.40% | 100 | 1.70 | 101.70 | 1.70% |
| 5.50% | 100 | – | 100.00 | 0.00% |
| 5.60% | 100 | – | 100.00 | 0.00% |
| 5.70% | 100 | – | 100.00 | 0.00% |
| 5.80% | 100 | – | 100.00 | 0.00% |
| 5.90% | 100 | – | 100.00 | 0.00% |
| 6.00% | 100 | – | 100.00 | 0.00% |

The basic structure entails utilizing the coupon on a 1-year security that is foregone to purchase a 1-year call on the 30-year Treasury bond to generate the bond price exposure.

**Exhibit 4.24**
**Principal-protected Bond-linked Note — Example 2**

| | |
|---|---|
| Issuer | AA-rated issuer |
| Amount | ¥5 billion |
| Maturity | 1 year |
| Issue Price | 100.00 |
| Coupon | Calculated in accordance with the following formula: |

$$2.23 \times (1 - (JGB(f) / JGB(i)))$$

|                         | Where                                                    |
|-------------------------|----------------------------------------------------------|
|                         | JGB is the Japanese Government Bond futures contract.     |
|                         | JGB (i) is initially equal to 124.00 and is adjusted on each JGB futures contract maturity by adding the spread between the closing price of the maturing contract and the closing price of the next listed contract. |
|                         | JGB (f) is the official closing price of each contract.   |
| Minimum Redemption      | 100.00                                                   |

In the 1990s, the increased interest in emerging markets lead to adaptation of these structures to emerging markets bonds. **Exhibit 4.25** sets out an example of a structure with an embedded forward on an emerging market bond index. The investor's principal investment is at risk in this structure with return being contingent on the performance of the index. **Exhibit 4.26** sets out an example of a transaction combining a zero-coupon bond issue with a call on a basket of emerging market bonds, designed to allow investors to create asymmetric exposure to emerging market debt. **Exhibit 4.27** on page 168 sets out a second example of this type of structure.

**Exhibit 4.25**
**Emerging Market Bond-linked Note — Example 1**

| Issuer             | AA-rated issuer                                        |
|--------------------|-------------------------------------------------------|
| Amount             | US$10 million                                         |
| Maturity           | 3 years                                               |
| Issue Price        | 100.00                                                |
| Coupon             | 0.00% pa                                              |
| Redemption Value   | Redemption amount is based on the following formula:  |
|                    | $$\text{Amount} \times \text{Index}/131.8$$           |
|                    | Where                                                 |
|                    | Index is the J.P. Morgan Emerging Local Markets Index (in US$) on the Value Date |
| Minimum Redemption | 0.00                                                  |
| Value Date         | 5 business days before maturity                       |

**Exhibit 4.26**
**Emerging Market Bond-linked Note — Example 2**

In early 1995, following a major sell-off in emerging markets a number of structured notes linked to emerging market securities, usually Brady bonds, were issued. The following note was typical of the type of securities issued:

| | |
|---|---|
| Issuer | AAA or AA-rated |
| Maturity | 1 year |
| Coupon | 0% |
| Principal Redemption | The higher of 100 + (Final Basket Price – 48%) or Minimum Redemption |
| Minimum Redemption | 100% |
| Basket | 40% Par bond of Latin country A |
| | 30% Par bond of Latin country B |
| | 30% Par bond of Latin country C |
| Current Basket Price | 48% |

The note combines a zero-coupon bond with a call option on a basket of three Brady bonds. The call option is engineered through the linking of the redemption value to the price of the Brady bonds. The call option being financed through the forgone interest on the note.

The issue was designed to allow investors to increase exposure on a risk-averse basis to emerging market debt following the Mexican crisis where emerging market Brady bond spreads widened between 100 and 400 bps, bringing the spreads to their highest levels for many years.

The economics of the transaction were as follows:

• The 1-year yield on AAA- or AA-rated notes at the time of issue was around 7.00 to 7.25% pa. The breakeven price on the note to equate the return to that on a conventional note was around 93.25/93.50.
• The breakeven price increase on the basket such that the noteholder would earn the yield on 1-year securities was around 14.58/15.10% pa implying a final basket price of 55-55.25% pa.

---

**Exhibit 4.27**
**Emerging Market Bond-linked Note — Example 3**

| | |
|---|---|
| Issuer | AA-rated issuer |
| Amount | US$25 million |
| Maturity | 3 years |
| Issue Price | 100.00 |
| Coupon | 1.00% pa |
| Redemption Value | Redemption amount is based on the following formula: |
| | 100 + [Amount × Max (0; Index — 82.25%)] |
| | Where |
| | Index is the value of the Security Basket calculated on Value Date |
| Security Basket | The value of the Security Basket is calculated as the product of the price of the Reference Bonds multiplied by their weight. |

| Reference Bond | Reference Bond | Weight |
|---|---|---|
| | Latin country A | 30% |
| | Latin country B | 20% |
| | Latin country C | 10% |
| | Asian country D | 20% |
| | Eastern European country E | 20% |

| | |
|---|---|
| Minimum Redemption | 100.00 |
| Value Date | 5 business days before maturity |

---

## 4.4    Swap Rate-indexed Notes

The concept of securities with redemption values linked to bond prices has been extended to notes whose redemption values are linked to *interest rate swap rates*. The use of swap rates reflects:

* The benchmark function performed by these rates in certain markets where the underlying government bond market is less liquid and efficient in pricing.
* The ease of hedging the derivative element embedded in the structure.

The incorporation of swap rates does not alter the underlying logic of the transactions from that described in the previous section. The basic structure entailing embedded forwards or options remains identical.

· The swap rates are usually determined for the purposes of these transactions by either reference to a screen quotation service or a dealer polling mechanism from a group of reference dealers.

Exhibit **4.28** sets out an example of a note linked to Swedish Krona (Skr) swap rates.

---

**Exhibit 4.28**
**Swap Rate-linked Note — Example 1**

| | |
|---|---|
| Issuer | Swedish Export Credit |
| Amount | Skr200 million |
| Maturity | 1 year |
| Issue Price | 100 |
| Coupon | 9.50% pa (annual bond basis) |
| Redemption | 100 plus 15 times (7.85% pa less 3-year Skr swap offered yield) |
| Minimum Redemption | 0 |

---

The Note effectively embeds a 1-year forward start 3-year Skr interest swap where the investor receives fixed rate and pays floating rates within the transaction.[18] The investor's payout reflects the movements in this rate:
- If the 3-year swap rate goes to 6.85% pa at maturity, then the investor receives a redemption payout equivalent to 115% of par.
- If the 3-year swap rate goes to 7.95% pa at maturity, then the investor receives a redemption payout equivalent to 98.5% of par.

The investor achieves both an exposure to the 3-year sector of the yield curve on a forward basis and an above-market yield. The above-market yield represents the present value of the difference between the forward swap rate embedded in the note and actual market forward swap rates.

**Exhibit 4.29** sets out an example of a note linked to Sterling (£). **Exhibit 4.30** sets out the hedging structure for the transaction.

The return profile of the transaction reflects the embedded option on £ swap rates (effectively an option on a £ swap). As £ rates decline from current levels the investor's return increases. However, increases in swap rates do not translate

---

[18] Please note the number by which the yield difference at maturity is multiplied is a mechanism for equating the yield movement to price terms together with a leverage factor. The PVBP of a 3-year swap at the relevant yield level is around 3 (that is, a 1 bps movement in yield results in a 3 bps change in the value of the swap). This means that the transaction is effectively leveraged 5 times. In effect, the investor is entering into forward swaps for a notional principal amount equalling 5 times the face value of the note (SKR 1,000 million).

**Exhibit 4.29**
**Swap Rate-linked Note — Example 2**

| | |
|---|---|
| Issuer | AA-rated institution |
| Amount | US$10 million |
| Maturity | 18 months |
| Issue Price | 100 |
| Coupon | 0% pa (annual bond basis) |
| Redemption | 100 plus 5 times (7.70% pa less 2-year £ swap offered yield) paid in US$ |
| Minimum Redemption | 100 |

*Source:* Lehman Brothers International.

**Exhibit 4.30**
**Swap Rate-linked Note Hedging Structure**

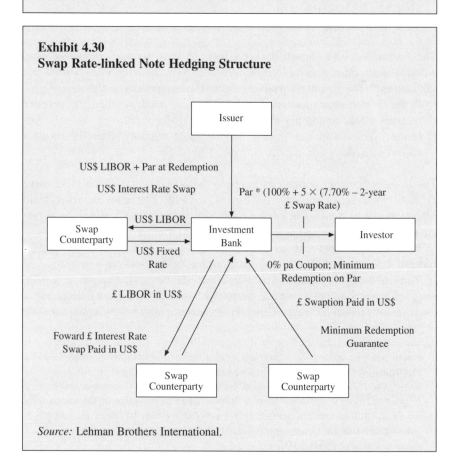

*Source:* Lehman Brothers International.

into losses for the investor because of the minimum redemption feature. The investor finances the purchase of the option on the swap through the foregone coupon on the note itself.

The transaction while similar to the Skr note described above has a number of differences:

- The investor does not risk principal but only the coupon as the minimum payout is restricted to par.
- The transaction is fully currency-protected with the £ exposure being fully hedged back into US$.

The coupon at risk structure effectively requires a forward (1-year forward into a 2-year swap) £ swap where the investor receives fixed rates combined with a swaption to pay the fixed rate (for two years, 1-year forward) purchased by the investor to be embedded in the swap. The swaption is designed to provide the guaranteed return of principal. The strike on the swaption relative to the forward swap rate and the swaption premium in conjunction with the cost of currency protection will be adjusted to equate to the coupon foregone by the investor to generate the transaction economics.

The currency-protected structure is created by incorporating quanto options in the structure. The quanto structure, also referred to as a quantity-adjusting option, ensures that the £ values are translated into US$ at a pre-agreed rate.[19]

In the mid- to late-1990s, these types of swap-linked structures were commonly utilized to seek to monetize expectations of convergence in interest rates as between European countries planning to become part of the monetary union and become foundation members in the Euro. The basic expectation was that interest rates in the participating countries should converge. This would basically entail the interest rates in Italy, Spain and Portugal declining towards the level of interest rates in Germany.

In order to take advantage of this expectation, a number of note structures linked to the forward rates in these currencies were created. The basic concept was to receive the forward swap rate in the high interest rate currency and pay the forward swap rate in the lower interest rate currency. These swaps were then embedded in the note principal redemption. Other structures involved options to create asymmetric exposures to expected rate movements. The structures required a currency protection element to be incorporated to ensure that the values in each currency were translated into the other currency at a pre-agreed exchange rate as above.

---

[19] For a discussion of quanto options see Das, Satyajit (1996) *Exotic Options*; LBC Information Services, Sydney at Chapter 12; see also Chapter 13.

Two examples are set out in **Exhibit 4.31** and **Exhibit 4.32**. The first structure is linked to the spread between 10-year lira and DM swap rates. The investor receives a return where the spread is above 2.00% pa and suffers a loss where the spread is below 0.50% pa. The second structure is a principal protected note where the interest is linked to the spread between European Currency Unit (Ecu) and DM rates. The investor receives enhanced coupons where the spread increases. The investor receives a lower return where the spread diminishes. In both cases, the investor created a position that resulted in gains if the planned monetary union did not proceed. The European Economic and Monetary Union (EMU), which was implemented in January 1999, was expected to result in interest rates between member currencies converging.

---

**Exhibit 4.31**
**Swap Rate-linked Note — Example 3**

| | |
|---|---|
| Issuer | AA-rated issuer |
| Amount | DM50 million |
| Maturity | 2 years |
| Issue Price | 100 |
| Interest Rate | 0% pa |
| Redemption Value | Redemption value is calculated in accordance with: |
| | Amount $\times$ Factor |
| Factor | 100% – 7 $\times$ Max. [0; 0.50% pa – Index] + 7 $\times$ Max. [0; Index – 2.00% pa] |
| | Where |
| | Index = Lira 10-year swap rate – DM 10-year swap rate |

---

**Exhibit 4.32**
**Swap Rate-linked Note — Example 4**

| | |
|---|---|
| Issuer | AA-rated issuer |
| Amount | DM50 million |
| Maturity | 2 years |
| Issue Price | 100 |
| Redemption Value | 100.00 |

| Coupon | Interest is calculated in accordance with: Amount × Factor |
|---|---|
| Factor | 4.45% pa + (7 × Index) |
| | Where |
| | Index = Ecu 2-year swap rate – DM 2-year swap rate |
| Minimum Coupon | 0.00% pa |

The concept of notes linked to swap rate differences between currencies is generic and has been extended beyond the special context of the EMU. The basic concept of these transactions based on spreads between currencies has also been extended to the spread between two points of the swap curve *in the same currency* as well as the *swap spread itself.*

**Exhibit 4.33** sets out a swap spread-based structure based in non-European currencies. The transaction is linked to the spread between yen and US$ swap rates. The investor has created an exposure that will benefit from a decrease in the spread between 10-year US$ and yen swap rates.

**Exhibit 4.34** and **Exhibit 4.35** set out transactions where the return is linked to the shape of the swap curve. In the first example, the investor benefits from an increase in the slope of the sterling swap curve. The benefit is capped at a spread of around 80 bps. At this level, the investor receives an effective return of around 9.54% pa. The investors return if the spread remains at the level prevailing at the time of entry into the transaction (5 bps pa), the investor receives a below-market return of 5.62% pa. These structures were designed to enable investors to position for a steepening in the sterling yield curve that was exceptionally flat between three and 15 years during this period. The second transaction is a derivative structure where the investor is taking a position that the difference between the swap curve slope in DM relative to sterling will decrease. If the difference between the two slopes is above 2.10% pa, then the investor receives no return. The return to the investor increases by around 1.00% pa for each 0.10% pa reduction in the slope difference. The maximum return to the investor is where the slope differentials between the currencies is zero.

**Exhibit 4.36** sets out the terms of a transaction where the return is linked to changes in the US$ swap spread. The investor return improves (deteriorates) as the swap spread decreases below (increases above) 80 bps. The investor has effectively entered into a forward on the swap spread that is embedded in the bond structure.

**Exhibit 4.33**
**Swap Rate-linked Note — Example 5**

| | |
|---|---|
| Issuer | AA-rated issuer |
| Amount | US$25 million |
| Maturity | 1 year |
| Issue Price | 100 |
| Interest Rate | 0% pa |
| Redemption Value | Redemption value is calculated in accordance with: |
| | Amount × Factor |
| Factor | 11.5 × [4.20% pa – Index] |
| | Where |
| | Index = US$ 10-year swap rate – ¥ 10-year swap rate |
| Minimum Redemption | 100.00 |

**Exhibit 4.34**
**Swap Rate-linked Note — Example 6**

| | |
|---|---|
| Issuer | AA-rated issuer |
| Amount | Lira 50 billion |
| Maturity | 2 years |
| Issue Price | 100 |
| Interest Rate | 0% pa |
| Redemption Value | Redemption value is calculated in accordance with: |
| | Amount × Factor |
| Factor | 12.05 – 10 × Index |
| | Where |
| | Index = £ 10-year swap rate – £ 5-year swap rate |
| Minimum Redemption | 100.00 |
| Maximum Redemption | 120.00 |

**Exhibit 4.35**
**Swap Rate-linked Note — Example 7**

| | |
|---|---|
| Issuer | AA-rated issuer |
| Amount | Lira 50 billion |
| Maturity | 3 years |
| Issue Price | 100 |
| Interest Rate | 0% pa |
| Redemption Value | 100 |
| Coupon | Interest is calculated in accordance with: |
| | Amount × Factor |
| Factor | 12.00% – 10 × (Index – 0.95%) |
| | Where |
| | Index = (DM 5-year swap rate – DM 3-month LIBOR) – (£ 5-year swap rate – £ 5-year swap rate) |
| Maximum Coupon | 21.00% pa |
| Minimum Coupon | 0.00% pa |

**Exhibit 4.36**
**Swap Spread-linked Note — Example 8**

| | |
|---|---|
| Issuer | AA-rated issuer |
| Amount | US$25 million |
| Maturity | 2 years |
| Issue Price | 100 |
| Interest Rate | 5.00% pa |
| Redemption Value | Redemption value is calculated in accordance with: |
| | Amount × Factor |
| Factor | 10 × [0.80% pa – Index] |
| | Where |
| | Index = US$ 10-year swap rate – US$ 10-year Treasury bond rate |
| Minimum Redemption | 0.00 |

## 5.   Capped and Collared Floating Rate Notes

### 5.1   Evolution

Capped and collared FRNs have been undertaken at various periods commencing in the mid-1980s. The issue of these instruments and investor interest in these instruments has coincided with positive yield curves and opportunities to extract value from the sale of options on short-term interest rates.

### 5.2   Capped FRNs[20]

Capped FRN and certificate of deposit (CD) issues, typically, are structured as 7- to 12-year FRN or 2- to 5-year CD issues with ceilings on interest payments. The issues are undertaken by highly rated borrowers, primarily banks or sovereign entities. Investors in the issues, in return for accepting a cap or maximum rate on their yield, received a higher than normal current coupon or margin on the FRNs and CDs.

Capped FRN and CD issues were initially undertaken in June 1985 in US dollars in the Euromarkets. The capped FRN concept has also been extended beyond US$ with a series of issues in a wide variety of currencies. Variations include delayed cap FRNs where the maximum interest rates do not operate for the first three to four years. A variation on the capped FRN structure was the maximum rate notes (MRNs). MRNs involved the issue of fixed-rate debt combined with a nominated cap rate on a floating rate index (such as 6-month LIBOR). If 6-month LIBOR exceeds the cap rate, the fixed-rate coupon decreases by the same amount. Functionally, MRNs operate in the same way as capped FRNs.

The cap, which is structurally identical to a put option on the price of a short-term security priced off the underlying short-term interest rate index, is sold to third parties with the proceeds of the sale, the option premium, in effect, lowering the issuer's borrowing cost, usually below market rates. Where the market rates exceed the capped rate, the investor's return is limited to the specified maximum rate allowing the purchaser of the cap to receive the difference between the cap and market rate from the issuer, thereby allowing it to establish a known maximum cost of funding.

The detailed structure of the transaction is more complex. For example, the Banque Indosuez transaction, arranged by Shearson Lehman Brothers, which opened this market, was an issue of 12-year US$200 million FRNs carrying an

---

[20] See Sowanick, Thomas J. and Tally, John G. (August 28, 1985) Floating Rate Notes With Interest Rate Caps; Merrill Lynch Capital Markets Securities Research Division, New York; Grant, Charles "Can Caps Beat Swaps" (July 1985) *Euromoney* 12-13.

interest coupon of 0.375% over 3-month LIMEAN.[21] The FRN coupon was
capped at 13.0625%. It should be noted that the cap level on LIMEAN is
equivalent to 12.6875% (13.0625% pa minus the 0.375% pa margin).

Shearson arranged for the sale of the cap (with a strike of 12.6875% pa on
LIMEAN) to a US corporation. Indosuez pays out LIMEAN plus 0.375%, or
13.0625% to the holders of the FRNs unless 3-month LIMEAN exceeds
12.6875% pa. For example, if LIMEAN go to 14.0625%, Indosuez pays
13.0625% to the FRN holders and 1.375% to Shearson who passes it on to the
purchaser of the cap to compensate it for rates rising above the cap level.
Indosuez is compensated for the cap by a payment of 0.375% pa of the principal
amount (effectively, the option premium). Indosuez wanted this flow as a
continuous quarterly flow, although it could have received it as a discounted
lump sum. This brought Indosuez's cost of funds down to LIMEAN. To avoid
any credit risk, the purchaser of the cap paid Shearson a lump sum that was
reinvested in some US Treasury zero-coupon securities which produced the
quarterly income stream equivalent to 0.375% pa. The structure of such a
transaction is set out in **Exhibit 4.37**.

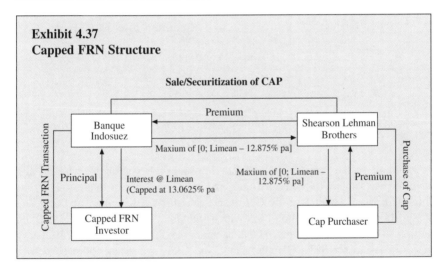

**Exhibit 4.37**
**Capped FRN Structure**

The structure of the capped FRN and its derivatives is that the issue was
engineered such that the investors created out-of-the-money caps. Analytically,
the investor has written a series of put options expiring every three or six months
until maturity on the underlying index. The premium paid to the investor is the

---

[21] LIMEAN is the London interbank mean rate (being the arithmetic average of the
LIBOR and London interbank bid rate (LIBID). This has traditionally been around
6.25 bps below LIBOR.

higher spread on the FRN. Studies undertaken to evaluate the pricing structure have concluded that the values implied for the caps are low compared with theoretical values derived from historical levels of volatility. This undervaluation provided a significant arbitrage opportunity whereby certain organisations active in trading caps purchased these caps stripped from the FRNs or CDs to effectively hedge their risk exposures in their interest rate cap portfolios.

The capped FRN structure has been utilized extensively in yen. **Exhibit 4.38** sets out an example of this structure.

---

**Exhibit 4.38**
**Capped Yen FRN**

| Issuer | A-rated issuer | |
|---|---|---|
| Amount | ¥5 billion | |
| Maturity | 5 years | |
| Interest | Yen 6-month LIBOR | |
| Maximum Interest | **Year** | **Maximum Interest (% pa)** |
| | 1 | 1.50 |
| | 2 | 2.00 |
| | 3 | 2.50 |
| | 4 | 3.00 |
| | 5 | 3.50 |
| Interest Coupon | Semi-annual | |

---

A variation on the capped FRN was the mini-max FRN structure whereby the investor was subject to both maximum and minimum rates of interest. The first mini-max issue, undertaken by Goldman Sachs for the Kingdom of Denmark, was a 10-year US$250 million FRN with a coupon of 10.1875% pa over LIBOR subject to a minimum rate of 10.00% pa and a maximum rate of 11.875% pa. A series of issues for SEK, Commerzbank, and Christiana Bank followed before investor interest evaporated. Just as the maximum or cap interest rate was identical to a series of caps or put options, the minimum interest rate was analytically identical to a floor or a series of call options. These options, which were granted by the issuer in return for the investor accepting a maximum rate of interest on the security, were then presumably stripped off and sold separately. In the case of these mini-max issues, in a number of cases, the issuer eliminated any exposure under the call options or floors granted by in turn purchasing a floor from a financial intermediary. The mini-max FRN concept re-emerged in 1992-93 in the form of collared FRNs discussed in the next section.

## 5.3 Collared FRNs

### 5.3.1 Background/Origins

The collared FRN structure has its origins in the capped FRN and mini-max FRN transactions completed in the mid-1980s. The collared FRN market emerged around August 1992 when Kidder Peabody, the US investment bank, reintroduced the concept with issues for, among others, J.P. Morgan and Credit Local de France.

In an environment of low nominal interest rates and a steep positively shaped yield curve, investors seeking higher short-term money market interest rates created demand for a series of issues of FRNs with both a minimum and maximum interest rate. These structures, which effectively combined a normal FRN with an interest rate collar (a purchased cap and sold floor on the relevant interest rate index), were used to extract value from the positively shaped yield curves.

### 5.3.2 Structure

The basic structure of the collared FRN entails a normal FRN structure with an interest coupon related to US$ LIBOR (either 3- or 6-month). The interest rate coupon is subject to a minimum and maximum interest rate level of 5% pa and 10% pa respectively. The initial issues were undertaken for maturities of 10 years.

The initial transactions undertaken were subordinated FRNs (designed to be treated as Tier II Capital for BIS capital adequacy purposes). However, a number of subsequent issues were senior rather than subordinated issue structures.

**Exhibit 4.39** sets out the term of the J.P. Morgan issue, one of their first transactions to be undertaken.

---

**Exhibit 4.39**
**Collared FRN Structure**

| | |
|---|---|
| Issuer | J.P. Morgan and Co. Inc. |
| Amount | US$200 million of subordinated FRNs |
| Maturity | 10 years (due August 19, 2002) |
| Interest rate | 3-month LIBID[22] flat |
| Fixed Reoffer Price | 99.85 |

---

[22] LIBID is the London interbank bid rate. This has traditionally been 12.5 bps below LIBOR.

| Minimum Interest | 5% |
| Maximum Interest | 10% |
| Amortisation | Bullet |
| Call option | None |
| Listing | Luxembourg |
| Governing Law | New York |
| Denominations | US$5,000, US$100,000 |
| Commissions | 0.50% (management and underwriting 0.25%; selling 0.25%) |
| Payment | August, 18 |
| Outstanding Rating | Aa2 (Moody's), AA+ (S&P) |
| Lead Manager | Kidder Peabody Intl (books) |
| Co-lead Managers | J.P. Morgan Securities, Merrill Lynch Intl, Salomon Brothers Intl, CSFB |
| Co-managers | Lehman Brother Intl, Goldman Sachs Intl, Morgan Stanley Intl |
| Premarket Price | 100.10, 100.25 |

*Source: International Financing Review Issue 940, (August 1992): 56.*

### 5.3.3   Economics

The basic economics of the collared FRN is driven by the fact that it combines a standard FRN transaction with a US$ LIBOR interest rate cap and floor. Based on the structure described, the investor purchases a package consisting of:

- A normal 10-year US$ LIBOR-related coupon FRN.
- Sells a cap on US$ LIBOR at the maximum interest rate (say, 10% pa).
- Purchases a US$ interest rate floor at the minimum interest rate level (say, 5% pa).

The sale of the cap and purchase of the floor equates to, effectively, a sold interest rate collar on US$ LIBOR.

The position of the issuer is the exact opposite of that of the investor. The issuer has borrowed utilizing a US$ LIBOR-based FRN, while simultaneously purchasing a US$ LIBOR interest rate cap and selling a US$ LIBOR-based floor (a purchased interest rate collar on US$ LIBOR).

**Exhibit 4.40** sets out the structure of the collared FRN decomposed into the relevant components.

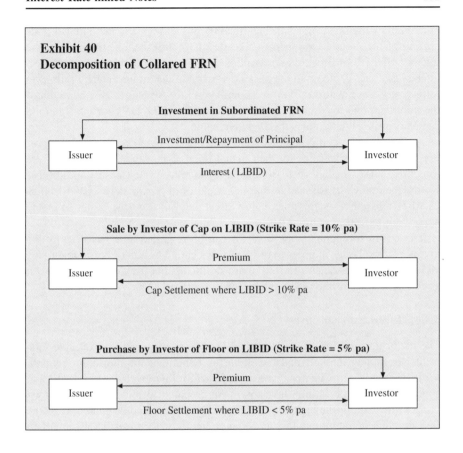

**Exhibit 40**
**Decomposition of Collared FRN**

Investment in Subordinated FRN

Investment/Repayment of Principal

Issuer          Investor

Interest ( LIBID)

Sale by Investor of Cap on LIBID (Strike Rate = 10% pa)

Premium

Issuer          Investor

Cap Settlement where LIBID > 10% pa

Purchase by Investor of Floor on LIBID (Strike Rate = 5% pa)

Premium

Issuer          Investor

Floor Settlement where LIBID < 5% pa

As described in detail below, the issuer hedges this exposure under the collar by onselling the cap and purchasing the floor to generate normal US$ LIBOR-based funding.

The economics of the transaction are driven by the shape of the US dollar yield curve. The strongly positive nature of the yield curve means that forward rates in US dollars are significantly above the prevailing rates for particular maturities. For example, the rate for US$ 3- or 6-month LIBOR in 3, 6, 9, 12 and so on, months is significantly above the prevailing LIBOR or bank borrowing rates for the corresponding maturity. This merely reflects the steepness of the yield curve itself.

The steepness of the yield curve and the fact that the US$ LIBOR forward rates implied from the curve are significantly above the observed yield curve dictates the respective values of the cap and floor that, in turn, dictate the economics of the transaction. The fact that forward US$ LIBOR rates are significantly above current yield curve rates means that the US$ LIBOR floors purchased by the investors while significantly in-the-money in the initial periods are out-of-the-money for much of the life of the transaction. In contrast, the higher US$ LIBOR forward rates implied in the yield curve dictate that the US$ interest rate cap is closer to the strike price of the maximum interest rate level (effectively, the cap strike level) of the collared FRN structure. This relativity of the minimum and maximum rates (effectively, the strike rates for the floor and cap respectively) determines their relative value.

At the time these transactions were undertaken, based on the yield curves prevailing, the market price for the cap and floor suggest that the investors were foregoing approximately 25 to 50 bps pa in value from the transaction. In other words, the collared FRN had an implied yield of approximately LIBOR minus 25 to 50 bps pa. This foregone value effectively allowed the issuer to create attractively priced funding as described in detail below.

The return foregone by the investor can be regarded as a payment by the investor to the issuer in order to provide an incentive to him or her to undertake an issue providing the customized return profile sought by the investor, as well as compensating for the credit enhancement provided.

### 5.3.4  Investor Perspective

The major demand for these collared FRNs was from money market investors, primarily money market funds, seeking the benefit of the minimum coupon. With US$ short-term interest rates at historically low levels and, at that time, appearing still to be falling, investors were prepared to trade off the foregone profit of the cap for the high short-term current coupon income generated by the floor implicit in the minimum interest level. In effect, the investors were willing to sell the cap, at a lower than theoretical value level, as firstly, they placed a greater importance on current income and, secondly, their expectations of forward interest rates on US$ LIBOR were significantly below those implied by the current yield curve.

### 5.3.5  Issuer Perspective

From the perspective of the issuer, these transactions were fully hedged into normal US$ LIBOR-based funding, typically, at relatively attractive borrowing rates. The issuer had effectively purchased a US$ interest rate cap at the maximum rate and sold the investor an interest rate floor at the minimum interest rate. The issuer hedged its exposure by simultaneously onselling the interest rate cap and purchasing a corresponding interest rate floor to immunize itself from the risk of the transaction. The hedging interest rate cap and floor transactions were undertaken generally by the issuer directly with the arranger of the transaction or alternatively a third-party derivatives trader.

The attractive funding cost for the issuer was generated by the fact that, as noted above, the investors were valuing the collar element of the transaction at a level that was lower than the economic value of the separate interest rate cap and floor. This allowed issuers to typically onsell the interest rate cap and purchase the interest rate floor for premiums that generated a net cash inflow to the issuer that reduced their borrowing costs.

From the issuer's perspective, the transactions were particularly attractive as they generated attractively priced funding for long terms, typically, 10 years, at a time when arbitrage opportunities in traditional bond markets were relatively scarce. An additional advantage, particularly for banks, was the capacity to structure a number of these transactions as subordinated issues, thereby allowing these institutions to raise cost-effective Tier II capital to enhance their capital adequacy positions.

### 5.3.6 Market Evolution and Product Variations

The market developed extremely rapidly after the re-emergence of this market in the early 1990s. As the market developed, a number of variations on the basic product concept also emerged. These variations focused on a number of elements of the transactions:

• Variations on the interest formula utilized.
• Transactions in currencies other than the US dollar.
• Securitization of the option elements of the transaction.
• Development of a whole new class of transactions.

Initially, the collared FRN market operated around the basic formula described above with minor variations for the differences in credit quality of the issuer, as well as fluctuations in the price of the cap or floor element reflecting changes in the shape of the US dollar yield curve. However, as the arbitrage margins in such transactions narrowed, a number of transactions sought to maximize available opportunities with changes in the interest rate formula utilized.

The first such variation was to adjust the maximum interest rate level. In order to extract more value from the shape of the forward US$ LIBOR yield curve, the maximum interest rate was "tiered" with the rate increasing over time. For example, in a transaction completed for Abbey National Treasury Services Plc in late August 1992, the maximum interest rate was set at 6% pa in years 1 and 2, 7% in years 3 and 4, and 8% in year 5. A similar structure was utilized in an issue for Bayerische Hypotheken und Wechsel Bank with the maximum interest rate rising from 7% pa to 9% pa, albeit with a lower minimum interest rate of 4% pa. A central feature of these transactions requiring the tiered maximum interest rate was the issuer's desire for shorter maturities. This necessitated adjustments to the maximum interest rate level to generate premiums from the sale of interest rate caps to subsidize the floor of purchases required.

The other major change in the interest rate formula of such instruments emerged later in September 1992 as changes in the yield curve shape dictated a reduction in the maximum interest rate to levels of around 8-8.25% pa to extract the required value from the forward rates in the yield curve. The lower band level was repeated in March 1993 as the flatter shape of the US$ yield curve forced a lowering of the maximum interest rate or cap strike level to generate the necessary premiums to allow these transactions to proceed.

A further variation was to undertake transactions where the underlying interest rate was a term constant maturity or swap rate (such as a 10-year swap rate) rather than the traditional short-term money market rates.

As the market evolved, an interesting product variation focused on securitizing the option elements of the structure. Under this arrangement, the issue of FRNs was combined with a maximum interest rate, but was sold in conjunction with the issue by the borrower of floor certificates that were detachable. The floor certificates were effectively the minimum interest rate element of the transaction and allowed the investor to freely trade in the floor certificates quite separate from the capped FRN itself.

**Exhibit 4.41** sets out an example of this particular variation detailing the terms of an issue for the World Bank completed in March 1993.

---

**Exhibit 4.41**
**Collared FRN with Securitized Floor Structure**

*Capped FRN*

| | |
|---|---|
| Issuer | World Bank |
| Amount | DM 200 million of FRNs |
| Maturity | 10 years (due April 28, 2003) |
| Coupon | 6-month LIBOR plus 0.25% payable semi-annually on April 28, and October 28 |
| Maximum Interest | 7.25% as from the beginning of the fifth interest period |
| First Interest determination Date | April 26 |
| Issue Price | 100% |
| Amortisation | Bullet |
| Call Option | None |
| Listing | Frankfurt SE |

| | |
|---|---|
| Denominations | DM10,000 and DM250,000 (global note) |
| Commissions | 0.20% (management and underwriting combined 0.10%, selling 0.10%) |
| Launch Date | March 11, 1993 |
| Payment | April 28, 1993 |
| Lead Manager | Commerzbank (books) |
| Co-managers | ABN Amro Bank, BBL, Bayerische Landesbank, Bayerische Vereinsbank, CSFB Effectenbank, Deutsche Bank, Kidder Peabody Intl, Merrill Lynch Bank AG, J.P. Morgan GmbH, Morgan Stanley GmbH, Paribas GmbH, Salomon Brothers AG, Sanwa Bank (Deutschland), Schweizerische Bankgesellschaft (Deutschland), Schweizerischer Bankverein (Deutschland), Trinkaus & Burkhardt, WestLB |
| Premarket Price | 99.80, 99.90 |

### Floor Certificates

| | |
|---|---|
| Issuer | World Bank |
| Number | 20,000 certificates |
| Exercise | Each certificate entitles the holder to payment on April 28, and October 28, corresponding to the positive difference between 7% and 6-month LIBOR. Each certificate relates to DM10,000. |
| Issue Price | DM695 per certificate |
| Expiration | April 28, 2003 |
| Selling Concession | 0.25% |
| Listing | Frankfurt SE |
| Launch Date | March 11, 1993 |
| Payment Date | April 28, 1993 |
| Lead Manager | Commerzbank (books) |
| Premarket Price | DM720, 740 |

*Source: International Financing Review* Issue 970, (1993 March): 72.

The structure is interesting for a number of other features including:

- The deferral of the maximum interest level, which only operates from the beginning of the fifth interest rate period (effectively, 2.5 years into the term of the 10-year transaction). This reflected the fact that DM LIBOR was higher than the maximum rate at the time of issue.

- The maximum interest rate, which is lower than the then prevailing DM LIBOR rate, reflecting the inverse slope of the DM yield curve and the different pattern of forward DM LIBOR rates implied.
- The structure of the floor certificates, which have a strike rate at a level of 7% (which is unusually close to the maximum interest rate level) and operate for the full life of the transaction, again reflecting the particular shape of the DM yield curve.

The concept of securitized floors in conjunction with an issue of FRNs (without the cap) has been utilized in the sterling market with the issue of FRNs with detachable Additional Detachable Interest Rights (ADIRs). The first issue for Britannia Building Society, arranged by Samuel Montagu in June 1993, entailed a £100 million FRN at 3-month £ LIBOR plus 15 bps in combination with ADIRs that entitled the holder to receive 5% pa less 3-month £ LIBOR where £ LIBOR is less than 5% pa. The ADIRs were effectively floors on £ LIBOR with a strike price equivalent to 5% pa and, in structure, securitized the minimum coupon on the FRN. The ADIR structure was utilized to create additional value for the issuer to allow a higher price for the minimum coupon element to be realized. In addition, the use of ADIRs avoided potential *ultra vires* problems regarding the capacity of the UK Building Society issuer to separately sell a 5% floor.

A number of variations entailing hybrid products has also evolved. Principal among these are 1-way or ratchet FRNs, as well as a variety of structures linked to the 10-year Constant Maturity Treasury (CMT) rate (known as step-up recovery FRNs (SURFs)).[23] These product variations seek to take advantage of the prevailing interest rate environment in a manner similar to collared FRNs. They extract value from the higher forward US$ LIBOR rates implicit in the steep yield curve that is translated into a higher current income level through the purchase of a floor by the investor.

The 1-way or ratchet FRN offers investors a yield around 3- or 6-month US$ LIBOR plus 35 bps, with a floor equal to the previous coupon and a cap equal to the previous coupon plus 25bps. The floor locks in any increase in LIBOR while the cap allows LIBOR to rise moderately. Effectively, the structure creates a "ratcheting" return for the investor. For example, at the time these transactions were undertaken around late November/early December 1992, the first interest payment was set at around 4.2875% pa. This effectively means that given that the interest rate on the issue can rise by 0.25% for 20 semi-annual interest periods, the issue had an increasing cap that peaks at 9.2875% pa for the last interest rate period. **Exhibit 4.42** sets out the terms of a typical ratchet FRN issue.

---

[23] See Chapter 5.

**Exhibit 4.42**
**Ratchet FRN Structure**

| | |
|---|---|
| Issuer | Credit Local de France |
| Amount | US$100 million |
| Maturity | 5 years |
| Coupon | 3-month LIBOR plus 0.35% |
| | The coupon cannot be increased by more than 0.25% per interest reset and cannot be decreased. |
| Issue Price | 101.625 |
| Fixed Reoffer Price | 100 |
| Amortisation | Bullet |
| Call Option | None |
| Put Option | None |
| Listing | Luxembourg |
| Denominations | US$10,000, US$100,000, US$1 million |
| Commissions | 1.875% (management and underwriting 0.05%; selling 1.825%) |
| Payment | December 23 |
| Swap | Into a variety of fixed-rate European currencies |
| Outstanding Rating | Aaa (Moody's), AAA (S&P) |
| Lead Managers | Morgan Stanley International (books) |
| Co-managers | Daiwa Europe, Merrill Lynch |
| Premarket Price | 99.95 |

Source: *International Financing Review* Issue 958, (1992 December): 58.

The value in the ratchet structure is driven by the interaction in the premium levels of the tiered cap relative to that of the tiered floor that operates in such transactions. This type of structure yields the most economic value for the issuer where the slope of the yield curve and the pattern of forward rates implied are at a level where the interest rate caps sold by the investor through the ratchet structure are substantially more in-the-money or closer to the strike price of the ratcheting caps, while the corresponding floors are to a large degree out-of-the-money.

The put and call options created by the capped, mini-max, and so on, issues were, in fact, bought, substantially, by institutions active in the creation and sale of interest rate options, usually in the form of floor, cap, or collar agreements. The securitized options were purchased to match out the portfolio risk exposures of the market makers, allowing them to unwind (or reverse out of) other less efficient hedges.

## 6.    Bond Index-linked Notes[24]

An emerging class of interest rate-linked notes are fixed interest bonds where the return, both principal and interest, is linked to the total return on a specified bond price index.[25]

The principal building block of a bond index note is a bond index swap. **Exhibit 4.43** sets out the structure of a bond index swap. **Exhibit 4.44** on page 189 sets out example of a bond index swap. **Exhibit 4.45**, also on page 189, sets out the return computation mechanics.

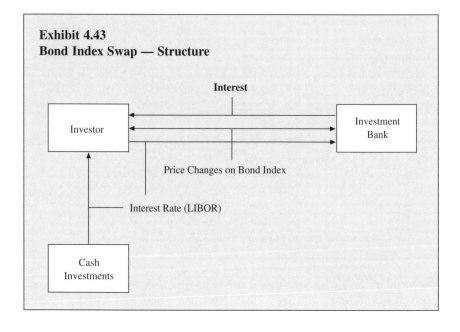

**Exhibit 4.43**
**Bond Index Swap — Structure**

---

[24]  See Efraty, Ravit (March 1995) "An Introduction to Index Swaps and Notes"; Salomon Brothers US Derivatives Research Fixed Income Derivatives, New York.

[25]  A variety of bond price indexes is published by a variety of investment banks, including Salomon Brothers, Lehman Brothers, Goldman Sachs, J.P. Morgan, and so on. The indexes are available on a variety of underlying bond universes—for example, investment grade, high-yield, emerging market, specific currency markets, and so on.

**Exhibit 4.44**
**Bond Index Swap — Terms**

*Total Return Swap On Bond Index*

| | |
|---|---|
| Amount | US$100 million |
| Maturity | 1 year |
| Investor Receives | Total return of [nominated index] |
| Investor Pays | 1-month LIBOR plus [margin] |
| Payment/Resets | All payments and index resets are monthly. |

*Total Return Swap on Currency (DM)) Sector of Index*

| | |
|---|---|
| Amount | US$100 million |
| Maturity | 1 year |
| Investor Receives | [(End period US$/DM)/(Beginning period US$/DM) times (1 + Total return on DM sector of [nominated index] – 1 |
| Investor Pays | 1-month LIBOR plus [margin] |
| Payment/Resets | All payments and index resets are monthly. |

**Exhibit 4.45**
**Bond Index Swap — Return Computation[26]**

Index returns are calculated on several bases: local currency terms, base currency terms, unhedged, and currency-hedged terms.

The local currency return is calculated as follows:

Total rate of return      =  [(End period value/Beginning period value) – 1] × 100

Where:

Beginning period value  =  (Beginning price + Beginning accrued interest) × Beginning par amount outstanding

---

[26] This is based on Efraty, Ravit (March 1995) "An Introduction to Index Swaps and Notes"; Salomon Brothers US Derivatives Research Fixed Income Derivatives, New York.

End period value          = (End price + End accrued) × (Beginning par
                            amount outstanding – Principal repayments)
                            + Coupon payments + Principal payments
                            + Reinvestment income

The local currency sector return is the weighted average of individual
bond returns using each bond's beginning of month market value as its
weight.

The base currency returns is calculated by multiplying the local
currency return by the end of period exchange rate divided by the
beginning of period currency exchange rate.

The calculation of the next total return payment of a currency hedged
return is as follows:

Total rate of return      = [(End period value/Beginning
                            period value) – 1] × 100

Where:

Beginning period value  = ((Beginning price + Beginning accrued
                          interest) × Beginning par amount
                          outstanding)) × (Beginning of period spot
                          exchange rate)

End period value          = [(Yield for forward settlement at end of
                          1 month + Expected change in accrued
                          Interest over 1 month + Cash flow and
                          reinvestment income) × Beginning of period
                          1-month forward exchange rate] + [Change
                          in market value of principal amount due to
                          yield change × [End of period spot exchange
                          rate]

The currency hedged base currency sector return is the weighted average
of individual bond returns using each bond's beginning of month market
value as its weight.

**Exhibit 4.46** sets out the structure of a bond index linked note. The note
combines the purchase of a floating-rate asset with entry into a bond index swap.

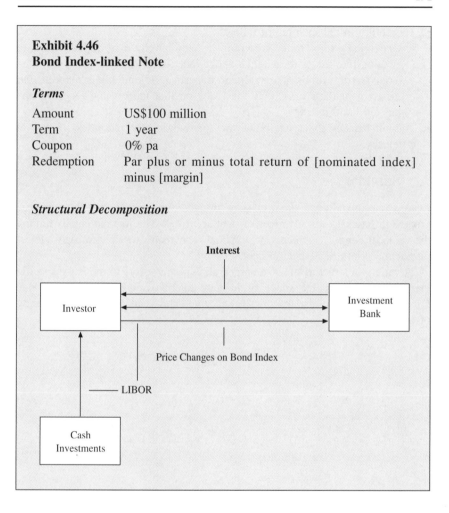

**Exhibit 4.46**
**Bond Index-linked Note**

*Terms*

| | |
|---|---|
| Amount | US$100 million |
| Term | 1 year |
| Coupon | 0% pa |
| Redemption | Par plus or minus total return of [nominated index] minus [margin] |

*Structural Decomposition*

The major attraction of these bond index-linked notes (as with the swap itself) includes:

• The ability to gain diversified exposure to selected bond markets. This is achieved without the difficulties with physical replication of an index, including tracking errors and rebalancing costs.
• Lower operational costs through avoiding physical purchase of securities, including back office, custody, and settlement costs.
• Potential tax benefits for some investors unable to recover withholding tax on bonds in certain markets.
• Ability to short bond markets without the need to liquidate physical holdings.

- The ability to enhance return through:
  - Receiving index returns combined with purchase of higher yielding floating rate assets to generate above-index returns.
  - Transferring funds management expertise in one bond market into different markets by paying the index on that market and receiving the desired bond index.
- The off-balance-sheet nature of the transaction that increases its capital efficiency.

## 7.  Summary

Interest rate linked notes are a class of structured notes that embody a specific linkage to interest rates or prices of debt securities. The linkage entails linking the value of coupon payments or principal repayments to an identified interest rate or the prices of a specific debt security.

A variety of structures have emerged allowing investors to monetize specific views in relation to the shape of forward interest rates and/or interest rate volatility. The structures are now well accepted and available in a wide variety of currencies.

# 5

# Constant Maturity Treasury and Swap Rate Notes

## 1.  Introduction

The concept of derivatives and structured notes based around Constant Maturity Treasury (CMT) rates and Constant Maturity Swap (CMS) rates is a relatively new phenomenon in capital markets. The central objectives of these instruments is their use in hedging and taking positions on:
*   Medium-to-long-term portion of the yield curve in any currency.
*   The spread between interest rates at different points in the yield curve (effectively, the slope or shape of the yield curve).

In this chapter, the structure and applications of CMT/CMS-based instruments is examined. The concept of CMT and CMS rates and the basic "building block" CMT/CMS instruments are first considered. The next section examines the different types of CMT/CMS note structures. In subsequent sections, the pricing, valuation, and hedging, as well as the market for these types of instruments is examined.

## 2.  CMT/CMS Rates and Instruments

### 2.1  CMT/CMS Rates

The concept of CMT/CMS rates[1] focuses on an interest rate on securities with specified maturities. For example, yields on treasury securities at "constant maturity" are interpolated by the US Treasury from the daily yield curve. This curve, which relates the yield on a security to its time to maturity, based on the closing market bid yields on actively traded treasury securities in the over-the-

---

[1]  See Smithson Charles "ABC Of CMT" (September 1995) *Risk* 30-31

counter market. These market yields are calculated from composites of quotations reported by five leading US government securities dealers to the Federal Reserve Bank of New York. The constant maturity yield values are read from the yield curve at fixed maturities: currently 1-, 2-, 3-, 5-, 7-, 10- and 30-years. According to the Federal Reserve, this method would provide a yield for a 10-year maturity, for example, even if no outstanding security has exactly 10 years remaining to maturity. **Exhibit 5.1** sets out the manner in which the CMT rates, as published by the Federal Reserve, are determined.

---

**Exhibit 5.1**
**CMT Rates**

*CMT Rates*

CMT rates are equivalent to the par yield for a US Government Treasury security with an exact maturity of one, two, three, five, seven, 10, 20 or 30 years.

*Methodology*

The Federal Reserve of New York polls five primary dealers (selected from the over 30 primary dealers) for closing bids for "on the run" issues. This poll is conducted daily, when the market is open, at 3:30 PM.

The bids are utilized to construct a complete Treasury yield curve. Cubic spline methodology is used to interpolate between data points. The CMT rates for each maturity are then interpolated from this yield curve.

*Dissemination of CMT Rates*

The Treasury posts the calculated rates in a number of ways:
- The CMT rates are available from the Commerce Department's economic bulletin board after 4:30 PM on the relevant day. A number of commercial data services disseminate the rates from the Commerce Department.
- The CMT rates are also published by the Federal Reserve Bank in its weekly H-15 Statistical Release.

---

CMT rates are used predominantly in the US. In other markets, the concept of CMS rates has evolved to mean, typically, the interest rate swap rate for the relevant maturity assuming a generic structure for the underlying swap transaction.

The use of CMS rates reflects the following factors:

- The central role played by swap rates in financial markets in a number of markets where these rates are utilized as the major market interest rate indicator.
- The level of liquidity of swap rates relative to other fixed income benchmark rates.
- The constant maturity feature of swap rates. The maturity for a generic swap is, inherently, a constant maturity as it is for the relevant maturity from the start date irrespective of the start date selected. This contrasts with Treasury securities that, by their nature, have fixed maturities and the remaining life to maturity diminishes over time.

CMT/CMS rates generally facilitate hedging and the trading of pure interest rates for a selected maturity, without reducing term to maturity associated with physical securities. A further advantage of using CMT/CMS rates is that in the case of options on term rates, the fixed and constant maturity feature avoids some of the difficulties in pricing options on physical debt securities, particularly bonds, such as a declining maturity, and a declining volatility reflecting the pull of the bond's price to par.[2]

## 2.2   CMT and CMS Instruments[3]

The major CMT/CMS instruments are, in fact, the basic derivative building blocks: forwards and options on CMT rates or spreads (for convenience, in the rest of this book, the term CMT is used to indicate CMT- or CMS-based structures). The two major formats are:
- **Yield curve swaps** (also known as CMT swaps) — effectively, a portfolio of forwards allowing the counterparties to take positions on the forward spread between two nominated CMT rates.
- **Options on yield curve spreads** — effectively, call and put options on the forward spread between two nominated CMT rates.

---

[2]   See Chapter 2, Appendix A.

[3]   For a discussion of yield curve products see Bennet, Rosemary "Creative Solutions for Interest Rate Uncertainty" (August 1993) *Euromoney* 50-52; Cornog, Peggy "Hidden Powers of the Yield Curve" (1994) *Corporate Finance, Risk Management & Derivatives Yearbook* 57-60; Klotz, Rick, Shah, Nilesh V., and Efraty, Ravit A. (May 26, 1994) Structured Note Strategies: Alternatives to LIBOR Based Floating Rate Notes; Salomon Brothers Fixed Income Derivatives Research, New York; Britt, Patrick E. "CMT Plays" (December 14, 1994) *IFR Swaps Weekly* 9; Patyne, Hans and McCarroll, Veronique "Beating The Positive Yield Curve" (1995) *Corporate Finance, Risk Management & Derivatives Yearbook* 30-32; Dago, Virginie and Lauwick, Vincent "Taking Advantage Of The Steep Yield Curve" (1996) *Corporate Finance, Risk Management & Derivatives Yearbook* 18-22.

Appendix A sets out the detailed structure of a yield curve swap. Appendix B sets out the technique for pricing such transactions by decomposing such transactions into portfolios of forwards.

Yield curve options are, in fact, a category of spread options. Spread options refer to an option structure where the underlying asset is the differential between the prices of two underlying assets. The spread option payout is determined by the difference if positive (negative) for a call (put) between the identified indexes.

Spread options are a special type of multi-factor options. Multi-factor options refer to a special class of options whose primary distinguishing characteristic is that the option payout is based on the relationship between more than one asset. This is in contrast to conventional options that are based on the price or performance of a single asset. Spread options like other multi-factor options have two sources of price risk, dictated by the multiple underlying assets on which the option contract is structured.[4]

The general terminology in regard to such options is as follows:[5]

- Call options are used to buy the yield curve. This is equivalent to a long position in the shorter maturity security and a short position in the longer maturity security (the amounts are volatility — matched using duration, Present Value of 1 Basis Point (PVBP) or Dollar Value of 1 Basis Point (DVO1) methods, to equate the relative price sensitivities of the different securities to yield movements). This position will allow the purchaser to gain from a steepening of the shape of the yield curve where short rates rise less or fall more than longer rates.
- Put options are used to sell the yield curve. This is equivalent to a short position in the shorter maturity security and a long position in the longer maturity security (the amounts are volatility-matched). This position will allow the purchaser to gain from a flattening of the shape of the yield curve where short rates rise more or fall less than longer rates.

**Appendix C** sets out a technique for pricing spread/yield curve options.

## 3.   Structures

The CMT note structures typically found are, in effect, securities, usually floating rate securities such as a LIBOR-based FRN, combined with a yield

---

[4]   See Das, Satyajit (1996) *Exotic Option*; LBC Information Services, Sydney at Chapter 12.

[5]   The terminology for these options in common with other exotic structures is far from standardized.

curve swap or yield curve option based on CMT rates. As noted above, these structures usually are attractive to counterparties seeking to hedge or trade yield curve risks.

The major types of structures available are:

- CMT-based FRNs.
- CMT-based Yield Curve Notes.
- CMT Option Notes.

Each of these is discussed below. Variations on these structures are also frequent but the basic structural features identified are largely consistent. Consistent with the general structural features of these instruments, the notes can be designed to incorporate additional leverage by increasing the notional principal of the derivative component embedded in the security.

## 3.1   CMT FRNs

CMT-based floaters emerged originally in the US market in an environment of tightening monetary policy and an extremely steep yield curve. The steepness of the yield curve made a LIBOR-based FRN unattractive, while lengthening the term of the investment in an environment of expected increasing interest rates exposed portfolios to a risk of capital loss. In this environment, a FRN priced off the CMT rate emerged as an attractive alternative format of floating rate investment.

**Exhibit 5.2** sets out the terms of a typical 5-year FRN whose coupon is priced off of the 2-year CMT rates (CMT2). Functionally, the CMT2 FRN can be decomposed into an investment by the investor in a AAA-rated 5-year FRN yielding 3-month LIBOR minus 10 bps and the simultaneous entry by the investor into a 5-year yield curve swap where the investor pays 3-month LIBOR and receives CMT2 − 24 bps. **Exhibit 5.3** sets out the structure in a diagrammatic format.

---

**Exhibit 5.2
CMT FRN**

| | |
|---|---|
| Issuer | AAA-rated issuer |
| Amount | US$100 to 400 million |
| Maturity | 5 years |
| Index | 2-year Constant Maturity Treasury (CMT2) |
| Coupon | CMT − 34 bps reset quarterly |

---

**Exhibit 5.3**
**CMT FRN Structure**

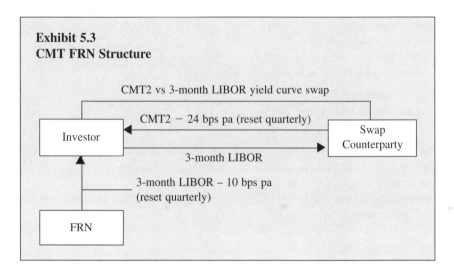

The CMT-based FRN offers a higher return to the investor relative to a LIBOR-based FRN investor. This return advantage was around 75-80 bps at the time of entry into this transaction based on a comparable yield on a LIBOR-based FRN of LIBOR minus 10 bps. The investor is assuming the risk that the spread between 3-month LIBOR and CMT2 will not decrease or even if the curve flattens that the spread will not narrow to an extent that will reduce the return performance of the CMT2 FRN below that of the LIBOR FRN. The spread must decrease to a level below 34 bps before the CMT2 FRN underperforms the LIBOR FRN.

At the time this transaction was undertaken, the spread between CMT2 and LIBOR was 94 bps. Two-year forward rates implied a spread of 3 bps, that is a decrease of 91 bps. The investor is monetizing its expectation that the implied narrowing of the yield curve spread (flattening) overestimates the actual narrowing that will occur. As long as the decrease in the spread does not occur at the rate or to the level implied by the current yield curve, the CMT2 FRN will outperform the LIBOR FRN.

### 3.2   CMT Yield Curve Notes

CMT yield curve notes were another category of structures entailing derivative return characteristics based on CMT rates to also emerge in the low nominal interest rate and steep yield curve environment of the early 1990s. An example of this innovation is the Step-Up Recovery FRNs (SURFs), also referred to as a Deleveraged FRN (referred to hereinafter as a Deleveraged FRN).

The Deleveraged FRN entails a floating rate bond where the interest return is linked to the return on the theoretical constant maturity 10-year Treasury bond rate. The coupon rate is linked to a specific CMT rate. In contrast to the type of CMT FRN described above, which pays CMT minus a margin, a CMT Deleveraged FRN pays a coupon calculated as:

Leverage factor × CMT plus/minus a margin

The leverage factor is set between 0 and 100%.

The structure can be decomposed in a number of ways:

- A fixed-rate bond with an embedded yield curve swap where the notional principal of the yield curve swap is equal to the notional principal of the note multiplied the leverage factor.
- A fixed-rate bond and a position in a CMT FRN where the amount of the investment in the bond is equal to in percentage terms to one minus the leverage factor and the position in the CMT FRN is equal to the leverage factor.

The major feature in terms of return characteristic of this structure is that the coupon does not increase or decrease as rapidly as the CMT index, participating only partially (in proportion to the leverage factor) in the movement of the relevant index.

It is possible to analyze the comparative return of three instruments: a fixed-rate note, a CMT FRN returning a coupon of CMT minus a spread, and a Deleveraged FRN (leverage factor of 50%). The analysis indicates that for low absolute CMT rates, the Deleveraged FRN provides returns superior to that of the CMT FRN. For higher absolute values of CMT rate, the CMT FRN outperforms the Deleveraged FRN.

The return characteristics can be manipulated by lowering the leverage factor that has the effect of increasing the initial coupon rate on the transaction. This increase is accomplished at the risk of reduction in potential increases in CMT rates. The increase in initial coupon achievable is a function of the steepness of the yield curve. The steeper the curve the greater the increase for a given change in leverage factor.

The investor will typically select the maturity of the CMT rate consistent with the investor's views on the shape of the yield curve and its evolution over the investment horizon. The Deleveraged FRN will outperform a LIBOR-based FRN at commencement as its initial coupon will be higher. However, outperformance over the investment horizon will depend upon the performance of the selected maturity FRN rate. If the differential between the selected CMT rate and short-term rates flattens less than the decrease implied by the forward rates derived from the current yield curve, then the superior performance is likely to be sustained.

In order to lower the risk of the coupon becoming low on the Deleveraged FRNs, a number of these structures incorporates a floor component that ensures that the coupon cannot go below an agreed level. This protection is achieved by embedding a floor on CMT rates within the note.

A detailed analysis of the Deleveraged FRN structure together with the accompanying swap arrangements, which incorporate a yield curve swap, is set out in **Exhibit 5.4**.

---

**Exhibit 5.4**
**Step-up Recovery FRN (SURF)/ Deleveraged FRN**

In early 1993, a series of structured FRNs—introduced as SURFs or Deleveraged FRNs—were issued in the Eurobond market. The first issues were undertaken for the World Bank and Eurofima by Lehman Brothers. The issues in the Eurobond market followed approximately US$1 billion of issues in the US domestic market.

***Structure***

The basic structure is a floating rate bond where the interest rate is calculated in accordance with a formula linked to the theoretical 10-year US Treasury bond rate.

The terms of the World Bank transaction are summarized below:

| | |
|---|---|
| Issuer | World Bank |
| Amount | US$100 million |
| Maturity | 5 years (due March 17, 1998). |
| Coupon | (Constant Maturity Treasury × 0.5) plus 1.45% |
| | CMT is a theoretical 10-year Treasury yield |
| Minimum Coupon | 4.60% pa |
| Maximum Coupon | 25.00% pa |
| Issue/Fixed Re-offer Price | 100.00 |
| Amortisation | Bullet |
| Call Option | None |
| Put Option | None |
| Listing | Luxembourg |
| Denominations | US$1,000, US$10,000, US$100,000 |
| Commission | 0.40% (management and underwriting 0.15%; selling 0.25%). |
| Payment | March 17, 1993 |
| Swap | Into floating-rate DM |
| Lead Managers | Lehman Brothers Intl (books) |

| Co-lead Managers | CSFB, Kidder Peabody Intl, Merrill Lynch Intl, Salomon Brothers Intl, SBC. |
| Pre-market Price | 100, 100.15. |

*Source: International Financing Review* Issue 967 (1993 February): 59.

The return to investors is dependent on the CMT yield. The table below sets out the absolute return on the Deleveraged FRN (inclusive of the minimum coupon level) on the transaction:

| 10-year CMT Yield (% pa) | Deleveraged CMT Yield (% pa) |
| --- | --- |
| 4.000 | 4.600 |
| 4.500 | 4.600 |
| 5.000 | 4.600 |
| 5.500 | 4.600 |
| 6.000 | 4.600 |
| 6.500 | 4.700 |
| 7.000 | 4.950 |
| 7.500 | 5.200 |
| 8.000 | 5.450 |
| 8.500 | 5.700 |
| 9.000 | 5.950 |
| 9.500 | 6.200 |
| 10.000 | 6.450 |
| 10.500 | 6.700 |
| 11.000 | 6.950 |
| 11.500 | 7.200 |
| 12.000 | 7.450 |
| 12.500 | 7.700 |
| 13.000 | 7.950 |
| 13.500 | 8.200 |
| 14.000 | 8.450 |
| 14.500 | 8.700 |
| 15.000 | 8.950 |
| 15.500 | 9.200 |
| 16.000 | 9.450 |
| 16.500 | 9.700 |
| 17.000 | 9.950 |

The table below sets out the yield curve risk in the transaction by comparing the return on the Deleveraged FRN with LIBOR and deriving the breakeven CMT rate needed to equate the two returns.

| LIBOR (% pa) | Breakeven (10-year CMT) (% pa) | Deleveraged FRN Yield (% pa) | Breakeven LIBOR-CMT Spread (bps pa) |
|---|---|---|---|
| 2.000 | 1.100 | 2.000 | −90.0 |
| 2.500 | 2.100 | 2.500 | −40.0 |
| 3.000 | 3.100 | 3.000 | 10.0 |
| 3.250 | 3.600 | 3.250 | 35.0 |
| 3.500 | 4.100 | 3.500 | 60.0 |
| 4.000 | 5.100 | 4.000 | 110.0 |
| 4.500 | 6.100 | 4.500 | 160.0 |
| 5.000 | 7.100 | 5.000 | 210.0 |
| 5.500 | 8.100 | 5.500 | 260.0 |
| 6.000 | 9.100 | 6.000 | 310.0 |
| 6.500 | 10.100 | 6.500 | 360.0 |
| 7.000 | 11.100 | 7.000 | 410.0 |
| 7.500 | 12.100 | 7.500 | 460.0 |
| 8.000 | 13.100 | 8.000 | 510.0 |
| 8.500 | 14.100 | 8.500 | 560.0 |
| 9.000 | 15.100 | 9.000 | 610.0 |
| 9.500 | 16.100 | 9.500 | 660.0 |
| 10.000 | 17.100 | 10.000 | 710.0 |
| 10.500 | 18.100 | 10.500 | 760.0 |
| 11.000 | 19.100 | 11.000 | 810.0 |
| 11.500 | 20.100 | 11.500 | 860.0 |
| 12.000 | 21.100 | 12.000 | 910.0 |
| 12.500 | 22.100 | 12.500 | 960.0 |
| 13.000 | 23.100 | 13.000 | 1010.0 |

For a LIBOR-based investor, the return on the Deleveraged FRN is attractive. For example, on the World Bank transaction, the CMT on the day of launch was just below 6.30% pa, meaning that the bonds would pay their minimum interest rate of 4.6% pa. This compared to 3-month dollar LIBOR of around 3.25% pa. The return to the investor over the life of the transaction will continue to be attractive where the shape of the US$ yield curve remains positive. Based on a price formula of [(CMT × 0.5) + 1.45% pa], the investor's return on a Deleveraged FRN continues to be superior to LIBOR where the CMT-LIBOR rate differential is not less than approximately at the time of the issue (ignoring the minimum coupon level). The degree of yield curve steepness needed for the Deleveraged FRN to outperform a LIBOR-based FRN increases as the LIBOR level increases.

The minimum or floor rate means that where the CMT rate is less than 6.30% pa, then the investor receives the minimum rate. This means that for CMT levels lower than or equal to 6.30% pa, LIBOR has to be below 4.60% pa (a yield spread of 170 bps) for the Deleveraged FRN to outperform a LIBOR-based FRN.

In essence, the Deleveraged FRN will outperform LIBOR-based FRNs where the yield curve remains positive and relatively steep. The major risk to the investor is a flattening or inversion of the US$ yield curve.

*Derivative Structure*

The issuer of the Deleveraged FRN will, typically, seek to insulate itself from the full impact of the coupon structure. The issuer will seek to swap the issue into US$ LIBOR-based funding.

The swap structure entails two separate transactions:

* A 5-year yield curve swap on 50% (equivalent to the leverage factor) of the total amount of the Deleveraged FRN issue where the issuer receives CMT minus a margin and pay US$ LIBOR.
* A conventional 5-year US$ interest rate swap where the issuer receives fixed rates and pay US$ LIBOR.

Algebraically, the position is as follows:

Net borrowing cost = Deleveraged FRN coupon − Yield curve
Swap payment − Swap payments.

This translates into:

$$-[CMT \times 0.5 + M(S)] + 0.5 [CMT - M(YCS) - LIBOR] + 0.5 [SR - LIBOR]$$

Where:

M(S)      = Deleveraged FRN margin
M(YCS)    = Yield curve swap margin
SR        = Swap rate

The equation simplifies to:

$$- \text{LIBOR} - M(S) + 0.5\,(SR - M(YCS))$$

Assuming a transaction of US$100 million where:

M(S)      = +145 bps
M(YCS)    = −155 bps
SR        = 650 bps (or 6.50% pa)

The net borrowing cost is:

$$\text{LIBOR} - [145 + 0.5\,(650 - 155)] = \text{LIBOR} - 102.5 \text{ bps}$$

This is equivalent to a borrowing cost of LIBOR − 102.5 bps.

This cost does not include the cost of the floor at 4.6% pa designed to insulate the issuer from the risk of the minimum rate in the Deleveraged FRN. This floor is on the 10-year CMT rate rather than on 6-month LIBOR, reflecting the interest formula of the Deleveraged FRN structure. Given the steeply positive shape of the US$ yield curve, the bulk of the value in the floor is in the initial periods. The higher forward rates implicit in the yield curve dictate that the floors as structured are initially in-the-money. However, the longer dated floors are substantially out-of-the-money and are consequently relatively inexpensive.

In the above case the issuer has available, assuming a sub-LIBOR target of 50 bps pa, 52.5 bps pa (or 2.19% pa flat in present value) to cover the floor premium.

The 25% cap is more intriguing. CMT rates would have to rise above 47.1% pa for the Deleveraged FRN coupon to reach the cap level. The 25% pa cap, which the issuer can sell, is also not of any significant value and therefore does not assist in reducing the cost of the floor premium. One theory is that the Euromarket transactions were priced in accordance with US domestic transactions where such a cap was necessitated to avoid the cost of the Deleveraged FRN rising above legal upper limits on borrowing cost (for example, Fannie Mae has an official 24% pa cap on its borrowing cost).

The swap arrangements underlying the Deleveraged FRN issue highlight the price dynamics. The Deleveraged FRN pricing depends on the interaction of the following variables:

> • Price for yield curve swaps.
> • Price for interest rate swaps.
> • Cost of the CMT floors.
>
> The variables reflect the prevailing yield curve shapes in the relevant markets.
>
> Variations on the above structure have been undertaken. Seven-year transactions with a higher minimum rate (5.00% pa) emerged reflecting market opportunities as the US$ yield curve shifted.

A variation on this structure is the CMT-based *superfloaters*, which entails a leverage factor greater than 100%. The higher leverage factor has the following effect: the initial coupon is lowered (although it may still be above LIBOR but the structure provides greater upside participation for a rise in the CMT rate.

### 3.3   CMT Option Notes

The CMT Option Notes typically take the form of notes combined with the sale by the investor of a call or put option on the relevant CMT rates to monetise expectations on yield curve movements. The transactions, as noted above, can be structured either as a conventional option trade, embedded in a yield curve swap or as a structured note.

Assume an investor expects that the yield spread between the 2-year CMT rate (CMT2) and 10-year CMT rate (CMT10) will steepen. The investor's expectations are based on historical rate movements that are characterized by steepening in this portion of the yield curve during periods of falling interest rates while in a rising rate environment this portion of the yield curve has flattened.

In order to capture value from the expected rate movements, the investor can buy interest rate floors on CMT2 and sell interest rate floors on CMT5. The interest rate floors represent calls on the price of the relevant securities of the particular maturity. The implementation of this strategy is shown in three transaction formats:

• Option trades (**Exhibit 5.5**).
• Embedded CMT floor options in a yield curve swap (**Exhibit 5.6**).
• Structured Note (**Exhibit 5.7**).

**Exhibit 5.5**
**CMT Floor Transaction**

| | |
|---|---|
| Investor Buys | Floor on CMT2 with strike price at 5.20% pa (Spot CMT2 = 5.50% pa) |
| Investor Sells | Floor on CMT10 with strike price at 5.65% pa (Spot CMT10 = 5.80% pa) |
| Option Expiration | 2 years |
| Floor Reset Frequency | Quarterly |
| Net Premium Paid | 0.00% |

**Exhibit 5.6**
**Yield Curve Swap with Embedded CMT Floor Options**

| | |
|---|---|
| Investor Pays | 3-month LIBOR (payable and reset quarterly on actual/360-day count basis) |
| Investor Receives | CMT2 − 10 bps + Max [5.20% − CMT2; 0] − Max. [5.65% − CMT10;0] (payable and reset quarterly) |
| Maturity | 2 years |

**Exhibit 5.7**
**Structured Note with Embedded CMT Floor Options**

| | |
|---|---|
| Issuer | AAA-rated issuer |
| Issue Price | 100 |
| Maturity | 2 years |
| Coupon | CMT2 − 20 bps + Max. [5.20% − CMT2; 0] — Max. [5.65% − CMT10; 0] |
| Payment/Reset | Payable and reset quarterly |
| Minimum Coupon | 0.00% |

The essential value dynamics of these transactions are identical. The option transaction is utilized to examine the returns from this strategy.

The option transaction will be profitable for the investor in circumstances *except where* the CMT10 rallies below 5.65% pa and the spread between

CMT10 and CMT2 is less than 45 bps (the difference between the strike rates of the two options). The investor has thus isolated a limited set of transactions where the transactions can result in a loss. The transaction would be predicated typically on the basis that the scenario where the investor would sustain a loss has occurred infrequently (based on historical data).

The transaction results in neither gain nor loss to the investor where the rates are unchanged, or where both options are out-of-the-money (CMT2 is higher than 5.20% pa and CMT10 is greater than 5.65% pa). The return to the investor where both options are in-the-money will vary with the slope of the yield curve. Where the yield curve steepens and rates increase, the CMT2 may be in-the-money but the CMT2 floor will be out-of-the-money.

The same transaction can be embedded in either a yield curve swap or combined with a security in the form of a structured note. In each case, the options are incorporated into the other instrument. In the case of the yield curve swap, the pricing reflects the combined values of the yield curve swap (receive CMT2 – 10 bps against payment of 3-month LIBOR). In the case of the structured note, the pricing reflects the structure that combines a FRN yielding 3-month LIBOR – 10 bps and the CMT Floor embedded yield curve swap.

## 4.    Pricing, Valuation, and Hedging

As is evident from the discussion to date, the pricing of CMT-based products is based on decomposition of each instrument into the underlying components: typically, a fixed- or floating-rate bond, a CMT forward, and/or a CMT option. The elements are then valued separately and the values combined to derive the value of the combined product.

These principles are easily demonstrated using the CMT Yield Curve Note or Deleveraged FRN structure. Pricing this security requires in effect determination of the spread that, at transaction commencement, will equate the *expected* transaction cash flows (all cash flows are floating, therefore are not known with certainty although implied rates are available) to the initial value of the security, say, par. This calculation is performed by deriving the forward LIBOR and CMT rates for the relevant maturity from the *current* yield curve. The implicit spread (reflecting the fact the investor is paying rates priced off one point in the yield curve and receiving rates priced off another point of the maturity spectrum) is then calculated and discounted to the present using applicable discount rates. This allows the margin to be determined.

The major refinement to this approach required is the need to adjust for the relative price sensitivity of the two rates that given the term difference are likely to be present. The coupon payments on the Deleveraged FRN and, by implication, the embedded yield curve swap are projected using the implied forward rates incorporating convexity-based adjustments.

The hedging follows the approach to pricing/valuation. The CMT forward structures are hedged by trading in instruments to replicate the forward rates utilised in the structure. For example, a yield curve swap would be hedged by trading in LIBOR forwards (in the form of FRAs or futures contracts where available; for example, in US$ this would be the Eurodollar contract) and the corresponding CMT forwards.

The major problem with the creation of the hedge is the replication of the CMT forwards, particularly where the maturity of the forwards is significant. The following possible approaches are available:

- Trading in the physical bonds that are funded to the relevant forward dates to replicate the forward.
- Use of bond futures contracts, where available.
- Use of other derivatives such as interest rate swaps.

Trading in the underlying physical bonds is balance sheet- and capital-intensive. This is combined with potential difficulties in funding the bonds for the requisite maturities through the repo market that creates an interest rate risk for the trader. The use of bond futures is attractive as it eliminates the balance sheet and capital use problems. However, the limited range of contracts available and the level of liquidity of individual contracts (particularly, in the relevant contract maturities where the maturity of the forward sought to be hedged is long) may well generate significant basis risks in hedging. Similarly, the use of interest rate swaps, effectively forward start interest rate swaps requires an assumption of the risk in changes between the swap and underlying bond rate (the swap spread). This basis risk is clearly not a factor of CMS-based products.

CMT spread options are usually created dynamically through trading in the underlying assets. Consistent with normal delta hedging approaches the amount of the model portfolio held is adjusted continuously to synthetically replicate the returns on the put option.

Spread options cannot usually be efficiently replicated by trading in options on the underlying options. The portfolio of options is generally more expensive reflecting the separate payoff that allows each option to be separately exercised to maximise the value of individual options. This reflects the fact that the yield curve option is insensitive to absolute rate levels while the option portfolio is generally sensitive to the overall absolute level of rates.

## 5.   Market

The market for CMT-based products developed in response to demand for instruments, either in derivative or structured note form, which allowed investors to hedge or position for interest rate movements, particularly changes in yield curve shape as distinct from absolute rate movements.

An additional impetus came from the potential value that could be created from utilizing the forward *term* interest rates embedded in the yield curve. The low nominal interest rates and positive slope of the yield curve that prevailed through the 1990s in a number of currencies also created demand for these structures. The investment environment was dominated by the search for returns and strategies based on capturing value from the forward rates, which created additional demand for these types of structures. A further source of demand related to the use of CMT-based products by fixed income portfolio managers to replicate the performance of benchmark indexes against which their performance was indexed.

The advantages of CMT-based instruments derived from a number of key factors:

• Fixed and certain maturity of the interest rate utilized.
• Capacity to avoid issues relating to physical debt securities, such as coupon effects, the movement away from par value as yields change relative to yield, and the diminishing term to maturity.

These advantages allowed CMT-based products to emerge as a superior alternative for the type of transactions described to express the interest rate expectations identified. In this regard, CMT-based transactions had advantages relative to physical transactions that could be used to monetize similar strategies including lower transaction costs, greater transparency of pricing and the opportunity for off-balance sheet structures.

A significant use of CMT-based products is their use in hedging in mortgage-backed securities. CMT structures, particularly CMT caps, are increasingly utilized to hedge pre-payment risk on mortgages and mortgage-backed security portfolios. This reflects in part research that has highlighted the fact that the pattern of prepayment of mortgages is correlated to medium-term rates as well as the shape of the yield curve.[6]

The CMT market itself is substantially US$ and US domestic investor-focused. CMT-based products, usually in the form of structured notes, such as the Deleveraged note structures, have been successfully marketed to non-US investors, primarily European and Japanese/Far Eastern investors, primarily denominated in US$. However, the volumes of these non-US transactions remain modest.

In currencies other than US$, the concept of CMT-based transactions is replaced, substantially, by CMS-based transactions, for the reasons identified above. Transactions involving CMS rates have been completed in yen, sterling,

---

[6] For example, see Cataldo, James "Welcome To The CMT Jungle" (November 1996) *Derivatives Strategy* 20-26.

A$ and a number of European currencies (since 1999 in Euros). The rationale for these transactions is substantially similar to those applicable in US$.

In recent times, other countries (France and Germany) have introduced their own CMT equivalents. In France, the TEC 10 Index (the CMT yield) is the redemption yield on the 10-year notional French OAT (calculated by Le Comite de Normalisation Obligataire daily by a dealer poll mechanism). A TEC 5 Index is also available, being linked to the redemption yield on a 5-year notional French OAT. The TEC indexes have become the basis of both issuance (the French government issues a 10-year bond with coupons linked to the TEC index and other issuers have also issued bonds indexed to the TEC index) and derivatives (yield curve swaps and option on the index).[7] The German equivalent is the REX Index. The REX Index provides benchmarks for all German government securities with maturities ranging from six months to 10 years and six months. As with the TEC index, securities issues and derivatives linked to the REX indexes are available.[8] The range of products and typical applications are very similar to those using US$ CMT instruments. However, the size of the market and the range of products are less developed than in US dollar.[9] **Exhibit 5.8** sets out an example of a DM FRN linked to the REX Index.

---

**Exhibit 5.8**
**REX-linked Structured Note**

| | |
|---|---|
| Issuer | AA-rated issuer |
| Amount | DM18 million |
| Issue Price | 100 |
| Redemption | 100 |
| Maturity | 10 years |
| Coupon | Year 1: 4.90% pa |
| | Year 2 to 10: 90% of REX10 |
| | Where REX10 is the closing Deutsche Rentenindex with a maturity of 10 years, 2 business days prior to the relevant interest rate period |
| Payment/Reset | Payable and reset annually |
| Minimum Coupon | 0.00% |

---

[7]   See Saunderson, Emily "Vive Le TEC" (November 1997) *Risk* 38-40.
[8]   See Muller, Jochen and Pedersen, Morten Bjerregaard "REX Floaters" (November 23, 1998) *Derivatives Week* 6.
[9]   The prospects for both these indexes following the introduction of the Euro in 1 January 1999 is not clear.

## 6. Summary

CMT-based transactions represent an innovative mechanism for capturing returns from interest rate expectations, primarily changes in the shape of the yield curve. Transactions involving forwards, options on the CMT forwards and/ or the implied forward spread can be structured to hedge exposures to these rate movements or to position to take advantage of anticipated movements. Transactions structured as pure derivatives or embedded in structured notes are feasible. The greater efficiency of these structures, relative to undertaking physical transactions to express these views, has provided part of the impetus to the development of this market. US$ CMT and, its counterpart in non-US$-based markets, CMS-based products are now a permanent feature of the instrument set available in many markets.

## Appendix A

## Yield Curve Swaps

### 1. Yield Curve Swaps — Concept

A yield curve swap is a floating-for-floating interest rate swap (similar conceptually to a basis swap). Under the structure, the swap counterparty:

- Pays (receives) one interest rate as set by one part of the yield curve, say, US$ 3- or 6-month LIBOR.
- Receives (pays) another interest rate as at another point of the yield curve, say, the 10- or 30-year US$ Treasury yield plus/minus a spread.

Both rates are reset either quarterly or semi-annually and the term of the yield curve swap ranges from one to 10 years.

The yield curve swap was introduced in late 1980s. Conceptually, the transaction is similar to the basis swap except in so far as one of the interest indexes is a long-term rate, although it is reset frequently.

Yield curve swaps have the following characteristics:

- They are generally insensitive to the absolute level of interest rates.
- Yield curve swaps are very sensitive to the shape of the yield curve.

Yield curve swaps create an exposure to the slope of the yield curve. Under a typical arrangement, where the counterparty receives the 10- or 30-year Treasury yield and pays US$ LIBOR, if the yield curve steepens (flattens or inverts) its net receipt under the yield curve swap will increase (decrease). **Exhibit 5.9** sets out the structure of a yield curve swap diagrammatically. **Exhibit 5.10** sets out an example of the mechanics of the yield curve swap.

**Exhibit 5.9**
**Yield Curve Swap – Structure**

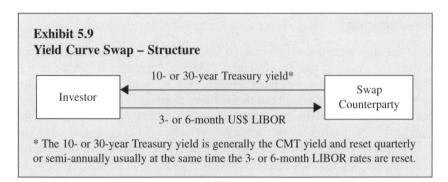

* The 10- or 30-year Treasury yield is generally the CMT yield and reset quarterly or semi-annually usually at the same time the 3- or 6-month LIBOR rates are reset.

---

**Exhibit 5.10**
**Yield Curve Swap – Payment Calculations**

Investor A enters into a 5-year yield curve swap to pay 6-month LIBOR and receive the 10-year Treasury plus five basis points.

| | |
|---|---|
| Trade Date | January 10, 2000 |
| 1st Rate-setting Date | January 11, 2000 (next business day) |
| Effective Date | January 13, 2000 (2 business days later) |
| 2nd Rate-setting Date | July 11, 2000 (6 months after 1st rate setting) |
| First Payment Date | July 13, 2000 (6 months after effective date) |

The 10-year rate utilized will be the Constant Maturity Treasury (CMT) rate for the relevant term as calculated by the US Treasury and the Federal Reserve Bank of New York by a process of interpolation from the existing yield curve (refer to **Exhibit 5.1**). Both LIBOR and the US Treasury rate are set as of the rate-setting date. The Treasury rate will not be known until the following Tuesday, after the release of the Fed H-15 report with calculation of the first payment being made until the release of the report.

The structure of the yield curve swap will be as follows:

| | |
|---|---|
| Treasury Maturity | 10 years |
| Payments per Year | 2 |
| Term | 5 years |
| Swap Maturity Date | 13 January 2005 |
| Notional Principal | $100 million |
| Current 6-month LIBOR | 9.56% pa (calculated on an actual/360-day basis) |
| Current 10-year Treasury | 9.23% pa (calculated on a semi-annual bond equivalent basis) |
| Yield Curve Swap Spread | 5 bps |

Each payment date the Investor receives the following payment:

US$100 million × (10-year CMT rate + spread) × actual days in period/365

The customer pays the following:

US$100 million × US$ 6-month LIBOR × actual days in period/360.

Using the above formulas, the first payment to the customer is as follows (for the 181-day period January 13, 2000 and July 13, 2000):

US$100 million × (9.23% + 0.05%) × 181/365 − US$100 million × 9.56% × 181/360 = $204,693.

The customer pays this amount on the first payment date, July 13, 2000.

## 2.  Applications

Yield curve swaps allow the counterparty receiving the term rate to price of the long rather than the short end of the yield curve. The major application of this type of arrangement includes:

- Investors converting the return on a floating-rate asset from a short-term rate index to a long-term rate by receiving the term rate and paying out US$ LIBOR, which is matched by the income from the underlying floating rate asset.
- Hedging liabilities floating off the 10- or 30-year Treasury bond rate. These types of exposures are incurred by insurance companies and the yield curve swap payment received under such transactions offsets the liability floating off the long-term rate thus converting it into a LIBOR-based liability. An example of this type of liability is US insurance companies Guaranteed Investment Contracts (GICs) whose return is pegged to the 10-year Treasury rate.
- An index diversification technique for investors to convert floating-rate assets away from short-term indexes to long-term indexes.
- Positioning or trading the shape of the yield curve. For example, an investor expecting the yield curve to steepen would receive the 10-year or 30-year rate and pay short-term rates or vice versa. Similar strategies can be developed for borrowers.

Yield curve swaps developed rapidly to become commonly utilized products, particularly among investors, in the US$ swap market. Subsequently, it has been applied in a number of other markets allowing investors of a liability managers and financial institutions to take advantage of the prevailing shape of the yield curve.

A number of variations on the standard yield curve swap structure have also emerged. Yield curve swaps, as between various term interest rates (for example, 5-year against 10-year, and so on) have been undertaken. A major variation has been the emergence of options on yield curve shapes. This type of instrument, effectively, allows traders, borrowers, and investors to buy and sell volatility on the *shape* of the yield curve.

## Appendix B

## Pricing Yield Curve Swaps

### 1.   Approach

The economics of yield curve swaps is driven largely by the shape of the yield curve in the relevant currency. The pricing of such transactions derives from the implicit forward rates embodied in the yield curve. In effect, the transaction pricing is generated by calculating the implied *term* forward interest rates (for example, the 10-year rate in 6, 12, 18, and so on months) relative to the implied short 6-month rates implied in the same yield curve (for example, the 6-month rate is six, 12, 18, and so on months). The interaction of these two sets of implied forward rates determines the margin above or below the term interest rate component of the yield curve swap.

### 2.   Valuation Dynamics

The dynamics of value of a yield curve is purely a function of the shape of the two forward curves (say, the 3- or 6-month LIBOR forwards and the term rate forwards, say, the 10- or 30-year rate) and the *implied* forward spread.

In an upward-sloping or positive yield curve, the short-term forwards will, typically, increase at a faster rate than the longer term forwards. This will reflect the mathematics of forward rates whereby the lower rate for the shorter maturity must be compensated for by the higher implied forward rate to equate the rate for the longer maturity to prevent yield curve arbitrage. The fact that the higher rate can be earned over a longer period in the case of a term security rather than over a short period dictates the relative rate of increase. This pattern of increase will inherently *imply* a contraction in the yield spread between the two rates suggesting a *flattening* of the yield curve. In the case of a negatively sloped yield curve, the opposite will be the case with the shape of the yield curve projected to steepen with short forward rates declining at a faster rate than term forward rates.

## 3.    Example

This section sets out the valuation and pricing of a series of yield curve swaps utilizing the same yield curve.

**Exhibit 5.11** sets out the yield curve and the 3-month and 10-year forwards implied by the yield curve.[10] **Exhibit 5.12** on page 223 sets out this data in a graphical form. The implied forward rates are then utilized to calculate the spread for the yield curve swaps.

**Exhibit 5.11**
**Yield Curve and Forwards**

| Years | Interest Rates (% pa) | 3-month LIBOR Forward Rates (% pa) | 10-year CMT Forward Rates (% pa) | Forward Differential (% pa) |
|-------|-------|-------|-------|-------|
| 0.00  |       | 3.2500 | 5.8500 | 2.6000 |
| 0.25  | 3.25  | 3.5502 | 5.9214 | 2.3712 |
| 0.50  | 3.40  | 3.7025 | 5.9854 | 2.2829 |
| 0.75  | 3.50  | 3.9028 | 6.0452 | 2.1424 |
| 1.00  | 3.60  | 4.2238 | 6.1002 | 1.8764 |
| 1.25  | 3.73  | 4.4745 | 6.1477 | 1.6732 |
| 1.50  | 3.85  | 4.7337 | 6.1891 | 1.4554 |
| 1.75  | 3.98  | 4.9946 | 6.2238 | 1.2292 |
| 2.00  | 4.10  | 4.9980 | 6.2519 | 1.2540 |
| 2.25  | 4.20  | 5.1988 | 6.2807 | 1.0819 |
| 2.50  | 4.30  | 5.4108 | 6.3047 | 0.8938 |
| 2.75  | 4.40  | 5.6243 | 6.3233 | 0.6990 |
| 3.00  | 4.50  | 5.2277 | 6.3367 | 1.1090 |
| 3.25  | 4.56  | 5.3404 | 6.3607 | 1.0202 |
| 3.50  | 4.61  | 5.4618 | 6.3820 | 0.9202 |
| 3.75  | 4.67  | 5.5841 | 6.4004 | 0.8163 |

---

[10] The interest rates utilized for the purpose of valuation will need to be made consistent in terms of compounding and day-count bases. This is particularly important for yield curve products as the CMT side is often paid quarterly whereas the market convention is to quote the rate on a semi-annual basis.

**Exhibit 5.11 (continued)**
**Yield Curve and Forwards**

| Years | Interest Rates (% pa) | 3-month LIBOR Forward Rates (% pa) | 10-year CMT Forward Rates (% pa) | Forward Differential (% pa) |
|-------|------|---------|---------|---------|
| 4.00  | 4.72 | 5.6770  | 6.4159  | 0.7389  |
| 4.25  | 4.78 | 5.7898  | 6.4294  | 0.6396  |
| 4.50  | 4.84 | 5.9139  | 6.4404  | 0.5265  |
| 4.75  | 4.89 | 6.0393  | 6.4485  | 0.4092  |
| 5.00  | 4.95 | 6.3934  | 6.4538  | 0.0604  |
| 5.25  | 5.02 | 6.5318  | 6.4465  | -0.0854 |
| 5.50  | 5.09 | 6.6871  | 6.4357  | -0.2513 |
| 5.75  | 5.16 | 6.8435  | 6.4214  | -0.4221 |
| 6.00  | 5.23 | 6.9451  | 6.4036  | -0.5415 |
| 6.25  | 5.29 | 7.0838  | 6.3829  | -0.7009 |
| 6.50  | 5.36 | 7.2423  | 6.3588  | -0.8834 |
| 6.75  | 5.43 | 7.4021  | 6.3313  | -1.0708 |
| 7.00  | 5.50 | 6.3423  | 6.3002  | -0.0421 |
| 7.25  | 5.53 | 6.4008  | 6.2951  | -0.1056 |
| 7.50  | 5.56 | 6.4689  | 6.2887  | -0.1802 |
| 7.75  | 5.59 | 6.5376  | 6.2809  | -0.2567 |
| 8.00  | 5.62 | 6.5754  | 6.2716  | -0.3038 |
| 8.25  | 5.65 | 6.6340  | 6.2612  | -0.3728 |
| 8.50  | 5.67 | 6.7034  | 6.2494  | -0.4540 |
| 8.75  | 5.70 | 6.7620  | 6.2362  | -0.5258 |
| 9.00  | 5.73 | 6.8090  | 6.2218  | -0.5872 |
| 9.25  | 5.76 | 6.8676  | 6.2060  | -0.6616 |
| 9.50  | 5.79 | 6.9384  | 6.1889  | -0.7495 |
| 9.75  | 5.82 | 7.0229  | 6.1704  | -0.8525 |
| 10.00 | 5.85 | 6.0536  | 6.1503  | 0.0966  |

### Exhibit 5.12
### Yield Curve and Forwards – Graph

The underlying rates including the 3-month LIBOR and 10-year CMT forwards are set out below:

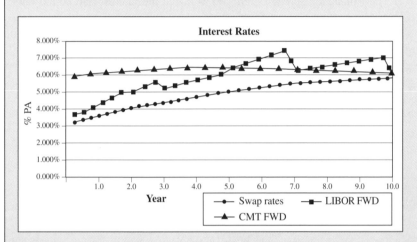

The differential (10-year CMT minus 3-month LIBOR) implied by the forwards is set out below:

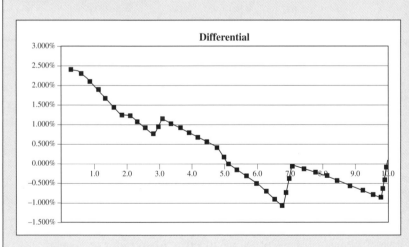

The determination of the spread on the yield curve swap is undertaken utilizing the following steps:

- The forwards as at each pricing date of the yield curve swap is identified to calculate the implied forward spread.
- The implied forward spread is then adjusted in two ways:
  1. The annualized spread is reduced to match the interest rate period under the swaps (quarterly).
  2. The quarterly forward spread is discounted back to the commencement of the transaction using zero-coupon swap rates for each maturity.
- The discounted spread is then amortized over the term of the yield curve swap to calculate the margin on the transaction.

**Exhibit 5.13** sets out the above calculation for a 1-year yield curve swap.

---

**Exhibit 5.13**
**Pricing/Valuation of 1-year CMT Yield Curve Swap**

The table below sets out the cash flows of the yield curve swap using the implied forward rates:

| Days | Discount Rates (% pa) | CMT Forward Rates (% pa) | LIBOR Forward Rates (% pa) | CMT-LIBOR Differential (% pa) | CMT-LIBOR Differential (% pa over Number of Days) | NPV Of Differential (% pa) |
|------|------|------|------|------|------|------|
| 92   | 3.25 | 5.8500 | 3.2500 | 2.6000 | 0.6553 | 0.6501 |
| 184  | 3.40 | 5.9214 | 3.5502 | 2.3712 | 0.5977 | 0.5877 |
| 275  | 3.50 | 5.9854 | 3.7025 | 2.2829 | 0.5692 | 0.5546 |
| 366  | 3.60 | 6.0452 | 3.9028 | 2.1424 | 0.5341 | 0.5155 |
|      |      |        |        | **Total** | 2.3563 | 2.3079 |

The discounted implied spread is then translated into an annualized margin equivalent to 2.36% pa.

In this case, given the upward-sloping nature of the yield curve, the implied decrease in the 3-month, 10-year spread dictates that the spread on the yield curve swap is negative. That is, the receiver of the 10-year rate will receive the 10-year rate reset quarterly reduced by the margin. In the case of a negative shape of the yield curve, the spread is received by the party receiving the term rate reflecting the implied increase in the spread.

---

# 4. Convexity Adjustment[11]

The value of a yield curve swap is affected by:
- The *implied* interest rate differential as at the relevant forward dates.
- The convexity position inherent in the structure.

The valuation/pricing methodology outlined above only deals with the implied interest rate differential. A separate adjustment must be made for the convexity effect.[12]

The convexity impact relates to the fact that the CMT payment is calculated in a linear fashion using the relevant index while the underlying instrument itself is convex. This difference is exacerbated by the fact that the yield curve swap itself may be hedged using the underlying convex instrument. A different way of conceptualizing the problem is to identify that the CMT payoff does not relate to a single zero-coupon rate but a series of payments related to the relevant rate on pre-agreed payment dates. Where the derivative (in this case the forward) is structured so that its payoffs correspond to the payment pattern on the underlying instrument (bond or swap), then it is appropriate to set the expected rate used to calculate the implied spread to the derived forward rate. Where the payoffs do not follow the same payment pattern, as in the case of CMT-based products, then a convexity adjustment to the forward rate is required. This difference must be dealt with in the pricing.

The linearity of the payment on the CMT side of the swap and the convexity of the underlying instrument lead to a benefit for the receiver of CMT rates under the swap. The exact same factor affects the valuation of CMS-based yield curve transactions. This must be reflected in the pricing.

There are a number of ways to make this convexity adjustment.[13] **Exhibit 5.14** sets out one form of convexity adjustment.

---

[11] The convexity adjustment in relation to CMT or yield curve swaps is similar to that impacting upon arrears reset structures, see Chapter 4.

[12] For a detailed discussion of the convexity adjustment, see Hull, John (1997) *Futures, Options* and *Other Derivatives*, Prentice Hall, Upper Saddle River, NJ at 406-411; Coleman, Thomas S. "Convexity Adjustment for Constant Maturity Swaps and LIBOR-in-Arrears Swaps" (Winter 1995) *Derivatives Quarterly* 19-27; Brotherton-Ratcliffe, R. and Iben, B. "Yield Curve Applications of Swap Products" in Schwartz, R. and Smith, C (editors) (1993) *Advanced Strategies In Financial Risk Management*, New York Institute of Finance at Chapter 15.

[13] See Coleman, Thomas S. "Convexity Adjustment for Constant Maturity Swaps and LIBOR-in-Arrears Swaps" (Winter 1995) *Derivatives Quarterly* 19-27; Brotherton-Ratcliffe, R. and Iben, B. "Yield Curve Applications of Swap Products" in Schwartz, R. and Smith, C (editors) (1993) *Advanced Strategies in Financial Risk Management*, New York Institute of Finance at Chapter 15.

**Exhibit 5.14**
**Convexity Adjustment**

Brotherton-Ratcliffe and Iben[14] show that the convexity adjustment that must be made to the forward rate (F) is:

$$-0.5 \; F^2 \; \sigma^2 \; T \; [P''(F)/ \; P'(F)]$$

Where:

F     = forward CMT rate
$\sigma$     = volatility
T     = time to maturity of the forward
P (F) = the price at time t of a security that provides coupons equal to the forward CMT rate over the life of the bond as a function of yield (Y)
P'(F) = first derivative of the price of bond (P) with respect to yield (Y)
P''(F) = second derivative of the price of bond (P) with respect to yield (Y)

This means that the adjusted forward rate should be:

$$F \; - \; 0.5 \; F^2 \; \sigma^2 \; T \; [P''(F)/ \; P'(F)]$$

The application of this adjustment can be illustrated with an example. Assume the following:

F  = 6% pa
Y  = 6% pa
$\sigma$  = 15% pa

Assume that the instrument provides a payoff in three years time-linked to the 3-year rate.

The value of the instrument is given by:

$$P(Y) = F/(1 + Y) + F/(1 + Y)^2 + (1 + F)/(1 + Y)^3$$

The first and second derivatives are given by:

$$P'(F) = -F/(1 + Y)^2 - 2F/(1 + Y)^3 - 3(1 + F)/(1 + Y)^4 = -2.6730$$
$$P''(F) = 2/(1 + Y)^3 + 6\,F/(1 + Y)^4 + 12(1 + F)/(1 + Y)^5 = 11.4695$$

The convexity adjustment is given by:

---

[14]  See Brotherton-Ratcliffe, R. and Iben, B. "Yield Curve Applications of Swap Products" in Schwartz, R. and Smith, C. (editors) (1993) *Advanced Strategies In Financial Risk Management*; New York Institute of Finance at Chapter 15.

$-0.5 \times 0.06^2 \times 0.15^2 \times 3 \times (11.4695 / -2.6730) = 0.0005$ or 5 bps

This means that a forward rate of 6.05% pa (rather than 6.00% pa) should be used in the valuation.

The convexity effect increases the value of the receiving CMT payments under the CMT-based yield curve swap. This means that the swap has a higher value relative to the valuation generated by simply pricing of the forward curve. This means that the CMT payments will generally be reduced than that implied by the forward rates (before adjusting for convexity). This allows the expected values of the transaction to be equated at the time of entry into the transaction.

# Appendix C

# Valuation and Hedging of Spread Options[15]

## 1. Key Parameters

The key determinants of value in spread options are the forward yield spread and the volatility of this parameter. Other parameter inputs include the strike yield spread and the time to expiry (both givens) and the risk-free rate (effectively the discount factor). These parameters are readily available.

## 2. Forward Spread

The spread option structure is effectively an option on the forward yield spread between the nominated securities. The forward yield spread is economically the differential between the forward rates of the two securities as at the option expiration date. The forward rates are estimated using the current spot yield for the security and the financing rate (repo, LIBOR and so on) to the option maturity. Technically, the forward rate estimated using this technique is not exactly equal to the security's forward yield at the theoretical forward price because the security has a non-zero convexity, but particularly for short dated options, the difference is not material.

The dynamics of the value of spread options is based on the relationship between forward rates on shorter versus longer maturity securities in different yield curve environments. The differential between the implied forward rates is

---

[15] For a discussion of the pricing of spread options, see Bhansali, Vinneer (1998) *Pricing and Managing Exotic and Hybrid Options*; McGraw-Hill, New York at Chapters 1 and 3; Ravindran, K. (1998) *Customized Derivatives*; McGraw-Hill, New York at 68-79; 274-279.

largely dictated by the fact that the difference between spot and forward rates for shorter term securities are greater than the difference between the spot and forward rates for longer term securities. This creates substantial changes in the implied forward yield spread relative to the spot yield spread creating value creation opportunities.

Importantly, the underlying pricing dynamic of spread options dictates that the price of the option prior to expiration is sensitive to both the spot rates for the relevant securities and the financing rate to expiration, which in combination determines the forward spread.

## 3.   Volatility Estimation

The volatility of the forward spread is complex. It is in effect made up of the volatility of the underlying securities and the correlation between yield movements between the two securities.

This results in a number of ways to model the volatility of the forward spread:

- The historical volatility of the spread between the actual two securities.
- The historical volatility of the spread between two securities having constant maturities equivalent to the actual underlying securities (2-year CMT against 30-year CMT).
- The estimated yield spread volatility based on the average yield of each security, the historical yield volatility of each security, and the historical correlation between the two.
- The estimated expected future yield spread based the actual yields on the securities at transaction date, the implied volatility of options on each security, and an estimate of the future correlation coefficient.

## 4.   Valuation Approach

### 4.1   Overview

The spread option is then priced using one of a variety of models. A number of separate approaches exist to the valuation of spread options themselves.[16]

---

[16]   See Garman, Mark "Spread the Load" (December 1992) *Risk* vol. 5 no. 11 68-84; McDermott, Scott "A Survey of Spread Options For Fixed Income Investors" in Klein, Robert A. and Lederman, Jess (editors) (1993) *The Handbook of Derivatives & Synthetics*; Probus Publishing: Chicago, Illinois at Chapter 4; Ravindran, K. "Low Fat Spreads" (October 1993) *Risk* vol. 6 no. 10 66-67; Ravindran, K. "Exotic Options" in Dattatreya, Ravi E. and Hotta, Kensuke (1994) *Advanced Interest Rate and Currency Swaps: State-of-the Art Products, Strategies & Risk Management Applications*; Probus Publishing: Chicago, Illinois at Chapter 5.

These include:

• Modeling the spread itself as an asset price.
• Modeling the option as an exchange option.
• Utilizing multi (two) factor options models.

The advantage of the first approach is its relative simplicity. However, the approach creates significant problems. It assumes that the probability that the spread will ever become negative is nil. This may be a reasonably tractable assumption where the absolute spread (yield on a risky security is compared to the yield on a risk-free security) is concerned. This is clearly inconsistent where relative credit spreads (between two securities) are concerned, where negative spreads are feasible. This problem is introduced by the implicit assumption of the log normal distribution of the spread as an asset price.

In addition, the log normal assumption suggests that spread fluctuation size would increase for large spreads and decrease for small ones—the proportionality impact—however, this is not supported by evidence. One possible means of coping with the difficulties posed by the assumption of log normality (particularly in respect of the spread price being negative) is to assume a normal as opposed to log normal distribution where volatility is calculated on the *absolute price change* annualized standard deviation.

The other two approaches incorporate both the separate volatility of the underlying assets and the correlation between the two assets to derive the spread option value. This approach is preferable in that it does not suffer the same restrictions as the first approach.

## 4.2 Spread/Option Pricing Models

An example of a closed-form option pricing model for these instruments adapting the approach of Black's commodity option pricing model[17] is set out in **Exhibit 5.15** on page 224.[18] An example of a calculation of the value of a spread/option using this type of model is set in **Exhibit 5.16** on page 224[19]

---

[17] See Black, Fischer "The Pricing of Commodity Contracts" (March 1976) *Journal of Financial Economics* 3 167-179.

[18] For an adaptation specifically to spread options, see McDermott, Scott "A Survey of Spread Options For Fixed Income Investors" in Klein, Robert A. and Lederman, Jess (editors) (1993) *The Handbook of Derivatives & Synthetics*; Probus Publishing: Chicago, Illinios at Chapter 4; see also Gamze, Michael S. and McCann, Karen "A Simplified Approach To Valuing An Option On A Leveraged Spread: The Bankers Trust, Proctor & Gamble Example" (Summer 1995) *Derivatives Quarterly* 44-53.

[19] For other single factor approaches see Bhansali, Vineer (1998) *Pricing and Managing Exotic and Hybrid Options*; McGraw-Hill, New York at 29-33.

**Exhibit 5.15**
**Spread/Option Pricing Formula**

The pricing of a call option is:

$$C_t = e^{-rt} [(S_t - K) N (h) + \sigma\sqrt{t\ N'(h)}]$$

Where:

$$h = (1/\sigma \sqrt{t}) (S_t - K)$$

Where:

K    = strike yield spread
$S_t$    = forward yield spread at time t
$\sigma$    = volatility (standard deviation of yield spread)
r    = risk-free rate
t    = time to option maturity
N(h)  = standard normal distribution

The equivalent pricing for a put option is:

$$P_t = e^{-rt} [(K - S_t)(1 - N (h)) + \sigma\sqrt{r\ N'(h)}]$$

Where:

$$h = (1/\sigma \sqrt{t}) (S_t - K)$$

*Source:* McDermott, Scott. "A Survey of Spread Options For Fixed Income Investors" in. Klein, Robert A. and Lederman, Jess (editors) *The Handbook of Derivatives & Synthetics.* Probus Publishing, Chicago, Illinios, 1993 Chapter 4.

---

**Exhibit 5.16**
**Spread/Option Pricing – Example**

Assume the following parameters for a spread option: the trade date is April 15, 2002; option expires on October 15, 2002 (six months); the current forward spread is 85 bps; the option is struck at a spread of 90 bps; the spread volatility is 65% pa; and the risk-free rate is 5.75% pa.

The option price is calculated below:

**Pricing Inputs**

| | |
|---|---:|
| Underlying Asset Price | 85.00 |
| Strike Price | 90.00 |
| Trade Date | 15-Apr-2002 |
| Expiry Date | 15-Oct-2002 |
| Volatility | 65.00% |
| Risk-free Rate | 5.75% |
| Number of Steps (Binomial Model) | 500 |

| Option Premium | Black | | Binomial | |
|---|---|---|---|---|
| **Model Outputs** | **Call** | **Put** | **Call** | **Put** |
| Option Premium | 13.16 | 18.02 | 13.23 | 18.13 |
| Option Premium (% of Asset Price) | 15.48% | 21.20% | 15.56% | 21.33% |

European option prices are calculated using an adapted Black model while the American option prices are calculated using a binomial model.

Approaches incorporating the separate volatility and correlations fall into a number of groups: exchange option structures, bivariate binomial schemes, or other numerical structures.

Spread options can be equated to exchange options in certain circumstances and valued utilizing techniques similar to those applicable to minimum/maximum option structures. William Magrabe provides a valuation model for valuing an exchange option where both assets are denominated in the same currency[20] (see **Exhibit 5.17**).[21]

---

[20] See Margrabe, William "The Value Of An Option To Exchange One Asset For Another" (1978) *Journal of Finance* vol. 33 177-186; for a version of this model that shows where the second asset is denominated in a foreign currency, see Brotherton-Ratcliffe, R. and Iben, Ben "Yield Curve Applications Of Swap Products" in Schwartz, R. and Smith, C (editors) (1993) *Advanced Strategies in Financial Risk Management*; New York Institute Of Finance: New York at Chapter 15.

[21] For an adaptation of the Margrabe approach, see Bhansali, Vineer (1998) *Pricing and Managing Exotic and Hybrid Options*; McGraw-Hill, New York at 69-79.

**Exhibit 5.17**
**Exchange Option Pricing Model[22]**

$$S_2 e^{-q2t} N(d1) - S_1{}^{-q1t} N (d2)$$

Where
$$d1 = [\ln (S_2 / S_1) + (q1 - q2 + \sigma^2/ 2) t]/\sigma\sqrt{t}$$
$$d2 = d1 - \sigma\sqrt{t}$$
$$\sigma = \sqrt{(\sigma 1^2 + \sigma 2^2 - 2 \rho \sigma 1\sigma 2)}$$

Where
$S_1 ; S_2$ = Spot price of assets 1 and 2
q1;q2  = Yields on assets 1 and 2
$\sigma 1;\sigma 2$  = Volatility of assets 1 and 2
$\rho$       = Correlation between asset 1 and 2
$\tau$       = time to expiry

*Source:* Margrabe, William. "The Value Of An Option To Exchange One Asset For Another." *Journal of Finance* vol. 33 (1978): 177-186

Researchers have suggested binomial types model to price spread options.[23] Other numerical models include approaches that factor in the joint density of the terminal prices of the underlying assets into the product of univariate marginal and conditional densities to derive the available analytic expression for the integral of the option payoffs.[24] Monte Carlo approaches are also feasible.[25]

---

[22] For an American version see Rubinstein, Mark "One For Another" (July/August 1991) *Risk* 30-32.

[23] See Ravindran, K. "Exotic Options" in Dattatreya, Ravi E. and Hotta, Kensuke (1994) *Advanced Interest Rate and Currency Swaps: State-of-the Art Products, Strategies & Risk Management Applications*; Probus Publishing: Chicago, Illinois at Chapter 5; Ravindran, K. (1998) *Customized Derivatives: A Step-by-Step Guide to Using Exotic Options, Swaps and Other Customized Derivatives*; McGraw-Hill, New York at 274-278.

[24] See Pearson. Neil D. "An Efficient Approach for Pricing Spread Options" (Fall 1995) *The Journal of Derivatives* 76-91.

[25] See Ravindran, K. (1998) *Customized Derivatives: A Step-by-Step Guide to Using Exotic Options, Swaps and Other Customised Derivatives*; McGraw-Hill, New York at 331-332.

## 5.   Hedging/Trading Spread Options

Spread options are usually created dynamically through trading in the underlying assets. Consistent with normal delta hedging approaches the amount of the model portfolio held is adjusted continuously to synthetically replicate the returns on the put option.

Spread options cannot usually be efficiently replicated by trading in options on the underlying assets. The portfolio of options is generally more expensive, reflecting the separate payoffs that allow each option to be separately exercised to maximize the value of individual options. This reflects the fact that the yield curve option is insensitive to absolute rate levels while the option portfolio is generally sensitive to the overall absolute level of rates.[26]

It should be noted that the one factor approach creates significant hedging difficulties. This reflects the fact that this type of model indicates a single delta governing synthetic replication or hedging of the spread option.

The two-factor model will usually entail binomial lattice structures simulating the price fluctuations in the two relevant assets. The two-factor approach creates more complex valuation parameters including two deltas, multiple (cross) gammas and at least two vegas. It requires, for computation purposes as already noted, the volatility of both assets involved in the spread and the correlation coefficient between them.

A particularly significant factor of spread options, when priced utilizing multi-factor options approaches, is the phenomenon of a negative vega. This reflects the fact that lower volatility levels can, under certain circumstances, result in higher option premiums. This reflects the fact that if the volatility of one asset diminishes (at least, with other variables held constant) the diminished volatility in one asset price performance can *increase* the value of the spread option as it increases the possibility of the spread increasing or decreasing. Hence, the negative vega. This phenomenon is not unique to spread options and is, in fact, present in several multi-factor option structures.

---

[26]   This is often expressed as the fact that the $ duration of the option portfolio is not zero while the $ duration of the yield spread option is zero.

# 6
# Index Amortizing Notes and Related Derivatives

## 1. Introduction

Index Amortizing Notes (IANs) are typically fixed interest securities whose essential feature is that the principal amount of the transaction may amortize at a prespecified rate depending on the occurrence of specific movements in a nominated market rate. This market rate usually is a specified interest rate, such as LIBOR.

Index amortizing products include structured investments (IANs) or pure derivative (off-balance sheet) transactions such as Index Amortizing Rate (IAR) swaps. The essential elements of the transaction are identical irrespective of the format utilized.

IANs and IAR swaps are essentially cross-market derivative products creating a relationship between changes in a specified market variable and cash flows in another instrument (the rate of amortization of principal or notional principal).

IAN and IAR swaps developed around the late 1980s. The structures proved popular with fixed income investors in the 1990s in an environment of low nominal interest rates, steep positively sloped yield curves and narrow spreads. The product, originally developed in US$, continues to be an important innovation with special importance in the US market, although the concept has been adopted in a number of other markets.

## 2. Concept

### 2.1 Structure[1]

As noted above, an index amortizing product entails a transaction (structured note or swap) whose rate of amortization is linked to changes in a specific rate index. An example of the terms and conditions of a typical IAN is summarized in **Exhibit 6.1**. An example of the terms and conditions of a typical IAR swap is summarized in **Exhibit 6.2**.

---

**Exhibit 6.1**
**Index Amortization Note**

Assume an investor seeks a structured investment that can be met through the following IAN transaction.

*General*

| | |
|---|---|
| Issuer | AAA/AA-rated institution |
| Amount | US$100 million |
| Maturity | 5 years (Original) |
| Interest Coupon | 5.50% pa (2-year Treasury note (4.20%) plus (say) 130 bps |

*Index Amortization Features*

| | |
|---|---|
| Lock-out Period | 2 years (eight quarters). No amortization during this period. |
| Reference Index | 3-month LIBOR set 5 days prior to each quarter or interest rate payment date |
| Current Index Level | 3.50% pa |
| Amortization Table | The principal amount of the note will amortize in accordance with the table set out below. |
| | If future movements fall between the points indicated on the matrix, then the amortization rate is determined by linear interpolation between the nearest points on the matrix. Any unamortized |

---

[1]  See Cheung, Kin S. and Konenigsberg, Mark (September 4, 1992) Index Amortizing Notes; Salomon Brothers United States Derivatives Research, New York; McDermott, Scott and Huie, Marcus (February 1993) "Index Amortization Swaps And Notes"; Goldman Sachs Fixed Income Research, New York; Petersen, Bjorn and Raghavan, Vijay R. "Index Amortizing Swaps" in Dattreyava, Ravi E. and Hotta, Kensuke (editors) (1994) "Advanced Interest Rate And Currency Swaps"; Probus Publishing: Chicago, Illinios at Chapter 3; Williams, Christopher J., Twomey, Melinda M., Latif, Hasan, Usher, Bruce M., Hsia, Ming Jiao, and Calabrisotto, Dianne "Fixed Income Hybrid and Synthetic Securities" in Dattreyava, Ravi E. and Hotta, Kensuke (editors) (1994) *Advanced Interest Rate And Currency Swaps*; Probus Publishing, Chicago at Chapter 6.

principal outstanding is repaid in full as at the maturity.

| Reference Index (% pa) | Amortization of Remaining Balance | Average Life (years) |
|---|---|---|
| 3.50 (unchanged or below current index level) | 100% | 2 |
| 4.50 (current index level plus 100 bps) | 12% | 3.5 |
| 5.50 (current index level plus 200 bps) | 3% | 4.5 |
| 6.50 (current index level plus 300 bps or more) | 0% | 5 |

Clean-up provision    The Note matures if the outstanding principal amount reaches 10% or less of the original principal amount.

The mechanics of the calculation of the amount of amortization of principal is as follows. If, for example, the rate of interest rises from 3.50% pa to 4.00% pa (a rise of 50 bps), then 56% of principal is amortized [(100% +12%) × 50 bps/100 bps].

**Exhibit 6.2**
**Index Amortization Rate Swap**

Assume a transaction where a counterparty pays fixed rate and receives floating rate (LIBOR) on a 5-year transaction with the following characteristics:

*General*

| | |
|---|---|
| Notional amount | US$100 million |
| Maturity | 5 years (original) |
| Fixed Rate | 5.50% pa (2-year US Treasury (4.35% pa) + 115 bps). |
| Floating Rate | 3-month LIBOR |

*Index Amortization Features*

Lock-out Period         2 years (eight quarters). No amortization during
                        this period.
Reference Index         3-month LIBOR set 5 days prior to each quarter or
                        interest rate payment date
Current Index Level     5.25% pa
Amortization Table      The notional principal amount of the swap will
                        amortize in accordance with the table set out
                        below. Linear interpolation will be used where
                        interest rates change by an amount in between the
                        levels set out in the table.

| Reference Index (% pa) | Amortization of Remaining Balance | Average Life (years) |
| --- | --- | --- |
| 2.25 (300 bps or more below current index level) | 100 | 2 |
| 3.25 (200 bps below current index level) | 100 | 2 |
| 4.25 (100 bps below current index level) | 100 | 2 |
| 5.25 (at current index level) | 100 | 2 |
| 6.25 (100 bps above current index level) | 80 | 3 |
| 7.25 (200 bps above current index level) | 30 | 4 |
| 8.25 (300 bps or more above current index level) | 0 | 5 |

Clean-up provision      The swap matures if the outstanding notional
                        amount reaches 10% or less of the original
                        notional principal amount.

The mechanics of the calculation of notional principal outstanding under
this swap is set out below.

If rates rise 100 bps from the initial base rate of 5.25% on the first reset
after the initial lock-up period, the new principal amount will be $80
million, derived as follows:

> Initial principal – (initial principal × annual amortization rate)/number of periods per year (in this case, four) = $100 million – ($100 million × 80%)/4 = $80 million
>
> Subsequent principal amounts will depend on the next reset rate and will be calculated on the remaining principal amount until the new principal reaches 10% of the original, when the clean-up provision takes effect.

In practice, the two structures are often closely inter-related with the IAN being specifically structured for the requirement of an investor with the issuer being insulated from the index amortizing features of the transaction through the entry, by the issuer, into an IAR swap with a derivatives dealer to hedge its index amortizing exposure. This type of structure is set out in **Exhibit 6.3**.

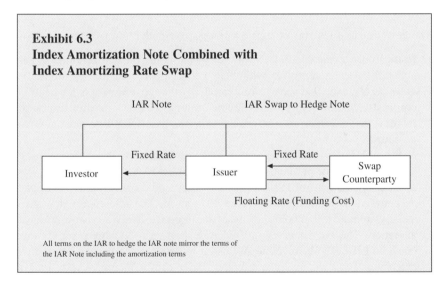

**Exhibit 6.3**
**Index Amortization Note Combined with**
**Index Amortizing Rate Swap**

IAR Note                          IAR Swap to Hedge Note

Investor ← Fixed Rate ← Issuer ← Fixed Rate ← Swap Counterparty

Floating Rate (Funding Cost)

All terms on the IAR to hedge the IAR note mirror the terms of the IAR Note including the amortization terms

In the IAN transaction identified, the investor entered into a structured investment where the maximum maturity of the investment is five years. However, the investment may have an actual maturity of between two and five years depending on the performance of 3-month LIBOR. The minimum investment period is predicated on the lock-out period that dictates that the note cannot be amortized for the first two years. The 5-year maximum maturity is dictated by the absolute final maturity specified whereby any principal outstanding not amortized as at that date is repaid.

The exact maturity of the note is determined by the behavior of the reference index (3-month LIBOR) consistent with the amortization matrix specified. If the 3-month LIBOR remains at or falls below its current level of 3.50% pa, then the note will amortize in full after two years. In contrast, if the 3-month LIBOR rises by equal to or more than 300 bps (to 6.50% pa), then the note principal does not amortize at all until final maturity. In between these two rate levels, the rate of amortization is gradual in accordance with the agreed schedule. As discussed in more detail below, this transaction structure specifies amortization as a percentage of the note's outstanding balance.

The structure of the IAR swap is very similar to the IAN structure. The major difference is that the transaction is structured as a standard fixed for floating swap with the notional principal of the swap declining in accordance with a structure which is similar to that applicable to the IAN.

## 2.2 Structural Features

The key structural features of such a transaction include:

- **Issuer** (only applicable to IAN format) — the issuer of such instruments has generally been a borrower with high credit quality. In the US domestic market, issuance has been dominated by the government agencies. In contrast, IAR structures have been undertaken by a wide variety of institutions in order to synthesize specific asset liability management positions.
- **Reference index** — the reference index is central to the structure as it determines the rate of amortization and the effective life of the security. The reference index is agreed as between the issuer and the investor in a IAN and as between the counterparties in an IAR swap. The reference index also, usually, applies throughout the life of the transaction and is not capable of alteration. The typical index utilized is a short-term or money market rate (such as LIBOR). However, as discussed in detail in the context of product extensions and variations, the reference index can be intermediate or longer term interest rates such as 5- or 10-year CMT yields. Non-interest rate indexes, such as currency rates are also feasible. The selection of reference index will be predicated on the investor or counterparty's rate expectations and requirements, for example, to create exposure to one or other portion of the yield curve.
- **Amortization table** — the amortization table agreed determines the amortization amount and the amortization rate for given movements in the reference index. It embodies the maturity risk of the structure in that the average life of the transaction is determined by the rate of amortization. The amortization amount can be expressed in two separate formats:

1. Percentage of the IAN's remaining balance or the IAR swap's remaining notional principal; or,
2. Percentage of the transaction's original balance.

   The amortization table is designed to generate the required average life characteristics of the transaction. In practice, it is generated by choosing interest rate scenarios at each interest period and utilizing a process of trial and error to determine the amortization rate as a percentage of outstanding principal to match the desired average life schedule for various assumed reference index rate movements.[2]

- **Lock-out period** — the lock-out period provides the IAN investor or the fixed-rate receiver in an IAR swap with a specified period of protection against prepayment of principal. This reflects the fact that irrespective of the direction and magnitude of reference index movements during the lock-out period, no amortization is allowable.

- **Maturity** — the maturity of an index amortization transaction by implication is the final date by which time unless previously amortized the IAN principal is repaid. The maturity has a similar significance for an IAR transaction insofar as it signifies the termination of the swap unless previously terminated through the amortization of notional principal.

- **Clean-up provision** — the clean-up provision places an obligation on the issuer in an IAN to call the note where the outstanding balance falls below a nominated de minimus level, typically, 10 to 15%. It is designed, for practical purposes, to terminate the transaction where the balance outstanding is not meaningful. For an IAR swap, the concept is very similar with the swap being automatically terminated on any payment date where the notional principal falls below the nominated level.

- **Average life** — the average life of the transaction (calculated in a manner consistent with standard fixed interest market convention) is indicated to provide a measure of the term and interest rate risk of the structure.

## 2.3 Transaction Economics

The essential economic rationale of the transaction is driven by the fact that the investor in an IAN or the fixed-rate receiver in an IAR swap receives a higher fixed rate, relative to a similar but non-index amortizing structure. This additional return represents the capture of return designed to compensate for the prepayment risk assumed. This risk can be effectively modelled as the sale of

---

[2] For an example of how the amortization rate is calculated see Petersen, Bjorn and Raghavan, Vijay R. "Index Amortizing Swaps" in Dattreyava, Ravi E. and Hotta, Kensuke (editors) (1994) "Advanced Interest Rate And Currency Swaps"; Probus Publishing: Chicago, Illinios at 58, 59.

options on the relevant reference index. The economics are driven by the optionality embedded in this structure that is discussed in detail below.

Transactions utilizing index amortizing structures developed in the low nominal rate and steep yield curve environment, primarily in US$, that existed in the early 1990s. This interest rate environment created opportunities for investors to undertake structured investments with maturity uncertainty through the linkage to the movements in the reference index to generate enhanced yields. The primary benefit to investors was the capacity to earn higher returns in combination with a relatively short maturity, particularly where short-term rates stayed low, maximizing the rate of amortization under these structures.

The economic logic of the IAR swap was more complex. Receipt of the fixed rate under an IAR swap combined with an investment in a LIBOR-based FRN allowed the synthetic creation of an IAN investment. In contrast, the rationale of these transactions for liability managers was that in a very steep yield curve environment borrowers seeking to price their debt at the short end of the yield curve (that is, floating-rate borrowers), the IAR swap could lower their interest cost significantly by issuing debt in longer maturities (five to 10 years) and swapping it into a floating-rate basis. The benefit in this case was the result of the fact that the fixed rates received were higher than for conventional swaps.

A significant feature of index amortizing structure is the negative convexity of this instrument. Convexity is a measure of the rate of change in the price of an instrument for a given change in interest rates. Generally, a fixed income security has positive convexity, whereby the price of the instrument increases when interest rates fall.[3] This holds true where the investor in the security does not grant, through any feature of the instrument, any option element.

An index amortizing instrument features negative convexity in that the price of the instrument will, generally, decline as interest rates fall. This reflects the specific feature that the rate of amortization of principal or face value under the structure is highest when the reference index, short-term interest rates, declines. **Exhibit 6.4** sets out the negative convexity feature of an index amortization structure.

---

[3]  Convexity can be defined as the change in duration of a fixed interest security due to a change in interest rates where duration measures the weighted average term of cash flows of the fixed interest instrument and effectively provides a measure of its interest rate sensitivity (the relationship of change in price to the change in its yield). See discussion in Chapter 16.

**Exhibit 6.4**
**Index Amortization Structure — Convexity Dynamics**

The convexity of an interest rate product describes the rate of change in its price for a movement in interest rates. If the rate of change is linear (it changes price in a constant ratio whether rates move up or down), the product has no convexity. As shown in the graph, fixed-rate bonds and swaps (receiving fixed) have positive convexity. When rates rise, the rate of change in their price is slower relative to the interest rate move than when rates fall. Buying options will increase the convexity of an instrument or a portfolio. Certain instruments, including mortgage instruments and their synthetic structure that replicate these instruments, have negative convexity. When rates rise their price change is faster relative to the interest rate move than when rates fall. Selling options will reduce the convexity of an instrument or portfolio. IAN and IAR swaps (receiving fixed) have negative convexity since they effectively involve the sale of put options to the fixed payer.

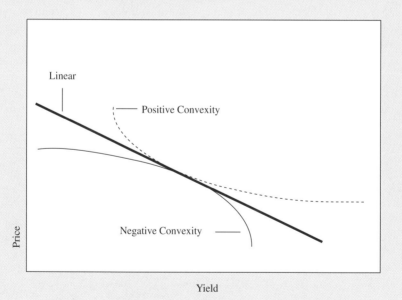

## 3. Applications

### 3.1 Yield Enhancement

The central feature of IAN and IAR swap structures (for the fixed-rate receiver) is the yield enhancement provided by such structured investments. As noted above, this yield enhancement is obtained in return for assuming maturity risk in terms of the extension or shortening of the life of the instrument. This yield enhancement, which is effected through the sale of interest rate options, is analogous to investments in mortgage-backed securities (MBS). MBS securities exhibit similar behavior to index amortizing structures. Lower interest rates trigger prepayment on the underlying mortgages with a resultant shortening in the life of the MBS investment. Both structures share an exposure to interest rate-driven prepayment risk.

However, the two structures also have significant differences in terms of features. In particular, as discussed below, index amortizing structures provide competitive returns under certain market conditions. In addition, index amortizing structures have certain superior features to MBS transactions providing investors with the capacity to diversify and customize credit risk and prepayment risk. They also have greater control over the average life ranges and greater flexibility. **Exhibit 6.5** summarizes the major differences in features as between MBS and index amortizing structures.

**Exhibit 6.5**
**Index Amortization Structures and Mortgage-backed Securities —**
**Comparison of Features**

| Feature | MBS/CMO Transactions | IAN/IAR Swaps |
|---|---|---|
| Interest rate exposure | Exposure to mortgage refinancing rates | Exposure to reference index |
| Prepayment/ Amortization risk | Prepayment is only capable of estimation as it is | Prepayment is capable of being specifically structured |
| | a function of complex factors including:<br>1. Yield curve shape<br>2. Demographics<br>3. Mortgage financing alternatives | and is certain being a function of only the movements in the reference index |
| Option exposure | Investor sells prepayment options | Investor sells call and put options on reference index |

| Feature | MBS/CMO Transactions | IAN/IAR Swaps |
|---------|---------------------|---------------|
| Nature of maturity exposure | Greater uncertainty as a result of:<br>1. Prepayment predictions<br>2. Absence of lock-up and clean-up provisions<br>3. Risk of unusual prepayment scenarios | Greater certainty as a result of:<br>1. Specific reference index-based prepayment model<br>2. Lock-out period and final maturity provides well-defined term boundaries<br>3. Clean-up provisions prevents typical MBS "tail" |
| Customization — prepayment risk | Linkage only to mortgage rates | Capacity to link to specific rate that because of imperfect correlation with mortgage rates allows diversification of prepayment risk |
| Customization — credit risk | Credit risk is linked to mortgage pool and security structure | Credit risk can be precisely structured to allow greater diversification of credit risk |

## 3.2   Liability Applications

The liability management applications of index amortizing structures are more varied. They fall, generally, into two separate categories:

- Borrowers utilizing the higher fixed rate receivable under an IAR swap to generate cheaper floating rate funding.
- Borrowers using IANs or paying fixed-in IAR swaps to create customized risk profiles consistent with interest rate expectations.

The first application developed in the steep yield curve environment, primarily in US$, that existed in late 1991 and 1992. These transactions involved IAR swaps. The rationale of these transactions was that in a very steep yield curve environment, borrowers were seeking to price their debt at the short end of the yield curve (that is, they preferred to be floating-rate borrowers). In the yield curve environment that prevailed, borrowers could lower their interest cost by up to 200-250 basis points by issuing debt in longer maturities (five to 10 years) and swapping it into a floating-rate basis.

For the borrower, the benefits of this type of strategy included:

- The substantial savings on interest cost.
- The lack of liquidity risk as the underlying debt was medium to long term.
- The interest rate savings (generated by the shape of the yield curve) gave the borrower protection against a future increase in the absolute interest rate levels or a change in the shape of the yield curve.

However, this strategy became disadvantaged by the fact that interest rate swap spreads in US dollars fell sharply to historically low levels at this time. The IAR structure allowed borrowers to receive at higher interest rate swap spreads. Under the arrangement, the borrower had the following cash flows:

- The borrower received a fixed rate from the swap counterparty.
- The borrower paid a floating rate payment to the swap counterparty usually, based on US$ LIBOR or US$ CP.

The final maturity of the swap was between 7 and 15 years (typically, around 10-12 years). At the commencement of the transaction, an agreed amortization schedule was agreed to, based on the prevailing level of either short-term rates (LIBOR or T-Bills) or CMT Treasury rates (see discussion below on product extensions) and on a stated final maturity.

For the first five years (the lock-up period), the swap operated as a regular interest rate swap. After the expiry of the lock-up period, the IAR swap amortized in a manner consistent with the pre-agreed amortization structure. The variable amortization structure resulted in a quicker (slower) amortization depending on whether 10-year rates increase (decrease). The major advantage of this type of structure was the increase in the swap spread achievable. For example, in late 1991, it was possible utilizing this structure to increase the swap spread over Treasury for maturities of 10 to 12 years by an additional 25 to 30 bps pa.

The transaction structure had some appeal to borrowers as it was viewed as being self-hedging from an economic perspective. This is because if 10-year interest rates fell, the borrower benefited from lower interest costs creating additional cash flows that coincided with the slower amortization of debt and the higher effective cost of borrowing.

As noted above, the fixed rate under the IAR swap was higher than for a conventional interest rate swap of the same maturity, reflecting the fact that the receiver of fixed rates had written a series of options on interest rate swaps, the premium in respect of which is embedded in the higher swap rate.

The second application entailed issuers and payers of fixed rates under IAR swaps. These liability managers utilized these structures to essentially create interest rate-sensitive hedges for underlying liability portfolios to engineer interest rate exposure hedges. For these counterparties, if the reference index fell, the term of the liability or interest rate hedge automatically shortened. In contrast, as rates rose, then the term of liability or hedge lengthened until it reached the final maturity of the transaction affording these liability managers protection as the reference index increased. In effect, the higher coupon cost of the borrowing or hedge reflected the cost of the options purchased to create this interest rate-sensitive hedge structure.

## 4. Valuation and Hedging Issues

### 4.1 Performance Characteristics

The central valuation issue of index amortizing structures relates to the options on the reference index sold by the investor or fixed-rate receiver to enhance yield. The valuation problem is best analyzed with reference to the performance characteristics of these instruments.

The index amortizing structure provides above-market returns where interest rates remain static or decline from current levels. In a typical structure, the amortization rate is based of the current level of the reference index with rises above the index resulting in an increasing average life. This performance characteristic reflects the fact that only where rates perform in the identified manner does the investor or fixed-rate receiver enjoy returns above the market returns prevailing at the time of entry into the transaction. For example, in the transactions set out in **Exhibits 6.1** and **6.2**, the investor and fixed-rate receiver enjoyed higher fixed rates relative to the underlying 2-year Treasury note or swap rate prevailing at that time for a non-index amortizing transaction. As the reference index increases, the average life of the transaction increases with the result that the investor or fixed-rate receiver suffers an erosion of value from two separate sources:

- As the average life of the transaction increases, in a positively sloped yield curve environment, the return from the transaction decreases, at least in a spread sense as the reference rate level moves up the yield curve.
- As the absolute level of rates rise as the reference index increases, the actual value of the investment and the swap falls reflecting the higher interest rates.[4]

The performance characteristics of index amortizing instruments reflect the implicit interest rate outlook embedded in the options sold which embody the expectation that interest rates will not rise at the rate implied by the positively sloped yield curve. This expectation has two separate implications: firstly, it increases the value capture facilitated by the sale of the options; and, secondly, it

---

[4] The fall in value assumes a degree of correlation between rises in the reference index and the rates used to discount the cash flows associated with the transaction.

reflects the expectation on the part of the investor or fixed-rate receiver regarding the possible exercise of those options to lengthen the average life of the instrument.

There are three separate elements to the relationship between the amortization rates embodied in an index amortization structure and the structure of forward rates:[5]

- **Absolute level of forward rates of the reference index** — in a positively sloped yield curve environment, implied forward rates lie above the physical yield curve. The steeper the slope of the yield curve, the higher the momentum of the forward rate curve with the implied forward rates being at progressively higher levels above the current yield curve. This was the actual swap curve and implied yield curve prevailing during the period when index amortizing structures were at the height of utilization. Implied forward rates are poor predictors of *actual* LIBOR rates based on historical evidence. Over the relevant period, forward 3-month LIBOR has consistently been different from actual 3-month LIBOR; that is, the forward curve has over- or underestimated actual spot LIBOR rates. The extent of over- or underestimation is also substantial. Index amortizing structures allow the investor or fixed-rate receiver to monetize the expectation that actual LIBOR rates will not rise at the rate or to the levels implied by the yield curve. This reflects the fact that the index amortizing structure will generally outperform a conventional nonamortizing instrument with an average life equal to the base case average life of the index amortizing structure under this rate scenario.
- **Volatility of the reference index rates** — the index amortizing structures entail the sale of options on the underlying reference index. As the investor or fixed-rate receiver is the seller of options, a fall (rise) in the volatility of the reference index will benefit the value of the instrument. The level of volatility will also impact on the premium received from the sale of the options sold and will determine, in part, the incremental return generated from the assumption of maturity risk. Investors in IANs or fixed-rate receivers in IAR swaps will maximize the value of the structure where they enter into the transactions during periods of high implied volatility of the reference index rate on the expectation that the level of volatility will decline.
- **Yield curve shape risk** — the value of an index amortizing instrument is a function of the interaction of two separate interest rates: the reference index (LIBOR) and the term interest rate that will determine the value of the future

---

[5]  The analysis of performance characteristics of an index amortizing structure is illustrated using a LIBOR reference index-based instrument—in practice, the major interest rate index utilized.

cash flows under the structure upon extension or reduction of the average life. This creates an exposure to the changes in the shape of the yield curve. While the amortization and the average life of the transaction is driven by the movements in LIBOR, changes in term rates and in the shape of the yield curve can impact upon the investor or fixed-rate receiver. For example, in a scenario where the yield curve flattens (LIBOR rises while term rates fall), the underlying fixed-rate instrument may increase in value. The increase in value may be accentuated by the lengthening in the average life of the transaction triggered by the rise in LIBOR. Conversely, a steepening yield curve will negatively affect the value of the instrument as a result of a shortening of the average life and the impact on the value of the cash flows from the higher term interest rates. The change in the yield curve shape will also impact upon the forward rate structure and the corresponding values of the options sold by the investor or fixed-rate receiver. In a scenario of curve flattening, the value of these options may change in a manner favorable to the investor or fixed-rate receiver.

The exact interaction of the above factors in the value and performance of an index amortizing structure will depend on the individual structure. In practice, a key determinant will be the base level of the reference index. A higher base rate will usually require a greater amortization speed and a shorter average life.

The actual performance of an index amortizing instrument can be inferred by utilizing simulation approaches and modeling its behavior under certain scenarios. Two researchers[6] examined the performance of a 5-year final maturity/2-year lock-out and a 5-year final maturity/3-year lock-out structure for a 3-month LIBOR index amortizing instrument with different base rates assuming LIBOR rates increased at (1) levels slower than implied by forward rates, (2) a rate consistent with the implied forwards, and (3) levels greater than that implied by the forward rates. For each scenario, the average life and the gains or losses were computed. The results are summarized in **Exhibit 6.6**.

**Exhibit 6.6**

[6] See Petersen, Bjorn and Raghavan, Vijay R. "Index Amortizing Swaps" in Dattreyava, Ravi E. and Hotta, Kensuke (editors) (1994) *Advanced Interest Rate And Currency Swap*; Probus Publishing: Chicago, Illinios at 59-63.

**Comparative Performance of Indexed Amortizing Structure Under Different Interest Rate Paths**

| Base rate | Slower Than Forward | | Forward Curve | | Faster Than Forward | |
| | Average Life (years) | Gain ($ million) | Average Life (years) | Gain ($ million) | Average Life (years) | Gain ($ million) |
|---|---|---|---|---|---|---|
| **5/2 Structure** | | | | | | |
| 5.375 | 2.00 | 3.7 | 2.54 | 2.3 | 3.70 | −1.3 |
| 4.875 | 2.00 | 3.9 | 3.52 | 2.1 | 4.23 | −0.4 |
| 4.375 | 2.16 | 4.3 | 4.04 | 2.0 | 4.67 | −0.8 |
| 4.125 | 2.74 | 5.4 | 4.31 | 2.2 | 4.84 | −1.0 |
| 3.875 | 3.35 | 5.9 | 4.54 | 1.7 | 4.95 | −1.2 |
| 3.625 | 3.58 | 6.1 | 4.76 | 1.5 | 5.00 | −1.3 |
| 3.375 | 3.84 | 6.1 | 4.91 | 1.3 | 5.00 | −1.4 |
| **5/3 Structure** | | | | | | |
| 5.375 | 3.00 | 4.8 | 4.12 | 1.5 | 4.39 | −1.1 |
| 4.875 | 3.15 | 5.2 | 4.19 | 1.4 | 4.39 | −1.6 |
| 4.375 | 3.88 | 6.1 | 4.51 | 1.2 | 4.98 | −1.9 |
| 4.125 | 3.88 | 6.1 | 4.70 | 1.1 | 5.00 | −1.9 |
| 3.875 | 4.11 | 6.1 | 4.88 | 0.9 | 5.00 | −1.9 |
| 3.625 | 4.26 | 6.1 | 4.98 | 0.7 | 5.00 | −2.0 |
| 3.375 | 4.42 | 6.1 | 5.00 | 0.7 | 5.00 | −2.0 |

*Source:* Petersen, Bjorn and Raghavan, Vijay R. "Index Amortizing Swaps" in Dattreyava, Ravi E. and Hotta, Kensuke (editors) *Advanced Interest Rate And Currency Swaps*; Probus Publishing, Chicago, Illinios, 1994: 61.

The analysis concludes that:

• Increasing base rates decrease average lives because of the increased speed of amortization.
• Average lives tend to be higher for higher versus lower rate increases.
• Average lives increase with increases in the lock-out period.
• The gains and losses are consistent with the average life behavior with gains tending to increase with lower base rates (higher average lives) at least where rates increase slower than implied by the forward curve. However, higher than implied rate rises contribute to higher losses consistent with the extension risk.

The analysis, while specific to the actual market conditions upon which it is based, highlights the complex performance dynamics in index amortization structures. The essential element of structuring such an instrument requires a trade-off between the amortization rate and the selected base rate. For a given scenario, accelerating the amortization speed (either by utilizing higher base rates or quicker amortization rates) decreases the average life and the breakeven fixed rate. The yield enhancement level can be increased by increasing the option value of embedded options sold. This is achieved by an optimal choice of the base rate level and by increasing the time period from lock-out to final maturity. The higher option value captured reflects the increased uncertainty in the duration of the instrument. **Exhibit 6.7** sets out an example of the trade-off between the level of yield enhancement achieved in one specific instance.

---

**Exhibit 6.7**
**Relationship Between Return and Base Reference Index Rate**

| Reference Index — Base Level | Fixed Rate Coupon (bps spread to 2-year Treasury Note Yield) | Average Life (years) |
|:---:|:---:|:---:|
| 3.5 | 167 | 4.67 |
| 4.0 | 170 | 4.42 |
| 4.5 | 171 | 4.12 |
| 5.5 | 160 | 3.34 |
| 6.5 | 123 | 2.70 |

The above relationships between return enhancement levels and base rates on the reference index are based on a 5-year final maturity/2-year lock-out index amortization note. The average life is based on a probability-weighted Monte Carlo simulation of future interest rate scenarios.

*Source:* McDermott, Scott and Huie, Marcus. "Index Amortization Swaps And Notes." Goldman Sachs Fixed Income Research, New York, February 1993: 8.

---

**4.2 Valuation and Hedging**

The valuation and the corresponding mechanism for hedging are a function of the decomposition into and pricing of the option elements in an index amortizing transaction. These structures can be characterized as effectively callable bonds or swaps where the call feature is triggered by movements in specific rate movements in the reference index.

The value of the index amortizing instrument is driven by the valuation of the embedded interest rate options. **Exhibit 6.7** sets out an example of the trade-off between the level of yield enhancement achieved in one specific instance. The table highlights the fact that the highest level of return enhancement is achieved when the amortization schedule is centred around the implied forward rate to maximize the premium value captured from the sale of options.

This is evident from the actual increase in return enhancement as the base rate level of the reference index is increased. This reflects the fact that where the base rate is 3.50% pa (6.50% pa) the transaction has a long (short) average life against which call options representing the prepayment risk (put options representing the extension risk) have been sold. The transaction with a base rate level of 4.50% pa represents an intermediate average life security with both prepayment and extension risk. In effect, the IAN investor or fixed-rate receiver in an IAR swap has sold an at-the-money straddle capturing a higher premium level that results in the higher level of return enhancement achieved.

The valuation of the identified options is complex, reflecting a number of factors:

- The exercise of the option is determined with reference to the reference index while the value of the amortization is dependent on the term interest rate to the maturity of the transaction as of the relevant amortization date. This requires the term structure of interest rates or the yield curve shape to be known as at each amortization date.
- The principal reduction at a given amortization date is dependent on not only the term structure of interest rates on that date but on the unamortized principal as at that date. This means that the structure requires a history of interest rates (that is, it is path-dependent).

The valuation of these options requires a trade-off between computational simplicity and accurate estimation of the values of the optionality involved. The following approaches have evolved:

- **Simple one-factor models** — these types of models assume all yields along the yield curve are correlated.
- **Term structure models** — these models belong to the class of options used to price interest rate options generally. Typically, these models introduce a second factor to allow generation of a more complete yield curve to more accurately model term structure movements. A number of models are available. Each of these models make specific assumptions regarding the term structure of interest rates.[7]

---

[7]   See discussion of debt option pricing in Appendix A to Chapter 2.

- **Simulation models** — these approaches involve using typically Monte Carlo simulation procedures to generate arbitrage-free paths consistent with given yield and volatility structures. The cash flows generated on these paths are then discounted back to determine the value of the structure.

The relative merits of the identified approaches are subject to dispute and discussion. The simple one-factor models, while simple in computational terms, may be inaccurate in practice, because of the simplified yield curve structure assumed.

The term structure models assume the ability to appropriately calibrate the term structure variables in the model. This assumes the existence of a liquid market and availability of pricing information that allows the correlation between different parts of the yield curve to be tested and adjusted. The difficulty lies in the absence of such markets. However, the emergence of markets such as those for yield curve products hold longer term promise to enable such calibration as these market segments gain in liquidity. The use of historical data to determine the relationships is inherently risky given the nonstationary nature of these correlations.

The identified estimation problems mean that in some instances the advantage of the introduction of a second factor to determine term structure may introduce, of itself, distortions. The errors inherent in assuming a more simplified term structure (as in a single factor model) may be less significant for particular structures such as short (two to three years) average life structures (see discussion below). However, for longer dated structures the need for a term structure model is more important.

The use of simulation approaches is attractive. However, the major disadvantage is the computational and data intensity of such approaches that makes them slower and less than ideal from a practical standpoint.

In practice, the pricing of index amortizing structures is driven by procedures that have regard for the manner in which these transactions are hedged by traders and dealers in these instruments. Consistency of hedging and pricing dictate the need to adjust the valuation model for index amortization products to the following traded market rates and volatility:

- The swap yield curve and the implied forward rates therein.
- Short-term interest rate option volatility.
- Volatility on option on interest rate swaps/swaptions.

The calibration of the valuation model, irrespective of the model utilized, to these variables merely reflects the use of US$ Eurodollar futures contracts (FRAs in other currencies), interest rate swaps, caps/floors and swaptions to hedge portfolios of index amortizing instruments.

Hedging portfolios of index amortizing products is similar to the procedures utilized for other similarly traded financial instruments. The hedging technique utilized seeks to find the price or value sensitivity of an index amortizing structure to each of the relevant rate and volatility inputs. This is usually done by utilizing the valuation model and perturbing each pricing parameter separately to identify the price sensitivity of the structure. The index amortizing instrument is then hedged utilizing a dynamic hedging approach. This involves establishing and periodically rebalancing positions in a set of the identified instruments to match the sensitivity of the index amortizing structure to that of the hedges.

The hedging costs, consistent with dynamic hedging techniques generally, are derived from the cost of trading in the underlying hedge instruments and hedge rebalancing costs. A major factor in determining hedge costs is the relative stability of the hedge to index amortizing product relationships. The relative stability or instability of this relationship, particularly for larger or jumpy (discontinuous) rate movements is an important determinant of both hedge cost and performance.

The hedge structures are based on the standard hedge measures such as delta, gamma, and vega. In general, the delta or absolute price sensitivity of index amortizing structures exhibits the following pattern:

- Corresponds to that of an equivalent fixed interest security during the lock-out period.
- The delta of an index amortizing structure is particularly sensitive to the underlying rate movements after the end of the lock-out period.
- The delta of an index amortizing structure becomes gradually lower than that for a fixed interest security, reflecting the expected lower principal as a result of the expected amortization.

Index amortizing structures have relatively lower gammas. Index amortizing structures have vegas significantly different from zero, reflecting the embedded options in the structure. The corresponding fixed interest security has zero vega as its value is not affected by volatility changes as it does not entail any option elements. For 2-factor term structure models, two vegas are relevant, reflecting the sensitivity to both a uniform change in the volatility curve and the change in the shape of the volatility curve.[8]

---

[8]   See discussion in Hull, John and White, Alan "Finding The Keys" (September 1993) *Risk* vol 6 no 9 109-112.

## 5.    Product Extensions and Variations

The market for index amortizing structures has spawned a number of variations and product extensions. These include:

- The various off-balance sheet methods of structuring index amortizing cash flow features.
- Variations in each of the key elements including:
  1. Alternative coupon structures.
  2. The use of alternative reference indexes.
  3. Shorter maturity index amortizing instruments.
  4. Alternative amortization schedules.
  5. The use of alternative credit structures.
- The creation of structures featuring embedded exotic options.
- Index amortization linked to alternative noninterest reference indexes.

### 5.1    Off-balance Sheet Index Amortizing Instruments

As noted above, both on- and off-balance sheet structures for index amortizing instruments have emerged. The major off-balance sheet format of these instruments has been the IAR swap (described previously). The IAR swap is clearly the equivalent of an IAN transaction provided that the face value of the transaction is invested in a floating rate investment that yields at least LIBOR flat. The principal amortization is replicated by the reduction in the notional amount of the IAR swap.

The use of these off-balance sheet variations were motivated by a variety of considerations including:

- Absence of impact on the balance sheet with the resultant lack of impact on balance sheet ratios while facilitating the investor's capacity to improve returns through the higher return available on index amortizing structures.
- The differential status of IAR swaps from a capital adequacy standpoint for financial institutions whereby the swap required a lower capital level to be held against it than for a corresponding IAN.[9]
- The ability to further boost the return on the transaction by investing in floating-rate assets that provided a return in excess of LIBOR. This was achieved in part by, in effect, altering the nature of the credit risk on the actual investment. In this regard, the IAR swap structure assisted in extending the range of credit risk available in index amortizing instruments (see discussion below).

---

[9]  Similar advantages may apply to insurance companies where a risk-adjusted capital framework is applicable.

## 5.2   Variations in Key Structural Features

### 5.2.1   Coupon Variations

Index amortizing structures entailing a zero-coupon format have been undertaken.[10] The zero-coupon index amortizing structure is identical in all respects with more conventional coupon-paying transactions featuring the early amortization provision where the reference index declines, the minimum and maximum maturity and the lock-out period during which no amortization occurs. The investor receives compensation for the prepayment risk assumed through a higher discount in the price of the security.

The major motivation of this coupon adjustment was to replicate the Principal Only (PO) structures in the US mortgage market. In periods where demand for PO structure from MBS investors is high, reflecting the requirement for either high duration assets or to hedge interest-only (IO) structures, zero-coupon indexed amortizing structures were created to meet this demand. The classic advantages of index amortizing structures over MBS transactions are also applicable.

### 5.2.2   Shorter Maturity Index Amortization Instruments

Maturity variation in index amortizing instruments have also evolved. In late 1994, index amortizing transactions, featuring a 3-year life with a 1-year lock-out and total amortization after one year if rates decreased, emerged. The typical terms for such a transaction (in the IAN format) are summarized in **Exhibit 6.8**.

| **Exhibit 6.8** **Short Maturity Index Amortization Note** | |
|---|---|
| ***General*** | |
| Issuer | AAA- or AA-rated institution |
| Amount | US$100 million |
| Maturity | 3 years (Original) |
| Interest Coupon | 7.125% pa (1-year Treasury Note plus 100 bps) |

---

[10]   See for example Salomon Brothers Variable Maturity Strips (VMS) Product.

*Index Amortization Features*

| | |
|---|---|
| Lock-out Period | 1 year (4 quarters). No amortization during this period. |
| Reference Index | 3-month LIBOR set 5 days prior to each quarter or interest rate payment date |
| Current Index Level | 6.25% pa |
| Amortization Table | The Principal Amount of the Note will amortize in accordance with the table set out below. |

| Reference Index (% pa) | Amortization of Remaining Balance | Average Life (years) |
|---|---|---|
| 6.25 (unchanged or below current index level) | 100 | 1 |
| 7.50 (current index level plus 125 bps) | 100 | 1 |
| 7.75 (current index level plus 150 bps) | 15.70 | 2 |
| 8.25 (current index level plus 200 bps or more) | 0 | 3 |

The shorter term maturity index amortizing transactions were motivated by market conditions where implied volatility in LIBOR caps and options on swaps rose. As noted above, cap volatility (a 1-year option to enter into a 2-year swap and a 2-year 3-month LIBOR cap) are close surrogates for the volatility of the option embedded in the short maturity (3-year/noncall 1-year) index amortizing transaction identified. For example, in 1995, the implied volatility of a 1-year option into a 2-year swap rose to 19.5% (from 16.5% earlier in the year) and 2-year cap volatility rose in the same period by some 2.5% to 21.0%. This rise in volatility allowed investors in short maturity IANs and receivers of fixed-in IAR swaps to sell volatility at higher levels allowing generation of increased premium levels that increased their return levels on these structures.

For example, the IAN transaction described in **Exhibit 6.8** would have provided the investor with a return equivalent to around 100 bps over 1-year Treasury bills and also 55-60 bps and 25-30 bps over the 1- and 3-year swap rate. The higher return combined with an expectation of the impending end to the tightening of US monetary policy created demand for these structures.

### 5.2.3   Index Amortization Linked to Alternative Reference Indexes

The transactions identified have focused to date on amortizing schedules linked to LIBOR as the reference index rate. One common variation entails linking the amortization to an alternative index such as the 5- or 10-year Treasury bond rate (the Constant Maturity Treasury (CMT) rate is usually used). The Constant Maturity Swap (CMS) rate can also be utilized as the term interest rate alternative to LIBOR as the basis for amortization.

The use of CMT in preference to LIBOR as the reference index reflects the trade-off between the typically lower level of volatility in term rates relative to LIBOR, the greater relationship between 5- and 10-year CMT rates and MBS transactions, and the desire by the investor to customize the structure to expectation about the future path of LIBOR and CMT rates.

The lower volatility of CMT rates that constitutes a disadvantage in the case of an investor or fixed-rate receiver can actually be an advantage in the case where the relevant investor *pays* fixed rate in an IAR (going short an IAN) to hedge a portfolio of MBS. The lower volatility translates into a lower cost, as represented by the fixed rate paid, of the hedge. Similarly, the closer correlation of CMT rates to MBS rates may assist in such a hedge.

### 5.2.4   Alternative Amortization Schedules

An important variation to the structural features of index amortization transactions is the incorporation of alternative amortization schedules. The most important of these is the reverse index amortization structure where the principal of the IAN or notional principal in the case of IAR swaps *increases* as the reference rate declines. The typical terms for such a transaction (in the IAN format) are summarized in **Exhibit 6.9**.

---

**Exhibit 6.9**
**Reverse Index Amortization Note**

*General*

| | |
|---|---|
| Issuer | AAA- or AA-rated institution |
| Amount | US$100 million |
| Maturity | 7 years (Original) |
| Interest Coupon | 6.25% pa (3-year Treasury Note minus 30 bps) |

---

*Index Amortization Features*

| | |
|---|---|
| Lock-out Period | 3 years (12 quarters) |
| Reference Index | 3-year CMT set 5 days prior to each quarter or interest rate payment date |
| Current Index Level | 6.375% pa |
| Amortization Table | The Principal Amount of the Note will increase in accordance with the table set out below. |

| Reference Index (% pa) | Amortization of Remaining Balance | Average Life (years) |
|---|---|---|
| 4.375 (current index level minus 200 bps) | 0 | 7 |
| 5.375 (current index level minus 100 bps) | 17 | 5 |
| 5.875 (current index level minus 50 bps) | 33 | 4 |
| 6.375 (current index or current index plus 100 bps or more) | 100 | 3 |

The change in amortization, in effect, creates positive convexity (rather than the negative convexity of traditional index amortizing formats) that can be structured in a manner consistent with the investor's specific requirements. The investor is effectively buying call options on the reference index. In the example, the call options are on the CMT rate. The lower coupon reflects the cost of this option purchased.

The primary motivation of reverse index amortization structures is the positive convexity acquired, reflecting the increasing average life as the reference index falls. This allows the structure to be utilized to hedge existing MBS investment portfolios that have negative convexity reflecting the prepayment risk in a falling interest rate environment.

### 5.2.5 Alternative Credit Issuers

Further enhancement of returns on index amortizing products can be achieved by altering the credit risk of the structure. This is achieved by substituting a lower rated issuer in the case of an IAN or altering the nature of the underlying floating rate investment in the case of an IAR swap.

The principle type of credit enhancement through the change of the credit risk on IAN transactions was through the introduction of corporate IANs. The basic features of the structure were identical to the generic features of index amortizing products.

The corporate issuance fell into two distinct categories: arbitrage funding by high-quality credits (who insulated the issuer from the prepayment risk with a matching IAR swap, as set out above) and issuers willing to assume the prepayment risk. The first type of transaction did not offer as great a level of additional return as the second class of transaction. The second group of issuers were prepared to take the prepayment risk as a form of economic interest rate hedge. The additional coupon constituted the effective cost of the hedge. The hedge served to reduce the issuer's average life of fixed-rate debt as rates declined allowing refinancing while extending to the agreed final maturity where rates rose effectively hedging the issuer from the impact of higher interest rates. This type of issuance tended to utilize the CMT rates as the reference index in order to reduce the effective cost of the hedge for the issuer.

For the issuer and the investor, index amortizing structures issued by corporations were analogous to callable bonds with a number of differences:

• When a note is called, in the case of a callable bond, the entire issue is redeemed whereas with a corporate IAN the bond principal is amortized gradually in most cases.
• The issuer has no discretion in relation to the repayment with the IAN.
• The linkage to a reference index may mean that there is imperfect correlation between the rate-driving amortization of the IAN and the issuer's refinancing rates (effectively, the credit spread).

An alternative means for enhancing the returns in an index amortizing product entails the use of term repurchase agreements or other higher yielding assets, such as asset-swapped securities, in combination with IAR swaps.

In the US, the use of government agencies as the issuer in IAN issues dictated that the investor was sacrificing return for the government credit risk of the transaction. Some investors utilized term repurchase agreements, for example, which provide higher returns than government debt to improve the return on the transaction.

### 5.3    Exotic Option Embedded Index Amortization Products

Structures incorporating exotic optionality have also evolved. The most common type of transaction is the knockout index amortization structures, which incorporates barrier options on the reference index.[11]

---

[11] For a discussion of barrier options, see Das, Satyajit (1996) *Exotic Options*; LBC Information Services, Sydney at Chapter 7.

In a normal index amortization product, the principal or notional principal amortizes as a function of changes in the prespecified index. In contrast, in a knockout index amortization structure, the amortization is also dependent on the level of the reference index attained on a specific date before the end of the lockout period (in effect the knockout date). If the index is below an agreed level (in effect the knockout strike level) on or by that date, then the principal will amortize in full after lock-out irrespective of future levels of the index. Amortization will follow the agreed schedule only where the index is at or above the outstrike level (the price that triggers the knockout feature of the transaction) before the knockout date.

The rationale for the knockout feature was demanded by investors who had an expectation that rates would remain low or decrease over the near future but were more uncertain about the path of interest rates beyond that time horizon.

The impact of using a barrier option effectively reduces the premium captured by the investor as the option sold may become inoperative where interest rates fall to below the knockout strike (the outstrike rate). **Exhibit 6.10** sets out an example of the price dynamics of the knockout index amortizing structure. The conventional index amortizing structure would have generated a return for the investor over the 2-year Treasury rate, but with the addition of a knockout feature the coupon received falls as the strike increases, approaching the 2-year swap rate reflecting the increasing likelihood of the transaction having an average life equal to the lock-out period.

---

**Exhibit 6.10**
**Knockout Index Amortization Note**
**Conventional Index Amortization Product**

*General*

| | |
|---|---|
| Issuer | AAA- or AA-rated institution |
| Amount | US$100 million |
| Maturity | 5 years (Original) |
| Interest Coupon | 5.50% pa |

*Index Amortization Features*

| | |
|---|---|
| Lock-out Period | 2 years (8 quarters) |
| Reference Index | 3-month LIBOR set 5 days prior to each quarter or interest rate payment date |
| Amortization Table | The principal amount of the Note will increase in accordance with the table set out below. |

| Reference Index (Current Index +/- bps) | Average Life (years) |
|:---:|:---:|
| -300 | 2 |
| -200 | 2 |
| -100 | 2 |
| 0 | 2 |
| +100 | 3 |
| +200 | 4 |
| +300 | 5 |
| +400 | 5 |

**Knockout Index Amortization Product**

All terms are the same as above except coupons that are contingent on the knockout level selected.

| Knockout Strike Level on 3 month LIBOR (% pa) | Coupon Level (% pa) |
|:---:|:---:|
| 3 | 5.50 |
| 4 | 5.20 |
| 5 | 4.80 |
| 6 | 4.40 |

## 6.  Market for Index Amortizing Products

The market for index amortizing products developed in an environment of low nominal interest rates and steep positively sloped yield curves in US$. The driving force behind the development of these instruments was the investor's desire for enhancement of yield. Index amortizing products competed with both physical securities, such as MBS investments and callable bonds,[12] and derivative-based structured notes, including capped and collared FRNs, reverse FRNs, arrears reset structures[13] and a range or accrual notes,[14] to provide investors with the required yield levels commensurate with the risk parameters specified.

The market evolved rapidly into one where investors were willing to assume prepayment risk through the sale of optionality viewed index amortizing

---

[12]  See Chapters 2 and 3.
[13]  See Chapter 4.
[14]  See Chapter 13.

products and MBS products as directly comparable investments. The dynamics of the market, consistent with this premise, revolved around the competing features of the two instruments and the relative value that could be extracted from either structure at any point in time.

The two instruments were broadly comparable and movements in pricing parameters such as interest rate volatility on LIBOR (which was an important element in the valuation of index amortizing structures) allowed investors to create the required investment, either through direct investment in MBS or indirectly through the index amortization product, at the highest possible return levels.

Examples of the relative performance characteristics of index amortizing products relative to comparable MBS securities (Collateralized Mortgage Obligations (CMOs), is summarized in **Exhibit 6.11**.

---

**Exhibit 6.11**
**Comparison of Return Characteristics of CMOs vs Index Amortization Notes**

An alternative means of comparing the relative performance of CMO and IAN investments is to directly compare market prices for comparable transactions from both investment classes.

The two investment types compared are:

- A portfolio of FNMA CMOs.
- A portfolio of IAN transactions with a 5-year final maturity and a 2-year lock-out period.

In comparing the two transactions, the following points should be noted:

- **Credit differentials** — the comparison is sensitive to the credit underlying the IAN (in effect, the issuer). In this case, an A-rated industrial or financial credit is utilized. Given that an A-rated issuer would normally fund at, say, LIBOR flat versus a government agency (FNMA) that would expect to fund at a lower cost (say, LIBOR minus 25 bps or more), the comparison must be adjusted for the credit differential as between the two transactions (that is, IAN returns should be reduced by around 25 bps).
- **Volatility assumption in CMO prepayment** — the comparison is based on utilizing the option-adjusted spread (OAS) of the CMOs. In the table below the OAS represents the spread over Treasury forward rates assuming a 12% volatility for short rates (a commonly utilized assumption in the MBS market). The over or underestimation of this

volatility may impact on the returns calculated. A higher volatility
would reduce the return for both CMOs and IANs. In practice, a higher
volatility may be appropriate for IAN and IAR Swaps reflecting the use
of LIBOR as the relevant amortization benchmark in contrast to CMOs
that are linked to mortgage refinancing rates.

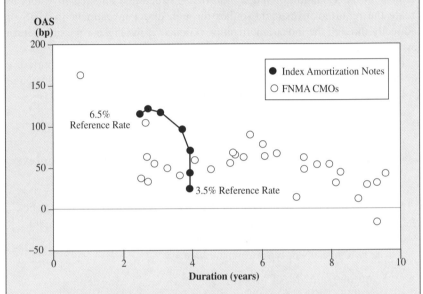

*Source:* McDermott, Scott and Huie, Marcus. "Index Amortization Swaps And
Notes." Goldman Sachs Fixed Income Research, New York, (February 1993): 10.

The emergence of index amortizing structures allows investors who traditionally
have not undertaken MBS investments to synthesize the prepayment risk profile
of such transactions without the need to assume the complex credit risks and
other features of direct MBS. These investors included both asset managers and
financial institutions.

The development of the product allowed increased utilization of this structure
by investors to also hedge prepayment risk in appropriate interest rate
environments, as well by liability managers to hedge interest rate risk. The later
applications, while not insignificant, have not been major factors in the market
for index amortizing products.

The initial market for index amortizing structures was in US$. The US
market continues to be the major component of the global market for these
products. However, the concept has been applied in other currency markets. In

these markets, the ability to synthetically create the prepayment risk profile of a MBS investment where a physical market for such securities is not available has been a factor in the use of such structures. However, the penetration of such products outside the US$ market has been modest.

Increasing applications of the concept of amortization of principal, with its inherent liquidity impact, where the prepayment profile is linked to a different underlying asset, has emerged. Transactions entailing amortization linked to exchange rates and commodity prices have emerged in the context of highly structured and customized risk management applications for corporations. An example of this type of transaction is set out in **Exhibit 6.12**. These cross-market hedges with their rich inter-relationships to underlying economic exposures and their management represent significant opportunities for the further logical development of the market in these types of instruments.

---

**Exhibit 6.12**
**Index Amortization Note Linked to Currency Movements**

Assume a US company is a major exporter with strong foreign sales (in yen). Growth in export sales has created increased working capital requirements that must be financed. The company seeks to borrow on a fixed-rate basis in US$ to take advantage of low US$ interest rates. However, it seeks protection from a higher US$/yen exchange rate that could reduce its export competitiveness and its foreign yen sales, thereby reducing its working capital funding requirement.

The company has two hedging options:
1. US$ interest rate swap that is callable.
2. Index amortization swap (IAS) where amortization is linked to the US$/yen rate.

Under the first option, the position is as follows:

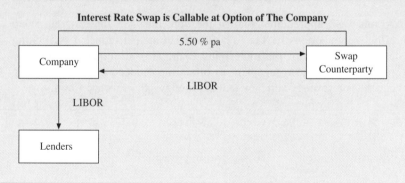

**Interest Rate Swap is Callable at Option of The Company**

The swap is for five years and can be terminated at any time. However, the company may be incurring additional cost (the premium for the option on the swap) that may not be required.

Under the second option, the position is as follows:

**IAS Swap Principal Amortizes Based on US$/yen Movements**

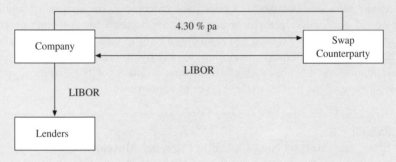

The IAS swap would link amortization of the principal amount of the swap to movements in the US$/yen in accordance with the following schedule:

| US$/Yen Spot Rate | Average Life of US$ Interest Rate Swap | Early Repayment Rate (as % of Original Notional Principal) |
|---|---|---|
| 140.55 | 2 | 100 |
| 128.33 | 3 | 11 |
| 118.41 | 4 | 5 |
| 110.00 | 5 | 0 |

As the US$ appreciates against the yen, the US$ interest rate swap effectively shortens its life (the notional principal reduces) facilitating early repayment of the underlying loan. This structure provides the required hedging arrangement to offset the reduced need for working capital as a stronger currency reduces foreign sales revenue flows.

## 7. Summary

Index amortizing products entail the design of notes or their off-balance sheet equivalent instruments, whereby the investor receives an enhanced return in return for accepting a prepayment risk that is linked to the performance of an interest rate index. In an environment of low and falling interest rates these structures have provided investors with significantly enhanced returns with the securities being amortized and prepaid. The economic logic of such transactions seeks to capture value from the forward interest rate curve that in a steeply positive yield curve environment is above the spot yield curve implying an increasing pattern of interest rates. Index amortizing instruments seek to derive value from these forward rates through the sale of options on these forward rates that are then used to enhance the yields on the investment.

# 7
# Currency-linked Structured Notes

## 1. Overview

Currency-linked notes are a class of structured notes that embody a specific linkage to foreign exchange values or currency rates. The linkage entails linking the value of coupon payments or principal repayments to an identified currency.

There are a number of types of currency-linked note structures:

- **Dual-currency structures** — these notes are a specific subset of currency-linked note structures entailing denominating the coupon of a security in a fixed income security in a currency *different* from that of the principal of that security.
- **Currency-linked structures** — these include a very wide range of note structures entailing engineering a specific currency derivative, either a forward or option, in the coupon or principal component of a conventional fixed interest security to create a specific exposure to currency movements.

In this chapter, the structures identified are analyzed in terms of their structural features, value dynamics for investors, pricing, and trading/hedging.[1] Currency-

---

[1] For a discussion of these structures, see Cunningham, Michael M. (1987) Selected Analysis of Recently Issued Index-Linked and Option Embedded Securities; unpublished research paper presented to course on Swap Financing, Centre for Studies in Money, Banking and Finance, Macquarie University; Das, Satyajit "Option Swaps: Securitising Options Embedded in Securities Issues" *Journal of International Securities Markets* (Summer 1988) 117-138; Das, Satyajit (1994) Swaps and Financial Derivatives; LBC Information Services, Sydney; McGraw-Hill, Chicago at Chapter 15; Koh, Kenny (1986) Option Or Forward Swap-related Financing Structures, unpublished research paper presented to course on Swap Financing, Centre for Studies in Money, Banking and Finance, Macquarie University.

linked notes that embed exotic options within the structure are also increasingly common. These structures are discussed in Chapter 12.

## 2.   Dual-currency Notes

### 2.1   Concept

A dual-currency bond involves an issue where the interest coupon is denominated in a different currency to the underlying principal of the bond. For example, a dual-currency US$/Swfr bond may be structured to have interest payable in Swiss francs and the principal in US$ or vice versa.

There are two basic structures:

- **Dual-currency bonds** — this is usually taken to be a bond where the bond is structured for, say, a yen investor, with an initial investment in yen, interest coupons in yen, and *a principal redemption in a foreign currency, say, US$.*
- **Reverse dual-currency bonds** — this is usually taken to be a bond where the bond is structured for a yen investor with an initial investment in yen, principal redemption in yen, and *interest coupons denominated in a foreign currency, say, A$.*

The fundamental difference between the two structures is the nature and extent of foreign exchange risk assumed within the structure. In a dual-currency bond, the currency risk is on the full principal value of the investment. In a reverse dual-currency bond, the currency risk is on the interest coupons only.[2]

### 2.2   Economics and Structure

The structure of a dual-currency note effectively combines the following elements:

- A fixed interest bond.
- A single or a series of currency forward contracts to convert the coupon flows into the desired currency.

An example of a dual-currency bond is set out in **Exhibit 7.1**. The example described is one of the earliest dual-currency bonds undertaken (around 1980 to 1985). The initial transactions were Swiss franc (Swfr) bonds where the

---

[2]   See Jones, W.R. (1987) Dual-currency Bonds; unpublished research paper presented to course on Capital Raising, Centre for Studies in Money, Banking and Finance, Macquarie University; Rosenberg, M.R. "The Pricing of Dual-currency Bonds" (November 1985) *Intermarket* 40-52; Crabbe, M. "Are Two Currencies Better Than One" (October 1985) *Euromoney* 206-207; Sender, H. "The Dual-currency Phenomenon" (April 1986) *Institutional Investor* 254-257.

redemption was in US$. These bonds typically were of long maturity (eight to 10 years) and carried coupons around 100 to 200 bps higher than comparable Swfr bonds. The US$ redemption structure was at an implied US$/Swfr rate of between 1.60 to 1.90 that compared to the US$1: Swfr 2.00 spot rate prevailing at the time of issue. The concept was quickly extended to yen bonds where the principal redemption was in US$. **Exhibit 7.1** sets out an example of such a ¥/US$ dual-currency bond.

---

**Exhibit 7.1**
**Dual-currency Note**

| | |
|---|---|
| Issuer | AA-rated financial institution |
| Term | 5 years |
| Principal Amount | ¥25,000 million |
| Coupon | 7.75% pa payable annually in yen |
| Redemption Amount | US$115.956 million (payable in US$) |

---

In the example, the investor makes a yen investment and receives yen coupons. The principal of the bond is redeemed in US$. The coupon on the dual-currency bond was around 100 to 150 bps above yields on comparable yen securities. The implied exchange rate on redemption was US$1: ¥215.60. This was below the prevailing spot rate that was around US$1: ¥235.

The instrument was targeted at a Japanese investor and has the following characteristics:

• The investor has *no currency exposure on the coupon payments of the note.* This reflects the fact that the note pays interest in yen.
• The investor receives a coupon that is *higher* than the comparable yen interest rate for a comparable investment.
• The investor has a *currency exposure on the principal amount of the investment.* This reflects the fact that the principal redemption is in US$ (a currency other than the home currency of the investor).

**Exhibit 7.2** on page 267 sets out the return profile of the investor under different currency (US$/¥) scenarios. The analysis illustrates the economic characteristics of the security:

• If the US$/¥ exchange rate at maturity is the same as the embedded redemption exchange rate, then the realized return to the investor is equivalent to the coupon rate of 7.75% pa.
• If the dual-currency note US$ principal is hedged back to yen through the entry into a forward contract to sell US$/purchase yen at the prevailing

forward rate at the time of entry into the transaction, then the investor return is around 6.28% pa. This is approximately equivalent to the yen return on a comparable *yen-denominated* conventional security with comparable characteristics reflecting the fact that it is, once the US$ principal amount is hedged into yen, economically a yen security.

- If the US$/¥ exchange rate remains at the level prevailing at the time of entry into the transaction, then the investor return is 9.38% pa.
- If the US$ depreciates over the life of the security vis-à-vis the yen at a rate of 5% pa, then the return to the investor is around 5.05% pa (representing a reduction in yield of around 120 bps against a yen investment).

The analysis of the performance of the security illustrates its economic nature. The additional yield from the dual-currency note structure is generated from the combination of the bond with a currency forward. In the above example, the additional return of around 100-150 bps is derived from the fact that the US$ is at a substantial discount relative to yen in the forward market, reflecting the higher interest rates in US$ relative to yen. The additional coupon represents the value of this discount that is captured by the investor and then amortised across the coupons of the bond. In addition, the embedded forward is *off market*; that is, an additional source of value. In effect, the investor is purchasing US$ forward at the embedded redemption exchange rate of ¥215.60. At the time of entry into this transaction the implied forward (based on interest rate differentials between the currencies) was around US$1:¥198-203. This means that the investor is purchasing US$ at an above-market rate. The extra payment can be used to enhance the coupon of the dual-currency bond itself.

The structure entails the investor having a position in the forward US$/¥ exchange rate. The position monetises the expectation that the forward rates *overestimate* the depreciation in the US$ relative to the yen. Given that the currency forwards are essentially a product of the prevailing interest rate differential, the dual-currency note entails two specific positions: firstly, on movements in the US$/¥ spot rate; and, secondly, in the interest rate differential. To the extent that the *actual spot* US$/¥ rates are *above* the implied forward rates, the investor will realise a higher economic return from the investment.

In effect, the dual-currency note structure is designed to engineer an exposure to the path of currency rates. This allows the investor seeking to monetize a view that the spot rates as at the relevant dates will actually prove to be different from that implied by the forward currency rate structure.

## Exhibit 7.2
## Economics of Dual-currency Note

The table below sets out the issue's cash flows together with the realized return to the investor under four US$/¥ exchange rate scenarios:

- The US$/¥ rate at maturity coincides with the embedded redemption exchange rate of US$1 = ¥15.60.
- The prevailing US$/¥ forward rates.
- The US$/¥ rate remains at the level at the time of issue of US$1 = ¥236.80.
- A steady depreciation of the US$/¥ exchange rate by 5% pa.

### Issue Cash Flows

| | Dual-currency Bond | | Case 1: Embedded Redemption Exchange Rate | | Case 2: Forward Exchange Rate | |
|---|---|---|---|---|---|---|
| Period (Years) | Principal & Interest (¥) | Principal Redemption (US$) | ¥/US$ Rate | Bond Cash Flows (¥) | ¥/US$ Rate | Bond Cash Flows (¥) |
| 0 | −25,000,000,000 | | | −25,000,000,000 | | −25,000,000,000 |
| 1 | 1,937,500,000 | | | 1,937,500,000 | | 1,937,500,000 |
| 2 | 1,937,500,000 | | | 1,937,500,000 | | 1,937,500,000 |
| 3 | 1,937,500,000 | | | 1,937,500,000 | | 1,937,500,000 |
| 4 | 1,937,500,000 | | | 1,937,500,000 | | 1,937,500,000 |
| 5 | 1,937,500,000 | 115,956,000 | 215.60 | 26,937,500,000 | 197.60 | 24,850,405,600 |
| | | | Realized ¥ Yield | 7.750% | Realized ¥ Yield | 6.28% |

| | Dual-currency Bond | | Case 3: Spot Exchange Rate at Commencement | | Case 4: 5% pa Depreciation in Exchange Rate | |
|---|---|---|---|---|---|---|
| Period (Years) | Principal & Interest (¥) | Principal Redemption (US$) | ¥/US$ Rate | Bond Cash Flows (¥) | ¥/US$ Rate | Bond Cash Flows (¥) |
| 0 | −25,000,000,000 | | | −25,000,000,000 | 236.8000 | −25,000,000,000 |
| 1 | 1,937,500,000 | | | 1,937,500,000 | 224.9600 | 1,937,500,000 |
| 2 | 1,937,500,000 | | | 1,937,500,000 | 213.7120 | 1,937,500,000 |
| 3 | 1,937,500,000 | | | 1,937,500,000 | 203.0264 | 1,937,500,000 |
| 4 | 1,937,500,000 | | | 1,937,500,000 | 192.8751 | 1,937,500,000 |
| 5 | 1,937,500,000 | 115,956,000 | 236.80 | 29,395,880,800 | 183.2313 | 23,184,271,638 |
| | | | Realized ¥ Yield | 9.38% | Realized ¥ Yield | 5.03% |

An example of a reverse dual-currency bond is set out in **Exhibit 7.3**. In this example, the principal of the bond is set in yen while the coupon of the bond is denominated in A$. The coupon on the bond is calculated as the yield applied to the A$ equivalent of the yen principal at the spot rate applicable at the start of the transaction.

---

**Exhibit 7.3**
**Dual-currency Note**

| | |
|---|---|
| Issuer | AA-rated financial institution |
| Term | 10 years |
| Principal Amount | ¥20,000 million |
| Coupon | 8.00% pa payable annually. |
| | The coupon is payable in A$ calculated on the A$ equivalent of the yen principal amount at the A$/¥ rate at the time of issue (assumed to be A$1 = ¥118) equal to A$169,491,525. This equates to an annual cash flow of A$13,559,322. |
| Redemption Amount | ¥20,000 million (payable in yen). |

---

The instrument that is targeted at a Japanese investor has the following characteristics:

• The investor has *no currency exposure on the principal face value of the note.* This reflects the fact that the note redeems in yen.
• The investor receives a coupon that is *higher* than the comparable yen interest rate for a comparable investment.
• The investor has a *currency exposure on the interest coupons.* This reflects the fact that the coupons are payable in A$ (a currency other than the home currency of the investor).

**Exhibit 7.4** sets out the return profile of the investor under different currency (A$/¥) scenarios. The analysis illustrates the economic characteristics of the security:

• If the A$/¥ exchange rate remains at the level prevailing at the start of the transaction, the realized return to the investor is equivalent to the coupon rate of 8% pa.
• If the dual-currency note A$ coupons are hedged back to yen through the entry into a series of forward contracts to sell A$/purchase yen, then the investor return is around 5.787% pa. This is approximately equivalent to the yen return on a comparable *yen-denominated* conventional security with

comparable characteristics reflecting the fact that it is, once the A$ coupons are hedged into yen, economically a yen security.

- If the A$ depreciates over the life of the security vis-à-vis the yen at a rate of 5% pa, then the return to the investor is around 6.392% pa (representing additional yield of around 51 bps against a yen investment).

---

**Exhibit 7.4**
**Economics of Dual-currency Note**

The table below sets out the issue cash flows together with the realized return to the investor under three A$/¥ exchange rate scenarios:

- The A$/¥ rate remains at the level at the time of issue of A$1 = ¥118;
- The prevailing A$/¥ forward rates.
- A steady depreciation of the A$/¥ exchange rate by 5% pa.

| | Bond Cash Flows | | Realized Return to Investors | | Realized Return to Investors | | Realized Return to Investors | |
|---|---|---|---|---|---|---|---|---|
| | | | Case 1: Steady Currency | | Case 2: Forward Currency Rates | | Case 3: 5% Depreciation | |
| (Period Years) | Principal ¥ | Interest A$ | ¥/A$ Rate | Bond Cash Flows (in ¥) | ¥/A$ Rate | Bond Cash Flows (in ¥) | ¥/A$ Rate | Bond Cash Flows (in ¥) |
| 0 | −20,000,000,000 | | 118.00 | −20,000,000,000 | 118.00 | −20,000,000,000 | 118.0000 | −20,000,000,000 |
| 1 | | 13,559,322 | 118.00 | 1,600,000,000 | 109.35 | 1,482,730,506 | 112.1000 | 1,520,000,000 |
| 2 | | 13,559,322 | 118.00 | 1,600,000,000 | 101.55 | 1,376,936,365 | 106.4950 | 1,444,000,000 |
| 3 | | 13,559,322 | 118.00 | 1,600,000,000 | 94.23 | 1,277,681,719 | 101.1703 | 1,371,800,000 |
| 4 | | 13,559,322 | 118.00 | 1,600,000,000 | 86.94 | 1,178,804,337 | 96.1117 | 1,303,210,000 |
| 5 | | 13,559,322 | 118.00 | 1,600,000,000 | 81.27 | 1,178,804,337 | 91.3062 | 1,303,210,000 |
| 6 | | 13,559,322 | 118.00 | 1,600,000,000 | 75.85 | 1,101,984,082 | 86.7408 | 1,238,049,500 |
| 7 | | 13,559,322 | 118.00 | 1,600,000,000 | 70.84 | 1,028,539,295 | 82.4038 | 1,176,147,025 |
| 8 | | 13,559,322 | 118.00 | 1,600,000,000 | 65.48 | 960,483,943 | 78.2836 | 1,117,339,674 |
| 9 | | 13,559,322 | 118.00 | 1,600,000,000 | 60.89 | 887,826,856 | 74.3694 | 1,061,472,690 |
| 10 | 20,000,000,000 | 13,559,322 | 118.00 | 21,600,000,000 | 56.39 | 20,764,671,668 | 70.6510 | 20,957,979,103 |
| | | | Realized ¥ Yield | 8.000% | | 5.787% | | 6.392% |

---

The analysis of the performance of the security illustrates its economic nature. The additional yield from the dual-currency note structure is generated from the combination of the bond with the currency forwards. In the above example, the additional of around 221 bps is derived from the fact that the A$ is at a substantial discount relative to yen in the forward market reflecting the higher interest rates in A$ relative to yen. The additional coupon represents the value of this discount that is captured by the investor and then amortized across the coupons of the bond.

The structure entails the investor having a position in the forward A\$/¥ exchange rate. The position monetises the expectation that the forward rates *overestimate* the depreciation in the A\$ relative to the yen. Given that the currency forwards are essentially a product of the prevailing interest rate differential, the dual-currency note entails two specific positions: firstly, on movements in the A\$ spot rate; and, secondly, in the interest rate differential. To the extent that the *actual spot* A\$/¥ rates are *above* the implied forward rates, the investor will realize a higher economic return from the investment.

In effect, the dual-currency note structure is designed to engineer an exposure to the path of currency rates where the investor is seeking to monetise the view that the spot rates as at the relevant dates will actually prove to be different from that implied by the forward currency rate structure. This is not substantially different from the positions in respect of the forward interest rate curve embedded in a number of the interest rate-linked note structures discussed in Chapters 4 and 5.

### 2.3   Pricing, Trading, and Hedging Dual-currency Notes

The creation of a dual-currency note structure requires both the engineering of the currency exposure for the investor and the immunization of the issuer from that exposure. The issuer will generally seek to enter into a series of derivative transactions that eliminates the specific currency exposure and provides a guaranteed rate of funding. The structure of the derivative transactions against a dual-currency issue entails a number of separate steps usually involving separate currency or interest rate swaps and a series of currency forward or LTFX[3] contracts.

For example, for the yen/US\$ dual-currency issue (coupons denominated in yen and principal in US\$), the issuer would enter into a LTFX contract to hedge the US\$ to yen create a synthetic yen liability that could then be swapped into floating rate US\$ through a currency swap. In the case of a reverse dual-currency bond issue (A\$ coupon and yen principal), the derivative structure would include a series of A\$/¥ LTFX contracts to hedge the A\$ coupons to yen to create a yen liability that would then be swapped into floating rate US\$ through a currency swap.

**Exhibit 7.5** sets out the mechanics of hedging the ¥/US\$ dual-currency bond issue. **Exhibit 7.6** on page 272 sets out the mechanics of hedging the ¥/A\$ reverse dual-currency bond issue.

---

[3]   LTFX equates to Long Term Foreign Exchange and is sometimes used in connection with forward foreign exchange contracts with longer maturates (say, beyond 1 year).

**Exhibit 7.5**
**Hedging a Dual-currency Note Transaction**

Assume Bank B is asked to price a ¥/US$ dual-currency swap in connection with the following issue:

| | |
|---|---|
| Issuer | AA-rated financial institution |
| Term | 5 years |
| Principal Amount | ¥25,000 million |
| Coupon | 7.75% pa payable annually in yen |
| Redemption Amount | US$115.956 million (payable in US$) |

The issuer of the bond wishes to be completely immunized from the dual-currency characteristics of the transaction, seeking to use it as a basis for generating sub-LIBOR US$ floating rate funding. B enters into a structured currency swap whereby the issuer:

- At closing, pays the ¥25 billion proceeds to B in return for receiving the equivalent amount of US$105,529,759 (based on a spot exchange rate of US$1 = ¥236.90).
- Over the life of the transaction, A pays US$ 6-month LIBOR minus a margin (see below) semi-annually in return for receiving ¥1,937,500,000 being the exact yen coupon due to the bond-holders thereby eliminating any currency exposure.
- At maturity the initial exchange is reversed with the issuer paying US$105,529,759 to B in return for receiving US$115,956,000 covering the redemption of the dual-currency issue. In practice, there would only be a net settlement on this part of the transaction.

In order to hedge its exposure under the transaction with the issuer, B will enter into two sets of transactions:

- A US$/¥ LTFX contract selling US$115,956,000/buying the equivalent yen for value in year 5 matching the maturity of the dual-currency bond issue. This transaction is undertaken at the prevailing US$/¥ forward rate of US$1: ¥197.60.
- A conventional yen fixed US$ floating LIBOR swap under which it receives yen at the market rate of 7.00% pa and pays US$ 6-month LIBOR minus margin.

The LTFX contract creates a synthetic yen liability at 6.28% pa as set out in table below.

| Period (years) | Principal & Interest (¥) | Principal Redemption (US$) | ¥/US$ Rate | Bond Cash Flows (¥) |
|---|---|---|---|---|
| 0 | −25,000,000,000 | | | −25,000,000,000 |
| 1 | 1,937,500,000 | | | 1,937,500,000 |
| 2 | 1,937,500,000 | | | 1,937,500,000 |
| 3 | 1,937,500,000 | | | 1,937,500,000 |
| 4 | 1,937,500,000 | | | 1,937,500,000 |
| 5 | 1,937,500,000 | 115,956,000 | 197.60 | 24,850,405,600 |
| | | | Realized ¥ | |
| | | | Yield | 6.28% |

The transaction has the effect of creating a sub-LIBOR funding for the issuer at US$ LIBOR minus 79 bps pa (assuming the full benefit is passed on to the issuer). This is calculated as follows:

B receives        Yen at 7.00% pa annual
B pays            Yen at 6.28% pa annual
Yen Surplus       Yen 72 bps pa

The yen surplus of 72 bps pa translates into 79 bps pa in US$. This is based on a currency conversion factor whereby ¥1 bps is equal to US$1.1 bps.[4]

**Exhibit 7.6**
**Hedging Reverse Dual-currency Note Transaction**

Assume Bank B is asked to price a ¥/A$ dual-currency swap in connection with the following issue:

Issuer            AA-rated financial institution
Term              10 years
Principal Amount  ¥20,000 million
Coupon            8.00% pa payable annually.
                  The coupon is payable in A$ calculated on the A$ equivalent of the yen principal amount at the A$/yen rate at the time of issue (assumed to be A$1: ¥118) equal to A$169,491,525. This equates to an annual cash flow of A$13,559,322.

---

[4]  For details of the calculation of currency conversion factors (also known as foreign exchange basis points) see Das, Satyajit (1994) *Swaps And Financial Derivatives*; LBC Information, Sydney; McGraw-Hill, Chicago at 179-183.

Redemption Amount    ¥20,000 million (payable in yen).

The issuer of the bond wishes to be completely immunized from the dual-currency characteristics of the transaction, seeking to use it as a basis for generating sub-LIBOR US$ floating rate funding. B enters into a structured currency swap whereby the issuer:

- At closing, pays the ¥20 billion proceeds to B in return for receiving the equivalent amount of US$129,728,814 (based on a spot exchange rate of US$1: ¥154.17).
- Over the life of the transaction, A pays US$ 6-month LIBOR minus a margin (say 20 bps pa) semi-annually in return for receiving A$13,559,322 being the exact A$ coupon due to the bond holders thereby eliminating any currency exposure.
- At maturity the initial exchange is reversed with the issuer paying US$129,728,814 to B in return for receiving ¥20 billion covering the redemption of the dual-currency issue.

In order to hedge its exposure under the transaction with the issuer, B will enter into two sets of transactions:
- A conventional yen-fixed US$ floating LIBOR swap under which it receives yen at the market rate of 5.78% pa and pays US$ 6-month LIBOR minus 20 bps.
- A series of A$/¥ LTFX contracts selling ¥1,156 million/buying the equivalent A$.

The structure of the hedge and the detailed cash flows from the viewpoint of B are summarized below in the table.

| Years | Swap Payments | | Swap Receipts | ¥/US$ Swap Receive ¥ at 5.780% pa | Pay US$ LIBOR | Net Flows ¥ | A$ |
|---|---|---|---|---|---|---|---|
| 0 | ¥ | 20,000,000,000 | US$ −129,728,814 | −20,000,000,000 | 129,728,814 | | |
| 1 | A$ | −13,559,322 | US$ LIBOR — Margin | 1,156,000,000 | (LIBOR — Margin) | 1,156,000,000 | −13,559,322 |
| 2 | A$ | −13,559,322 | US$ LIBOR — Margin | 1,156,000,000 | (LIBOR — Margin) | 1,156,000,000 | −13,559,322 |
| 3 | A$ | −13,559,322 | US$ LIBOR — Margin | 1,156,000,000 | (LIBOR — Margin) | 1,156,000,000 | −13,559,322 |
| 4 | A$ | −13,559,322 | US$ LIBOR — Margin | 1,156,000,000 | (LIBOR — Margin) | 1,156,000,000 | −13,559,322 |
| 5 | A$ | −13,559,322 | US$ LIBOR — Margin | 1,156,000,000 | (LIBOR — Margin) | 1,156,000,000 | −13,559,322 |
| 6 | A$ | −13,559,322 | US$ LIBOR — Margin | 1,156,000,000 | (LIBOR — Margin) | 1,156,000,000 | −13,559,322 |
| 7 | A$ | −13,559,322 | US$ LIBOR — Margin | 1,156,000,000 | (LIBOR — Margin) | 1,156,000,000 | −13,559,322 |
| 8 | A$ | −13,559,322 | US$ LIBOR — Margin | 1,156,000,000 | (LIBOR — Margin) | 1,156,000,000 | −13,559,322 |
| 9 | A$ | −13,559,322 | US$ LIBOR — Margin | 1,156,000,000 | (LIBOR — Margin) | 1,156,000,000 | −13,559,322 |
| 10 | A$ | −13,559,322 | US$ LIBOR — Margin | 1,156,000,000 | (LIBOR — Margin) | 1,156,000,000 | −13,559,322 |
| | ¥ | −20,000,000,000 | US$ 129,728,814 | 20,000,000,000 | −129,728,814 | | |

| Years | Net Flows ¥ | Net Flows A$ | Zero-coupon Interest Rates ¥ | Zero-coupon Interest Rates A$ | LTFX Rates (A$:Yen) | Net Cash Flow A$ | Present Value A$ |
|---|---|---|---|---|---|---|---|
| 0 | | | | | 118.0000 | | |
| 1 | 1,156,000,000 | −13,559,322 | 6.840% | 15.290% | 109.3514 | −2,987,896 | −2,591,635 |
| 2 | 1,156,000,000 | −13,559,322 | 6.720% | 15.040% | 101.5491 | −2,175,661 | −1,643,969 |
| 3 | 1,156,000,000 | −13,559,322 | 6.590% | 14.890% | 94.2290 | −1,291,340 | −851,518 |
| 4 | 1,156,000,000 | −13,559,322 | 6.340% | 14.780% | 86.9368 | −262,309 | −151,129 |
| 5 | 1,156,000,000 | −13,559,322 | 6.290% | 14.520% | 81.2713 | 664,637 | 337,425 |
| 6 | 1,156,000,000 | −13,559,322 | 6.250% | 14.370% | 75.8548 | 1,680,325 | 750,794 |
| 7 | 1,156,000,000 | −13,559,322 | 6.180% | 14.210% | 70.8357 | 2,760,135 | 1,088,934 |
| 8 | 1,156,000,000 | −13,559,322 | 6.020% | 14.120% | 65.4772 | 4,095,670 | 1,423,741 |
| 9 | 1,156,000,000 | −13,559,322 | 5.910% | 13.990% | 60.8855 | 5,427,134 | 1,670,205 |
| 10 | 1,156,000,000 | −13,559,322 | 5.840% | 13.950% | 56.3945 | 6,939,118 | 1,880,014 |
| | | | | | | Net Cash Flow | 1,912,861 |

The ¥/US$ currency swap (which matches the US$ floating cash flows) leaves B with net cash flows where it is long yen (¥1,156.0 million) and short A$ (A$13,559,322) on each bond coupon date. The LTFX contracts are designed to cover this exposure. The LTFX contracts result in a distinctive pattern of cash flows. B is short A$ in the early years (reflecting the fact that the yen surplus does not at the relevant LTFX rate cover the A$ outflow) and long A$ in later years (reflecting the falling A$/¥ LTFX rates that result from the interest rate differential between A$ and yen). In essence, B has to fund this shortfall in the early years and recover the shortfall together with the funding cost from the surplus in late years. Based on the assumed zero-coupon interest rates, B generates a profit (on a PV basis) of A$1,912,861 from this transaction. This profit is additional to any earning generated by B from the ¥/US$ swap on the LTFX contracts (presumably, the bid-offer) or the dual-currency issue itself.

*Source:* This example draws on Maxwell G. W. Morley. "Swapping An Australian Dollar/Yen Dual-currency Bond Issue" in Satyajit Das (editor). *The Global Swap Market.* IFR Publishing, London, 1991.

The dual-currency bond swap layers a complex initial transaction with a series of foreign exchange and swap transactions basically designed to generate, at least initially, cost-effective floating rate US$ funding.

## 2.4   Market for Dual-currency Notes

The market for dual-currency notes has evolved significantly over the period since inception. The earliest transactions, undertaken in the 1970s, were designed to allow investors, particularly in Europe, to take positions in currency markets that would otherwise have been difficult for these investors to assume. The concept has been applied sporadically since that time but has been expanded to encompass a broader range of applications:

- **Regulatory arbitrage** — the fact that the dual-currency bond can be decomposed into a zero-coupon bond and an annuity bond (in different currencies) can be utilized to arbitrage tax rules in certain jurisdictions.
- **Income vs capital distinction** — the structure can also be used be overcome income capital distinctions. The Japanese investor targeted dual-currency transactions are often predicated on specific regulatory issues. Under Japanese insurance laws, Japanese life insurers are only allowed to distribute dividends/bonuses from the income on investments. Realized capital gains or losses, as well as foreign exchange gains or losses, are charged to reserves and capital accounts. These items were excluded from any calculation of income out of which distribution could be made. This dictated that the insurers sought to increase yield or income on the portfolios to allow higher rates of distribution. The dual-currency structures are consistent with this objective. Higher income is received over the life of the investment. The expected loss embedded in the structure (for example, in a dual-currency structure from the embedded redemption exchange rate) economically offsets this higher early income but may be classified as a foreign exchange or capital item and therefore not included in the determination of income available for distribution.
- **Higher yield** — the structure has been utilized to generate higher yielding securities with limited currency exposure. In the case of a dual-currency structure, the exposure is on the redemption face value but not on the coupons. In a reverse dual-currency structure the currency exposure is only in relation to the coupons with the principal amount being protected.
- **Forward currency rate monetization** — use of dual-currency structures to monetize expectations in relation to the forward currency rate curve.

The major emphasis in relation to dual-currency notes in recent times has been the second and third objectives outlined above, although the other objectives are also relevant. Examples of recent dual-currency issues are set out in **Exhibit 7.7**. These transactions were aimed primarily at Japanese investors seeking additional yield and prepared to trade off currency risk on the coupons in return for that additional yield[5]. In more recent time, there has been increasing interest in dual-currency structures from European investors.[6]

---

[5] "Yen moves Unsettle Yield Hunters" (June 1997) *Risk* 35.

[6] See Mahtani, Arun "Dual-currency Bonds Provoke Derivative Headache" (June 27, 1998) *International Financing Review* Issue 1239 114.

**Exhibit 7.7**
**Dual-currency Notes**

*DM/¥ Reverse Dual-currency Note*

| | |
|---|---|
| Issuer | AA-rated borrower |
| Amount | ¥100 billion |
| Maturity | 10 years |
| Coupon | 4.45% pa payable in DM |
| Redemption Amount: | ¥100 billion |

*A$/¥ Dual-currency Note*

| | |
|---|---|
| Issuer | AA-rated borrower |
| Amount | ¥10 billion |
| Maturity | 4 years |
| Coupon | 6.20% pa payable in yen |
| Redemption Amount | A$108.932 million (fixed redemption exchange rate of A$1:¥91.80) |

*A$/¥ Reverse Dual-currency Note*

| | |
|---|---|
| Issuer | AA-rated borrower |
| Amount | ¥50 billion |
| Maturity | 2 years |
| Coupon | 5.90% payable in A$ |
| Redemption Amount | ¥50 billion |

*Lira/US$ Reverse Dual-currency Note*

| | |
|---|---|
| Issuer | AA-rated borrower |
| Amount | US$100 million |
| Lira Notional Amount | The equivalent of the US$ Notional Amount at the Lira/US$ exchange rate. |
| Issue Price | 100% |
| Maturity | 10 years |
| Coupon | 7.85% pa payable in Italian lira of the Lira Notional Amount on an annual basis calculated on a bond basis. |
| Redemption Amount | US$100 million |
| Lira/US$ Exchange Rate | The exchange rate on the date the transaction is undertaken Lira1678:US$1. |

As opportunities for yield enhancement from dual-currency structures diminished, a number of alternative structures have evolved.[7] These include:

- **Callable reverse dual-currency structures** — this structure combines a dual-currency bond with embedded interest rate optionality through incorporation of a call option. **Exhibit 7.8** sets out an example of this structure. In the first case an European option is incorporated. In the second case, a Bermudan call option is embedded. In both cases, the investor has sold an option in exchange for a higher coupon. The coupons on these structures provided between 5 and 10 bps additional yield over and above a normal dual-currency structure to the investor. The enhanced yield is in exchange for the call risk assumed by the investor. The call risk under these types of structures is a mixture of currency and interest rate risk. The call may be triggered by changes in interest rate and/or currency rates. If early redemption occurs, then the investor forgoes future coupons denominated in foreign currency. From the viewpoint of a yen-based investor (the example assumes a yen-based investor), this may represent an acceptable risk. This is because the redemption would provide the investor with yen proceeds that could then be reinvested in yen assets. The issuer in these issues is fully hedged through a swap entered into with the arranger. The structure creates significant hedging risks. The hedging of these long-dated options is problematic. This is particularly the case with the structures that incorporate a Bermudan option. Typically, the arranger would seek to enter into a long-dated Bermudan currency option with a derivative dealer. The market for such options is illiquid. Often, the structures are hedged with shorter dated options leaving the trader with a volatility spread position. The linkage of currency and interest rate risk creates additional complexity because of the need to incorporate the correlation between the two in pricing and hedging the structure.
- **Variable-currency coupon or dual-currency bonds with embedded currency options** — this structure entails a dual-currency structure with embedded optionality. The issuer in these structures is allowed to select the coupon currency. The applicable rate is set at the time of issue. The selection is usually between two or more currencies. Examples of this structure are set out in **Exhibit 7.9**. The structure embeds an exchange or best-of option[8] within the note allowing the issuer to pay the coupon that has the lowest value at the time of payment. The investor in this case is selling a series of

---

[7]   See "Structured Derivatives As An Investment Vehicle" (September 1995) *Asiamoney* 52-55.

[8]   These are particular types of exotic options; refer to Das, Satyajit (1996) *Exotic Options*; LBC Information Services at Chapter 8.

*options on the currency pair or pairs* with the premium received being used to enhance the yield on the security. The option sold is contingent both on currency value *and* the embedded interest rate in the relevant currency. The issuer would typically on-sell the option and immunize itself from any exposure to the option payoffs.

---

**Exhibit 7.8**
**Callable Reverse Dual-currency Note**

*Transaction 1 — European Call*

| | |
|---|---|
| Issuer | AAA-rated financial institution |
| Amount | ¥10 billion |
| Maturity | 10 years |
| Redemption Amount | ¥10 billion |
| Coupon | A fixed amount of DM5,590,900 (calculated as 3.43% pa based on a DM principal amount of DM163 million). |
| Call Option | The issuer has the right to call the note with 21 days' notice on the coupon date at year 2. |

*Transaction 2 — Bermudan Call*

| | |
|---|---|
| Issuer | AAA-rated financial institution |
| Amount | ¥10 billion |
| Maturity | 10 years |
| Redemption Amount | ¥10 billion |
| Coupon | A fixed amount of DM5,590,900 (calculated as 3.43% pa based on a DM principal amount of DM163 million). |
| Call Option | The issuer has the right to call the note with 21 days, notice on any coupon date after year 2. |

---

**Exhibit 7.9**
**Dual-currency Note with Embedded Currency Options**

*Transaction 1*

| | |
|---|---|
| Issuer | AAA-rated financial institution |
| Amount | ¥10 billion |
| Maturity | 10 years |

| | |
|---|---|
| Redemption Amount | ¥10 billion |
| Coupon | On each interest payments date, the Issuer has the option of paying:<br>1. A fixed amount of ¥343 million (equivalent to 3.43% pa); or<br>2. A fixed amount of DM5,590,900 (calculated as 3.43% pa based on a DM principal amount of DM163 million. |
| *Transaction 2* | |
| Issuer | AA-rated financial institutions |
| Amount | ¥10 billion |
| Maturity | 10 years |
| Issue Price | 100.50 |
| Redemption Amount | ¥10 billion |
| Coupon: | On each interest payments date, the Issuer has the option of paying:<br>1. In A$ at a rate of 5.86% pa calculated on a specified A$ principal; or<br>2. In DM at a rate of 5.31% pa calculated on a specified DM principal; or<br>3. In US$ at a rate of 6.61% pa calculated on a specified US$ principal.[9] |

## 3. Currency-linked Notes

### 3.1 Overview

Dual-currency notes represent a special subset of currency-linked instruments. The currency-linked note structure represents a broader range of instruments that are characterized by the (now familiar) creation of a linkage between the coupon and/or the principal of the note with a nominated exchange rate. The mechanics of that linkage are the same as those identified previously in connection with interest rate-linked notes. However, there are some distinguishing features of the market for currency-linked securities.

The major distinguishing feature is the nature of the underlying debt utilized. Currency-linked structures exist in a wide variety of formats including:

---

[9] The specified principal in each of the currencies is calculated as the spot value of the relevant currency against yen based on the spot rate as at the date of issue.

- Conventional fixed and floating securities.
- Syndicated loans.
- Off balance sheet pure derivative formats combined with underlying funding.

In addition to the standard format of structured notes, increasingly syndicated loan transactions with embedded currency positions have been used. These have often been structured as off-balance format, as well as embedded in the loan. This type of transaction typically took the following form:

- The borrower arranged a fixed-rate financing for a term of, say, five years.
- Simultaneously, the borrower would enter into a swap with a counterparty whereby the borrower would agree to receive a fixed rate in the currency of the financing (say, US$) and pay a floating rate in its selected currency (say, yen) at a rate of, say, yen LIBOR minus a margin per annum.
- Typically, following the first interest period at every interest rate reset date, the counterparty has the right to receive interest at *either* yen LIBOR minus, say, 50 bps or US$ LIBOR minus 50 bps.

The counterparty has a one-time election to switch its interest receipts to US$ LIBOR. In the event that the counterparty elects to exercise this option, then it would be forced to receive US$ LIBOR for the remaining term of the swap. It is not able to switch from yen to US$ and reverse the selection during the life of the loan.

This structure effectively embeds a yen put/US$ call option into the currency swap. The borrower has written the yen put/US$ call. In the event that the yen declines in value relative to the US$, the swap counterparty will make an election under its swap to receive US$ thereby crystallising the foreign exchange gain. The premium due to the borrower for creating this option is embedded into the swap structure by way of a lower margin under the relevant floating-rate indexes.

A particular feature of this type of arrangement is that the option is very complex, reflecting the fact that the amounts in both currencies are dependent on the relevant interest rates in yen and US$. In essence, it is an option on an uncertain amount (often referred to as a quanto) and poses hedging problems similar to those identified in the context of index differential swaps.[10]

The off-balance-sheet structure is almost identical to the loan with this structure embedded in the format for interest payments.

A number of variations on this type of structure exist, including arrangements whereby the swap counterparty has an independent and separate election as to the currency of its receipt *as at each interest rate reset date*. This merely means that the borrower is creating a series as distinct from a single option. In another

---

[10]  See Chapter 13.

variation, the borrower may grant the swap counterparty a "one-off" option to switch as at specified time during the life of the transaction, such as the first interest rate reset period (which is analogous to an option on a currency swap).

An interesting aspect of these transactions is the fact that the motivation for this class of transactions was *issuer-driven* rather than investor-driven (as is the case with structured note format). The issuer motivations included:

- Lowering borrowing cost through increase in foreign exchange risk.
- Structures utilized to exploit to the natural currency portfolio positions with known cash inflows or outflows in the relevant currencies entailing monetization of the expectations regarding future currency movements.

In the remainder of this chapter, the focus is on the conventional structured note with engineered linkages of interest coupon or principal to currency movements.

The initial focus is on a series of transactions from the mid-1980s that introduced this type of security in capital markets. The transactions, while dated, are nevertheless useful examples of the key dynamics of structuring and value applicable in relation to these securities. It is fair to say these transactions created the basic template that all currency-linked securities subsequently have largely followed. Subsequently, the focus is on more recent transactions that highlight the modern structure of currency-linked notes.

## 3.2 Indexed Currency Option Notes

In 1985, an issue of indexed currency option notes (ICONs) saw for the first time the combination of a conventional fixed-rate debt issue with a currency option.[11] The ICON structure is very similar, conceptually, to and, in fact, predated the interest rate-linked structures described in Chapter 4.

The initial issue, for the Long Term Credit Bank of Japan, entailed the issuer paying the investor a higher than usual coupon, in return for which the investor creates what is effectively a currency option. The investor, in that case, granted a European-style 10-year US$ put/¥ call option with a strike price of ¥169.

The redemption structure of the ICON effectively simulated the characteristics of a call option on yen (a put option on US$ relative to yen). The investor (the grantor of the option) suffered a loss as the yen strengthens relative to the US$ and conversely the purchaser gaining. The currency option was implicit in the redemption terms of the issue whereby notes were to be redeemed at par (100) if the yen and US$ rate were equal to ¥169 or more at maturity. If

---

[11] See French, Martin "Bowing Before The ICON" (December 1985) *Euromoney* 85-87; Rosenberg, M.R. "Dual-currency yen Redemption Bonds: Combining The Features of 'Heaven And Hell' (ICON) Bonds with Traditional Dual-currency Bonds" (February 24, 1986) Merrill Lynch Currency & Bond Market Trends vol. 2 no. 7 1-3.

the US$ was below ¥169 at maturity, then the redemption amount received by the investor was reduced on a sliding discount from par. Analytically, the investor had granted a foreign currency option in exchange for the higher coupon on the transaction (approximately 55 to 65 bps pa) that represented the option premium.

The net result of the transaction is that the issuer, Long Term Credit Bank of Japan, had purchased a 10-year European put option on the US$ against the yen with the strike price of US$1/¥169 from the investors in the security. Given that it was interested in securitising the option and using the proceeds from the sale to reduce its borrowing costs, the issuer is likely to sell the option position to a financial intermediary, such as the originator of the transaction. The purchaser will compensate the issuer for the option either in the form of an up-front payment or, usually, through an annuity payment that will be designed to lower the all-in funding costs of the issuer. This will usually be built into the accompanying swap for the transaction.

The financial intermediary purchasing the option has a number of alternatives to securitize this currency option:

- The intermediary can, in turn, sell this currency option.
- Given that the market for long-dated currency options was limited at the time the issue was undertaken, as an alternative to selling the option on identical terms, the intermediary could write short-term US$ put options against the yen and roll the position at maturity of each series of options. In this case, while the high level of premium for short-term options may allow the financial intermediary to recover the price it pays for the option in a relatively short time, there would be significant cash flow mismatches. This suggests that it may not be able to ensure a profit from the transaction and, in fact, it may even incur a loss if exchange rates move substantially against it, given that it cannot effectively exercise the currency option securitized through the ICON issue.
- Alternatively, the financial intermediary can utilize the US$ put option position as part of the hedge for a straight Euro yen debt issue for a counterparty who wants US$ funding.

The final structure noted proved the most attractive means of securitizing the option. This structure is set out, in the case of the ICON issue, in **Exhibit 7.10**.

**Exhibit 7.10**
**Indexed Currency Option Note (ICON)**

*Issue Structure*

The ICON issue was lead-managed by Bankers Trust (BT) for the Long Term Credit Bank of Japan (LTCB). The issue was for US$120 million for 10 years with a coupon of 11.50% pa.

The redemption value was calculated according to the following formula if the yen strengthened beyond ¥169/US$1:

$$R = US\$120,000,000[1-((169-S)/S)]$$
Where
R = Redemption value in US$
S = ¥/US$ spot exchange rate on November 21, 1995

If the ¥/US$ exchange rate was weaker than ¥169/US$1, investors would receive the face value of the notes.

*Derivatives Hedge*

Under the terms of the accompanying US$ interest rate swap, LTCB achieved an all-in cost of approximately LIBOR minus 40-45 bps pa. The swap structure effectively securitizes the currency option. BT purchases this US$ put option against the yen on US$120 million at a strike price of ¥169/US$1.

To securitize the option position:
• BT arranged either directly or indirectly for a yen issue at 6.65% pa for 10 years for ¥24,240 million.
• BT exchanged the issue proceeds for US$120 million on the spot market.
• BT hedged the interest commitments forward leaving the capital redemption unhedged and charged the counterparty 10.70% pa for the US$120 million loan.

*Transaction Economics*

The profits dynamics of the transaction are as follows:
    Assumptions:

• 10-year US Treasury bond rate is 10.50% pa.
• Yen risk-free rate (the 10-year Japanese government bond) is 6.50% pa.
• ¥/US$ spot exchange rate as at November 1985 was ¥202/US$1.

- Forward exchange rates were:
  - 1 year forward      ¥194.6878/US$1
  - 2 year forward      ¥187.64/US$1
  - 3 year forward      ¥180.8476/US$1
  - 4 year forward      ¥174.3013/US$1
  - 5 year forward      ¥167.9918/US$1
  - 6 year forward      ¥161.911/US$1
  - 7 year forward      ¥156.05/US$1
  - 8 year forward      ¥150.401/US$1
  - 9 year forward      ¥144.956/US$1
  - 10 year forward     ¥139.956/US$1

At maturity, the worst case exchange rate BT had to repay its yen commitment was ¥169/US$1. Therefore the shortfall in the amount of yen on that date in the worst case was: ¥24,240,000,000 − ¥20,280,000,000 = ¥3,960,000,000. This shortfall translate into an annual payment of ¥293,454,573. Therefore, BT had to hedge the interest payment of: ¥1,611,960,000 + ¥293,454,573 = ¥1,905,414,573 forward annually.

Cash flows from the ¥24,240 million debt issue were as follows:

| Year | Yen Interest Commitment (¥) | Annuity for Capital Redemption (¥) | US$ Amount to Hedge Cash Flows (US$) | Counterparty Interest Payments (US$) | BT's Profits (US$) |
|------|------|------|------|------|------|
| 0 | 24,240,000,000 | @yen202 /US$1 | 120,000,000 | | |
| 1 | 1,611,960,000 | 293,454,573 | 9,787,026 | 12,840,000 | 3,052,974 |
| 2 | 1,611,960,000 | 293,454,573 | 10,154,629 | 12,840,000 | 2,685,371 |
| 3 | 1,611,960,000 | 293,454,573 | 10,536,024 | 12,840,000 | 2,303,976 |
| 4 | 1,611,960,000 | 293,454,573 | 10,931,729 | 12,840,000 | 1,908,271 |
| 5 | 1,611,960,000 | 293,454,573 | 11,342,307 | 12,840,000 | 1,497,693 |
| 6 | 1,611,960,000 | 293,454,573 | 11,768,284 | 12,840,000 | 1,071,716 |
| 7 | 1,611,960,000 | 293,454,573 | 12,210,282 | 12,840,000 | 629,718 |
| 8 | 1,611,960,000 | 293,454,573 | 12,668,896 | 12,840,000 | 171,104 |
| 9 | 1,611,960,000 | 293,454,573 | 13,144,779 | 12,840,000 | −304,779 |
| 10 | 1,611,960,000 | 293,454,573 | 13,638,443 | 12,840,000 | −798,443 |
| | 24,240,000,000 | −3,960,000,000 | @¥169/US$1 | 120,000,000 | |

BT's profits from the above transaction, at a discount rate of 10.50% pa, after ten years, would have been US$25,564,688, equivalent to a US$1,566,024 annuity over 10 years.

This annuity is used to reduce LTCB's borrowing cost from US$13,800,000 (11.50% of US$120 million) to US$12,233,976 pa (US$13,800,000 – US$1,566,024). This translated to an effective interest rate of US$12,233,976/US$120,000,000 or 10.20% pa, a rate under the equivalent US Treasury rate if all the profits are distributed to the issuer (an unlikely scenario).

A variation on this basic structure was undertaken in an issue for IBM (nicknamed "Heaven and Hell"). Under this structure in return for taking a risk of loss if the yen strengthened beyond US$1/¥169, the investor would receive a higher redemption payment if the yen was weaker than US$1/¥169 at maturity. This contrasted with the ICON structure above where the investor did not receive any benefit over and above the premium and could have potentially suffered a loss equivalent to the *full principal amount of the investment* (which gave rise to the term the "Hell" bond).

The redemption arrangements analytically constitute a yen call/US$ put granted by the investor and the simultaneous purchase of a yen put/US$ call by the investor. Both options have a strike rate of US$1/¥169 and a term of 10 years creating effectively a long US$/short yen 10-year forward position.

In the IBM transaction the issue was structured in two tranches: a fixed-rate and a floating-rate issue. In the fixed (floating) rate portion, the investor received approximately 70 bps pa (25 bps pa) in extra yield in return for the variable redemption arrangement. In this structure, the currency position created was securitized in a manner very similar to that used for the ICON issue. Both options again were capable of being traded separately or combined into a synthetic currency forward position to reduce the overall borrowing cost of its issues.

The detailed structure of the Heaven and Hell issue and accompanying currency-linked swap is set out in **Exhibit 7.11** on page 286. These structures were rapidly commoditized. They came to be known as Principal Exchange Rate Linked Securities (PERLS). **Exhibit 7.12** on page 288 sets out the generalized structure and related hedges.

**Exhibit 7.11**
**Heaven and Hell Notes**

*Issue Structure*

The first issue of Heaven and Hell notes was arranged by Nomura International for IBM Credit Corporation. The IBM issue was to raise US$50 million for 10 years, with a maturity date of December 4, 1995. To entice investors to invest in this bond, IBM had to pay a rich coupon of 10.75% pa, payable in US$, which was equivalent to 84 bps over US Treasuries. In a prior comparable issue, IBM had only paid 14 bps over US Treasuries for a straight Eurodollar issue. The redemption amount for the issue, payable in US$, varied according to the following formula:

$$R = US\$50,000,000[1 + ((S - 169)/S)]$$

Where:

R = Redemption value in US$
S = ¥/US$ spot exchange rate on November 21, 1995

If the ¥/US$ exchange rate at maturity was stronger than ¥84.5/US$1, investors will get no principal return.

*Derivatives Hedge*

IBM securitizes the currency position implicit in the transaction to Nomura in return for payments that effectively lower its cost of funds.

From the IBM Heaven and Hell debt issue, Nomura has a short US$ position in 10 years' time at a forward price of ¥169/US$1 for US$50 million. To utilize this forward position effectively, Nomura issued yen 10,212,500,000 at 6.70% pa for a counterparty who wanted 10-year US$ funds. Nomura exchanged the yen proceeds on the spot market, hedged the interest commitments forward and left the final capital redemption amount unhedged. Nomura charged the counterparty approximately 10.25% pa for the US$ funds.

*Transaction Economics*

The profit dynamics of the issue are as follows:
    Assume:

- Yen 10-year risk-free interest rate is 6.50% pa.
- 10-year US Treasury interest rate is 10.00% pa.
- ¥/US$ spot exchange rate is ¥204.25/US$1.

- Forward exchange rates were:
  | | |
  |---|---|
  | 1 year forward | ¥197.751/US$1 |
  | 2 year forward | ¥191.459/US$1 |
  | 3 year forward | ¥185.367/US$1 |
  | 4 year forward | ¥179.469/US$1 |
  | 5 year forward | ¥173.759/US$1 |
  | 6 year forward | ¥168.230/US$1 |
  | 7 year forward | ¥162.877/US$1 |
  | 8 year forward | ¥157.695/US$1 |
  | 9 year forward | ¥152.677/US$1 |
  | 10 year forward | ¥147.819/US$1 |

At maturity, Nomura exchanged the US$ into yen at the rate of ¥169/US$1. This gave Nomura ¥8,450,000,000 to repay the ¥10,212,500,000 loan, leaving a shortfall of ¥1,762,500,000. This shortfall translated into an annual payment of ¥130,609,517 at the risk-free rate of 6.50% pa. Nomura therefore had to enter into an annual forward agreement to hedge ¥814,847,017 annually (¥684,237,500 + ¥130,609,517).

The cash flows involved are as follows:

| Year | Yen Interest Commitment (¥) | Annuity for Capital Redemption (¥) | US$ Amount to Hedge Cash Flows (US$) | Counterparty Interest Payments (US$) | Nomura's Profits (US$) |
|---|---|---|---|---|---|
| 0 | 10,212,500,000 | @¥204.25/US$1 | | 50,000,000 | |
| 1 | 684,237,500 | 130,609,517 | 4,120,571 | 5,125,000 | 1,004,429 |
| 2 | 684,237,500 | 130,609,517 | 4,255,987 | 5,125,000 | 869,013 |
| 3 | 684,237,500 | 130,609,517 | 4,395,858 | 5,125,000 | 729,142 |
| 4 | 684,237,500 | 130,609,517 | 4,540,322 | 5,125,000 | 584,678 |
| 5 | 684,237,500 | 130,609,517 | 4,689,524 | 5,125,000 | 435,476 |
| 6 | 684,237,500 | 130,609,517 | 4,843,649 | 5,125,000 | 281,351 |
| 7 | 684,237,500 | 130,609,517 | 5,002,837 | 5,125,000 | 122,168 |
| 8 | 684,237,500 | 130,609,517 | 5,167,234 | 5,125,000 | –42,234 |
| 9 | 684,237,500 | 130,609,517 | 5,337,065 | 5,125,000 | –212,065 |
| 10 | 684,237,500 | 130,609,517 | 5,512,465 | 5,125,000 | –387,465 |
| | 10,212,500,000 | –1,762,500,000 | @¥169/US$1 | 50,000,000 | |

Nomura's profits from the above transaction, using a discount rate of 10.00% pa, at the end of 10 years, would be US$7,291,912, equivalent to a US$457,534 annuity over 10 years. The annuity is used to reduce IBM's annual interest cost of US$5,375,000 (10.75% of US$50 million) to US$4,917,467 (US$5,375,000 – US$457,533). This would reduce IBM's interest cost down to US$4,917,467/US$50,000,000 = 9.835% (a rate below US Treasuries). However, because investors of the IBM Heaven and Hell issue also purchased a US$ put option with a strike price of ¥84.5/US$1, Nomura is left with a residual foreign currency risk should the yen/US$ exchange rate strengthen beyond ¥84.5/US$1. Nomura could leave this position unhedged or hedge this residual exposure by buying a US$ put option with a strike price of ¥84.5/US$1 or it could delta hedge the position to create a synthetic option.

**Exhibit 7.12**
**Principal Exchange Rate-linked Securities (PERLS)**

*Issue Structure*

The PERLS structure is a generalization of the ICON concept. The typical components include:

- A US$-denominated bond typically five years in maturity.
- A coupon that is significantly higher than the coupon payable on an equivalent conventional bond at the time of issue. The coupon increment initially was around 250 bps. Subsequently, the coupon increment has declined to around 50-100 bps.
- Principal redemption is linked to a nominated exchange rate (say, US$/yen) at the maturity date.

The normal redemption formula for a PERLS would be:

Principal Redemption = Face Value $\times$ [1 – ((FS – S)/S)]

Where:

S = Spot yen/US$ rate as at issue date
FS = Spot yen/US$ rate at the bond maturity date

The principal redemption structure, effectively, embeds a currency forward into the note. Any desired exposure can be generated. In the above example, an investor requirement to increase exposure to an appreciation of the US$ is achieved through incorporation of a currency forward to purchase US$/sell yen. The coupon increment is generated by structuring the forward at an off-market rate. The value of the forward (resulting from this adjustment in the rate) is used to create the annuity to enhance the return on the bond.

The effect of the redemption linkage is to create the following return payoff for the investor. The investor receives a boosted running yield. At maturity, using the above example, the investor will receive further enhancement of return (potentially, unlimited) where the US$ appreciates vis-à-vis the yen *above the embedded rate*. However, if the US$ decreases in value, then the investor suffers a potential loss of principal. The investor could suffer a loss equal to the face value of the transaction (typically, in the absence of any leverage, where the spot rate at maturity is equal to or below the spot rate at the commencement of the transaction).

The structure combines:

- A fixed interest bond.
- An off-market currency forward.
- An out-of-the money yen call/US$ put.

The option is necessary to limit the losses on the forward (in the event of a fall in the value of the US$ below the spot rate at commencement) to the *face value of the bond*. The strike of the option would be set at, in this example, at half the current spot rate.

### *Derivatives Hedge*

The issuer of a PERLS would be immunized from the impact of the embedded currency forward through the entry into the following transactions:

- A currency forward to sell yen/buy US$ for value as at the maturity of the note. The currency forward would generate a gain (loss) where the yen depreciated (appreciated) offsetting the loss (gain) resulting from the increase (decrease) in the redemption amount. The principal amount of this forward should be the US$ (reflecting the currency of the bond) principal amount adjusted by the ratio of the spot rate to the 5-year outright forward rate. In effect, the issuer is required to sell forward the *current* yen equivalent of the US$ principal amount rather than the forward yen equivalent of this US$ amount.
- Purchase of the yen call/US$ put with a strike price equal to half the current spot rate and an expiry coinciding with the maturity of the Note. The call would show gains where the yen appreciated beyond the strike offsetting losses on the currency forward that would exceed the gain resulting from the decrease in the redemption amount that is constrained to 100% of the face value of the bond. The principal

amount of the option must be set at an amount larger than the face value of the transaction. In this example, the option face value must be set on *two times the US$ principal value of the Note* in order to hedge the yen principal amount at the appreciated ¥/US$ exchange rate.

The entry into the hedges would insulate the issuer from the embedded currency derivative elements creating a fixed-rate bond. This fixed-rate liability could be converted into a floating rate borrowing in US$ or a fixed- or floating-rate liability in other currencies through interest rate or currency swap transactions as required.

The fundamental elements of these transactions were the full linkage of *principal* to the currency movement. The value extracted from the forward discount or premium was built into the higher coupon on these notes. Additional yield enhancement was often created by engineering the currency forward at an *off-market rate* with the intrinsic value of the derivative position *at commencement* being used to further increase the running yield.

### 3.3   Indexed Currency Option Notes — The Variations

The ICON/PERLS-type structure that yielded currency positions that were securitized and on-sold was extended in a number of directions, for example:

- Variability linked to currency rates has been extended to coupon amounts thereby creating a stream of currency options.
- Mini-max notes where the variable redemption amount operates *only* if the currency rates are outside a stated band.
- Inclusion of ICON features in dual-currency issues.
- Variable redemption structures linked to both currency and interest rates.

The ingenuity of these currency-linked variable redemption bonds and also their creators, primarily, the Japanese securities houses, is best illustrated by two examples. **Exhibit 7.13** sets out the intricate and elegant combination of an issue by OKB and BFCE that allowed simultaneous foreign currency options to be securitized. **Exhibit 7.14** on page 294 sets out the structure of "duet" bonds where the linkage to currency rates has been extended to coupon amounts.[12]

---

[12]   For more detailed discussion of these transactions, see Das, Satyajit "Option Swaps: Securitising Options Embedded in Securities Issues" *Journal of International Securities Markets* (Summer 1988) 117-138.

## Exhibit 7.13
## Yen/US$ Variable Redemption Reverse Dual-currency Note

*Issue Structure*

On April 15, 1986, Oesterreichische Kontrollbank (OKB) issued a ¥20 billion, 10-year variable redemption bond. The coupon was 8.00% pa payable in yen. Redemption was in US$ based on the following formula:

R = US$114,155,252 × [1 + (S − 169)/S]

Where:

R = Redemption amount in US$
S = ¥/US$ spot exchange rate at maturity of the bonds

If the yen strengthens beyond ¥84.5/US$1, then investors will not receive their principal back.

On the same date, Nomura also lead managed a reverse dual-currency bond issue worth ¥20 billion, with a maturity of 10 years for Banque Francaise du Commerce Exterieur (BFCE). This issue involved BFCE paying a 7.50% pa coupon, payable in US$ at a fixed exchange rate of ¥179/US$1. The redemption amount, payable in yen, was at par as long as exchange rates were above ¥84.5/US$1, declining below par if the yen strengthened beyond ¥84.5/US$1. The foreign currency positions implicit in the two issues were securitized by Nomura.

*Derivatives Hedge*

The OKB and BFCE issues complemented one another as the redemption amount in the OKB issue was in US$ while the redemption amount of the BFCE issue was payable in yen. The redemption formula of both issues *jointly* gave a short US$ position at a forward price of ¥169/US$1.

Interest payment of the OKB issue was in US$ but that of the BFCE issue was in yen. Therefore, if BFCE wanted US$ funding, Nomura had to hedge the yen interest commitments of the BFCE issue forward. To capitalize on the short US$ position obtained from both issues, Nomura would not have hedges the capital redemption of OKB's yen redemption amount forward.

*Transaction Economics*

The profit dynamics of the transaction are as follows:
  Assume:

- Yen 10-year risk-free interest rate is 6.50% pa.
- US 10-year Treasury interest rate is 8.50% pa.
- ¥/US$ spot exchange rate is ¥175.2/US$1.

- Forward exchange rates were:
  1 year forward     ¥171.97/US$1
  2 year forward     ¥168.80/US$1
  3 year forward     ¥165.65/US$1
  4 year forward     ¥162.63/US$1
  5 year forward     ¥159.64/US$1
  6 year forward     ¥156.69/US$1
  7 year forward     ¥153.81/US$1
  8 year forward     ¥150.97/US$1
  9 year forward     ¥148.19/US$1
  10 year forward    ¥145.46/US$1

Interest flows for BFCE were as follows: assuming OKB paid Nomura the equivalent of 8.30% pa (a rate under US Treasuries), BFCE paid an interest flow to Nomura of US$9,474,886 [(¥20 billion/175.2) × 8.30%]. Nomura paid investors US$8,379,888 [(¥20 billion × 7.50%)/¥179/US$1]. Therefore, Nomura obtained an annual profit of US$1,094,998 from this part of the transaction.

Interest flows for OKB are as follows: assuming it paid Nomura the equivalent of US$8.30% pa, BFCE paid Nomura US$9,474,886 [(¥20 billion/175.2) × 8.30%] and Nomura paid investors ¥1,600,000,000 [¥20 billion × 8.00%]. Nomura will have to hedge this obligation forward to limit any losses.

The interest flows under the OKB transaction are as set out below.

| Year | OKB Yen Interest Commitment (¥) | US$ Amount to Hedge Cash Flows (US$) | OKB's Interest Payments (US$) | Nomura's Profits (US$) |
|---|---|---|---|---|
| 1 | 1,600,000,000 | 9,303,949 | 9,474,886 | 170,937 |
| 2 | 1,600,000,000 | 9,478,673 | 9,474,886 | −3,787 |
| 3 | 1,600,000,000 | 9,656,588 | 9,474,886 | −181,722 |
| 4 | 1,600,000,000 | 9,838,283 | 9,474,886 | −363,417 |
| 5 | 1,600,000,000 | 10,022,551 | 9,474,886 | −547,685 |
| 6 | 1,600,000,000 | 10,211,245 | 9,474,886 | −736,379 |
| 7 | 1,600,000,000 | 10,402,445 | 9,474,886 | −927,579 |
| 8 | 1,600,000,000 | 10,598,132 | 9,474,886 | −1,123,266 |
| 9 | 1,600,000,000 | 10,796,950 | 9,474,886 | −1,322,084 |
| 10 | 1,600,000,000 | 10,999,588 | 9,474,886 | −1,524,722 |

Nomura's net profit position from the two transactions was:

| Year | Profit from BFCE (US$) | Profit from OKB (US$) | Net Profit (US$) |
|------|------------------------|------------------------|------------------|
| 1    | 1,094,998              | 170,937                | 1,265,935        |
| 2    | 1,094,998              | -3,787                 | 1,091,211        |
| 3    | 1,094,998              | -181,722               | 913,276          |
| 4    | 1,094,998              | -363,417               | 731,581          |
| 5    | 1,094,998              | -547,685               | 547,313          |
| 6    | 1,094,998              | -736,379               | 358,619          |
| 7    | 1,094,998              | -927,579               | 167,419          |
| 8    | 1,094,998              | -1,123,266             | -28,268          |
| 9    | 1,094,998              | -1,322,084             | -227,086         |
| 10   | 1,094,998              | -1,524,722             | -429,724         |

At the US$ risk-free interest rate of 8.50% pa, the compounded value of this net profit cash flow at year 10 is US$8,368,408.

The redemption amount that OKB and BFCE paid Nomura at maturity was equal to US$228,310,504 (US$114,155,252 × 2). The premium from the OKB issue was ¥300,000,000 and for BFCE it was ¥350,000,000. This totals to US$3,710,045 at ¥175/US$1 (both issues were made at a premium to par).

Total amount of cash available to Nomura to repay investors was US$240,388,957 [US$8,368,408 (Nomura's profit) + US$228,310,504 (principal repayments in US$ by OKB and BFC) + US$3,710,045 (issue premium)].

The amount owed by Nomura to investors of both issues at maturity if the spot exchange rate is weaker than ¥84.5/US$1 depended on the following formula:

R = ¥20 billion/179 [1 + ((S − 169)/S)] + ¥20 billion/S

Where:

R = Redemption amount in US$
S = ¥/US$ spot exchange rate at maturity

Therefore, Nomura's profit is as follows:

| Spot Rate (S) | Cash Available to Nomura (US$) | Redemption Amount (US$) | Gain (US$) |
|---|---|---|---|
| 300 | 240,388,957 | 227,188,083 | 13,200,874 |
| 200 | 240,388,957 | 229,050,280 | 11,338,677 |
| 150 | 240,388,957 | 230,912,477 | 9,476,480 |
| 100 | 240,388,957 | 234,636,872 | 5,752,085 |
| 90 | 240,388,957 | 235,878,337 | 4,510,620 |
| 85 | 240,388,957 | 236,608,610 | 3,780,347 |
| 84.5 | 240,388,957 | 236,686,391 | 3,702,566 |
| 80 | 240,388,957 | 235,937,500 | 4,451,457 |
| 60 | 240,388,957 | 197,222,222 | 43,166,735 |

From the above profit table, we observe that it was possible for Nomura to reduce the cost of borrowing of both entities to below US Treasuries and still not incur a loss on the capital redemption amount at maturity.

**Exhibit 7.14**
**Duet Bond**

*Issue Structure*

The first duet bond was issued for the Kingdom of Denmark and managed by Dai-Ichi Kangyo Bank (DKB). It was a 5-year debt issue worth US$100 million issued on August 8, 1986.

The coupon, payable in US$, was based on the following formula:

$$C = \$100,000,0000 \times 0.165 - [(¥16,300,000,000 \times 0.065)/S]$$

Where:

C = Coupon payable in US$
S = ¥/US$ exchange rate at coupon date

The capital redemption amount, also payable in US$, was calculated using the following formula:

$$R = \$100,000,0000 \times 2 - [(¥16,300,000,000/S]$$

Where:

R = Redemption amount in US$
S = ¥/US$ exchange rate at the maturity of the bonds

From the formula, it is clear that Denmark had an exposure to the ¥/US$ exchange rate on each coupon date and at maturity of the bonds. These currency positions were securitized by DKB.

## Derivatives Hedge

Under the swap structure, Denmark effectively sold the currency positions implicit in the structure to DKB. DKB assumed an annual exposure to yen coupon payments as a result of the duet bond's coupon payment formula. In addition, DKB had a short US$ forward exposure for US$100 million in five years' time at a forward rate of ¥163/US$1.

To capitalize on this position, DKB arranged a yen issue, for a counterparty wanting US$ funding, with an annual coupon payment equivalent to ¥1,059,500,000. If the yen interest rate on the issue was 5.20% pa, then DKB would have issued ¥20,375 million principal amount of bonds.

The duet bond, because of the amount issued, would only support US$100 million or ¥16,300 million of the yen issue to be perfectly hedged. Therefore, ¥4,075 million from the yen issue will be unhedged. DKB had to undertake a 5-year forward agreement to purchase yen to hedge this exposure.

## Transactions Economics

The profit dynamics of this transaction were as follows:
Assume:

- The 5-year yen interest rate was 5.00% pa.
- The 5-year US$ interest rate was 7.50% pa.
- The spot exchange rate was ¥163/US$1.
- The 5-year forward rate was ¥144.9078/US$1.

Therefore, DKB required US$28,121,329 (¥4,075,000,000/¥144.9078) to hedge the ¥4,075,000,000 yen forward exposure.

If DKB charged the counterparty 7.70% pa for US$ funding, the borrower therefore paid DKB US$9,625,000 (7.70% of US$125,000,000) and DKB was committed to pay ¥1,059,500,000 (5.20% of ¥20,375,000,000 at ¥163/US$1) for the straight yen debt. The duet bond coupon formula covered this, leaving DKB with US$3,125,000 (US$9,625,000 − US$6,500,000) annually for the next five years. This accumulated to

US$18,151,222 at the end of five years at the interest rate of 7.50% pa.

At maturity, DKB had US$125 million to pay off the ¥20,375 million straight yen debt. The duet bond hedged ¥16,300 million (equivalent to US$100 million) and the forward agreement hedged the remaining ¥4,075 million. This amount was covered by the US$18,151,222 from the coupon receipts and US$25 million from the capital redemption amount. This left DKB with US$15,029,893 (US$25,000,000 + US$18,151,222 – US$28,121,329) profits at maturity.

This profit at maturity (US$15,029,893) would be used to reduce the duet bond's interest cost. The US$15,029,893 plus the US$1,625,000 premium from the issue of duet bonds would give an annuity of US$2,989,260 over five years at 7.50% pa. Interest cost of the duet bond was US$10,000,000 (10.00% of US$100,000,000). Effective interest cost of the bond after deducting the annuity was 7.02% pa [(US$10,000,000 – US$2,989,260)/US$100,000,000]. This was a rate under the equivalent US Treasury bond rate, if the full benefit is passed on to the borrower.

### 3.4   Currency-linked Bonds — Evolution

Currency-linked notes continue to be structured and issued. The structures incorporate embedded currency forward or option position. The implicit currency forward or option positions embedded in security issues are hedged in the market to insulate the issuer from exposure to the currency elements of the transaction.

The demand for capital market issues with such embedded elements fluctuates. However, from time to time, investor demand for particular currency-related characteristics is evident. The basic structures used are the types of transaction already outlined. Some more recent example of these types of transactions are set in this section. **Exhibit 7.15** sets out an example of a currency-linked transaction where the underlying debt is short-dated commercial paper that is packaged with a participating currency forward.[13] **Exhibits 7.16, 7.17** and **7.18** set out examples of bonds with engineered linkages to exchange rates. **Exhibit 7.19** sets examples of bonds designed to create exposure to emerging market currencies.

The distinguishing features of these transactions include the:

---

[13]   See Kimelman, Nancy, Callahan, James, and Demafeliz, Salvador (September 23, 1986) Performance Indexed Paper — A Foreign Currency-Indexed Money Market Instrument; Salomon Brothers Inc., New York.

- Shorter maturity.
- Linkage that places the coupon at risk rather than the principal of the transaction.
- Guaranteed minimum coupon.

In part, these changes reflect broader changes in the structured note market generally.

Specific structures have their own evolving dynamic. The structures depicted in **Exhibit 7.17** and **7.18** for example, involving primarily yen and more infrequently European currencies, are designed to create asymmetric currency exposures through the embedded option. **Exhibit 7.19** sets out examples of bonds where the payoffs are linked to the price performance of emerging market currencies primarily to give the investor exposure to the relevant currency (often also the higher yields available in the local currency) without the necessity to purchase local currency securities.

---

**Exhibit 7.15**
**Currency-linked Commercial Paper**

A typical currency-linked commercial paper (either domestic US or Euro) issue may be structured as follows:

| | |
|---|---|
| Issuer | A1+/P1 rated issuer |
| Amount | (multiples of) US$1 million |
| Maturity | 90 days |
| Coupon | Indexed to the currency (calculated two days prior to maturity) subject to the Minimum and Maximum Coupon. |
| Minimum Coupon | 2.50% pa |
| Maximum Coupon | 6.00% pa |

The investor selects the Minimum Return and the issuer (in effect, the dealer/investment bank acting on behalf of the issuer) establishes the maximum rate. In this example, the rates were based on US$/¥ range of US$1 equals ¥1.46/1.60.

Where the yen appreciates against the US$, the investor receives a return in excess of that available on conventional commercial paper of the relevant maturity. If the yen depreciates, then the return to the investor will be below that on equivalent commercial paper, subject to the minimum return of 2.50%.

The diagram below sets out the investor's return profile from this transaction:

---

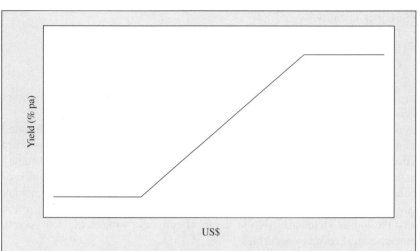

The payoff profile illustrates the nature of the currency exposure created. The structure effectively combines the following:

- Investment in 90-day commercial paper.
- Selling the US$ principal and interest forward to the maturity of the commercial paper.
- Repurchasing US$ back via a Range Forward contract.[14]

The issuer of the currency-indexed commercial paper hedges its currency exposure by offsetting its position with the dealer/investment bank through the entry into a contract to sell US$/buy yen forward for value the maturity date of the commercial paper and entry into a Range Forward contract to sell yen/buy US$ (the currency range in the Range Forward is set to that embedded in the issue).

At maturity, if the yen appreciates (depreciates), then the Range Forward will provide additional US$ gains that are passed through to the investor (losses that lower the return to the investor). The investor's loss is limited as the floor on the Range Forward guarantees the agreed Minimum Coupon.

---

[14]  A Range Forward contract is basically a zero-cost currency option collar entailing the simultaneous sale and purchase of two currency options with different strikes but the same maturity.

**Exhibit 7.16**
**DM/US$ Currency-linked Notes**

| | |
|---|---|
| Issuer | AAA-rated institution |
| Amount | US$100 million |
| Maturity | 1 year |
| Issue Price | 100% of Face Value |
| Redemption Value | 100% of Face Value |
| Coupon (annual) | Calculated in accordance with the following formula: |
| | $2.00\% + [100 \times (Index - 1.46)/Index]$ |
| | Where |
| | Index = DM/US$ rate on the Index Set Date |
| Index Set Date | 2 days before maturity |
| Minimum Coupon | 2.00% pa |
| Maximum Coupon | 10.75% pa |

The Note can be decomposed into the following components:

• A 1-year fixed interest bond.
• A 1-year put spread (denominated in US$) on DM as follows:
  1. Purchased DM put at US$/DM1.4600.
  2. Sold DM put at US$/DM1.6000.

The investor's return profile is as follows:

• US$/DM above 1.60, return equivalent to 10.75% pa.
• US$/DM below 1.46, return equivalent to 2.00% pa.
• US$/DM between 1.46 and 1.64, return as per the following table:

| US$/DM Exchange Rate at Maturity | Coupon (% pa) |
|:---:|:---:|
| 1.46 | 2.00 |
| 1.48 | 3.35 |
| 1.50 | 4.67 |
| 1.52 | 5.95 |
| 1.54 | 7.19 |
| 1.56 | 8.41 |
| 1.58 | 9.59 |

Based on a 1-year Treasury rate of 5.75% pa, the Investor requires the US$ to strengthen to around US$/DM1.52 to generate returns above this benchmark.

**Exhibit 7.17**
**US$/Yen Currency-linked Notes**

| | |
|---|---|
| Issuer | AAA-rated institution |
| Amount | US$100 million |
| Maturity | 1 year |
| Issue Price | 100% of Face Value |
| Redemption Value | 100% of Face Value |
| Coupon | Calculated in accordance with the following formula:<br>2.85% + (Index − 102.00)<br>Where<br>Index = ¥/US$ rate on the Index Set Date |
| Index Set Date | 2 days before maturity |
| Minimum Coupon | 2.50% pa |
| Maximum Coupon | 12.50% pa |
| Interest Basis | 30/360 annual payment |

The Note can be decomposed into the following components:

- A 1-year fixed interest bond.
- A 1-year put spread (denominated in US$) on yen as follows:
  1. Purchased yen put at US$/¥102.00
  2. Sold yen put at US$/¥112.00

The investor's return profile is as follows:

- US$/¥ above 112, return equivalent to 12.50% pa.
- US$/¥ below 102, return equivalent to 2.50% pa.
- US$/¥ between 102 and 112, return as per the formula. For example, if US$/¥ is equal to 107, then the Investor receives 7.50% pa (2.50 + (107 − 102)).

Based on a 1-year Treasury rate of 5.75% pa, the investor requires the US$ to strengthen above to US$/¥105.25 to generate returns above this benchmark.

**Exhibit 7.18**
**US$/Yen Currency-linked Notes**

The period of persistently low interest rates in yen that has prevailed since the mid-1990s has encouraged the design of a number of currency-linked structure for yen-based investors. These structures have been designed to provide investors with a higher yield than would be available directly in return for assuming currency risk. A typical structure from this period is described below:

| | |
|---|---|
| Issuer | AAA-rated institution |
| Amount | ¥5 billion |
| Maturity | 10 years |
| Issue Price | 100% of Face Value |
| Redemption Value | 100% of Face Value |
| Interest Coupon | Payable annually calculated in accordance with the following formula: 8.40% × (Index/120) — 4.90% Where: Index = ¥/US$ rate on the Index Set Date |
| Index Set Date | 2 days before each interest rate payment date |
| Minimum Coupon | 0.00% pa |
| Interest Basis | 30/360 day count basis payable in yen |

Under the structure, the investor receives an annual coupon linked to movements in the ¥/US$ exchange rate. Where the ¥/US$ rate is above 120, then the investor receives a coupon in excess of 3.50% pa. Where the ¥/US$ rate is below 120, then the investor receives a coupon below 3.50% pa. Where the ¥/US$ exchange rate is at or below 70, then the investor receives no interest. The investor's principal investment denominated in yen is not at risk and is returned at maturity.

The structure entails that the investor has entered into the following transactions:

• Purchase of a yen note.
• A series of yen/US$ forwards whereby the investor purchases US$/sells yen for value each of the interest coupon dates. This component creates the linkage to currency fluctuations.
• A series of US$ put/yen call options at a strike of ¥70 with expiry dates corresponding to each of the interest rate payment dates. The options are designed to ensure that the coupon on the bond does not become negative.

The value dynamics of the structure were driven by the fact that the currency forwards are at off-market rates.

**Exhibit 7.19**
**Emerging Market Currency-linked Notes**

The increased investment and trading interest in emerging markets that manifested itself through the 1990s created demand for currency-linked notes where interest and/or principal was indexed to the local currency unit. Such transactions were driven by a variety of considerations. These were in addition to the traditional factors motivating structured note transactions. They included:

- The regulatory environment including the existence of currency controls that restricted trading in some of these currencies.
- The low credit quality of issuers and counterparties in some of these jurisdictions.
- The presence of convertibility risk, including the risk of imposition of restrictions on funds transfers.
- The lack of liquidity in the domestic markets and uncertainty regarding the efficacy of the trading and settlement mechanisms in these jurisdictions.

These factors made it attractive for traders and investors to use structured notes to access these markets and create exposure to the local currency and local currency interest rates. Transactions were undertaken in a wide variety of currencies including Asian currencies (Korean won, Thai baht, Indonesian rupiah, Indian rupee, and so on), Central and Latin American currencies (for example, Mexican peso and Brazilian Reals) and Eastern European currencies (for example, Polish zloty and Czech koruna). Such transactions were also undertaken in some Southern European currencies (for example, Spanish peseta, Portuguese escudo and Greek drachma).

The basic structures entailed embedded forwards to create the relevant underlying currency exposure or embedding options to create asymmetric risk exposures to the local currencies. A number of examples of these types of transactions are set out below.

*Example 1 — Indian Rupee-linked Note*

| | |
|---|---|
| Issuer | AAA-rated institution |
| Amount | US$25 million |
| Maturity | 6 months |
| Issue Price | 100% of Face Value |
| Interest Coupon | Payable at maturity calculated in accordance with the following formula: |

|                    | Amount × 22.00% × (40.00/Index) × 182/365 |
| --- | --- |
| Redemption Value   | Amount × (40.00/Index) |
| Index              | US$/Rupee rate on the Index Set Date |
| Index Set Date     | 2 days before maturity |
| Minimum Coupon     | 0.00% pa |
| Minimum Redemption | 0.00 |
| Interest Basis     | Actual/365 day count basis payable in US$ |

The structure creates a linkage between the coupon and principal received and the US$/rupee exchange rate. The structure entails the purchase of a US$ note and simultaneous entry into a currency forward where the investor sells US$/buys rupees at US$1: Rs40.00.

The effect of the transaction is to replicate a local currency (Indian rupee) investment with full currency exposure. The investor gains where the Rupee appreciates but suffers losses where the rupee devalues.

*Example 2 — Portuguese Escudo (Esc)-linked Note*

| Issuer           | AAA-rated institution |
| --- | --- |
| Amount           | DM20 million |
| Maturity         | 6 months |
| Issue Price      | 100% of Face Value |
| Interest Coupon  | Payable at maturity calculated in accordance with the following formula: Amount × [0.50% + 50 × Max. (0, Index − 110)] × 182/365 |
| Redemption Value | 100% |
| Index            | DM/Esc exchange rate on the Index Set Date |
| Index Set Date   | 2 days before maturity |
| Minimum Coupon   | 0.50% pa |
| Interest Basis   | Actual/365 day count basis payable in DM |

The structure entails a principal-protected DM investment where the coupon is linked to the DM/Esc exchange rates. The investor is guaranteed a minimum coupon of 0.50% pa with participation in any appreciation in the DM against the Esc. The structure entails the investor purchasing a DM bond and forgoing all but 0.50% of the coupon with the foregone coupon being used to purchase a DM call/Esc put to create the desired currency linkage.

*Example 3 — Japanese Yen/Thai Baht (Bt)-linked Note*

| | |
|---|---|
| Issuer | AAA-rated institution |
| Amount | US$20 million |
| Maturity | 1 year |
| Issue Price | 95% of face value |
| Interest Coupon | 0% |
| Redemption Value | 100% + Adjustment factor |
| Adjustment Factor | 160% × Amount × [(yen payout) + (5 × baht payout)] |
| Yen Payout | (¥/US$ on Index Set Date − 120)/¥/US$ on Index Set Date. The yen Payout cannot be less than 0. |
| THB Payout | (25 − Bt/US$ on Index Set Date)/Bt/US$ on Index Set Date |
| Index Set Date | 2 days before maturity |
| Interest Basis | Actual/365-day count basis payable in DM |

The structure creates a simultaneous exposure to yen and baht. The investor benefits where the yen weakens against the US$ and the baht strengthens against the US$. The exposure in respect of the yen is asymmetric with the investor having limited exposure to a decline in the US$ because of the minimum constraint condition. However, the investor has an outright forward position on the Bt/US$ exchange rate. If the baht fall below 28.57 (a decline in value of 12.5%), then the investor suffers a loss of it principal investment. In fact, the Asian monetary crisis that commenced in July 1997 resulted in many of these types of structures inflicting large losses on investors.

## 4.   Summary

Currency-linked notes are a class of structured notes that embody a specific linkage to foreign exchange or currency values. The linkage entails linking the value of coupon payments or principal repayments to an identified exchange rate.

A variety of structures has emerged allowing investors to monetise specific views in relation to the shape of forward currency rates and/or currency volatility. The structures are now well accepted and available in a wide variety of currencies.

# 8

# Commodity-linked Notes

## 1. Overview

Commodity-linked notes[1] are a class of structured notes that embody a specific linkage to commodity prices. The linkage entails linking the value of coupon payments or principal repayments to an identified commodity or commodity index.

In this chapter, the key dynamics of commodity-linked notes—including the evolution of commodity-linked investment; the types of commodity-linked notes and the structuring, pricing and trading of these securities—are discussed.

## 2. Commodity Investment

### 2.1 Overview

Commodity-linked transactions are distinct from transactions involving linkages to other financial market asset prices (for example, interest rates, currency values or equity prices). This difference relates to two specific factors:

- Commodities and commodity prices impact upon the *nonfinancial* aspects of businesses (in terms of revenues and input costs).
- Commodity investment is driven by different factors from those that drive investment in other financial assets.

In this section, these aspects of commodity investments and markets are examined.

Commodity-linked transactions have a significant history. However, the market for commodity-linked instruments has evolved radically since inception.

---

[1] The author would like to thank Robert Greer (Chase Manhattan) for his helpful comments on an earlier draft of this chapter in relation to commodity indexes and commodities as an asset class. The author would like to thank Steve Strongin and Melanie Petsch (Goldman Sachs); Adam de Chiara and Dan Raab (AIG International); Mark Fulton, James Bourke, and Paul Brownsey (Salomon Smith Barney); and Tanweer Kabir and Jesse Foo (Merrill Lynch) for assitance with data in relation to this chapter.

The demand for *financial* investment in commodities and commodity-linked securities has primarily been driven by:

* **Speculation** — investors seeking to speculate on future price movements of the underlying commodity.
* **Inflation protection** — investors seeking "inflation proof" investments in an attempt to preserve the purchasing power of their monetary assets, particularly under conditions of high inflation.
* *Pure* **commodity exposure** — investors seeking *pure* commodity exposure that is not obtainable efficiently through equity investments (which filter the direct commodity exposure).
* **Commodities as a separate asset class** — investors seeking exposure to commodities in a diversified portfolio where commodity assets are treated as a unique asset class.

The demand for commodity investment for speculative purposes is a constant feature of commodity markets. This interest derives from both retail and institutional investors. Retail interest is widespread, in particular in areas where commodities, such as precious metals, are seen as a type of savings. This is particularly evident in Asia, the Middle East and Latin America. Institutional investment has been dominated by hedge funds and institutional funds invested through registered CTAs who trade on commodity futures markets.[2]

During the inflationary period of the 1970s and 1980s, a variety of commodity-linked structures evolved in response to the demand for effectively priced inflation-linked securities. These types of investment were sought by investors seeking to protect the value of their investment capital *in real terms*. However, interest in commodity-linked structures as a mechanism for preservation of purchasing power has become less important as the price inflation pressures have reduced in the 1990s.

In more recent times, the market for *financial* as distinguished from *industrial* investment in commodities has been driven by:

* The emergence of commodities as a unique and separate asset class within institutional investor portfolios.
* Investor demand for *pure price* exposure to commodities.

A factor in the demand for commodity-linked investment has also been the psychological element implicit in owning monetary assets supported by tangible commodities that in some way is seen to safeguard the future redemption of the bonds. This has been a factor particularly in retail investment in commodities and

---

[2]    See Locke, Jane "Hedge Funds Go Mining" (May 1994) *Risk* 45-52; "Commodity Markets Welcome Funds" (November 19, 1994) *International Financing Review* Issue 1057 108; van Duyn, Aline "Diversify But The Herd Will Follow (December 1994) *Euromoney* 8; Parsley, Mark "Commodity Comeback" (July 1996) *Euromoney* 12.

investment originating from politically unstable or hyper-inflationary environments. An additional factor has been the demand for commodity-linked investments from Islamic investors who face significant religious restrictions on investment choice.

Within this framework, commodity investment has evolved. The original format for commodity investment was investment in the *stocks* of companies involved in resources (commodity producers and users). Increasingly, direct investment in the commodity itself has emerged as the favored form of creating the price exposure. This reflects the increased awareness that resource-based stocks price movements are strongly correlated to movements in equity prices generally. This means that the commodity price exposure obtained through the stock investment is imperfect (that is, there is significant *basis risk* in the approach). This problem reflects a number of factors including:

- Firm-specific factors such as the quality of the resource, cost position, degree of vertical integration, management quality, and other strategic considerations.
- The commodity hedging policies followed by the firm.
- Corporate restructuring activity (mergers and acquisitions) that might impact on the commodity price exposure.
- Financial structure whereby an increase in interest rates unrelated to commodity prices will affect the performance of a leveraged firm.

The fact that a commodity firm may have investments in a range of (unrelated) commodities may also make it difficult to obtain *pure* price exposure *to a single commodity*.

The lack of disclosure or informational transparency in relation to many of these factors also compounds the problems.

## 2.2 Commodities as an Asset Class[3]

The concept of an asset class relates to a set of investments that exhibit similar and distinctive investment characteristics (primarily, return, volatility of return,

---

[3] See O'Hara, Maureen "Consumption Bonds and Consumption Risks" (March 1984) *Journal of Finance* vol. XXXIX no. 1 193-206; Ankrim, E. and Hensel, C. "Commodities in Asset Allocation" (May/June 1993) *Financial Analysts Journal*; Shimko, D. and Masters, Blythe (September 1994) Commodities — A Suitable Asset Class; J.P. Morgan, New York; Strongin, S. and Cohen, A.J. (September 1994) *The Case for Commodities*; Goldman Sachs: New York; Towers Perrin (1994) Investment In Commodities: An Option For Pension Funds; Towers Perrin: Melbourne, Australia; Strongin, Steven and Petsch, Melanie "Commodity Investing: Long-Run Returns And The Function Of Passive Capital" (Fall 1995) *Derivatives Quarterly* 56-64; Huberman, Gur "The Desirability Of Investment in Commodities Via Commodity Futures" (Fall 1995) *Derivatives Quarterly* 67; Greer, Robert J. "What Is An Asset Class, Anyway?" (Winter 1997) *Journal Of Portfolio Management* 86-91; see also Robinson, Danielle "Beat The Downturn" (May 1994) *Euromoney* 132.

and relationship of return to returns from other investment assets). Moreover, the identical investment characteristics are not displayed by other asset classes.

The typical characteristics of an asset class include:

- yield
- price return
- volatility; and
- liquidity.

In examining the performance of commodities as an asset class it is important to differentiate between physical commodity investments (investment in commodity assets) and *paper* commodities (investment in commodity assets created synthetically using derivatives). In practice, all commodities but particularly *paper* commodity assets display all of the requisite characteristics identified above.

Commodity investments provide yield-like returns. In the case of physical commodities, this return can be generated by lending out the commodity itself.[4] In the case of commodity exposure synthesized by derivatives such as commodity futures contracts, the return is from several sources:

- Interest income from the cash cover for the futures contract.[5]
- The roll yield being the difference between the spot price of the commodity and the futures price. The roll yield is captured by selling spot or the near month futures contract and buying the far month futures contract. Where the market is in contango (futures prices at a premium to the spot price), the investor earns a negative roll yield. Where the market is in backwardation (futures price at a discount to the spot price), the investor earns a positive roll yield.[6]

Commodities also display price returns. The price returns on commodity assets are complex. The basic component of price return is commodity price changes. This may be in the form of changes in the price of the physical asset itself or in the price of the derivative contract that is driven by the underlying commodity price.

An interesting aspect of commodity price returns is driven by the mean-reverting nature of some commodity prices. This contrasts with other financial asset prices that do not demonstrate such characteristics. This behavior reflects the

---

[4]   In practice, this is possible only in a few commodities such as gold.

[5]   This assumes that the position is unleveraged with the position in the futures contract being matched by a cash investment equivalent in value to the dollar value of the commodities underlying the futures contract.

[6]   See Das, Satyajit "Commodity Swaps: Forward March" (February 1993) *Risk* 41-49.

nature of commodities as consumable items and the inter-relationship between supply and demand for commodities and commodity price. In effect, commodity supply and demand changes constantly to meet market conditions. For example, an increase in price will encourage increased production (increasing supply) and decreased consumption as users seek substitutes or economize where possible in consumption levels (decreasing demand). This will over time place pressure on the price that will reduce to equilibrate supply and demand at the new levels. A decrease in price will have similar results but in the opposite direction.

This pattern of price behavior allows trading strategies to be implemented to earn returns from this mean-reversion process. The simplest manner of testing this hypothesis is to construct an equal *dollar-weighted* commodity portfolio. At regular intervals, the portfolio is rebalanced by selling commodities that have increased in value and purchasing commodities that have decreased in value. The rebalancing is designed to maintain the dollar weighting of the portfolio components. Some researchers have found that this strategy is successful in boosting returns. This highlights the capacity for active management of commodity assets to enhance returns.

Commodity prices also exhibit a skew in returns over certain periods of time. Commodities appear to exhibit a positive skew more often than other financial assets. This is driven by the fact that unexpected changes in price tend to be positive in nature.

Commodity prices display volatility. The volatility of commodity prices is significant and (often) higher than for equity portfolios.[7] Commodity indexes (see discussion below) display lower volatility reflecting the diversification effect of the portfolio.

Commodity volatility has some distinctive characteristics relative to say equity investments. Equity portfolios demonstrate positive beta (B); that is, they are characterized by directional harmony or cross-correlations. Commodities in contrast do not demonstrate similar behavior; they are characterized by lower cross-correlations. This reflects the different price drivers of individual commodities.

Commodity markets are also characterized by liquidity. Generally, with minor exceptions such as precious metals and energy products, physical commodity markets are relatively low in liquidity. However, the commodity derivative market is more liquid and compares favorably with financial asset markets.

In summary, commodity investments appear to demonstrate all the characteristics of a distinct asset class. **Exhibit 8.1** sets out the returns and price volatility of commodity investments.

---

[7] This is particularly the case for *individual commodities* to *individual stocks*.

**Exhibit 8.1**
**Commodity Returns and Volatility**[8]

The following table sets out the annualized total returns and annualized
volatility of commodity assets and other financial assets.

| | | | | Returns (% pa) | | | |
|---|---|---|---|---|---|---|---|
| Index | CPCI | GSCI | DJ-AIG | S&P | SSB Bonds | ML Bonds | CPI |
| Dec 83 – Jan 91 | 11.73 | 16.05 | | 14.98 | 13.97 | 11.22 | 4.52 |
| Jan 91 – Jul 99 | 4.95 | 0.90 | –2.49 | 19.86 | 9.35 | 7.59 | 2.82 |

| | | | | Volatility (% pa) | | | |
|---|---|---|---|---|---|---|---|
| Index | CPCI | GSCI | DJ-AIG | S&P Bonds | SSB Bonds | ML | CPI |
| Dec 83-Jan 91 | 4.70 | 3.76 | | 4.92 | 3.40 | 1.29 | 0.10 |
| Jan 91-Jul 99 | 3.90 | 5.12 | 3.07 | 3.87 | 2.33 | 1.06 | 0.12 |

*Notes:*
1. CPCI is the Chase Physical Commodity Total Return Index. GSCI is the
   Goldman Sachs Commodity Total Return Index. S&P is the S&P 500
   Accumulation/Total Returns Index. The SSB Bonds is the Salomon Smith
   Barney Total Return Treasury Bond Index. ML Bonds is the Merrill Lynch
   Total Return Treasury Bond index. CPI is the US Consumer Price Index.
2. Returns are calculated as monthly % pa returns that are then annualized for the
   periods December 31, 1983 to January 31, 1991 and January 31, 1991 to July
   31, 1999.
3. Volatility is calculated as the annualized standard deviation of the monthly
   index changes.

The positive expected return and price volatility would of itself make it desirable
to add commodity investments as a separate investment asset. However, the
major benefits of commodity investment derive from additional sources of value
created from adding commodities to an investment portfolio. These additional
sources of value relate to:

---

[8]   The choice of periods is driven by the fact that it was 1984 that the indexes first
      included crude oil (this is now the largest single component of many indexes). The
      second sub-period is driven by the fact that the DJ-AIG index only covers the period
      from January 1991.

- The diversification benefit provided by commodity investment because of the pattern of correlation between commodity returns and returns on traditional investment assets.
- The special value drivers affecting commodity investment, such as inflation.

Exhibit 8.2 sets out the correlation between returns on commodity holdings and returns on other asset classes.

---

### Exhibit 8.2
### Commodity Return Correlations

The following table sets out the correlation between returns on commodities and other financial assets, as well as macroeconomic indicators.

| | CPCI – Total Return | CPCI – Excess Return | GSCI – Total Return | GSCI – Excess Return | DJ-AIG – Total Return | DJ-AIG – Excess Return | S&P | SSB Bond Index | ML Bond Index | CPI |
|---|---|---|---|---|---|---|---|---|---|---|
| CPCI – Total Return | 1 | | | | | | | | | |
| CPCI – Excess Return | 0.999 | 1 | | | | | | | | |
| GSCI – Total Return | 0.891 | 0.888 | 1 | | | | | | | |
| GSCI – Excess Return | 0.892 | 0.890 | 0.999 | 1 | | | | | | |
| DJ-AIG – Total Return | 0.481 | 0.483 | 0.444 | 0.445 | 1 | | | | | |
| DJ-AIG – Excess Return | 0.482 | 0.483 | 0.445 | 0.446 | 1.000 | 1 | | | | |
| S&P | –0.045 | –0.045 | –0.034 | –0.034 | –0.133 | –0.130 | 1 | | | |
| SSB Bond Index | –0.186 | –0.191 | –0.078 | –0.083 | –0.159 | –0.156 | 0.302 | 1 | | |
| ML Bond Index | –0.121 | –0.128 | –0.047 | –0.054 | –0.145 | –0.141 | 0.304 | 0.936 | 1 | |
| CPI | 0.023 | 0.007 | 0.060 | 0.044 | –0.014 | –0.014 | –0.085 | 0.053 | 0.113 | 1 |

Notes:
1. CPCI is the Chase Physical Commodity Total Return and Excess Return Index. GSCI is the Goldman Sachs Commodity Total Return and Excess Return Index. DJ-AIG is the Dow Jones-AIG Commodity Total Return and Excess Return Index. S&P is the S&P 500 Accumulation/Total Returns Index. The SSB Bonds is the Salomon Smith Barney Total Return Treasury Bond Index. ML Bonds is the Merrill Lynch Total Return Treasury Bond index. CPI is the US Consumer Price Index.
2. All correlation is based on data for the period December 31, 1983 to July 1999, except for correlation involving the Dow Jones-AIG Commodity Index, which is for the period January 1991 to July 1999.
3. Correlation is calculated using ordinary least squares methodology on the % changes in the relevant indexes.

The analysis shows the weak correlation of commodity prices and inflation (particularly, changes in the rate of inflation) and commodity prices and stock prices. It also shows the negative correlation with bond returns.[9] This means that the addition of commodity investments can enhance portfolio performance in a number of ways:

- Reduction of volatility of real returns.
- Reduction of the overall volatility of the portfolio.
- Generation of returns comparable to those on stocks and bonds.
- Act as an inflation hedge.

In summary, commodity investments appear to provide financial investors with attractive total returns, volatility of returns, and (some) liquidity. From a portfolio perspective, the investment characteristics of commodities is enhanced because of its (generally) negative correlation to returns on financial assets and positive correlation to inflation. The first relationship enables portfolio managers to diversify their risks improving returns for a given level of risk or reducing risk for a given level of return. The second relationship enables these assets to perform well during periods of inflation stabilizing portfolio returns.

## 2.3   Commodity Indexes

### 2.3.1   Concept

An increasing element of the commodity-linked market is the interest in *commodity indexes*.[10] Similar in conception to other indexes, including equity indexes, the ability to provide diversified exposure to *commodity prices in general on a diversified basis* has encouraged the advent of transactions where the linkage is to an index. The benchmarking of commodity portfolios to these indexes for the purpose of performance measurement has also encouraged

---

[9]   Other research has shown the positive correlation of commodity prices and inflation (particularly, changes in the rate of inflation) and the negative correlation with stock and bond returns.

[10]   The concept of an investable commodity index that is treated as a separate asset class was first suggested by Greer, Robert J. "Conservative Commodities: A Key Inflation Hedge" (Summer 1978) *Journal of Portfolio Management*. For a discussion of commodity indexes see Greer, Robert J. "Institutional Use Of Physical Commodity Indices" in Smith, Kathleen Tener and Kennison, Pam (1996) *Commodity Derivatives and Finance*; Euromoney Publications, London at Chapter 9; Reed, Nick "Fruit Of The Boom" (February 1995) Risk vol. 8 no. 2 31-35; van Duyn, Aline "First Pick Your Index" (January 1995) *Euromoney* 39-41.

transactions based on the index. **Exhibit 8.3** sets out some of the available commodity indexes.[11]

---

**Exhibit 8.3**
**Commodity Indexes**

Chase Physical Commodity Index (CPCI)
Commodity Research Bureau Index (CRB)
Dow Jones-AIG Commodity Index (DJ-AIGCI)
Goldman Sachs Commodity Index (GSCI)

---

### 2.3.2 *Characteristics*

A commodity index is essentially designed to represent and track price changes in a basket of commodities or commodity futures contracts. The underlying logic is that the returns on the index approximate the returns to an investor holding an unleveraged position in the assets underlying the basket.

The essential drivers of commodity indexes are:

• Indexes allow diversified exposure to commodities to be engineered.
• The index can be used as a performance benchmark for commodity investments.

In practice, commodity indexes are important in commodity markets as derivative transactions (futures contracts, as well as forwards and options) and structured notes based on the *index* rather than *specific commodities* have become increasingly popular.

The difference between the different indexes are based on a variety of design factors including:

• **Index composition** — the various commodity indexes are either narrow or broad based. Narrow-based indexes typically cover major commodities, primarily energy and metals. Broad-based indexes cover these commodities but extend their coverage to a large variety of commodities including "softs" (grains, livestock, and other agricultural products). Narrow-based indexes aim to be sector specific and focus on liquid commodities with a direct link to industrial production and GDP. Narrow-based indexes also seek to avoid exposure to factors such as weather conditions. Broad-based indexes are focused on a widely based exposure to *all commodities that are economically*

---

[11] Other indexes that are used include: Bankers Trust Commodity Index (BTCI); J.P. Morgan Commodity Index (JPMCI); Lehman Brothers Commodity Index (LBCI); and Merrill Lynch Energy And Metals Index (ENMET).

*significant.* Broad-based indexes, while more difficult to replicate, will generally provide more accurate protection against inflation and exposure to the low cross-correlations between commodities. The underlying assets in a commodity basket may also vary. Some indexes use *physical commodities* while others use *futures contracts on the commodity*. The difference is driven by the relative liquidity and price transparency of the relevant commodity markets.

- **Index weights** may be based on:
  1. Economic weights — based on fundamental economic data (such as world production quantities or values).
  2. Equal weights — based on fixed weights.
  3. Market weights — based on relative trading volumes in futures markets (on futures contracts on the commodity).
  4. Optimized weights — based on econometric models that seek to optimize nominated criteria (such as level of returns, volatility of returns, correlations to inflation, and so on) over the selected time period
- **Index rebalancing** — entails two separate factors: the mechanics of rolling futures contracts and rebalancing the portfolio weighting. Where the commodity index is based on commodity futures contracts, the futures contract will mature and must then be rolled forward into a more distant maturity. This rolling process is the mechanism that allows capture of the convenience yield in the commodity markets. The other element of index rebalancing necessitates adjusting the positions in individual commodities based on factors such as value changes and the emergence of new commodities (for example, electricity or telecommunications capacity). There are two basic approaches:
  1. Fixed weights — consistent exposure is maintained, based on fixed quantities of commodities in the basket.
  2. Value weights — which requires constant rebalancing with investors effectively selling (buying) commodities that have risen (fallen) in value.
- **Return calculation** — returns may be calculated on an arithmetic or geometric basis. The use of geometric returns prevents domination of index value changes by higher priced commodities.
- **Leveraged versus unleveraged returns** — a leveraged commodity index is typically based on futures contracts. This reflects the fact that trading in futures requires minimal commitment of capital (the initial and variation margins). This will have the effect of enhancing the returns as price changes will be relative to low levels of employed investment capital. Unleveraged indexes assume either:
  1. Investment in cash or physical commodity assets.
  2. Investment in futures contracts, but with fully matched cash investment equal to the underlying value of the contract (the cash earns risk-free returns).

- **Total return versus excess returns** — the commodity index returns are calculated in two ways:
  1. Total return — representing the total rate of return of the index.
  2. Excess return — representing the total returns minus the return on Treasury bills.

### 2.3.3   Comparison of Indexes

**Exhibit 8.4** sets out a brief comparison of the various commodity indexes. **Exhibit 8.5** sets out a brief comparison of the relative performance of these indexes.

**Exhibit 8.4**
**Commodity Indexes — Comparison**

| Index | CRB | CPCI | GSCI | Dow Jones–AIG |
|---|---|---|---|---|
| Composition | Broad | Broad | Broad | Broad |
| Major Sectors | Major sectors are energy, livestock, grains, industrial metals, precious metals and softs | Major sectors are energy, livestock, grains, industrial metals, precious metals and softs | Major sectors are energy, livestock, grains, industrial metals, precious metals and softs | Major sectors are energy, livestock, grains, industrial metals, precious metals and softs |
| Weighting | Equal | Economic | Economic | Liquidity; Economic |
| Rebalancing | Value; Static | Value; Dynamic | Quantity; Dynamic | Value; Dynamic |
| Returns | Geometric | Arithmetic | Arithmetic | Arithmetic |

## 2.4   Structure of Commodity Markets

The identified factors have created a rapid growth in demand for commodity-linked investment instruments. The growth in this source of commodity demand is evidenced by the fact that a significant portion of commodity trading is now *investor driven*.

However, financial and portfolio investors face substantial difficulties in effecting commodity investments. These include storage and related (insurance, transport, and so on) costs and difficulties in leasing or lending out the commodity holding. These factors have encouraged the development of a *paper*

**Exhibit 8.5**
**Commodity Indexes — Performance**

| Commodity Index | Annual Return (% pa) Dec 1983- Jan 1991 | Volatility (% pa) Dec 1983- Jan 1999 | Annual Return (% pa) Jan 1991- July 1999 | Volatility (% pa) Jan 1991- July 1999 | Correlation (%) with Changes in Inflation | Correlation (%) with Stocks (S&P) | Correlation (%) with Bonds (SSB Inflation) |
|---|---|---|---|---|---|---|---|
| CPCI | 11.73 | 4.70 | 4.95 | 3.90 | 0.023 | –0.045 | –0.186 |
| Dow Jones-AIG | | | –2.49 | 3.07 | –0.014 | –0.133 | –0.159 |
| GSCI | 16.05 | 3.76 | 0.90 | 5.12 | 0.060 | –0.034 | –0.078 |

*Notes:*
1. CPCI is the Chase Physical Commodity Total Return Index. GSCI is the Goldman Sachs Commodity Total Return Index. DJ-AIG is the Dow Jones-AIG Commodity Total Return Index. S&P is the S&P 500 Accumulation/Total Returns Index. The SSB Bonds is the Salomon Smith Barney Total Return Treasury Bond Index. CPI is the US Consumer Price Index.
2. All analysis is based on data for the period December 31, 1983 to July 31, 1999 except for analysis involving the Dow Jones-AIG Commodity Index, which is for the period January 1991 to July 1999.
3. Returns are calculated as monthly % pa returns that are then annualized.
4. Volatility is calculated as the annualized standard deviation of the monthly index changes.
5. Correlation is calculated using ordinary least-squares methodology on the % changes in the relevant indexes.

commodity market that strongly emphasises commodity-linked notes (or pure off-balance sheet structures) as the mechanism for creating the required exposure to commodity prices.

The investment demand for commodity-linked product has been met from two sources: firstly, issue of commodity-linked debt from commodity producers (and, less frequently, commodity users); and, secondly, structured notes with commodity price linkages.

The issuers of commodity-linked bonds were, originally, commodity producers or users motivated by the following reasons:

• Creating hedges against underlying commodity positions entailing the future sale or purchase of the relevant commodity.

- Commodity producers utilizing the value of their commodity resources as the basis of raising capital to finance extraction and production.
- Transfer potential profits or gains from appreciation or depreciation in the commodity price to investors in return for lower borrowing costs.

The original type of commodity-linked bonds, which did not necessitate or involve commodity derivatives, were based on matching investor demand and issuers with underlying positions in the relevant commodity. However, it rapidly became evident that demand for commodity-linked securities out-stripped borrower interest in issuing such instruments. This necessitated the creation of *purely financial* commodity transactions in the form of commodity price-linked structured notes that allowed issuers to offer investors the desired commodity exposure while simultaneously insulating themselves from the risk of commodity price movements through specially structured derivative transactions.

The central focus of these purely financial commodity transactions was arbitrage issuers who were willing to undertake issues of commodity-linked transactions on the basis that their own commodity exposure was hedged by the derivative dealer. Central to this type of "new" commodity-linked bond structure was the transference of specific derivative positions in the underlying commodity from one segment of the capital market to another. The more common commodity derivative structures are set out in **Appendix A** in this chapter.

## 3. Commodity-linked Notes — Structural Alternatives[12]

The types of commodity-linked notes are predicated upon the evolution of commodity investments described above. The principal structural models are:

- Commodity-based financing transactions.
- Commodity-linked structured notes.

---

[12] See Budd, Nicholas "A Future Role For Commodity-linked Securities" (November 1982*) The Banker* 49-57; Budd, Nicholas "The Future Of Commodity Indexed Financing" (July-August 1983) *Harvard Business Review* 44-50; Fehon, C.M. "Commodity-linked Financing" (June 1993) *The Australian Corporate Treasurer* 9-11; Koh, Kenny (1986) Reasons for Using and the Pricing of Commodity-linked Bonds, unpublished research paper presented to course on Capital Raising, Centre for Studies in Money, Banking and Finance, Macquarie University; J.P. Morgan & Co. Inc. (1992) Commodity-linked Finance; *Euromoney Publications*: London; Lassiter, Leslie "Commodities Blueprint For Corporate Finance" (March 1991) *Euromoney* 95-98; Priovolus, Theophilos and Duncan, Ronald C. (editors) (1991) *Commodity Risk Management and Finance*; Oxford University Press: Oxford; Roche, Julian (1993) *Commodity-linked Derivatives*; IFR Publishing: London; White, Daniel L. "Next In Corporate Finance: Index-linked Loans" (September-October 1981) *Harvard Business Review* 14-22; for a valuation perspective see Schwartz, Eduardo "The Pricing Of Commodity-linked Bonds" (May 1982) *Journal of Finance* vol. 37 no. 2 525-541.

The distinguishing characteristics of the two types of transactions relate to the underlying issuer and the commodity exposure that is embodied. Commodity-based financing relates to the issue of debt linked to commodities where the linkage is predicated upon the position *of the issuer* in the underlying commodity.

Commodity-linked structured notes are issues of debt where the commodity price exposure is deliberately engineered into the return profile of the instrument and where the issuer has no position in the commodity being insulated from this exposure through derivative transactions completed with a derivatives dealer. Each of these structural models are discussed below.

The earliest issues of commodity-linked structured notes were undertaken in the Swiss franc capital market in the mid-1980s with a number of issues of Swiss franc notes with attached oil warrants being completed. The second phase of issuance of these types of securities was in the late 1980s with a substantial number of issues denominated in US dollars linked to oil prices being completed.

A special type of commodity-linked security transaction has been the issue of warrants on the price of a variety of commodities, primarily energy commodities. These issues of warrants have been structured as either naked warrants or warrants issued in conjunction with debt. In a number of cases, the issue of warrants linked to debt has been in transactions designed to take advantage of substantial spreads between retail and wholesale market prices for commodity options. In general, the issuer of these warrants has been a financial institution seeking to satisfy investor demand for instruments sensitive to commodity price movements. The financial institutions have hedged their own exposure under the derivative transactions by purchasing offsetting instruments in the wholesale market or by undertaking synthetic option hedging transactions.

The major types of commodities utilized in commodity-linked transactions are summarized in **Exhibit 8.6**. The market for commodity-linked notes/financing has been historically biased in favor of precious metals, base metals, and energy. However, in recent years, there has been increasing diversity in the range of commodities utilized.

---

**Exhibit 8.6**
**Commodities Utilized in**
**Commodity-linked Financing/Structured Notes**

*Precious Metals*
Gold
Silver
Platinum

*Metals*
Copper
Aluminium
Lead
Nickel
Tin
Zinc

*Energy Products*
Crude Oils (WTI; Brent etc.)
Products (jet fuel; gasoline; diesel; heating oil etc.)
Natural gas
Coal
Electricity

*Forestry Products*
Pulp
Timber

*Agricultural Products*
Cereals (wheat, corn, soybeans)
Cocoa
Coffee
Sugar
Livestock
Cotton
Wool

# 4. Commodity-based Financing Transactions

## 4.1 Overview

There are a number of possible types of commodity-based financing structures:

- Debt repayable with a fixed amount of the commodity (or the monetary equivalent at market value).
- Debt where the investor receives a premium return based on commodity price appreciation above a prenominated level (structured either as a convertible bond where the bond can be converted into a predetermined amount of the commodity or through warrants to purchase the product at a known strike price).

## 4.2   Debt Indexed to a Fixed Amount Of Commodity

Debt repayable with a fixed amount of commodity generally takes the form of indexing, either principal and/or interest in a fixed income security to the relevant commodity. A change in the commodity price has a proportional effect on the dollar amount of interest or principal due, effectively representing the market value of the underlying commodity.

### 4.2.1   Commodity Loans

The basic structure of a commodity loan transaction can be illustrated with a gold loan transaction.[13] **Exhibit 8.7** sets out the structure of a gold loan.

---

**Exhibit 8.7**
**Commodity (Gold) Loan Transaction**

*Structure*

The steps in a gold loan are as follows:

- The gold producer borrows an agreed amount of the gold.
- The gold is simultaneously sold to the dealer thereby raising cash for the producer.
- At a future date, the producer repays the gold loan by transferring the amount of gold borrowed plus an interest amount *in physical gold* (the gold-borrowing interest or lease rate—the offered side).

This is set out in the diagram below:

---

[13] For a discussion of the gold market see Cross, Jessica (1994) *New Frontiers in Gold: The Derivatives Revolution*; Rosendale Press, London; Manuell, Guy "Risk Management Techniques For Gold Producers" (December 1995) *Financial Derivatives & Risk Management* Issue 4 23-31; see also Street, Michael "Considerations In Gold Mine Project Financing" (June 1983) *JASSA* 19-22; Chant, Warren "Gold-related Finance" (July 1984) *The Chartered Accountant In Australia* 30-31; Cox, Ian (1994) The Gold Borrowing Market: A Decade Of Growth; Research study no. 5, World Gold Council.

### Structure of Gold Loan

**At Commencement**

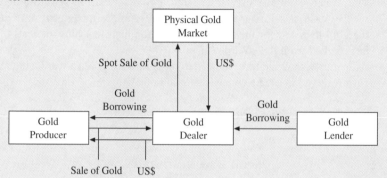

**At Maturity**

### Hedging Structure

The gold dealer covers the gold borrowing in one of two ways:

### Option 1

- The gold lent is borrowed (typically from a central bank) in return for payment of a fee, the gold-borrowing rate (or bid lease rate).
- The sale of the gold in the spot market raises cash that is advanced to the gold producer.
- The gold received at the maturity of the gold loan is used to return the borrowed gold plus interest to the gold lender.

This structure is set out in the above diagram.

### Option 2

- The dealer does not physically borrow or lend and then sell the gold. Instead, the dealer lends the US dollars equivalent (based on the spot price) of the amount of gold that is then funded by borrowing the equivalent amount of funds by way of an interbank deposit that is raised.

- The dealer simultaneously enters into a gold forward to sell gold and receive cash at a forward date coinciding with the repayment date of the gold loan and for the amount of gold (amount lent plus interest) to be received from the gold producer.
- At maturity, the gold received is delivered into the gold forward and the cash received is used to repay the cash borrowing.

This structure is set out below:

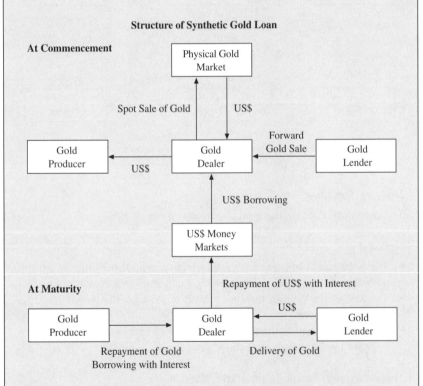

**Structure of Synthetic Gold Loan**

In effect, the gold loan combines a US dollar loan with an embedded gold forward. The structure of a typical gold forward (which underlies the structure of a gold loan) is set out in the diagram below.

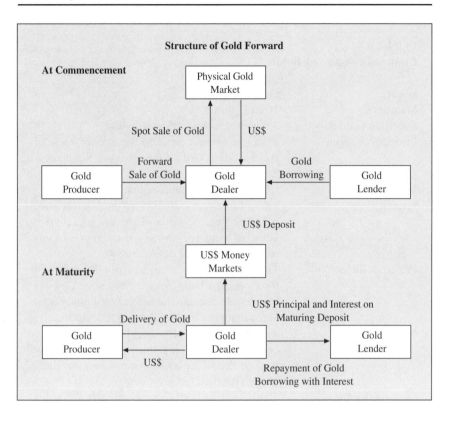

The commodity loan structure is most commonly utilized in the gold market. This reflects the availability of a large number of counterparties (mainly central banks) willing to lend gold. This was driven by the fact that central banks held substantial gold reserves and were seeking to generate returns on these investments. The absence of a similar available source of commodity available for borrowing in other markets has meant that the commodity loan structure has not developed as a form of financing.

### 4.2.2  Debt Repayable in Commodity

An issue by Refinement International, in February 1981, entailing the issue of bonds indexed to the price of gold is typical of this structure. The issue that carried a coupon of 3.25% pa had both principal and interest payable in multiples of 100 ounces of gold. The terms and conditions applicable to a typical example of this particular type of commodity-linked financing is set out in **Exhibit 8.8**.

**Exhibit 8.8**
**Commodity-indexed Bonds**

| | |
|---|---|
| Issuer | Gold Producer |
| Maturity | 10 to 15 years |
| Specified Gold Amount | An agreed amount of gold bullion. |
| Principal Amount | Principal amount equal to the market value of the Specified Gold Amount as at the date of issue. |
| Interest Rate | [ ]% of the Principal Amount. |
| Interest | Interest is payable in US$ at the Interest Rate calculated on the basis of the average market value of gold for an agreed number of days prior to the interest payment. |
| Principal Redemption | The bonds will be redeemed in US$ based on the Specified Gold Amount calculated on the basis of the average market value of gold for an agreed number of days prior to redemption. |
| Security Interest | The bonds are fully secured primarily by certificates obligating third parties to deliver gold or the issuer to maintain inventory equal to the Specified Gold Amount. |
| Optional Payment | To the extent that a bond holder aggregates interest entitlements or bonds representing an agreed minimum amount of gold (say, 1,000 ounces) or integral multiples thereof, the holder may elect to receive such interest or redemption in gold bullion. |
| Call Option | The issuer may call the bond: |

1. At any time after five years at the average of market value of the Specified Gold Amount at the time of redemption; or
2. At any time if the average market value of the Specified Gold Amount at the time of redemption, if the average market price of gold over a period of 60 days trades at or above 200% of the market price of gold at the time of issue.

These types of transactions are conceptually very similar to commodity loans (such as gold loans). This can be illustrated with a more recent example of this type of transaction entailing the issue of gold indexed by Poseidon Gold, a large Australian gold producer.

Traditionally, gold producers, such as Poseidon Gold, would finance themselves through a gold loan transaction. In the case of Poseidon, the gold producer wanted to undertake a long-term funding. If the transaction was structured as a gold loan, the company faced the following difficulties:

- Access to credit lines for a long-term gold loan (10 years) would be restricted.
- The gold lease rate[14] while low (around 1% pa) for shorter maturities is sharply higher rising to 3 to 5% pa for longer maturities thereby increasing the cost of capital for the borrower.

The alternative would have been to borrow shorter term and roll the borrowing, creating an exposure to fluctuations in both interest rates and gold-leasing rates.

Under these circumstances, Poseidon issued gold-indexed bonds that had both coupons and principal redemption values indexed to the gold price. In effect, Poseidon had sold forward and the investor had bought forward the specified amounts of gold. The transaction combines a US$ bond with these embedded gold forwards. The principal terms and economics of the issue are summarized in **Exhibit 8.9**.

---

**Exhibit 8.9**
**Gold-indexed Bond**

| | |
|---|---|
| Issuer | Posgold Finance Limited |
| Guarantor | Poseidon Gold Limited |
| Amount of Gold | 500,000 troy ounces |
| Maturity | 10 years (due 2004) |
| Amount | US$194,376,00 (calculated as the Specified Amount of Gold at US$390.19—being the gold price as at the time of issue—multiplied by the issue price). A total of 20,000 bonds were issued, each representing 25 troy ounces of gold. |
| Issue Price | 99.6315 |

---

[14] The gold lease rate is generally calculated as the gold forward premium to spot (the carry) adjusted for the pure interest cost of carry for the relevant maturity.

| | |
|---|---|
| Interest Rate | Years 1-5: 0.33125 ounces of gold per bond. |
| | Years 6-10: 0.47500 ounces of gold per bond. |
| Interest Payments | Interest is payable in US$ semi-annually at the Interest Rate calculated on the basis of the average market value of gold for three days prior to the interest payment date. |
| Principal Redemption | The bonds will be redeemed in US$ based on the Specified Amount of Gold calculated on the basis of the average market value of gold for 20 days prior to redemption. |
| Put Option | The holders have the option to redeem the bonds at 99.75% of the Redemption Amount after five years. |

The major attraction for investors was the capacity afforded by the gold-indexed bond to create a term exposure *directly* to gold while earning a running return on the investment. The practical advantages of the security structure of the investment are also relevant. From the perspective of the issuer, the bond acts as a hedge against its underlying gold risk, with increasing servicing costs of the bond being offset by rises in cash flows from increased revenues from its gold production and sales. In addition, it offers term funding at attractive fixed rates for gold and allows diversification of funding sources.[15]

The return to the investor (interest payments and redemption amounts) based on hypothetical reference gold prices (US$/ounce) is set out in the **Exhibit 8.10**.

**Exhibit 8.10**
**Gold-indexed Bonds — Returns**

| | |
|---|---|
| Denomination of Bond (oz) | 25 |
| Gold Price At Issue (US$/oz) | 390.19 |
| Issue Price | 99.6135% |
| Bond Face Value | $9,717.05 |

---

[15] See Manuell, Guy "Risk Management Techniques For Gold Producers" (December 1995) *Financial Derivatives & Risk Management* Issue 4 23-31.

| | Interest Payments (US$/Bond) | | Redemption Amount (US$/bond) | | Yield (% pa) | |
|---|---|---|---|---|---|---|
| | Years 1-5 | Years 6-10 | At put | At Maturity | To Put | To Maturity |
| Gold Amount (oz) Gold Price (US$/oz) | 0.33125 | 0.475 | 99.75% | 100% | | |
| 90.19 | $29.88 | $42.84 | $2,249.11 | $2,254.75 | -25.94% | -12.40% |
| 190.19 | $63.00 | $90.34 | $4,742.86 | $4,754.75 | -12.02% | -4.74% |
| 290.19 | $96.13 | $137.84 | $7,236.61 | $7,254.75 | -3.55% | -0.14% |
| 390.19 | $129.25 | $185.34 | $9,730.36 | $9,754.75 | 2.69% | 3.22% |
| 490.19 | $162.38 | $232.84 | $12,224.11 | $12,254.75 | 7.67% | 5.91% |
| 590.19 | $195.50 | $280.34 | $14,717.86 | $14,754.75 | 11.86% | 8.17% |
| 690.19 | $228.63 | $327.84 | $17,211.61 | $17,254.75 | 15.48% | 10.14% |
| 790.19 | $261.75 | $375.34 | $19,705.36 | $19,754.75 | 18.70% | 11.88% |

Other structures have included commodity financing indexed to floating prices. An example of this structure is an issue in 1980 undertaken by the Petro-Lewis Corporation for US$52 million where the principal is the nominal face value amount, but *the interest* is indexed to the market value of oil subject to a 1% maximum annual adjustment. The interest indexation (in effect, an embedded commodity fixed-for-floating oil swap in the loan) effectively offsets the fluctuations in the company's cash flows as a result of movements in the price of oil.

**Exhibit 8.11** sets out an example of a structure where the commodity indexation is applied to a transaction involving a commodity consumer embedding a forward purchase within the financing to provide an economic hedge against future purchases of the commodity.

**Exhibit 8.11**
**Commodity-indexed Loan for Commodity Consumer**

Assume a consumer of a commodity seeks a hedge for its commodity price exposure in the form of a commodity-indexed loan. The terms of such a loan or note would be as follows:

| Principal Amount | US$50 million |
|---|---|
| Term | 5 years |
| Repayment | In full at maturity |
| Commodity Index | Fuel Oil Index |
| Fixed Commodity Price | US$20/barrel |

Under the transaction, the borrower receives US$50 million at the start of the financing. This is the cash equivalent of an agreed US$20 barrel basis price (that is, the notional commodity position is 2,500,000 barrels equivalent).

The borrower's principal repayment is linked to movements in fuel oil price in accordance to the following formula:

Principal repayment − [(Index price (at maturity) − Fixed commodity price) × Notional commodity position]

Assuming the fuel oil price has moved to US$25/barrel, the cash amount due as principal repayment is:

US$50,000,000 − [(US$25/barrel − US$20/barrel) × 2,500,000]
= US$37,500,00

The principal repayment in this case is US$12,500,000 less than the face value of the loan. The savings provide a hedge against the increased cost of the higher cost (based on higher oil prices) of fuel oil for the borrower. Partial indexation structures are also feasible.

The major benefits of the debt-indexed to fixed amount of commodity structure include:

- **Additional security for lenders** — this takes the form of reduction in the volatility of the producer's cash flows and its exposure to commodity prices, as well as the security interest that can be created in the underlying commodity.
- **Economic hedge** — the commodity price linkage (in effect, a sale of the commodity forward by the producer) provides an economic hedge to the commodity producer. This type of hedge may be more effective in several respects. It may take longer in maturity than pure derivative markets (for example, exchange traded commodity futures and option or OTC transactions) and may be more credit efficient. The latter is the result of combining the hedge with the financing that effectively collateralizes the hedge facilitating the limitation of exposure of the seller to the buyer.
- **Nonrecourse structure** — it may be possible to structure these transactions on a nonrecourse basis, limiting recourse to reserves and production of specific commodities.

- **Lower cost of capital** — these structures may allow lower cost of capital in several respects. The features identified, particularly the security aspects and the nonrecourse structure, may enhance the credit-enabling lower cost funding. A second source of lower cost finance may be the lower commodity interest rates. Extreme care should be taken in comparing *commodity* interest rates to *nominal* interest rates. Commodity interest rates, while superficially lower, are only comparable to nominal interest rates upon conversion into monetary terms that are then translated into yield-to-maturity comparables. Opportunities to lower the cost of funding can, however, exist in certain circumstance where the shape of the forward commodity price curve allows the effective normal interest rate cost to be lowered.[16]

### 4.3   Debt with Commodity-linked Appreciation Potential

Debt with commodity-linked appreciation potential is a separate class of commodity-linked financing in which the investor provides funding at a lower cost of capital in exchange for a premium return if the commodity price increases above a predetermined level. This usually, economically entails a combination of a call option or multiple options on the relevant commodity with an issue of debt.

This type of financing entails the following structure:

- A bond convertible or loan into a specified amount of the commodity or indexed to the market value of that amount at the option of the holder.
- A bond, loan or preferred stock issue with a warrant attached granting the holder the right to purchase a specified amount of that amount at the option of the holder.
- A bond issue or loan where the interest payable increases if the price of the commodity exceeds a predetermined level.

Among the earliest of the first type of transactions were two issues undertaken in early 1980 by Sunshine Mining of the US that entailed the issue of US$25 million of 8.50% pa coupon 15-year silver-backed bonds. The bonds were to be redeemed at maturity at par or the market price of silver, whichever was higher. Each US$1,000 bond was redeemable either at par or the market price of 15 ounces of silver. This represented a premium of about 25% above the then current value of silver. The second issue entailed a premium of around 20%.[17] **Exhibit 8.12** sets out the terms and conditions of an issue similar to that of the Sunshine Mining issue.

---

[16]  See Das, Satyajit "Commodity Swaps: Forward March" *Risk* (February 1993) vol. 6 no. 2 41-49.

[17]  See Brauer, Greggory and Ravichandran, R "How Sweet Is Silver" (Summer 1986) *Journal of Portfolio Management* 33-42.

**Exhibit 8.12**
**Commodity-indexed Bonds with Conversion Feature**

| | |
|---|---|
| Issuer | Silver producer |
| Maturity | 10 to 15 years |
| Specified Amount of Silver | The amount of silver underlying each bond. |
| Indexed Principal Amount | For each US$1,000 Face Amount Bond, the greater of: US$1,000; or a specified average of the specified amount of silver. |
| Redemption Value | Indexed principal amount |
| Payments in Silver | If the indexed principal amount is greater than US$1,000, The issuer has the option of delivering the specified amount of silver to holder in satisfaction of the indexed principal amount. |
| Interest Payments | [ ]% pa on US$ value of the specified amount of silver at the time of issue (the effective coupon would be at a significant discount to prevailing market rates for the issuer). |
| Call Option | Callable at the option of the issuer: 1. At the indexed principal amount after 5 years: or 2. If the indexed principal amount is US$2,000 or more for a period of 30 consecutive calender days. |
| Sinking Fund | 7% of the amount of the original issue will be called or redeemed each year. |

The attraction for the issuer was a relatively low nominal interest rate payable on the bonds (8.50% pa rather than the prevailing market interest rate of around 13-14% pa). The borrower absorbed the redemption risk of the issue. This reflected the fact that if the price of silver went up, thereby increasing the redemption price of the bonds, Sunshine Mining's revenues would have also appreciated reflecting the higher market value of its production. If, however, the price of silver stagnated or fell, the company would have borrowed money at a rate of interest substantially below market levels at the time of issue.

An example of the second type of structure, effectively, debt or stock combined with commodity warrants, is the issue undertaken in 1981 by Echo Bay Mines entailing the issue of preferred shares with gold warrants. Each share (maturing in 1989) was issued with four warrants (exercisable annually commencing in 1986 and expiring in 1989), each entitling the holder to purchase a total of 0.0706 troy ounces of gold. **Exhibit 8.13** sets out the terms and conditions typically applicable to these issues.

Another example of this type of structure entailing debt combined with oil warrants undertaken by Standard Oil is described in **Exhibit 8.14**. **Exhibit 8.15** on page 333 sets out an example of a commodity-linked financing structure used by American Barrick for financing its gold production.

---

**Exhibit 8.13**
**Preferred Stock Issue with Commodity Warrants**

| | |
|---|---|
| Issuer | Commodity producer |
| Issue | Issue of cumulative redeemable voting preferred shares with detachable gold purchase warrants. |
| Price | US$50 per unit made up as follows: |
| | 1. US$25 for the preferred share. |
| | 2. US$25 is a prepayment on account of the purchase price for gold under the four gold purchase warrants. |
| Dividends | Fixed cumulative preferential dividends payable either quarterly or semi-annually. |
| Redemption | Mandatory redemption after five to 10 years at issue price inclusive of any premium on issue. |
| Voting | Generally nonvoting (except where dividends are missed or other conditions are not complied with). |
| Gold Warrants | Each detachable warrant will entitle: |
| | 1. The holder to purchase from the issuer an agreed amount of gold at a specified strike price; or |
| | 2. The holder will receive the US$ equivalent of the gold price as at the date of exercise and the specified strike price on the relevant amount of gold. |
| | Upon exercise (in option 1) the holder will be required to pay the balance of the purchase price for gold. |
| | The gold purchase warrants will trade separately from the underlying preferred shares. |

**Exhibit 8.14**
**Standard Oil — Crude Oil-linked Bonds**

An example of this type of structure was a series of issues undertaken in the middle of 1986 by the Standard Oil Company, the US arm of British Petroleum.

Under the structure, Standard Oil issued:

US$300 million 15-year, 6.30% coupon bonds priced at 74.70% of face value.

Simultaneously, detachable oil-indexed notes were issued as follows:

- US$37.5 million due December 1990; and
- US$37.5 million due March 1992.

The oil-indexed notes have a strike price of US$25 per barrel (based on West Texas Intermediate Crude oil (WTI)). The oil-indexed warrants were capped at a WTI market price of US$40 per barrel.

The result of the transaction is that Standard Oil borrows US$224.1 million (being effectively the discounted proceeds of the US$300 million face value bonds) at normal market rates. Simultaneously, it receives US$75 million in return for the issue of the oil-indexed notes (effectively call options on oil) to investors. This US$75 million can be treated as reducing the cost of the 15-year bond issue or can be utilized to retire other debt.

For the investor in the oil-index notes, if the WTI price is US$25 or below, the options will expire unexercised and the investor will receive the face value of the notes from Standard Oil. In the event that WTI is above US$25 per barrel, the investor will receive an indexed amount reflecting the appreciation in the oil price equating to the appreciation in the value of the call option.

From the perspective of Standard Oil, it achieves a lower cost of funding through the sale of the WTI call options. In the event that oil prices appreciate, its cost of borrowing increases, reflecting the higher redemption payout under the oil-indexed notes. However, this added borrowing cost should be offset by the increased revenue and earnings resulting from the higher oil price.

**Exhibit 8.15**
**Gold-indexed Financing**

In 1984, American Barrick raised US$17 million to finance expansion of one of its mines through the Barrick-Cullaton Gold Trust. The Trust effectively was a commodity-indexed financing structure.

The structure was as follows:

• Investors invested in the Trust.
• Investors received returns calculated as follows:
  1. 3% of mine output when the price of gold was equal to or below US$399/ounce.
  2. A rising percentage of production capped at 10% of production when gold was at US$1,000/ounce.

The essential structure of the Trust for the investors was as follows:
1. The investor owns 0.03 ounces of gold per trust unit.
2. The investor has purchased put options on gold with a strike price of US$400/ounce.
3. The investor has purchased 0.1167 call options with an exercise price of US$400/ounce.
4. The investor has sold 0.1167 call options with an exercise price of US$1,000/ounce.
5. The investor has purchased 0.07 call option with an exercise price of US$1,000/ounce.

The combination of 1 and 2 ensures that if the gold price is below US$400/ounce, then the investor receives US$12.00 (US$400 × 0.03). Transactions 3 and 4 are essentially a call spread. If the gold price is at US$1,000/ounce, the investor receives US$100 (US$1,000 × 10%). This compares to the return of US$30 (US$1,000 × 0.03) on the gold owned. The US$70 surplus return is generated by the embedded call option [0.1167 being US$70/US$600] that provides the incremental return. Transaction 5 provides any incremental return above US$1,000/ounce.

The investor also has an exposure to the production levels at the mine.

The dynamics of the structure are interesting. At low gold prices, the structure results in low servicing costs for the mine. At increasing gold price levels, the servicing costs increase as the incremental returns are triggered. However, the mine's higher cash flows from increased revenues cover this higher servicing cost. In effect, the structure provides the investor with direct participation in gold price and mine production.

---

For the mine, the structure provides an inherent low-cost source of funding and lowers its servicing risk where gold prices are low or mine production is low.

American Barrick used this structure in 1984 to finance US$40 million for its Camflo mine. In that transaction, trust investors received a return of 8% when the gold price was US$365/ounce. The rate increased or decreased 1% for every US$35/ounce change in the gold price capped at a maximum price of US$1,500/ounce.

---

A number of variations on the basic structure have emerged. The most significant of these is one that was designed to allow producers of lower credit standing to raise funds from capital markets. These structures combined a zero-coupon collateral structure for the principal of the financing (effectively using a portion of the funds raised) with call options on both the commodity *and* the shares of the producer. **Exhibit 8.16** sets out an example of this type of structure.

The major attraction of these commodity-linked financing structures for the producers was the lower cost of funds and access to capital markets facilitated by these types of arrangements. This benefit is obtained in exchange for the following cost:

• The producer reduces his upside profit potential to an increase in the price of the commodity above the strike level.
• The producer only is hedged economically against falls in the price of the commodity to the extent of the lower interest rate. The producer does not have a guaranteed minimum price for its product.

---

**Exhibit 8.16**
**Zero-coupon-secured Commodity Convertible Bond**

| | |
|---|---|
| Issuer | Special purpose vehicle |
| Guarantor | Balmoral Resources N.L. Perth (for 50% of coupon only). |
| Type | Collateralized bonds exchangeable for gold bullion and convertible into shares of the Guarantor. |
| Amount | (up to) US$20 million |
| Collateral | 50% of issue proceeds will be invested in US$ zero-coupon bonds |

| Maturity | 7 years (due July 1, 1994) |
|---|---|
| Coupon | 3% pa |
| Issue Price | 100 |
| Conversion Period | Throughout the life of the bond. |
| Exchange for Gold | Each bond is exchangeable into 100 grams of fine gold (in fact the amount equivalent to the then current market value of the equivalent amount of gold bullion). |
| Conversion for Shares | Each bond is convertible into the shares of the guarantor at a conversion price equivalent to a 27% premium (equivalent to A$0.7160/share) at a fixed exchange rate set as at closing. |
| Denomination | Equivalent to 100 grams of gold (approximately US$1,700). |
| Amortisation | Bullet |
| Call Option | None |
| Listing | Luxembourg Stock Exchange |
| Commissions | 2.25% |
| Lead Manager: | Bank Gutzwiller Kurz Bungener (Overseas) |

*Source: International Financing Review Issue, 677. (June 13, 1987): 1976.*

## 4.4   Commodity-linked Financings — Variations

The structures of commodity-linked financing described have been extended in recent times to encompass a very broad range of transactions. The variations have in fact encompassed two specific trends:

• The use of commodity linkages in syndicated loans and other financing.
• The integration of commodity hedges in funding arrangements.

A number of syndicated loan transactions for emerging market credits (such as Algeria and China) have been undertaken. Commodity, primarily oil, options have been utilized to reduce the margin on these syndicated loan transactions.

**Exhibit 8.17** sets out the details of an aluminium-linked financing for a Middle East aluminium producer that combines commodity derivatives within the loan structure to provide an economic hedge against aluminium price fluctuations. **Exhibit 8.18** on page 338 sets out details of another aluminium-linked transaction where the commodity hedge is structured in both loan and pure derivative forms.

**Exhibit 8.17**
**Dubal Aluminium Company — Aluminium-linked Financing**

In February 1995, Dubai-based Dubal Aluminium Company (Dubal) completed a US$250 million 5-year aluminium-linked loan through Merrill Lynch.

Dubal owns and operates a 250,000-ton aluminium smelter in Dubai. The funds were required in connection with a planned increase in its production by 127,600 tons. The total project cost was around US$503 million with approximately half to be funded from internal resources.

The terms of the loan were as follows:

*General*

| | |
|---|---|
| Borrower | Dubal Aluminium Company Limited |
| Type | Aluminium-linked loan |

*Loan*

| | |
|---|---|
| Amount | US$250 million |
| Term | 5 years (maturing March 15, 2000) |
| Average Life | 3.75 years |
| Interest Rate | LIBOR plus 50 bps pa |
| Repayment | 6 equal installments beginning 2.5 years after drawdown. |
| | Each repayment instalment is for a notional US$41,666,667 with the exact amount calculated as: 1.15 × US$41,666,667 minus protection. |
| Protection | Sum of each of the previous six monthly calculations of the following formula: |
| | (US$1,500 per metric tonne – Aluminium price) × Volume pricing periods to commence January 1, 1997 and end December 31, 1999. The aluminium price can never be greater than US$1,750 per metric ton. |
| Aluminium Price | The arithmetic average of the LME Official cash settlement prices for business days during the relevant month. |
| Volume | 10,400 metric tonnes. Total loan repayment can never be less than zero. |
| Drawdown: | In one lump sum on March 15, 1995. |

*Swap*

| | |
|---|---|
| Swap Parties | Merrill Lynch and the lending banks |
| Swap Notional Amount | Amount of each lending banks' participation |
| Swap Start Date | March 15, 1995 |
| Swap Maturity Date | March 15, 2000 |
| Payment to Merrill Lynch by Lending Banks | The lending banks' respective share of the repayment installments due from the borrower under the loan. |
| Payment by Merrill Lynch to Lending Banks | The lending banks' respective share of the notional principal repayment installment under the loan. |

The effect of the transaction is to link the loan repayments to the price of aluminium, subject to the cap of US$1,750 per ton. This is designed to hedge the borrower's cash flow risk in the event of a decline in the market price of aluminium.

The hedge is achieved by the repayment formula that explicitly links the amount to be repaid as at each repayment date to the price of aluminium. If the price of aluminium falls, the borrower repays *less* than US$41,666,667. If the aluminium price remains high, the borrower will repay an amount greater than US$41,666,667 subject to a cap of US$63,516,667. The higher repayments would be offset by the stronger cash flows at these higher aluminium prices.

The lending banks do not have exposure to the aluminium price risk. Their exposure is offset through the swap arrangement with Merrill Lynch. Lenders pay the payment due from the borrower and receive the amount of the fixed repayment installment under the loan.

The transaction entails a series of options on the aluminium prices that guarantees a minimum price to the borrower. The borrower effectively has purchased puts on aluminium that have been financed by the sale of call that caps the benefit from higher aluminium prices.

*Source: International Financing Review, 1069 (February 18, 1995): 50.*

**Exhibit 8.18**
**VAW — Aluminium-linked Financing**

In 1992, VAW, the German company, entered into a series of innovative transactions in relation to the financing of the third pot line in the Tomago Aluminium smelter in NSW.

There were two transactions:

- A loan linked to aluminium prices arranged by Bankers Trust.
- A derivative (an interest rate-aluminium swap) entered into by Citibank.

Full details of the transactions have never been made public. However, it appears that both transactions entailed embedded aluminium derivatives designed to manage the cash flow and commodity price risk of the borrower.

The first entailed a US$ financing whereby the interest rate was indexed to the spot aluminium price bounded by a range (maximum and minimum prices). The transaction entailed a combination of:

- An aluminium swap where VAW sold a certain quantity of aluminium at an agreed flat price to be cash settled against actual future spot prices of aluminium.
- A series of put and call options on aluminium against US$.

The second transaction entailed VAW entering into an interest rate swap where it was paying an interest rate margin above or below the company's normal LIBOR margin with the actual margin payable being indexed to the spot aluminium price. The net effect of the transaction was to produce a lower LIBOR margin for the borrower unless the future spot price exceeded an agreed strike price. The transaction was engineered as an aluminium swap whereby the company sells a certain quantity of aluminium forward at an agreed flat price for a series of future delivery dates. The net cash settlement amounts being used to reduce or increase net interest costs.

The second transaction is very similar to the first but effectively unbundles the funding and commodity hedge aspects of the structure allowing VAW to separately access its most efficient form of funding. Both transactions were engineered to fit the company's future aluminium price expectations and to create a risk-reward profile consistent with its exact objectives.

## 5.   Commodity-linked Notes

### 5.1   Overview

Commodity-based financing transactions, as noted previously, are predicated on the underlying position of the issuer in the relevant commodity. This type of structure does not, as noted above, require inclusion of any derivative transaction to securitize the commodity element in the issue or to insulate the issuer from commodity price risk.

The second type of commodity-linked transaction (the commodity-linked structured note where the issuer is insulated from the commodity price movements) is fundamentally different in the following respects:

* The issuer utilizes the transaction as a means for generating lower cost funding in its desired currency (generally, at a nominated margin under US$ LIBOR). Accordingly, the issuer seeks complete insulation from the commodity price elements of the transaction that is shifted through a series of derivative transactions to the derivative dealer and ultimately to the commodity derivative sector of the capital market.
* Unlike the commodity-linked financing structures described above, the investor absorbs the risk of the commodity price movement by either creating a forward or option on the relevant commodity in favor of the issuer of the security. The accompanying derivative transaction securitizes this derivative element by selling it in another sector of the capital market. This effectively creates a lower cost borrowing for the issuer by arbitraging the price paid to the investor for the derivative element relative to the value obtainable for the forward or option on the commodity price in the capital market.

The impetus for these types of transactions came from a number of sources:

* The fact that investors seeking exposure to commodity risk were unenthusiastic about the credit risk of the general universe of commodity producers. The commodity-linked structured note format with its emphasis on high credit quality issuers was ideal in separating the commodity price exposure from the credit risk aspects of such transactions.
* Investor requirement for flexibility, in terms of maturity, quantum, and type/ degree of exposure to the commodity could not be readily accommodated within the commodity-based financing format. The commodity-linked structured note format is well suited to decoupling the investor requirements from issuer requirements with the dealer or arranger utilizing other markets, such as the commodity spot and derivatives markets, to manage mismatchs between the two.
* Issuer requirements of flexibility. A number of issuers found the commodity-based financing format, particularly where it entailed a capital markets

transaction, such as a bond issue, inflexible where the transaction was required to be restructured at a later date. This led to two developments. The first resulted in a move away from public markets to bank financing (primarily, syndicated bank loans). The second was an emphasis on commodity derivatives, in its pure off-balance-sheet format, to manage derivative price risk.[18] Both developments encouraged the growth of commodity-linked structured notes as the preferred methodology for investors creating exposure to commodity price.

Commodity-linked structured notes entail a number of specific types of structures:

• **Commodity forward-linked structures** — this type of transaction entails a fixed interest security combined with a commodity forward or swap position.

• **Commodity option-linked structures** — this type of transaction entails a fixed interest security combined with a commodity option.

### 5.2    Commodity Forward-linked Notes

**Exhibit 8.19** sets out an example of a commodity forward-linked structure. The transaction described was undertaken by the Swedish Export Credit Agency (SEK) where the redemption price is linked to movements in the price of silver. In this structure, the investor enters into a forward position in silver to purchase a commodity at a price significantly above the effective forward price of silver prevailing in the over-the-counter or exchange traded market. This allows SEK to generate attractively priced funding. **Exhibit 8.20** on page 342 sets out the trading and hedging of derivatives element embedded in this issue.

---

**Exhibit 8.19**
**Silver-linked Structured Note**

*Structure of Commodity-linked Issue*

The example outlined below is based on an issue undertaken by Svensk Export Kredit (SEK) named BISONs (Bull Index Silver Opportunity Notes). The terms of the commodity-linked issue are summarized below:

---

[18] See Das, Satyajit "Oil and Commodity Swaps" *Journal of International Securities Markets* (Autumn 1990) vol. 4 227-250.

*Terms of Commodity-linked Issue*

| | |
|---|---|
| Amount (US$) | 100,000,000 |
| Term (years) | 1 |
| Coupon (% pa) | 6.50 |
| Redemption | Amount [1 + (SPM − 4.46)/4.46)] |
| | Where: |
| | SPM = Silver price (US$/ounce) at maturity |
| Swap Rate For Term (% pa) 6.78 | |

Under the terms of the issue, the issuer undertakes for US$100.0 million for one year. This borrowing carries a coupon of 6.50% pa.

The issue is structured to include a variable redemption feature whereby the redemption amount payable by the borrower is linked to movements in the price of silver. The table below sets out the redemption payment to be made by the issuer to the investor based upon a range of market prices of silver at the maturity of the issue.

*Investors Return Profile*

| SPM | Redemption Amount (US$) | Redemption Amount (%) | Return (% pa) |
|---|---|---|---|
| 1.46 | 32,735,426 | 32.7354 | −60.76 |
| 1.96 | 43,946,188 | 43.9462 | −49.55 |
| 2.46 | 55,156,951 | 55.1570 | −38.34 |
| 2.96 | 66,367,713 | 66.3677 | −27.13 |
| 3.46 | 77,578,475 | 77.5785 | −15.92 |
| 3.96 | 88,789,238 | 88.7892 | −4.71 |
| 4.46 | 100,000,000 | 100.0000 | 6.50 |
| 4.96 | 111,210,762 | 111.2108 | 17.71 |
| 5.46 | 122,421,525 | 122.4215 | 28.92 |
| 5.96 | 133,632,287 | 133.6323 | 40.13 |
| 6.46 | 144,843,049 | 144.8430 | 51.34 |
| 6.96 | 156,053,812 | 156.0538 | 62.55 |
| 7.46 | 167,264,574 | 167.2646 | 73.76 |
| 7.96 | 178,475,336 | 178.4753 | 84.98 |
| 8.46 | 189,686,099 | 189.6861 | 96.19 |

From the perspective of the investor, an investment in these notes combines two specific elements:

- Investment in the US$100.0 million debt instrument that pays 6.50% pa.
- A forward position in silver whereby the investor agrees to purchase (or is long) silver at US$4.46 per ounce for delivery at the maturity of the notes (that is, one year forward).

Consequently, the investor's return is linked to the prevailing price of silver at maturity. For example, the investor will only realize 6.50% pa (nominal return on the debt instrument) where the price of silver at maturity is US$4.46 per ounce. In the event that the price of silver is below the embedded forward price of US$4.46 per ounce, the investor's return will be lower than 6.50% pa and, conversely, if the price of silver is above US$4.46 per ounce, the investor's return will be correspondingly higher. The rates of return accruing to the investor at varying closing prices of silver at maturity are summarized above.

---

**Exhibit 8.20**
**Silver-indexed Structured Note — Hedging Structure**

The economics and hedging structure of the issue of BISONs (described in **Exhibit 8.19**) is set out below.

*Economics of the Transaction*

The economics of the transaction derive, substantially, from the fact that the forward price embedded in the redemption structure is *above* the forward price prevailing for silver at the time of issue.

At the time of issue, the price of silver was as follows:

US$4.16 per ounce (spot).
US$4.40 per ounce (1-year forward price based on 1-year Comex futures).

The "off-market" forward rate embedded in the security (US$4.46 per ounce) generates an arbitrage gain that forms the basis of the borrowing cost saving to the issuer and the profit to the intermediary arranging the transaction.

The amount of this arbitrage gain is US$1,345,291. This gain derives from the fact that the issuer (or the intermediary arranging the derivative hedge) can "lock in" the US$0.06 difference in the forward prices. In order to achieve this, the party seeking to implement the hedge would purchase 22,421,525 ounces of silver (calculated as US$100.0 million/ US$4.46 per ounce) for delivery one year forward coinciding with the maturity of the notes. This transaction could be undertaken as an over-the-counter forward contract with a commodities dealer or, alternatively, as a futures transaction on Comex.

The issuer or the intermediary, which is long silver in the forward market, has a corresponding short position (at a forward price of US$4.46 per ounce) under the structure of the security (see detailed cash flow under the swap). This effectively locks in a gain of US$1,345,291 (being US$0.06 times 22,451,525 ounces).

The rationale for the investor purchasing silver forward at a rate some 1.36% above the actual forward price, which drives the arbitrage process, may be predicated on a number of factors:

- The investor may be a consumer or trader who anticipates having to purchase the relevant amount of silver in one year and wishes to create a hedge against its position in the underlying commodity.
- The investor anticipates a sharp recovery in silver prices and is willing to pay a premium for an instrument specifically structured to provide a return geared to this commodity outlook.

The US$ interest rate swap itself would typically be hedged using "strip" of Eurodollar futures contracts or FRAs.

### Forward Silver Hedge

In additional to the US$ interest rate swap outlined above, the swap counterparty would enter into an agreement whereby it would cover the issuer's difference in cash flow between the actual amount borrowed (US$100.0 million being the par value of the bonds) and the redemption amount (calculated in accordance with the silver-linked redemption formula).

These cash flows are more complex:

- In the event that the silver price at maturity of the notes is above the US$4.46 per ounce, then swap counterparty will make a payment to the issuer. The issuer, in turn, will repay to the investor the principal borrowed (US$100.0 million) plus the redemption payment received from the swap counterparty. For example, if the silver price at maturity is equaled to US$4.96 per ounce, then the redemption value of the bonds will be US$111,210,762. The issuer will repay the US$100.0 million received from the investor at the commencement of the transaction together with the US$11,210,762 received from the swap counterparty.
- In the event that the silver price at maturity is less than US$4.46 per ounce, then the issuer will repay the redemption amount of less than par (that is, less than US$100.0 million) to the investor. The difference

between the par value of the bond and the redemption amount is paid to the swap counterparty. For example, if the silver price at maturity is equal to US$3.96 per ounce, then the issuer will repay US$88,789,238 to the investor (in accordance with the redemption formula) and make a payment of US$11,210,762 to the swap counterparty.

For the swap counterparty, the redemption cash flow payments are offset by its forward silver hedge. It has entered into a contract for the forward purchase of silver to match its position whereby it is selling silver forward to the issuer to cover the embedded forward silver contract in the commodity-linked security.

These cash flows are set out in the table below.

*Case 1: Silver price at maturity equal to US$4.46 per ounce*

| | Bond Cash Flows | | Interest Rate Swaps | | Silver Hedge | | |
|---|---|---|---|---|---|---|---|
| Years | Interest | Principal | Payment | Receipts | Redemption Payment | Forward Silver Hedge (at US$4.40 per ounce) | Net Cash Flow |
| **0.5** | | | | | | | |
| **1.0** | 6,500,000 | 100,000,000 | (7,033,585) | 7,033,585 | 0 | 1,345,291 | 1,345,291 |

*Case 2: Silver price at maturity equal to US$4.96 per ounce*

| | Bond Cash Flows | | Interest Rate Swaps | | Silver Hedge | | |
|---|---|---|---|---|---|---|---|
| Years | Interest | Principal | Payment | Receipts | Redemption Payment | Forward Silver Hedge (at US$4.40 per ounce) | Net Cash Flow |
| **0.5** | | | | | | | |
| **1.0** | 6,500,000 | 100,000,000 | (7,033,585) | 7,033,585 | (11,210,762) | 12,556,054 | 1,345,291 |

*Case 3: Silver price at maturity equal to US$3.96 per ounce*

| | Bond Cash Flows | | Interest Rate Swaps | | Silver Hedge | | |
|---|---|---|---|---|---|---|---|
| Years | Interest | Principal | Payment | Receipts | Redemption Payment | Forward Silver Hedge (at US$4.40 per ounce) | Net Cash Flow |
| **0.5** | | | | | | | |
| **1.0** | 6,500,000 | 100,000,000 | (7,033,585) | 7,033,585 | 11210,762 | 9,865,471 | 1,345,291 |

The overall position is summarized in the diagram below.

## Commodity-linked Swap Structure

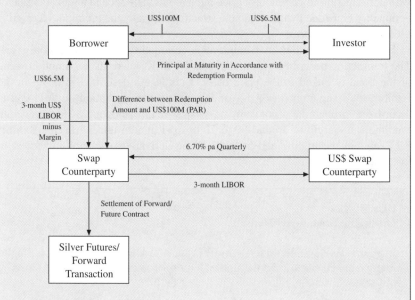

### *Arbitrage Gain*

The US$0.06 per ounce difference between the forward price achieved by the swap counterparty in its forward/futures hedge relative to a forward price embedded in the security and corresponding swap will result in a net gain to the swap counterparty. This gain (refer the diagram above) will reflect the net cash flow difference between the gain on the futures hedge position and the payment to be made to the issuer or the payment received from the issuer relative to the loss under the futures hedge.

This arbitrage gain is available for the following purposes:

- Profit to the swap counterparty.
- To further lower the interest cost of the issuer.

In practice, this arbitrage gain would be shared between swap counterparty and the issuer. Assuming an equal share between the swap counterparty and the issuer (that is, US$672,645 each), the issuer's cost of funds from this transaction can be reduced by an additional approximately 66.34 bps pa. This would result in the borrower achieving a borrowing cost in the vicinity of 3-month US$ LIBOR less 1.19% pa.

## 5.3   Commodity Option-based Notes

Commodity option-based transactions are of two types. The first entails the use of foregone coupons to purchase a commodity option that provides the investor with participation in commodity price movements. The second entails the sale of optionality embedded within the note structure whereby the premium received is used to enhance returns.

**Exhibit 8.21** sets out an example of a commodity option-based note issue. The transaction described was undertaken by SEK where the redemption value of the bond is linked to the price of WTI crude. As described in detail in the Exhibit, the issue embodies a 1-year European-style put option on WTI that is securitized through the accompanying swap structure allowing SEK to generate funding at a margin of around 60 to 70 bps per annum under LIBOR. **Exhibit 8.22** sets out the trading and hedging of the derivatives element embedded in this issue.

---

**Exhibit 8.21**
**Oil-linked Structured Note**

In April 1989, SEK undertook an issue of FUELS (Fixed US dollar Energy-linked Securities) through Salomon Brothers. The principal terms of the issue were as follows:

| | |
|---|---|
| Amount | US$100 million |
| Maturity | 1 year |
| Coupon | 20% pa |
| Issue Price | 100.875 |
| Commissions | 0.875% |
| Redemption | The redemption value of the bonds was linked to the following formula: |

- If the price of the oil index at maturity was greater than the redemption strike price of the oil index, then the redemption value is par.
- If the price of the oil index is below the redemption strike price per barrel then the bond-holder will receive less than par on his or her principal determined as below per US$1,000 bond:
  1,000 × (Redemption strike/Reference price)

For the purpose of the redemption formula:
*Reference* (Crude Type): West Texas Intermediate (WTI).

---

*Redemption strike setting:* The New York Mercantile Exchange Settlement Price per barrel on April 19, 1989 for the WTI light sweet crude oil futures contract for delivery during the month of June 1989, as quoted in the price source multiplied by a factor of 0.89. Approximately US$17.50.

*Reference price:* The arithmetic average of New York Mercantile Exchange Settlement Prices for WTI light sweet crude oil futures contract for delivery during the month of June 1990, as quoted in the price source, for the three New York Mercantile trading days immediately preceding but excluding two days prior to the maturity date.

*Price source: The Wall Street Journal.*

*Settlement:* Cash payment as per redemption formula above.

The redemption formula embodied a 1-year European-style put option on WTI at a strike price of around US$17.50 per barrel. The put option was granted by the investor in favor of the issuer.

---

**Exhibit 8.22**
**Oil-indexed Structured Note — Hedging Structure**

The issue of FUELS (described in **Exhibit 8.21**) would be hedged as follows.

The issuer on sold the 1-year WTI European put to the arranger/swap counterparty (Salomon Brothers or its related entity Phibro Energy). The proceeds from the sale of the option allowing the issuer to reduce its costs below LIBOR.

The structure of the swap was as follows:

- The basic structure was that of a 1-year US$ interest rate swap. The swap counterparty pays 20% pa and receives US$ LIBOR minus a margin, quarterly or semi-annually.
- At maturity:
  - If the reference price for WTI is above redemption strike price (US$17.50), then there are no cash flows under the swap and the issuer repays the bond-holder the par value of the bonds.
  - If the reference price for WTI is below redemption strike price (say,

US$15.00), then the cash flows will be as follows. The issuer repays the bond-holder in accordance with the redemption formula 85.714% of par [calculated as follows: 1,000 × (15.00/17.50) = 857.14]. This is equivalent to US$85,714,286. The difference between par and the redemption value of US$14,285,714 is paid by the issuer to the swap counterparty representing the value of the option at maturity.

The volatility implicit in the embedded put option sold by the investor was estimated at around 23% pa. This compares to prevailing market levels for the volatility on comparable options of around 30% pa. This represents a difference in premium levels of approximately US$2.0-2.5 million. If the full benefit of this margin on the option is passed on by the swap counterparty to the issuer, SEK achieves a funding cost of around 8.30-8.80% pa, compared to 1-year LIBOR of 10.8125% pa. It is understood that SEK achieved funding of around 60-70 bps under LIBOR.

## 5.4   Commodity Index-based Notes

As noted above, there is increasing focus on utilizing commodity indexes as the basis for commodity transactions. **Exhibits 8.23**, **8.24** and **8.25** set out examples of two transactions involving the GSCI.

---

**Exhibit 8.23**
**Commodity Index-linked Structured Note — Example 1**

| | |
|---|---|
| Issuer | Swedish Export Credit |
| Amount | US$100 million |
| Maturity | 3 years |
| Coupon | Zero |
| Issue Price | 100.875 |
| Fixed Price Re-offer | 99.75 |
| Redemption | Indexed principal amount (IPA) calculated as follows: <br> IPA = FA × [0.9557 × (GSCI Ending Value/ 2590.81) <br><br> Where: |

FA = Face Value of Note
GSCI ending value = GSCI 15 days before maturity
In no event shall the IPA be less than zero.

The following table sets out for assumed GSCI values the return to the investor:

| GSCI Value | % of Face Value | IPA (per US$100,000 Face Amount) | Pretax Return (% pa Compounded Annually |
|---|---|---|---|
| 1200 | 44.27 | 44,270 | −23.79 |
| 1400 | 51.64 | 51,640 | −19.77 |
| 1600 | 59.02 | 59,020 | −16.12 |
| 1800 | 66.40 | 66,400 | −12.76 |
| 2000 | 73.78 | 73,780 | −9.64 |
| 2200 | 81.15 | 81,150 | −6.72 |
| 2400 | 88.53 | 88,530 | −3.98 |
| 2600 | 95.91 | 95,910 | −1.38 |
| 2800 | 103.29 | 103,290 | 1.08 |

**Exhibit 8.24**
**Commodity Index-linked Structured Note — Example 2**

| | |
|---|---|
| Issuer | Swedish Export Credit |
| Amount | US$75 million |
| Maturity | 3 years |
| Coupon | Zero |
| Issue Price | 100.875 |
| Fixed Price Re-offer | 99.75 |
| Redemption | 100 + [100% × (GSCI Excess Return − Spot)/ Spot] |
| Minimum Redemption | 100 |
| Strike | 400 |
| Commissions | 1.375% |

---

**Exhibit 8.25**
**Commodity Index-linked Structured Note — Example 3**

| | |
|---|---|
| Issuer | AAA rated |
| Amount | US$25 million |
| Maturity | 1 year 6 months |
| Coupon | Zero |
| Issue Price | 100 |
| Redemption | 100 + 80% × (Basket – Spot)/Spot) |
| | Where |
| | Basket = (GSAG-ER × 0.17178) + (GSCI-ER × 0.12923) |
| | GSAG-ER is the Goldman Sachs Agriculture Excess Return Index |
| | GSCI-ER is the Goldman Sachs Commodity Index Excess Return Index |
| Strike | 101 |
| Minimum Redemption | 100 |

*Source:* (November 14, 1997) *MTNWeek*

---

The first transaction entails the entry by the investor into a forward on the GSCI combined with a zero-coupon bond. The second transaction entails the combination of a call option on the index and a zero-coupon bond to create an asymmetric exposure to commodity prices. The call in this case was set out of-the-money by around 5% requiring a 20% increase in the index in order to equate to the return on a conventional fixed-rate investment for the equivalent period. The third transaction is similar to the second transaction. This transaction is partially on the GSCI sub index that covers agricultural items such as corn, wheat, soybeans, sugar, cotton, coffee, and cocoa. At the time of entry into the transaction, the GSAG-ER was around 191.19 and GSCI-ER was around 510.67—that translates into an initial basket value of 98.84. This means that the indexes need to increase by around 2.2% to generate positive returns for the investor. The investor receives 80% of any return above the agreed strike.

## 6. Summary

The increased level of interest in commodity investment derives from the emergence of commodities as a specific asset class within investment portfolios. The capacity of commodity investments to enhance portfolio performance by either allowing increased expected return for a given level of risk or reducing risk for a given level of return within a portfolio diversification framework has increased institutional investment participation in commodity investment.

The difficulty with physical direct investment in commodities has prompted the use of synthetic mechanisms for acquiring commodity exposure. Commodity-linked investments have emerged as one of the principal mechanisms for acquiring this exposure.

Commodity-linked transactions encompass a broad range of transactions including commodity-linked financing and commodity-linked structured notes. Commodity-linked financing, which entail structures predicated on the underlying commodity position of the issuer (typically, a commodity producer or consumer), has traditionally been the preferred format. Commodity-linked structured notes, where the issuer is totally insulated from the commodity price risk, have now emerged as the predominant type of commodity-linked bonds utilized.

# Appendix A

# Commodity Derivative Products[19]

## 1.   Commodity Forwards and Swaps

Commodity forwards entail agreements to purchase or sell a commodity as at a forward date. Economically, commodity forwards are simply forward contracts where the underlying asset is a commodity. The underlying commodity can be an individual commodity or a basket of commodities (typically a commodity index such as the Commodity Research Bureau (CRB) Index or the Goldman Sachs Commodity Index (GSCI)).

In practice, commodity forwards take two formats: commodity forwards or commodity swaps (economically a portfolio of forwards on the underlying commodity or index). Commodity forwards are structured as outright forward contracts or commodity futures. A variety of structured commodity forwards are also utilized. **Exhibit 8.26** sets out an example of a structured spot-deferred forward contract.

---

[19] For a more detailed discussion, see Das, Satyajit (1994) *Swaps & Financial Derivatives*; LBC Information Services, Sydney; McGraw-Hill, Chicago at Chapter 16.

**Exhibit 8.26**
**Spot-deferred Commodity Contract**

Assume a gold producer (X) wishes to hedge its gold production by selling it forward. Projected gold production is 100,000 ounces per annum for each of the next two years. It has the choice of two types of contracts:

- A standard forward contract.
- A spot-deferred contract.

Assume the following price parameters:

Spot Gold Price          US$300 per ounce
1-year Interest Rate     6.00% pa
1-year Gold Lease Rate   1.00% pa

The 1-year forward price is calculated as follows:

$$US\$300 \times (1 + (0.06 - 0.01))^1 = US\$315$$

Assume at the end of one year the gold price is at US$350 per ounce. The outcomes under the two different hedging options are discussed below.

*Standard Forward Contract*

If X had entered into a forward at US$315/ounce, then the contract would be settled in one of the following ways:

- Delivery — X would deliver 100,000 ounces of gold in return for receipt of US$31.5 million (US$315 × 100,000 ounces).
- Cash settlement — X would cash settle the gold forward by making a payment of US$3.5 million ((US$350-US$315) × 100,000). This represents the loss as a result of the movement in the gold price. The cash settlement would be combined with a sale in the spot market of the gold production. The sale would net US$35 million (US$350 × 100,000). The sale proceeds adjusted for the cash settlement on the forward would result in total revenue of US$31.5 million (equating to the hedged price).

Irrespective of the settlement protocol adopted, the gold producer suffers an economic loss relative to current market price reporting revenue of US$31.5 million as against the market value of production of US$35 million. The accounting and tax income reported is US$31.5 million.

### Spot-deferred Contract

As an alternative to the standard forward contract, X could have entered into a spot-deferred gold forward contract. The contract would operate as follows:

- The contract is for two years.
- The amount covered is 100,000 ounces per year for the 2-year term, in effect a forward sale of 200,000 ounces over the term of the contract.
- The contract provides X with a choice of delivering 100,000 ounces at the end of years 1 and 2, or deferring delivery at the end of year 1 and delivering 100,000 ounces at the end of year 2.
- The pricing of the contract is structured so that the gold delivered at the end of year 1 receives the current forward price (US$315 per ounce). In the event that the delivery option is not exercised at the end of year 1, then a new spot-deferred contract price is determined for the end of year 2 based on market rates at the end of year 1.

Assume the same situation prevails as described above with gold prices reaching US$350 per ounce at the end of year 1. In that case X would in all probability choose not to deliver at the forward price (as it is lower than the current spot price). X would enter therefore into the following transactions:

- X would sell 100,000 ounces receiving US$35 million (US$350 × 100,000).
- X would defer delivery on the spot-deferred contract and reset the forward price at the end of year 2 as provided for under the spot deferred contract.

The new forward price would be calculated so that the economics of the transaction are such that the present value of a deferral is exactly identical to that of immediate delivery.

Assume the following parameters at the end of one year:

| | |
|---|---|
| Spot Gold Price | US$350 per ounce |
| 1-year Interest Rates | 5.00% pa |
| 1-year Gold Lease Rate | 1.25% pa |
| 1-year Financing Rate | 6.00% pa (the 1-year interest rate plus a risk margin of 1.00% pa) |

The calculation of the new forward price is the actual forward price adjusted for the cost of financing the loss on the initial forward determined as follows:

US$350 $\times$ (1 + (0.05 − 0.0125))$^1$ − (US$350 − US$315) $\times$ (1 + 0.06)$^1$ = US$326.03

The contract would have to be settled as at the end of year 2.

*Comparison of Standard- and Spot-deferred Forwards*

The actual income recorded under the two contract structures is different:

| Revenue Recognised | Year 1 | Year 2 |
|---|---|---|
| Under standard forward | US$31.500 m | US$36.313 m |
| Under spot-deferred contract | US$35.000 m | US$32.603 m |

Please note that the income for year 2 under the standard forward contract is calculated as the forward price for delivery at year 2 as at the end of year 1 (US$350 $\times$ (1 + (0.05 — 0.0125))$^1$ = US$363.13). In effect, it is assumed that the forward will be rolled forward at the end of year 1. The two income streams are equivalent in present value terms. The spot-deferred transaction in this case was for two years. However, longer term contracts are also feasible. Such contracts increase the flexibility of the parties in terms of bringing income to account.

Commodity swaps are a common format in which these transactions are structured. A fixed-for-floating commodity price swap is an agreement whereby a consumer (producer) fixes the purchase (sale) price of its commodity relative to an agreed established market pricing benchmark for the commodity for an agreed period of time. **Exhibit 8.27** sets out in diagrammatic form the basic structure of a fixed-for-floating commodity price swap. In the example set out the commodity utilized is oil.[20]

---

[20] Oil is used for illustrative purposes only. The transaction would operate similarly irrespective of the underlying commodity.

**Exhibit 8.27**
**Fixed-for-floating Commodity Price Swap**

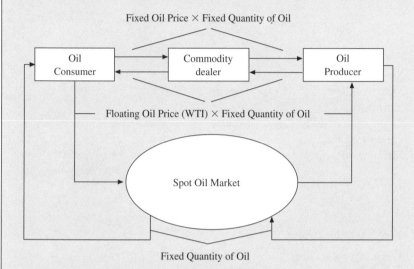

In the example, in order to manage its exposure to oil price fluctuations, an oil producer enters into an oil price swap to lock in a fixed price for WTI crude oil. The opposite side of this oil price swap is taken by an oil consumer seeking to lock in a fixed price for its oil purchases over an identical period. The oil producer and oil user agree to exchange cash flows (denominated in US$) whereby the oil producer receives a fixed price on a pre-agreed volume of oil and agrees to pay a floating oil price index (nominated to be the WTI Price Index) on an identical volume. The consumer enters into an identical transaction but in reverse. The counterparties agree that settlement will be on a cash basis based on spot WTI prices on a monthly basis. The transaction effectively allows both the oil producer and oil user to lock in a price on an agreed volume of oil priced off the WTI Index.

**Exhibit 8.28** sets out typical terms of a conventional fixed-for-floating commodity price swap.

**Exhibit 8.28**
**Commodity Fixed-for-floating Price Swap**

*General*

| | |
|---|---|
| Notional Quantity per Calculation Period | 100,000 barrels |
| Commodity | WTI Light Sweet Crude Oil |
| Trade Date | January 15, 2001 |
| Effective Date | January 22, 2001 |
| Termination Date | July 22, 2001 |
| Calculation Periods | Monthly |
| Period End Date | 22nd of each month |
| Settlement/Payment Date | 5 business days after the period end date subject to the modified following business day convention |
| Settlement Basis | Daily average of the commodity reference price |

*Fixed Amount Details*

| | |
|---|---|
| Fixed Price Payer | [Company] |
| Fixed Price | $18 per barrel |

*Floating Amount Details*

| | |
|---|---|
| Floating Price Payer | [Bank] |
| Commodity Reference Price | WTI (as defined in 1993 ISDA commodity derivatives definition) |

A number of essential features of the fixed-for-floating commodity price swap structure should be noted:

• The commodity price swap is purely financial; that is, there is no physical exchange of commodities between the counterparties. The transaction assumes that both parties continue to operate in the spot market for the commodity normally to purchase or sell the required amount of oil or other commodities being swapped. The commodity price swap itself is totally independent of these underlying physical transactions and the purchaser or seller in the spot transaction does not enter into contractual relationships with the commodity swap counterparty and, in fact, would not necessarily be aware that the commodity swap had been undertaken.

- The financial settlement undertaken is on a net basis only. The amounts owed to and from each counterparty are netted as at each settlement date with the party owing the greater amount paying the difference to the other party. There are no intermediate cash flows and the commodity price swap would not generally be subject to any margin or mark-to-market requirement.
- The settlement under a commodity swap is usually based on the difference between the contracted price and the *average of the periodic (daily, weekly, and so on) price of the reference asset*. This contrasts with derivatives in interest rates, currency, and equity where settlement is against the price of the commodity on the relevant date. The use of the average mechanism is designed primarily to match the underlying purchases or sales of the commodity by the purchaser or seller in the spot market. This would have the effect of better matching the cash flows and creating a better hedge.

## 2.   Commodity Options

Commodity options' underlying asset is a commodity or commodity index. In all fundamental aspects, commodity options are identical to conventional options. They exhibit the same behavior and have similar applications to options generally. They are used primarily to manage risk or generate premium income through asymmetric risk exposures to the underlying asset price movements.

Commodity options in the OTC market are sometimes packaged as commodity caps and floor contracts, the cap being a series of put options on the commodity itself and the floor being a series of call options on the commodity. The cap and floor structures are commonly used to manage ongoing price exposures to the underlying commodity.

Commodity options are often structured as average rate options (a form of exotic option). Under the average rate option structure, the option pay is calculated through a comparison of the strike price of the option and the average price of the underlying commodity as sampled over the relevant period. This is in contrast to traditional option contracts where the payoff is determined by a comparison to strike price and the *final* price of the underlying asset. As with commodity swaps, the average rate mechanism is designed to allow a better match to the underlying cash transaction and provide a superior hedge.

# 9
# Equity-linked Notes (1): Convertible Debt and Debt-with-equity Warrant Issues

## 1. Equity-linked Structured Notes

Equity-linked structured notes may be defined as fixed income securities where the interest coupons and/or principal of the instrument is linked to the movements in equity prices. The underlying equity prices may be the values of individual equity securities or equity market indexes. As with other types of structured notes, the equity-linked structured notes can typically be decomposed into two essential instruments: a fixed income security and an equity derivative embedded in the security.

The structures, design, applications, valuation, and market for equity-linked structured notes are examined in this and the following two chapters. This chapter discusses convertible debt and debt-with-equity warrants issues. Chapter 10 examines hybrids and variations on the traditional equity-linked note structures. Chapter 11 analyzes equity index-linked note products. This chapter and Chapter 10 focus, primarily, on equity-linked notes where the underlying equity instrument is an individual stock. Chapter 11 focuses predominantly on equity market index-linked note structures. The other differentiating factor among the chapters is that this and Chapter 10 emphasize instruments where the issuer is usually the entity whose equity securities are the basis of the transaction and the structure is designed to facilitate the raising of capital for the issuer. In contrast, the structures discussed in Chapter 11 focus on instruments where the issuer is not the entity whose equity is incorporated in the issue and the exposure to the underlying equity element is specifically hedged through derivative transactions to immunize the issuer from the equity price exposure.

The structure of this chapter is as follows: the evolution of the structure of equity notes, particularly the shift in emphasis from individual equities to equity market indexes is first considered. The structure of traditional equity notes, convertible debt, and debt-with-equity warrants is then examined. The structure of these instruments, implications for issuers and investors, valuation techniques, trading characteristics, and the differences between convertible debt and debt-with-equity warrants are examined.

## 2. Evolution of the Market for Equity-linked Notes

Equity-linked notes and equity derivatives have a long history. These instruments, together with traditional interest rate-linked securities such as callable bonds, represent one of the oldest and most enduring forms of structured notes. Traditional forms of equity derivatives include equity options, and, more recently, exchange traded options on individual stocks, as well as futures and options contracts on equity indexes. Traditional forms of equity-linked notes include convertible debt securities and issues of debt-with-equity warrants.

The market for equity-linked notes has undergone a significant evolution over recent years. The major elements of this change include:

- Traditional equity notes consistent with the format of traditional equity derivatives has emphasized individual equity securities. Modern equity notes increasingly emphasize equity market indexes.
- Traditional forms of equity notes were developed as a means for providing equity capital-raising opportunities for corporations as part of customized financing strategies. Modern equity-linked structured notes, insofar as they relate to individual corporations, are usually incorporated in the process of debt fund raising through the new issue arbitrage techniques where the issuer is completely insulated from the impact of the embedded equity element.
- Modern equity-structured notes that tend to be equity market index-oriented are directed primarily towards investors/portfolio managers rather than corporations.

The development of modern, as distinct from traditional, equity-linked notes reflects a number of factors:

- Investors can utilize these instruments to simulate purchase of an entire equity index as an alternative to direct investment in the relevant equity market with return and cost benefits.
- Equity index-linked notes, which replicate the characteristics of derivative instruments, allow investors to circumvent investment constraints prohibiting entry into forward or option transaction on equities.
- These instruments allow investors to create highly customized structures creating a specific pattern of exposure to the relevant equity index.

- The structures are also capable of being customized in terms of exposure to exchange rates allowing investors to maintain currency exposure on foreign equity investments or to partially hedge or eliminate the foreign currency risk on the investment.
- Index instruments are attractive to investors who are primarily passive asset managers seeking exposure to the relevant equity market index.

A substantial portion of the attraction of these instruments focuses on the alternative to direct investment in the underlying equity markets. The major advantages relating to simulated, as distinct from direct, investment in equity markets are considered in Chapter 11.

## 3.  Forms of Equity-linked Issues

Offerings of debt that include an equity-linked element (to an individual equity security such as a particular stock) constitute an often complex hybrid security that has been of continuing interest to issuers and investors.

There are basically two forms of equity-linked securities:

- **Convertible securities** — a convertible security is an issue of debt combined with a nondetachable option to convert the debt security, at the holder's option, into the common stock (or less frequently into other class of equity securities) of the issuer in accordance with the terms specified in the issue.
- **Debt-with-equity warrants** — an issue of debt-with-equity warrants represents the offering of debt securities in combination with detachable equity options exercisable into the equity securities of the issuer at the option of the holder of the warrant. The debt-with-equity warrants package viewed as a single transaction is equivalent to a convertible bond.

A popular variation is exchangeable debt securities and exchangeable units of debt with warrants. The major difference between exchangeable securities and convertible securities is the fact that exchangeable debt can be exercized into the common ordinary shares of a company *other than the issuer*. For example, a convertible issue by XYZ company exercisable into the ordinary shares of XYZ would be categorized as a convertible security issue whereas it would be classified as an exchangeable security issue if the convertible were to be capable of conversion into the ordinary shares of ABC corporation.[1]

The underlying security need not necessarily be debt. Convertible preference share issues are also feasible (generally referred to as convertible preferred stock).

---

[1]  Exchangeable debt structures are discussed in detail in Chapter 10.

## 4.   Structure of Equity-linked Issues

### 4.1   Issue Structures

The major terms and conditions of a typical issue of convertible debt are set out in **Exhibit 9.1**. The major terms and conditions of a typical issue of debt-with-equity warrants are summarized in **Exhibit 9.2**.

---

**Exhibit 9.1**
**Convertible Debt Issue —Terms and Conditions**

| | |
|---|---|
| Issuer | ABC Company Ltd |
| Guarantor | [if applicable] |
| Amount | US$500 million of subordinated convertible bonds |
| Maturity | 10 years (due July 6, 2010) |
| Coupon | 4.00% pa annually |
| Issue Price | 100 |
| Redemption Price | 100 |
| Conversion | Each US$10,000 bond is convertible at the option of the bond-holder during the conversion period into 657.89 shares of ABC Company Ltd. |
| Conversion Price | £9.50 |
| Conversion Premium | 21.79% over the closing share price of £7.80 |
| Conversion Period | September 6, 2000 to June 30, 2010 |
| Conversion Exchange Rate | £1: US$1.60 |
| Denominations | US$10,000 |
| Amortisation | Bullet |
| Call Options | Noncallable for the first four years and then callable at 105% of face value declining by 1% per annum to 100% of face value subject to 130% test. |
| Commissions | 2.5% (management and underwriting 1%; selling 1.5%) |
| Payment | July 6, 2000 |

---

**Exhibit 9.2**
**Debt Issue with Equity Warrants — Terms and Conditions**

| | |
|---|---|
| Issuer | ABC Company Ltd |
| Guarantor | [if applicable] |

*Bonds*

| | |
|---|---|
| Amount | US$500 million of bonds |
| Maturity | 10 years (due July 6, 2010) |
| Coupon | 4.00% pa |
| Issue Price | 100 |
| Redemption Price | 100 |
| Denominations | US$10,000 |
| Amortisation | Bullet |
| Call Options | Noncallable for the first four years and then callable at 105% of face value declining by 1% per annum to 100% of face value. |

*Warrants*

| | |
|---|---|
| Warrants | Each warrant is exercisable into the issuer's shares at the warrant strike price at the option of the bond-holder during the exercise period at the exercise price. |
| Warrants per Bond | 658 warrants per each US$10,000 bond |
| Exercise Price | £9.50 (representing a conversion premium of 21.79% over the closing share price of £7.80) |
| Exercise Period | September 6, 2000 to June 30, 2010 |

*General*

| | |
|---|---|
| Commissions | 1.875% |
| Payment | July 6, 2000 |

## 4.2   Primary Issue Terms

### 4.2.1   Overview

The primary terms of an equity-linked issue requiring consideration include:

• Issue economics (namely, conversion rights, interest coupon, and maturity).
• Subordination issues.

- Redemption provisions.
- Call provisions.
- Dilution considerations.
- Participation rights in new equity issues.
- Change of control considerations.

For issuers, regulatory considerations, under the relevant Companies or Securities Code, the Stock Exchange Listing Regulations, and the Income Tax legislation, are relevant in determining the detailed structure of the issue. These aspects are jurisdiction specific and are beyond the scope of this text.

Some key terms associated with convertible securities are set out in **Exhibit 9.3**.

---

**Exhibit 9.3**
**Convertible Debt Terminology**

**Conversion premium** — the percentage by which the price of a convertible bond exceeds its conversion value calculated as:

(Convertible price — Conversion value)/Conversion value

**Conversion price** — the share price at which the face value of the bond may be exchanged into shares (effectively the strike price of the embedded equity option) calculated as:

Par value of convertible bond/Conversion ratio

**Conversion ratio** — the number of shares for which each convertible bond of specified face value can be exchanged is calculated as:

Face value of bond/Conversion price

**Conversion value** — the equity value of the convertible bond calculated as:

Current share price × Conversion ratio

**Income Pickup** — the amount by which the yield to maturity on the convertible bond exceeds the dividend yield on the underlying shares calculated as:

Yield on convertible – Dividend yield on ordinary shares

**Investment value (also know as the bond floor)** — the effective price at which the convertible would trade if there was no conversion option. In effect this is the level at which a nonconvertible bond of the same maturity and credit risk would trade.

---

> **Parity** — the theoretical price at which there is no conversion premium, which is equal to the conversion value.

### 4.2.2   Conversion Rights

The key economic element of a convertible issue is the right to convert the bond into the underlying equity. The convertible bond entails the bond-holder having the right to convert the bonds into the issuer's shares at any time within a nominated period. The conversion rights are usually described in terms of a conversion ratio (the number of shares that each bond can be converted into). In the example in **Exhibit 9.1**, the bond-holder is awarded the right to convert each US$10,000 into 657.89 shares.

Almost all equity-linked structures entail the issue of deferred equity at a premium to the current market price for the underlying equity. This conversion premium is the amount by which the implicit conversion share price exceeds the current market price. The conversion share price as a mechanical matter is usually set at the agreed premium (which is usually within an indicative range announced at the time of launch adjusted in accordance with market reception) over the closing market price of the shares on a specified day. The conversion premium is typically set at a level of 15-25% above the prevailing market price of the underlying shares.

The structure of a convertible issue, where the underlying equity securities are denominated in a currency different from that of the currency of the convertible bond, requires the conversion exchange rate to be fixed. This is usually set at the spot exchange rate as of the pricing date when the issue terms are set. The setting of a fixed conversion exchange rate is designed to ensure that the face value of each bond is exactly exchangeable into a fixed number of shares.

The mechanics of the calculation are as follows (using the example set out in **Exhibit 9.1**):

The share price of ABC Company on the pricing date is £7.80. Using a premium of 21.79%, this equates to a conversion price of £9.50 per share. The £ share price is now converted to a US$ equivalent price of US$15.20 (£9.50/share × £1 = US$1.60). The face value of the bonds (US$10,000) is then divided by the US$ conversion share price (US$15.20) to establish the conversion ration of 657.89 shares per US$10,000 bonds.

Where the currency of the underlying shares is the same as the currency of the convertible bond issue, it is not necessary to convert the conversion share price into the currency of the bond (in effect, the conversion exchange rate used is equal to one).

The mechanics of the debt-with-equity warrants issue is somewhat different. The equity warrants are separate equity options that can be exercised quite independently of the underlying debt issue. The conversion price (incorporating the premium) is embodied in the exercise price of the option rather than in the conversion ration. As discussed in more detail below, the number of warrants need not necessarily equate to the face value of the issued bonds. The conversion exchange rate is also not fixed in an issue of debt-with-equity warrants. This results from the fact that the exercise of the equity warrants requires the exchange of cash (in the currency of the equity securities) for the underlying equity at the time of exchange rather than the effective tender of the bond or debt issue as consideration for the equity.

### 4.2.3   Interest Coupon

The coupon on the convertible bonds (dividends where the host issue is in the form of preferred stock) is generally set at a level below what the issuer would have to pay on conventional nonconvertible debt of equivalent maturity and seniority. In general terms, coupons on convertible bonds and dividends on preferred convertibles have tended to be set at around 2.00 to 4.00% pa below the equivalent debt rate.

In economic terms, the issuer has issued bonds that can be exchanged into the equity of the issuer. The embedded conversion right equates to an American exercise call option on the issuer's shares with a strike price equal to the conversion price (in the above example £9.50 per share) and an expiry date equal to the maturity of the issue. The premium payable for the option is used to lower the interest rate on the bond or dividend coupon rate.

In determining the pricing of an issue, there is a natural trade-off between the conversion premium and the coupon. In the case of convertibles, the value of any implicit currency option where the underlying equity is in a different currency to that of the issue may also influence the pricing decision. In the case of an issue of warrants, the convenience of the detachability is also relevant.

In practice, the bond coupon or preferred dividend on the convertible is set at a rate above the dividend rate on ordinary shares or common stock. The coupon or dividend rate on average exceeds the ordinary share dividend rate (in yield or rate of return terms) by around 2.00-4.00% pa. This is designed to ensure a yield advantage on the convertible securities relative to the ordinary shares designed to attract a different clientele (equity income investors) and/or prevent early conversion into the underlying equity.

The coupon on the debt component of the debt-with-equity warrants issues is more variable and not subject to the considerations identified in relation to convertible securities. This reflects the fact that the debt component is quite separate from the equity options. In practice, the debt and equity elements are separately traded, allowing greater flexibility and choice in the structure of the debt issue.

### 4.2.4  Maturity

Convertible securities have a wide range of maturities. Historically, convertible bonds had maturities of up to 20 years. In more recent periods, the maturity profile has shortened with maturities between five and 10 years becoming more common. Convertible preferred stock issues are normally either for 10 years (usually structured as an option or a mandatory conversion feature) or perpetual (that is, with no fixed maturity). The maturities of the debt component of a debt-with-equity warrant issue is more varied in terms of maturity for the reasons outlined above. There is also no requirement to match the term of the debt with the final exercise date of the equity warrants.

### 4.2.5  Subordination Issues

The debt component of an equity-linked issue can rank pari passu with other unsecured debt of the issuer or alternatively can be subordinated. A significant proportion of the universe of convertible issues is subordinated. This means that the convertible ranks behind senior creditors in the case of liquidation or bankruptcy of the issuer. The principal advantages of subordination is the convertible issue as it ranks behind other creditors is seen as more akin to equity and hence viewed as strengthening the balance sheet of the issuer. It is however unusual to subordinate the debt component of an equity warrants transaction.

Convertible preferred stock naturally ranks behind all debt reflecting its equity nature. However, it ranks ahead of ordinary shares in the capital structure. In the US domestic market, further stratification by the creation of senior and junior subordinated or preferred stock is also feasible.

### 4.2.6  Redemption Provisions

Convertible bond and convertible preferred stock can usually be redeemed in one of two ways:

• The bond-holder converts the issue, exchanging the bonds or preferred stock for underlying shares. This conversion has the impact of vitiating the debt and replacing it with equity on the balance sheet of the issuer. The conversion does not generate any new cash flow for the issuer.
• The bond-holder does not convert, requiring the issuer to repay the face value of the issue in full at maturity.

In the case of debt-with-equity warrants issues, the debt component must always be repaid at maturity. However, the issuer receives a cash injection in the event of exercise of the equity warrants. The cash injection received is equal to the number of warrants multiplied by the exercise price.

In the case of some convertibles, a sinking fund provision may be incorporated to retire a portion of the issue before maturity. This is usually done by open market purchases (purchases in the secondary market on pre-arranged dates) or lottery (random selection of bonds that are then redeemed at face value). The presence of a sinking fund tends to reduce the value of the conversion option. The use of sinking funds has become less common in recent years, reflecting in part the general shortening of maturities in the equity-linked securities markets.

An important issue in relation to convertible securities is that upon conversion no adjustment is made for an accrued interest or dividend entitlement. In effect, the investor sacrifices any accrued interest or dividend entitlement upon conversion.[2]

### 4.2.7  Call Options

Convertible issues incorporate call options allowing prepayment of the issue. This may also allow the issuer to force conversion of the issue. The typical structure involves a noncall period after which the issue can be called. The typical call structure is as follows:

- The issuer is prohibited from calling the issue during a specified period (usually three years, though it can range between two and five years) (the non-call period or the call protection period). This can take two forms. Hard call protection where the issuer cannot call the convertible bond for any reason. Soft call protection where the issuer cannot call the bond except where the closing price of the stock is above say 130% of the conversion price (the range is 130-150%) on 20 to 30 consecutive trading days.
- After the initial call protection period, the issuer will generally have the right to call the bond irrespective of the share price. The call will typically be at a premium to the face value of the bonds. The premium usually reduces with a reduction in the remaining maturity of the bonds.

Where the call is exercised and the underlying shares have appreciated significantly, the bond investor will generally be forced to convert to protect the economic value of the gain achieved. This may actually be achieved by the bond-holder converting into the underlying equity and simultaneously selling the shares to lock in the profit on the transaction.

The call provisions for preferred stock and the debt component of debt-with-equity warrants issues are not as standardized as the provision for convertible bonds.

---

[2]  This provision is often referred to as the "screw clause".

### 4.2.8  Dilution Consideration

The dilution considerations associated with an equity-linked issue exist at two levels:

• For existing shareholders.
• For the investors in the equity-linked issue.

Any equity-linked issue will dilute (depending on the conversion basis) existing shareholders' interest to the extent that they forego any pro rata right to take up the issue. The extent of any dilution will reflect the proceeds of any sale of entitlement to subscribe (if applicable), whether or not the equity-linked issue is actually converted and the pricing of the equity option element. For some companies, a solution to the issue of dilution often lies in a financing package that enables major shareholders to take up a pro rata entitlement to the equity-linked issue.

The theoretical dilution is expressed as the effective dilution in the event that the entire convertible issue is converted into common stock:

Dilution = (Number of outstanding shares + Number of shares issued upon potential conversion)/[Number of outstanding shares + (Number of outstanding shares + Number of shares issued upon potential conversion)]

In the absence of express protection, the investor in the equity-linked issue may suffer from a reduction in the value of the conversion right as a result of recapitalization actions taken by the issuer. Specific protection is provided through anti-dilution clauses. These clauses vary greatly in their detail but usually provide protection against:

• Bonus and rights issues.
• Consolidations and subdivisions of capital.
• Issue of shares at less than market price, including issues pursuant to dividend reinvestment plans, share election plans and employee share schemes.
• Issues of options to purchase shares at less than market price.
• Capitalization of profits or reserves and capital distribution.

The manner in which the investor's conversion rights are protected varies depending on the impact of securities, stock exchange, and tax regulations. There are two general possibilities:

• Provision can be made for adjustment to the conversion ratio (and by implication the conversion price).
• Investors in the equity-linked issue can be given participatory rights in new equity issues by the issuer.

Where changes in conversion price are required, the trust deed will specify the mechanics of the adjustment, including rounding and carry forward of minor adjustments, as well as exemptions where a transaction involves a small percentage of existing capital.

### 4.2.9  Participation Rights in New Issues

In certain jurisdictions, it is common practice to provide investors in equity-linked issues with the right to participate in rights issues of securities made to existing shareholders of the issuer. However, generally only a notional entitlement to bonus issues accrues with the entitlement being realized only upon conversion into the underlying shares. As discussed above, participatory rights are given to investors as an anti-dilution measure.[3]

### 4.2.10  Change of Control Considerations

An actual or potential change of corporate control has major implications for investors in equity-linked securities, particularly convertibles and equity warrants. The actual approach to change of control is substantially dependent on the applicable securities legislation and its impact on mergers, acquisitions, and other forms of corporate restructuring.

The general approach to change of control issues is to avoid the potential risk of being "locked in". The objective of these provisions is to allow the investor to exit the holding at face value in the event of corporate actions that have the potential to reduce the value of the convertible bond occurring.

This takes the form of investors being given the right to convert or redeem their securities where:

- A party becomes entitled to a specific proportion, generally in excess of 30-40%, of the issuer's voting shares.
- A majority of the directors being or likely to be imminently replaced.
- A sale of all or a major portion on the issuer's assets.
- A restructuring entailing a sale of a large portion (say 50%) of the issuer's voting stock.
- A restructuring that entails the distribution in cash, securities, or assets of a large portion (say 30%) of the value of the shares prior to the restructuring.

---

[3]  This is particularly true of domestic Australia equity-linked transactions as the provisions of tax legislation technically prevent adjustment to the conversion price. The difficulty is that rights issues at a discount to market price reduce the share price growth experienced by the issuer and tend to reduce the prospect of the equity-linked security being converted. See Beaven, John R. & Johnston, T. Campbell "Australian Convertible Issues" (September 1984) *International Financial Law Review* 33-35.

The approach that has gained in importance is the right to immediately convert or a provision that enables the investor to put the convertible bond back to the issuer at a prespecified price if a specified event occurs.

# 5.    Economics of Equity-linked Issues

## 5.1    Implications for Issuers

From the perspective of issuers, the utilization of convertible securities reflects the transaction economics, the impact of taxation factors, the desire to broaden the investor base for its securities, and to diversify the range of financing instruments utilized. The major factors underlying the utilization by issuers of convertible debt include:

- **Cost-effective funding** — issuers, because interest payments are tax-deductible, may find it attractive to issue equity-linked securities such as convertible debt. The main advantage of a convertible to an issuer is its *lower coupon* relative to an issue of conventional debt securities. For some issuers this is the overriding consideration, although there are advantages, such as longer maturities relative to straight debt. The true economic cost to the issuer is clearly not solely the coupon but the equity that may be called upon to be issued upon conversion.
- **Source of balance sheet equity financing** — an equity-linked financing may be regarded externally as equity thereby having less of a detrimental effect on the firm's debt-to-equity ratio than would a corresponding issue of straight debt. The exact treatment of equity-linked debt varies depending on the exact structure. Traditional convertibles are treated as debt but where long-term and subordinated may receive some equity like credit from banks and financial institutions. Rating agencies will generally not treat such transactions as equity. However, certain structured equity-linked issues, primarily mandatory convertible structures, may receive equity treatment from both lenders and rating agencies.[4]
- **Lower level of equity dilution** — convertibles also represent the sale of ordinary shares at a fixed conversion price that usually represents a premium over the current market price of the share. Convertibles are a form of delayed equity financing assuming that conversion does take place or can be forced. The fact that the equity underlying the equity-linked issue can be sold at a premium over common stock price and then forced in certain circumstances to convert means that fewer shares need be sold and less dilution need result than from a normal offering of common stock. As equity hybrids represent a

---

[4]    See discussion in Chapter 10.

deferred rather than immediate equity, it is not required to be serviced until conversion.[5] Because of their popularity among certain classes of international investors, convertibles targeted to these markets can be offered at attractive terms relative to the terms achievable in the issuer's domestic markets. Euro-convertibles, for example, may have the added advantage that as they are sold outside the issuer's domestic market. This may create less selling pressure on the underlying ordinary shares than a domestic convertible issue which may prompt investors to sell stock in order to buy convertible bonds. The absence of this selling pressure with an Euro-convertible may allow an issuer to get a higher effective conversion price than could have been obtained in the domestic market.

- **Diversification of investor base** — various investors, because of different risk profiles and tax positions, will find investment in convertible debt to be more effective than direct equity investments.

The major costs of issuing equity-linked debt include:

- **Potential dilution** — the major cost of issuing equity-linked securities is the fact that they require the issuer to potentially give up equity and as a result to dilute existing shareholders' economic interests. Earnings must be reported on two bases: primary — all shares outstanding, and fully diluted (all shares outstanding plus those potentially outstanding as a result of the conversion of equity-linked securities).
- **Failure to convert** — there is a risk that the issue is not converted prior to maturity. Failure to convert might be the result of market factors (a fall in equity prices generally) or the performance of the shares of the issuer. The failure to convert might also result from the deterioration of the currency of the shares relative to the currency of the convertible (an effective fall in the share price *in foreign currency terms*). The risk of nonconversion creates both liquidity and a balance sheet management problem for the issuer. The existence of an unconverted convertible sometimes also makes the issue of new equity more difficult. The failure to convert and the resulting impact on liquidity and the balance sheet can be very significant as set out in **Exhibit 9.4**.

---

[5]  In jurisdictions characterized by an integrated tax system where corporate tax paid is credited to investors in relation to dividends paid, this also means that no tax credits are utilized until conversion is affected as no dividends are paid on the convertible or warrants until conversion.

**Exhibit 9.4**

**Nonconversion Risk on Convertible — The Emerging Market Experience 1997-1998**

In 1997, following the Asian monetary crisis, a large number of borrowers that had issued convertible debt experienced this problem. These borrowers had issued US$ denominated convertible issues. The issues were not hedged back into the issuer's domestic currency. The absence of hedging was driven by the following factors:

- The belief that the Asian currencies (in particular, the Indonesian rupiah, Malaysian ringgit, and the Thai baht) were linked to the US$.
- The difficulty in hedging a convertible because of the uncertainty of whether or not the issue will be converted and therefore the need to be repaid.
- The view that the prospects for the country and the economy were positive and as a result the shares price was likely to appreciate and lead to conversion eliminating the foreign currency exposure.

In July 1997, the value of the Thai baht collapsed, triggering collapses in other Asian currencies. The fall in value was significant with the currencies falling by between 50 and 80%. The collapse in currency values was accompanied by a sharp fall in equity market prices. The combined effect of depreciation in the currency and equity prices was to make the equity conversion option far out-of-the-money reducing the prospect of conversion.

The reduced chance of conversion combined with the depreciation in the local currency created large foreign exchange translation losses on the outstanding US$ convertible debt. This loss was now likely to be realized when the convertible debt was due for repayment in the likely case of nonconversion. The large currency losses combined with in some cases the inability to refinance the maturing convertible debt precipitated major financial problems for these borrowers. The inability to refinance was as a result of the withdrawal of capital from emerging markets as investors and banks became concerned by the deteriorating economic position of these countries and issuers.

The risk and losses were exacerbated by the fact that the issues were often relatively short in maturity (three to five years). This meant that there was not enough time for the markets (equity and currency) to recover either to reduce the foreign exchange loss or improve the prospects of conversion.

## 5.2    Implications for Investors

Convertibles and other forms of equity-linked securities offer a number of advantages to the investor:

- **Limited risk equity exposure** — equity-linked issues combine the certainty of a bond, with the right to participate in the capital appreciation of a company's ordinary shares. This is particularly suited to investors seeking a defensive form of equity exposure to a particular issuer. Convertible notes thus provide a middle ground between the relative stability of a fixed interest investment and the relative volatility of an equity security.

- **Income advantage to ordinary equity** — an advantage of investment in convertible notes is that the notes usually will have a higher yield at least in the early years of their term relative to corresponding dividend yields on ordinary shares. It may also be suited to certain income-oriented equity investors seeking equity exposure with certain minimum income requirements.

- **Trading opportunities** — for speculators, convertibles provide an active trading medium. Equity-linked notes can experience sharp price increases. But convertibles have risks in common with other volatile securities. Although they provide bond value protection, this is by definition below that of straight bonds because of the lower than market coupons they carry, if an issuer's share price falls, its convertible securities may also drop sharply. Often, a falling share price is symptomatic of a company's deteriorating credit standing. This would typically depress bond value as well as equity value.

- **Taxation factors** — the varying taxation treatment applicable to different investors may also tend to make convertible notes more attractive to some groups. For example, depending on the specific tax regime that is applicable:
  1. Tax-paying investors who are taxed at the same rate on both dividends and interest will generally be indifferent as between the two types of income.
  2. Tax-free institutions will be indifferent between shares and convertible notes from a taxation point of view although if the dividends carry a tax credit that makes them free of tax an inability to utilize the credit may create a bias in favour of convertibles.
  3. Companies subject to tax who pay tax on interest but receive a rebate of tax on dividends will naturally avoid investment in convertible notes.
  4. Under an integrated tax system, it may be attractive to certain companies to issue convertible notes where otherwise they could not pay tax-free dividend income. Similarly, as noted above, convertible notes may be a very attractive investment medium for nontaxpaying investors who would be unable to utilize the tax credit.

International investors in convertibles may also enjoy significant tax benefits. The attraction to overseas investors of convertibles derives from issue structures such as Euro-convertible issues that are issued free from withholding tax, providing international investors with an opportunity to invest without any withholding tax penalty.

# 6.    Pricing Equity-linked Issues

### 6.1    Pricing Approaches

There are a number of valuation mechanisms for equity-linked securities, such as convertibles/debt-with-equity warrants.

Factors relevant in pricing such securities include:

- The future evolution of the price of the underlying shares.
- The yield on comparable debt of equivalent maturity and credit risk, the convertible coupon and yield sacrifice required to purchase the convertible or equity-linked security.
- The income advantage offered through acquiring the convertible security rather than the dividend on the number of shares that would be obtained through a conversion.
- The number of years over which the conversion option subsists.

From the viewpoint of the investor, a convertible security is worth at a minimum its parity value or its investment value—whichever is higher. The convertible should in most circumstances have a higher value than this minimum value, reflecting the embedded equity option that will have a residual time or volatility value.

In practice, convertible valuation focuses on a set of different techniques. These approaches can be classified into two separate categories of valuation techniques:

- **Relative value measures** — these measures focus on comparing the relative investment merits of a number of comparable equity-linked securities. The most common relative value approaches include the payback approach and the required rate of growth in the share price.
- **Absolute value measures** — these measures seek to determine the unique and standalone value of the equity-linked security. This approach requires the bifurcation of the instrument into its separate debt and equity components, and the valuation of these elements separately.

## 6.2    Relative Value Approaches

### 6.2.1    Payback Method

This method looks at the difference between the interest yield on the convertible bond and the dividend yield on the shares to determine how long it would take for the extra income on the convertibles to account for the premium paid for the convertible securities. There are a number of variations on this method:

- **Simple payback** — this looks at the number of years that it takes for the convertible investor to recover the extra cost of the convertible (the conversion premium) from the additional income (the income on the convertible relative to the income on the equivalent shares). From the viewpoint of the investor, a shorter payback period is preferred. Typically, convertible investors look for a payback period of three to five years. The sought for payback period is also affected by the call options in the issue.
- **Adjusted payback** — this is identical to simple payback with the adjustment that the income advantage utilized is the actual cash flow difference between the coupon on the convertible bond and dividend income rather than the percentage difference between the coupon and the dividend yield. This is designed to take into account the different market values in the convertible and the shares. This approach has a different outcome only where the convertible is trading at market price away from par or face value in the secondary market.
- **Discounted payback** — this approach is to compare the expected income stream from the convertible note (up to a chosen conversion date) and the expected income stream from the shares. The comparison is made using the present value of the two different income streams. The method involves calculating the present value of all interest payments to be received up until the chosen conversion date and subtracting the present value of all expected dividends up to the same date. Purchase of the convertible notes is justified if the present value of the extra income received from the convertible notes relative to the shares is greater than the premium on the convertible notes

The main limitation of the simple and adjusted payback approach is that it takes no account of the time value of money. The payback period method also does not take into account the timing of interest and dividend payments during the payback period, or the tax effect of the higher income stream from the notes. It also ignores the possibility of growth in dividends and capital growth in the share price. Even if the model were adjusted for the timing of cash flows and adjusted for taxation, it would still suffer from the disadvantage of all payback methods in that some arbitrary cut-off period must be set by the investor and all cash flows after this cut-off point are therefore ignored. The method essentially focuses only on the downside risk of not recovering the premium paid for the notes.

This discounted payback approach is most attractive for investors in two categories:

• Investors who have decided to invest in a particular company. The present value analysis assists in determining whether such an investor should invest in ordinary shares or in convertible notes and later convert into ordinary shares.
• Investors already holding a particular stock. The present value analysis indicates whether gains can be made by switching out of the stock into the convertible notes and later converting back into ordinary shares.

The main assumptions using this approach to valuing a convertible note include:

• The approach requires that an estimate be made of the future dividend flows.
• The approach also requires the choice of a discount rate to establish the present value of the future streams of dividends and interest.
• A "horizon date" for investment in each convertible note issue must be assumed.
• It primarily establishes a value of the equity-linked security relative to the underlying equity security.

### 6.2.2   Required Rate of Growth in Share Price Method

This method of evaluating investment in convertible notes calculates what compound annual rate of growth in the share price over the remaining life of the note is required to account for the premium paid on the purchase of the convertible note. If the investor's expectation of the rate at which the share price will increase is greater than this required rate then the convertible notes should be bought. If the investor's expectation of the rate at which the share price will increase is less than this required rate then the convertible notes should not be bought.

The limitations in this approach include:

• Like the payback period, this method takes no account of the timing or relative riskiness of cash flows in that the investor is paying out cash for the premium now which is expected to be made up by way of a return (the capital growth in the share price) to be received some time in the future.
• The method requires that a forecast be made of the growth in the share price for up to 10 years into the future.
• This method assumes that investors have a long time horizon. Specifically, it

assumes that investors are willing to hold the notes over the remaining term to redemption.

**Exhibit 9.5** sets out examples of the valuation of a convertible security using the relative value measures identified.

---

**Exhibit 9.5**
**Relative Valuation Methods — Example**

Assume the following market information:

| Ordinary Share/Common Stock | |
|---|---|
| Price | $21.00 |
| Dividends/Share | $0.50 |
| Dividend Yield | 2.38% |

| **Convertible Bond** | |
|---|---|
| Maturity (years) | 5 |
| Current Market Price (%) | 96% |
| Current Price (per bond) | $960.00 |
| Bond Face Value | $1,000.00 |
| Conversion Ratio | 40 |
| Conversion Price | $25.00 |
| Conversion Premium | 19.0% |
| Coupon | 5.75% |

| **Interest Rates** | |
|---|---|
| Risk free Rates | 5.50% |
| Credit Margin | 1.50% |
| Risk-adjusted Rates | 7.00% |

Based on the above, the payback and the required share price, growth is calculated in the table below:

| **Convertible Economics** | |
|---|---|
| Parity Value | $840.00 |
| Conversion Premium ($) | $120.00 |
| Conversion Premium (%) | 14.3% |
| Income Pickup ($) | $37.50 |
| Income Pickup (%) | 3.369% |

| Payback Method | |
|---|---|
| Simple (years) | 4.24 |
| Adjusted (years) | 3.20 |
| **Discounted Payback** | |
| Discounted Dividend Stream | $93.72 |
| Discounted Coupon Stream | $226.33 |
| Discounted Income Advantage | $132.61 |
| Income Advantage/Conversion Premium | $12.61 |
| **Required Share Price Growth** | |
| % Growth | 19.0% |
| % pa Growth | 3.5% |

## 6.3    Absolute Value Measures — Separate Valuation of Equity Option and Debt

### 6.3.1    Overview

Under this approach, the convertible or debt-with-equity warrants is treated as a mixture of the following elements:

- Straight debt (with a coupon rate and a maturity date).
- An equity option to purchase the issuer's equity at a stated price on stated date(s).

The separate elements of the package are individually valued. The debt portion is valued utilizing the normal present value/internal rate of return approach to valuing fixed income securities. The discount rate relevant would be the normal yield on a comparable straight debt offering by the issuer. The equity option element would be valued utilizing either one of the available equity option pricing models (such as Black-Scholes or a binomial model) or utilizing a market value of a comparable option, such as an exchange traded option on the issuer's equity securities.[6]

---

[6]    For a discussion of the bond/equity option valuation technique, see Brennan, Michael and Schwartz, Eduardo "Convertible Bonds: Valuation and Optimal Strategies for Call and Conversion" (December 1977) *Journal of Finance* vol. 32 no. 5 1699-1716; Ho, Thomas S.Y. and Pfeffer, David M. "Convertible Bonds: Model, Value Attribution, and Analytics" (September/October 1996) *Financial Analysts Journal* 35-44; Nelken, Izzy "A Convertible Primer" (1997) *Financial Products* Issue 70 14-19.

A shorthand method of valuing such securities is to utilize the value of the debt component to "back out" an implied price for the equity conversion rights. This equity conversion right is then compared to the expected value of the relevant option.[7]

**Exhibit 9.6** sets out the key determinants of the value of the convertible bond. **Exhibit 9.7** sets out the behaviour of the value of a convertible bond.

**Exhibit 9.6**
**Key Determinants of Convertible Bond Value**

| Determinant | Impact on Convertible Bond Value of Increase in Variable | Pricing Model |
|---|---|---|
| **Bond** | | Internal rate of return/ bond pricing model |
| Coupon | Increase | |
| Risk-free rate | Decrease | |
| Credit spread | Decrease | |
| **Equity Option** | | Option pricing model |
| Share price | Increase | |
| Dividend yield | Decrease | |
| Maturity | Increase | |
| Conversion premium | Decrease | |
| Share volatility | Increase | |
| Risk-free rate | Decrease | |
| **Other Factors** | | Subjective |
| Liquidity | Increase | |
| Stock borrowing and lending | Increase | |

---

[7] The backed-out price is useful in comparing the relative investment attractiveness of issued equity-linked securities, particularly convertibles. However, this approach is not helpful in pricing a new issue except where a similar security, previously issued, is trading in the secondary market.

**Exhibit 9.7**
**Behavior of Convertible Bond Values**

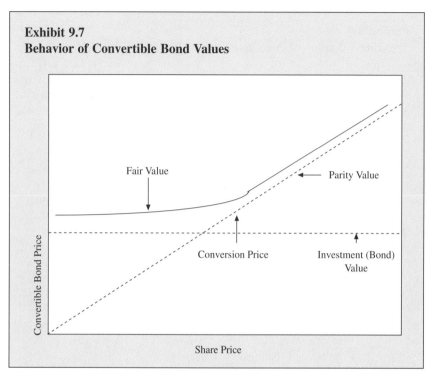

The behavior of the convertible bond price (discussed in more detail below) follows the following pattern:

• Where the equity option is out-of-the-money, the instrument behaves similarly to a debt instrument with the primary determinant of value being the bond price, and it is most sensitive to changes in interest rates and the credit spread for the issuer.

• Where the equity option is in-the-money, the instrument behaves more like the underlying shares with the major determinant of value being the performance of the underlying share price.

**Exhibit 9.8** sets out an example of the valuation of a convertible bond using the separate valuation of debt and equity components.

**Exhibit 9.8**
**Separate Valuation of Debt and Equity Elements — Example**

The following example summarizes the separate valuation of a convertible, utilizing the separate valuation of the debt and equity components. The following assumptions are made:

- The shares are denominated in A$ while the issue is undertaken in US$. The spot exchange rate assumed is A$1 = US$.70.
- The valuation is at launch for a new issue.
- The bond is valued using a standard yield model.
- The equity option component is valued using a binomial model assuming a constant dividend yield rate.

The valuation of the convertible is as follows:

| | |
|---|---|
| Par Value | $1,000 |
| Coupon | 4.7500% |
| Frequency | 1 |
| Settlement Date | 15-Jan-00 |
| Maturity Date | 15-Jan-10 |
| Conversion Premium | 20.00% |
| Conversion Share Price | $17.64 |
| Share Per Bond | 56.69 |
| Final Exercise Date | 7-Jan-10 |
| Yield To Maturity | 7.0000% |
| Credit Spread | 1.5000% |
| Share Price | $21.00 |
| Exchange Rate (A$1 = US$) | $0.7000 |
| Foreign Currency Share Price | $14.70 |
| Dividend (per share) | $0.75 |
| Risk-free Rate | 5.5000% |
| Volatility | 18.00% |
| **Bond** | |
| Clean Price | 841.9694 |
| Accrued Interest | 0 |
| Total Bond | 841.9694 |
| **Option** | |
| Per Share | 2.45 |
| Total Option Value | $138.76 |

| Convertible | |
|---|---|
| Excludes Accrued Interest | $980.72 |
| Includes Accrued Interest | $980.72 |

As is evident, the theoretical value of the convertible bond is approximately 98% of face value. The same issue is now priced at a future date with different market parameters:

| | |
|---|---|
| Par Value | $1,000 |
| Coupon | 4.7500% |
| Frequency | 1 |
| Settlement Date | 1-Dec-02 |
| Maturity Date | 15-Jan-10 |
| Conversion Premium | 20.00% |
| Conversion Share Price | $17.64 |
| Share (per bond) | 56.69 |
| Exercise Date | 7-Jan-10 |
| Yield to Maturity | 7.3000% |
| Credit Spread | 1.2000% |
| Share Price | $17.50 |
| Exchange Rate | $0.6800 |
| Foreign Currency Share Price | $11.90 |
| Dividend (per share) | $0.85 |
| Risk-free Rate | 6.1000% |
| Volatility | 15.00% |
| **Bond** | |
| Clean Price | 861.97 |
| Accrued Interest | 41.64 |
| Total Bond | 903.62 |
| **Option** | |
| Per Share | 0.51 |
| Total Option Value | $28.88 |
| Convertible | |
| Excludes Accrued Interest | $890.85 |
| Includes Accrued Interest | $932.49 |

The valuation of a debt-with-equity warrants package would follow the same basic logic.

### 6.3.2   Model Issues

The use of this approach in practice needs to be adjusted to reflect a variety of factors. These include both model problems and the specific features of the security.[8]

Specific model problems include the assumption of a constant dividend rate, constant stock volatility, constant interest rate, and constant credit spread. An additional model problem is the assumption of the lack of correlation between interest rate, equity prices, and (in the case of a foreign currency-denominated convertible bond) the exchange rate. The most significant feature of the security requiring adjustment is the embedded call option, common to most convertibles. The issuer's ability to call the issue effectively reduces the value of the call option as it eliminates the remaining time value of the embedded equity option element.

The above one-factor model is inadequate to incorporate all of the above considerations. In practice, a number of multiple-factor models are used for valuation. These models ideally would specify the inputs as follows:

• Stochastic processes would be specified for the stock price, dividends, term structure of interest rates, credit spread and exchange rate.
• Correlations (stochastic or fixed) would be specified between the variables.

In practice, such a complex modeling task is not economic. Consequently, more advanced valuation models utilize stochastic models for the interest rate term structure and the stock price. Correlations are generally not incorporated. A binomial or Monte Carlo process is utilized combining an interest rate tree and an interest tree in order to capture the valuation effect of interest rates (applicable to the remaining term structure to maturity) and equity price movements. This type of two-factor models allows more effective capture of the call behavior of the convertible and the interaction of the bond and equity values.

However, the complexity of the interaction between the various parameters makes valuation imprecise and the model risk of such valuation approaches is very high. For example, the sensitivity of the value of convertible to the credit spread and currency risk are not insignificant but often not effectively modeled.[9]

---

[8]   See for example Nelken, Izzy "Reassessing The Reset" (October 1998) *AsiaRisk* 36-39.

[9]   For a discussion of some of the problems of equity-linked security pricing, see Das, Satyajit "Pricing & Risk Management of Equity Derivatives Transactions: Part 1" (1998) *Financial Products* Issue 87 18-23; "Pricing & Risk Management of Equity Derivatives Transactions: Part 2" (1998) *Financial Products* Issue 89 18-26.

# 7.  Equity-linked Securities — Trading Characteristics

## 7.1  Overview

Equity-linked bonds share the characteristics of both bonds and shares. They also have values (bond value and conversion value) deriving from these shared characteristics. The trading behavior of these securities reflects the interaction of the two underlying securities.

The interaction of the bond and equity securities is most readily seen in the context of convertible securities. The trading behavior of debt-with-equity-linked securities is dominated by the fact that the equity warrants are, generally, stripped off or detached from the bond and traded separately. Consequently, each component is traded independently, consistent with the trading characteristics of the debt or equity element.

## 7.2  Convertible Securities — Trading Characteristics

The behavior of the convertible bond can be analyzed from the viewpoint of both investors and issuer. **Exhibit 9.9** sets out the trading behaviour of a convertible security from the perspective of an investor.

---

**Exhibit 9.9**
**Convertible Securities — Trading Behavior**

A hypothetical 15-year convertible offering by ABC Corporation Ltd (ABC) can be used to provide a good illustration of the trading characteristics of the instrument in general.

Assume an issue of US$8% coupon subordinated debentures convertible into the ordinary shares of the issuer, ABC, at the price (conversion price) of A$23.125 per share. This implies that each bond valued at US$1,000 can be exchanged into 51.92 common shares (US$1,000 divided by A$23.125 at a fixed exchange rate of US$1 = A$1.2007 (A$1 = 0.8328).

The conversion value is the number of shares issuable upon conversion multiplied by the latest stock price for the company's common shares. If the stock were selling for A$25 per share, then the conversion value would be US$1,081.04 (51.92 times A$25 at the specified exchange rate) per convertible bond (or a price of 108.1%). If the stock price fell to A$20, then conversion value would be US$864.83 (51.92 times A$20 at the fixed exchange rate) per bond (or a price of 86.48%). Fluctuations in the exchange rate would manifest themselves as changes in the US$ parity value of the bond.

---

There is, however, a limit to how far a convertible's price can fall, because of the support provided by its bond value. Assuming that general interest rate levels dictated a yield to maturity for a 15-year nonconvertible or straight US$ bond of 9%, the bond value of the convertible (based on its 8% coupon) would indicate a price of 92.07%, and with a conversion value of 86.48% the convertible bond would quite possibly trade at 93-94%. This would happen because investors believed that the conversion right still had some worth (for example, share price and conversion value might rise in the future). Assuming, in another instance, that the share price increased to A$22.50 (indicating a conversion value of $972. 93 or price of 97. 29%) while the bond value remained the same, the convertible might then trade in the 99-100% range. This premium would occur because investors felt that the bond characteristics of the convertible still had value as a form on insurance against future share price declines. This trading premium, in economic terms, equates to the time value of the embedded equity option.

The trading premium of a convertible is greatest when the two values, bond and conversion, are closest together. As they move apart, they are seen by investors as providing each other less benefit. In the last example, if the conversion value indicated a price of 99-100%, but the bond value dropped to 45-55%, the insurance provided by the bond characteristics would be less and the trading premium would be correspondingly reduced.

The premium is most dramatically cut back when a convertible is trading at or above par when the issuer has the right to call its convertible. Issuers use opportunities such as these to force conversion into their common stock. If, for instance, the common stock price of ABC increased to A$30 per share, the securities would be trading at or just above 129.72%, on the basis of conversion value. Assuming that the company had the right to call the securities at 104%, and announced its intention to do so, holders of the bonds would be forced to convert them into shares rather than incur the 19.8% loss [calculated as 129.72%–104% divided by 129.72%]. Many issuers in fact have every intention of forcing conversion of their convertibles after they have reached an appropriate price. In this way, equity can be raised for their companies. Investors are also aware of these intentions and therefore in advance of an expected call convertibles trade at only a very modest premium if any at all over the conversion value.

In certain instances, convertibles may even trade at a slight discount from conversion value. This reflects the loss of accrued interest (if any) and the expected transaction expenses of conversion borne by investors. If the discount were to widen beyond a particular point, this would introduce trading possibilities. For instance, one could buy the convertible and convert immediately into common shares, buying them in effect at a discount, and simultaneously sell short the same number of shares at the then current market price. An investor would receive revenues from the sale of the shares at market value while making delivery on the short sale with shares purchased at a discount. The difference would be his or her profit. Market price fluctuations of the bonds or the common shares would be inconsequential, as the two parts of the transaction would be handled at the same time.

The above example focuses on the trading characteristics of a convertible as an equity-linked security. In recent times, there has been increased interest in trading convertible bonds *as a fixed income security*.[10] This has been the case in particular in relation to convertible where the embedded equity option has little value as a result of a decline in the price of the underlying stock to levels well below the strike price of the option. Under these conditions, convertible and fixed income arbitrage traders have looked to unbundle the security and repackage it through an asset swap.[11]

This form of trading has taken two forms:

- **Convertible arbitrage** — this structure entails a trader purchasing a convertible and separating the transaction into a conventional fixed income bond and the embedded equity option. The equity option is onsold to an equity derivative counterparty and the bond cash flows reprofiled into a floating rate bond. The yield achievable is higher than would be available from a direct investment in a comparable bond issued by the underlying issuer.

- **Convertible and credit arbitrage** — this structure is the same as the above form of convertible arbitrage with an added feature. The additional feature is that the trader will typically purchase protection against the risk of default by the issuer in the form of a credit default swap.[12] This has the effect of creating a fixed income security where the underlying credit risk is transformed from that of the issuer to that of the counterparty providing

---

[10]  See Mahtani, Arun "Asset Swappers, Bond Investors Target Convertibles" (March 13, 1999) *International Financing Review* Issue 1274 at 75.

[11]  For a discussion of asset swaps, see Das, Satyajit (1994) *Swaps And Financial Derivatives*; LBC Information Services, Sydney; McGraw-Hill, Chicago at Chapter 18.

[12]  For a discussion of credit derivatives, see Das, Satyajit (editor) (1998) *Credit Derivatives*; John Wiley & Sons, Singapore.

credit protection. The motivation is again the return achievable from this transaction relative to that on a comparable transaction where the underlying credit is the provider of credit protection.

The major drivers underlying these forms of transactions include:

• **Returns** — the yields available from these transactions have been very attractive on a relative value basis. This higher return as in the case of standard convertible arbitrage is relative to returns relative to those available on comparable securities issued by the issuer or equivalent credit or relative to returns available on the credit risk of the seller of credit protection or equivalent risk. As relative value groups in financial institutions and hedge funds systematically traded away pricing discrepancies in the conventional fixed income markets, the pricing anomalies in pricing equity-linked securities were the center of trading focus. These pricing anomalies related to both the pricing of the bond itself (including any embedded optionality) and also the equity component.

• **Availability of investments** — the lack of availability of fixed income securities issued by the relevant issuer also contributed to the development of this type of transaction. Investors seeking *fixed income exposure* to a particularly issuer may have been constrained by the lack of availability of securities issued by that particular issuer. Where the issuer has outstanding convertibles, the capacity to asset swap these securities to create a fixed income investor has proved attractive. For example, the lack of European corporate bond issuance in the period 1998-2000 contrasts with the significant volume of convertible and exchangeable bond issuance by European issuers. This created the opportunity to synthesize the credit risk of these issuers through convertible asset swaps. The risk is sold in two possible formats. The first form is as a conventional asset swap where the investor creates a floating rate investment returning a margin relative to LIBOR (in the currency of the investor's choice) by combining the purchase of the convertible, sale of the equity option back to the trader, and entry into an interest rate or currency swap. The second form entails assuming the credit risk indirectly through the sale of credit protection under a credit default swap. Under the second format, the trader purchases the convertible, sells the equity option to another trader, and purchases credit protection from the investor wanting to create credit exposure to the issuer. The trader is left with a substantially hedged position and an arbitrage profit. The investor can assume the credit risk is a funded (credit-linked note) or unfunded form (credit default swap).

The transactions are not free of risk. The presence of the equity option and the call features of the convertible (where the drivers are both the equity price and interest rates) all make this type of transaction more complex than conventional asset swaps. These risks require the swap structure to be customized to the underlying asset to avoid any residual risk of the transaction. For the investor in the asset swap, the major residual issue is the uncertainty regarding the duration of the investment.[13]

**Exhibit 9.10** sets out the detailed structure of a convertible asset swap transaction.

---

**Exhibit 9.10**
**Convertible Bond Asset Swap**

Assume the investor purchases the following convertible bond:

| | |
|---|---|
| Issuer | A Company |
| Maturity | November 15, 2010 |
| Face Value Amount | US$10 million |
| Coupon | 3.00% pa payable annually (30/360 bond basis) |
| Current Price | 73.75 plus accrued interest 2.35 |
| Trade Date | August 22, 2001 |
| Settlement Date | August 27, 2001 |
| Purchase Price | US$7,609,412 |

The investor purchases the bond, sells the equity option to the trader and enters into an interest rate swap to convert the cash flows into a synthetic floating rate note paying a margin over LIBOR. The cash flows of the swap are as follows:

- *Initial cash flows* — there are no initial cash flows unless the investor wants to adjust the amount invested to a round amount.[14]
- *Periodic payments* — the following exchanges take place over the life of the bond:
  1. On each annual coupon date of the convertible, the investor passes through to the swap counterparty the coupons on the convertible (US$30,000 calculated as 3.00% on US$30,000). Typically, the investor passes through the complete coupon, including the initial full coupon despite the fact that the swap commences only a short

---

[13] See Das, Satyajit "Pricing & Risk Management of Equity Derivatives Transactions: Part 1" (1998) *Financial Products* Issue 87 18-23; "Pricing & Risk Management of Equity Derivatives Transactions: Part 2" (1998) *Financial Products* Issue 89 18-26.

[14] For a discussion of the detailed structure of asset swaps, see Das, Satyajit (1994) *Swaps And Financial Derivatives*; LBC Information Services, Sydney; McGraw-Hill, Chicago at 571-574.

time prior to the first coupon payment. The swap counterparty adjusts for this extra receipt in the margin paid on the floating rate side of the swap.

2. Every quarter (February 15, May 15, August 15, and November 15, commencing November 15, 2001 and ending November 15, 2010 unless terminated early), the investor receives a payment equivalent to 3-month US$ LIBOR plus a margin (say, 95 bps).[15]

- *Final termination* — unless terminated early, the investor receives from the counterparty the purchase price paid for the convertible bond at the commencement of the asset swap and pays to the counterparty the US$10 million face value of the maturing convertible bond.
- *Early termination* — if the bond is converted or called prior to final maturity, the investor receives from the counterparty the purchase price paid for the convertible bond at the commencement of the asset swap and pays to the counterparty the amount received from the call of the convertible bond or transfers ownership of the convertible or the stock received as a result of conversion. The investor must also terminate the swap (accordingly, the swap must be capable of being terminated at any time).

The following diagram sets out the transaction cash flows:

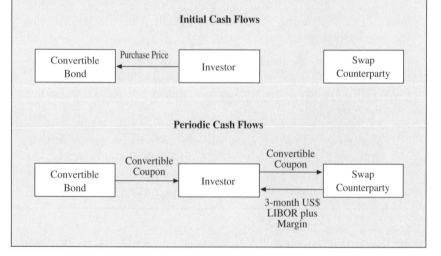

**Initial Cash Flows**

**Periodic Cash Flows**

---

[15] Interest payments can be priced of US$ 3-month LIBOR, swapped into fixed rate or swapped into a currency of the investor's choice.

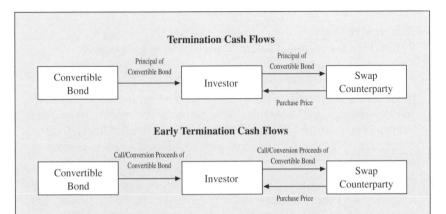

The result of the transaction is that the investor has synthesized a floating rate investment at a return of US$ LIBOR plus 95 bps. This compares to a return on a conventional bond issued by the issuer of comparable maturity that would swap into US$ LIBOR plus 71 bps. This represents an additional return of 24 bps pa that is in return for the sale of the embedded equity option and assuming the call risk on the underlying convertible bond. In case of conversion or call, the swap counterparty has the right to effectively terminate the asset swap.

In the case of a convertible and credit arbitrage transaction, the mechanics would be similar. The major differences would be as follows:

• The trader would hold the convertible bond, sell the equity option, and enter into the swap.
• The trader would enter into a transaction with the investor whereby the investor paid the spread (95 bps pa) to the investor in return for the investor agreeing to assume any loss on the convertible bond in the event that the issuer defaulted on its obligations. The term of the credit default swap would be until maturity or termination by conversion or call. The return could also be structured as the coupon on a credit-linked note issued by the trader to the investor.

The above analysis focuses on investor trading in convertible securities. In practice, issuers may also consider a range of strategies in managing outstanding convertible issues. These trading strategies revolve around the call option available and the ability of the issuer to call the issue to either force conversion or take advantage of attractive refinancing opportunities. **Exhibit 9.11** sets out examples of strategies available to an issuer to optimize the value of the call option on a convertible issue.

**Exhibit 9.11**
**Convertible Securities — Issuer Management of Call Option**

*Forced or Induced Conversion*

If the shares underlying the convertible are trading at a level above the conversion price, the convertible issuer can call the security (where the convertible is outside the call protection period), effectively forcing conversion. The forced conversion can be effected under two separate scenarios:

• **Forced conversion** — where the convertible is callable, the shares are trading well above the conversion price and the issuer has an after-tax coupon cost on the convertible that exceeds the cash cost of dividends on the equivalent underlying shares that would be issued after conversion, the issuer should force conversion by calling the bond. This reflects the fact that the convertible under these circumstances is basically an equity substitute. The forced conversion enables the issuer to achieve balance sheet recognition of the funding as equity rather than debt, reducing its leverage as well as savings in cash flow used to service its financing.

• **Induced conversion** — where the convertible is not currently callable but the share price is trading significantly above the conversion price and where the issuer would achieve cash flow savings through the payment of dividends rather than the convertible coupon, the issuer may use a variety of strategies to *induce* conversion. The typical technique is to temporarily reduce the conversion price to provide an economic incentive to convert. This reduction is usually only available for a short period (30 days). Investors have to convert on the more advantageous terms within this window period. At the end of the window, the conversion terms are reset to the original terms of the convertible. The adjusted conversion terms are usually designed to offer an incentive (around 10-20% premium to the previous price of the convertible) to encourage the investors to convert.

In seeking to force conversion, the issuer needs to be sensitive to a number of factors:

• **Timing of the call** — the issuer will generally seek to time the call to be just prior to the interest payment date in order to save the issuer the full coupon payment. As noted above, the coupon payment is forgone by the investor upon conversion. As long as the issue is sufficiently in-the-money, the investor will convert to protect its economic gains on the issue that is reduced by the lost coupon.

- **Conversion risk** — where a call notice is issued the issuer is exposed to the performance of its share price between the date of the call notice and the redemption date on which the bond must be repaid or converted. This reflects the fact that if the share price falls, investors may not convert, exposing the issuer to the liquidity risk of having to finance the repayment of the bond. This risk may be significant where the share price is trading slightly above the call price or the share market is volatile. For investors who are not likely to hold the shares upon conversion, the conversion decision will necessarily include an estimate of the price at which the share (which may be a large parcel) can be liquidated, as well as the transaction cost of the sale. Where markets are volatile and the risk on the sale is large, investors in this position may need the shares to trade at a sufficient margin over the call price to cover the costs and risk. In practice, these risks are dealt with in two different ways. The issuer may only call the convertible when the underlying conversion value is significantly greater than the call price to reduce the liquidity risk. Alternatively, the issuer can enter into an underwriting arrangement (often referred to as a call underwriting) with an investment bank. Under the terms of such an arrangement, the investment bank agrees to purchase any shares that are not converted at the initial conversion price. The investment bank may then re-offer the shares to the market at the current market price. The underwriting is designed to ensure that the issuer will not need to make cash redemption of the convertible bonds.
- **Signaling aspects** — the decision by an issuer to call may inadvertently signal to the market a weaker future financial performance outlook necessitating a strengthening of the balance sheet. An issuer seeking to take advantage of significant cash flow savings from inducing conversions may need to clearly communicate the benefits to investors to minimize any adverse signaling effects.

## Refinancing

It may be economically beneficial to call a convertible even where the convertible is out-of-the-money with the share price trading below the conversion price. This reflects a potential saving from a refinancing of the convertible debt with either straight debt or a new convertible bond. The primary motivation in this situation is the reduction in after-tax interest expense. The analysis of any potential decision to call in these circumstances is driven by the net present value savings between the existing issue and the refinancing transaction taking into account any refinancing costs.

### 7.3    Debt-with-equity Warrants — Trading Characteristics

Like convertibles, equity warrants allow a reduction of the coupon on the bond, and permit an issuer to sell equity ahead of the market. They are unlike convertibles in that the warrants have a separate identity from the bond.

Almost all warrants may be detached from their bonds and traded freely in a secondary market, usually at a premium over their exercise value (their value when converted into common shares). When warrants are exercised, outside capital is usually used to buy the shares. This practice is different from a convertible, where it is the principal amount of the security itself that is used to purchase shares. Thus, while the conversion of convertible securities necessitates the transfer of debt capital into an equal amount of equity capital, leaving the absolute amount of capital unchanged, the exercise of warrants can inject new equity capital into a corporation while allowing the bonds that once carried the warrants to remain outstanding.

The bond component of a debt-with-equity warrants issue (often referred to as the corpus or host bond) when trading in the secondary market will be quoted on two different bases: cum-warrant (that is, with the equity warrants attached), or, ex-warrant (that is, without the equity warrants). Generally speaking, warrant bonds are traded on an ex-warrant basis and will be valued in the secondary markets as straight nonequity-linked bonds.[16]

Investors are attracted to warrants because of the chance they give to participate in the appreciation of a corporation's common stock. Warrants provide leverage, low-dollar cash outlay, greater price volatility per dollar of investment, and thus appeal to investors and speculators. For example, assume a warrant that is valued at $4 can be used to purchase the common stock of a company at $10 per share. If the market price of the common stock increases from $9 to $15, the warrant would jump in value to about $8 ($15 less $10 exercise price plus premium). The warrant would thus gain in price by 100% while the common stock, to which it is linked, would increase by only 66.7%.

## 8.    Convertible Debt vs Debt-with-equity Warrants — A Comparison

The differences between convertible debt and issues of debt-with-equity warrants are important.

---

[16]    In practice, the host bond, which usually trades at a substantial discount reflecting the lower coupon on the bond, is repackaged through an asset swap transaction and placed with investors as a floating rate note; see Das, Satyajit (1994) *Swaps And Financial Derivatives*; LBC Information Services, Sydney; McGraw-Hill, Chicago at Chapter 18.

Convertible issues consist of debt securities that give the holders of the debt the right to convert their debt claim against the borrower into an equity claim. Characteristic features of such issues include:

- The conversion rights are inseparable from the debt claim. The holder cannot end up with both debt and equity arising from the same issue, and the borrower receives no extra cash injection upon conversion.
- Since debt and conversion components are physically inseparable, when the share price is low, the convertible will trade on pure yield considerations just like a straight bond, while when the share price rises, the convertible will tend to rise in price as the value of the shares into which it is convertible goes up with a higher yield on the bond keeping its price above the shares. Eventually the convertible will trade like a higher yielding version of the underlying equity.
- If a convertible is converted, then the underlying debt will never have to be repaid.
- The "equity content" of a convertible is almost always 100%; that is, the number of shares times the conversion price is equal to the face value of bond.
- The exchange rate used on conversion between currency of the debt and currency of the shares (when the two are different) is fixed. However (in the unlikely event), if it is not fixed, some compensating payment must be made between the bond-holder and the borrower upon conversion, to make up for the difference between the number of shares times the conversion price in equity currency and bond value in bond currency.
- The interest rate on a convertible is usually fixed higher than the dividend rate on the shares. This is to prevent a holder converting almost immediately the share price reaches the exercise price. Given this higher yield on the convertible bonds, holders will prefer convertible bonds to equity, and conversion will usually be deferred until the dividend rate on the share has caught up with the coupon on the bonds.
- Convertibles frequently carry call provisions, effectively forcing conversion if exercised when the bonds are at a premium to par (see previous discussion).

Issues of debt-with-equity warrants, in contrast, have the following features:

- Warrants are usually separable from the underlying debt. An investor can dispose of either warrants or debt and keep the other. The borrower receives extra cash upon the exercise by investors of warrants.
- Since the component parts are physically separable, an issue with warrants will usually trade around a price consisting of the underlying debt valued on a straight yield basis, plus a warrant valuation.
- The warrant content may be less than, equal to, or greater than the bond value; that is, a borrower has more flexibility as to how much equity incentive to provide investors to induce subscription for the debt.

- The exchange rate used for exercising of a warrant is usually not fixed. The right to buy shares is expressed in terms of a fixed price in the home currency of those shares; that is, the investor gets no implicit exchange rate option on the currency of the shares.
- The debt component of a warrant issue always has to be repaid at maturity regardless of whether the warrants are exercised.
- It is not usually possible for the borrower to force conversion by calling the issue, since the warrants are detachable from the debt (the debt itself may embody call provisions and, of course, may be called).
- The warrants themselves carry no yield only anticipation of profit if the share price goes up. The warrant's value lies in the opportunity of participating in future share price rises, with a lower commitment of cash than for buying the shares.

For potential issuers examining the two structures as alternative forms of raising capital, the following considerations are relevant:

- A warrant can give extra cash upon conversion, a convertible does not.
- A warrant's associated debt will always have to be repaid, unlike a convertible if converted.
- If having cheap debt on the balance sheet is desirable, regardless of what happens to the equity component, the warrants have an advantage (the cheap debt is not extinguished by conversion).
- Exchange rate considerations probably make warrants relatively more attractive to strong currency borrowers (avoids dilution for existing shareholders if the currency of the debt in a convertible goes down) and the convertibles more attractive to weak currency borrowers (the appreciating debt will not have to be repaid if holders convert).
- Convertibles are probably more predictable in conversion behaviour and conversion can be forced (only worthwhile if bonds are at premium and share price over conversion price). Provided the share price has gone up since issue, and the bond is trading at a premium, convertibles permit forced conversion (by calling the issue); it is not generally possible to force holders to exercise their warrants. If assurance of equity sometime in next few years is a factor in the issue decision, convertibles may be advisable.
- Since the debt is separable from the equity component, a warrant-linked issue is capable of being hedged or otherwise managed where the underlying currency exposure is of concern. A convertible issue because the underlying debt may be extinguished as a result of conversion is difficult to hedge. The risk attached to this hedging difficulty is discussed above (see **Exhibit 9.4** on page 373.

## 9.  Summary

Equity-linked securities, in particular, convertibles, and debt-with-equity warrant issues are an interesting means of raising capital on attractive terms while achieving diversification of the issuer's investor base. The convertible note market, both domestic and internationally, and in particular the Euromarket for such issues, has emerged as a mature and increasingly liquid market allowing companies to raise relatively large amounts of capital for medium to long terms.

### Selected References

Aldred, P. *Convertibles and Warrants.* Euromoney Publications, 1987.

Blanton, Peter B., Dickson, Tyler G. and Weiseneck, Larry S. "The Issuer's Guide To Convertible And Equity-Linked Securities," Salomon Brothers Financial Equity Capital Markets/Syndicate, New York, October 1993.

Connolly, Kevin and Philips, George. *Japanese Warrant Markets.* MacMillan Publishers, England, 1992.

Das, Satyajit. "Equity-linked Issues for Australian Corporations." *The Australian Corporate Treasurer,* December 1987. 1-6 and *The Australian Corporate Treasurer,* February 1988: 8-11.

Gunn III, Gilman C. "Convertible Eurobonds: An Introduction." *Journal of International Securities Markets,* Summer 1988: 97–112.

Jones, E. Philip and Mason, Scott P. "Equity-linked Debt" *Midland Corporate Finance Journal* vol. 3 no. 4. Winter 1986: 46-58.

Phillips, George A. *Japanese Warrants—Second Edition.* IFR Publishing, London, 1989.

Price, Quintin. *Warrants, Options and Convertibles.* IFR Publishing, London, 1990.

Redmayne, Julian. *Convertibles—An International Perspective.* Euromoney Books, London, 1998.

Senner, Madis. *Japanese Euroderivatives.* Euromoney Books, London, 1989.

# 10
# Equity-linked Notes (2) — Structural Variations

## 1. Equity-linked Structured Notes

Equity-linked structured notes may be defined as fixed income securities where the interest coupons and/or principal of the instrument is linked to the movements in equity prices. As with other types of structured notes, equity-linked structured notes can typically be decomposed into two essential instruments: a fixed income security and an equity derivative embedded in the security.

The structures, design, applications, valuation, and market for traditional equity-linked structured notes, such as convertible debt and debt with equity warrant issues, were examined in Chapter 9. This chapter examines variations on the traditional equity-linked note structures. This chapter, as in Chapter 9, focuses primarily on equity-linked notes where the underlying equity instrument is an individual stock.

## 2. Structural Variations in Equity-linked Notes — Overview

Over recent years, a number of important variations on the basic convertible/ debt with equity warrant structure have been developed to satisfy issuer and investor requirements.[1] **Exhibit 10.1** sets out an overview of many of these structural variations. The structural variations identified in the table while

---

[1] For an overview of innovations in equity-linked instruments, see Smithson, Charles "Hybrid Securities" (April 1996) *Risk* vol. 9 no. 4 18-19; Nicholls, Mark "Winning New Converts" (April 1996) *Risk* vol. 9 no. 4 44-46; Ball, Matthew "How To Exploit The Convert's New Versatility" (April 1997) *Corporate Finance* 22-28; Cox, T. Anne, Harrington III, Preston M., and Elliot, Anne (January 27, 1998) "Convertible Special Report — Convertible Structures: Building Further Innovations 1998 Update"; Global Convertibles Research Group, Merrill Lynch.

analytically distinct are often combined in the context of a single issue. For example, issues of Liquid Yield Option Notes (LYONs$^{TM®}$) that are zero-coupon convertible structures effectively represent a combination of coupon variations and embedded debt optionality (call and put options on the debt).

---

**Exhibit 10.1**
**Convertible Debt/Debt-with-equity Warrants —**
**Hierarchy of Structural Variations**

| Dimension | Structure |
|---|---|
| Underlying fixed income Instrument | • Debt<br>• Preference capital/Shares or preferred stock |
| Coupon | • Low coupon<br>• Zero-coupon<br>• Deep discount |
| Conversion premium | • Variable (step-up or step-down structures) |
| Mandatory conversion | • Equity notes/Equity commitment notes<br>• Variable strike structures<br>• Equity option-based structures (limited appreciation structures; structured mandatory convertibles) |
| Underlying equity securities | • Exchangeable bonds<br>• Going public bonds<br>• Synthetic equity conversions |
| Debt optionality | • Puttable (fixed or flexible) |
| Structured optionality | • Embedded structured/Exotic equity option structures |
| Synthetic convertibles | • Synthetic convertible/Reverse convertible and trust-based structured issues |

---

The principal motivations of these structural variations include:

• **Cost/return considerations** — a number of structures are predicated on lowering the economic cost or increasing the return to the investor in these instruments. For example, the various coupon configurations are often designed to generate improved returns for the investor, usually on an after-tax basis. The enhanced yield is reflected in a commensurately adjusted coupon cost for the issuer. The major adjustment to cost/return of these structures is generally achieved by modifying the equity component and/or the risk of the instrument. Attempts at modifying the equity content are usually sought through:

- Adjustment, usually progressive, to the conversion price where the gradual increase is designed to lower the level of dilution as the share price grows over time.
- Utilization of multiple or exotic options to place a limit on the gain captured by the equity investor in the convertible or equity warrant.

- **Risk considerations** — risk adjustments focus on either modifying the exposure of the investor or reducing the risk of nonconversion for the issuer. Risk adjustments designed to modify the exposure of the investor are generally structured as reductions in the conversion premium or embedding a put option in the convertible. The adjustment in conversion premium is designed to allow the investor to have a greater chance of capturing value from the equity option. The embedded put option allows the investor to redeem the investment at pre-agreed dates at a yield comparable to a debt return for the period. This means that the investor has a debt investment with equity participation without necessarily sacrificing the yield difference between debt yields and the convertible yield for the full life of the issue. The reduction of conversion risk usually is achieved through mandatory convertible structures. The principal objective is the minimisation of the cash flow claim from redemption and the impact on leverage from nonconversion of the equity-linked structure.

- **Balance sheet considerations** — balance sheet factors are typically relevant to issuers. The major concern is the treatment of the equity-linked security as part of the permanent capital base or shareholder's funds/equity base of the entity for accounting, regulatory, ratings, and covenant purposes. Mandatory convertible structures are generally attempts to focus on these issues.

- **Asset liability considerations** — asset liability considerations are relevant to both investors and issuers. Investors may, for example, wish to ensure significant call protection in relation to an equity-linked transaction to maximize the value of the embedded equity option. Coupon variations, particularly the discount coupon structures, often are designed among other factors to provide this call protection. Issuer asset liability consideration, are broader ranging, including:
  - Balance sheet treatment for these instruments (as noted above).
  - Structuring dispositions on an optimal economic basis through use of exchangeable securities.

- **Managing the initial public offering risk** — through the use of certain types of exchangeable securities convertible into the shares to be offered in the future.

• **Tax or regulatory considerations** — tax considerations include the use of coupon variations or exchangeable debt to manage the tax profile of investors and issuers, as well as structures designed to change the tax nature of financial claims.

• **Alignment of issuer and investor interests** — differences in interests between issuers and convertible investors include:

1. Ensuring that shareholders cannot dilute the convertible investors (the claims dilution issue).
2. Shareholders cannot increase the risk of the firm by undertaking risky investments (the asset substitution issue).
3. Risk of the firm not investing in profitable projects due to earning volatility (the under investment issue).

The inclusion of a put option attempts to reduce the debt dilution and asset substitution problem. Some of the mandatory convertible structures that recapture equity participation above a pre-agreed level is designed to help reduce the problem of potential under-investment.

The above considerations are not mutually exclusive and many of the structural variations are based on a combination of these factors. The innovative structures are also a function of market conditions. The structures often represent complex attempts to access markets under conditions of difficulty when traditional instrument formats would preclude issuance activity or to provide investors with instruments that meet specific objectives. For example, in the 1990s, the low level of nominal interest rates lead investors to seek higher yielding investment opportunities spawning a number of structures such as some of the mandatory convertibles noted.

## 3. Variations on the Underlying Fixed Income Instruments

### 3.1 Convertible Preference Shares/Preferred Stock

One of the fundamental variations in convertible/debt-with-equity warrants issues is the structure of the host fixed instrument. The major choices include:

• Debt either on a senior or subordinated basis.
• Preferred or preference stock/shares.

Debt has been the traditional basis for equity-linked transactions. However, the use of preference stock has become an increasing feature of these structures. The common characteristics of debt and certain types of preference capital, such as fixed term, fixed coupon, absence of voting rights (except in limited circumstances), and lack of dilution, dictate that a variety of equity-linked structures can be used with both types of instruments as the underlying instruments.

The traditional convertible preference share/preferred stock issue is very similar to the structure of a conventional convertible issue. The major features relating to the use of preference shares relative to debt include:

- **Balance sheet treatment** — the preference shares may be accorded equity treatment under certain circumstances from the date of issue.
- **Treatment of servicing charge** — the dividend coupon may be lower than the coupon on a debt convertible that may have cash flow benefits for the issuer, particularly where the issuer is in a nontax-paying position and not able to take advantage of the interest deduction for tax purposes. There may be additional benefits in relation to the lowering of interest expense for reporting purposes, including improvements in interest coverage ratios.[2]
- **Treatment of dividend income** — the dividend income may be treated more advantageously for the investor depending on the tax system applicable.

## 3.2 Convertible Preference Shares/Preferred Stock — Structural Variations

### 3.2.1 Overview

A number of variations on the traditional convertible preference share/preferred stock structure have emerged. The central focus of these innovations has been the preservation of the balance sheet benefit while seeking tax deductibility on the servicing cost of the servicing charge on the shares themselves. Most of these innovations have been in the US domestic market.[3] These structures are known as: Monthly Income Pay Securities (MIPS) (Goldman Sachs); Quarterly Income Pay Securities (QUIPS) (Goldman Sachs); Term Convertible Securities (TECONS) (J.P. Morgan); Term Income Deferrable Equity Securities (TIDES) (CS First Boston); and Trust Originated Preferred Securities (TOPrS) (Merrill Lynch).

### 3.2.2 Structure

The basic structure involves the interposition of a trust or special-purpose subsidiary in the issue process. The structure is set out in **Exhibit 10.2**.

---

[2] Analysts often adjust for the substitution of dividends for interest by incorporating dividend payments that are akin to debt in interest coverage or fixed charges coverage ratios.

[3] See Cox, T. Anne, Harrington III, Preston M., and Elliot, Anne (January 27, 1998) "Convertible Special Report — Convertible Structures: Building Further Innovations 1998 Update;" Global Convertibles Research Group, Merrill Lynch at 17-22.

**Exhibit 10.2**
**Convertible Trust Preferred Stock Issue Structure**

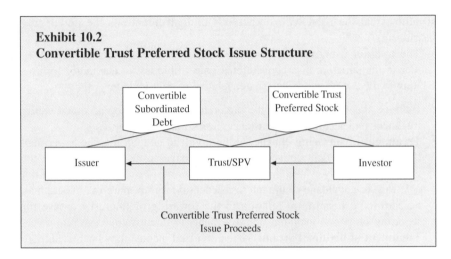

The essential steps are as follows:

- The issuer establishes a trust or special purpose entity (generally this is a trust vehicle).
- The trust issues convertible trust-preferred stock to the investor.
- The proceeds of the issue are used by the trust to purchase convertible subordinated debentures with terms matching that of the convertible preferred stock issue.
- The issuer owns all the common securities in the trust allowing consolidation under US law of the securities onto the issuer's balance sheet.

In the issues undertaken in the US, the interposed entity is a Delaware statutory business trust. In earlier versions of the convertible trust-preferred issues such as the MIPS issues, the interposed entity was a special purpose subsidiary in the form of a limited partnership. The issuer is the general partner in the limited partnership. Under this structure according to US law, holders of the convertible preferred stock issue had to lodge Schedule K returns.

### 3.2.3   Terms and Conditions of Convertible Trust-preferred Stock Issues

The terms and conditions of the convertible trust-preferred issues are as follows:

- The shares have a par value of US$50.
- The maturity of the shares is up to 30 years with possible extension options. There is usually a 3- to 5-year call protection period.
- The preferred stock is convertible at any time at the holder's option into the issuer's shares at a premium of 20-25%.
- The convertible preferred stock pays a quarterly dividend that is typically set at 4-7% pa over the issuer's dividend on its ordinary shares.

The issuer is permitted to defer interest payments on the convertible subordinated debt issue. This is permitted for up to five years (20 consecutive quarters). The dividend accrues during the deferral period and is compounded quarterly. During any period of interest deferral the issuer cannot pay dividends on its own common or preferred stock, ensuring that the convertible trust securities are essentially at the same level in the issuer's capital structure.

### *3.2.4   Economics and Applications of Convertible Trust-preferred Stock Issues*

From the viewpoint of the issuer, the structure achieves several objectives:

• The issuer does not show the convertible subordinated *debt* on its balance sheet. The trust structure is consolidated and the convertible preferred stock issue is shown as a minority interest in the balance sheet of the issuer. This enables the issuer to get a larger equity credit for the structure in balance sheet/rating agency terms.

• The issuer's servicing charge is deductible for tax purposes as it is allowed to deduct the interest on the convertible subordinated debt sold to the trust.

From the investor's perspective, the structure is similar to traditional convertible preferred stock transactions. The major difference is that in the US market the structure is less attractive than a traditional convertible preferred issue; as for a taxable corporate investor the dividend received deduction is not available. However, the loss of the tax benefit is usually reflected in the higher yield on these structures.

These types of issues have been attractive to issuers seeking a form convertible issue that provides the balance sheet benefit of equity but allows the servicing charge to be deducted. The structure has also been used in certain more specialized situations:

• Corporations with existing issues on nondeductible convertible preferred stock issues have found it economical to exchange outstanding standard convertible preferred stock issues for convertible trust-preferred stock.

• Issuers whose convertible preferred issues are not capable of being forced into conversion because the share price is trading below the conversion price can offer to exchange the outstanding convertible preferred for convertible trust-preferred stock. The primary objective is to reduce the cash flow servicing cost by attaining tax deductibility for the dividends.

## 4.   Variations on Coupon

### 4.1   Overview

Variations in the coupon applicable to equity-linked securities relate both to the quantum and to the structure through which the economic yield to the investor is created.

The quantum issue is particularly relevant in relation to the level of dividends paid on the underlying equity. A number of transactions have been undertaken utilizing low coupons to effectively use the equity-linked structure to replicate an investment in the equity security into which the host is convertible.

The other major structural variation entails issuing the host fixed income security at a discount to effectively provide the yield component through a discount as distinct from coupon. The major drivers in this structuring include the tax treatment of the discount for the issuer and investor, as well as the effective protection that this structure provides against early call of the security.

### 4.2   Low Coupon Structures

The use of low coupon structures to replicate near-equity exposure can be demonstrated by the example of an issue of convertible debt for Texas Instruments set out in **Exhibit 10.3**.

---

**Exhibit 10.3**
**Low Coupon Convertible Issue**

In 1987, Texas Instruments undertook a 15-year US$300 million issue that carried a coupon of 2.75% pa and a conversion premium of 8%.[4] The issue carried a put option at the election of the investor at par after seven years. The issue was also callable at the option of the issuer after a call protection period of three years conditional upon the underlying stock having traded at 140% of issue price. The issue terms compared to a coupon of around 6.00% pa and a conversion premium of 20% that was available on a comparable issue utilizing a conventional format. At the time of issue, Texas Instruments shares were quoted at a price-earning ratio of around 127 times and carried a dividend yield of around 1% pa.

The low coupon issue structure entailed a higher than usual equity component (effectively, the embedded call option had a higher delta) that translates into a larger equity premium. The larger premium enables the lower than usual coupon.

The higher equity content means that the convertible's trading behavior is closely linked to that of the underlying equity. This provides the investor with a high equity exposure that is combined with an investment value floor represented by the bond value component. The bond value floor in this case is at a lower level reflecting the fact that the coupon discount to

---

[4]   See "Texas Convertible Driving Into The Euromarkets" (October 1987) *Corporate Finance* 4.

market rate is higher. The coupon is nevertheless higher than the comparable dividend on the stock.

The major economic advantages of the structure include:

- The ability to target income investors seeking equity exposure but requiring higher running returns than provided by the dividend yield. This type of structure allows targeting of these investors without the necessity to increase the overall dividend payout.
- The appeal to equity investors receiving a more advantageous treatment for interest income than dividend income. This may be for dividend withholding tax where the coupons may be free and clear of withholding tax, whereas dividends would have attracted a withholding.
- The high equity content allows access to relatively aggressive investors who wish to participate in the equity growth, but who are unenthusiastic at investing at the prevailing valuation levels in the absence of some protection against a sharp shift in the value of the underlying equity securities.

## 4.3   Zero-coupon Structures — Liquid Yield Option Notes (LYONs$^{TM®}$)

### 4.3.1   Structure

The most significant example of a zero-coupon-based convertible or equity-linked note is that of LYONs$^{TM®}$. LYONs$^{TM®}$ combine a zero-coupon bond with the features of a convertible security that is both callable (at the option of the issuer) and puttable (at the option of the investor). The individual components of the security are not novel. However, the combination of these separate features in a single transaction is the defining feature of the instrument.[5]

The key features of a LYONs$^{TM®}$ issue include:

- **Maturity** — generally around 15 to 20 years.
- **Coupon** — like all zero-coupon bonds, the LYONs$^{TM®}$ structure pays no interest until it is redeemed at or before maturity. The difference between the issue price and the redemption price represents the accrued interest. The zero-coupon bonds have typically been priced at around 20% to 40% of face value to produce an yield to maturity of around 4-7% pa.

---

[5]   See Cox, T. Anne, Harrington III, Preston M. and Elliot, Anne (January 27, 1998) "Convertible Special Report — Convertible Structures: Building Further Innovations 1998 Update"; Global Convertibles Research Group, Merrill Lynch at 13-16.

- **Conversion option** — the LYONs<sup>TM®</sup> may be converted by the holder into stock of the issuing corporation within a specified time period and at a specified conversion price (which is embedded by allowing exchange of the bonds for a fixed number of shares). Initial conversion premiums have been in the range of 10-20%. Some issues have included an option for the issuer to deliver the cash equivalent of the conversion value instead of delivering the actual shares.
- **Put options** — the bond also has embedded a series of put options allowing investors to terminate the transaction by requiring the issuer to repurchase the bonds at fixed prices at specified dates. The repurchase prices are set at a level that ensures that the investor receives a return akin to that of debt for the relevant maturity. Put options may be met in cash (*hard* puts) and those that may be satisfied with cash, stock, subordinated debt, or a combination (*soft* puts).
- **Call options** — the bond can also be prepaid by the issuer, at its option, at specified times. The call prices are set at a level that is designed to penalize the issuer and discourage early exercise of the call.

**Exhibit 10.4** sets out the terms and structure of an issue of LYONs<sup>TM®</sup>. The issue detailed in this case is the original issue of LYONs<sup>TM®</sup> that was undertaken on April 12, 1985. **Exhibit 10.5** on page 410 sets out the terms of a more recent issue of LYONs<sup>TM®</sup> undertaken for Roche.

---

**Exhibit 10.4**
**Liquid Yield Option Notes — Terms and Conditions (1)**

| | |
|---|---|
| Issuer | Waste Management, Inc. |
| Amount | US$1,000 million face value of securities |
| Issue Date | April 12, 1985 |
| Maturity | Around 16 years (January 21, 2001) |
| Coupon | 0% pa |
| Initial Offering Price | US$250 per US$1,000 bond |
| Yield To Maturity | 9% pa |
| Investor's Conversion Option | At any time prior to maturity, the investor may convert each bond into 4.36 Waste Management, Inc. shares. |
| Conversion Price | The conversion price at issue is US$57.34 per share (calculated as the Initial offering price/ Number of shares per bond). This represents a premium of 9.74% against the current price of US$52.25. |

| Investor Put Option | The investor has the right to put the bond to the issuer beginning on June 30, 1988 and on each subsequent anniversary date at predetermined exercise prices that increase in accordance with the attached table. |
| Issuer Call Option | The issuer has the right to call the bond at fixed exercise prices that increase in accordance with the attached table. |

### Table of Put And Call Prices

| Date | Put Price (US$ per US$1,000 Face Value Bond) | Yield to Put (% pa) | Call Price (US$ per US$1,000 Face Value Bond) | Yield to Call (% pa) |
|---|---|---|---|---|
| Issuance | | | 272.50 | |
| June 30, 1986 | | | 297.83 | 14.92 |
| June 30, 1987 | | | 321.13 | 11.62 |
| June 30, 1988 | 301.87 | 6 | 346.77 | 10.44 |
| June 30, 1989 | 333.51 | 7 | 374.99 | 9.85 |
| June 30, 1990 | 375.58 | 8 | 406.00 | 9.51 |
| June 30, 1991 | 431.08 | 9 | 440.08 | 9.30 |
| June 30, 1992 | 470.75 | 9 | 477.50 | 9.17 |
| June 30, 1993 | 514.07 | 9 | 518.57 | 9.08 |
| June 30, 1994 | 561.38 | 9 | 563.63 | 9.02 |
| June 30, 1995 | 613.04 | 9 | 613.04 | 9 |
| June 30, 1996 | 669.45 | 9 | 669.45 | 9 |
| June 30, 1997 | 731.06 | 9 | 731.06 | 9 |
| June 30, 1998 | 798.34 | 9 | 798.34 | 9 |
| June 30, 1999 | 871.80 | 9 | 871.80 | 9 |
| June 30, 2000 | 952.03 | 9 | 952.03 | 9 |
| Maturity | | | 1,000 | 9 |

*Source:* McConnell, John and Schwartz, Eduardo. "The Origins of LYONs[TM]": A Case Study in Financial Innovation." *Journal of Applied Finance* vol. 4 no. 4 (Winter 1992) at 46-47.

**Exhibit 10.5**
**Liquid Yield Option Notes — Terms and Conditions (2)**

| | |
|---|---|
| Issuer | Roche Holdings Ltd |
| Amount | US$2,150 million face value of securities |
| Issue Date | April 21, 1995 |
| Maturity | 15 years |
| Coupon | 0% pa |
| Initial Offering Price | 35.628 |
| Yield To Maturity | 7% pa |
| Investor's Conversion Option | At any time prior to maturity, the investor may convert each bond into Roche Genuussscheine American Depositary Securities (ADS) at a predetermined number per bond. |
| Conversion Price | The conversion price at issue represents a premium of 30% against the current price of the underlying equity rising to 265% at maturity. |
| Investor Put Option | The investor has the right to put the bond to the issuer at year 4 at an effective yield to put of 5.5% pa and at year 8 at an effective yield to put of 7% pa. |
| Issuer Call Option | The issuer has the right to call the bond after year 8 at accreted value at the original issue yield. |

### 4.3.2   Benefits for Issuers

The major attraction to the issuer of a LYONs[TM®] is that the issuer of the security is not required to make cash coupon payments. The conservation of cash may be enhanced by the fact that the issuer is allowed under the tax laws in a number of jurisdictions to accrue the deductible original issue discount. This generates significant cash flow benefits as the accrued but unpaid interest reduces tax liabilities. Most importantly, these tax benefits may not be recaptured upon exchange of the LYONs[TM®] for the equity of the issuer. The issuer receives continuous tax benefits after issuance until the holder exchanges the LYONs[TM®] for shares, if it occurs. As a result, the net present value of the transaction to the issuer continues to increase the longer the notes remain outstanding.

The most important advantage to the issuer is the fact that the zero-coupon structure embeds an increasing strike price on the equity option included in the issue. This increase is achieved by the fact that if exchange is undertaken then the investor forgoes the accrued discount on the LYONs<sup>TM®</sup> (effectively the interest accruing at the original yield to maturity of the security). This allows the investor to reduce the effective dilution impact of the issue of equity upon conversion. This reduces the effective cost of the transaction.

### 4.3.3  Benefits for Investors

The economics of an investment in a LYONs<sup>TM®</sup> issue shows the following characteristics:

*   The conversion option of the issue only becomes valuable *if the rate of the appreciation in the equity exceeds the accretion of the discount on the debt component of the LYONs*<sup>TM®</sup>. In essence, the initial conversion premium steadily increases.
*   The structure is also less sensitive to interest rates changes because of the embedded put option that provides significant price support on the bond.

These characteristics tend to give LYONs<sup>TM®</sup> structures a low equity content and a high degree of price stability making them closer to bonds in their price and investment performance.

The development of the LYONs<sup>TM®</sup> structure can be traced to an observation by Mr Lee Cole of Merrill Lynch that individual retail investors' investment activity followed a discernible pattern. Investors appeared to maintain large balances in cash (in vehicles such Cash Management Accounts) while purchasing call options on the equity stocks. This strategy entailed effectively risking a proportion of the interest of the interest earnings from the cash investments (traditionally, a low-risk investment, both in terms of credit risk and interest rate risk) to create some exposure to the equity market using options. This strategy was low risk and ensured preservation of investment capital.[6]

The LYONs<sup>TM®</sup> structure sought to address these specific investment requirements. LYONs<sup>TM®</sup> traditional appeal to individual investors is founded on the following:

*   The investor receives an embedded long-term option on the equity underlying the issue. This allows the investor to achieve significant savings in transaction costs effectively allowing maintenance of an option position for the term of the issue, which is generally 10-15 years, without incurring ongoing trading costs.

---

[6]  For an interesting discussion of the origins of LYONs<sup>TM®</sup> and as a case study in product innovation, see McConnell, John and Schwartz, Eduardo "The Origins Of LYONs<sup>TM®</sup>: A Case Study In Financial Innovation (Winter 1992) *Journal of Applied Finance* vol. 4 no. 4 40-47.

- A high level of principal protection through the embedded put options that reduces the investors exposure to interest rate increases.

The LYONs$^{TM®}$ structures typically also have better call protection than comparable conventional convertible or equity-linked structures. The reduction in option trading costs and the higher level of principal protection is traded off against the increasing call option strike price that is attractive to the issuer.

The appeal to retail investors of this structure that seeks to replicate, more efficiently, an underlying investment paradigm that is practiced proved to be very successful. A typical LYONs$^{TM®}$ issue is generally placed some 60% with individual investors and some 40% with institutional investors.

The institutional demand for LYONs$^{TM®}$ structures is based on the fact that it is a very attractive security for investors who practice portfolio insurance. This entails creating upside exposure to a stock while limiting the risk of adverse market movements. This strategy that is analogous to the individual investor strategy identified above is effectively replicated by the LYONs$^{TM®}$ eliciting institutional investor participation in these securities.

### 4.3.4   Pricing Considerations

The pricing of a LYONs$^{TM®}$ relies on the valuation of the individual components of the structure. However, the model is adjusted for the interaction of the individual elements. The call option and the equity conversion option reduce the value of the put option because it reduces the expected life of the put. Similarly, the conversion option value is reduced by the existence of the issuer's call option and put option because these reduce the probability of conversion.

A simple approach to the valuation of a LYONs$^{TM®}$ structures models the issue as a combination of a 5-year zero-coupon bond and 5-year equity call option. This simplification is predicated on the behavior of the underlying elements. The investor is unlikely to convert earlier than is necessary as conversion will result in a loss of the time value of the embedded equity option. The critical conversion date is the first call date as the investor is exposed to the risk of the issuer forcing conversion if the stock has performed well. Even if the stock has not performed well but interest rates have fallen, there is a possibility that the issuer will refinance the issue at lower cost. The behavior of the issue is also constrained by the investor's put option at the end of five years. The fact that the put option ensures that the investor will receive the accreted value after five years means that if interest rates rise and/or the stock has not performed then the investor will exercise the put.[7]

---

[7]   The calls and puts prior to five years are not considered as they are set at prices that penalize the issuer and investor if exercised.

A model predicated on incorporating these interactions and the traditional option valuation parameters for the individual elements combined with the bond valuation is available.[8] **Exhibit 10.6** sets out the application of this approach. The numerical model is used to value the LYONs[TM®] transactions set out in **Exhibit 10.4** and sets out the sensitivity of the price to fluctuations in the various parameters.

---

**Exhibit 10.6**
**Valuation of Liquid Yield Option Notes**

*Initial Valuation*

| | |
|---|---|
| Stock Price | US$52.25 |
| Stock Price Volatility | 30.0% |
| Dividend Yield | 1.6% |
| LYONs[TM®] Maturity | 15 years |
| Face Value | US$1,000 per bond |
| Conversion Ratio | 4.36 shares per bond |
| Call Options | Refer to **Exhibit 10.4** |
| Put Options | Refer to **Exhibit 10.4** |
| LYONs[TM®] Value | US$262.75 |

*Valuation Sensitivity*

| Change in Parameter | LYON Value (US$ per bond) | Effect of Change in Bond Value |
|---|---|---|
| Basic Features | 262.70 | |
| Stock Price to US$56.00 | 271.68 | +8.98 |
| Stock Price Volatility to 40% | 271.89 | +9.19 |
| Dividend Yield to 3.0% | 260.78 | -1.92 |
| Interest Rate to 13.21% | 252.38 | -10.32 |
| Without Call | 283.29 | +20.59 |
| Without Put | 215.04 | -47.77 |

*Source:* McConnell, John and Schwartz, Eduardo. "The Origins of LYONs[TM®]: A Case Study In Financial Innovation." *Journal of Applied Finance* vol. 4 no. 4 (Winter 1992): 40-47 at 46-47.

---

[8]   See McConnell, John J. and Schwartz Edwardo S. "LYONs[TM®] Taming" (July 1986) *Journal of Finance* 561-576.

The model can also be utilized to derive the critical conversion price at which the investor becomes indifferent to holding the LYONs$^{TM®}$ (Winter 1992) and exchanging the bond for the underlying equity stock. **Exhibit 10.7** sets out these prices for the same issue. The analysis indicates that the breakeven conversion price increases over much of the life of the issue and declines at the end. This reflects the interaction of two separate factors:

- The optimal conversion price falls because the reduction in time to maturity effectively lowers the value of the equity option (this is present in all convertibles).
- The conversion price (the option strike) is also increased through the increase in redemption price while holding the conversion ration constant. This further reduces the value of the conversion option.

---

**Exhibit 10.7**
**Breakeven Conversion Price**

| *Date* | *Breakeven Conversion Share Price (US$/share)* |
|---|---|
| Issuance | 129.50 |
| June 30 1985 | 132.00 |
| June 30 1986 | 145.50 |
| June 30 1987 | 158.50 |
| June 30 1988 | 173.50 |
| June 30 1989 | 194.50 |
| June 30 1990 | 217.00 |
| June 30 1991 | 238.50 |
| June 30 1992 | 257.00 |
| June 30 1993 | 273.00 |
| June 30 1994 | 287.00 |
| June 30 1995 | 301.50 |
| June 30 1996 | 316.00 |
| June 30 1997 | 329.50 |
| June 30 1998 | 339.00 |
| June 30 1999 | 340.00 |
| June 30 2000 | 317.50 |
| Maturity | 229.36 |

*Source:* McConnell, John and Schwartz, Eduardo. "The Origins of LYONs$^{TM®}$: A Case Study In Financial Innovation." *Journal of Applied Finance* vol. 4 no. 4 (Winter 1992): 40-47 at 47.

### 4.3.5  Product Variations

The LYONs[TM®] format has spawned a number of structural variations. One of the most interesting is the geared zero-coupon convertible format that has primarily been used by French borrowers. **Exhibit 10.8** sets out an example of the geared convertible structure.

---

**Exhibit 10.8**
**Geared Zero-coupon Convertible Structure[9]**

The geared zero-coupon convertible structure incorporates the following:

* It is issued as the issuer's senior debt.
* The final maturity is between four and five years.
* The issue bears no coupon.
* The issue is redeemed at final maturity at a redemption price between 100% and a maximum cap (typically set at 180-190%). The redemption amount is indexed to the issuer's share price and generally will be set at 125-130% of the increase in the share price of the issuer over the life of the issue, subject to the floor (100%) and call (180-190%).

The geared zero-coupon convertible format is similar to LYONs[TM®] in the following respect:

* The zero-coupon.
* The principal protection of the structure.
* The relatively short effective maturity assuming the first put date on the LYONs[TM®] is generally similar to the final maturity of the geared zero-coupon convertible.

The major differences include:

* The absence of a conversion premium in the geared zero-coupon convertible.
* The geared zero-coupon structure is noncallable.
* The geared zero-coupon convertible offers no return other than by the appreciation in the equity whereas the LYONs[TM®] structure incorporates a minimum rate of earning through the discount to face value at which the security is sold.

---

[9]  See McGuire, Simon "Capital Markets: Geared Zero-Coupon Convertible" Goldman Sachs *Euroconvertible Focus* 7-10.

- The participation in the increase in the underlying equity value is greater under geared zero-coupon convertible issues. This is because the bond will outperform the shares up to the cap because of the gearing factor.
- The upside on a geared zero-coupon convertible is limited by the cap.

The major attraction of this structure for the issuer is that it provides:

- A limitation on dilution (set by the cap).
- The opportunity for the issuer to hedge the equity dilution risk through the purchase by the issuer of a call option on its equity to cover the redemption payment. The issuer would also sell a call at the cap level to partially fund the call struck at the money. The economics of the transaction, inclusive of the hedge, should be similar to the issue of nonconvertible debt though in practice the issues of geared zero-coupon convertibles typically provided a lower cost of funding for the issuer.

The structure allows issuers to potentially issue debt that provides its investors with an equity exposure to fluctuations in its share price without equity dilution (if the structure is hedged). This opens the way for issues of convertibles by issuers who would not otherwise issue convertible or equity-linked securities. The structure also, because of the immunization to dilution, encourages the issue of convertibles irrespective of the level of the share price.

The investor attraction lies primarily in the gearing to equity rises, the absence of a conversion premium and the short final maturity making it an interesting means to capture an expected rise in equity value within a range allowing significant outperformance on portfolio return with capital protection.

## 4.4 Deep Discount Structures

A variation on the zero-coupon convertible structures entails the issue of convertible at a deep discount. **Exhibit 10.9** sets out an example of this type of structure.

**Exhibit 10.9**
**Deep Discount Convertible Issue**

In 1995, Sandoz undertook a deep discount convertible issue as part of a package of equity-linked funding that included a US$600 million and Swfr 600 million convertibles.

The US$ convertible was structured as follows:

| | |
|---|---|
| Maturity | 7 years |
| Coupon | 2% pa |
| Issue Price | 81.17% |
| Conversion Premium | 20.26% initial conversion premium rising to an effective conversion premium at maturity of 48%. |
| Call Provision | Noncallable for three years. |
| | Callable in years 4 and 5 at the accreted value if the underlying share price exceeds 130% of the accreted conversion price for at least 30 days. |
| | Redeemable after year 5 at accreted value. |

The advantages of the overall structure include:

- A lower coupon.
- A lower number of shares and a lower level of equity dilution.
- The absence of the put option usually provided in a LYONs[TM®] structure.
- The deferral of conversion.

The structure also provides protection against currency fluctuations arising from the fact that the underlying shares are denominated in a currency different to that of the underlying shares. In this example, as the US$ depreciates versus the Swfr, the effective Swfr conversion price falls, potentially inducing earlier conversion and increasing the issuer's cost of equity. The deep discount structure reduces this problem as the effective conversion price rises providing protection against a weaker US$.

*Source:* "A Skillful Balancing Act." *Corporate Finance.* (December 1995): 18-19.

The major advantage of this structure for the issuer includes the higher effective share price as the discount accrues and the resulting lower dilution. The primary advantage for the investor appears to be the potentially advantageous treatment of the discount for taxation purposes and the higher degree of call protection afforded by these structures reflecting the fact that the bond is callable at prices above par, increasing the effective call premium payable.

## 5.   Variations on Conversion Premium

The traditional convertible or equity-linked structure embodies a fixed conversion premium. This has a number of implications:

*   The value of any increase in the value of the issuer's equity above the premium accrues to the investor. This is in effect the dilution effect that results in a shift of value from existing shareholders to the convertible holders (to the extent that the latter group did not or had no entitlement to take up the convertible securities pro rata to their shareholding).
*   The failure of the share price to perform and exceed the conversion premium as anticipated may result in nonconversion requiring cash redemption of the bond. This results in a call on cash flow or the need to refinance the obligations. It also alters the financial risk of the issuer through the change in leverage through the failure to receive the equity injection embedded in the convertible.

The latter may occur as a result of general economic and market factors that are beyond the control of the issuer.

There have been a number of responses to these problems. The first issue has been dealt with by structures where the conversion price increases over time. This structure is often referred to as a reset convertible. It is also known as a "step-up" convertible issue or a "step-up conversion premium" issue. The increase is structured in one of the following ways:

*   **Direct step-up conversion price** — by explicitly lowering the conversion ratio, effectively increasing the conversion premium, and the strike price of the equity option, in accordance with an agreed schedule.
*   **Indirect step-up conversion price** — by implicitly increasing the effective strike price in structures such as the LYONs$^{TM®}$ structure or the discount structures described above.

The reduced value of the equity option component dictates that these structures will generally have higher coupons or effective interest costs than conventional convertible or equity-linked structures.

The second issue is dealt with by structures where the effective conversion price is refixed at a lower level upon the occurrence of a specified event. This event generally is a fall in the value of the underlying shares. The refixing can be structured in a number of ways:

*   A single refixing or progressive series of pricing adjustments based on pre-agreed refixing dates.
*   The conversion price adjustment is based on a pre-agreed reduction or set with reference to the share price as at the refixing date.

- The sampling period for share prices is based on a single or small number of observations, or on a trailing monthly average formula.
- In cases where the convertible is denominated in a foreign currency (relative to the base currency of the issuer's shares), there may also be a conversion rate refix based on adverse movements in the currency that may reduce the chance of conversion.

**Exhibit 10.10** sets out an example of this type of structure.

---

**Exhibit 10.10**
**Step-down Coupon Convertible Issue**

| | |
|---|---|
| Issuer | ABC Company |
| Amount | US$100 million convertible bonds |
| Maturity | 5 years |
| Coupon | 2% pa payable semi-annually |
| Issue Price | 100 |
| Conversion Price | ¥943 |
| Conversion Premium | 2.5% over the ¥920 closing share price |
| Conversion Exchange Rate | US$1 = ¥120 |
| Refixing | If the average share of the selling prices of the shares for five consecutive days leading up to and including one year from issue and/or two years after issue (respectively the first and second setting dates) multiplied by 1.025 rounded up to the nearest 1 yen is at least 1 yen less than the respective conversion price in effect on the first and/or second setting date, the conversion price will be revised downward to the greater of that amount and 80% of the conversion price in effect on the first setting date, rounded upward to the nearest yen on or from one year from issue and/or two years after issue (the first and second effective dates). In the event that the conversion price is revised, if the US$/¥ exchange rate on the first or second setting date is higher than the fixed exchange rate in yen in effect on the first or second setting dates, the fixed exchange rate in yen |

|                | shall, on the and from the first or second setting date be revised upward to the exchange rate in yen. In the event that the conversion price is not revised, if the current exchange rate in yen is higher than the fixed exchange rate in yen in effect and the share price in US$ at the current exchange rate is less than the conversion price, the exchange rate will be revised upward to the exchange rate in yen as follows:<br>Revised fixed foreign exchange rate<br>= Current exchange rate × Conversion price ÷ the current share price. |
| Call Options   | At the company's option after three years and annually thereafter at 105 (at year 3), and 102 (at year 4). |

The additional protection afforded investors is recognized in this structure by way of a higher equity option value[10] or allowing access to convertible markets for issuers who would for reason of their outlook or performance or the outlook of equity markets generally be precluded from issuing.

The pricing of the reset structures is analogous to that of pricing a path-dependent option. This reflects the fact that it is necessary to adjust the conversion price of the convertible over time in addition to incorporating the evolution of the underlying stock price and interest rate fluctuations.[11] The reset structure generally trades at values consistent with conventional convertibles where the share prices are well above the *original* conversion price (the reset feature has little value) or where the share price is very low (the reset feature has been triggered but the shares have a low value). In between these prices, the values of a reset convertible and a conventional convertible can vary significantly, reflecting the value of the reset feature. The impact of the reset feature is to limit the loss of value of the embedded call option on the underlying equity as the stock price falls. This is because a fall in stock price below a

---

[10] Structurally, the refixing feature is analogous to a Lookback Option (a type of path-dependent exotic option) on the equity of the issuer that effectively allows the investor to lower the call option strike price with reference to the path of equity prices. See Das, Satyajit (1996) *Exotic Options*; LBC Information Services, Sydney at Chapter 4.

[11] For an example of pricing approaches, see Nelken, Izzy "Reassessing The Reset" (October 1998) *AsiaRisk* 36-39.

certain price level triggers a reset of the conversion price. At an extremely low stock price, the lowering of the conversion price is increasingly offset by the high risk of bankruptcy that manifests itself as an increase in the credit spread on the issue.

## 6.  Mandatory Conversion Structures

### 6.1  Overview

Traditional equity-linked structures suffer from the inherent risk that the exchange into the underlying equity does not occur. This risk derives from the performance of the individual equity stock or broader market factors that dictate non conversion.

This risk has a number of implications including:

- The reluctance of analysts, regulatory authorities, and rating agencies to treat these structures as equity or part of the permanent capital base of the firm at least until conversion.
- The problems of financial planning in that the leverage of the firm and the future claims on cash flows are unpredictable.

One approach to this problem is the adjustment to the conversion price discussed above. A more general approach is the mandatory convertible structure that is specifically designed to address the issues identified. The major differentiation between the two structures is that in the conversion price refixing structure conversion is made *more likely but not guaranteed* while the mandatory conversion format ensures that conversion *must* take place.

The mandatory convertible format takes a number of structural forms:

- Equity notes and equity commitment notes.
- Variable strike conversion structures.
- Limited appreciation mandatory convertible structures.
- Structured high-yield mandatory convertible structures.

The structural variations are dictated by the tension between providing the required incentives to investors to accept the mandatory conversion feature reducing the principal protection characteristic of equity-linked issues generally and the desire by the issuer to minimize the economic cost of this feature, in particular the degree of dilution.

### 6.2  Equity Notes and Equity Commitment Notes

These types of mandatory convertible securities were primary utilized by banks as a major source of primary capital funding in the early 1980s. The basic structure of these mandatory convertible issues entails the issue of a conventional debt instrument with specific conditions as to the source of funding out of which redemption of the security may be effected.

The basic impetus for these structures included:

* Qualification, under certain conditions, as primary capital for US bank regulatory purposes (refer **Exhibit 10.11**).
* Treatment as debt for income tax purposes allowing a lower cost of capital through the deductibility of the servicing charge as interest.
* Depressed bank stock prices that made banks reluctant to sell new equity in traditional forms at low price-earnings multiples and stock-to-book-value measures

---

**Exhibit 10.11**
**Guidelines for Issuance of Equity Notes and Equity Commitment Notes Qualifying As Primary Capital**

The following US Federal Reserve guidelines were applicable to the issuance of equity notes and equity commitment notes at the time of issue of these instruments in 1982. These guidelines have substantially been superseded by the various capital adequacy accords introduced subsequently, primarily the 1988 BIS Capital Adequacy Accord and the 1995 Capital Accord to Incorporate Market Risk.

The capital guidelines operational at the time of issue established the following specific criteria for both equity notes and equity commitment notes to satisfy to ensure eligibility as capital:

* The notes must have a maturity not exceeding 12 years.
* The issuer may redeem the notes prior to maturity only:
  - with the proceeds of the sale of equity stock; or
  - with the approval of the appropriate federal regulator.
* The investor cannot accelerate the payment of principal except in the event of the issuer's bankruptcy, insolvency, or reorganization.
* The note must be subordinated in right of payment to the issuer's senior indebtedness.

The following additional criteria were applicable to equity commitment notes:

* The issuer must establish a special segregated fund ("the special fund") that is funded only with the proceeds of the sale of equity stock. This special fund will be the sole source of repayment of the notes prior to

maturity. At maturity, the equity commitment notes can be repaid from any source if the special fund has not been sufficiently funded. (The special fund concept is also applicable to equity note structures as most equity note issues incorporated a voluntary special fund.)

- The issuer is obligated to pay into the special fund out of the proceeds of the sale of stock as follows:
  - one-third of the principal amount by the time of expiry of one-third of the term of the notes; and
  - two-thirds of the principal amount by the time of expiry of two-thirds of the term of the notes.
- The amount of the equity commitment note treated as capital is reduced as the issuer sells equity stock. The issuer was required to earmark equity proceeds for the special fund during the quarter of issue.

The following additional criteria were applicable to equity notes:

- The stock purchase contract could only be separated from the note if the holder of the contract provided sufficient collateral (the stock purchase contract was the obligation of the holder of the equity note to purchase equity stock or to accept equity stock in payment of the note).
- The stock purchase contract must require the purchase of equity stock at maturity.

The transactions that qualified as sale of stock for the purpose of the special fund were usually taken to encompass:

- Issuance of equity by private placement or rights offering.
- Equity sold pursuant to any dividend or interest reinvestment plan.
- Equity issued upon exercise of equity options.
- Equity issued in exchange for assets to the extent that the cash in an amount equal to the fair market value of the purchased assets is deposited in the special fund equity issued upon conversion of non-primary capital securities (for example, convertible notes).

There are two basic types of mandatory convertibles: equity commitment notes and equity notes.

Equity commitment notes are required to be repaid from the proceeds of a fund that is created through the sale of, or exchange for other property of, equity securities qualifying as primary capital. The issuer is required to fund an amount equal to one-third of the capital amount by the end of one-third of the life of the debt instrument, two-thirds of the principal amount by the end of two-thirds of the life of the debt instrument, and the full amount of principal by maturity.

Equity notes, in contrast, are repayable from the proceeds of an optional fund from the sale of equity securities qualifying as primary capital on behalf of debt holders or, if equity cannot be so sold, by delivery of equity securities qualifying as primary capital to debt holders.

While originally utilized by banks, the mandatory convertible structure has infrequently been extended to nonbank issuers. In 1986, for example, a French company Thomson CSF issued a US$100 million internationally targeted equity note issue with a maturity of 10 years carrying a coupon of 8%. Under the structure utilized, the holder had no choice whether or not to convert the notes into Thomson's equity — only a choice as to the date of conversion.

### 6.3   Variable Strike Conversion Structures

An alternative approach to the mandatory conversion structure entails the issuer undertaking to deliver to the investor at maturity equity securities for an amount equal to the face value of the maturing debt. The amount delivered is based on the *then current market value of the equity securities being delivered*. This is undertaken in the event that the convertible security has not been exchanged for the underlying equity. In effect, the structure entails the issuer providing the investors with the quantity of equity stock that can be sold in the market at prevailing prices to economically equate to the value of the maturing host debt.

**Exhibit 10.12** sets out the terms and conditions of a variable strike mandatory convertible issue for a Japanese bank. **Exhibit 10.13** sets out the terms and conditions of a mandatory converting preference share issue of a type undertaken for Australian companies.

---

**Exhibit 10.12**
**Mandatory Convertible Issue — Example 1**

| | |
|---|---|
| Issuer | Luxembourg Subsidiary of Sakura Bank |
| Type of Issue | Convertible preference share convertible into the ordinary shares of Sakura Bank at any time by investors at their option. |
| Guarantor | Sakura Bank on a preferred basis |
| Amount | ¥100 billion (US$758 million) |
| Maturity | 3 years and 3 months |
| Dividend Coupon | 6.75% pa |
| Conversion Options | *Prior to maturity*: At any time at a 15% premium *At Maturity*: If unconverted prior to maturity, investors will be mandatorily converted at maturity. The number of shares issuable will be a |

---

|                    | function of Sakura Bank's share price at maturity calculated as follows: No. of shares issuable = ¥100 billion/Share price at maturity where the share price at maturity is an average of Sakura Bank's closing share price for 30 days prior to maturity, subject to a minimum of 35% of the conversion price in effect prior to maturity. |
|--------------------|---|
| Issuer Call Options | At maturity only, at 100% in cash or standard tax call if withholding taxes are imposed. |

*Source:* McGuire, Simon. "Capital Markets: Bank Mandatory Convertibles." Goldman Sachs *Euroconvertible Focus* 10-12.

**Exhibit 10.13**
**Mandatory Convertible Issue — Example 2**

| | |
|---|---|
| Issuer | ABC Company Limited |
| Type of Issue | Issue of converting preference shares |
| Amount | A$500 million |
| Maturity (final conversion date) | 3.5 years |
| Issue Price | A$1.55 (A$0.50 par and A$1.05 premium) |
| Dividend Coupon | 8% pa cumulative preference dividend on issue price payable half yearly in arrears. |
| Ranking | In priority to ordinary shares for payments of dividends and for return of capital (including premium) on a winding up with no rights to participate in surplus. |
| Voting Rights | Holders may only vote on proposals directly affecting the rights under the preference shares and in certain limited circumstances. |
| Conversion | The preference shares are not redeemable and will convert into ordinary shares on or before the final conversion date. |
| Early Conversion | At the issuer's option:<br>• After 3 years; or<br>• In the event of certain takeover offers for the issuer.<br>At the holder's option: |

|                         | • In the event of a failure to pay dividends on the preference shares.<br>• In the event of certain takeover offers for the issuer; and<br>• Upon certain other limited events. |
|-------------------------|--------------------------------------------------------------------------|
| Conversion Mechanism    | On conversion, each converting preference shares will become one ordinary share. In addition, in certain circumstances, further ordinary shares may be allotted.<br>• If the market price of ordinary shares over a period prior to the relevant conversion date is A\$1.72 or more, then each converting preference share will become one ordinary share and no additional shares will be allotted.<br>• If the market price of ordinary shares over a period prior to the relevant conversion date is less than A\$1.72, then each converting preference share will become one ordinary share and additional shares will be allotted in accordance with the following formula, subject to a maximum of 2.1 further ordinary shares.<br><br>$AS = IP/RP - 1$<br>Where<br>$AS$ = additional ordinary shares to be allotted<br>$IP$ = issue price subject to adjustment for bonus and rights issues, capital reconstructions, and so on.<br>$RP$ = 90% of the weighted average sales price of ordinary shares during 20 business days immediately preceding the conversion date. |

The two issues have a number of common characteristics:

• The underlying security is a preference share allowing immediate recognition as capital. In the case of the Sakura Bank issue, coupons are also only payable to the extent that the Bank has sufficient distributable reserves in order to qualify as Tier 1 capital.
• The issues are not redeemable in cash (except at the option of the issuer in the case of the Sakura Bank issue).

- The issue is redeemable through delivery of stock with a market value equal to the par or issue value of the convertible preference share if unconverted.

The structure offers the investor an attractive investment in the following regard:

- An option on the underlying equity. The investor captures any potential appreciation over and above the conversion premium or price.
- Limited downside risk as the issue provides the principal protection of debt.
- The coupon is typically structured at an attractive level, significantly above the dividend yield on the underlying equity.

The structure increases the risk for the investor insofar as the holder must sell the shares received at maturity to obtain the cash due at maturity. The second issue incorporates an effective discount of 10% to the market price at the time near delivery of the shares at maturity in order to provide the investor with additional protection against the risk of realization of cash from the sale of the shares deliverable at maturity.

Economically, the structure entails the purchase of a share by the investor combined with a purchase of a put option struck at the issue price and the simultaneous sale of a second put at the minimum conversion price. The minimum conversion price is incorporated to either comply with regulatory requirements such as the restriction on issue of equity at less than the par value of the shares or to place a limit on the equity dilution of the transaction.

The major issuer interest in these types of issues has been from distressed or weaker issuers, particularly those undergoing financial reconstruction. The structure facilitates access to equity investors where that access would otherwise be difficult because of the performance of the issuer at the time of issue.

The advantage of immediate recognition as equity allows improvement of the issuer's financial position to be achieved while issuing equity at a premium to the market. The alternative may have been an issue of equity at a substantial discount to market value if this option was available at all. The major risk of this structure is the risk of additional equity dilution in the event that the equity price fails to perform as expected and the mandatory convertible remains unconverted at maturity necessitating delivery of additional shares to the investor.

Issues of mandatory convertibles using variable strike conversion structures have been undertaken successfully in a number of markets including Japan and Australia. Variations on the structures have been undertaken in the US and Europe. While targeted primarily at equity investors, these structures have attracted interest from fixed income investors who have purchased the security and stripped out and on-sold the equity option component to synthesize an attractive debt like investment.

**Exhibit 10.14** sets out a recent example of this type of transaction undertaken in Europe.

**Exhibit 10.14**
**Mandatory Convertible Issue — Example 3**

In May 1997, Daimler Benz undertook a successful issue of mandatory convertible notes through Deutsche Morgan Grenfell and Goldman Sachs. The issue terms were as follows:

| | |
|---|---|
| Instrument | Subordinated mandatory convertible notes |
| Amount | DM1,543.32 million |
| Maturity | 5 years and 1 month |
| Coupon | 5.75% pa payable semi-annually |
| Subscription Price | DM130.70 (US$79.67) for existing shareholders |
| | DM139.50 (US$80.99) for new investors |
| Conversion Period | From payment till 10 days prior to maturity |
| Conversion Premium | 16% |
| Conversion Exchange Rate | US$1 = DM1.7225 |
| Maximum Conversion Price | DM151.62 (16% above the subscription price) |
| Minimum Conversion Price | DM104.56 (20% below the subscription price) |
| Amortisation | Bullet |
| Put Option | None |
| Call Option | None |

The offering structure is designed to provide the issuer with equity funding irrespective of the price performance of the issuer's shares as follows:

- If the issuer's share price is below the minimum conversion price, the investor will receive 1.25 shares per note.
- If the issuer's share price is above the maximum conversion price, the investor will receive 0.862 shares per note.
- If the issuer's share price is above the minimum conversion price and below the maximum conversion price, the conversion ratio alters based on the market price of the share at maturity (calculated as the average price of the shares in a 20-day period prior to maturity). The conversion ratio declines from 1.25 to 0.862 shares.

The structure dictates that the investor is protected against any decline in the share price of the issuer up to 20% from the initial price. The investor also does not participate in the upside of the shares for the first 16% of any increase from the initial price.[12]

---

[12] The structure has certain similarities to the Structured High Yield Mandatory Convertible Issue structures discussed below.

## 6.4  Limited Appreciation Mandatory Convertible Structures

### 6.4.1  Structure[13]

The major disadvantage of the mandatory convertible structures identified above is the risk of additional and, in some cases, unquantifiable dilution. A number of attempts have been undertaken to place limitations on the dilution impact to enhance the attractiveness of the format for issuers. The major structure of this type is the limited or capped appreciation mandatory convertible issue introduced in the early 1990s. These are issues of convertible stock that convert on a mandatory basis into ordinary shares at maturity offering investors limited upside participation on the underlying shares (up to a cap of around 30-35% above the share price at the time of issue).

These structures are marketed under a variety of titles including: Preferred Equity Redemption Cumulative Stock (PERCS) (Morgan Stanley); Yield Enhanced Securities (YES) (Goldman Sachs); Mandatory Conversion Premium Dividend Preferred Stock (MCDPS) (Merrill Lynch); Targeted Growth Enhanced Terms Securities (TARGETS) (Sun Co.); Common Linked Higher Income Participating Debt Securities (CHIPS) (Bear Stearns); Equity-linked Debt Securities (ELKS) (Salomon Smith Barney); Enhanced Yield-equity Securities (EYES) (Merrill Lynch); Performance Equity-linked Redemption Quarterly Pay Securities (PERQS) (Morgan Stanley); and Yield-enhanced Equity-linked Debt Securities (YEELDS) (Lehman Brothers). The issues fall into two categories:

- **Company-issued** (PERCS, MCDPS, TARGETS, YES) — that is, the issue is undertaken by the company itself directly.
- **Synthetic** (all others) — that the security is issued by an investment bank rather than the company itself.[14]

The essential features of limited appreciation mandatory convertibles (for convenience these structures are referred to on occasion as PERCs in the text) are as follows:

---

[13]  See Cox, T. Anne, Harrington III, Preston M. and Elliot, Anne (January 27, 1998) "Convertible Special Report — Convertible Structures: Building Further Innovations 1998 Update"; Global Convertibles Research Group, Merrill Lynch at 22-27; Arzca, Enrique R. "PERCs, DECS, And Other Mandatory Convertibles" (Spring 1997) *Journal of Applied Corporate Finance* vol. 10 no. 1 54-63; McGuire, Simon "Capital Markets: PERCing Through The Looking Glass", Goldman Sachs Euroconvertible Focus 10-12; McGuire, Simon "Capital Markets: Euro Yes?" Goldman Sachs *Euroconvertible Focus* 10-13.

[14]  See discussion below regarding synthetic equity-linked issues.

- Issues of preferred shares.
- Typical maturity is three years.
- The dividend on the preferred shares is paid quarterly. The dividend is set significantly higher than the dividend on the underlying ordinary shares (in the order of 3-4% above the dividend on ordinary shares).
- The securities are issued at the prevailing market price of the shares with no premium. The securities convert at maturity automatically into ordinary shares. Conversion is on a one-for-one basis as between the convertible preferred stock and the underlying stock unless the share price has appreciated above a pre-agreed level set at the time of issue. This cap is set at around 30-35% above the price of the stock at the time of the issue. Where the share price is above the cap level, the preference shares convert into a fraction of an ordinary share with a market value equal to the cap.
- The securities are callable at the option of the issuer at a declining price payable in shares.

**Exhibit 10.15** sets out the typical terms of the limited appreciation mandatory convertible securities issues undertaken in the early 1990s when issuance of these securities was at their most active levels. **Exhibit 10.16** sets out the terms of a specific issue of PERCS by K-Mart. **Exhibit 10.17** sets the investor return profile on the K-Mart issue.

---

**Exhibit 10.15**
**Limited Appreciation Mandatory Convertible Securities Issues —**
**Typical Terms**

| | |
|---|---|
| Issuers | Issuers with restriction to equity capital access but requiring large new equity injections. |
| Amounts | US$100 to US$1,000 million |
| Maturity | 3 years |
| Dividend Yield | Around 7.75 to 8.00% pa |
| Conversion Premium | Zero |
| Conversion | Mandatory at maturity into 1 share (or cash at the issuer's option) unless share price above cap; conversion above cap is into a fraction of a share with market value equivalent to the cap price. |
| Cap | Typically, 30-45% (effectively 130-145% of issue price). |
| Call Option | Callable at any time for cash or stock at cap price plus premium. The call premium declines to 0% at maturity. |

**Exhibit 10.16**
**PERCS Issues — Terms for an Issue by K-Mart**

| | |
|---|---|
| Issuer | K-Mart Corporation |
| Security | Depositary shares representing one-quarter share of Series A preferred stock. |
| Amounts | US$1,012 million |
| Issue Price | US$44.00 (the price of ordinary shares at time of issue) |
| Maturity | 3 years (due September 15, 1994) |
| Dividend Yield | Around 7.75% pa (compared to ordinary share dividends of US$0.44 per share or 4.00% pa). |
| Conversion Premium | Zero |
| Conversion | Mandatory at maturity into one share (or cash at the issuer's option) unless share price above cap; conversion above cap is into a fraction of a share with market value equivalent to the cap price. |
| Cap | 30% (effectively 130% of issue price) |
| Call Option | Callable at any time for stock at with a market value equal to the call price. |
| Call Price | US$62.15 initially declining in equal increments to US$57.20 plus accrued dividends. |

**Exhibit 10.17**
**K-Mart PERCS Issues — Investor Return Profile**

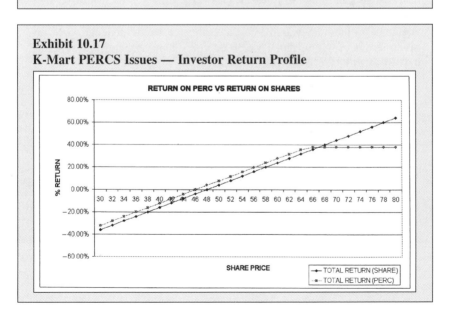

### 6.4.2   Applications

The limited appreciation mandatory convertible securities structure is applicable to issuers requiring a current equity infusion but who are of the view that their share price is significantly undervalued. In terms of signalling theory, an issue of limited appreciation mandatory convertible securities conveys an explicit signal that the issuer considers that its equity securities are significantly undervalued. Issues of limited appreciation mandatory convertible securities are more expensive in terms of servicing cost reflecting the higher dividend rate. This additional cost is recovered, if the share price expectation is realized, as the reduction in the number of ordinary shares issued will more than offset the higher short-term servicing cost. **Exhibit 10.18** sets out the cost savings achieved by Avon in one issue. Limited appreciation mandatory convertible securities issues have also been used to manage the equity dilution created through employee stock option programs. **Exhibit 10.19** sets out an example of this type of transaction.

---

**Exhibit 10.18**
**Limited Appreciation Mandatory Convertible Securities Issues —
Issuer Economics**

In 1988, Avon issued 18 million limited appreciation mandatory convertible securities (an issue of YES) at US$23.875 each in exchange for 18 million shares of common stock trading at the same price. The dividend on the YES was 8.38% pa (compared to the dividend yield on Avon shares of 4.19% pa). The cap on conversion at maturity was set at US$31.50 (132% of issue price).

The issue matured on June 3, 1991. Avon's share price had risen to US$44.75 well above the cap. Avon issued 0.72 shares of common stock to investor per YES.

Avon's savings were equivalent to 0.28 shares on 18 million YES — that is equivalent to US$226 million. This saving can be compared to the additional dividend cost of around US$54 million over the life of the YES issue resulting in net savings to the company of US$172 million.

*Source:* McGuire, Simon. "Capital Markets: Euro Yes?" Goldman Sachs *Euroconvertible Focus* 10-13.

---

**Exhibit 10.19**
**Limited Appreciation Mandatory Convertible Securities —**
**Equity Dilution Management**

In December 1996, Microsoft undertook a highly structured limited appreciation mandatory convertible securities issue.[15] The transaction was structured as follows:

| | |
|---|---|
| Instrument | Convertible exchangeable principal-protected preferred stock (EPPPS) |
| Amount | US$1 billion |
| Maturity | 3 years |
| Coupon | 2.75% (US$2.196/share) |
| Conversion Rights | Investors can convert into Microsoft shares subject to the conversion cap and floor although Microsoft has the right to cash settle the transaction. |
| Conversion Cap | Investor's return is capped at 28% (US$102.24) above the share price at issue (US$79.875) if the share price is above the issue price. |
| Conversion Floor | Investors will receive US$79.875 or its equivalent in shares if the share price at maturity is below US$79.875. |

The transaction appears to have been motivated by the desire of Microsoft to manage the dilution caused by employees exercising their option. Microsoft has a stock option program for its employees that is regarded as an important technique from attracting and retaining personnel of the appropriate calibre. However, the stock option program as employees exercise their options has a significant dilution effect.

The EPPPS issue was used to manage this dilution in a number of ways:

* The proceeds were used to repurchase shares.
* The cap on conversion is effectively a call on its shares purchased by Microsoft that is designed to hedge the dilution through the options as the stock price rises.
* The principal protection feature is effectively a short put position on its shares created by Microsoft that has the effect of complementing its buy-back program

---

[15] See "Microsoft Stops The Dilution" (April 1997) *Corporate Finance* 28.

The issue was successful, being significantly oversubscribed. A major attraction for investors was the ability of equity income investors to purchase exposure to Microsoft (which pays no dividends) on an income-producing basis.

Investor demand for limited appreciation mandatory convertible securities-type investment structures has derived from income-oriented equity investors, willing to trade off capital gains in return for income, such as certain types of mutual funds and individual retail investors.

The major attraction of these structures in the market environment that prevailed in the early 1990s was the yield that was significantly above that on cash, convertible, or other securities. In this environment, the limited appreciation mandatory convertible securities structure was attractive to investors seeking improved running yields with neutral to modest appreciation expectations on equity prices.

The structure of limited appreciation mandatory convertible securities also enables investors to construct synthetic fixed income investments. For example, certain arbitrage accounts purchase limited appreciation mandatory convertible securities and simultaneously purchase a put at the share price at issue to create high-yielding cash investments.

The limited appreciation mandatory convertible securities structure will typically outperform an investment in the underlying equity on a total return basis for a wide range of equity price appreciation outcomes. The only circumstance in which the limited appreciation mandatory convertible securities format underperforms the underlying equity is where the equity price increases substantially above the cap levels and/or the dividend yield on the underlying equity is increased, reducing the income advantage.

### 6.4.3. Valuation and Trading

#### 6.4.3.1 Pricing and Valuation

Analytically, an issue of limited appreciation mandatory convertible securities can be unbundled into its component parts:

- The purchase of the underlying shares.
- The simultaneous sale of an out-of-the-money call option on the shares at a strike equal to the cap level with an expiry coinciding with the expiry date of the security.

The proceeds from the sale of the call are used to increase the dividend level by being reinvested in the transaction.

**Exhibit 10.20** sets out an example of the pricing and valuation of an issue of limited appreciation mandatory convertible securities. **Exhibit 10.21** sets out the valuation of an issue of limited appreciation mandatory convertible securities using a theoretical option pricing model.

---

**Exhibit 10.20**
**Limited Appreciation Mandatory Convertible Securities Issues —**
**Valuation and Trading Performance**

Assume ABC Corporation issues a 3-year limited appreciation mandatory convertible securities that has a 8.25% pa coupon with a stock price of US$10. The limited appreciation mandatory convertible securities have a cap of 35%. The underlying shares pay no dividend.

Discounting this income advantage over three years yields a value of US$2.10. In return for this income the investor in the limited appreciation mandatory convertible securities is selling a 3-year call on ABC stock, struck at the cap price of US$13.50. The value of this option is around US$1.66 (assuming equity stock volatility of around 31%).

The issuer is therefore receiving US$2.10 (in present value terms) in return for selling a call worth US$1.66.

This implies the following relationship:

Limited appreciation mandatory convertible securities valuation = Value of common stock + value of additional income − value of 3-year call

Based on the above, it is possible to deduce that the limited appreciation mandatory convertible securities will in a scenario of increasing equity prices outperform the underlying equity unless the equity price increases by more than 18.5% pa over the three years. If the share price falls, then the limited appreciation mandatory convertible securities will outperform the shares because of the income advantage unless the fall in value of the underlying equity securities is at a rate in excess of the income advantage.

For example, in the above example, if the shares fall by 35% after one year, the theoretical value of the limited appreciation mandatory convertible securities would be US$8.02 versus an equity share value of US$6.58—an advantage of around 20%. The depreciation is partially offset by the dividend of 8.25% that will boost the limited appreciation mandatory convertible securities value to US$8.855, reducing the loss on the limited appreciation mandatory convertible securities to around 12.5%. If the stock price increases by 35% after one year, then the value of the limited appreciation mandatory convertible securities would be around

US$12.20 (an increase of 20.5%). Inclusive of the dividend, the limited appreciation mandatory convertible securities value of US$13.035 would equate to a gain of 28.7% or 82% of the appreciation in the share value.

Over a 2-year horizon, if the stock value is down 35%, the theoretical limited appreciation mandatory convertible securities value is US$7.39 (a fall of 27%). Adjusted for the dividends, the limited appreciation mandatory convertible securities value is around US$9.06 (a decline of 10.5%). If the stock value increases by 35%, the fair value of the limited appreciation mandatory convertible securities would be US$12.50 (an increase of 23.48%). Inclusive of dividends the increase relative to the equity is around 40%. The only case when the limited appreciation mandatory convertible securities, in this example, underperforms the equity significantly is where there is a sharp upward movement in the value of the equity.

*Source:* McGuire, Simon. "Capital Markets: PERCing Through The Looking Glass." Goldman Sachs *Euroconvertible Focus* 10-12.

The actual experience in the valuation and trading of PERCS is largely consistent with the theory. In practice, the issues of PERCS were in general issued at a premium to the theoretical fair value. However, because of the nature of the long-dated underlying equity options embedded in the structure, there are a number of valuation difficulties. These relate to estimation of the appropriate volatility for the underlying equity stocks, as well as projection of the expected dividends.

**Exhibit 10.21**
**Limited Appreciation Mandatory Convertible Securities Issues —**
**Theoretical Valuation**

Assume the following:

| | |
|---|---|
| Issue Date | 1-Jan-2001 |
| Maturity | 1-Jan-2005 |
| Maturity (years) | 4 |
| Dividend Rate | 7.50% pa |
| Conversion Premium | 0.00% |
| Conversion Ratio | 1.00 |
| Conversion Cap | 30.00% |
| Share Price (at issue) | $50.00 |

| | |
|---|---|
| Dividends (/share) | $2.00 |
| Current Dividend Yield | 4.00% |
| Option Volatility | 25.00% |
| Interest Rate | 6.50% |

Based on the above input the following prices can be derived:

| | |
|---|---|
| Option Premium ($) | $5.92 |
| Option Premium (%) | 11.84% |
| Amortized Premium | 3.45% |
| Implied Coupon | 7.45% |

This implies a value of the limited appreciation mandatory convertible security of $50.08.

### 6.4.3.2 Managing the Call Option

The issuer of a limited appreciation mandatory convertible security has the right to call the issue at any time prior to maturity. The predetermined call prices are set at a level that ensures that the investor receives payment for the remaining dividend advantage of the issue over ordinary shares. The call prices are also calculated assuming a constant dividend rate and are not adjusted for any decrease in the stock dividend. This means that the issuer has little or no economic reason to call the issue early. The only condition under which early call becomes economic is where the stock price is well above the cap level and the issuer anticipates a future decline in the share price.

Where the call is exercised, the investor receives payment in ordinary shares rather than cash with the number of shares determined as follows:

Shares delivered = (Call price + accrued and unpaid dividends)/
                    Current market price

Current market price is based typically on an averaging mechanism whereby the closing stock price for around five days ending two days prior to the notice date. This is subject to the condition that if the stock price on the trading day immediately preceding the 5-day period is less than 95% of the 5-day average, then the current market price will be the next day's closing price.

The averaging process can create problems whereby the holder receives shares worth an amount significantly different from the call price. This derives from the fact that the issuer can choose the most economically opportune time to exercise the call although the 95% rule serves to protect the investor. The issuer usually has between 15 and 60 days after the notice date as delivery date for the ordinary shares and the delivery date is fixed at the time of notice of the call.

*6.4.3.3 Managing Conversion Risk*

The conversion process of a limited appreciation mandatory convertible security entails certain risks that require careful management. As the issue approaches maturity, the issuer must manage to competing factors:

- The economic advantage of calling the issue early to avoid paying incremental dividends.
- Not calling the issue in the expectation of a rise in the share price that will result in fewer shares being delivered at maturity.

Conversion also may create liquidity problems and price pressure in the market for the issuer's shares. As additional shares are issued at conversion, investors that are not long-term holders of the stock will seek to liquidate their position. This has the potential to overhang the market and create downward-pricing pressures on the stock price.

### 6.4.4 *Product Variations*

Product variations include:

- **Tax-effective structures** — in October 1996, SunAmerica issued US$375 million of tax-deductible PERCS units. The transaction achieved tax deductibility by embedding a forward contract for common stock of the company sold to equity investors with the proceeds from the purchase contracts being used to buy US Treasury Notes on behalf of the investors to collateralize the purchase contract. The return to the investor is based on the interest on the Treasury Notes plus a supplement paid by the issuer. In addition, the issuer placed US$375 million of 6.20% pa notes to fixed income investors. At maturity, the issuer uses the proceeds from the forward purchase contract to repay the fixed income notes. The structure provided the issuer with tax deductibility of the interest on the notes, as well as equity treatment for the amount raised (because of the forward equity sale that effectively repaid the notes).[16]
- **Flexible cap structures** — these are structures where the preferred share converts into one share up to a capped level (giving the investor 100% participation up to the capped level) and a fixed portion, say, 50% above the cap level (giving the investor 50% of any additional participation). The investor is effectively long one unit of the shares and short a call at the cap level on 50% of the issue. The benefit to the issuer is lower dilution while achieving immediate equity treatment. The benefit for the investor is the higher income received as a result of the call premium received.

---

[16] Arzca, Enrique R. "PERCS, DECS, And Other Mandatory Convertibles" (Spring 1997) *Journal of Applied Corporate Finance* vol. 10 no. 1 54-63 at 55-56.

## 6.5    Structured High-yield Mandatory Convertible Securities[17]

### 6.5.1    Structure

A popular form of equity hybrid that has been utilized is structured high-yield mandatory convertible securities. This type of issue entails the issue of preference stock that pays a significantly higher dividend coupon than ordinary shares and is convertible on a mandatory basis into ordinary shares at maturity. Unlike the limited appreciation convertible structure, they contain no cap on equity participation once the share price has exceeded a pre-specified limit.

The structured high-yield mandatory convertible securities are known variously as: Automatically Converting Equity Securities (ACES) (Goldman Sachs); Dividend Enhanced Convertible Securities (DECS) (Salomon Smith Barney); Mandatory Adjustable Redeemable Convertible Securities (MARCS) (UBS Securities); Preferred Redeemable Increased Dividend Equity Securities (PRIDES) (Merrill Lynch); Preferred Equity Participation Securities (PEPS) (Morgan Stanley); and Stock Appreciation Income Linked Securities (SAILS) (CS First Boston)).

The structured high-yield mandatory convertible securities typically have the following characteristics:

- Preferred shares issued at the price of the ordinary shares at the date of issue.
- Maturity of around three or four years.
- Carry fixed dividends, payable quarterly, at a significantly higher yield (around 5-6% pa) above that on dividends on ordinary shares.
- At maturity the convertible preferred stock is automatically converted into ordinary shares. The conversion ratio at maturity is dependent on the price of the ordinary shares at maturity. The effective conversion premium is around 20-25% above the market share price at the time of issue.
- The issue typically has three years of call protection. The issuer has the right to call the issue and force mandatory conversion during the last year of the life of the ACES. In the case of early call, the issuer may have to reset the conversion ratio to ensure that the minimum value of the shares received is equivalent to the sum of the initial price of the common shares at issue and the value of unpaid preference dividends between the call date and the scheduled final maturity.

---

[17]    See Cox, T. Anne, Harrington III, Preston M. and Elliot, Anne (January 27, 1998) "Convertible Special Report — Convertible Structures: Building Further Innovations 1998 Update"; Global Convertibles Research Group, Merrill Lynch at 28-33; Arzca, Enrique R. "PERCS, DECS, And Other Mandatory Convertibles" (Spring 1997) *Journal of Applied Corporate Finance* vol. 10 no. 1 54-63; Iyer, Anand S. and MacInnes, Andrew (January 19, 1994) The Investor's Guide To DECS"; Salomon Brothers, New York.

**Exhibit 10.22** sets out an example of an issue of ACES detailing the typical terms of this type of structure.

---

**Exhibit 10.22**
**ACES Issue — Terms for an Issue by Boise Cascade**

| | |
|---|---|
| Issuer | Boise Cascade |
| Issue Type | Preferred G ACES |
| Issue Price | US$21.125 (equal to the share price at the time of issue) |
| Dividend on ACES | US$1.584 per ACES paid quarterly, equivalent to a yield of 7.5% pa (compared to a dividend rate on ordinary shares of US$0.60 per share or 2.8% pa paid quarterly). |
| Mandatory Conversion Date | September 15, 1997 |
| Conversion Ratio | |
|   At Maturity | Based on the following formula: |
| | • One share per ACES if Boise Cascade share price is US$21.125 or less; or |
| | • Between 1 share and 0.8010 shares if Boise Cascade shares are between US$21.125 and US$26.375, such that the value of shares received per ACES is US$21.125; or |
| | • 0.801 shares if Boise Cascade share price is above US$26.375. |
| Call Option | Callable from July 15, 1997 onwards. Call paid in stock with a value based on the maximum of parity and US$21.225. |

*Source:* "ACES: Confusion Creates Opportunity." Goldman Sachs *Global Convertible Review* 15-22.

---

**Exhibit 10.23** sets out the return profile of the investor in the ACES issue example in **Exhibit 10.22**.

The first graph shows the performance of the shares compared to the performance on the high-yield mandatory convertible issue in terms of responsiveness to pure share price movements. The second graph shows the performance comparison incorporating the dividends on the shares and the mandatory convertible issue.

The payoff shows clearly the performance structure of the instrument:

- If the share price closes below the issue price, then the investor receives one share and the return performance tracks that of the share.
- If the share price closes between the initial price and the conversion price (a premium over the market stock price), then the investor converts on a sliding scale designed to give the investor shares to the value equivalent of the initial issue price of the preferred stock. This equates to a nil participation in any appreciation in the shares and the issue lags the performance of the ordinary shares.
- If the share price rises above the conversion price, the investor receives a fixed number of shares in accordance with a pre-agreed ratio (calculated as 1/(1 + conversion premium at issue). The issue performance now tracks the performance of the ordinary shares but based on the pre-agreed conversion ratio. As this ratio is less than one (where the conversion premium is greater than 0), then the issue underperforms the share price.
- In all cases, the investor benefits from the high coupon which dictates that the high-yield mandatory convertible underperforms the share price if the share price rises above the conversion price but outperforms the shares if the share price falls below the issue price.

**Exhibit 10.23**
**ACES Issue — Return Payoffs**

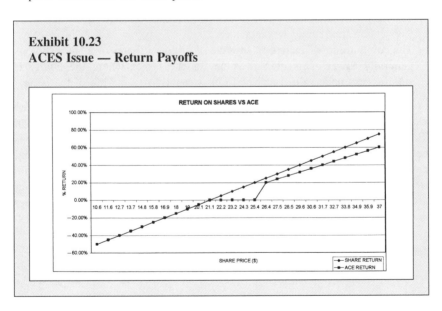

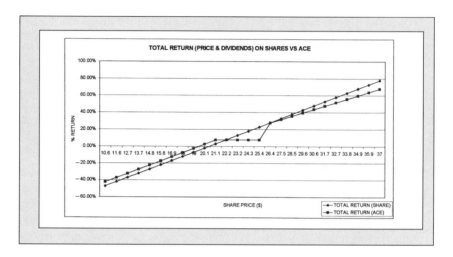

### 6.5.2  Applications

The major benefits of the high-yield mandatory convertible structure to issuers include:

- The mandatory future conversion feature ensures immediate equity treatment.
- Conversion into equity is guaranteed.
- The equity dilution relative to an issue of ordinary shares or a convertible is generally lower. This creates value for the issuer where the equity is significantly undervalued and performs strongly over the life of the issue.

From the viewpoint of the investor, the major attraction is the high dividend yield combined with a high level of exposure to the equity price of the issuer. The structure closely replicates the underlying shares except where the price is between the issue price and the conversion price. Compared to traditional convertible preferred stock issues, the high-yield mandatory convertible structure has a greater downside risk that is compensated for by the higher dividend yield. In essence, the structure enables the investor to create a higher dividend yield version of the underlying shares.

### 6.5.3  Pricing and Trading

#### 6.5.3.1  Pricing Economics

The structure basically, in return terms, will perform as follows:

- The high-yield mandatory convertible securities will significantly outperform the ordinary shares in terms of income. The capital value performance will be as follows:

- Identical to the equity if the share price falls.
- Zero capital return if the shares have risen by less than a predetermined amount (generally, 15-25%) over the term of the high-yield mandatory convertible securities.
- Participation at a pre-agreed ration in any share price appreciation over the pre-agreed level.

Structurally, the high-yield mandatory convertible securities issue can be decomposed from the viewpoint of the investor into three distinct transactions:

- Purchase of equity.
- Sale of one at-the-money call and purchase of part of an out-of-the money call struck at the upper price band at which the investor participates in any appreciation (the proportion of the call is 0.801 in the example in **Exhibit 10.22**). The calls both have an expiry equal to the final maturity of the security.[18]

### 6.5.3.2  Pricing Approaches/Sensitivities

The high-yield mandatory convertible structure is usually priced in one of two ways:

- **Call spread method** (identified above) — the sale of the at-the-money call and the simultaneous purchase of the out-of-the money call results in a net premium receipt for the investor that is used to enhance the yield on the high-yield mandatory convertible securities. Analytically, the relationship (in relation to the example in **Exhibit 10.22**) should be as follows:

   Present value of incremental income on high-yield mandatory convertible securities relative to underlying equity = premium on 1 call short at strike of US$21.125 less premium on 0.801 calls purchased at strike of US$26.375.

- **Convertible security/bought-put combination** — this entails decomposition of the transaction into a short maturity security plus a sold put that has a strike price equal to the issue price of the security that is the same as the market price of the shares at launch.

---

[18] From the point of view of the issuer, the structure is effectively a monetised collar against a holding in the underlying stock (whether it is the issuer's own stock or shares in a third party into which the investor can exchange into. The issuer's long stock and long call (at the prevailing market price) is equivalent to a synthetic long put position (using put call parity). The sold call (out-of-the-money) is the other component of the collar.

**Exhibit 10.23** below sets out the pricing of a high-yield mandatory convertible structure using the call spread method.

---

**Exhibit 10.23**
**High-yield Mandatory Convertible Securities Issues — Theoretical Valuation**

Assume the following:

| | | |
|---|---|---|
| Issue Date | | 1-Jan-2001 |
| Maturity | | 1-Jan-2005 |
| Maturity (years) | | 4 |
| Dividend Rate | | 6.25% |
| Conversion Premium | | 25.00% |
| Conversion Ratio | | |
| If Share Price Below | $50.00 | 1.00 |
| If Share Price Above $50.00 and Below | $62.50 | 0.800 |
| If Share Price Above | $62.50 | 0.800 |
| Share Price (at issue) | | $50.00 |
| Dividends (/share) | | $2.00 |
| Current Dividend Yield | | 4.00% |
| Option Volatility | | 20.00% |
| Interest Rate | | 5.00% |

Based on the above input the following prices can be derived:

| | |
|---|---|
| Net Option Premium ($) | $3.72 |
| Net Option Premium (%) | 7.44% |
| Amortized Premium | 2.10% |
| Implied Coupon | 6.10% |

This implies a value of the high-yield mandatory convertible security of $50.26.

---

The sensitivity of high-yield mandatory convertible structures to changes in market-pricing parameters is as follows:

- **Stock price** — the price is very sensitive to the price of the underlying shares reflecting the very high equity content of the structure.
- **Stock price volatility** — the structure is not very sensitive to shifts in stock volatility because of the offsetting (sold and bought) option positions.

However, the structure is sensitive to the changes in the shape of the volatility smile reflecting the different strike prices.[19]

- **Interest rates** — the structure is less sensitive to interest rates than a traditional convertible because of the mandatory conversion feature of the structure. The major interest sensitivity derives from the fact that changes in interest rates will affect the value of the enhanced dividend income steam, as well as the pricing of the options.

### 6.5.3.3  Conversion and Redemption Issues

The holder of these securities generally has the option to exchange for the minimum conversion ratio prior to maturity. Early conversion is unlikely except where the dividend stream on the underlying stock has increased above that on the high-yield mandatory convertible structure.

The issuer also has a call option usually at the end of three years at pre-specified premiums to the issue price plus accrued dividends. Where the share price has fallen, the issuer will usually not call the issue as the terms of the call would require the investor to receive the number of shares required to recoup the initial investment causing excess dilution. However, if the share price is trading above the conversion price then the issuer may redeem to achieve a cash flow saving by avoiding paying the high dividend rate.

### 6.5.4  Product Variations

A number of variations on the basic high-yield mandatory convertible structure have evolved:

- **Principal protected structures** — these structures are designed so that in the event that the share price falls below the issue price, the investor receives more than one share up to a pre-specified maximum number. In effect, the investor is protected from the first, say, 20% of any price decline. This is achieved economically by the investor buying a put at the issue price and selling an out-of-the money put at the level at which the protection is terminated. It has the impact of lowering the yield on the issue to finance the put-spread purchase. The investment profile of this structure is closer to a conventional convertible structure as it provides downside price protection on the shares (to the agreed level).[20]

---

[19] For a discussion of the volatility smile, see Das, Satyajit "Estimating Volatility" in Das, Satyajit (editor) (1997) *Risk Management and Financial Derivatives: A Guide to the Mathematics*"; McGraw-Hill, Chicago; MacMillan Press, London; LBC Information Services, Sydney at 307-355.

[20] An example of this structure is Merrill Lynch's RESET PRIDES issues.

• **Exchangeable structures** — the structure can be designed as an exchangeable bond (see discussion below) to effect divestiture of equity holdings. They are more attractive in the sense that conversion and sale is guaranteed while providing the opportunity to sell the stake at a premium to current market price and defer capital gain recognition until exchange.

The most interesting variation on the basic structure of a high-yield mandatory convertible security is the Participating Hybrid Option Note Exchangeable Securities (PHONES) launched in early 1999. The structure utilizes US tax regulations to create an attractive monetization structure for issuers seeking to engineer a tax-effective synthetic disposition of a shareholding in another company. **Exhibit 10.24** sets out an analysis of this structure.

---

**Exhibit 10.24**
**High-yield Mandatory Convertible Securities Issues —**
**PHONES Structure**[21]

*Structure*
The basic structure is as follows:

| | |
|---|---|
| Type Of Instrument | Contingent payment debt or PHONES |
| Issuer | Entity with position in shares of a third party (the exchange shares). This holding has typically been a large holding with a low cost base and significant accreted profits that would trigger a taxable gain if the underlying stock were sold. |
| Amount | $ [Variable] |
| Issue Price | Current price of the exchange shares. |
| Maturity | 30 years |
| Coupon Payments | 1.75 to 2.00% pa plus an amount replicating the dividends on the exchange shares. |
| Other Distributions | Any other distributions on the exchange shares are replicated in payments on the PHONES. |
| Deferral Payments | The issuer has the right to defer any payments for periods of up to five years. |
| Redemption Amount | The maximum of: |
| | • The issue price (designated as the contingent principal amount). |

---

[21] For an analysis of the PHONES structure, see Sheppard, Lee "Rethinking DECS and New Ways To Carve Out Debt" (April 19, 1999) *Tax Notes* 347-352.

| | • The market value of the exchange shares plus any deferred payments. |
|---|---|
| Call Option | The issuer has the right to redeem the PHONES at annual intervals for an amount equal to the greater of the issue price or the market value of the exchange shares plus any deferred payments plus an additional premium for early redemption. |
| Put Option | The investor has the right to redeem the PHONES at annual intervals for an amount of 95% of the market value of the exchange shares at the time of exchange. |

Early examples of these types of transactions included an issue by Comcast Corporation into 26.6 million AT&T shares (acquired as consideration when AT&T acquired Tele-Communications Inc.) and an issue by Tribune Co. into 11 million America Online Inc. shares (acquired in the course of a joint venture).

***Transaction Economics***

The basic transaction structure can be decomposed into the following components:

• A low coupon bond.
• A low exercise price option into the underlying shares.

The low exercise price is driven by the very long maturity of the transaction. A call struck at the current market price has a strike price effectively at around 17% of the *implied forward stock price at the end of 30 years.*[22]

The economic structure of the transaction is as follows:

• From the viewpoint of the issuer — the PHONES is effectively an economic disposition of the position in the underlying stock. The low exercise price option has a theoretically high probability of exercise.
• From the viewpoint of the investor — the PHONES represent an economic investment in the underlying stock with an enhanced coupon.

The economic structure is reinforced by the straight pass through of dividends and other distributions on the underlying exchange shares. It is

---

[22] Assuming interest rates of around 6.00% pa. The implied delta of such an option would be close to 1.00 (implying that the option position was akin to a long or short position in the underlying asset).

also reinforced by the structure of the call and put options that are designed to create a disincentive for early termination of the transaction.

The transaction economics are driven by the taxation treatment of the structure under US tax regulations.[23] The tax drivers of the transaction appear to be as follows:

- The issue of PHONES is not regarded generally as a sale of the underlying equity therefore avoiding triggering of the tax liability (if any) on the sale of the shares. This appears based on the fact that the issuer bears the risk of price falls on the underlying shares below the current market price at the time of issue.
- The issuer as holder of the shares continues to enjoy any tax benefits on the underlying shares (such as any available dividend received deduction, and so on).
- The PHONES themselves are treated as a contingent payment debt carrying below-market rates of interest. This means that investors will have to include in income not only the income actually received but an amount designed to equate the yield to a *market yield* (this was determined as 8.125% pa in the Tribune transaction and 9.30% pa in the Comcast transaction).[24] In a symmetric application of this regulation, the issuers obtain a *tax deduction* for both the actual payments and the amount designed to equate the PHONES yield to the determined market yield. The net result is that the investors (if they are taxpayers) have a high current taxable (but not cash) income and corresponding tax liabilities. In contrast, issuers have a high current tax (but not cash) expense and a corresponding large tax deduction.

The tax-driven transaction economics means that the structure is attractive to non-tax-paying investors. For these investors, the PHONES transaction

---

[23] The US tax position is extremely complex and this discussion is a very brief summary of the anticipated position. This does not purport to be definitive and interested parties should seek detailed advice from their tax advisers. The position stated is based on the discussion in Sheppard, Lee "Rethinking DECS and New Ways To Carve Out Debt" (April 19, 1999) *Tax Notes* 347-352.

[24] The higher determined equivalent market yield for the Comcast issue was driven in part by the fact that this particular issue structure allowed the term of the PHONES to be automatically extended to 60 years at the end of the initial maturity of 30 years, provided the underlying AT&T shares have appreciated by 50% over the initial term of the issue (an annual compound appreciation rate of 1.35% pa). The Tribune phone issue did not include this extension feature.

is identical to ownership of the underlying shares with enhanced income. The additional tax liability from the additional imputed earning is not an issue as the investor is not in a tax-paying position. For the issuer, the structure generates large tax deductions from the imputed expense (which is not paid in cash) that shelters the issuer's ultimate capital gain on any disposition of the underlying shareholding.

The economic advantages (driven by the potential tax benefits) for the issuer are the basis of the enhanced return offered to the investor in the PHONES transaction.

## 7. Variations in Underlying Equity Securities

### 7.1 Overview

The traditional equity-linked structure entails conversion of the host debt into the equity securities of the issuer or a related entity (typically, the parent or holding company). Equity-linked structures entailing the exchange of the debt into the equity of a third party is also feasible.

There are three separate types of these structures:

- **Exchangeable debt** — issues of securities convertible into the ordinary shares of a company that the issuer is seeking to divest itself of are popular as deferred divestment structures.
- **Going public bonds** — issues of securities exchangeable for equity securities to be issued in the future generally in an initial public offering (IPO).
- **Synthetic convertibles** — issues of securities convertible into the ordinary shares of the issuer where the issuer hedges the embedded equity option in order to avoid the impact of equity dilution.[25]
- **Synthetic equity** — issues of convertibles into equity securities or indexes unrelated to the equity securities of the issuer.

---

[25] This type of synthetic convertible should be distinguished from the synthetic equity-linked structures discussed below. These types of synthetic convertibles are issued by an entity seeking to raise funds whereas the second type of synthetic convertibles are issued by investment banks/dealers where the underlying entity whose stock is utilized does not wish to raise funds.

## 7.2  Exchangeable Bonds[26]

### 7.2.1  Overview

The term exchangeable debt usually refers to a transaction where the borrower issues debt securities that are convertible into the equity of a nonrelated third-party entity in which the issuing company holds equity securities.

The earliest identifiable issue of exchangeable debt was undertaken in November 1971 by International Paper Company, with the debt exchangeable into the common stock of CR Bard Inc. In recent times, these transactions have gained popularity as an alternative means of divesting corporate equity holdings or to reduce the holding cost associated with the purchase of an equity stake in an unrelated corporation.

### 7.2.2  Exchangeable Debt — Structure

Exchangeable debt securities are similar to conventional equity-linked securities, such as convertible bonds. The distinguishing feature of exchangeable debt is that an exchangeable bond is convertible into, typically, the ordinary shares of a company other than the issuer of the bond (hence, the term exchangeable rather than convertible).

This similarity dictates that exchangeable debt securities feature a number of characteristics that are similar to those found in conventional convertible bonds. For example, the terms of an exchangeable bond issue would closely follow those of a convertible security. The major difference, relative to a conventional convertible bond, is that:

- The issuer of the bond is responsible for servicing of the interest coupon on the exchangeable debt and, unless converted, repayment of the principal value of the bond.
- The potential for capital appreciation of the issue is contingent on the performance of the ordinary shares of the company into which the exchangeable debt is convertible.

The principal features of an exchangeable debt issue include:

- An issue of senior or subordinated, secured or unsecured debt securities (although quasi-equity securities such as preference shares have also been used). The debt instrument used in the exchangeable structure can be either a bond or debenture in registered or bearer form. The rights of the investor are generally unsecured and unsubordinated, although secured and/or subordinated structures are feasible.

---

[26] See Das, Satyajit "Exchangeable Debt" (Winter 1989) *Journal of International Securities Markets* vol. 3 409-425; and (Spring 1990) vol. 4 91-98.

- The debt securities are exchangeable during specified periods (usually, any time prior to maturity) into the ordinary shares (or other specified equity securities) of a third party, the latter being typically a publicly listed company, which is unrelated to the issuer.[27]
- The issuing company (or companies) associated with the issuer hold or are in the process of acquiring the relevant equity securities in the third-party company.
- The capacity to exchange the debt securities may be subject to an option for the issuer to pay cash as a substitute for delivery of the relevant shares. The cash option is calculated according to an agreed formula that is related to the market price of the underlying equity securities as at the time of conversion, in order to leave the investor in the same economic position as if he or she had converted into the relevant shares.
- The price at which the debt securities can be exchanged for the equity securities of the third-party company represents a premium to the prevailing market price at the time the issue is undertaken. This premium is variable ranging from between 110% to 130% of the market price of the shares at the time of issue. As in all convertible or equity-linked structures, there is an explicit trade-off between the level of the premium and the coupon on the debt securities. Typically, the higher the level of the premium upon exchange, the higher the interest rate on the exchangeable debt securities or, its equivalent, the lower the discount to the issuer's normal equivalent cost of debt.
- The equity securities subject to the exchange arrangement have, typically, all been publicly listed companies. While there are no technical reasons that an exchangeable issue convertible into the shares of a private company should not be possible, in practice, it is difficult to conceive of such a transaction because of the underlying lack of liquidity and the market-determined price of such equities. The only exception to this is the going public and synthetic convertible structures discussed below.
- It is possible for the issuer effectively to secure or enhance the creditworthiness of the issue by lodging the shares with a trustee under custody and/or escrow arrangements. Where the issuer itself is a less creditworthy entity, the structure may enhance the marketability of the instrument through use of the higher credit standing of the company into whose equities the bond is exchangeable. The structure effectively involves the value inherent in the equities owned as a means of securing or enhancing the credit of the issuer in accessing funds.

---

[27] Issues of convertible debt are often undertaken via special-purpose vehicles (for tax, accounting and/or regulatory reasons) with conversion into the shares of the ultimate holding company. These transactions are not authentic exchangeable share issues.

- Issuers have often sought to retain the option either to pay cash to those investors seeking to exchange the debt securities for the underlying equity or alternatively to buy back the shares from the investor following the exchange. Economically, the presence of a cash option limits the investor's potential gain to the difference (at the time of conversion) between the market price of the shares and the predetermined exchange price. It effectively prevents the investor from capturing any further appreciation in the shares following exchange. In essence, it assumes that the investor would, following exchange, immediately dispose of the acquired shares in the market at the then-prevailing price for these securities.

Exchangeable issues have been undertaken in a wide range of currencies and there is theoretically no restriction (subject to investor acceptance) on the currencies in which such transactions may be launched. It is also feasible to undertake issues in a currency different from the currency denomination of the underlying equity securities. For example, an exchangeable bond issue denominated in US$ where the underlying equity securities are denominated in A$ is feasible, provided the conversion exchange rate is fixed at the time the issue is launched.[28]

### 7.2.3 Exchangeable Debt — Cash Flow Characteristics

The cash flow characteristics of an issue of exchangeable debt are as follows:

- At the commencement of the transaction, when it is launched, the issuer receives the cash equivalent to the face value of the issue (less any underwriting fees and issue expenses). The main feature of this initial cash flow is that because the issue is launched at a premium to the prevailing market price of the shares, the amount raised is in excess of that required to fund the purchase of the relevant equity stake. In a typical transaction, the proceeds of the exchangeable debt issue may be required to replace existing funding used to finance the holding in the relevant company.
- Over the life of the exchangeable debt transaction, there are two relevant sets of cash flows:
  - The cash flows and related rights contingent upon the issuer maintaining the beneficial rights to the underlying exchange shares.
  - The cash flows relating to the actual issue of exchangeable debt.
- The exchangeable debt transaction will typically be terminated in one of two ways:

---

[28] The conversion exchange rate would need to be set at the start of the transaction as in a standard convertible where the underlying equity is in a currency other than that of the issue; refer to Chapter 9.

– By the investor exchanging the debt securities prior to maturity for the underlying exchange shares.

– The maturity of the exchangeable debt issue whereupon it must be repaid.

As the issuer continues to maintain its beneficial interests in the shares into which the exchangeable debt can be exercised, it continues to enjoy:

• The rights of ownership including voting rights, rights to participate in the management of the company, and so on.

• Rights contingent upon ownership including participation in bonus share issues, share splits, as well as pre-emptive rights such as the right to participate in any new issue of equity or quasi-equity securities undertaken by the company.

• Receipt of dividends including any increase in dividends.

• Any return of capital.

A critical feature resulting from the continued beneficial interest enjoyed by the issuer in the exchange shares is the right to receive dividends that can then, at least partially, go towards servicing the interest obligations on the exchangeable debt. An important aspect of this right to receive dividends is the opportunity to enjoy any increase in the dividend payout rate during the time the exchangeable debt securities remain unconverted.

The primary implication of the exchangeable debt securities in terms of cash flow is the requirement for the issuer to make interest payments at the agreed interest rate on the face value of the exchangeable debt issue that remains unconverted. In practice, the fact that the interest rate on exchangeable debt is typically lower than that on ordinary debt, as a result of the exchange feature, will mean that the gap (or deficiency in cash flow) between dividend receipts and interest payments on funding required to support the holding of the equities, is reduced.

Where the investor exchanges the debt securities for the exchange shares, the issuer's debt is extinguished and beneficial ownership of the exchange shares is transferred to the investor. The only exception to this situation is where the issuer has the option to pay cash for or to repurchase the exchange shares. In this case, the issuer faces a refinancing requirement to fund the payment to the investor at the time of conversion.

Where the exchangeable debt issue matures without the investor converting the debt into the exchange shares, the issuer is required to repay the face value of the exchangeable debt. This will typically require the issuer either to refinance in order to raise the required amount of funds to make the repayment; or, alternatively, the issuer can dispose of the exchange shares in order to provide at least part of the cash required to repay the maturing exchangeable debt securities.

## 7.2.4   Exchangeable Debt — Applications

### 7.2.4.1   Overview

In overall terms, the use of exchangeable debt in corporate finance applications by issuers or as part of investment strategies by investors is consistent with the use of convertibles and other equity-linked note transactions.

The issue of exchangeable debt securities is, at its simplest, merely another alternative form of capital raising available to an organization. A company may have acquired a significant holding of shares in a third company through a planned investment, or as part of corporate restructuring activity, including an attempted or aborted takeover. The company has the alternative of financing its equity holding through the issuance of exchangeable debt securities without having to dispose of its shareholding immediately.

The major distinguishing feature of exchangeable debt as a capital-raising instrument is that it allows the issuing company effectively to capture a premium over the value of the equity securities held. This is because the exchangeable debt, as is the case for conventional convertible bonds, is issued at a premium over the current market value of the exchange shares. In addition, when the exchange shares demonstrate higher levels of volatility than the issuing company's own shares, the value of the option on the exchange shares will be greater and this will translate into either a higher premium on the exchangeable debt issue or a lower interest coupon.

An exchangeable debt transaction is generally most attractive where the exchange shares have significant appreciation potential. Debt exchangeable into the shares of a corporation not expected to issue convertible debt securities or, alternatively, that has no outstanding equity-linked securities, can also prove particularly attractive to investors.

From an investor perspective, exchangeable debt securities are similar in most ways to conventional convertible issues. Consequently, the attractiveness or otherwise of exchangeable debt securities as an investment is usually determined on the basis of criteria similar to those used to assessing conventional convertible issues.

However, exchangeable debt has a number of significant differences to conventional convertibles that affect their value as investments. The major one is that the issuing company is obligated to make the interest payments and the capital appreciation potential is determined by the performance of the exchange shares. As a result, the risk profile of exchangeable debt is more complex. This division of risk between two separate companies can create complex valuation issues. This will be the case for example where the two companies belong to two distinct and separate industry groups.

The use of exchangeable debt securities is confined predominantly to two situations:

- The divestiture of corporate equity holdings.
- Finance equity stakes in nonrelated companies.

### 7.2.4.2   Exchangeable Debt as a Divestiture Structure

Where the issuing company wishes to divest itself of an existing shareholding, an issue of exchangeable debt can help substantially to improve, under certain conditions, the terms under which the company sells its holding. Where the issuing company holds an equity stake in another company, changing business and strategic considerations may dictate the need to divest itself of that shareholding. Under such circumstances, the company has the following options:

- Continue to hold (and finance) the shares.
- Effect an immediate sale of its shares.
- Undertake an issue of debt today and dispose of its equity holding in the future.
- Launch an issue of exchangeable debt.

The specific impact of these various alternatives on the company seeking to divest itself from its shareholding is very different.

Where the company continues to hold its shares, the economic value of this alternative is the present value of dividends received, as well as the present value of the future disposition proceeds of its shareholding, adjusted for its cost of financing its equity stake. Under this alternative, both the asset and the offsetting liability are reflected in the company's balance sheet, potentially reducing its debt capacity.

Where the divesting corporation seeks an immediate sale of its equity holding, there are a number of alternative methods of achieving the sale, including:

- A negotiated private sale to a third party.
- A block trade on a stock exchange (assuming the securities are listed).
- A private placement or public offering of the relevant equity securities.

The economics of this alternative are straightforward. The cash received from the sale could be used in the company's business or to repay outstanding debt. However, depending on a variety of factors, including equity market conditions and the size of the equity holding, an immediate sale may be inconsistent with achieving the best possible value for the shares.

For example, if the shareholding is particularly large, any sale or placement of the stake may have to be achieved at a discount to the prevailing market price. Furthermore, the sale would normally trigger a taxable gain or loss, depending on the relationship between the sale price and the acquisition price of the shares, upon the sale being effected. Depending on the tax jurisdiction, this may create a significant tax liability for ordinary income or capital gains tax.

Combined with the future sale of the shares, the sale of debt by the issuing company is similar to the first and fourth options listed above. However, the major distinction is that the issue of debt is undertaken upon normal market terms and the interest cost of funding the equity stake continues to impact negatively on issuing company's credit standing, interest coverage, and other financial ratios. In addition, depending on the interest cost on its debt relative to the dividend yield on its equity stake, the company may incur a negative spread or annual funding cost until the sale of the shares is effected.

The use of exchangeable debt is broadly similar to the third above-listed alternative. The major differences are that the inclusion of a premium relative to market price for the exchange shares results in an additional initial cash flow to the issuer that can presumably go toward general corporate purposes or to retire additional debt. In addition, an exchangeable issue will have a coupon lower than a conventional issue of debt by the issuing company that effectively lowers the carrying cost of the equity stake. A further advantage is that the debt does not have to be redeemed if the investor exchanges the securities for the exchange shares.

As discussed in greater detail below, the use of exchangeable debt to effect divestiture can generate superior economics under certain conditions. These benefits are primarily a result of the premium on the exchange shares that captures some of the appreciation potential of the equity stake and the deferral of any tax liability resulting from the sale of the underlying equity until exchange is effected. Benefits may also accrue from continued control of the underlying shares, as well as participation in dividends including growth in the dividend rate and such ancillary benefits as rights issues, capital returns, and bonus share issues.

One problem with exchangeable debt transactions is that depending on the relativity of the interest rate on the exchangeable debt and the dividend flow received on the equity stake, the company may continue to incur a negative spread, albeit a smaller one than where the stake is funded by ordinary debt. The exchangeable debt also appears on the balance sheet of the issuer. It continues to rely on available credit lines to the borrower and is part of the debt burden of the issuing company.

The major risk with exchangeable debt is that of nonconversion of the issue. For example, if the exchange shares perform poorly, investors may redeem the debt securities at maturity rather than exchange them for the underlying equity. However, as illustrated below, even where the debt securities are not exchanged and the issuing company is forced to sell the shares at maturity, the economics of the transaction can be superior to alternative methods of divestiture. One structural variation seeking to address this problem of potential nonconversion is the high-yield mandatory convertible structure discussed above. Issues of *exchangeable* ACES, DECS, and PRIDES, for example, have been undertaken.

An example of this type of application of exchangeable debt is a celebrated issue by IBM undertaken in February 1986. **Exhibit 10.25** outlines the principal terms of this transaction.

---

**Exhibit 10.25**
**Exchangeable Debt Issue —**
**IBM Debt Securities Exchangeable into Intel Shares**

In that transaction, IBM issued US$300 million worth of subordinated 10-year debentures exchangeable into the capital stock of Intel Corporation. IBM was Intel's largest customer and, conversely, Intel is one of the most significant suppliers of components to IBM. Based, in part, on this business relationship, IBM originally purchased approximately 19.4% of outstanding Intel ordinary shares in the period between 1983 and 1984. Subsequently, the performance of Intel led IBM to divest itself of a significant portion of its shareholding in the stock, despite continuation between the two companies of close and productive relationships in many aspects of their respective businesses. The 1986 issue was exchangeable into an aggregate of 7,792,208 shares in Intel stock (or approximately 6.7% of Intel's outstanding shares).

The terms of the issue are summarized below:

| | |
|---|---|
| Issuer | International Business Machines Corporation |
| Amount | US$300 million of exchangeable subordinated debentures exchangeable for capital stock of the Intel Corporation. |
| Maturity | 10 years (due March 1, 1996) |
| Coupon | 6.375% pa. |
| Issue Price | 100 |
| Conversion Period | From closing date to maturity |
| Conversion Premium | Approx. 33.0% over the share price at fixing of US$28.75; a conversion price of US$38.50 |
| Denominations | US$5,000 |
| Amortisation | Bullet |
| Call Option | From closing at 105, declining after March 1989 by 10% pa. subject to the 130% rule. |
| Listing | Luxembourg |
| Governing Law | New York |
| Commission | 2.5% (Management and underwriting 1%; selling 1.5%) |
| Lead Managers | Morgan Stanley (books) |

Through this structure IBM divested itself of its holding in Intel and was able to release it at a premium rather than the discount it would have had to accept had it sold the shares directly in the market. It also added value to a conventional fundraising transaction and significantly reduced its interest costs.

A number of similar exchangeable transactions have been undertaken in recent years. Two significant transactions undertaken by Bell Atlantic are described in **Exhibit 10.26**. Other transactions undertaken include:

- An exchangeable 5- and 7-year bond issue denominated in Swfr, US$, and Euros for US$2.1 billion equivalent by Swiss Life Insurance & Pensions exercisable into the shares of Glaxo Wellcome, Mannesmann, Novartis, Unilever, Royal Dutch/Shell, and UBS.[29] The 6-tranche issue was undertaken at an average yield to maturity of 2.4% pa with conversion premiums ranging from 25.1% to 28.1%. The issuer retained the option to provide investors in the exchangeable bond with cash equivalent instead of the stock itself. The issue was used to raise lower cost debt by the company to finance potential European acquisitions.[30]

- An exchangeable bond issue for French francs 2.1 billion by the French cable TV operator Canal+ exchangeable into the shares of Italian company Mediaset. The shares in Mediaset were acquired by Canal+ when it merged with Dutch Group Nethold. The French company did not view the shares in Mediaset as a strategic shareholding and wanted to dispose of the holding as soon as possible in early 1997. However, the sale was impeded by the fact that the merger was not due to be finalized until April 1997. This meant that Canal+ could not sell the shares until such date, and a hedge of the equity price would have been difficult because of the large size of the stake and the relative illiquidity of the Italian company's shares. Sale of the Mediaset shares was also restricted by a lock-up agreement whereby the banks involved in the IPO of Mediaset were prevented from selling shares or related options, warrants, or convertible securities for a period of 270 days from the date of the IPO. The exchangeable issue was undertaken in advance of completion of the merger. In the event that the merger was not completed by August 1997 the exchangeable converted into a straight bond issue paying a coupon of 50 bps over the 2001 BTAN. The issue also included an unusual

---

[29] The issue was arranged by Warburg Dillion Read and entitled Guaranteed Exchangeable Monetisation of Multiple Shares (GEMMS).

[30] See Lanchner, David "Bonds That Act As Equity Options" (June 1998) *Global Finance* 16.

conversion feature. On conversion, Canal+ was obliged to offer the Mediaset shares to holders of pre-emptive rights on the stock. If these investors took up the shares under their preemption rights, then the investors in the exchangeable receive a cash settlement based on the value of the Mediaset shares. If these investors failed to purchase the shares, then the investors would be delivered the shares.[31]

• An issue by Fullerton Global (acting on behalf of the Singapore Government) into Singapore Telecom stock and an issue by Allianz into Deutsche Bank shares.[32]

---

**Exhibit 10.26**
**Exchangeable Debt Issue — Bell Atlantic**

*Exchangeable into New Zealand Telecom*

In February 1998, Bell Atlantic issued a US$2.46 billion issue exchangeable into New Zealand Telecom shares.[33] The transaction that was the largest exchangeable bond to that time was designed to divest Bell Atlantic of part of its stake in New Zealand Telecom.[34]

The transaction history relates to the privatization sale in 1990 by the New Zealand government of New Zealand Telecom. Bell Atlantic and Ameritech each purchased 49.8% of the Telecom Corporation, New Zealand. Under the terms of the transaction, both purchasers were required to reduce their shareholding to 24.95% of the company through either private or public sales. Bell Atlantic achieved the required reduction in its stake through the exchangeable issue. Ameritech sold its shares on a partly paid basis (50% of the purchase price payable at issue and the remaining 50% payable one year later).

The terms of the exchangeable bond issue were as follows:

Issuer/Guarantor                    Bell Atlantic Corporation

---

[31] See "Structure Frees Canal+ From Lock-Up" (December 1997) *Corporate Finance* 56.

[32] See Cooper, Graham "Equity Issuers Toast Record Year" (May 1998) *Risk* 13.

[33] See Gailey, Colin "Bell Atlantic Trades Off The CUFS" (April 1998) *AsiaMoney* 9-12.

[34] The largest exchangeable debt transaction ever attempted prior to this transaction was a 3-tranche issue denominated in US dollars, sterling, and Australian dollars valued at approximately A$1.06 billion. Launched by Merrill Lynch Capital Markets on behalf of Bell Resources, it was exchangeable into the shares of BHP Limited. Emerging as it did, however, in October 1987, this ambitious issue was withdrawn following the stock market crash.

| Issue Structure | Exchangeable into existing ordinary shares of New Zealand Telecom. |
|---|---|
| Amount | US$2.46 billion |
| Maturity | 5 years |
| Coupon | 5.75% pa |
| Exchange Price/Premium | NZ$7.98 per share representing a premium of 20% |
| Exchange Period | Any time after 18 months. |
| Exchange Structure | The issuer can deliver shares or pay the cash equivalent of the shares. |
| Call Option | 3-year noncall period |
| Lead Manager | SBC Warburg Dillion Read |

The issue was utilized to monetize Bell Atlantic's shareholding in New Zealand Telecom. The structure enables Bell Atlantic to achieve a premium to the current market price. A direct sale may have resulted in lower proceeds reflecting the size of the position, the relative liquidity of the Australian and New Zealand stock markets, and the stock overhang as both shareholders moved to liquidate their positions. The issue was successful at attracting around US$15 billion of demand.

### Exchangeable into Cable & Wireless Shares

Subsequently, in August 1998, Bell Atlantic undertook an even larger exchangeable issue into Cable and Wireless Communication Plc shares. The terms of the issue were as follows:

| Issuer/Guarantor | Bell Atlantic Financial Services Inc/Bell Atlantic Corporation. |
|---|---|
| Issue Structure | Exchangeable into existing ordinary shares of Cable and Wireless Communication Plc. |
| Amount | US$3.18 billion |
| Maturity | 7 years |
| Coupon | 4.25% pa |
| Exchange Price/Premium | GBP 7.00 per share representing a premium of 28%. |
| Exchange Structure | The issuer can deliver shares or pay the cash equivalent of the shares. |
| Call Option | Four-year noncall period then callable at any time at the accreted value plus accrued interest. |
| Lead Manager | Warburg Dillion Read/Morgan Stanley Dean Witter |

### 7.2.4.3 Exchangeable Debt as a Funding Mechanism for Equity Holdings

The second application of exchangeable debt — namely, funding equity stakes in other companies — is predicated on a similar logic. The equity stakes being funded are typically either:

* Long-term strategic shareholdings.
* Equity stakes acquired as part of an attempted takeover or other corporate restructuring activity.

The alternatives available to the issuing company in this case are more limited. The company can either fund its equity stake through conventional debt or equity financing, or alternatively it can issue exchangeable debt. Since, unlike the divestiture case, the issuing company will want to have the option of retaining control of the shares, a critical characteristic of exchangeable debt issues will be an ability to either buy back the exchange shares, or to make a cash payment to investors in lieu of exchanging the debt securities for the exchange shares.

The most significant benefit from the perspective of the issuing company is a reduction in the holding cost of the equity stake. However, it would be erroneous to suggest that the use of exchangeable debt is cheaper. This is because the final cost of the issue depends largely on the capital value of the exchange shares. For example, where the underlying exchange shares increase in value significantly and the issuing company wishes to retain control of the shares, the cash outflows on repurchase of the exchange shares or any cash payments in lieu of exchange will increase the cost of the issue significantly above the initial interest cost of the exchangeable debt issue itself. In some cases, this additional cost will eliminate any initial advantage gained from reducing the interest cost of holding the shares.

The use of exchangeable debt may also increase or decrease the strategic alternatives available to and overall flexibility of the issuing company. For example, in certain situations, it is conceivable that the use of exchangeable debt actually enhances the strategic position of the issuer. Where the equity stake is acquired as part of an attempted takeover, the issuing company can, through exchangeable debt, create the opportunity to divest itself out of its equity stake where the exchange shares continue to appreciate enabling it naturally to abort its attempted takeover. This may occur when a bidding war erupts that the issuing company does not wish to participate in, or an if a "white knight" moves in and is prepared to pay a significant premium above the issuing company's bid. Alternatively, the issuing company, particularly given its reduced holding costs (at least in nominal coupon terms), can maintain its equity holding in circumstances in which it wishes to continue to pursue the relevant company.

The economic value issues identified have resulted in a number of structural variations in the basic exchangeable structure designed to enhance the application of these formats to finance equity holdings. Some of the mandatory convertible structures described above are attempts to deal with this issue.

In other situations, however, the use of exchangeable debt can limit flexibility. For example, the issue of exchangeable debt may mean that the issuing company cannot divest itself of the borrowed shares. It may still be called upon to deliver the exchange shares to investors wishing to convert under the exchangeable debt structure. This restriction is usually countered by allowing the issuer to retire the bonds (typically at a declining premium) during the life of the transaction.

The major attraction to the use of exchangeable debt to fund equity shareholdings is that takeover activity itself, by definition, causes an increase in volatility and, in the eyes of some investors, in the capital appreciation potential of the underlying shares. Such greater volatility or capital appreciation potential translates into the higher conversion premium or a more significant cost saving to the issuing company. In addition, where the exchange shares themselves are of a large and substantial entity, they may be effectively used as a form of credit enhancement for the underlying issue. This ability for the issuing company to enhance its own access to funding through the use of the exchange shares will prove an attractive feature when the company is smaller or of a lower financial standing than the organization it is seeking to take over.

An example of this type of application is provided by two issues undertaken by finance vehicles associated with Australia's Bond Corporation. The issues are discussed in **Exhibit 10.27**.

---

**Exhibit 10.27**
**Exchangeable Debt Issue —**
**Bond Finance (Europe) Limited Debt Securities Exchangeable into Allied Lyons Shares**

These two deals were launched in March and June 1988, following the purchase by Bond of a substantial stake in Allied Lyons of the UK to fund the acquisition and maintenance of what was described as a "long-term strategic stake" in the British brewing company. The fact that there was substantial takeover speculation surrounding Allied Lyons, and the fact that Allied Lyons itself had no convertible or other equity-linked securities outstanding, contributed to the success of both issues.

The terms of the issue are as follows:

## Issue 1

| | |
|---|---|
| Issuer | Bond Finance (Europe) |
| Guarantor | Bond Corporations Holdings Ltd |
| Amount | £125 million (increased from £100 million) of notes convertible into the stock of Allied Lyons — the shares are held in trust for the bond-holders |
| Maturity | 10 years (due March 30, 1998) |
| Coupon | 6% |
| Issue Price | 100 |
| Conversion Period | From closing date to maturity date. |
| Conversion Premium | Around 17% over the share price at fixing of 362 p, with a conversion price of 420 p (the cap). There is a cash option at the borrower's option. |
| Denomination | £1,000; £10,000 |
| Amortisation | Bullet |
| Put Option | On March 30, 1993, at 127-1/4 (yield to put 10.43%) |
| Call option | From closing at 105, declining by 1% per annum, subject to the 130% rule. |
| Listing | Luxembourg |
| Governing Law | English |
| Commission | 2-1/2% (management and underwriting 1%; selling 1-1/2%). |
| Lead Managers | Merrill Lynch Capital Markets (joint lead), Salomon Brothers (joint books). |

## Issue 2

| | |
|---|---|
| Issuer | Bond Finance (Europe) |
| Guarantor | Bond Corporation Holdings Ltd on a subordinated basis. |
| Amount | £100 million of bonds convertible into shares of Allied Lyons. |
| Maturity | 10 years (due July 6, 1998) |
| Coupon | 6% |
| Issue Price | 100 |
| Conversion Period | The bonds are convertible from 90 days at a price of 485 p with a cash alternative. |
| Conversion Premium | 10.5% |
| Denomination | £1,000 and £5,000 |
| Amortisation | Bullet |
| Put Option | On July 6, 1993 at 127.13 (yield to put 10.41%). |

| Call Option | After four months at 105, decreasing by 1% per annum to par, subject to the 30% rule prior to 1993. |
| Listing | Luxembourg |
| Governing Law | English |
| Commissions | 2-1/2% (management 0.5%; underwriting 0.5%; selling 1-1/2%). |
| Lead Managers | Salomon Brothers (books), Merrill Lynch. |

The rationale behind these two transactions by Bond Corporation was complex. They enabled the Australian corporate to fund its Allied Lyons shareholding on a long-term basis and to lower its funding cost to approximately 1% pa (according to market sources and after taking dividend income into account).

An advantage common to both applications is that where the issuing company holds a substantial stake in the relevant shares, an exchangeable debt issue to fund its holding proves an alternative to an outright sale of the shares. This is because the issuing company can continue to boost its reported earnings by equity accounting or consolidating (if relevant) a pro-rata portion of that company's earnings. The net improvement to the financial position of the company is enhanced by the fact that the cost of funding the equity stake is generally substantially reduced.

For financial accounting purposes, the exchangeable debt is carried on the company's balance sheet as normal borrowing. If the debentures are converted, then the company will report a gain or loss on the sale of the stock to the extent the book value of the debt varies from the book value of the exchange shares. Because the debt is not convertible into the issuing company's shares, the exchangeable debt would never be ordinary share equivalents for purposes of calculating primary and fully diluted earnings per share. In some instances, however, net income may be reduced and the debt may be slightly dilutive in calculating the company's primary and fully diluted earnings per share, if applicable.

### 7.2.5  Exchangeable Debt — Economics

#### 7.2.5.1  Overview

There are two separate aspects to the economics of exchangeable debt securities:

• The pricing of exchangeable debt issues.

- The economics of such a transaction from the perspective of the issuing company, in particular, as a comparison to alternative methods of divestiture or of funding the equity holding.

### 7.2.5.2 Exchangeable Debt — Pricing

The pricing of an exchangeable debt issue is not dissimilar to that of pricing a conventional convertible bond or equity warrants issue. Similar considerations are therefore relevant. However, exchangeable debt issues have a number of special features that must be incorporated in the pricing decision.

A major difference clearly is that the implicit equity option is exercisable into the shares of a company other than that of the issuer. Consequently, the value of the equity option itself will be a function of the capital appreciation potential and price volatility of the exchange shares, rather than the shares of the issuing company.

One must also consider the potential pricing impact of the fact that the issuing company has an equity stake in the company whose shares are subject to the exchange arrangements. For example, the mere fact that the issuing company has acquired an equity stake, thereby putting the company "into play", may in fact alter the price performance and the volatility of the exchange shares. Conversely, where the acquisition of the equity stake is defensive in origin and is designed to protect the share register of the company, the volatility of the exchange shares and its potential price performance may be diminished and this will translate into a lower equity option value. These complex inter-relationships between the acquisition of the equity stake and the value of the exchangeable transaction are important.

There is also a complex interaction between the rationale for the exchangeable debt issue and its pricing. The considerations that determine the trade-off between the exchange premium and the coupon on the exchangeable debt issue are influenced by the motivation for the exchangeable debt issue in the first place.

Where the issue is undertaken with the specific purpose of disposing of an equity stake held by the issuing company, the pricing of the transaction would typically reflect the following considerations:

- The optimal combination of exchange premium and lower interest coupon that maximizes the transaction economics. This will generally dictate the highest possible exchange premium to create the highest possible capital gain on exchange.
- The issuer will not necessarily be interested in either purchasing the shares back or paying the cash equivalent for the shares at the end of the term.
- The economics of such transactions will typically dictate that the issuing company will want the bonds to remain unexchanged for the longest period of time, again dictating a higher exchange premium.

If the rationale for an exchangeable debt issue is to fund an equity stake in a company, the issuer is likely to be motivated by quite different considerations. If the issuing company has acquired the equity stake as part of a takeover or merger strategy, then it will probably have a relatively short-term focus, say, the first 12 to 24 months of the life of the exchangeable bonds. Where the issuing company is seeking to acquire the company in which it has built up an equity stake, then the issuer will be most concerned with reducing holding cost until a takeover can be launched.

Consequently, the issuing company will seek to balance the following considerations:

- The lowest possible interest coupon on the bond.
- An appropriate balance of exchange premium and coupon level, such as to allow the company to issue a sufficient quantity of bonds to fund the required proportion of its equity stake, as well as an exchange premium level that balances the conflicting objectives of the issuer and the investor. For example, the exchange premium may have to be set at the lower end of a possible range to stimulate investors to take a position either in the exchange company, a position in the takeover/merger battle, the currency of the exchange shares, or some combination of these three factors. Conversely, the issuing company will not want to set the exchange premium too low. This is because it will typically seek to repurchase the shares if the investor exercises its exchange rights, and its cost will be determined by the difference between the market price of the shares and the exchange price.
- An additional consideration in pricing exchangeable debt issues is the inclusion of the cash alternative, at the option of the issuer. Effectively, if the issuer chooses to exercise this option, it merely elects to pay a cash equivalent upon surrender of the bond, as opposed to delivering the exchange shares. Practically, this mechanism assumes that the investor would in case if it exercised its exchange option immediately sell the acquired exchange shares at the prevailing market price to realize its capital gain. However, under these circumstances, the investor is deprived of any potential further appreciation in the capital value of the exchange shares subsequent to the exchange. This process of "capping" out the profit to the investor will typically be translated into a lower exchange premium or higher coupon on the exchangeable bond.

### 7.2.5.3 Exchangeable Debt — Economics

The economics of an exchangeable debt transaction relate to the value to the issuing company (in net present value terms) of launching this type of instrument as against an alternative set of transactions, such as straight debt or immediate sale of the shares. The relative economics of exchangeable debt issues differs markedly depending on the type of application.

Where the exchangeable debt transaction is involved in the divestiture of an existing equity holding, the issuing company will be concerned to maximize the value received in net present value terms of the disposition of its shares. Alternatively, where it seeks to fund its equity stake in the exchange company, the issuer will typically be concerned to minimize its holding costs over the life of the transaction.

In both cases, the economic value of the transaction is closely related to the cash-flow consequences of the exchangeable debt issue. The major components of these cash flows include:

- The exchange premium.
- The interest coupon on the exchangeable debt, and particularly how it compares with the normal borrowing cost of the corporation.
- The dividend receipts on the exchange shares, including the dividend growth rate.
- The future value of the exchange shares that will determine whether or not the exchangeable debt securities are converted and if there is a cash option, the repurchase price of the exchange shares to the issuer.
- The tax consequences of the various cash inflows and outflows. They include the tax treatment on the dividend receipts and the interest payable on the exchangeable debt, as well as any tax liability on any capital gain upon exchange (if any), and the timing of any capital gains tax liability.

In this type of transaction, the cash flow consists of proceeds of the issue, the after-tax dividends less the after-tax interest payments, and the cash flow generated by reinvesting funds in the business. The future period cash flow consists of proceeds from the sale of the equity holding less any taxation liability (such as capital gains tax) less the cash needed for the redemption of debt.

The tax position will vary between jurisdictions. Generally, prior to conversion all dividends received by the company on the stock will be taxable (subject to any dividend rebate, dividend received deduction, or any imputed tax credit for taxes already paid on the income being paid out as dividends). The interest payments on the issue of exchangeable debt, as well as any associated borrowing expenses, will be deductible to the issuing company.

Tax treatment in the case of conversion will depend on whether there is a tax on capital gains in the relevant jurisdiction. If the debentures are converted and there is a capital gains tax, then there will usually be a taxable gain or loss for the company to the extent the proceeds of the issue exceed the company's acquisition price in the stock. This tax will only be payable when exchange is effected.

The economics of typical exchangeable debt transactions are set out in **Appendix A,** which provides an analysis of the economics of two transactions. One transaction is where the issuing company seeks to divest itself of its shareholding. The second transaction is an exchangeable debt transaction where the issuing company is seeking to fund its equity stake in a company that it wants to acquire.

### 7.2.6 The Market for Exchangeable Debt[35]

#### 7.2.6.1 Overview

As mentioned above, the first public issue of exchangeable bonds was launched as early as November 1971 by International Paper Company (and was exchangeable into the common stock of CR Bard Inc.). The concept has been used with increasing frequency in recent years. The increased appeal of exchangeable bonds is arguably related to the upsurge in corporate restructuring activity. At least two additional factors had a role as well:

- Closer focus in corporate restructuring on maximizing the financial benefits through the use of financial engineering techniques.
- The changing nature of corporate restructuring activity, which has seen smaller, entrepreneurial corporations become active in takeover and merger activity involving companies often many times their size. This change in the nature of takeover/merger offers has forced the bidding corporations to develop alternative mechanisms for financing equity stakes in target companies.

A major feature of the market is the spread of the concept beyond the US and the Euromarkets to domestic capital markets in both developed and emerging countries. An additional relevant feature is increased experimentation with variations on the basic exchangeable debt concept (see discussion below).

#### 7.2.6.2 Types of Exchangeable Issues

Exchangeable debt issues can be divided into two broad categories: issues launched and offered in the US and issues offered outside the US, primarily in Europe or elsewhere. In the case of the second category of issues, the bonds cannot specifically be offered for sale in the US, as they are not registered pursuant to the requirements of US securities laws. There are a number of

---

[35] For a discussion of the structural features of the market for exchangeable debt, see Das, Satyajit "Exchangeable Debt" (Winter 1989) *Journal of International Securities Markets* (Winter 1989) vol. 3 409-425; and (Spring 1990) vol. 4 91-98; Nizzola, Adrian (August 1988) "An Analysis of Exchangeable Bond Issues" unpublished research paper submitted in connection with a course on Mergers and Acquisitions: Corporate Restructuring conducted at Macquarie University, Sydney, Australia.

structural differences between the two categories of exchangeable debt issues which merit comment. The main areas of difference include:

- **Issuer** — The typical issuer of US exchangeable bonds is generally incorporated in the United States and a company of substance thereby eliminating the requirement for a guarantee. In contrast, in many of the European issues, the issuer is a wholly owned subsidiary of the guarantor, generally a finance company incorporated in a tax haven. This requires the on-lending of funds from the issuer to the guarantor or some other subsidiary of the guarantor. In a few cases, the issuing vehicle is only 50%-owned by the guarantor or an associated company. This structure was designed to avoid consolidating the debt raised through the exchangeable issue, on the guaranteeing group's balance sheet.
- **Form and denomination and status** — US exchangeable issues are launched in denominations of US$1,000 in registered form. The rights of the bond-holders are generally subordinated to senior debt of the issuer. European exchangeable bonds are issued in bearer form and in some cases in registered form, in denominations of 1,000, 5,000, or 10,000 currency units (for example, US$, £, and so on). In contrast to US exchangeable bonds, the status of obligations of a European issuer varies across individual transactions. In the case of exchangeable bonds, where the issue was guaranteed, the bonds and coupons constitute either direct, unsecured (except in some cases for the exchange rights) unsubordinated obligations of the issuer, or, direct, unsecured obligations of the issuer, subordinated to senior debt.
- **Exchange rights** — US issues are generally exchangeable into common stock of US publicly listed companies owned by the issuer. In contrast, in European exchangeable issues the exchange property involves the ordinary shares of public companies listed in the US, UK, Australia, and other countries. In European exchangeable deals, the issuing company is not necessarily the owner of the exchange shares. This absence of requirement of ownership is particularly useful where, for example, the transfer costs (including brokerage and stamp duty) or the tax consequences of any transfer from the company owning the shares to the issuer, are significant. Other advantages include avoiding the administrative problems of running funds through the issuer simultaneously with drawdown of the issue in order to pay other associated companies for the transfer of the shares. It is typical for both US and European exchangeable bonds to be exchangeable by the bond-holder generally at any time prior to maturity subject to any option reserved by the issuer to pay cash.
- **Cash options** — The option to pay cash for or purchase the exchange shares is generally either set at the market value of the shares at the time they are

delivered for exchange or at the exchange price for the shares. The practical distinction between paying the market price or the exchange price for the exchange shares is firstly that in the latter case the payout on the share by the issuer is known and secondly there is no upside for the bond-holder if the market price exceeds the exchange price. When the market price is opted for, however, the opportunity for the bond-holder to profit from any move in the market price above the exchange shares is subject to the issuer's option to force redemption, although possibly at a premium (see below). The option for the issuer not to provide the shares but to pay cash instead was not historically a typical provision of US exchangeable transactions, although it has become increasingly common. However, where it did exist, the right was to pay the price prevailing on the appropriate stock market at the time of exchange. In some European issues, in the event of the delivery or transfer of the exchange shares to the bond-holder being unlawful, the issuer was required to pay either:

– The cash equivalent of the exchange price;
– The current market value; or
– The principal amount of the bond, plus or minus any excess or shortfall between the principal amount of the bond and the market price of the exchange shares.

There are a number of unique features common to some US issues. In addition to the issuer's option to pay cash instead of providing shares in exchange, there is the option to provide equity in the issuer. Hence, the instrument could be categorized as a straight bond, an exchangeable bond, or a convertible bond, in each case at the option of the issuer. In some US transactions the issuer reserved the right to increase the coupon if it thought it would discourage exchange and it was in the best interest of the issuer. In another variation, the issue is not only secured against the exchange shares, but in addition the repayment of the first six interest payments are secured by using a portion of the gross proceeds of the issue to purchase US government securities with the same maturity as the interest payment.

• **Security and custody** — The security and custody arrangements with respect to the exchange shares can be categorized into three main classes. The shares can be either:

– Held in trust by a trustee for the benefit of the bond-holders in accordance with the terms of a deed of trust;
– Held in escrow or in custody under the terms of an escrow agreement; or
– The owner of the exchange shares can undertake to hold the required number of securities free and clear from any encumbrance.

In US exchangeable issues, the mechanics of exchange are generally such that the title to the shares available for exchange did not pass from the issuer to, say, for example, the escrow or custody agent. The shares are merely deposited prior to the issue with an escrow agent who holds them to the issuer's order to be released only on specified circumstances. Such circumstances include, for example, the surrender of the bond with the escrow agent for exchange into the exchange shares. Title to the securities did not pass and the shares were not secured for the benefit of the debenture holders. In a number of European exchangeable issues, the shares are transferred to the trustee to effectively secure or collateralize the issue. Where the obligations of the issuer are secured against the exchange shares, the issuer will have recourse in the event of default, albeit through the trustee to the exchange property. In some European issues, the issuer does not own the exchange shares that were beneficially owned by wholly owned subsidiaries of the guarantor. In order to provide some comfort to bond-holders that the necessary exchange shares would be available on surrender of the bond, the issuer is given an irrevocable option by the beneficial owners to purchase the exchange shares at the exchange price. This is automatically exercised each time a bond was surrendered for exchange.

• **Redemption features** — Unlike their European counterparts, the US issues often provide some form of mandatory redemption of the bonds or a sinking fund prior to maturity. The mechanics of the sinking fund were basically the same, requiring annual redemption of either a fixed amount or a percentage of the principal sufficient to redeem between 50% and 75% of the issue prior to final maturity. Any bonds exchanged, otherwise redeemed or acquired by the issuer could be credited into the fund. In all cases, there was no restriction on the purchase of the bonds by the issuer in the open market. Both European and US exchangeable issues provide the issuer with the option to redeem some or all of the bonds after a given point in time, generally three years after the issue, at declining premiums. In most cases, the issuer is also entitled to force redemption (usually at a premium) of all or some of the bonds prior to that if either:

  – The value of the shares has risen above a given level relative to the exchange price, generally between 130% and 150%;
  – There was a change in the tax laws affecting the issuer; or
  – In the event of a takeover offer for the exchange shares.

  There are a number of significant points of distinction between US and European exchangeable issues in the context of redemption of the bonds:

  1. In relation to US issues, the issuer can redeem all or part of the bonds, whereas in European issues, at least by non-US issuers, it is typical that the issuer could redeem all but not some of the bonds.
  2. The option for the issuer to redeem in whole or in part in the event of a takeover offer for the exchange shares tends also to be unique to US issuers. This option enables the issuer to accept any offer for the exchange shares by requiring it to redeem the appropriate number of

bonds (at par or at a premium, depending upon the issue). This is subject, however, to the holder's right to exchange the bond within a given period of time from the notice of redemption (generally 15 days). This provision means that any benefit flowing from a takeover offer (where the price offered exceeded the redemption premium on the bond multiplied by the exchange price) was available to the issuer and not the bond-holder.

- **Corporate restructuring events** — In the event of a takeover offer for the exchange company, most of the European issuers reserve the right to accept or reject the offer. Any securities, cash or other consideration, received for the exchange shares become available to the bond-holder on exchange in lieu of the shares. This is to be compared with US issues, which require the issuer to redeem the bonds, possibly at a premium, before being entitled to tender the equivalent number of exchange shares into the offer. Significantly, some European issues go further than simply giving the issuer the option to accept or reject any takeover offer by specifying that in doing so, the issuer may act contrary to the best interests of the bond-holders. In most European exchangeable issues the issuer is entitled to merge or consolidate with, and, in some cases, sell substantially all of its assets to another company on certain provisos, the principal one being that the new entity assumes the issuer's obligations. In US issues, the bond-holder is given certain rights in the event either of the merger, consolidation, or sale of substantially all of the assets of the exchange company. Basically, the bond-holder is treated as if he or she held the exchange shares to which he or she was entitled prior to the transaction in question. The investor would then on exchange receive the number of shares in the new corporation it would have received if it held the exchange shares at the time of the merger, consolidation, or sale.
- **Rights of issuers and bond-holders** — In both US and European exchangeable issues, the issuer was entitled to all cash dividends paid on the exchange shares, interest earned on any debt securities held as exchange property, and to vote on the exchange shares. In voting on the shares, some issues included the caveat that in doing so the issuer or guarantor (as appropriate) may act contrary to the best interests of the bond-holder. In the case of bonus issues by the exchange company, rather than have the bonus shares added to the shares available for exchange as in European issues, the exchange premium in US issues is proportionally adjusted. Under this mechanism, there is no assurance at the time of exchange that the issuer will have the additional shares. As there is no prohibition on the issuer dealing with these bonus shares, one assumes that the issuer could deal with those shares as it wished. In the event of a transferable rights issue by the exchange company, the typical provision in US exchangeable issues is that the issuer or escrow agent must sell his or her rights for cash and invest the proceeds

at the issuer's direction. Any interest received was for the issuer's account. In the event of a nontransferable rights issue, however, the escrow agent was generally required to distribute the rights pro-rata to the bond-holders at the time of exchange. In the event of a rights issue by the exchange company, the typical UK or Australian issuer is required to sell or procure the sale of sufficient rights to enable the purchase of the balance. The purchased rights are then included as exchange property. In the event of a bonus issue, the bonus shares are simply added to the exchange property. The issuer, guarantor, or subsidiary are in all cases entitled to purchase the bonds on the market and at any price. In the case of US-based issues of European exchangeable issues, the rights of the issuer in the event of a bonus or rights issue followed similar lines to US issues. As far as bond-holders' rights are concerned, US and European exchangeable issues appoint either a trustee or an escrow or custody agent. The significant distinction between the two is that the escrow agent is likely to be the agent of the issuer and not the bond-holder. A trustee, however, is the representative of the bond-holders and in the case of secured issues, of the issuer to the extent beneficial title in the exchange shares is retained by the issuer.

### 7.2.6.3  Structural Variations

Debt with attached but detachable equity warrants is one alternative to exchangeable debt securities. The sale of units of debt and separate exchange warrants achieves the benefits of the standard exchangeable structure with a few significant differences.

The primary difference derives from the fact that exercise of the warrants results in a change of ownership of the relevant equity securities from the divesting corporation to the investor, and creates an additional cash inflow. However, the original debt is not extinguished and the units of debt are still required to be redeemed. Consequently, the future cash flow is similar to the sell debt today/future sale of equity holding option; that is, it consists of the proceeds of the sale, less any tax liability, less the cash needed for the redemption of debt.

The appeal of debt with equity warrants will depend on the relative pricing of the exchangeable debt and debt-cum-equity warrant alternatives. The debt-cum-equity warrants option could also be attractive where the divesting corporation preferred to borrow funds for a known period at a lower interest rate than would be required for a straight debt issue of the same maturity.

**Exhibit 10.28** sets out the structure of an issue by a company associated with Elders IXL, entailing the issue of bonds in combination with warrants exchangeable into the shares of Goodman Fielder Wattie Ltd, in which Elders-IXL has a substantial shareholding.

**Exhibit 10.28**
**Exchangeable Warrants Transaction**

Elders-IXL (Elders), a major Australian industrial, mining, and food conglomerate, held a 10.8% shareholding in Goodman Fielder Wattie (GFW). Elders entered into the following multi-part structure designed to lower the cost of financing its shareholding in GFW.[36]

The structure involved a series of transactions:

1. Long Term Bond Trust (LTBT), a special purpose vehicle was used to borrows from a group of bank on the following terms:

   | | |
   |---|---|
   | Facility Type | Medium-term loan |
   | Amount | US$260 million |
   | Term | 6 years |
   | Interest Rate | LIBOR plus 50 bps |
   | Repayment | Bullet |
   | Availability | 3 days after signing |
   | Participation Fee | 0.125% flat |
   | Lead Manager | Bankers Trust |

2. The loan was secured by a charge over GFW shares, as well as an indirect guarantee by Elders-IXL Ltd via its guarantee of Elders-IXL Treasury (Aust) Ltd.
3. LTBT uses the loan proceed to purchase 1,050 FRNs issued by Avilock Ltd (Avilock), a special-purpose vehicle company, established to acquire and hold GFW shares for Elders. Each FRN had a face value of US$247,619.05 bearing a coupon of LIBOR plus 51 bps.
4. Avilock issues options over approximately 105 million GFW shares it holds to investors at a strike price of A$3.07, an expiry date of six years and receives, in return, a premium of 3% flat.
5. Elders places its GFW shares in Avilock and in return, Avilock takes up U$260 million of FRNs issued by Elders-IXL Treasury (Aust) Ltd (Elders' borrowing vehicle, guaranteed by Elders-IXL Ltd. These bonds will attract interest at around LIBOR minus 250 bps (reportedly)).

The transaction is set out in the attached diagram.

---

[36] See (November 26, 1988) *International Financing Review* Issue 752 3826.

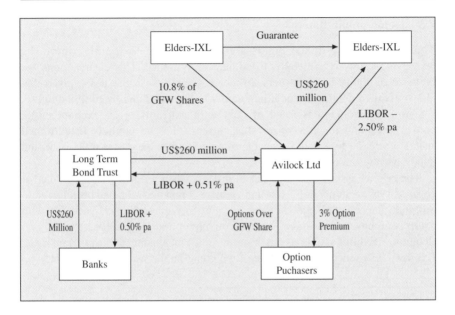

Credit Suisse First Boston (CSFB) initially applied the exchangeable principle to two preferred issues in 1985 for Jardine Matheson and News Corporation. The preferred stock (150,000 shares for Jardine and 200,000 for News Corporation) were exercisable, respectively, into the ordinary shares of Hong Kong Land and Reuters, in which the issuers had substantial shareholdings.

The use of preference capital as the host debt achieves a number of objectives. The main benefit of exchangeable preferred shares over ordinary exchangeable debt is its balance sheet treatment. As liabilities, straight exchangeable bonds can either be senior or subordinated debt. Exchangeable preferred shares create a class of equity ranking after debt and above common shares. Where the issuer issues its preference shares through a subsidiary, so the equity on consolidation into the group appears as minority interests on the balance sheet. The parent company guarantees the issue on a subordinated basis, preserving its status as nominal equity.

Preferred share issues also may have tax advantages. Some issues have been undertaken through a subsidiary based in a tax-advantaged jurisdictions to enable investors to receive preferred dividends free of withholding tax.

One of the major difficulties with exchangeable debt is that conversion or exercise of the warrants cannot be forced, except in very restricted circumstances. This necessarily means that the corporation seeking to divest itself of its equity holdings may not, primarily through a loss of market value of that equity holding, achieve its sale objective. Mandatory conversion structures can be incorporated in the exchangeable concept to reduce this risk.

## 7.3    Going-public Bonds

Traditional equity-linked bonds are exchangeable for equity where the underlying equity is, generally, listed and freely traded. This clearly limits the universe of equity-linked issuers. In recent years, a structure has evolved that allows issue of debt convertible into equity to be issued and listed in the future.

The basic concept is issue of debt with warrants or an exchangeable/ convertible bond for a company that currently has no publicly listed/traded shares where the host debt is capable of exercise into the equity upon issue and listing usually through an IPO.

The original issues were undertaken in 1988 when following the stock market crash of 1987, a number of Swiss and German companies who had been forced to postpone planned public flotation due to equity market conditions issued debt with equity warrants. The warrants were effectively options to purchase shares upon flotation.[37] **Exhibit 10.29** sets out the terms of a typical going public warrant issue. **Exhibit 10.30** sets out the structure of the going-public warrant transaction.

---

**Exhibit 10.29**
**Going-public Warrant Issue**

| | |
|---|---|
| Issuer | ABS Pumpen AG |
| Amount | SFR 25 million with going public option coupons. |
| Maturity | 5 years (due September 9, 1993) |
| Coupon | 3.25% pa payable annually |
| Issue Price | 100% (plus 0.30% Federal stamp duty) |
| Warrants | Each note is issued with one going-public option coupon. If the borrower goes public during the life of the bonds the coupon can be exchanged for equity warrants allowing the purchase of at least DM 37,000 of common or priority shares of AB Pumpen AG. |
| Redemption | At 110.80% to yield 5.2% if the option coupon has not been exchanged or if the going public has not taken place. At par if the going-public option coupon has been exchanged for warrants. |
| Warrant Coverage | 60% |
| Exercise Period | 2 years after going public |
| Exercise Price | Going public price (no premium) |
| Denominations | SFR 50,000 |

---

[37]    See "Going Public Privately — The German Way" (May 1989) *Corporate Finance* 51.

Commissions          1.75%
Amortisation         Bullet
Call Option          None — except in the event that the German
                     withholding tax on investment income is above 10%.
                     If this is the case, the borrower has the right to call
                     the transaction at par as from August 25, 1989 and on
                     any coupon payment date.
Listing              None
Lead Manager         Bank Julius Baer

*Source:* (August 27, 1988) International Financing Review Issue 739.

**Exhibit 10.30**
**Structure Of Going-public Warrant Issue**

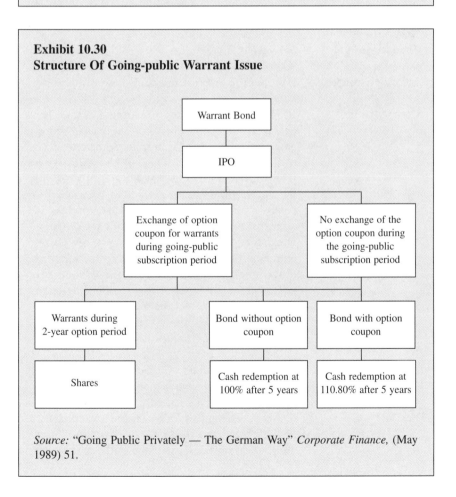

*Source:* "Going Public Privately — The German Way" *Corporate Finance,* (May 1989) 51.

The structure subsequently re-emerged in Asia in the period 1993 to 1995 in the form of a going-public exchangeable or convertible security as a form of pre-initial public offering (IPO) finance. The terms of a typical transaction are set out in **Exhibit 10.31**. There are some differences between the two structures but the essential dynamics are similar.

---

**Exhibit 10.31**
**Going-public Exchangeable Note — Indicative Terms and Conditions**

| | |
|---|---|
| Issuer | [Party requiring funds] |
| Guarantor | Creditworthy guarantor |
| Security | Unsecured [and subordinated (if required)] obligation of issuer and guarantor |
| Issue Size | [Up to US$250 million] |
| Final Maturity | 3-5 years |
| Issue Price | 100% |
| Indicative Coupon | [Discount to interest rate and close to dividend rate.] |
| Complying IPO | It is the current intention of the issuer [or guarantor] to procurean IPO of [designated entity] on or before [2 to 3] years from the date of issue of the Notes. Such an IPO will be a complying IPO; namely, an IPO by way of offer of shares to the public for subscription and/or purchase for cash (with warrants or other securities, if appropriate) on a specified stock exchange meeting certain conditions relating to offer size, minimum distribution, managers, marketing, and other conditions. However, the issuer [or guarantor] is not obliged to effect an IPO or to ensure that an IPO will be a complying IPO and there can be no assurance that an IPO will occur on or before [2 to 3] years from the date of issue of the Notes. |
| IPO Exchange | Upon the occurrence of a Complying IPO, each Note will be exchangeable on a mandatory basis for the shares of the issued under the complying IPO at a discount of [5 to 15]% discount to the IPO price within a [6- to 12- month] period after the IPO. Mandatory exchange will occur at the |

---

| | |
|---|---|
| Optional Exchange | end of this [6-to-12] month period. In the event that an IPO Exchange is not effected as a result of the nonoccurrence of an IPO within the set period for an IPO or the IPO is not a complying IPO, the noteholders have the right, at their option, to exchange the Notes into the ordinary shares of [designated entity] at a price based on [ ] times audited earning on a fully diluted basis. |
| Put Option | In the event that the IPO Exchange is not effected as a result of the nonoccurrence of an IPO within the set period for an IPO or the IPO is not a complying IPO and the optional exchange is not effected, the noteholders have the right, at their option, to require the issuer to repurchase the Notes at the corresponding price plus accrued interest: |
| | Date      Put Price |
| | [Dates]      [Put prices are set at a premium to provide investors with a return comparable to debt rates at the time of issue.] |
| Listing | [Optional] |

The attraction for issuers is:

• The capacity to access quasi-equity capital without the need to undertake the IPO until market conditions are more favorable. This allows significant value capture where the market value of the firm improves and can be captured through the deferred public offering.
• The capacity to access low coupon funding prior to the IPO.
• Tax deductibility of interest payments.
• The exposure to potential investors through the going public transaction that may facilitate the share issue when undertaken.

The attraction for investors is the capacity to obtain equity exposure to companies on a debt-protected basis. The terms of the going-public typically also offer significant economic incentives to the investor allowing them to obtain access to the IPO on preferential terms or access to the underlying equity on attractive terms.

A similar product that has emerged in the US domestic market combines the features of a bridge loan to a company expecting to complete an IPO in the near future. An example is the BT.Alex Brown product Equity-linked Venture Investment Securities (ELVIS). The structure entails the issue by the borrower |of high-yield bonds with equity warrants. The coupon steps-up after a set period in the event that the issuer fails to undertake the planned IPO. The coupon steps-up at regular intervals until maturity if the IPO is not effected. The structure is designed to be part of the final round of venture capital funding prior to an IPO. The issuer gains cheaper financing and limits the equity appreciation potential of the venture capitalist (through the number of equity warrants issued). Investors gain access to the company pre-IPO but are able to be compensated by the higher coupon in case of any delay in the IPO and also benefits from the potential liquidity on the bridge funding because of the tradeable instrument used.[38]

In an interesting variation on the basic structure of going-public bonds, Vivendi, an European company, issued a convertible that was capable of conversion into either *existing* shares of the issuer or *news* shares of an IPO of Vivendi Environnement (if this takes place).[39] The issue arranged by SG and Goldman Sachs was for Euro 2.6 billion (plus an over allotment option of Euro 400 million) for a term of just under six years. The issue had a coupon of 1.50% pa and was redeemable at a premium (in the case of nonconversion) to yield around 2.54% pa (a yield about 79 bps pa below French OATS). The special aspect of the issue was the conversion option. The convertible bonds allowed the investor to convert into the following securities:

- If the IPO of Vivendi Environnement occurs during the term of the bond, then investors have the option of converting the bonds into the IPO shares at a 5.00% discount to the offering price.
- If the IPO does not take place or even if it does take place, then investors have the option of converting the bonds into Vivendi shares at an issue premium of 29.1% to the price of the stock at the time of issue.

The dual option embedded within the structure provided the investor with an interesting play on both the share price performance of the issuer or the IPO.

---

[38] See Rutter, James "Crossing Capital Market Volatility" (July 1998) *Euromoney* 140-142.

[39] See "Vivendi Enters The Record Books" (April 17, 1999) *International Financing Review* Issue 1279 96.

## 7.4  Synthetic Conversions

Synthetic convertibles entails issues of securities convertible into the ordinary shares of the issuer where the issuer hedges the embedded equity option in order to avoid the impact of equity dilution. The structure can be illustrated with an example.

In 1998, Nestlé undertook a 7-year US$250 million synthetic convertible issue.[40] The issue was undertaken by Nestlé's Australian subsidiary. The issue was structured as a normal convertible with the investor able to convert the bond into Nestlé shares. The embedded equity option reduced the interest cost of the structure to 1.50% pa (well below prevailing market interest rates). The distinguishing feature of the structure was that the issuer entered into a hedging arrangement for the equity option with the arranger of the convertible (Credit Suisse First Boston (CSFB)). Under the terms of the hedge, CSFB would supply the stock to meet the requirement for Nestlé shares where investors exercise their conversion option under the bond. In effect, Nestlé has purchased a call option on its own stock from CSFB to hedge the equity dilution risk on the convertible. CSFB delta hedges the exposure under the transaction.

The effect of the transaction is to allow Nestlé to be able to meet investor demand for a convertible bond without the need to issue additional equity. The hedging arrangement entails CSFB purchasing stock in the market and delivering it to Nestlé to ensure any conversion and therefore issue of equity is exactly offset by the corresponding reduction of shares on issue. The transaction enabled Nestlé to a lower its cost of funding without incurring any equity dilution risk.

## 7.5  Synthetic Equity Conversions

In a number of cases the option of exchange into equity, either currently or at some time in the future, is not available. This may reflect the nature of the entity and its constitution that prevents issue of equity. The concept of a synthetic equity conversion represents an attempt to deal with this problem.

The structure is best illustrated with an example. In 1995, Rabobank, the Dutch bank, launched a novel Dutch guilder denominated convertible that uses a stock index for conversion. The structure was necessitated by the fact that the issuer was a joint stock cooperative society with individual Rabobanks being members making conversion into the bank's own stock impracticable. The structure uses the Top Five Dutch Index that is compiled by the European Option Exchange and relates to the five largest corporations. The terms of the issue are summarized in **Exhibit 10.32**

---

[40]  See "Synthetic Convertible Bonds" (March 1999) *Global Finance* at 19.

**Exhibit 10.32**
**Synthetic Equity Convertible Structure**

| | |
|---|---|
| Issuer | Rabobank Netherlands |
| Amount | G200 million of convertible senior bonds |
| Maturity | 10 years (due January 23, 2006) |
| Coupon | 4.25% payable annually |
| Issue Price | 102% |
| Conversion | The bonds are convertible into the weighted Top Five Dutch Index that is made up of shares from Azko, Royal Dutch, Unilever, KLM, and Philips. Investors have the right to seek redemption in the form of cash settlement or share delivery. |
| Conversion Ratio | 1,000 divided by the strike price of Dfl 980 |
| Conversion Price | Dfl 980, corresponding to a 20% premium |
| Conversion Date | January 23, 2006 |
| Amortisation | Bullet |
| Call Option | For tax reasons |
| Listing | Amsterdam SE |
| Lead Manager | Rabo Securities |

*Source: International Financing Review* Issue 1112 (December 16, 1995): 92.

The convertible is in a sense indistinguishable from the equity index-linked structured notes discussed in Chapter 11. The sole difference is the investor's right to seek redemption in cash or through delivery of shares.

An alternative form of synthetic equity has been used in Australia. The transaction involved the issue of primary capital notes or performance-linked notes primarily by building societies. These institutions are mutual in nature and under their charter are unable to issue. The primary capital or performance notes were cash-settled instruments where the payoff was linked to the financial performance of the issuer as measured by a series of financial statement-based indicia. The investor traded off this participation in the financial performance of the issuer for a lower coupon just as in the case of a convertible. The lack of transparency and the indirect nature of the participation in the underlying equity values prevented these structures from gaining in popularity.

## 8.   Embedded Debt Optionality — Puttable Convertibles

The concept of debt options embedded in an equity-linked structure is evident in a variety of structures. A very common structure entails the incorporation of a put option in the convertible allowing the investor to redeem the bond prior to maturity. The put structure generally entails a put at a premium to the par value of the bond. This is designed to provide an enhanced return to the investor closer to the yield to maturity on a comparable bond for the term to put. **Exhibit 10.33** sets out an example of the typical terms and conditions of a premium put convertible.

---

**Exhibit 10.33**
**Puttable Convertible Structure**

| | |
|---|---|
| Issuer | ABC Company Ltd |
| Amount | US$250 million |
| Maturity | 15 years |
| Coupon | 5.75% pa payable annually |
| Conversion Premium | 18-22% |
| Investor Put Option | On the fifth anniversary at 119.45% of face value to yield approximately 9% pa. |
| Early Redemption | Issuer may redeem the bonds: |
| | 1. At any time at a price of 105% of par value if redeemed prior to the first coupon date and declining by 1% thereafter on each coupon date to par value on the fifth coupon date if the price of the issuer's shares trade at 130% of the conversion price for specified period. |
| | 2. At any time for tax reasons at par plus accrued interest. |
| Commissions | 2.50% |
| Status | Subordinated |
| Listing | London or Luxembourg |

---

The premium put structure seeks to address the following issues:
- The investor sacrifices interest income in return for the equity option embedded in the note. The failure of the underlying equity to increase in value may significantly lower the effective return over the investor's holding period.
- Underperformance of the equity (either through firm-specific or market-wide factors) may decrease the equity content leading the convertible to trade at a discount, impede liquidity, and result in capital losses to the investor.
- The lower coupon on equity-linked structures increases the exposure to increases in interest rates.

The premium structure enhances the attractiveness of the convertible issue by reducing the sensitivity of the value of the security to rises in rates, as well as allowing the preservation of the capital value where the equity underperforms expectations.

From the viewpoint of the issuer, the inclusion of the put allows access to equity markets under difficult conditions such as an environment of rising interest rates and flat equity values. This is because the embedded put mitigates the investor's risk in these conditions. In the context of an individual issuer, the inclusion of the put will generally allow increased size of issue, as well as an increase in the nominal maturity of the structure.

The risk of the put is that the issuer may face a substantial refinancing risk as at the put date. This risk became apparent in relation to a number of UK issuers whose premium put convertibles were put back under the terms of the issue following the October 1987 stock market crash and the resultant decrease in equity prices. Similar difficulties were experienced with emerging market convertible issuers in 1997 and 1998 as the global monetary crisis led to falls in equity prices prompting investors to exercise the put options to redeem their investment. These exceptional situations served to highlight the difficulties created by circumstances outside the control of the issuer under this format. The presence of this risk has prompted, for example, the requirement by accountants to provide for the accreted value of the put option.

In an effort to reduce the risk of the put, a flexible put format structure has evolved. This structure has generally found favor with issuers and will generally avoid the need to provide for the put in the early life of the issue. The flexible put is designed to preserve the benefit of the puttable structure (low cost, higher conversion premium, and broader investor distribution) while limiting the risk of nonconversion.

The structure entails a put at, say, year 5 (of a 15-year issue) at a premium. However, the issuer would be granted the capacity to alter the structure, in terms of modifications or extra rights, prior to the put date. These changes would economically be utilized if the risk of nonconversion and exercise of the put increases. These rights include:

- Leave the issue terms unaltered.
- Activate a second premium put at, say, year 10 or a third premium put at maturity.
- Allow setting of the yield (effectively embedded in the premium) at the second or third put dates at a level designed to provide a strong economic incentive to defer redemption. The alteration of yield is usually constrained by a provision that the yield cannot be dropped below the original coupon level.
- Increase the interest rate on the convertible from year 5 onwards.

- To resell any convertible put as at the put date if economically viable through a dealer/investment bank.
- To restrict or abolish the issuer's forced conversion right (incorporated in the call) to reflect any new put option granted and/or to enhance the remaining equity option value in the security.

The range of modification rights is designed to provide a flexible range of alternatives for the issuer to provide economic incentives against redemption via the premium put. The structure focuses on:

- Providing the investor with additional income by increasing the coupon.
- Grant of extra redemption rights at levels to include extra capital gain guarantees (the premium on the put).
- Increase the equity option value by limiting the forced conversion rights of the issuer.

The economic effects of the flexible put structure can be considered with an example in **Exhibit 10.34**.

---

**Exhibit 10.34**
**Flexible Puttable Convertible Structure Economics**

Assume a convertible with the following characteristics:

| | |
|---|---|
| Maturity | 15 years |
| Coupon | 6% pa |
| Conversion Premium | 15% |
| Initial Put Yield (after 5 years) | 10.5% pa (put price 127.75%) |

The investor is assumed to exercise the put if the intrinsic value of the convertible as restructured exceeds the relevant put price. The economics of the put option can be gauged from the annual price increase in the underlying shares required to avoid put risk or redemption.

| Scenario | Annual Price Increase Required to Avoid Put Risk/Redemption (% pa) |
|---|---|
| A. Issuer retains the initial 5-year put and does not exercise any further rights. | 7.99 |
| B. Issuer grants another put option after 10 years at a price of 173.46 (10.50% pa yield). | 7.15 |

**Exhibit 10.34 (cont.)**

| Scenario | Annual Price Increase Required to Avoid Put Risk/Redemption (% pa) |
| --- | --- |
| C. As with B above, except issuer pays the put yield from year 5 annually by way of a higher coupon, thereby freezing the put price at 127.75. | 3.92 |
| D. Issuer grants a put option at year 10 at 127.75 and pays a higher coupon annually from year 5. | 2.60 |
| E. Issuer grants a put option at year 10 at 127.75 and foregoes three years of call options with no increased coupon. | 2.60 |

The structure of payoffs from the flexible put structure compares with the required share price appreciation under a nonputtable convertible issue on similar terms of around 0.94% pa.

This illustrates that the flexible put structure can be used to reduce its exposure to the put over the 15-year term of the issue. This reduction is achieved at the cost of increased interest cost or higher put price.

## 9.  Embedded Structured Optionality

The concept of exotic option embedded notes is explored in detail in Chapter 15. There have, however, been a number of issue of equity-linked notes exchangeable into the equity securities of an issuer where the concept of the highly structured optionality, including incorporation of exotic options, has been creatively deployed. The primary objective has been the alteration of the risk-reward balance as between the issuer and the investor. The structures are best illustrated via examples of transactions undertaken by Roche in the period 1991 to 1994, and a similar transaction for Benetton in 1993.

**Exhibit 10.35** sets out the structure of the debt with bull spread warrants issue undertaken by Roche in 1991. **Exhibit 10.36** sets out the payoff to the investor under the structure. The issue was exercisable into existing Roche bearer shares.[41]

---

[41]  See "Dashing Debut Offering From Roche" (May 1991) *Corporate Finance* 6-8; Chew, Lilian "SBC's Roche Prescription" (May 1991) *Risk* 4.

**Exhibit 10.35**
**Debt with Bull Call Equity Warrants — Structure**

In 1991, the Swiss pharmaceutical company Roche issued the following issue to refinance part of a US$2 billion loan used in connection with the acquisition of a bio-technology company Genetech. The issue terms were as follows:

| | |
|---|---|
| Amount | US$1 billion |
| Maturity | 10 years |
| Coupon | 3.50% pa payable annually |
| Equity Warrant Structure | Each US$10,000 bond was issued with 73 bull spread warrants with an expiry date of 3 years. The warrants will pay as follows on exercise: |

1. If the closing price of Roche bearer shares is less than or equal to Swfr7,000, the investors will receive Swfr7,000; or
2. If the closing price of Roche bearer shares is above Swfr7,000, the investor receives 1 bearer share or at Roche's option Swfr10,000.

Roche Share Price
(at issue date)                Swfr7,490

**Exhibit 10.36**
**Bull Call Equity Warrants — Return Profile**

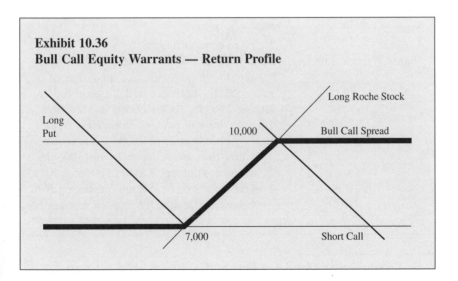

The issue entails the investors receiving equity participation in a highly structured form. The investor is effectively purchasing a put at Swfr7,000 and selling a call at Swfr10,000 on the underlying equity combined with a purchase of the underlying equity itself. The return on the equity warrants is as follows:

• If Roche share prices fall, the investor will exercise the put option at Swfr7,000 assuring a return on investment of around 7.80%.
• If Roche share prices rise, then the issuer will exercise its option to pay the investor out at Swfr10,000 capping the investor return at 9.9%.

The attraction to the issuer of the structure was the lower equity content required compared to a more traditional equity warrants transaction. The investor demand was primarily derived from Swiss investors seeking returns above minimum legal investment returns while creating a degree of equity exposure to Roche.

**Exhibit 10.37** sets out the 1993 transaction entailing the issue of debt with knock-out warrants. **Exhibit 10.38** sets out the payoff to the investor of this structure.[42]

---

**Exhibit 10.37**
**Debt with Knockout Equity Warrants — Structure (1)**

In 1993, the Swiss pharmaceutical company Roche undertook another issue to refinance part of a US$2 billion loan used in connection with the acquisition of a bio-technology company Genetech. The issue terms were as follows:

| | |
|---|---|
| Amount | US$1 billion |
| Maturity | 7 years |
| Coupon | 2.75% pa payable annually |
| Equity Warrant Structure | Each US$10,000 bond was issued with 46 knockout warrants with an expiry date of 3 years. Sixty warrants will be required to acquire 1 Roche genussscheine in May 1996. The warrants will pay as follows on exercise: |
| | 1. If the closing price of Roche genussscheine is less than or equal to Swfr4,500, the investors will receive Swfr4,500; or |
| | 2. If the closing price of Roche genussscheine is above Swfr4,500, the investor receives 1 |

---

42  See Cooper, Graham "Knock Out Drug Issue" (May 1993) *Risk* vol. 6 no. 5 6-7.

genussscheine or at Roche's option
Swfr6,000. If the underlying genussscheine
reaches Swfr5,000 during the 3-year life of
the warrant, then 1 above is knocked out.

Roche Genussscheine
Price (at issue date)                Swfr4,100

**Exhibit 10.38**
**Knockout Equity Warrants — Return Profile (1)**

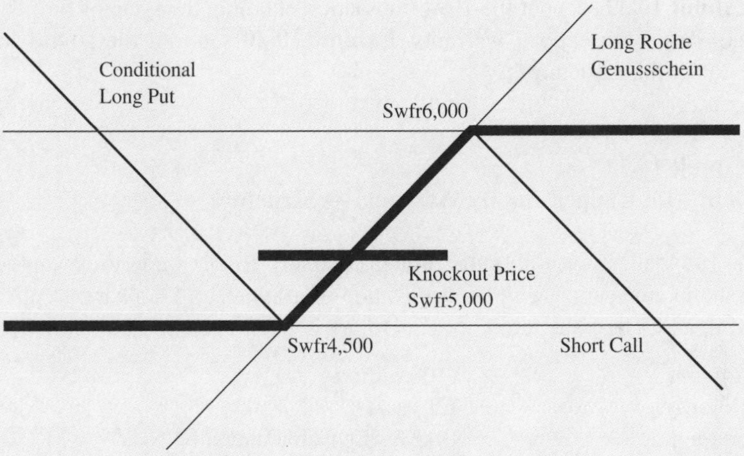

The structure is similar to the first transaction with the added advantage to Roche that in the event that the equity securities had risen by 25% the put feature effective becomes de-activated. The inclusion of the knockout put, in preference to the conventional put used in the first transaction, effectively lowered its cost allowing the investor a lower cost entry into the warrants.

The issuer interest was driven by the desire to control the equity cost of the issue as in the first transaction while allowing access to medium-term funding at low coupon costs. The effective equity coverage of the issue was around 21% of issue value. The issue cost is capable of being further reduced if the equity securities increase in value above the call price of Swfr6,000. This reduction in cost would be achieved by Roche selling equity in the market at a higher price and using the proceeds to pay out the warrant holders at the capped payout level.

The investor demand, as with the first structure, was predominantly conservative Swiss holders of Roche equity switching from the underlying equity to a less risky structure of equity exposure. The issue also appealed to institutional investors required to achieve a minimum return on investments of 4% pa. The warrant structure provides the investor with the following return profile:

- The put at Swfr4,500, provided it is not knocked out, guarantees an annualized return of 4.57% pa (around the yield on Swiss National bonds for a similar maturity at the time of issue).
- The call at Swfr6,000 allows a maximum return of 14.74% pa.

The put structure may have tax benefits for the investor insofar as any profits resulting from the sale or exercise of the warrants may qualify for treatment as a tax-free capital gain.

**Exhibit 10.39** sets out the 1994 transaction entailing the issue of further debt in this case with capped warrants. **Exhibit 10.40** sets out the payoff to the investor of this structure.[43]

---

**Exhibit 10.39
Debt with Capped Equity Warrants — Structure**

In 1994, the Swiss pharmaceutical company Roche undertook another issue in connection with the acquisition of a Syntex, a US pharmaceutical company. The issue terms were as follows:

| | |
|---|---|
| Amount | ¥100 billion |
| Maturity | 7.5 years |
| Coupon | 1.00% pa payable annually |
| Equity Warrant Structure | Each ¥1 million bond was issued with 69 capped warrants with an expiry date of July 15, 1998. One hundred warrants will be required to acquire 1 Roche genussscheine. The warrants will pay as follows on exercise: if the closing price of Roche genussscheine is above Swfr4,784, the investor receives 1 genussscheine or at Roche's option Swfr7,100. |
| Roche Genussscheine Price (at issue date) | Swfr5,880 |

---

[43] See "A ¥100 billion Sleight Of Hand" (November 1994) *Corporate Finance* 5-6.

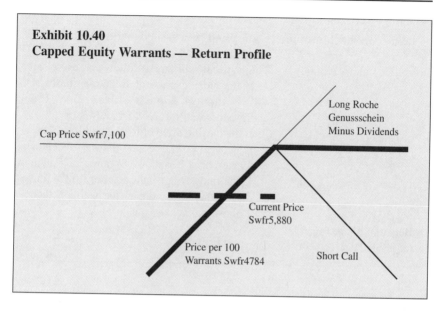

**Exhibit 10.40**
**Capped Equity Warrants — Return Profile**

Cap Price Swfr7,100

Long Roche
Genussschein
Minus Dividends

Current Price
Swfr5,880

Price per 100
Warrants Swfr4784

Short Call

The issue in this case was undertaken with the warrants being offered to investors at around Swfr4,784 per genussscheine (representing an 18% discount to current market price of Swfr5,880). The structure entails the investor purchasing an in-the-money warrant and funding it with the sale of an out-of-the money call option that curtails the potential return from the option. The structure's appeal to the issuer lies primarily in its management of the equity dilution through the capped warrant payoff structure.

**Exhibit 10.41** sets out the 1993 transaction for Benetton entailing the issue of debt with knockout warrants. **Exhibit 10.42** sets out the payoff to the investor of this structure.[44]

**Exhibit 10.41**
**Debt with Knockout Equity Warrants — Structure (2)**

In 1993, the Italian clothing manufacturer Benetton issued a debt with knockout warrants package. The issue terms were as follows:

Amount        Lira 200 billion (US$124.4 million)
Maturity       5 years
Coupon        4.5% pa payable annually

---

[44] See "Benetton Styles A New Lira Bond" (August 1993) *Corporate Finance* 8.

| Equity Warrant Structure | Each bond was issued with 63 knockout warrants with an expiry date of three years. The warrants will pay as follows on exercise: |
|---|---|
| | 1. If the closing price of Benetton shares is less than or equal to Lira21,543, the investors will receive Lira21,543; or |
| | 2. If the closing price of Roche genussscheine is above Lira21,543, the investor receives 1 share or at Benetton's option Lira29,973. If the underlying share reaches Lira24,353 during the 3-year life of the warrant, then 1 above is knocked out |
| Benetton Share Price (at issue date) | Lira18,733 |

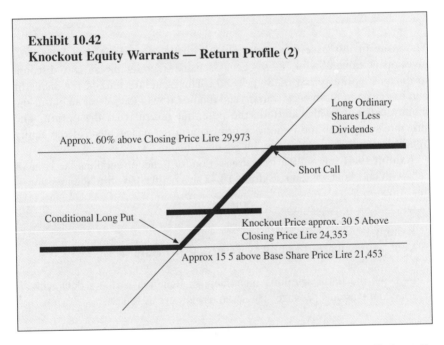

**Exhibit 10.42**
**Knockout Equity Warrants — Return Profile (2)**

The transaction that is similar to the Roche transaction already detailed entails the issue of debt in combination with a transaction where the investor purchases the underlying equity and purchases a knockout put (to guarantee the erosion of value provided the share value at no time rises above 30% of the share price at the time of issue and selling a call option with a strike some 60% above the current price of the shares.

The appeal of the structure for the issuer was its ability to limit the economic cost and the dilution effect in view of its expectation of a rise in its share price over the term of the warrants. The investor appeal lay in the ability of the structure to provide structured equity exposure on a low-risk basis with the possibility of equity participation for up to 60% of any rise in Benetton shares over a 3-year time horizon.

## 10. Miscellaneous Variations

There are a number of other variations on the basic equity-linked structures including:

- **Credit-enhanced issues** — the underlying concept is to enhance the credit of the issuer by having the issue supported by a guarantee or letter of credit from a highly credit-rated bank (typically A+ or better). The guarantee only covers the payment of interest and principal (in the case of nonconversion). As the issue is guaranteed it receives the higher rating of the credit support bank. **Exhibit 10.43** sets out the basic structure. The major advantages to the issuer include larger issue sizes, ability to use a wider variety of structure (such as zero-coupon, higher conversion premium, and aggressive call features), and a wider investor base because of the enhanced credit. The disadvantages include the cost of the credit enhancement and the higher issue costs arising from the structural complexity.

- **Multi-currency issues** — the structure entails a large issue being simultaneously placed in a number of currencies in different markets on similar terms but denominated in the currency of each market. The structure was used very successfully by Elder-IXL Limited in 1986[45] to raise very substantial amounts of capital. The multi-currency structure enabled the issuer to avoid issuing a large amount of equity at a heavily discounted price, to raise a substantial amount of quasi-equity funding at competitive pricing, it enabled access to the broadest possible investor base, and it facilitated the execution of extremely large equity-linked transactions. **Exhibit 10.44** sets out the terms of the issues. The initial transaction (which raised £300 million in October 1986) was followed by a second transaction in January 1997 that raised £275 million. The second transaction was similar to the first transaction with two differences (a lower premium, 10%, and a fifth currency — Dutch guilders).

---

[45]  See the Harvard Business School Case Study Elders-IXL Ltd 1986 (9-288-042) that gives the background to and structure of the issue.

- **Exchangeable capital units** — this issue represents hybrid structures that have evolved in response to the specific requirement of issuer, primarily banks, to manage their capital bases. **Exhibit 10.45** sets out the details of an exchangeable capital units issue undertaken by National Australia Bank.

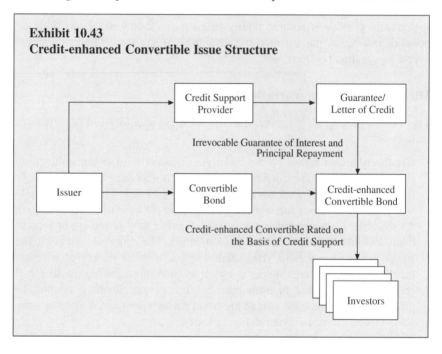

**Exhibit 10.43**
**Credit-enhanced Convertible Issue Structure**

**Exhibit 10.44**
**Multi-currency Convertible Issue**

|  | US$ Tranche | DM Tranche | £ Tranche | Swfr Tranche |
|---|---|---|---|---|
| Guarantor | Elders-IXL Limited on a subordinated basis | Elders-IXL Limited on a subordinated basis | Elders-IXL Limited on a subordinated basis | Elders-IXL Limited on a subordinated basis |
| Maturity | 12 years (November 5, 1998) | 12 years (November 5, 1998) | 12 years (November 5, 1998) | 12 years (November 5,1998) |
| Conversion Premium | A$6.00 (20.72% over the October 10, 1986 closing price of the shares A$4.97) | A$6.00 (20.72% over the October 10, 1986 closing price of the shares A$4.97) | A$6.00 (20.72% over the October 10, 1986 closing price of the shares A$4.97) | A$6.00 (20.72% over the October 10, 1986 closing price of the shares A$4.97) |

| Amount | US$175 million | DM200 million | £40 million | Swfr200 million |
|---|---|---|---|---|
| Coupon | 5.25% pa | 3.00% pa | 8.00% pa | 2.50% pa |
| Conversion Price | Each bond is convertible into 261.23 shares | Each bond is convertible into 130.39 shares | Each bond is convertible into 373.11 shares | Each bond is convertible into 800 shares |
| Conversion Period | November 6 1986 to October 27, 1998 | November 6 1986 to October 23, 1998 | November 6 1986 to October 27, 1998 | November 6 1986 to October 27, 1998 |
| Exchange Rate (A$1=) | US$0.6380 | US$1.2782 | £0.4467 | Swfr1.0417 |
| Denominations | US$1,000 bearer and registered | DM1,000 and 10,000 | £1,000 bearer and registered | Swfr1,000 |
| Amortisation | Bullet | Bullet | Bullet | Bullet |
| Put Option | At 125 on November 5 1993 to yield 8.05% pa to put date | At 123 on November 5 1993 to yield 5.76% pa to put date | At 124 on November 5 1993 to yield 10.49% pa to put date | At 120 on November 5 1993 to yield 4.96% pa to put date |
| Call Option | At 106% on or after 30 days after the exchange date declining by 1% pa to 100 on November 5, 1992 but not before 1993 unless the closing price for ordinary shares exceeds 130% of the conversion price for a specified period. | At 101% in 1991, at 100% in 1990, and if the closing price for ordinary shares exceeds 130% of the conversion price for a specified period. | At 106% on or after 30 days after the exchange date declining by 1% pa to 100 on November 5, 1992, but not before 1993 unless the closing price for ordinary shares exceeds 130% of the conversion price for a specified period. | Forced conversion at 106% at any time decreasing by 1% pa if the closing price for ordinary shares exceeds 130% of the conversion price for a specified period. |
| Listing | Luxembourg | Frankfurt | Luxembourg | Zurich, Basle, Geneva, Lausanne, Berne |
| Governing Law | English | Germany | English | Switzerland |
| Fees | 1.50% | 2.50% | 2.50% | 2.875% |

**Exhibit 10.45**
**Exchangeable Units Issue**

In March 1997, National Australia Bank (NAB) raised US$1 billion
through Exchangeable Capital Units (ECUs).[46] The NAB, while domiciled
in Australia, generates approximately half of its revenue outside of
Australia, primarily in Europe and to a lesser extent in the US. The terms
of the issue were as follows:

| | |
|---|---|
| Issuer | National Australia Capital Securities (UK)/ National Australia Capital Securities (Jersey). |
| Guarantor | National Australia Bank on an unconditional, subordinated basis. |
| Amount | US$875 million |
| Number of Units | 35 million (5 million over allotment option) of ECUs at an issue price of US$25 each together with a purchase contract that entitles the holder to exchange the ECUs into ordinary shares/American Depositary Receipts (ADRs) of the guarantor. |
| Maturity | Undated |
| Coupon | 7.875% pa |
| Conversion Option | 1. Holders are entitled to exchange the ECUs at any time into the ordinary shares of the guarantor or at the guarantor's option to cash equivalent of such shares based on the market prices at the time of exchange. |
| | 2. The issuer can at any time in whole but not in part convert the ECUs into 7.875% non-cumulative preference shares issued by the guarantor on a 1 for 1 basis. The preference shares issued under such an exchange will be convertible at the option of the holder into the ordinary shares of the guarantor or at the option of the issuer after the fifth anniversary of the issues of ECUs into the ordinary shares of the guarantor or the cash equivalent based on the market prices at the time of conversion. |

---

[46]  See "A Cost Effective Capital Restructuring" (May 1997) *AsiaMoney* 13-14.

| Conversion Price | 1.635 for ordinary shares and 0.327 for ADRs subject to certain anti-dilution adjustments. |
|---|---|
| Conversion Premium | 21% |
| Conversion Period | Undated |
| Call Option | After 10 years |
| Listing | New York and Luxembourg |
| Governing Law | New York |
| Fees | 2.75% |
| Arranger | Merrill Lynch |

The structure of the ECUs is complex but can be analyzed as follows:

- **Base issue** — The base issue is a perpetual US$-denominated debt issue that pays a coupon of 7.875% pa. For the NAB, the interest expense is tax deductible as long as the securities are not converted into either preference shares or ordinary shares.
- **Conversion right (holder)** — The holder has the right, as in a normal convertible, to exchange the ECUs for ordinary shares at a premium of 21% to the prevailing share price.
- **Conversion right (issuer)** — The holder has the right to convert the ECUs for convertible noncumulative preference shares. This option is designed to enable the issuer to convert Tier 2 capital (the ECUs are initially treated as subordinated debt on the balance sheet) to Tier 1 capital.
- **Cash payment options** — The issuer also has the right at the end of five years to pay the cash equivalent instead of issuing ordinary shares to preference shareholders who wish to convert into ordinary shares. The issuer can make a special cash offer to acquire any outstanding preference shares for the equivalent of the principal and any outstanding interest. Shareholders who do not wish to accept the cash offer will be forced to convert into ordinary shares at the conversion ratio allowing, economically, the NAB to limit any dividend payment to preference shareholders at the end of 10 years.

The issue had a number of advantages for the issuer:

- It allowed it to control its capital base in terms of Tier 1 and Tier 2 capital.
- It provided cost-efficient capital — while in the balance sheet as subordinated debt it incured an effective after-tax cost well below that of equity.

> • It also allowed NAB to target overseas investors diversifying its
> predominantly domestic shareholding base. The pricing on the issue
> reflected its overseas appeal resulting in a significant reduction in the
> issuer's cost of equity. This was achieved by using the proceeds of the
> issue to repurchase ordinary shares from domestic holders.
>
> The investor appeal of the issue derived from the high nominal yield for a
> well-rated credit (the issue was rated (A1/A+).

## 11. Synthetic Equity-linked Structures

### 11.1 Overview

Increasingly, equity-linked structures are devised and issued *synthetically*. This
indicates that the transaction does not entail an issue by the issuer whose equity
underlies the transaction. Instead, the issue is undertaken by an investment bank
or using a special-purpose financing vehicle.

This trend reflects a variety of factors including:

• The demand from equity and fixed income investors for structured product
  devised to satisfy specific investor requirements for return and risk.
• The inability or unwillingness of issuers to meet the demands of the
  investors.
• Advances in financial engineering and structuring techniques.

The concept of synthetic equity has evolved primarily in the US and European
markets. It encompasses a wide range of transactions.

### 11.2 Synthetic Structured Equity

#### 11.2.1 Concept

Several synthetic equity issue structures have been utilized. Structured Yield
Products Exchangeable for Stock (STRYPES) (designed by Merrill Lynch) is an
example of this type of approach.[47] It is essentially a financial structure that is
used to facilitate an equity-linked issue. The key element of the structure is the
interposition of a special purpose issuance vehicle between the issuer and the
investor.

---

[47] See Cox, T. Anne, Harrington III, Preston M., and Elliot, Anne (January 27, 1998)
"Convertible Special Report — Convertible Structures: Building Further Innovations
1998 Update"; Global Convertibles Research Group, Merrill Lynch at 41-42.

### *11.2.2 Structure*

The basic structure operates as follows:

- The issuer enters into a forward sale of its equity securities to a special-purpose vehicle (typically, in the US, this is an investment bank or a trust; outside the US, this is a special-purpose company).
- The special-purpose vehicle issues the equity-linked securities to investors.
- At maturity, the special purpose vehicle purchases the shares from the issuer and pays the proceeds of the issue to the issuer.

**Exhibit 10.46** sets out the structure of a synthetic structured equity issue using the Structured Yield Products Exchangeable for Stock (STRYPES) format.

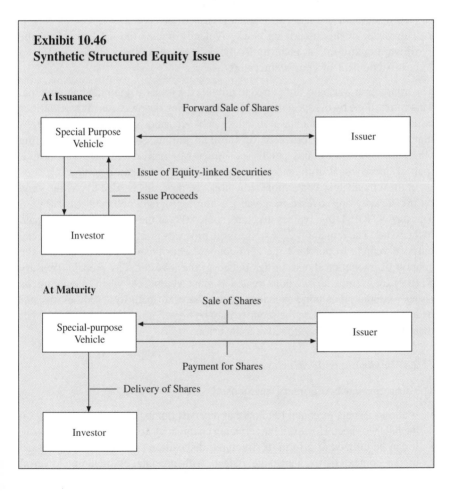

**Exhibit 10.46**
**Synthetic Structured Equity Issue**

**At Issuance**

Forward Sale of Shares

Special Purpose Vehicle — Issuer

Issue of Equity-linked Securities

Issue Proceeds

Investor

**At Maturity**

Sale of Shares

Special-purpose Vehicle — Issuer

Payment for Shares

Delivery of Shares

Investor

The equity-linked security issued by the special-purpose vehicle can take any desired form. However, in practice, the issue undertaken is a mandatory convertible structure. This is to ensure conversion into equity at maturity to match the obligations under the forward equity purchase contract. A common structure used is one of the mandatory convertible structures described in the section on structured high-yield mandatory convertible structures.

Several aspects of the structure require analysis:

- If the equity-linked securities are issued through an investment bank, then the investor accepts the credit risk on the investment bank as the issuer of the securities. If the equity-linked securities are issued through a trust or special-purpose company, then the cash raised can be usually invested in debt securities (such as US Treasury notes) to collateralize the issue in part or full (see discussion in regard to releasing cash to the issuer)
- The issuer of the underlying equity typically retains the right to satisfy the forward equity sale at maturity by the delivery of ordinary shares or effect a cash settlement of equivalent value.

The transaction is usually structured to provide the issuer with immediate funding. This can be done by the special-purpose vehicle using the proceeds of the securities issued to investors to purchase offsetting debt securities issued by the issuer. At maturity, the maturing proceeds on the debt purchased are used to meet the obligations under the equity purchase contract. Alternatively, the issuer receives a (partial) prepayment of the payment required under the forward contract.

In most mandatory convertible structures, the proceeds needed to pay the yield on the security are covered in advance using high-grade collateral (usually US Treasury STRIPs). In a typical structure, some 80% of the issue proceeds are paid to the issuer. The remaining 20% of the issue proceeds is retained within the special purpose vehicle to purchase the zero-coupon securities (STRIPs) that fund the coupon payments on the securities issued to the investor. The prepaid Treasury STRIPs are in some jurisdictions treated as reduced proceeds when calculating the issuer's capital gains upon exchange of the shares at maturity. From an investor perspective, the coupon on the security may be treated as a return of capital rather than interest that may be attractive to investors.

### 11.2.3 Implications of Structure

The structure has two primary functions:

- It allows issuers to obtain funding that receives immediate equity treatment on the balance sheet. However, the servicing charge may be deductible to the issuer.
- It can be utilized as a form of structured disposition (such as those discussed in the context of exchangeable issues) with advantages including deferral of tax, receipt of current proceeds, a cash settlement option and minimal market impact.

## 12. Summary

The variations on the basic equity-linked structures have evolved in response to issuer and investor demand. They entail refinements designed to achieve particular corporate finance and asset-liability management objectives and adjustments to the risk-reward trade-offs as between the issuer and the investor. The structures also represent attempts to broaden both issuer and investor participation in the market and in particular to facilitating access under market condition that traditionally would prevent such access.

## Appendix A

## Exchangeable Debt — Economics

This Appendix focuses on the practical economics of exchangeable debt.

### 1.  The Divestment Case

#### 1.1   Assumptions

Assume the issuing company (A) has acquired a holding of 20 million shares ("the exchange shares") in the exchange company (B). The average cost price of the exchange shares is US$4.50. The current market price of the exchange share is US$5.00. The exchange shares pay after-tax dividends of US$0.20 per share and these dividends are expected to grow at a rate of 5% pa.

Company A wishes to divest itself of its holding of the exchange shares for strategic reasons. It opts for an exchangeable debt transaction on the following basis:

| | |
|---|---|
| Exchange premium | 20% |
| Issue amount | US$120 million |
| Issue costs | 2.5% |
| Interest rate | 8.00% pa |

Also assume that A's conventional borrowing cost for a similar amount and term would be 12.00% pa. The corporate tax rate (applicable to A) is 40% and the capital gains tax rate is 25%.

#### 1.2   Economics: Assuming Exchange is Effected

**Table 1** on page 503 sets out the economics of the transaction, assuming the price performance of the exchange shares is such that exchange takes place.

The analysis indicates that the exchangeable debt transaction has superior economics to an immediate sale of the shares. This gain is created by the premium-to-market implicit in the exchangeable issue and the deferral of capital gains tax liability. The advantage of the exchangeable issue is significant early on, but diminishes as the requirement to fund the deficiency between the dividends received and interest paid erodes the advantage over time. The NPV advantage increases in the later years as the growth in dividend receipts creates a surplus after servicing interest payments.

### 1.3    Economics: Assuming Exchange is Not Effected

**Table 2** on page 504 sets out the economics of the transaction, assuming the price performance of the exchange shares is such that exchange does not take place and the exchangeable debt must be redeemed. It is assumed that the exchange shares are worth US$4.00 at the maturity of the exchangeable debt issue and are sold to partially fund the redemption. It is also assumed that the capital loss on sale is deductible to the issuing company.

The analysis shows that the exchangeable debt transaction features inferior economics to an immediate sale of shares. The exchangeable debt issue has superior economics to a deferred sale of shares (at maturity). This is the result of the company having use of the funds for 10 years and the time value of money which dictates that the deficiency requiring funding at maturity (the difference between the amount received from the sale of shares and the face value of exchangeable debt to be redeemed) is a relatively small amount in NPV terms.

### 1.4    Sensitivity Analysis

The sensitivity of the NPV result to variations in key assumptions is summarized in **Table 3** on page 505 In each case, one of the variables was varied while all other variables were held constant at the level used in the assumed base case (see above). In the no-exchange case the future share price is assumed to be US$6.00 per share (the original strike price); at this level the investor is indifferent between conversion and open market purchase of the stock (assuming no transactions costs). The economic sensitivity of the economics was analyzed for variations in the following parameters:

1. Exchange premium.
2. Interest rate.
3. Dividend rate and dividend growth rates.
4. Tax rate, including changes in the capital gains rate.
5. The alternative borrowing cost of the issuing companies.
6. The price of the exchange shares at maturity.

**Table 1**

| Year | NPV Factors | Issue Proceeds | After-tax Issue Costs | Interest Payments | Total Exchangeable Cash Flow Pre-tax | Total Exchangeable Cash Flow After-tax | Dividends | Total Cash Flow | NPV of Total Cash Flow | Cumulative NPV of Exchangeable Bond | Result of Sale | NPV Advantage of Exchangeable Over Spot Sale ($) | NPV Advantage of Exchangeable Over Spot Sale (%) |
|---|---|---|---|---|---|---|---|---|---|---|---|---|---|
| 0 | 1.000 | 120,000,000 | -1,800,000 | | | 118,200,000 | | 118,200,000.00 | 118,200,000.00 | 110,700,000 | 97,500,000 | 13,200,000 | 13.54% |
| 1 | 0.933 | | | 3,840,000 | -9,600,000 | -5,760,000 | 4,200,000 | -1,560,000.00 | -1,455,223.88 | 109,748,507 | 97,500,000 | 12,248,507 | 12.56% |
| 2 | 0.870 | | | 3,840,000 | -9,600,000 | -5,760,000 | 4,410,000 | -1,350,000.00 | -1,174,746.60 | 109,043,660 | 97,500,000 | 11,543,660 | 11.84% |
| 3 | 0.812 | | | 3,840,000 | -9,600,000 | -5,760,000 | 4,630,500 | -1,129,500.00 | -916,857.58 | 108,565,140 | 97,500,000 | 11,065,140 | 11.35% |
| 4 | 0.757 | | | 3,840,000 | -9,600,000 | -5,760,000 | 4,862,025 | -897,975.00 | -679,962.72 | 108,294,075 | 97,500,000 | 10,794,075 | 11.07% |
| 5 | 0.706 | | | 3,840,000 | -9,600,000 | -5,760,000 | 5,105,126 | -654,873.75 | -462,576.60 | 108,212,933 | 97,500,000 | 10,712,933 | 10.99% |
| 6 | 0.659 | | | 3,840,000 | -9,600,000 | -5,760,000 | 5,360,383 | -399,617.44 | -263,315.07 | 108,305,433 | 97,500,000 | 10,805,433 | 11.08% |
| 7 | 0.615 | | | 3,840,000 | -9,600,000 | -5,760,000 | 5,628,402 | -131,598.31 | -80,888.51 | 108,556,463 | 97,500,000 | 11,056,463 | 11.34% |
| 8 | 0.573 | | | 3,840,000 | -9,600,000 | -5,760,000 | 5,909,822 | 149,821.78 | 85,904.65 | 108,951,992 | 97,500,000 | 11,451,992 | 11.75% |
| 9 | 0.535 | | | 3,840,000 | -9,600,000 | -5,760,000 | 6,205,313 | 445,312.86 | 238,183.77 | 109,479,005 | 97,500,000 | 11,979,005 | 12.29% |
| 10 | 0.499 | | | 3,840,000 | -9,600,000 | -5,760,000 | 6,515,579 | 755,578.51 | 376,991.66 | 110,125,426 | 97,500,000 | 12,625,426 | 12.95% |

*Notes:*

1. Issue proceeds are adjusted for issue expenses that are assumed to be tax deductible at the corporate tax rate in the year of issue.
2. Initial dividend is escalated at dividend growth rate and is assumed to be paid at the end of each year.
3. Assumes exchangeable coupon is fully deductible at the corporate tax rate.
4. Discount rate used is the alternative borrowing cost adjusted for the corporate tax rate.
5. Cumulative NPV is cumulation of NPV of exchangeable cash flows adjusted for the capital gains tax payable upon exchange at the applicable capital gains tax rate.
6. Result of sale is calculated as the sale proceeds at commencement of the exchangeable transaction adjusted for capital gains tax liability at the capital gains tax rate.

**Table 2**

| Year | NPV Factors | Issue Proceeds | After-tax Issue Costs | Interest Payments | Total Exchangeable Cash Flow | | Dividends | Total Cash Flow | NPV of Total Cash Flow | Cumulative NPV of Exchangeable Bond | Result of Sale | NPV Advantage of Exchangeable Over Spot Sale ($) | NPV Advantage of Exchangeable Over Spot Sale (%) |
|---|---|---|---|---|---|---|---|---|---|---|---|---|---|
| | | | | | Pre-tax | After-tax | | | | | | | |
| 0 | 1.000 | 120,000,000 | -1,800,000 | | | 118,200,000 | | 118,200,000.00 | 118,200,000.00 | 118,200,000 | 97,500,000 | 20,700,000 | 21.23% |
| 1 | 0.933 | | | -9,600,000 | 3,840,000 | -5,760,000 | 4,200,000 | -1,560,000.00 | -1,455,223.88 | 116,744,776 | | | |
| 2 | 0.870 | | | -9,600,000 | 3,840,000 | -5,760,000 | 4,410,000 | -1,350,000.00 | -1,174,746.60 | 115,570,030 | | | |
| 3 | 0.812 | | | -9,600,000 | 3,840,000 | -5,760,000 | 4,630,500 | -1,129,500.00 | -916,857.58 | 114,653,172 | | | |
| 4 | 0.757 | | | -9,600,000 | 3,840,000 | -5,760,000 | 4,862,025 | -897,975.00 | -679,962.72 | 113,973,209 | | | |
| 5 | 0.706 | | | -9,600,000 | 3,840,000 | -5,760,000 | 5,105,126 | -654,873.75 | -462,576.60 | 113,510,633 | | | |
| 6 | 0.659 | | | -9,600,000 | 3,840,000 | -5,760,000 | 5,360,383 | -399,617.44 | -263,315.07 | 113,247,318 | | | |
| 7 | 0.615 | | | -9,600,000 | 3,840,000 | -5,760,000 | 5,628,402 | -131,598.31 | -80,888.51 | 113,166,429 | | | |
| 8 | 0.573 | | | -9,600,000 | 3,840,000 | -5,760,000 | 5,909,822 | 149,821.78 | 85,904.65 | 113,252,334 | | | |
| 9 | 0.535 | | | -9,600,000 | 3,840,000 | -5,760,000 | 6,205,313 | 445,312.86 | 238,183.77 | 113,490,517 | | | |
| 10 | 0.499 | (120,000,000) | | -9,600,000 | 3,840,000 | -125,760,000 | 6,515,579 | -119,244,421.49 | -59,496,335.49 | 53,994,182 | 41,162,912 | 12,831,270 | 31.17% |

*Notes:*
1. All assumptions as in Table 1 except as specified below.
2. Exchangeable debt is assumed to be repaid in full at maturity.
3. Result of sale assumes that capital loss is fully deductible in the year in which it is incurred.
4. Sale is assumed to be effected at the assumed future price of the shares.
5. The share sale proceeds are made available to fund the repayment of the exchangeable at maturity to the full extent received.

## Table 3

| Case | Assuming Exchange (after year) | Assuming Exchange (after year) | Assuming Exchange (after year) | Assuming No Exchange (relative to sale at year) | Assuming No Exchange (relative to sale at year) |
|---|---|---|---|---|---|
| | 1 | 2 | 5 | 0 | 10 |
| **Base** | 12.56 | 10.99 | 12.95 | 21.23 | 31.17 |
| **Sensitivities** | | | | | |
| **Premium Variations** | | | | | |
| Lower Premium (15%) | 8.94 | 7.85 | 10.25 | 16.18 | 29.33 |
| Higher Premium (25%) | 16.19 | 14.13 | 15.65 | 26.28 | 33.02 |
| **Interest Rate Variations** | | | | | |
| Lower Coupon (6%) | 13.94 | 17.01 | 23.23 | 21.23 | 55.52 |
| Higher Coupon (10%) | 11.18 | 4.96 | 2.67 | 21.23 | 6.83 |
| **Dividend Variations** | | | | | |
| Lower Dividend (15c/Share) | 11.56 | 6.17 | 3.78 | 21.23 | 9.46 |
| Higher Dividend (25c/share) | 13.57 | 15.89 | 22.12 | 21.23 | 52.89 |
| Lower Growth Rate (4%) | 12.52 | 10.45 | 11.14 | 21.23 | 26.88 |
| Higher Growth Rate (6%) | 12.60 | 11.54 | 14.86 | 21.23 | 35.71 |
| **Tax Variations** | | | | | |
| Lower Corporate Tax (30%) | 11.44 | 7.21 | 6.64 | 20.92 | 45.97 |
| Higher Corporate Tax (50%) | 13.70 | 14.99 | 19.96 | 21.54 | 17.54 |
| Lower Capital Gains Tax (0%) | 16.74 | 13.51 | 13.87 | 18.20 | 35.27 |
| Higher Capital Gains Tax (40% | 9.95 | 9.41 | 12.38 | 23.13 | 28.83 |
| **Issuer Debt Cost** | | | | | |
| Lower Debt Cost (10%) | 12.46 | 10.54 | 12.41 | 21.23 | 1.55 |
| Higher Debt Cost (14%) | 12.66 | 11.41 | 13.44 | 21.23 | 63.96 |
| **Future Price of Exchange Share** | | | | | |
| US$2/share | | | | 21.23 | 106.13 |
| US$3/share | | | | 21.23 | 60.32 |
| US$4/share | | | | 21.23 | 31.17 |
| US$5/share | | | | 21.23 | 10.99 |

*Notes:*
1. All calculations (for the exchange case) are based on a comparison of the NPV of the exchangeable transaction as at the relevant year compared to the NPV of an immediate sale of the shares.
2. All calculations (for the no exchange case) are based on a comparison of the NPV of the exchangeable transaction over the full term compared to the NPV of a sale at either year 0 or year 10.

The sensitivity analysis indicates that where the exchange takes place the economics of the exchangeable transaction improves (deteriorates) where:

- The premium is higher (lower).
- The coupon on the exchangeable is lower (higher).
- The dividend rate is higher (lower).
- The dividend growth rate is higher (lower).
- The corporate tax rate is higher (lower).
- The capital gains tax is lower (higher).
- The issuer's alternative borrowing cost is higher (lower).

The transaction economics varies significantly, depending on the timing of exchange.

The sensitivity analysis indicates a similar pattern where exchange does not take place.

### 1.5   The Funding Equity Holding Case

Assume the same basic circumstances as above, except as specifically varied below.

**Table 4** sets out the economics of the transactions, including a comparison of the cash flow resulting from funding the shareholding with debt, as well as exchangeable debt.

**Table 4**

**Exchangeable Debt Cash Flows**

| Year | NPV Factors | Dividends | Issue Proceeds | After-tax Issue Costs | | Interest Payments | | Total Exchangeable Cash Flow | Exchangeable Funding — Total Cash Flow |
|------|------------|-----------|----------------|-----------------------|---|---------|---------|------------------------------|----------------------------------------|
| | | | | Pre-tax | After-tax | | | | |
| 0 | 1.000 | | 120,000,000 | –1,800,000 | | | | 118,200,000 | 118,200,000.00 |
| 1 | 0.933 | 4,200,000 | | | | –9,600,000 | 3,840,000 | –5,760,000 | –1,560,000.00 |
| 2 | 0.870 | 4,410,000 | | | | –9,600,000 | 3,840,000 | –5,760,000 | –1,350,000.00 |
| 3 | 0.812 | 4,630,500 | | | | –9,600,000 | 3,840,000 | –5,760,000 | –1,129,500.00 |
| 4 | 0.757 | 4,862,025 | | | | –9,600,000 | 3,840,000 | –5,760,000 | –897,975.00 |
| 5 | 0.706 | 5,105,126 | | | | –9,600,000 | 3,840,000 | –5,760,000 | –654,873.75 |
| 6 | 0.659 | 5,360,383 | | | | –9,600,000 | 3,840,000 | –5,760,000 | –399,617.44 |
| 7 | 0.615 | 5,628,402 | | | | –9,600,000 | 3,840,000 | –5,760,000 | –131,598.31 |
| 8 | 0.573 | 5,909,822 | | | | –9,600,000 | 3,840,000 | –5,760,000 | 149,821.78 |
| 9 | 0.535 | 6,205,313 | | | | –9,600,000 | 3,840,000 | –5,760,000 | 445,312.86 |
| 10 | 0.499 | 6,515,579 | (120,000,000) | | | –9,600,000 | 3,840,000 | –125,760,000 | –119,244,421.49 |

**Debt Cash Flows**

| Year | NPV Factors | Dividends | Issue Proceeds | After-tax Issue Costs | Interest Payments | | Total Exchangeable Cash Flow | Exchangeable Funding — Total Cash Flow |
|------|-------------|-----------|----------------|-----------------------|-------------------|---|------------------------------|----------------------------------------|
| | | | | Pre-tax | After-tax | | | |
| 0 | 1.000 | | 100,000,000 | -1,500,000 | | | 98,500,000 | 98,500,000 |
| 1 | 0.933 | 4,200,000 | | | -12,000,000 | 4,800,000 | -7,200,000 | -3,000,000 |
| 2 | 0.870 | 4,410,000 | | | -12,000,000 | 4,800,000 | -7,200,000 | -2,790,000 |
| 3 | 0.812 | 4,630,500 | | | -12,000,000 | 4,800,000 | -7,200,000 | -2,569,500 |
| 4 | 0.757 | 4,862,025 | | | -12,000,000 | 4,800,000 | -7,200,000 | -2,337,975 |
| 5 | 0.706 | 5,105,126 | | | -12,000,000 | 4,800,000 | -7,200,000 | -2,094,874 |
| 6 | 0.659 | 5,360,383 | | | -12,000,000 | 4,800,000 | -7,200,000 | -1,839,617 |
| 7 | 0.615 | 5,628,402 | | | -12,000,000 | 4,800,000 | -7,200,000 | -1,571,598 |
| 8 | 0.573 | 5,909,822 | | | -12,000,000 | 4,800,000 | -7,200,000 | -1,290,178 |
| 9 | 0.535 | 6,205,313 | | | -12,000,000 | 4,800,000 | -7,200,000 | -994,687 |
| 10 | 0.499 | 6,515,579 | -100,000,000 | | -12,000,000 | 4,800,000 | -107,200,000 | -100,684,421 |

The analysis indicates that the exchangeable debt transaction results in a distinctive pattern of cash flows to A:

- A higher initial cash flow receipt, in excess of the market value of the shares (representing the premium) that must, if the exchangeable debt, issue is redeemed in due course at maturity, be repaid.
- A lower net (after-dividend receipts) cash servicing cost as a result of the lower coupon.

The effective cost to the borrower is dependent on:

- Whether the exchangeable debt is converted into the exchange shares; and
- Whether the transaction provides a cash payout or repurchase option.

**Table 5** sets out the effective cost to the borrower at the end of each year, assuming the transaction is terminated. The net (after-dividend) after-tax cost is calculated under the following assumptions:

- The debt is assumed to be repayable in full at face value at the end of each year.
- The exchangeable debt is assumed to be callable (without premium for reasons of simplicity) at the end of each year.
- The transaction provides for the borrower to cash out the investor by making a payout representing the difference between the strike price under the exchangeable and the prevailing market price of the exchange shares.

The analysis indicates that while exchangeable debt is more cost-effective where the exchangeable debt is converted or the price of exchange shares does not rise above the effective strike price, the exchangeable debt transaction is considerably more expensive where the borrower must make cash payouts to repurchase the shares.

**Table 5**

**Comparison of Debt Versus Exchangeable Structure**

| Year | NPV Factors | Exchangeable Funding — Total Cash Flow | Borrowing — Total Cash Flow | Difference Between Borrowing And Exchangeable Debt | NPV of Funding Advantage | Cumulative NPV of Funding Advantage |
|---|---|---|---|---|---|---|
| 0 | 1.000 | 118,200,000.00 | 98,500,000 | 19,700,000 | 19,700,000 | 19,700,000 |
| 1 | 0.933 | -1,560,000.00 | -3,000,000 | 1,440,000 | 1,343,284 | 21,043,284 |
| 2 | 0.870 | -1,350,000.00 | -2,790,000 | 1,440,000 | 1,253,063 | 22,296,347 |
| 3 | 0.812 | -1,129,500.00 | -2,569,500 | 1,440,000 | 1,168,902 | 23,465,249 |
| 4 | 0.757 | -897,975.00 | -2,337,975 | 1,440,000 | 1,090,394 | 24,555,642 |
| 5 | 0.706 | -654,873.75 | -2,094,874 | 1,440,000 | 1,017,158 | 25,572,801 |
| 6 | 0.659 | -399,617.44 | -1,839,617 | 1,440,000 | 948,842 | 26,521,643 |
| 7 | 0.615 | -131,598.31 | -1,571,598 | 1,440,000 | 885,114 | 27,406,756 |
| 8 | 0.573 | 149,821.78 | -1,290,178 | 1,440,000 | 825,666 | 28,232,422 |
| 9 | 0.535 | 445,312.86 | -994,687 | 1,440,000 | 770,210 | 29,002,632 |
| 10 | 0.499 | -119,244,421.49 | -100,684,421 | (18,560,000) | (9,260,408) | 19,742,224 |

**Table 5**

The following table sets out the comparison of net effective cost of exchangeable debt compared to conventional borrowing (in % pa) at prescribed share values.

| Year | Effective Borrowing Cost | Share Price < US$6 | Share Price US$8 | Share Price US$10 |
|---|---|---|---|---|
| 1 | 4.57 | 2.84 | 36.68 | 70.52 |
| 3 | 3.32 | 1.64 | 11.67 | 20.15 |
| 5 | 2.90 | 1.25 | 7.11 | 11.90 |
| 7 | 2.58 | 0.96 | 5.11 | 8.45 |
| 10 | 2.13 | 0.56 | 3.48 | 5.80 |

Notes:
1. All costs are calculated after taking into account the dividends received that are used to partially offset the interest outflows.
2. Calculated as the internal rate of return on after-tax cash flows.
3. Assume full borrowing is repayable without penalty.
4. Assume the exchangeable is callable at par without premium.
5. Where the market price of the exchange shares exceeds US$6 (the implicit strike price) of the exchangeable debt, the borrower is assumed to make a payment equivalent to the difference between market price and US$6 to the investor in addition to the par value of the bond.

# 11
# Equity-linked Notes (3) — Equity Index-linked Notes

## 1. Overview

Equity index-linked structured notes[1] may be defined as fixed income securities where the interest coupons and/or principal of the instrument is linked to the movements in *equity market indexes*. Chapter 9 and Chapter 10 focused primarily on equity-linked notes where the underlying equity instrument is an individual stock. This chapter focuses predominantly on equity market index-linked note structures.

The major differentiating factor of equity index-linked structures includes:

- The issuer is not usually the entity whose equity securities are the basis of the transaction and the structure is not designed to facilitate the raising of equity capital for the issuer.
- The exposure to the underlying equity element is specifically hedged through derivative transactions to immunize the issuer from the equity price exposure.

## 2. Equity Index-linked Structures — Rationale

### 2.1 Overview

The major differences between traditional equity-linked issue structures and more recent equity-index note structure derivatives as previously noted include:

---

[1] For an analysis of international equity trading costs, see Allen, Julie A. and Showers, Janet L. (April 1991) Equity Indexed Linked Derivatives — An Investor's Guide; Salomon Brothers, Bond Portfolio Analysis Group, New York; (1993) Equity Investment Across Borders: Cutting The Costs; Swiss Bank Corporation, Basel, Switzerland at 2-6; Hutchinson, Jr, Daniel L. "Global Trends In Exchange Listed Derivatives" (December 1996) *Financial Derivatives & Risk Management* Issue 8 9-19 at 18-19; Willoughby, Jack "Trade Secrets" (November 1997) *Institutional Investor* 65-71.

- Traditional equity-linked notes focus on individual stocks rather than market indexes.
- Traditional forms of equity notes were developed primarily as a means for providing equity capital-raising opportunities for corporations as part of customized financing strategies.
- Equity index-linked notes, insofar as they relate to individual corporations, are usually incorporated in the process of *debt* fundraising through new issue arbitrage techniques.
- Equity index-linked notes are directed primarily towards investors rather than issuers.

The development of the market for equity index-linked notes reflects a number of factors:

- Investors can utilize these instruments to simulate the purchase of an entire equity index as an alternative to direct investment in the relevant equity market with (often significant) return and cost benefits.
- Index instruments are directed to investors who are primarily passive asset managers seeking exposure to the relevant equity market index.
- These instruments allow investors to create highly customized structures creating a specific pattern of exposure to the relevant equity index.
- The structures are also capable of being customized in terms of exposure to exchange rates allowing investors to maintain currency exposure on foreign equity investments or to eliminate the foreign currency risk on the investment.
- Equity index-linked structures may allow investors to circumvent investment constraints (particularly in emerging markets).

The attraction of these instruments is that they represent an alternative to direct investment in the underlying equity markets. The major advantages relating to simulated as distinct from direct investment in equity markets include:

- Asset allocation approaches to equity portfolio management.
- Return enhancement.
- Structured returns.
- Enhanced efficiencies in cross-border investments.

The attraction of these structures is equally relevant to institutional and individual retail investors. The advantages of notes are particularly relevant to individual retail investors who typically would encounter significant transaction costs in achieving the equity investment profile created through notes directly. This has created a significant market for these types of instruments.

The structures described in this chapter are capable of utilization with reference to individual equity securities and a number of transactions utilizing these structures have emerged to complement the larger equity index-related market.

The identified benefits are equally available from traditional equity derivative transactions. These include exchange traded products (equity index futures contracts and equity index options) and over-the-counter products (equity index swaps and equity index options). The benefits relating to the use of equity-linked *structured notes* are related to the benefits of structured notes generally. In particular, the capacity to create a fully funded investment, the avoidance of the need to directly transact in derivatives, and the credit enhancement aspects of equity-linked notes are specially important.

## 2.2 Asset Allocation Strategies

Institutional investors currently use asset allocation approaches to investment. Under these strategies the required return on their portfolios is sought to be achieved through the identification of particular asset classes/markets in which to invest. The emphasis is on relative value of the *asset or market* as distinct from *specific security* selection.

In relation to equity markets, the investment strategy of these investors is focused on purchasing shares in order to create a portfolio *that replicates the return on an index*. The trend towards index replication is also influenced by the process of investment performance evaluation whereby investment returns are measured *relative to the performance of the benchmark index*. Equity index-linked notes are particularly suitable for this type of investment strategy as they facilitate the purchase of an entire index *with a single transaction*.

Individual or retail investors may also benefit from replicating the underlying equity index. The major benefit for this group of investors derives from the ability to create a diversified exposure to equity securities. However, the ability to create such a diversified portfolio directly is not usually available to retail investors. This is because the amount of individual investments may make it difficult to diversify the portfolio fully. Alternatively, the transaction costs of diversification are very high for individuals. Equity-linked notes are attractive to retail investors as they enable the creation of diversified exposure to an entire index with relatively low minimum capital investments and minimal transaction costs.

This benefit of equity-indexed structures is particularly evident in relation to international or cross-border investments.

**Exhibit 11.1** summarizes some of the most common equity market indexes utilized in equity-linked derivative transaction. Increasingly, a number of emerging market equity indexes, primarily, in Latin America, Asia, and Southern Africa, are also utilized.

Other indexes utilized for these type of transactions include global indexes. These include indexes such as the Financial Times (FT) Actuaries World Indices, the Morgan Stanley Capital International (MSCI) market indices, or in the case of emerging markets the IFC Emerging Market Index. The global market indices provide broad-based equity exposure to a wide range of equity markets. Each of the global indices provides a broad range of sub-indices that provide exposure to a specific *geographic* subset of the equity market covered within the overall index. Example of this type of subindex include the FT-Actuaries Europe Pacific Index or the MSCI Europe and Far East (EAFE) Index.

**Exhibit 11.1**
**Major Global Equity Market Indexes**

| Country | Index | Description |
| --- | --- | --- |
| Australia | All-Ordinaries Index | All-Ordinaries Index. Capitalization-weighted index of more than 250 companies, mostly industrial. |
| Canada | TSE-35 | Toronto Stock Exchange 35 Index. Capitalization-weighted index of 35 stocks. |
| Europe | Euro-Stoxx | Capitalization-weighted index of the 50 largest capitalized and liquid stocks from the 11 countries of the EMU. |
| France | CAC-40 | Capitalization-weighted index based on 40 of the 100 most highly capitalized companies listed on the forward segment of the official list. Calculated by the Societe des Bourses Francais. |
| Germany | DAX | Deutsche Aktien Index. Capitalization-weighted, total rate-of-return index of 30 blue-chip stocks. |
| Great Britain | FTSE-100 | Financial Times Stock Exchange 100-Share Index. Based on the 100 largest companies by market capitalization. |
| Hong Kong | Hang Seng | Capitalization-weighted index of 33 stocks, including four financial, nine property, six utility, and 14 commerce and industry. |
| Italy | MIB | Capitalization-weighted index of 30 large capitalization and liquid companies traded on the Italian Stock Exchange. |
| Japan | TOPIX | Tokyo Price Index. Capitalization-weighted index of all shares listed on the first section of the Tokyo Stock Exchange. |
| Japan | NIKKEI-225 | Price-weighted index of 225 Japanese blue-chip stocks that are traded on the first section of the Tokyo Stock Exchange. |
| Netherlands | EOE | European Options Exchange Dutch Stock Index. Based on prices quoted on the Amsterdam Stock Exchange for 25 leading Dutch stocks. |
| Spain | FIEX | Capitalization-weighted index of the 35 most liquid companies quoted on the four Spanish stock exchanges (Barcelona, Bilbao, Madrid, and Valencia). |
| Switzerland | SMI | Swiss Market Index. Capitalization-weighted index currently consisting of 22 Swiss companies. |
| United States | S&P 500 | Standard & Poor's Index of 500 widely held common stocks, including 400 industrial, 40 public utility, 40 financial, and 20 transportation issues. |

## 2.3    Return Enhancement

### 2.3.1   Sources of Return Enhancement

The use of equity-indexed notes can result under certain circumstances in improved returns to the investor. This return improvement derives from the following sources:

- Depending upon the shape of the forward curve for equity index prices in the relevant market, simulated investment through equity-indexed transactions may result in higher net returns relative to direct equity investment.
- Improved returns may also be achieved reducing the cost that would typically be incurred by an investor in replicating an index through direct equity investments, including the cost of stamp taxes, portfolio rebalancing costs, and so on.
- Tax benefits such as reducing the impact of withholding taxes on dividends, reallocating tax credits on dividend income to other parties to whom these benefits are more attractive or avoiding problems of foreign source income and other forms of international taxation.

In practice, the second and third sources of return enhancement are particularly important.

### 2.3.2   Equity Investment Cost[2]

**Exhibit 11.2** sets out an estimate of cost associated with direct equity ownership in a number of major markets. **Exhibit 11.3** on page 515 summarizes the result of a recent survey of execution costs.

An additional cost for international investors is the impact of taxes. The most obvious tax impact is the loss suffered through the imposition of dividend withholding taxes. Typically, cross-border dividend payment will result in the deduction of withholding tax from the dividend payment. This has the immediate effect of reducing the return to the foreign investor. The tax withheld may be recovered but there will at a minimum be a loss as a result of the delay in recovery of the tax credit. In some cases, the dividend withholding tax may not be recoverable. For example, a tax-exempt investor may not qualify for a tax

---

[2]  For an analysis of international equity trading costs, see Allen, Julie A. and Showers, Janet L. (April 1991) Equity Indexed Linked Derivatives — An Investor's Guide; Salomon Brothers, Bond Portfolio Analysis Group, New York; (1993) Equity Investment Across Borders: Cutting The Costs; Swiss Bank Corporation, Basel, Switzerland at 2-6; Hutchinson, Jr, Daniel L. "Global Trends In Exchange-Listed Derivatives" (December 1996) *Financial Derivatives & Risk Management* Issue 8 9-19 at 18-19; Willoughby, Jack "Trade Secrets" (November 1997) *Institutional Investor* 65-71.

refund of the tax withheld. **Exhibit 11.4** on page 516 summarizes the impact of dividend-withholding taxes.

An additional tax effect may derive from the fact that the dividend may have significant tax effects. For example, in an integrated tax system the receipt of the dividend paid out of taxed income may be entitled to tax paid *by the company*. This is designed to avoid the double taxation of income as between the corporate entity and the ultimate shareholder. The impact of this system is that dividend receipt is completely or substantially free of tax to the shareholder. Foreign shareholders generally do not receive the benefit of this tax credit. Consequently, the economic value of the tax credit may be maximized if it can be transferred to a local shareholder that can take full advantage of the tax credit. The foreign shareholder may benefit from this transaction by the local shareholder passing on the tax benefit in an alternative form.

---

**Exhibit 11.2**
**Costs of Direct Equity Investment in Major Equity Markets**

| Country | USA | Japan | UK | Germany | Switzerland | France | Netherlands | Canada | Hong Kong | Australia |
|---|---|---|---|---|---|---|---|---|---|---|
| **Round Trip Costs** | | | | | | | | | | |
| Commission | 0.13% | 0.13% | 0.20% | 0.20% | 0.20% | 0.20% | 0.20% | 0.20% | 0.20% | 0.20% |
| Market Impact | 0.56% | 1.00% | 0.80% | 1.00% | 1.00% | 0.80% | 1.00% | 0.85% | 0.75% | 0.80% |
| Taxes | | 0.30% | 0.50% | | | | | | 0.30% | 0.30% |
| Total | 0.69% | 1.43% | 1.50% | 1.20% | 1.20% | 1.00% | 1.20% | 1.05% | 1.25% | 1.30% |
| **Annual Costs** | | | | | | | | | | |
| Custody | 0.05% | 0.10% | 0.10% | 0.10% | 0.10% | 0.10% | 0.10% | 0.10% | 0.10% | 0.10% |
| Rebalancing Costs | 0.07% | 0.14% | 0.15% | 0.12% | 0.12% | 0.10% | 0.12% | 0.11% | 0.13% | 0.13% |
| Total | 0.12% | 0.24% | 0.25% | 0.22% | 0.22% | 0.20% | 0.22% | 0.21% | 0.23% | 0.23% |
| **Total Costs** | | | | | | | | | | |
| **1-year Holding Period** | 0.84% | 1.68% | 1.86% | 1.47% | 1.46% | 1.24% | 1.47% | 1.32% | 1.56% | 1.61% |
| **3-year Holding Period** | 0.37% | 0.73% | 0.82% | 0.65% | 0.65% | 0.56% | 0.65% | 0.60% | 0.70% | 0.72% |

*Notes:*
1. The round trip costs are taken to include commissions for a buy-sell transaction. The round trip costs are for a portfolio of physical shares.

2. Market impact costs are taken to be the cost of executing the transaction (effectively the market bid-offer spread). The market impact is dependent upon the size of the transaction. The estimates are for reasonable size transactions in the relevant markets.

3. Taxes refer to stamp duties and other transaction taxes incurred in transferring shares.

4. Custody cost refers to the cost of a foreign investor using custodial services. The costs may in reality be lower reflecting the potential for revenue from stock lending transactions.

5. Rebalancing costs are calculated as the cost of trading in the stocks in the index to match changes in index definitions. For convenience these are assumed to be equivalent to trading costs (round trip costs) on 10% of the portfolio.

6. Total costs are the sum of round trip costs (amortized over one or three years at the interest rate in the currency) and annual costs.

*Source:* Estimates are derived with assistance from Salomon Smith Barney.

## Exhibit 11.3
## Costs of Physical Stock Transactions

| Market | Average Price of Stock Traded (US$) | Average Commissions (bps) | Average Fees (bps) | Average Market Impact (bps) | Total Trading Cost (bps) |
|---|---|---|---|---|---|
| New York |  |  |  |  |  |
| Stock Exchange | 38.92 | 13.3 | 0.0 | 20.8 | 34.1 |
| Over-the-counter | 32.34 | 1.2 | 0.0 | 50.7 | 51.9 |
| International |  |  |  |  |  |
| (30 countries) | 7.30 | 25.7 | 11.4 | 12.7 | 49.8 |

*Source:* Elkins/McSherry Co. as quoted in Willoughby, Jack. "Trade Secrets." *Institutional Investor* (November 1997): 65-71 at 67.

**Exhibit 11.4**
**Impact of Dividend Withholding Taxes**

| Country | Index | Dividend Yield | Withholding Tax Rate | Net Loss |
|---------|-------|----------------|----------------------|----------|
| USA | S&P 500 | 2.00% | 15.00% | 0.30% |
| Japan | NIKKEI 225 | 0.75% | 15.00% | 0.11% |
| UK | FTSE | 3.25% | 15.00% | 0.49% |
| Germany | DAX | 1.70% | 10.00% | 0.17% |
| Switzerland | SMI | 2.10% | 15.00% | 0.32% |
| France | CAC | 1.90% | 15.00% | 0.29% |
| Netherlands | EOE | 3.10% | 15.00% | 0.47% |
| Canada | TORONTO 35 | 2.90% | 15.00% | 0.44% |
| Australia | ALL-ORD | 3.20% | 15.00% | 0.48% |
| Hong Kong | HANG SENG | 3.00% | 0.00% | 0.00% |

### 2.3.3    Return Enhancement Utilizing Derivatives

As noted above, the advantages of equity-linked notes are substantially driven by the general advantages of equity derivative transactions. In particular, the capacity to utilize equity derivatives to lower the cost of equity investment is significant. The ability to synthesize equity index exposure using equity index futures contracts or equity swaps is well recognized.

These transactions take the following form:

- The investor invests in a cash asset that yields an interest return.
- The investor enters into:
  1. A purchased equity index futures contract on the relevant index; or
  2. Receives the equity index return on the relevant index in return for paying an interest return.

The derivative transaction is renewed at maturity until such time as the investor wishes to discontinue the investment in the equity market.

The combined transaction creates a synthetic equity index investment for the investor.

The advantages of such an investment structure includes:

- Enhanced returns *relative to direct investment in the stocks underlying the equity index.*

- Full replication of the index.
- Absence of tracking error and rebalancing risk.

The most significant driver of derivative-based equity investment is the enhanced returns available. **Exhibit 11.5** sets out the relative costs of trading stocks and replicating the index by trading in equity index futures. **Exhibit 11.6** sets the costs of trading equity index futures in a variety of markets. **Exhibit 11.7** sets out the cost differentials as between physical stocks and equity index futures. **Exhibit 11.8** sets out the net gain achieved potentially through replicating the performance of a number of equity indexes through an equity swap. The analysis overall highlights the significant cost savings and consequential enhanced returns available by replicating equity indexes using derivative structures (either pure derivatives or structured notes).

---

**Exhibit 11.5**
**Relative Costs of Trading Stocks Versus Equity Futures — US Market**

The following tables set out a comparison of trading a US$200 million portfolio of stocks or an equivalent 548 S&P 500 equity futures contracts. The table below sets out a comparison of relative liquidity:

|  | NYSE | S&P 500 Futures |
|---|---|---|
| Average daily volume | 425 million shares | 75,000 contracts |
| Approximate unit value | US$46/shares | US$365,000 /contract |
| Total dollar value | US$19.55 billion | US$13.7 billion |

The table below sets out a comparison of market impact:

| | Equity Portfolio | | | S&P 500 Futures | | |
|---|---|---|---|---|---|---|
| | Last | Bid | Ask | Last | Bid | Ask |
| Market | 730.00 | 728.75 | 731.25 | 732.30 | 732.20 | 732.40 |
| Bid/ask spread | 2.50 index points | | | 0.2 index points | | |
| Dollar value | US$685,000 | | | US$54,800 | | |

The table below sets out a comparison of commissions:

|  | **NYSE** | **S&P 500 Futures** |
|---|---|---|
| Volume | 4.384 million shares | 548 contracts |
| Cost per unit | US$0.03/share | US$12.50/contract |
| Round trip cost | US$130,000 | US$6,850 |

*Source:* Hutchinson, Jr, Daniel L. "Global Trends In Exchange Listed Derivatives." *Financial Derivatives & Risk Management* Issue 8 (December 1996): 9-19 at 19.

**Exhibit 11.6**
**Relative Costs of Trading Equity Futures — Multiple Markets**

| Country | USA | Japan | UK | Germany | Switzerland | France | Netherlands | Canada | Hong Kong | Australia |
|---|---|---|---|---|---|---|---|---|---|---|
| **Roll Frequency (/Year)** | 4 | 4 | 4 | 4 | 12 | 12 | 12 | 4 | 12 | 4 |
| **Round Trip Cost** | 0.01% | 0.04% | 0.02% | 0.02% | 0.05% | 0.04% | 0.10% | 0.04% | 0.05% | 0.05% |
| **Roll Costs** | 0.05% | 0.15% | 0.08% | 0.07% | 0.10% | 0.15% | 0.15% | 0.05% | 0.15% | 0.10% |
| **Annual Cost** | 0.24% | 0.76% | 0.40% | 0.36% | 1.80% | 2.28% | 3.00% | 0.36% | 2.40% | 0.60% |
| **Spread To Fair Market Value** | | | | | | | | | | |
| **– 1 Standard Deviation** | –0.25% | –0.25% | –0.25% | –1.00% | –0.50% | –1.25% | –0.50% | –0.20% | –0.25% | –0.75% |
| **Mean** | 0.10% | 0.15% | 0.15% | –0.60% | 0.10% | –0.75% | 0.10% | 0.10% | 0.50% | 0.30% |
| **+ 1 Standard Deviation** | 0.40% | 0.75% | 0.60% | –0.10% | 1.00% | –0.25% | 1.00% | 0.40% | 1.25% | 1.25% |
| **Total Costs** | | | | | | | | | | |
| **– 1 Standard Deviation** | –0.01% | 0.51% | 0.15% | –0.64% | 1.30% | 1.03% | 2.50% | 0.16% | 2.15% | –0.15% |
| **Mean** | 0.34% | 0.91% | 0.55% | –0.24% | 1.90% | 1.53% | 3.10% | 0.46% | 2.90% | 0.90% |
| **+ 1 Standard Deviation** | 0.64% | 1.51% | 1.00% | 0.26% | 2.80% | 2.03% | 4.00% | 0.76% | 3.65% | 1.85% |

*Notes:*
1. Roll frequency refers to the number of contracts listed and traded in a calender year.

2. Round trip costs refer to the cost of trading a buy-sell contract.
3. Roll costs refer to the estimated average cost of rolling the contract from the near-month futures contract to the next listed contract month.
4. Annual cost is the sum of the round trip cost and roll costs multiplied by the number of rolls in a single year to create an annual equivalent cost.
5. Spread to fair market value represents the expected deviation from theoretical futures values given as a mean, as well as plus/minus one standard deviation.
6. Total costs are the sum of annual costs and spread to fair market value.

*Source:* The approach used here is that in Hutchinson, Jr, Daniel L. "Global Trends In Exchange Listed Derivatives." *Financial Derivatives & Risk Management* Issue 8 (December 1996): 9-19 at 18. The cost data has been updated to reflect more recent information.

**Exhibit 11.7**
**Relative Costs of Trading Stocks vs Equity Futures —**
**Multiple Markets**

| Country | USA | Japan | UK | Germany | Switzerland | France | Netherlands | Canada | Hong Kong | Australia |
|---|---|---|---|---|---|---|---|---|---|---|
| **Physical Stock Costs** | 0.84% | 1.68% | 1.86% | 1.47% | 1.46% | 1.24% | 1.47% | 1.32% | 1.56% | 1.61% |
| **Index Futures Costs** | 0.34% | 0.91% | 0.55% | –0.24% | 1.90% | 1.53% | 3.10% | 0.46% | 2.90% | 0.90% |
| **Cost Differential** | 0.50% | 0.77% | 1.31% | 1.71% | –0.44% | –0.29% | –1.63% | 0.86% | –1.34% | 0.71% |
| **Breakeven (years)** | 2.5 | 1.8 | 3.4 | – | 0.8 | 0.8 | 0.5 | 2.9 | 0.5 | 1.8 |

*Notes:*
1. Physical costs refer to the cost of trading stock using a holding period of one year.
2. Index futures costs refer to the cost of trading index futures to replicate a 1-year exposure to the underlying equity market.
3. Cost differential refers to the difference between physical stock trading costs and index futures costs.
4. The breakeven calculation derives the required holding period in years required to equate the costs of physical stock ownership and replication using index futures.

**Exhibit 11.8**
**Relative Performance of Trading Stocks Versus Equity Swaps**

| Country | Index | Equity Swap Price | Withholding Tax Loss | Stock Costs | Net Gain |
|---------|-------|-------------------|----------------------|-------------|----------|
| USA | S&P 500 | –0.30% | 0.30% | 0.84% | 0.84% |
| Japan | NIKKEI | –0.40% | 0.11% | 1.68% | 1.39% |
| UK | FTSE | –0.75% | 0.49% | 1.86% | 1.59% |
| Germany | DAX | 0.40% | 0.17% | 1.47% | 2.04% |
| Switzerland | SMI | 0.30% | 0.32% | 1.46% | 2.08% |
| France | CAC | 0.15% | 0.29% | 1.24% | 1.68% |
| Netherlands | AEX | –0.20% | 0.47% | 1.47% | 1.73% |
| Canada | TORONTO 35 | –0.40% | 0.44% | 1.32% | 1.36% |
| Australia | ALL-ORD | –0.50% | 0.48% | 1.61% | 1.59% |
| Hong Kong | HANG SENG | –0.90% | 0.00% | 1.56% | 0.66% |

*Notes:*
1. The equity swap price is stated as the return above or below the equity index level paid by the counterparty to the investor seeking to replicate exposure to the index.
2. The withholding tax loss and stock ownership costs (for a 1-year holding period) are derived from the previous analysis.
3. The net gain reflects the difference (relative to the index) achieved via the equity swap as against physical stock investment to replicate the index.

## 2.4   Structured Returns

A major factor underpinning the development of these types of transactions in equity markets is the capacity to customize the pattern of returns from the relevant investment. Investment managers can utilize these specially tailored structures to position portfolios to profit from anticipated moves in equity market values, often within the constraints of investment portfolio management guidelines.

An additional factor is the capacity of these structures to be tailored to the foreign exchange risk management requirements of individual investors. Returns from investment in foreign equity markets, which are increasing, are a function of changes in value in both the equity market and in the exchange rate. Investment managers increasingly seek to customize their degree of exposure to the currency element of foreign equity market investments. The process of positioning currency hedges to achieve these objectives is more easily encompassed within equity index-linked notes.

### 2.5   Cross-border Investments

Equity index-linked notes are particularly useful where the investor is undertaking investments in foreign markets. The use of these types of instruments enables the investor to avoid some of the physical transactions that would otherwise be undertaken and resultant costs incurred including foreign exchange transactions, rebalancing of the portfolio, tracking error, reinvestment of dividend income, as well as the avoidance of costs of custodial arrangements to hold the equities and stamp taxes, and so on.

These factors are particularly important in emerging market where these costs are relatively high. In addition, there are regulatory factors (inability for foreign investors to purchase stock) or regulatory risk (risk of currency controls and inconvertibility) attached to such investments. Synthetic investment strategies are attractive alternatives to direct investment under those circumstances.

## 3.   Equity Index-linked Notes — Building Blocks

Equity index-linked notes are usually constituted from a number of identifiable building blocks. This is consistent with the approach to constructing all structured note products. The key elements of the structure include:
- A fixed income security, typically a zero-coupon bond.
- An equity index-based derivative, generally a forward on the relevant equity index[3] or an option on the equity index.

**Appendix A** to this chapter sets out the structure and mechanics of equity derivatives.

## 4.   Types of Structure

The equity index-linked security structures[4] that have evolved fall into two types of transactions:

- Yield-enhancement structures.
- Principal-protected structures.

---

[3]   Increasingly, the equity index forward embedded in the note is an equity index swap transaction (effectively, a portfolio of forward contracts on the index).

[4]   For a discussion of these types of products, see Allen, Julie A. and Showers, Janet L. (April 1991) Equity Indexed Linked Derivatives — An Investor's Guide; Salomon Brothers, Bond Portfolio Analysis Group, New York; Baubonis, Charles, Gastineau, Gary, and Purcell, David "The Banker's Guide To Equity-linked Certificates Of Deposit" (Winter 1993) *The Journal of Derivatives* 87-95; (1993) Equity Investment Across Borders: Cutting The Costs; Swiss Bank Corporation, Basel, Switzerland.

The yield-enhancement structures entail the use of equity index forwards or options in combination with fixed income securities to enhance the coupon return. The major attraction of this structure is the higher yield. The higher return is typically generated through the use of off-market prices on the forwards to create a future cash flow or the capture of premium on the sale of the option that is then used to increase the coupon.

The second structure entails the creation of very structured equity exposures by combining *purchased* options on the relevant equity index with a fixed income instrument. The option premium is typically funded by foregone income or interest coupon or risking a small portion of the principal of the transaction. The primary objective of these structures is the creation of limited risk exposure to the equity market typically in highly structured format.

Yield-enhancement structures have been generally targeted at institutional investors and to a more limited degree at less risk averse high net worth individual investors. The principal-protected structures are targeted at individual retail investment accounts that are concerned to preserve invested capital. These structures have also created interest among capital stable investment funds and portfolio-insured investment asset managers.

A variety of structures based on the basic transaction types described have also developed primarily in response to investor requirements for structured exposure to equity markets. These structures have been predicated on either the demand for customized return profile or the presence of regulatory factors.

## 5.    Equity-linked Notes — Yield-enhancement Structures

As noted above, the yield enhancement-based structures entail the combination of either off-market forwards or sale of options on the relevant equity index. There have been several types of transactions of this class undertaken.

### 5.1    Bull-bear Structures

One specific type of this transaction entails the issue of bull-bear bonds. Bull and bear bonds in all currencies have been structured to include offsetting tranches with the redemption value of each tranche being directly linked either positively (in the case of the bull bond) or inversely (in the case of the bear bond) to the value of the relevant index.

From the viewpoint of the investor in a bull or bear bond, the fact that the redemption value upon maturity is determined by the level of the relevant index at some point of time in the future allows the investor to participate in index movements consistent with its expectations. It is however important to note that in almost all bull and bear bonds the structure embodies a cap on the final pay out as well as a floor. The typical structure entails structuring the actual forward on the index at a level above or below the forward price to create a positive cash flow that can be used to enhance the coupon of the note.

From the perspective of the issuer, there is no underlying risk to movements in the relevant index. This is because the two tranches are designed to be perfectly offsetting and to provide the issuer with a known fixed stream of cash flow payments into the future. The issuer effectively assumes no risk to movements in the relevant index as changes in the redemption value of one tranche (say the bull tranche) are offset by the asymmetric changes in the redemption value generated by the other tranche (in our example, the bear tranche).

An example of the type of stock index bull-bear issue involving the Nikkei Keisan Shimbun Index on the Tokyo Stock Exchange is set out in **Exhibit 11.9**.

---

**Exhibit 11.9**
**Yen Bull and Bear Bonds Linked to the Nikkei Stock Index**

AB Svensk Exportkredit (SEK) on July 25, 1986 issued a series of yen bull and bear bonds. The SEK issue involved two tranches, each for five years. The bull tranche involved an issue of ¥10,000 million and paid a rich coupon of 8.00% pa to compensate investors for the additional risks that they have undertaken. The redemption value of the bonds was indexed to the *Nikkei Keisan Shimbun* index in the following manner:

For the bull bonds: $R = ¥10,000,000,000 (I + (I - 26,067)/22,720))$
For the bear bonds: $R = ¥10,000,000,000 (I + (I - 19,373)/22,720))$

Where:

R = redemption value in yen
I = Nikkei stock average at maturity of the bonds

R is subject also to the following constraint:

If I is greater than 28,461 at maturity, $R = ¥6,000,000,000$
If I is less than 16,979 at maturity, $R = ¥11,054,000,000$

SEK's net position is a function of the underlying forward positions on the Nikkei index created. These positions are hedged, presumably, with Daiwa Securities, the lead manager of the issue.

For Daiwa, the bull bonds represent a 5-year (European) bear option spread where Daiwa purchased a call with a strike price of 28,461 and wrote a call with a strike price of 16,979, both of which expire in five years. The bear bonds resemble a bull spread for Daiwa where the strike price of the purchased call is 16,979 and the strike price of the written call is 28,461. The offsetting nature of the two tranches allows Daiwa to stay perfectly hedged with no exposure to the stock index.

Mathematically, this can be represented as follows:

Redemption value of both the bull and bear tranches where I is the index at maturity is:

¥10,000,000,000 × [(1 − (I − 19,373)/22,720)) + (1 + (I − 26,067)/22,720)]
= ¥10,000,000,000 × [(1 − (22,720 − 19,373)/22,720)) + (1 + (22,720 − 26,067)/22,720)]
= ¥10,000,000,000 × (38,746/22,720) = ¥17,053,697,183

Therefore, the net cash flow accruing to Daiwa from the combined transactions is:

¥20,000,000,000 − ¥17,053,697,183 = ¥2,946,302,817

For example, if the Nikkei Index is greater than 28,461 then the cash flow is:

For bear bond   ¥10,000,000,000 − ¥6,000,000,000 = ¥4,000,000,000
For bull bond   ¥10,000,000,000 − ¥11,054,000,000 = ¥1,054,000,000
Net cash surplus for Daiwa = ¥2,946,000,000

If the Nikkei Index is less than 16,979 then the cash flow is:

For bear bond   ¥10,000,000,000 − ¥11,054,000,000 = ¥1,054,000,000
For bull bond   ¥10,000,000,000 − ¥6,000,000,000 = ¥4,000,000,000
Net cash surplus for Daiwa = ¥2,946,000,000

The value dynamics of the issue are as follows:

- The bull bear bonds pay a rich yen coupon of 8.00% pa that in yen terms is ¥20,000,000,000 × 8.00% = ¥1,600,000,000.
- At a 5-year yen risk free rate of 6.50% pa the profit of ¥2,946,000,000 translates into an annuity of ¥517,419,347 for five years.
- Therefore, effective interest cost to SEK is ¥1,600,000,000 − ¥517,419,347 = ¥1,082,580,653, which translates into 5.413% pa (¥1,082,580,653/¥20,000,000,000).

From the above derivation, it is evident that the bull and bear structure can reduce interest cost to below the yen risk-free rate. In fact, the all-in cost achieved represented a savings of approximately 55 bps pa on a comparable Euroyen issue. SEK, desiring floating rate US$ funding, undertook a ¥/US$ currency swap generating funds at an attractive margin under LIBOR.

From the perspective of the issuer, the only reason for undertaking a bull or bear bond is that the overall locked-in fixed cost of funds generated is significantly lower than that achievable by a conventional transaction in the relevant market. The issuer takes no final redemption risk (although the investor does) and is able to lock in a cheaper cost of borrowing no matter what the level of the relevant index is upon maturity. This lower cost of borrowing achievable through the bull or bear bond can be translated across markets. The issuer can effectively swap out of the currency or interest rate basis of the underlying bull or bear transaction to generate an attractive cost of funds in its desired currency or interest rate basis.

It is important to note that, from the viewpoint of the issuer, there is nothing apart from the relative cost to distinguish a bull or bear transaction from a conventional borrowing and the derivative transaction is entirely conventional. The only variation from a standard derivative transaction may flow from differential coupons, and so on. (relative to market levels). For example, in the issue for SEK, the coupon on the bonds was an above-market 8.00% pa (relative to the market rate that would have had to be paid by SEK of 6.00% pa). This higher coupon was compensated for by an effective redemption value at maturity of less than par (once the offsetting tranches were taken into account). If SEK had desired to undertake a swap against this bond issue then the peculiar high coupon cash flow structure would have had to be matched under the corresponding swap.

It is also important to note that several important variations on the basic bull and bear structure is feasible. These include undertaking a transaction where the maturity of the bond is longer than the period over which the final payout to be distributed to the investors in the various tranches is determined. For example, a number of transactions have been undertaken on the basis that on a 5-year maturity bond the final redemption amount is determined by the movement in the index for a period of say one year. Under this structure, if the index appreciates, the bull tranche investor has a higher redemption value that crystallizes and is guaranteed after one year although not payable until maturity of the bond. Conversely, the exact opposite applies to an investor in the bear tranche.

## 5.2    Embedded Sold Optionality Structures

The other predominant form of yield-enhancement structure is the note with an embedded sold option position. The premium on the option is incorporated in the enhanced coupon of the transaction. **Exhibit 11.10** sets out an example of a Nikkei Index-linked Bond of this type to illustrate the major structural elements.

The structure described entails the sale of a call on the equity index with the premium being reinvested in the bond to generate a significantly above-market coupon in return for the investor assuming the market risk of the option. As with all option embedded structures, the optionality embedded entails a spread with an option being purchased to ensure that the option payout does not exceed the face value of the bond.

**Exhibit 11.11** sets out the hedging of the structure, which entails stripping out the embedded call option and securitizing it as well as, in the case examined, the entry into a currency swap to hedge the currency and interest rate elements of the transaction.

---

**Exhibit 11.10**
**Nikkei Index-linked Note**

*1.   Terms of Issue*
The principal terms of the issue are as follows:

| | |
|---|---|
| Issuer | AA-rated financial institution |
| Principal | ¥5 billion |
| Coupon | 16.50% pa payable annually on a bond basis |
| Issue Price | 100.25% |
| Fees | 0.25% |
| Maturity | 1 year |
| Redemption | In yen at maturity based on: |
| | 100 — [((Nikkei at maturity — Nikkei at launch)/Nikkei at launch) × 100] |
| Maximum Redemption Amount | 100% |
| Minimum Redemption Amount | 0% |

*2.   Structure of Issue*
The payoff structure (stated as % of principal) of the issue (assuming the Nikkei Index at launch was 22,950) is set out in the table below:

---

| Nikkei Index At Maturity (index value) | At Maturity (% of start) | Bond Redemption (% of face value) | Coupon (%) | Total Redemption (% of face value) | Rate of Return (% pa) |
|---|---|---|---|---|---|
| 11,475 | 50 | 100 | 16.50 | 116.500 | 16.50 |
| 13,770 | 60 | 100 | 16.50 | 116.500 | 16.50 |
| 16,065 | 70 | 100 | 16.50 | 116.500 | 16.50 |
| 18,360 | 80 | 100 | 16.50 | 116.500 | 16.50 |
| 20,655 | 90 | 100 | 16.50 | 116.500 | 16.50 |
| 22,950 | 100 | 100 | 16.50 | 116.500 | 16.50 |
| 25,245 | 110 | 90 | 16.50 | 106.500 | 6.50 |
| 27,540 | 120 | 80 | 16.50 | 96.500 | -3.50 |
| 29,835 | 130 | 70 | 16.50 | 86.500 | -13.50 |
| 32,130 | 140 | 60 | 16.50 | 76.500 | -23.50 |
| 34,425 | 150 | 50 | 16.50 | 66.500 | -33.50 |
| 36,720 | 160 | 40 | 16.50 | 56.500 | -43.50 |
| 39,015 | 170 | 30 | 16.50 | 46.500 | -53.50 |
| 41,310 | 180 | 20 | 16.50 | 36.500 | -63.50 |
| 43,605 | 190 | 10 | 16.50 | 26.500 | -73.50 |
| 45,900 | 200 | 0 | 16.50 | 16.500 | -83.50 |

Under the structure, the investor writes a call on the Nikkei 225 Index embedded in the bond (via the redemption formula) in favor of the issuer in return for the higher coupon. The option is struck at the level of the Nikkei index at the time of launch. If the Nikkei Index rises above the strike rate (the Nikkei Index at launch), then the principal repaid to the investor is reduced in accordance with the formula effectively representing the payout under the sold call option.

The sale of the call is combined with the repurchase of the call at a strike price set at 200% of launch. This is designed to prevent the payout on the option exceeding the face value amount of the note.

**Exhibit 11.11**
**Nikkei Index-linked Note-hedging Structure**

The derivative structure required to hedge the issuer from exposure to fluctuations in the equity index is effectively embodied in the note structure set out in **Exhibit 11.10**. The hedging structure entails two separate components:

- The ¥/US$ currency swap to convert the issue into floating rate US$ funding. The arranger of the note issue is assumed to be the counterparty to the currency swap.
- The stripping out and on-sale of the Nikkei Index call option.

### 1. *Yen/US$ Currency Swap*

Assume the rate structure at the time of launch is as follows:
- US$/¥ rate (1-month forward) is US$1: ¥133.50
- US$/¥ swap rate (1-year swap; 1-month forward start):
  Counterparty pays yen 8.09% pa (30/360-day basis)
  Counterparty receives US$ LIBOR less 0.25% pa (the issuer's sub-LIBOR target).

### 2. *Nikkei Index Call*

At the time of launch, the arranger procures a buyer for the 13-month Nikkei Index Call Option to be sold in return for receipt of a premium of 8.25% (flat).

### 3. *Combined Cash Flows*

The combined cash flows (as between the issue and the arranger) are as follows:

### Day 1 Payment Date

The issuer receives ¥5,012,500,000 (representing issue proceeds inclusive of the issue premium) from the issuer. The arranger receives ¥12,500,000 representing the issue fees out of the proceeds.

The issuer is party to the following payments with the arranger:

- Issuer pays to the arranger ¥5,000,000,000.
- Issuer receives from the arranger US$37,453,184 (the US$ principal amount).

The arranger, in turn, enters into two separate contracts:

- A conventional ¥/US$ currency swap (to match the cash flow between the arranger and the issuer).
- An option sale agreement whereunder the option buyer pays an amount of ¥412,500,000 (US$3,089,888) to the arranger (representing the option premium). The option premium is then reinvested (typically via the currency swap) to generate the total yen coupon payment under the issue.

**Day 183 (six months after launch) US$ Interest Payment**
Issuer pays arranger (who in turn makes a corresponding payment to swap counterparty) US$ interest at the rate of 6-month LIBOR less 0.25% pa (on the US$ principal amount).

**Day 365 (maturity) US$ Interest Payment**
Issuer pays arranger US$ interest at rate of 6-month LIBOR less 0.25% pa.

**Day 365 (maturity) Principal/Redemption Payments**
**Case 1: Nikkei Index Below Strike Level**

Arranger undertakes following payments:

• The bond redemption amount is 100% of original face value. There is no payment obligation to the option buyer.
• Pays to issuer ¥5,825,000,000 (representing ¥5,000,000,000 (principal) and ¥825,000,000 (interest at 16.50% pa)).
• Receives from issuer US$37,453,184.

These cash flows are matched by offsetting cash flows with the swap counterparty.

The issuer uses the yen received to fulfil its obligation to the investor under the terms of the bond.

**Day 365 (maturity) Principal/Redemption Payments**
**Case 2: Nikkei Index Above Strike Level**

The bond redemption amount is less than 100% of original face value. The Nikkei Index call option is in-the-money and the option buyer is entitled to receive a payment under the option contract (based on a cash settlement arrangement).

The cash flows are the same as for Case 1 with the following adjustments:

• The arranger reduces the payment to the issuer. The amount of the payment is adjusted in accordance with the redemption formula with the issuer receiving exactly the yen amount corresponding to its obligation to the investor.
• The balance of the yen (the difference between the face value of the bond and the actual amount owed to the investor in terms of the redemption formula) is paid to the option buyer under the settlement terms of the option.

For example, if the Nikkei Index at maturity is 29,835 (130% of launch level), the arranger makes the following payments:

- To the issuer          ¥3,500,000,000 (70% of ¥5,000,000,000)
- To the option buyer     ¥1,500,000,000 (30% of ¥ 5,000,000,000).

The above arrangement ensures that the issuer and the arranger are protected from the fluctuations in the value of the option that are borne by the investor.

The structure of the cash flows are set out in diagrammatic form below:

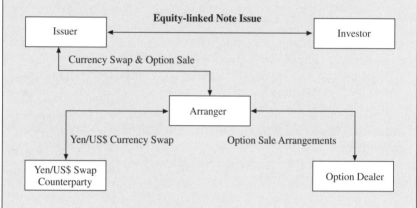

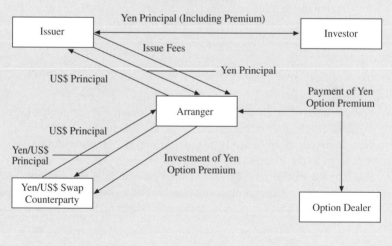

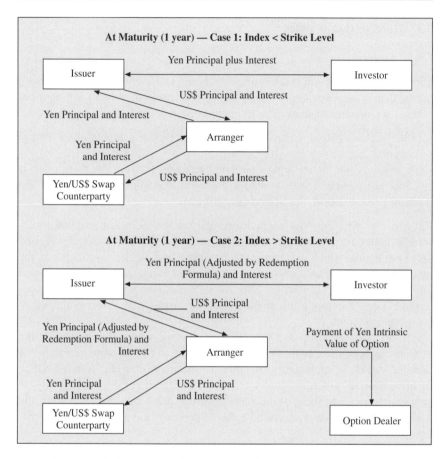

A number of variations are feasible on the basic structure:

- Leveraging the structure through the sale of additional options to increase the premium capture to increase the running yield. The extent of the additional enhancement feasible will depend on the relative value of the two options required to be traded as the strike of the option being purchased will increase as more options are sold.
- De-leveraging the structure by reducing the number of options sold.
- Limiting the capital loss by purchasing the put at a level that ensures return of some but not all the capital. In the extreme case, the principal could be fully guaranteed with only *the coupon amount* being risked.

The variations are designed to trade-off the level of yield enhancement against the risk of loss from unfavorable movements in the underlying index. One of the main variations on the basic structure of sold optionality is the reverse convertible structure discussed in the next section

## 5.3 Reverse Convertibles

### 5.3.1 Concept

The basic concept of a reverse convertible bond[5] is an issue of debt that pays a higher than market coupon in return for the investor in the bond granting a put option on a nominated share. The transaction operates as follows:

- The investor makes an investment and receives the higher than market coupon.
- At maturity, the issuer repays the bond either in cash (if the share price is above the agreed strike) or with a predetermined number of shares (if the share price is below the agreed put strike).

Reverse convertibles were originally developed in 1993.[6] The original issues were structured to enable the investor to sell an *out-of-the-money* (by around 10%) put option, which was viewed by the investor as a price level at which the investor would increase exposure to the relevant stock (effectively a targeted buy or cash-covered put write). The stocks underlying such transaction were popular large capitalization stocks, such as Coca-Cola, Pfizer, Johnson & Johnson, and so on.

The market spread in the late 1990s to Europe where the interest in the product has been more retail focused.[7] The market in Europe was driven by low nominal yields and high equity volatility. The structure enabled the construction of high coupon structures that were attractive for investors seeking higher coupon returns.[8] The focus of the market is the Benelux countries, Germany and Switzerland. The reverse convertible issues generally have been on large well-known companies.

The structure has also been used in Asia. A typical structure, as at the end of 1995, would entail an issue of, say, a 6-month note with an embedded European put option on a Hong Kong stock. The embedded put option would be struck at a price of around 90% of the prevailing market price of the equity stock. The yield on these notes, depending on the underlying stock involved, was around 11 to 13% pa. The attraction of these instruments includes the high yield available.

---

[5]   See Andrew Webb "Reverse Convertibles: Drive-By Deals" (September 10, 1998) *Financial Products* Issue 97 18-20.

[6]   Bankers Trust is reported to have originated the structure.

[7]   For example, Warburg Dillion Read introduced this structure as Geld oder Aktien Lieferung (GOAL) meaning cash or share delivery for the German and Swiss markets.

[8]   For example in 1998, these structures were designed to offer yields of 7.00 to 11.50% pa at a time when German interest rates were around 3.50% pa and Swiss interest rates were around 1.00 to 2.00% pa.

However, the principal attraction of these structures was the investor willingness to take *delivery* of the stock, in the case of exercise of the put option. The investors were willing to purchase the underlying equity at the relevant entry prices. The product was used both by individual retail investors and portfolio managers.

### 5.3.2 Structure

**Exhibit 11.12** sets out the typical terms of synthetic reverse convertible issues.

---

**Exhibit 11.12**
**Reverse Convertibles**

| | |
|---|---|
| Issuer | Highly rated bank or frequent issuer. |
| Amount | To be agreed in US$ or specified currency. |
| Maturity | 1 year |
| Coupon | Agreed yield well above the prevailing market return in the relevant current. |
| Redemption | At the issuer's option either at par or in the form of 1 registered share in ABC Company if the stock price is below say Swfr 2,100. |
| Denomination | Swfr 2,100 |

---

The key structural aspects are as follows:

- **Issuer** — the issuers of reverse convertible bonds have typically been highly rated (AA or better) investment banks or frequent issuers.
- **Maturity** — the issues have generally been for maturity up to three years with a concentration in shorter maturities.
- **Coupon** — the coupon is purely driven by the put option premium that is added to the market yield. The premium depends upon the strike of the option, as well as term and volatility of the underlying stock. In most cases, the put has been written at-the-money or significantly in the money relative to the forward price of the stock to generate higher coupons for the investors.
- **Strike price of the embedded put option** — the embedded put option is usually structured at a strike price below the current market price of the stock (say around 90-95% of the prevailing market price). This is designed to enable the investor to obtain stock at below levels prevailing in the market at the time of issue where the issuer exercises the put option.

The embedded put option will generally be stripped out and sold into the OTC market or alternatively held by the investment bank as a hedge within its own option portfolio. In the case of issues by frequent issuers, the arranger has typically entered into a derivative transaction to hedge out the issuer's cash flows (effectively purchasing the put from the issuer) to guarantee the issuer a known and attractive cost of funds.

### 5.3.3 Economics

The economic structure of the issues combines from the viewpoint of the investor a combination of:

- An investment in a bond
- The sale of a European-style put option on the shares of the underlying equity

The valuation reflects the simple combination of these two elements. The pricing dynamics reflect a variety of factors including:

- The strike price relative to the current stock price.
- The volatility of the share price, as well as the term structure of volatility and any skews in the volatility surface.
- The term structure of interest rates.

The short-term nature of the market reflects in part the above pricing dynamics. As maturity of the reverse convertible increases, the value of the embedded option does not increase sufficiently to allow the issuer to provide the additional coupon to attract the investor. The additional yield has to be generated by adjustments to the strike price (setting it in-the-money to increase the premium). This tends to be unattractive to investors as the risk of exercise increases.

The reverse convertible outperforms an equivalent bond investment provided the share price on the underlying shares does not fall below the strike on the embedded put option. The issue will underperform the bond where the share price falls below the strike price.

### 5.3.4 Variations

Structural variations include:

- Incorporation of a redemption option hereby the issuer can deliver a mixture of cash and a specified selection of shares. **Exhibit 11.13** sets out an example of this type of structure where the investor can receive a basket of shares representing the relevant interest or the cash equivalent.
- Inclusion of an amortizing structure whereby the notes amortize in prenominated installments. **Exhibit 11.14** sets out an example of this type of structure.

- Double triggers where the embedded put option can only be triggered by two conditions: usually the fact that the stock or index price is below the nominated initial value *and* on any day the relevant stock or index reaches a certain minimum value below the nominated initial value. These structures are generally based around exotic options such as barrier options that are triggered upon the occurrence of a specific price event.
- The capacity to repay using *one* from *a selection of nominated equities*. This is effectively the sale of a worst of option entailing greater risk to the investor.

---

**Exhibit 11.13**
**Reverse Convertibles — Variations: Example 1**

The structure set out below enables the issuer to deliver cash equivalent of the stocks under the reverse convertible structure rather than the shares themselves:

| | |
|---|---|
| Issuer | AA or better rated |
| Amount | Euro 25 million |
| Maturity | 2 years |
| Issue Price | 100.00 |
| Interest Rate | 10.00% pa payable annually |
| Redemption | At the option of the issuer as: |

- 100%; or
- By delivery of the total share amount or the cash equivalent of the total share amount calculated as:

$$\text{Amount}/1{,}000{,}000 \times \text{Share amount}$$

Where:

Share amount in respect of each Euro Stoxx 50 constituent shares is calculated as a number of such shares equal to the weighting in the index multiplied by a conversion factor of 283.12.

The structure provides the investor with a high current coupon. The investor assumes the risk that if the Euro Stoxx index declines the investor receives less than the face value of the security either in stocks or cash equivalent. Where the investor receives cash the loss is crystallized and there is no prospect of recovery of value from any future appreciation in the stocks/index. This can be corrected if at the time of maturity the investor purchases the underlying stock equal to the original cash value of the index.

**Exhibit 11.14**
**Reverse Convertibles — Variations: Example 2**

The structure below sets out an amortizing reverse convertible transaction:

| | |
|---|---|
| Issuer | AAA rated |
| Amount | Euro 50 million |
| Issue price | 100% |
| Maturity | 5 years |
| Interest | 6-month Euro Euribor plus 4.00% pa payable semi-annually. |
| Redemption | The notes will amortize in installments on each interest date in accordance with the following: |

- If closing level ≥ initial level, redemption will be 100.00% of the principal.
- If closing level < initial level, redemption will be by delivery of 12 Michelin shares per Euro 5,400 denomination.

Where:

Closing level is the closing price per Michelin share on the Paris Stock Exchange five business days before each interest date.
Initial level is equal to Euro 45.00375.

Under this structure, investors receive a high coupon in return for assuming the risk of a redemption amount below par. In a conventional bullet-amortizing reverse convertible, investors are exposed to the share value on a single date at maturity. The amortizing structure means that the issue matures and is repaid in 10 amortizing instalments. Investors will receive a redemption installment lower than 100.00% of the redemption amount only for the semi-annual periods where the share value falls. This has the effect of distributing the risk over the redemption dates of the note.

*Source: MTNWeek* (April 30, 1999).

# 6.    Equity Index-linked Notes — Principal-protected Structures

## 6.1    Overview

Principal-protected equity index-linked structures are targeted at risk averse investors seeking preservation of capital while creating a low risk exposure to the underlying equity index. The basic component of these transaction is a fixed income bond where the coupon or return is foregone and utilized to buy an option that creates the required exposure to the index. In this section, the structure and hedging of these types of notes is considered together with structural variations and the performance of these notes.

### 6.2 Principal-protected Note Structure

The basic structure consists of short- to medium-term investment that provides protection against a decline in market values while maintaining some exposure to the market in the case of appreciation. This necessitates the combination of a call option on the index with the underlying bond.

An example of a principal-protected equity index-linked note is set out in **Exhibit 11.15**. The transaction described is the issue of A$50 million of All Ordinary Share Price Riskless Index Notes (ASPRINs) issued by the New South Wales Treasury Corporation in November 1986. The hedging structure of the issue is set out in **Exhibit 11.16**. The basic structured depicted forms the basic template for all such transactions.

---

**Exhibit 11.15**
**Principal-protected Equity Index-linked Note — Example 1**

In November of 1986, Bankers Trust Australia Limited (BTAL) launched an issue of A$50 million of All Ordinaries Share Price Riskless Index Notes (ASPRINs) on the following terms:

| | |
|---|---|
| Issuer | New South Wales Treasury Corporation (guaranteed by the New South Wales Government). |
| Amount | A$50 million |
| Maturity | 4 years (due December 21, 1990) |
| Coupon | 0% pa |
| Issue Price | 100 |
| Redemption Price | In accordance with the following formula: FV × Index (at maturity)/Index (at launch). |

Where:

FV = face value amount
Index (at maturity) = All Ordinaries Index at close of business December 20, 1990
Index (at launch) = All Ordinaries Index at time of issue set at 1372.00

Minimum
Redemption Price  100

From the viewpoint of the investor, the transaction operates as follows:

- The investor is guaranteed return of its initial investment. That is, if A$ 100 is invested at maturity, then the investor receives at least A$ 100.
- The investor's final cash receipt, that is, the redemption amount, is linked to the All Ordinaries Share Price Index. If the index appreciates over a stated level (1,372) and stands at this level upon maturity of the security, then the investor receives a redemption amount that is calculated as the face value amount multiplied by the All Ordinaries Index at maturity divided by the initial share index level of 1,372. For example, if the index doubles over the 4-year life of the bonds, investors simply double the original investment. If the index declines under the strike price, investors will receive back their original investment.

In substance, the investor has bought a 4-year European call option on the All-Ordinaries Index with a strike price of 1,372. The effective cost of the call is the income forgone on the funds invested.

This income forgone can be stated as the interest income on equivalent 4-year comparable risk-fixed interest investments (around 14.70/14.75% pa). In theoretical terms, the effective cost equates to the say 14.70% pa forgone, interest that is equivalent to a A$ option cost of 42.83% of face value or A$21.42 million for the A$50 million call.

**Exhibit 11.16**
**Principal-protected Equity Index-linked Note — Hedging Structure**

The hedging structure for the ASPRINS issue entails a series of derivative transactions designed to convert the exposure under the note into a conventional debt issue.

Under the structure of the issue, the issuer saves approximately 14.70% pa; that is, the full coupon on conventional debt. However, the issuer assumes a final redemption risk as it has an exposure to the level of the All Ordinaries Share Price Index at maturity. The issuer uses a portion of its saving on interest cost to purchase an option that effectively hedges its exposure of the final redemption amount on the securities. This is done through the purchase of an (European) option on the All Ordinaries Index at a strike price of 1,372 with an expiry date in four years. The options were arranged by BTAL and were apparently written by institutional investors. BTAL provided the New South Wales Treasury Corporation with the option and in turn purchased an offsetting option from the institutions. The institutions granting the option undertook the transaction as part of a program of covered call writing against their equity portfolios.

The structure of the transaction for the issuer was as follows:

- New South Wales Treasury Corporation paid, it is estimated, 41% of face value (A$20.5 million) to BTAL to cover its exposure under the equity index call.
- This effectively leaves New South Wales' Treasury with a 4-year-zero coupon borrowing (face value A$50 million with a present value or net proceeds of A$29.5 million (59% of face value)).
- This equates to an effective yield of 14.10% pa. This represents an estimated saving of approximately 60 bps pa on its normal cost of funding.
- At maturity, New South Wales Treasury Corporation repaid A$50 million to the investors if the All Ordinaries Share Price Index was below 1372.0. If the index was above 1372.0, then BTAL made payments to the issuer covering the additional amounts as calculated under the redemption formula payable by New South Wales Treasury Corporation to the investor.

The issuer, if it wished to eliminate its exposure to the zero-coupon structure of the borrowing, could enter into a further derivative transaction (a zero-coupon interest rate swap). This would eliminate its exposure to the pattern of coupons under the borrowing and restructure its exposure into a par coupon bond.[9]

The economic basis of the ASPRINs issue was the differential value placed on the 4-year equity index call by the investor (the purchaser of the option) and the equity portfolio fund managers (the ultimate grantor of the option). The value of the call option on the index (stated in % terms) is estimated as follows:

---

[9]   See Das, Satyajit (1994) *Swaps & Financial Derivatives*; LBC Information Services, Sydney; McGraw-Hill, Chicago at Chapter 12.

| Assumed Volatility (% pa) | Dividend Rates (% pa) | | | | |
|---|---|---|---|---|---|
| | 0.00 | 1.00 | 2.00 | 3.00 | 4.00 |
| 20 | 41.98 | 38.77 | 35.68 | **32.72** | **29.90** |
| 25 | 43.51 | 40.41 | 37.43 | **34.57** | **31.85** |
| 30 | 45.40 | 42.37 | 39.47 | 36.69 | 34.02 |

The option fair value estimated is based on the following assumptions:

Market Index (at launch/closing)    1,372
Strike                              1,372
Time to Expiry                      4 years
Risk Free Rate                      13.90% (4-year government bond rate)

As is evident, the option price is sensitive to the assumed market dividend rate and volatility level. Based on an assumed market volatility level of 20-25%, and a market dividend rate of around 3-4% pa, it is possible to establish a range of values for the option of 29.90-34.57%.

The investors in the ASPRINs transaction are clearly paying around 30% more for the call option on the market index, relative to its estimated fair value. Assuming that the institution granting the option priced the option at close to its theoretical price, then there is a maximum arbitrage margin of around 9-11% to be divided between the issuer and the arranger of the transaction.

**Exhibit 11.17** sets out an example of a principal-protected note where the underlying index (the S&P 500) is denominated in a currency (US$) other than that of the underlying bond (A$). An additional difference between the structure is the variation in the participation rate (110% versus 100%). In effect, the investor participates in any appreciation in the index at a rate that is *1.1 times* any increase. This reflects the fact that the *face value of calls* embedded in the note is equivalent to the participation rate (110%) of the *face value of the note*.

**Exhibit 11.18** highlights the trade-off between coupon and participation levels utilizing the transaction described in **Exhibit 11.17** as an example.

**Exhibit 11.17**
**Principal-protected Equity Index-linked Note — Example 2**

Issuer                  AAA- or AA-rated issuer
Issue Price             100%

| | |
|---|---|
| Amount | A$100 million |
| Maturity | 5 years |
| Coupon | 3 to 3.25% pa (paid annually in A$) |
| Underlying Index | S&P 500 |
| Market Participation | 110% of the percentage increase of the index payable in US$. |
| A$/US$ Exchange Rate (issue date) | A$1: US$0.78 |
| Redemption Amount | At maturity, the note will redeem as follows: In A$ — the issue amount of A$100 million; plus: In US$ — increase in the underlying index calculated as follows: Market participation × [(Underlying index (at maturity) – Underlying index (at issue date)/ Underlying index (at issue date)] × [Amount] × [A$/US$ Exchange Rate (issue date)] |

In this example, if the S&P 500 had risen 10% at maturity, the investor's return would be as follows:

• Return of A$100 million investment.
• Receipt of US$8.58 million (being 11% of US$78 million being the US$ value of the initial investment based on the exchange rate at the issue date).

The return on investment would equate to a A$ return (principal plus interest) equal to A$11 million if it was assumed that the exchange rate remained unchanged.

**Exhibit 11.18**
**Principal-protected Equity Index-linked Note — Example 2 — Sensitivities**

| Maturity (years) | Coupon (% pa) | Participation Rate (%) |
|---|---|---|
| 1 | 0.00 | 80 |
| 2 | 0.75 to 1.00 | 100 |
| 3 | 2.25 to 2.50 | 100 |
| 5 | 3.00 to 3.25 | 110 |

The essential elements of principal protection entail the combination of a call option on the index with the bond. The call premium is funded from the coupon available. The issuer of the note, in common with most structured note issue formats, is generally immunized from the market risk of the structure. This is achieved through the simultaneous entry by the issuer into a derivative transaction with typically the arranger to cover the equity exposure (through the purchase of the call option on the underlying index). The derivative transaction has the effect of converting the issuer's exposure into a fixed-rate debt issue for the relevant maturity that can be transformed in terms of currency or interest rate through additional derivative transactions as required.

**Exhibit 11.19** sets out the essential structural design of the principal protected note in a general framework. **Exhibit 11.20** sets out the general hedging structure for these types of notes.

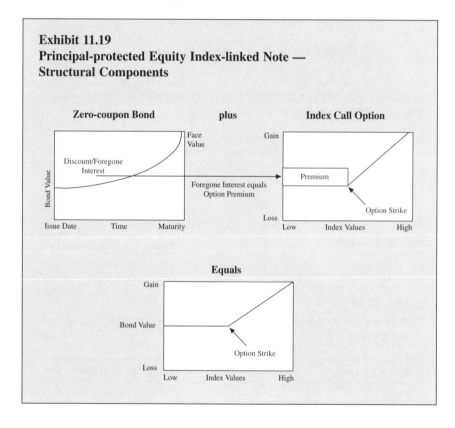

**Exhibit 11.19**
**Principal-protected Equity Index-linked Note —**
**Structural Components**

**Exhibit 11.20**
**Principal-protected Equity Index-linked Note — Hedging Structure**

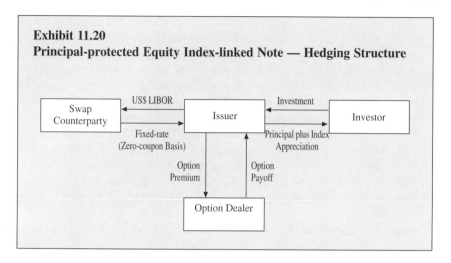

### 6.3   Principal-protected Notes — Structural Variations

The basic principal-protected equity-linked note structure entails a note with a lower than market coupon that has a guaranteed return of principal while providing the investor with asymmetric exposure to the equity market through the mechanism of the embedded call option. The exposure is, in the standard arrangement, equivalent to 100% of the face value of the note.

A number of variations on the basic structures have also evolved. These variations have evolved in response to a number of factors including:

- The investor requirement for a minimum coupon level.
- The investor requirement for a certain level of participation in any movement in the index.
- Investor willingness to sacrifice *total protection* of transaction principal.
- The available level of coupon income that can be used to purchase the required option.
- The cost of the option.

The variations that have evolved to reconcile the above factors include:

- **Variable participation structures** — where the level of participation relative to the face value of the bond is varied. This entails the use of a gearing element into the principal indexation process whereby the value of the security changes by a multiple (usually higher or lower than one) for a move in the underlying equity market index. The participation level is lowered usually to accommodate a higher coupon level or the relative cost of the option to the coupon available. The participation level may be increased through increasing the volume of options embedded to increase the sensitivity of the note to equity market movements. The higher level of option premium to be financed is funded through a lower coupon or, where the coupon available is insufficient by reducing the level of principal protection (usually to a level lower than 100% of the face value, say, 90%). **Exhibit 11.21** sets out the return profile of a principal-protected participating equity index-linked note. **Exhibit 11.22** sets out an example of a principal-protected participating note. The transaction described is an issue of Protected Equity Participation Securities (PEPS) linked to the price performance of an *individual equity stock* (in this case Nestlé)[10] where return of principal is guaranteed at 100% but participation in any appreciation is limited to 82% of any increase. This reflects in this case the inability to finance more than 0.82 call option per note out of the coupon income available.

- **Capped participation level** — where the note principal is 100% guaranteed and where the participation level is 100%, in cases where the coupon available is insufficient to meet the amount of premium to be financed, a mechanism for reducing the option premium is the use of an option spread. This entails the purchase of a call option at a strike level set at-the-money and the sale of a call option at a strike level that is out-of-the-money. Both options have the same expiry date. The second option restricts the return to the investor to a maximum of the difference between the par value of the note and the strike price of the out-of-the-money option. The premium received for the second option effectively lowers the option cost that allows the *net* premium to be funded from the available coupon. **Exhibit 11.23** on page 546 sets out the return profile of a principal-protected capped return equity index-linked note. **Exhibit 11.24** on page 547 sets out an example of a principal-protected capped equity-linked note. The transaction described is an issue of GROIs where the performance of the individual notes is linked to the performance of the FTSE-100. Three separate tranches were offered each offering a choice of guaranteed income and return trade-offs. The issues effectively embed a call spread to create the required return profile. The strike of the base option (lower strike) is also set above the current spot value of the index to lower the net premium cost in this issue. The number of options in the call spread is varied to create the trade-off between coupon income and index participation.

- **Less than 100% principal guarantee** — where the coupon available is insufficient to engineer the degree of exposure to the underlying index, the investor may be prepared to utilize a portion of the principal to purchase the required quantum of optionality. This is usually done by guaranteeing the principal return at a level of between 70 and 90% of face value. **Exhibit**

---

[10] Identical structures involving an equity index are clearly feasible.

**11.25** on page 548 sets out an example of an issue of Protected Index Participation (PIP) units creating a return profile linked to the performance of the Swiss stock market through the SMI index. The structure described entails a guaranteed return at a level lower than par (95%). This allows the creation of a higher degree of participation in any index appreciation (in this case 96%) than would have been permissible given the coupon available, based on prevailing market rates, to finance the purchase of the option.

**Exhibit 11.21**
**Principal-protected Participating Equity Index-linked Note — Return Profile**

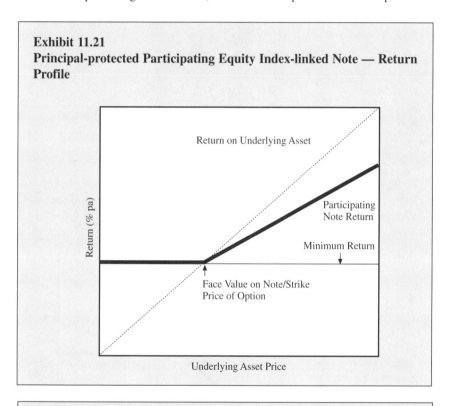

**Exhibit 11.22**
**Principal-protected Participating Equity-linked Notes**

| Issuer | Swiss Bank Corporation (Luxembourg) |
|---|---|
| Amount | (Up to) 10,000 Protected Equity Participation Securities (PEPS). |
| Maturity | 18 months |
| Underlying Securities | Each PEPS is on 1 underlying bearer share of Nestlé SA. |
| Exercise Price | Swfr 9,590 |

| Participation Percentage | 82% |
| --- | --- |
| Exercise | If at maturity the price of the underlying security is greater than the exercise price, then investors will receive the initial outlay, calculated as the initial outlay plus the participation percentage of the increase in the price of the underlying security. If at maturity the price of the underlying security is below the exercise price, then investors will receive the initial outlay. |
| Issue Price | 100% (plus 0.165% of stamp tax, cantonal, and stock exchange fees) |
| Lead Manager | Swiss Bank Corporation |

*Source: International Financing Review* Issue 926 (April 25, 1992): 71.

**Exhibit 11.23**
**Principal-protected Capped Return Equity Index-linked Note —**
**Return Profile**

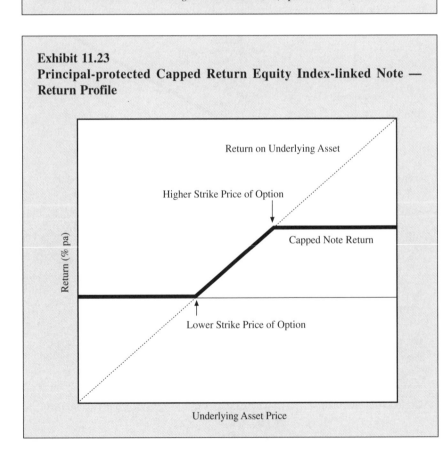

**Exhibit 11.24**
**Principal-protected Capped Return Equity Index-linked Note**

In February 1992, Swiss Bank Corporation issued 1-year GROIs linked to the performance of the UK stock market, through the FTSE-100 index. The terms of the issue were as follows:

| | |
|---|---|
| Issuer | Swiss Bank Corporation |
| Amount | £20 million |
| Maturity | 1 year |
| Interest | Zero |
| Underlying Equity Index | FTSE-100 |
| Initial Value of Index | 2,552.90 |
| Redemption Value | |

| | Minimum Return (underlying index is less than 2,680.55 at maturity) | Maximum Return (underlying index is greater than 3,344.30 at maturity) |
|---|---|---|
| Tranche A | 7% | 13.0% |
| Tranche B | 4% | 20.3% |
| Tranche C | 0% | 30.1% |

The GROI issue was structured to enable investors to select between the different offered payout profiles. Each tranche structure offered a minimum return irrespective of the value of the FTSE-100 index at maturity. In addition the issue offered a returns linked to the performance of the equity index. These returns commenced once the FTSE-100 exceeded the 2,680.55 level (the initial index level). The return was capped at a preset maximum level that was activated when the FTSE-100 reached 3,344.30 (the maximum index level).

Economically, the structure entails a combination of the following elements:

• A 1-year £ note issued by the issuer.
• A call spread on the FTSE-100 as follows:
  Purchase a call at the initial index level.
  Sell a call at the maximum index level.
• The net premium on the call spread is funded by the investor from the interest payable on the note.

The capped payment structure is created by the call spread structure. The pattern of payoffs as between the tranches is varied by adjusting the *number* of call options utilized. In order to increase the maximum level, the number of calls is increased with the additional premium payable further reducing the guaranteed minimum level of return on the note.

**Exhibit 11.25**
**Minimum Principal Guaranteed Equity Index-linked Note**

| | |
|---|---|
| Issuer | Swiss Bank Corporation (Luxembourg) |
| Amount | Swfr50 million of Protected Index Participation (PIP) units. |
| Maturity | 1 year |
| Issue Price | 100% |
| Coupon | Zero |
| Denominations | Swfr5,000 |
| Underlying Index | SMI |
| Exercise Price | Swfr2,590 (at the money) |
| Participation Percentage | 96% |
| Exercise | If at maturity the value of the underlying index is greater than the exercise price, then investors will receive the initial outlay, calculated as the initial outlay plus the participation percentage of the increase in the value of the underlying index. If at maturity the price of the underlying security is below the exercise price, then investors will receive the guaranteed redemption amount. |
| Guaranteed Redemption Amount | 95% or Swfr4,750 per note |
| Lead Manager | Swiss Bank Corporation |

*Source: International Financing Review* Issue 1050 (October 31, 1994): 99.

The demand for highly structured equity exposure has prompted the creation of specific equity-linked note structures with highly customized returns. The customization of return can take a variety of formats. The major types require incorporation of *multiple* option strategies or exotic options within the note structure.

**Exhibit 11.26** sets out an example of an equity-linked note incorporating multiple options. The transaction involving the German DAX index combines a bond and four separate options (a Condor option spread strategy). The central feature of the bond is the coupon of 9.00% pa; that is, at a level some 4.80% pa above the return available on comparable 2-year bank bonds for comparable issuers. The higher return to the investor in the bond reflects the sale of options embedded in the redemption arrangements the premium on which is used to enhance the return on the structure. The return to the investor will be in the range −6.46% pa (worst case) to 9.00% pa (best case). Return of principal of 70% is effectively guaranteed. This type of structure entails incorporating highly customized option transactions to create a specific return profile consistent with the investor's expectations regarding the expected value movements in the underlying index.

---

**Exhibit 11.26**
**Issue of Equity Index-linked Option Spread Notes**

In late 1995, WestDeutsche Landesbank Girozentrale, following on from earlier issues of similar structure, undertook an issue of Condor Bonds. The essential terms of the issue are as follows:

| | |
|---|---|
| Issuer | WestDeutsche Landesbank Girozentrale |
| Amount | DM100 million |
| Maturity | 2 years |
| Coupon | 9.00% pa payable annually |
| Issue Price | 99.90% of face value |
| Redemption | The principal at redemption is calculated as follows: |

1. at 100% or par, if the DAX index is between 1,900 and 2,550 on the reference date (some eight days before maturity); or
2. if the DAX is above 2,550:
   20,300 less six times the DAX on the reference date, subject to a minimum redemption level of DM3,500 per DM5,000 bond; or
3. if the DAX is below 1,900:
   6 times the DAX on the reference date less 6,400, subject to a minimum redemption level of DM3,500 per DM5,000 bond; or

The central feature of the bond is the coupon that of 9.00% pa. This is 4.80% pa above the return available on comparable 2-year bank bonds for comparable issuers. The higher return to the investor in the bond reflects the sale of options embedded in the redemption arrangements, the premium on which is used to enhance the return on the structure.

The options embedded are as follows:

- Sold call on the DAX with a strike of 2,550 that is effectively capped by a purchased call with a strike of 2,800.
- Sold puts on the DAX with a strike of 1,900 that is effectively capped by a purchased put with a strike of 1,650.

The structure is leveraged with the options sold being some six times the face value of the bond (DM5,000).

The combination of options allows the maximum capture of premium to the investor. The combination of the call and put spreads creates the specific payment profile whereby the redemption fluctuates between 70% and 100%.

From the investor's perspective, the attraction of the structure is the enhanced yield available that is offset by the risk of some capital loss if the DAX moves outside the boundaries specified. The return to the investor will be in the range −6.46% pa (worst case) to 9.00% pa (best case). Return of principal of 70% is effectively guaranteed. The structure that embodies an option combination behaves in a manner that is not dissimilar to a digital option embedded in the bond.

**Exhibit 11.27** sets out an example of a different type of highly customized equity-linked structure. In this case, the investor receives a return linked to the performance of the Japanese Nikkei 225 Index *denominated in A$*. The investor's principal is guaranteed and the return is asymmetric. The structure entails the combination of a fixed interest security with a quanto call option. The quanto option is a type of multifactor exotic option.[11] The major feature of this type of option is that it is designed to primarily have a *principal amount* or *face value* that is linked to a market variable. In this case, the call option on the Nikkei option is quanto-ed to enable any positive return on the option (resulting from the appreciation of the index) to be converted *at a pre-agreed A$/¥ exchange rate*. This quantity-adjusting feature of the option allows the yen denominated increases in the underlying index to be captured in A$ terms.

---

[11] For a discussion of quanto options, see Das, Satyajit (1996) *Exotic Options*; LBC Information Services, Sydney at Chapter 12.

**Exhibit 11.27**
**Issue of Currency-protected Equity Index-linked Note**

| | |
|---|---|
| Issuer | AAA- or AA-rated issuer |
| Issue Price | 100% |
| Amount | A$100 million |
| Maturity | 5 years |
| Coupon | 0 to 0.25% pa (paid annually in A$) |
| Underlying Index | Nikkei 225 |
| Market Participation | 115% of the percentage increase of the index payable in A$. |
| A$/US$ Exchange Rate (issue date) | A$1 = US$ 0.78 |
| Redemption Amount | At maturity, the note will redeem as follows: In A$ – the issue amount of A$100 million; Plus: In A$ – increase in the underlying index calculated as follows: Market participation × [(Underlying index (at maturity) – Underlying index (at issue date))/ Underlying index (at issue date)] × [Amount] |

In this example, if the Nikkei 225 had risen 10% at maturity, the investor's return would be as follows:

- Return of A$100 million investment.
- Receipt of A$11.5 million (being 10% of the initial investment adjusted by the market participation factor).

The return on investment would equate to an *A$* return (principal plus interest) equal to A$11.5 million irrespective of whether the exchange rate remained unchanged.

Other equity structures with embedded exotic optionality are feasible. For example, structures where the performance of the underlying security is linked to not one but a variety of indexes have been completed. For example, the investor may receive a return based on the most favorable movement within a specified basket of indexes.[12]

---

[12] Some of these types of note structures are discussed in Chapter 13.

## 6.4    Principal-protected Notes — Performance

The structures identified highlight the intrinsic attraction of these principal-protected structures to risk-averse investor's seeking to create exposure to equity markets. The flexibility in structures available allows considerable customization to fit risk-return trade-offs for individual investors.

These advantages have led to a rapid increase in the use of these structures in both developed and emerging markets. Issues have been targeted to both US domestic and European markets, as well as Asian markets. A significant portion of the demand for these instruments has been driven by individual investors. There is also interest from institutional investors in these structures. The institutional interest derives, in part, from evidence that these types of instruments offer significant advantages over traditional defensive investments, primarily fixed income investments.

Based on research, these instruments appear to offer attractive risk-return profiles. **Exhibit 11.28** sets out the comparative returns for investments in principal-protected equity-linked notes relative to debt and equity returns for the overlapping 5-year periods between 1948 and 1993. The pattern of investment returns shows the predictable outcome that these instruments outperform stocks when stock markets decline and underperform when stock markets rise. The returns are on average greater than that available on traditional debt investments. The US research is consistent with the results from other markets such as France, Germany, Switzerland, and the UK.[13]

The empirical evidence is both predictable and consistent with the practice of portfolio insurance type concepts of investment management. This has encouraged capital stable investors to utilize this particular investment structure within asset portfolios.

---

**Exhibit 11.28
Comparative Investment Returns —
Principal-protected Equity Index-linked Note vs
Debt and Equity Returns**

| Investment | Average Annual Return (% pa) |
|---|---|
| Treasury Bill | 4.81 |
| 5-year Treasury Note | 5.42 |
| Equity-linked Note | 8.33 |
| S&P 500 | 9.93 |

---

[13]  See Baubonis, Charles, Gastineau, Gary, and Purcell, David "The Banker's Guide To Equity-linked Certificates Of Deposit" (Winter 1993) *The Journal of Derivatives* 87-95.

Notes:
1. The above investment results are for overlapping 5-year periods between 1948 and 1993.
2. The return on equity-linked notes is based on equity-linked Certificates of Deposit adjusted for a 2.5% sales fee. The equity-linked structure assumes a 100% principal guaranteed structure and a 100% participation in the S&P 500 index. If the interest available is greater than that required to purchase a 100% participation in the index, any surplus is paid out as an interest coupon.
3. The dividend-adjusted S&P 500 returns are after adjustment for a present value management fee of 2%.

Source: Baubonis, Charles, Gastineau, Gary, and Purcell, David "The Banker's Guide To Equity-linked Certificates Of Deposit." The Journal of Derivatives 87-95 (Winter 1993): 91-92.

## 7.  Equity-linked Notes — Regulatory Arbitrage Structures

Regulation-driven structures are customized to individual investor requirements. However, one prominent theme in these types of note structures is the presence of foreign investment restrictions on share ownership.

**Exhibit 11.29** sets out the terms and conditions of an issue of QanMacs undertaken by Macquarie Bank Limited (an Australian investment bank). The issue is effectively designed to allow investors to replicate an economic equivalent of an investment in the shares of Qantas Limited (Qantas) (an Australian company whose principal business is aviation). The security is effectively a 5-year note with an embedded 5-year equity swap on the underlying equity.

The background and context of the issue is illustrative of these regulation-driven structures. In July 1995, the Australian government launched an initial public offering of 75% of the capital of Qantas as part of its privatization. The government had earlier completed a trade sale of 25% of the airline to British Airways by way of a trade sale. The initial public offering was subject to a restriction that dictated that a majority of the shares (that is, in excess of 50% of the shares) must be held by Australian residents. This was designed to ensure satisfaction of the conditions applicable under air and landing rights treaties in place between Australia and other jurisdictions that substantially determined the airlines network activities. The float that was successful saw foreign interest in excess of around the 24% level permitted (given British Airways was a nonresident). This required foreign shareholders to divest their shareholding to enable compliance with the ownership restriction.

The QanMacs issue was launched against this background. The issue structure enabled the investor to economically replicate its investment in Qantas with the exception of voting rights. The fact that the underlying shares were held by Australian residents allowed the airline to satisfy the ownership requirement. The legal owner of the shares effectively transferred its ownership of the shares to the investors indirectly through the equity-linked notes.

The exact structure by which this issue was hedged is not known. However, a possible arrangement whereby the issuer, Macquarie Bank, issues the note and hedges itself through the entry into an offsetting equity swap on the underlying Qantas shares is set out in **Exhibit 11.30**.

The structure used in the QanMacs issue is equally applicable to other markets where similar ownership restrictions are applicable. Example include many emerging markets where foreign ownership is restricted by an absolute ceiling level or certain industries where social, economic, or political factors dictate foreign or other ownership restrictions. The structure described can be utilized to avoid the impact of these limitations on direct equity exposure to these entities.

---

**Exhibit 11.29**
**QanMacs Issue — Terms and Conditions**

| | |
|---|---|
| Issuer | Macquarie Bank Limited |
| Type Of Issue | Unsecured Notes with a payoff and yield profile equal to Qantas Limited (Qantas) ordinary shares. |
| Rating | A (Standard & Poor's) |
| Amount | A$100 million |
| Maturity | 5 years subject to extension for further periods up to 75 years. |
| Face Value | A$2.00 |
| Issue Price | Prevailing price for Qantas shares plus A$0.05. |
| Fees | 0% |
| Stamp Duty | 0% |
| Interest | 100% of Qantas share dividend paid in A$. |
| Interest Payment Dates | Same as Qantas dividend dates. |
| Redemption | At maturity at redemption price. |
| Redemption Price | Lesser of face value and weighted average Qantas share price over 30 days prior to maturity. |
| Repurchase | Optional at each interest payment date at repurchase price or, if remaining unrepurchased, at maturity. |

| Repurchase Price | Weighted average Qantas share price over the 20 days prior to repurchase (or 30 days prior to maturity). |
| Fees On Repurchase | 0.75% |
| Listing | Australian Stock Exchange |
| Governing Law | New South Wales, Australia |
| Other Conditions | Exemption from withholding tax has been applied for and the notes will have full entitlement to the rights and distributions of Qantas stock, except for voting rights. |

**Exhibit 11.30**
**QanMacs Issue — Possible Hedging Structure**

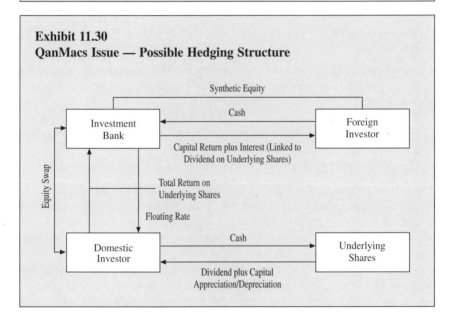

## 8.   Equity-linked Notes — Market Structure

The market for equity index-linked notes developed in response to investor demand for tailored exposure to specific anticipated equity market movements. The earliest examples of these types of transactions were driven by demand, primarily from Japanese and continental European investors, for forward or option positions in the underlying equity market index. These investors were not able to take positions in the relevant derivative instruments due to investment restrictions. This prohibition necessitated the development of notes embedding equity index derivatives to meet the investor requirements.

The initial demand was for yield-enhancement structures to enhance the coupon return. The major attraction of this structure is the higher yield. As notes above, yield-enhancement structures generally were targeted at institutional investors and to a more limited degree at less risk-averse high net worth individual investors. However, over time principal-protected structures became the dominant form of equity-linked notes structures. The primary objective of these structures is the creation of limited risk exposure to the equity market typically in highly structured format. This made the principal-protected structures very attractive individual retail investment accounts. This reflected the primary concern of these investors to preserve invested capital. These structures also created interest among capital stable investment funds and portfolio-insured investment asset managers. Investor requirements for structured exposure to equity markets have also been a driver of the market.

However, in recent years (around 1997-1998), the dynamics of the market underwent a significant change.[14] This change was driven by a number of factors:

- The continued appreciation of global equity markets saw a shift of investment from these types of principal-protected low-risk investments to direct equity investments.
- The sharp increase in equity market volatility following the Asian monetary crisis in 1997 with market volatility increasing to levels some two times the levels that had prevailed previously.
- The fall in interest rates in developed countries to historically low levels.

The primary impact of these developments was the increased difficulty in structuring principal-protected equity-linked notes. This reflected the combination of two factors: the lower interest amount available to fund the coupon and the higher cost of the options themselves (reflecting the higher implied volatility of equity markets.

The market response to these difficulties was varied. The demand for principal-protected equity-linked products continued to be strong. The primary focus was to adapt the products to the new trading environment. The structures developed included:

- **Capped or variable participation structures** — these structures effectively vary or limit the return to the investor (refer **Exhibit 11.22** and **11.24** above). The investor received partial participation in the movement in the equity index. Alternatively, the investor received full participation in the rise in the

---

[14] See "Structured Equity Products" in (March 1999) *Equity Derivatives Yearbook Volume 1*; Risk Publications at 6-7; "Equity-linked Structured Products" in (March 1999) *Equity Derivatives Yearbook Volume 1*; Risk Publications at 11-12; Dunbar, Nicholas "Guaranteed Products: The New Generation" (April 1999) *Risk* 6.

equity index for a nominated rise (say, 20%). The investor received limited or no further participation in any rise in the index value above this level. The first structure entailed the investor purchasing an option for *less than the face value of the note*. This lowered the option cost. The second structure involved an option spread whereby the investor both purchased and sold an option. The sale of the option worked to reduce the impact of the higher option price. This is because the net option premium paid was lower. However, the structure of volatility assisted the investor. The structure of volatility reflects a phenomenon referred to as the volatility smile.[15] This refers to the fact that the implied volatility of out-of-the-money options is greater than the implied volatility of at-the-money options. Historically, equity-linked note structures entail the investors purchasing at-the-money volatility. The introduction of the capped payoff structures meant that the investors were *sellers of out-of-the-money volatility*. The shape of the volatility smile therefore worked in favor of the investor reducing the net cost of the options.[16]

- **Sold volatility structures** — the higher volatility encouraged investors to sell volatility directly. This was primarily in the form of reverse convertible structure where the investor was basically selling put options on the index (see **Exhibit 11.12** above). Investors were attracted by the ability to earn significant running yields while having the risk of having the security redeemed in shares if the market suffered a correction. The original issues were structured to enable the investor to sell an *out-of-the-money* (by around 10%) put option that was viewed by the investor as a price level at which the investor would increase exposure to the relevant stock (effectively a targeted buy or cash covered put write). The market spread in the late 1990s to Europe where the interest in the product has been more retail-focused.[17] The retail investors were motivated by the very high nominal yields available and the possibility in the case of a decline in the value of the underlying shares of acquiring these at a price below the market price at the time the transaction is entered into.[18] The focus of the market is the Benelux countries, Germany

---

[15] For a discussion of the volatility smile, see Das, Satyajit "Option Pricing — Volatility Estimation" in Das, Satyajit (1997) *Risk Management & Financial Derivatives: A Guide To The Mathematics*; LBC Information Services, Sydney; McGraw-Hill, Chicago; MacMillan Publishing, England at Chapter 8.

[16] The use of these structures ultimately impacted upon the shape of the volatility smile — the so-called skew.

[17] For example, Warburg Dillion Read introduced this structure as Geld oder Aktien Lieferung (GOAL), meaning cash or share delivery for the German and Swiss markets.

[18] For example, in 1998, these structures were designed to offer yields of 7.00 to 11.50% pa at a time when German interest rates were around 3.50% pa and Swiss interest rates were around 1.00 to 2.00% pa.

and Switzerland. The structure has also been used in Asia. The attraction of these instruments for Asian investors includes the high yield available. However, an attraction of these structures was the investor willingness to take *delivery* of the stock, in the case of exercise of the put option. The investors were willing to purchase the underlying equity at the relevant entry prices. The product was used both by individual retail investors and portfolio managers, as well as dealers who used these structures to cover exposures under covered warrant issues at times.

• **Exotic option structures** — investors also started to utilize exotic option-based structures to reduce the premium for the purchased option. Investors increasingly also sought to monetize expectations of relative performance (or correlation) through these structures. The principal structures used were average rate options, correlation-based products (basket options) and barrier option products to lower the effective cost of the option. In the case of barrier options, the higher volatility favored the investor as it significantly lowered the cost of knock-out options. Other structures included "best of" and "worst of" structures where the note returned the best performance among two or more indexes.[19]

• **Hybrid structures** — a variety of complex hybrid structures also evolved including:

 1. **Callable equity-index notes** — these structures entailed principal-protected equity-linked notes that provides investors with full participation in changes in a nominated index. The special feature of the callable structure was the ability of the issuer to call the bond at pre-agreed dates before final maturity. The call was usually at a premium to the issue price of the bond. The structures are usually designed to offer the investor an attractive rate of interest in the event of the bond being called (relative to market rates prevailing at the time of issue). The structure embedded both an equity option and an interest rate option (effectively an embedded swaption or option on an interest rate swap). The investor also assumes a position on the correlation between equity prices and interest rate movements. The callable structure entails effectively the investor purchasing an option (where the strike is at-the-money) and selling a portion of the upside on the option (in the event the call option is exercised). As with capped structures, the callable equity index-linked bond is designed to take advantage of the skew shape or smile in equity-

---

[19] Some of these structures are discussed in Chapter 13. For a discussion of exotic options generally, see Das, Satyajit (1996) *Exotic Options*; LBC Information Services, Sydney.

implied volatility. **Exhibit 11.31** sets out an example of a callable equity index-linked bonds.[20]

2. **Equity index volatility notes** — these structures entail the investor investing directly in expectations of changes in implied volatility. These typically involve embedding equity volatility swaps in a fixed income bond.[21]

The most developed market for equity index-linked product is Europe. The market is characterized by strong retail investor participation with some institutional investor participation. The market is characterized by a wide range of products and structures. The UK equity index-linked product market is dominated by the UK life bond market. This market is based around capital guaranteed structures designed to provide a minimum total return (interest coupons plus redemption amount). Typical structures involve the use of leveraged call spreads to structure this type of return profile.

The US and Asian markets for equity-linked products is less developed. The US market is dominated by equity-linked variable annuity products issued by insurance companies. The basic structure is a capital guaranteed equity-linked note repackaged within an insurance policy. A parallel retail market (mainly focused around high net worth individuals marketed through private banking channels) for equity index-linked notes has also developed.

The Asian market is more varied. The Japanese market consists of an institutional component (mainly life insurance companies) and a retail component. The institutional component has focused yield enhancement structures. The major objective is to boost interest income in a period of low and declining nominal rates. The institutional component has also focused on regulation-driven structures, including the conversion of capital gains into income and also overcoming restrictions on transacting derivatives. Retail investment is modest but rapidly growing. The major focus is principal-protected structures that offer equity participation. A popular focus has been structures that provide Japanese investors with exposure to foreign equity markets. The remainder of Asia is focused on high net worth individual investors and principal-guaranteed equity-linked structures.

---

[20] For another example, see Dunbar, Nicholas "Guaranteed Products: The New Generation" (April 1999) *Risk* 6.

[21] For a discussion of volatility swaps, see Gross, Leon, Mesrich, Joe, and Fairman, Randall (January 1998) Introducing Volatility Swaps; Salomon Smith Barney, New York; Gross, Leon "Volatility Swaps" (2 March 1998) *Derivatives Week* 6-7; Carr, Peter and Madan, Dilip "Introducing The Covariance Swap" (February 1999) *Risk* 47-51; Demeterfi, Kresimir, Derman, Emanuel, Kamal, Michael, and Zou, Joseph "A Guide To Variance Swaps" (June 1999) *Risk* 54-59.

**Exhibit 11.31**
**Callable Equity Index-linked Notes**

| | |
|---|---|
| Issuer | AAA/AA issuer |
| Principal Amount | US$20 million |
| Maturity | 5 years |
| Interest Rate | 0.00% pa |
| Issue Price | 100% |
| Redemption Price | Principal amount + Capital adjustment |
| Capital Adjustment | Principal amount × Maximum [0; (index value (at maturity) − Index value (at commencement)/Index value (at commencement)]. Where index value (at commencement) is the value of the nominated equity index value at the start of the transaction. Index value (at maturity) is the value of the equity index value at maturity of the note |
| Call Option | The Note is callable at the option of the issuer as follows: |

| Year | Redemption Price |
|---|---|
| 3 | 125% of face value (7.72% pa) |
| 4 | 135% of face value (7.79% pa) |

## 9. Summary

Equity index-linked structured notes have developed to complement more traditional equity-linked structures. The major differentiating quality of these structures is the linkage to a market-wide index rather than the equity of the issuer and the complete insulation of the issuer from any price exposure to the underlying equity risk of the transaction. The development of these instruments is driven primarily by investor demand, both institutional and individual, for highly customized forms of equity exposure. This demand has seen the development of several types of transactions, including transactions designed to create higher running yield for the investor or alternative structures entailing the sacrifice of yield to finance the acquisition of options to create limited risk exposure to equity markets. Alternative structures designed primarily to avoid the impact of regulatory restrictions on direct equity ownership through synthetic equity instruments have also developed.

# Appendix A
# Equity Derivatives[22]

## 1.  Equity Options/Equity Warrants

Equity options are economically options where the underlying asset is an equity stock or equity index. Equity options are largely identical with options in all other aspects and have the same types of applications.

Equity warrants are equity options that are structured as securities issued by the grantor of the option itself. The structuring of an equity warrant as a *security* has a number of implications:

• The warrant as a security is capable of being listed on an exchange and traded in a manner consistent with other securities.
• The security structure eliminates the bilateral nature of a typical option contract, enabling the transfer of the option through purchase or sale of the warrant (effectively allowing multilateral trading in the option).

## 2.  Equity Forwards and Swaps

### 2.1  Structure

Equity forwards entail agreements to purchase or sell an equity security as at a forward date. Economically, equity forwards are simply forward contracts where the underlying asset is an equity security. The underlying equity security can be an individual stock or a basket of stocks (typically the market index).

In practice, equity forwards take two formats: equity forwards or equity swaps (economically a portfolio of forwards on the underlying equity security or index). Equity forwards are generally undertaken in the form of a futures contract on the market index. Equity swaps are the more common format in which these transactions are structured in the OTC market.

---

[22] For a more detailed discussion, see Das, Satyajit (1994) *Swaps & Financial Derivatives*; LBC Information Services, Sydney; McGraw-Hill, Chicago at Chapter 17; Das, Satyajit "Equity Swaps and Related Derivative Products" (Winter 1992) *Journal of International Securities Markets* vol. 6 349-370; Allen, Julie A. and Showers, Janet L. (April 1991) Equity Indexed Linked Derivatives — An Investor's Guide; Salomon Brothers, Bond Portfolio Analysis Group, New York; Watson, John (editor) (1993) *The Equity Derivatives Handbook*; Euromoney Publications, London; Francis, Jack Clark, Toy, William W., and Whittaker, J. Gregg (editors) (1995) *The Handbook of Equity Derivatives*; Irwin Professional Publishing, Chicago.

An equity index swap entails a contractual agreement to exchange a stream of payments linked to the performance of an equity market index against a stream of payments based on a short-term interest rate index. **Exhibit 11.32** sets out the structure of a typical equity index swap.

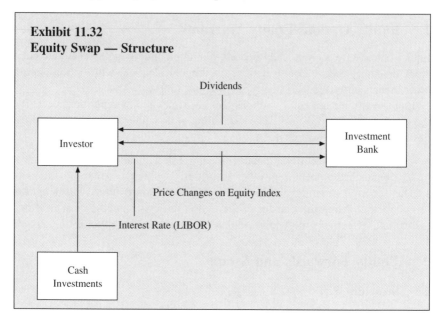

**Exhibit 11.32**
**Equity Swap — Structure**

## 2.2   Key Terms and Conditions

Key aspects of the swap include:
- **Notional principal** — in an equity swap, the payments are based on a notional principal amount but no principal is actually exchanged. The notional principal amount is utilized for calculating the payment amounts. An equity index swap can be based on either a variable or fixed notional principal amounts. Typically, such swaps are structured with variable notional principal amounts that increase or decrease by the index return payment made or received. This type of structure is utilized to simulate the cash flows of a direct equity investment in the relevant market. Where a fixed notional principal amount is utilized, the principal amount is set on the swap settlement date and remains unchanged throughout the life of the swap. This type of structure simulates direct equity investment where the investor seeks to keep the equity investment constant. Therefore, the investor is required to liquidate part of the equity portfolio whenever the market rises and invest more in the underlying equities whenever the market falls to maintain the investment in the index constant.

- **Equity market index** — the party entering into the equity index swap will, typically, pay or receive the return on the equity market index. The investor receives the total return of the index. This is defined as a percentage change in the capital value of the index and the dividend return on the securities underlying the index. The dividend return on the index is paid to the investor. The capital movement is more complex. The investor receives a return where the return on the index is positive. The investor will, in contrast, be required to make a payment to the counterparty in addition to the floating rate payment (where it is the equity index return receiver under this equity index swap) where the return over the period is negative.

- **Interest rates** — the party receiving (paying) the equity market index will as its other cash flow stream pay (receive) an amount calculated with reference to a nominated money market index plus or minus a spread (specified as a number of basis points). The actual spread or margin reflects the equity index forward pricing and depends on market conditions, such as the prices in the futures market in the equity market index and the particular structure of the transaction. In a typical transaction, the floating rate index will be the relevant money market index in the currency in which the swap is denominated and utilized.

- **Payments** — exchanges are based on agreed reset frequency (typically, quarterly or semi-annual) and agreed maturity or termination date.

- **Currency** — the streams of cash flows can be denominated in the same or in different currencies. In an equity index swap in a single currency, the index return is determined in the currency selected. In an equity index swap that is structured as a cross-currency transaction, the return associated with the transaction incorporates both the change in the index and the change in exchange rates between the index and swap currencies. The investor has the option of maintaining its exposure to the currency of the equity market index. Alternatively, the investor may hedge this foreign currency exposure by requesting currency-hedged return payments. In this case, the return to the investor will be based on movements in the index adjusted for the cost of hedging the index returns back into the investor's specified currency. The currency-hedged equity swap structures incorporate, in effect, adjusting/compensating principal or quanto options.

The typical terms for a generic equity index swap are set out in **Exhibit 11.33**.

**Exhibit 11.33**
**Equity Swap — Terms and Conditions**

*General Terms*

| | |
|---|---|
| Trade Date | January 19, 2001 |
| Effective Date | January 22, 2001 |
| Termination Date | January 22, 2002, subject to adjustment in accordance with the [preceding/succeeding/ modified succeeding] Business Day Convention. |
| Index | S&P 500 |
| Exchange | NYSE |

*Equity Payments*

| | |
|---|---|
| Equity Amount Payer | [Investment Bank] |
| Equity Notional Amount | US$10 million |
| Equity Notional Reset | Applicable |
| Equity Payment Dates | 3rd business day following each valuation day |
| Type of Return | Total Return |
| Initial Price | 1,050 |
| Valuation Time | The close of trading on the Exchange in New York. |
| Valuation Dates | Quarterly commencing April 19, 2001 and ending January 19, 2002 subject to adjustment in accordance with the [preceding/succeeding/ modified succeeding] Business Day Convention. |
| Dividend Amount | The dividend amount will be an aggregate amount including all dividends declared and paid on all stock in the index during any quarter prorated based on the Equity Notional Amount. |
| Dividend Reinvestment | Not applicable |

*Floating Rate Amounts*

| | |
|---|---|
| Floating Rate Payer | [Investor] |
| Notional Amount | Equity Notional Amount |
| Payment Dates | Quarterly commencing April 22, 2001 and ending January 22, 2002 subject to adjustment in accordance with the [preceding/succeeding/ modified succeeding] Business Day Convention. |
| Floating Rate | US$ LIBOR |

| Designated Maturity | 3-month |
| Spread | 50 basis points |
| Floating Rate Day Fraction | 365/360 |
| Reset Dates | January 20, 2001 and two business days prior to the payment dates. |

## 2.3   Equity Swaps — Types

The alternative types of equity index swap structures are dictated by variations in the following:

* Variable or fixed notional principal.
* Single or cross-currency.
* Currency exposure of equity market index—hedged or unhedged.

**Exhibit 11.34** sets out an example of a variable notional principal single currency equity index swap. **Exhibit 11.35** on page 568 sets out the structure of a fixed notional principal, single currency swap. **Exhibit 11.36** on page 569 sets out the structure of a variable notional principal, cross-currency equity index swap. **Exhibit 11.37** on page 573 sets out the structure of a variable notional principal, cross-currency swap where the equity index return is currency hedged.[23] The currency-hedged equity swap structure incorporates adjusting/compensating principal or quanto options.[24]

---

**Exhibit 11.34**
**Equity Swap Cash Flows — Single Currency Variable Notional Principal**

*1.   Assumptions*

Assume an investor enters into the following equity swap to convert a portfolio of FX floating rate assets into an equity index-linked investment. The terms of the swap are as follows:

| Initial Notional Principal | FX100 million |
| Term | 2-year (quarterly settlement) |

---

[23]   In order to generalize the example, a hypothetical equity index (equity index) and a hypothetical currency (FX) are utilized.

[24]   See discussion in Chapter 13. See also Das, Satyajit (1996) *Exotic Options*; LBC Information Services, Sydney at Chapter 12.

Investor Pays                    FX LIBOR — 0.10% pa
Investor Receives                Equity index

All swap cash flows are denominated FX. The cash flows under this swap (based on assumed equity index and FX LIBOR rates) are attached. All cash flows (in terms of receipts and payment) are analyzed from the viewpoint of the bank counterparty (this is the case in **Exhibit 11.34** to **Exhibit 11.37** inclusive).

The methodology utilized in calculating the equity swap cash flows is summarized below.[25]

### 2. First Settlement

The first settlement under the swap is effected on May 2, 2002. The floating rate payment by the investor is calculated as follows:

Principal amount floating rate × Number of days/360 =
FX100,000,000 × 9.45% × 90/360 = FX2,362,500

The payment linked to the equity index is calculated as follows:

Principal amount × (Index (t + 1) − Index (t))/Index (t) =
FX100,000,000 × (1,912.5 − 1,900.6)/1,900.6 = FX626,118

The margin calculation is similar to the floating rate payment:

FX100,000,000 × 0.10% pa × 90/360 = FX25,000

The net payment by the investor (to the counterparty) is:

FX2,362,500 − FX626,118 − FX25,000 = FX1,711,382.

The payment flows on all subsequent settlement dates are calculated in an identical manner.

### 3. Variable Notional Principal

The concept of variable notional principal is predicated on the concept that the investor purchases FX100 million of the equity index and does not add to or liquidate the investment and reinvests all dividends in the index over the term of the swap.

---

[25] Please note that as the equity index assumes reinvestment of all dividends, the dividend cash flows are not shown separately. For an index where the dividend flows are not reinvested, it will be necessary to calculate the dividends separately and for the investment bank to pay these to the investor based on the notional principal of the transaction.

This, in practical terms, operates as follows:

- At the beginning of the swap, the investor purchases FX100,000,000 of assets yielding, at least, FX LIBOR. Through the swap, the investor has an equivalent purchase of FX100,000,000 of shares in the equity index.
- As at the first settlement date, the FX LIBOR income on the FX100,000,000 of floating rate assets matches the outflow under the swap. The cash inflow of FX626,118 (representing the appreciation of the index) is utilized to purchase an additional FX626,118 of assets, increasing the notional principal under the transaction to FX100,626,118.
- The notional principal under the swap is adjusted as at each payment date. The notional principal increases, that is, additional floating rate assets are purchased, where the index return is positive. The notional principal decreases, that is, floating rate assets are sold, where the index return is negative.
- At maturity, the swap payments (interest and index return) are calculated as normal. However, in addition, the floating rate assets mature or are sold for face value of FX102,099,377 (the notional principal as at November 2, 2003 — the penultimate payment date). This together with the last index return payment of FX115,753 generates a total investment value of FX102,215,090 that equates the terminal value of an investment in the equity index over the 2-year period.

The table below illustrates how the swap operates, as described above.

## Equity Swap Cash Flows — Single Currency Variable Notional Principal

| Date | Days | Cumulative Days | Years | Equity Index | FX LIBOR (FX) | Notional Principal (FX) | Equity Swap Flows | | | Net Payment |
| | | | | | | | Equity Index (FX) | Margin (FX) | FX LIBOR (FX) | |
|---|---|---|---|---|---|---|---|---|---|---|
| 02-Feb-02 | | | | 1,900.6 | 9.450% | 100,000,000 | | | | |
| 02-May-02 | 90 | 90 | 0.25 | 1,912.5 | 9.375% | 100,626,118 | −626,118 | −25,000 | 2,362,500 | 1,711,382 |
| 02-Aug-02 | 92 | 182 | 0.50 | 1,875.9 | 9.250% | 98,700,410 | 1,925,708 | −25,716 | 2,410,834 | 4,310,826 |
| 02-Nov-02 | 92 | 274 | 0.75 | 1,860.5 | 9.480% | 97,890,140 | 810,270 | −25,223 | 2,333,168 | 3,118,215 |
| 02-Feb-03 | 92 | 366 | 1.00 | 1,885.4 | 9.100% | 99,200,253 | −1,310,113 | −25,016 | 2,371,552 | 1,036,423 |
| 02-May-03 | 89 | 455 | 1.25 | 1,885.8 | 8.520% | 99,221,299 | −21,046 | −24,525 | 2,231,730 | 2,186,160 |
| 02-Aug-03 | 92 | 547 | 1.50 | 1,892.7 | 8.240% | 99,584,342 | −363,043 | −25,357 | 2,160,378 | 1,771,979 |
| 02-Nov-03 | 92 | 639 | 1.75 | 1,940.5 | 8.010% | 102,099,337 | −2,514,995 | −25,449 | 2,097,025 | −443,420 |
| 02-Feb-04 | 92 | 731 | 2.00 | 1,942.7 | | 102,215,090 | −115,753 | −26,092 | 2,089,973 | 1,948,128 |

**Exhibit 11.35**
**Equity Swap Cash Flows — Single Currency Fixed Notional Principal**

*1.  Assumptions*

Assume the same transaction structure as in **Exhibit 11.34** with the exception that the swap is on a fixed notional principal amount; that is, the investor seeks a constant asset allocation strategy requiring the FX100,000,000 principal of the swap to be constant.

The cash flows under this swap structure are attached. The methodology used to calculate the equity swap cash flow is summarized below.

*2.  First and Subsequent Settlement*

The first settlement under the swap effected on May 2, 2002 is as in **Exhibit 11.34** entailing a payment by the investor to the counterparty of FX1,711,382. However, at this date, the notional principal amount is not reset (as in **Exhibit 11.34**) and remains at FX100,000,000. This means that the cash flows as at the second settlement date of August 2, 2002 are as follows:

Floating Payment   FX100,000,000 × 9.375% × 92/360
                   = FX2,395,833
Index Return       FX100,000,000 (1,875.9 — 1,912.5)/1,912.5
                   = FX (1,913,725)
Spread             FX100,000,000 × 0.10% × 92/360 = FX25,556

The net payment by the investor to the counterparty is FX4,284,003 (note the difference to the settlement amount in **Exhibit 11.34**).

As at each settlement date, the FX LIBOR and equity index rates are reset to the new levels. The principal amount is never reset.

*3.  Fixed Notional Principal*

The concept of fixed notional principal is predicated on maintaining the level of exposure to the equity market at a constant level. This, in practical terms, operates as follows:

- At the beginning of the swap, the investor purchases FX100,000,000 of assets yielding FX LIBOR.
- As at the first settlement, the FX LIBOR receipt matches the equivalent outflow under the swap. The cash inflow of FX626,118 (representing the appreciation of the index) means that the investment in the index is valued at FX100,626,118. In order to maintain the equity index

investment level at FX100,000,000, part of the equity is sold, in conceptual terms, and would, in the case of direct investment in the index provide the investor with cash (the cash inflow under the equity swap corresponding to this).

- The notional principal stays constant as at each settlement date. Where the index return is positive, the investor receives a cash inflow (conceptually, the proceeds of the sale of part of the equity investment). Where the index return is negative, the investor experiences a cash outflow (conceptually, additional investment in the index to maintain the investment constant).

- At maturity, the investor receives FX100,000,000 from the maturing floating rate assets or from the sale of these assets. In addition, the investor receives FX113,373, reflecting the index return in the period November 2, 2003 to February 2, 2004. This amount equates to the market value of the investment in the equity index that could be realized through liquidation of the equivalent equity investment.

The table below illustrates how the swap operates, as described above.

**Equity Swap Cash Flows — Single Currency Fixed Notional Principal**

| Date | Days | Cumulative Days | Years | Equity Index | FX LIBOR | Notional Principal | Equity Swap Flows | | | | Net Payment |
|------|------|------|------|------|------|------|------|------|------|------|------|
| | | | | | | | Equity Index | Margin | FX LIBOR | | |
| | | | | | | (FX) | (FX) | (FX) | (FX) | | (FX) |
| 02-Feb-02 | | | | 1,900.6 | 9.450% | 100,000,000 | | | | | |
| 02-May-02 | 90 | 90 | 0.25 | 1,912.5 | 9.375% | 100,000,000 | −626,118 | −25,000 | 2,362,500 | | 1,711,382 |
| 02-Aug-02 | 92 | 182 | 0.50 | 1,875.9 | 9.250% | 100,000,000 | 1,913,725 | −25,556 | 2,395,833 | | 4,284,003 |
| 02-Nov-02 | 92 | 274 | 0.75 | 1,860.5 | 9.480% | 100,000,000 | 820,939 | −25,556 | 2,363,889 | | 3,159,273 |
| 02-Feb-03 | 92 | 366 | 1.00 | 1,885.4 | 9.100% | 100,000,000 | −1,338,350 | −25,556 | 2,422,667 | | 1,058,761 |
| 02-May-03 | 89 | 455 | 1.25 | 1,885.8 | 8.520% | 100,000,000 | −21,216 | −24,722 | 2,249,722 | | 2,203,784 |
| 02-Aug-03 | 92 | 547 | 1.50 | 1,892.7 | 8.240% | 100,000,000 | −365,892 | −25,556 | 2,177,333 | | 1,785,885 |
| 02-Nov-03 | 92 | 639 | 1.75 | 1,940.5 | 8.010% | 100,000,000 | −2,525,493 | −25,556 | 2,105,778 | | −445,270 |
| 02-Feb-04 | 92 | 731 | 2.00 | 1,942.7 | | 100,000,000 | −113,373 | −25,556 | 2,047,000 | | 1,908,072 |

**Exhibit 11.36**
**Equity Swap Cash Flows — Cross-currency Variable Notional Principal**

*1. Assumptions*

Assume an investor enters into the following equity swap to convert a portfolio of US$ floating rate assets into an equity index-linked investment denominated in FX. The terms of the swap are as follows:

| Initial Notional Principal | FX100 million |
| Term | 2 years (quarterly settlement) |
| Investor Pays | US$ LIBOR |
| Investor Receives | Equity Index + 0.15% pa |
| Exchange Rate at Commencement | US$1 = DM1.6425 |

The cross-currency nature of this transaction adds an extra layer of complexity. In the single currency (FX), variable notional principal transaction (described in **Exhibit 11.34**), the market value of the swap was adjusted as at each settlement date by the return or the equity index. Most importantly, the FX principal amounts for both the floating rate and the equity index payments were the same.

In the cross-currency equity swap, the process is similar but because of changes in the US$/FX exchange rate over the life of the swap the US$ principal amount is likely to diverge from the FX principal amount. This requires the market value of the swap to be adjusted as at each settlement date. This adjustment reflects the equity index return (in FX) plus the change in value of the US$ principal over the period. This additional payment is made or received by the investor. In this case, if the FX appreciates (depreciates) against the US$ relative to the level prevailing at the commencement of the transaction, then the investor receives (makes) the payment from (to) the counterparty.

The cash flows under this swap are attached. The methodology utilized in calculating the equity swap cash flow is summarized below.

### 2. Initial Principal Amounts

The initial FX notional principal amount is specified at FX100,000,000. The corresponding US$ notional principal amount is determined by converting the FX notional principal amount to US$ at the US$/FX rate current at the commencement of the transaction.

Assuming an exchange rate of US$1 = FX1.6425, the US$ notional principal amount would be set at US$60,882,801.

On each subsequent settlement date, the notional principal amount is adjusted as follows:

- The FX notional principal is adjusted by the equity index return.
- The US$ notional principal is reset to equate to the FX notional principal amount at the exchange rate prevailing at the settlement date.

### 3. First Settlement

The first settlement under the swap is effected on May 2, 2002 and is calculated as follows:

US$ Floating Rate   US$60,882,801 × 4.375% × 90/360
= US$665,906

US$ Spread          US$60,882,801 × 0.15% × 90/360 = US$22,831

Index Return        FX100,000,000 × (1,912.5 − 1,900.6)/1,900.6
= FX626,118

The investor pays US$643,075 (US$665,906-US$22,831) and receives FX626,118 from the counterparty.

The principal amounts are adjusted as follows:

* FX notional principal is reset at FX100,626,118.
* US$ notional principal is reset as per the following calculation: FX100,626,118 @ US$1:DM1.7870 = US$56,310,083.

The difference between the original US$ notional principal and new reset US$ notional principal is made up of:

* Movement in the original US$ notional principal = US$4,923,092.
* Movement in the equity index = US$(350,374).
* Total = US$4,572,718.

The exchange rate loss represented by the movement in the original principal (US$4,923,092) is paid by the investor to the counterparty.

The payment calculations for the next period are based on the reset FX and US$ notional principal amounts calculated above.

The payment flows in all subsequent periods are determined in an identical manner.

### 4. Variable Notional Principal

The concept of variable notional principal is identical to that set out in **Exhibit 11.34** and assumes the reinvestment of dividends in the equity index and no change in investment during the term of the swap.

This, in practical terms, operates as follows:

* At the beginning of the swap, the investor invests in US$60,882,801 of floating rate US$ LIBOR yielding assets. Through the swap the investor has an equivalent purchase of FX100,000,000 of shares in the equity index.

- As at the first settlement date, the US$ LIBOR receipt offsets the equivalent payment under the swap. There is, in addition, a positive cash flow of FX626,118 (representing the return on the index) and a cash outflow of US$4,923,092 (representing the appreciation of the US$). The investor adjusts the US$ notional principal value of the floating rate assets by selling US$4,572,718 of these assets. This amount is paid to the counterparty, leaving the investor with no net cash flow.
- On subsequent settlement dates, the process is repeated. The US$ LIBOR payments are matched. Where the equity index return plus the change in the US$ value of the FX investment is positive (negative), the investors purchases (sells) US$ floating rate assets to equate the value of the US$ floating rate assets to equal the FX market value of the index at the settlement date.
- At maturity, the final swap payments (interest and index return) are calculated as normal. The investor has a total cash position of:

| US$ Floating Rate Assets | US$61,444,444 |
|---|---|
| US$ Floating Rate Assets | US$61,119,028 |
| US$ Principal Adjustment | US$3,114,590 |
| Total | US$64,233,618 |
| Equity Index Return | FX115,753 (US$72,825) |

This equates to a total of US$64,306,442 or FX102,215,090 that is equal to the terminal value of an investment in the equity index over the 2-year period.

The table below illustrates how the swap operates, as described above.

## Equity Swap Cash Flows — Cross Currency Variable Notional Principal

| Date | Days | Cumulative Days | Years | Equity Index | US$ LIBOR | US$/FX | FX Cash Flows Principal | FX Cash Flows Equity Index | US$ Cash Flows Principal | US$ Cash Flows US$ LIBOR | US$ Cash Flows Spread | Principal Adjustment |
|---|---|---|---|---|---|---|---|---|---|---|---|---|
| | | | | | | (FX) | (FX) | (FX) | (US$) | (US$) | (US$) | (US$) |
| 02-Feb-02 | | | | 1,900.6 | 4.375% | 1.6425 | 100,000,000 | | 60,882,801 | | | |
| 02-May-02 | 90 | 90 | 0.25 | 1,912.5 | 4.450% | 1.7870 | 100,626,118 | 626,118 | 56,310,083 | 665,906 | 22,831 | 4,923,092 |
| 02-Aug-02 | 92 | 182 | 0.50 | 1,875.9 | 4.750% | 1.8795 | 98,700,410 | -1,925,708 | 52,514,185 | 640,371 | 21,586 | 2,771,313 |
| 02-Nov-02 | 92 | 274 | 0.75 | 1,860.5 | 5.120% | 1.8802 | 97,890,140 | -810,270 | 52,063,685 | 637,464 | 20,130 | 19,551 |
| 02-Feb-03 | 92 | 366 | 1.00 | 1,885.4 | 4.975% | 1.8647 | 99,200,253 | 1,310,113 | 53,199,041 | 681,224 | 19,958 | -432,770 |
| 02-May-03 | 89 | 455 | 1.25 | 1,885.8 | 5.250% | 1.8380 | 99,221,299 | 21,046 | 53,983,296 | 654,311 | 19,728 | -772,804 |
| 02-Aug-03 | 92 | 547 | 1.50 | 1,892.7 | 5.280% | 1.6820 | 99,584,342 | 363,043 | 59,205,911 | 724,276 | 20,694 | -5,006,774 |
| 02-Nov-03 | 92 | 639 | 1.75 | 1,940.5 | 5.750% | 1.6705 | 102,099,337 | 2,514,995 | 61,119,028 | 829,146 | 22,696 | -407,583 |
| 02-Feb-04 | 92 | 731 | 2.00 | 1,942.7 | | 1.5895 | 102,215,090 | 115,753 | 64,306,442 | 898,110 | 23,429 | -3,114,590 |

**Exhibit 11.37**
**Equity Swap Cash Flows — Currency-hedged Variable Notional Principal**

*1. Assumptions*

Assume the same structure as in **Exhibit 11.36** with the exception that the investor is insulated by the counterparty from movements in the US$/FX exchange rate. In return for absorbing the exchange risk of the transaction, the swap margin is adjusted to *minus* 0.60% pa.

The margin adjustment reflects the cost of hedging the currency risk (representing the prevailing interest rate differential in favour of the FX). An additional cost element of the transaction is the fact that the required forward currency contracts must be structured as quantity adjusting and off-market reflecting the uncertainty as to future FX cash flows to be hedged (which are dependent on the level of the equity index).

Assume that the variable notional principal amount is set at US$100,000,000. The cash flows under this swap structure are attached. The methodology used to calculate the equity swap cash flows is summarized below.

*2. First Payment*

The first settlement under the swap effected on May 2, 2002 will entail the following cash flows:

| | |
|---|---|
| Floating Payments | US$100,000,000 × 4.375% × 90/360 |
| | = US$1,093,750 |
| Index Return | US$100,000,000 × (1,912.5 – 1,900.6)/1,900.6 |
| | = US$626,118 |
| Spread | US$100,000,000 × 0.60% × 90/360 |
| | = US$150,000 |

The net payment by the investor to the counterparty is US$617,632.

The index for the subsequent settlement period is set at the level prevailing on May 2, 2002. The notional principal amount is set at US$100,626,118. This process is repeated as at each settlement date.

*3. Variable Notional Principal*

This type of transaction functions as a combination of a variable notional principal investment in the equity index (dividends reinvested and no change in investment over the swap term) and a (quantity adjusting) currency forward contract to convert FX to US$ in two years at the initial exchange rate.

This, in practical terms, operates as follows:

• At the beginning of the swap, the investor purchases US$100,000,000 of assets paying interest at US$ LIBOR. Through the swap, the investor purchases an equivalent number of shares in the equity index (@ US$1.6425 = FX164,250,000).

• On the first payment date, the US$ floating rate interest flows from the investment and the swap offset each other. There is a positive index return equivalent to US$626,118 that is used to purchase additional floating rate assets increasing the notional principal underlying the swap. Through the swap, the investor has an investment in the equity index of FX165,278,399 that, if converted at the initial exchange rate, is equal to US$100,626,118.

• On subsequent settlement dates, the pattern is repeated. The US$ interest rate cash flows continue to be offsetting. Where the index return is positive (negative), additional US$ floating rate assets have to be purchased (sold) to equate the value of the US$ floating rate investments to the market value of the index, converted to US$ at the initial exchange rate.

• At maturity, the interest flows and return on index are calculated as for all settlement dates. The US$ assets mature or are liquidated for US$102,104,193, which together with the final payment of US$110,897 equates to the value of the corresponding equity maturity value of FX167,888,285, which at the original, currency-hedged rate, is equal to US$102,215,090.

The table below illustrates how the swap operates, as described above.

## Equity Swap Cash Flows — Currency Hedged Variable Notional Principal

| Date | Days | Cumulative Days | Years | Equity Index | US$ LIBOR | US$/FX | Principal | Equity Index | US$ LIBOR | Spread US$ | Net Payment US$ |
|---|---|---|---|---|---|---|---|---|---|---|---|
| 02-Feb-02 | | | | 1,900.6 | 4.375% | 1.6425 | 100,000,000 | | | | |
| 02-May-02 | 90 | 90 | 0.25 | 1,912.5 | 4.450% | 1.7870 | 100,626,118 | –626,118 | 1,093,750 | 150,000 | 617,632 |
| 02-Aug-02 | 92 | 182 | 0.50 | 1,875.9 | 4.750% | 1.8795 | 98,700,410 | 1,925,708 | 1,144,343 | 154,293 | 3,224,344 |
| 02-Nov-02 | 92 | 274 | 0.75 | 1,860.5 | 5.120% | 1.8802 | 97,890,140 | 810,270 | 1,198,113 | 151,341 | 2,159,724 |
| 02-Feb-03 | 92 | 366 | 1.00 | 1,885.4 | 4.975% | 1.8647 | 99,200,253 | –1,310,113 | 1,280,838 | 150,098 | 120,824 |
| 02-May-03 | 89 | 455 | 1.25 | 1,885.8 | 5.250% | 1.8380 | 99,221,299 | –21,046 | 1,220,094 | 147,147 | 1,346,195 |
| 02-Aug-03 | 92 | 547 | 1.50 | 1,892.7 | 5.480% | 1.6820 | 99,584,342 | –363,043 | 1,331,219 | 152,139 | 1,120,315 |
| 02-Nov-03 | 92 | 639 | 1.75 | 1,940.5 | 5.750% | 1.6820 | 102,099,337 | –2,514,995 | 1,394,623 | 152,696 | –967,676 |
| 02-Feb-04 | 92 | 731 | 2.00 | 1,942.7 | | 1.6820 | 102,215,090 | –115,753 | 1,500,293 | 156,552 | 1,541,092 |

## 2.4   Equity Swaps — Applications

Equity swaps are primarily utilized as a means for acquiring or divesting equity exposure. Investors typically utilize equity swaps to hedge holdings of equities or to synthesize an investment in the index. Corporations generally utilize such structures to acquire exposure to the share price movement of a specific company to hedge the price risk in the context of a merger or the share price movement of the company itself to synthesize a share repurchase. Investors will typically transact equity swaps on the *equity index*. Corporations will generally seek to transact equity swaps on *individual stocks*.

In both cases, the use of equity swaps rather than trading in the underlying equity (particularly equity index transactions) may have economic benefits. These include lower transaction costs (avoidance of stamp taxes, lower bid-offer spreads, absence of custodial costs) and tax benefits (allowing transfer of any tax incidents of share ownership to the party likely to value it most highly *without equity price risk* and potential withholding tax benefits).

## 2.5   Equity Swaps — Pricing

An equity swap is, in its basic form, equivalent to a portfolio of forward contracts on the relevant equity index. Consequently, the technique for pricing and valuing commodity swaps is, substantively, also applicable to the pricing of equity swap transactions.

In practice, the pricing of equity swap transactions is driven, to a large degree, by the means through which a dealer or market-maker in such instruments can hedge its own exposure. Typically, the market-maker in equity swaps will hedge the exposure in one or other of the following markets:

* Hedged in the futures market on the relevant stock market index.
* Replication of the index by the market-maker who will transact in the underlying physical shares constituting the index.
* Matching the transaction with an exact but offsetting counterparty.

In practice, the predominant technique for hedging equity swap positions is the futures market in the relevant stock price index (at least, where index futures are available). In the absence of an index futures market, actual replication of the physical index can be utilized, although it is usually expensive.

The pricing of equity swaps hedged in the relevant stock index futures is a function of a number of factors:

* The liquidity in the futures market and, in particular, the liquidity in contracts other than near-month contract. In practice, in a number of futures markets liquidity is confined to the near-month stock index futures contract. This

necessitates the execution of "stack"' hedges.[26] Under this approach, a term equity index swap may be hedged by the market-maker taking an offsetting position in the liquid near-month futures contract. The market-maker then periodically rolls the contract upon expiry assuming the risk of changes in the inter-contracts/inter-month spread between the relevant stock index futures contracts.

- Shape of the futures price curve in the relevant stock index. In practice, the capacity to arbitrage equity market indexes will generally ensure that it approximates the forward price behavior of typical financial assets although backwardation in equity market index futures is not unknown nor indeed uncommon.

Establishment of a hedge in the equity index futures contracts will require an estimate of a number of factors including:

- Market impact of establishment rolling and closing of the futures position.
- Basis risk between the equity swap and the futures contracts in which the position is hedged.
- Cost of rolling futures contracts, in particular where, as noted above, a stack hedge entailing hedging a term swap in the near month liquid stock index futures contract is utilized (in this regard, it is useful to note that the relationship between contract months and, consequently, cost of rolling positions in futures markets is notoriously volatile and difficult to predict).
- Cost of financing initial deposit and of margin payments.
- Dealer's estimate of the risk of the hedge itself.

**Exhibit 11.38** sets out an example of pricing a single currency equity swap.

---

**Exhibit 11.38**
**Single Currency Equity Swap Pricing**

Assume the dealer is asked to price the following 1-year swap:

Notional Principal        $1,000,000
Term                      (Approximately) 1 year

The swap is to be hedged in equity index futures. To assist in this process the dealer structures the swap with a stub (broken) period at the start. This

---

[26]   See Das, Satyajit (1994) *Swaps & Financial Derivatives*; LBC Information Services, Sydney; McGraw-Hill, Chicago at Chapter 35.

enables the swap settlement dates to be aligned to the equity futures contract dates. This results in the equity swap having a maturity of slightly in excess of one year.

In order to hedge the equity swap, the dealer first determines the equivalent equity index units (by dividing the notional principal by the current level of the index:

Stock Index Level    2,200.0
Index Units          454.55

The structure of the swap will be that the dealer pays the equity index plus the dividends on the index stocks to the investor. In return the dealer receives from the investor money market rates in the relevant currency. The dealer hedges by purchases equity index futures and sells interest rate futures on the relevant money market index. The transaction cash flows are summarized in the attached cash flow table.

As with any swap, the discounted *net* cash flows under the swap must equal zero at the commencement of the swap. In this case, this requires an adjustment to be incorporated in the swap pricing to adjust for the fact that the swap value as projected is not zero at commencement. As the swap has a negatives net present value to the dealer, the dealer must recover the equivalent of $6,353 over the life of the swap. This equates to a margin of approximately 75 bps pa. This is payable by the investor. In practice, it is recovered either by the dealer paying the equity index return less 75 bps pa or the dealer receiving the money market return plus 75 bps pa from the investor.

## Single Currency Equity Swap Pricing Cash Flows

| Time | | Interest Rates | | Equity Index Prices | | | Equity Swap Cash Flows | | | |
|---|---|---|---|---|---|---|---|---|---|---|
| Number of Days | Days in Period | Zero Rates (% pa) | Forward Rates (% pa) | Forward Price (Index Points) | Adjusted Forward Prices (% pa) | Equity Index ($) | Money Market ($) | Net ($) | Net Present Values ($) |
| | | | | 2,200.00 | 2,200.00 | | | | |
| 47 | 47 | 6.6000% | 6.6000% | 2,218.18 | 2,208.18 | 3,718 | (8,498) | (4,780) | (4,741) |
| 138 | 91 | 7.0300% | 7.2528% | 2,257.24 | 2,247.24 | 17,609 | (18,082) | (472) | (460) |
| 230 | 92 | 6.8100% | 6.4808% | 2,293.25 | 2,283.25 | 15,953 | (16,335) | (381) | (366) |
| 322 | 92 | 6.4500% | 5.5553% | 2,324.72 | 2,314.72 | 13,720 | (14,002) | (281) | (268) |
| 412 | 90 | 6.7800% | 7.9691% | 2,369.09 | 2,359.09 | 19,085 | (19,649) | (563) | (517) |
| | | | | | | | Total | (6,353) | |

*Notes:*
1. All cash flows are calculated on the basis of a 365-day year. Positive cash flows refer to cash inflows. Negative cash flows refer to cash outflows.
2. The number of days refers to the days from commencement of the transaction.
3. Days-in period refers to the numbers of days in a specific period of the swap.
4. Zero and forward rates are for the currency in which the equity index is denominated and the currency of the swap.
5. Equity index prices are the actual equity index futures prices where the contract is trading. Where the contract is not trading the theoretical equity index futures price is used.
6. The adjusted forward price reflects an adjustment of minus 10 index points per quarter. This is designed to cover the roll risk of the dealer in the event that the futures contracts trade away from their theoretical values.
7. The equity index cash flows are calculated as the cash flows under the equity swap using the adjusted forward prices for the equity index.
8. The money market cash flows are calculated by accruing on the notional principal at the forward rate for the relevant period.
9. The net cash flows refer to net position of the dealer after paying the equity flows and receiving the money market cash flows.
10. The net present values are calculated as the net cash flows discounted at the zero rates.

Additional factors are relevant to pricing equity swaps where they are cross-currency or currency-hedged. In the case of cross-currency equity swaps, the base price of an equity swap in a single currency will be adjusted by the price of a cross-currency floating-to-floating swap. This may create value or reduce value in this specific transaction.

In the case of currency hedge structures, the cost of hedging will incorporate, among other things:

• Interest differentials between the currencies.
• Yield curve shape between the relevant currencies.
• Nature of the currency exposure to be hedged.

In regard to the nature of the currency exposure being hedged, where the investor seeks to capture a totally currency risk-free return on a foreign equity market index, in its home currency, the necessity for a quantity-adjusting currency hedge creates additional costs. Such hedges, often referred to as quanto options require the hedge to operate in respect of *an uncertain amount*. In the context of capturing hedged-equity market returns, the actual return component (the amount) is unknown and therefore a fixed-quantity hedge cannot be structured. The cost of such quantity adjusting or quanto hedges is driven by the need to structure dynamic and correlation-based hedges. The costs of these quanto options or hedges are incorporated into the currency-hedged structures of equity swaps.[27]

---

[27] For a discussion of pricing and hedging quanto options see, Das, Satyajit (1996) *Exotic Options*; LBC Information Services, Sydney at Chapter 12.

# 12
# Credit-linked Notes

## 1. Credit-linked Notes — Overview

Credit-linked notes[1] are a relatively recent addition to the universe of structured note products. These instruments entail the combination of a fixed income security with an embedded credit derivative. The credit-linked note is designed to allow the investor to capture value from movements in the value of an underlying bond or loan, credit spreads or default risk itself.

Credit-linked notes are part of a class of transactions of credit derivatives involving the isolation and separate trading in aspects of credit risk. In this chapter, the background to, structure and applications of credit-linked structured notes are examined.

## 2. Credit Derivatives — Overview

The emergence of credit derivatives must be understood against a background of a progressive redefinition of risk and financial derivatives. This change may ultimately prove to be as important as the advent of derivatives themselves and their use in capital markets.

The concept of financial derivatives is increasingly becoming one of trading *attributes* of assets. The move to combine the trading, sales, distribution, and risk management of physical assets; and that of derivatives on those assets and the broader trends in the measurement, quantification, and management of market risk all reflect this important shift in focus.

A simple asset, such as a physical bond, is a complex bundle of attributes. These attributes include:

---

[1]   For a detailed discussion of credit derivatives and credit-linked notes, see Das, Satyajit (editor) (2000) *Credit Derivatives and Credit-Linked Notes — Second Edition*; John Wiley & Sons, Singapore Chapters 1, 2, 3, and 4.

- **Liquidity** — represented by the investment of funds and the ultimate return of the investment where the amount and timing of the cash flows (principal and interest) determines the return on or value of the investment.
- **Interest rates/debt prices** — where the return is represented by fluctuations in the asset price representing the present value of cash flows driven by interest rate movements or changes in the discount rate. The discount rate applicable, which combines a risk-free rate and a risk margin (to compensate for credit risk), is utilized in valuing the cash flows. The risk in this case also includes exposure to a series of discount rates (the zero curve) (in effect the risk of yield curve shape changes) that will interact with the movement of time (maturity and term structure risk).
- **Currency** — reflecting changes in the value of the currency in which the cash flows are paid.
- **Contingent elements** — relating to embedded option features such as embedded prepayment or other rights.
- **Default risk** — relating to the exposure to the potential failure of the issuer to perform its obligations under the contract.

Derivatives above all else facilitate the *separate* trading of *individual* attributes of the asset *in isolation* from the asset itself. In the above case, traditional derivatives, involving interest rates and currencies, can be utilized to manage the risk of many of the attributes embedded in this security. However, these traditional derivatives do not, except indirectly, allow the separate trading of two risks—the risk of changes in the risk margin and the risk of default. These attributes are both aspects of the credit risk of the security or the issuer. Traditionally, these risks have been treated as impacting upon the price of the *overall* security. Consequently, exposure to these risks is managed through trading in the *asset or security* itself. Credit derivatives are specifically designed to allow the separate trading in and management of these risks.

*Credit derivatives may be defined as a specific class of financial instruments whose value is derived from an underlying market value driven by the credit risk of private or government entities, other than the counterparties to the credit derivatives transaction itself.* The last component of the definition is critical. In essence, it captures the role of credit derivatives in trading the credit risk of a particular entity (credit spread or price fluctuations arising from changes in credit quality, including default) by two parties who may, in some cases, have no commercial or financial relationship with the entity whose credit risk is being traded. Credit derivatives are, in essence, traditional derivatives (forwards and options, both on a standalone basis or embedded in the from of structured notes) reengineered to have a credit orientation.

The principal feature of these instruments is that they separate and isolate credit risk, facilitating the trading of credit risk with the purpose of:

- Replicating credit risk.
- Transferring credit risk.
- Hedging credit risk.

Credit derivatives also create new mechanisms for taking on credit risk in nontraditional formats within defined risk/reward parameters.

The principal demand for credit derivative products have, to date, been from banks/financial institutions and institutional investors. The use of credit derivatives by banks has been motivated by the desire to hedge or assume credit risk, improve portfolio diversification (synthetically) and to improve the management of credit portfolios.

Investor demand is motivated by a mixture of factors:

- The ability to add value to portfolios through trading in credit as a separate dimension. This particularly entails assumption of specific types of credit risk *without the acquisition of the credit asset itself.*
- The opportunity to manage the credit risk of investments.
- The inability of traditional institutional investors and asset managers to participate in the loan markets, in part, as a result of the absence of the necessary origination and loan administration infrastructure.
- The ability to arbitrage the pricing of credit risk in and between separate market sectors.

In the longer term, it is probable that credit derivatives will dictate a profound change in the activity of both these groups:[2]

- Institutional investors will add credit risk as *a separate and distinct* asset class that will be managed within general asset-allocation frameworks.
- Banks will alter their role into that of the *originator* of credit assets that are then distributed to investors.

Corporate use of credit derivatives is also likely to develop as a mechanism for the management of financing risk or project risk (particularly in emerging markets), increasing the range of business counterparties, as well as insulating against default of major suppliers or purchasers.

The potential for credit derivatives to become a vital component of capital markets is clear. However, the market is still in its development phase. Significant infrastructure problems await final resolution:

- The standardization of terms and documentary conventions.
- The treatment of credit derivatives from the viewpoint of regulatory capital and credit risk.

---

[2] See Das, Satyajit "The Credit Revolution" (September 1999) *Futures & OTC World* 52-61.

- The pricing and valuation of credit risk and credit derivatives.
- The accounting and taxation of such transactions.

## 3.  Credit Derivatives Instruments

The principal products, usually referred to as credit derivatives, encompass three instruments:

- Total return or loan swaps.
- Credit spread products.
- Credit default products.

Total return swaps are adaptations of the traditional swap format to *synthetically* create loan or credit asset-like investments for investors. The defining characteristic of these structures is that they are off-balance sheet and do not necessitate entry into loan arrangements (in the traditional sense) and the concomitant obligation to fund.

Credit spread products are generally forwards or options on the credit risk margins on credit sensitive assets (primarily loans or assets). These instruments allow the separate trading of this attribute of assets for the purpose of risk reduction, speculation, or return enhancement.

Total return swaps and credit spread products can be regarded as replication products as they allow the synthetic creation of certain positions. These positions can be created in the physical market but the derivative format offers significant advantages in terms of efficiency and transaction cost savings.

Credit default products are not dissimilar in structure to put options on credit-sensitive assets. They are usually structured as instruments that pay an agreed payoff (either fixed or calculated with reference to a specific mechanism) upon the occurrence of a specific event—generally the payment default of the subject credit. The credit default products thus allow the transfer and assumption of *pure credit risk,* in relation to the event of default of a nominated issuer.

**Appendix A** details the structure and features of the key building block credit derivative structures.

## 4.  Credit-linked Notes

### 4.1  Structure

Credit-linked notes entail the combination of a fixed income security with an embedded credit derivative. The credit-linked note enables the investor to replicate exposure to the credit risk inherent in a bond or a loan without the necessity of undertaking a direct investment in the security itself. The credit-linked note is designed to allow the investor to capture value from movements in the value of an underlying loan asset or bond, credit spreads, or default risk itself.

The reengineering of credit derivatives into a structured note format is motivated by the traditional factors that dictate the use of these structures generally. However, there are a number of additional factors that are also relevant including:

- The capacity to participate in markets that traditionally have excluded participation by such investors as the bank loan market.
- The ability to assume exposure to credit risk where *the performance obligation* (that is, the issuer) is separate in a credit sense from *the underlying credit risk,* allowing investment in assets or asset classes that traditionally have not been available.
- The capacity to create formats for rated investment in traditionally unrated assets.
- The ability to add credit risk—as a unique and specific asset class or risk factor—to investment portfolios.

These factors occur in addition to the more conventional advantages of these structures, such as customization of exposure and structured forms of tradeable risk.

## 4.2.   Credit-linked Notes — Types

There are a large variety of credit-linked notes transactions. **Exhibit 12.1** sets out a classification of the types of credit-linked notes.

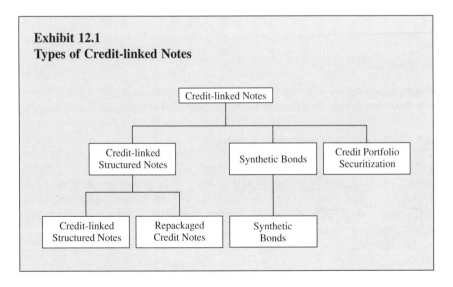

**Exhibit 12.1
Types of Credit-linked Notes**

The various types of credit-linked notes include:

• **Credit-linked structured notes** — these are traditional types of structured notes where a fixed income security is combined with a credit derivative (a total return swap, credit default swap, or credit spread forward or option). These structured notes feature a linkage of either coupon or principal to the underlying credit risk component specified by the investor. A high quality issuer (AAA- or AA-rated) issues the notes. The issuer in turn hedges out its exposure fully with a back-to-back credit derivative transaction with a dealer.

• **Repackaged credit notes** — this involves using a special purpose issuance vehicle or asset repackaging structure to create credit-linked structured notes. The repackaging vehicle purchases securities in the secondary market and then reprofiles the cash flows and the credit risk of the underlying securities by entering into derivatives transactions with a dealer. The repackaged cash flows are then bundled up as a security and placed with investors. The repackaged credit notes are similar to and complement credit-linked structured notes and asset swap transactions.

• **Synthetic bonds** — this entails the issue of "corporate" or "sovereign" debt out of a special purpose issuance or asset repackaging vehicle where the underlying credit risk exposure is created through a combination of cash securities and credit derivative transaction. The synthetic bond is designed to replicate the characteristics of a fixed interest security issued by the underlying issuer. These transactions are typically similar to repackaging transactions utilizing credit derivatives identified above.

• **Credit portfolio securitization** — this entails repackaging *portfolios* of credit risk (both from loans/securities and counterparty risk on derivatives/ off-balance sheet transactions) utilizing securitization concepts into multiple tranches of securities that are then sold to investors. The issuer of the securities reduces or eliminates the credit risk to existing obligors through the issues.

There is naturally some overlap among the structures. The principles used to construct and hedge the different types of notes also are similar.

### 4.3 Utilization of Credit-linked Notes

Investors have been the principal users of credit-linked notes. The major attraction of this format for credit derivatives is the capacity to create synthetic exposure to the underlying cash market asset without the need to undertake an actual physical investment in the relevant security. The fact that this can be done using an acceptable and traditional securities format is especially attractive.

The advantage of being able to avoid direct investment derives from a number of different sources. In developed capital markets, the advantages derive primarily from the capacity to avoid withholding taxes, eliminate the requirement for custody, and minimization of foreign exchange transactions. However, in high-yield/noninvestment grade securities and emerging markets the advantages derive from a wider range of factors:

- The regulatory framework that may prevent investors directly purchasing the underlying security.
- The presence of often complex and cumbersome procedures to obtain approval in order to make a direct investment.
- The lack of underlying securities of the type (term, and so on) sought by the investors.
- The difficulties of trading in the underlying market including lack of liquidity and high transaction costs.
- Lack of development of the infrastructure of investment (particularly, for foreign investors) including the absence of well-developed settlement, custody, and foreign exchange markets.

The difficulties of direct investment co-exist with increased demand for investment in the high-yield and emerging markets. This demand is driven by:

- The search for higher investment returns in an environment of low nominal returns and low spreads.
- The volatility of asset prices and credit spreads in these markets that provides significant trading opportunities.
- The attractive longer term prospects of these market segments that may be less efficient and less fully arbitraged than more developed markets, therefore offering relative value opportunities.
- The need for diversification of credit risk.
- The increased search for currency diversification within investment portfolios.

The combination of increased demand for foreign investment and the presence of these significant barriers to direct investment has encouraged the development of the market for credit-linked notes to allow *economic* investment in the underlying asset without the necessity to make direct investments in these markets. The use of credit default notes to overcome the absence of suitable cash investments can also be devised. The capacity to create customized and highly structured risk reward profiles within these structures is also attractive.

The identified advantages are particularly important to credit-linked notes and repackaged credit assets. However, the synthetic bonds and credit portfolio securitization are driven by different considerations including:

- Banks and financial institutions with portfolios of credit risks seeking to hedge and restructure its risk profiles. These transactions enable the issuers to hedge the credit risk of individual counterparties or an entire credit portfolio.

- Investors seeking credit risk may find these structures to be more attractive on a relative value basis or offering higher liquidity than comparable securities issued by individual issuers.

## 5. Credit-linked Structured Notes

The major types of credit-linked structured notes[3] include:
- Total return swap-embedded notes.
- Credit spread-linked notes.
- Credit default-linked notes.

A central feature of credit-linked notes is the capacity to create exposures to unrated credits through the introduction of a rated issuer and engineering the exposure to the unrated underlying loan asset synthetically. The key issue in this regard is the basis of the rating.

There are two possible approaches:

- A separation of the performance obligation (the risk on the issuer) and the market risk element (effectively the exposure to the reference credit asset).
- A rating based on the credit risk of *both* the issuer and the reference credit using the so-called *expected loss* approach.

The first approach is consistent with the approach utilized in connection with structured notes with other embedded risk factors (such as interest rate, currency, and commodity). The position of the rating agencies is evolving in this regard. The major rating agencies generally favor the second approach arguing that it more correctly portrays the investment credit risk profile.[4]

## 6. Total Return Credit-linked Notes

### 6.1 Structure

The principal object of total return credit-linked notes is the simulation of an investment in the underlying loan asset (bank loan or bond) or an index based on

---

[3]    See Das, Satyajit Credit-linked Notes — Structured Notes: Parts 1 and 2 (March 23, 1999) *Financial Products* Issue 110 20-24 & (9 April 1999) *Financial Products* Issue 111 16 – 23.

[4]    For a detailed analysis of the rating of credit-linked notes, see Das, Satyajit (editor) (2000) *Credit Derivatives and Credit-linked Notes*; John Wiley & Sons, Singapore, Chapter 16; see also Pimbley, Joseph "Credit Derivatives And Credit Ratings" (March 1996) *Financial Derivatives and Risk*; Efrat, Isaac, Gluck, Jeremy, and Powar, David (July 3, 1997) Moody's Refines Its Approach to Rating Structured Notes; Moody's Investor Service — Global Investors Service, New York Management.

a basket of the underlying loan assets. The structure also allows a separation of the risk profile with direct credit risk on the issuer and the underlying market risk exposure to the high-yield issuers underlying the index.

**Exhibit 12.2** sets out an example of a total rate of return credit-linked note.

---

**Exhibit 12.2**
**Total Return Swap-indexed Note**

| | |
|---|---|
| Issuer | AA/AAA-rated institution |
| Principal Amount | US$50 million |
| Maturity (years) | The earlier of |
| | 1. One (1) year from commencement date. |
| | 2. The next succeeding payment date following occurrence of a credit event on the underlying credit asset. |
| Underlying Credit Asset | Loan to ABC Corporation dated March 15, 2001, or 8% pa 2012 15 March bonds issued by ABC Corporation. |
| Coupon | 3-month LIBOR plus margin payable quarterly on an actual/360-day basis. |
| Margin | [250] bps pa |
| Principal Redemption | At par plus capital price adjustment subject to the minimum redemption level. |
| Minimum Redemption Level | 0% |
| Capital Price Adjustment | Principal amount times Change (either positive or negative) in the Price of the underlying credit asset. The price of the underlying credit asset change is calculated as (Current price – Initial price)/Initial price. |
| Initial Price | 100.00 |
| Current Price | The [bid or offer] price of the underlying credit asset as calculated by the calculation agent in accordance with the calculation method at 11.00 AM (New York time) two business days prior to each payment dates. |
| Calculation Method | 1. In the sole opinion of the calculation agent; or |
| | 2. By dealer poll under which the calculation agent will poll at least 4 and no more than six dealers in the loan and utilize the quoted |

|  | prices to determine an average price for the loan; or<br>3. By reference to a screen or quote service. |
|---|---|
| Calculation Agent | [Dealer] |

The structure can be decomposed into two separate transactions that are combined in the note:
1. An investment by the investor in a floating rate asset (such a LIBOR-based FRN).
2. The simultaneous entry by the investor into a total return swap where the investor pays the floating interest rate index (LIBOR) and receives the total return on the underlying loan asset.

The issuer will, in this case, enter into the total return swap to eliminate any exposure to fluctuations in the index and allow generation of a known cost of funds (consistent with its funding cost objectives).

**Exhibit 12.3** sets out the construction of this type of structure. The first part shows the construction on the transaction from the viewpoint of the issuer. The second part shows the transaction components from the perspective of the investor.

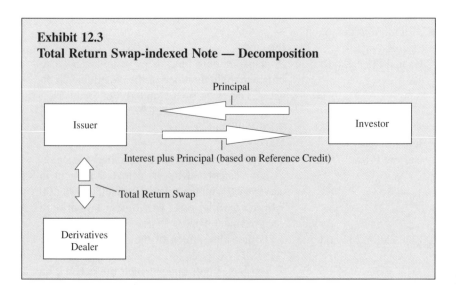

**Exhibit 12.3**
**Total Return Swap-indexed Note — Decomposition**

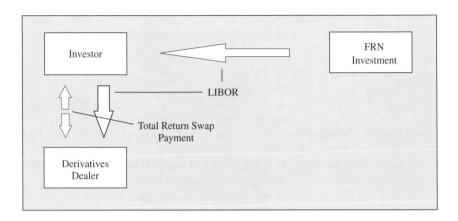

Two aspects of this type of note merit comment: the ability to introduce leverage and the capacity to effectively short sell the relevant loan or bond market to capture value from a decline in the price of loans from either a deterioration in the credit or increase in credit spreads.

In the above case, the transaction could readily be structured to incorporate leverage. This would be achieved by embedding a *higher* face value of total return swaps relative to the face value of the underlying floating rate cash investment in the note structure.

**Exhibit 12.4** sets out an example of a structure that features eight times leverage. Note that the coupon is calculated as leverage factor times the coupon on the total return swap plus leverage factor minus one times LIBOR. This reflects the fact that the LIBOR payment on 1/Leverage factor is effectively funded by the cash investment in the FRN.

**Exhibit 12.4**
**Leveraged Total Return Swap-indexed Note**

| | |
|---|---|
| Issuer | AA/AAA-rated institution |
| Principal Amount | US$50 million |
| Maturity (years) | The earlier of: |
| | 1. One (1) year from commencement date. |
| | 2. The next succeeding payment date following occurrence of a credit event on the underlying credit asset. |
| Underlying Credit Asset | Loan to ABC Corporation dated March 15, 2001 or 8% pa 2012 15 March Bonds issued by ABC Corporation |

| Coupon | (Leverage factor times Margin) plus 3-month LIBOR payable quarterly on an actual/360-day basis. |
|---|---|
| Margin | [250] bps pa |
| Principal Redemption | At par plus capital price adjustment subject to the minimum redemption level. |
| Minimum Redemption Level | 0% |
| Capital Price Adjustment | [Leverage factor] times Principal amount × Change (either positive or negative) in the Price of the underlying credit asset. The price of the underlying credit asset change is calculated as (Current price – Initial price)/Initial price. |
| Leverage Factor | 8 |
| Initial Price | 100.00 |
| Current Price | The [bid or offer] price of the underlying credit asset as calculated by the calculation agent in accordance with the calculation method at 11.00 AM (New York time) two business days prior to each payment dates. |
| Calculation Method | 1. In the sole opinion of the calculation agent; or |
| | 2. By dealer poll under which the calculation agent will poll at least four and no more than six dealers in the loan and utilize the quoted prices to determine an average price for the loan; or |
| | 3. By reference to a screen or quote service. |
| Calculation Agent | [Dealer] |

**Exhibit 12.5** sets in diagram form the construction and hedging of the leveraged note.

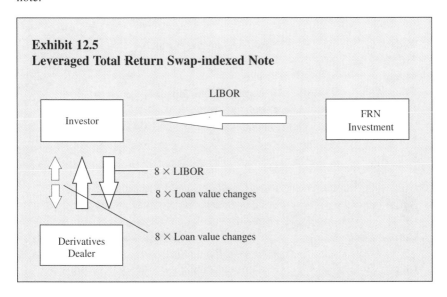

**Exhibit 12.5**
**Leveraged Total Return Swap-indexed Note**

Use of leverage requires caution as fluctuations in the value may have the effect of eroding the capital value of the underlying FRN in full. Consequently, in order to hedge the leveraged note it is necessary to combine the total return loan swap on the larger total principal with an option to effectively cap the losses at a level that equates to total loss of principal. This is designed to avoid negative redemption values under the note. This aspect of construction of leveraged structures is also relevant to leveraged versions of other types of credit-linked notes including credit-linked notes, as well credit default-linked notes.

Shorting the loan market is traditionally difficult to achieve in the physical market because of the difficulty of borrowing nongovernment bonds for the purposes of creating the short sale. The ability to utilize the embedded total rate of return loan swap to create the short position is advantageous in this respect.

## 6.2 Product Variations

**Exhibit 12.6** sets out an example of credit-linked note where the investor has specific exposure to a high-yield index. **Exhibit 12.7** sets out an example of a transaction where the investor has specific exposure to an emerging market index.

**Exhibit 12.6**
**High Yield-indexed Note**

| | |
|---|---|
| Issuer | AAA/AA-rated institution |
| Principal Amount | US$50 million |
| Maturity | 3 years |
| Coupon | 3-month LIBOR plus 200 bps |
| Principal Redemption | Principal amount plus Leverage factor × Change in underlying credit asset |
| Minimum Redemption Level | 0% |
| Leverage Factor | 3 |
| Underlying Credit Asset | Nominated high-yield bond index |
| Initial Price | Price of underlying credit asset as at the date of issue. |
| Current Price | The [bid or offer] price of the underlying credit asset as at the maturity. |
| Change In the Underlying Credit Asset | Percentage change in the underlying credit Asset as calculated from the initial price and the final price. |

**Exhibit 12.7**
**Emerging Market-indexed Note**

| | |
|---|---|
| Issuer | AA-rated issuer |
| Amount | US$10 million |
| Maturity | 3 years |
| Issue Price | 100.00 |
| Coupon | 0.00% pa |
| Redemption Value | Redemption amount is based on the following formula: Amount × Index/131.8 Where: Index is the J.P. Morgan Emerging Local Markets Index (in US$) on the value date. |
| Minimum Redemption | 0.00 |
| Value Date | 5 business days before maturity |

In these cases, the note structure allows the investor the following advantages:

- Assumption of a diversified exposure to the high-yield sector that allows reduction of the specific risk of individual counterparties.
- The benefits of a liquid and tradeable instrument on the index.
- Avoidance of the difficulties that would be associated with directly replicating the index.
- The leverage inherent in this transaction that entails embedding additional total return index swaps or entering into a total return swap with a larger notional principal amount. This is optional depending on the requirement of the investor.
- The ability to short sell the index.

The capacity to effectively short sell loan assets can be illustrated with the following example. Assume an investor holds an illiquid emerging market or high-yield bond and is concerned about the price exposure arising primarily from potential deterioration in the credit outlook for the issuer. The traditional physical solution to deal with this problem would be to either:

- Sell the securities that would give rise to immediate realization of a capital gain or loss (that may have tax and other implications).
- Short sell the securities that may be difficult to engineer as a result of the unavailability of securities to borrow, as well as the risks and ongoing management of the short position.

A potential synthetic solution would be to purchase a total rate of return credit-linked note either on the security or an index—the corresponding emerging market or high-yield index—that is correlated in its price behavior to the securities held. The note has embedded within the structure a total return swap where the investor, effectively, receives the floating rate of interest (LIBOR) and *pays* the total rate of return on the security or index.

   This, effectively, provides a hedge for the investor while potentially overcoming the problems of the transaction costs in the physical market and the practical difficulties of shorting the securities.

## 7.   Credit Spread Notes

### 7.1   Structure

The use of credit spread notes allows the creation of highly specific and structured exposure to *the credit spread* without the need to either have direct credit exposure to the counterparty whose credit spread underlies the transaction and any absolute exposure to interest rate risk. The ability to mismatch or vary the duration of the underlying investment and the credit spread to which exposure is sought is also a potential source of additional value.

**Exhibit 12.8** sets out an example of a credit spread note. The structure seeks to monetize the investor's expectations in respect of the implied forward credit spread. The investor gains if the spread decreases and loses if the spread increases.

---

**Exhibit 12.8**
**Credit Spread-linked Notes—Example 1**

| | |
|---|---|
| Issuer | AAA/AA-rated institution |
| Principal Amount | US$50 million |
| Term | 3 years |
| Issue Price | 100 |
| Coupon | 3-month LIBOR plus 125 bps |
| Reference Security | [Identified] bonds issued by [sovereign state] |
| Reference Treasury | |
| Benchmark | [Identified US Treasury Bond] |
| Principal Redemption | Face value + [(Spread duration factor = 5) × (120 bps – Credit spread)]. |
| Credit Spread | Defined as the yield at maturity of the reference security minus yield at maturity of the reference treasury benchmark. |

---

Analytically, a fixed income bond is combined with a credit spread forward (where the investor purchases the spread) in this structure. **Exhibit 12.9** sets out the detailed construction and hedging of the structure.

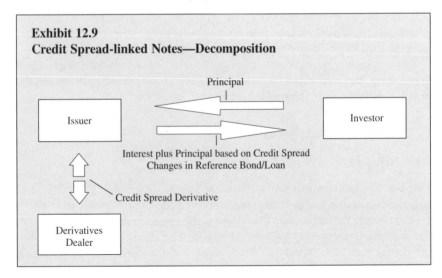

**Exhibit 12.9**
**Credit Spread-linked Notes—Decomposition**

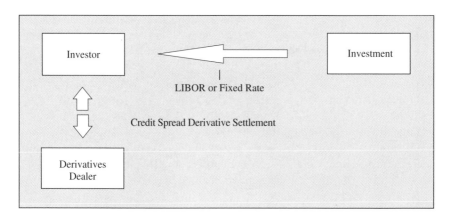

The face value amount of the credit spread forward can be higher than the face value of the note to create leverage, if required. Additional yield on the note can be engineered by structuring the spread forward at an off-market rate. For example, the transaction can be structured such that the investor can buy the spread forward at a price relative to the forward price (above the theoretical forward price) which creates an intrinsic value that is then present-valued and used to enhance the yield on the security.

## 7.2 Product Variations

**Exhibit 12.10** sets out an example of a credit spread note where the return profile is linked to the performance of the credit spread relative to US Treasuries of a sovereign issue. The rationale of the transaction is that the investor assumes an exposure to the credit spread and seeks to monetize the expectation that the spread will stay within the identified range. The investor benefits if the spread stays within the range. If the credit spread increases or decreases outside the range, then the investor receives a minimum coupon but clearly suffers a reduction in return.[5]

---

[5] This structure is focused on the credit spread at maturity. An alternative that is also common entails the coupon being determined *daily*, depending on whether the spread is within or outside the nominated range.

**Exhibit 12.10**
**Credit Spread-linked Notes — Example 2**

| | |
|---|---|
| Issuer | AAA/AA-rated institution |
| Principal Amount | US$50 million |
| Term | 3 years |
| Issue Price | 100 |
| Coupon | Zero |
| Reference Security | [7.25% September 2031] bonds issued by [Sovereign State] |
| Reference Treasury Benchmark | [Identified US Treasury Bond 6.25% February 2031] |
| Principal Redemption | If credit spread at maturity is between 95 and 140 bps, then at 126% of face value (implied yield to maturity of 8.01% pa). If credit spread at maturity is below 95 or above 140 bps, then at 109% of face value (implied yield to maturity of 2.91% pa) |
| Credit Spread | Defined as the yield at maturity of the reference security minus yield at maturity of the reference treasury benchmark |

The structure effectively can be decomposed into a digital put and call option on the credit spread with the premium received for the sale of these options being used to enhance the return on the Note. The digital payout on the embedded options has the effect of lowering the return to the note investor in case the spread is outside the nominated range triggering either the call or put option on the spread. The issuer in turn on sells the embedded option to hedge its own exposure and reduce its cost of funds to its target level.[6]

**Exhibit 12.11** sets out an example of a credit spread note where the underlying securities are emerging market issues. In this structure, the investor uses the foregone coupon to purchase a call option on a basket of four countries, which is then embedded in the note. The structure links redemption to changes in four Brady bonds. The return profile provide for unlimited potential gains but with an assured return of principal.

---

[6] The structure is modelled on the Range or Accrual Note structure which evolved in the early 1990s see Chapter 13; Satyajit Das (1996) *Exotic Options*; LBC Information Services Chapter 13.

---

**Exhibit 12.11**
**Credit Spread-linked Note — Example 3**

In early 1995, following a major sell-off in emerging markets a number of structured notes linked to emerging market securities, usually Brady bonds, were issued. The following note was typical of the securities issued:

| | |
|---|---|
| Issuer | AAA- or AA-rated |
| Maturity | 1 year |
| Coupon | 0% |
| Principal Redemption | The higher of: |
| | 100 + (Final basket price − 48%) or Minimum redemption |
| Minimum Redemption | 100% |
| Basket | 40% par bond of Latin country A |
| | 30% par bond of Latin country B |
| | 30% par bond of Latin country C |
| Current Basket Price | 48% |

The note combines a zero-coupon note with a call option on a basket of three Brady bonds. The call option is engineered through the linking of the redemption value to the price of the Brady bonds. The call option is financed through the forgone interest on the note.

The issue was designed to allow investors to increase exposure on a risk-averse basis to emerging market debt following the Mexican crisis where emerging market Brady bond spreads widened between 100 and 400 bps bringing the spreads to their highest levels for many years.

The economics of the transaction was as follows:

• The 1-year yield on AAA- or AA-rated notes at the time of issue was around 7.00 to 7.25% pa. The breakeven price on the note to equate the return to that on a conventional note was around 93.25/93.50.
• The breakeven price increase on the basket such that the noteholder would earn the yield on 1-year securities was around 14.60/15.10%, implying a final basket price of 55-55.25%.

---

These notes have been frequently structured and used in the context of emerging market bonds where the credit spreads can be extremely volatile. The major investors have included institutional investors seeking exposure to the emerging market sector without the need to assume direct credit exposure to emerging market issuers. An added advantage is the ability to avoid the risks of trading in emerging market debt.

# 8.   Credit Default Notes

## 8.1   Structure

Credit default notes are primarily used to assume or reduce counterparty default exposure. Investors have traditionally used credit default structures *to assume* credit default exposure to generate premium income to enhance yield. However, structures that entail shifting of credit exposure while less common are also feasible.

**Exhibit 12.12** sets out an example of a credit default note. The note structure depicted sets out a note linked to a single issuer credit. The credit default note is constructed by combining a cash investment with a default swap.

| | |
|---|---|
| **Exhibit 12.12** | |
| **Credit Default-linked Note — Example 1** | |
| | |
| Issuer | AAA/AA-rated institution |
| Principal Amount | US$50 million |
| Term | 5 years |
| Issue Price | 100 or Face Value |
| Coupon | LIBOR plus 150 bps |
| Reference Security | [Identified bond or loan of nominated borrower.] |
| Principal Redemption | If no credit event has occurred before or as at maturity, then at face value. If a credit event has occurred before or as at maturity, then par minus default payment. |
| Credit Event | Any of the following with respect to nominated borrower: |
| | 1. Failure to pay interest or principal on any senior debt security. |
| | 2. Event of bankruptcy. |
| | 3. Cross-default or cross-acceleration on any senior unsecured obligation. |
| | 4. Restructuring event. |
| Default Payment | Any one of the following. |
| | 1. An agreed US$ amount equal to [60]% of the principal amount. |

2. Change in price of the reference security as between the issue date and date an agreed period after default as determined by a poll of selected dealers in the reference security.
3. Payment of par or the price of the security as at issue date in exchange for delivery of the defaulted reference security.

The notes are structurally created from the combination of a fixed interest security (fixed or floating coupon) and the entry by the investor into a credit default swap where the investor is the provider of default protection. The default payment or recovery rate is engineered into the principal redemption structure. The issuer enters into an offsetting default swap with a counterparty to eliminate its default risk position and generate a known cost of funds for the issuer.

The payment for the default swap is used to generate the return above the underlying interest rate on the credit default-linked note. In the event of default, the principal repayment to the investor is reduced by the amount of the default payment (effectively the loss suffered as a result of the occurrence of the credit event). The default payment can be calculated either as a fixed amount or an amount reflecting the actual recovery amount (calculated using changes in the value of the underlying bond following default using a dealer polling mechanism). The calculation mechanics are identical to those applicable to credit default swaps.

**Exhibit 12.13** sets out the construction and hedging of a typical default note.

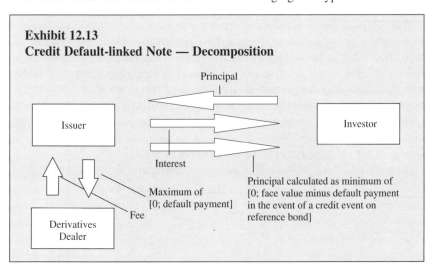

**Exhibit 12.13**
**Credit Default-linked Note — Decomposition**

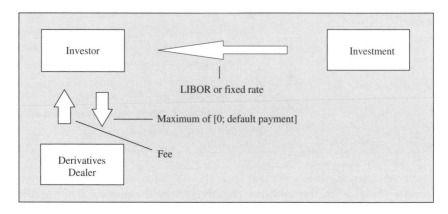

The major advantages of the structure include:

• Providing yield enhancement in return for assuming the risk of default.
• Allows utilization of credit risk assumption capacity that might not otherwise be capable of being utilized through the absence of available investments.
• Separation of default risk and principal credit risk that are attributable to different underlying issuers.
• Ability to create capped and known loss profile in the event of default.

The structure has some significant credit enhancement aspects. The fact that the credit default swap is embedded in the note that is purchased by the investor dictates that the performance obligation to make the default payment in the case of default under the reference asset is *fully cash collateralized*. This results from the fact that in the event of default the issuer merely adjusts the payment to the investor reducing the principal repayment by the default payment obligation.

This allows substitution of the *credit of the issuer* for the *credit of the investor* in the provision of default protection. This significantly broadens the range of institutions able to provide credit default protection through the unbundling of the assumption of default risk from the actual counterparty credit risk of the party providing default protection. By extending this concept to the synthetic bond framework (discussed in detail below), high-quality collateral (government or high credit rated (AA/AA or better) bonds) can be utilized to significantly increase the range of providers of default protection *irrespective of the credit quality of the entity or person providing the protection*.

**Exhibit 12.14** sets out an additional example of credit default-linked notes.

**Exhibit 12.14**
**Credit Default-linked Note — Example 2**

| | |
|---|---|
| Issuer | AAA/AA-rated institution |
| Principal Amount | US$20 million |
| Maturity | 3 months |
| Issue Price | 96.65% of principal amount |
| Coupon | 0.00% pa |
| Reference Security | Republic of Korea 8.75% April 15, 2003 |
| Principal Redemption | If no credit event has occurred before or as at maturity, then at face value. If a credit event has occurred before or as at maturity, then default payment. |
| Credit Event | Any of the following with respect to reference security. |
| | 1. Failure to pay interest or principal on any senior debt security. |
| | 2. Cross-default or cross-acceleration on any senior unsecured obligation. |
| | 3. Debt moratorium, suspension of interest or principal repayments on debt or any material restructuring event. |
| Default Payment | The issuer will deliver reference securities to the value of the principal amount to the noteholder. |

## 8.2 Product Variations

One variation on the credit default note structure to emerge is the *callable* credit default note. **Exhibit 12.15** sets out the detailed structure of this type of credit-linked note.

**Exhibit 12.15**
**Callable Credit Default-linked Note**

This structure entails a security where the final maturity of the note is, say, five years. The redemption of the note is linked to a reference asset and in the event of default the principal repaid is adjusted by the amount of the agreed default payment. The major differences in the callable versus the noncallable structure are the following additional features:

- The note can be called annually or sometimes semi-annually or quarterly (upon provision of appropriate notice) at *the option of the issuer*.
- In the event, the note is not called, then the coupon on the security increases by a preset amount.
- The call and the increase in coupon mechanism is repeated as at the specified date during the life of the note until final maturity unless the note is called at any of the call dates.

In effect the issuer (in practice, the ultimate buyer of default protection through the credit default swap used by the issuer to hedge its own exposure) can continue as of each call date to maintain protection against the cost of default of the underlying credit *but at an increasing cost*. This increasing cost of protection is embedded in the higher coupons.

Economically, this type of structure can be used to secure protection against default over the near term with the option to extend but at higher cost. The investor is, in turn, the receiver of increased remuneration for assumption of the default risk. In effect, if the note is *not* called, than it is probable that the credit risk of the underlying credit asset has increased but the investor receives additional income, by way of higher yield, to compensate for the increased default risk.

In practice, this structure was used extensively by banks, in particular Japanese banks, to purchase protection against credit risk on certain obligations. However, most of these transactions were not designed to achieve real transfer of risk. They were intended as period and risk management strategies with the issuers exercising the call at the earliest opportunity.[7]

Exhibit 12.16 sets out an example of a credit default note where the investor is guaranteed return of principal but risks the coupon through linkage to a default event. Exhibit 12.17 sets out an additional example of this structure. It also introduces the addition of a leverage factor that modulates the exposure in line with the investor's desired risk profile.

---

[7] For example, see Mahtani, Arun "Credit Derivatives Bolster Balance Sheets" (November 21, 1998) *International Financing Review* Issue 1260 91.

**Exhibit 12.16**
**Principal Guaranteed Credit Default-linked Note — Example 1**

| | |
|---|---|
| Issuer | AAA/AA-rated institution |
| Principal Amount | US$20 million |
| Term | 5 years |
| Issue Price | 100 or face value |
| Coupon | • If there is no credit event, then US$ LIBOR plus 125 bps. |
| | • If there is a credit event, then coupon terminates. |
| Reference Security | [Identified bond or loan of nominated emerging market borrower.] |
| Principal Redemption | Principal amount. If there is a credit event then the principal amount is repayable immediately. |
| Credit Event | Any of the following with respect to reference security. |
| | 1. Failure to pay interest or principal on any senior debt security. |
| | 2. Cross-default or cross acceleration on any senior unsecured obligation. |
| | 3. Debt moratorium, suspension of interest or principal repayments on debt- or any material-restructuring event. |

**Exhibit 12.17**
**Principal Guaranteed Credit Default-linked Note — Example 2**

| | |
|---|---|
| Issuer | AAA/AA-rated institution |
| Principal Amount | US$50 million |
| Term | 3 years |
| Issue Price | 100 |
| Coupon | 4.50% pa; coupon terminates upon occurrence of credit event. |
| Reference Security | [Identified bond or loan of nominated emerging market borrower.] |
| Principal Redemption | Greater of face value or face value plus [Market value of reference security × Factor]. |

| Credit Event | Any of the following with respect to reference security :<br>1. Failure to pay interest or principal on any senior debt security.<br>2. Cross-default or cross acceleration on any senior unsecured obligation.<br>3. Debt moratorium, suspension of interest or principal repayments on debt, or any material-restructuring event. |
|---|---|

A similar structure that has developed to allow risk-averse investors to assume credit risk with guaranteed principal returns entails a note where:

- The capital value of the note is returned at maturity.
- The investor participates in any upside performance of the underlying credit asset (loan or security) as captured by the increase in price of the asset above a pre-agreed level.

The note has the return profile of a call option on the underlying credit asset. The note is constructed as either a risk-free bond combined with a call on the underlying asset or the purchase of the loan that is hedged by the purchase of a default put on the asset. In each case the option is paid for by the foregone or reduced income from the underlying assets. This type of investment has been attractive for investors seeking to invest in higher risk loan transactions within a low-risk format. **Exhibit 12.18** sets out an example of this type of structure.

---

**Exhibit 12.18**
**Principal Guaranteed Credit Default-linked Note — Example 3**

| | |
|---|---|
| Issuer | AAA/AA-rated institution |
| Principal Amount | US$20 million |
| Maturity | 5 Years |
| Issue Price | 100 |
| Coupon | • If there is no credit event, then 0.00% pa.<br>• If there is a credit event, then 5.75% pa (accruing from issue date to the date of the credit event). |
| Redemption Value | • If there is no credit event, then 150% of principal amount. |

---

| | |
|---|---|
| | • If there is a credit event, then 100% of principal amount (payable at maturity). |
| Reference Security | [Identified bond or loan of nominated emerging market borrower.] |
| Credit Event | Any of the following with respect to reference security:<br>1. Failure to pay interest or principal on any senior debt security.<br>2. Cross-default or cross-acceleration on any senior unsecured obligation.<br>3. Debt moratorium, suspension of interest or principal repayments on debt, or any material-restructuring event. |

Other variants on the basic credit default note structures include the use of basket credit default notes linked to the first to default within the basket to enhance yield. For example, an investor seeking to enhance yield within an AA-rating constraint would generally seek relative value within the universe of available asset within this credit category. An alternative would be to invest in a basket credit default note where the default event is indexed to multiple (say, 3 to 4) AA-rated sovereign issuers. The investor receives an enhanced return (say, around 10 to 15 bps) relative to the return *on any individual asset*. This higher return compensates the investor for the higher risk as the default payment can be triggered by default on the *first* of the three names to default.[8]

Another example of a basket credit note may entail an investor seeking to increase exposure to a particular sovereign issuer within the constraint that it will withdraw *from the sector* upon reduction in the credit rating or from an increase in bond spreads. The traditional physical solution would be to purchase the relevant securities and sell the portfolio upon the occurrence of the relevant credit event.

Two possible derivative solutions, entailing basket credit default notes are also potentially available:

• Purchase a basket credit default note linked to the reference sovereign assets with the investor's risk linked to the first to incur the credit event.
• Purchase the physical securities and simultaneously purchase a basket credit default note on a first-to-default basis where the exposure under the note is capable of being extinguished by delivery of the underlying physical securities at an agreed price.

---

[8]  See detailed discussion in Chapter 1.

**Exhibit 12.19** sets an example of a credit default note where the reference credit is an emerging market nation with the return of principal being contingent on performance on external credit obligations and on continuation of currency convertibility. Another interesting feature of this issue is the shortness of tenor of the issue. **Exhibit 12.20** and **Exhibit 12.21** sets out additional examples of this type of structure.

---

**Exhibit 12.19**
**Credit Default-linked Note — Default/Inconvertibility Structure**
**Example 1**

In 1995, following the financial crisis in Mexico, a special type of short-term security was issued. The credit derivative-embedded structure issued by a number of issuers was designed to allow investors to monetize their expectation that Mexico would continue to meet its credit obligations and that the convertibility of the Mexican peso would continue. The typical structure of these transactions was as follows:

| | |
|---|---|
| Issuer | A1+/P1-rated issuer |
| Principal Amount | (up to) US$20 million |
| Maturity | Between 30 and 90 days |
| Coupon | Zero |
| Issue Price | Issued at discount to give investor-required yield to maturity. |
| Credit Event | Any default on any reference security or inconvertibility of the Mexican peso into US$. |
| Reference Credit | Government of Mexico |
| Reference Security | Cetes, Tesobonos, Bondes, Ajustabones, or other securities issued or guaranteed by the reference credit. |
| Principal Redemption | If there is no credit event, at par (100%). If there is a credit event, the issuer can satisfy its obligations under the note by delivery of any of the reference securities or its cash equivalent. |

These short-dated securities were priced to yield the equivalent of LIBOR plus 350 to 450 bps, depending on market conditions. The investors received significant yield enhancement in return for their willingness to risk the principal investment to the risk of credit default by the Mexican government or the restriction of currency convertibility (between the Mexican peso and the US$) by the Mexican authorities.

**Exhibit 12.20**
**Credit Default-linked Note — Default/Inconvertibility Structure**
**Example 2**

| | |
|---|---|
| Issuer | AA-rated issuer |
| Principal Amount | (up to) US$75 million |
| Maturity | 2 years |
| Coupon | 8.00% pa payable semi-annually |
| Issue Price | 100.00 |
| Credit Event | • The Government of Brazil restricts the convertibility of the Brazilian Real into US$. |
| | • Default, rescheduling, moratorium or suspension of payments on Government of Brazil debt. |
| | • War, civil strife, or similar event occurs involving Brazil. |
| Interest Payments and Principal Redemption | • If there is no credit event, the payment of interest as scheduled and redemption of principal at par (100%). |
| | • If there is a credit event, then the issuer can defer its payment obligation under the note until 10 days after cessation of such a credit event or satisfy its obligations under the note by delivery of any Real-denominated securities issued by the Government of Brazil. |

The investors received significant yield enhancement in return for their willingness to risk deferral of payments on the investment in the event of default by the Brazilian government or the restriction of currency convertibility (between the Real and the US$).

---

**Exhibit 12.21**
**Credit Default-linked Note — Default/Inconvertibility Structure**
**Example 3**

| | |
|---|---|
| Issuer | A-rated issuer |
| Principal Amount | (up to) US$50 million |
| Maturity | 1 year |

| | |
|---|---|
| Coupon | 0.00% pa |
| Issue Price | 88.00% |
| Final Redemption | • If there is no credit event, then: Principal amount × (1530/FX), where FX is the US$/ Lebanese pound exchange rate. |
| | • If there is a credit event, then final redemption will be in Lebanese pounds in an amount equal to Principal amount × US$: L£1532. |
| Credit Event | The Government of Lebanon restricts the convertibility of the Lebanese pound into US$. |

The investors received significant yield enhancement (a return of 13.64% pa) and the ability to gain from any appreciation in the Lebanese pound against the US$. The risk of the investment is that the investor may receive nonconvertible Lebanese pounds as payment where restrictions on currency convertibility (between the Lebanese pound and the US$) is imposed.

Similar structures have emerged in recent years to facilitate synthetic investor exposure to Eastern European domestic. Significant regulatory and administrative burdens in making investments in and holding domestic securities in these markets has encouraged the use of these types of structures to gain effective economic exposure to the domestic securities.[9] **Exhibit 12.22** sets out details of one example of these types of synthetic emerging market-structured notes as applied to Eastern Europe. **Exhibit 12.23** sets out details of an additional example as applied in Asia.

**Exhibit 12.22**
**Synthetic Emerging Market-structured Notes**
**Example 1**

An example of this type of structure includes investments in short-dated notes linked to Russian GKOs, effectively Treasury bills. In 1996, the Russian capital markets were deregulated to allow foreign investment in fixed interest securities. This was facilitated by the introduction of the S

---

[9]  See Kim, Theodore "Open All Hours" (April 1997) *Euromoney* 109-111; Kim, Ted "No KO for GKOs" (August 1997) *Futures & Options World* 15-17.

account for foreign fixed income investment. Previous to this initiative, foreign investors were unable to repatriate the proceeds from the GKO (effectively Treasury bills) and OFZ sovereign debt markets. However, the establishment of the S account was administratively complex. This encouraged foreign investment indirectly through the use of structured notes where the price performance of the note was linked to the underlying GKO securities.

The transactions were typically structured as follows:

- The investor invested US$ and received an interest rate and principal redemption based on the underlying GKO settled *in US$*. The return received by the investor reflected the interest rate on the GKO, as well as the final principal repayment (in the absence of default) converted from roubles into US$ *at the currency rate at maturity*.
- The structure of the transaction transferred the credit risk, interest rate risk, and currency risk to the investor. The structure effectively replicated an investment in the GKO itself.
- The seller of the structured note (typically an investment bank with an S account) hedged its risk by purchasing the GKO itself and transferring the economic risk and returns through the issue of the notes.

The impact of these types of transactions can be seen in the following statistics:

- The GKO market increased to approximately US$60 billion by end 1997 with foreign investment representing around 50% of total outstandings.
- GKO interest rates fell from around 40% pa to a pre-crisis low of 16.75% pa, in part due to the impact of foreign participation.[10]

The structure has also been used in other markets. For example, set out below is a representative structured note that passed through Polish government Treasury bill risk to the investor. The structure is designed, as above, to allow investors who might not otherwise be able to invest to participate in the market.

| | |
|---|---|
| Issuer | Investment bank |
| Maturity | 3 months |
| Amount | (multiples of) US$5 million equivalent |

---

[10] The default by Russia on its debt in 1998 created significant problems with the large volume of GKO-linked structured notes on issue.

| Redemption | Amount $\times$ (1 + Interest rate) $\times$ Currency adjustment |
|---|---|
| Interest Rate | Polish zloty 3-month Treasury bBill yield (on an actual/360-day basis) plus/minus a margin |
| Currency Adjustment | (0.45 $\times$ US\$1/US\$2) + (0.35 $\times$ DM 1/DM 2) + (0.10 $\times$ £1/£2) + (0.05 $\times$ Ffr1/Ffr2) + (0.05 $\times$ Swfr2/Swfr2) |

The note effectively is a US\$-settled investment that replicates an investment in Polish zloty Treasury bills. The currency adjustment is designed to embed a basket-weighted forward currency position in the Note matching the Polish zloty basket peg in order to reduce the currency risk of the investment.

**Exhibit 12.23**
**Synthetic Emerging Market-structured Notes**
**Example 2**

The structure set out below is a representative structured note that passed through The Philippines government Treasury bill risk to the investor. The structure is designed, as above, to allow investors who might not otherwise be able to invest to participate in the market.

| Issuer | Investment bank |
|---|---|
| Maturity | 2 years |
| Amount | (multiples of) US\$5 million equivalent |
| Issue Price | 100 |
| Interest Rate | • If there is no credit event, then US\$ 6-month LIBOR plus 150 bps.<br>• If there is a credit event, then default payment will apply. |
| Principal Redemption | • If there is no credit event, then amount in US\$.<br>• If there is a credit event, then default payment will apply. |
| Reference Credit | Bangko Sentral ng Philpinas (BSP) (the Central Bank of the Republic of Philippines) |

| | |
|---|---|
| Reference Securities | Treasury bills issued by BSP equal to the Amount. |
| Credit Event | • Default, rescheduling, moratorium, suspension of payments or material restructuring of BSP or Republic of Philippines debt. |
| | • BSP restricts the convertibility of The Philippines peso into US$. |
| Default Payment | The issuer will not be required to pay any unpaid interest rate coupons or principal amount. The issuer will have the option to: |
| | 1. Deliver the reference securities to the investor; or |
| | 2. Pay the net proceeds that would result from the sale of the reference securities. |

The note effectively is a US$-settled investment that replicates an investment in Treasury bills issued by the Central Bank of the Republic of Philippines.

## 9. Repackaged Credit-linked Notes

Repackaged credit-linked notes[11] are a special class of credit-linked structured notes. They involve using a special-purpose issuance vehicle or asset repackaging structure to repackage the credit risk of securities to create credit-linked structured notes. The repackaging vehicle purchases securities in the secondary market and then reprofiles the cash flows and the credit risk of the underlying securities by entering into derivatives transactions with a dealer. The repackaged cash flows are then bundled up as a security and placed with investors.[12]

The motivations underlying repackaged notes and repackaging vehicles are similar to that underlying the market for credit-linked notes generally. These include:

---

[11] See Das, Satyajit "Credit-linked Notes: Repackaged Notes And Repackaging Vehicles: Part 1" (May 6, 1999) *Financial Products* Issue 113 16-21; "Credit-linked Notes: Repackaged Notes and Repackaging Vehicles: Part 2" (June 4, 1999) *Financial Products* Issue 115 16-22.

[12] See Chapter 1 for a detailed discussion of repackaging vehicles.

- Investor demand for credit risk that is not directly available in the market.
- Relative value considerations under which the credit exposure can be created at a more attractive value through structured notes.
- Regulatory and market considerations that favor indirect assumption of the credit exposure relative to direct investment in the security.

However, the demand for repackaged credit assets *over traditional structured notes* is predicated upon the following additional factors:

- The lack of requirement to compensate the issuer for issuing the structured note (effectively the sub-LIBOR margin requirement).
- Relative value considerations whereby the repackaging structure has the inherent opportunity to allow purchase of under-valued securities in the secondary market to collateralize the structure reducing the cost.
- Greater flexibility to structure investments, consistent with investor requirements, without the restriction of needing to satisfy the requirements of the note issuer.[13]
- Enhanced freedom to select the credit and issuer profile of the underlying securities, which allows both customization of issuer risk and diversifies the universe of issuers of structured notes.

These factors (in particular, the first two factors) have greatly contributed to the development of repackaged notes generally. Repackaged credit notes complement and compete with credit-linked structured notes.

## 9.1 Concept

The concept of repackaged credit-linked notes is based firmly on the asset swap/ asset repackaging principles outlined above. The rationale is to deliberately create credit exposure to selected counterparties using a credit derivative contract. The process is identical to that described. Assets are bought in the secondary market lodged in a repackaging vehicle. The repackaging vehicle enters into credit derivative transactions to reprofile the credit risk on the asset. The repackaging vehicle then issues a security to the investor consistent with the investor's requirements. The distinguishing feature of repackaged credit-linked notes is the focus on reprofiling the *credit risk* of the underlying securities. This reprofiling is typically achieved with either total return swaps or credit default swaps.

---

[13] This is relevant despite the fact that the issuer is perfectly insulated from the impact of the embedded derivative and is fully hedged back into LIBOR-based funding at an attractive cost.

The market for repackaged credit-linked notes is extremely large. It functions as a mechanism for enabling investors to access credit risk in a manner consistent with investment requirements and risk-reward profiles. The asset repackaging market, in performing this function, allows the reprofiling of credit risk and facilitates the transfer of credit risk between market segments. It also brings increased transparency and consistency to credit risk-pricing in capital markets.

## 9.2 Types

In general, there are two types of repackaged credit-linked note transactions:

- Creation of exposure to high-quality credits (referred to here as asset credit swaps) — this is done by buying an asset in the secondary market and entering into a credit derivatives transaction to *reduce* the risk to the obligor/ issuer of the underlying security. The repackaged security enables the investor to acquire exposure to the derivatives counterparty (via the credit derivative). The repackaged security generates a return that is lower than that on the underlying security but higher than the normal return that would be available on an equivalent security for *the higher rated* credit (the derivatives counterparty). This type of transaction may be motivated by relative value considerations whereby the asset swap is used to arbitrage the valuation of different credits in the capital market.
- Creation of exposure to a selected credit(s) (referred to here as synthetic credit assets) — this is done by purchasing high-quality collateral assets that are then converted through a credit derivative to provide exposure to a selected credit nominated by the investor. The repackaged security in this case provides the investor with indirect exposure to the selected underlying credit. This type of transaction is motivated by the ability of the investor to access the underlying asset (which may not be available in the cash market), the ability to circumvent regulatory and legal constraints on the investment, the capacity to structure the exposure in a manner desired by the investor or relative value considerations.

**Exhibit 12.24** sets out an example of the structures of an asset credit swap.

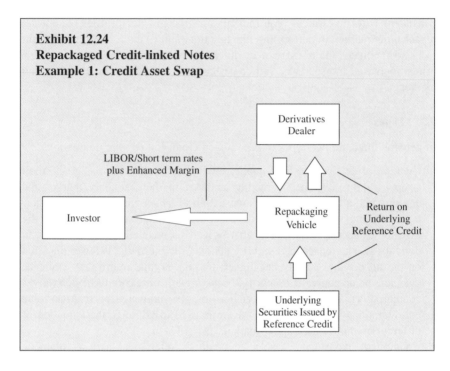

Exhibit 12.24
Repackaged Credit-linked Notes
Example 1: Credit Asset Swap

The mechanics of the transaction are as follows:

- The underlying securities issued by the reference credit are purchased by the repackaging vehicle.
- The vehicle enters into a total return swap with the derivative dealer. Under the swap, the dealer receives the return on the underlying securities and pays LIBOR plus a margin the repackaging vehicle.
- At maturity, the derivatives dealer pays par to the vehicle (unless it is in default) and receives the maturing proceeds of the underlying securities unless the obligor on the underlying securities is in default in which case it receives the liquidation proceeds.

The credit risk transfer of the repackaging structure is important to recognize. The objective is to immunize the investor from any credit exposure to the underlying asset. However, the repackaging structure inevitably creates an exposure to the underlying securities *and* the derivatives counterparty. In this structure, to avoid any exposure to the underlying securities, the obligation of the derivative counterparty to pay is *absolute*, irrespective of the performance of the obligor. In effect, the derivative counterparty's obligation to pay the LIBOR plus margin stream is unconditional. The derivatives counterparty has an entitlement to receive the return on the underlying securities (both interest and principal). In this way, the only exposure assumed by the investor is to the higher rated derivatives counterparty.

**Exhibit 12.25** sets out the structure of the construction of a synthetic credit asset.

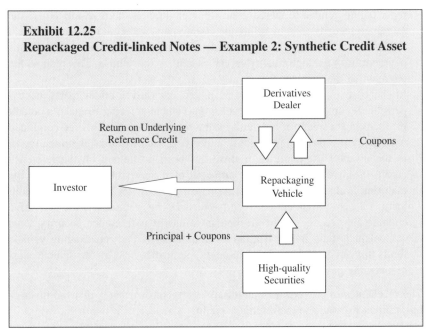

**Exhibit 12.25**
**Repackaged Credit-linked Notes — Example 2: Synthetic Credit Asset**

The mechanics of the structure are as follows:

- The repackaging vehicle purchases high-quality securities in the market.
- The repackaging vehicle enters into a credit derivative transaction with a derivative counterparty. This can be a total return swap or a credit default swap linked to reference credit or reference security.
- The repackaging vehicle issues securities that pay a return to the investor that equates to the return on the reference security. The security issued by the repackaging vehicle at maturity pays out the principal value of the transaction, but in the event of default pays out the post-default value of the reference securities calculated through either a screen price, dealer poll, or as calculated by deducting a pre-agreed quantification of the expected loss on default.

The cash flow structure of the synthetic credit asset structure is dependent on the type of credit derivative embedded:

- In the case where a total return swap is used, the return on the underlying high-quality securities is paid thorough to the derivatives counterparty. In return, the counterparty pays the return on the reference security. This return corresponds to the return received by the investor on the note. At maturity, the counterparty effects a cash settlement with the repackaging vehicle based on the change in value of the reference security. Where the reference security increases in value, the counterparty pays the net settlement amount to the repackaging vehicle to increase the value paid out to the investor. Where the reference security falls in value, the counterparty receives the net settlement amount from the repackaging vehicle. The repackaging vehicle funds this payment from the high-quality securities held by the vehicle. This reduces the payment to the investor.
- In the case of a credit default swap, the derivatives counterparty pays a periodic fee in return for the repackaging vehicle agreeing to make a default payment in the event of a default by the reference credit. This fee combined with the return on the high-quality underlying securities makes up the return to the investor. At maturity, if there has been no default on the reference credit, the investor receives the principal of its investment financed by the maturing high-quality securities. If there is default on the reference credit, there is a cash settlement between the repackaging vehicle and the derivative counterparty based on the decline in value in a reference security. This settlement is paid to the derivatives counterparty. The repackaging vehicle funds this payment from the high-quality securities held by the vehicle. This reduces the payment to the investor.

The mechanics of the synthetic credit asset structures ensures that the investor has a direct exposure to the reference credit.

## 9.3 Examples

In this section, some examples of repackaged credit assets are set out. The principal focus is on synthetic credit assets. The asset credit swaps are more straightforward transactions that are designed to pay a floating rate return on a high-quality underlying credit targeted to, in general, money market investors looking for a yield pick-up. However, one example of a repackaging of longer term securities for investors seeking short-term exposure is set out. The synthetic credit asset structures discussed are focused on synthetizing exposures to reference credits in a manner that is nontraditional. The examples described here are in addition to the more traditional structures of credit-linked structured

---

[14] For an indication of the size of the market in these types of notes, see Mahtani, Arun "Synthetic Structures Facilitate Leverages Loan Boom (November 28, 1998), *International Financing Review* Issue 1261 85.

notes described above. These types of credit-linked notes can and are structured using repackaging vehicles in addition to the more traditional direct issuance structures.[14]

**Exhibit 12.26** sets out an example of a transaction to create short-term exposure to underlying assets that have longer maturities.

---

**Exhibit 12.26**
**Repackaged Credit Assets — Example 1**

A form of repackaging that has been popular has been the restructuring of the cash flows of assets with a longer maturity into a structured note where the investor has exposure to the asset for a shorter term. Generally, these transactions have been structured as follows:

- The repackaging vehicle purchases the longer dated security.
- The repackaging vehicle enters into a credit spread swap with a derivatives counterparty for a period of, say, one year corresponding to the maturity *of the structured note issued by the repackaging vehicle.* Under the terms of the swap, which is equivalent to a forward on the spread on the security, at maturity:
  1. The derivatives counterparty pays a settlement amount equal to the amount of any depreciation in the value of the security in the event that the value of the security falls.
  2. The derivatives counterparty receives a settlement amount equal to the amount any appreciation in the value of the security in the event of the value of the security increasing.
- The repackaging vehicle may also enter into additional derivatives transaction (usually an interest or currency swap) with the derivatives counterparty to reprofile the cash flow of the underlying security into the desired framework (generally, US$ floating rate LIBOR).
- The repackaging vehicle issues a structured note for a maturity that is identical to that of the credit spread swap. The structured note is collateralized by the underlying longer dated security and the credit spread swap.
- The structured note pays a return to the investor equivalent to US$ LIBOR plus a spread generated off the coupon on the security and interest rate/currency swap.
- At maturity, the structured note pays out at par. This is achieved as follows:
  1. The underlying securities are liquidated in the market.
  2. The credit spread swap is settled with the derivative counterparty with the repackaging vehicle paying (receiving) cash in the event of

an increase (decline) in the value of the underlying security. Where the repackaging vehicle has to make the payment, the payment is financed by the excess of liquidation value over the amount required to redeem the structured note at par.

3. The combination of the liquidation amount and the credit spread swap settlement equates to the total cash available for payment to the investor.

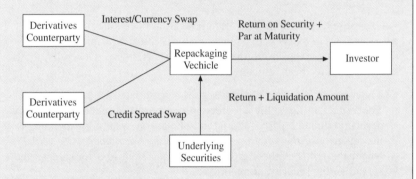

The investor's risk in this type of transaction is on the underlying asset and the derivatives counterparty. The transaction enables the investor to complete the maturity spectrum of investments using the credit spread swap to hedge the market risk on sale as on the underlying longer dated asset as at maturity of the shorter structured note.

Exhibit 12.27 sets out an example of using a repackaging vehicle to create diversified exposure to a portfolio of bonds/credits.

**Exhibit 12.27**
**Repackaged Credit Assets — Example 2**

The objective in this case is to create an investment where the investor has exposure to a diversified portfolio of securities. The transaction is structured as follows:

• The repackaging vehicle issues a structured note to the investor.
• The cash proceeds of the note are used to make an investment in high-quality bonds.

- The repackaging vehicle enters into a series of total return swaps with a derivative counterparty to gain exposure to a variety of bonds/credits. The total return swaps have total notional principal equivalent to the value of the investments in the high-quality bonds that are used to fully collateralize the swaps.
- The structured note returns to the investor (usually) a floating rate return calculated as LIBOR plus a margin. The return is equivalent to the payments received under the total return swaps. The return from the underlying high-quality bond investments is used to fund the floating rate payments under the total return swaps.
- At maturity, the structured note pays out the value of the securities underlying the total return swaps. An appreciation in value adds to the pool of funds generated from the liquidation of the high-quality collateral pool and is available for distribution to the investor. Any depreciation in the value of the securities underlying the total return swaps is funded by the collateral pool and reduces the payment to the investor in the structured note.

The structure is designed to allow an investor through the investment in the structured note issued by the repackaging vehicle to obtain economic exposure to the diversified portfolio of securities. The major benefits include the higher level of diversification that is obtained as a result of the lower threshold size of total return swaps (versus investment in the bonds) and the elimination of administration costs of managing a portfolio of securities.

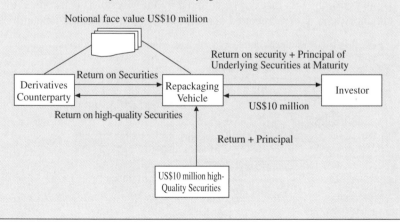

**Exhibit 12.28** sets out an example of a transaction where the repackaging vehicle creates exposure to one or more credits *on a leveraged basis.*

---

**Exhibit 12.28**
**Repackaged Credit Assets — Example 3**

The objective of this type of structure is to create leveraged exposure to a portfolio of securities or loans. The essential transaction dynamics are exactly the same as that identified in **Exhibit 12.27**. The only additional element is that the total return swap entered into is for a notional principal *greater than* the face value of the collateral.

The structure will operate as follows:

- As in the previous case, the repackaging vehicle uses the proceeds of the issue of structured notes to purchase high-quality securities that are then used to collateralize the total return swaps.
- The collateral will represent approximately 10-20% of the notional principal of the total return swaps entered.
- The structured note redeems at maturity as in the previous example. However, the investor can only lose the principal face value of the structured note *not the notional value of the total return swaps entered into* (that is, there is an effective put on the value of the underlying securities written by the counterparty to the total return swap in favour of the repackaging vehicle).

The investor has exposure to both the collateral and the securities underlying the total return swaps.

The rationale for the structure is the very high returns an investor can generate from the leverage embedded in the transactions. However, unlike traditional forms of leverage (such as purchasing the underlying securities on margin), the loss that can be suffered by the investor is constrained to the face value of the structured notes (effectively, the collateral amount).

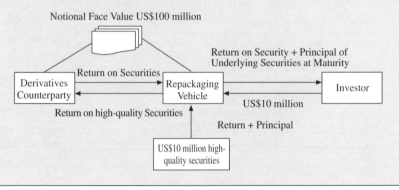

Several total return swaps on different underlying securities

Notional Face Value US$100 million

Return on Securities

Return on Security + Principal of
Underlying Securities at Maturity

Derivatives Counterparty → Repackaging Vehicle → Investor

Return on high-quality Securities

US$10 million

Return + Principal

US$10 million high-quality securities

**Exhibit 12.29** sets out an example of using a repackaging vehicle to create a first-to-default security.

---

**Exhibit 12.29**
**Repackaged Assets — Example 4**

The underlying concept in this case is to create a higher yielding structured note through leveraged exposure to multiple credit risks through a first-to-default basket.

The structure will operate as follows:

- The repackaging vehicle issues a structured note for, say, face value of US$10 million.
- The proceeds of the note are invested in high-quality securities.
- The repackaging vehicle enters into a credit default swap on a first-to-default basis with a counterparty. The first to default swap operates as follows:
  1. The repackaging vehicle receives a fee in return for assuming the credit risk on a portfolio of securities (say, US$40 million made up of four securities of US$10 million).
  2. In the event of default on *any* of the securities, the first default swap is triggered and the *defaulted security* is put to the repackaging vehicle.
  3. The repackaging vehicle uses the proceeds from the sale of the high-quality securities to purchase the defaulted securities.
- The investor in the structured note receives the return on the portfolio of high-quality collateral together with the fee under the credit default swap.
- At maturity, where there has been no default, the settlement under the structured note is at par from the proceeds of the maturing high-quality collateral. In the event of default, the investor can physically settle (by receiving delivery of the defaulted bonds) or cash settle (the repackaging vehicle selling the defaulted bonds at the post-default price in the market).

A number of variations are feasible. For example, the credit default swap may be structured on the basis of a pre-agreed default loss amount (an assumed recovery rate). This would mean that instead of physical delivery of the defaulted security the repackaging vehicle would make a pre-agreed payment (the loss or par minus the recovery rate assumed) to the derivatives counterparty. This structure has the advantage of a known loss in the event of default for the investor.

The rationale for the structure is that the investor provides first loss protection on a first-to-default basis on a portfolio of securities allowing the monetization of expectations on default risk. The structure enables the value to be released to the investor by way of enhanced return on the note.

An additional driver for these transactions has been the ability to use these structures to create securities that may not be available in the market. For example, assume the investor is seeking a B-rated investment that is unavailable. However, the investor can synthesize the B credit rating exposure by purchasing a first-to-default note of the type described where the first-to-default portfolio consists of say four BB-rated securities. The combined risk of the portfolio on a first-to-default basis is higher than the risk of default on any individual security. This higher risk equates to a single B-type exposure.[15] This allows the creation of specific types of credit exposures unavailable directly in the market.

**Exhibit 12.30** sets out an example of transactions involving a recovery rate expectations using a repackaging vehicle to structure it as a note.

---

**Exhibit 12.30**
**Repackaged Credit Assets — Example 5**

This type of structure is designed to create a higher yielding investment by monetizing expectations on recovery rates. The structure operates as follows:

- The repackaging vehicle issues a structured note to the investor. The return on the note is linked to the price performance on a specified reference security.
- The repackaging vehicle pays an enhanced return to the investor while there is no event of default on the underlying securities.
- In the event of default, the investor suffers a loss equal to the full face value of the note. The investor has no right to take physical delivery of the underlying reference security. The investor does not have any

---

[15] Assume a BB-rated issuer has a 2% likelihood of defaulting over a 1-year holding period. Assuming zero default correlations, the probability of *any one* of the four issuers defaulting can be approximated as $1 - (1-0.02)^4$ that equates to 0.08 or 8.00%. This is equivalent to the approximate likelihood of default on a B-rated issuer over a 1-year time horizon. The 1-year time horizon reflects the maturity of the structured note and the term of first-to-default credit swap.

recourse against the issuer of the structured note or the repackaging vehicle in terms of any recovery value on the defaulted securities.

In effect, the structure provides the investor in the note an enhanced return predicated on the investor giving up *any recovery value on the underlying security*. The repackaging vehicle generates the enhanced return by using the structured note proceeds to purchase the reference security. Simultaneously, the repackaging vehicle enters into a credit derivative transaction with a counterparty that agrees to purchase the asset in the event of default at nominal value (say, US$0.01 per US$1 million face value of bonds) in the event of default. The counterparty pays a periodic fee for that right that is passed onto the investor in the structured note.

The process of repackaging has been applied increasingly to the leveraged loan market. These transactions combine the techniques of repackaging and portfolio securitization. An example of this type of transaction is Synthetic Equity Loan Securitization (SEQUILS) and Morgan Intermediated Collateralized Loan Obligations (CLO) Securities (MINCS) transactions introduced in 1999 by J.P. Morgan. **Exhibit 12.31** sets out a description of the structure.

**Exhibit 12.31**
**Repackaged Credit Assets — SEQUILS/MINCS Structure**

In April 1999, J.P. Morgan launched the SEQUILS/MINCS transactions.[16] The objective of the transaction was to allow investors to invest in leveraged loans.
The structure operates as follows:

- SEQUILS and MINCS are special-purpose vehicles.
- SEQUILS issues US$712.5 million in AA-rated senior notes. The proceeds are used to purchase leveraged loans from the primary market, the secondary market and from J.P. Morgan's own portfolio.
- SEQUILs enters into a credit default swap on US$114 million (16% of the total portfolio) with J.P. Morgan. SEQUILS pays a fee out of the

---

[16] See Mahtani, Arun "JPM Launches Next Generation Credit Vehicle" (April 17, 1999) *International Financing Review* Issue 1279 99.

interest income received from the underlying portfolio of leveraged loans. The credit enhancement provided through the credit default swap enables the portfolio to achieve the high investment grade ratings on the notes issued out of the SEQUILS vehicle.

- J.P. Morgan in turn enters into a transaction with MINCS to reduce the credit risk assumed under its credit default swap with SEQUILS. This is done through the issue of credit-linked notes by J.P. Morgan to MINCS. The payments on the credit-linked notes are linked to the credit performance of the underlying leveraged loan portfolio in SEQUILS. MINCS finances the purchase of these credit-linked notes through the issue of US$114 million of BBB-rated notes to investors.
- The transaction operates as follows:
  1. In the event there is no default on the underlying loans, SEQUILS receives the interest on the loans that is used to make payments to investors in the notes and J.P. Morgan under the credit default swap. J.P. Morgan uses the fee received to make payment to MINCS that in turn uses the receipts to finance payments to noteholders. At maturity, the cash flow from maturing loans is used to make principal repayments to SEQUILS noteholders. At maturity, J.P. Morgan repays the principal of the credit-linked notes to MINC that in turns repays the noteholders in MINCS.
  2. In the event of default on the underlying loans, SEQUILS claims under the credit default swap with J.P. Morgan (to a maximum of US$114 million). J.P. Morgan covers any default payment to SEQUILS by reducing the principal repaid to MINCS under the credit-linked notes. MINCS in turn reduces the principal paid on the notes issued to investors by MINCS.

The structure of the notes issued is as follows:

- All notes issued by SEQUILS and MINCS are floating rate notes with a legal final maturity of 12 years.
- Notes issued by SEQUILS were offered as a standard structured AA-rated issue to investors at a small yield premium to comparable issues.
- Notes issued by MINCS were offered to investors at an expected return of LIBOR plus 400 bps. The expected coupon was LIBOR plus 150 bps and a potential return of LIBOR plus 550/600 bps.

The SEQUILS/MINCS vehicle structures were cash flow-based. This contrasts with market value-based structures. The cash flow-based structures rely on expected cash flows generated from the underlying asset pool. In contrast, market value structures rely on changes in market values of the underlying assets.[17] Cash flow-based structures are more stable in high-stress scenarios where market values may move in a very volatile manner.

The objective of the structure was to provide investor access to a diversified portfolio of leveraged loans. The structure also effectively bifurcates the returns—SEQUILS investors obtain exposure to the lower risk component while MINCS investors obtain exposure to the higher risk elements through assuming the *first loss position.*[18]

# 10. Synthetic Bonds

## 10.1 Structure

Synthetic bonds entail the issue of "corporate" or "sovereign" debt out of a special-purpose issuance or asset-repackaging vehicle where the underlying credit risk exposure is created through a combination of cash securities and credit derivative transaction. The synthetic bond is designed to replicate the characteristics of a fixed interest security issued by the underlying issuer.

These transactions are typically similar to asset repackaging transactions involving the use of a special-purpose repackaging vehicle. The central concept of these structures is their ability to create securities (trust receipts or bonds/ notes) that represent either repackaged cash flows which approximate a conventional bond created through repackaging that are sold to investors. The securities are rated by one or more of the major rating agencies and the trust receipt is tradeable to facilitate liquidity.

The distinguishing characteristics of these transactions, which differentiate the synthetic bond transactions from typical repackaged credit-linked note transactions, are:

- The transactions are driven by the desire by the counterparty (usually a bank/ financial institution) to shed risk to the relevant credit. This contrasts with the typical asset-repackaging transactions that tend to be driven by investors seeking exposure to a particular underlying obligation or wishing to create the exposure in a structured manner.

---

[17] See discussion in relation to CBOs/CLOs below.

[18] MINCS investors are approximately six times leveraged to the performance of the portfolio. This is not dissimilar to the logic of the BISTRO structure discussed in Chapter 4.

- The size of the transactions. Typical synthetic bond transactions have been significant (US$400 million plus). This contrasts with typical asset repackaging that are in the range US$10-50 (on average).
- The synthetic bond is designed as public or quasi-public issue that is expected to trade in the secondary market. Asset repackaging are generally structured as private placements that are to be held to maturity. In the event that the investor needs secondary market liquidity, in the case of a typical asset repackaging, this is achieved by restructuring the security into a format (a US$ LIBOR-based FRN) by reverse engineering the derivative components.

## 10.2 Examples of Synthetic Bonds

There have been a number of examples of synthetic bonds. The most notable examples of these transactions involves J.P. Morgan who issued two synthetic bonds[19] to open this market: a $594 million transaction where the underlying credit exposure is to Wal-Mart, the US retailing corporation; and, a US$460 million transaction where the underlying exposure is to Walt Disney, the US entertainment company.[20] Other transactions are thought to have been completed including one for BAT. **Exhibit 12.32** sets out the structure, including the construction and hedging of the Wal-Mart synthetic bond.

---

**Exhibit 12.32**
**Example of Synthetic Bond Transaction**

*Transaction*

In late 1996, J.P. Morgan arranged an issue of a synthetic bond where the underlying credit was Wal-Mart. The unique feature of the transaction was that the transaction was completed *independent* of the participation of Wal-Mart itself, insofar as Wal-Mart did not issue the bonds nor guarantee the payment of interest and/or principal.

The transaction details was as follows:

---

[19] See Irving, Richard "Credit Notes In Record Deals" (January 1997) *Risk* vol. 10 no. 19.

[20] The second transaction for Walt Disney was originally not confirmed although is mentioned in press reporting see "More Credit To JP Morgan" (February 5, 1997) *IFR Financial Products* 16-17.

| Issuer | A special-purpose trust |
|---|---|
| Underlying Credit Risk | Wal-Mart |
| Amount | US$594 million (issued as US$576 million in notes and US$18 million in subordinated certificates. |
| Maturity | 10-year final with amortization giving an average life of 5.8 years. |
| Yield | Treasury plus 65 bps |
| Market | Rule 144 A issue |

The transaction operates as follows:

• The investor purchases the note for value.
• The investor receives repayment of interest and principal, provided Wal-Mart is not in default.
• In the event of default, the investor receives repayment of principal equivalent to the recovery value of Wal-Mart debt.

The relevant default event under the terms of this transaction is the default of Wal-Mart under a referenced credit obligation. The specific terms of default of Wal-Mart were as follows:

• Payment default or event of bankruptcy or insolvency (as established by publicly available information); *and*
• The satisfaction of a materiality test whereby the definition of default required any event of default was not have been deemed to have occurred unless the spread on Wal-Mart public debt increased by a prespecified amount (believed to be 150 bps pa). This was designed to ensure that there was no spurious triggering of the default.

A specified process establishes the recovery value of Wal-Mart debt. It was linked to the traded market value of existing Wal-Mart bonds. The process required a dealer poll of five market-makers in the reference obligations. The poll is to be conducted every two weeks for three months following default. The investor has the option of requiring either early redemption based on a dealer poll conducted as soon as possible after default or redemption based on actual recovery values within an 18-month period. In the event that the 18-month period proves insufficient to derive actual recovery values, the recovery value is calculated using a dealer poll mechanism at the end of 18 months. This process was designed to replicate the *actual payoffs* where the investor held physical bonds issued by Wal-Mart as closely as possible.

## Construction

The construction of the synthetic bond is feasible in one of two ways:

- **Structure 1** — This would entail collateralizing the issuing vehicle with floating rate securities purchased from the proceeds of the synthetic bond issue itself. The securities that generate floating rate returns (LIBOR plus or minus a margin) could be either floating rate securities or fixed-rate bonds that are swapped using an interest rate swap. The issuing vehicle would simultaneously enter into a total rate of return swap where it pays a floating rate (LIBOR plus/minus a margin) and receives the return on the Wal-Mart bonds or debt. The combined cash flows effectively create the cash flow and credit risk profile described above.
- **Structure 2** — This structure is identical to the first with the exception that the credit risk profile is created by the entry by the trust into a credit default swap whereby it receives a fee (payable per annum) in return for agreeing to make a payment based on the recovery rate following default of Wal-Mart debt. The compensation received for assuming the default risk effectively enhances the return to the investor over and above the return on the collateral held in the trust.

The quality of the collateral in this case need only be of a credit quality sufficient to ensure that the rating of the structure equates to that of the underlying credit on a combined basis.

It is understood that the Wal-Mart transaction was constructed using a combination of the above techniques.

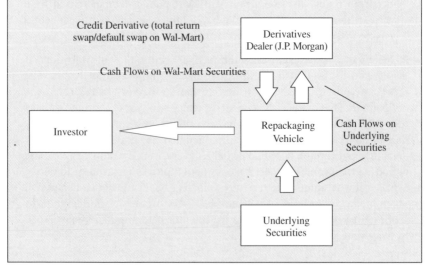

## 10.3  Risks of Synthetic Bonds

The structure of synthetic bonds (consistent with repackaged credit-linked notes involving asset repackaging vehicles) entails three levels of risk:
1. Risk to the reference credit.
2. Risk to the underlying collateral.
3. Risk to the credit derivative counterparty.

The primary objective of structuring is to create exposure only to the reference credit. The risk to the other two risk elements is sought to be minimized. This is sought to be achieved in a number of ways:

• Utilizing high-quality collateral such as US Treasury securities or AAA-rated securities.
• The risk to the derivative counterparty is similarly managed by transacting with AAA- or AA-rated counterparties.
• Credit enhancement may also be used in the form of cash/high-quality collateral being used to manage the credit risk on the derivative. One approach that has been used is the concept of a contingency derivative counterparty that steps into the position of the derivatives counterparty in the event of default to perform the originally contracted obligations under the swap.

## 10.4  Implications of Synthetic Bonds

The issue of these synthetic bonds raises both a series of difficulties for the underlying credits and opportunities for intermediaries. The problems relate to the fact that the underlying credit effectively suffers a diminution in its control of the market in *its own debt securities*. For example, the Wal-Mart transaction was priced at a yield spread to Treasuries of 65 bps (at issue) that compares favorably to publicly traded Wal-Mart debt that trades at approximately 40/45 bps spreads to Treasuries. This discrepancy, which is partially attributable to inherent additional risks of the synthetic bond structure, may create pricing pressures, as well as constraining the issuers access to the underlying credit market.

The opportunities for intermediaries relate to the prospect of synthetically repackaging credit exposure in the form of bank debt or other types of financial transactions into a format that is capable of distribution in public markets to investors. The major advantage in this context is the opportunity to separate the *issuer's* desire to undertake the transactions from the creation of publicly tradeable obligations allowing the investors to create the required exposure through the embedded credit derivative.

# 11. Credit Portfolio Securitization Structures[21]

Credit-linked notes entail the combination of a fixed income security with an embedded credit derivative. The credit-linked note enables the investor to replicate exposure to a bond or a loan without the necessity of undertaking a direct investment in the security itself. The credit-linked note is designed to allow the investor to capture value from movements in the value of an underlying loan asset or bond, credit spreads, or default risk itself. Both credit-linked structured notes and repackaged credit-linked notes represent this type of technology.

Credit portfolio securitization entails repackaging *portfolios* of credit risk (both from loans/securities and counterparty risk on derivatives/off balance sheet transactions). It utilizes securitization concepts to repackage credit risk into multiple tranches of securities that are then distributed to investors. The issue of the securities is designed to reduce or eliminate the credit risk to existing obligors. While building on existing credit-linked note technology, credit portfolio securitization structures are characterized by a number of distinctive features:

- The transaction encompasses a *portfolio* of credit risks rather than an individual counterparty credit risk.
- The transaction is *issuer driven*, being primarily motivated to transfer credit risk and also in some cases access funding.
- The credit portfolio securitization structures are predicated upon credit derivatives techniques (in particular, credit-linked note technology) and asset repackaging structures, *as well as* securitization technology (particularly the techniques commonly used in Collateralized Bond Obligations (CBOs) and Collateralized Loan Obligations (CLOs) transactions).

The key driving forces underlying the development of these structures include:

- **Capital management** — the reduction of the regulatory capital committed to support loan portfolios, particularly the low-yielding loans to highly rated corporations.
- **Balance sheet management** — the ability to shift assets off-balance sheet and enhance return on equity through these structures.
- **Funding** — for lower rated banks (such as the Japanese banks suffering from the affect of the Japanese funding premium), these structures have been an effective mechanism for raising funding.[22]

---

[21] Earlier version on this chapter were published as Das, Satyajit "Credit-linked Notes: Credit Portfolio Securitization Structures; Part One" (November 1999) FOW 57-64; "Credit-linked Notes: Credit Portfolio Securitization Structures: Part Two" (December 1999) FOW 35-43.

[22] See Paul-Choudhury, Sumit "Fables of Reconstructions" (March 1998) *Credit Risk Supplement to Risk* 20-24; Rutter, James "Selling The Securitization Story" (May 1998) *Euromoney* 8-10.

- **Credit risk management** — these structures can be effective in transferring the credit or counterparty risk of assets with certain credit quality or particular credit characteristics from the financial institution's balance sheet enabling more effective risk management.
- **Management of client relationships** — these structures allow banks and financial institutions to continue to maintain relationships with clients, even where that relationship would normally create concentration of credit risk, because it allows the bank to shed or manage its exposure through these techniques.

From the point of view of investors, the appeal of these securitized structure include:

- **Access to assets/risks** — these structures allow investors to access diversified portfolios of corporate risk in a highly effective format. They have also allowed diversification of the range of highly rated assets (AAA/AA) available for investment.
- **Performance history** — the performance history in respect of portfolio defaults and erosion of returns (in CBOs/CLOs) has been favorable, encouraging institutional investor participation in the market.[23]
- **Returns** — the credit spreads available on these types of transactions have been attractive compared with those of equivalent risk, providing relative value investors with a significant yield enhancement opportunity
- **Liquidity** — the market has developed in terms of secondary market trading and liquidity, and offers an investment alternative to the less liquid corporate bond market.

In essence, the credit portfolio securitization structure represents an evolution of the more common credit derivative applications of credit risk management. It represents a shift in focus to *portfolio level* and *strategic* applications. These include:

- Management of systemic or portfolio credit risk include creating strategic short positions to reduce systemic credit risk.
- Transferring credit risk without undertaking loan sales, assignments, or participations by using synthetic sales and securitization techniques.
- Banks seeking to manage the institution's credit ratings and portfolio credit quality.
- Management of regulatory capital and managing concentration risk.

---

[23] The emerging market collapse has resulted in increased scrutiny of the risks of these structures, see Spinner, Karen "CDOs Under Fire" (November 1998) *Derivatives Strategy* 18- 25.

# 12. CBO/CLO Techniques

## 12.1 Market History

CBO structures originally were developed around 1987. However, the market did not show significant volume until the mid-1990s when the segment emerged as one of the fastest growing areas of the bond market and asset-backed securities.

The original driver for the market was the repackaging of high-yield bonds for placement with investors. A major factor underlying the development of the market was insurance companies who found that their holdings of high-yield bonds were problematic for two reasons: the lack of liquidity of some of these securities and the application of the National Association of Insurance Commissioners' (NAIC) reserve-weighted reserve requirements made these securities very expensive to hold. In response to these pressures, the insurance companies repackaged these high-yield assets into CBOs enabling the riskier tranches to be transferred to their holding companies (which were not subject the reserve requirements). The insurance companies continued to hold the repackaged higher credit quality securitized debt that was subject to lower capital requirements.[24]

In a precursor to the more recent activity in the market, CLO structures also emerged in connection with banks with problem loans who sought to securitize these loans using asset-backed structures.

However, there was only limited interest in these structures. In the 1990s, the factors identified above became more important encouraging rapid development of the market.

## 12.2 Concept

In concept,[25] CBOs and CLOs represent an application of traditional concepts of securitization and asset-backed securities (ABS) to bonds and commercial loans.

CBO/CLO structures are similar to ABS structures:

---

[24] The reserve requirements are as follows: NAIC 1 — 1%; NAIC 2 — 2%; NAIC 3 — 5%; NAIC 4 — 10%.

[25] For an overview see Feinne, Linda, Papa, Albert, Craighead, Bradford, and Arsenault, Brian (September 19, 1997) CBOs/CLOs: An Expanding Securitization Product; J.P. Morgan Securities Inc; Lawrence, Richter Quinn "Slicing Up Bank Loans" (December 22, 1997) *Investment Dealers' Digest*; (December 18, 1997) Bank Collateralized Loan Obligations: An Overview; *Fitch Research Structured Finance Asset-Backed Special Report*; (November 4, 1996) CLOs Meet Investor Appetite for Loans; *Fitch Research Structured Finance Special Report*.

- A standalone special-purpose issuing vehicle (SPV) is established. The vehicle is bankruptcy remote to the loan originator.
- The SPV purchases a portfolio of assets (bonds or loans) from the originator(s).
- The SPV funds the purchase through an issue of several tranches of securities and a residual equity portion.
- The securities issued are rated on the basis of the credit quality of the asset pool and the credit is enhanced through the use of several types of types of credit enhancement.
- The investors rely on the cash flow from the underlying asset pool to receive interest and principal payments.

The structure of a CBO and CLO are set out in **Exhibit 12.33** and **Exhibit 12.34**.

**Exhibit 12.33**
**CBO Structure**

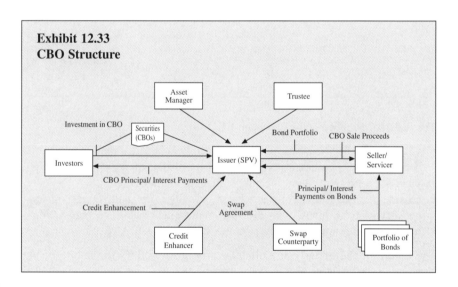

**Exhibit 12.34**
**CLO Structure**

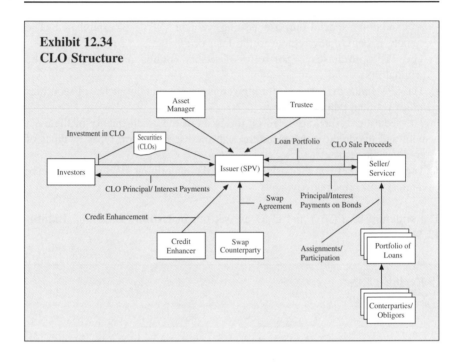

The differences between the CBO and CLO structures are as follows:

• **CBOs** — the SPV issues a mix of investment grade and noninvestment grade debt against a purchased collateral pool consisting of typically US$ high-yield securities and, more recently, emerging market debt.

• **CLOs** — while structurally similar to the CBO, the underlying collateral consists of bank loans, typically investment grade but some high-yielding noninvestment grade loans may be included.

The nature of the underlying collateral pool also dictates the nature of the structure to some degree. For instance, the ability to transfer bonds into the SPV is relatively straightforward. However, the transfer of loan assets, essentially bi-lateral loan obligation, is more problematic. It will require assignments of or participations in the loans to be entered into by the SPV. These may require the consent and agreement of the obligor.

### 12.3  Structural Dynamics

There are several structural issues in these types of structures:

• **Single versus master trust structure** — traditional CBO/CLO structures utilize a single-purpose vehicle. However, recent CLO transactions have been structured using a master trust structure that permits the issue of multiple series out of a single vehicle.

*   **Revolving structure** — some CBO/CLO transactions include:
    1.  A ramp-up period — this refers to a period during which the initial collateral is purchased by the SPV.
    2.  A revolving period — during which the collections on the underlying asset pool are reinvested in *new* assets, followed by a period in which the bond principal is repaid.
*   **Management of asset pool** — typical CBO/CLO transactions nominate a manager (usually for CBOs this is an asset manager with expertise in the underlying assets and for CLOs the originator of the assets or a related entity) to actively manage the asset pool.
*   **Cash flow versus market value structures** — there are basically two types of CBO/CLO structures:
    1.  Cash flow structures — where all payments to the investors in the securities are met from and secured over the cash flows from the underlying collateral asset pool.
    2.  Market value structures — where reliance is placed on periodic (daily or weekly) mark-to-market values of the collateral portfolio. If the market value of collateral assets declines below threshold levels some portion of the collateral is sold and some notes retired to allow the over collateralization level to be preserved.

Cash flow structures are used for both CBOs and CLOs. In contrast, market value structures are used generally only with CBOs. Market value structures are generally designed to allow inclusion of certain assets that are currently nonincome producing, such as distressed bonds, but that are attractive from a return perspective. The structures also require different levels of trading. The cash flow structures requires only limited trading by the manager of the asset pool within prescribed investment guidelines. The market value structure requires more active trading.

## 12.4 Rating Issues

The rating[26] of CBO/CLOs is based on the techniques used to evaluate other structured transactions, such as ABS transactions generally. The generic approach by the rating agencies is based on the following criteria:

---

[26] See Falcone, Yvonne Fu and Gluck, Jeremy (April 3, 1998) *Moody's Approach to Rating Market Value CDOS*; Moody's Investor Service Global Credit Research; (March 17, 1997) *CBO/CLO Rating Criteria; Fitch Research Structured Finance Asset-Backed Special Report*; (February 1998) CBO/CLO Criteria Update: Market Innovations: *Standard & Poor's Structured Finance Ratings Asset Backed Securities.*

- **Asset quality** — this examines the credit quality of the collateral assets in terms of repayment ability, diversification of the portfolio (default quality) and asset maturity.
- **Cash flow analysis** — this focuses on timing of cash flows and any mismatch between cash inflows and outflows, and the impact of reduced cash flows from default on any portfolio asset.
- **Market risk** — this examines any interest rate or currency mismatch as between the cash flow from the asset pool and the required payments on the securities to be issued and the derivative transactions in place to manage these risks. This analysis will include evaluation of the credit quality of the counterparty to any derivative transaction.
- **Legal risks** — this includes review of legal structure to ensure insulation from bankruptcy of the SPV, the effectiveness of transfer of title to the collateral, legal enforceability of the contracts, and other legal issues associated with the structure.
- **Asset manager** — this analyzes the ability of the asset manager to perform the ongoing management of the asset portfolio and the credit quality of the asset manager.[27]

The ratings will depend on the evaluation of the following:

- **Expected credit losses** — a major component of the risk of the CBO/CLO securities is the level of expected credit losses for the assets in the portfolio. This is a function of:
  1. The expected default rate — each obligor is assigned a rating to establish a default probability that is based on historical default rates and maturity.
  2. Timing of defaults — the timing of defaults and the impact of differences in default timing are considered.
  3. Recovery rates or default severity — this focuses on the level of recovery following default and the timing of any such recovery. This is estimated based on historical data of defaults and recoveries.
- **Stress testing** — the rating process emphasizes stressing the asset portfolio in terms of default rates, default timing, and recovery rates and recovery timing with a view to analyzing the ability of the asset portfolio to meet the obligations issued by the SPV.
- **Credit enhancement** — the structure will incorporate one or more types of credit enhancement. The level and type of credit enhancement will be determined by the rating desired on the securities issued by the SPV. Typical types of credit enhancement include:

---

[27] See the analysis in (December 8, 1997) *Management of CBOs/CLOs*; Fitch Research Structured Finance Special Report.

1. Subordination/over-collateralization — over collateralization entails creating an excess of assets (collateral) over liabilities (the highly rated debt tranches). This is achieved through tranching the debt—that is, issuing different series of debt with different payment priorities; in particular, the issuance of subordinated debt and equity tranches. The tranching ensures that there is over-collateralization of the more highly rated tranches. The lower rated subordinated debt bears a higher risk of loss that is compensated for by the higher return received.
2. Payment structure — the allocation of cash flow from the asset pool to repayment of the issued securities is also used to engineer the credit risk. Common techniques include:
   • Sequential pay — this requires repayment of senior debt in full before payment of more junior tranches of debt.
   • Fast pay/slow pay — this requires a more rapid paydown of senior debt than that on more junior debt.
3. Excess spread — there is usually a surplus of cash flow from assets over the level that is required to service the securities on issue. This excess spread can be maintained within the SPV to build up reserves against future credit losses and liquidity risks to provide additional protection for bond-holders.
4. Cash reserves — a cash reserve account (held in the form of highly rated securities) can be created by overfunding the structure to enhance the credit quality of the structure.
5. Financial guarantees — this involves a third-party financial guarantee or insurance policy typically provided by a monoline insurer (known as the insurance wrap). This transfers the risk of the assets to a guarantor, typically the highly rated (AAA) insurance company, who guarantees timely payment of principal and interest.
6. Other — this would include variations on the above, as well as guarantees of collateral or noteholder payments, liquidity puts on bond payment dates, or credit default swaps.

Within the rating framework, the rating agency will typically require certain specified tests to be met:

• **Collateral quality tests** — this entails ensuring that the asset portfolio complies with certain criteria:
  1. Diversity test — a minimum level of diversity (issuer, industry, and country) must be maintained.
  2. Maximum maturity profile — a minimum amount of principal must be available for amortization of the bonds on each payment date.
  3. Weighted average rating factor — a minimum average-weighted average credit rating for the asset portfolio is specified

These tests must be satisfied initially and over the life of the structure in the case of a revolving structure where the asset manager has the ability to sell and purchase assets from the pool in purchasing new assets for the pool.

- **Coverage tests** — these tests are designed to ensure that specified levels of over-collateralization are maintained for CBO/CLO notes. These tests include:
    1. Par value tests — the principal outstanding on the asset portfolio must exceed or equal the level of outstanding bonds.
    2. Interest coverage ratio — the interest due to the bond-holders will be payable from the interest to be received from the asset portfolio during the collection period.

In the event of breach early amortization of the notes may be necessitated.

The above describes the overall approach adopted in establishing the rating of CBO/CLO securities. There are obviously differences of emphasis between different rating agencies in relation to their analysis.

There are a number of additional issues with regard to the rating of CLOs. These relate to:

- The documentation of the loan is less standardized than for bonds and can be more complex.
- Loan terms can vary in terms of principal repayments, interest payment dates, interest rates payable, and so on. In addition, loan terms can be renegotiated or restructured by mutual agreement between the lender and borrower.
- The secondary market for loans is less liquid than the bond market.
- The mechanism for transfer of the lender's rights in the loan to the SPV is more problematic.

In practice, it is the last issue that creates the greatest problems in a CLO transaction. Unlike CBOs, where the transfer of the interest in the bonds can be effected relatively simply (by delivery in case of a bearer bond or registration of a transfer of the interest in case of a registered bond), there are a number of means for transferring the seller's interest in a loan. These include:

- **Participations** — this represents a right to receive the cash flows of the referenced loan. However, if the sale is undertaken without the knowledge and agreement of the borrower, the participation creates a contractual relationship only between the seller (the original lender) and the SPV (as buyer). This means that if the seller becomes insolvent, the SPV may be an unsecured creditor in bankruptcy *of the selling lender* without direct recourse to the borrower. This will generally have a rating impact on the structure and will create a rating linkage between the rating *of the seller* and the rating of the notes.[28] For US banks an additional complication is the right of set-off. Under law, the Federal Deposit Insurance Corporation may in the event of insolvency of a bank reduce the amount of any outstanding loan by the amount of any deposit held by the amount of the deposit held by the institution. This would have the effect of diminishing the cash flows due to the SPV. This risk can be managed by contractual waivers of rights to set off or by tracking a set-off exposure.

- **Assignment** — these represent the full legal assignment of the rights of the seller in the loan. This requires notification and (in some cases) approval of the borrower. This allows a direct contractual nexus to be established as between the SPV (as buyer) and the borrower.

The advantage of nondisclosure dictates that sponsors prefer assignments. However, the legal problems with participations favor assignments. Some hybrid structures have also developed:

- **Contingent assignments** — whereby the selling bank would only be obligated to assign in the event of decline in *its credit rating* below an agreed threshold.
- **Credit derivatives/credit-linked notes** — whereby the risk on the loan is transferred synthetically using credit derivatives technology. This approach is detailed below.

## 12.5 Types of CBO/CLOs

The CBO/CLO market can be classified into two distinct market segments that are differentiated by the motivation/objectives of the sponsor. These are:

- **Arbitrage structures** — these are generally secondary market transactions initiated by an investment bank or trading entity designed to take advantage of relative value opportunities in the market. Undervalued assets are purchased and repackaged to lock in a value differential that is realized by the sponsor as the spread between the cash flow from the asset portfolio and the servicing requirements on the bond issued to finance the purchase. Assets

---

[28] There is a notable exception to this general rule. The NationsBank Commercial Loan Master Trust has a rating of the highest rated tranche of AAA higher than that of NationsBank, the sponsor bank, which is rated AA-. Fitch IBCA based this rating on a review of the security interest in each eligible loan, the legal documentation, and the enforceability of the security interest in the event of the insolvency of the sponsor banks. It concluded that the default risk of the relevant securities was substantially independent of the seller's insolvency. The current position for US federally regulated banks appears to be that where the asset transfer is structured as a participation with a back-up first perfected security interest then the rights of the purchaser under the participation will be protected in the event of an insolvency of the selling bank under the FIRREA regulations.

will typically include high-yield bonds and emerging market bonds. Some more recent structures may include high-yield bank loans. The senior higher rated tranches are sold to normal asset investors while the subordinated junior tranches are targeted at investors seeking a leveraged exposure to a pool of assets.

• **Balance sheet structures** — these are transactions that have been driven by the desire to obtain regulatory capital relief, access funding, and reduce balance sheet size. The underlying assets have been bank loans, primarily investment grade. In these transactions, the sponsor bank has generally held the first loss or equity component of the structure. This has forced the sponsor bank to focus on investment grade loans in order to reduce the size of the equity component required to be contributed and to ensure favorable regulatory capital treatment. These structures have also attracted insurance companies. These companies, as noted above, have used CBO/CLO techniques to retranche existing assets to obtain capital relief in terms of reserves to be held against assets.

In the remainder of this chapter, the focus is on the balance sheet structures. This is done through analysis of a series of transactions. First, a classical CLO transaction is analyzed. Second, a credit-linked note-based CLO transaction is examined. Finally, a synthetic credit portfolio securitization structure is considered. The objective is to explore the structural dynamics in terms of the capacity of each of the structures to meet the objectives of the sponsor bank.

## 13.  Transaction Examples

### 13.1  Classical CLO Transactions

The first major collateralized loan transaction completed was by National Westminister Bank Plc (NatWest) of the UK. The transaction—Repeat Offering Securitization Entity Funding (ROSE)—represented the securitization of a US$5 billion portfolio of corporate loans from NatWest's balance sheet.[29] The structure of the transaction is set out in **Exhibit 12.35**.

---

[29]  See Caplen, Brian "Will NatWest's Deal Backfire?" (October 1996) *Euromoney* 38-40; Hagger, Euan and Ball, Matthew "How Sweet is NatWest's ROSE?" (November 1998) *Corporate Finance* 22-26.

## Exhibit 12.35
## CLO Structure — ROSE Transactions

*Overview*

ROSE Funding is a securitization collateralized by a portfolio of US$5 billion of NatWest's corporate loans. The transaction was completed in November 1996 and was for a period of five years. The transaction appears to have been designed to free capital by selling down a portion of the Bank's low-yielding corporate loan portfolio.

*Structure*

The overall structure is set out in the diagram below:

**ROSE Structure**[30]

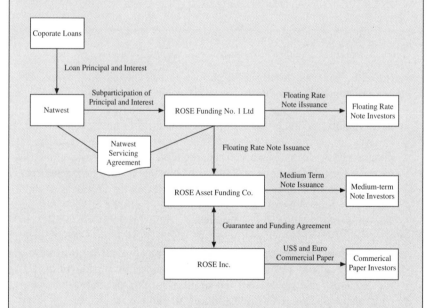

*Source:* "R.O.S.E. Funding." Fitch Research Structured Finance New Issue (27 January 1997).

---

[30] The description of the structures is based on (January 27, 1997) R.O.S.E. Funding; Fitch Research Structured Finance New Issue.

The basic structure was as follows:

1. ROSE purchased a portfolio of US$ and £ loans from NatWest (see details of asset portfolio below).
2. ROSE financed this purchase through the issue of multiple tranches of securities:

| Tranche | Rating | US$ million | £ million | Pricing (Margin over US$ or £ LIBOR) |
|---------|--------|-------------|-----------|--------------------------------------|
| Senior Class A1 | AA | 750 | 600 | 8 bps |
| Senior Class A2 | AA | 750 | 600 | 18 bps |
| Senior Class A3 | AA | 500 | 600 | 22 bps |
| Mezzanine A4 | A | 25 | 16 | 40 bps |
| Mezzanine A5 | BBB | 27 | 18 | 65 bps |
| Class | Unrated | 100 | | |

Several structural aspects of the transaction should be noted:

- R.O.S.E. purchased sub-participations in drawn and undrawn loan commitments entered into by NatWest. Under the sub-participations, R.O.S.E. paid to NatWest the total US$ and £ amounts of the loans sub-participated and received from NatWest all amounts received by NatWest under the loans. The sub-participations do not represent a purchase of the loans themselves and the legal title to the loans remains with NatWest. R.O.S.E. does not have recourse to NatWest for payment defaults under the loans. It is also understood that the identities of the underlying loan obligors were not disclosed.
- The loan portfolio includes revolving credit facilities. R.O.S.E. is structured so that repayments under revolving facilities are maintained in a cash pool from which further advances under revolving facilities.
- During an initial period of 18 months (the substitution period), R.O.S.E. may use funds from redemptions to purchase substitute sub-participations if the relevant loan meets all eligible criteria.
- After the completion of the substitution period, the notes will be subject to mandatory redemption in accordance with the following priorities:

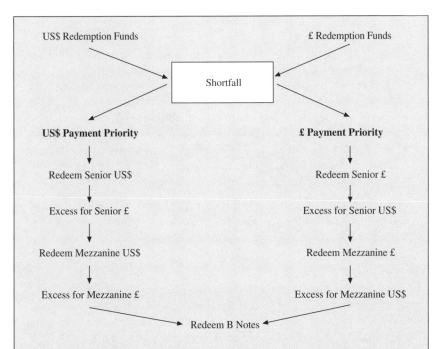

*Source:* "R.O.S.E. Funding." Fitch Research Structured Finance New Issue (January 27, 1997).

### Asset Portfolio

The asset portfolio consisted of some 201 loans with a value of US$4.97 billion entered into by NatWest. The characteristics of the loans were as follows:

- **Types** — numerous structures including revolving facilities, term loans, and so on.
- **Maturity** — all loans had a maturity of five years or less.

The rating of the asset portfolio was predicated on the following:

- **Obligor credit quality** — this was based on an analysis of the NatWest internal credit-scoring system by comparing internal ratings with rating agency categories and compared actual default experience with external studies.
- **Diversification** — the portfolio was geographically diversified (13 countries including UK (60%), US (27%), and other investment-grade countries (13%)). The industry exposure was also well diversified with

the largest exposure to any one industry totalling 7.79% (food industry). The portfolio was also well diversified in terms of individual obligors with the largest single obligor being £75 million.

- **Market risk profile** — this consists of basis risk (mismatches between the interest rates received and the interest rate obligations on the CLOs in terms of interest rate benchmarks) and currency risk (multi-currency options). The basis risk is managed through a swap with NatWest that fully hedged any mismatch. The currency risk is managed by NatWest and through conversion of any drawing other than in US$ or £ into the one of those two currencies.

NatWest operates as a loan administrator. The rating agencies conducted due diligence on NatWest's capabilities in administering the transaction. This was an important element in rating the transaction.

### Credit Enhancement

The major form of credit enhancement was the use of subordinated tranches of securities. The credit enhancement levels (effectively the sizes of the lower rated tranches of securities) were based on stress tests conducted by the rating agencies. The stress test focused on default probabilities, recovery rates, and timing and obligor concentration levels within the portfolio.

---

As noted above, a number of similar transactions have also been completed subsequently. These are thought to include transactions for US banks (NationsBank, Citibank), European banks (ABN-Amro), and Japanese banks (IBJ, Tokyo Mitsubishi, DKB, and Sumitomo Bank). These transactions are all predicated on a similar approach although individual transactions are characterized by (often significant) structural differences.

The classical CLO-type transactions assist the sponsor banks in achieving the following objectives:

- Credit risk reduction at both an economic level (reducing exposures to selected clients, often freeing up lines to large clients) and at a regulatory capital level (reducing the level of regulatory capital by lowering risk assets). The overall exposure is typically reduced to the level of the equity component of the transaction retained by the sponsor bank.
- Improved balance sheet management by removing assets off-balance sheet (other than the equity component) and assisting in improving certain accounting/performance ratios.
- Increasing the diversification of funding sources by allowing capital market

access in the form of funding through the ABS market, effectively separating the credit quality of the *sponsor bank* from the funding that relies on the quality of the *collateral assets*.

However, the CLO structure, as described, may suffer from some significant disadvantages from the viewpoint of certain banks:

- The bank's asset portfolio may be unsuitable for securitization where there is a predominance of nonfunded types of exposures—revolving credits, unfunded commitments, and counterparty exposure on market value instruments such as derivatives.
- The transfer of the loan obligations without advising the borrower or the cooperation of the borrower may be difficult in some jurisdictions. The potential for damage to the client relationship may limit the utility of the structure.
- Economic and regulatory capital requirement may be unchanged as the sponsor bank retains in a typical transaction the major component of the credit risk in the form of the equity tranche. Under regulatory guidelines there is an advantage in minimizing the equity or first loss component of the transaction in order to allow the bank to benefit from the low-level recourse rules (see discussion below). This means that in practice there is a tendency to focus on *investment-grade* loan commitments in these transactions, lowering their value to banks.
- The actual cost of funding achieved through these transactions may be unattractive for banks with a low cost of funds. The comparative cost of funds is evident from the table below:

| Type | Rating | Spread (bps to 3-month LIBOR) | Rating | Spread (bps to 3-month LIBOR) |
|------|--------|-------------------------------|--------|-------------------------------|
| Collateralized Mortgage-backed Securities | AA | 25-30 | BBB | 80-90 |
| Corporates | AA | 0-5 | BBB | 50-70 |
| Credit Card Asset-backed Securities | AA | 10-15 | BBB | 100-120 |
| Collateralized Loan Obligations | AA | 18-23 | BBB | 110-160 |
| Collateralized Bond Obligations | AA | 35-45 | BBB | 130-180 |

*Source:* Feinne, Linda, Papa, Albert, Craighead, Bradford, and Arsenault, Brian. "CBOs/CLOs: An Expanding Securitization Product." J.P. Morgan Securities Inc (September 19, 1997): 5.

Other issues may include:

- The cost and long time needed (around four to six months) to complete a CLO.
- The need to change bank loan administration operations to accommodate the CLO operation.

## 13.2  Credit-linked Note CLO Transactions

In 1997, a variation on the traditional CLO was introduced with the credit-linked note CLO transaction. Swiss Bank Corporation launched the first transaction— SBC Glacier Limited. It was followed by a transaction for Credit Suisse, launched by CSFB—Triangle.

The concept underlying these transactions is the use of credit-linked notes to transfer the credit exposure from the sponsor bank to the SPV and to use the credit-linked note itself as the collateral for the issue of securities. The credit-linked note is structured normally. It is issued by the CLO sponsor and references the payment obligations of an individual obligor under a loan or other transaction. The defining element is the use of the credit-linked note to transfer the credit risk and hedge the sponsor bank's credit exposure *without the transfer of the actual loan or contract.*

**Exhibit 12.36** describes the structure of the SBC Glacier transaction.[31]

---

**Exhibit 12.36**
**Credit-linked Note CLO Transaction — SBC Glacier Transaction**[32]

*Overview*

SBC completed the Glacier transaction in September 1997. The transaction for a total of approximately US$1.7 billion was successful with the issue of bonds being oversubscribed. The transaction was predicated on transferring the risk on a portfolio of corporate loans to enable the bank to reduce the capital held against the loan in order to improve the bank's return on risk capital. The interesting aspect of the transaction is its combination of CLO and credit derivative technology.

Following the success of the initial transaction, Credit Suisse completed

---

[31] See Lee, Peter "SBC Taps Its Credit Pool For Cash" (October 1997) *Euromoney* 16; Chow, Robert "A New Leaf for the ROSE" (January 1998) *Institutional Investor* 74-75.

[32] The description of the structure is based on SBC Glacier Finance Ltd (November 1997) Standard & Poor's Structured Finance.

a similar larger transaction—Triangle. This transaction was motivated by similar factors as the SBC Glacier transaction. A number of transactions have subsequently been completed based on the template developed.

*Structure*

SBC Glacier Finance Limited (Glacier) is a Cayman Island-incorporated limited liability company that acts as the issuer of the CLO securities. It is SPV that is bankruptcy remote to SBC. The issuer is structured a Master Trust Facility enabling Glacier to undertake further CLO issues for SBC

The overall structure of the transaction is set out in the diagram below:

Bonds Issued Collateralized by Credit-linked Notes

The transaction operates as follows:

- Glacier issues two series of notes each totaling US$870 million in floating rate and zero-coupon notes. The notes are expected to mature in five and seven years. The notes were issued in the following tranches:

| Type | Series 1997 – 1 | Series 1997 — 2 |
|------|-----------------|-----------------|
| Class A | US$798.225 m floating rate notes | US$798.225 m floating rate notes |
| Class B | US$36.105 m floating rate notes | US$29.58 m floating rate notes |
| Class C | US$20.88 m floating rate notes | US$10.44 m floating rate notes |
| Class D | US$10.875 m floating rate notes | US$26.1 m floating rate notes |
| Class E | US$3.915 m zero-coupon rates | US$5.655 m zero-coupon rates |

- The proceeds of the notes are used to purchase credit-linked notes issued by SBC under its MTN program. As described in more detail below, the credit-linked notes are linked to the credit risk of SBC's corporate customers. These credit-linked notes constitute the collateral for the notes issued by Glacier.
- The notes issued by Glacier are direct and limited recourse obligations guaranteed by SBC (acting through its New York Branch) payable solely from the collateral consisting of the credit-linked notes.
- The investors in the Glacier notes receive repayments of interest and principal derived from the corporate loans underlying the credit-linked notes. SBC acts as administrator of the loan facilities to collect and pass through payments.
- In the event of losses on the underlying loan obligations, investors in the Glacier notes bear the losses. These losses are calculated as the face value of the credit-linked notes less the post-credit event redemption amounts paid upon the defaulted obligations. This is calculated as the post-default market value of the reference security nominated under the credit-linked notes or a fixed percentage (51%). The allocated principal and interest are paid on each payment date sequentially within a series in accordance with a specified priority structure to protect the highest ranking Class A notes.

The structure also incorporates a number of special features:

- **Asset transfer** — the loans and commitments undertaken by SBC that underlie the credit-linked notes are not transferred to Glacier but continue to remain on SBC's balance sheet. SBC receives cash from the sale of credit-linked notes that can effectively be utilized to finance the loans (retiring existing borrowing).
- **Revolving structure** — the collateral asset portfolio is dynamic in structure. The proceeds of the issue are used to purchase the initial portfolio of credit-linked notes. However, the credit-linked notes are optionally redeemable at par on every quarterly interest payment date. Where credit-linked notes are redeemed or mature or there are additional issues of notes, Glacier can purchase additional credit-linked notes within the specified collateral guidelines (see below). This dynamic feature is available during the revolving period that continues until the earlier of an amortization event or expected maturity. This feature is designed to allow SBC to adjust its credit hedge. Where the loan has been repaid or the exposure on derivatives contract has changed due to market price movements, the existing credit-linked note

may not match SBC's underlying credit exposure. SBC then repays the relevant credit-linked note and issues of a new credit-linked note which matches the current exposure profile.

*Asset Portfolio*

The underlying asset portfolio consists as already noted of credit-linked notes issued by SBC referencing underlying corporate loans that have been entered into by SBC. The characteristics of the credit-linked notes included:

- They are US$-denominated senior unsecured debt obligation of SBC acting through its New York Branch issued under its medium-term note program.
- Each credit-linked notes references a specified individual borrower or counterparty. SBC establishes the face value of the credit-linked note based on its estimate of credit exposure to the underlying obligor under either a loan or a derivative transaction.
- Each credit-linked note pays a floating rate of interest based on 3-month LIBOR plus a designated spread. The credit-linked notes all have a bullet maturity.
- Each credit-linked note has both an optional redemption (at par on any quarterly interest payment date) and a mandatory redemption date that is triggered by a default or credit event occurring on the underlying reference obligation.
- Credit event in respect of the notes and a reference obligor is defined as payment default, bankruptcy, insolvency, debt restructuring, or a similar event.
- In the event of default, the recovery amount is calculated in one of two ways:
  1. **Reference security note** — this is calculated as the average bid price on the basis of quotations from five dealers on the specified senior unsecured security of the reference obligor payable on a redemption date 25 business days after the credit event.
  2. **Fixed percentage notes** — this is specified as 51% of the face value of the notes (effectively a pre-estimate of the recovery rate) payable on a redemption date five business days after the credit event.

The rating agencies placed stringent guidelines on the composition of the credit quality of the underlying asset portfolio of credit-linked notes. These criteria must be satisfied both initially when the initial collateral is purchased and also in the event of further purchases of credit-linked notes.

The guidelines are as follows:

- Minimum SBC internal rating of C9 (around a B) on reference obligor at the time of credit-linked note purchase.
- Maximum concentration limits:
  1. 8% for any single industry.
  2. 5% aggregate exposure to countries with a sovereign rating of less than AA–.
  3. 2% to any single obligor.
  4. 50% for aggregate exposures to obligors with an SBC internal rating of C5 to C9 (effectively below BBB-; that is, noninvestment grade).
- Maturity limit of:
  1. Weighted average credit-linked maturity of no more than 4.25 years.
  2. Maturity date of each credit-linked note at the time of acquisition must not exceed the expected maturity date of the last maturing series.
- Minimum 25% in fixed percentage notes.
- Credit-linked portfolio must total 106% of all but the principal outstanding of the last maturing series.

The rating of the asset portfolio of credit-linked notes was predicated on the following:

- The **credit rating** of SBC (AA+).
- **Obligor credit quality** — this was based on an analysis of the SBC's internal credit scoring system by comparing internal ratings with rating agency categories and compared actual default experience with external studies. The guidelines also restrict the types of underlying obligor risks that can be purchased through the credit-linked notes.
- **Diversification and maturity profile** — the portfolio was structured to maintain a high degree of diversification and limit maturity through the portfolio collateral guidelines.
- **Interest rate risk profile** — Glacier at closing entered into an interest rate swap with SBC designed to cover the risk of narrowing spreads between performing credit-linked note assets and note liabilities. This was structured as basis swap whereby:
  1. SBC paid Glacier quarterly an amount equal to the positive difference between the weighted average rate on Glacier's notes and the weighted average rate on the performing (nondefaulted) credit-linked notes. This was based on the notional amount equal to the weighted average principal amount of performing credit-linked note collateral.

2. Glacier paid SBC where the weighted average performing credit-linked note rate exceeds the weighted average note rate, an amount equal to any excess spread over 0.25% on the notional amount.

SBC operates as an administrator of credit-linked note collateral portfolios and ensures the portfolio is managed in accordance with the collateral guidelines. The rating agency (Standard & Poor's) maintains continuous surveillance based on a monitoring process.

### Credit Enhancement

The credit enhancement embedded in the CLO structure included:

- **Subordination** — approximately 8.25% of each series of notes was subordinated to provide credit enhancement to the more highly rated tranches.
- **Early amortization provisions** — both series had early amortization triggers based on adverse changes in portfolio credit quality (as evidenced by charge-offs exceeding 2% of the initial principal balance) and accompanying negative carry from post-default cash recoveries. These are designed to protect investors.

The use of credit-linked notes in a CLO transactions represents an interesting combination of securitization and credit derivatives technology.

The major benefits of the structure include:

- The ability to avoid the issues in respect of perfecting the asset transfer without the necessity of an assignment. This has numerous aspects including avoiding any impediment to the client relationship, the maintenance of confidentiality in respect of the client, and also simplification of the legal issues in terms of perfection of the security (which now is focused on the credit-linked note).
- The ability for the sponsor bank to hedge and manage credit risk through the credit-linked note. This should achieve reductions for the bank in terms of both economic capital and regulatory capital. The regulatory capital relief will be achieved if the criteria in respect of normal default swaps are satisfied.

However, some of the disadvantages in respect of the CLO structure identified above persist. The actual cost of funding achieved through these transactions may be unattractive for banks with low cost of funds. This will depend on the implicit rate on the credit-linked note after stripping out the embedded credit default swap transaction and the rate demanded by investors in the securities issued collateralized by the credit-linked notes. In particular, the potential funding disadvantage will be governed by the extent to which these notes are treated as different from ABS transactions.

In addition, the balance sheet benefits of the classical CLO structure are not achieved as the underlying transactions continue to remain on the balance sheet of the sponsor bank despite the fact that the credit-linked note effectively transfers the credit risk to the SPV and thence to the investors.

The credit-linked note CLO structure also introduces new issues:

- The transaction is fundamentally dependent on the credit standing *of the issuer of the credit-linked notes* — the sponsor bank. This is because there is no effective separation of the underlying credit obligation in the portfolio of the selling bank. In effect, there is full performance risk on the seller. This dictates that the structure is restricted inevitably to sponsor banks with a strong issuer credit rating. This is necessary because the rating agencies will treat the credit-linked notes as a primary debt obligation of the sponsor bank, which is contractually obligated to pass through the credit-linked note's underlying reference obligations payments to the CLO SPV. This effectively limits the rating of the highest rating tranche of CLO securities to that of the sponsor bank.
- The ability to create the required credit-linked notes themselves may be subject to practical limitations. The necessity to link loss estimates to reference securities means that the universe of obligors to which this technique can be applied is restricted primarily to those with some liquid outstanding traded securities, although the use of fixed recovery amount notes can overcome this problem to some degree.

### 13.3 Synthetic Credit Portfolio Securitization

In December 1997, J.P. Morgan completed an innovative synthetic transaction that highlighted the potential for synthetic portfolio securitization using credit default swaps. The transaction—Broad Index Secured Trust Offering (BISTRO)—was effectively a massive capital market securitization of a US\$9.722 billion credit default swap executed by J.P. Morgan against its underlying corporate credit exposures. The transaction was designed to hedge the bank's credit risk to these obligors.[33]

**Exhibit 12.37** sets out the structure and details of the BISTRO transaction.[34]

---

[33] See Paul-Choudhury, Sumit "BISTRO Opens For Business" (January 1998) *Risk* 8-9.
[34] See Efrat, Isaac (August 21, 1998) BISTRO Trust 1997-1000; Moody's Investors Service Structured Finance New Issue Report.

## Exhibit 12.37
## Synthetic Credit Portfolio Securitization — BISTRO Transaction

*Overview*

In December 1997, J.P. Morgan, through BISTRO, an SPV, launched a US$700 million issue of credit-linked notes. In effect, BISTRO issued bonds to finance a collateral pool of US$ Treasury securities that were used to collateralize a credit default swap entered into by BISTRO with J.P. Morgan. Under the terms of the swap, J.P. Morgan hedged the credit exposure on US$9.722 billion of credit exposure to its corporate customers. The innovative structure differs from the classical CLO or credit-linked note CLO in that it transfers the *pure* credit risk of the underlying credit exposures without providing any financing for J.P. Morgan and has no balance sheet impact.

*Structure*

The overall structure of the BISTRO transaction is set out in the diagram below:

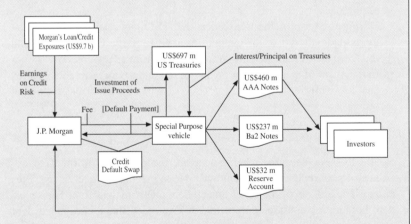

The specific steps entailed in the transaction are as follows:

• BISTRO issues US$697 million of 5-year notes in two tranches:

| Type | Senior Notes | Subordinated Notes |
|------|:---:|:---:|
| Amount (US$ million) | 460 | 237 |
| Rating | AAA | Ba2 |
| Yield (Spread bps over US$ Treasuries) | 60 | 375 |

- The issue proceeds were used by BISTRO to purchase US Treasury notes.
- BISTRO enters into a 5-year credit default swap on a portfolio of credit exposure with a total notional face value of US$9.722 billion with J.P. Morgan. The swap is structured so that in return for a fee BISTRO assumes the default risk on this portfolio that is static and consists of identified reference entities. BISTRO's obligations under the credit default swap are collateralized by a pledge of the US Treasury Notes.
- BISTRO also holds a US$32 million reserve account funded for five years. This represents the equivalent of the equity component of the transaction. It is refundable to J.P. Morgan in the event it is not required.
- During the term of the transaction, BISTRO pays out the coupons on the issued debt out of the coupon received from the US Treasuries and the fee on the credit default swap received from J.P. Morgan.
- In the event of a credit event on any of the underlying reference credits, any loss suffered (net of any recovery) will be met in the following order:
  1. Reserve account.
  2. The Treasury collateral pool.

Where losses exceed the reserve account, the drawings on the Treasury collateral pool reduce the amount available to meet repayment of the notes issued. The holders of the subordinated debt meet any loss first. The senior debt holders incur losses only after losses exceed the subordinated debt amount.

- The loss amount on the underlying reference credits is calculated as either:
  1. The average work-out recovery value.
  2. Physical delivery of senior unsecured claims against individual reference credits.
- Any default payment is made at maturity; that is, after five years.

## Risk Profile

The risk profile of the credit portfolio after the BISTRO transaction is set out below:

### Risk Readjustment through Synthetic Securitization

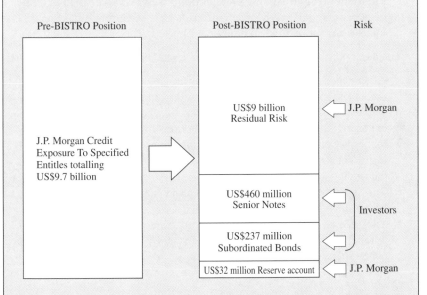

Pre-BISTRO Position          Post-BISTRO Position          Risk

J.P. Morgan Credit Exposure To Specified Entitles totalling US$9.7 billion

US$9 billion Residual Risk ⟵ J.P. Morgan

US$460 million Senior Notes ⟵

US$237 million Subordinated Bonds ⟵ Investors

US$32 million Reserve account ⟵ J.P. Morgan

As is evident, under the structure, J.P. Morgan retains the following risk on its underlying credit portfolio:

- First loss piece of US$32 million (0.33%).
- Final loss piece of US$ (92.5%).

The first loss component is equivalent to the expected loss on the credit portfolio. The next US$697 million (7.17%) is borne by the BISTRO subordinated and senior noteholders in that order. The final loss piece represent losses exceeding US$729 million. This is borne by J.P. Morgan. However, based on the fact that the Senior Notes are rated AAA, the risk of this loss is obviously remote.

## Asset Portfolio

The credit portfolio in respect of which J.P. Morgan purchased protection has the following characteristics:

- **Obligor credit quality** — the portfolio was of relatively high credit-quality obligors. The weighted average credit quality was A2/A. The lowest credit quality was A3/BBB+. As a proportion of the overall portfolio, A3 obligors represent 22.7% of the portfolio and BBB+ obligors represent 4.4% of the portfolio.
- **Portfolio diversification** — the portfolio was well diversified in terms of geography (80.4% US; 2.3% Canada; 17.3% Europe); industry (29 industries); and individual obligors (307).

The asset portfolio was characterized by some interesting features:

- All obligors were identified in the prospectus, both by name and amount of exposure (not exceeding a maximum of US$37 million).
- The asset portfolio included obligors to whom J.P. Morgan had no exposure. This effectively creates a short credit position for J.P. Morgan that either enables the bank to undertake transactions with that obligor in the future on fully credit hedged basis or to profit from changes in the pricing of the obligor's credit risk.
- The asset portfolio is completely static and cannot be altered during the life of the transaction.
- The credit exposure could be derived from any type of transaction ranging from drawn loans, unfunded standby loan commitments, and counterparty exposures on derivatives.

### Credit Enhancement

The credit enhancement within the structure is primarily based on the following:

- The first loss retention by J.P. Morgan.
- The senior subordinated tranche structure of the issue.

### Investor Perspective

The BISTRO securities were placed successfully in a difficult market in December 1997. The major attraction for investors in the transaction included:

- The ability to earn attractive returns on a relative value basis on the notes compared to equivalent rated securities.
- The absence of prepayment risk and no extension risk unlike comparable ABS transactions.

The most significant appeal of the BISTRO notes was that the inherent risk on the underlying portfolio was to a high-grade universe of obligors.

This was particularly attractive in the subordinated tranche as in effect the investor was taking a leveraged exposure to this high-grade obligor universe to generate extra yield from the consequent lower rating. This compared favourably in terms of risk to taking *direct exposure* to lower rated corporate credits. This is particularly so as at the end of the credit cycle where the BISTRO subordinated notes may well offer more attractive returns and lower risk than comparable conventional corporate bonds of equivalent rating.

An interesting aspect of the investor analysis of the BISTRO securities was the disclosure of the underlying obligors and the static nature of the portfolio. This contrasts with the aggregate disclosure in terms of broad portfolio characteristics and the revolving and dynamic nature of more conventional CLO structures. This allows the investor to base the investment decision on both the ratings analysis and its own analysis of the underlying asset portfolio.

The synthetic securitization structure represented by the BISTRO transaction is significantly different to the more traditional CLO structures and the variants on CLO structures. These include:

- **Credit risk reduction** — traditional CLOs achieve both economic and regulatory capital release by reducing risk. The regulatory capital reduction is contingent on certain conditions being met (see discussion below). The synthetic securitization structures achieve *economic* risk reduction. However, they may not achieve regulatory capital reduction.
- **Balance sheet management** — unlike traditional CLOs, the synthetic securitization structures do not have any balance sheet management implications. This is because they shift the credit risk of the underlying transaction through the credit default swap but the assets remain on the sponsor bank's balance sheet.
- **Funding** — the synthetic securitization, unlike traditional CLOs, also does not generate funding. As the underlying asset/transaction is not transferred or credit-linked notes referenced to it are not issued, no financing is created. This means the synthetic securitizations do not allow access to new sources of funding. However, for highly rated banks, it means that the CLO disadvantage of a higher funding cost relative to the sponsor bank's own cost of funds is avoided.

A significant benefit of the synthetic securitization structure is that it significantly reduces the amount of securities required to be placed with capital market investors. This is because the transaction does not necessitate the total collateral portfolio being purchased or financed. The quantum of securities sold is dependent on the level of capital needed to be raised to collateralize the underlying credit default swap. In the BISTRO transaction, this was only US$697 million (US$729 million inclusive of the reserve account) on a portfolio of US$9.722 billion.

The structure has proved attractive and popular.[35] J.P. Morgan is estimated to have issued approximately US$2 billion in synthetic CLO BISTRO offerings covering the credit risk of portfolios totalling in excess of US$20 billion during 1998.[36] Other dealers and investment banks have launched similar structures. Warburg Dillion Read launched one of these structures in October 1998. The structure—Eisberg Finance—is similar structurally to BISTRO format of synthetic CLO.[37] The initial issue was for five years and for an amount of US$211.25 million (3 tranches: US$82.5 million AAA/Aaa; US$65 million A/A2; US$63.75 million BB/Ba2). All tranches were floating rate being priced off LIBOR. The issue was used to securitize a US$2.5 billion credit default swap hedging a part of the corporate loan portfolio for United Bank of Switzerland AG, the parent of Warburg Dillion Read.[38] A similar structure was used by Credit Suisse First Boston in the Triangle II transaction.

In an interesting variation on the concept, in late 1998 J.P. Morgan and Commerzbank completed synthetic securitization transactions of *mortgage portfolios*. The transactions utilized credit default swaps to transfer the default risk on mortgages to institutional investors. The J.P. Morgan transaction (reported to be around US$1.5 billion) was undertaken on behalf of a German bank. The Commerzbank transaction (reported to be around US$1.0 billion) was in respect of its own portfolio. The transactions were very similar in structure to the basic synthetic securitization format described and were driven by the desire to achieve regulatory capital relief.[39]

A number of other synthetic securitization structures have also been completed. Citibank engineered a transaction on behalf of a European bank.[40]

---

[35] See Mahtani, Arun "Synthetic CLOs Move to the Fore" (October 3, 1998) *International Financing Review* Issue 1253 77.

[36] See Booth, Tamzin "The Good, the Bad and the Ugly" (January 1999) *Institutional Investor* 65-66 at 66.

[37] One noteworthy difference was the withholding of the identity of the obligors whose loans, and so on, was covered by the credit default swap. In addition, the Eisberg structure, unlike BISTRO, retains the capacity to dynamically manage the credit pool.

[38] See "Warburg Launches Tip of Eisberg" (October 10, 1998) *International Financing Review* Issue 1254 39.

[39] See "First Synthetic Securitizations Surface" (January 25, 1999) *Derivatives Week* vol. VIII no. 4 1,14.

[40] See "European Credit Risk Hedge" (March 1999) *Global Finance* at 27.

The banks sought to transfer the risk on approximately DM6 billion of corporate risk in the form of term loans, undrawn commitments, letters of credit, and guarantees. The European bank did not want funding. The major motivation of the transaction was the transfer of the credit risk. The transaction was complicated by the fact that a portion of risk assets was from small- to medium-sized unrated obligors. In addition, the bank was subject to stringent bank secrecy laws and transfer of assets would have required the cooperation of obligors. To avoid these difficulties, the European bank segregated the portfolio into several rated tranches. The bank then entered into two series of transactions:

- Entry into a credit default swap with Citibank in respect of the AAA-rated tranche (93% of the portfolio).
- Hedging credit risk through the sale of credit-linked notes to Citibank and third-party investors in respect of the AA- and BBB-rated tranches.

The European bank continued to hold the risk on the unrated assets.

The result of the transaction was to transfer a substantial portion of the economic credit risk, obtain regulatory capital relief, and avoid payment of high funding costs of CLOs.

In a separate transaction, Gerling Credit Insurance (an affiliate of Gerling Konzern AG, an insurance company) hedged the credit risk on small- to medium-sized company exposures through an issue arranged by Goldman Sachs.[41] The Euro-denominated transaction entailed the issue of a series of 3-year credit-linked FRNs. There were three classes of notes rated Aa2, A2, and Baa2. The payoffs on the FRNs were linked to a reference portfolio of over 90,000 obligors in Europe. The investor's returns were contingent on annual insolvency rates remaining below nominated levels. If annual solvency rates exceed 2.1%, 2.6% or 3.3%, then the principal and coupons in each of the three classes of notes decline according to the extent of any excess in accordance to a formula. In addition, if the cumulative losses exceed 5.4%, 5.9% or 6.6%, then the principal and coupons in each of the three classes of notes also decline according to the extent of any excess in accordance to a formula. The solvency index is compiled by Dun and Bradstreet. The major driver for the transaction is the ability to hedge the credit exposure on a large diverse unrated universe of obligors on a cost-effective basis.

Other transactions known to have been undertaken include transactions for KBC[42] and BNP[43] in Europe.

---

[41] See Rhode, William "Credit, The Final Frontier" (May 1999) *Risk* 7.

[42] See (August 10-16, 1999) *Financial Products* 1-2.

[43] See (July 27–August 2, 1999) *Financial Products* 3; for a perspective on European synthetic CLOs see Parolai, Richard and Lewis, Jonothan "The Mechanics of European Synthetic CLOs" (August 3-9, 1999) Financial Products 8-9.

Synthetic securitizations have been also used in the Asia-Pacific—primarily Australia.[44]

The European synthetic securitizations are similar to the BISTRO transactions described above. However, there are significant differences. These differences are driven by a number of factors. The major driver is the regulatory capital treatment. An example of these structures is set out in **Exhibit 12.38**.

---

**Exhibit 12.38**
**Synthetic Credit Portfolio Securitization – C*Star Transaction**[45]

*Overview*

In June 1999, Citibank/Salomon Smith Barney launched a synthetic securitization—C*Strategic Asset Redeployment Program 1999-1 Limited (C*Star). The transaction represented the first public synthetic securitization of a European credit portfolio. The transaction was repeated in November 1999 with C*Star 1999-2 Corp and also in a transaction for a credit portfolio involving Banca Commercial Italiana (SCALA 1 Limited). Similar transactions have been used by a number of other European banks, including Deutsche Bank.

*Structure*

The basic structure of C*Star is similar to the BISTRO transaction described in **Exhibit 12.37**. However, there are a number of interesting differences driven primarily by regulatory considerations.

The basic structure is as follows:

• Citibank assembled a portfolio of Euro 4 billion of corporate credit risk.
• Citibank hedged its risk on this portfolio through a series of separate transactions:
    1. Citibank retained the first loss portion of Euro 40 million (1% of the portfolio).
    2. Citibank entered into a credit default swap with C*Star, an SPV-domiciled in Jersey, covering Euro 280 million of credit risk (7% of

---

[44] See Wood, Duncan "CBA Secures First For Credit Risk Exposure" (August 1999) *AsiaRisk* 8; see discussion of Asian potential for synthetic securitization in "Asian Banks Get Taste For Synthetic CLOs) (October 9, 1999) *International Financing Review* Issue 1304 97.

[45] See Murra, Francesca "C*Star Points The Way Forward" (September 1999) *International Securitisation Review* Issue 40; I am grateful to Herman Watzinger of Citibank/ Salomon Smith Barney for providing information on the above transaction.

the portfolio). This swap is collateralised with German government bonds (see below).

3. Citibank entered into a credit default with OECD banks covering Euro 3,680 million (92% of the portfolio).

- C*Star issued the following tranches 10-year notes:
  1. Euro 100 million Class A notes (rated AAA/ Aaa) bearing interest at Euribor + 21 bps (2.5% of the portfolio).
  2. Euro 128 million Class B notes (rated A/A2) bearing interest at Euribor + 48 bps (3.2% of the portfolio).
  3. Euro 52 million Class C notes (rated BB/ Ba2) bearing interest at Euribor + 48 bps (1.3% of the portfolio).

The Euro 280 million proceeds of the Note issue were invested in German government bonds to collateralise the credit default swap with Citibank.

The risk transfer within this structure is set out below:

**C*STAR Transaction**

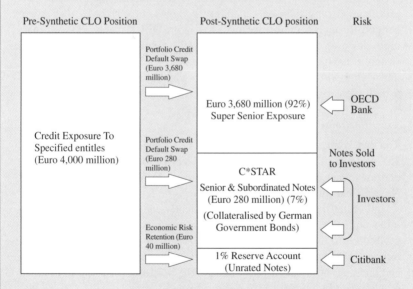

The transaction structure dictated that Citibank bore the first 1% of losses. The investors in the C$STAR notes bore the next 7% of credit losses. The remaining 92% of loss (usually referred to as the super AAA tranche—

reflected the fact that the risk was very low in a ratings sense) was borne by the OECD bank counterparties to the credit default swap.

The C*STAR structure was very similar to the BISTRO structure and had similar advantages including:

- **Credit risk transfer** – Citibank shed credit exposure to the underlying counterparties.
- **Cost-effective risk transfer** – the fact that Citibank retained the underlying transactions and only the risk was hedged meant that the higher funding spread on the transaction was only paid on about 7% of the total portfolio. Given that the coupon on the AAA/Aaa tranche was around 21 bps and assumed a funding cost for a highly rated bank of around LIBOR minus 15 bps, this translated into a cost saving of around 36 bps pa.
- **Separation of underlying transaction from credit hedge** – this enabled a wide variety of transactions to be hedged.

The differences between BISTRO and C*STAR relate primarily to the super AAA tranche. In BISTRO, this is retained by the sponsor bank (although it may then be separately hedged). In C*STAR, this risk is hedged through a credit default swap with OECD banks. The primary motivation of this structure is BIS credit capital relief. The C*STAR structure enables a reduction in risk capital to 20% from 100% for the underlying portfolio. The credit default swap on the super AAA tranche is usually attractively priced reflecting the very low risk on this tranche.

*Asset Portfolio*

The underlying portfolio of Euro 4 billion consisted of 164 transactions to 152 obligors. The transactions were primarily loans of which 67% were undrawn. The obligors were primarily from Europe (excluding Greece), Norway and Switzerland.

Individual obligors were not specifically identified. The structure is rated with the rating being based on a mixture of external ratings and Citibank's internal credit ratings (mapped to rating agency external ratings). Approximately 40% of the portfolio has to have ratings at all time and the other 60% has mapped ratings. The portfolio is subject to limits on industry and individual obligor concentration limits.

*Credit Enhancement*

The structure uses the sponsor-retained first loss provision and the tranched notes to enhance the credit structure of the portfolio.

## 14.  Regulatory Capital Considerations

As is evident, a significant driving factor behind these transactions is the regulatory capital treatment of credit risk.[46] In this section, the current position of the different structures is considered.

The basic regulatory capital position in respect of credit risk in terms of the BIS credit capital accord as expressed in the risk-weighting calculations is as follows:

• Term loans and the funded component of revolving credit facilities to a corporate counterparty are 100% risk weighted.
• Unfunded commitments have a risk weighting of 50%.

Where the credit risk is sought to be eliminated/hedged, the bank can enter into three classes of transactions:

• Participations and assignments.
• Securitizations, such as CLOs.
• Credit derivatives, such as credit default swaps.

The impact of these types of risk reduction transactions varies in terms of its regulatory treatment. Participations and assignments reduce the risk weighting of both funded loans and unfunded commitments to 0%.

The treatment of securitization transactions is more complex. For example, US regulators (the Federal Reserve Board, FDIC and OCC) apply the so-called low-level recourse rules. Under this approach, in bank securitization transactions, capital must be held against the retained first loss position. Retention of a first loss position of more than 8% results in treatment of the transaction as a financing rather than a sale. This results in the requirement to hold capital equal to 8% of the underlying pool. Retention of a first loss position of less than 8% allows capital to be reduce proportionally to the face value of the retained position.

Recent inter-agency proposals, which would be applicable to both a bank's own securitization and third-party securitization transactions, would alter the treatment as follows:

• AAA-rated second loss positions would be 20% risk weighted.
• Other investment grade positions would be risk weighted at either 100% of par amount or 50% of the underlying pool from which the risk of loss derives.

---

[46] For a consideration of the regulatory treatment of credit derivatives, see Das, Satyajit (editor) (2000) *Credit Derivatives and Credit-linked Notes*; John Wiley & Sons, Singapore at Chapters 19.

- Below investment grade recourse provisions would be 100% risk weighted based on the entire pool from which the risk of loss derives.

Securitizations, such as the CLO structures described, have been effective means for reducing risk. However, in order to achieve favorable regulatory capital treatment, the first loss retained loss position must be less than 8%. This can typically only be achieved where the underlying portfolio is investment grade.[47]

This means that CLO transactions are difficult to justify economically because of the high funding cost for banks with access to low-cost funding except as a mechanism for creating regulatory relief. It has the perverse aspect of allowing banks to shed lower risk assets and create higher levels of credit risk on their retained assets. In effect, this is a form of credit capital arbitrage that forces the existing credit capital guidelines to reflect lower risk weighting for investment grade risk.

Bank regulators generally allow regulatory capital relief where credit derivatives are utilized to hedge credit exposure. Under the current position,[48] the treatment of credit defaults swaps is as follows:

- **Banking book** — where the transaction is in the banking book, where protection is sold, the credit exposure assumed is treated as analogous to that on a letter of credit or guarantee and risk weighted according to the reference credit rather than the counterparty. Where protection is purchased and the transaction provides virtually complete protection (that is, the notional principal, seniority of debt, maturity, and obligations are matched) and certainty of the recovery amount, the protection afforded is recognized through the reduction of the counterparty risk-weighting to that of the seller of protection. This means that where the seller of protection is an OECD bank, the risk weight declines for a corporate 100% risk-weighted asset from 100% to 20% (for a funded obligation) or 50% to 10% (for commitments).
- **Trading book** — where the credit default swap is in the trading book, the transaction is treated as follows under the market risk capital guidelines (not the credit capital rules):
  1. The transaction must be marked-to-market.
  2. Capital must be held against the general market risk (effectively the VAR of the transaction), specific risks, and counterparty credit risk.

---

[47] In a typical CLO transaction, the size of the unrated first loss piece for an investment grade portfolio would be in the region of 3% where the mezzanine tranche of debt to be issued against the asset pool is sought to be rated investment grade (BBB).

[48] This is problematic insofar as there is no definitive regulations on the treatment of credit derivatives. The statements reflect discussion /guidance papers published by regulators.

3. Market risk can be calculated either by reference to internal models or using the BIS standard model.
4. Specific risk charges (which in practice are the most problematic) are designed to cover the change in the value of reference asset that is unique to the issuer and in effect represents unsystematic or diversifiable risk. It can also be calculated using either internal models or standard models.
5. Counterparty credit risk is only applicable to the buyer of protection under a credit default swap. It is calculated as the mark-to-market amount (if positive) and an add-on factor for potential future exposure.

If specific risk is not modeled, the standardized specific risk charges are as follows:

| Category | Remaining Term to Maturity | Weighting Factor | Conventional Risk Weighting Equivalence |
|---|---|---|---|
| **Government** | Not applicable | 0 | 0 |
| **Qualifying (debt of OECD** | | | |
| **banks; government agencies;** | < 6 months | 0.25 | 3.125 |
| **investment grade corporates)** | 6-24 months | 1.00 | 12.5 |
| | > 24 months | 1.60 | 20 |
| **Other** | Not applicable | 8.00 | 100 |

The standardized rules allow offsets only where the structure, maturity and reference asset is identical.

The counterparty risk add-ons are as follows:

- Equity conversion factors for investment grade reference assets.
- Commodity conversion for non-investment grade reference assets.

These factors (as a % of notional principal) are:

| Maturity | Equity | Commodity |
|---|---|---|
| < 1 year | 6 | 10 |
| 1-5 years | 8 | 12 |
| > 5 years | 10 | 15 |

The treatment of credit derivatives is relevant to both the credit-linked note CLO structure and the synthetic securitization structures.

In the case of the credit-linked note structure, provided the virtually complete protection test is satisfied, regulatory capital relief on the assets on which the risk is transferred should be achieved. The low-level recourse test may also have to be satisfied.

However, the synthetic securitization structures, such as BISTRO, do not necessarily *prima facie* achieve regulatory capital relief. This is despite the fact that it may act as an economic hedge of the credit risk on the underlying transaction. This is because based on the current risk-based capital rules, the mismatch in collateral underlying the credit default swap dictates that the reduction in risk weighting to 0% is only available *on the notional amount of the Treasury collateral*.

In practice, additional capital relief may be possible by structuring the transaction as an internal credit default swap between the banking book and the trading book *within the sponsor bank*. Under this structure, the banking book achieves at least a reduction in the risk weighting. In the trading book, the credit default swap is subject to mark-to-market and the risk capital rules. If the transaction has been economically efficiently structured, this would enable the regulatory capital relief to be achieved. This is because the retained risk in a transaction like BISTRO would be minimal in terms of economic risk models. However, it is far from clear whether this strategy is one that would be accepted by regulators who have yet to indicate their position on such transactions.

The capital requirements for credit-linked notes is subject to considerable uncertainty. The Basle Committee on Banking Supervision issued its paper on reformation of the existing Capital Adequacy Accord in June 1999.[49] The paper proposed significant reform of the original 1988 Capital Accord (originally published in July 1988).

The key element of the proposed amendments was the alteration in the credit risk weighting in banking book assets. Under the proposed systems, the approach taken was:

- A more carefully differentiated set of risk weighting for sovereigns, banks, corporations and securitization vehicles.
- Reliance upon external credit ratings and potentially internal credit scoring techniques.

The proposed risk-weighting system is summarized in **Exhibit 12.39**.

---

[49] See (June 1999) A New Capital Adequacy Framework; consultative paper issued by Committee on Banking Supervision, Basle.

**Exhibit 12.39**
**BIS Risk Weightings — Proposed**

| Credit Rating | AA– or above | A+ to A– | BBB+ to BBB– | BB+ to B– | B– and below | Unrated |
|---|---|---|---|---|---|---|
| Sovereign | 0% | 20% | 50% | 100% | 150% | 100% |
| Bank (Option 1) | 20% | 50% | 100% | 100% | 150% | 100% |
| Bank (Option 2) | 20% | 50% | 50% | 100% | 150% | 50% |
| Corporate | 20% | 100% | 100% | 100% | 150% | 100% |
| Securitization SPV | 20% | 50% | 100% | 150% | Full deduction | Full deduction |

The proposals were predicated on the principle that securitization can serve as an efficient way to redistribute credit risk. The Committee regarded securitization as a potential arbitrage technique that is employed to avoid maintaining capital commensurate with the risk exposure of a given financial entity.

The primary proposal was that securitization tranches should be weighted in accordance with the risk-weighting categorization set out in **Exhibit 12.38**. The most important change was that holdings of securitization tranches rated B+ or below and all unrated tranches would be deducted in full from capital.

The current regulatory position for synthetic securitization transactions (referred to as Synthetic CLOs in the regulatory guidelines) is not settled. The US Federal Reserve and OCC issued guidelines in November 1999.[50] The approach taken covered the treatment of sponsor banks and investors in notes issued under these structures. The Guidelines appeared to apply to the banking book.

The treatment of investors in notes issued under synthetic securitization transactions was relatively straightforward. Investor in notes must assign risk weights appropriate to risk-weighted assets underlying the notes.

The regulatory position for synthetic securitization was based on classification into three separate types of transactions:

---

[50] See Pelham, Mark "US Regulators Address Synthetic CLOs" (November 23-29, 1999) Financial Products 1,11; Cass, Dwight "Fed Issues CLO Guidelines" (December 1999) Risk 11.

- **Transaction 1** — this entails a banking organization hedging the *whole* notional amount of reference asset portfolio through synthetic CLO. The proposed regulatory treatment required the cash proceeds to be treated as collateral and the capital required to be reduced to collateral risk weighting.
- **Transaction 2** — this covers a banking organization hedging *part* of the notional amount of reference asset portfolio through a synthetic CLO. The bank retains a high-quality risk position (that is, it absorbs loss in excess of the junior loss position). The proposed treatment was that there would be a reduction in capital on the part hedged with synthetic CLO (to collateral risk weight). There is a requirement that capital be held against the high-quality (super senior) position.
- **Transaction 3** — this covers a banking organization hedging *part* of the notional amount of reference asset portfolio through a synthetic CLO. The bank retains first loss risk position. The proposed treatment was for capital to be the higher of:
  1. *Approach 1*: hold $-for-$ capital against loss retained but no capital against additional risk.
  2. *Approach 2*: hold 8% against loss retained, with second loss position viewed as completely collateralized (at collateral risk weight).

## 15. Credit Portfolio Securitization Structures — Comparison

The pressure to manage capital (both economic and regulatory) while preserving relationships with clients has led banks to examine a variety of financial structures to shed credit exposure. Traditionally, this has taken the form of securitization transactions, including CLO structures. However, increasingly, alternatives to securitization usually involving credit derivative structures have emerged. These have included the credit-linked note CLO structures (SBC Glacier and Triangle) and synthetic securitization using credit default swaps (BISTRO).

The evolution of the structures has created competitive alternatives for banks seeking to manage the capital committed to credit exposure assumed in servicing their corporate relationships. **Exhibit 12.40** sets out the comparative features of the competing structures.

**Exhibit 12.40**
**Comparison of CLO, Credit-linked Note CLO and Synthetic Securitization**

| Feature | CLO | Credit-linked Note CLO | Synthetic Securitization |
|---|---|---|---|
| Asset Transfer Mechanism | Assignment or participation | Credit-linked note | Credit default swap |
| Economic Capital | Risk is reduced by the amount of assets transferred less the first loss position retained. | Risk is reduced to the extent that the credit-linked note hedges the underlying credit exposure less any equity piece in the CLO retained. | Risk is reduced to the extent that the credit exposure is transferred less the first loss position assumed (which is less than that needed for CLO) and to the extent that losses exceed the protection purchased triggering the final loss position retained by the sponsor bank. |
| Regulatory Capital | Relief available dependent on quantum of first loss position. | Relief available dependent on the extent the credit-linked notes provides virtually complete protection. | Limited relief available *prima facie* but may be able to be achieved by structuring. |
| Balance Sheet Impact | Assets are transferred off-balance sheet. | Assets remain on balance sheet. | Assets remain on balance sheet. |
| Funding | Funding generated as a result of the sale. | Funding generated as a result of sale of credit-linked notes. | No funding generated. |
| Client Relationship | Clients may need to be advised where an assignment is required. Client particulars are not usually disclosed in the offering document. | Clients do not need to be advised. Client particulars are not usually disclosed in the offering document. | Clients do not need to be advised. Client particulars disclosure optional in the offering document. |

| Feature | CLO | Credit-linked Note CLO | Synthetic Securitization |
|---|---|---|---|
| **Credit Rating of Selling Bank** | Important in rating where participation structure is used; not important where assignment structure is used. | Important in rating. | Not relevant. |
| **Amount of Securities** | Equal to approximately face value of loans sold. | Equal to approximately face value of loans sold. | Equal to the level required to shed economic risk but will generally be significantly lower than face value of asset hedged. |

The emerging structures also highlight the deficiencies of the existing BIS credit risk capital regulations. The discrepancies between economic capital and regulatory capital have been exposed by the use of the structure identified. The current position means that often transactions that reduce economic credit risk may not achieve regulatory capital relief. The divergence is clearly inefficient. The solution will require a revision of credit capital standards and will in all probability see the introduction of model-based approaches to credit risk analogous to those in use in relation to market risk.

## 16. Summary

The structured note concept has been readily adapted to credit-linked structures. A wide variety of credit-linked structured notes have been issued. In addition to the traditional benefits of structured notes, credit-linked structured notes through its embedded cash collateral feature greatly broadens the range of counterparties able to sell or provide credit protection in financial markets.

Repackaged credit-linked notes have emerged as a special category of credit-linked structured notes. They involve using a special-purpose issuance vehicle or asset repackaging structure to repackage the credit risk of securities to create credit-linked structured notes. Synthetic bonds are an extension of the basic repackaging concept being designed to allow bank and financial institutions to repackage credit risk for the purpose of selling it down in capital markets.

The concept of structured notes has evolved rapidly in response to bank demands for instruments to manage credit risk and capital (both economic and regulatory). The market has evolved a variety of financial structures (credit portfolio securitization structures) to shed credit exposure. These structures, which are often hybrids, employ concepts from securitization, credit derivative, and structured note markets.

# Appendix A

# Credit Derivative Instruments

## 1.   Credit Derivatives — Definition

Credit derivatives may be defined as a specific class of financial instruments the value of which is derived from an underlying market value that is driven by the credit risk of private or government entities, other than the counterparties to the credit derivatives transaction itself. The last component of the definition is critical. In essence, it captures the role of credit derivatives in trading the credit risk of a particular entity (credit spread or price fluctuations arising from changes in credit quality, including default) by two parties who may, in some cases, have no commercial or financial relationship with the entity whose credit risk is being traded. Credit derivative are, in essence, traditional derivatives (forwards and options, both on a standalone basis or embedded in the from of structured notes) reengineered to have a credit orientation.

The principal feature of these instruments is that they separate and isolate credit risk, facilitating the trading of credit risk with the purpose of:

- Replicating credit risk.
- Transferring credit risk.
- Hedging credit risk.

Credit derivatives also create new mechanisms for taking on credit risk in nontraditional formats within defined risk/reward parameters.

**Exhibit 12.41** sets out the product groupings of credit derivative instruments.

**Exhibit 12.41**
**Product Hierarchy**

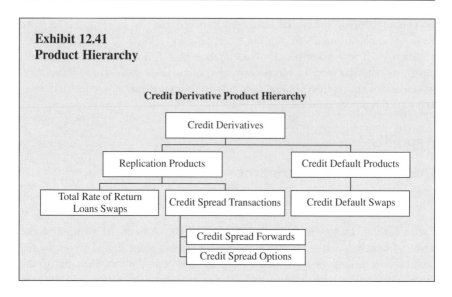

The principal products, usually referred to as credit derivatives, encompass three instruments:

- Total rate of return or total return swaps (also known as loan swaps) (referred to as "total return swaps").
- Credit spread products.
- Credit default products.

Total return swaps are adaptations of the traditional swap format to *synthetically* create loan or credit asset-like investments for investors or hedge or short credit risk. The defining characteristic of these structures is that they are off-balance sheet and do not necessitate entry into loan or bond purchase arrangements (in the traditional sense) and the concomitant obligation to fund.

Credit spread products are generally forwards or options on the credit risk margins on credit-sensitive assets (primarily bonds, loans, or other credit assets). These instruments allow the separate trading of this attribute of assets for the purpose of risk reduction, speculation, or return enhancement.

Total return swaps and credit spread products can be regarded as replication products as they allow the synthetic creation of certain positions. These positions can be created in the physical market but the derivative format offers significant advantages in terms of efficiency and transaction cost savings.

Credit default products, which are not dissimilar in structure to put options on credit-sensitive assets, are usually structured as instruments that pay an agreed payoff (either fixed or calculated with reference to a specific mechanism) upon the occurrence of a specific event—generally the payment default of the subject credit. The credit default products thus allow the transfer and assumption of *pure credit risk,* in relation to the event of default of a nominated issuer (however, defined).

The market for credit derivatives is segmented as between the following sectors:

- Investment grade credits.
- Noninvestment grade/high-yield credits.
- Distressed credit assets.
- Emerging marker credits.

Predictably, given the relatively low risk of default of investment grade issuers, the principal products germane to this group are the replication products (particularly, the credit spread products). However, credit-concentration problems, for example, in derivatives trading by dealers with high-quality investment grade credits, may necessitate the use of credit default products for these counterparties.

The other three sectors encompass both the replication and credit default products. The availability of credit derivative products adds an interesting dimension to these market segments for the following reasons:

- The value in these markets is influenced significantly by credit factors.
- Value shifts, such as the spread decreases or increases experienced in emerging market credits or bond or loan price fluctuations driven by changing expectations of the risk of default or recovery rates in the event of default, are principally credit driven.
- The underlying credits may be of a credit standing that would not be acceptable to the investor whereas a higher rated counterparty providing the opportunity to create exposure to the credit underlying indirectly may be an acceptable format.
- Regulatory and legal constraints may make it difficult to take the credit exposure directly necessitating the use of synthetic means for creating the position sought.

## 2. Total Return Swaps

### 2.1 Structure

The central concept of this credit derivative structure is the replication of *the total performance of a loan asset.* The basic structure of a total return swap is set out in **Exhibit 12.42**.

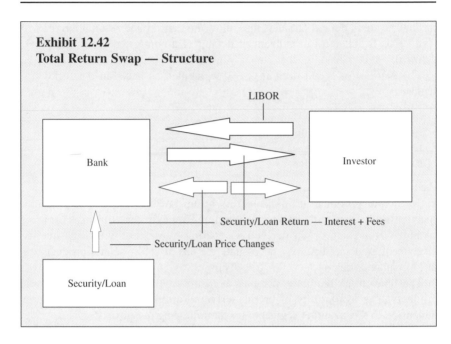

**Exhibit 12.42**
**Total Return Swap — Structure**

The key elements of the structure include:
- The investor assumes all risk and cash flow of the underlying asset. The phrase investor is used to merely differentiate the parties; in reality, both parties may well be banks. The phrase loan is used generically to cover all credit assets including bonds, loans, and so on; most transactions use *traded* bonds and *traded* loans as the underlying asset.
- The bank passes through all payments of the underlying asset.
- The investor in return effectively makes a payment akin to a funding cost.
- The investor bears the full risk of capital price fluctuations on the underlying asset. This risk is structured as payments by the investor to the bank where the price of the underlying asset decreases and payments by the bank to the investor where the price of the underlying asset increases. This adjustment is made at specified times through the life of the transaction in accordance with an agreed mechanism based on the *actual* market price of the underlying security.

The investor may fully fund the total return swap (in effect, eliminating all leverage) by investing cash equivalent to the notional principal of the transaction in an asset yielding a return related to money market interest rates that matches its payments to the bank. **Exhibit 12.43** sets out this particular structure.

The quotation convention for total rate of return swaps is for the return to be paid or received against the payment or receipt of the money market return *plus or minus* a margin. The margin is used to adjust the return to the purchaser of the underlying bond or loan asset.

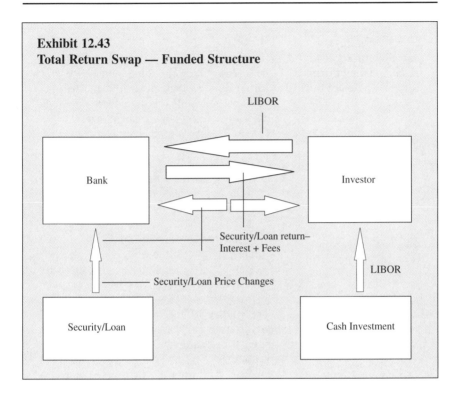

**Exhibit 12.43**
**Total Return Swap — Funded Structure**

## 2.2 Key Terms

**Exhibit 12.44** sets out an abbreviated term sheet/confirmation of a total return swap.[51]

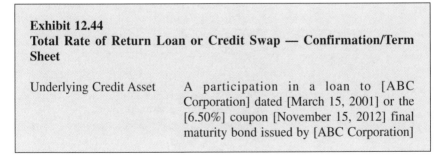

**Exhibit 12.44**
**Total Rate of Return Loan or Credit Swap — Confirmation/Term Sheet**

| | |
|---|---|
| Underlying Credit Asset | A participation in a loan to [ABC Corporation] dated [March 15, 2001] or the [6.50%] coupon [November 15, 2012] final maturity bond issued by [ABC Corporation] |

---

[51] For a detailed analysis of terms sheets and documentation issues of total return swap, see Das, Satyajit (editor) (2000) *Credit Derivatives and Credit-linked Notes*; John Wiley & Sons, Singapore at Chapters 17.

| | |
|---|---|
| Total Return Payer | [Bank] |
| Total Return Receiver | [Investor] |
| Initial Notional Principal | US$ [20] million times the initial price |
| Current Notional Principal | Initial notional principal adjusted for any principal reductions in the underlying credit asset since the commencement date. |
| Commencement Date | Five business days after entry into transaction. |
| Maturity Date | The earlier of: |
| | 1. One (1) year from commencement date. |
| | 2. The next succeeding payment date following repayment of the full principal and interest due on the underlying credit asset. |
| | 3. Occurrence of a credit event on the underlying credit asset. |
| | 4. Default or termination event caused by total return payer and total return receiver. |
| Initial Price | [100.00] |
| Current Price | The [bid or offer] price of the underlying credit asset as calculated by the calculation agent in accordance with the valcuation method at 11.00 AM (New York time) [five] business days prior to the final settlement. |
| Total Return Payment | All coupons and fees on the underlying credit asset received by the total return payer. |
| Total Return Payment Date | Two (2) business days after total return payments are received. |
| Floating Rate Payment | 3-month LIBOR plus floating rate margin calculated on the current notional principal. LIBOR is as quoted on Telerate page 375, two business days prior to each the commencement of each floating rate interest period. |
| Floating Rate Margin | [0.50]% pa |
| Floating Rate Payment Date | Quarterly in arrears commencing three months after the commencement date. |
| Total Return Payments | The total return payer pays to the total return receiver the total return payment on the total return payment date. |
| Floating Rate Payments | The total return receiver pays the floating rate payment to the total return payer on the floating rate payment date. |

| | |
|---|---|
| Final Settlement | On maturity date, the total return receiver will, at its option, receive from the total return payer, either:<br>1. Cash settlement calculated as: (Current price – Initial price)/Initial price times the current notional principal amount: and, the final total return payment. In the event the cash settlement amount is negative, then the total return receiver will make the payment to the total return payer.<br>2. Physical delivery of the underlying credit asset including any existing cash or successor debt in exchange for payment to the total return payer of the current notional principal times the initial price plus the final total return payment. |
| Credit Event | [Bankruptcy or insolvency event], [failure to pay or payment default above a nominated minimum amount that stays uncured for a nominated period], [restructuring event as defined], or[credit downgrading] affecting the underlying credit asset or [ABC Corporation]. |
| Collateral (optional) | 10% of the initial notional principal being US$[2.0] million in cash or US government securities. The transaction is to be marked-to-market and the collateral requirement may be adjusted on a [daily/weekly/monthly] basis. |
| Calculation Agent | [Bank] |
| Calculation Method: | 1. In the sole opinion of the calculation agent; or<br>2. By dealer poll under which the calculation agent will poll at least four and no more than six dealers in the loan on agreed dates and utilize the quoted prices to determine an average price for the underlying credit asset; or<br>3. By reference to a screen or quote service. [Select one of the above calculation methods.] |

The key terms of the structure include:

- **Reference bond/loan or underlying credit asset** — the typical total return swap is referenced to any widely quoted and traded bond or loan. This is essential to allow the price of the asset to be determined from an objective source. This requirement has meant that most swaps are based on traded obligations. In cases, where an illiquid and nontraded loan assets is utilized, the term of the loan asset and the total return swap must coincide with the final price of the loan becoming the *actual final principal repayment* made by the borrower.
- **Notional amount** — the transaction is based on a notional principal amount. No initial exchange is undertaken. The notional principal reduces in line with any amortization of the underlying bond or loan.
- **Term** — total return swaps are typically for relatively short terms of around six months to one year although longer terms are not unknown. In practice, the documented term typically is, say, three years with the provision on each annual anniversary of the transaction to terminate the swap at the option *of either* party. This type of structure provides the flexibility of a 1-year renewable annually, which has the added benefit of reducing the documentation costs in such a swap. The term of the total return swap need not coincide with the maturity of the underlying credit asset. The swap also terminates in case of a credit event on the underlying bond or loan, as well as the default by either party to the total return swap itself. Where there is a credit event on the underlying bond or loan, there may be an additional requirement for Materiality conditions to be met (see discussion below in the context of credit default swaps).
- **Asset price** — the initial price is agreed as between the parties based on where the asset price is currently trading. In the case of a new bond or loan, the initial price will be set at or close to 100% or par value. In case of an existing bond or loan, it will be the prevailing market price (which may be greater than or lower than the face or par value). The current price is required to calculate the final settlement under the transaction. This will be at maturity in the absence of default on the underlying bond or loan or default by either party to the total return swap. It may also be needed to calculate the mark-to-market value of the swap for the purpose of valuation or collateral calculations. The current loan price is determined in one of a number of ways, including:
  1. Independent quotes obtained from dealers in the asset over an agreed period that are then averaged.
  2. Publicly available (screen or quote services) price information on the asset.
  3. The dealer's own quote.

The problem of determination of the loan or security price is common to both total return swaps and credit default swaps. This matter is discussed later in the context of credit default structures.

- **Payments** — under the total return swap structure, the investor receives the following payments:
  1. Interest payments.
  2. Any loan fees, including commitment fees.

The investor pays:

> LIBOR (or the equivalent money market interest rate in the relevant currency) plus or minus an agreed margin.

All payments are calculated on the notional principal adjusted for any amortization or repayments on the underlying bond or loan. Payments are usually made quarterly on the floating rate money market side while loan payments are passed through as close as possible to actual receipt. The payments may be netted when they are on the same date.

- **Final Settlement** — At maturity, upon default on the underlying loan or bond or default by one of the counterparties to the total return swap, a price settlement based on the change in the value of the bond or loan is made. The price used is that determined in accordance with the relevant price calculation mechanism agreed. In the case of an appreciation in the loan price, the investor receives a payment equal to the change in value of the loan. In the case of depreciation in the loan price, the investor *makes* a payment equal to the change in the value of the loan. While it usual to make the loan value settlement at maturity or default, as noted above, more frequent adjustments effectively marking the loan to market, including as at each payment date, can be made.

The above structure assumes a total return swap indexed to a single loan. Total return swaps indexed to a basket or a specified loan index are also feasible. A total return swap indexed to a specific loan index would be structurally similar to a bond index swap.[52] Total return swaps linked to a loan index are gradually increasing despite some problems including:

- The illiquidity of the index itself.
- Occasional divergences between loan trading and index values that make these structures difficult to hedge.

However, the index structures have the advantage of creating diversified exposure that may be sought by investors seeking either to hedge or assume exposure to the credit risk of the assets.

---

[52] See Chapter 4.

Indexes used include the Lehman Brothers Corporate Loan Index, as well as various indexes published by other investment banks/dealers including Salomon Brothers, Goldman Sachs, J.P. Morgan, and so on. An interesting index in this regard is the Citicorp/IFR European Impaired Loan Index,[53] which tracks a basket of distressed of impaired loan assets.

## 2.3  Transaction Rationale

The explicit rationale of the total return swap is to facilitate the purchase of or investment in (or sale or divestment of) credit assets (bond or loan) in a synthetic format. The receiver of the total return under the total return swap structure has full exposure to the underlying credit asset. The payer of the total return under the total return swap structure effectively *short sells* or hedges its exposure to the underlying asset. It is important to note that the total return swap transfers the *full* risk of the underlying asset covering:

*   **Credit spread risk** (effectively credit improvement of deterioration short of default) — this is achieved by the final payment mechanism where there is a payment between the counterparties to the transaction reflecting the price change in the underlying bond or loan. As this price change would reflect market changes in credit spread, this risk would effectively have been assumed and transferred under the structure.
*   **Default risk** — this is also achieved through the final payment mechanism. In the event of default, the total return swap final payment will reflect the impact of default through the fall in price of the underlying bond or loan (effectively, the expected recovery level on the asset). The final payment mechanism will therefore effectively indemnify the payer under the total return swap against any loss as a result of default through the receipt of the difference between the price at the commencement of the transaction and the price following default. The receiver in the total return swap correspondingly will bear the loss upon default via the payment to be made.

The total return swap structure is similar to and achieves the same *economic* outcome as a number of types of transactions involving the physical asset including:

*   Sale of the asset.
*   A sub-participation transaction.
*   A repurchase (repo) arrangement.

---

[53]  See (January 20, 1996) *International Financing Review* Issue 1116 76.

The advantages of the total return swap include:

- The off-balance-sheet nature of the structure.
- The capacity to short sell the loan market to hedge or position credit assets.
- Potential cost of funding advantages.
- The ability, because of the off-balance-sheet nature of the structure, to leverage the exposure by utilizing a fraction of asset value as collateral to leverage the credit view.
- The separation of the transaction from the underlying security or loan transaction that effectively allows the defacto transfer of the credit risk to be affected without the consent of the issuer or borrower. This also allows the transfer of the economic rights relating to the obligation to be undertaken in complete confidentiality.
- The ability to separate the maturity of the exposure from that of the underlying credit asset.

Advantages such as the off-balance-sheet nature of the transaction and potential funding cost advantages provide significant benefits for banks and investors with lower credit ratings and higher funding costs in certain markets. The identified advantages of the structure are especially attractive to certain institutional investors seeking to participate in loan markets. These entities may lack the essential infrastructure to undertake such transactions or suffer from significant barriers to trading credit default risk as part of broad macro-economic views or suffer high funding costs in holding such assets. Hedge funds have been a significant component of this last group.

The structure of total return swaps also creates certain issues. There is no direct relationship or contractual nexus between the borrower and the investor assuming the economic risk exposure to the bond or loan. This means that there may be problems of confidentiality or representation in the case of default, distress short of default requiring restructuring of liabilities or dispute resolution.

Confidentiality issues may arise in respect of confidential financial and other information that is not publicly provided by the borrower to the *lender on record* (as distinct from the economic risk holder of the bond or loan). This is because the investor in the bond or loan through the total return swap may not be able to access this information without breach of the confidentiality provisions. In the event of default or other matters requiring creditors to meet to agree to a restructuring of the obligation or amendment to the terms of the original bond or borrowing, the investor via the total return swap may not be entitled to be directly represented at any such meeting or be able to participate in such a process to protect its economic interests. It may be forced to rely on the lender of record to act *on its behal*f, presumably based on its advised intentions and views in relation to the matter.

## 3.    Credit Spread Products

### 3.1    Structure

Credit spreads represent the margin relative to the risk-free rate designed to compensate the investor for the risk of default on the underlying security. The credit spread itself is calculated as:

Credit spread =   Yield of security or loan – Yield of corresponding
                             risk-free security

Two general formats of credit spread derivatives exist:

•   Credit spread relative to the risk-free benchmark (the absolute spread).
•   Credit spreads between *two* credit-sensitive assets (the relative spread).

Both linear (forward) and nonlinear (option) format of investments are available. **Exhibit 12.45** sets out the structure of a credit spread swap.

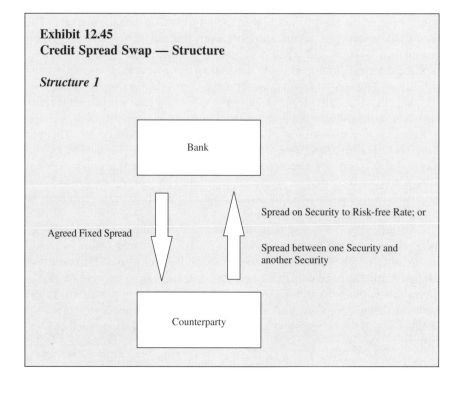

**Exhibit 12.45**
**Credit Spread Swap — Structure**

*Structure 1*

Bank

Agreed Fixed Spread

Spread on Security to Risk-free Rate; or

Spread between one Security and another Security

Counterparty

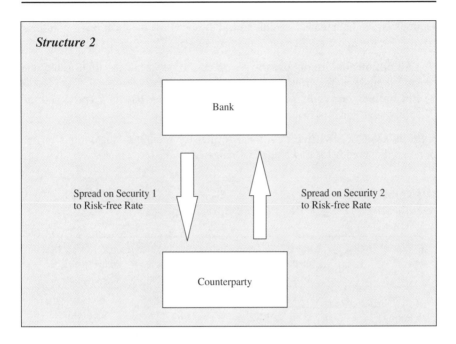

**Structure 2**

Bank

Spread on Security 1
to Risk-free Rate

Spread on Security 2
to Risk-free Rate

Counterparty

In the transaction depicted, under Structure 1 (the absolute spread case), the counterparty gains if the spread between the nominated security and either a risk-free security or other risky security decreases. If the spread increases, the counterparty suffers a loss of value. In Structure 2 (the relative spread case), the counterparty gains (loses) where the spread on the second security decreases (increases) relative to that on the first security. The relative spread transaction, in reality, is merely the absolute spread case where the counterparty enters into two credit spreads swaps where the risk-free component is offset and eliminated.

In practice, the most common structure utilized is that of a spread between a security (bond or loan) and the risk-free rate. In practice, often the asset swap[54] spread to US$ LIBOR (or less frequently the LIBOR or equivalent in the relevant currency) is utilized. This is the case despite the fact that LIBOR itself is not strictly a *risk-free rate*.

The credit spread swap structurally is a forward on the credit spread. In reality, it does not need to be structured as a swap or exchange of cash flow. It is capable of being structured as a simple forward akin to a Forward Rate Agreement (FRA) where at maturity of the contract there is a net cash settlement based on the difference between the agreed spread and the actual spread.

---

[54]  For a detailed discussion of asset swaps, see Das, Satyajit (1994) *Swaps & Financial Derivatives*; LBC Information Services, Sydney; McGraw-Hill, Chicago at Chapter 18.

Options on credit spreads or credit spread swaps allow the creation of nonlinear payoffs on the underlying credit spread movement. The types of options are:

- **Call options on credit spreads** — where the buyer has the right to buy the spread and benefits from a decreasing spread.
- **Put options on credit spreads** — where the buyer has the right to sell the spread and benefits from an increase in the spread.

**Exhibit 12.46** sets out the traditional format for premiums for options on the bond credit spreads for a hypothetical range of securities.

**Exhibit 12.46**
**Indicative Pricing of Bond Credit Spread Options**

| Type of Option | European call options on the spreads at the strike spread | European call options on the spreads at the strike spread | European call options on the spreads at the strike spread |
|---|---|---|---|
| Issuer | A Corporation | B Corporation | C Corporation |
| Rating | Baa3/BBB- | A2/A | Baa2/BBB |
| Underlying Bond Issue | 8.000% July 15, 2031 | 6.875% January 15, 2006 | 8.625% April 15, 2012 |
| Reference Treasury | 6.25% August 2031 | 6.25% February 2006 | 6.25% August 2012 |
| Spot Spread (bps) | 180 | 80 | 160 |
| Strike Spread (bps) | 150 | 70 | 140 |
| Premium (bps) | 28 | 6 | 10 |

| Type of Option | European call options on the spreads at the strike spread | European call options on the spreads at the strike spread | European call options on the spreads at the strike spread |
|---|---|---|---|
| Issuer | A Corporation | B Corporation | C Corporation |
| Rating | Baa3/BBB- | A2/A | Baa2/BBB |
| Underlying Bond Issue | 8.000% July 15, 2031 | 6.875% January 15, 2006 | 8.625% April 15, 2012 |
| Reference Treasury | 6.25% August 2031 | 6.25% February 2006 | 6.25% August 2012 |
| Spot Spread (bps) | 180 | 80 | 160 |
| Strike Spread (bps) | 220 | 95 | 180 |
| Premium (bps) | 35 | 15 | 40 |

## 3.2    Spread Duration

Credit spread products entail the use of the concept of spread duration. Spread duration can be defined as the sensitivity of the capital value of a security to a movement in the credit spread. It represents the effective change in the capital price of the bond reflecting the impact of a change in the spread on the discount rate used to calculate the present value of the security. It therefore captures the impact of the spread changes *over the full life of the security* in the present value price of the cash flows.

It is typically calculated by measuring the change in the value of the underlying bond price for a change in credit spread of, say, 1 bp at current yield levels. **Exhibit 12.47** sets out an example of the calculation of spread duration.

---

**Exhibit 12.47**
**Calculation of Spread Duration**

Assume the following security:

| | |
|---|---|
| Issuer | Company A |
| Term | 10 years |
| Coupon | 7.25% pa payable semi-annually |
| Yield | 7.55% pa (semi-annual) |
| Spread (to Treasury) | 64 bps over reference Treasury bond that is yielding 6.91% pa. |

The spread duration of the security is 6.8. This signifies that for 0.01% pa (1 bps pa) change in yield at current yield levels, the value of the underlying bond will change by 0.068% (6.8 bps).

The sensitivity of the spread duration (expresses as bps change in price) to changes in yield and spread levels is summarized in the table below:

| Yield Level (% pa Treasury yield) | 5.91 | 6.91 | 7.91 |
|---|---|---|---|
| Spread to Treasury (bps pa) | | | |
| 34 | 7.7 | 7.0 | 6.4 |
| 64 | 7.5 | 6.8 | 6.3 |
| 94 | 7.3 | 6.7 | 6.1 |

Spread duration is also maturity sensitive as set out in the table below:

---

| Maturity (years) | 1 | 3 | 5 | 7 | 10 | 20 | 30 |
|---|---|---|---|---|---|---|---|
| Coupon (% pa semi-annual) | 8.00 | 8.00 | 8.00 | 8.00 | 8.00 | 8.00 | 8.00 |
| Yield Level (% pa Treasury yield) | 8.00 | 8.00 | 8.00 | 8.00 | 8.00 | 8.00 | 8.00 |
| Spread to Treasury (bps pa) | 50 | 50 | 50 | 50 | 50 | 50 | 50 |
| Spread Duration (bps in price) | .9 | 2.6 | 4.0 | 5.1 | 6.5 | 9.2 | 10.3 |

It should be noted that spread duration is characterized by convexity; that is, the spread duration alters at different yield levels and with changes in the level of credit spread. It is feasible to adjust for the convexity of the credit spread.[55]

## 3.3  Transaction Rationale

The central concept of credit spread-oriented credit derivatives is the isolation of and capture of value from:

- Relative credit value changes independent of changes in interest rates.
- Trading forward credit spread expectations.
- Trading the term structure of credit spreads.

The central concept underlying credit spread products is the ability to use credit spread derivatives to trade, hedge, or monetize expectations on *future credit spreads*.

The key dimension related to trading and hedging credit spreads is the term structure and volatility of credit spreads.[56]

The forward credit spread is calculated as follows:

1. Identify the spot price of the security and the risk-free benchmark security.
2. The forward prices of both securities are calculated and converted to the corresponding forward yield.
3. The forward credit spread is taken as the forward security yield minus the forward risk-free rate.

---

[55] For a discussion of adjustments for convexity in pricing derivatives, see Hull, John (1996) *Futures, Options, and Other Derivative Securities*; Prentice Hall, Upper Saddle River NJ at 408-409; Brotherton-Ratcliffe, R. and Iben, B. "Yield Curve Applications of Swap Products" in Schwartz, Robert and Smith Jr, Clifford (1993) *Advanced Strategies in Financial Risk Management*; New York Institute of Finance, New York at Chapter 15.

[56] For a more detailed discussion of credit spreads and the mathematics of credit spreads, see Das, Satyajit (editor) (2000) *Credit Derivatives and Credit-linked Notes*; John Wiley & Sons, Singapore at Chapters Chapter 6.

From a theoretical perspective, the credit spread should increase in line with increasing default risk and maturity. In practice, the mathematics of the calculation indicates that in the case of a positive-sloped yield curve that the forward credit spreads increase. This merely reflects the inherent mathematics of the calculation of forward prices and yields whereby the slope of the forward rates on the security increase at a faster rate that the forwards on the risk-free rate reflecting the increasing credit spread.

The implied forward credit spreads, in practice, seem to exhibit the following characteristics:

- They do not appear to accurately reflect investor expectations.
- The forward credit spreads appear to be poor indicators of futures spot spreads.

The forward credit spreads also appear to be relatively more volatile than the underlying securities. This higher spread volatility reflects the following:

- Lower absolute level of spread.
- Imperfect correlation between the security and risk-free rate.[57]

These factors allow the use of credit spread forwards or options for the following purposes:
- Trading credit spread as an isolated variable.
- Trading the credit spread without assuming the interest rate risk.
- Structuring specific risk-reward profiles on credit spreads.

In contrast to total return swaps that transfer both the spread risk and the default risk, credit spread forwards and options only transfer the risk of changes in the credit spread. In reality, the transfer of spread risk may provide default protection as the spread could be expected to increase following default. The credit spread forward also provides a symmetric payoff with participants benefiting from improvements in the credit and suffering a loss from adverse changes in the spread.

The use of credit spread products rather than physical transactions to replicate the positions is favored by the fact that the transactions are off-balance-sheet and generally have lower transactional costs.

**Exhibits 12.48** and **12.49** on pages 690 and 691 set an example of using credit spread derivatives. **Exhibit 12.50** on page 692 sets out an example of a credit spread derivative transaction involving emerging market securities.

---

[57] For a discussion of the volatility of credit spreads, see Das, Satyajit (editor) (2000) *Credit Derivatives and Credit-linked Notes*; John Wiley & Sons, Singapore at Chapters in Chapter 6.

**Exhibit 12.48**
**Credit Spread Forward — Example 1**

Assume the widening of credit spreads on bonds issued by ABC Company allowed the structuring of the following transaction:

| | |
|---|---|
| Notional Amount | (up to) US$10 million |
| Maturity | 1 year |
| Payoff of Spread Rate at | |
| Maturity | 4.9 × (Strike spread – Final spread) × Notional principal |
| Strike Spread | 150 bps |
| Final Spread | Reference yield – Reference treasury yield |
| Issuer | ABC Corporation |
| Reference Yield | Issuer's 7.75% of February 15, 2006 |
| Reference Treasury Yield | US Treasury 6.00% of May 15, 2006 |

The investor entering into the transaction effectively receives the fixed-strike spread and pays the floating credit spread on the credit spread swap. The result of these transactions is that the investor receives a fixed percentage of the notional amount for every basis point (the spread duration) that the spread on the issuer's bonds decreases relative to the strike spread of 150 bps. If the spread increases, then the investor pays a fixed amount per basis point of the widening spread.

The transaction effectively segregates the spread duration of the underlying 8-year corporate bond from its interest rate risk. This type of transaction would be undertaken in an environment where spreads for these bonds had increased and were expected to decline over the 1-year time horizon of the transaction.

The breakeven analysis for the investor in this type of transaction is set out below:

| Final Spread (bps) | 75 | 100 | 125 | 150 | 175 | 200 | 225 |
|---|---|---|---|---|---|---|---|
| Payoff on Spread Agreement | 3.675 | 2.45 | 1.225 | 0 | –1.225 | –2.45 | 3.675 |
| (% of notional amount) | | | | | | | |

The investor benefits under the structure as long as the spread on the spreads tightens from the spot level of, say, 150 bps (the forward is set at the spot spread level).

The spread forward may be combined with an investment in a 1-year security. The yield on the combination of a 1-year investment and the spread forward may provide a return in excess of the return on the security. Given the symmetric nature of the instrument, the investor would suffer losses where the spread continues to widen.

In an interesting variation, a number of these structures are combined with an option that effectively guarantees the investor a minimum spread on the investment (say, at 4.00% pa). This is achieved through embedding an option on the spread in the structure that limits the downside from a continued increase in the credit spread.

**Exhibit 12.49**
**Credit Spread Option — Example 1**

Assume an investor perceives that the credit spread on bonds issued by ABC Company is likely to narrow over a 1-year period. The investor can monetize its expectations by selling the following put option on the credit spread:

| | |
|---|---|
| Notional Amount | (up to) US$25 million |
| Expiry Date | 1 year |
| Option Premium | 0.75% flat |
| Current Offer Spread (bps) | 85 |
| Strike Spread (bps) | 100 |
| Reference Bond | ABC Company's 7.75% 10-year bonds |
| Reference Treasury | Current US Treasury benchmark 10-year (as agreed by the parties). |
| Reference Spread | Yield of reference bonds – yield of reference treasury |
| Option Payoff | The purchaser of the option has the right to put the reference bonds to the seller of the option at the strike spread over the yield on the reference treasury at the expiry date. |

Under the terms of the transaction, the investor is selling an out-the-money forward spread option whereby the purchaser can sell the reference securities of the issuer to the investor at a spread of 100 bps over the relevant Treasury benchmark. The investor receives 75 bps in premium for the sale of this option.

Based on spread duration of the ABC Company bonds at maturity of the option (that is, the price of the bond changes 6.81% for each 100 bps change in the spread), the investor's breakeven level is around 11 bps. This is calculated as the premium divided by the spread duration. This breakeven point is some 26 bps above the spot spread.[58] This means that the spread on the bonds would have to increase to a spread in excess of 27 bps above current levels (around 32% increase *in the spread*) before the investor suffered a loss.

The investors would through this trade be seeking to monetize their neutral to positive view on the credit spread outlook. The sale of put option may be superior to an outright position in the bonds for the following reasons:

- The absence of direct interest rate risk.
- The capture of return from the high volatility of the spread relative to the volatility on the underlying bonds.
- The ability through the strike level to adjust the spread level at which the bonds are acquired if the put option is exercised.

The purchaser in this case obtains protection against an increase in the spread on these bonds above the strike level.

---

**Exhibit 12.50**
**Credit Spread Forward — Example 2**

In the aftermath of the emerging market sell-off in early 1995, the mispricing in relative value terms of various emerging market securities created interesting trading opportunities. For example, the following transaction, involving a credit spread forward, is designed to take advantage of the relative pricing of two types of Brady Bonds of an emerging market issuer. As of early 1995, the following bonds were trading as follows:

---

[58] It is not strictly correct to view this option as being out-of-the-money. The in- or out-of-the-money nature of the option is determined by looking at the implied *forward* credit spread (*not* the current spot spread).

| Security | Stripped Yield (% pa) | Stripped Spread (bps pa) | Stripped Duration (years) |
|---|---|---|---|
| Bond 1 (around 26 years final maturity) | 15.84 | 943 | 3.5 |
| Bond 2 (around 9 years final maturity) | 14.42 | 870 | 4.1 |

The current spread of 142 bps between the two securities is at the upper end of the range over the past 12-24 months. Given the similar stripped duration between the two securities, an investor, who believes that the two bonds should trade closer together, could monetize this expectation with the following transaction:

| | |
|---|---|
| Notional Amount | US$10 million |
| Maturity | 6 months |
| Payment | Notional amount × (Current spread – Final spread) × Average of stripped spread duration of the two bonds |
| Payment Flows | If the payment is positive, then the dealer pays the investor. If the payment is negative, then the investor pays the dealer. |
| Final Spread | Bond 1 stripped yield at maturity – Bond 2 stripped yield at maturity. |
| Bond 1 | [Issuer; type of bond; coupon; final maturity.] |
| Bond 2 | [Issuer; type of bond; coupon; final maturity.] |
| Bond 1 Stripped Yield Calculation | For Bond 1, the stripped yield is the semi-annual yield to maturity of cash flows resulting from a long position in the Bond and a short position in the US Treasury zero corresponding to its final maturity. |
| Bond 2 Stripped Yield Calculation | For Bond, the yield to maturity is calculated by using a coupon bonds amortizing similar to the bond and a price that is the sum of the offer price on the bonds and the unwind value of an interest rate swap to pay LIBOR plus an agreed margin and receive the coupon. |

The spread indexed swap outlined allows the investor to profit (lose) from a narrowing (widening) of the spread between the two securities.

## 4.   Credit Default Products

### 4.1   Structure

Credit default products are designed to isolate the risk of default on credit obligations. These instruments can be structured as:

- Credit default swaps.
- Credit default options.
- Indemnity agreements.

The exact structure is often regulation or jurisdiction driven. However, the essential elements are common to all forms of the transaction. The underlying default risk sought to be traded is capable of a high level of definition, including:

- Static exposures (such as bonds or loans) or dynamic exposures (such as those occurring in market value-driven instruments, primarily, derivatives) can be isolated and transferred.
- All obligations or a nominated subset of credit assets of the issuer can be identified. This categorization may be by seniority of debt or by market of issue (bank versus bond/public markets).
- The instrument can be linked to an individual credit or a basket of credits to create a specific or diversified exposure to default risk.

**Exhibit 12.51** sets out a diagrammatic structure of a credit default swap. **Exhibit 12.52** sets out an example of a credit default swap. The transaction would operate as follows: if there were a credit event by the reference credit then, in this example, the bank providing protection would pay to the counterparty (the bank seeking protection) the agreed default payment. In effect, the counterparty has acquired protection from the risk of default of the reference credit and, in return, pays a periodic fee to the bank.

**Exhibit 12.51**
**Credit Default Swap — Structure**

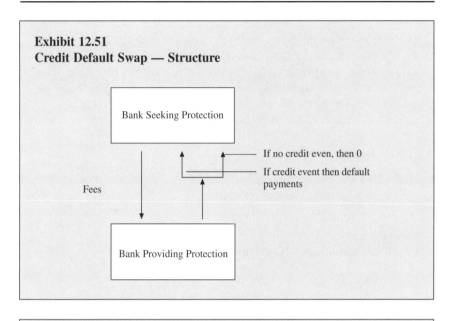

Bank Seeking Protection

If no credit even, then 0

If credit event then default payments

Fees

Bank Providing Protection

---

**Exhibit 12.52**
**Credit Default Swap**

Assume investors owned long maturity bonds that were issued by a company (ABC Company). The issuers bonds have seen a widening of credit spreads with 3-year spreads currently quoted at 115 bps and 12-year spreads at 203 bps. The investor could, if concerned with a shorter term default risk, hedge with the following credit default swap:

| | |
|---|---|
| Maturity | 3 years |
| Reference Credit | ABC Company |
| Reference Bond | ABC Company 8.50% 3-year bond |
| Credit Event | On the first business day following a default on its senior debt or a bankruptcy filing by reference credit. |
| Default Payment | Notional amount × [100% – Fair market value of reference bond after default] |
| Default Swap Premium | 3.20% (flat) payable by the entity purchasing protection. |
| Payment of Default Payment | The default payment is payable by the entity providing protection upon the occurrence of a credit event. |

The transaction would have allowed the investor to hedge its exposure to default by reference credit. An investor purchasing the underlying 12-year bond could have hedged its default risk for the first three years and still enjoyed a positive spread on reference credit 12-year bonds of around 80 bps over Treasuries.

## 4.2   Key Terms

**Exhibit 12.53** sets out an abbreviated form of term sheet/confirmation utilized in connection with these types of transactions.[59]

**Exhibit 12.53**
**Credit Default Swap — Confirmation/Term Sheet**

| | |
|---|---|
| Buyer of Protection | A Bank, London Branch |
| Seller of Protection | X Bank |
| Reference Entity | [ABC Corporation] and any successors. |
| Calculation Amount | US$ [10,000,000] |
| Trade Date | [Date of entry into transaction.] |
| Effective Date | [3-5] business days after trade date |
| Scheduled Termination Date | 1 year from effective date |
| Termination Date | The scheduled termination date; or [5-10] business days following the occurrence of a credit event [and the materiality requirement exists] as evidenced by the delivery by either the seller of protection or the buyer of protection of a credit event notice, provided that this is on or before the scheduled termination date. |
| Fixed-rate Payer | Buyer of protection. |
| Fixed-rate | [1.00]% pa (calculated on a 365/360-day count basis) |
| Fixed-rate Payment Dates | Quarterly in arrears with the fixed rate payer paying the fixed rate up to the termination date. |

---

[59] For a detailed analysis of terms sheets and documentation issues of credit default swap, see Das, Satyajit (editor) (2000) *Credit Derivatives and Credit-linked Notes*; John Wiley & Sons, Singapore at Chapters 17.

| | |
|---|---|
| Floating-rate Payer | Seller of protection. |
| Floating-rate Payment | If there is no credit event prior to the scheduled termination date, then there is no payment. If there is a credit event prior to the scheduled termination date, then the floating rate payer will either<br>a) make a cash settlement; or<br>b) undertake a physical settlement. |
| Floating-rate Payment Dates | Following termination date, as specified in cash settlement or physical settlement. |
| Cash Settlement | Floating-rate payer pays:<br>a) Variable amount — calculated as Calculation amount × Percentage change in price<br>Where:<br>Percentage change in price is equal to (Initial price – Final price)/Initial price<br>b) Fixed Amount — being [60]% of the calculation amount. The floating rate payment is due and payable [5] business days after the final price calculation date. |
| Physical Settlement | Floating-rate payer pays:<br>Calculation amount × Initial price<br>Fixed-rate payer delivers:<br>Face value equivalent to the calculation amount of the deliverable obligations.<br>Where:<br>Deliverable obligations means the reference asset or where delivery of the reference asset is illegal or prohibited by regulation any obligation of the reference entity where the traded bond or loan obligation is (a) of equivalent priority in payment with the reference asset, (b) denominated in US$, (c) repayable in an amount equal to the principal amount and is not repayable in an amount determined by any formula or index, and (d) a maturity not exceeding [10] years. Physical |

| | |
|---|---|
| | settlement must be affected [10 to 20] business days after the termination date in the event of the occurrence of a credit event. |
| Reference Asset | Means the following obligation: Issuer/Borrower: [ABC Corporation] Maturity: [November 15, 2012] Coupon: [ 6.50]% pa CUSIP/ISIN: [ ] Original issue amount: US$ [500] million If the amount of the reference asset (or a substitute asset) is, in the reasonable opinion of the calculation agent, materially reduced, the calculation agent may substitute an alternative reference asset (the substitute asset) issued or guaranteed by the reference entity of the same credit quality as the reference asset. |
| Initial Price | [94]% of face or par value, excluding accrued interest. |
| Final Price | Means the price determined by the calculation agent determined by the calculation agent in accordance with the calculation method. |
| Initial Spread (to US$ LIBOR on an asset swap basis) | 0.85% pa |
| Final Spread (to US$ LIBOR on an asset swap basis) | The spread of the reference asset to US$ LIBOR on an asset swap basis calculated by the calculation agent on the calculation date(s) after the termination date in the event of the occurrence of a Credit Event. |
| Credit Event | Credit event means the existence of at least one of the following events: a) Failure to pay — the failure by the reference entity to make a due and payable payment exceeding US$ [10] million on any obligation after giving effect to an applicable grace period not exceeding [5] business days. |

b) Cross default — the occurrence of a default event or similar event in respect of the reference entity under any obligation in any amount exceeding US$ [10] million that has resulted in such obligations becoming capable of being declared due and payable before their original due date.

c) Bankruptcy — the occurrence of any event set forth in Section 5(a) (vii) of the ISDA Multi-currency Cross Border Master Agreement 1992 Edition with respect to the reference entity.

d) Restructuring — waiver, deferral, restructuring, rescheduling, standstill agreement, debt or payment moratorium, obligation exchange, or other adjustment occurs with respect to any obligation of the reference entity and the effect of such that the terms of such obligations are overall materially less favoured from an economic, credit, or risk perspective to any holder of such obligation.

e) Rating downgrade [optional] — the reference is downgraded by either Moody's Investor Service or Standard & Poor's rating service to a long-term senior debt rating below BBB-/Baa3. Where obligation(s) means any external obligation whether present or future contingent or otherwise as principal, surety, or otherwise for payment or repayment of money incurred by the reference entity.

| | |
|---|---|
| Credit Event Notice | Means an irrevocable notice that sets out the occurrence of a credit event based on publicly available information. |
| Publicly Available Information | Means information that has been published or electronically displayed by at least two (2) internationally recognized financial |

| | |
|---|---|
| | news sources. However, if either the buyer of protection or the seller of protection is cited as the source for the information then such information shall be deemed not to be publicly available information. |
| Materiality Requirement [Optional] | The materiality requirement is taken to exist if after the termination date in the event of the occurrence of a credit event the final spread exceeds the initial spread by [1.50]% pa on [any one/majority/all] the calculation dates. |
| Business Days | London and New York as adjusted by the Modified Following business day convention. |
| Calculation Agent | [X Bank] |
| Calculation Method | The final price will be determined as the arithmetic average of the [bid] prices provided to the calculation agent by [4 to 6] dealers on the calculation date(s). |
| Calculation Dates | [10 to 20] business days after the termination date in the event of the occurrence of a credit event; or [4 to 6] successive samples provided over a [4- to 6-] week period after the termination date in the event of the occurrence of a credit event. |
| Dealers | [list agreed dealer panel members] |
| Documentation | Standard ISDA documentation |
| Governing Law | [London or New York] |

The key terms and conditions of the credit default swap include:

- **Reference entity** — this is in effect the reference obligor the occurrence of a credit event in respect of which triggers the payout under the swap. The concept of reference entity is unique to credit default swaps. In the case of both total return swaps and credit spread transactions, a reference asset is needed. In contrast, in the case of a credit default swap, a reference entity concept is required. A reference asset is only required where there is cash settlement (based on the post default price of the bond or loan) or physical settlement. It may also be needed to determine materiality.
- **Reference asset** — the relevant traded bond or loan asset issued or guaranteed by the reference credit must be nominated. The initial price of the

asset must be agreed as between the parties as at the commencement of the transaction. This is particularly important where the default payment is based on the post-default price of the security. The initial spread to US$ LIBOR on an asset swap basis is also agreed to enable determination of materiality where this is a condition of the transaction.

- **Transaction dates** — the key transaction dates include: the *trade date* on which the effective terms of the transaction are agreed between the buyer and seller of protection; the *effective date* (usually three to five business days after the trade date) on which the transaction becomes effective; and the *termination date* on which the transaction ends. The effective date is important in that credit protection is only valid commencing on that date and any credit event that occurs prior to that date is not covered. Termination is usually after the agreed period of credit protection or where there is a credit event prior to the scheduled maturity the date of the credit event.
- **Credit event** — the occurrence of the credit event triggers the obligation of the seller of default protection to make the default payment to the purchaser of default protection. There are a number of possibilities:
  1. Payment default on obligations above a nominated threshold (say, in excess of US$10 million) after expiration of a specific grace period (say, two to five business days).
  2. Cross-default or cross-acceleration on other obligations.
  3. Bankruptcy or insolvency event.
  4. Restructuring, administration or Chapter 11, or equivalent bankruptcy protection filing by the issuer.
  5. Ratings downgrade below agreed threshold.

Given the heterogenous nature of credit obligations (sometimes even for the same borrower), there are significant difficulties in defining the credit events. Reflecting the early stage of market evolution, there is also a lack of standard practices. However, in general, Items 1, 2, 3, and 4 are commonly used as the nominated credit or default event based on their importance, transparency, and lack of ambiguity.

- **Materiality** — the default event is usually linked to some concept of materiality to avoid an inadvertent or unintended triggering of a credit event. The concept of materiality is based on a *minimum* change in either the price of the bond or loan, or in the spread of the bond or loan relative to a benchmark rate such as US$ LIBOR or US Treasury bonds. The market practice has evolved around the concept of an increase in the asset swap spread (over US$ LIBOR) by a prespecified amount (say, 150 bps). This is calculated by specifying the spread at the time of entry into the credit default swap and then comparing the initial spread to the prevailing market spread *following* a credit event. This provision is designed to ensure that there has been a *true* credit event triggering the requirement to make the default payment and to avoid the possibility of triggering a credit event when there has not, in reality, been an event of default. Materiality is usually determined simultaneously with the post-default price sampling used to determine the settlement payment. It is important to note that where materiality is a requirement it is not an independent trigger, but must co-exist with the credit event to trigger the default payment. The materiality provision is controversial with considerable debate about its desirability and efficacy between major market practitioners.

- **Publicly available information** — the existence of a credit event is usually determined on the basis of publicly available information. This is required because it is assumed that either seller or buyer of protection has a contractual relationship with the reference entity and therefore will only become aware of the occurrence of a credit event from public sources of information. This approach is standard to all credit default swaps and total return swaps. The standard requirement is for a minimum of two reputable information sources. Information from interested parties is excluded to ensure that there is no conflict of interest. In order to avoid problems, a dispute resolution process is usually incorporated. **Exhibit 12.54** sets out the structure of this process in a diagrammatic form.

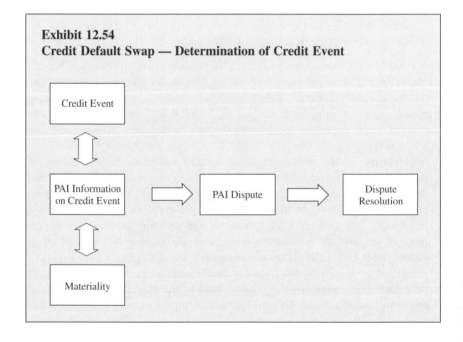

**Exhibit 12.54**
**Credit Default Swap — Determination of Credit Event**

- **Default payment** — following a credit event, the buyer of protection is compensated by the receipt of a payment from the seller of protection designed to match the erosion of value in the underlying bond or loan arising from the credit event. There are at least three possible types of default payment:
  1. Post-default price — the transaction principal times the percentage change in the reference asset, as determined by dealer poll or from price quote services. Typically, (up to) six dealers are polled either on a single date or on a pre-agreed frequency over a (up to) 3-month period following the credit event. The post default price reflects the market price or the average of the prices obtained.
  2. Fixed payout — pre-agreed fixed percentage of notional principal.
  3. Physical settlement — payment of par or initial price by the default protection provider in exchange for delivery of defaulted credit asset.

In practice, Options 1 and 3 predominate. Where Options 1 and 3 are used, they may be used in conjunction with the choice of a default payment mechanism resting with the buyer of protection. The choice usually must be made at a pre-specified time around the time the post-default price is established. However, limitations on the universe of available liquid and publicly traded securities, as well as concerns about the effectiveness and transparency of dealer polls or market prices has led to the use of Options 2. Where fixed payouts are used, they are typically based on historical loss experience in cases of default. These statistics may be internal to the organization or derived from rating agency statistics. The evidence of loss experience, somewhat predictably, points to average losses upon default being related to the seniority of the obligation and the secured or unsecured nature of the exposure.[60] Possible loss ratios include:

| | |
|---|---|
| Secured Obligations | 20-30% |
| Unsecured Senior Obligations | 40-60% |

The use of physical settlement assumes the availability of adequate face value of the reference asset. In the event that there are insufficient securities available or there are legal or regulatory impediments to physical settlement, a process of substitution is provided with the cash settlement option as a final option. The market standard for substitutability allows for any US$-denominated standard obligation (bond or loan) of equivalent seniority with a maturity of up to 10 years.

- **Payment timing** — the timing of settlement varies between the different default payment structures. The simplest timing is for the fixed payout option.

---

[60] For a discussion of recovery statistics, see Das, Satyajit (editor) (2000) *Credit Derivatives and Credit-linked Notes*; John Wiley & Sons, Singapore at Chapters 6 and 10.

This takes place an agreed number of business days after the termination of the agreement as a result of the occurrence of a credit event has been established. The post-default price and the physical settlement option are more complex. Where the post-default price mechanism is used, payment is made an agreed number of days after the post-default price has been made. Where physical settlement is used, the timing is around 10 to 20 business days from the termination arising from the occurrence of the credit event.

- **Payment for credit/default protection** — the buyer of default protection pays a premium. This premium is usually structured as a pa fee paid quarterly or semi-annually. This is expressed as the fixed rate in the default swap and is accrued up to the termination date. In certain transactions, this fee is paid as a lump-sum up-front amount. This amount is calculated as the fixed pa fee discounted back to the effective date at an agreed interest rate. The lump-sum up-front amount structure is primarily utilized to avoid credit exposure for the protection seller to the protection buyer. Where this structure is utilized, there is an adjustment or "claw back" provision requiring the protection seller to repay the unamortized amount of the fee in the event of an early termination of the swap.

Several of the key terms and conditions of credit default derivatives require comment. The two other terms that, in practice, create the greatest difficulties are the definition of the credit event, determination of the occurrence of a credit event, and the calculation of the default payment.[61] The definition of these terms impact not only on credit default swaps but also, as noted above on total return loan swaps (where the fluctuations in loan value are transferred as between the counterparties and therefor the loan value must be calculated periodically).

The definition of default as noted above is confined to payment defaults as well as certain reasonably clear events of financial distress. In practice, the definition of default usually combines a trigger credit event, the existence of *public information* regarding the credit event, and, increasingly, the concept of materiality.

In examining the definition of default event, a distinction between private sector and sovereign obligors is essential. The discussion on credit events to date has focused on private sector obligors. Where the obligor is sovereign while many of the same types of default events are relevant, there are additional factors that must be considered. For example, the concept of a bankruptcy-

---

[61] For detailed discussion of the definition of these terms, see Das, Satyajit (editor) (2000) *Credit Derivatives and Credit-linked Notes*; John Wiley & Sons, Singapore at Chapter 12. See also Brown, Claude "Credit Derivative Payout Mechanisms" (March 5, 1997) *IFR Financial Products* Issue 61 18-22.

driven credit event is less applicable. Typical credit event for sovereign obligors include:

- Payment default.
- Cross-default or cross-acceleration on other obligations.
- Ratings downgrade below an agreed threshold.

Additional credit events would generally include:

- Debt moratorium or suspension of payment obligations or similar action.
- Restructuring of the obligation where the new terms are materially less favorable to the lenders.

The possibility of differential treatment of different types of obligations (public versus bank, domestic versus international, local versus foreign currency) also has the potential to create significant problems.

The calculation of default payment presents greater problems. The fixed-payout structure is the only default mechanism that is relatively free from doubt. The need to work out a post-default value to effect a cash settlement or physical settlement presents a series of problems.

The calculation of a post-default value assumes:

- A tradeable and reasonably liquid loan or bond.
- A transparent and objective polling process.

In reality, the first condition is generally satisfied through avoidance of variable payout structures where the underlying bond or loan is not sufficiently traded or liquid. The second condition is met in practice through a series of provisions:

- A sufficient number of dealers are included in the dealer poll.
- The prices must be for a size comparable to the relevant transaction.
- There is usually some provision for excluding quotes that are *too* high or low or where the bid-offer spread is unrealistically high.
- The inclusion of a series of polls rather than reliance on a single poll (often referred to as anniversary polling). Under these structures, an agreed sequence of polls are conducted with intervals of one week or two weeks between polls for a fixed period. This has the difficulty of extending the amount of time before actual settlement is affected.

There is also a need to include a provision to deferring the valuation where a satisfactory poll is not conducted. **Exhibit 12.55** sets out a typical time line of events in establishing a default payment.

Physical delivery avoids some of these difficulties. However, it creates different problems including:

- The availability of the underlying securities to be delivered.

- The ability to legal effect a secure and effective transfer of the *defaulted* securities.

The lack of certainty on both these points means there is usually provision to deliver *substitute* securities (usually preagreed) or to revert to a dealer poll mechanism.

These choices and the problems they create in structuring these types of transactions are very real. For example, the fixed payout structure that has the considerable advantage of avoiding some of the mechanical difficulties identified, creates economic risks for the counterparties as the agreed payout may not provide a true hedge for the party seeking to hedge the underlying risk.

The final problem regarding the default payment relates to the necessity of selecting one of these mechanisms. This can be agreed at the commencement of the transaction or at the time that the credit even has occurred. The potential for disagreement on the mechanism for setting the default payment is substantial.

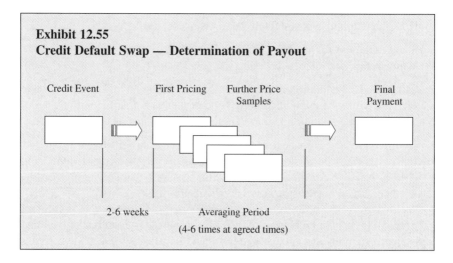

**Exhibit 12.55**
**Credit Default Swap — Determination of Payout**

### 4.3    Transaction Rationale

The principal application of credit default structures is the transfer of credit risk. It is used primarily by financial institutions to manage credit risk arising from intermediation activities. Investment applications include the ability to both transfer or, more commonly, *assume* credit risk synthetically to enhance portfolio return.

Principal applications include:

- Management of concentration risk within credit portfolios, particularly improvements in the diversification of portfolios.
- Adjustment of term requirements of credit by aligning supply of credit assets with internal constraints on the maximum term of an investment funds.
- Synthesis of credit risks with highly structured return profiles or to create credit risk-affected investments that are not directly available.
- Creation of and investment in nonfunded and off-balance-sheet credit exposures.
- Predetermination of and trading in recovery rates that are not generally available in capital markets.
- Management of return on credit risk including optimizing returns unaffected by funding constraints or balance sheet restrictions.

In considering the role of credit default swaps, it important to note the difference between these transactions and total return swap or credit spread transactions. Credit default swaps transfer price risk on the underlying bond or loan *in the event of a credit event*. However, the credit default swap does not transfer any price risk arising from *changes in credit quality falling short of default*. This is because there is no settlement between the parties unless there is a credit event. In contrast, both total return swaps and credit spread forwards transfer the risk of price changes as the result of changes in credit quality falling short of default as embodied in changes in credit spread and hence in the price of the bond or loan.

## 5.  Product Variations

The product structures within credit derivatives have evolved rapidly. Two variations that have emerged as important in the context of credit-linked notes is first-to-default baskets and convertibility derivatives are described below.[62]

### 5.1  First-to-default Basket

The first-to-default basket[63] concept is based on a credit default-based on a *basket* of underlying assets with different issuers. **Exhibit 12.56** sets out an example of a basket-linked credit default swap.

---

[62] For other variations, see Das, Satyajit (editor) (2000) *Credit Derivatives and Credit-linked Notes*; John Wiley & Sons, Singapore at Chapter 1.

[63] For a more detailed discussion of the structure and value dynamics of first-to-default baskets, see Das, Satyajit (editor) (2000) *Credit Derivatives and Credit-linked Notes*; John Wiley & Sons, Singapore, Chapter 5.

**Exhibit 12.56**
**Basket-linked Credit Default Swap**

| | |
|---|---|
| Counterparties | [Dealer] and [Investor] |
| Notional Principal | US$50 million |
| Adjustment Of Notional Principal | In the event that any of the issuers makes an early repayment in respect of an underlying credit asset, the notional principal will be reset on the next payment date to reflect the outstanding value of the remaining bonds. |
| Maturity | 5 years from commencement date |
| Commencement Date | 5 business days |
| Payments | Dealer pays enhanced payments. Investor pays interest payments. |
| Enhanced Payments | 3-month LIBOR plus 0.35% paid quarterly on an actual/360-day basis. |
| Interest Payments | 3-month LIBOR paid quarterly on an actual/360-day basis. |
| Underlying Credit Assets | **Issuer**    **Maturity** |
| | Entity A    December 2000 |
| | Entity B    June 1999 |
| | Entity C    April 2000 |
| | Entity D    December 2000 |
| | [Average coupon: LIBOR plus [20] bps pa] |
| Event Of Default | If any one of the issuers files for bankruptcy protection or incurs a payment default on any debt that remains uncured for five business days, the swap will be terminated and the investor will pay the termination payment to the dealer who will pay to the investor the termination asset. |
| Termination Payment | Equal to the notional principal |
| Termination Asset | The defaulted underlying credit assets to the amount of face value equal to the notional principal. |
| Calculation Agent | [Dealer] |

The critical aspect of these transactions is the concept of *first-to-default*. This effectively entails that the relevant credit event that triggers the default payment or physical settlement under the transaction in respect of the underlying credit assets is the *first* default of *any* of the credit assets included in the basket of credits.

The rationale for a first-to-default basket is that the combination of credit risks in the structure creates a lower credit quality than the individual credit standing of the credit assets. This reflects the combination of two factors:

- The low default correlations between the credit assets included in the basket.
- The fact that there is an element of inherent leverage in the structure. Effectively, in a US$50 million transaction on four underlying credit assets, the provider of default protection on a first-to-default basis provides protection *on any of the four assets* up to a face value of US$50 million. The seller of default protection is providing protection on *US$200 million of credit assets* at least until one of the entities defaults.

In practice, the earliest first-to-default structures entailed high-quality underlying credit assets such as Scandinavian sovereign issuers and other large European borrowers. The motivation for these transactions was the need for commercial and investment banks to hedge large credit exposures to these entities. These credit exposures related to capital market activity, such as interest rate and currency swaps, standby credit facilities to support funding of these borrowers, and limits to facilitate trading in securities issued by these entities.

The providers of protection under these structures were primarily institutional investors seeking higher yields on high-quality securities. The higher yield obtained on these first-to-default baskets was attractive to investors who did not properly quantify the additional marginal risk of the structure or because they were indifferent to the risks as the underlying credit assets were eligible investments for these investors *on a standalone purchase basis.* Far Eastern investors, including Japanese institutions, European and Middle Eastern investors were the major providers of these types of credit default protection. The attraction of these structures from the perspective of the parties purchasing protection was that these structures enabled them to reduce large credit concentrations within their portfolios at an attractive cost.

In more recent times, the structure has been used primarily with Japanese banks and emerging markets credits. The emergence of significant credit problems within the Japanese banking system in the mid-1990s prompted a significant volume of transactions that primarily entailed the sale of default risk on the weaker Japanese financial institutions through these first-to-default credit structures. The driving force was the necessity to reduce the large credit concentration within bank portfolios to this group of obligors. The protection was provided by Far Eastern investors, including *better capitalized* Japanese financial institutions, primarily institutional investors, as well as investors in other markets *with low levels of exposure to Japanese bank risk.*

The emerging market transactions involved trading baskets of Latin, South-

East Asian and, more recently, Eastern European risk. The underlying rationale of these transactions was for large international money centre commercial and investment banks active in these markets to diversify or trade out of large risk concentration to particular counterparties to allow them to continue to transact business with these counterparties. The providers of default protection was again institutional investors and hedge funds willing to take the default risk to these issuers/counterparties.

In all these types of transactions, a major driving force of these transactions was the fact that the format for the transfer of credit risk created in the first-to-default basket was attractive for the investors assuming the default risk. The structures embedded in notes/securities provided an elegant mechanism for creating the desired exposure while allowing the investors to generate incremental *yield* that provides out-performance relative to the underlying benchmarks against which the performance of these investors was measured.

In reality, the first-to-default basket structures are essentially predicated on allowing providers of protection to trade default correlation. As default correlation has historically not been easy to trade, the ability to trade it and to use this factor to generate incremental income were the major drivers of the structure. The capacity to create hidden leverage was also attractive.

## 5.2   Currency Inconvertibility Agreements

A number of structures that deal with specific aspects of sovereign risk in financial transactions have emerged. In the main, these structures are utilized in relation to emerging markets transactions. This reflects both the higher level of sovereign risk evident in such transactions and the central role played by sovereign risk in emerging market trading.

There are various levels of credit risk in transactions involving emerging markets. They range from: regulatory risk; market risk (currency, interest rate, and equity price risk); counterparty default risk; and sovereign risk.

The sovereign risk element involves a series of risks including the inconvertibility of the currency or nontransferability of the currency. For example, a borrower with foreign currency debt or other payment obligation may not be able to exchange local currency to meet these obligations even where it has the cash resources to make the relevant transfer. This risk is a central concern of foreign investors in emerging market (both direct and portfolio equity investors and purchasers of debt securities). It is also a concern for traders in emerging market debt and financial products, including emerging market securities and derivative contracts. Currency inconvertibility agreements have emerged as a mechanism for dealing with these types of risks.

The aspect of sovereign risk most commonly dealt with in the credit derivatives market is the risk of currency inconvertibility or restrictions placed on the free flow of funds. This reflects the fact that this is a central concern of foreign investors and the fact that structures linked to default have certain problems in the context of emerging market transactions and sovereign risk generally. In particular, there are a number of events short of actual default that have a material impact on transactions involving emerging market debt. In addition, the actual event of default on sovereign debt is likely to be somewhat remote.

In this context, several types of currency inconvertibility agreements have emerged in the context of credit derivatives more generally. **Exhibit 12.57** sets out an example of one possible transaction structure. Structures where this element is embedded in a security are also utilized. **Exhibit 12.58** on page 713 sets out the structure of a inconvertibility agreement in diagrammatic form.

---

**Exhibit 12.57**
**Currency Inconvertibility Agreement — Example**

Assume an investor has investments in an emerging market (in the form of debt issued by nonsovereign issuers located in the relevant jurisdiction). The investor is concerned about the risk of inconvertibility and transfer of funds and decides to hedge the currency conversion risk on its investments. The specific exposure under consideration is that the issuer may be prevented by government regulations from converting local currency into the foreign currency (say, US$ or other hard currency in which the debt obligation is denominated) in order to make payments to the investor.

The currency inconvertibility transaction is structured as follows:

- The agreement is structured to provide protection for a fixed period, say, one year against currency inconvertibility in the relevant jurisdiction on a specified face value amount that is related to the amount of the investor's exposure by way of its investment (say, US$25 million). The exact under security or investment does not need to be defined as the protection is not necessarily related to the underlying investment.
- The investor pays a premium to the provider of protection of, say, 1.00% pa based on the face value (US$25 million), equivalent to US$250,000.
- The payoffs under the currency inconvertibility agreement are as follows:
  1. If during the 1-year tenor of the agreement, there is no currency inconvertibility event, then the investor receives no benefit and the agreement expires normally.
  2. If during the 1-year tenor of the agreement, there is a currency

---

inconvertibility event that is continuing at the maturity of the agreement or alternative upon the occurrence of the inconvertibility event (usually two business days after exercise), the investor receives the benefit of currency inconvertibility protection as follows:

- The investor receives the face value of the contract (US$25 million) from the party providing protection (usually in New York).
- In return, the investor pays the equivalent amount of local currency of the emerging market country in the emerging market location at the then current prevailing exchange rate (the rate determination mechanism is prescribed).

The inconvertibility event will generally be defined to include the imposition of regulations (described in broad terms) that have the effect of:

- Preventing or making illegal the conversion of the local currency into foreign currency.
- Preventing or making illegal the payment of the local currency to accounts outside the jurisdiction and/or transferring any funds outside the jurisdiction.
- Prohibiting the receipt of or repatriation outside the jurisdiction of any capital, principal of any security, interest, dividend, capital gain, or proceeds of the sale on any assets owned by foreign persons or entities.
- Making the US$ unavailable in any legal exchange market in the jurisdiction in accordance with normal commercial practice.

Additional events that would trigger the inconvertibility event would include:

- A general banking moratorium of suspension of payments by banks or government entities in the jurisdictions.
- A general expropriation, confiscation, nationalization, or other compulsory acquisition or similar action by the government of the jurisdiction that derives OECD banks of all or substantially all of their assets in the jurisdiction.
- Any war, revolution, insurrection, or hostile act that has the effect of preventing convertibility of the local currency or transfer of funds to overseas accounts.

The rate at which the conversion is undertaken is usually the exchange rate as at the date of settlement. The rate used is usually either the Central

Bank-published rates or, in the absence of such a rate or where it is manifestly incorrect a rate determined by a poll of dealers or in some other commercially realistic method under the circumstances.

The effect of the transaction is to enable the investor seeking protection against restriction on currency conversion that might impact unfavorably on its ability to receive payment in hard currency or to transfer funds out of the emerging market country despite the imposition of currency controls.

**Exhibit 12.58**
**Currency Inconvertibility Agreement — Structure**

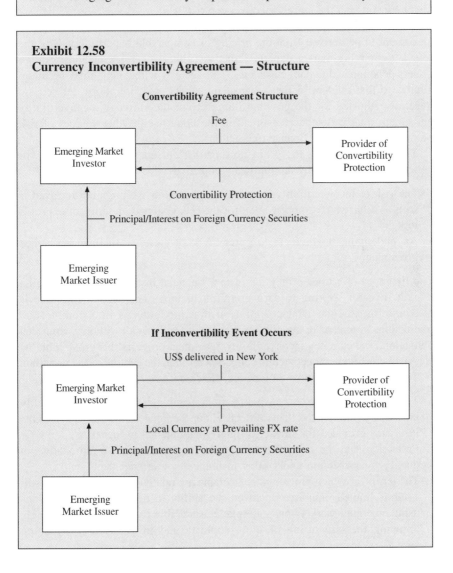

Convertibility Agreement Structure

Fee

Emerging Market Investor → Provider of Convertibility Protection

Convertibility Protection

Principal/Interest on Foreign Currency Securities

Emerging Market Issuer

If Inconvertibility Event Occurs

US$ delivered in New York

Emerging Market Investor → Provider of Convertibility Protection

Local Currency at Prevailing FX rate

Principal/Interest on Foreign Currency Securities

Emerging Market Issuer

The parties providing the currency inconvertibility protection in effect assume the risk of the local currency obligation, at least in relation to currency convertibility. The risk assumed is not significantly different from that in purchasing a foreign currency-denominated security issued by an issuer located in an emerging market country. The transaction effectively separates the credit risk from the currency conversion risk. This separation is important, for example, in the case of issuers such as subsidiaries of large creditworthy multinationals where the credit risk is low (perhaps by reason of parent company credit support) but the currency conversion risk is high.

This relationship allows the pricing of the currency inconvertibility agreement to be derived from the pricing of comparable maturity bonds of the relevant emerging market country issued by either sovereign or nonsovereign issuers denominated in hard currencies. This security will exhibit a risk premium similar to that evident in these transactions. The risk premiums derived are generally adjusted for the possible illiquidity of the currency inconvertibility agreement relative to the investment in the bond itself. Other sources of risk premiums include trade finance transactions.

The party providing the protection against currency inconvertibility will generally be motivated by the following objectives:

- The risk of inconvertibility is seen as slight and/or the premium received is seen as a fair value compensation for the risk assumed, in terms of expected loss.
- An underlying requirement to purchase local currency to finance planned investments.

The first type of rationale may motivate a financial institution or an emerging market investor seeking to earn premium income. The second rationale is relevant for an industrial corporation that has entered into commercial transactions to undertake the relevant investment and cannot withdraw from that obligation. The currency inconvertibility agreement provides this group with the ability to effectively monetize this obligation through the capture of the premium.

These types of structures, in practice, are characterized by the following:

- They tend to be more expensive than comparable export credit or officially provided sovereign risk. This reflects either the noncommercial nature of the insurance provided the impact of inter-governmental influence.
- Protection may be available for transactions that would traditionally not qualify for protection under other insurance-type arrangements.
- The terms for which protection is available are relative short. The market still exhibits limited liquidity. However, the ability to hedge these transactions using emerging market bonds, despite considerable basis risk, is increasingly allowing the structuring of quite sophisticated instruments for hedging aspects of sovereign risk.

# Selected References

BZW. "An Investor's Guide Credit Derivatives." *Derivatives Strategy Credit Derivatives Supplement* (June 1997): 1-8.

Chase Manhattan Bank. "Credit Derivatives: A Primer." *Asiamoney Derivatives Guide* (April 1997): 2-5.

*Credit Derivatives: Applications for Risk Management*. Euromoney Books, London, 1998.

Fallon, William. "Credit Where Credit's Due." *Risk* vol. 7 no. 3 (March 1994): 9-11.

Ghose, Ronit, (editor) *Credit Derivatives: Key Issues*. British Bankers Association, London, 1997.

Howard, Kerrin. "An Introduction To Credit Derivatives." *Derivatives Quarterly* (Winter 1995): 28-37.

Iacono, Frank. "Credit Derivatives" in Schwartz, Robert J. and Smith Jr, Clifford W. (editors) *Derivatives Handbook: Risk Management and Control*. John Wiley & Sons, Inc., New York 1997: Chapter 2.

Masters, Blythe. "A Credit Derivatives Primer" *Derivatives Strategy* (May 1996): 42-44.

Masters, Blythe and Reoch, Rob. *Credit Derivatives: Structures and Applications*. J.P. Morgan, New York and London (March 1996).

Masters, Blythe and Reoch, Rob. *Credit Derivatives: An Innovation in Negotiable Exposure*; J.P. Morgan, New York and London (March 1996).

Nelken, Izzy. *Implementing Credit Derivatives*. McGraw-Hill, New York, 1999.

Reoch, Rob and Masters, Blythe. "Credit Swaps: An Innovation In Negotiable Exposure." *Capital Market Strategies* 7 (March 1996): 3-8.

Scott-Quinn, Brian and Walmsley, Julian K. *The Impact of Credit Derivatives on Securities Markets*. International Securities Market Association, Zurich, 1998.

Smith, Bradley E. "Total Return Swaps." *Capital Market Strategies* 3 (1994): 37-39.

Smithson, Charles with Holappa, Hal. "Credit Derivatives." *Risk* vol. 8 no. 12 (December 1995): 38-39.

Storrow, Jamie. *Credit Derivatives: Key Issues — 2nd Edition*. British Bankers Association, London, 1999.

Tavakoli, Janet M. *Credit Derivatives: A Guide To Instruments And Applications*. John Wiley & Sons, Inc., New York, 1999.

Whittaker, Greg J. and Kumar, Sumita "Credit Derivatives: A Primer" in Atsuo Konishi and Ravi Dattatreya, (editors) "*The Handbook of Derivative Instruments*" (Irwin Publishing, 1996): 595-614.

# 13
# Exotic Option-embedded Structured Notes

## 1. Overview

A central element in the development of structured notes is the ability to use these instruments to provide investors with customised risk-return profiles. This element is equally applicable across all asset classes. The emergence of exotic options[1] in capital markets is also motivated by the increased desire of market participants to increasingly refine the risk-return profiles *within instrument structures*. The combination of the two formats is therefore almost inevitable.

In this Chapter, exotic option embedded structured notes are considered. The objective is to examine the use of exotic optionality to enhance the customization capabilities of structured notes. The use of exotic options is examined across all asset classes with examples being drawn from debt,

---

[1] In this chapter, the exotic options utilized in the context of engineering structured notes are briefly described. However, there is no detailed discussion of the pricing, trading and hedging of these instruments, except insofar as they impact specifically on the structured note. For a more detailed consideration of the exotic option *in itself*, see: Das, Satyajit (1996) *Exotic Options*; LBC Information Services, Sydney; Tompkins, Robert (1994) *Options Explained*; Macmillan Press Limited, England; Nelken, Israel (editor) (1996) *The Handbook Of Exotic Options*; Irwin Professional Publishing, Chicago; Ravindran, K. (1998) *Customised Derivatives*; McGraw-Hill, New York; Bhansali, Vineer (1998) *Pricing and Managing Exotic And Hybrid Options*; McGraw-Hill, New York; (1992) *From Black-Scholes To Black Holes — New Frontiers In Options*; Risk Publications, London; Jarrow, Robert (editor) (1995) *Over The Rainbow — Developments In Exotic Options and Complex Swaps*; Risk Publications, London; Wilmott, P., Dewynne, J., and Howison, S. (1994) *Option Pricing: Mathematical Models and Computation*; Oxford Financial Press, Oxford.

currency, equity, and commodity. The concept of exotic optionality is first considered. Individual structured note instruments, incorporating different types of exotic options, are then examined.

## 2. Exotic Options

Exotic options can be defined as:

> *Any option whose characteristics, including strike price calculations/ determinations, payoff characteristics, premium payment terms or activation/expiration mechanisms vary from standard call and put options or where the underlying asset involves combined or multiple underlying assets.*

Exotic options (also referred to as third-generation risk-management products) are primarily focused on varying one or more elements of the fundamental structure of an option contract. This can be illustrated by examples:

- In the case of an average rate option, the dimension that is altered is the payoff determination. The option payoff is calculated through a comparison of the strike price of the option and the average price of the underlying commodity as sampled over the relevant period. This is in contrast to the traditional option contract where the payoff is determined by a comparison to strike price and the *final* price of the underlying asset.
- In the case of a barrier option, the existence of the option is itself contingent upon a specified event occurring. Typically, a barrier option will only be activated if the underlying asset price reaches some specified level or, in the case of a knock-out, will continue to remain active unless the asset price achieves the nominated level.

**Exhibit 13.1** sets out a classification of exotic options.[2]

---

[2] The categorisation used is that in Chase Securities Inc. "Mundane Problems, Exotic Solutions" (August 1992) *Euromoney* 42-48.

**Exhibit 13.1**
**Categorisation Of Exotic Options**

Exotic options can be classified into five categories:

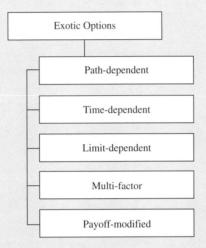

Each category can then itself be further classified into different types of
options. Path-dependent options consist of the following types of options:

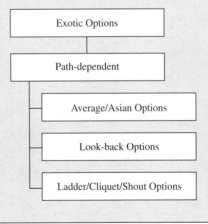

Time-dependent options consist of the following types of options:

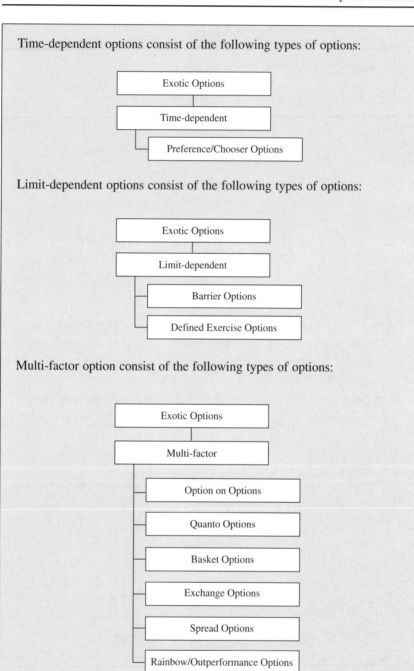

Limit-dependent options consist of the following types of options:

Multi-factor option consist of the following types of options:

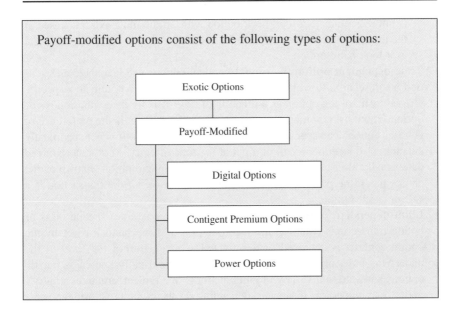

Payoff-modified options consist of the following types of options:

The various types of exotic option instruments that can be identified can be categorized into a number of categories:

- **Path-dependent options** — path-dependent options are characterized by payoffs that are a function of the particular path that asset prices follow over the life of the relevant option. The path of the underlying asset price can determine not only the payoff but can determine the structure of the option. Path-dependent structures include:
  1. **Average rate (or Asian) options** — where, as noted above, the payoff upon settlement is determined by comparing the strike price with the average of the spot asset price over a specific period during the life of the option.
  2. **Average strike rate option** — where the strike rate itself is not fixed and the payoff is determined through a comparison of the underlying price of expiration with the strike price computed as the average of the underlying asset price over a specified period.
  3. **Look-back options** — that refers to an option where the purchaser has the right at expiration to set the strike price of the option at the most favorable price for the asset that has occurred during a specified time. In the case of a look-back call (put), the buyer can choose to purchase (sell) the underlying asset at the lowest (highest) price that has occurred over a specified period; typically, the life of the option.
  4. **Ladder options** — where the strike price of the option is periodically reset based on the underlying evolution of the asset price. A ladder option

is not dissimilar to a look-back option with, in the most extreme cases, if the amount of reset is set to infinity, the ladder option becoming identical to a look-back option.

- **Time-dependent options** — time-dependent options can be characterized as options in relation to which the purchaser has the right to nominate a specific characteristic of the option as a function of time, usually the expiration of the option. The most common type of time-dependent option is the preference or chooser option. The specific feature of this option is that it is not specifically characterized as either a call or a put at the time of entry. At a predetermined date usually after commencement but no later than expiration (known as the choice date), the purchaser can nominate whether or not the transaction is a call or a put option.

- **Limit-dependent options** — limit-dependent options are a special class of option transactions entailing the incorporation of a mechanism whereby the option contract is activated or deactivated as a function of the level of the underlying asset price. These types of options are usually known as barrier options and sold in a variety of combinations. In a typical structure, a barrier option may appear or disappear, depending on the contractual arrangements agreed, based on the performance, in price terms, of the underlying asset. Barrier options are in a sense both limit and path-dependent.

- **Multi-factor options** — multi factor options typically involve a pattern of payoffs based on the relationship between multiple assets, as opposed to the price in the case of a traditional option for single assets. A variety of structures exist including:
  1. **Compound options** — are in essence options on options where the holder has the right but not obligation to buy or sell another predetermined option at a pre-agreed price.
  2. **Basket options** — the payout under the contract is related to the cumulative performance of a basket of underlying assets.
  3. **Exchange options** — give the purchaser the right to exchange one asset for another.
  4. **Quanto options** — the option contract is denominated in a currency other than that of the underlying asset to which exposure is sought or being hedged. The quanto contract will typically allow the quantity or notional principal of the transaction to be adjusted reflecting the fact that the face amount of the currency cover required fluctuates to cover changes in the foreign currency value of the underlying asset.
  5. **Rainbow options** — the payout relationship is based on the relationship between multiple assets as opposed to a price of a single asset. Typical structures include spread options or better of two or worst of asset options (often known as out performance options).

- **Payoff-modified options** — payoff-modified options entail adjustment to the linear and smooth payoffs that are associated with conventional options. The major types include:

1. **Digital options** — where the payout under the option contract is discontinuous with the payout being a fixed pre-determined amount payable if the strike price is reached irrespective of how much the option is in-the-money.

2. **Contingent premium** — this class of instrument entails the linking of the option premium to be paid to the writer to the asset price performance. In the classical structure of the contingent premium option, no premium is payable at the commencement of the transaction with the premium only becoming due and payable at expiration and only if the option expires in money. Technically, the contingent premium structure is a combination of a conventional option and a digital option.

3. **Power (or exponential) options** — unlike a standard option return, which is a clear linear function of the difference between the underlying asset price at exercise or at maturity, in the case of a power option, the option payoff is a defined function of the difference, usually raised to a power, for example, higher than one.

The exotic option structures identified are predicated on the achievement of one or more of the following objectives:

- **Reduction in option premium** — effectively to lower the cost of creating the option position.
- **Alteration in risk profile** — this can take one of a number of forms:
  1. **Increased probability of gain** — by ensuring the capacity to restructure the strike, type, or other aspect of the option to ensure that it has economic value at exercise.
  2. **Quantification of loss** — by ensuring *the option writer's* potential payout if the option expires in-the-money at maturity is known at the time the option is traded, or ensuring the premium on the option is *only payable* by the buyer under defined conditions.
  3. **Optimal exercise timing** — by ensuring that the option pays out the maximum value or near to this value of the option irrespective of whether the option is exercised at the optimal time.
- **Asset liability matching** — the option payoff profile matches the underlying asset or liability required to be altered or managed through the transaction.

The capacity of exotic options to reduce option premiums and also alter risk profiles makes them particularly suitable for use within structured notes. In practice, the major types used in designing structured notes include average rate options, ladder options, barrier options, basket options, and digital options.

## 3.   Path-dependent Option-embedded Structures

### 3.1   Overview

Path dependent options are usually incorporated within structured notes to achieve the following objectives:

* The use of path-dependency, particularly using average rate options, to reduce the cost of the option.
* The use of path-dependency, using look-back or more usually ladder options, to enhance the return profile.

### 3.2   Average Rate Option-embedded Note

A number of structured notes have been designed to incorporate an embedded average rate option. For example, Citicorp issued 5-year certificates of deposit in the US domestic market that are 100% principal guaranteed and return the investor double the *average* increase in the S&P 500 index over the life of the security. This structure incorporates *an average rate option* on the index rather than the traditional *European option* on the index.

The major advantages of this structure include:

* **Lower cost of the option** — the lower cost of the average rate option relative to the corresponding series of European option reflects:
    1. The volatility relevant is that of the average asset price.
    2. The moving average of the asset price tends to be less volatile than the asset price itself

This lower cost (up to 30 to 40%) allows the investor's degree of participation in any appreciation of the index to be enhanced.

* **Lower exercise risk of the structure** — the lower exercise risk derives from the fact that the holder of the option is not exposed *solely* to the value of the index *at maturity* (the expiry of the option). The return to the holder is based *average value of the index over the life of the option*. This dictates a payoff to the option holder where the index has on average outperformed the strike price of the option.

The structure also has disadvantages. The average rate option will not generally give a return commensurate with the total appreciation in the market as the average will lag by definition the increase particularly in a steadily rising market.

The major use of the average rate options has been in structured notes targeted to individual retail investors.

**Exhibit 13.2** sets out an example of a structured note that embeds an average rate option on a stock index. **Exhibit 13.3** sets out an example of a structure that embeds a *partial* average rate option on a stock index.

---

**Exhibit 13.2**
**Average Rate Option-embedded Note — Example 1**

The terms of the transaction are as follows:

| | |
|---|---|
| Issuer | AAA/ AA-rated issuer |
| Amount | US$20 million |
| Maturity | 8 years |
| Issue Price | 100% |
| Coupon | 0.00% |
| Redemption Price | 100% plus maximum [20%; 100% × {(Average index value/Initial index value) − 1} |
| Initial Index Value | S&P 500 index level at commencement of transaction. |
| Average Index Value | Arithmetic average of S&P 500 index level on March 15, June 15, September 15, and December 15 of each year commencing on the first quarter following commencement of the transaction and also two business days before the maturity date. |

The investor is guaranteed to receive a minimum yield of 2.31% pa (based on the minimum guaranteed level of 120% of investment. The investor receives the appreciation of the index above the initial level based on the quarterly S&P 500 price levels over the term of the transaction.

---

**Exhibit 13.3**
**Average Rate Option-embedded Note — Example 2**

The terms of the transaction are as follows:

| | |
|---|---|
| Issuer | AAA/ AA-rated issuer |
| Amount | US$20 million |
| Maturity | 5 years |
| Issue Price | 100% |
| Coupon | 0.00% |

| Redemption Price | 100% plus maximum [20%; 100% × {(Average index value/Initial index value) − 1} |
|---|---|
| Initial Index Value | S&P 500 index level at commencement of transaction. |
| Average Index Value | Arithmetic average of S&P 500 index level on March 15, June 15, September 15, and December 15 of the last year of the transaction and also two business days before the maturity date. |

The investor is guaranteed to receive a minimum yield of 3.71% pa (based on the minimum guaranteed level of 120% of investment. The investor receives the appreciation of the index above the initial level based on the quarterly S&P 500 price levels over the final year of the transaction. The structure uses a partial average structure with the investor having full participation in any increase in market values until the commencement of the averaging period.

### 3.3    Ladder Option-embedded Note

The concept of path dependency in option structures is a source of value to option users. In a nonpath-dependent option, the evolution of the asset price does not impact on the payoff profile of the option. The effect of introducing path dependency can be seen from a consideration of some of the more important path-dependent structures:

- **Average rate (Asian) options** (discussed above) — where the asset price on which the option payoff is based is the *average price* of the asset as distinct from the *final* asset price. The average asset price is inherently path-dependent, being a function of the series of asset prices over the relevant period.
- **Look-back options** — where the exercise price is based on the best asset price over a nominated period (usually the period to expiry) allowing the purchaser to set an exercise price at the lowest (highest) asset price attained over the look-back period for a call (put) option. The exercise price under this structure is path-dependent, being a function of the price evolution of the asset.

The demand for path-dependent structures is governed by a number of factors:

- The fact that the value of option will rarely be at its optimal at the maturity of the option.

- Demand for structures that inherently optimize option value by (generally) passive exercise rules being embedded within the option. This demand can be motivated by the type of investor (retail investment products) or asset liability matching requirements (regular streams of cash flows that often motivate the use of average rate options).

The advantage of optimal exercise characteristics can only be achieved at a cost to the purchaser. The look-back option structure is ideal for the purchaser who wishes to ensure a very high probability of a positive payoff for the option but is generally extremely expensive. A number of structures have developed that seek to use the concept of path dependency and extend it to provide many benefits of such structures but with a lower cost.

Ladder options entail a special type of path-dependent option where the *strike price* is periodically reset (automatically) when the asset underlying the option trades through pre-specified asset price levels. For example, in the case of a ladder call on an asset with an initial strike price of $100 and ladder re-set levels set at $5 intervals, if the price rises above $105, then the strike price is automatically reset to $105 thereby locking in the $5 price appreciation. The major attraction of the ladder option structures is its automatic capability to lock in gains from movements in asset prices increasing the probability of optimal exercise of the option at a cost that is favourable relative to other comparable option products such as look-back options. In fact, one means of characterising ladder option is as a *discrete* look-back option.

**Exhibit 13.4** sets out an example of an equity-linked Eurobond issue, undertaken by Banque Paribas and BNP, incorporating a ladder option on the CAC-40 French stock market index. The structure ensured that where the value of the index rose above 125% of the commencing index value and 25% increments above that level up to 250%, the gain (being the difference between the ladder level attained and the commencing index value) is preserved *irrespective of the final value of the index*. For example, if the index achieves a high of between 176% and 199% of the initial index value, then the investor receives a return of 75% of the investment in addition to return of principal. There is no cap on the return to the investor with the investor receiving the full value of the appreciation above the final threshold of 250% of the initial index value. The structure was attractive to investors compared to available alternative equity-linked structures that were capped at 160% to 190%. In addition, the embedded ladder option ensures that the investor is not exposed to short-term volatility in the value of the index. The investor does not need to optimise the realization of the investment as the payoffs under the note are based on longer term trends in the value of the index and any appreciation was automatically preserved through the ladder levels. The issuer insulated itself from the exposure to the embedded options by purchasing corresponding ladder options on the CAC-40. **Exhibit 13.5** sets out an example of a similar structure in Italian Lira.

The ladder option itself can be replicated by purchasing a conventional 8-year European style call option on the stock index struck at the initial value of the index and combining it with a series of put option which were triggered as the ladder levels were reached.[3] **Exhibit 13.6** sets out a replication methodology for the creation of the ladder option.

---

**Exhibit 13.4**
**Ladder Option-embedded Note — Example 1**

In February 1992, Credit Foncier de France (CFF) issued an equity index-linked Eurobond on the following terms:

| | |
|---|---|
| Issuer | Credit Foncier de France |
| Amount | French franc 500 million |
| Type of Issue | Equity index-linked Eurobond |
| Maturity | Zero |
| Redemption Value | Par |
| Underlying Index | CAC-40 |
| Option Thresholds (Ladders Levels) | Six ladder levels commencing at 125% of the initial value of the underlying index in 25% increments up to a maximum of 250%. |
| Return | The investor will receive the following return: |

- If the underlying index is below the level at commencement of the transaction, then the investor will receive no return.
- If the underlying index is above the level at commencement of the transaction, then the investor will receive the percentage appreciation in the index subject to the condition that where any ladder level has been achieved during the life of the bond, the return to the investor will not fall below the percentage difference between the ladder level achieved and the commencement value of the index although it may increase above the minimum value achieved.

*Source:* Brady, Simon "Deal of The Month" *Euromoney* (February 1992): 16

---

[3] These are effectively barrier options on the index, specifically up-and-in knock in barrier options.

**Exhibit 13.5**
**Ladder Option-embedded Note — Example 5**

The terms of the issue are as follows:

| | |
|---|---|
| Issuer | AAA/AA-rated issuer |
| Amount | Italian lira 10,000 million |
| Maturity | 8 years |
| Issue Price | 100% |
| Coupon | 0.00% |
| Redemption Value | Amount + {Amount × Maximum [35%; 80% × Maximum [(((Final index value/Initial index value) – 1); ((Highest ladder level/Initial index value) – 1)} |
| Initial Index Value | Value of the Swiss Market Index (SMI) at commencement of the transaction. |
| Final Index value | Value of the SMI at maturity of the transaction. |
| Highest Ladder Level | The highest level reached by the SMI during the period from issue date to maturity of the transaction based on set ladder levels of 150%, 200%, 250%, and 300% of the initial index value. |

The investor has guaranteed return of its principal investment and receives a minimum return of 3.82% pa. In the event that the SMI increases to at least 150% of its initial value, then the investor receives 80% of price appreciation based on the higher of the final price attained and the highest ladder level breached.

---

**Exhibit 13.6**
**Construction of a Ladder Option**

The following example illustrates the mechanism by which a ladder option can be constructed. In this case, the ladder is on a stock index that is assumed to be trading at a level of 500.00. The option with a strike price of the spot level of the index (500.00) is structured with one ladder level of 5%, which corresponds to index levels of 525. The option is for a life of six months and the purchaser is guaranteed a payout of the ladder levels (that is, 5%) in the event where the index *trades* above those levels even if the index level *at maturity* is below the relevant ladder level or option strike price. If the index is above the upper ladder level, then the purchaser benefits to the full extent that the index exceeds the strike price.

The construction of the ladder option requires the following decomposition, entailing a series of standard and barrier options on the index:

1. Purchase a European 6-month call option with a strike of 500.
2. Sell a 6-month European put option with a strike of 500.
3. Purchase a knock-out put with a strike level of 500 and an outstrike level of 525.
4. Purchase a European 6-month put option with a strike of 525.
5. Sell a 6-month knock-out put option with a strike of 525 with an out strike level of 525.

The operation of this set of options can be analysed as follows:

- If the index value of 525 (the ladder level) is not reached over the life of the option, then Options 2, 3, 4, and 5 either expire unexercised or cancel themselves out leaving only Option 1. This means that the transaction has the normal payoff of a European option.
- If the index value of 525 (the ladder level) is reached, then Option 3 and 5 are knocked out. Options 1 and 2 combine to create a synthetic long position. The combination of the synthetic long position and the purchased put at the index level of 525 (Option 4) locks in a minimum value of 25 (525-500) where the asset price at maturity is below 525. It also enables the holder to participate in any rise above 525 through the synthetic long position that is then sold at maturity.

In essence, the structure combines a call option with a series of put spreads/knock-out put spreads. The process can be repeated to create additional steps in the ladder if required. Additional ladder levels are created by adding additional put spreads/knock-out put spreads at the relevant ladder levels. The ladder option value itself is the total premiums paid and received in creating the structure. The structure is capable of being packaged as an over-the-counter product or embedded in a fixed interest security in the form of a structured note.

# 4.    Limit-dependent Option-embedded Structures

## 4.1    Overview

Barrier options represent a special class of options where the contract is characterized by a feature that the option, typically, European, becomes operational or is extinguished if the asset price reaches a specified level. Technically, barrier options are a class of path-dependent options. However, they give rise to some unique features that justify considering them a separate class in their own right.

The economic benefits of the barrier option structure derive from the fact that it usually attracts lower premiums relative to conventional options. This lower premium amount reflects the possibility that the option will be extinguished or not activated. This lower premium typically allows barrier options to be utilized to provide structured protection to hedgers and investors at modest cost. The reduction in cost relative to conventional options is dependent upon a number of factors including the relationship between the spot price or forward price level, the barrier level, and the maturity of the option.

In the case of structured notes, the lower premium is critical in lowering the cost of any embedded option. For example, the lower option premium allows a higher degree of participation in the movement in the relevant asset to be created for a given coupon or principal sacrifice. The barrier feature may, however, significantly reduce the participation in any market value shift that results in the barrier level being attained. This dictates that the structure is most attractive where the investor expects a modest market move, at least less than the barrier level, to achieve the maximum benefits from the incorporation of this type of exotic optionality.

## 4.2    Barrier-embedded Notes

Some examples of barrier embedded notes will illustrate the use of barrier options within structured note formats. **Exhibit 13.7** sets out the terms of an FRN incorporating embedded interest rate barrier options on a short-term interest rate index. The note is attractive to investors seeking to monetize an expectation regarding the *future path* of LIBOR. This is done through the sale of barrier options on the forward rates. This type of structure is used particularly in an environment of a steep yield curve, declining bond yields, and narrow credit spreads.

**Exhibit 13.7**
**FRN Incorporating Interest Rate Barrier Option**

| | |
|---|---|
| Issuer | AAA-rated issuer |
| Amount | US$100 million |
| Maturity | 3 years |
| Issue Price | 100 |
| Floating Coupon | 3-month LIBOR plus 37.5 bps pa payable quarterly |
| Barrier Coupon | 1.50% pa payable quarterly |
| Commencement Level | 40 bps over current 3 month LIBOR |
| Current 3 Month LIBOR | 3.50% pa |
| Step Up | 1.00% pa (effectively 25 bps per quarterly interest period) |

The return to the investor under this structure is predicated on the interaction of the spread, the barrier level, and the conversion coupon. In the example, the barrier is set at a level (the commencement level) of 40 bps over LIBOR that then increases at a fixed increment rate of 25 bps per period. The structure entails a trade-off between the floating coupon margin and the conversion coupon. The higher is the desired conversion coupon, the lower the corresponding enhancement to the margin relative to LIBOR.

The coupon payable where the barrier level is not reached is the floating coupon. The barrier coupon is the fixed-rate payable where the barrier is reached. Where LIBOR plus the spread does not exceed the barrier level on a reset date, the FRN pays LIBOR plus the spread of 37.5 bps. If the barrier is reached, then the next coupon is the barrier level and the fixed conversion coupon of 1.50% pa is paid for all subsequent periods. In effect, the security behaves like a high-margin FRN *unless LIBOR reaches the barrier level* when it becomes a fixed-rate note with a 1.50% pa coupon.

The investor, under this note, achieves an enhanced return as long as LIBOR does not increase by 140 bps pa over one year and 340 bps over three years. As the barrier levels are set above the implied LIBOR forwards, the investor will benefit from the sale of the barrier option where LIBOR reaches the forwards or exceeds them by a small margin. The additional spread relative to a normal FRN ensures that the barrier FRN outperforms the conventional FRN where the barrier level is not breached until well into the term of the note. As the rate of increase rises and the barrier level is breached at earlier dates the relative advantage of the barrier floater decreases. The breakeven rate of increase is around 30-40 bps and a barrier breach time of 12 to 18 months. Accordingly, the additional enhanced return on the barrier FRN is preserved as long as LIBOR increases at a rate of less than the breakeven level per quarter. If the increase in LIBOR exceeds this level the return on the barrier FRN falls sharply, reflecting the lower conversion coupon.

An alternative method of analysis of the breakeven slope as between the barrier FRN and the conventional FRN is to consider the case where LIBOR stays at current levels for, say, (up to) three to four quarters and subsequently increases at a constant rate. Predictably, the slope of the breakeven rate *increases* the greater the number of quarters that the interest rate curve stays static. This signifies that if LIBOR is initially constant, then it will have to increase at a higher constant rate to reach the barrier level. An initial period of static interest rates thus significantly enhances the benefits of the structure to the investors.

**Exhibit 13.8** sets out an example of a structured note entailing a sold barrier option on currency values. **Exhibit 13.9** sets out an example of a structured note embedding a sold barrier option on equity index values.

---

**Exhibit 13.8**
**FRN Incorporating Currency Barrier Option**

The terms of the issue are as follows:

| | |
|---|---|
| Issuer | AAA/AA-rated issuer |
| Amount | US$25 million |
| Maturity | 1 year |
| Issue Price | 100% |
| Coupon Rate | 10.50% pa |
| Redemption Value | Redemption (per US$1 million) will be: |
| | 1. If the exchange rate does not trade above Yen 130 at any time over the term of the note and the exchange rate at maturity is below ¥110, then US$1 million. |
| | 2. If the exchange rate trades above ¥130 at any time over the term of the note and the exchange rate at maturity is above ¥110, then ¥110 million per US$1 million. |
| Exchange Rate | US$/¥ spot exchange rate |

The basic dynamics of the structure is that the investor receives a higher coupon in relation to available market rates through the sale of a knock-in put option on the US$/¥ exchange rate. The knock-in put option has a strike of US$1: ¥110 and an instrike (or trigger) of US$1: ¥130. If the Yen trades above ¥130, then the put is activated. However, as with any option, the put does not provide a payoff for the investor unless the ¥ value *at maturity (not the knock in date)* is below the strike level of ¥110. If the option is triggered and the yen is trading below ¥110, then the investor receives *less valuable yen (in US$ terms)* through the redemption. The higher coupon incorporates the premium received for the sale of the barrier option. From the investor's point of view, the structure creates a specific risk to the US$/¥ exchange rate. The specific risk is that the yen weakens beyond ¥130 and remains at that level at the maturity of the note.

---

**Exhibit 13.9**
**FRN Incorporating Equity Barrier Option — Example 1**

The terms of the issue are as follows:

| | |
|---|---|
| Issuer | AAA/AA-rated issuer |
| Amount | Euro 25 million |
| Maturity | 1 year |
| Issue Price | 100% |
| Coupon | 10.00% pa |
| Redemption Price | Redemption will be as follows: |
| | 1. If the index value falls below the barrier index value at any time over the term of the transaction and the final index value is lower than the initial index value at maturity, then calculated as: Amount × Final index value/ initial index value. |
| | 2. If the index value remains above the barrier index value at all times over the term of the transaction, or the final index value is above the initial index value, then 100%. |
| Index Value | Nominated equity index |
| Initial Index Value | The value of the nominated equity index at commencement of the transaction. |
| Barrier Index Value | 75% of the value of the initial index. |
| Final Index Value | The value of a nominated equity index at maturity of the transaction. |

The structure is a variation on the reverse convertible structure[4] and incorporates a barrier equity option.

The investor receives a higher coupon in relation to available market rates through the sale of a knock-in put option on the relevant equity index. The knock-in put option has a strike equal to the current value of the index and an instrike (or trigger) some 25% below the current index level. If the equity trades below 75% of the current equity index level, then the put is activated. However, as with any option, the put does not provide a payoff for the investor unless the index value *at maturity (not the knock in date)* is below the strike level. If the option is triggered and the equity index is trading below the starting value of the index, then the investor receives a redemption amount of less than 100% of the initial investment. The higher coupon incorporates the premium received for the sale of the barrier option. From the investor's point of view, the structure creates a specific risk to the equity index. The specific risk is that the index weakens to a level at least 25% below its starting level and remains at that level at the maturity of the note.

The lower option premium of a barrier option can also be utilized to create very attractive structures. In these structures the lower cost of the option allows the construction of structured notes where a barrier option is embedded within the structure. For example, in the Hong Kong market, in mid-1995, a 1-year at-the-money up and out knock-out call option on the Hang Seng index struck at the current index level with the outstrike (or knock-out level set at 40% above the spot index level) where the premium was rebateable in full upon the option being knocked out had a premium cost around 30 to 35% lower than that on a conventional European option with similar specifications.

This allowed structuring of 1-year equity-index-linked notes on the Hang Seng index with 100% principal guarantee and 100% participation in any appreciation in the index up to the knock-out level of around 50% above the prevailing spot level of the index. If at a time during the life of the note, the index rose to or above the knock-out level, the investor would receive 106% of par at maturity. The structure was specifically targeted at investor's seeking to monetize a view that the Hong Kong stock market would rebound moderately, but concerned about a sustained and sharp decline in the equity market.[5]

**Exhibit 13.10** sets out an example of a structured note that incorporates a purchased equity index option with barrier features.

---

[4] See Chapter 11.

[5] "Equity Linked Bonds" in (September 1995) *AsiaMoney Derivatives Guide* 56-58.

**Exhibit 13.10**
**FRN Incorporating Equity Barrier Option — Example 2**

The terms of the issue are as follows:

| | |
|---|---|
| Issuer | AAA/AA-rated issuer |
| Amount | Euro 25 million |
| Maturity | 1 year |
| Issue Price | 100% |
| Coupon | 0.00% pa |
| Redemption Price | Redemption will be as follows: |
| | 1. If index value trades above barrier index value at any time over the term of the transaction, then 102.50% of amount. |
| | 2. If index value trades below barrier index value at all times over the term of the transaction, then in accordance with the following formula: Amount + Amount × [Maximum (0; ((Final index value/Initial index value) − 1)]. |
| Index Value | Nominated equity index. |
| Initial Index Value | The value of a nominated equity index at commencement of the transaction. |
| Barrier Index Value | 130% of the value of the initial index. |
| Final Index Value | The value of a nominated equity index at maturity of the transaction. |

The structure incorporates a purchased barrier call option with a premium rebate feature. The barrier call option on the equity index has a strike equal to the initial index value with an outstrike (trigger) of 130% of initial value. In the event the option is knocked out, then the premium paid for the option is rebated (paid back to purchaser). Under the structure, the investor uses the available coupon to purchase the option. In the event, the equity index rises above the barrier level (130% of current equity index values) then the call is knocked out and the investor receives only the return of the premium. The investor effectively earns a money-market equivalent return. If the equity index appreciates by less than 30% over the 1-year term of this security, then the investor receives the equity appreciation (up to a maximum return of 29.99%). The structure effectively limits the investor's risk to a decline in the index.

## 4.3 Defined-exercise Option-embedded Notes

Traditional barrier options are activated or extinguished by the behavior of the price of the asset that underlies the actual option contract. Defined exercise (or cross-barrier) options entail option structures where a second variable determines whether the option is knocked-in or knocked-out.[6]

An example of a defined exercise option is an interest rate derivative, such as a cap agreement that pays the difference between the strike and the current market *only if a nominated variable such as a commodity or currency value is below or above a nominated levels.* For example, a 5-year interest rate cap on US$ 3-month LIBOR with a strike level of 6.50% pa that pays out the difference between 3-month LIBOR and the strike level (where LIBOR is above 6.50% pa) if aluminium prices are below US$1,800 per tonne.

The major benefits of the defined exercise option includes:

• The problem of inefficient exercise where the option must be exercised even though it is uneconomic to undertake the exercise.
• The option exercise is conditional such that the option can only be exercised where both conditions are fulfilled, effectively reducing the expected payoff to the seller of the option.
• The option embeds the correlation between the two indexes in addition to the volatility and forward prices of both assets.

This allows both the lowering of the cost of the option or alternatively the creation of a highly specific exposure for the investor in a structured note incorporating this form of exotic option. Indexed or defined callable notes (hereinafter defined callable notes) represent a variety of structured note where a multi-factor option is incorporated in a structured note.

**Exhibit 13.11** sets out an example of a defined callable structured note. The structure of a defined callable note is a bond that is callable if the underlying index is below the strike at the call date. In the above example, the note is callable unless US$ 3-month LIBOR increases some 200 bps above the spot rate over 12 months. The note becomes a 1-year note yielding around 90 to 100 bps over the current 1-year Treasury rate if 3-month LIBOR does not increase at the specified rate. Alternatively, it extends into a 3-year note yielding 5-10 bps over the current 3-year Treasury rate if 3-month LIBOR increases by the requisite amount.

---

[6] See Heynen, Ronald and Kat, Harry "Crossing Barriers" (June 1994) *Risk* vol. 7 no. 6 46-51.

**Exhibit 13.11**
**Indexed or Defined Callable Note**

| | |
|---|---|
| Issuer | AAA-rated issuer |
| Amount | US$100 million |
| Maturity | 3 years |
| Issue Price | 100% |
| Coupon | 7.375% pa payable quarterly on a bond basis (around 90 bps over the 1-year Treasury and 5-10 bps over the 3 year Treasury). |
| Call Date | In one year if the underlying index is below the strike level. |
| Underlying Index | 3-month LIBOR |
| Strike Level | 7.50% pa (200 bps over current 3-month LIBOR of 5.50% pa) |

The typical pattern of this structure is driven by the trade-off between the coupon of the defined callable note and the strike level on the underlying index. The higher coupon that is designed to compensate the investor for the embedded option risk demonstrates the following behavior:

- Where the strike level is low, the note behaves like a 3-year note reflecting the fact that the probability of the strike level being breached is very high (reflecting the fact that the strike level is below the *implied* 3-month LIBOR forward rate). The transaction is one of a 3-year note and a sold deep-out-of-the money defined call option.
- Where the strike level is high, the note behaves like a 1-year note reflecting the low probability of the strike level being attained and the transaction is effectively a 1-year note with a sold deep-out-of-the money defined call option. In this and the previous case, the options have low value resulting in limited yield enhancement with the note interest approximating that for a conventional transaction for the equivalent maturity.
- The maximum coupon is achieved at a strike level set at around 100 to 150 bps over spot 3-month LIBOR where the value of the embedded option is maximized.

The exercise of the call option follows the following pattern:

- The call is driven by the behavior of 3-month LIBOR (the underlying index) rather than *the 2-year Treasury rate* as at the call date.
- This means the call exercise may be *inefficient* in that the issuer may be

forced to prepay the note even where it is economically disadvantageous to do so. This would occur where the 2-year Treasury rate is at a level that does not allow the note to be refinanced at a lower rate.

- *Efficient* exercise is effected only where 3-month LIBOR is above the strike level *and* 2-year Treasury rates are below the coupon of the note.

The most efficient rate at which exercise is effected is dependent on the forward rates for both Treasury rates and 3-month LIBOR, the volatility of the two rates and the correlation between the two rates.

From the viewpoint of the issuer, the call option is transferred through the offsetting sale of a defined purchase call that is designed to generate lower cost funds for the issuer albeit with uncertainty of final maturity—one or three years.

The investor views this type of security as a shorter term (corresponding to the call date) security *with extension risk.*[7] The risk of extension is lowered by setting the strike level that is above the anticipated path of increase in LIBOR over the relevant period. The extension risk can be quantified by considering the interest scenario and expected volatility. The risk of extension is related to the mean and the standard deviation of the distribution of the underlying index (in the above case, 3-month LIBOR). If the distribution is assumed to be log normal, the expected interest rate scenario can be used as the mean of the distribution and volatility as the standard deviation of the distribution. The probability of extension increases with the increase in the mean. In the example considered, if the mean future rate is the forward 3-month LIBOR and volatility is around 15% pa, the probability of extension, that is, an increase in 3-month LIBOR of 200 bps over one year, is around 1.75 to 2%. If the mean LIBOR rate is the implied forward rate rises to much higher levels, then the probability of extension increases quite rapidly.

The extension risk behavior is as follows:

- If the mean is lower than the strike, then higher volatility increases the risk of extension, for example, volatility increases where the mean at current LIBOR will increase the risk of extension. This reflects the fact that the increase in volatility increases the probability of the index finishing above the strike level.
- If the mean is above the strike, then higher volatility may decrease the risk of extension where the mean is at the implied forward rate that will decrease the risk of extension. This reflects the fact the higher mean will dictate that the higher volatility increases the probability of the rate finishing below the strike level.

---

[7] This is similar to the approach with various types of other structured notes (IARs and callable bonds); see Chapter 2, 3, and 6.

A defined callable note can incorporate either European or American exercise rule. In the case of any American style exercise, the note is callable at any time after a noncall period if the underlying index is above the strike price *on any interest payment date prior to maturity.*

The behavior of the coupon on a defined call note comparing the yield-enhancement effect of either exercise feature is quite complex. The coupon on American defined call options appears to *decline* where the strike is set well above the spot 3-month LIBOR level. This lower option premium is reflected in the lower coupon as the investor effectively sells the option embedded in the bond.

The lower option value is evident if the following line of reasoning is considered. This example considers the call behavior in a European and American defined call bond where the strike level is set at higher above spot. If 3 month LIBOR is below strike, both bonds are called. If 3-month LIBOR rises by more than the nominated level, then the notes are not called. The investor in the case of a European defined call note may have a 2-year bond that is trading below par depending on the rise of 2-year rates relative to the rise in 3-month LIBOR rates. However, for the investor in the American-defined call bonds, if rate falls below the strike level, then the bond will be called at par allowing this note to trade at a value above that of the comparable European-defined call bond. This protection feature means that the option value is lower as the continuous exercise feature favours the note holder.

# 5.  Multi-factor Option-embedded Structures

## 5.1  Overview

Multifactor options refer to a special class of exotic options whose primary distinguishing characteristic is that the option payout is based on the relationship between more than one asset. This is in contrast to conventional options that are based on the price or performance of a single asset. Multifactor options have two sources of price risk, dictated by the multiple underlying assets on which the option contract is structured. The essential features characterizing multi factor options as a class are that these structures allow participants in capital markets to:

- Capture the volatility of each of the underlying asset prices.
- Trade/manage the correlation between the prices, as well as the volatility of the assets.

From the perspective of structured note design, the major attraction of multifactor options is that these types of exotic options allow the creation of structures with a number of benefits:

- The creation of specific exposure to a market sector or asset grouping *in combination* through a *single* transaction.

- The creation of structured exposure to a market variable, for example, the relative price movements of two or more assets. This can be structured to either enhance the level of premium income generated to allow higher degrees of yield enhancement or to create customized risk-reward profiles.
- The reprofiling of market asset prices into a second currency through the use of quanto options to provide market price exposures not directly available, for example, an index value in a foreign currency.
- The use of the imperfect correlation between asset price changes to lower the cost of options, for example, basket options, to allow structured note investors more efficient and cost-effective mechanisms for creating exposure to the asset.

In this section, some applications of multifactor options, in particular, basket, exchange, best/worst of and quanto options are considered in their use in structured note transactions.

## 5.2    Basket-linked Notes

Basket-linked notes are structured notes with an embedded basket option. Such structures have often been used to express diversified views on related assets or markets on a cost-effective basis.

A basket option is a type of exotic option whose payout is related to the cumulative performance of a specified basket of underlying assets. Typical examples include baskets of currencies and equity stocks. For example, in the case of a currency basket, an index is created that represents the base currency value of a predetermined portfolio of currency positions. The strike price of the option is set relative to the index allowing the option buyer to hedge against the base currency value of the portfolio falling below a certain point while retaining the potential to gain if the portfolio rises in value.

The key structural feature of the basket option is that it is identical to purchasing an option on the individual basket of components. However, a premium on the basket option should, except in very limited circumstances, be lower than the option premium on the individual components. This lower premium allows basket options to be designed to hedge complex exposures of corporate treasurers or investment fund managers.

The premium of basket options reflects the correlation between the components of the basket. The overall premium is dictated by the level of covariance within the basket components. Depending on the nature of the covariance, basket volatility is in general terms lower than for the individual components. In the event that the correlations between basket components are imperfect, then moves in the value of one component will tend to be neutralized by opposite movements of another. Consequently, unless all the components are highly correlated the option will be cheaper than a series of individual currency options.

Exhibit 13.12 sets out an example of an equity basket-linked structured note.

---

**Exhibit 13.12**
**Equity Basket-linked Note**

The terms of the transaction are as follows:

| | |
|---|---|
| Issuer | AAA/AA-rated issuer |
| Amount | US$20 million |
| Maturity | 5 years |
| Issue Price | 86.26% |
| Coupon | 0.00% |
| Redemption | 100% plus basket appreciation factor. |
| Basket Appreciation Factor | Amount × Maximum [0; ((Final basket price − Initial basket price)/Initial basket price)] |
| Basket | The basket consists of one each of the following shares: Novartis; Roche; Zeneca; BP; Royal Dutch/Shell; ICI; Merck; Exxon; Mobil. |
| Initial Basket Price | Refers to the sum of the prices of each of the nine stocks at the commencement date of the transaction converted into US$ at the spot exchange rate. |
| Final Basket Price | Refers to the sum of the prices of each of the nine stocks at the maturity date of the transaction converted into US$ at the maturity exchange rate. |
| Spot Exchange Rate | The spot exchange rate between the currency of the share and the US$ as at the commencement of the transaction. |
| Maturity Exchange Rate | The spot exchange rate between the currency of the share and the US$ as at the maturity of the transaction. |

The structure of the transaction provides the investor with an exposure to a basket of pharmaceutical and oil/chemical shares. The investors purchases the following:

• A zero-coupon bond.
• A European exercise call option on the basket of stocks.

The European exercise basket option includes exposure to nine stocks in a number of markets traded in different currencies. The initial value of the basket is based on the current price of the stock converted into US$ at the spot exchange rate at the commencement of the transaction. The final value of the basket is based on the value of the stocks at maturity converted at the *maturity* exchange rate.

The major features of the option structure includes:

*   Exposure to the currency values in which the individual stocks are quoted or traded.
*   The lower cost of the option reflecting the imperfect correlation between the stock in the basket (in particular, the impact of both currency and stock prices, which should ensure imperfect correlations).

The structure guarantees the investor a minimum income of 3.00% pa and allows participation in any appreciation in the basket of shares. The investor's principal is guaranteed. The major advantage for the investor is that the cheaper cost of the option enables creation of a higher level of exposure to the underlying stocks for a given amount of forgone interest income. The disadvantage is that the underperformance of any one stock or currency in the basket will impair returns.

A number of variations on the basic structure are feasible. These include embedding call features or quanto options (see discussion below) within the structure. **Exhibit 13.13** sets out an example of a quanto-ed equity basket-linked structured note. **Exhibit 13.14** on page 745 sets an example of an equity linked basket that combines a basket option with an embedded interest rate call. **Exhibit 13.15** on page 746 sets out an example of a basket-linked note structure utilized to express investors' views on European interest rate markets.

**Exhibit 13.13**
**Quanto Equity Basket-linked Note**

The terms of the transaction are as follows:

| | |
|---|---|
| Issuer | AAA/AA-rated issuer |
| Amount | US$20 million |
| Maturity | 2 years |
| Issue Price | 100% |

| Coupon | 0.00% |
|---|---|
| Redemption | 100% plus basket appreciation factor. |
| Basket Appreciation Factor | Amount × 0.70 × Maximum [0; ((Final basket price – Initial basket price)/Initial basket price)] Basket The basket consists of one of the following shares: Lloyds TSB; Bank of Scotland; ABN-Amro; ING; Paribas; AXA-UAP; Deutsche Bank; Commerzbank; Allianz; UBS; Credit Suisse; BBV. |
| Initial Basket Price | Refers to the sum of the prices of each of the 12 stocks at the commencement date of the transaction converted into US$ at the spot exchange rate. |
| Final Basket Price | Refers to the sum of the prices of each of the 12 stocks at the maturity date of the transaction converted into US$ at the fixed exchange rate. |
| Spot Exchange Rate | The spot exchange rate between the currency of the share and the US$ as at the commencement of the transaction. |
| Fixed Exchange Rate | The spot exchange rate between the currency of the share and the US$ as at the commencement of the transaction. |

The structure set out above is similar to that described in **Exhibit 13.12**. The major differences are:

- Exposure is to a basket of UK/European banking and financial sector stocks.
- The exposure to the currency in which the share is traded is eliminated through embedding quanto options within the basket. This has the effect of allowing any appreciation in the stocks being translated back into the base currency (US$) *at a fixed exchange rate*. This enables the investor to eliminate any currency exposure leaving pure equity exposure.
- The cost of the quanto options reduces the available return to the investor. This is in the form of a zero interest return although principal is guaranteed. The level of participation in any appreciation in the index is also reduced to 70%.

**Exhibit 13.14**
**Callable Equity Basket-linked Note**

The terms of the transaction are as follows:

| | |
|---|---|
| Issuer | AAA/AA-rated issuer |
| Amount | US$20 million |
| Maturity | 7 years |
| Issue Price | 100% |
| Coupon | 0.00% |
| Redemption | 100% plus basket appreciation factor |
| Basket Appreciation Factor | Amount $\times$ 1.00 $\times$ Maximum [0; ((Final basket price – Initial basket price)/Initial basket price)] The basket consists of the following: |

| Country | Index | Weighting (%) |
|---|---|---|
| UK | FTSE | 7.50 |
| Germany | DAX | 7.50 |
| France | CAC | 7.50 |
| The Netherlands | EOE | 5.00 |
| Italy | MIB | 5.00 |
| Spain | IBEX | 2.50 |
| **Europe** | | **35.00** |
| Japan | TOPIX | 20.00 |
| Australia | AOI | 10.00 |
| Hong Kong | Hang Seng | 5.00 |
| **Asia-Pacific** | | **35.00** |
| USA | S&P 500 | 30.00 |
| **USA** | | **30.00** |
| **Total** | | **100.00** |

| | |
|---|---|
| Initial Basket Price | Refers to the value of the basket at the commencement date of the transaction converted into US$ at the spot exchange rate. |
| Final Basket Price | Refers to the value of the basket at the maturity date of the transaction converted into US$ at the maturity exchange rate. |
| Spot Exchange Rate | The spot exchange rate between the currency of the share and the US$ as at the commencement of the transaction. |
| Maturity Exchange Rate | The spot exchange rate between the currency of the share and the US$ as at the maturity of the transaction. |

| Call Options | The issuer has the right to call the Note as follows: |
| --- | --- |

| Call Date | Call Price |
| --- | --- |
| 3 years | 135% |
| 5 years | 170% |

The structure set out above is similar to that described in **Exhibit 13.12**. The major differences are that:

• Exposure is to a basket of global equity market indexes.
• Exposure to the currency in which the share is traded is not hedged.

The interesting feature in this structure is the call option. The call option if exercised would provide a yield to the investor as follows:

• 3 years — 10.52% pa
• 5 years — 11.20% pa.

In both cases, the return to the investor is well in excess of returns available on fixed interest securities for comparable maturities.

   The presence of the call means that the bond will be called if the underlying basket appreciates by more than 35% after three years (70% after five years). In effect, the investor has bought a Bermudan call option (7-year maturity with strike at initial basket price with exercise dates after three, five and seven years) and sold a Bermudan basket call option (5-year maturity with a strike at 130% of initial basket price at the first exercise date of three years and a strike at 170% of initial basket price at its 5-year maturity). The effective call spreads at three and five years have the effect of truncating the return to the investor. The call options described are complex and difficult to price and hedge. This relates to the path-dependent nature of the option payoffs.

---

**Exhibit 13.15**
**Interest Rate Basket-linked Note**

The transaction structure described emerged in the aftermath of the September 1992 European exchange rate mechanism ("ERM") crisis and the subsequent (in August 1993) widening of the ERM bands. Against a background of general expectations of lower or declining rates, albeit with some volatility particularly in the higher yielding European community currencies, a number of investors sought to purchase structured notes that created a diversified view on declines in European rates. The diversified structure, embedded in the basket-linked note, was designed to lower the risk of market events *in any one market* affecting the investors strategy.

The terms of the transaction are as follows:

| | |
|---|---|
| Issuer | AAA-rated institution |
| Amount | US$100 million |
| Maturity | 3 years |
| Issue Price | 100% |
| Coupon | 5.25% pa payable annually |
| Redemption | 100% + 15 × (Average of basket at commencement − Average of basket at maturity) |
| Basket | Swedish Kroner (Skr), Italian lira (L), Spanish Pesetas (Pta) and French francs (FFr) at 3-year constant maturity swap rates. |

The principal of the note described pays out the average of Skr, L, FFr and FFR 3-year rates. The rates used are the CMS rates. Each basis point fall of the basket average increases the redemption payment by 15 bps. The structure effectively combines a bond with the forward purchase by the investor of the basket. There is an embedded option to prevent the redemption from becoming negative.

The return to the investor in this transaction is driven by the path of the selected basket rates and reflects:

- The actual movements in each yield curve relative to the implied forward 3-year rates in each currency.
- The degree of risk sought. The leverage factor included in this case gears the investor's return, presumably reflecting the desire to enhance sensitivity to market movements. A more risk-averse structure could be engineered to guarantee a minimum redemption amount. The minimum redemption is incorporated by arranging the purchase of a put on the price of the basket (call on yield) to offset the risk of rising rates. The purchase put converts the transaction into a synthetic call purchase.
- The currency protection of the structure, whereby all payments are in US$. In effect, the incorporation of a quanto option to eliminate the currency risk of the structure.

The basic structure incorporates no optionality. However, a variation on the structure embeds a call option on the basket. The coupon level is reduced to finance the purchase of a call option that provides asymmetric exposure to a fall in interest rates on a diversified basis. The basket option pricing would reflect the impact of volatility of the individual currency CMS rates and the correlations between the changes. The volatility of the average will be highest for highly correlated rates. A decline in correlations will reduce the volatility. This means that the basket volatility will be substantially a function of the degree of correlation between the basket elements that will influence the option pricing. The design of the basket that incorporates interest rate markets in disparate currencies is designed to reduce the correlation to effectively lower the cost of the option to allow a higher level of effective exposure to the basket to be created at a lower cost.

### 5.3    Worst-of/Best-of or Exchange Structures

Worst-of or best-of options and exchange options are sometimes combined with fixed-rate bonds to create return profiles for investors related to the *relative price performance* of two or more assets.

A worst-of/best-of option is an option contract whose payout depends on the relative performance on two assets. In a typical structure, the option contract pays out the maximum (minimum) price performance as between two assets in the case of a call (put) option. The option structure can be extended to more than two assets. An exchange option specifically refers to an option structure whereby the purchaser has the right to exchange one asset for another.

An example of a multi-asset-based note may entail using a worst-of multi-asset option to provide additional yield enhancement in a structured note. Assume a 12-month structured note that has embedded a put option on a particular stock with a strike set at 90% of the current stock price. The put option premium increases the yield on this note to around 12% pa (compared to a market yield of around 6% pa). A similar structured note that has an embedded put (at the same 90% of current stock price strike) on a second less volatile stock will yield around 9% pa. However, assume the investor is willing to embed a worst-of multi-asset option. Under this structure, the investor can under the note be exercised *if either of the two stocks* were to be in-the-money at maturity. The increased risk assumed by the investor is compensated by the higher option premium received that enables the return on the note to be increased to around 15.00% pa.

**Exhibit 13.16** sets out an example of a structure with an embedded outperformance option. **Exhibit 13.17** sets out an example of a structure with an embedded exchange option.

**Exhibit 13.16**
**Out Performance Option-embedded Note**

The terms of the structure are as follows:

| | |
|---|---|
| Issuer | AAA/AA-rated issuer |
| Amount | L100 billion |
| Maturity | 3 years |
| Issue Price | 100.00% |
| Coupon | 0.00% |
| Redemption | Amount + (Amount × Adjustment factor) |
| Adjustment Factor | Maximum [0; Final stock price/Initial stock price − Final index price/Initial index price. |
| Initial Stock Price | Price of nominated stock at commencement date. |
| Final Stock Price | Price of nominated stock at maturity date. |
| Initial Index Price | Price of MIB index at commencement date. |
| Final Index Price | Price of MIB index at maturity date. |

The structure provides a return to the investor based on the superior performance of the nominated stock relative to changes in the general market index. This will provide a payoff irrespective of whether the stock and the market increase or decrease *in absolute value terms*.

---

**Exhibit 13.17**
**Exchange Option-embedded Note**

Consider the Double Index Bull ("DIB") note, which is suited to investors who believe that two indices will rally over a given term. The note typically pays no coupon and has a redemption value linked to the lowest value of the two indices at maturity. More exactly, the redemption value is:

Gearing × Min. [Index (1), Index (2)]

Where:

Index (1) and Index (2) are the dollar values of the two indices on the maturity date of the note. Gearing is the degree of leverage of the note.

Generally, the two indices are standardised to have identical forward values.

This structure is closely related to the best-of note, whose redemption value is linked to the highest value of the two indices and defined as:

Gearing × Max. [Index (1), Index (2)]

The important difference between the two notes lies in the ownership of the embedded option. This may be seen by restating the redemption profile for each. In the case of the DIB note, the redemption payoff may be decomposed as follows:

Gearing × Min. [Index (1), Index (2)] =
Gearing × [Index (1) – Max. (Index (1) – Index (2), 0)]

Likewise, the payoff of the best-of note may be decomposed as follows:

Gearing × Min. [Index (1), Index (2)] =
Gearing *[Index (1) + Max. (Index (2) – Index (1), 0)]

Embedded in the DIB note is the sale, on the part of the investor, of an exchange option. The option premium is used to increase the gearing of the note. On the other hand, the best-of note embeds the purchase of an exchange option. The option premium, in this case, decreases the gearing of the note. As a result, the DIB note will pay in excess of 100% of the upside of the minimum of the two indices, whereas the best-of note will pay less than 100% of the maximum of the two indices.

For example, consider an investor who has a bullish view on both oil and gold. In such a case, it is possible to structure a note with a US$20 million face value and 3-year term, which pays no coupon and has a redemption value of 107% of the minimum value of 44,444 ounces of gold and 1,975,268 barrels of oil. The payoff of the note for various gold and oil scenarios is provided in the Table below.

**Redemption Amount (US$ million)**

| Oil Price US$ /Barrel) | Price of Gold (US$ per ounce) | | | | | | | | | |
|---|---|---|---|---|---|---|---|---|---|---|
| | 375 | 400 | 425 | 450 | 475 | 500 | 525 | 550 | 575 | 600 |
| 16 | 17.83 | 18.41 | 18.41 | 18.41 | 18.41 | 18.41 | 18.41 | 18.41 | 18.41 | 18.41 |
| 17 | 17.83 | 19.02 | 19.56 | 19.56 | 19.56 | 19.56 | 19.56 | 19.56 | 19.56 | 19.56 |
| 18 | 17.83 | 19.02 | 20.21 | 20.71 | 20.71 | 20.71 | 20.71 | 20.71 | 20.71 | 20.71 |
| 19 | 17.83 | 19.02 | 20.21 | 21.40 | 21.86 | 21.86 | 21.86 | 21.86 | 21.86 | 21.86 |
| 20 | 17.83 | 19.02 | 20.21 | 21.40 | 22.59 | 23.01 | 23.01 | 23.01 | 23.01 | 23.01 |
| 21 | 17.83 | 19.02 | 20.21 | 21.40 | 22.59 | 23.78 | 24.16 | 24.16 | 24.16 | 24.16 |
| 22 | 17.83 | 19.02 | 20.21 | 21.40 | 22.59 | 23.78 | 24.97 | 24.97 | 25.31 | 25.31 |
| 23 | 17.83 | 19.02 | 20.21 | 21.40 | 22.59 | 23.78 | 24.97 | 26.16 | 26.46 | 26.46 |

The investor receives full principal repayment if the price of oil per barrel is greater than US$17.38 and the price of gold per ounce is greater than US$420.57. For an investor who is bullish on both indices, this structure offers a higher expected return than an equal weighted portfolio in the two indices. Specifically, this transaction will provide a return of 17.70% if both indices rally 10%.

Source: Broer, Sydney, Durland, Michael, Engel, Mark, and Vohra, Anil "Double Index Bull Note" *IFR Swaps Weekly* Issue 66 (April 27, 1994): 10.

## 5.4  Quanto Notes

### 5.4.1  Overview

Quanto options refer to an option on an uncertain underlying amount where the amount being hedged is driven by movements in a separate financial market variable. A quanto option is in essence a derivative product denominated in a currency other than that of an underlying asset to which exposure is sought to be hedged. Quanto options usually refer to quantity-adjusting options based on the variable notional principal of the contract.

Major examples of this class of product include:

• Currency-hedged equity options or equity market indexes.
• Currency-hedged fixed income products.
• Currency-hedged differentials or spreads between various equity and/or fixed income markets.

The classical example of a quanto option relates to an investor (base currency US$) seeking to invest in the Japanese stock market. A quanto option in this case would entail an option on the Nikkei stock index denominated in US$ whose payoff is characterised by the total return on the Nikkei stock index converted to US$ at an agreed exchange rate, say, the spot exchange rate prevailing at the start of the option contract. The structure allows the investor to create an exposure to the underlying asset free from exchange risk.

The critical element in this concept is that the foreign exchange exposure component of this transaction is variable. The amount to be hedged will depend on the return on the Nikkei index. Consequently, the option writer must convert the returns from the index from its original currency (yen) into US$ as at each payment date. Traditional forward contracts cannot be used as the quantity required to be hedged is unknown. The quantity to be hedged, which must match the receipts from the index, must reflect the correlation between changes in value in the stock index (the Nikkei) and fluctuations in the value of the yen against the dollar. An additional feature of the contract will be that if the forward market is at a premium or discount to spot in currencies, the shape of the forward curve must also be taken into account and the forwards transacted will be typically off market.

The economics of quanto products is driven by the capacity of this instrument to utilize the correlation between the currency and the underlying asset return to create a total hedge of the underlying risk profile. This hedge structure has two primary benefits:

• It creates a specific exposure to the underlying asset return free of currency risk.
• It overcomes the deficiency of traditional hedging instruments in terms of an uncertain notional amount to be hedged.

Quanto options have been used in a variety of formats such as those described. In the context of structured notes, the incorporation of quanto option is primarily utilized to re-profile asset returns in currency terms including:

• The combination of quanto options with call options on other assets (for example, foreign equity) to create customised exposures to equity market movements in the investor's chosen currency.
• Index differential note structures that entail notes with embedded differential swaps that use quanto options to hedge the currency risk on interest differentials between money market rates in two currencies.[8]

An example of the first structure is set out in Chapter 11. The concept of index differential notes is discussed below.

### 5.4.2    Index Differential Notes

Index differential structures are utilized by investors seeking to increase returns on money market interest-related investment assets. Asset managers willing to take positions on interest rate differentials between currencies have utilized

---

[8]    See Das, Satyajit (1994) *Swaps and Financial Derivatives*; LBC Information Services, Sydney; McGraw-Hill, Chicago at 363-387; Das, Satyajit "Differential Swaps — Differential Strip-Down" (May 1992) *Risk* vol. 5 no. 6 65-72; Das, Satyajit "Differential Operators" (July-August 1992) *Risk* vol. 5 no. 7 51-53; Das, Satyajit "Differential Swaps" in Hotta, Kensuke and Dattatreya, Ravi E. (editors) (1994) *Recent Advances in Interest Rate and Currency Swaps*: New Products and Strategies; Probus Publishing, Chicago; Das, Satyajit "Differential/ Quanto Swaps" in Parekh, Naru (editor) (1995) *Financial Engineering: Risk Management in Practice*; Euromoney Publications, London; Das, Satyajit "Differential Swaps" in Jarrow, Robert (editor) (1995) *Over The Rainbow*; Risk Publications, London.

differential swaps or notes with embedded index differential swaps for the following reasons:

- Enhance returns on investment assets in currencies where money market rates have dropped to relatively low levels, such as US$ short-term investments in 1991-1993, in yen in the period since 1995, and in Euros and other European currencies in 1999.
- Take positions in interest rate differentials *as between any two currencies* without incurring currency exposures. For example, an investment manager with a primarily US$ investment portfolio could seek to take advantage of anticipated movements in the differential between £ and yen interest rates by entering into a £/¥ differential swap (where all payments are in US$) to create the required exposure to £/¥ interest differentials.

The basic building block of all index differential structures is the index differential swap. The differential swap structure is designed to allow financial managers to capture existing and expected differentials in floating or money market rates between alternative currencies without incurring any foreign exchange exposure. In a typical differential swap, the party entering into the transaction will:

- Agree to receive payment in a particular currency on a specific principal amount for a specified term at the prevailing floating money market rate in that currency.
- In exchange, it will make payments on the same principal amount, in the same currency for the same term based on the prevailing floating money market rate in an alternative or different currency.

The major features of this arrangement include:

- Both payments and receipts (which are based on the same notional principal amount) are on a floating rate basis with the rate being reset at specified intervals (usually quarterly or semi-annually).
- All payments under the transaction are made in the counterparty's nominated currency thereby eliminating any foreign exchange exposure.
- Consistent with its status as a single currency transaction, no exchange of principal amounts is required.

**Exhibit 13.18** sets out the structure of a standard index differential swap. **Appendix A** to this chapter sets out the detailed structure of index differential swap and **Appendix B** sets out the methodology for pricing these transactions.

Investors typically would enter into a differential swap whereby it would receive the higher money market rate (DM 6-month LIBOR minus differential swap spread (in US$) in the example used) and pay the lower money market rate (US$ 6-month LIBOR in the above example). Under this structure, the US$ 6-

month LIBOR flows would be matched by the return accruing to the investor from its underlying US$ investment asset. The overall return to the investor would be based on DM 6-month LIBOR rates. Accordingly, the investor would benefit from utilising the differential swaps where DM 6-month LIBOR minus the differential swap margin exceeded US$ 6-month LIBOR over the life of the transaction. **Exhibit 13.19** sets out an example of a differential swap structure that can be utilized by an asset manager.

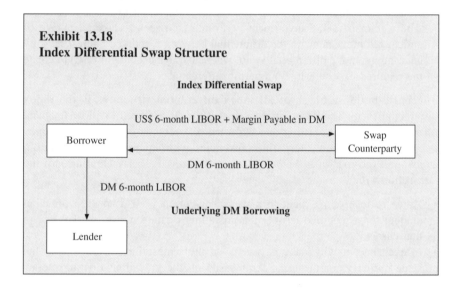

**Exhibit 13.18**
**Index Differential Swap Structure**

Index Differential Swap

US$ 6-month LIBOR + Margin Payable in DM

Borrower

Swap
Counterparty

DM 6-month LIBOR

DM 6-month LIBOR

**Underlying DM Borrowing**

Lender

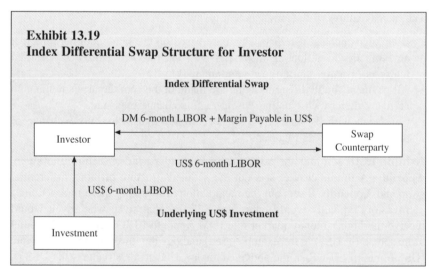

**Exhibit 13.19**
**Index Differential Swap Structure for Investor**

Index Differential Swap

DM 6-month LIBOR + Margin Payable in US$

Investor

Swap
Counterparty

US$ 6-month LIBOR

US$ 6-month LIBOR

**Underlying US$ Investment**

Investment

As an alternative to entering into the differential swap, investors can benefit from the structural advantages of this type of transaction by purchasing securities where the differential swap cash flow profile is embedded into the bond to provide the anticipated interest rate differential benefit.

A number of security issues (primarily private placements and a few public issues) have been undertaken with embedded differential swap characteristics. In a typical issue, the borrower issues securities (say, in US$) that carry an interest coupon in a high short-term rate currency (say, DM 6-month LIBOR minus a spread). The borrower, in turn, enters into a differential swap with a bank to convert its payments stream linked to DM 6-month LIBOR to a US$ 6-month LIBOR-related payment at a margin below its normal funding costs. **Exhibit 13.20** sets out an example of this type of structure.

Differential swap transactions can also be embedded in inverse FRN issues. **Exhibit 13.21** sets out an example of this structure. In such a transaction, the investor would receive an interest rate on its investment of, say, 18.00% pa minus US$ LIBOR plus a margin, with all payments being in A$. The issuer of the A$ Reverse FRN would convert its borrowing onto a conventional basis by entering into two swaps:

- A differential swap under which it pays US$ LIBOR plus a margin and receives A$ LIBOR (all payments in A$).
- A conventional A$ interest rate swap on *double the total amount of the face value of the reverse FRN* whereby it receives a fixed A$ rate (say, 2 × 9.50%pa = 19.00% pa) and pays A$ LIBOR (2 × A$ LIBOR).

The result of these swaps would be to leave the issuer with a borrowing (equivalent to the face value of the FRN) at a margin under A$ LIBOR (in this example, 1.00% pa).

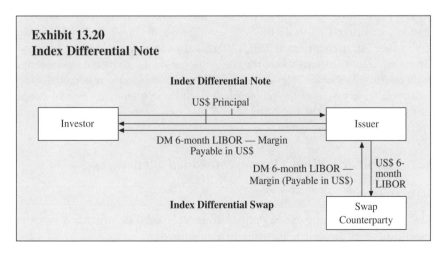

**Exhibit 13.20**
**Index Differential Note**

**Index Differential Note**

US$ Principal

Investor

DM 6-month LIBOR — Margin
Payable in US$

Issuer

DM 6-month LIBOR —
Margin (Payable in US$)

US$ 6-
month
LIBOR

**Index Differential Swap**

Swap
Counterparty

**Exhibit 13.21**
**Inverse FRN with Embedded Index Differential Structure**

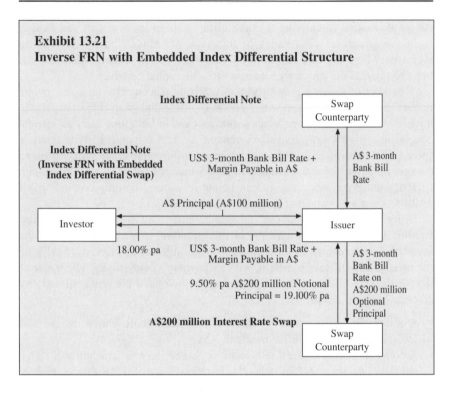

A central aspect of differential swaps is that entry into these types of transactions is predicated on the counterparty assuming an interest rate risk position across currencies. The transaction is by its inherent nature not free of risk as changes in interest rate differentials will increase the cost of borrowing or reduce the return to investors utilising such transactions. Differential swaps can by their very nature be utilized to trade the shape of the yield curve as between two currencies. For example, an existing differential swap position can be traded and unwound to lock in gains where the change in the yield differential (in the long-term interest rates in the relevant currencies that determine the differential swap margin) alter in favour of the counterparty. An issue in trading differential swaps is the relatively higher bid-offer spread that may increase the cost of such trading in these instruments.

# 6.    Payoff Modified Option-embedded Structures

## 6.1    Overview

One of major types of exotic options commonly used in structured notes is payoff-modified structures, particularly digital options.

Digital options are options whose payouts are discontinuous. Normal options have smooth payout profiles (that is, the further the option is in the money, the higher the option payoff to the purchaser). In contrast, digital options have fixed payouts, the payout being an agreed amount or nothing, providing certain conditions are met. In the typical structure of a digital option, if the strike price is reached, the payouts are fixed predetermined amounts no matter by how much the option is in the money. The simplest structure for a digital option entails a path independent structure whereby a call (put) pays nothing if the underlying asset price finishes below (above) the strike price or pays a predetermined constant amount if the underlying asset price finishes above (below) the strike price. These options are often referred to as cash-or-nothing or all-or-nothing options.

The payoff of a digital option structure is set out in **Exhibit 13.22**. The structure indicates the particular payoff profile of this option contract highlighting the truncated payoff (representing the digitised payout amount) and the limited loss profile represented by the premium paid.

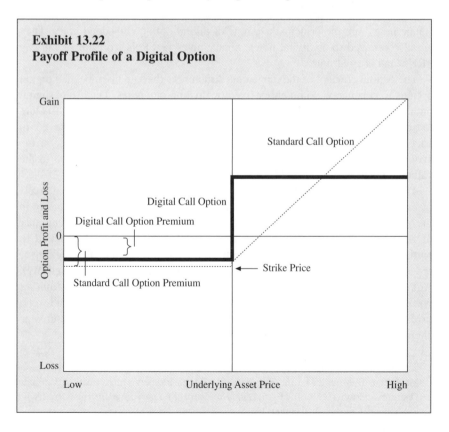

**Exhibit 13.22**
**Payoff Profile of a Digital Option**

The structure is particularly attractive to option grantors or writers because the digital structure means a known and limited loss in the event the option is exercised. This known loss profile makes these options ideal for use in structured note transactions as they allow easy quantification of the loss profile, allowing minimum return or maximum loss values in relation to principal risked to be determined.

For the purchaser, the major advantage of a digital option is that the option payoff is a known constant amount. This amount may be related to some fundamental amount related to the underlying hedging transaction. In addition, it overcomes the problem of a purchaser where the option expires at or slightly in the money and the resultant payoff does not cover the cost of the option premium paid to purchase the option contract. A number of examples of structured notes incorporating digital and power options are considered below.

## 6.2   Digital Option-embedded Notes

### 6.2.1   Range Notes - Concept

Range notes[9] are the principal example of digital option embedded notes. They are also referred to as digital notes, binary notes or FRNs, corridor or fairway FRNs, and accrual notes.

The central concept of the range note structure is the sale of embedded digital options to enhance yield on either fixed or floating rate notes. The use of digital options with their defined loss profile allows the customisation of the structure to exactly attune the level of risk relative to the return enhancement achieved. In particular, these structures are used to monetize investor expectations on the *evolution or path* of future asset prices or value, particularly in relation to the values implied by the current forward rates.

The structure evolved in an environment characterised by low nominal levels of interest rates, positive (often steep) yield curves, and significant volatility in the term structure of the interest rates. The period was characterised by a number of financial variables that appeared, at least for a period, to be locked in particular trading ranges (in part through the actions of central bank's seeking to reduce the impact of volatility on investment and macro-economic activity). Against this background, a number of investors, primarily money market portfolio managers (experiencing unprecedented pressures on their return levels) invested in range notes, which emerged with a variety of other structures as alternative forms of investment for asset managers.

---

[9]   See Smithson, Charles (1995) *Managing Financial Risk — 1995 Yearbook*; Chase Manhattan Bank at 134-136; Das, Satyajit "Range Floaters" in Konishi, Atsuo and Dattatreya, Ravi (Editors) (1996) *The Handbook of Derivative Instruments*; Irwin Publishing, Chicago at Chapter 12.

## 6.2.2    Range Note — Structure

### 6.2.2.1    Structural Features

The most common structure range note is a FRN with an embedded range feature. The basic concept of a range FRN embodies a number of elements:

- It is a floating rate security paying a return relative to the normal money market index (for example, US$ LIBOR).
- The range FRN typically pays an above-market or richer coupon than conventional FRNs.
- The coupon payment on the FRN is conditional on a specific financial market variable fixing within a set range as at specific points in time.

The last two elements require additional explanation. The financial market variables that were initially utilized in range FRNs were typically interest rates (see discussion below). Under this arrangement, the range FRN would pay an above-market coupon relative to LIBOR only for each day that LIBOR fixed within a set range.

The timing and denomination of the range vary as between transactions:

- The LIBOR range is typically set at the outset of the issue, although there are variations on this (see discussion below).
- The actual dates on which LIBOR fixes must be within the set range also vary. There are two general formulas:
    1. **Periodic set** — the relevant financial market variable, say, LIBOR, must set within the specified range, at the start of each reset period that coincides with the interest period on the FRN—three or six months.
    2. **Daily set** — where the financial market variable fixes are on a daily basis. On each day that the financial market variable sets outside the rate, the coupon on the range FRN is 0% pa. In contrast, when the financial market variable sets within the rate range on the relevant day, the range FRN pays the normal above-market coupon relative to LIBOR.

The terms of a typical transaction are set out in **Exhibit 13.23**.

---

**Exhibit 13.23**
**Interest Rate Range Note**

| | |
|---|---|
| Issuer | AAA/AA-rated issuer |
| Amount | US$100 million |
| Term | 2 years |
| Issue Price | 100 |

| Redemption Price | 100 |
| Coupon | [3-month US$ LIBOR + Margin% pa] × Accrual factor/Number of days. |
| Margin | 1.00% pa |
| Number of Days | 360 |
| Accrual Factor | The number of days during the relevant interest rate period that US$ 3-month LIBOR is fixed within the range set out below: |

| Period | Maximum Rate (% pa) | Minimum Rate (% pa) |
| --- | --- | --- |
| 0-6   months | 4.00 | 3.00 |
| 6-12   months | 4.75 | 3.00 |
| 12-18 months | 5.50 | 3.00 |
| 18-24 months | 6.00 | 3.00 |

In the case of a range FRN structure based on the periodic set approach, the coupon *for the full interest rate period* would be set at either the nominated coupon or zero. The rate would depend on whether the relevant benchmark rate would be set within or outside the range as at a specific date at the start of the interest rate period.

In the case when counterparties wish to gain the cash flow and return profile of a range FRN without the necessity of purchasing the underlying security, this return profile can be constructed through an "accrual swap". Under this type of swap structure, the swap trader may pay an investor a floating rate (say, LIBOR) plus a margin in return for receiving fixed rates or floating rates when a nominated financial market variable sets within a specified range. This would enable an existing investor to swap either a fixed or floating rate asset into a range FRN structure. Alternatively, a liability manager could structure a swap where his or her LIBOR receipts under a fixed-floating interest rate swap have a pay-off profile matching that of a range FRN. In effect, this lowers the fixed cost of paying under an interest rate swap to seek to manage the cost of the organisation's debt portfolio.

### 6.2.2.2   Reverse Engineering

By a process of reverse engineering the transaction, its component parts are easily discernible. The range FRN consists of:

- A conventional FRN.
- Sold digital options on the relevant financial market variable (in the above example, US$ 3-month LIBOR rates). In effect, the investor sells a series of

digital options. The digital options are sold either on specific dates during the term of the Note (the periodic set structure) or daily (the daily set structure). The above-market coupon effectively equates to the premium captured for sale of the digital option. The loss of coupon on the days that the relevant financial market variable is outside the range nominated represents the fixed or digitised payout under the digital option that is owing from the investor to the purchaser of the digital option.

The objectives of both issuers and investors are relatively clear. The issuer will typically seek to be insulated usually via the arranger or another derivatives dealer from the exposure under the digital option. This will require the issuer to onsell the digital option and receive a premium for the sale. Typically, the proceeds received from the sale will lower the cost of the issuer to or below its target borrowing costs.

From the perspective of the investor, the major attraction of range FRNs is the higher coupon. The higher coupon is designed to increase portfolio earnings with the capture of the premium for the sale of the digital option. The economic logic behind investment in range FRNs assumes that rates will continue to move in a relatively narrow range (a state that biologists refer to as "homeostasis"— whereby organisms regulate their activities such that their temperature does not fluctuate wildly).[10] Investors derive their enhanced return by creating digital options that reflect this underlying economic view.

The second order economic logic underlying the investment is the fact that the value in the digital option derives from the pattern of forward rates implied in the yield curve. In part, if the investor is of the view that the implied forward rates are likely to be higher than actual realized short-term rates, then the value transferred as a result of the sale of the digital option will be greater than the realized value of the options. Under this approach, the investors who expect that the forward rates implied by the curve are higher than actual likely realized rates can structure range FRNs that are designed to capture the spread between its expectations and the forward curve.

Investors in range note structures often derive a breakeven point of the strategy. This is calculated in terms of the number of days that the underlying market variable has to stay within the range for the instrument to return at least the prevailing money market interest rate for the relevant period. For example in the example set out in **Exhibit 13.23**, assuming US$ 3-month LIBOR is trading at 3.50% pa, the breakeven point would be as follows:

Breakeven number of days = (US$3 month LIBOR rate × Number of days in interest rate period)/(US$ 3-month LIBOR plus Margin) = (3.50 × 91)/(4.50) = 71 days (or 78% of the period)

---

[10] See "Fashion and Homeostasis" (March 2, 1994) *IFR Swaps Weekly* Issue 58.

## 6.3   Pricing And Hedging

Pricing and hedging of range FRNs revolves around the decomposition of the structure into its components. The pricing process requires a two stage approach:

- The conversion of the FRN component into a fixed-rate instrument (either through swapping the floating rate payments to fixed or, alternatively, by utilizing FRA's /futures to convert the future payments to fixed payments).
- The valuation of the digital option itself.

The conversion of the floating rate payment into a fixed-rate dollar equivalent is needed to create a net uniform series (NUS) of cash flows (that is, the dollar amount of the FRN payments as implied by the current yield curve are calculated). This process is necessary to arrive at the exact digitised payout under the digital option that will be specified as the payout. In a number of structures, the corridor structure entails a fixed-rate bond in which case the payments are known in dollar amounts eliminating the need for this step in the pricing.

The pricing of the digital option is more complex. The premium on a digital option is predicated on:

- The fact that the payoff of the digital option tends to be switched completely one way or the other, depending on whether underlying asset price satisfies that condition.
- The payoff under the option provided it is in-the-money is fixed and discreet. This is in contrast to the payoff profile under a normal option that is continuous and variable in proportion to asset price changes provided the option expires in-the-money.
- The value of the option derives from two specific probabilities:
  1. The probability that the option will expire in-the-money.
  2. Whether the asset price, if the option expires in-the-money, will be at a level above or below a level whereby the intrinsic value of the option exceeds or is lower than the digitised payout.

It is possible to utilize a variation on Black-Scholes to value a digital option. Several authors have shown how to value digitised options in a Black-Scholes environment.[11]

The dynamics of the premium for digital options are dependent on the interaction of the following variables:

---

[11]   Rubinstein, Mark and Reiner, Eric "Unscrambling the Binary Code" (October 1991) *Risk* vol. 4 no. 9 75-83; see also Turnbull, Stuart "The Price is Right" (April 1992) *Risk* vol. 5 no. 4 56-57; Kat, Harry M. "Contingent Premium Options" (Summer 1994) *Journal of Derivatives* 44-54.

- The digitized payout, which is a function of the coupon on the debt security (as the payout cannot be larger than this amount).
- The premium value of the digital options, which is a function of:
  1. The nominated range.
  2. The volatility of the underlying asset (in the example, interest rates).
  3. The pattern of forward prices of the asset (in the case of interest rates, the shape of the forward yield curve as implied by the current term structure of interest rates). This reflects the option value insofar as the options may be further in- or out-of-the-money.

In the context of range notes, the value of the embedded digital options is impacted upon primarily by the strike level and the volatility of the underlying index. The two factors act in concert to influence the value of the option.

For example, if the strike level is set *below* the implied forward levels of the index, the value of the digital option and the incremental spread that can be generated from investing the premium to enhance the coupon is low. This reflects the fact that the structure of implied forward rates imply the digital option will not be exercised and the range note will pay the coupon. Under these circumstances, an increase in volatility has the effect of increasing the risk of the note breaching the strike level and not paying a coupon that increases the required spread on the range note (that is, an increase in the digital option premium). If the strike level is set *above* the implied forward levels of the index, the value of the digital option and the incremental spread that can be generated from investing the premium to enhance the coupon is higher. This reflects the fact that the structure of implied forward rates imply that the digital option will be exercised and the range note will not pay the coupon. Under these circumstances, an increase in volatility has the effect of decreasing the risk of the note not paying a coupon that decreases the required spread on the range note (that is, a decrease in the digital option premium).

The behavior of the digital option premium is similar to the behavior of delta (or the hedge ratio) of a conventional option. Delta increases or decreases, depending on whether the option is in-the-money or out-of-the money. This reflects the fact that the boundary condition for the hedge ratio is discontinuous.

## 6.4 Range Note — Structural Variations

### 6.4.1 Market Evolution

Range FRNs originally emerged in 1993. The majority of transactions were undertaken in US$. In early 1994, with US$ short-term interest rates moving up, the traditional formula of a range FRN linked to US$ LIBOR rates became increasingly unattractive. However, the drive for returns at higher yields continued to favour investment in floating rate investments with enhanced returns prompting a series of product variations.

These variations fall into a number of categories:

- Adjustments to the traditional range FRN structure, including amendments to sampling period, a one-sided exposure to value shifts, and refinement to the risk of large value shifts in the index and currency hedged structure.
- Extensions to the basic concept, incorporating a broader range of underlying indexes and currency-hedged structures.

### 6.4.2    Range Note Variations — Sampling Period Adjustments

This variation reflected concern from investors that they were significantly exposed under the range FRN pricing formula to LIBOR sets on specific days. This concern led to the evolution of the daily accrual formula with the LIBOR fixes being undertaken on a daily date to measure relative to the range. This allowed the investor to reduce its exposure to specific fixing dates.

### 6.4.3    Range Note Variations — Risk Exposure Adjustments

A number of variations focus on adjusting the risk to the seller of the embedded digital options. The refinements to the risk of the structure focus principally on:

- Adjusting the risk exposure to isolate the risk of an increase or decrease of the value of the index. This is been usually structured as an accrual note or binary FRN.
- Limiting the exposure to a large shift in the underlying index that would result in the note not paying any coupon at all over the entire life of the note. This is structured as a range or accrual note where the digital option feature is only applicable for part of the life of the note or as a constant spread structure where the strike levels can be adjusted during the life of the transaction.

**Exhibit 13.24** sets out an example of an accrual note FRN where the coupon on the FRN varies as a function of LIBOR rates. In this example, the accrual note outperforms a conventional FRN if LIBOR rates are *only above* certain nominated levels. The investor uses this structure to monetize expectations that interest rates will rise more rapidly than anticipated by the current implied forward curve. The investor gives up coupon in circumstances that are considered improbable in return for enhanced return in situations considered more likely.

**Exhibit 13.25** on page 766 sets out an example of an accrual note where the higher returns are generated for the investor where return is enhanced if the forward rates anticipate a more rapid rise in interest rates than expected.

The desire to customise the expectations regarding the evolution of asset prices to limit risk may take the form of limiting exposure to a shorter period than the life of the note. In the examples considered to date, the digital options were sold usually either periodically or daily throughout the life of the note. Where, for example, the investor only wishes to take a position on the level of rates for the next year, a semi-accrual note structure can be used.

**Exhibit 13.26** on page 767 sets out an example of a semi-accrual note where the accrual period (the period in which the digital options are sold) covers only one year in the life of a 5-year note. The transaction is similar to the accrual notes described previously except that the time horizon is reduced to one year. If the investor's view is realized, then the structure returns an enhanced yield over the term of the note. If the investor's view is not realized, then the returns under the structure are reduced.

The economics of the semi-accrual structure are interesting. The 5-year structure returns a coupon of 6.00% pa or 100 bps above the 5-year Treasury rate. Utilizing the same strike levels, a 1-year final maturity accrual note would yield a return equivalent to around 50-60 bps pa over the 1-year Treasury note. The incremental yield in the shorter maturity structure is reduced because the payout is a function of the coupons sacrificed. In the semi-accrual structure, the value of the digital options are a function of the average exercise value of the options, which in the longer maturity version corresponds to selling an option with a larger fixed payout or a larger number of options with the same fixed payout. The semi-accrual note, therefore, behaves like a more leveraged version of the conventional accrual note structure.

**Exhibit 13.27** on page 767 sets out a semi-accrual note structure where the return on 1-year note is linked to the performance of a specified 5-year Treasury Note over a 3-month period. If the 5-year Treasury Note trades in a range of 5.39% pa to 5.89% pa, the semi-accrual note pays a coupon of 9.50% pa. The note is structured with a minimum coupon of 3.00% pa if the 5-year Treasury Note trades outside the range of 5.14% pa and 6.14% pa during the following three months.

---

**Exhibit 13.24**
**Accrual Note FRN — Example 1**

| | |
|---|---|
| Issuer | AAA/AA–Rated Issuer |
| Amount | US$100 million |
| Issue Price | 100% |
| Maturity | 5 years |
| Coupon | • For first 6 months: 5.50% pa |
| (payable semi-annually) | • For remaining life: |

|                        | 1. If underlying index is above or equal to strike level—LIBOR plus 100 bps. |                |               |
|                        | 2. If underlying index is below strike level—0%. |                |               |
| Underlying Index       | 6 month US$ LIBOR |                |               |
| Strike Levels          | **Reset Dates (years)** | **Strike Level (% pa)** | **LIBOR Forward Rate (% pa)** |
|                        | 0.5 | 4.00 | 4.63 |
|                        | 1.0 | 4.50 | 4.98 |
|                        | 1.5 | 5.00 | 5.27 |
|                        | 2.0 | 5.25 | 5.41 |
|                        | 2.5 | 5.50 | 5.57 |
|                        | 3.0 | 5.75 | 5.81 |
|                        | 3.5 | 6.00 | 6.12 |
|                        | 4.0 | 6.25 | 6.45 |
|                        | 4.5 | 6.25 | 6.68 |

**Exhibit 13.25**
**Accrual FRN — Example 2**

| Issuer          | AAA/AA-rated issuer |
|-----------------|---------------------|
| Amount          | US$100 million |
| Issue Price     | 100% |
| Maturity        | 3 years |
| Redemption      | 100% |
| Coupon          | • If underlying index is below strike level—3-month LIBOR plus 75 bps. |
|                 | • If underlying index is above strike level—0%. |
| Coupon Payments | Coupon is calculated daily and paid quarterly, based on a actual/360-day basis. |
| Underlying Index | 3-month LIBOR |
| Strike Levels   | **Reset Date (months)** | **Strike Level (% pa)** |
|                 | 0 to 6 | 5.00 |
|                 | 6 to 12 | 5.50 |
|                 | 12 to 18 | 6.00 |
|                 | 18 to 24 | 6.50 |
|                 | 24 to 30 | 6.50 |
|                 | 30 to 36 | 6.50 |

**Exhibit 13.26**
**Semi-accrual Note — Example 1**

| | |
|---|---|
| Issuer | AAA/AA-rated issuer |
| Amount | US$100 million |
| Issue Price | 100% |
| Maturity | 5 years |
| Redemption | 100% |
| Coupon | Year 1: 6.00% subject to accrual provision. |
| | Year 2: 6.00% × Accrual percentage. |
| Coupon Payments | Coupon is calculated daily and paid quarterly based on a bond basis. |
| Accrual Provision | The coupon will accrue for each day that LIBOR is at or below the strike level. |
| Accrual Percentage | The percentage of days within the first year that the underlying index is at or below the strike level. |
| Underlying Index | 3-month LIBOR |

| Strike Levels | **Reset Date (months)** | **Strike Level (% pa)** |
|---|---|---|
| | 0 to 3 | 4.50 |
| | 3 to 6 | 4.75 |
| | 6 to 9 | 5.00 |
| | 9 to 12 | 5.25 |

---

**Exhibit 13.27**
**Semi-accrual Note — Example 2**

| | |
|---|---|
| Issuer | AAA/AA-rated issuer |
| Amount | US$100 million |
| Issue Price | 100 |
| Maturity | 1 year |
| Redemption | 100% |
| Coupon | Coupon will be determined by reference to the yield level of underlying index trading over following 3-month period. |
| Coupon Payments | Coupon is paid quarterly based on a bond basis. |
| Underlying Index | Current on the run-specified US 5-year Treasury Note. |
| Current Level of Underlying Index | 5.64% pa |

| Coupon and Strike Levels | Strike Level (Current level of index +/- bps) | Coupon (% pa) |
|---|---|---|
| | 25 | 9.00 |
| | 30 | 8.00 |
| | 35 | 7.00 |
| | 40 | 6.00 |
| | 45 | 5.00 |
| | 50 | 4.00 |
| | Outside Above Ranges | 3.00 |

The range or accrual note structures expose the investor to the risk that a sudden increase or decrease in prices may cause the coupon of the note to set at zero. The constant spread structure embodied a changing range spread to provide additional protection for the investor in a higher volatility environment. This structure was originally offered by J.P. Morgan and known as "Constant Spread Range Index Bonds" (CS-RIBS). Other versions of this structure are known by a variety of names such as choice notes or ratchet notes.

The structure requires the investor to nominate a range of parameters:

- Reference rate, the range, the observation frequency (daily, weekly, monthly, or quarterly).
- Form (the product is available for both debt security or as a swap).
- Coupon frequency—the reset frequency.
- Minimum coupon.

The return is determined by whether the observed nominated financial market variable (say, interest rates) falls within the nominated range. For example, if the target rate is 3-month LIBOR and every observation falls within the range, then the return is, say, 3-month LIBOR plus 1.00% pa. However, if only 90% of the observations fall within the range, the return is 90% × the base rate:

$$(0.9 \times (3\text{-month LIBOR} + 1.00\% \text{ pa.}))$$

The major feature of the constant spread range structure is that the target range *is adjusted at the beginning of each period*. The target range set at the rate at the beginning of each interest period is the maximum set according to the nominated range. In effect, the target range floats together with the reference rate in contrast with traditional range FRNs, which presets the target range for each period at the commencement of the transaction.

The additional return generated from these transactions is lower than those generated by traditional range FRNs, reflecting the lower value of the digital options that in turn reflects the lower risk to the investor of this structure. The typical range chosen is 50 bps above and 25 bps below the reference. Transactions tend to be for shorter maturity, particularly one to three years. In certain transactions, the constant spread option is applicable only for part of the life of the security.

**Exhibit 13.28** sets out an example of this type of structure.

---

**Exhibit 13.28**
**Ratchet Accrual Note**

| | |
|---|---|
| Issuer | AAA/AA-rated issuer |
| Amount | US$25 million |
| Maturity | 1 year |
| Issue Price | 100% |
| Redemption Price | 100% |
| Reference Rate | US$ 10-year CMT rate |
| Coupon | US$ 1-year LIBOR plus margin payable at maturity. The coupon will accrue for each day that the reference rate is within initial range or following a ratchet event the adjusted range: |

| | Maximum Rate (% pa) | Minimum Rate (% pa) |
|---|---|---|
| Initial Range | 5.80 | 5.20 |
| Adjusted Range | 6.20 | 5.10 |

| | |
|---|---|
| Margin | 1.50% pa (initial margin) or following a ratchet event 0.65% pa (ratchet margin). |
| Ratchet Event | If the reference rate touches the initial range on any day, then: |

- The margin will be adjusted from the initial margin to the ratchet margin for all subsequent days; and
- The initial range will be replaced by the adjusted range over the remaining term of the Note.

---

A number of other hybrid structures has evolved. **Exhibit 13.29** sets out a callable range note structure. **Exhibit 13.30** sets out a collared FRN structure with an embedded digital option.

**Exhibit 13.29**
**Callable Range Note**

The terms of the issue are as follows:

| | |
|---|---|
| Issuer | AAA/AA-rated issuer |
| Amount | US$25 million |
| Term | 3 years |
| Issue Price | 100 |
| Redemption Price | 100 |
| Coupon | [3-month US$ LIBOR + Margin% pa] × Accrual factor/Number of days payable quarterly |
| Margin | 1.10% pa |
| Number of Days | 360 |
| Accrual Factor | The number of days during the relevant interest rate period that US$ 3-month LIBOR is fixed within the range: Maximum rate — 7.00% pa Minimum rate — 5.00% pa. |
| Minimum Coupon | 0.00% |
| Call Option | The issue is callable at the option of the issuer after one year and each subsequent coupon payment date. |

The structure is similar to the structure of a normal range FRN. The additional feature is the ability of the issuer to call the issue after 1-year and quarterly thereafter. The value of the digital option is greater than for a conventional digital option enabling the issuer to enhance its return, at least for the period to call. In effect, the issuer (in reality the purchaser of the digital option) will terminate the option (effectively selling them back to the investor) in the event that the value of the digital option as at a call date is lower than the original value. This will be the case where interest rates and implied forward rates are shift in a manner where the implied value of option declines.

**Exhibit 13.30**
**Digital Collared Note**

The terms of the issue are as follows:

| | |
|---|---|
| Issuer | AAA/AA-rated issuer |
| Amount | Euro 12.5 million |
| Term | 6 months |
| Issue Price | 100% |
| Redemption Price | 100% |
| Coupon | 0.10% + (125% × Minimum [3.75%; Maximum {0, (6m Swiss Franc (CHK) LIBOR − 1.62%)/ 1.62%}]) payable in accordance with an actual/ 360 basis at maturity |

*Source:* MTNWeek (April 30, 1999).

Under the structure, the investor will receive an interest equal to the percentage surplus of 6-month Swiss franc LIBOR over 1.62% pa, geared by a factor of 1.25, plus 10 bps. The formula will yield a maximum interest of 4.79% pa and a minimum of 0.10% pa.

The final coupon will outperform the Swiss Franc LIBOR if the latter sets above 1.64% pa. If LIBOR fixes at or below 1.62% pa, then investors will receive the minimum coupon of 0.10% pa. The following graph shows the return structure for different levels of the 6-month Swiss Franc LIBOR.

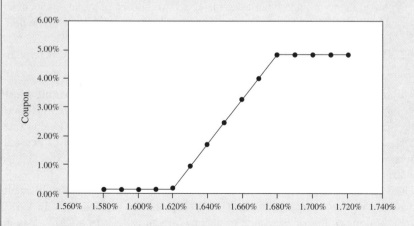

The structure can be decomposed as follows:

- Investor purchases an FRN.
- The investor sells:
    1. A normal cap with a strike of 1.69% pa (on 80% of the face value of the Note (100%/125%).
    2. A digital floor at a strike of 1.62% pa (on 125% of the face value).

The premium from the digital floor and cap increases the yield on the floater provided rates stay above 1.62% pa and below 1.69% pa. If rates are below 1.62% pa the binary payoff, which is the equivalent of the expected LIBOR (as implied by the forward rates), and the premium received less 0.10% pa reduces the return to the minimum coupon. If rates rise above 1.69% pa, then the investor gives up all the upside above 1.69% pa. The issuer hedges by reversing the original elements of the trade with the arranger.

### 6.4.4   Range Note Variations — Index Variations

The other major group of variations relates to the underlying asset utilized. The variations include:

- **Interest rate utilized** — range FRN structures linked to term interest rates (typically 5- or 10-year CMT's). The linkage to longer term rates was linked to an expectation that the yield curve would flatten with increases in interest rates and volatility being focused at the shorter end of the yield curve.
- **Alternative asset markets** — increasingly, the range FRN concept is applied to abroad range of underlying asset markets. Two classes of variations include:
    1. **Alternative asset market range or accrual structures** — where the note is linked to financial assets other than interest rates.
    2. **Quanto range structures** — whereby the range FRN is hedged through a quanto currency option into a third currency.

**Exhibit 13.28** (above) sets out a structure linked to CMT rates. **Exhibit 13.31** sets out an example of a CMT-linked accrual note linked to 10-year CMT rates. The structure described can be structured on either a fixed rate or floating rate basis. The structure is largely identical with that of other range or accrual structures with the major difference being the ability to monetize expectations on *term* interest rates through digital options on these indexes.

The major advantage of the CMT-based accrual structures is the different volatility and the corresponding level and shape of the implied forward CMT curve. The major use of the range or accrual structures based on CMT rates in risk management applications are in the context of mortgage portfolio management. These structures can be an effective means to recover interest income on a mortgage portfolio (or fee income on mortgage servicing rights) that is relinquished due to accelerating prepayments. Income that is foregone as yields fall and prepayments rates accelerate can be replaced by the higher return on these structures. This type of application requires the maturity, index rate, and strike level to be matched to the anticipated prepayment behavior of the underlying mortgage portfolio.

**Exhibit 13.31**
**CMT Accrual Note**

| | |
|---|---|
| Issuer | AAA/AA-rated issuer |
| Amount | US$100 million |
| Maturity | 1 year |
| Issue Price | 100% |
| Redemption | 100% |
| Coupon | 10-year CMT + 30 bps subject to accrual conditions |
| Coupon Payments | Coupon is calculated daily and paid quarterly based on an actual/actual basis. |
| Accrual Provision | The coupon will accrue for each day that the underlying index is at or below the strike level. |
| Underlying Index | 10-year CMT rate |

| Strike Levels | Reset Date (months) | Strike Level (% pa) |
|---|---|---|
| | 0 to 3 | 5.50 |
| | 3 to 6 | 5.70 |
| | 6 to 9 | 5.85 |
| | 9 to 12 | 6.00 |

Several examples of range structures in other asset markets are set out in the remainder of this Section. The logic of the range notes based on alternative assets is identical to that for the interest rate-linked range notes. The major difference is the digital option is based on currency values, commodity prices, and equity index values, rather than interest rates.

**Exhibits 13.32, Exhibit 13.33** and **Exhibit 13.34** on page 775 set out examples of range note structures linked to currency values. **Exhibit 13.35** on page 776 sets out examples of a variation on the traditional structure involving currencies entailing a double or super range. **Exhibit 13.36** on page 778 sets out an example of a range note structure linked to commodity values. **Exhibit 13.37** on page 778 sets out an example of a structure linked to equity market index values. **Exhibit 13.38** on page 793 sets out an example of a range note structure based on interest rate differentials between two currencies.

An example of a quanto option embedded range note is a transaction undertaken by Creditanstalt for Osterreichische Postsovarksse. The transaction is based on a range on 3-month Italian lire interest rates with the currency risk hedged through the quanto option into US$. The 1-year transaction pays a coupon of 4.50% in US$. The range nominated was: 7.50-9.00% pa for the first six months; 6.50-8.50% pa in the second six months.

---

**Exhibit 13.32**
**Currency Range Note — Example 1**

The terms of the issue are as follows:

| | |
|---|---|
| Issuer | AAA/AA-rated issuer |
| Amount | Yen equivalent of US$25 million |
| Maturity | 1 year |
| Issue Price | 100% |
| Redemption Price | 100% |
| Underlying Index | US$/¥ |
| Spot Reference Rate of Underlying Index | US$1: ¥120.50 |
| Range | Maximum: 125; Minimum: 116 |
| Reference Interest Rate | 1-year yen deposit rates were 0.75% pa. |
| Interest | Payable in yen at maturity in accordance to the following formula: |

1. If the underlying index never trades outside the selected range during the period to maturity, the interest rate is 2.5% pa.
2. If the underlying index trades at or outside the upper or lower boundary of the range at any time during the period to maturity, the interest rate is 0.25% pa.

The structure of the issue is identical to interest rate-based range notes. In this case, the note pays a higher than market return if the US$/¥ rate stays in a narrow range around the current spot price. Unlike the interest rate range notes, the currency range note entails the investor selling *a single* digital option on the currency. This option is typically structured as a 1-touch payment at maturity digital option with a maturity identical to that of the note.

**Exhibit 13.33**
**Currency Range Note — Example 2**

The terms of the issue are as follows:

| | |
|---|---|
| Issuer | AAA/AA-rated issuer |
| Amount | US$25 million |
| Maturity | 1 year |
| Issue Price | 100% |
| Principal Redemption | 100% |
| Underlying Index | £/US$ |
| Spot Reference Rate of Underlying Index | £1: US$1.5950 |
| Range | Maximum: 1.6458 Minimum: 1.5250 |
| Reference Interest Rate | 1-year US$ deposit rates were 5.50% pa |
| Interest | Payable in US$ maturity in accordance to the following formula: |

1. If the underlying index never trades outside the selected range during the period to maturity, the interest rate is 14.00% pa.
2. If the underlying index trades at or outside the upper or lower boundary of the range at any time during the period to maturity, the interest rate is 1.00% pa.

The structure is similar to that depicted in **Exhibit 13.32**.

---

**Exhibit 13.34**
**Currency Range Note — Example 3**

The terms of the issue are as follows:

| | |
|---|---|
| Issuer | AAA/AA-rated issuer |
| Amount | US$100 million |
| Maturity | 1 year |
| Issue Price | 100% |
| Principal Redemption | 100% |
| Underlying Index | US$/Thai baht |
| Spot Reference Rate of Underlying Index | US$1: Bt24.65 |

| Limit | 25.50 |
|---|---|
| Interest | Payable in US$ or Thai baht at maturity in accordance to the following formula: |

1. If the underlying index remains below the limit at all times during the period to maturity, the interest rate is 13.0% pa.
2. If the underlying index is at or above the limit at any time during the period to maturity, the interest rate is 0% pa.

The structure is similar to that depicted in **Exhibit 13.32**. The major difference is that the linkage is to an emerging market currency. In addition, the structure is based on a single digital option rather than multiple digital options. The structure described is typical of those issued in Asia in the period preceding the Asian monetary crisis that commenced in 1997.

---

**Exhibit 13.35**
**Currency Super or Double Range Note**

*Structure*
The terms of these issues are structured as follows:

*Issue 1*

| Issuer | AAA/AA-rated issuer |
|---|---|
| Amount | Italian lira 10,000 million |
| Maturity | 18 months |
| Issue Price | 100% |
| Coupon | 3.75% pa |
| Underlying Index | US$/L |
| Redemption Price | • If the underlying index is within range 975 and 1,035 during the term of the transaction at all times, then 112.38%. |
| | • If the underlying index is within range 955 and 1,055 during the term of the transaction at any time, then 102.84%. |

*Source: MTNWeek* (December 6, 1996).

*Issue 2*

| | |
|---|---|
| Issuer | AAA/AA-rated issuer |
| Amount | US$10 million |
| Maturity | 6 months |
| Issue Price | 100% |
| Principal Redemption | 100% |
| Underlying Index | US$/Swiss Franc |
| Narrow Range | The number of business days where the underlying index is between the range specified below divided by the business days in the relevant period: Maximum—1.48; Minimum—1.42. |
| Wide Range | The number of business days where the underlying index is between the range specified below divided by the business days in the relevant period: Maximum—1.52; Minimum—1.35. |
| Interest | [11.40% × Narrow range] + [3.80% × Wide range] |

*Source: MTNWeek* (December 12, 1997).

*Economics*

The super or double range notes structure generates higher returns for the investor where the underlying asset price (currency values) remains within a narrow range. In the event that the asset price moves outside the narrow range, the investor receives a lower return as long as the asset price stays within a second range *that is wider*. It is only if the asset price moves outside the second wider range than the investor receives a nominal or no return on the structure. The structure is similar to ratchet structures described above. The structure is created by trading a package of digital options. The investor sells digital calls and puts at the narrower and wider ranges. The investor also simultaneously repurchases the digital calls and puts at the narrower range with a different digital payout. The combination of digital options creates the payoff profile.

**Exhibit 13.36**
**Commodity Range Note**

| | |
|---|---|
| Issuer | AAA/AA-rated issuer |
| Amount | US$10 million |
| Issue Price | Par |
| Maturity | 1 year |
| Principal Redemption | Par |
| Underlying Index | Aluminium price as quoted on the London Metal Exchange AM Cash Fixing. |
| Spot Reference Rate of Underlying Index | US$1,800 per ton |
| Range | High: US$2,065 per ton |
| | Low: US$1,800 per ton |
| Reference Interest Rate | 1-year US$ interest rates were 6.00% pa |
| Interest Rate | • 10.50% pa for every business day the underlying index is in the range. |
| | • 0.00% pa for every business day the underlying is at or outside the range. |

**Exhibit 13.37**
**Equity Range Note**

Assume short-term Deutschemark rates are expected to come down and DM-based investors are looking to enhance the yield on their short-term assets. The investor can to enter into an accruing corridor swap that benefits from the linkage of the German and French stock markets. Specifically, the swap will have a high payoff if the difference between the DAX Index (that is, the German Equity Index) and the CAC Index (that is, the French Equity Index) trades within a range.

For an investor who would like the above view to be expressed in a bond, the indicative terms of such a bond are set out below:

| | |
|---|---|
| Issuer | AAA/AA-rated issuer |
| Issue Size | DM 20 million |
| Maturity | 1 year |
| Issue Price | 100% |
| Coupon | [8% × b/B] payable in DM. Where: b = number of business days on which the difference between the closing levels of the DAX Index and the CAC Index |

| | remains between −200 and +200; and B = the total number of business days. |
|---|---|
| Interest Rate Basis | The coupon is quoted on an annual 30/360-day basis. |

The 8% pa coupon represents a 2.85% pa pick-up relative to a comparable straight 1-year AA-rated note yielding around 5.15% pa at the time of issue.

A basis for entering into the swap lies in the high historical correlation of the movements of the DAX and the CAC. The difference at the time of issue between the DAX and the CAC equals 83. The DAX-CAC spread traded with a standard deviation of below 130 throughout each of the last four years and within a range of 300 points throughout three of the last four years.

The DAX-CAC spread (based on weekly figures) over the period prior to the issue of the note is as follows:

| Period | Low | High | Range | Mean | Standard Deviation |
|---|---|---|---|---|---|
| 3/8/90-26/7/91 | −294 | +1 | 295 | −151 | 62 |
| 2/8/91-24/7/92 | −315 | −99 | 216 | −204 | 56 |
| 31/7/92-30/7/93 | −364 | −139 | 225 | −252 | 50 |
| 23/7/93-22/7/94 | −283 | +164 | 447 | −64 | 129 |

*Source:* Bloomberg

A rationale for the transaction is the fundamental view that the German and French equity markets would move away from their current focus on inflation and instead will focus more on corporate earnings. In that scenario, the movements of the DAX and the CAC should be highly correlated, due to the fact that the economies of Germany and France are closely intertwined and interdependent, and are therefore likely to experience similar developments in their respective corporate earnings levels.

In the transaction, the investor accrues a high fixed-rate for each day that the spread trades within a predefined range. For each day that the spread trades outside of the predefined range, the investor does not accrue a coupon.

*Source:* van der Maas, Paul "The German French Pact" *IFR Swaps Weekly* Issue 80 (August 3, 1994): 12.

**Exhibit 13.38**
**Spread-based Range Note**

The terms of the issue are as follows:

| | |
|---|---|
| Issuer | AAA/AA-rated issuer |
| Amount | Italian Lira 20 billion |
| Maturity | 2 years |
| Issue Price | 100% |
| Principal Redemption | 100% |
| Underlying Index | The spread between the 5-year DM swap rate and the 5-year £ swap rate. |
| Range 1 | The number of business days where the underlying index is within the range specified below: Maximum—250 bps pa. Minimum—150 bps pa. |
| Range 2 | The number of business days where the underlying index is outside the range specified below: Maximum—250 bps pa. Minimum—150 bps pa. |
| Interest | [7.55% × Range 1/360] + [0.50% × Range 2/360] |

*Source: MTNWeek* (October 24, 1997).

The issue provides the investor with an enhanced return where the spread between the 5-year DM swap rate and the 5-year £ swap rates traded within the range of 150 to 250 bps pa. The structure was designed for investors with the view that interest rates between euro bloc countries and the UK would diverge after monetary union in 1999. The spread at the time the transaction was undertaken was 154 bps pa. In the event that the spread moved outside the range, the investor received a low nominal return. The structure embedded digital call and put options on the spread between the two rates.

## 6.5    Power Option-embedded Notes

The concept of modified or discontinuous payoffs is central to digital options. Transactions that feature embedded digital structures can also be extended to alter payoffs in a manner designed to increase the return profile to the option purchaser. The major example of this type of return enhancement in options is a special group of structures that are referred to as exponential options. These options are often also referred to power, polynomial, or squared options. The nomenclature is usually reflective of the design of the instrument where the option return is expressed as a power of the underlying asset, for example, $LIBOR^2$, and so on.

The central feature of a power option relates to the payoff at maturity. While a standard option return is a clear linear function of the difference between the underlying asset price at exercise or at maturity, in the case of a power option, the option payoff is a defined function of the difference, usually raised to a power, for example, higher than one. For example, a power option with a strike price of 100 whose return is squared would provide the purchaser with a return, if the option expires in the money, which is equal to the asset price less the exercise price multiplied by itself. For an expiry asset price of 105, the power option pay-off would equal 25 (calculated as $(105-100)^2$), which compares to the payoff of an equivalent standard option of 5.

This type of return design in a power option is not dissimilar to the payoff modification inherent in digital or binary option structures. In those structures, the linear and continuous payoffs of standard options are replaced with an agreed payoff amount that is fixed by agreement between the seller and the buyer of the option. However, unlike a digital or binary option, in the case of a power structure, the payoff of the option is amplified by the introduction of the exponent rather than restricted to the agreed amount.

The modification of the payoff profile has a number of implications for the purchaser and seller of the power option:

• For the purchaser, the power feature has the effect of increasing the sensitivity of the option's payoff for relatively small movements in the underlying asset price. This enhances the return that may allow the option purchaser to recover its premium payment for a small favourable movement in the underlying asset price or, similarly, increase its degree of protection for a particular specified directional movement in the underlying asset price.

• For the power option seller, the power feature increases the risk as the potential payout is increased proportional to the exponent utilized for a given movement to the underlying asset price. In effect, the writer is asked to increase the level of *insurance* protection offered to the option purchaser as the market movement in the asset price increases the option buyer's desire for protection.

• The alteration in the payoff is reflected in the option premium that is higher than that usually required for an identical standard option. The higher premium reflects the higher risk of the payoff structure to the writer.

A power option can be regarded as a series of options with different strike prices where the *number* of options increases the further into-the-money the option moves. This allows power options to be hedged and priced with a hedge constituted from a series of options with a mix of different strike prices and maturities and a mix of purchased and sold positions. The hedge portfolio is constructed, taking into account the sensitivity of the option to movements in the underlying asset price. A second method of decomposition would entail re-stating a power option (say, a call) as a standard call option combined with barrier options. In this case, the barriers would be structured as a series of knock-in options with a strike equal to the strike of the standard call and instrike levels corresponding to a series of asset prices reflecting the appreciation of the asset. The power option would then be priced and hedged as the combination of the different options.

Structures featuring embedded power options within a fixed interest security in the form of a structured note have emerged. This type of structure is designed to allow investors or borrowers to trade in the power option where for regulatory or other reasons it cannot utilize these instruments directly. **Exhibit 13.39** illustrates these particular transaction formats with the example of three warrant issues undertaken in Germany in 1995. The three warrant issues cover debt, equity, and currency asset classes, and are, in substance, a power option spread with the warrant purchasers both purchasing and selling the relevant options— the sale effectively capping the purchaser's returns.

The rationale for the warrant transactions is illuminating. The transactions were motivated, at least in part, by the investors' expectations of a small move in the underlying asset price. For example, in the currency tranche, the maximum payoff is set at DM25, which would require an appreciation in the US$ to DM1.70 (an increase of 17.24%). In contrast, the power warrant would provide a similar return to the option purchaser for an increase in the US$ to DM1.50 (an increase of 3.45%). The amplification of the return provided by the power feature allowed investors to maximise the expected return of its expectations in a low-risk manner. The structure also allows a relatively defensive investment strategy, allowing the warrant buyer to benefit from modest market movements.

---

**Exhibit 13.39**
**Power Option-embedded Note**

The following issues were undertaken by Trinkhaus & Burkhardt, the German merchant banking arm of HSBC Markets, in May 1995. All warrant were listed on the Berlin, Dusseldorf, Frankfurt, Hamburg, and Stuttgart stock exchanges. All warrants were denominated in DM. The issue of warrants was divided into three tranches:

*1. 10-year Bund Tranche*

The Bund tranche was structured as follows:

- Three tranches with strike prices ranging from 101%, 102%, and 103% of par.
- European style exercise on March 4, 1996.
- Payouts as follows:
  **Strike   Payout (based on underlying notional value of DM100)**
  101%   (Change in bond price above strike)$^2$ capped at DM 9 per warrant
  102%   (Change in bond price above strike)$^2$ capped at DM 16 per warrant
  103%   (Change in bond price above strike)$^2$ capped at DM 16 per warrant

*2. DAX Warrants*

The DAX tranche was structured as follows:

- Strike price 2,000.
- European style exercise on May 23, 1996.
- Payouts as (Change in DAX above strike)$^2$ capped at DM25 per warrant based on an underlying warrant value of DM100 (implying a capped DAX level of 2,500).

*3. US$/DM Warrants*

The DM currency tranche was structured as follows:

- Two tranches with strike prices of US$/DM at 1.45 and 1.55.
- European-style exercise on June 17, 1996.
- Payouts as 100 × (positive difference between spot above strike)$^2$ capped at DM 25 per warrant based on an underlying warrant value of US$100.

Source: *International Financing Review* Issue 1095 (August 19, 1995): 88.

# 7.   Summary

Exotic options have emerged as a specific class of risk management instruments allowing transformation of the payoff profiles of options to more accurately attune them to the requirements of investors. The combination of exotic options and fixed income securities in the structured note format allows a higher degree of refinement of the risk reward trade-offs in structured notes to be achieved. This makes the incorporation of exotic optionality attractive in the design and engineering of structured note products.

# Appendix A

# Index Differential Swap Structures

## 1. Concept

The differential swap structure is designed to allow financial managers to capture existing and expected differentials in floating or money market rates between alternative currencies without incurring any foreign exchange exposure. In a typical differential swap, the party entering into the transaction will:

• Agree to receive payment in a particular currency on a specific principal amount for a specified term at the prevailing floating money market rate in that currency.
• In exchange, it will make payments on the same principal amount, in the same currency, for the same term, based on the prevailing floating money market rate in an alternative or different currency.

The major features of this arrangement include:

• Both payments and receipts (which are based on the same notional principal amount) are on a floating rate basis, with the rate being reset at specified intervals (usually quarterly or semi-annually).
• All payments under the transaction are made in the counterparty's nominated currency thereby eliminating any foreign exchange exposure.
• Consistent with its status as a single currency transaction, no exchange of principal amounts is required.

## 2. Example

The following numerical example illustrates the concept utilizing a transaction whereby a borrower elects to enter into a DM/US$ differential swap seeking to benefit from the fact that floating money market rates in the US$ sector are currently well below equivalent floating money market rates in the DM sector.

**Exhibit 13.40** sets out the structure of this differential swap. The counterparty enters into a differential swap for a term of three years in which it agrees to pay interest in DM that will be calculated by applying the nominal 6-month US$ LIBOR rate to a notional principal amount of DM 160 million (based on an exchange rate of US$1: DM1.60, equivalent to US $100 million). The counterparty will receive interest in DM that will be calculated by applying the nominal 6-month DM LIBOR rate to DM160 million.

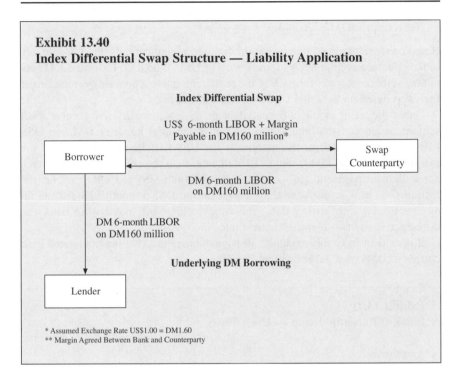

**Exhibit 13.40**
**Index Differential Swap Structure — Liability Application**

**Index Differential Swap**

US$ 6-month LIBOR + Margin
Payable in DM160 million*

Borrower → Swap Counterparty

DM 6-month LIBOR
on DM160 million

DM 6-month LIBOR
on DM160 million

**Underlying DM Borrowing**

Lender

\* Assumed Exchange Rate US$1.00 = DM1.60
\*\* Margin Agreed Between Bank and Counterparty

The counterparty, under this differential swap, will pay interest under this transaction at a rate equivalent to the 6-month US$ LIBOR rate plus a margin (assumed to be 194 bps in DM). The margin represents, primarily, the differential between interest rates of the relevant maturity (three years) in US$ and DM markets, as well as the hedging costs to the bank. The derivation of this margin is discussed below in **Appendix B**.

The cash flows under this differential swap transaction from the perspective of the counterparty is summarised in **Exhibit 13.41**.

At the end of each interest period (semi-annually), the counterparty makes payments on DM160 million at the 6-month US$ LIBOR rate (plus the differential swap margin) and receives payment on DM160.0m at the 6-month DM LIBOR rate. The net settlement amount calculation is as follows:

Settlement calculation — September 1, 2002:

Counterparty pays: DM160,000,000 @ US$ 6-month LIBOR plus margin (4.25% + 1.94% = 6.19%) × 184/360 days = DM5,062,044

Counterparty receives: DM160,000,000 @ DM 6-month LIBOR (9.50%) × 184/360 days = DM7,768,889

Net receipt = DM2,706,844

Based on these assumed rates, as at the first settlement date, the bank would pay
to the counterparty the net settlement sum of DM 2,706,844. **Exhibit 13.41** sets
out the settlement sums for each of the remaining interest periods over the life of
the swap based on assumed US$ and DM LIBOR rates.

Under the terms of this differential swap, the counterparty will receive a net
settlement amount that equates to the net differential between DM and US$
LIBOR rates adjusted for the margin. If the US$ LIBOR rate inclusive of the
margin is below the DM 6-month LIBOR rate, then the counterparty receives a
net settlement payment. Conversely, if the 6-month US$ LIBOR rate plus the
margin rises to a level above the then prevailing DM 6-month LIBOR rate on
any particular rate setting date, the counterparty will pay to the bank the
difference in the two nominal interest rates in DM.

It is evident from this example, all payments are made in the nominated base
currency (DM) on a net settlement basis.

---

**Exhibit 13.41**
**Index Differential Swap — Cash Flows**

*Assumptions*

| | |
|---|---|
| Structure | Pay US$ LIBOR |
| | Receive DM LIBOR |
| FX Currency | US$100,000,000 |
| Base Currency | DM 160,000,000 |
| Exchange Rate | US$1: DM1.6000 |
| Term (years): | 3 |
| Start Date | March 1, 2002 |
| Maturity Date | March 1, 2005 |

The (assumed) floating rates are as follows:

| Semi-annual Period | 1 | 2 | 3 | 4 | 5 | 6 |
|---|---|---|---|---|---|---|
| 6-month US$ LIBOR | 4.25% | 4.38% | 4.13% | 4.75% | 5.13% | 5.50% |
| 6-month DM LIBOR | 9.50% | 9.35% | 9.62% | 9.00% | 8.63% | 8.25% |
| Differential | 5.25% | 4.98% | 5.50% | 4.25% | 3.50% | 2.75% |
| Pricing Margin | 1.94% | 1.94% | 1.94% | 1.94% | 1.94% | 1.94% |
| US$ LIBOR + Margin | 6.19% | 6.32% | 6.07% | 6.69% | 7.07% | 7.44% |

*Cash Flows*

The transaction cash flows based on the above parameters are as follows:

| Period | Days | Counterparty Payments (DM) | Counterparty Receipts (DM) | Net Receipt (+) or Payment (−) (DM) |
|--------|------|------|------|------|
| 01-Mar-02 | | | | |
| 01-Sep-02 | 184 | 5,062,044 | 7,768,889 | 2,706,844 |
| 01-Mar-03 | 181 | 5,080,067 | 7,521,556 | 2,441,489 |
| 01-Sep-03 | 184 | 4,959,822 | 7,867,022 | 2,907,200 |
| 01-Mar-04 | 181 | 5,381,733 | 7,240,000 | 1,858,267 |
| 01-Sep-04 | 184 | 5,777,600 | 7,053,333 | 1,275,733 |
| 01-Mar-05 | 181 | 5,985,067 | 6,636,667 | 651,600 |

From the viewpoint of the counterparty (assumed to be a DM borrower) the transaction results in the following:

- The borrower has created a DM liability with nominal US$ 6-month LIBOR rate as the interest benchmark. This, necessarily, means that it benefits where US$ 6-month LIBOR rates are below DM 6-month LIBOR rates by more than the margin.
- From mechanical perspective, this reduction in interest cost is achieved by the net settlement amounts under the swap that reduce the borrower's interest payments under its underlying DM borrowing.
- The borrower has achieved a conversion of its DM based liability to a US$-based liability without incurring any foreign exchange exposure as all its payments continue to be in DM.

An identical transaction could be utilized by an asset manager to convert an underlying US$ asset yielding a floating rate of return linked to US$ LIBOR into a US$ asset yielding a return linked to DM 6-month LIBOR.

Under this transaction structure, the base currency would be restructured to be US$100 million (equating to DM 160 million at the assumed exchange rate). The investor would pay US$ 6-month LIBOR on US$100 million and receive DM 6-month LIBOR *less* a specified margin on US$100 million in US$. Under the terms of this transaction, all payments would be in US$ to insulate the investor from any foreign exchange risk. Such a transaction would allow the investor to benefit from the positive differential between DM floating rates and US$ floating rates while maintaining its underlying US$ investment position. **Exhibit 13.42** sets out the structure of a investor-oriented transaction.

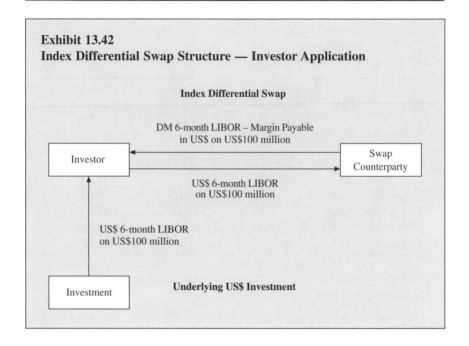

Exhibit 13.42
Index Differential Swap Structure — Investor Application

Index Differential Swap

# Appendix B

# Pricing Index Differential Swap Structures

## 1.  Overview

The pricing of an index differential swap transaction is derived from the techniques utilized by the bank to hedge its own exposures as a result of entering into a transaction with its counterparty. In this Appendix the pricing of and hedging structure for an index differential structure is set out.

In substance, the index differential swap can be decomposed into a series of forwards on money market interest rates in the two respective currencies and a foreign exchange exposure management problem. The trading in the forwards is designed to capture the *current implied interest rate differential* from the current yield curves. This is done using interest rate forwards (futures (if available), FRAs, or interest rate swaps) in the respective currencies. The foreign exchange exposure problem relates to translating the implied differential into a single currency. The exposure, as described below, is uncertain in quantum and direction and must be hedged using a quanto option.

## 2. Hedge Structure

The essential structure of the hedge for a differential swap entails two discrete steps:

- Entry by the bank into two separate interest rate swap transactions to generate the cash flow stream of a differential swap.
- Management of a complex series of foreign exchange exposures that are created in structuring the hedge.

Each of these two steps is considered in detail below. The analysis of pricing and hedging considerations is based on the numerical example of the DM/US$ differential swap discussed in **Appendix A**.

In order to hedge its underlying position, the bank would enter into two 3-year interest rate swaps to replicate the cash flows of the differential swap. These swaps to be entered into by the bank would be as follows:

- A 3-year DM 160 million interest rate swap under which the bank:
  1. Pays 8.70% pa on DM160 million (payable semi-annually on an actual/365-day basis).
  2. Receives DM 6-month LIBOR on DM160 million.
- A 3-year US$100 million interest rate swap in which the bank:
  1. Pays US$ 6-month LIBOR on US$100 million.
  2. Receives 7.20% pa on US$100 million (payable semi-annually on an actual/365-day basis).

The fixed rate on the US$ and DM swaps are the prevailing market interest rate swap rates. The currency parities between the US$ and DM interest rate swaps is established by the assumed US$/DM exchange of US$1:DM1.60 (the market rate at the time the transaction is entered into).

The overall hedging structure is illustrated in **Exhibit 13.43**.

**Exhibit 13.43**
**Interest Rate Differential Swap Hedging Structure — Overview**

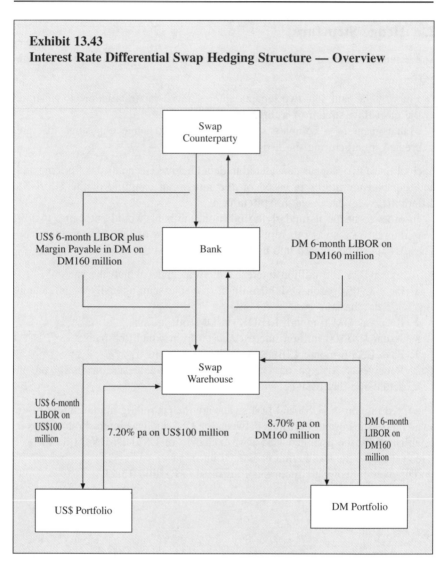

For analytical purposes, the structure of the hedge can be simplified in two steps:

- In order to assist in deriving the spread over US$ LIBOR payable by the counterparty, the US$ interest rate swap is restructured to an off-market rate basis. The fixed rate under the US$ swap is restructured to match the fixed coupon of 8.70% pa payable under the corresponding DM interest rate swap. This necessitates the bank paying the present valued equivalent of 1.50% pa at the commencement of the swap. The up-front payment required to restructure the swap is US$3,983,900 (equivalent DM6,374,239). **Exhibit 13.44** sets out the derivation of this up-front payment.[12]

- Two sets of cash flows completely offset each other in the hedge. The DM 6-month LIBOR received on DM160 million by the swap warehouse is exactly matched by the corresponding payments required to be made to the counterparty. These cash flows that cancel or offset each other can be ignored for the purposes for the hedge and are eliminated.

**Exhibit 13.44** sets out the cash flow structure of the hedge following completion of these two steps.

---

**Exhibit 13.44**
**Derivation of Up-front Payment On Off-market**
**US$ Interest Rate Swap**

| Period | Days | US$ Payments (at market rate of 7.20% pa) | US$ Payments (at off-market rate of 8.70% Pa) | Payments Difference | Present Value of Payment Differences |
|--------|------|------|------|------|------|
| | | (US$) | (US$) | (US$) | (US$) |
| 01-Mar-02 | | | | | −3,983,900 |
| 01-Sep-02 | 184 | 3,629,589 | 4,385,753 | −756,164 | |
| 01-Mar-03 | 181 | 3,570,411 | 4,314,247 | −743,836 | |
| 01-Sep-03 | 184 | 3,629,589 | 4,385,753 | −756,164 | |
| 01-Mar-04 | 181 | 3,570,411 | 4,314,247 | −743,836 | |
| 01-Sep-04 | 184 | 3,629,589 | 4,385,753 | −756,164 | |
| 01-Mar-04 | 181 | 3,570,411 | 4,314,247 | −743,836 | |

---

[12] Please note that for convenience the swap rate has been utilized to present value the cash flow differences as between the 8.70% pa fixed-rate payments required and the on market rate of 7.20% pa. In practice, zero-coupon rates would be utilized adjusted for the fact that the US$ swap portfolio is essentially accepting a deposit over the life of the transaction that is repaid in the form of annuity by way of the higher coupon under the US$ interest rate swap requiring assumption of a reinvestment risk on these cash flows.

**Exhibit 13.45**
**Interest Rate Differential Swap Hedging Structure —**
**Adjusted Structure**

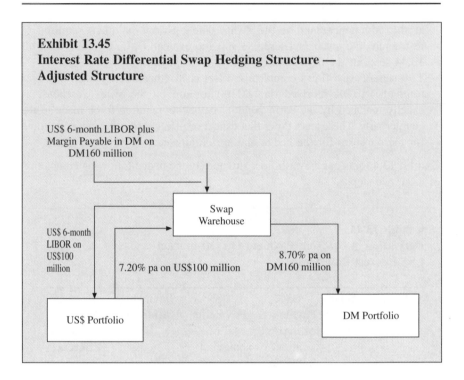

## 3.  Foreign Exchange Risk Management

### 3.1  Nature of Exposure

The bank under the terms of the differential swap has a complex foreign exchange exposure to movements in the US$/DM interest rates reflecting the fact that the bank has a series of US$ and DM cash flows to manage.

The unique aspect of this currency risk management position is that:

- The bank's US$ and DM net cash flows as at each settlement date is determined by an exogenous factor—US$ 6-month LIBOR (which is not known until the rate is set at the commencement of the relevant interest period).
- The nature of the exposure to the US$/DM rate *changes* depending upon the nominal level of 6-month US$ LIBOR.

**Exhibit 13.46** analyses the net cash flow exposures experienced by the bank (within its swap portfolio) as at the first settlement. Please note that while this discussion focuses on the first settlement date only, a similar problem exists in respect of each of the remaining five interest periods and settlement dates.

## Exhibit 13.46
## Foreign Exchange Risk Analysis

### Case 1: US$ 6-month LIBOR < 8.70% pa

| US$ LIBOR (% pa) | Receipts (DEM) | Payments (DEM) | Payments (US$) | Receipts (US$) | Net DEM Flow (DEM) | Net US$ (US$) | FX Rate Flow | Net Cash Flow (US$) |
|---|---|---|---|---|---|---|---|---|
| 4.25% | 3,475,556 | -7,017,205 | -2,172,222 | 4,385,753 | -3,541,650 | 2,213,531 | 1.6000 | 0 |
| 4.25% | 3,475,556 | -7,017,205 | -2,172,222 | 4,385,753 | -3,541,650 | 2,213,531 | 2.0000 | 442,706 |
| 4.25% | 3,475,556 | -7,017,205 | -2,172,222 | 4,385,753 | -3,541,650 | 2,213,531 | 1.8000 | 245,948 |
| 4.25% | 3,475,556 | -7,017,205 | -2,172,222 | 4,385,753 | -3,541,650 | 2,213,531 | 1.4000 | -316,219 |
| 4.25% | 3,475,556 | -7,017,205 | -2,172,222 | 4,385,753 | -3,541,650 | 2,213,531 | 1.2000 | -737,844 |

### Case 2: US$ 6-month LIBOR > 8.70% pa

| US$ LIBOR (% pa) | Receipts (DEM) | Payments (DEM) | Payments (US$) | Receipts (US$) | Net DEM Flow (DEM) | Net US$ (US$) | FX Rate Flow | Net Cash Flow (US$) |
|---|---|---|---|---|---|---|---|---|
| 10.50% | 8,586,667 | -7,017,205 | -5,366,667 | 4,385,753 | 1,569,461 | -980,913 | 1.6000 | 0 |
| 10.50% | 8,586,667 | -7,017,205 | -5,366,667 | 4,385,753 | 1,569,461 | -980,913 | 2.0000 | -196,183 |
| 10.50% | 8,586,667 | -7,017,205 | -5,366,667 | 4,385,753 | 1,569,461 | -980,913 | 1.8000 | -108,990 |
| 10.50% | 8,586,667 | -7,017,205 | -5,366,667 | 4,385,753 | 1,569,461 | -980,913 | 1.4000 | 140,130 |
| 10.50% | 8,586,667 | -7,017,205 | -5,366,667 | 4,385,753 | 1,569,461 | -980,913 | 1.2000 | 326,971 |

### FX Hedge Position Analysis

| US$ LIBOR Rate (% pa) | 4.250 | 5.250 | 6.250 | 7.250 | 8.250 | 9.250 | 10.250 | 10.500 |
|---|---|---|---|---|---|---|---|---|
| US$ Cash Flows | 2,213,531 | 1,702,420 | 1,191,309 | 680,198 | 169,087 | -342,024 | -853,135 | -980,913 |
| DEM Cash Flows | -3,541,650 | -2,723,872 | -1,906,094 | -1,088,317 | -270,539 | 547,239 | 1,365,017 | 1,569,461 |
| Breakeven Exchange Rate | 1.6000 | 1.6000 | 1.6000 | 1.6000 | 1.6000 | 1.6000 | 1.6000 | 1.6000 |

As evident from a review of **Exhibit 13.46**, if US$ 6-month LIBOR is less than 8.70% pa (the fixed-rate payable under the DM swap), then the bank will have a net receipt of US$ that will be needed to fund a net DM outflow. Conversely, if US$ 6-month LIBOR exceeds 8.70% pa, then the bank has a net DM inflow that is required to fund a net US$ outflow. Consequently, the bank's swap portfolio, in hedging its exposure under the differential swap, is required to make a number of payments in one currency (either DM or US$) while receiving the equivalent cash flow in the other currency. The bank must manage this complex foreign exchange exposure.

In analyzing the complex foreign exchange exposures generated by the hedge structure, any exposure in regard to the *margin* over US$ 6-month LIBOR payable by the counterparty in DM is ignored. In practice, part of the margin (see below) will represent an annuity designed to recover the upfront US$ payment made as part of restructuring the cash flows of the US$ interest rate swap to equate the fixed-rate payable under the DM interest rate swap. In practice, this exposure can be eliminated quite simply by the following strategies:

- The swap structure could have been realigned by reducing the DM coupon to equate to the US$ interest rate swap coupon of 7.20% pa.
- Alternatively, the DM equivalent of the US$ payment to the US$ swap portfolio could have been borrowed from the DM swap portfolio with the borrowing being repaid by the margin payable by the counterparty (in DM).

This exposure is ignored in the remainder of this analysis.

If US$ 6-month LIBOR is less than 8.70% pa, then the bank has a net positive US$ cash flow that is utilized to fund a net cash outflow. If US$ 6-month LIBOR (for the first settlement) is set at 4.25% pa, then the bank has a net US$ inflow of US$2,213,531 and a net DM outflow of DM 3,541,650. If the US$/DM exchange rate remains at US$1:DM1.6000 (the rate of the commencement of the transaction), then the bank's net cash flow position is zero; that is, the DM equivalent of the net US$ inflow exactly matches the bank's DM shortfall. However, the bank has a currency gain if the DM depreciates against the US$ and has a currency loss if the DM appreciates against the US$. The cash flows realized by the bank under alternative currency rate are summarised in **Exhibit 13.46**.

The bank's exposure to an appreciating DM is *reversed* where US$ 6-month LIBOR is greater than 8.70% pa. Where US$ 6-month LIBOR is greater than 8.70% pa, the bank has a net US$ outflow that must be funded from a net DM cash surplus. As a consequence, the bank's exposure is to a depreciating DM relative to the US$.

The difficulty in managing this exposure is the inherent linkage between the nature of the underlying currency exposure to the US$ 6-month LIBOR rate for any interest period during the life of the differential swap. This exposure can be managed in one of a number of ways:

- The exposure can be left unhedged.
- The exposure can be managed on an opportunistic basis as a trading position in line with currency value expectations.
- The exposure can be hedged statically assuming certain known cash flow ranges.
- The exposure can be managed dynamically incorporating the correlation between the two variables (US$ LIBOR and US$/DM in this example).

In practice, this exposure is hedged in either a static or a dynamic framework. Quanto option based pricing approaches are utilized by major financial institutions active as differential swap market makers.

### 3.2 Foreign Exchange Exposure Management — Static Model

Under the static replication model, the risk is treated as one that is similar to those incurred under currency options and hedged through the use of foreign exchange options.

To structure the currency option hedge it is necessary to make assumptions regarding the anticipated maximum and minimum future level of the 6-month US$ LIBOR rate over the life of the differential swap transaction. This is because the exact quantum of the cash flows to be hedged is generated by the actual level of US$ 6-month LIBOR as at any rate set date.

For the purpose of illustration, assume that it is anticipated that US$ 6-month LIBOR will never be set below 4.25% pa or above 10.50% pa over the three year term of the differential swap. Utilizing this assumption, to fully hedge against losses, the bank would need to purchase the following options:

- **Purchase of DM call/US$ put option** — the bank would purchase a series of six DM call options (with maturities corresponding with the payment date under the differential swap structure) at a strike price equal to the prevailing spot rate of US$1:DM1.6000. The bank would purchase the DM call on approximately 2.21% of the US$100 million notional principal amount. The amount of DM calls required is calculated by taking the difference between the assumed minimum LIBOR rate and the breakeven US$ 6-month LIBOR rate (which equates to the US$ swap rate payable under the swap) to generate the US$ cash inflow.
- **Purchase of DM Put/US$ call** — to hedge its exposure where US$ 6-month LIBOR is greater than 8.70% pa, the bank would purchase a series of six DM put options with a strike price of US$1:DM1.6000. The bank would purchase DM puts on approximately 0.98% of the US$100.0m notional principal amount of the transaction.

As is evident, the structure of this currency hedge is inefficient. In general, the hedger will be overhedged as it is hedging against both a rise and a fall in the currency and in reality only one option will be required. The effectiveness of the hedge also depends on the forecasting accuracy of the minimum and maximum US$ 6-month LIBOR rates over the life of the differential swap. For example, even if the bank is accurate in prescribing the minimum and maximum levels of US$ 6-month LIBOR over the swap, there will be certain circumstances, such as when the US$ LIBOR rate is within the range, where the hedge will not be accurate. It is possible, however, that the hedger will be underhedged. For example, where the maximum or minimum is exceeded by a large amount, the face value of the hedge might be insufficient.

In the above example, in periods in which US$ 6-month LIBOR is between the minimum level assumed (4.25% pa) and the breakeven rate (8.70% pa), if the DM strengthens against the US$, the DM call/US$ put option purchased by the bank will generate a higher gain than the actual cash flow loss incurred by the bank under the swap. Similarly, the bank will be over-hedged where US$ 6-month LIBOR is between 8.70% pa and the assumed maximum of 10.50% pa and the US$ strengthens. An approach to avoid overhedging is for the amount of the options required to be calculated on the maximum and minimum rates that US$ 6-month LIBOR is expected to *average* over the life of the transaction, rather than the lowest and highest possible US$ 6-month LIBOR rate over the term of the transaction.

In summary, the static hedging model while it allows modelling of the risk does not provide an efficient hedge.

### 3.3    Foreign Exchange Exposure Management — Dynamic Model

The problem in structuring the hedge, which lowers hedge efficiency, is the inherent assumption that movements in the US$ 6-month LIBOR rate are *not* correlated to movements in the US$/DM exchange rate. In practice, there will be some correlation between movements in US$ 6-month LIBOR rate and the US$/DM rate that will necessarily influence the *actual* exposure under the differential swap.

Correlation-based hedging techniques (incorporating quanto options) can be designed to improve the efficiency of the currency hedge necessitated by the differential swap. Improving the efficiency of the currency risk management process necessarily minimises the cost of implementing and maintaining the hedge. For example, if it is assumed that increases in US$ LIBOR are likely to coincide with a stronger US$, the hedge structure could be adjusted to lower the effective level of protection against a depreciation of the US$ against the DM. This could entail the bank purchasing a lower face value amount of DM call/ US$ put option (in the extreme case, this exposure could be left unhedged).

The correlation concepts underlying the derivation of the option value are common to quanto (or quantity adjusting) options. The central feature of these instruments is the uncertainty underlying the value or amount of cash flow required to be hedged.

This type of transaction is equivalent to a purchase of a relevant option on the index and the simultaneous entry into a derivative transaction to hedge the return into its base currency usually at rates prevailing at the commencement of the transaction. Given the uncertainty in the value of the index and therefore the maturity value of the option, the currency hedge must be structured to cater for the uncertainty of the value to be hedged. In effect, the hedge needs to recognize the correlation between the change in value of the index and the movements in the currency relativities. The problem in the case of the index differential swaps where the underlying currency exposure is linked to the interest rate relativities as between the currencies.

Mathematical pricing models for valuing quanto options or derivatives of this type have been developed.[13] The approach to pricing quanto options is to utilize the correlation between the relevant variables as a parameter in the pricing of the option. For example, in the context of the currency-hedged structures, the relevant correlation is that between the returns on the relevant currency values and the return on the foreign market index in the currency of the index. In the case of index differential swaps, the relevant correlation is that between the relevant currencies and the interest rate in the relevant currency (effectively, the foreign currency, US$ LIBOR in the above example). A problem underlying this approach to pricing is the need to assume stability of the relationship between the variables.

Utilizing the quanto option methodology to price the currency risk management component of such transactions requires the separation of the risks of differential swaps into specific components (which are consistent with the approach discussed above):[14]

• Exchange rate risk based on current yield curves in the relevant currencies and exchange rates.
• A contingent exposure based on future yield curves.

---

[13] See Reiner, Eric "Quanto Mechanics" (March 1992) *Risk* vol. 5 no. 3 59-63; Rubinstein, Mark "Two Into One" (May 1991) *Risk* vol. 4 no. 5 49; Jamshidian, Farshid "Price Differentials" (July 1993) *Risk* vol. 6 no. 7 48-51 and "Corralling Quantos" (March 1994) *Risk* vol. 7 no. 3 71-75.

[14] See, for example, Letter to the Editor by Putley, Jeremy (Lehmann Brothers, New York) (1993) (March) *Risk* vol. 6, no. 3, 12.

As above, this approach seeks to manage and hedge the exchange rate and interest rate risks of differential swaps separately, the rationale being that this facilitates more efficient management of these risks.

Under this approach, the amounts to be received and paid under the differential swaps are determined utilizing the forward rates in the relevant currencies implied by the respective yield curves. For example, in the example utilized previously, the 6-month DM LIBOR and the 6-month US$ LIBOR implied at the relevant points in time (for example, six, 12, 18, and so on, months in the future) from the existing yield curve would be determined. The determination of the forward rates would allow the differential to be paid or received under the differential swap to be established. The interest rate exposures is hedged using forwards in the respective currencies.

Once the net payments are established, the net amounts of a particular currency to be paid or received can be present valued to a current sum with the resultant payable or receivable amount being hedged by:

• Purchase of the required quanto options.
• An offsetting spot position in the currency that is then dynamically adjusted as the yield curve in both currencies changes and the currency rates alter.

This procedure allows the interest rate exposure and the currency exposure of the transaction to be hedged.

An alternative is not to specifically hedge the interest rate exposure but to hedge dynamically where the contingent exchange rate risk that is driven by changes in interest rate risks is immunised if required through option transactions. This approach described only enables a perfectly immunised position to be created instantaneously at a given point in time. Maintenance of the hedge requires future transaction costs to be incurred that will be driven by the volatility of interest rates, foreign exchange rates, and most importantly the correlation between these variables. The major difficulty with this approach is that the risk of interest rates movements and currencies are, for all practical purposes, closely related and there are limited opportunities for hedging this correlation with liquid instruments.

An alternative method of hedging would entail utilising securities with the embedded differential swap positions as a potential instrument to immunise exposures entered into by financial institutions in transacting differential swaps. However, the limited level of outstanding differential bonds greatly restricts the opportunities to manage portfolio exposures in such transactions in this manner. Another potential avenue of hedging these transaction exposures is the emerging market in spread differential options.

The complexity of hedging and pricing differential swap transactions has, in practice, led to a multiplicity of approaches to the management of the underlying risks of such transactions. The concern about the methodology for pricing and hedging such transactions has been exacerbated by persistent rumours of large profits and losses incurred by major providers of such instruments. This is in addition to concern regarding the difficulties in hedging such exposures, particularly in periods of increased volatility in markets. For institutions active in financial derivatives generally who are large traders/providers of index differential swap products, a portfolio approach to risk management has generally been assumed. Under this approach, the risk of differential swap transactions is aggregated into portfolios of other interest rate and currency transactions, and the net position hedged.

## 4.  Margin on Interest Rate Differential Swap Transaction

The actual margin payable under the differential swap requires the amortisation over the life of the transaction of the following items:

*   The up-front payment required to be made by the bank to rewrite one of the interest rate swap coupons.
*   The cost of purchasing or creating the options designed to hedge the foreign exchange exposure.

In the above example, the total cost that must be amortised over the life of the transaction is as follows:[15]

*   Up-front payment in respect of US$ interest rate swap: US$3,983,900.
*   Option premiums: US$1,051,938.

This total cost of US$5,035,838 (DM8,057,341) is amortised over the six payments (three years of semi-annual payments) and equates to approximately 194 bps pa payable semi-annually over US$ LIBOR payable in DM.

Based on these calculations, the pricing of the differential swap requires the counterparty to pay US$ 6-month LIBOR plus 194 bps pa on a notional principal amount of DM160 million in return for receiving DM 6-month LIBOR on DM160 million. Accordingly, the counterparty would benefit from the transaction as long as US$ 6-month LIBOR was, at least, 194 bps pa below DM 6-month LIBOR over the term of this transaction.

In general, pricing of a differential swap will closely approximate the net difference in swap rates in the relevant currencies for the maturities relevant to the desired term of the differential swap plus the cost of hedging the currency risk entailed for the bank in the transaction. The cost of hedging will depend upon a variety of factors, including the assumptions regarding the future path of the relevant floating rate index and the exact structure of the currency hedge.

---

[15]  For reasons of simplicity, the option cost of the static hedge has been used.

The cost of hedging the currency risk will generally depend on the shape of the yield curve of the two relevant currencies. The wider the interest differential between the two currencies over the life of the transaction, the higher the hedging costs (or benefits). The importance of this factor relates to the fact that the strike price of the relevant options will be set at the prevailing spot rate at the commencement of the transaction. However, the prevailing forward rate (determined by interest differentials) will dictate whether the options are in or out-of-the-money and, therefore, their relative cost.

For example, in the above example, because of the positive interest rate differential in favour of the DM, forward rates for the purchase of DM against sales of the US$ will be lower than the prevailing spot rate of US$1: DM1.60. This means that DM call/US$ puts with the strike rise of DM1.60 required to be purchased will be out-of-the-money options, thereby, reducing the cost of the option. Conversely, the DM put/US$ calls required to hedge the bank's cashflow mismatch where US$ 6-month LIBOR is greater than 8.70% pa will be in-the-money commensurately increasing the cost.

Consequently, the pricing of the differential swap in terms of the margin components will be most favourable where the net difference in swap rates between the two respective currencies for the relevant maturities is low and the shape of the yield curve for the two currencies means that the cost of hedging the currency risks is minimal.

# 14
# Inflation-indexed Notes and Related Derivatives

## 1. Overview

In recent years, notes and securities linked to price inflation have emerged as an important class of transactions in the capital markets. A number of related derivative products have also emerged.

Inflation-indexed notes[1] are a class of structured notes that embody a specific linkage to price inflation. The linkage entails linking the value of coupon payments or principal repayments to an identified price index. In a sense, inflation-indexed notes can be regarded as being related to or a specific subset of commodity-linked notes. The relationship is derived from the inter-relationship between commodity prices and inflation.

In this chapter, the key dynamics of inflation-indexed notes are discussed including the concept, structure, valuation, and applications of inflation-indexed securities and related derivatives. The structure of this chapter is as follows: the basic concept is first discussed; the structural features of inflation-indexed securities and derivatives are then outlined; valuation and pricing structures are then detailed; and applications are analyzed.

## 2. Concept

All investments are designed to generate returns that, at least at a minimum, preserve the *purchasing power* of the investment. Inflation-indexed securities explicitly link the return on the investment to levels of inflation with the objective of preserving the real value of the investment and providing an additional *return* (over and above the inflation adjustment) to the investor. These securities provide

[1] The author would like to thank Vinay Kolhatkar and Sean Carmody for their very helpful comments on an earlier draft of this chapter.

inflation protection by indexing the future cash flows of the security through an adjustment mechanism that creates a specific linkage to changes in a prescribed price index. Derivatives linked to inflation have also emerged.

The key feature of inflation-indexed structures (security or derivatives) is the positive dependence between the level of inflation and the cash flows under the transaction (the higher the level of price inflation, the higher the return to the investor). The essential objective of this structure is the preservation of the real yield on the investments.

There are close similarities between conventional fixed and floating interest rate securities and inflation-indexed structures. For instance, a fixed interest security will carry a coupon that is designed to provide investors with compensation for both *expected inflation* and a real rate of return. Similarly, a floating rate security will carry a margin over an interest rate that is reset periodically. The movements in the underlying interest rate will reflect changes in inflationary expectations providing the investor with both a real rate of return plus compensation for inflation. In contrast, the inflation-linked security has a real rate that is fixed for the life of the transaction and periodic inflation compensation explicitly linked to and determined by the *actual* inflation level over the life of the security.

The key differences between conventional securities and inflation-indexed securities are:

- The explicit adjustment for actual (as distinct from expected) price inflation through a direct linkage between the coupon and inflation.
- A pre-agreed and fixed real rate of return.

The capacity of inflation-indexed securities to provide protection against inflation is subject to certain practical limitations:

- **Identification of an appropriate inflation index** — there are significant problems in establishing whether one or other index *accurately* measures changes in price levels. The problem is compounded by the fact that available price indices vary significantly.
- **Index calculation** — in practice, inflation indices are periodically adjusted. These adjustments that are mostly unpredictable create uncertainty about the efficacy of the inflation compensation. For example, the treatment of one-off effects such as the introduction of a value-added tax, good and services tax, or changes in the calculation methodology has the potential to impact upon the inflation rate.
- **Indexation lag** — inflation or price change indices are generally available with a lag (in the order of several months). This means that price adjustments are not synchronized fully with actual levels of prevailing inflation. This also erodes the efficiency of the inflation compensation.
- **Taxation effects** — the tax treatment of the returns on the inflation-adjusted

returns (see discussion below) may dictate an *after-tax* outcome that does not provide a satisfactory inflation compensation element. This is particularly so where the inflation indexation component is taxed.

## 3. Inflation-indexed Securities

Several structures for inflation-indexed securities have emerged. The principal types in use include:

1. **Inflation-indexed coupon bond** — this structure is a conventional bond with a bullet maturity with a coupon paid either quarterly or semi-annually. Each coupon consists of a fixed real rate component, as well as an inflation component for the relevant period. The fixed real rate coupon is pre-agreed at the time of issue. The inflation component is calculated periodically over the life of the security.
2. **Capital-indexed bond** — this structure is a conventional fixed-rate bond with a bullet maturity. The coupon paid on the bond is a pre-agreed real rate of return. On each coupon payment date, an indexation adjustment is made as follows:
   - The bond principal is indexed; that is, the principal value is adjusted by the inflation level applicable ("the capital adjustment"). This accretion to the principal is *not paid* to the bond-holder at the time of calculation.
   - The real rate of interest is then used to calculate an additional interest amount based on the capital adjustment ("the interest indexation amount"). This interest indexation amount is paid to the bond-holder as part of the periodic interest payment.
   - The accumulated capital adjustment is paid to the bond-holder at maturity. The capital-indexed bond is in effect a normal coupon bond paying the real rate of interest with the cash flows (both principal and interest) being indexed to inflation.
3. **Indexed annuity bond** — this structure consists of an amortizing bond where the principal and interest (calculated as the real rate of interest) is repaid by level instalments. The periodic payments (both principal and interest) are adjusted for inflation. The capital adjustment and the interest adjustment are paid to the bond-holder as at each interest payment date.

All structures incorporate a zero floor element whereby if the quarter-on-quarter inflation falls below zero (deflation) the bond value does not decrease but there is an adjustment as of a future period.

**Exhibit 14.1** sets out the cash flows of each structure. The cash flows of each bond are set out based on a face value amount of $1,000, 15-year final maturity, and a real rate of return of 3.50%. Future inflation rates are assumed for the purpose of calculation. For each bond structure, the average inflation rate and pretax internal rate of return (IRR) (effectively, the yield-to-maturity) is also calculated.

In practice, different structures are utilized in different markets. The capital-indexed bond has emerged as probably the most common structure. The structure effectively capitalizes the *entire* inflation component of a nominal interest bond in addition to the repayment of normal principal. However, the credit risk issues implicit in this type of structure limits issuance to sovereign or quasi-sovereign issuers. The inflation-indexed coupon bond is by far the simplest structure but has not proved popular. This reflects the fact that it is in reality analogous to a floating interest rate bond. The indexed annuity bond has also not proved popular because of its complexity although some lower credit quality utility issuers have used the structure.

**Exhibit 14.2** on page 806 sets out a brief comparison of types of inflation-indexed bonds traded in different markets. In addition to the markets listed, small markets for inflation-indexed securities exist in Denmark and also in a number of emerging markets. Several emerging markets with high inflation rates have issued inflation-indexed debt. This has been motivated by the capacity to raise funds in otherwise difficult circumstances, achieve longer maturities, and introduce an inherent monetary discipline on the economy. These issues have been undertaken in South America (Brazil, Chile, Argentina, and Mexico), Eastern Europe (Poland, and Hungary), and the Middle East (Turkey and Israel).

---

**Exhibit 14.1**
**Bond Structures**

*1. Coupon-indexed Bond*

| Years | Inflation Rate | Inflation Index | Bond Cash Flows ($) Principal | Bond Cash Flows ($) Interest | Bond Cash Flows ($) Total |
|-------|---------------|-----------------|-----------|----------|-------|
| 0     |               | 100.00          | −1,000    |          | −1,000 |
| 1     | 2.00%         | 102.00          |           | 55.00    | 55    |
| 2     | 1.20%         | 103.22          |           | 47.00    | 47    |
| 3     | 0.50%         | 103.74          |           | 40.00    | 40    |
| 4     | 1.10%         | 104.88          |           | 46.00    | 46    |
| 5     | 1.35%         | 106.30          |           | 48.50    | 49    |
| 6     | 2.20%         | 108.64          |           | 57.00    | 57    |
| 7     | 2.75%         | 111.62          |           | 62.50    | 63    |
| 8     | 3.00%         | 114.97          |           | 65.00    | 65    |
| 9     | 2.90%         | 118.31          |           | 64.00    | 64    |
| 10    | 2.75%         | 121.56          |           | 62.50    | 63    |

| Years | Inflation Rate | Inflation Index | Bond Cash Flows ($) Principal | Bond Cash Flows ($) Interest | Bond Cash Flows ($) Total |
|---|---|---|---|---|---|
| 11 | 2.80% | 124.96 | | 63.00 | 63 |
| 12 | 3.00% | 128.71 | | 65.00 | 65 |
| 13 | 2.10% | 131.41 | | 56.00 | 56 |
| 14 | 1.95% | 133.98 | | 54.50 | 55 |
| 15 | 1.75% | 136.32 | 1,000 | 52.50 | 1,053 |
| Average | 2.09% | | | IRR | 5.50% |

## 2. Capital-indexed Bond

| Years | Inflation Rate | Inflation Index | Principal Indexation | Principal | Real Interest | Interest Indexation | Total |
|---|---|---|---|---|---|---|---|
| 0 | | 100.00 | −1,000 | | | | −1,000 |
| 1 | 2.00% | 102.00 | | | 35.00 | 0.70 | 36 |
| 2 | 1.20% | 103.22 | | | 35.00 | 1.13 | 36 |
| 3 | 0.50% | 103.74 | | | 35.00 | 1.31 | 36 |
| 4 | 1.10% | 104.88 | | | 35.00 | 1.71 | 37 |
| 5 | 1.35% | 106.30 | | | 35.00 | 2.20 | 37 |
| 6 | 2.20% | 108.64 | | | 35.00 | 3.02 | 38 |
| 7 | 2.75% | 111.62 | | | 35.00 | 4.07 | 39 |
| 8 | 3.00% | 114.97 | | | 35.00 | 5.24 | 40 |
| 9 | 2.90% | 118.31 | | | 35.00 | 6.41 | 41 |
| 10 | 2.75% | 121.56 | | | 35.00 | 7.55 | 43 |
| 11 | 2.80% | 124.96 | | | 35.00 | 8.74 | 44 |
| 12 | 3.00% | 128.71 | | | 35.00 | 10.05 | 45 |
| 13 | 2.10% | 131.41 | | | 35.00 | 11.00 | 46 |
| 14 | 1.95% | 133.98 | | | 35.00 | 11.89 | 47 |
| 15 | 1.75% | 136.32 | 1,000 | 363 | 35.00 | 12.71 | 1,411 |
| Average | 2.09% | | | | | IRR | 5.60%[2] |

---

[2] The calculated IRR is the best possible result. If inflation is below zero in a given year, although the average inflation rate remains unaltered, then there could be a variation in the return as the adjustment in later years is not present valued.

## 3.   Indexed Annuity Bond

| Years | Inflation Rate | Inflation Index | Bond Cash Flows ($) | | | | | | |
|---|---|---|---|---|---|---|---|---|---|
| | | | Bond Cash Flows | Principal Balance | Interest Payment | Principal Repayment | Indexation Payment-Principal | Indexation Payment-Interest | Total Payments |
| 0 | | 100.00 | −1,000 | 1,000. | | | | | −1,000.00 |
| 1 | 2.00% | 102.00 | 86.83 | 948.17 | 35.00 | 51.83 | 20.00 | 0.70 | 107.53 |
| 2 | 1.20% | 103.22 | 86.83 | 894.54 | 33.19 | 53.64 | 11.38 | 0.40 | 98.60 |
| 3 | 0.50% | 103.74 | 86.83 | 839.02 | 31.31 | 55.52 | 4.47 | 0.16 | 91.45 |
| 4 | 1.10% | 104.88 | 86.83 | 781.56 | 29.37 | 57.46 | 9.23 | 0.32 | 96.38 |
| 5 | 1.35% | 106.30 | 86.83 | 722.09 | 27.35 | 59.47 | 10.55 | 0.37 | 97.75 |
| 6 | 2.20% | 108.64 | 86.83 | 660.54 | 25.27 | 61.55 | 15.89 | 0.56 | 103.27 |
| 7 | 2.75% | 111.62 | 86.83 | 596.83 | 23.12 | 63.71 | 18.16 | 0.64 | 105.63 |
| 8 | 3.00% | 114.97 | 86.83 | 530.90 | 20.89 | 65.94 | 17.90 | 0.63 | 105.36 |
| 9 | 2.90% | 118.31 | 86.83 | 462.65 | 18.58 | 68.24 | 15.40 | 0.54 | 102.76 |
| 10 | 2.75% | 121.56 | 86.83 | 392.02 | 16.19 | 70.63 | 12.72 | 0.45 | 99.99 |
| 11 | 2.80% | 124.96 | 86.83 | 318.92 | 13.72 | 73.10 | 10.98 | 0.38 | 98.19 |
| 12 | 3.00% | 128.71 | 86.83 | 243.25 | 11.16 | 75.66 | 9.57 | 0.33 | 96.73 |
| 13 | 2.10% | 131.41 | 86.83 | 164.94 | 8.51 | 78.31 | 5.11 | 0.18 | 92.11 |
| 14 | 1.95% | 133.98 | 86.83 | 83.89 | 5.77 | 81.05 | 3.22 | 0.11 | 90.15 |
| 15 | 1.75% | 136.32 | 86.83 | 0 | 2.94 | 83.89 | 1.47 | 0.05 | 88.34 |
| Average 2.09% | | | | | | | | IRR | 5.39% |

## Exhibit 14.2
## Inflation-indexed Bond Markets

| Market | Issuer(s) | Bond Structure | Indexation/Quotations |
|---|---|---|---|
| US | US Treasury; other Federal Agencies, banks and non-bank issuers | Capital-indexed bond | Linked to CPI with 3-month lag. Contracted real rate determined by auction. |
| Canada | Bank of Canada | Capital-indexed bond | Linked to CPI with 3-month lag. Contracted real rate determined by auction. |
| UK | Bank of England | Capital-indexed bond | Linked to all items RPI with 8-month lag. Contracted real rate determined by Dutch auction. |

| Market | Issuer(s) | Bond Structure | Indexation/Quotations |
|--------|-----------|----------------|----------------------|
| Australia | Commonwealth and State Governments; private sector issuers | Capital-indexed bond; Indexed annuity structures | Linked to CPI with two-quarter lag for capital-indexed bonds. Indexed annuities typically do not have a complex lag formula. Contracted real rate determined by tender system. |
| New Zealand | New Zealand Government | Capital-indexed bond | Linked to All Groups CPI with two-quarter lag. Contracted real rate determined by dutch auction. |
| Sweden | National Debt Office | Capital-indexed bond | Linked to CPI with three-month lag. Issued via permanent tap system. |

*Source:* (1997) *The HSBC Markets Guide to Global Inflation Protection Bonds*; HSBC Markets.

## 4.   Inflation-indexed Derivatives

### 4.1   Overview

In addition to inflation-indexed securities, a parallel market in inflation-linked derivatives has emerged. The derivative market has focused primarily on over-the-counter market structures such as inflation swaps and options (caps and floors on inflation levels).[3]

The market has developed as a complement to the securities market. The market has several functions:

- It enables inflation-linked securities to be converted into conventional securities by transferring the inflation-linked component through the swap and the reverse.
- It enables off-balance-sheet creation of exposure to inflation or hedges against inflation to be created.
- It allows asymmetric risk transfer of inflation price risk and creation of structured exposure to this risk.

---

[3]   For an excellent discussion of inflation swaps and option structures, see Carmody, Sean and Glover, James "CPI Linked Derivatives" (August 1998) *The Australian Corporate Treasurer* 23-25.

## 4.2   Inflation-indexed Swaps

Inflation-indexed swaps (often referred to as real-rate swaps) are designed to restructure inflation-linked cash flows to nominal interest rate basis or vice versa. The inflation-indexed swaps can be structured in a number of ways:
1. To replicate a capital-indexed bond.
2. To swap all inflation-indexed cash flows for either fixed indexation cash flows (inflation swap) or constant cash flows (constant cash flow swap).[4]

In practice, the first structure is used only in connection with inflation-indexed bonds that are swapped to nominal interest rate returns. The majority of inflation swaps are based on the second structure. A major rationale for this structural preference is that this format avoids any need to index the notional principal of the swap. If the traditional capital-indexed structure is used, a large component of the inflation indexation is paid *at the maturity of the swap*. This has several implications:
- The accounting and taxation treatment is complex.
- Credit risk of the swap is significantly increased.
- There is a significant deferral of cash flow.

**Exhibit 14.3** sets out the structure of an inflation swap or a constant cash flow swap.

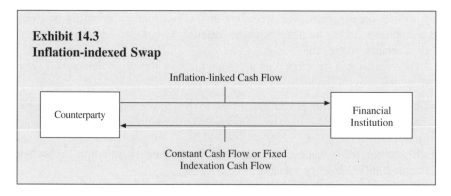

**Exhibit 14.3
Inflation-indexed Swap**

Inflation-linked Cash Flow

Counterparty

Financial
Institution

Constant Cash Flow or Fixed
Indexation Cash Flow

In a fixed indexation or inflation swap, the cash flows are as follows:
- The counterparty pays the inflation-linked cash flow.
- The counterparty receives the fixed indexation cash flows.

---

[4]   This is similar to the inflation-indexed bond structure.

The cash flows for a 1-year quarterly swap are set out in the table below:

| Time Period (years) | Inflation-linked Cash Flow | Fixed Indexation Cash Flow |
|---|---|---|
| 0.25 | $P_0 \times (1 + CPI_1)$ | $P_0 \times (1 + R)^{0.25}$ |
| 0.50 | $P_0 \times (1 + CPI_1) \times (1 + CPI_2)$ | $P_0 \times (1 + R)^{0.50}$ |
| 0.75 | $P_0 \times (1 + CPI_1) \times (1 + CPI_2) \times (1 + CPI_3)$ | $P_0 \times (1 + R)^{0.75}$ |
| 1.00 | $P_0 \times (1 + CPI_1) \times (1 + CPI_2) \times (1 + CPI_3) \times (1 + CPI_4)$ | $P_0 \times (1 + R)^{1.00}$ |

The terms in the table are as follows:

$P_0$ = Notional principal of the swap
$CPI_n$ = Inflation index at time n
R = fair value of the fixed indexation rate of the swap, which equates the present values of the two sides of the swap.

Several aspects of the transaction should be noted:

• The transaction is purely notional and no exchange of principal is effected.
• The inflation index is calculated with a lag.
• The inflation rates are compounded.
• The fair value of the swap is based on using the implied forward inflation rate derived from the combination of the market prices of inflation-indexed securities and nominal securities.

The net effect of the transaction is to swap variable and unknown inflation indexation cash flows for fixed and known indexation payments effectively locking in forward inflation rates.

In a constant cash flow inflation swap, the cash flows are as follows:

• The counterparty pays the inflation-linked cash flow.
• The counterparty receives the constant cash flows.

The cash flows for a 1-year quarterly swap are set out in the table below:

| Time Period (years) | Inflation-linked Cash Flow | Fixed Indexation Cash Flow |
|---|---|---|
| 0.25 | $P_0 \times (1 + CPI_1)$ | $P_0 \times (1 + Q)$ |
| 0.50 | $P_0 \times (1 + CPI_1) \times (1 + CPI_2)$ | $P_0 \times (1 + Q)$ |
| 0.75 | $P_0 \times (1 + CPI_1) \times (1 + CPI_2) \times (1 + CPI_3)$ | $P_0 \times (1 + Q)$ |
| 1.00 | $P_0 \times (1 + CPI_1) \times (1 + CPI_2) \times (1 + CPI_3) \times (1 + CPI_4)$ | $P_0 \times (1 + Q)$ |

The terms in the table are as follows:

$P_0$    = Notional principal of the swap
$CPI_n$ = Inflation index at time n
$Q$      = the fixed interest charge payable

Several aspects of the transaction should be noted:

- The transaction is purely notional and no exchange of principal is effected.
- The inflation index is calculated with a lag.
- The inflation rates are compounded.
- The fair value of the swap is based on equating the present value of cash flows on the swap. The inflation-indexed cash flows are determined using the implied forward inflation rate derived from market prices of inflation-indexed securities. The constant cash flows are derived using the implied forward interest rates from the swap or equivalent interest rate curve. This process is designed to ensure the absence of the opportunity to arbitrage that would otherwise exist in nominal and real government securities.

The net effect of the transaction is to swap inflation-indexed cash flows for nominal fixed interest payments. In practice, a nominal floating rate against inflation-indexed cash flows swap can be generated by combining the constant cash flow swap with a conventional fixed-for-floating interest rate swap.

### 4.3   Inflation-indexed Options

Inflation-indexed options, in the form of caps and floors, have also emerged. The basic structures are as follows:

- The inflation cap operates to provide protection against inflation above the strike cap rate. No payments are indexed as long as price inflation as calculated by the underlying index is below the strike inflation level. If the inflation level reaches above the strike level, then the buyer benefits through indexation *above the strike level*. This is calculated as the indexation cash flow at the actual inflation level minus the indexation cash flow at the strike inflation level.
- The inflation floor operates to provide protection against inflation falling below a strike floor rate. The payments are indexed in accordance with market price inflation levels as long as inflation levels are above the strike inflation level. If inflation falls below the strike level, then the buyer benefits through indexation at the strike level. This is calculated as the indexation cash flow at the strike inflation level minus the indexation cash flow at the actual inflation level. A common floor structure is where the floor strike is set at zero inflation level. This is to ensure that the cash flows from the underlying transaction cannot fall.

A variant on the above is the net inflation floor structure. The structure is based on the fact that the traditional floor will have an inherently compounding effect. The net floor structure removes the compounding effect. The inflation index is always reset at the maximum index level attained. This dictates that the inflation index level remains constant if the inflation level falls below the strike of the inflation floor until the index increases above the floor level. The net floor structure will provide the buyer with lower payouts than a compounding floor resulting in a lower cost to the buyer.

# 5.   Structural Issues

The structures of inflation-indexed securities and derivatives create complex accounting, taxation and credit risk issues.

The accounting and taxation issues are evident in the treatment of the indexed component of the cash flows of these transactions. One issue relates to the characterization of these issues as either capital or interest in substance. This impacts upon:

- **Income statement** — it is not clear whether the accrued but unpaid capital indexation amount in a capital-indexed bond is to be treated as interest (therefore accrued as income for the bond-holder or as an expense for the issuer (if nongovernmental)). The additional complication is that there is a separation between the timing of calculation and payment that creates a divergence between cash and accrual records.
- **Balance sheet** — the classification of the accrued but unpaid capital indexation amount affects the reported balance sheet. If treated as interest in the income statement, then the amount is included in shareholders funds. However, if treated as capital, then it may be treated as an accretion to the *face value* of the security affecting the reported investment or debt of the entity.

The treatment for tax purposes is also focused on the interest/capital dichotomy, as well as the timing difference between cash receipt and the determination of the indexation amount.

The difficulties identified are exacerbated in the case of an index annuity bond structure. This reflects the fact that the inflation adjustment is on the outstanding balance covering both the preservation of the real value of the principal and an additional interest payment required to create an inflation-adjusted return on the unamortized balance.

These complexities have the potential to create significant timing differences between actual cash flows and the recording and treatment of the inflation-indexed transaction for accounting and tax purposes. It is possible that these complexities and distortions impair investment and trading in these types of instruments.

The credit risk of inflation-indexed structures may be significantly greater than that for conventional transactions of the same maturity. The difference arises, most seriously, where the structure has a capital-indexed structure that defers the payment of the capital indexation amount *till maturity*. The risk is directly related to the tenor of the bond. However, this risk is present, albeit at a lower level, in an index annuity bond. The investor is in effect deferring a significant proportion of the cash flow (the accumulated inflation adjustment). This necessarily means that in the event of default by the issuer, the investor's loss is significantly higher than the commencement face value of the transaction. The additional risk is evident from the analysis in **Exhibit 14.4**.

---

**Exhibit 14.4**
**Inflation-indexed Securities — Credit Risk**

The peak outstanding (effectively, the face value credit exposure) of a capital-indexed bond and an indexed-annuity bond is set out in the table below. The exposure calculation assumes:

Face value        = 100
Constant real rate = 5%
Inflation         = 4% pa

| Maturity (years) | Peak Outstanding Under Capital-indexed Bond | Peak Outstanding Under Indexed Annuity Bond |
|---|---|---|
| 10 | 149.9 | 99.0 |
| 15 | 182.3 | 99.8 |
| 20 | 221.9 | 101.9 |
| 30 | 328.4 | 122.7 |

The exposure is highly sensitive to inflation levels. The table below shows the sensitivity of the exposure to changes in inflation rates. The exposure calculation assumes:

Face value        = 100
Constant real rate = 5%
Inflation         = 4% pa

| Maturity (years) | Peak Outstanding Under Capital-indexed Bond | Peak Outstanding Under Indexed Annuity Bond |
|:---:|:---:|:---:|
| 3.0 | 157.7 | 99.6 |
| 4.0 | 182.3 | 99.8 |
| 8.0 | 321.1 | 109.5 |
| 12.0 | 823.9 | 172.6 |

*Source:* Vineburg, Stephen and Kolhatkar, Vinay "Inflation-indexed Securities." *Financial Derivatives and Risk Management.* 7 41-49 (September 1996): 47.

Similar considerations affect inflation derivatives, particularly inflation swaps. As noted above, this problem is most significant in a swap that seeks to replicate the cash flows of capital-indexed structures. This is one of the reasons that the inflation derivative structures have generally evolved to the inflation swap or the constant cash flow swap structure described above.

The higher credit risk of inflation-indexed structures limits the type of issuer generally acceptable to investors in these instruments.

# 6.   Valuation

## 6.1   Real Rates of Return

The central concept in pricing and valuation of inflation-indexed transaction, in particular, inflation-indexed securities, is the *real rate of return*. In this section, the emphasis is on the pricing of inflation-indexed securities. Inflation derivative structures are priced off the inflation-indexed securities market prices.

The Fisher equation provides the basis of the relationship between nominal rates on interest and real rates of return.[5] The relationship is:

$$(1 + R_N) = (1 + R_R) \times (1 + h) \times (1 + u)$$

---

[5]   In theory, the real rate of return should equal the return on real investment that in a portfolio framework is determined by the point of tangency with the consumer's aggregate indifference curve in a mean variance context; that is, the point at which the consumer's marginal rate of compensation between risk and return is equated to the expected real economic production; see Seigel. J.J. and Warner, J.B. "Indexation, The Risk-free Asset, And Capital Market Equilibrium" (1977) *Journal of Finance* vol. 32 no. 4 1101-1107.

Where:

$R_N$ = nominal interest rate
$R_R$ = expected real interest rate
h  = expected inflation
u  = risk premium for uncertainty of expected inflation estimate

The dynamics of real versus nominal returns are illustrated in **Exhibit 14.5**. The analysis highlights that with no indexation lags, the values of inflation-indexed bonds are a function of real rates. However, where there are indexation lags, the values of inflation-indexed bonds are affected also by changes in the inflation level.

---

**Exhibit 14.5**
**Real vs Nominal Returns**

Assume the following data:

$R_R$ (expected real interest rate) = 3.00% pa
h (expected inflation) = 2.50% pa
u (risk premium for uncertainty of expected inflation estimate) = 0.50% pa

The nominal interest rate implied is 6.10% pa for a 1-year security. Also assume an indexed bond with a contractual real interest rate of 3.00% pa. The following table shows the *realized returns* of these securities:

| | | Actual Rates of Inflation | | | | |
| | | **2.00%** | **3.00%** | **4.00%** | **5.00%** | **6.00%** |
|---|---|---|---|---|---|---|
| Conventional bond | Nominal return | 6.10% | 6.10% | 6.10% | 6.10% | 6.10% |
| | Real return | 4.02% | 3.01% | 2.02% | 1.05% | 0.10% |
| Inflation-indexed bond | Nominal return | 5.06% | 6.09% | 7.12% | 8.15% | 9.18% |
| | Real return | 3.00% | 3.00% | 3.00% | 3.00% | 3.00% |

As is evident, the conventional nominal interest bond exhibits a declining *real* return as inflation rates increase above the *expected* inflation rate. In contrast, the indexed bonds provide a constant *real* return as the interest amount adjusts to changes in price levels.

The above analysis assumes that there are *no time lags* in the inflation indexation mechanism. The following table shows the nominal and

---

realized returns on both the conventional and the inflation-indexed securities where there is a single period time lag and the previous inflation rate is 2.50% (the indexed coupon is therefor 5.58% pa):

| | | Actual Rates of Inflation | | | | |
| | | 2.00% | 3.00% | 4.00% | 5.00% | 6.00% |
|---|---|---|---|---|---|---|
| Conventional bond | Nominal return | 6.10% | 6.10% | 6.10% | 6.10% | 6.10% |
| | Real return | 4.02% | 3.01% | 2.02% | 1.05% | 0.10% |
| Inflation-indexed bond | Nominal return | 5.58% | 5.58% | 5.58% | 5.58% | 5.58% |
| | Real return | 3.50% | 2.50% | 1.51% | 0.55% | -0.40% |

The analysis shows that where actual inflation rates are higher the impact of the lag effectively reduces the real rate on the indexed security, as well as on the conventional bond.

## 6.2 Securities Valuation

The predominant market convention for quotation for inflation-indexed securities is based on the real interest rate or real yield to maturity. This reflects the theory that the value of inflation-indexed securities should be driven by changes in the expected real rate of return. In practice, the link between real rates and inflation-indexed securities values is more complex, reflecting factors such as the indexation lags, interest accrual factors, the specific structure of the security, and institutional/market factors.

The general valuation approach is driven by the different sets of cash flows associated with the security:

| Type of Cash Flow/Payment | Payment Characteristic |
|---|---|
| Original real interest payments and original principal repayment | Known at issuance/ known at pricing date |
| Indexation payments (interest and capital) over life of security until the present | Unknown at issuance/ known at pricing date |
| Indexation payments (interest and capital) over remaining life of security | Unknown at issuance/ unknown at pricing date |

The generalized pricing approach is to discount the two known sets of cash flows with a nominated discount rate. The present value amount calculated is the price or value of the security. The internal rate of return that equates the price to the future known cash flows is the effective real rate of return or yield to maturity that is quoted or used in trading. The expected future inflation rate is not utilized to calculate the value of the security.

This approach is applied to the different structures as follows:

• **Inflation-indexed coupon bond** — this type of bond is effectively similar to a FRN security. In contrast to the other types of inflation-linked securities, this structure has a relatively small dependence on inflation rates. For valuation purposes, it is usual to assume the *most recent* or *last* inflation statistic available for all future coupon payments. The bond coupons therefore are fixed at the assumed fixed inflation rate plus the guaranteed real rate. These fixed cash flows are then discounted back as the current *market* real rate of return.[6] Therefore, the bond trades at a discount (premium) when market real rates are above (below) the guaranteed real rate under the transaction. Where the bond is traded and the price is available, the current price and fixed future cash flows can be used to derive an implied real rate on the issue.

• **Capital-indexed bond** — the pricing formula for a capital-indexed bond is set out in **Exhibit 14.6**. A pricing example is set out in **Exhibit 14.7**.

• **Indexed annuity bond** — the pricing formula for a capital-indexed bond is set out in **Exhibit 14.8** on page 816. A pricing example is set out in **Exhibit 14.9** on page 819.[7]

---

**Exhibit 14.6**
**Pricing Formula — Capital-indexed Bond**

Price per \$100 face value $= V^{f/d} [g (c + a_n)$
$$+ 100 V^n] [(K_t (1 + P/100)^{-f/d})/100]$$

Where:
$i$ = annual real yield % pa/(100 × number of coupon per year)
$V = 1/(1 + i)$
$f$ = number of days from settlement date to the next coupon date

---

[6]   This is similar to the valuation of FRNs based on the last LIBOR rate.
[7]   The pricing formulas used is that in use in the Australian inflation-indexed bond market. The pricing formula used in other markets are broadly similar although some of the pricing conventions may vary.

d = number of days between last coupon date and the next coupon date

p = average change in CPI over two quarters ending in two quarters prior to that in which the next coupon occurs

g = 0 if ex-interest (7-day ex-interest currently applies); 1 if cum-interest

$K_{(t-1)}$ = the nominal value of the (indexed) principal at the previous coupon date

$K_{(t)}$ = the nominal value of the (indexed) principal at the next coupon date

g = the percentage coupon per quarter

n = the number of full coupon periods between the next coupon date and the date of maturity

$a_n$ = $(1 - v^n)/i$

*Source:* Vineburg, Stephen and Kolhatkar, Vinay "Inflation-indexed Securities" *Financial Derivatives and Risk Management.* 7 (September 1996): 41-49 at 44.

---

**Exhibit 14.7**
**Pricing Example — Capital Index Bond**

Assume the following pricing details:

| | |
|---|---|
| Maturity | 20-Aug-2010 |
| Settlement | 25-Jan-96 (day after December CPI release) |
| Real Yield | 4.680% (quoted/traded yield) |

The price of the bond is as follows:

$$\text{Price} = 0.988435306909 \; \frac{26}{92} [1*(1 + 41.9376827097)$$

$$+ \; 100*.988435306958] \; \frac{108.95\left[1 + \frac{1.26}{100}\right]}{100} \; \frac{-26}{92}$$

Price = 101.576

*Source:* Vineburg, Stephen and Kolhatkar, Vinay "Inflation-indexed Securities" *Financial Derivatives and Risk Management.* 7 (September 1996): 41-49 at 44.

**Exhibit 14.8**
**Pricing Formula — Indexed Annuity Bond**

Value on coupon date/issue
Price per \$100 face value = $[Bj * a_n]$

Value when Bj unknown

Price per \$100 face value = $\left(\dfrac{v}{p}\right)\dfrac{f}{d}[Bj - 1 * q * (z + a_n)]$

Value when Bj known

Price per \$100 face value = $\left(\dfrac{v}{q}\right)\dfrac{f}{d}[Bj * (z + a_n)]$

Where:

$i$ = traded real yield % pa/(100 * number of coupon pa)

$v$ = $1/(1 + i)$

$f$ = the number of days from settlement date to the next coupon date

$d$ = the number of days between last coupon date and the next coupon date

$q$ = the per-period inflation factor

$Bj$ = the next annuity payment at time $j$ = $B(j - 1) \times CPI(j - 1)$ = Bo $\times CPI(j)/(CPI(o)$

$Bj\text{-}1$ = the previous annuity payment (or Bo prior to the first annuity payment)

$Bo$ = the base annuity payment

$n$ = the number of full coupon periods between the next coupon date and the date of maturity

$z$ = 0 if ex-interest (7-day ex-interest currently applies); 1 if cum-interest

$a_n$ = $(1 - v^n)/i$

*Source:* Vineburg, Stephen and Kolhatkar, Vinay "Inflation-indexed Securities" *Financial Derivatives and Risk Management.* 7 (September 1996): 41-49 at 45.

**Exhibit 14.9**
**Pricing Example — Indexed Annuity Bond**

Assume the following:

| | |
|---|---|
| Maturity | 15-Dec-2010 |
| Issue Date | 25-Feb-96 (after December CPA release) |
| Real Yield | 4.75% (Quoted/Traded yield) |

The price of the bond is calculated under two scenarios:

**Scenario 1: Hypothetically CPI December quarter not released yet.**

Use formula B when CPI in previous quarter is not yet known.

q = the per-period inflation factor = $CPI(j)/CPII(j - 1)$
  Where:
  CPI(o) = or is the CPI for the full calendar quarter prior to issue = 114.7
  CPI(j) is the highest CPI released from CPI(o) to the settlement date
  CPI(j − 1) is the highest CPI released from CPI(o) to the second latest released CPI as at settlement date
  = Next coupon occurs on 15-Mar-96; that is, March 96 quarter. Highest and latest release in June 95 quarter.
  Thus:
  CPI(j) is the Consumer Price Index for September 95 = 117.6
  CPI(j − 1) is the Consumer Price Index for June 95 = 116.2
  = 117.6/116.2
  = 1.01204819277
Bj − 1 = the previous annuity payment (or Bo prior to the first annuity payment) = 2.394037
  Z = 1 because cum-interest (7-day interest currently applies)
  $a_n = (1 - v^n)/i = (1 - 0.988264360716^{59})/0.011875 = 42.2461008131$

$$Price = \left[\frac{0.988264360716}{1.01204819277}\right]^{\frac{50}{91}} [2.394037 * 1.01204819277 *$$

(1 + 42.2461008131)]

Price = 103.420

---

**Scenario 2: December CPI is 118.2 ie 0.5%**

Use formula C when CPI(t) is known.

q = the per period inflation factor = CPI(j)/CPI(j - 1)
Where: CPI(o) is the CPI for the full calendar quarter prior to issue

*Source:* Vineburg, Stephen and Kolhatkar, Vinay "Inflation-indexed Securities"
*Financial Derivatives and Risk Management.* 7 (September 1996): 41-49 at 45.

---

### 6.3    Nominal vs Real Rate Curve

The critical element utilized in pricing or valuation of inflation-indexed securities is the expected real rate of return or real yield to maturity. In practice, the derivation of the implied real rate of return creates significant challenges.

In theoretical terms, the derivation of a real-rate zero-coupon curve is not significantly different to the construction of a *nominal* interest rate zero-coupon curve.[8] Where there is a reasonably liquid market with a sufficient range of inflation-indexed securities with differing maturities, the real zero curve should be capable of derivation. However, in practice, the limited market data limits this approach.

In practice, two approaches are available:

• Using assumptions about the shape of the real rate curve to approximate it's zero-coupon equivalent.[9]
• Utilize a term structure model to derive the real rate yield curve and the implied forward inflation rates.

---

[8]    For a description of the techniques for the derivation of zero-coupon curves, see Das, Satyajit (with Roger Cohen) "Interest Rate And Yield Curve Modelling: An Introduction" in Das, Satyajit (editor) (1997) *Risk Management and Financial Derivatives: A Guide to the Mathematics*; LBC Information Services, Sydney; MacMillan, England; McGraw-Hill, Chicago at Chapter 3.

[9]    Little is known about the term structure of real rates. One view is that the real rate term structure should be relatively flat with the Australian experience suggesting that the curve is flat to slightly negative with a small decline in real yields (approximately 6-8 bps for every five years in maturity). This may reflect investor preferences for longer maturities and/or liquidity/trading consideration; see Vineburg, Stephen and Kolhatkar, Vinay "Inflation-indexed Securities" (September 1996) *Financial Derivatives and Risk Management* 7 41-49 at 44,45.

The second approach has the advantage that it allows the valuation of options (either embedded in the security or specific over-the-counter structures). An example of a generic term structure model has been published.[10] The model constructs a real return yield curve using an observable set of real rates (from traded inflation-indexed bonds). The implied inflation term structure is calculated by solving simultaneous equations of price as a function of the nominal discount factor and an assumed interpolation method. The approach in effect assumes investors have specified inflation expectations based on assumed inflation rates that are embedded in the nominal interest rate structure and in the prices of inflation-indexed securities.

This curve can then be used within a Hull-White interest term structure model framework to value options on such securities. The model can be calibrated to recover available market prices of securities and options within an arbitrage-free framework.

This approach has a number of merits:

- It uses a single model of real returns based on available market real yields.
- The implied forward inflation rates are derived directly from available market instruments.
- It is flexible and allows a consistent pricing methodology to be applied to inflation-indexed securities and inflation derivatives including options.

However, the approach also has some limitations:

- Absence of or limitations in the number of available securities/instruments in the market that may limit the ability to apply this approach. Gaps and discontinuity in the market may require assumptions and estimates to be made that are difficult to validate.
- The depth and liquidity in the underlying market may be limited making the approach flawed. For example, the market prices may embody liquidity premiums that may not have been properly modeled.
- The issue of issuer credit risk may be relevant where nongovernmental issuers issue the inflation-indexed bonds.
- The impact of tax and accounting factors on the market prices are difficult to isolate.
- Considerable uncertainty exists about the underlying relationship between real yields, nominal yields, and inflationary expectations.

In practice, the concept of the breakeven inflation rate has become an important concept in the trading of such securities. The breakeven return refers to the level

---

[10] See Moss, Doug and Preston, Benjamin "Profiting From Inflation" (February 1997) *AsiaRisk* 37-39.

of actual inflation that would equate the return available on a fixed-rate nominal interest security with the same maturity. This breakeven inflation rate is calculated as follows by rearranging the Fisher relationship:

$$h_{be} = (1+ R_N)/(1 + R_R)$$

Where:

$h_{be}$ = breakeven inflation rate
$R_N$ = nominal interest rate
$R_R$ = expected real interest rate

This approach assumes that inflation expectations are implicit in the nominal yield curve. The breakeven rate uses an assumed real rate to derive the implied inflation expectation. This allows comparisons between *expected* and *implied* inflation expectation to be used to assess the relative value of inflation-indexed bonds.

## 6.4  Price Sensitivity

The price sensitivity of inflation-indexed securities may be measured in a manner similar to that used with conventional securities. The concept of duration can be used to measure the relative price risk of such transactions.

As described previously, the value of an inflation-linked bond is driven by the indexation for inflation to the date of valuation and the expected real return over the remaining life of the security. In the case of inflation-indexed securities, the duration and modified duration of these bonds are calculated with regard to changes in the real rate or real yield to maturity. This is done by taking the known cash flows to derive the duration of the security. This approach, as with valuation, does not require assumption about future inflation.

Inflation-indexed securities will generally have a duration that is greater than that for a conventional bond for an equivalent maturity. This reflects the fact that the cash flows and the principal of an index-linked bond increases with inflation and the deferred payment structure used in structures such as capital-indexed bonds. However, the duration of inflation-indexed bonds (with respect to real yields) is not directly comparable with the duration of conventional bonds (with respect to nominal yields).

**Exhibit 14.10** sets out the dynamics of the real rate duration of inflation-indexed securities.

**Exhibit 14.10**
**Inflation-indexed Securities — Real Rate Duration**

Assume the following terms:

Face Value      100
Coupon Rate     5.00%
Real Yield      5.00% pa

The following table sets out the duration of both capital-indexed bonds and index-amortizing bonds with different maturities:

| Maturity (years) | Capital-indexed Bond | Index Amortizing Bond |
|:---:|:---:|:---:|
| 10 | 7.9 | 4.7 |
| 15 | 10.6 | 6.7 |
| 20 | 12.8 | 8.5 |
| 50 | 18.6 | 15.7 |

*Source:* Vineburg, Stephen and Kolhatkar, Vinay "Inflation-indexed Securities" *Financial Derivatives and Risk Management* 7 (September 1996): 41-49 at 45.

## 6.5   Derivatives Pricing

As noted above, inflation derivatives are generally priced off the underlying market prices for inflation-indexed securities. This reflects both the role of the inflation-indexed securities market as a source of market information of expected real rates and expected future inflation rates, and as the hedging medium for inflation derivative trading.

In practice, inflation derivatives are focused on the valuation of structures that seek to either lock in future real rates of return and/or future inflation expectations. This means that the derivatives must be priced so that the expected cash flows of the transaction as at commencement are equal on a present value basis. This requires the estimate of forward inflation rates and expected real rates to be stripped out traded market instruments. This is calculated using the techniques described above. Once the forward inflation rates and expected real rates are stripped out, it is a relatively simple matter to derive the cash flows of the proposed transactions. The cash flows are then discounted to the start of the transaction with the pricing being set to equate the two sets of cash flows.[11]

---

[11]  This assumes that that any uncertainty premium is known.

The hedging of such transactions is more problematic. The market is not at a true trading stage and in general transactions are counterparty-matched transactions or transactions that are hedged using an underlying inflation-indexed security. Where the transaction relies on trading in the underlying inflation-indexed bonds, the type of transaction is dictated by the availability of the hedge.[12] Hedge availability may be restricted in a number of ways:

- The restricted availability of borrowing facilities for inflation-indexed securities may constrain short selling. This dictates that the dealer financial institution may typically prefer to pay inflation-indexed returns versus receipt of a fixed or floating nominal rate.
- The pattern of cash flows of the underlying inflation-linked bond used to hedge the derivative may be significantly different from the derivative cash flows. This requires the dealer to undertake separate transactions to engineer the cash flow match required.

In practice, this has dictated two types of inflation derivative trading. Firstly, matched trades as between two counterparties with the dealer facilitating the transactions and managing any timing or cash flow mismatch. Secondly, inflation trades where the dealer purchases the underlying inflation-indexed bond and enters into an inflation swap to convert the inflation-indexed cash flows to nominal interest cash flows. This effectively allows the dealer to pay an investor inflation-linked cash flow under the swap. For example, the second type of transaction has been common in markets (such as Australia) where there has been significant inflation-linked bond issuance connected with infrastructure projects. These bonds have been purchased by financial institutions that have entered into the inflation swap to convert the inflation-indexed cash flows to nominal interest rates at an attractive credit spread. **Exhibit 14.11** and **Exhibit 14.12** set out examples of these structures.

---

[12]  The hedging difficulties add significantly to the cost of inflation swaps (for example, up to 50-60 bps pa in the UK); see Irving, Richard "Inflation Swappers Savour US Boost" (October 1996) *Risk* vol 9 no 10 6; Locke, Jane "Growing Attractions" (July 1994) *Risk* vol. 7 no. 7 6-7.

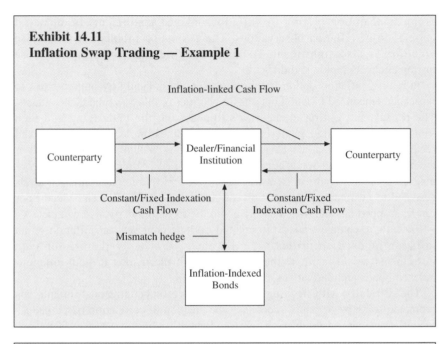

**Exhibit 14.11**
**Inflation Swap Trading — Example 1**

Inflation-linked Cash Flow

Counterparty → Dealer/Financial Institution → Counterparty

Constant/Fixed Indexation Cash Flow         Constant/Fixed Indexation Cash Flow

Mismatch hedge ———

Inflation-Indexed Bonds

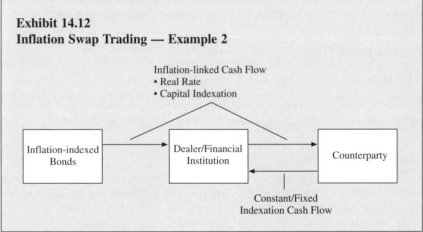

**Exhibit 14.12**
**Inflation Swap Trading — Example 2**

Inflation-linked Cash Flow
• Real Rate
• Capital Indexation

Inflation-indexed Bonds → Dealer/Financial Institution → Counterparty

Constant/Fixed Indexation Cash Flow

The above approach to pricing is focused on inflation swaps. Inflation options present different challenges for both pricing and hedging.

Inflation floors and caps are generally priced within a general derivative pricing framework. The valuation of options on inflation-indexed securities at fixed real yield levels can be attempted using traditional option pricing models. However, most pricing is undertaken using Monte Carlo techniques. A special problem of option pricing on inflation-indexed instruments is the serial correlation of inflation observations. The estimation problem of real return volatility is also significant. Dynamic hedging and replication of these instruments is complex and difficult.

In reality, inflation option trading is driven significantly by opportunities to repackage embedded inflation options in securities or other commercial contracts. The repackaged option element is stripped from the underlying and then transferred and traded in derivative form. For example, inflation-indexed securities in several markets have embedded options enabling the issuer to call or the investor to put the bonds at pre-specified real rates. Similarly, some inflation-indexed revenue streams in infrastructure projects have minimum inflation levels designed to guarantee the project revenues at a base level. This embedded floor can be stripped out and traded separately in the form of a derivative contract.

To date, exchange traded futures and options contracts on inflation or on inflation-indexed securities have not emerged. The availability of such instruments would facilitate the development of the market in both inflation-indexed bonds and derivatives.

The difficulty with hedging and the absence of hedging instruments has prompted some participants to consider the creation of correlation-based hedges for inflation-indexed products. This would entail trading in a basket of interest rate, equity, currency, and commodity contracts (futures/options or over-the-counter derivatives) to hedge positions in inflation-indexed instruments

# 7.　Applications

## 7.1　Issuers

The major issuers of inflation-linked securities have been governments and other public entities. The major motivation for this group of issuers includes:

- The demonstration of a commitment to inflation control (this naturally only applies to governments).
- The lower nominal cost to the issuer on the inflation-indexed bonds reflecting the avoidance of the need to pay an inflation uncertainty risk premium as the real rate is guaranteed.
- The longer maturity achievable using inflation-indexed bonds.

Other factors have included the desire to foster a market in inflation-indexed products to assist investment managers to develop long-term saving and retirement income products. This has been a part of the desire by various governments to encourage private pension schemes.

In certain emerging market countries, inflation-indexed securities have been issued to ensure positive real rates of return in high or hyper-inflationary environments.

However, parallel to the government issuer market, interest in private issuance of inflation-linked debt has developed.[13] This private issuance falls into two categories:

- **Arbitrage issuers** — these are generally highly rated, frequent capital market borrowers who issue inflation-indexed bonds and simultaneously enter into an inflation swap to convert the funding into either a fixed or floating rate basis at a relatively attractive cost. This issuance is driven on the issue side by either a demand supply imbalance on the new issue side whereby investor demand is met by the issue or a pricing discrepancy between the inflation swap market and the inflation-indexed bond market. The inflation swaps are mainly undertaken against the position of dealers or investors along an inflation-indexed bond that is sought to be converted into a nominal return investment (see **Exhibit 14.12** above).
- **Inflation-indexed revenue issuers** — these are generally issuers with a natural inflation-indexed revenue stream seeking to match the income and expense basis of their operations. These include utilities (electricity, gas, pipelines, water, airports, and so on), specific separate infrastructure projects (toll roads, bridge, mass transit systems, railroads and other transportation systems, and so on) and property (property leases). The major attraction of inflation-indexed bond issuance for these issuers includes: the revenue-expense hedging, lower nominal financing cost (because of the absence of the inflation uncertainty risk premium), and the longer maturity funding achievable (up to 25-30 years in certain markets for inflation-indexed debt that compares to about 12-15 for normal project debt).

In practice, there are certain inherent limitations in the new issuance market:

- The credit risk profile of inflation-indexed debt creates a natural limitation on the type and range of issuer. Alternatively, the credit risk premium demanded for lower credit quality may be significantly higher than for a conventional bond thereby reducing or eliminating any cost advantage of the inflation-indexed financing.
- The potential for inflation-indexed revenue issuers is naturally restricted. Equity investors in infrastructure projects are motivated, partially, by the impact of inflation on the revenues and earning of such investments. The investment dynamic of infrastructure projects is driven by an initial large capital outlay followed by a long-term, rising earnings stream (the earnings stream is very revenue-sensitive because of the low variable cost component). This makes the project economics highly sensitive to rates of inflation as

---

[13] See Ogden, Joan "When Companies Can Use Inflation-indexed Bonds" (March 1997) *Global Finance* 72.

increasing prices (through the in-built pricing mechanism that is directly or implicitly price-inflation related—typically, price inflation minus a productivity factor). Investors are therefore reluctant to hedge the inflation risk (at least, all of it) as it effectively limits their equity returns from the investment.

- The inflexibility of inflation-linked debt (right to call, and so on) relative to conventional debt instruments also makes these instruments unattractive to inflation-indexed revenue issuers.
- The relative illiquidity and early stage of development of the market for inflation-indexed debt may result in the pricing of these forms of debt, reflecting a liquidity premium that vitiates any price advantage.

However, despite these difficulties a significant nongovernment-issuer market in inflation-indexed bonds exists in certain jurisdictions, such as Australia.

## 7.2 Investors

Investors in inflation-indexed bonds have been traditional investor groups including pension funds, insurance companies, and other fixed income investors. In addition, a number of specialist mutual funds/unit trusts have been established to invest in inflation-indexed securities.

Investor participation in inflation-indexed markets is driven by two primary factors:

- The inherent exposure to changes in inflation risk in certain investment products offered by fund managers.
- The fact that inflation bonds may function as a separate asset class allowing additional portfolio diversification opportunities.

Other reasons for investing in inflation-indexed securities include: trading implied real rates or implied inflation rates, the longer duration of these securities, and relative value strategies devised around environments where inflation-indexed securities are likely to outperform conventional nominal interest securities.

In practice, investor participation has been restricted by a number of factors:

- Lack of size of the market and the early stage of development of the market.
- Lack of liquidity in these securities.
- Complexity of structure and pricing/valuation issues.
- Accounting and tax treatment issues.

In recent times, the low actual inflation levels and therefore low nominal returns on inflation-indexed bonds has also limited investment interest in these securities.

## 7.3 Investment Inflation Risk

Investment managers have inherent inflation risks. For example, the liabilities of pension and superannuation funds, workers compensation insurers, and disability insurers are linked directly to inflation or indirectly linked to inflation through linkages to salary or other income levels. A good example of this type of risk is the obligation of some pension plans to pay either a lump-sum benefit based on final salary or inflation-linked pensions or annuities for fixed or indefinite periods (typically life) to fund beneficiaries upon retirement.

The liability in these cases is a function of the *actual* inflation levels between the time of determination of the rate of payment into the fund or premium and the timing of the payout. The ability of the fund investments to meet these liabilities is inherently linked to the difference between the expected level of inflation and the actual level of price inflation. The extreme risk in the situation identified is the underfunding of the future obligations whereby the value of the investments is insufficient to cover the liabilities. This risk is referred to as "surplus risk" (the actuarial surplus refers to the excess of fund asset market value over the present value of expected/projected fund liabilities). Inflation-indexed securities and derivatives can be utilized to hedge these risks.

**Exhibit 14.13** sets out an interesting transaction based around the hedging of investment inflation risk.

---

**Exhibit 14.13**
**Inflation Index Investment Hedge**

In 1995, Midland Bank undertook a 20-year £ inflation-indexed bond issue.[14] The issue was structured to pay an annual coupon of 4.1% pa indexed for inflation subject to a cap on the inflation level of 5.0%. The bond was priced at around 90 (a discount of 10% to face value).

The bond was successfully targeted at pension plans that either guaranteed their beneficiaries a fixed annual increase of either 3% pa or an increase linked to the UK inflation rate as measured by the RPI (retail price index) capped at 5.00% pa. These guarantee schemes create significant exposures to the rate of inflation for the investment funds.

However, the risk is difficult to hedge. Trading in traditional UK inflation-indexed gilts is not fully effective as the pension fund's maximum exposure to inflation rates is capped at 5.00%. This means that the indexed gilt is an expensive hedge. Where inflation is above 5.00% pa

---

[14] See Irving, Richard "HSBC Caps the Bank" (June 1995) *Risk* 7-8.

the fund may find itself over-invested in a low-yielding investment. In contrast, the capped bond issue provides a superior and cost-effective hedge as it exactly matches the cash flow profile of the pension fund's liabilities.

The economics of the hedge are interesting. At the time of the transaction, UK-indexed gilts offered a real return of 3.61% pa. The capped indexed bond offered significantly higher returns through the combination of the issue discount and the higher real coupon. The improved economics are driven by the premium received for the embedded call sold by the investor to the issuer and the credit risk differential between the issuer and the government risk on the index-linked gilt.

## 7.4    Inflation Bonds as a Separate Asset Class[15]

There is a continuing debate as to whether inflation-indexed securities constitute a separate asset class.[16] If inflation-indexed securities are an asset class distinct from and separate to conventional debt securities, then investment portfolios would benefit in terms of risk and return performance from the addition of these instruments to the overall portfolio.

Investments are generally regarded as having three characteristics: returns (income and price changes), risk (in the form of price volatility), and correlation to other investment assets. Inflation-linked securities are characterized by:

- **Returns** — inflation-indexed securities offer slightly lower nominal returns compared to conventional securities in periods where actual inflation coincides with expected inflation as embedded in the nominal return conventional securities. The lower return reflects the absence of the risk premium for uncertainty of expected inflation. The inflation-indexed security will underperform a conventional security where inflation falls but will outperform a conventional security where inflation is higher than expected.
- **Volatility** — inflation-indexed securities have lower volatility than conventional securities. This reflects the adjustment to the cash flows where inflation levels rise.
- **Correlation** — the relationship between inflation-indexed securities and other asset classes is dependent on inflation levels. In periods of stable

---

[15]  For a discussion of the definition of a separate asset class, see Chapter 8.

[16]  For an analysis of this issue, see Borutta, Hansjorg "Real Bonds—The Real McCoy" (1997) SBC Prospects 1 12-17; Lamm, R. McFall "Inflation Protected And Insurance Linked Securities Portfolios" (June 1998) *The Australian Corporate Treasurer* 9-12.

inflation, the behavior of inflation-indexed bonds is similar to that of conventional securities and the correlation between inflation-indexed securities and other asset classes is very similar to that of conventional securities. Where there are changes in inflation, the correlation relationship changes. For example, if inflation rises, then inflation-indexed securities are likely to be negatively correlated to nominal interest rate securities and also have a low or negative correlation with other asset classes.

The analysis indicates that inflation-indexed securities will be characterized in a stable inflation environment by similar returns to conventional securities, lower volatility, and low or negative correlation with conventional bonds and other assets where inflation levels rise. This would be consistent with the thesis that adding inflation-indexed bonds as an investment asset to a portfolio has the potential to enhance return (for a given level of risk) or decrease risk (for a given level of return). In both these environments, the risk may be defined in terms of the correlation relationship to an equity index such as the S&P 500 or to the MSCI index. If the risk is reduced by matching assets and liabilities, then the potential benefits to investors such as pension funds are very significant.

**Exhibit 14.14** and **Exhibit 14.15** on page 833 set out two examples of the potential impact of including inflation-indexed securities in an investment portfolio.[17]

---

**Exhibit 14.14**
**Inflation-indexed Securities in Investment Portfolios — Example 1**

In order to assess the potential role of inflation-indexed securities in a portfolio context, it is necessary to assume expected returns, volatility and correlations. The assumed levels for these parameters are set out in **Table 1**.

The forecast return, volatility and correlation estimates can be used to generate optimal portfolios. The optimum asset allocations using the forecasts for two purely domestic US portfolios are set out in **Table 2**.

The analysis indicates that by adding insurance-linked securities and insurance-linked bonds and removing bonds, it may be possible to add return without significantly altering the risk level of the portfolio.

If other asset classes are added, such as corporate bonds, international equities, commodities, emerging market debt, and emerging market

---

[17] Care should be taken in interpreting the results as the results are very sensitive to assumed returns, volatility, and correlations.

equities, then the portfolio, before adding inflation-indexed securities and insurance-linked bonds, exhibits higher (2-3% pa) returns for the same level of risk relative to the purely domestic portfolio. The introduction of inflation-indexed securities and insurance-linked bonds increases returns for a given level of risk but not to the same degree as for the purely domestic portfolio.

*Source:* Lamm, R. McFall "Inflation-protected And Insurance-linked Securities Portfolios" *The Australian Corporate Treasurer* (June 1998): 9-12 at 10-12.

## Table 1: Returns, Volatility and Correlations

| Asset Class | Commodities | S&P | EAFE | Emerging Market Equities | Cash | Treasury Bonds | Corporate Bonds | Emerging Market Debt | Real Estate | Inflation-Indexed Securities | Insurance Linked-Securities |
|---|---|---|---|---|---|---|---|---|---|---|---|
| Returns (% pa) | 5.0 | 10.0 | 12.0 | 20.0 | 5.0 | 7.0 | 7.5 | 10 | 3.0 | 6.8 | 7.0 |
| Volatility (% entire period) | 30 | 20 | 25 | 40 | 1.5 | 10.0 | 11 | 15 | 4.0 | 7.5 | 11 |
| Sharpe Ratio | 0.16 | 0.50 | 0.50 | 0.50 | 3.33 | 0.70 | 0.68 | 0.63 | 0.75 | 0.91 | 0.64 |
| **Correlations** | | | | | | | | | | | |
| Commodities | 1.00 | -0.53 | -0.54 | -0.39 | 0.37 | -0.15 | -0.20 | -0.10 | -0.20 | -0.10 | 0.00 |
| S&P | | 1.00 | 0.46 | 0.30 | 0.15 | 0.44 | 0.53 | 0.30 | 0.25 | 0.30 | 0.00 |
| EAFE | | | 1.00 | 0.12 | -0.10 | 0.43 | 0.43 | 0.17 | 0.15 | 0.30 | 0.00 |
| Emerging Market Equities | | | | 1.00 | 0.10 | 0.15 | 0.15 | -0.30 | 0.10 | 0.10 | 0.00 |
| Cash | | | | | 1.00 | 0.06 | 0.05 | 0.21 | 0.00 | 0.00 | 0.00 |
| Treasury Bonds | | | | | | 1.00 | 0.97 | 0.21 | -0.30 | 0.50 | 0.00 |
| Corporate Bonds | | | | | | | 1.00 | 0.23 | -0.30 | 0.50 | 0.00 |
| Emerging Market Debt | | | | | | | | 1.00 | -0.10 | 0.10 | 0.00 |
| Real Estate | | | | | | | | | 1.00 | -0.25 | 0.00 |
| Inflation-indexed Securities | | | | | | | | | | 1.00 | 0.00 |
| Insurance-linked Securities | | | | | | | | | | | 1.00 |

*Source:* BT Global Economic Research.

## Table 2: Optimal Asset Allocations for Purely Domestic Portfolios

| Portfolio Return | Equities | Cash | Bonds | Portfolio Volatility | Equities | Cash | Bonds | Inflation-indexed Securities | Insurance-linked Bonds | Portfolio Volatility |
|---|---|---|---|---|---|---|---|---|---|---|
| (%) | (%) | (%) | (%) | (%) | (%) | (%) | (%) | (%) | (%) | (%) |
| 5.0 | 0 | 99 | 1 | 1.5 | 0 | 99 | 0 | 1 | 0 | 1.5 |
| 5.5 | 8 | 87 | 5 | 2.1 | 4 | 80 | 0 | 9 | 6 | 1.8 |
| 6.0 | 18 | 75 | 7 | 3.3 | 11 | 64 | 0 | 15 | 11 | 2.7 |
| 6.5 | 28 | 63 | 9 | 4.5 | 18 | 48 | 0 | 20 | 15 | 3.7 |
| 7.0 | 38 | 51 | 11 | 5.8 | 25 | 31 | 0 | 24 | 19 | 4.8 |
| 7.5 | 48 | 39 | 13 | 7.1 | 32 | 15 | 0 | 29 | 24 | 5.9 |
| 8.0 | 58 | 27 | 15 | 8.4 | 40 | 0 | 0 | 32 | 28 | 7.0 |
| 8.5 | 68 | 15 | 17 | 9.7 | 57 | 0 | 0 | 17 | 26 | 8.4 |
| 9.0 | 78 | 3 | 19 | 10.9 | 74 | 0 | 0 | 1 | 25 | 10.0 |
| 9.5 | 94 | 0 | 6 | 12.4 | 91 | 0 | 0 | 0 | 9 | 12.0 |
| 10.0 | 100 | 0 | 0 | 15.0 | 100 | 0 | 0 | 0 | 0 | 15.0 |

*Source:* BT Global Economic Research.

## Exhibit 14.15
## Inflation-indexed Securities in Investment Portfolios — Example 2

The impact of introducing inflation-indexed bonds into a global portfolio for £ investors in the period January 1988 to September 1996 was undertaken by SBC. The proportion on inflation-indexed securities was changed from 0% to 50% to 100% in three different portfolios—an income portfolio, a yield portfolio, and a balanced portfolio. The results are summarized below:

### Income portfolio

Benchmark weights in the portfolio are:

Global Equities  = 0%
Domestic Bonds = 45%
World Bonds    = 15%
Cash        = 40%

| Domestic Bonds (weights in %) | | Sharpe Ratio[18] | | |
| Nominal | Index-linked | All Maturities | 5-year Maturity | Maturities Over Five Years |
| --- | --- | --- | --- | --- |
| 100 | 0 | 0.08 | 0.08 | 0.08 |
| 50 | 50 | 0.00 | –0.34 | 0.00 |
| 0 | 100 | –0.08 | –0.25 | –0.08 |

*Yield portfolio*

Benchmark weights in the portfolio are:

Global Equities  = 20%
Domestic Bonds = 45%
World Bonds      = 15%
Cash                  = 20%

| Domestic Bonds (weights in %) | | Sharpe Ratio | | |
| Nominal | Index-linked | All Maturities | 5-year Maturity | Maturities Over Five Years |
| --- | --- | --- | --- | --- |
| 100 | 0 | 0.29 | 0.29 | 0.29 |
| 50 | 50 | 0.24 | 0.25 | 0.23 |
| 0 | 100 | 0.18 | 0.17 | 0.17 |

*Balanced Portfolio*

Benchmark weights in the portfolio are:

Global Equities  = 45%
Domestic Bonds = 33.75%
World Bonds      = 11.25%
Cash                  = 10%

| Domestic Bonds (weights in %) | | Sharpe Ratio | | |
| Nominal | Index-linked | All Maturities | 5-year Maturity | Maturities Over Five Years |
| --- | --- | --- | --- | --- |
| 100 | 0 | 0.35 | 0.35 | 0.35 |
| 50 | 50 | 0.33 | 0.34 | 0.33 |
| 0 | 100 | 0.30 | 0.30 | 0.30 |

---

[18] The Sharpe Ratio measures the excess return over the risk-free rate divided by the amount of risk (measured by volatility of returns).

The analysis indicates that under none of the strategies would adding inflation-indexed securities have significantly improved portfolio performance. The portfolios with higher portion of bonds are more affected by the addition of inflation-indexed bonds. This reflects the high correlation between nominal and inflation-indexed bonds and the similarity of risk under certain inflation environments. Where the portfolios have a lower portion invested in bonds, the addition of inflation bonds assists in reducing risk through diversification reflecting the lower correlations between inflation-linked bonds and other asset classes.

*Source:* Hansjorg Borutta "Real Bonds—The Real McCoy" *SBC Prospects.* 1 (1997): 12-17.

## 7.5   Inflation Risk Hedging[19]

As noted above, industrial companies often have a significant level of exposure to inflation levels. This can be on revenue (effectively, the linkage of revenue to price inflation) or expense (effectively, the linkage of expenses to price inflation). Sectors with inflation-indexation elements include:

- Utilities (electricity, gas, pipelines, water, airports, and so on).
- Healthcare (health cost reimbursement from private insurers and governments).
- Specific infrastructure projects (toll roads, bridge, mass transit, railroads, and other transportation systems).
- Property (property leases).

This means that providers of these services have revenue-side risks linked to changes in inflation levels. This also means that *purchasers* of these services also have expense-side risks linked to inflation levels. The latter element implies that there are very few companies that do not have some degree of exposure to changes in price levels either directly or indirectly. Some companies may have risks on both revenue and expense sides. For example, a retailer whose primary activity is buying wholesale and selling retail is naturally exposed to inflation on the margin.

---

[19]   See Carmody, Sean and Glover, James "CPI-linked Derivatives" (August 1998) *The Australian Corporate Treasurer* 23-25; Alaton, Peter "Swap Markets: A Real Rate Swap" (December 1997*) Risk Magazine—Nordic Markets Supplement* 12-13; "Locking In The Inflation Rate" (February 1998) *AsiaMoney* 8;"Prebon Writes First Standalone Inflation Hedge" (1 May 1996) *Financial Products* Issue 41 20.

The exposure to price inflation levels creates risk only where there is a mismatch between inflation-linked revenue flows and noninflation-linked expenses or vice versa. Increasingly, organizations have become sensitive to this risk and have sought to manage this risk in a manner similar to other financial risks.

This inflation risk management has taken a number of forms. Entities with inflation-linked revenues, as noted above, have examined the possibility of issuing inflation-linked bonds to better match revenues and expenses. In contrast, entities with inflation-linked expenses have examined the use of inflation derivatives, particularly inflation swaps, to hedge their inflation risks.

The demand for derivative-based inflation risk management is driven by a variety of factors:

• The off-balance sheet nature of the hedge that avoids the need to invest (regulatory) capital in and hold bonds on-balance sheet.
• The ability to customize the hedge in terms of maturity and structure.

The dynamics of the market are varied as between jurisdictions. The Australian market illustrates the pattern of activity:[20]

• Payers of inflation-indexed returns have been typically:
  1. Entities with inflation-linked expenses seeking to either lock in the nominal cost in interest rate terms or by fixing the future inflation rates at market-implied inflation rates.
  2. Entities with inflation-indexed revenues seeking to hedge streams of inflation-indexed income into a fixed stream either in interest rate terms or by fixing the future inflation rates.
  3. Financial institutions, primarily banks, who have purchased inflation-indexed securities (primarily, issued by special-purpose infrastructure companies) that are then swapped into nominal returns over a floating index rate at a margin that is at a level considered attractive for the project risk taken.
  4. Receivers of inflation-indexed returns have been fund managers with underlying inflation exposures on their liabilities or arbitrage issuers of inflation-indexed bonds.

---

[20] See Daly, Troy "Index-linked Opportunities" (August 1997) *Risk—Australia & New Zealand Supplement* 5; Webb, Andrew "A Tale of Two Markets?" (January 1998) *Futures & Options World* 15-17.

# 8. Summary

Inflation-indexed instruments have been in existence for some 15 years. Increasingly, there is interest in these securities as an attractive alternative investment. There is also parallel interest in the inflation derivative structures as a mechanism for the management of price-inflation risk. While liquidity and volumes are relatively modest, the market is showing growth both in terms of new issuance (both government and private) and inflation derivatives. Low rates of inflation have to some extent restricted the growth in these markets. However, with inflation rates at very low levels in historic terms, the increased risk of rises in inflation over the longer term may encourage consideration of these types of instruments.

# 15
# Insurance-linked Notes and Derivatives

## 1. Overview

In recent years, notes and securities linked to insurance risk[1] have emerged as a class of transactions in the capital markets. A number of related derivative products have also emerged. The development of insurance derivatives is driven by the application of derivative *technology* to *new* asset classes.

The trading of financial instruments linked to insurance risk commenced in the early 1990s[2] and is currently showing strong growth. These instruments that take the form of option contracts or structured notes have payoffs linked to property catastrophe risk. Insurance-indexed notes embody a specific linkage to losses arising from claims against insurers as a result of some natural event such as a hurricane, storm, earthquake, or similar event. The linkage entails linking the value of coupon payments or principal repayments to an identified event. They are designed to allow insurance companies to hedge their exposure to the risk of losses arising from payouts under certain types of insurance events. These financial instruments are usually purchased by investors who in return for a fee assume the risk of the catastrophe event and the loss incurred by the insurer. These new products have emerged as an

---

[1]  An earlier version of this chapter was published as "Insurance Derivatives—Part One: Reinsurance Markets" (14 January 1999) *Financial Products* Issue 105 20-25; "Insurance Derivatives—Part Two: CAT Derivative Structures (February 11, 1999) *Financial Products* Issue 107 16-28; "Insurance Derivatives—Part Three: CAT Risk Pricing" (March 11, 1999) *Financial Products* Issue 109 18-25.

[2]  The possibility of securitization of insurance risk was first suggested in the 1970s, see Goshay, Robert and Sandor, Richard "An Inquiry Into the Feasibility Of A Reinsurance Futures Market" (1973) *Journal of Business Finance* vol. 5 no. 2 56-66.

important innovation that provides a link between the insurance industry and the capital markets.

In this chapter, insurance-derivative products are analyzed. The structure of this chapter is as follows: the structure of the insurance and reinsurance markets are examined; the types of hedging strategies available to manage insurance risk are then considered; the different types of insurance derivatives (CAT options, CAT bonds, recapitalization structures, and so on) are then analyzed; the pricing of insurance-derivative products is then discussed; and, finally, the interaction of capital markets and the insurance markets is analyzed.

## 2. Structure of Reinsurance Market

### 2.1 Market Structure

The structure of the insurance market is set out in **Exhibit 15.1**.

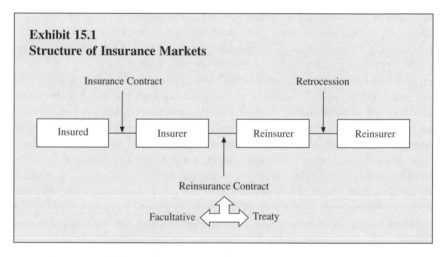

**Exhibit 15.1**
**Structure of Insurance Markets**

The market for insurance is traditionally divided into two quite separate although closely inter-related markets:

- **The primary market** — this consists of the transaction between the insured party (the party seeking protection through the insurance contract) and the insurer (the party providing the protection in return for the payment of the premium). This market focuses on the sale of various types of insurance policies such as various types of casualty policies covering the risk of loss to property and possessions (houses, contents, automobiles, and so on).
- **The reinsurance market** — this is the market where the insurers can pass on or cede the insurance risk (either all or part) to an insurer (unrelated to the

primary insurance contract). The reinsurance is transacted with the objective of reducing the primary insurer's risk. It may be entered into for a variety of reasons including: managing the volatility of the primary insurer's earnings as a result of losses suffered; increasing risk-bearing capacity of the primary insurer; or managing the use of the primary insurer's capital. The reinsurer charges a premium for assuming the reinsurance risk. This fee is referred to as the rate on line (ROL). The second component of the reinsurance market is the concept of retrocession. This is a process whereby the reinsurer may in turn pass on (retrocede) a portion of their *reinsurance risk* to other reinsurers (known as retrocessionaries).

The reinsurance process is based on a bilateral contract between the insurer and the reinsurer. The reinsurance contract is entered into either directly or through an insurance broker active in reinsurance.

## 2.2   Types of Cover

The reinsurance cover can be structured in a number of ways. This entails both different types of risks and the actual structure of the risk transfer.

The reinsurance contracts are structured on one of the following basis:

- **Treaty basis** — this relates to a contract that is written to cover an entire line or book of business of the ceding primary insurer.
- **Facultative basis** — this relates to a contract that is written to cover specific risks on a risk-by-risk basis where the reinsurer has the right to accept or reject *each individual risk* submitted for reinsurance coverage by the ceding primary insurer.

The actual structure of risk transfer may take a number of forms:

- **Proportional (prorata)** — under this structure, the reinsurer covers a specified proportion of the ceding primary insurer's loss as a result of the occurrence of a casualty event. The level of cover is calculated as an agreed fixed percentage of losses.
- **Excess of Loss** — under this structure, the reinsurer provides the ceding primary insurer with protection on a structured basis. This may take the form of assuming the risk of losses above an agreed upon amount (this may be specified as a US$ loss amount or a stated loss ratio (losses/premiums received). This structure usually provides the primary insurer with an agreed amount of protection above a minimum level (the agreed retention level). This threshold level is referred to as the attachment point. For example, a typical transaction might entail the primary insurer entering into an excess of loss policy whereby the reinsurer covers US$25 million of losses in excess of US$50 million. The primary insurer is required under this contract to bear

the first US$50 million of losses. If losses exceed this amount, then the reinsurer will bear losses up to US$25 million. Any losses in excess of US$75 million are borne by the primary reinsurer.[3]

These structures are primarily applicable to treaty basis reinsurance arrangements. Typical reinsurance contracts are for a period of one year.

Other structures include dual trigger policies. Under this structure, the ceding primary insurer is only indemnified against losses where it suffers a loss as a result of claims *and* some aggregate insurance industry loss index measure is above a certain level.

The structure of contracts highlights the fact that the reinsurance market is far from homogenous and a variety of structures are utilized to transfer and manage risk.

## 2.3 Reinsurance Cover

Insurance risks are of two distinct types:

- **High-frequency low-severity** — this refers to the types of insurance where individual events and resulting individual claims are small relative to the resources (capital and reserves) of the insurer. This typically covers most types of insurance claims and contracts.
- **Low-frequency high-severity** — this refers to the types of events where individual events and resulting claims while relatively infrequent have the potential for resulting in very significant claims on the insurer. These claims have the potential to have significant economic impact on the insurer in terms of the capacity of the entity to meet claims out of its capital and reserves. This type of risk generally relates to natural catastrophes such as earthquakes, hurricanes/typhoons, and other natural diasters.

Insurers manage high-frequency low-severity events by diversification of risks. Insurance premiums are based on actuarial assessments of risks and the operational costs on the insurance company. In contrast, the low-frequency high-severity types of risks present difficulties in management.

In examining insurance derivatives, it is important to note at the outset that the products that have emerged have focused on a narrow segment of the market—the market for reinsurance of property catastrophe insurance (specifically, claims against losses caused by catastrophic natural events such as hurricanes and earthquake). While conceptually there is no. reason that the basic

---

[3]    Many commentators have identified the similarity of the excess of loss structure to a call option spread. In effect, the primary insurer is buying a call option with a strike of US$50 million and selling a call with a strike of US$75 million.

concepts underlying insurance derivatives could not be extended to cover all types of reinsurance, it has not been used extensively in the management of these noncatastrophe risks to date. This reflects in part the impact of the following factors:

- The difficulties in managing catastrophe risk where aggregate exposure levels to a single event may be very large. This is particularly so in relation to the capital and reserves of an individual insurer or reinsurer, or of the market in total.
- The capacity of the reinsurance market to provide the required level of reinsurance coverage for such catastrophe events on a consistent basis at acceptable prices.
- The need in the absence of any appropriate risk transfer mechanisms for the insurer to hold significant levels of capital against these low-frequency low-severity risks.

The process of reinsurance is a mechanism for managing insurance risk. However, reinsurance cannot prevent claims and the resulting losses suffered by insurers. As is often stated, the impact of a number of large catastrophic natural events has inflicted large losses on the insurance and reinsurance markets. These losses have affected the earnings and the capital positions of property insurers. This aspect of the reinsurance market requires consideration of a number of issues: the amount of reinsurance cover available; the level of risk; barriers to managing reinsurance risk; and the level of reinsurance currently transacted.

The actual magnitude of catastrophe risk is difficult to accurately measure. However, the loss experience in the US market in recent years highlights the quantum of the risk. The total losses paid out by property insurers are in excess of US$60 billion.[4] In recent years, the following severe catastrophe events have taken place:

- Hurricane Andrew (1992) — losses of US$16 billion.
- Northbridge earthquake (1994) — losses of US$12.5 billion.

The above single event losses compare to *cumulative* losses over the previous decade of around US$25 billion.[5] In aggregate, in the 7-year period to 1995, total insured losses from natural disasters totaled around US$75 billion. This compares to total insured losses from natural diasters in the previous 25 years of

---

[4]    See Canter, Michael S., Cole, Joseph B., and Sandor, Richard L. "Catastrophe Options On The Chicago Board Of Trade" (September 1996) *Financial Derivatives and Risk Management* Issue 7 13-20 at 13.

[5]    See Froot, Kenneth A. (1997) *The Limited Financing of Catastrophe Risk: An Overview*; National Bureau of Economic Research Working Paper 6025.

around US$51 billion. The average loss per catastrophe event rose during this period from US$56 million to US$302 million.[6]

Risk-modeling increasingly suggests that the larger loss severity for any individual event is a permanent feature of catastrophe insurance. Single loss events of in excess of US$50 billion are now considered possible. This larger risk reflects a variety of demographic and geographic dynamics:

- Rapid population growth in coastal areas vulnerable to catastrophes. For example, the population growth in California (susceptible to earthquakes), Florida, and Texas (vulnerable to hurricanes) was roughly twice the overall growth in the US general population.[7]
- Increased purchase of insurance also exacerbates the risk. Between 1984 and 1993 the proportion of US households with insurance increased from 70% to 76% primarily as a result of a 46% increase in the proportion of renters with insurance.[8]
- The increasing evidence of human impact on weather patterns may have adversely changed the frequency and severity of natural catastrophes and disasters.

There is evidence that the increase in risk has not been matched by a commensurate increase in the amount of capital held against such risks. The total amount of capital available to support these risks is estimated at around US$250-300 billion, including both primary insurance company capital and reinsurance capital.[9] After adjustment for existing claims and liabilities (such as asbestos, tobacco, toxic hazards), one commentator estimates that there is approximately US$265 billion in capital to support insurance risks relating to around US$25,000-30,000 billion in property assets.[10] This imbalance between

---

[6] See Thackray, John "Insurance Derivatives Catch Fire" (December/January 1997) *Derivatives Strategy* 28-31 at 30.

[7] See Borden, Sara and Sarker, Asani "Securitizing Property Casualty Risk" (August 1996) *Current Issues in Economics And Finance*, Federal Reserve Bank of New York vol. 2 no. 9 1-6 at 2.

[8] See Borden, Sara and Sarker, Asani "Securitizing Property Casualty Risk" (August 1996) *Current Issues in Economics and Finance*, Federal Reserve Bank of New York vol. 2 no. 9 1-6 at 2.

[9] Reinsurance capital is estimated at around US$57 billion globally as at 1996. This consists of US reinsurers (US$27 billion), Bermudan reinsurers (US$6 billion), German reinsurers (US$7 billion), and the rest (US$17 billion); see (1996) *Global Reinsurance Highlights*: Standard and Poor's.

[10] See Canter, Michael S., Cole, Joseph B., and Sandor, Richard L. "Insurance Derivatives: A New Asset Class for the Capital Markets and a New Hedging Tool for the Insurance Industry" (Fall 1997) *Journal of Applied Corporate Finance* vol. 10 no. 3 69-83 at 69.

demand and supply for insurance risk capital has lead to the establishment of a number of new Bermuda-based reinsurers (introducing some additional US$6.5 billion in capital).

However, the imbalance remains significant. This is evident in the changing economics of the reinsurance market. The dynamics of the market have lead to a significant increase in the price of catastrophe insurance (average ROLs) and the risk retention levels as evidence by the attachment point levels:

• In 1992, US insurers provide approximately US$10 billion in catastrophe coverage of which US$8 billion was reinsured leaving a retained risk level of US$2 billion. The retained level is projected by industry bodies to have doubled in 1993.

• Between 1989 and 1995, the average ROL increased from 7.93% to 15.09%, based on one leading reinsurance brokers estimates. During the same period, the average attachment point for a single catastrophe also increased from US$1.14 billion to US$2.57 billion in industry losses.[11] Another study found that between 1985 and 1994 reinsurers raised reinsurance rates by 126%, their attachment points by 73% and that over 1990 to 1995 the maximum amount of coverage available to a single insurer decreased from US$251 million to US$240 million.[12]

Primary insurers of catastrophe risk can seek to manage the increasing risk through the following mechanisms:

• **Increased premiums** — in practice, insurers have limitations on the ability to manage catastrophe risk through premium increases as premium rates may be subject to regulations that restrict the timing and size of premium increases in high-risk areas.

• **Withdrawal from catastrophe risk underwriting** — in practice, the capacity to withdraw from specific types of insurance is also limited by legislation. For example, legislation in Florida limits the number of policies an insurance company can drop upon expiration of the policy. In California, legislation requires insurance companies to offer earthquake insurance with homeowners' insurance policies.[13]

---

[11] See Litzenberg, Robert H., Beagle-Hole, David R. and Reynolds, Craig E. " Assessing Reinsurance-linked Securities as a New Asset Class" (Special Issue 1996) *Journal of Portfolio Management* 76-86 at 78.

[12] See Borden, Sara and Sarker, Asani "Securitizing Property Casualty Risk" (August 1996*) Current Issues in Economics And Finance*, Federal Reserve Bank of New York vol. 2 no. 9 1-6 at 3.

[13] See Borden, Sara and Sarker, Asani "Securitizing Property Casualty Risk" (August 1996*) Current Issues in Economics And Finance*, Federal Reserve Bank of New York vol. 2 no. 9 1-6 at 3.

- **Risk diversification** — the diversification of risk across different types of exposure could be used to reduce aggregate risk. However, the evidence illustrates that the insurance companies are significantly diversified and benefits of additional diversification would be minimal.[14]

The problem of increased risk is compounded by the fact that the pass-through of catastrophe risk through the reinsurance risk covers at best a small part of the total risk. One study[15] found that there are very low levels of reinsurance in place against industry-wide catastrophe losses in excess of US$5 billion. The study found that the reinsurance coverage as measured as a % of exposure declines with the size of the catastrophe event. For example, the coverage level is less than 20% for events in excess of US$5 billion. The absence of efficient reinsurance of primary catastrophe risk *for a large event loss* is particularly noteworthy in that it is these types of events for which the need to reinsure is greatest. The study also found that the level of reinsurance coverage fell after major catastrophe events. The study suggested a number of possible explanations for the lack of reinsurance coverage including: high costs (due to scarcity of reinsurance capital, the exercise of market power by reinsurers, market inefficiencies, and moral hazard/adverse selection types of contracting problems); regulatory inefficiencies; and the presence of ex post financing by third parties such as governments.[16]

The above analysis is primarily based on the US market. However, anecdotal evidence suggests that the market patterns are broadly consistent with those found in other markets.

## 2.4   Reinsurance — Risk Dimensions

The primary risk in insurance contracts is the loss resulting from events against which the insurance is sought. However, there are additional risks including:

- **Credit risk** — this refers to the risk of loss from the possibility of nonpayment of amounts due from a reinsurer. Recent large catastrophe events have forced consideration of potential risk of nonperformance on the reinsurance contract.

---

[14] See Borden, Sara and Sarker, Asani "Securitizing Property Casualty Risk" (August 1996) *Current Issues in Economics And Finance*, Federal Reserve Bank of New York vol. 2 no. 9 1-6 at 3.

[15] See Froot, Kenneth A. (1997) *The Limited Financing of Catastrophe Risk: An Overview*; National Bureau of Economic Research Working Paper 6025 at 2-4.

[16] See Froot, Kenneth A. (1997) *The Limited Financing of Catastrophe Risk: An Overview*; National Bureau of Economic Research Working Paper 6025 at 4-17.

- **Basis risk** — this refers in financial contracts to the mismatch between the cash flows from one financial instrument and the cash flows from another contract entered into to hedge the exposure. In the reinsurance context, it refers to the risk of mismatch where the reinsurance contract is not calculated on the same basis as the insurer's claim payments. Traditional reinsurance contracts do not have significant basis risk as the reinsurance payments are based on the claim payments to be made by the primary insurer. This ensures that there is no. mismatch between the basis on which the reinsurance payoff is based and the claims to be hedged. Some of the synthetic reinsurance contract structures detailed in this paper, in contrast, entail basis risk. For example, financial reinsurance hedges based on *industry* losses rather than on the *insurer's* losses would only protect the individual insurer to the extent that the insurer's losses were correlated to industry loss experience.
- **Liquidity risk** — this refers to the ability of an insurer to access liquidity to meet its claims. Liquidity risk in a reinsurance context is the result of two separate risks:
  1. The ability to sell securities holdings to generate the cash needed to meet claims. This may, in the event of large catastrophe loss, be difficult as a large number of reinsurers and insurers need to liquidate assets that may exacerbate their losses as the requirement to trade quickly results in poor prices being achieved for the securities.
  2. The ability to raise *new* liquidity by issuing securities to recapitalize the insurance operations.
- **Adverse selection/moral hazard issues** — adverse selection and moral hazard issues are aspects of all contracting arrangements and represent a special case of agency costs. Adverse selection refers to the existence of a seller with private information about the products that allows it to selectively sell poor risks to the buyer. In the reinsurance context, this risk derives from the fact that the primary insurer may have superior information on the risk of its policies creating an incentive for it to seek to reinsure only higher risk portions of the portfolio. Moral hazard arises from the position where one party to a contract can take actions, which cannot be monitored by the other contractual party, to affect the value of the transactions. In reinsurance contracts, moral hazard arises from the fact that primary insurers may have no. incentive to reduce loss settlement practices *because the loss is borne by the reinsurer*. It may also arise from the fact that the reinsurer may have no. incentive to take actions designed to reduce future losses or take actions that increases losses *because the loss is borne by the reinsurer*. Traditional forms of reinsurance seek to control these risks in a variety of ways. These include: long-term reinsurance relationships; the reputation risk aspects; predefined cession rules (where the exposures assumed by the reinsurer is based merely on the firm's

underwriting preventing cherry picking of poor risks); and the practice of the insurer retaining a residual risk component.

The traditional reinsurance market has a number of established ways in which these risks are dealt with. The extent to which the reinsurance market can, in practice, deal with some of these risks (such as credit risk and liquidity risk) is limited. The emerging market in insurance derivatives to some extent overcomes some deficiencies in risk transfer. This is particular the case in respect of credit risk and liquidity risk. However, insurance derivatives structures introduce *additional* risk, primarily basis risk, that affect the risk transfer process. In addition, the insurance derivative structures may inherently be more exposed to adverse selection and moral hazard risks than traditional forms of reinsurance.

## 3.    Reinsurance as Optionality

The analogy between derivatives, particularly options, and insurance contracts is well recognized. Option payoffs have a certain similarity with those under an insurance contract. However, it is increasingly common to make the reverse analogy; that is, the ability to characterize insurance as an option contract.

The optionality in reinsurance contract exists at two levels:

- Reinsurance (at least in the form of a lump sum paid in the event that an attachment point is reached) approximates the payoffs on a digital or binary option (a specific type of option where the option payout is a pre-specified amount if an agreed strike is reached).
- Certain types of reinsurance, such as excess of loss cover (described above), are similar to a call option spread on a financial asset.

The ability to characterize or restate certain types of options as insurance is important for a number of reasons:

- The similarity to traditional financial contracts allows products linked to insurance risk to be created and traded.
- The relationship also facilitates the ability to devise investment and trading strategies, as well as allowing these instruments to be incorporated into investment portfolios.
- The similarity implies an approach to pricing and valuation that also allows the products to be created, hedged, and traded.

In part, the impetus for product innovation in insurance derivatives has derived from the inherent option elements in all insurance contracts.

# 4.   Hedging Strategy

In an environment of increasing catastrophe insurance risk and limitations on transferring this risk, insurance derivatives emerged in the 1990s as an alternative mechanism for managing this risk. The financial instruments that have emerged range from futures and option contracts traded on established futures exchanges and over-the-counter instruments including catastrophe swaps and catastrophe-linked bonds. The common elements in these products are:

• The cash flows are linked to claims arising from a catastrophe event.
• The use of these instruments by insurers to securitize catastrophe risk, allowing the transfer of these risks from insurers to investors who are paid a fee in return for assuming the risk of both the occurrence and costs of catastrophe events.

The instruments that have emerged effectively focus on three types of risk transfer mechanisms:[17]

• **Asset hedges** — these transactions are designed around investment in an asset designed to offset the claims arising from the catastrophe event. The major type of insurance derivative that functions as an asset hedge is the market for property catastrophe options (CAT options), which are traded on the CBOT. The options are designed to provide a payoff in the event of a catastrophe event that will offset the claims against the insurer as a result of the catastrophe event.
• **Liability hedges** — these are transactions that are designed to reduce risk through the creation of a liability, the value of which falls in the event of a catastrophe event. The underlying logic is that the catastrophe event results in a decline in the asset value of the insurer (reflecting the claims that must be met). The reduction in the value of the liability has the effect of offsetting the decline in the asset value. The major type of insurance derivative that functions as a liability hedge is the CAT bond. These are instruments issued by insurers where the repayment of interest and/or principal is contingent on the nonoccurrence of a catastrophe event. In the event that a catastrophe event occurs, the absence of requirement to make some payments on its debt achieves the required reduction in liability.
• **Other hedges** — these are transaction focused on different risk and can be classified into three separate types of transactions:
  1. **Recapitalization structures** — these are predicated on engineering the capability of the insurer to recapitalize its position through the issue of

---

[17] The classification adopted is similar but not identical to that in Doherty, Neil A. "Financial Innovation In The Management Of Catastrophe Risk" (Fall 1997) *Journal of Applied Corporate Finance* vol. 10 no. 3 84-95 at 85-86.

debt and/or equity *following a catastrophe event.* These derivatives take
the form of reverse convertibles or CAT equity or debt puts.

2. **Diversification structures** — these are predicated on the reduction of
   insurance risk through increasing the level of diversification of the risk
   portfolio. These derivatives take the form of CAT swaps that facilitate
   efficient reallocation of risk between insurers.

3. **Liquidity hedges** — these are predicated on reducing the risk of
   liquefaction of assets/investment portfolios. The objective is to allow the
   insurer to generate cash needed to meet claims without suffering potential
   difficulties from market illiquidity. These derivatives take the form of
   bonds incorporating a liquidity put contingent upon a catastrophe event.

The classification set out above is useful in that it allows analysis of the risks
that individual insurance derivative structures seek to address.

## 5. CAT Options

### 5.1 Introduction

CAT options are standardized instruments traded on the CBOT. The options
allow buyers and sellers to take positions on the claims of insurers resulting
from a property catastrophe event. For example, as detailed below, the buyer of
call CAT option receives a payoff if insurance loss claims exceed the amount
specified in the strike price. The CAT options are based on an index representing
an estimate of the insurer's total claim payments from catastrophes occurring
within a pre-specified loss period in a specified region. The CAT options are
designed to allow buyers and sellers, in turn, to hedge and assume catastrophe
risk and exposure to the resulting claims. These instruments are designed to
function as an alternative to reinsurance markets offering the advantages of
lower transaction costs, increased liquidity, and access for *noninsurers* to the
reinsurance markets.

### 5.2 History

The CAT options market commenced in December 1992 when the CBOT
introduced its first insurance derivative contract.[18] These contracts are

---

[18] For a review of the trading performance of the original contract see Cole, Joseph B.
and Cole, Richard L. "Opportunities For Hedging With Catastrophe Futures And
Options" in Klein, Robert A. and Lederman, Jess (editors) (1994) *The Handbook of
Derivatives & Synthetics: Innovations, Technologies and Strategies in the Global
Market*; Probus Publishing, Chicago Illinios 195-209; Irvine, Stephen "Making
Money From Catastrophes" (January 1995) *Euromoney* 9-10.

effectively options on specified insurance loss indices.[19] The option contracts were based on the concept of a settlement value based on the loss to premium ratio observed on an underlying pool of insurance contracts. The amount of premium received is known before the commencement of the trading period. The aggregate amount of losses experienced on the insurance contracts during a specified event horizon was calculated at the maturity of the option contract to determine the option payout.

The contracts were based initially on an index provided by the Insurance Services Office (ISO), which was based on the losses of around 25 companies that represented 23% of the property insurance industry. The ISO index proved to be problematic as it did not accurately reflect the loss experience of *all insurers*. The Northridge Earthquake highlighted this when the actual losses were not adequately reflected in the ISO index.[20] An additional problem with the ISO-based contract was the absence of information release by the ISO during the trading period.[21]

In September 1992, the CBOT commenced trading in a revised option contract on insurance risk. This contract was based on the Property Claims Services (PCS) Indices. The PCS indices track the aggregate amount of insured losses resulting from catastrophes occurring in given regions and risk periods. The PCS indices (described in more detail below) are considered a much broader reflection of the loss experience of the insurance industry. The PCS indexes enjoys the advantage that it covers a higher percentage of insurers, it uses multiple techniques to assess losses, and is relatively transparent (being available daily upon request, allowing contract values to be updated and valued).

## 5.3 Contract Details

As noted above the underlying asset of the CBOT insurance contract is the PCS indices. Details regarding the indices are summarized in **Exhibit 15.2**.

---

[19] An interesting feature of these contracts is that these are one of the few option contracts traded on an exchange where *there is no. underlying futures contract*.

[20] See Canter, Michael S., Cole, Joseph B., and Sandor, Richard L. "Catastrophe Options On The Chicago Board Of Trade" (September 1996) *Financial Derivatives and Risk Management* Issue 7 13-20 at 14.

[21] See Geman, Helyette "Insurance-Risk Securitization And CAT Insurance Derivatives" (September 1996) *Financial Derivatives and Risk Management* Issue 7 21-24 at 22.

**Exhibit 15.2**
**PCS Indices**

The PCS indices track aggregate insured losses from catastrophe events
that occur in given regions and over a specified risk periods.
The PCS indices cover the following regions:

| Region | States Covered | Risk Period | Contract Months |
|---|---|---|---|
| Florida | Florida | Quarterly | March; June; September; December |
| Texas | Texas | Quarterly | March; June; September; December |
| California | California | Annual | December |
| Eastern | Includes north-eastern and south-eastern states | Quarterly | March; June; September; December |
| North Eastern | Maine, New Hampshire, Vermont, Massachusetts, Connecticut, Rhode Island, New York, New Jersey, Pennsylvania, Delaware, Maryland, Washington DC | Quarterly | March; June; September; December |
| South Eastern | Vancouver, West Virginia, North Carolina, South Carolina, Atlanta, Florida, Alabama, Louisiana | Quarterly | March; June; September; December |
| Mid Western | Okalahoma, Arkansas, Tennessee, Kentucky, Ohio, Michigan, Indiana, Illinios, Wisconsin, Minnesota, North Dakota, South Dakota, Iowa, Nevada, Kansas, Missouri | Quarterly | March; June; September; December |
| Western | Hawaii, Alaska, Washington, Oregon, California, Nevada, Arizona, New Mexico, Utah, Colorado, Wyoming, Montana, Idaho | Annual | December |
| National | All 50 states plus Washington DC | Quarterly | March; June; September; December |

The process underlying the calculation of indices are as follows:

• After the occurrence of a catastrophe event (defined as an event that
  causes more than US$25 million of insured losses to personal property,
  vehicles, boats, and business interruptions), PCS estimates the insured
  property damage from a variety of sources:

1. Survey of a wide range of insurers regarding the US$ amount of claims expected to be received.
2. PCS' own information regarding the value of insured property in the region and, in some instances, it's own damage survey.
- Upon completion of its assessment, PCS released an official loss estimate for each of the states affected. The state losses were totalled to generate the regional and national indices. These loss indices represent the total losses incurred in the region during the risk period arising from the catastrophe.

Several concepts underlie the structure of the indices and the options based on them, including:
- **Index calculation** — each index is zero at the beginning of its risk period and increases by one point for every US$100 million of insured property damage that occurs in the time period.
- **The risk period** — this is the time period over which losses are aggregated. These fall into two categories:
  1. **Seasonal** — this is for catastrophes such as hurricanes and tornados, and comprises quarterly risk periods with option contracts being traded on a quarterly cycle (March, June, September, and December).
  2. **Nonseasonal** — this for nonseasonal catastrophes such as earthquakes, and entails annual risk periods with a single option contract being traded (December).
- **Loss development period** — the loss development period (LDP) is a 6 or 12-month period that follows each risk period. During the LDP, the PCS updates the amount of damage that occurred during the risk period. For example, if there were hurricanes in Florida in the third quarter of 2001 that resulted in an aggregate loss of US$5 billion, the September 2001 index would be set at 50 (US$5 billion divided by US$100 million). However, if during the December 2001 quarter information became available that the losses actually were US$7.5 billion, the September 2001 Florida PCS Index would be adjusted to 75. This change does not affect any other index.

The PCS option contracts themselves have the specifications outlined in **Exhibit 15.3**.

**Exhibit 15.3**
**PCS Option Contract Specifications**

The PCS option contracts have the following specifications:

| | |
|---|---|
| Underlying asset | PCS indices (5 regional; 3 state, 2 national) |
| Development period | Choice of 6 or 12 months |
| Small or large cap | Choice of small cap contracts (track aggregate estimated catastrophe losses between US$0 to US$20 billion) or large cap contracts (track aggregate estimated catastrophe losses between US$20 to US$50 billion) |
| Index values | Each index point has a cash value of US$200 (representing US$100 million in insured damage) |
| Strike prices | Listed in integral multiples of 5 points. Small cap contracts can have strike values between 5 and 195. Large cap contracts can have values between 200 and 495 |
| Premiums | Quoted in points and one-tenths of a point (US$20) |
| Settlement | Cash |

Under these specifications, some nine contracts reflecting the various indices are traded. Each contract entails a choice of development period (the LDP) and the small or large cap option:

- **LDP** — the development period is used to enable a more accurate assessment of the insured property damage to be completed. This serves to ensure that the indices are accurate reflections of the damages suffered with the insurer selecting the LDP that matches its underlying portfolio of insured risks. The majority of contracts traded have been 12-month LDP contracts.[22] Contracts are available for trading

---

[22] The potential impact of choice of LDP can be seen from the Northridge earthquake where the initial loss estimate of US$2.5billion was adjusted up to US$12.5 billion; see Canter, Michael S., Cole, Joseph B., and Sandor, Richard L. "Insurance Derivatives: A New Asset Class for the Capital Markets and a New Hedging Tool For The Insurance Industry" (Fall 1997) *Journal of Applied Corporate Finance* vol. 10 no. 3 69-83 at 71.

throughout the LDP phase. For example, a December 2001 12-month LDP contract would be traded through to December 2002 (12 months after maturity).

- **Small vs large caps** — each PCS contract can be as either a small- or large-cap contract. The difference is as noted above in the aggregate insured losses. They have the effect of limiting the losses to the option seller (in practice converting the options into option spreads). For example, the seller of a call on a regional September 2001 call with a strike of 125 will automatically have his or her loss limited to US$15,000 even if the PCS index value is 300 (equivalent to losses of US$30 billion). This reflects the fact that the call will settle at US$15,000 (calculated as 200 − 125 × US$200/point). Without this cap, the loss would have been US$35,000. The classification system limits the loss of the seller (and the gain of the buyer) to the US$20 billion and US$50 billion aggregate loss levels for small- and large-cap options respectively. The cap provisions are designed to protect sellers from suffering unlimited losses. They however limit the utility of these contracts for buyers who cannot achieve protection against very large losses.

As already noted, the PCS option contracts are all cash settled, based on an index point value of US$200 per point. The call owner receives the difference between the US$ index value and the US$ strike price value. The put owner receives the difference between the US$ strike price value and the US$ Index value.

## 5.4 Applications

The use of the PCS option contracts is illustrated by the following examples. The first example (**Exhibit 15.4**) examines a simple call purchase. The second example (**Exhibit 15.5** on page 857) examines a call spread strategy that is designed to replicate an excess of loss type of reinsurance layer.

---

**Exhibit 15.4**
**Application of PCS Contract — Call Purchase**

Assume that an insurer seeks to hedge against the property catastrophe risk assumed in course of its underwriting over and above a specified amount. This presumably reflects the ability of the insurer to absorb losses

---

arising from claims in the event of a catastrophe event where losses exceed the stated amount based on their available capital and reserves. Assume that on March 2001, the insurer purchases a 12-month LDP call on the December 2001 call on a regional index corresponding to its risk to cover this exposure in the period through to the end of 2001. The call has the following characteristics:

| | |
|---|---|
| Strike Price | 50 |
| Type | 12-month LDP |
| | Small cap (that is capped at a maximum loss amount of US$20 billion) |
| Maturity | December 2001 |
| Contracts | 1,000 |

The insurer pays a premium in return for the call (say, 2 points per contract or 2,000 points in total equivalent to US$400,000). The call payoff is as follows:

- If the index at maturity is below 50, then the insurer receives no payments (effectively the option expires out of the money).
- If at maturity the index is above 50, then the insurer receives a payment based on the index value (subject to the cap at 200 under the small cap contract rules). For example, if the index is at 70 at maturity, the insurer receives a payment of US$4 million (calculated as (70-50) × US$200/point × 1,000 contracts).

In the first instance, the premium paid is lost. In the second instance, the premium paid reduces the gain on the option contracts to US$3.6 million.

The option payment offsets any losses resulting from claims on the underlying property insurance portfolio. This is so to the extent that the loss on the insurer's portfolio matches the loss experience of the index.

An alternative more aggressive strategy would entail selling put options on the index. Under this strategy, the insurer would receive a payment initially that would increase capital and reserves. At maturity of the option contract, if the index was lower than the strike (lower losses), the insurer would suffer a loss on the option that is presumably offset by the lower loss experience on the underlying insurance underwriting portfolio. If the index is higher, then the option contract is not exercised. However, the insurer experiences higher losses on its insurance contracts that must be borne by the insurer once the premiums received under the sold put option contracts are exceeded.

**Exhibit 15.5**
**Application of PCS Contract — Call Spread Purchase**

In this example, the concept of using a call spread to synthetically manufacture a reinsurance layer is set out.

Assume an insurer has a high concentration of its exposure in a single region. The insurer's portfolio is structured as follows: it has only 1% of the insurance business in that region but 80% of its losses in relation to claims in that region. This may reflect the high catastrophe risk in that area arising from earthquake or hurricane risk. Assume that the insurer wishes to purchase reinsurance on US$50 million of risk in regard to catastrophe risk in this area. It wishes to structure this protection as a reinsurance layer of US$50 million above an excess of US$100 million.

Traditionally, the insurer would have purchased reinsurance based on a US$50 million policy based on an attachment point or excess of loss of US$100 million. Alternatively, the insurer could structure its reinsurance protection layer as a call spread on the PCS index option contract. The insurer would select the index that corresponds to the region in which protection is sought.

The structure is based on the following:

- The strike of the purchased calls is equal to:

  (Insurer's retained loss position/Insurer's market share)
  $\times$ (1/Loss experience adjustment factor)
  (US$100 million/0.01) $\times$ (1/0.8) = US$12,500 million

  This is equivalent to 125 index points (US$12.5 billion/US$100 million per point)

- The strike of the sold calls is equal to:

  (Insurer's retained loss position + Amount of reinsurance sought)/
  (Insurer's market share) $\times$ (1/Loss experience-adjustment factor)
  ((US$100 million + US$50 million)/0.01) $\times$ (1/0.8)
  = US$18,750 million

  This is equivalent to 187.5 index points (US$18.75 billion/US$100 million/point)

- The number of option contracts would be calculated as follows:

(Reinsurance amount/US$ amount of protection offered by each spread)
(US$50 million/((187.5 – 125) $\times$ US$200 per point) = 4,000 contracts

The call spread transaction would be structured as the purchase of 4,000 contracts of the 125/187.5 vertical call spread. The option maturity would be based on the assumed protection period required. In this case assume this was through till December 2001.

Assume the vertical spread costs the insurer five points per spread. This would equate to a total premium of US$4 million (calculated as US$200/ point × 5 × 4,000 contracts). This is equivalent to an ROL of 8.00% (calculated as US$4 million in premium cost on reinsurance protection of US$50 million).

The hedge payoff is set out in the table below:

| Industry Loss (US$ m) | PCS Index | Insurers' Loss (US$ m) | Bought Call Payoffs (US$ m) | Sold Call Payoffs (US$ m) | Total Hedge Payoffs (US$ m) | Hedge Cost (US$ m) | Net Loss (US$ m) |
|---|---|---|---|---|---|---|---|
| – | 0 | 0 | 0 | 0 | 0 | –4 | –4 |
| 1,000 | 10 | 8 | 0 | 0 | 0 | –4 | –12 |
| 2,000 | 20 | 16 | 0 | 0 | 0 | –4 | –20 |
| 3,000 | 30 | 24 | 0 | 0 | 0 | –4 | –28 |
| 4,000 | 40 | 32 | 0 | 0 | 0 | –4 | –36 |
| 5,000 | 50 | 40 | 0 | 0 | 0 | –4 | –44 |
| 6,000 | 60 | 48 | 0 | 0 | 0 | –4 | –52 |
| 7,000 | 70 | 56 | 0 | 0 | 0 | –4 | –60 |
| 8,000 | 80 | 64 | 0 | 0 | 0 | –4 | –68 |
| 9,000 | 90 | 72 | 0 | 0 | 0 | –4 | –76 |
| 10,000 | 100 | 80 | 0 | 0 | 0 | –4 | –84 |
| 11,000 | 110 | 88 | 0 | 0 | 0 | –4 | –92 |
| 12,000 | 120 | 96 | 0 | 0 | 0 | –4 | –100 |
| 13,000 | 130 | 104 | 4 | 0 | 4 | –4 | –104 |
| 14,000 | 140 | 112 | 12 | 0 | 12 | –4 | –104 |
| 15,000 | 150 | 120 | 20 | 0 | 20 | –4 | –104 |
| 16,000 | 160 | 128 | 28 | 0 | 28 | –4 | –104 |
| 17,000 | 170 | 136 | 36 | 0 | 36 | –4 | –104 |
| 18,000 | 180 | 144 | 44 | 0 | 44 | –4 | –104 |
| 19,000 | 190 | 152 | 52 | –2 | 50 | –4 | –106 |
| 20,000 | 200 | 160 | 60 | –10 | 50 | –4 | –114 |

> As is evident, the call spread operates to provide protection to the insurer totaling US$50 million where industry losses (on an index basis) are between 125 and 187.5. The call spread functions in a manner that is analogous to traditional reinsurance.

In practice, call spreads as a mechanism for creating synthetic reinsurance protection has proved to be the most common type of structure utilized. This reflects, in part, its similarity to *traditional* reinsurance structures.

Other potential applications include:

- **Adjusting the layer of risk assumed** — for example, an insurer exposed to, say, a catastrophe event of between US$4-6 billion may feel it is over-exposed to that risk. It may hedge that risk by buying a vertical call spread structure at 40/60 on an appropriate index while simultaneously selling a vertical call spread at 60/80. This has the effect of shifting *the composition* of its risk exposure so that it is now exposed to a different strata of insurance risk at a higher loss.
- **Increasing diversification** — for example, an insurer with insurance exposure in a particular region could purchase calls or call spreads on an index relevant to that index while simultaneously selling calls or call spreads on *another region* to which it has no. exposure. This has the effect of improving the diversification of the insurer's risks.
- **Combining with traditional reinsurance** — for example, if an insurer can only buy reinsurance at very high levels of retention, effectively exposing it to an unacceptable degree of loss, then it can supplement that with purchased call spreads at a lower level to reduce its retention level to a desired loss level. Alternatively, the insurer can sell a vertical spread corresponding to the purchased reinsurance contract and simultaneously sell a call spread with lower strikes to effectively adjust the retention levels and reinsurance coverage.

There are increasing signs that insurers are implementing these types of strategies. For example, Hanover Re through its subsidiary Insurance Corporation of Hanover is reported to have used PCS options to fill the gap between its desired retention level and the retention level available in the traditional reinsurance market.[23]

---

[23] Reported in (Third Quarter, 1996) CBOT Review as quoted in Canter, Michael S., Cole, Joseph B., and Sandor, Richard L. "Insurance Derivatives: A New Asset Class for the Capital Markets and a New Hedging Tool For The Insurance Industry" (Fall 1997) *Journal of Applied Corporate Finance* vol. 10 no. 3 69-83 at 73.

## 5.5  Market Experience

The CBOT PCS option market has enjoyed reasonable growth in recent years. Following the restructure of the contract, the open interest and trading volumes have grown. Key factors underlying the growth have included:

- A number of developments in the OTC market and in CAT bonds that have focused attention on insurance derivatives generally.
- Increased focus on the risk of loss as a result of catastrophe events that is periodically highlighted by the approach of hurricanes near major population centres.[24]

However, despite these developments PCS options have not become as significant a component of the reinsurance market as might be expected. This reflects a variety of factors:

- The relative efficiency of the reinsurance market and the fact that insurers receive favorable renewable terms often linked to claims experience.
- The relative lack of liquidity of the PCS contract that is gradually improving.
- The basis risk entailed in using an index to hedge a portfolio of specific insurance risks. This reflects the fact that the option payoffs reflect *industry* loss experience. The insurer using the contracts will contribute to the index but the degree of match between the contract payoffs and the primary insurer's losses will depend on the correlation between the two portfolios of risk.

The problem of basis risk is probably the most intractable issue for insurers using insurance derivatives to hedge. While it is common for hedgers in other parts of capital markets to accept basis risk, the fact that traditional reinsurance does *not* entail any basis risk has made this a primary point of focus for insurers.

However, the PCS option contracts have significant additional benefits that may in time counteract these problems:

- The increased transparency of the options market relative to the reinsurance market. The reinsurance market is less transparent and involves greater complexities of documentation, inefficiencies in funds transfer, and (sometimes complex) price negotiations. These difficulties are largely absent from the PCS market, which is standardized and accessible through electronic means.

---

[24]  For example, on September 5, 1997 Hurricane Fran approached the east coast of the US, triggering record volumes in PCS options contracts. Daily volume reached 1,898 contracts and open interest reached 4,789 contracts; see Thackray, John "Insurance Derivatives Catch Fire" (December/January 1997) *Derivatives Strategy* 28-31 at 29.

- The reduction in credit risk achieved through the use of traditional credit-enhancement techniques utilized by exchanges (deposits and margining provisions). This avoids the inherent credit exposure to the reinsurer under traditional reinsurance arrangements.
- The adverse selection and moral hazard risks in reinsurance contracting are largely eliminated in the PCS options market, reflecting the standardized nature of the instrument and the use of an industry-wide index.

The CBOT launch in 1999 listed catastrophe options encompassing various types of catastrophic risk. This will complement the existing index-based contracts and is designed to allow individual insurers to hedge more accurately and efficiently.[25]

# 6. OTC CAT Swaps and Options

## 6.1 OTC CAT Swaps

More recently, an OTC CAT swap market has emerged to complement the existing exchanged traded CAT options markets. **Exhibit 15.6** sets out an example of a CAT swap transaction.

---

**Exhibit 15.6**
**CAT Swap Transaction[26]**

In early 1998, Swiss Reinsurance entered into a swap to cover its risks under a reinsurance contract with Mitsui Marine & Fire Insurance. The structure of the swap was as follows:

- The notional principal of the transaction was US$30 million.
- The transaction was for a term of three years from April 1, 1998.
- Swiss Re Financial Products (SRFP) entered into the swap with a number of counterparties (believed to be capital markets investors).
- SRFP pays the investors LIBOR plus 375 bps.
- In return, the counterparties have an obligation to make payment to SRFP contingent on the occurrence of an earthquake in Japan registering 7.1 on the Richter scale. The payments are as follows:
  1. If there is no. earthquake of the type identified, then there is no. payment by the counterparties.

---

[25] See "A New Take on CAT Options" (February 1998) *Derivatives Strategy* 5-6.
[26] See Paul-Choudhury, Sumit "Swiss Re Swaps A 'Quake'" (May 1998) *Risk* vol. 11 no. 5 16; (May 8, 1998) Financial Products Issue 89 8-9.

> 2. If there is an earthquake of the type identified, then the counterparties must make a payment to SRFP that is dependent on the magnitude of the earthquake.
>
> The transaction was interesting in that the payments were not linked in any way to size of the claims made on the insurers as a result of the catastrophe.

The structure of the swap is similar to the PCS option contract, but also to an unfunded CAT bond.

## 6.2   OTC CAT Options

There are a number of types of option transactions that have also emerged. These include: CAT swaptions and dual trigger options.

### 6.2.1   CAT Swaption[27]

A CAT swaption entails in return for the payment of an annual fee the right to enter into a swap with a counterparty where the party entering into the transaction has access to a known amount of catastrophe protection, whereby it can share with the counterparty the performance of a pool of catastrophe insurance contracts. The essential element of the transaction is the fact that the reinsurance cost is fixed and known. This provides protection against either increases in reinsurance costs or a large industry loss.

An example of such a transaction is one undertaken by Hannover Reinsurance, arranged by Citibank.[28] The transaction was driven by the decline in catastrophe insurance rates to a level where it was difficult to underwrite new business. Hannover Reinsurance, one of the world's top five reinsurers, wanted to continue to expand its business but sought protection against a future rise in reinsurance risk premiums. The CAT swaption transaction entailed Hannover Reinsurance paying 50 bps pa in return for access to US$50 million in catastrophe protection at any time over a period of three and a half years. In the event that reinsurance premiums increased or there was a large industry loss, Hannover Reinsurance could trigger the swaption. This would give it access to the additional reinsurance protection, allowing it to share with the counterparties (understood to be investors) the performance (gain or loss) of an underlying pool

---

[27]  See also discussion below in relation to options on CAT bonds.
[28]  See "Catastrophe Risk Hedge" (March 1999) at 27.

of client catastrophe insurance contracts. The transaction had a number of advantages. There was no. basis risk as the transaction was based on insurer's own policy portfolio rather than a generalized loss index. The transaction gave investors the capacity to gain as well as indemnify Hannover Reinsurance against losses. This is because the risk and returns of policies was to be shared between the investors and the reinsurer. The transaction was significantly lower in cost than a CAT bond that would have at the time of issue cost around 300-400 bps pa.

### 6.2.2 Dual Trigger Options

Dual trigger options are hybrid instruments that combine financial and insurance risk.[29] The dual trigger option only pays out if *two separate* trigger events occur during the life of the option (one trigger event is usually an insurance event while the other is a financial market event).

An example of a dual trigger option may be a company with an insurance policy that combines an insurance event and a currency event. Assume a Japanese company with an earthquake protection insurance policy. The policy has an excess of US$5 million whereby the company bears the first US$5 million of losses. This excess is denominated in US$. This means that in the event of an earthquake the insured party has an exposure to the US$/¥ exchange rate. This could be addressed by a dual trigger policy as follows:

- If there is an earthquake *and* the US$/¥ exchange rate is below US$1: ¥140 (assume current rate is US$1: ¥120), then the excess is fixed at ¥700 million (effectively a guaranteed US$/¥ exchange rate of US$1: ¥140).
- If there is an earthquake *and* the US$/¥ exchange rate is above US$1: ¥140 (assume current rate is US$1: ¥120), then the excess is fixed at US$5 million.

The transaction effectively has a contingent currency option embedded within the insurance contract that is designed to protect the insured party from the exchange rate risk on the excess.

Other dual trigger structures have included a dual trigger option that only pays out if there is a catastrophe event and the value of the equity market falls by a nominated amount (say, 25%). The rationale of such transactions is that the catastrophe event triggers large claims that require the insurer to sell investments to raise liquidity or to issue equity to recapitalize the balance sheet. A fall in the equity market has an adverse effect on the ability of the insurer to access liquidity. The dual trigger option is designed to protect the insurer from the *combination* of events.

---

[29] See Belcher, Sophie "Dual Trigger Options" (September 29, 1997) *Derivatives Week* 6-7.

Dual trigger transactions can be structured as either insurance contracts with a financial risk protection element or (less likely) a financial option with an insurance element. Regulatory factor may affect the ability to structure contracts in a particular way.

Dual trigger option structures only offer value where the combined option is more cost effective than two separate transactions. The lower cost should derive from the nature of the correlation between the two events. However, in practice, this correlation between insurance events and financial risk is difficult to establish and price. The transactions are also difficult to hedge. The financial option component can be readily hedged. The insurance risk is not as easily able to be hedged.[30]

The market for dual trigger option structures is still relatively small and illiquid. Maturities and volumes available are limited.

# 7.   CAT Bonds

## 7.1   Concept

The CAT bond is conceptually a structured note where the coupon payment and/or principal repayment by the issuer is contingent upon the nonoccurrence of a specified event—typically, a catastrophe event such as a hurricane or earthquake. In essence, the CAT bond structure creates a direct nexus between payment of interest or principal and catastrophe.

CAT bonds issues are typically undertaken by an insurer to hedge its losses upon the occurrence of a catastrophe event. The issues are generally structured as follows:

1. The issuer of the bond is a special-purpose vehicle (SPV) that is generally located in a tax haven such as Bermuda for reasons of regulatory, taxation, and legal efficacy.
2. The insurer seeking reinsurance cover enters into a reinsurance contract with the SPV. The insurer pays a premium to the SPV in return for assuming the insurance risk.
3. The SPV issues the CAT bond to transfer the reinsurance risk assumed in the transaction to investors in the bonds.
4. The SPV utilizes the proceeds of the issue to purchase high-quality securities (generally, US Treasury securities are utilized).

---

[30]  For a discussion of pricing issues, see Arvantis, Angelo and Lasry, Jean-Michel "Hedging Under Asymmetry" (June 1999) *Risk* 62-67.

5. The SPV pays the CAT bond investors a coupon that is equivalent to the coupon on the US Treasury securities and the reinsurance premium received by the SPV.
6. The principal repayment is contingent on the occurrence of the specified catastrophe event:
   - If there is a catastrophe event (this is usually defined as the occurrence of the specified natural disaster causing losses exceeding the nominated attachment point in the relevant region over the agreed loss period), then the investors will lose principal up to the full face value of the transaction. The loss to the insurer will be paid out under the reinsurance contract by the SPV funded out of the US Treasury securities held.
   - If there is no. catastrophe event, then the principal will be repaid in full to the investor out of the maturing US Treasury investment pool.

The structure specified is generally driven by the following factor:

- Enabling the insurer to obtain reinsurance accounting treatment.
- Separation of the risks that are being securitized through the CAT bond from all other insurance risks held by the insurer.
- Tax and legal efficiency considerations.

The CAT bond structure, consistent with that of all structured notes more generally, is designed to achieve the following objectives:

- **Allow investors access to insurance-linked investments** — the packaging of the reinsurance risk into a fixed income security format allows investors who may otherwise be prevented from entering into transactions involving insurance risk participating in this structure.
- **Reduce credit risk of the transaction** — the credit risk on the reinsurance contract is reduced as the obligations to cover losses are fully collateralized by the US Treasury securities. In effect, the investors provide the insurer with the hedge against losses through the forgiveness of the issued debt. This is designed to allow the performance on the reinsurance provision to operate independently of the bond-holders' asset and ensure the absence of credit risk for the primary insurer.
- **Provide structured exposure to insurance risk** — as discussed in detail below, the CAT bond format allows the precise degree and level of exposure to the insurance event to be precisely structured to meet investor requirements.

An example of a CAT bond transaction is set out in **Exhibit 15.7.**

**Exhibit 15.7**
**CAT Bond — USAA Transaction**[31]

In June 1997, the United States Automobile Association (USAA), a Texas-based insurance company undertook a US$477 million issue of hurricane-linked bonds. The issue details were as follows:

| | |
| --- | --- |
| Issuer | Residential Re, an SPV established by USAA |
| Amount | US$477 million made up of two tranches: <br> • A1 tranche—US$163.8 million face value of principal guaranteed bonds. <br> • A2 tranche—US$313.2 million face value of principal at-risk bonds. |
| Coupon | A1 tranche—LIBOR + 282 bps; A2 tranche — LIBOR + 575 bps |
| Catastrophe event | A category 3, 4, or 5 hurricane that hits one of 20 US states or the District of Columbia (the region) between July 1, 1997 and December 15, 1997 (the protection period) causing claims against the USAA exceeding US$1 billion (the attachment point). The losses are calculated based on a LDP of six months |

The structure has several interesting features:

• The principal protection feature of the A1 tranche means that in the event of a catastrophe event the investors suffer a loss of interest but not principal. This is achieved through the issuer undertaking two separate transactions. The issuer writes a reinsurance contract on only around US$85 million. In the event of a catastrophe event the US$85 million is at risk to pay USAA claims. The remaining US$78 million is invested in US Treasury securities, which ensures that the investors principal will be returned in full out of the US Treasury collateral pool (in around 10 years). This component was designed to allow the transaction to be marketed to investors who could not invest in securities without a principal guaranteed structure.

---

[31] See Nusbaum, David "Hurricane Bond Storms Wall Street" (July 1997) *Risk* 6; Canter, Michael S., Cole, Joseph B., and Sandor, Richard L. "Insurance Derivatives: A New Asset Class for the Capital Markets and a New Hedging Tool for the Insurance Industry" (Fall 1997) *Journal of Applied Corporate Finance* vol. 10 no. 3 69-83 at 74–5.

- The A2 notes are effectively structured as a US$1.0 billion/US$1.5 billion call spread. The loss of principal is triggered when losses exceed US$1 billion. The investor in the A2 notes bears 62.6% of the losses up to a maximum loss of US$500 million. The principal is exhausted when losses reach US$1.5 billion.
- The losses are not based on an index but relate to the *loss experience of USAA* that reduces any basis risk in the hedge.

## 7.2   Development of CAT Bonds[32]

Exhibit 15.8 sets out a selected list of CAT bond issues undertaken in the period to October 1998.

**Exhibit 15.8**
**CAT Bond Issues**[33]

| Issue Date | Issuer | Amount (US$ million) | Underwriter |
|---|---|---|---|
| 1996 | ACE | 25 | Goldman Sachs |
| 1996 | USAA | 500 | Merrill Lynch |
| 1996 | CAT | 55 | Morgan Stanley |
| 1996 | AIG | 25 | AIG/Benfield-Ellinger |
| 1996 | Reliance | 40 | Sedgwick Lane Financial |

---

[32] For a description of the evolution of this market see Canter, Michael S., Cole, Joseph B., and Sandor, Richard L. "Insurance Derivatives: A New Asset Class for the Capital Markets and a New Hedging Tool for the Insurance Industry" (Fall 1997) *Journal of Applied Corporate Finance* vol. 10 no. 3 69-83 at 80-82; see also "Insurance Derivatives on the Richter Scale" (1997) *Financial Products* Issue 74 12-13; "An Earthquake in Insurance" (February 28, 1998) *The Economist* 75-77; Hanley, Mike "A Catastrophe Too Far" (July 1998) Risk Insurance Risk Special Report 12-16; Hunter, Robert "Preparing for Catastrophe" (November 1998) *Derivatives Strategy* 26-33.

[33] This list is based on "An Earthquake In Insurance" (February 28, 1998) *The Economist* at 76; Canter, Michael S., Cole, Joseph B., and Sandor, Richard L. "Insurance Derivatives: A New Asset Class for the Capital Markets and a New Hedging Tool for the Insurance Industry" (Fall 1997) *Journal of Applied Corporate Finance* vol. 10 no. 3 69-83; Hunter, Robert "Preparing For Catastrophe" (November 1998) Derivatives Strategy 26-33; "Alternative Risk Transfer (ART) for Corporations: A Passing Fashion or Risk Management For 21st Century?" (1999) Sigma, Swiss Re No. 2/1999 at 30.

| Issue Date | Issuer | Amount (US$ million) | Underwriter |
|---|---|---|---|
| 1996 | St Paul Re | 69 | Goldman Sachs |
| 1996 | Hanover Re | 100 | Citibank |
| 1997 | Tokio Marine & Fire | 100 | Swiss Re/Goldman Sachs |
| 1997 | Swiss Winterthur | 280 | CS First Boston |
| 1997 | Swiss Re | 137 | Swiss Re/CS First Boston |
| 1997 | USAA | 477 | Goldman Sachs/Merrill Lynch/ Lehman Brothers |
| 1998 | Tokyo Fire & Marine | 90 | Not known |
| 1998 | Trinity Re | 84 | Centre Solutions |
| 1998 | Reliance | 30 | Not known |
| 1998 | CAN | 8.5 | Not known |
| 1998 | USAA | 450 | Not known |
| 1998 | Yasuda Fire & Marine | 80 | Not known |
| 1998 | St Paul Re | 30 | Not known |
| 1998 | Constitution Re | 10 | Swiss Re |
| 1998 | Allianz | 150 | Goldman Sachs |
| 1998 | Centre Solutions | 54 | Goldman Sachs; Chase Securities; Donaldson Lufkin & Jenerette; Zurich Capital Markets |
| 1998 | Toyota Motor | 566 | Goldman Sachs |
| 1998 | Freddie Mac | 243 | Morgan Stanley Dean Witter |
| 1998 | National Provident Institution | GBP 260 | SBC Dillion Read; Goldman Sachs; Dresdner Kleinwort Benson |
| 1999 | US F&G | 50 | Goldman Sachs; EX Blanche Capital Markets |

The initial securitization efforts involving CAT bonds commenced in 1995. The market gained impetus in 1997 with a series of successful issues.

The initial issues such as those for ACE, USAA, and CAT were difficult. Investors did not accept the bonds that offered very high coupons (around Treasury bills plus 150 to 550 bps). This lack of acceptance was drive by a number of factors:

- A lack of understanding of insurance risk generally.
- An inability to model and price the catastrophe risk accurately.
- The problem that these individual securities did not represent a diversified portfolio of risks.
- The potential lack of liquidity in these securities.

A major effort to introduce these securities entailed an attempt to have the California Earthquake Authority (CEA) issue some US$1.5 billion of earthquake-linked bonds in late 1996. The issue was ultimately canceled when National Indemnity (a catastrophe reinsurer owned by Warren Buffet's Berkshire Hathaway) offered terms superior to the CAT bond in a traditional reinsurance.[34]

However, in late 1996/1997, there were a series of moderately sized successful issues that created confidence in the longer term prospects of the market. These included:

- A CAT bond transaction by Hanover Re that involved reinsurance of Japanese earthquake risk, Australian and Canadian earthquake and wind storm risk, European wind storms, and worldwide aviation disaster risk.
- A CAT bond issued by Reliance that involved transfer of aviation, marine, satellite, and property risks.
- A CAT bond issued by Swiss Winterthur that involved transfer of hail storm damage risk.
- A CAT bond issued by St Paul Re that allowed transfer of losses and gains of the insurer's worldwide property risk.
- A CAT bond issued by USAA (see description above).
- A CAT bond issued by Swiss Re that allowed transfer of Californian earthquake risk.
- A CAT bond issued by Trinity Re that allowed transfer of Florida Hurricane risk.

The structures themselves are diverse and reflect different objectives of the insurer seeking protection. A number of these transactions are examined in **Exhibit 15.9**, **Exhibit 15.10**, and **Exhibit 15.11**. The discussed transactions were important in introducing important innovations in CAT bonds.

---

[34] It has been argued that National Indemnity took this action to protect its lucrative catastrophe reinsurance business.

**Exhibit 15.9**
**CAT Bond — Portfolio SecuritizationTransaction**[35]

In late 1996, the sixth largest US reinsurer St Paul Re, the reinsurance arm of Minnesota-based St Paul Companies, issued a US$68.5 million CAT bond in a private placement transaction arranged by Goldman Sachs. The transaction structure was as follows:

1. St Paul Re established an SPV (George Town Re). The SPV is owned by a Cayman Island charitable trust and licensed as a reinsurer.
2. The SPV purchases a participation in St Paul Re's future business. This reflects the fact that catastrophe insurance is annually renewable. The structure is designed to provide investors in the SPV-issued bonds with the potential to participate in the earnings growth of St Paul Re's business.
3. The SPV issued two types of securities totaling US$68.5 million:
   - US$44.5 million of 10-year principal-protected notes. US$23.2 million of the issue proceed are used to purchase zero-coupon US treasuries (STRIPS) to cover the principal value of the bond at redemption. The coupon on the bond is contingent upon St Paul Re's underwriting performance.
   - US$24 million of nonvoting preference shares due to be redeemed in 2000 (a maturity of 3.5 years). The dividend payments and redemption value of the preference shares is dependent upon the St Paul Re's underwriting performance (measured as premium income + investment income – underwriting losses).

The principal-protected bond was rated AAA based on the US Treasury collateral. The unusual features of this transaction included:

- The fact that it was effectively a full-scale securitization of St Paul Re's reinsurance books rather than a specific risk indemnity.
- The multi-year structure that allowed investors to share in losses as well as gains (a quota share) in St Paul's worldwide property catastrophe business.
- The fact that the CAT bond performance was linked to St Paul's reinsurance portfolio (a portfolio diversified by region (North America, Caribbean, and Europe) and type of risk (earthquakes, hurricanes, fires, and shipwrecks) rather than an index or a specific risk that tends to be the basis of CAT bonds.

---

[35] See Sheperd, Bill "A Working Model for Securitsation Risk, Courtesy of St Paul Re" (January 1997) *Global Finance* 18.

**Exhibit 15.10**
**CAT Bond — Earthquake Protection Transaction**[36]

In late 1996, Swiss Re undertook an issue through CS First Boston of a CAT bond indexed to Californian earthquake risk. The issue was undertaken through SR Earthquake Fund, a Cayman Island reinsurer, established as an SPV to provide a 2-year reinsurance contract covering Swiss Re's property insurance exposure in respect of residential and commercial properties exposed to earthquake risk in California.

The structure of the bond was as follows:

| | |
|---|---|
| Amount | US$137 million in 3 tranches |
| Risk Covered | Californian earthquake risk for a period of two years |
| Loss Index | PCS Index |

The tranche structure of the bonds were as follows:

| Tranche | A | B | C |
|---|---|---|---|
| Amount | US$62 million | US$60 million | US$15 million |
| Principal Protection | 40% | 0% | 0% |
| Coupon | LIBOR + 255 bps | 10.5% | 12.0% |
| Rating | BBB– | BB | |

The way the loss was allocated was based on a series of loss triggers. If there is an earthquake in California that causes insured property damage (as measured by PCS) of the following amount, this results in a corresponding loss on the bonds:

- Greater than US$18.5 billion but less than US$21 billion — loss of 33% of capital.
- Greater than US$21.0 billion but less than US$24 billion — loss of 66% of capital.
- Greater than US$24 billion — loss of 100% of capital.

---

[36] See Canter, Michael S., Cole, Joseph B., and Sandor, Richard L. "Insurance Derivatives: A New Asset Class for the Capital Markets and a New Hedging Tool for the Insurance Industry" (Fall 1997) *Journal of Applied Corporate Finance* vol. 10 no. 3 69-83 at 81.

The Class A notes are structured (using the collateralization principles using zero-coupon securities seen in the USAA and St Paul Re transaction) such that investors will only lose 60% of their entire principal. The transaction was notable for a number of features:

- Moody's rated the transaction in a notable first for insurance derivatives.
- Around 20 investors purchased the issue.[37]

---

**Exhibit 15.11**
**CAT Bond — Storm Damage Transaction**[38]

In late 1996, Swiss Winterthur issued a public bond through CS First Boston to obtain coverage against potential losses from a hail storm in Switzerland.
The structure of the CAT bond was as follows:

- The issue was for an amount of Swfr399.5 million (US$280 million) — an increase from the original issue size of Swfr300 million.
- The issue was a 3-year subordinated convertible bond exchangeable into five Winterthur shares at a conversion premium of Swfr940. The convertible component of the transaction is largely conventional.
- The convertible pays a coupon of 2.25% pa. This is equivalent to an approximately 75 bps margin over the equivalent Swiss National Bond. However, the coupon is contingent upon a catastrophe event.

---

[37] In 1999, Oriental Land Company (the owner/operator of Tokyo Disneyland) issued a similar bond. The US$200 million had a life of five years, and was issued through a special-purpose vehicle Concentric Ltd. The issue arranged by Goldman Sachs had two parts. The first was a US$100 million bond under which the bond-holders would receive the repayment of the principal investment only if there was no earthquake registering above 6.5 on the Japanese equivalent of the Richter scale. If there was an earthquake above 6.5, then investors would lose US425 million of the bond principal. If there was an earthquake above 7.5, then the investors would lose the complete bond principal. The second part of the transaction, also for five years, would provide a US$100 million loan to finance reconstruction. See Baldwin, Dominic "A Niche In Earthquakes" (June 1999) *Risk* 17; Pelham, Mark "Fault Tolerance" (June 1999) *Futures and OTC World* 47.

[38] See Paul-Choudhury, Sumit "All Hail The Catastrophe Comeback" (February 1997) *Risk* vol. 10 no. 29; (April 1997) *Corporate Finance* 26.

> If there is the specified catastrophe event, then the coupon is not payable for that year.
> - The catastrophe event specified is if Winterthur has to make good on claims against hail storm damage to in excess of 6,000 vehicles in a single day.
>
> The risk assumed by the investors in the bond can be analyzed in a number of ways:
>
> - Such storms have only occurred two times in the past 10 years. However, the event cannot be considered remote. A storm in France in 1996, for example, damaged 14,000 new cars.[39]
> - Based on this 80% probability, investors could *on average* expect to receive 80% of 2.25% or 1.80%, which is around 30 bps over that on a conventional convertible.
>
> The bond has a number of unusual features:
>
> - The incorporation of catastrophe risk within the framework of a traditional convertible is noteworthy.
> - The isolation of a highly specific and unusual risk is also innovative.

### 7.3 Market Experience

The market for CAT bonds has enjoyed reasonable growth and has emerged as a mechanism for securitization of catastrophe risk. The recent transaction has established the viability of the instrument with investors being attracted by the volumes, increasing liquidity, pricing, and the ability to rate the structures.

CAT bonds offer many of the same advantages as CAT options. However, a number of special aspects of CAT bond transaction merit comment:

- The CAT bond structures in practice have proved expensive to undertake. The establishment of the SPV, the cost of obtaining a rating, and underwriting fees have proved to be significant costs.
- The structures available have proved to be flexible in a number of respects, including:
  1. The ability to use either PCS indexes or the insurer's own losses enabling basis risk to be minimized. There is, however, the problem of confidentiality, as in the latter case the insurer's loss experience may need to be publicly disclosed.

---

[39] For an analysis of events and claims see Winterthur's website (www.winterthur.com).

2. The ability to create excess of loss or quota share structures, as well as to customize to specific type of protection sought to be created.

3. The types of risk that can be transferred.

- The CAT bonds have proved more attractive to institutional investors relative to PCS options because of the fixed interest investment format that negates the need to enter into separate derivative transactions.
- The CAT bonds as fully funded investments do not provide the inherent leverage potential of the PCS CAT option contracts. This makes the options more attractive to investors seeking leveraged risk profiles.

### 7.4 Market Evolution — Weather-linked Derivatives[40]

The structure described in **Exhibits 15.10** and **15.11** above are interesting in that they entail specific exposure to weather events (earthquakes, windstorms and hail storms). In both cases, the structures have an insurance trigger to payouts. This means that the event that triggers the payout from bond-holders is the *insurance losses* resulting from the weather event rather than the weather event itself. However, in recent types, a market for weather derivatives has evolved. This market has seen the issue of weather-linked bonds.

The major difference between these structures and the CAT bond structures described above is that the payout trigger is the *weather event* itself *irrespective of insurance loss sustained*. In this regard, these structures actually provide *primary insurance* to parties exposed to the specific weather event, rather than *reinsurance cover* to insurers who have indemnified the risk-holders against the risk of loss from these events.

Types of weather risk coverage currently available includes:

- **Degree days** — a measure of variation of daily temperature against a standard reference temperature (generally, 65 degrees Fahrenheit or 18 degrees Centigrade). Transactions are done on both heating degree days (HDD) or cooling degree days (CDD).
- **Precipitation** — a measure of rainfall or snowfall above a certain level.

---

[40] For a discussion of weather derivatives, see Hunter, Robert "Weather Derivative" (May 1998) *Derivatives Strategy* 19-23; Davey, Emma "Weather Or Not" (July 1998) *Futures & OTC World* 47-48; Locke, Jane "Rainclouds Yield Silver Lining" (July 1998) *Risk Insurance Risk Special Report* 23; (October 1998) Weather Risk; *Risk and Energy Power Risk Management Special Report*, Risk Publications, London; Hunter, Robert "Managing Mother Nature" (February 1999) *Derivatives Strategy* 15-27; Conley, John "Risk Coverage Coup" (April 1999) *Global Finance* 28-32; (1999) Weather Risk; *Risk and Energy Power Risk Management Special Report*, Risk Publications, London.

- **Sunshine** — a measure of the number of hours of sunshine relative to a standard reference.
- **Wind speed** — a measure of wind speed relative to a standard reference.
- **Wave height** — a measure of wave height relative to a standard reference.

The interest in these weather parameters derives from their impact (adverse or favorable) to a variety of businesses including electricity generators and distributors, energy producers, agribusiness, food producers, transportation providers, and resort operators. These businesses are in addition to insurers who may want to hedge the risk of high claims from a specific weather event such as excessive precipitation, high wind speed, and so on.

The concept of CAT bonds and derivatives have been readily adapted to weather-linked structures. In a typical weather-linked bond the interest or principal repayment is linked to weather conditions (specified as a relevant meteorological index). A trigger level is agreed and if hit during the term of the bond it triggers payouts (forgone interest or principal repayments) to indemnify the issuer against losses as a result of the specific weather condition prevailing. Swaps and options on the weather conditions have also evolved.

An example of a weather-linked bond of this types is the wind speed-linked bond proposed. The structure for a Spanish entity entails the issue of a bond where the coupon is linked to average wind speeds. If wind speeds are lower than a specified benchmark, the coupon declines. The issuer uses wind to generate electricity. Therefore, the structure provides a natural hedge against lower revenues arising from lower than normal wind speeds.[41]

# 8.    Recapitalization Structures

The recapitalization structures are predicated on engineering the capability of the insurer to recapitalize its position through the issue of debt and/or equity *following a catastrophe event*. These derivatives take the form of reverse convertibles or CAT equity or debt puts.

The logic of these transactions is that where the insurer suffers a large loss as a result of a catastrophe event and the subsequent claims, it suffers a depletion of its capital and reserves and requires recapitalization. The recapitalization structures focus on *prefunding* this capital requirement.

---

[41]  See "Bright Outlook For European Weather Derivatives" (October 31, 1998) *International Financing Review* Issue 1257 87; Baldwin, Dominic and Payne, Beatrix "Spanish Deal In The Wind" (April 1999) *Risk* 6.

## 8.1 Reverse Convertibles[42]

A reverse convertible entails the issue of a convertible bond by the insurer.[43] The issue incorporates a conversion feature whereby the issuer, in certain circumstances, can force conversion of the bond into a predetermined amount of equity (a specified number of shares per bond). The circumstances under which conversion can be forced can be structured in one of two ways:

• **Share price** — where the share price falls below a certain level (which is usually set below the prevailing market value of the shares at the time of issue), the issuer can trigger conversion at its option. This structure provides the insurer with a hedge against any decline in its share price below the set level. This is available irrespective of the cause of the decline in share price.
• **Catastrophe event** — where the conversion option is dependent upon the occurrence of a catastrophe event, the level of industry losses based on an index, or losses suffered by the insurer or some combination of these events.

The share price-based trigger assumes that the share price is likely to decline following losses incurred as a result of a catastrophe event.

The economic value of the reverse convertible is the value difference between the value of the convertible debt at the time of conversion and the value of equity into which the bond may be converted. Theoretically, the value of the structure is the value of the issued debt plus the premium value of the out-of-the-money equity put option sold by the purchaser.

The value to the insurer of this structure is the ability to obtain equity financing at attractive levels relative to the market value of its equity after a catastrophe event. The insurer is also guaranteed funding as it operates on the principal of conversion *of the existing debt* (this is similar to a CAT bond structure that is based around the forgiveness of debt).

Investors may be attracted to this structure on the following basis:

• The higher yield reflecting the combination of the debt coupon and the equity put or catastrophe risk assumed.
• The ability to take up shares at a discount to market in conditions of distress following a catastrophe event where the insurer is seen as being sound with a strong strategic industry position.
• The fact that the reverse convertible may serve to protect the solvency of the insurer and thereby support the equity prices of the company.

---

[42] See Doherty, Neil A. "Financial Innovation in the Management of Catastrophe Risk" (Fall 1997) *Journal of Applied Corporate Finance* vol. 10 no. 3 84-95 at 90.

[43] The structure is very similar to the reverse convertible structures used in equity market generally, see Chapter 11.

## 8.2 CAT Equity Puts[44]

CAT equity puts are transactions whereby the insurer has the option to sell an agreed amount of shares at a predetermined price upon the occurrence of a trigger event. The transaction has a fixed maturity during which the equity put can be exercised. The trigger event is usually defined as a loss exceeding a prescribed amount but being below an upper level (the "exercise window").

The CAT equity put enables the insurer to raise equity capital at a fixed price in the event of a large catastrophe loss. The structure because of its link to the insurer's share price will not typically be exercised unless the post-loss share price of the insurer is below the strike price of the CAT equity put. Consequently, exercise will only be effected where the catastrophe loss event occurs *and* the share price declines.

Some aspects of the CAT equity put structure merit analysis:

- The basic equity option component approximates the structure of a standard equity option, This means it is capable of being priced accordingly. The only complication is the exercise trigger—the catastrophe loss event. This element is exceedingly difficult to model.
- The exercise window concept is used to limit the exposure of the CAT equity put seller. In the event of a very large loss, the insurer's loss may be very large resulting in a very large loss to the CAT equity put seller where the share price falls substantially below the strike (potentially to zero where the insurer becomes insolvent as a result of the losses sustained). The limitation serves to place a known maximum loss on the CAT equity put seller. This limits the value of the structure for insurers although it is not substantially different to the protection created through traditional reinsurance contracts or other insurance derivatives. The insurer's cost of the CAT equity put is lower as a result of this feature.

The CAT equity put was originally introduced by AON and Centre Re, and a number of transactions have been completed, including: US$50 million transaction for RLI insurance (October 1996); US$100 million for Horace Mann (February 1997; and US$100 million for La Salle Re (July 1997).[45]

## 8.3 CAT Bond Puts

The CAT bond puts are based on an identical premise to that of the CAT equity puts. However, in the case of a CAT bond put, it is structured as an event

---

[44] See Doherty, Neil A. "Financial Innovation In The Management Of Catastrophe Risk" (Fall 1997) *Journal of Applied Corporate Finance* vol. 10 no. 3 84-95 at 91-94.

[45] See "An Earthquake In Insurance" (February 28, 1998) *The Economist* at 76.

contingent borrowing. The structure of these instruments is illustrated using two transaction examples in **Exhibit 15.12**.

---

**Exhibit 15.12**
**CAT Bond Puts — Transaction Examples**

*1.  Nationwide Mutual Insurance Company*[46]

Nationwide Mutual Insurance Company undertook an issue of contingent surplus notes.[47] The transaction structure was as follows:

- Nationwide Trust, an SPV, was established and undertook an issue of US$400 million of bonds. The proceeds of these bonds were invested in US Treasury securities.
- Nationwide Mutual entered into a transaction with the Nationwide trust whereby it had the option to issue up to US$400 million in surplus notes to the Trust.
- The operation of the Trust will be as follows:
  - If Nationwide Mutual exercises it option to issue surplus notes to the Trust, the Trust would sell its US Treasury securities, and use the liquidity to purchase the surplus notes. This would result in the underlying collateral changing from US Treasury securities to Nationwide Mutual surplus notes.
  - If the option is not exercised, then the Trust continues to hold US Treasury securities to collateralize the Trust-issued bonds.
- The Trust pays a coupon above US Treasuries financed by the coupon received on the Treasury holdings plus fees paid by Nationwide Mutual for the contingent surplus note option. The coupon payments are not altered by the exercise of the option.

The investors in the Trust notes assume the risk that the underlying collateral of the trust may shift from US Treasury securities to Nationwide Mutual surplus notes. In return, investors receive higher coupon rates. For

---

[46]  See Borden, Sara and Sarker, Asani "Securitizing Property Casualty Risk" (August 1996) *Current Issues in Economics and Finance*, Federal Reserve Bank of New York vol. 2 no. 9 1-6 at 4; Punter, Alan "Contingent Surplus Notes" (July 28, 1997) *Derivatives Week* 6-7.

[47]  Mutual insurers who cannot undertake issue of equity securities issue surplus notes. The concept of surplus in the context of an insurance company is that of its statutory net worth. Surplus notes are usually designed as subordinated debt obligations. Insurers treat surplus notes as equity capital or surplus for statutory purposes.

Nationwide Mutual, the Trust acts as a guaranteed purchaser of its surplus notes. Therefore, in the case of a catastrophe event, Nationwide Mutual would have immediate and guaranteed access to liquidity through the exercise of its options under this structure. Importantly, there is no. explicit and specific linkage between the exercise rights on the surplus notes and any catastrophe event.

## 2. Reliance National[48]

In 1998, US insurer Reliance National entered into a CAT bond put transaction. The structure was as follows:

- The transaction covered a period of approximately three years (through to end 2000).
- Investors sold Reliance options under the terms of which Reliance National could sell an insurance-linked note to the investors at any time until the maturity of the facility. Investors receive a premium of 150 bps pa for writing the options.
- If Reliance exercise its options, then it would issue notes that pay a coupon of 837.5 bps over LIBOR from the date of exercise through till maturity. The capital of the issued notes will be linked to Reliance's insurance businesses. Capital repayment will be dependent upon the loss performance on US property, worldwide property, aviation cover, drilling rig cover, and satellite launch failure cover as measured by Swiss Re's Sigma loss index.

The transaction enables Reliance to guarantee its worst cost of reinsurance cover on these risks over the life of the transaction.

## 3. Allianz[49]

In late 1998, Allianz, the German insurance company, entered into a transaction designed to hedge against adverse changes in reinsurance rates. The transaction provided coverage for German windstorm and hail risks underwritten by Allianz's German operations. The transaction was arranged by Goldman Sachs.

---

[48] See (June 1998) *Risk* vol. 11 no. 6 no. 9 18.
[49] See "Allianz Sells CAT Options" (January 9, 1999) *International Financing Review* Issue 1265 at 90; "Holy Allianz, Batman, It's A CAT Bond Option!" (January 14, 1999) *Financial Products* Issue 105 at 6.

The structure of the transaction was as follows:

- Allianz paid a fee of 49 bps pa for 3-year put options on US$150 million of CAT bonds.
- The underlying CAT bonds have a 3-year term from the date of exercise. The CAT bonds carry a margin of 822 bps over LIBOR.

The transaction operates as follows:

- Any time within the 3-year option life, Allianz can trigger the option to sell notes to the investors who have sold the put options. This is likely to be in the event of a rise in reinsurance rates following a catastrophic loss year.
- In the event of the put option being triggered, investors in the notes receive a high rate of return but bear the underlying insurance risk.

The structure provides Allianz with a low-cost method for fixed-price contingent reinsurance cover. It reduces the insurer's exposure to higher reinsurance cots following windstorm or hail loss.

## 9.   CAT Diversification Swaps[50]

Diversification structures are predicated on the reduction of insurance risk through increasing the level of diversification of the risk portfolio. These derivatives take the form of CAT swaps that facilitate efficient re-allocation of risk between insurers.

The principal vehicle for CAT diversification swaps is the Catastrophe Risk Exchange (CATEX). This is a screen-based trading system that is designed to allow insurers to swap one form of catastrophe risk for another to increase the diversification of risk within insurer's underwriting portfolios.

CATEX is structured as follows:

- Participants in the swaps are limited to insurers, reinsurers, or registered self insurers.
- Each CATEX swap is a bilateral agreement that creates reciprocal reinsurance as between the counterparties.
- The swap will enable exchange of property catastrophe risk by allowing trading in blocks of insurance policies in different region of the US. The units

---

[50] See Paul-Choudhury, Sumit "New Cures For Catastrophes?" (September 1996) *Risk* vol. 9 no. 9 13; "Heading Off Catastrophe" (1996) *Global Finance Practices in Risk Management* 47-48.

of exchange are US$1 million of insured property risk. Risks are classified by location and type of peril (hurricane, earthquake, and so on). CATEX will report proportional relativities between different risks (for example, one unit of Californian earthquake risk may be equivalent to 1.5 units of Texas hurricane risk). The relativities—which are really the proportional relationships between different risks—will be determined by supply and demand.

The principal objective of CAT swaps on CATEX is to allow participants to improve diversification of risks by enabling trading in risks. Insurers over-exposed to a certain types of risk will have the opportunity to exchange that risk for a more acceptable risk, presumably one that the insurer is less exposed to.

Some aspects of CATEX swaps should also be noted:

- CATEX does not have in place clearinghouse arrangements to enhance the credit quality of counterparties. Consequently, each participant will have a counterparty credit exposure on the swap.
- The basis risk entailed in the swap will depend on the structure of each swap. The choice is between the loss experience of each insurer (no basis risk) or an industry aggregate (basis risk will exist depending on the similarity of the insurer's portfolio to the index).

## 10.  Liquidity Puts (Earthquake Bonds)

Liquidity hedges are predicated on reducing the risk of liquefaction of asset/investment portfolios. The objective is to allow the insurer to generate cash needed to meet claims without suffering potential difficulties from market illiquidity. These derivatives take the form of bonds incorporating a liquidity put contingent upon a catastrophe event. **Exhibit 15.13** sets out an example of an earthquake bond that illustrates this type of structure.

---

**Exhibit 15.13**
**Earthquake Bonds**

A number of Japanese property and casualty insurers have since the early 1980s purchased issues of earthquake bonds. The bonds were created by Nomura Securities, Lehman Brothers, and a number of other Japanese entities to basically guarantee the liquidity of Japanese insurers in the event of a major earthquake.

---

The typical structure can be illustrated by analysing the following transaction for AB Electrolux undertaken in March 1990:[51]

- The face value amount of the transaction was US$50 million.
- The maturity was seven years.
- The bond paid a coupon of 8.90% pa. This represented a saving of around 50 bps relative to the normal funding cost of the issuer at the time of the issue.
- The bond has an early redemption feature whereby the investor can put the bond to the issuer at any time at face value upon occurrence of a trigger event. The trigger event was defined as an earthquake of a specified magnitude in any of four Japanese cities (Tokyo, Osaka, Nagoya, or Shizuoka).

The bonds are believed to have been privately placed with a small number of Japanese insurers. Other transactions based on a similar structure have been completed for borrowers such as SEK. The dynamics of the structure are as follows:

- The issuer obtains cost-effective funding in return for assuming a maturity and liquidity risk (in the event of an early redemption).
- The investor, the insurer, obtains a guarantee of liquidity without loss of capital in the event of an earthquake.

It is understood that the 1995 Kobe earthquake triggered some of the redemption puts. However, it is reported that few insurers chose to exercise the put because of the above-market coupons on these bonds.

## 11.  Pricing CAT Risk

### 11.1  Pricing Approaches[52]

The ability to price catastrophe risk is fundamental to the ongoing development of the market for insurance derivatives. As is evident from the above discussion, insurers and reinsurers have a natural incentive to securitize their risk. However,

---

[51]  See (March 3, 1990) *International Financial Review* Issue 816 48; (October 1990) *Corporate Finance* 44.

[52]  For a good overview of insurance pricing approaches, see Briys, Eric, Bellalah, Mondher, Mai, Huu Minh, and De Varrene, Francois (1998) *Options, Futures and Exotic Derivatives*; John Wiley & Sons, Chichester at Chapter 10; for a market view see "Hit Or Miss" (July 1998) *Risk Insurance Risk Special Report* 24-28.

in order to attract *external* (that is, noninsurance) capital to bear catastrophe risk, the insurance risks must be both understood and capable of being priced by the capital markets *generally*. This is essential to allow investors, such as pension funds and mutual funds, to assume insurance risk. In this Section, a number of issues in pricing insurance risk are considered including: the approach to pricing; the pricing of traditional reinsurance risk; and the approach to pricing different classes of insurance derivatives (CAT options and CAT bonds).

Conceptually, insurance risk price is not dissimilar to option pricing. In an efficient market, the contract premium should equal the estimate of expected actuarial insurer losses covered by the contract. The issue is that these losses are difficult to estimate with certainty.

Traditional reinsurance pricing is based on a detailed analysis of the underwriting risk of the primary insurer. This analysis is based on the primary insurer's specific loss experience, its specific exposures, and underwriting procedures. This approach reflects the nature of traditional reinsurance with its emphasis upon indemnification of *specific losses suffered by the primary insurer*. Insurance derivatives have a focus on *aggregate losses* and *industry performance*. As observed above, derivatives and securitization of insurance risk based on specific primary insurer experience is feasible. This structure would require the counterparty or investor to analyze the primary insurer in a manner identical that of the traditional reinsurer.

Pricing aggregate insurance risk based on loss indexes requires different approaches. The fundamental approach is that adopted with all derivatives; that is, the determination of expected values based on the calculation of the distribution of possible losses (the probability of losses).

The current methodology of pricing insurance risk in terms of loss probability is based on two possible approaches:

* **Simulations** — this approach requires analysis of potential randomly generated catastrophe scenarios and their impact on property losses. This approach uses data about weather patterns, seismic events, as well as information on insured values, demographic patterns, and economic information to model the specific levels and possible distribution of insured losses to allow assessment of underwriting risks. This approach is used by a number of specialist firms (Applied Insurance Research (AIR), EQECAT, Risk Management Solutions (RMS), and Towers Perrin).
* **Historical loss experiences** — this approach uses historical loss data (generally taken as aggregate losses such as PCS loss index divided by a sum of earned premiums on lines of insurance that cover losses resulting from catastrophes) to generate loss distributions that are used to price the insurance risk. The approach collates historical data to create a distribution of losses that is then used either parametrically (assuming some statistical distribution)

or empirically (using the *actual* loss experience) to generate the probability of specific events and the resultant losses.

Both approaches are similar in that they seek to create a probability distribution of future catastrophe losses. The simulation approach raises several issues:

- The capacity to build a specific understanding of risk and its potential impact on insured loss levels.
- The approach is limited by the available recorded information on natural diasters. This necessitates a broad range of assumptions and judgements to enable the analysis to be undertaken.
- Typically, such models are time-consuming and expensive to run.

The historical loss experience also raises several issues:

- As both insurance losses and premiums are affected by demographic changes (increase and location), changes in terms and types of insurance coverage and changes in building costs, it is usually necessary to adjust the time series of loss data.[53] These adjustments introduce a number of assumptions into the process.
- The data typically include very few large catastrophe events, necessitating the application of statistical inference techniques. These are based on a parametric characterization of the probability distribution of future loss ratios to allow the creation of a continuous probability distribution from limited observations.
- The loss distributions are generally not normal in characteristic, creating problems of use in inferring future losses based on confidence levels.
- The approach generally is predicated on the future loss experience approximating past loss experience. This may or may not prove to be the case. Paradigm shifts in natural phenomenon are difficult to incorporate into this approach.

The primary issue with the differences between the approaches is that they may in practice produce very different results. This reflects the sensitivity of the result to the loss probability assumptions.

## 11.2  Pricing of Reinsurance

Traditional reinsurance contracts are priced from an analysis by the reinsurer of the primary insurer's specific loss experience, its specific exposures, and

---

[53] For example, it might be possible to adjust by regressing the logarithms of the loss ratios to some demographic measure (population) and using the result to adjust the raw loss ratio data; this approach is used in Litzenberg, Robert H., Beagle-Hole, David R., and Reynolds, Craig E. "Assessing Reinsurance-linked Securities as a New Asset Class" (Special Issue 1996) *Journal of Portfolio Management* 76-86.

underwriting procedures. The ROL (calculated as the reinsurance premium over the risk ceded) is set to cover the expected losses.

Two aspects of reinsurance pricing should be noted:

- The thesis that catastrophe reinsurance premiums are high.[54]
- The fact that reinsurance premiums tend to be particularly high following a major catastrophe event.[55]

The thesis that reinsurance premiums are higher than the fair value reflecting the expected loss has been argued on several bases:

- **Transactional** — for example, in a much-publicized transaction, the CEA purchased reinsurance from National Indemnity (NI). Under the reinsurance contract, CEA pays NI an average annual payment of 10.75% pa for the 4-year cover of US$1.05 billion. Based on a risk of loss of 1.7% pa, the chance of no. event is 93.4% ($(1.00 - 0.017)^4$) and the cumulative risk of loss is 6.6%. This means that NI is receiving (up to) US$451 million in premium (US$112.9 million pa), in return for assuming a risk of loss of US$1.05 billion. This equates to a premium of around 43% of the actual exposure assumed.[56] Based on the probabilities of loss calculated, NI is receiving (up to) US$451 million in return for expected losses under the transaction of US$69.6 million (US$1.05 billion times 6.6%).[57]

- **Theoretical** — it is arguable that catastrophe risk as embodied in CAT bonds is similar to a high-yield bond.[58] The investor in the CAT bond is compensated by the high return for assuming the risk of loss in the event of a catastrophe event occurring. The investor in a high-yield bond is compensated by the high return for the higher risk of loss deriving from the higher risk of default. Guy Carpenter, a reinsurance broker, has estimated that there is a 22% cumulative default probability on top-layer catastrophe

---

[54] See Froot, Kenneth A. (1997) The Limited Financing of Catastrophe Risk: An Overview; National Bureau of Economic Research Working Paper 6025.

[55] See Froot, Kenneth A. and Paul G. J. O'Connell (April 1997) On The Pricing Of Intermediated Risks: Theory And Application To Catastrophe Reinsurance; National Bureau of Economic Research Working Paper 6011.

[56] This assumes that all premiums are paid prior to a payout under the reinsurance contract.

[57] This example is cited in Froot, Kenneth A. (1997) The Limited Financing of Catastrophe Risk: An Overview; National Bureau of Economic Research Working Paper 6025 at 5.

[58] See Canter, Michael S., Cole, Joseph B., and Sandor, Richard L. "Insurance Derivatives: A New Asset Class for the Capital Markets and a New Hedging Tool for the Insurance Industry" (Fall 1997) *Journal of Applied Corporate Finance* vol. 10 no. 3 69-83 at 77.

reinsurance. This compares to a cumulative default probability of 40% on B-rated corporate bonds. The return on insurance risk is estimated at 9.20% pa over Treasuries over the last 10 years. The return on B-rated corporate bonds is estimated at 4.63% pa over Treasuries.[59] This highlights the seemingly high *risk-adjusted returns* available on reinsurance.

The high costs are thought to derive from the scarcity of reinsurance capital, the exercise of market power by reinsurers, market inefficiencies, and moral hazard/adverse selection types of contracting problems.[60] The rise of reinsurance premiums after a large catastrophe event is attributable to a variety of factors including: decreases in supply and increased cost of reinsurance capital.[61]

The high returns seemingly available may well attract increased modeling interest in reinsurance risk at the same time as it attracts investor capital. This analysis may well prove important in introducing greater rigour in pricing *reinsurance risk generally* and introduce a greater degree of transparency into reinsurance markets.

### 11.3  Pricing CAT Options

Some of the effort in pricing reinsurance risk has been focused on the specific problem of pricing CAT options, in particular the CAT spreads that replicate a layer of reinsurance. The models are based on modeling the dynamics of the stochastic process of the index of aggregate insured losses.[62]

---

[59]  Based on Froot, Kenneth A., Murphy, Brian, Stern, Aaron, and Usher, Stephen "The Emerging Asset Class: Insurance Risk", Guy Carpenter & Co. cited in Canter, Michael S., Cole, Joseph B., and Sandor, Richard L. "Insurance Derivatives: A New Asset Class for the Capital Markets and a New Hedging Tool for the Insurance Industry" (Fall 1997) *Journal of Applied Corporate Finance* vol. 10 no. 3 69-83 at 77.

[60]  See Froot, Kenneth A. (1997) The Limited Financing of Catastrophe Risk: An Overview; National Bureau of Economic Research Working Paper 6025; Froot, Kenneth A. and O'Connell, Paul G. J. (April 1997) On The Pricing Of Intermediated Risks: Theory And Application To Catastrophe Reinsurance; National Bureau of Economic Research Working Paper 6011.

[61]  See Froot, Kenneth A. and O'Connell, Paul G. J. (April 1997) On The Pricing of Intermediated Risks: Theory And Application To Catastrophe Reinsurance; National Bureau of Economic Research Working Paper 6011.

[62]  See Geman, Helyette "CAT Calls" (September 1994) *Risk* vol. 7 no. 9 86-89; Geman, Helyette "Insurance-risk Securitization And CAT Insurance Derivatives" (September 1996) *Financial Derivatives and Risk Management* Issue 7 21-24; Cummins, J. David and Geman, Helyette "Pricing Catastrophe Insurance Futures and Call Spreads: An Arbitrage approach" (March 1996) *Journal of Fixed income* 46-57; Tomas III, Michael J. "A Note On Pricing PCS Single-Event Options" (Spring 1998) *Derivatives Quarterly* 23-28.

The models use an instantaneous claim process combining a diffusion process with a jump component. This is consistent with traditional approaches in insurance modeling that use Poisson or compound Poisson process (es) to model the claims experience. This approach is designed to combine the Poisson process (for major catastrophe events) and the diffusion process (for the randomness in reporting and small loss events). This approach allows the derivation of the option premium using standard no-arbitrage conditions underlying traditional option valuation. The complexity of the process means that an exact closed form solution has not been found with Monte Carlo simulations being used to price the options.

In using the approach, the authors of the model have found:[63]

- The pricing model is sensitive to parameter changes but appears relatively robust implying that in a liquid market it should be feasible to derive prices from market prices allowing efficient pricing.
- It is necessary to run a large number of simulations (100,000) to obtain spread premiums with an error less than 1%. This is clearly expensive and slow in terms of calculation speed.

The pricing of these transactions is clearly at the early stages of development.[64]

## 11.4  Pricing and Rating CAT Bonds

The second class of insurance derivatives required to be priced is CAT bonds. Pricing of CAT bonds typically involves decomposition of the bond into a position in a bonds and a CAT option or options.[65] **Exhibit 15.14** sets out examples of pricing CAT bonds.

---

**Exhibit 15.14**
**Pricing CAT Bonds**[66]

Assume the relevant security is a 1-year CAT bond with the following payoffs:

- The investor invests US$100 million.

---

[63]  See Geman, Helyette "CAT Calls" (September 1994) *Risk* vol. 7 no. 9 86-89.

[64]  For a review of market experience, see Lane, Morton and Movachan, Oleg "The Perfume of the Premium II" (Spring 1999) *Derivatives Quarterly* 27-40.

[65]  See Litzenberg, Robert H., Beagle-Hole, David R., and Reynolds, Craig E. " Assessing Reinsurance-linked Securities as a New Asset Class" (Special Issue 1996) *Journal of Portfolio Management* 76-86 at 80-82.

- The investor receives a coupon of 14.00% pa (equivalent to 800 bps over the 1-year Treasury bill rate of 6.00% pa).
- The principal repayment is linked to a CAT aggregate loss index with the following payoffs:
  1. If the loss index is above a prescribed level (say a loss ratio of 25%), then the investor only receives repayment of 50% of the principal of the transaction.
  2. If the loss index is below a prescribed level (say a loss ratio of 25%), then the investor receives repayment of the full 100% of the principal of the transaction.

The security can be bifurcated into two separate transactions:

- A 1-year bond.
- A sold binary call on the aggregate loss index with a strike as the specified loss ratio level of 25% and a payout amount of US$50 million (50% of the face value of the bond).

The implicit reinsurance ROL can be calculated as follows:

- Calculate the present value of the coupon above the market rate (8.00% calculated as 14.00% pa – 6.00% pa) discounted at 6.00% pa; that is, equivalent to 7.55% pa. This equates to the implicit reinsurance premium.
- The implicit ROL is equal to the implicit reinsurance premium (7.55%) divided by the maximum of 50% of bond value that is equivalent to 15.10%.

The expected value of the exposure can be separately calculated as follows:

- Assume that the probability of a loss level exceeding 25% is around 8.00% pa (derived from one of the two approaches outlined above). This implies that there is a 92% probability that the bond value will be 100% and an 8% probability that the bond value will be 50% of face value.
- Based on these probabilities the expected value of the bond can be determined as 96% of face value (calculated as (92% × 100) + (8% ×

---

[66] The approach used in this example is that used in Litzenberg, Robert H., Beagle-Hole, David R., and Reynolds, Craig E. " Assessing Reinsurance-linked Securities as a New Asset Class" (Special Issue 1996) *Journal of Portfolio Management* 76-86 at 80-82. Please note that all parameters used in this example are assumed and are not reflective of current market rates or loss expectations.

50)). This implies an expected reinsurance loss of 4.00% that discounted for one year at 6.00% pa is equivalent to 3.77% of face value or an implicit ROL of 7.55% (3.77%/50%).

The expected value of the exposure allows the derivation of the breakeven ROL that on this occasion is lower than the actual implicit ROL of the transaction. The breakeven ROL, generally, will be lower than the implicit ROL. The difference represents the risk premium received by the investor for bearing the reinsurance CAT risk.

For CAT bonds with embedded CAT option spreads, the approach to valuation is identical with the bond being decomposed into a conventional bond and positions in two CAT binary options, each of which is valued using the approach outlined above.

A related issue is the rating of CAT bonds. The rating agencies utilize their own models to rate these securities. The rating approach typically blends the process of rating an asset-backed security (ABS) transaction with an evaluation of the insurance risk component.

The type of methodology used focuses on estimating expected loss and the other factors affecting bond performance.[67] The analysis concentrates on:

- The catastrophic event — which is modeled using computer simulation models.
- The conditional loss amount — refers to the loss level transfer point that must be exceeded before being borne by the investor.
- The structure of the transaction — any special transaction features that may influence loss.

The overall analysis process is set out in **Exhibit 15.15**.

---

[67] See (February 3, 1997) Structured Finance and Catastrophic Risk; Fitch Research Financial Institutions Special Report; Efrat, Isaac, Falcone, Yvonne, Gluck, Jeremy, Kwoh, Lawrence, Murray, Alan, and Pawar, David (September 12, 1997) Moody's Approach to the Rating of Catastrophe-linked Notes; Moody's Investors Service Global Credit Research, New York.

**Exhibit 15.15**
**Catastrophic Event-backed Bond Analysis**

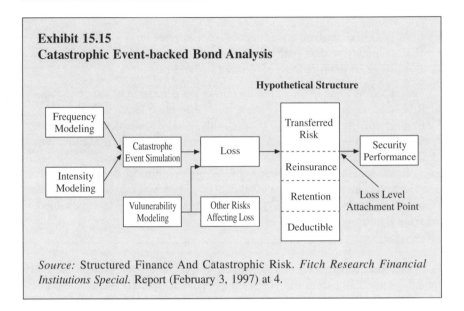

*Source:* Structured Finance And Catastrophic Risk. *Fitch Research Financial Institutions Special.* Report (February 3, 1997) at 4.

Key elements of the modeling include:

*   **Frequency modeling** — which addresses the likelihood of a long-term event occurrence within a probabilistic framework. This is undertaken with some form of stochastic analysis using probability distribution functions to simulate event occurrence (typical distributions are Poisson or Negative Binomial distributions).
*   **Intensity modeling** — which addresses the event's potential for destruction using dependency relationships between key variables that influence the amount of damage. For example, in the case of a hurricane, variables like peak wind speeds, storm pressure differentials, radius of maximum wind speeds, forward velocity of the storm, and angular storm to coastline positioning would all be modeled. For examples, in the case of an earthquake, variables like seismo-tectonic activity, attenuation of seismic activity, and soil condition would be modeled to generate the intensity of vibrations and peak ground acceleration that are the determinants of damage and the resultant insured losses.
*   **Vulnerability analysis** — which address the potential for damage in the event of the catastrophe occurring based on property specific attributes such as types of building and property. This entails deriving a damage factor (the statistical conditional amount of loss given the intensity of the event using a joint probability function, numerical techniques, or simulations).
*   **Aggregate loss distribution** — which is based on the distribution of frequency and intensity, and used to generate the aggregate loss distribution

to cover the relevant event. This may be done using a number of techniques such as Monte Carlo simulations, sampling techniques, and event trees.

• **Other factors** — which address a variety of issues including data quality, policy coverage, demand surge (the effect on regional prices of items such as construction cost inflation following a catastrophe), geographical concentrations, and loss management.

Once the distribution of the aggregate loss distribution is derived, then the rating is focused on the risk transfer mechanisms used. Structurally, most CAT bonds involve conditional loss amounts. A loss transfer point indicates the level of insured losses that must be breached before losses are borne by the investor. This provides the basis on which catastrophe events may be compared to ABS transactions. This is based on the fact that different events can be structured to have similar long-term expected losses *irrespective of the cause of the loss*. This reflects the fact that from a risk-return perspective, the investor should be indifferent as between different *types* of securities that have identical *expected loss* and *risk* characteristics. Using this approach the rating is derived by using the corporate bond market, with regards to its long-term expected performance in terms of expected loss as a comparative benchmark.

# 12. Capital Markets and Insurance Derivatives

## 12.1 Utilizing Capital Markets to Diversify Insurance Risk[68]

It is now fashionable to speak of the merger of capital and insurance markets. The developing inter-relationship between the two markets is at an early stage of evolution. The inter-relationship exists at two separate levels:
• The emergence of insurance risk as a tradeable asset in capital markets allowing insurers to increasingly transfer risk to traditional noninsurers.

---

[68] See Canter, Michael S., Cole, Joseph B., and Sandor, Richard L. "Catastrophe Options on the Chicago Board Of Trade" (September 1996) *Financial Derivatives and Risk Management* Issue 7 13-20; Canter, Michael S., Cole, Joseph B., and Sandor, Richard L. "Insurance Derivatives: A New Asset Class for the Capital Markets and a New Hedging Tool for the Insurance Industry" (Fall 1997) *Journal of Applied Corporate Finance* vol. 10 no. 3 69-83; Paul-Choudhury, Sumit "The Empire strikes Back" (June 1997) *Risk* vol. 10 no. 6 20-22; Clow, Robert "Coping With Catastrophe" (December 1996) *Institutional Investor* 143-150; Cooper, Graham "Protection Money" (September 1994) *Risk* vol. 7 no. 9 82-84; Doherty, Neil A. "Financial Innovation in the Management of Catastrophe Risk" (Fall 1997) *Journal of Applied Corporate Finance* vol. 10 no. 3 84-95; Dunbar, Nicholas "Trouble Indemnity" (December 1997) Futures & Options World 14; Elliot, Margaret "Convergence Or Collision" (December 1997) *Derivatives Strategy* 18-24; Fairlamb, David "Financial Alchemists" (April 1999)

- The increasing entry by insurance companies into capital markets, either in the adoption of capital market techniques in insurance or in the form of establishing business units that are active in conventional capital markets activities.

The emergence of insurance risk as a tradeable asset is driven by both supply- and demand-side considerations. The demand for additional risk transfer mechanisms for insurance risk, in particular, catastrophe risk, is driven by the cost and availability of capital to assume this risk. The supply-side argument is driven by several factors:

- Insured losses of US$50 billion arising from an earthquake and hurricane would absorb a significant portion (around 20%) of the capital of the primary and reinsurance capital. This compares to *daily fluctuations* in financial markets of a larger magnitude. The US capital market is estimated at around US$19,000 billion in capital value with the average daily standard deviation of US$133 billion.[69] This indicates that the risk of a large catastrophe would be readily absorbed into capital markets if the risk could be efficiently transferred and placed with a fully diversified group of investors.
- The fact that insurance risk as an unique asset class is poorly correlated to other more traditional investment assets allowing investors to improve the returns upon and increase the diversification of investment portfolios. An additional factor is that insurance risk seems to offer higher risk-adjusted returns than assets of comparable risk. This thesis is considered in detail below.

The proponents of the view that catastrophe risk is an investment asset argue that the emerging markets in insurance derivatives facilitate the deployment of capital from institutional and retail investors in insurance markets. They argue that the emerging instruments provide effective hedging mechanisms, higher

---

*Institutional Investor* 55-59; Leander, Ellen "When An Insurance Salesman is an Investment Banker" (March 1996) *Global Finance* 13-15; Piggot, Charles "Insurance Derivatives: Still Pioneer Territory" (July 1997) *Euromoney* 10; "Premium Products" (November 2, 1994) *Financial Products* Issue 5 14-17; Schut, Jan H. "Reinventing Reinsurance" (July 1995) *Institutional Investor* 135-139; Thackray, John "Insurance Derivatives Catch Fire" (December/January 1997) *Derivatives Strategy* 28-31; Webb, Andrew "Crisis Management" (June 4 1998) *Financial Products* Issue 92 16-17; Quinn, Lawrence Richter "Insure It All" (July 1999) *Derivatives Strategy* 23-27; Hunter, Robert "Securitizing Insurance Risk" (July 1999) *Derivatives Strategy* 28-31; "Reinventing Insurance: New Approaches To Risk" (July 1999) *Derivatives Strategy* 35-39.

[69] See Canter, Michael S., Cole, Joseph B., and Sandor, Richard L. "Insurance Derivatives: A New Asset Class for the Capital Markets and a New Hedging Tool for the Insurance Industry" (Fall 1997) Journal of Applied Corporate Finance vol. 10 no. 3 69-83 at 82.

efficiency, and price discovery and transparency of pricing in reinsurance contracts. The longer run benefits perceived include increased reinsurance capacity, lower pricing, and reduced pricing volatility.

The ultimate form of insurance market under this paradigm would be like the model depicted in **Exhibit 15.16**.

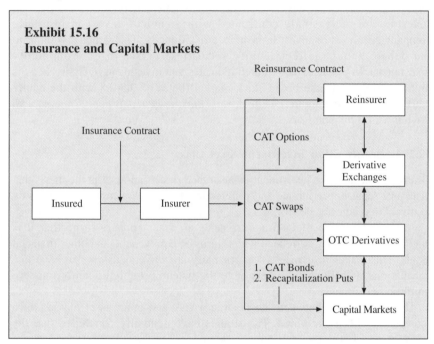

**Exhibit 15.16**
**Insurance and Capital Markets**

The arguments presented are logical but rely on the satisfaction of certain conditions. These include:

- The ability to create diversified insurance risk portfolios. The risk currently sought to be transferred is narrowly based (predominantly, US catastrophe risk) resulting in difficulties in investors acquiring a diversified portfolio of insurance risk.
- The efficient nature of the instruments themselves. The instruments exhibit certain basis risks and operational difficulties that impede efficient risk transfer.
- The ability to trade insurance risk in a liquid market setting. As already noted, the liquidity of insurance derivatives markets is still to be established.
- The ability to model and price insurance risk to an appropriate degree of precision. As noted above, the process of modeling and valuing insurance derivatives is at an early stage of development. The inability to confidently model and price the risk is a precondition to broad-based investor participation.

At a more fundamental level, the argument regarding deployment of investment capital assumes that there is limited involvement of investors in insurance risk. While this may be true in terms of direct assumption of catastrophe risk, there are significant amounts of investor capital committed to insurance *in the form of the equity securities issued by insurers and reinsurers*. In essence, the argument therefore is less about the investment as it is about the *mode* of investment. Investors are increasingly confronted with a choice—invest in insurance company securities or invest in insurance risk directly. This is not dissimilar to the debate about indirect (equity securities) versus direct commodity investments. In practice, the research indicates that investment in equity stock is highly correlated to the broad stock market (betas of 0.5-0.8 with the equity market indexes are common) while *actual catastrophe risk is not correlated with the returns on financial assets*.

## 12.2  Insurance as an Investment Asset Class

Central to the case for investment in insurance risk as an asset is the thesis that insurance represents a unique and differentiated asset class capable of inclusion in diversified investor portfolios.

A special feature of insurance risk as an asset appears to be that it is uncorrelated or poorly correlated with returns on equity, debt, and other financial assets. This makes insurance risk particularly attractive as assets that have low correlations with financial assets have the potential to significantly improve portfolio performance.

The correlations between the insurance risk and other asset classes have increasingly been examined. The studies have generally concluded that the correlations between insurance risk and other financial assets are not significantly different to zero. One study found that the adjusted historical loss ratios had a correlation of 0.058 with returns on the S&P 500 index and 0.105 with a government bond index between March 1955 and December 1994.[70] Another study found that annual percentage change in the PCS national index had a correlation of –0.5 with the S&P 500 between 1949 to 1997.[71] The correlation in each is small and not statistically different from zero.[72]

---

[70]  See Litzenberg, Robert H., Beagle-Hole, David R., and Reynolds, Craig E. "Assessing Reinsurance-linked Securities as a New Asset Class" (Special Issue 1996) *Journal of Portfolio Management* 76-86 at 83.

[71]  See Canter, Michael S., Cole, Joseph B., and Sandor, Richard L. "Insurance Derivatives: A New Asset Class for the Capital Markets and a New Hedging Tool for the Insurance Industry" (Fall 1997) *Journal of Applied Corporate Finance* vol. 10 no. 3 69-83 at 78.

[72]  See also Lamm, R. McFall "Inflation-protected and Insurance-linked Securities Portfolios" (June 1998) *The Australian Corporate Treasurer* 9-12.

Several studies have sought to analyze the impact of adding insurance risk to a diversified investment portfolio using different analytical frameworks:

- **Black Litterman Asset Allocation approach**[73] — this approach considers that the addition of a new security to a portfolio is attractive where it increases the portfolio's Sharpe ratio (the ratio of excess expected return (return less the risk-free rate) to volatility (standard deviation) of return). The study found that investors holding a portfolio corresponding to the S&P 500 index would find it attractive to hold 1% of the portfolio in a CAT investment provided that the returns on the CAT portfolio is at least 11 bps over the short-term rate. It would be attractive to hold 2% in CAT investments if the excess return was 22 bps over the short rate. For a bond portfolio, the excess returns are 3 bps over the short rate for a 1% holding and 5 bps for a 2% holding. Given the fact that current excess returns are significantly above these threshold levels, CAT investments increase the performance of a portfolio in which they are included.
- **Efficient frontier approach** — this approach focuses on all the optimal combinations of investments that provide the maximum return (as measured by holding period returns) for minimum risk (as measured by the standard deviation of returns). New assets are measured as to their ability to move the investor's portfolio closer to this efficient frontier. Insurance risk, because of the high returns available and also its zero correlation with the other assets in the portfolio, can simultaneously increase returns while reducing the risk. One estimate found that an addition of 2% catastrophe risk to a portfolio of 60% stock and 40% bonds increases expected returns by 1.25% while simultaneously reducing the standard deviation of the portfolio by 0.25%.[74]

The potential benefits, based on the historical loss data available, indicates that the addition of insurance risk to investment portfolios has significant benefits. This will undoubtedly assist in attracting investment in these markets in the longer term.

### 12.3 Impact of Derivatives Techniques on Insurance Markets

As noted above, the advent of insurance derivatives is prompting a greater convergence of capital markets and the insurance industry. This has taken the

---

[73] See Litzenberg, Robert H., Beagle-Hole, David R., and Reynolds, Craig E. " Assessing Reinsurance-linked Securities as a New Asset Class" (Special Issue 1996) *Journal of Portfolio Management* 76-86.

[74] A study by Guy Carpenter cited in Canter, Michael S., Cole, Joseph B., and Sandor, Richard L. "Insurance Derivatives: A New Asset Class for the Capital Markets and a New Hedging Tool for the Insurance Industry" (Fall 1997) *Journal of Applied Corporate Finance* vol. 10 no. 3 69-83 at 78.

form of increasing entry by insurance companies into capital markets, either in the adoption of capital market techniques in insurance or in the form of establishing business units that are active in conventional capital markets activities.

Underlying this trend are several broad themes:

- The increased redefinition of financial intermediation roles within capital markets generally.
- The inherent role of insurers in risk management that leads to an overlap with the activities of derivatives operations of financial intermediaries.
- The focus *by clients of both insurers and financial institutions* on integration of *all risks* for the purpose of both measurement and management.

The most tangible evidence of this convergence is the number of insurers who have established derivative products/capital markets operations. These include: AIG (AIG Financial Products; AIG Trading); General Re (General Re Financial Products); and Swiss Re (investment in CSFP). Earlier examples include Prudential (Prudential Global Funding). In addition, a number of insurers have utilized their high-quality credit standing (AAA/AA) to coventure with banks to enhance the credit quality of special-purpose derivative companies (SPDC) or derivative product companies (DPG).[75] Similarly, a number of investment banks have created special subsidiaries specializing in reinsurance derivatives.

The involvement of insurance companies in capital markets essentially is focused on several levels:

- Use of derivatives in the management of their own asset and (to a lesser extent) liability portfolios. This entails the use of traditional derivative techniques to manage the inherent equity, interest rate, currency, and commodity risks within this portfolio.
- Using insurance derivatives to transfer or acquire reinsurance risk or manage the portfolio of underwriting risks.
- Using established capital market technology to create new insurance products. For example, some insurers have begun to offer comprehensive risk insurance policies covering both traditional insurance-risks (property and casualty risk) and financial risk (currency exposures) requiring capital market/derivative skills to complement insurance underwriting expertise.

The special-purpose vehicles established by insurers are in fact organizational mechanisms for creating cells of specific expertise to assist with this process.

---

[75] See Das, Satyajit "Test Drive" (October 19, 1994) IFR *Financial Products* Issue 4 14-17; "A Comparative Analysis of Special Purpose Derivative Vehicles" (April 1995) *Capital Market Strategies* no. 5 33-37.

For example, the operation of these entities is focused on: insurance-linked products (primarily to create product to sell insurance risk such as CAT bonds); credit intermediation (managing the credit risk of the reinsurance market); and hybrid structures (combining different types of risk in complex insurance packages, often in a derivative format).[76]

Financial institution involvement is predicated upon the potential for securitization of and trading in insurance risk. It is also predicated on the interest by investors in these nontraditional alternative investments. However, the involvement is tempered in reality by the fact that these risks are difficult to trade and hedge within a market-making framework in a classical sense because of the absence of effective hedging mechanisms.

In the longer term, the convergence of capital markets and insurance may have more profound implications. The role of the primary insurer may be redefined as that of an *originator* of insurance risks that are then repackaged and sold to investors or to other insurers. This would parallel the development in mortgage markets where banks have had their role redefined as originators of mortgage assets that are primarily held in repackaged form by institutional investors in capital markets. However, these longer term evolutionary issues are contingent upon the continued development of the insurance derivatives markets and changes in the regulatory frame work governing the insurance industry overall.

## 13. Summary

The development of insurance derivatives represents a significant extension of derivative technology into the insurance industry. The ability to repackage insurance risk, primarily catastrophe risk to date, into structured notes (CAT bonds) or options (CAT options) allows these risks to be traded and therefore the underlying risk to be transferred and hedged. The establishment of insurance risk as a separate asset class and the empirical case for adding this risk to investment portfolios in order to enhance performance is gradually being secured, allowing broad-based investor participation in these markets. However, problems of instrument design, liquidity, the modeling of risk, and valuation issues are at an early stage of resolution. The market for insurance derivatives is at an early stage of development. Importantly, the essential linkages between capital markets and the insurance industry have now been built and will continue to develop.

---

[76] For example, see "Combined Is Prepared" (March 19, 1997) *Financial Products* Issue 62 16-17.

# 16
# Pricing and Valuation of Structured Note Transactions

## 1. Valuation Approach

### 1.1 Overview

The pricing and valuation of structured note transaction must by definition follow the inherent structure of the transaction. It must, as a consequence, follow the components of the transaction. These components will include, in a typical transaction, the following elements:

- A fixed or floating rate security.
- The embedded derivative component(s) that will be a forward or option on an identified financial market variable or asset.

The pricing and value of the instrument will reflect the sum of the value of the components.

This approach can be applied uniformly across all transaction structures. It can also be applied irrespective of the valuation context (that is, a new transaction, risk evaluation, secondary market pricing, and so on).

### 1.2 Pricing and Valuation of Components

The approach outlined utilizes existing valuation techniques *for the individual transaction components*. This means that the identified components are valued as follows:

- The fixed income component (either a fixed-rate bond or FRN) is priced using normal fixed income valuation techniques such as internal rate of return or yield to maturity.
- The derivative components are valued using the appropriate valuation technique:

1. **Forward components** — carry cost-based models.
2. **Option components** — using the relevant option pricing model.[1]

As discussed in greater detail below, the pricing or valuation of the structured note is the sum of the values of the individual components adjusted for some special factors.

A key aspect of this valuation approach is the ability to unbundle *any* structured note into its constituent elements. This is important from a number of reasons:

- It allows the transaction to be engineered by combining the individual elements. The trader enters into a series of transactions to create the desired structure. The decomposition is essential to the hedging process.
- It places boundary values to the instrument. This dictates that in an extreme case the transaction can be *reverse engineered* into the relevant elements. This allows the transaction to be repackaged and replaced with counterparties who are prepared to purchase or trade in the constituent elements. Given the generic nature of many of the components, the liquidity of the components will, typically, be greater than that for the structured note allowing an enhancement to the liquidity of the instrument (albeit at a price). The fact that the structured note must trade at a value *no lower* than that of its unbundled constituents also facilitates arbitrage (between the value of the structured note and the components) that assists in promoting the liquidity of these types of instruments.
- It overcomes the difficulty of seeking to price and manage the risk elements of the structured note *as a security* by breaking by the risks into discrete and separately hedgeable components.

### 1.3 Special Issues in Structured Note Valuation

The special issues in the pricing and valuation of structured notes relate, in general terms, two structural aspects of these instruments:

- Structured notes seek to isolate credit or default risk (the risk of failure to perform on the cash flow or payment obligations of the instrument) from market risk (the risk of fluctuations in the value of the instrument from

---

[1] Valuation models for derivative transactions are not discussed. For a good overview of derivative valuation techniques refer to: Hull, John (1997*) Options, Futures, and Other Securities — Third Edition*; Prentice Hall, Englewood Cliffs, NJ; Das, Satyajit (1994) Swaps and Financial Derivatives; LBC Information Services, Sydney, McGraw-Hill, Chicago; Das, Satyajit (editor) (1997) *Risk Management & Financial Derivatives: A Guide to the Mathematics*; LBC Information Services, Sydney; McGraw-Hill, Chicago; MacMillan Publishing, England.

changes in the value of the key market variables embedded in the instrument).

• A number of different value drivers (financial market variables) are combined typically within the structured note. For example, a commodity-linked note will combine an exposure to interest rates (on the fixed income component) and an exposure to the price of the relevant commodity (through the embedded derivative element).

These factors impact upon the valuation of these instruments in a number of ways. The isolation of credit risk and market risk dictates two value effects:

1. The typical structured note, as discussed in the context of the market for structured notes (see Chapter 18), is issued by high-quality (AA- or better rated) issuers. This dictates the risk of value fluctuations from credit quality is lower than for comparable traditional securities.
2. The fact that the structured note format uses the issuer's credit rating as a form of credit enhancement dictates that the cost of this enhancement charged by the issuer must be factored into the valuation (usually, expressed as the issuer's funding target).

The second consideration is not present where the structured note is created utilizing a special purpose repackaging vehicle.

The combination of value drivers requires capture of the correlation relationships between the fixed income component of the structured note (the bond value) and the embedded derivative component (the market or derivative value). It is unlikely that the two variables (the interest rates driving the bond value and the asset price driving the market or derivative value) are unrelated. For example, a change in commodity prices that will impact the value of the structured note may be accompanied by a change in interest rates (through the commodity price to inflation to interest rate linkages). This will either reinforce or offset partially the change in value of the structured note created by the shift in commodity prices alone.

Interestingly, the market values of structured notes frequently do not appear to totally incorporate the embedded correlation relationships. A factor in this is the relatively short tenor of structured note transactions where the market or derivative value element may dominate the value of the package (see discussion in Chapter 17 on the pattern of structured note issuance).

## 2. Valuation Context

In examining the process and issues related to pricing and valuing structured notes, it is useful to separate the process into a number of distinct contexts. This is dictated by the fact that the key areas of focus are different in each of these contexts. While the analytical basis will remain substantially the same in each of these valuation contexts, the nature of the analysis has significant differences of emphasis. This reflects in part the fact that each context emphasizes the different perspective of the issuer, investor, and the trader/structurer involved in engineering the transaction.

The three major contexts are as follows:

- Initial pricing.
- Risk evaluation.
- Secondary market pricing.

Each of these phases is considered in detail in the following sections.

### 3.    Structured Note Transactions — Initial Pricing

The initial pricing phase is focused on the structuring or construction of the security. The key participants are:

- **Investor** — who nominates the parameters of the transaction in terms of the issuer universe, the market risk to be assumed (the position sought to be taken in respect of the market variable sought to be traded), and the risk parameters (for example, interest or principal at risk/protected, minimum income requirement, time horizon at risk, and so on).
- **Issuer** — who nominates the target funding cost that will be determine the issuer's willingness to issue the security. This will incorporate the cost of credit enhancement required by the issuer.
- **Financial institution/dealer** — who must match investor and issuer requirements within the following constraints:
  1. The cost of the hedges that must be executed to engineer the structured note.
  2. The earnings sought to compensate for the creation, hedging, and ongoing risk and capital commitment required by the transaction (if relevant).

The key elements of the process can be summarized as follows:

- The issuer's funding target.
- The component values based on appropriate market value (including bid-offer spreads and other transaction costs).

The first element is difficult to specify scientifically. The issuers are opportunistic new issue arbitrage funders who will set benchmark funding costs based on the supply of financing opportunities on offer relevant to their financing requirements at a given point in time.

The process underlying this decision has been identified to be as follows:[2]

- Identify a base borrowing cost, usually taken as a direct FRN issue for the relevant maturity (effectively a zero-cost or base transaction).

- Identify the risks of the structured note or swapped transaction through a system of risk factors. This will incorporate the volatility of the relevant asset price as well as correlation between the relevant parameters. This risk should capture the credit risk of the transaction that will be recorded against the issuer and reflected in the capital allocated by the counterparty to the derivative transaction.
- The target cost for the issuer should be the base borrowing adjusted for the risks/capital cost of the transaction.

The second element is purely market driven, reflecting the cost of the constituent elements using appropriate market pricing parameters.

The value of the security is driven by these two factors. The difference between the market value of the structure and the price *paid by the investor* represents:

- Cost to the investor in the structure (including the regulatory arbitrage, credit enhancement, and so on, motivating entry into the transaction in the form of a structured note).
- Profit to the arranger in facilitating the transaction, as well as compensation for any hedging and underwriting risk assumed in the transaction.

**Exhibit 16.1** examines the pricing and initial valuation of a collared FRN transaction in the primary market.

---

**Exhibit 16.1**
**Pricing and Valuation of Capped FRN Transaction —**
**Primary Market**

*1. Transaction*

Assume the example of a collared FRN[3] that is being structured in response to investor demand. The potential issuer is an AA- rated financial institution that is willing to undertake the transaction on the basis that the arranger hedges out its expose to the embedded derivative elements and guarantees it an acceptable funding cost.

The components of the transaction are as follows:

1. A US$100 million 10-year subordinated FRN priced off LIBOR issued by the issuer.

---

[2]  See Yngwe, Peter "Derivative Applications: A Borrowers' Application" (1995) *Financial Derivatives & Risk Management* vol. 1 no. 1 pp 49-54.
[3]  A transaction similar to that set out in Chapter 1 and discussed in detail in Chapter 4.

2. A cap on 6-month LIBOR with a strike price of 10% pa sold by the investor and purchased by the issuer.
3. A floor on 6-month LIBOR with a strike price of 5% pa purchased by the investor and sold by the issuer.

The structure of the transaction will take the form of a privately placed issue of the FRNs to be documented under an existing Medium Term Note (MTN) program. The issue is expected to be placed with a small number (three-four) investors who have indicated interest in the transaction. The issuer will be hedged on its cap/floor exposure through the entry into a hedge with the arranger. Under the hedge the arranger will sell a floor to the issuer and purchase the embedded cap in the FRN to completely insulate the issuer from any market risk exposure under the cap or floor. This will be engineered so that where LIBOR rates are under 5% pa the issuer will receive from the arranger the difference between 5% pa and the LIBOR rate for the relevant interest period on a principal equal to the face value of the transaction. Where LIBOR rates are over 10% pa the issuer will pay to the issuer the difference between 5% pa and the LIBOR rate for the relevant interest period on a principal equal to the face value of the transaction.

## 2. Pricing and Valuation

The pricing and valuation of the transaction will reflect the value of the individual components. The only additional elements requiring identification to enable pricing of the transaction are the issuer's funding cost target and the arranger's fees in facilitating the issue.

Assume the prevailing market prices of the elements of the transaction are as follows:

- A subordinated FRN of the type identified is trading at around LIBOR plus 0.25% pa.
- The cap and floor prices are as follows:[4]
  Cap Price — 2.88% flat
  Floor Price — 1.64% flat.

---

[4]  The cap and floor prices are derived utilizing Black's Option Pricing Model utilizing the implied forward 6 month LIBOR rates calculated off the prevailing yield curve (which is steeply upward sloping with a spread between six month LIBOR (3.50% pa) and 10 year swap rates (7.10% pa) of approx. 360 bps) and based on volatility levels of 14% pa (for the floor) and 13% pa (for the cap). The different volatility reflect the bid and offer volatility levels which reflect the fact that the trader in hedging the issuer's exposure is purchasing the cap and selling the floor.

Assume the investor is willing to buy this asset at a coupon of LIBOR plus 0.0625% pa. The issuer's target is LIBOR minus 6.25 bps on this financing. Given a discount rate applicable over 10 years at 7.10% pa (payable semi-annually), the 12.5 bps pa reduction in cost to the issuer is equivalent to 88 bps in present value terms. The amount due to be received by the issuer from the arranger for the sold cap and bought floor transaction is equivalent to 124 bps (this is the net of the cap premium (288 bps) received and the floor premium (164 bps) paid by the arranger. This amount is realized when the arranger sells the cap into and buys the floor from the derivatives market. This leaves a surplus of 36 bps for the arranger after it has paid 88 bps (or 12.5 bps pa) to the issuer to enable it to achieve its target cost of funds.

This surplus is available to either:

- Be paid as fees to investors.
- Retained as profit by the arranger.

Assume in this case the arranger uses 10 bps of the surplus as management fees to be paid to the investor. The remaining 26 bps is available as remuneration to the arranger for facilitating this transaction.

# 4. Structured Note Transactions — Risk Evaluation

## 4.1 Overview

The risk evaluation context is most relevant to the investor seeking to evaluate the investment characteristics of an individual transaction. The pricing and valuation focus in this context seeks to identify the risk-return characteristics of the structured note from the viewpoint of an investor in terms of:

- Market risk.
- Cash flow risk.
- Liquidity risk.

This risk evaluation can encompass the evaluation of a transaction on a number of bases:

- Standalone versus portfolio basis.
- Hold to maturity versus active trading basis.

The risk evaluation process has a number of different components covering alternative methods of evaluation of the various risks identified.

A central element in this process is to ensure evaluation of all the risk elements of the transaction within a framework that allows the risks to be incorporated into the investors' overall portfolio management process.

## 4.2    Risk Evaluation Techniques

### 4.2.1    Overview

The major risk evaluation techniques utilized in this context are similar to those used in investment management of fixed income portfolios generally. They include:

*   **Duration concepts** — as a measure of the interest rate risk of the instrument.
*   **Market price sensitivity concepts** — utilizing the concept of the sensitivity of the instrument to the major pricing parameters.
*   **Scenario or simulation approaches** — based on either fixed (deterministic) combinations of market price events or probabilistic (stochastic) combinations of events to observe the value changes in the price of the instrument.

### 4.2.2    Duration-based Approaches

The concept of duration (in particular, modified duration) is commonly utilized to measure the interest rate sensitivity of a security or portfolio of cash flows. The concept of duration is outlined in **Appendix A.**

The use of duration as a measure of risk in structured notes requires significant adaptation of the concept reflecting the nature of the underlying security. For example, some commentators[5] suggest expansion of the concept to cover multiple valuation and risk analysis techniques predicated upon key rate duration based around the following:

*   Duration with respect to the interest rate applicable to the interest rate(s) used to value the fixed- or floating-rate host bond.
*   Duration with respect to the market rates relevant to the embedded derivative element. [This rate may be identical to the rate applicable to that identified above or may be a different rate to that used to value the bond component.]

In cases where the structured notes contain embedded optionality, the duration analysis is supplemented with measures of the sensitivity of the structured note to the option component with reference to traditional measures of option risk, such as delta, gamma, or vega.[6]

---

[5]    See Peng, Scott and Dattatreya, Ravi (1994) *The Structured Note Market*; Probus Publications, Chicago at 23-40.

[6]    For a discussion of the measurement of option risks, see Das, Satyajit "Option Pricing" and "Measuring Option Sensitivities" in Das, Satyajit (editor) (1997) *Risk Management & Financial Derivatives: A Guide to The Mathematics*; LBC Information Services, Sydney; McGraw-Hill, Chicago; MacMillan Publishing, England at Chapter 5 and 10.

In practice, this approach entails the following steps:

- Identify the rates determining the value of the structure, separating the rate affecting the bond component and that determining the embedded element.
- Measure sensitivity to *each rate* by measuring the key rate duration of the structured note by perturbing the yield curve by, say, 1 bps at the selected key points in the yield curve.
- [Optional] For structures with embedded option elements, calculate the price sensitivity of the option to changes in the rate determining the embedded component and volatility in that rate.

The approach outlined has a significant advantage in that it provides a measure of risk consistent with other components of fixed income portfolios. However, the approach has a number of disadvantages:

- It provides a reasonable measure of risk for structured notes with embedded exposure to *interest rates*. It does not provide a corresponding basis for the measure of risk in structured note transactions where the embedded component is related to a different asset class, for example, currency, commodity, equity, credit, and so on.
- It must be complemented by a measure of option risk where the embedded risk element has an option component.
- It does not provide a measure of the inter-relationship of risk; namely, the correlation risks relating to the interaction of the bond component with the market risk component.

### 4.2.3 Market Price Sensitivity Approaches

An alternative approach to risk evaluation focuses on measuring the market price sensitivity of the structured note within a general risk framework. Within this framework, the risk of the transaction is measured in terms of the traditional measure of market risk (the Greek alphabet of risk) as follows:

- **Absolute price (or rate) risk (delta $\Delta$)** — This measures the exposure of the price of the note to a given change in the price of underlying asset or instrument. The concept is identical to the concept of PVBP (present value of a basis point) or DVO1 (dollar value of 1 basis point). In the case of a structured note, there would be, generally, at least two deltas. The first delta will be with reference to the interest rate applicable to the bond component. The second or additional deltas will be with reference to the asset element underlying the embedded derivative element. Where the debt elements are valued using zero-coupon interest rates, which are perturbed at each point in the yield curve, the fixed interest elements (whether bond or embedded element) will have *multiple* deltas corresponding to each zero coupon rate.[7]

- **Convexity risk (gamma γ)** — This measures the exposure to a change of delta as a result of the change in the interest rate and the market price or rate element. There would also be cross-gammas reflecting the change in convexity as a result of changes in the underlying price elements and the correlation between the two components.

- **Volatility risk (vega κ)** — This measures the exposure to a change of the volatility of the price of the underlying asset price embedded in the structured note in price terms for, usually, a 1% change in volatility.

- **Time decay risk (theta τ)** — This represents the exposure in price terms of the structured note to a change of the maturity of the contract. The key elements will be the interest rate accrual on the fixed income components, as well as the impact of time decay on the embedded instrument.

- **Discount or riskless interest rate (rho ρ)** — This measures the exposure to a change in the rate used to discount future cash flows, usually the risk-free interest rate element used to value any embedded option element.

- **Correlation or basis risk** — This measures the exposure to changes in the correlation values between the interest rate of the bond component and the asset price element embedded.

The advantages of this market price sensitivity approach include:

- Uniformity and consistency of risk capture irrespective of the asset class of instrument embedded in the structured note.
- Total capture of risk of the instrument including correlation elements.

The disadvantage relates to primarily the potential inability to compare this risk measure to those utilized in traditional risk measurement approaches in the management of fixed income security portfolios.

### 4.2.4 Scenario/Simulation Approaches

An alternative set of risk evaluation tools focuses on simulation-type approaches. These fall into two classes:

- **Deterministic** — usually entailing the use of designated fixed sets of financial market rates to calculate the impact on the price of the structured note to measure its price sensitivity or risk profile.
- **Stochastic** — usually entailing the use of probability-based techniques, such

---

[7] For a discussion of the concept of multiple deltas, see Das, Satyajit (1994) *Swaps and Financial Derivatives*; LBC Information Services, Sydney, McGraw-Hill, Chicago at Chapter 33.

as Monte Carlo Simulations, to model the price of the structured note. This entails using potential distributions of the price elements (the bond interest rate, the embedded asset price element, and other relevant price drivers such as volatility). These distribution are based on spot prices, a volatility-based distribution centred on the implied forward price of the variable and the correlation between the elements. The distribution of price outcomes is used to determine the risk of the instrument. A common method is to identify the underlying movements that generate unacceptable price outcomes in the value of the security at any time during its life.

## 4.3   Risk Evaluation — In Practice

In practice, the approaches utilized will vary depending upon the type of risk measured. In this regard, it is usually important to identify the different risk elements:

- **Market risk** — reflecting potential changes in the price of the note in the event of changes in the key market variables that determine the value of the note.
- **Cash flow risk** — this is similar to market risk but focuses on the change in cash flow to the investor as a result of changes in market variables. In effect, this does not incorporate the *unrealized* and *future* changes in cash flow concentrating upon changes in the level of coupon payment during the life of the instrument and the principal repayment at maturity.
- **Liquidity risk** — reflecting the risk of loss (primarily, from transaction costs) from the need to sell the note prior to maturity.

The risk measures identified are above are all available to measure the *market* risk of transactions. The cash flow risk is best able to be identified using simulation approaches. The liquidity risk is more difficult to measure. In practice, it might be identified in qualitative terms only or by looking at the value loss by using the adjusted bid-offer spreads for all value elements reflecting unfavorable market conditions to quantity the potential loss.

## 4.4   Active versus Passive Investment Management — Risk Evaluation
##        Elements

Risk evaluation is inherently related to the type of investment management approach adopted in relation to the portfolio of structured notes or the portfolio in which the note is incorporated.

Passive portfolio management is assumed to be the management of a portfolio consistent with the objective of generating returns to match the relevant performance benchmark. This is achieved through the replication of the investment asset selection in the index. The replication may be complete or partial. It may also be either direct or indirect (usually synthetic entailing the application of derivative technology). Active portfolio management is assumed to be the management and trading of investment assets with the objective of generating returns relative to a benchmark or maximizing the total return of the portfolio (possibly, within some risk-return framework). The distinction is as much one of approach and in the activity levels in trading the underlying assets.

Structured notes can be utilized in both types of portfolios. For example, a structured note with an embedded forward or call option on an equity index can be incorporated in a passive portfolio to replicate tracking of the equity index performance. A structured note that incorporates yield curve positions combined with leverage can be incorporated into an active investment management portfolio to seek to create exposure to changes in the yield curve or to capture value from the implied forward shape of yield curves in order to increase investment returns.

The implications for risk measurement relate to the fact that in the case of the passive portfolio manager the focus of risk measurement is substantially the degree of *tracking error* representing the deviation from the portfolio manager's replication objectives. In the case of the active portfolio manager the focus of risk measurement is the general market risk of the instrument and potential movements in value of the structured note as a result of movements in the underlying rates/asset prices.

The implications flow to a large extent from the likelihood that the structured note designed for the passive investment manger will be held until maturity. This focuses on tracking risk (a subset of market risk) and cash flow risk. The active manager is more likely, at least in theory, to trade the note prior to maturity, presumably, to reflect changes in market rates that either allow capture and crystallization of the expected movement in rates/price or elimination of the risk. This means that the active manager emphasizes market and liquidity risk in the risk evaluation process.

# 5. Structured Note Transactions — Secondary Market Pricing

The final approach to pricing focuses on the pricing of transactions in the secondary market. The secondary market in this context is taken to mean the sale and purchase of structured notes *after* initial placement and *before* final maturity. The valuation in the secondary market will be provided typically by the dealer (at the investment bank or securities dealer) asked to provide a bid price to purchase the structured note.

The pricing and valuation approach in this context is predicated on establishing the value of a structured note at the time of the secondary market transaction. There are a number of mechanisms for determining value in this context:

- **Pricing the structured note as a security** — this entails the straight purchase and subsequent on-sale of the security to an end investor. The pricing in this case reflects the price the ultimate investor is willing to pay for the instrument.
- **Pricing on an issuer buy-back basis** — this entails enabling the original investor to *repurchase* the structured note.
- **Pricing on asset swap basis** — this entails unbundling the note into its constituent elements and stripping the note value to replace the instrument in the form of a fixed or floating bond with traditional fixed interest investors.

In theory the valuation on all three bases should be similar. In practice, the value arrived at will typically vary. This reflects the impact of a number of factors including segmentation of markets, the valuation parameters used to value individual elements of the transaction by different parties, the lot size factor, and the note maturity. These factors will typically be reflected in the supply and demand of the specific security and the market clearing price.

Pricing the structured note as a security entails the dealer making a price to the investor based on the *anticipated* price at which the dealer can on sell the note to *another investor*. The key element of the approach is that as the note is sold as a security no additional transactions (to strip out the derivative elements or repackage the asset) are required. The pricing logic will dictate that the dealer will bid the investor at a price reflecting the purchasing investor's valuation or price adjusted (reduced) by the dealer's profit margin.

In practice, structured notes are priced only as a security under limited circumstances. For example, there was an active market for collared FRNs in the early phase of the introduction of the product. This was characterized by excellent liquidity and tight bid-offer spreads for these instruments during this period.

Pricing on an issuer buy-back basis is predicated on two bases:

- Repurchase designed to generate significant arbitrage profits through pricing the structured note on an asset swap basis.
- Repurchase on a no- or low-gain basis designed primarily to provide liquidity to the investor and ensure an orderly after market in the securities.

In each case, the repurchase requires an asset swap pricing to reverse engineer the embedded derivative components. The major difference, in practice, is that in the first case the issuer seeks to earn the above-market return on its securities *in an approach that reflects the return an external investor would require to purchase the repackaged note* (as discussed below).

The issuer buy-back pricing should reflect the reversal of the credit enhancement built in to the transaction. The repurchase of the note and the cancellation or buy-out of the embedded derivative element should eliminate the use of capital and credit resources required by the original transaction structure. This should be reflected in the pricing. The additional factor that will impact on pricing is the opportunity cost in terms of the foregone funding cost saving over the remaining life of the transaction by the issuer.

The repurchase pricing on an asset swap basis is predicated on the reverse engineering of the transaction to create a synthetic asset (generally, a fixed-rate or more typically floating-rate note). This repackaged asset is placed with investors seeking a traditional investment. The pricing in this case requires the incorporation of:

- The cost of the derivative components *as at the time of repackaging.*
- The return required by the investor on the repackaged asset.

The return required by the investor will generally be higher than for a conventional asset of the type sought to be placed. This reflects the following considerations:

- The complexity of the structure (reflecting the elimination of the embedded derivative components).
- The capital and credit requirements of entering into the derivative transactions to eliminate the derivative generated market risk.
- Compensation for the relative illiquidity of the asset.

Other factors, in practice, that may impact upon the pricing of structured notes in the secondary market include:

- **Credit risk of issuer** — changes in credit quality may positively or negatively affect the pricing of the structured note.
- **Parcel size** — secondary market prices are affected adversely by the size of parcel offered. Sizes smaller than US$10 million will attract a penalty while parcel sizes in excess of around US$50-100 million, depending on market conditions, may be reflected in pricing pressure.
- **Maturity** — secondary market prices for long-dated structured notes are generally lower. The price adjustment for maturity, like the adjustment for parcel size reflects, firstly, the universe and preferences of purchasers of the asset (either in the original or repackaged format), and, secondly, the transaction costs associated with the repackaging transactions.
- **Market conditions** — in particular, supply and demand conditions for particular types of investments or structures can place temporary pressure on prices.

The relationship of the level of secondary market prices derived from the different valuation bases is interesting. The typical relationship is set out in **Exhibit 16.2.**

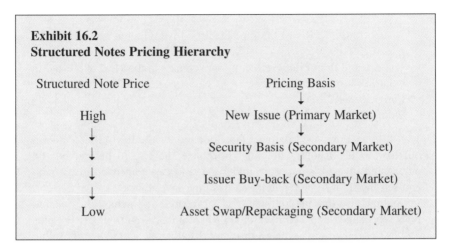

The importance of the different valuation techniques in the secondary market is also relevant. In practice, inevitably, asset swap/repackaging pricing is the most important. This reflects the depth and liquidity (in terms of number and range of investors) of the segment. This basis of pricing tends to place the floor price level for structured notes in the secondary market.

**Exhibit 16.3** sets out the pricing and valuation of a collared FRN transaction in the secondary market.

---

**Exhibit 16.3**
**Pricing and Valuation of Capped FRN Transaction —**
**Secondary Market**

*1. Assumptions*

This example focuses on the pricing and valuation of the capped FRN transaction detailed in **Exhibit 16.1** in the secondary market.

Assume the subordinated capped FRN was issued originally with a final maturity of 10 years and a coupon of LIBOR plus 0.0625% pa. The remaining maturity of this note is currently eight years. The investor now seeks to sell the capped FRN and seeks bids from the trader at the investment bank. The trader's bid to purchase the note is based on the premise that the note will be repackaged and placed as a straight FRN with traditional FRN investors.

*2. Pricing and Valuation*

The relevant pricing levels for the components are as follows:

- A subordinated FRN of the type identified is trading at around LIBOR plus 0.20% pa.
- The cap and floor prices reflecting movements in the yield curve and in volatility levels are as follows:
Cap price — 2.75% flat
Floor price — 0.82% flat.

The difference between the cap and floor price (193 bps) reflects a cash outflow to the trader who must purchase the cap to hedge out the purchasing investor's exposure under the sold cap embedded in the note and sell the floor to be repurchased from the investor.

Assume also that the investor who is prepared to purchase the collared FRN repackaged into a conventional FRN requires a return of LIBOR plus 35 bps (a premium of some 15 bps above that applicable to a comparable conventional FRN).

Utilizing the parameters outlined above, the pricing is determined as follows:

- The adjustment to the margin above LIBOR required to increase the coupon to the required 35 bps from the coupon of 6.25 bps equates to 28.75 bps pa or 178 bps in present value terms based on a discount rate of 6.40% pa payable semi-annually.
- The cost of hedging the cap and floor elements is 193 bps.
- The total cost of repackaging the note into a conventional FRN yielding LIBOR plus 35 bps is 371 bps.
- The trader's breakeven price would therefore be 96.29% of face value. Assuming a bid offer spread of 10 bps (in price terms), the trader would bid the investor at a price of 96.19% of face value.

Other required adjustments would include accrued interest and broken period calculation where the note is to be traded in between interest payment dates.

Prices for the cap and floor will be derived using the relevant bid-offer prices, reflecting the actual transactions required to be executed to repackage the risk of the transaction.

## 6.   Summary

The pricing and valuation of structured notes follows the separation of these structures into the relevant component elements and the pricing of the individual building blocks transactions. The valuation of the components follows traditional pricing techniques.

The complexity of the pricing and valuation of these types of instruments is related to capturing accurately and precisely all the risk elements and the correlation between the bond or fixed interest element and the embedded market risk element. Additional complexity is generated by the necessity of evaluating the risk of the structure from the perspective of the investing institution. In this regard, a major consideration is the requirement to match the risk of the structured note *with more general risk concepts utilized to measure the risk of fixed interest portfolios generally*. The final complexity is created by the availability of a variety of mechanisms for pricing such transactions in the secondary market.

# Appendix A

# Duration and Convexity[8]

## 1. Concept of Duration

Term to maturity is widely utilized as a measure of the length or maturity of securities. However, it is a highly deficient measure in that it only indicates when the final payment falls due. It ignores the time pattern of any payment received in the intermediate time span preceding the final payment. This deficiency of the concept of term to maturity can be overcome utilizing duration as a measure of the term and the risk of a security or set of cash flows.

## 2. Measurement of Duration

### 2.1 Overview

There are two types of duration:

- Macaulay's duration.
- Modified duration.

### 2.2 Macaulay's Duration

Duration, as proposed in 1938 by Frederick R. Macaulay, is the weighted average of the times in the future when cash flows (interest and principal payments) are to be received. Mathematically, duration can be measured as

---

[8] For a good overview of duration, see Bierwag, Gerald O. (1987) *Duration Analysis—Managing Interest Rate Risk*; Ballinger Publishing Company, Cambridge, Massachusetts; Cohen, Roger "Interest Rates" in Das, Satyajit (editor) (1997) *Risk Management & Financial Derivatives: A Guide To The Mathematics*; LBC Information Services, Sydney; McGraw-Hill, Chicago; MacMillan Publishing, England at Chapter 2.

follows:

$$D = \sum_{t=1}^{n} [(C_t \times t)/(1 + r)^t]/[(C_t)/(1 + r)^t]$$

Where:

D = duration
$C_t$ = cash flow (for example, interest and/or principal payments) at time t
t = length of time to the cash flow
n = length of time to final maturity
r = yield to maturity or discount rate

An example of the calculation of Macaulay's duration is set out in **Exhibit 16.4**.

---

**Exhibit 16.4**
**Macaulay's Duration — Calculation**

For example, assume a 5-year bond with a 6.00% pa coupon rate payable semi-annually and yielding 6.50% pa to maturity. Assume that interest payments are received at the end of each of the 10 semi-annual periods and that the principal payment is received at the end of the fifth year. The calculation of the duration of the bond is set out in the table below:

| Period | 0 | 1 | 2 | 3 | 4 | 5 | 6 | 7 | 8 | 9 | 10 | Sum |
|---|---|---|---|---|---|---|---|---|---|---|---|---|
| Coupon | | 3.000 | 3.000 | 3.000 | 3.000 | 3.000 | 3.000 | 3.000 | 3.000 | 3.000 | 3.000 | |
| Principal | | | | | | | | | | | 100.00 | |
| Total Cash Flows | | 3.000 | 3.000 | 3.000 | 3.000 | 3.000 | 3.000 | 3.000 | 3.000 | 3.000 | 103.00 | |
| Discount Factor | 1.000 | 0.969 | 0.938 | 0.909 | 0.880 | 0.852 | 0.825 | 0.799 | 0.774 | 0.750 | 0.726 | |
| $(C_t \times t)(1 + r)^t$ | | 2.906 | 5.628 | 8.177 | 10.559 | 12.783 | 14.857 | 16.788 | 18.582 | 20.247 | 748.060 | 858.586 |
| $C_t/(1 + r)^t$ | | 2.906 | 2.814 | 2.726 | 2.640 | 2.557 | 2.476 | 2.398 | 2.323 | 2.250 | 74.806 | 97.894 |

Duration in this case is calculated as: [858.586/97.894] = 8.77 semi-annual periods or 4.39 years.

For bonds with a series of cash flows, duration is less than the final maturity. If there is a single payment (a zero-coupon bond), then duration and maturity are equal.

As noted above, duration measures the weighted average of the times in the future when cash flows are to be received. Conceptually, it is the pivot or balancing point of the future cash flows. This is set out in diagrammatic form in **Exhibit 16.5.**[9]

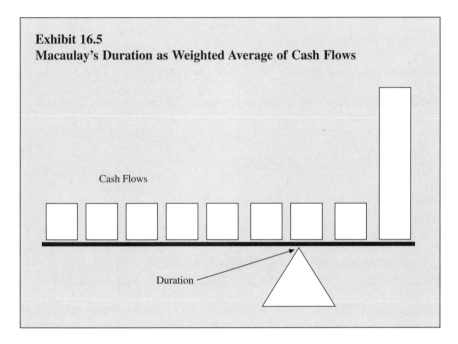

**Exhibit 16.5**
**Macaulay's Duration as Weighted Average of Cash Flows**

Cash Flows

Duration

In essence, Macaulay's duration creates a single index-type measure for any set of cash flows. This enables disparate sets of future cash flows to be compared. The essential risk measure is that longer duration is associated with greater risk, reflecting the greater interest rate sensitivity of cash flows.

## 2.3 Modified Duration

Modified duration was independently developed by Hicks in 1939 without any reference to Macaulay duration. Modified duration provides a particularly useful measure of the interest rate sensitivity or volatility of a given security. Mathematically, modified duration can be expressed as:

---

[9] I am indebted to Roger Cohen for pointing this out. The diagram is based on his insight, see Cohen, Roger "Interest Rates" in Das, Satyajit (editor) (1997) *Risk Management & Financial Derivatives: A Guide To The Mathematics*; LBC Information Services, Sydney; McGraw-Hill, Chicago; MacMillan Publishing, England at Chapter 2 at 37.

$D_{mod.} = D/(1 + r/f)$

Where:

D = Macaulay duration
r = yield to maturity (in decimal form)
f = frequency of cash flow payments per year
r/f = periodic yield (in decimal form).

For semi-annual coupon bonds, this formula becomes: $D_{mod.} = D/(1 + r/2 )$

**Exhibit 16.6** calculates the modified duration for the example discussed above.

---

**Exhibit 16.6**
**Modified Duration — Calculation**

Assume the same facts as in **Exhibit 16.5**:

Macaulay's duration is 4.39 years.
Yield to maturity is 6.50% pa semi-annually.

Modified duration is given by: $[4.39/(1 + .065/2)] = 4.25$

---

Mathematically, modified duration represents the first derivative of the price of the security with regard to yield to maturity. Modified duration can be used to estimate the percentage price volatility of a fixed income security. The relationship is as follows:

$\Delta P/P \times 100 = -D_{mod} \times \Delta R$

This implies that the percentage price change is equal to the negative modified duration multiplied by the yield change (in absolute percentage points).

For example, in **Exhibit 16.6**, the price volatility of the specified bond is 4.25%. This means that for an increase in rates of 10 bps, the price of the bond would be expected to decrease by 42.5 bps. This equates to the price volatility of the bond or its interest rate sensitivity. In practice, modified duration is the most commonly used duration measure of interest rate risk.

## 2.4    Duration and the Zero-coupon Rate Yield Curve

It is feasible in theory to calculate duration utilizing either normal conventional par (coupon) yields or zero-coupon interest rates for pure discount securities. For example, the original Macaulay formulation for reasons of computational convenience uses yield to maturity as the discount rate throughout rather than estimating interest rates for each future period and using them to discount the security payments to present value. However, it is not reasonable to assume that yields to maturity for different terms will always change by the same amount. This reflects the fact that yields to maturity are complex averages of the underlying zero-coupon yields. Consequently, in general a given shift in the zero-coupon rate curve will result in the yields to maturity at different maturities changing by different amounts.

To understand the interaction between duration and the zero-coupon rate yield curve, it is necessary to define the following terms:

- A zero-coupon rate, which is the rate of exchange between a cash flow now and a cash flow at a single date in the future; that is, the yield on a pure discount bond or zero-coupon security.
- A coupon or par yield to maturity, which is the standard internal rate of return formula that discounts all payments on a coupon bond at the same rate.

The difference between the two interest rates lies in the fact that actual realized returns only equal the normal redemption par yield to maturity if reinvestment rates on intermediate cash flows, typically the coupon, are actually equal to the redemption yield. In practice, reinvestment rates on coupon cash flows will rarely equal the redemption yield. Forward rates are the only true measure of the reinvestment rates and even then the forward rates implicit in the yield curve at any point in time do not guarantee that these reinvestment rates are actually achieved. In contrast, determining present values using zero-coupon rates, which are implicit in normal par redemption yields, do not involve any assumptions as to the reinvestment rate as no intermediate cash flows are involved.[10]

## 3. Behavior of Duration

The relationship among duration, maturity, and coupon is complex.[11] The general relationships are as follows:

---

[10] For a discussion of the derivation of zero-coupon rates and yield curves, see Das, Satyajit (with Cohen, Roger) "Interest Rates And Yield Curve Modelling: An Introduction" in Das, Satyajit (editor) (1997) *Risk Management & Financial Derivatives: A Guide To The Mathematics*; LBC Information Services, Sydney; McGraw-Hill, Chicago; MacMillan Publishing, England at Chapter 3.

[11] See Fisher, Lawrence and Weil, Roman L. "Coping with the Risk of Interest Rate Fluctuations: Returns to Bondholders from Naive and Optional Strategies'" (1971) 44 *Journal of Business* 418.

- There is an inverse relationship between coupon and duration. High coupon bonds effectively have shorter duration than lower (or zero) coupon bonds of the same maturity.
- As the term to maturity extends, the disparity between duration and maturity for a given coupon also increases.
- Duration falls when market yields rise because the present value of distant future payments falls relatively more than those closer to the present. As would be expected, when interest rates fall, duration rises for exactly the opposite reason.

**Exhibit 16.7** sets out the relationships using an example.

---

**Exhibit 16.7**
**Duration — Behavior**

Assume a bond with the following characteristics:

| | |
|---|---|
| Coupon | 6.00% pa payable semi-annually |
| Maturity | 10 years |
| Yield to Maturity | 6.25% pa semi-annually |

The table below calculates the price and duration of the bond:[12]

| | |
|---|---|
| Coupon | 6.00% |
| Maturity Date | 15-Feb-11 |
| Settlement Date | 15-Feb-01 |
| Yield | 6.25% |
| Price | 98.162 |
| Accrued Interest | 0.000 |
| Total Price | 98.162 |
| Macaulay Duration | 7.64 |
| Modified Duration | 7.41 |

The graphs below shows the relationships between duration and maturity, duration and coupon, and duration and yield.

---

12 All calculations are done using Add-In Software (Bond@nalyst, Options@nalyst, and Exotic@nalyst) supplied by Tech Hackers Inc.

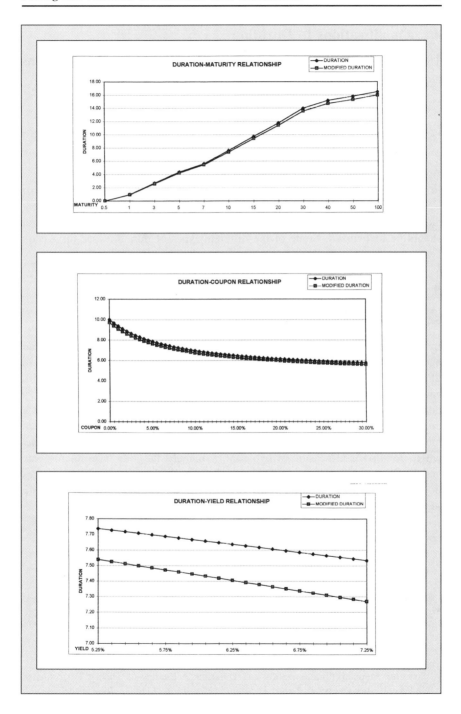

## 4.   Qualifications to Duration

There are a number of qualifications to the duration measure that must be recognized in any such immunization practice:

- Duration assumes a flat term structure of interest rates.
- Duration also assumes parallel shifts of the yield curve.
- Duration is a proxy for price risk only for relatively small changes in interest rates. Therefore, as market interest rates change, the duration of the relevant security also changes requiring adjustment of any offsetting hedge.

In using duration as a measure of interest rate risk or as basis for hedging (that is, immunization by assuming an offsetting asset or liability with an equivalent duration to reduce portfolio duration to zero), these weaknesses of duration should be recognized. Some of the different types of duration (see discussion below) are specifically designed to overcome the identified weaknesses.

## 5.   Types of Duration

### 5.1   Single versus Multiple Factor Duration

In the situation where the assumptions of flat term structure of interest rates and parallel shifts is violated, it would not be usually possible to effect immunization of interest rate risk by simply holding an offsetting asset or liability with equivalent duration. In response to this qualification to the duration measure, a number of multiple factor duration models have been developed to provide a more complex mapping of the stochastic processes governing interest rate movements. For example, one approach proposes a multifactor duration model where duration is a measure of two factors; namely, the long-term interest rate and the short-term interest rate. This approach implicitly seeks to model changes in the yield curve shape and the resultant effect on the duration of the relevant security.[13]

The difference between a single-factor model and a two-factor model is set out in **Exhibit 16.8.**

---

[13]   Schaefer, Stephen, "Immunization and Duration: A Review of Theory, Performance and Applications" (1984) 2 (no. 3) *Midland Corporate Finance Journal* 41-58.

**Exhibit 16.8**
**Duration — Single Factor vs Multiple Factor**

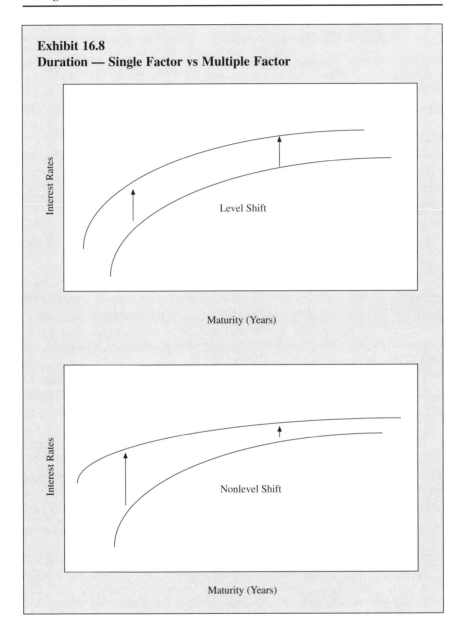

## 5.2  Key Rate Duration

Key rate duration[14] is a special form of multifactor duration introduced to allow the duration concept to be utilized to measure the risk of nonparallel movements in the yield curve. The concept revolves around the idea of measurement of the duration of a security with reference to *one key portion of the yield curve*. The key rates utilized can be either zero-coupon rates or par rates for the relevant risk class of instrument.

The application of the key rate duration approach entails a number of specific steps:

1. Identify the interest rates that affect the price of the instrument.
2. Specify the *key* rates that will be used to determine the price sensitivity of the instrument.
3. Calculate the impact on the price of the security of a 1 bp change in each key rate.

The key rate duration calculated measures the price change of the security for a change in the key rate. By repeating the calculation for each key rate in the specified yield curve, a series of price changes along the complete yield curve is determined. The process isolates the price sensitivity of the instrument for very small movements in the yield curve at each key segment as a result of the perturbation of the specified curve.[15]

The key rate duration of a note is, consistent with other forms of duration, dynamic with reference to changes in yield curves and also the effluxion of time.

# 6.  Present Value of a Basis Point (PVBP)

In practice, the PVBP of a cash flow or security is frequently used as a substitute for or complement to modified duration in measuring interest rate risk.

---

[14]  The concept of key rate duration was introduced by Dattatreya, Ravi "A Practical Approach to Asset/Liability Management" in Fabbozzi, Frank J. and Konishi, Atsuo (editors) (1991) *Asset/Liability Management*; Probus Publishing, Chicago; Ho, Thomas S.Y. "Key Rate Duration: Measures of Interest Rate Risk" (September 1992) *Journal of Fixed Income* 29-44.

[15]  The concept of key rate duration is similar to a cash-flow approach to measurement of interest rate risk and hedging, see Luedecke, Bernd P. "Measuring Displaying and Hedging The Market Risk On A Swap" in Das, Satyajit (editor) (1991) Global Swap Markets; IFR Publishing, London; see also Das, Satyajit (1994) *Swaps and Financial Derivatives*; LBC Information Services, Sydney, McGraw-Hill, Chicago at Chapter 33.

The concept of PVBP is the change in market value given a 0.01% pa increase in yield. It is also referred to as the dollar value of 1 basis point (DVO1).

The PVBP is calculated as follows:

PVBP  =  MV (r) – MV (r ± 0.01% pa)

Where:

MV  =  market value function
r  =  current market yield

PVBP is similar to duration and provides a measure of the interest rate sensitivity of future cash flows.

The characteristics and behavior of PVBP includes:

• PVBP generally increases as time to expiry increases.
• PVBP tends to be greater for lower coupon bonds
• PVBP is not constant. It changes with yield movements and the passing of time.

Like modified duration, PVBP is a standardized representation of the risk of a financial instrument (that is, the higher the PVBP the higher the risk). Like duration, PVBP can be used as the basis of hedging. This is done by PVBP matching. The PVBP of the position is determined and a sufficient number of, say, futures contracts are transacted to offset the PVBP (the hedge ratio). This creates a zero PVBP position or a position that is not sensitive to changes in interest rates.

## 7.  Convexity

As already noted, modified duration and PVBP is only accurate for small changes in the underlying rate or yield to maturity. This relates to the non-linearity of price movement for a given movement in yield. This is referred to as the convexity problem. **Exhibit 16.9** sets out the nonlinear relationship between price and yield for fixed income securities.

**Exhibit 16.9**
**Convexity Of Price-yield Relationship**

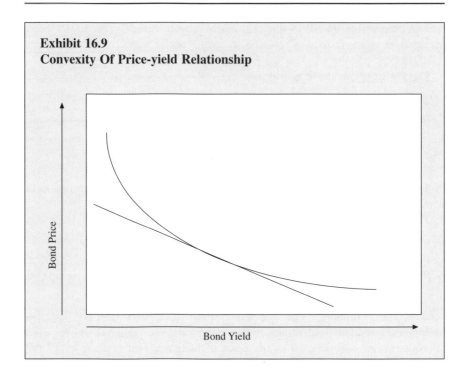

As is evident for a given movement in yield or interest rates, the quantum of the corresponding change in price (present value of the cash flow(s)) is different, depending upon the absolute rate level from which the rate displacement occurs and also the magnitude of the rate displacement. This reflects the fact that measures of price or interest rate risk such as modified duration and PVBP are measures of the rate of changes in the price of the security *as at the current yield or rate level.*[16]

Convexity measures the curvature of the price-yield relationship. It is a second order measure of price-yield sensitivity. It is the second derivative of price with respect to yield. In effect, the presence of convexity means that for a small displacement in rates modified duration/PVBP is a reasonable measure of price risk. However, for larger displacements the curvature of the price function needs to be approximated. This is usually done by a second order Taylor series approximation of the curve.

---

[16] Mathematically, as the first derivative modified duration or PVBP measures the rate of change at the current yield level. This equates to the slope of the tangent line to the price function at the current rate. As rates change, the slope of this line also changes.

The major significant of convexity is that it should be used in combination with modified duration to approximate percentage change in price given a percentage change in yield. This relationship is set out below:

$$\Delta \text{ Price/Price} = -D_{\text{mod}} \times \Delta \text{ Yield} + [\text{Convexity}/2 \times (\Delta \text{ yield})^2]$$

**Exhibit 16.10** sets out the use of this approach to more accurately measuring the interest rate risk of a security.

---

**Exhibit 16.10**
**Duration/Convexity Adjusted Risk Measurement**

Assume a bond with the following characteristics:

| | |
|---|---|
| Coupon | 6.00% pa payable semi-annually |
| Maturity | 10 years |
| Yield to Maturity | 6.25% pa semi-annually |

The table below calculates the price, duration, PVBP, and convexity of the bond:[17]

| | |
|---|---|
| Coupon | 6.00% |
| Maturity Date | 15-Feb-11 |
| Settlement Date | 15-Feb-01 |

| | |
|---|---|
| Yield | 6.25% |
| Price | 98.162 |
| Accrued Interest | 0.000 |
| Total Price | 98.162 |

| | |
|---|---|
| Macaulay Duration | 7.64 |
| Modified Duration | 7.41 |
| PVBP | 0.0727 |
| Convexity | 68.31 |

The table below compares the actual change in bond prices against forecast changes in bond prices using modified duration or modified duration adjusted for convexity:

---

[17] All calculations are done using Add-In Software (Bond@nalyst, Options@nalyst, and Exotic@nalyst) supplied by Tech Hackers Inc.

| Expected Change in Yield | 0.01% | 0.10% | 1.00% |
|---|---|---|---|
| Modified Duration | 7.41 | 7.41 | 7.41 |
| Convexity | 68.31 | 68.31 | 68.31 |
| Actual Price Change (based on change in bond price using current yield adjusted for expected change in yield) | –0.073 | –0.724 | –6.945 |
| Δ Price/Price (based on modified duration) | –0.074 | –0.741 | –7.405 |
| Δ Price/Price (based on modified duration adjusted for convexity) | –0.074 | –0.737 | –7.064 |
| Difference (actual price change vs modified duration) | 0.00 | 0.02 | 0.46 |
| $ Difference (per $1 million) | $14 | $170 | $4,604 |
| Difference (actual vs modified duration adjusted for convexity) | 0.00 | 0.01 | 0.12 |
| Difference (Per $1 million) | $14 | $135 | $1,188 |

As is evident, the modified duration measure *adjusted for convexity* is a more accurate measure of actual changes in bond prices for *large changes in yield* than modified duration itself.

## 8.  Interest Rate Risk Measurement using Duration, PVBP, and Convexity

The interest rate risk on the fixed-rate component of any security can be measured utilizing duration. The duration of the fixed rate on a note provides a measure of price volatility with respect to interest rate movements. It is feasible to hedge the interest rate risk component, utilizing duration as a measure of sensitivity of a position to movements in interest rates. Under this strategy, physical securities or futures contracts are held to offset potential changes in value on the bond with the level of hedge being determined by the duration factor. The basic duration hedging strategy is as follows:

Change in PV of hedging portfolio = –Change in PV of bond portfolio

The use of duration as a means of estimating interest rate risk varies as between a single factor model and a multifactor model. This relationship is set out in **Exhibit 16.11**.

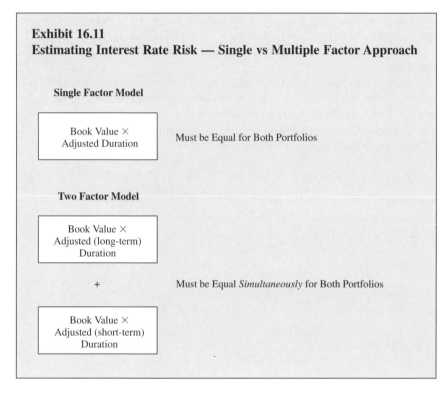

**Exhibit 16.11**
**Estimating Interest Rate Risk — Single vs Multiple Factor Approach**

The concept of duration-based hedging assumes that cash flows generated by the securities booked by a financial institution form a portfolio of assets and liabilities that will vary with interest rates and with maturity. The use of duration-based hedging seeks to solve the problem of ensuring solvency, irrespective of interest rate movements, by matching the duration of the asset and liability cash flow streams. The underlying assumption is that irrespective of interest rate movements and despite the fact that the cash flows are not perfectly matched, changes in values in the asset and liability portfolio would substantially offset each other.

The use of duration matching implicitly divides underlying market interest rate movements into two components:

• Systematic movements whereby rates for all maturities move in some statistically determined constant proportion to one or two index rates, such as the long and short interest rates, depending on whether single or multifactor duration measures are utilized.
• Nonsystematic movements that are the residual interest rate movement unexplained by movements in the indexes utilized. These are assumed to be randomly or normally distributed.

Duration matching only provides a formula to hedge away systematic market movements. Inefficiencies in hedge performance may result from the nonsystematic risk component that cannot be effectively hedged under this approach.

Duration matching is utilized in preference to maturity matching because it is usually felt to reduce basis risk. It can also overcome imperfections in the hedge market, such as unavailability of securities of the appropriate maturity. It may also reduce the actual expense of hedging as generally significantly lower levels of hedges will need to be maintained.

# 17
# Taxation & Accounting for Structured Notes
*PricewaterhouseCoopers*

## 1. Tax Treatment of Structured Notes — the US
*by Viva Hammer*

### 1.1 Introduction

The general US federal tax issues relating to structured notes and hybrid securities are summarized below. As the US federal tax system has developed very complex rules in this area, each instrument must be analyzed according to its specific terms, to determine the correct federal tax treatment. In addition, if the instrument is part of an overall transaction, the economics of the entire transaction could affect the US tax characterization of the instrument. Finally, this discussion does not address any state or local tax issues that may arise in connection with an investment in such instruments.

### 1.2 Tax Treatment — Generally

For US tax purposes, an instrument is generally treated as a unified item, based on its dominant characteristics. The first step in analyzing a derivative instrument is to determine its character based on its dominant characteristics. Some of the possible characterizations include: debt, equity, option, forward, swap.

Whether an instrument qualifies as debt or equity is a factual determination, based primarily on case law and rulings issued by the Internal Revenue Service (the Service). Debt is generally characterized as "an unqualified obligation to pay a sum certain at a reasonably close fixed maturity date along with a fixed percentage in interest payable regardless of the debtor's income or lack thereof."[1] Other factors that are relevant in making a debt/equity determination

---
[1]  Plumb, "The Federal Income Tax Significance of Corporate Debt: A Critical Analysis and a Proposal," 26 Tax L. Rev, 369, 404-405 n. 177 (1972).

include: (1) whether the holder is entitled to a form of participation in an underlying business as opposed to a return that is based upon more objective criteria, (2) whether the holder has any remedies upon default of payment under the instrument, (3) the debt/equity ratio of the issuer, and (4) the intent of the parties.

### 1.3    Tax Treatment — Debtor/Issuer

If an instrument is characterized as a debt instrument, interest is generally deductible at the time that it is either paid or accrued, depending on the debtor's method of accounting. For example, interest is generally deductible by a cash method taxpayer at the time that it is paid, whereas an accrual method taxpayer will generally be entitled to a deduction with respect to interest that has been calculated to have accrued over a given period of time.

The ability to deduct interest is subject to various restrictions depending on the type of debt instrument. For example, interest paid with respect to debt that is incurred to purchase tax-exempt securities is generally nondeductible. Furthermore, the deductibility of interest may also depend on the nature of the investor and the business context of the indebtedness; that is, whether the debtor is an individual or corporation, and whether the debt is related to the conduct of a trade or business. Finally, there are a number of other federal tax provisions that limit the ability to deduct interest, thus requiring an analysis of the overall transaction before determining the deductibility of interest paid with respect to a given debt instrument.

The amount and timing of interest deductions with respect to a particular instrument is generally governed by the terms and purchase price of the debt instrument. For example, if the debt instrument does not provide for stated interest payments, or the amount received at maturity is greater than the issue price, the debt instrument may have original issue discount (OID). If the instrument has OID, the obligor must generally deduct the aggregate daily portions of OID for each day that the debt is outstanding during a taxable year, thus causing the debtor to deduct interest on an accrual basis.

Of particular importance in analyzing a security with embedded derivatives, are the rules relating to contingent debt instruments (CDIs) and variable rate debt instruments (VRDIs). These rules govern the timing and treatment of interest and repayment of principal on debt instruments that qualify as either CDIs or VRDIs. As mentioned above, US federal tax rules will generally treat an instrument with an embedded derivative as a single integrated instrument, and derivatives are often used to create certain contingencies. As a result, a structured note must be carefully analyzed under these complex regimes in order to determine the proper characterization of the debt instrument.

The debtor may also enter into a transaction in order to hedge certain exposure or risk from the underlying instrument. As a result, US taxpayers may be entitled to integrate the hedge with the offsetting instrument for favorable US tax results.

The repayment of principal upon maturity of a debt instrument is generally not taxable. If, however, a debt instrument is sold prior to maturity, the seller will have a capital gain or loss equal to the difference between the purchase price of the instrument and the sales proceeds.

If a US taxpayer invests in a debt instrument that is either denominated in a foreign currency or whose terms are calculated by reference to one or more foreign currencies, the debt instrument may qualify as a Section 988 transaction, and as a result, will be subject to special timing and character rules. In general, a US taxpayer that invests in a foreign denominated bond will have to separately calculate the portion of gain or loss that is attributable to fluctuations in the underlying currency. In addition, gain or loss that is recognized with respect to the debt instrument will generally be ordinary gain or loss.

## 1.4   Tax Treatment — Creditor/Holder

A holder of a debt instrument generally recognizes interest income at the time that it is either received or accrued, depending on the creditor's method of accounting. For example, interest is generally includable by a cash method taxpayer at the time that it is received, whereas an accrual method taxpayer will generally have income with respect to interest that has been calculated to have accrued over a given period of time.

Similar to the timing of interest deductions, there are several US federal tax provisions that will affect the timing of income recognition. For example, a holder of a debt instrument with OID must include such OID in income over the term of the instrument as it accrues, using a yield-to-maturity calculation, regardless of its method of accounting. In addition, if the debt instrument is purchased for either a discount or a premium, the US tax law imposes timing and character rules with respect to the inclusion of these amounts.

If the debt instrument qualifies as either a CDI or a VRDI, the amount and timing of interest income that is includable by a holder of a debt instrument will be governed by the applicable regulatory provisions. In addition, the holder may enter into a transaction in order to hedge its exposure on the underlying instrument. As a result, the US taxpayer may be entitled to integrate the hedge with the offsetting instrument for favorable US tax results.

If a taxpayer disposes of a debt instrument prior to its maturity date, the taxpayer will generally recognize capital gain or loss. Return of principal upon maturity of a debt instrument, however, is generally not taxable.

If a US taxpayer invests in a debt instrument that is either denominated in a foreign currency or whose terms are calculated by reference to one or more foreign currencies, the debt instrument may qualify as a Section 988 transaction, and as a result, will be subject to special timing and character rules. In general, a US taxpayer that invests in a foreign denominated bond will have to separately calculate the portion of gain or loss that is attributable to fluctuations in the underlying currency. In addition, gain or loss that is recognized with respect to the debt instrument will generally be ordinary gain or loss.

## 2.   Tax Treatment of Structured Notes — the UK
*by Richard D. Clarke and Richard S. Collier*

### 2.1   Introduction

This section outlines the key taxation issues on generic *structured note* products from a UK perspective. For direct taxation, the UK tax system makes a fundamental distinction between income and capital, with separate provisions for each, largely consolidated in the *Income and Corporations Taxes Act 1988* and the *Taxation of Chargeable Gains Act 1992*. These consolidations are not comprehensive and much new legislation is to be found in the annual Finance Acts. For example, legislation in relation to foreign exchange, financial instruments, and debt contracts (the so-called "loan relationship rules") was enacted, essentially removing the income/capital distinction and seeking to tax all payments and receipts on revenue account. This legislation is contained within the Finance Acts of 1993, 1994 and 1996, respectively. It is the loan relationship rules contained within the Finance Act 1996 (FA96) that will be the focus of this analysis.

The basis of taxation in the UK differs widely according to the nature of the entities involved in a transaction and this analysis is therefore confined to typical companies resident in the UK for tax purposes. The tax implications of structured notes on taxpayers such as individuals, investment trusts, unit trusts, and the like, have not been discussed.

Please note that this section is not a comprehensive guide to the taxation of structured notes in the UK, but is intended to provide both issuers and investors with an outline of the key taxation issues to be considered. However, the implication of indirect taxes such as stamp duty and VAT (value-added tax) on generic structured note products has not been discussed.

### 2.2   General Tax Issues

For purposes of this discussion, the relevant taxation issues of a generic structured note product will be discussed under the following principles:

*   Status of entity for tax purposes.
*   Taxation of principal–loan relationship rules.

- Taxation of interest–distribution rules.
- Withholding taxes.

### 2.2.1  Status of Entity for Tax Purposes

To assess the tax result of a UK entity, the status of the company is important. Normally, companies are "trading" companies or "investment companies." Qualification as either a trading company or an investment company is important mainly to ensure that costs and expenses incurred by the company are tax deductible. Where a company is carrying on a financial trade or dealing in derivatives, it will usually be clear that the transaction forms part of the dealing activities of the company and the profit or loss arising from the transaction will broadly follow the accounts. In contrast, investment companies are subject to a very restrictive regime that applies to the deductions that an investment company may make in computing its profits subject to tax. Special-purpose vehicles (SPVs) are commonly used in structured note transactions, and pose yet another problem in the entity analysis. Where SPV's are used for isolated transactions only (for example, issuing a structured note and either lending on the proceeds or entering into a corresponding structured swap contract) it is doubtful if they would qualify as trading companies. It is possible that investment company status might be achieved but this may be of little use where a tax deduction was required in relation to payments made under structured swaps and other derivative contracts (see further below). The required trading status of a SPV would normally need to be secured by ensuring sufficient activity in the vehicle to guarantee this status or by specifically agreeing the status with the Revenue.

### 2.2.2  Taxation of Principal — Loan Relationship Rules

Structured notes are, by nature, tailored to meet the specific and often complex needs of the individual investor. Since these securities combine features of fixed income instruments with the characteristics of a derivative transaction, any *generic* description can vary widely from a tax perspective, making an overview discussion rather difficult. This is particularly the case because the different derivative characteristics of each note would, if treated independently from the underlying fixed income security, be dealt with under different legislation.

Nevertheless, on the basis that the notes in question are structured in the form of debt securities, their taxation in the UK should be relatively straightforward and fall within the "loan relationship rules" of FA96. The taxation of these notes should not therefore be excessively clouded by their embedded derivative characteristics, as the loan relationship rules provide that the instrument in question (or any part of it) cannot also be subject to tax under a different set of rules unless there is an express statutory provision.

A loan relationship will exist where one company stands in the position of a creditor or debtor in relation to a money debt and where that debt has arisen from the actual or deemed lending of money. A money debt is essentially a debt that fails to be settled by the payment of money, or by the transfer of a right to settlement under a money debt. Structured notes typically satisfy these conditions and should therefore be loan relationships for UK tax purposes.

In summary, the loan relationship legislation seeks to tax all profits and relieve all losses arising from the loan relationship on revenue account, rather than capital account. However, it is important to distinguish between relationships that are on trading or nontrading accounts. This includes profits and losses on principal.[2] The investor will therefore be taxed on the differential between the amounts originally invested and the redemption value of the structured notes. Likewise, the issuer will gain relief for any premium on redemption of the notes. The timing of taxability is determined by normal accountancy practice.

However, where the loan relationship is linked to the value of chargeable assets, provisions contained in FA96 seek to tax the capital element of the relationship on capital account. A loan relationship is linked to the value of chargeable assets when the redemption value of the security is calculated by direct reference to assets upon which chargeable gains would arise. Therefore, where underlying assets are not in the form of loan relationships, a tax mismatch could arise where the interest element of the debt remains within the loan relationship rules, but the principal is subject to capital gains tax on a realisation basis. Issuers may find this treatment less beneficial, as no deduction is available for any premium on redemption of the asset-linked debt securities.

### 2.2.3  Taxation of Interest — Distribution Rules

The loan relationship rules provide that interest payments and receipts should be taxed in accordance with normal accountancy practice as outlined in the previous section. The distribution rules override the loan relationship regime and apply to interest and other distributions in respect of securities where "the consideration given by the company for the use of the principal secured is to any extent dependent on the results of the company's business or any part of it".[3] This would result in the full amount of the interest paid under a structured note not to be deductible by the issuer, and treated as dividend income in the hands of the investor. These rules were designed to cover distributions of profit disguised

---

[2]  This is the case for typical companies resident in the UK. Individual investors will be taxed on the yield as income, but are, subject to many exclusions, liable to capital gains tax on the principal.

[3]  See s209(2)(e)(iii) of ICTA 1988.

as interest payments and can be an obstacle where the issuer has hedged the exposures under a structured note. A possible defence against the potential application of the distribution rules can be where an issuer has no net profits attributable to structured notes (with the exception of a margin/ arrangement fee), since the receipts on the reference assets would be matched with payments on structured notes. Hence, the return on structured notes is dependent upon performance of the reference assets and not the performance of the issuer's business.

Another circumstance where the distribution rules may apply to interest in respect of securities is where "consideration given by the company for the use of the principal secured represents more than a reasonable commercial return for the use of that principal."[4] Only the excessive element of the interest payment will be treated as a distribution. This is a fairly problematic issue, since it may be difficult to predict the level of return and whether that may exceed a normal commercial rate of return. Structured notes linked to, for example, equity instruments may be regarded as more aggressive and subject to this distribution rule than those linked to debt instruments.

### 2.2.4 *Withholding Tax Issues*

If the issuer of a structured note is a UK resident, coupon payments could be subject to a deduction of 20% UK income tax. An exception to this rule is where the issuer is a recognized bank and the interest is paid "in the ordinary course of banking business."[5]

Also, where the notes are in the form of quoted Eurobonds, no withholding tax will be imposed.[6] The provisions of this exception are as follows:

- The issuer must be a company.
- The notes must be listed on a recognised stock exchange.
- The notes must be in bearer form.
- The notes must carry a right to interest.

Depending on the commercial requirements of the structured note and the counterparties, there may be other ways of reducing or eliminating UK withholding tax.

(There are proposals by the EU to introduce a general withholding tax. This possibility should be addressed in the documentation of any structured note with an EU nexus.)

---

[4]  See s209(2)(d) of ICTA 1988.
[5]  Exception within s349(3)(b) of ICTA 1988.
[6]  See s124 of ICTA 1988.

## 3.    Generally Accepted Accounting Practice — the UK
*by Ian D. Wright*

United Kingdom Generally Accepted Accounting Practice (UK GAAP) is in a state of flux. The Accounting Standards Board published a discussion paper on the recognition and measurement of financial instruments in the mid-1990s and has since produced a lengthy standard in the form of Financial Reporting Standard (FRS) 13: Derivatives and other financial instruments: disclosures. However, that standard does not address including gains and losses on financial instruments in financial statements. Changes to the basis of measurement of financial instruments under UK GAAP are currently on hold awaiting the deliberations of the Joint Working Group of standard setters that is currently expected to produce a detailed exposure draft during the summer of 2000. That work is likely to have profound implications as it is widely predicted that it will propose that all financial instruments should be measured at fair value with all changes reported immediately in income: hedge accounting is expected to be outlawed.

In the interval, UK GAAP continues to rely upon work undertaken by the ASB when it developed FRS 4: Capital instruments. That standard addresses the accounting by issuers of complex capital instruments and applies to a wide range of instruments, including structured notes and similar hybrid securities. Further, in relation to holders of such securities, consideration needs to be given to specific industry guidance that takes the form of Statements Of Recommended Practice (SORP) covering investment entities and banks.

If the accounting issues are not addressed by these specific standards and guidance, consideration must be given to core principles contained within Company Law and to the accruals and prudence concepts contained in the soon to be revised Statement of Standard Accounting Practice (SSAP) 2: Disclosure of accounting policies. The revision is likely to lead to the prudence concept being downplayed in favour of neutrality (that is, an absence of systematic bias toward understating gains).

In UK GAAP, consideration also needs to be given to one further standard, FRS 5: Reporting the substance of transactions. Thus anti-abuse standard has a significant impact on structured finance products that involve special-purpose vehicles; they will often fall to be treated as subsidiaries or "quasi subsidiaries", and thus are fully consolidated into group financial statements.

Many complex instruments are in fact structured not just as one transaction but as a series of transactions that are undertaken at the same time and sometimes with the same counterparty. FRS 5 requires that a series of linked transactions be accounted for in relation to their overall commercial effect. This can often be clearly demonstrated where the combined product is promoted and contemplated as one integral item.

UK requirements that do not yet require all derivatives to be measured at fair value may be perceived to lag those of International Accounting Standards Committee and United States regulators. However, the recent arrival of FRS 13 has very significantly advanced the disclosure requirements. In particular, detailed narrative must be given covering the use of financial instruments, their role in risk management and thus for hedging, together with extensive tabular disclosures of interest rate and currency exposures. In addition, a table is required, comparing book and fair values by type of instrument that requires hedged components to be separated into constituent parts. This may need to be supplemented with further narrative, particularly about complex instruments with nonlinear features. Gone are the days that companies can enter into complex instruments and keep the details from investors and the capital markets.

## 3.1 Accounting by Issuers

FRS 4 provides that instruments used as a means of raising finance for the issuer must be categorized into one of two components. If the instrument takes the form of shares (including preference shares) then the instrument must be carried within shareholders funds to comply with Company Law. In all other circumstances an instrument must be carried as a liability in its entirety (split accounting required by IAS is not permitted in UK GAAP). Conversion of an instrument that converts into shares of the issuer may not be presumed in advance, even if it is thought highly likely.

A share that carries with it a preference over equity shares or some restrictions on dividends or capital on a winding up is classified as nonequity share capital for which there are complex additional disclosure requirements. In particular, there must be prominent disclosure of net assets into equity and nonequity funds. The amount for such nonequity share capital is intended to mimic the amount that would be reported as a liability if the instrument has the legal form of a debt rather than a share.

All debt instruments are required to be carried at their net issue proceeds plus finance costs less amounts paid. The same is true for nonequity instruments in relation to the supplementary disclosure required at the foot of the balance sheet. Finance costs in relation to debt instruments are all reported within interest and similar items on the face of the profit and loss account, while in relation to nonequity shares such costs must be reported within the "dividend" caption.

Finance costs are calculated as the difference between the issue proceeds from the instrument and the total payments (or any other transfers of economic benefits) that may be required to be made in accordance with the terms of the instrument. Such costs are allocated to accounting periods so as to achieve a constant rate on the carrying value (that is, inclusive of compounding interest). Thus for a zero-coupon bond, the gross interest increases each period as the carrying amount increases through the notional capitalization of prior-period finance costs.

Special provisions apply where the amount of the total payments to be made are dependent upon an index or some other uncertain future event. Such effects are only taken into account when they occur. For example, the increase in the capital obligation of a bond that is linked to, say, the FTSE 100 index is reflected as the index increases and is neither deferred over the remaining life of the instrument nor accrued in advance.

Many inventive structures for issuers involve the use of detailed contractual arrangements with special-purpose vehicles, such as orphan companies, trusts, and partnerships that are often located in tax havens. These structures are generally thinly capitalized and have banks, or their nominees, as registered owners or are structured with the ultimate beneficiaries being charities. FRS 5 requires that where such entities (known as quasi-subsidiaries) achieve the same economic result as if the entities are subsidiaries in their own right, then they should be accounted for as if they are subsidiaries. Thus group financial statements for issuers generally need to be prepared from the perspective that SPVs and SPEs are treated on a "look-through" basis. Special disclosures are required of the amounts so included within the group consolidation.

FRS 13s' requirements for narrative disclosures include a commentary to be given by issuers in relation to their use of complex financial instruments. For Boards of Directors and group treasury teams, keeping documentary evidence of their activities is especially important since this information forms part of the full financial statements subject to audit, rather than just in the management discussion and analysis or operating and financial review. In particular, the Directors will need to document and then explain their objectives, policies, and strategies in using any particularly complex instruments together with the details of any key features (unless the amounts involved are wholly immaterial to the entity).

While no specific guidance exists in relation to issuers, it is general practice under UK GAAP to use hedge accounting (match the gains or losses recognized under one instrument with the amounts that arise from another) where a capital instrument has been issued and there is some form of supplementary transaction. For example, hedge accounting is generally used where an interest rate swap transforms the interest rate exposure arising on a borrowing from a fixed rate to a floating rate or vice versa.

However, in practice there are limits to how far such principles can be extended and objections may well be raised where there is an absence of a very strong correlation between the variations in future cash flows or current market value of allegedly matching instruments. In particular, it is highly unlikely that hedge accounting can be claimed for written options, unless they are a strong match for another optional instrument undertaken at the same time that demonstrates a strong negative correlation with the written option. In the absence of such correlation, the potential liability under the written option should be separately marked-to-market as a provision required by FRS 12: Provisions, contingent liabilities and contingent assets (this standard exempts only those financial instruments that are carried at fair value).

## 3.2 Accounting by Investors

UK GAAP in relation to holders of complex instruments is much more difficult to summarize, in the absence of prescriptive standards in this area. Thus regard must be had to core accounting principles and to the provisions of company law. In essence there are two camps: fair value and amortized cost. Fair value accounting is used by a variety of special-purpose vehicles and in certain circumstances by banks.

Examples of special-purpose investment vehicles are Investment Trusts (in fact not a trust at all but instead a special type of company that is required by law to separate capital gains and losses from income and expense and may distribute income even if it has incurred a loss on capital) and Unit Trusts. The detailed accounting principles for both of these vehicles are incorporated in SORPs that require these entities carry such investments at fair value—generally mid-market. Income is then recorded in the income statement on an accruals basis (generally including amortization of any premium or discount) and fair value gains and losses are recognized in a capital account. However, the use of very complex financial instruments remains rare in such entities.

Fair value accounting is also used by banks where such assets are held within their trading books. In these circumstances, fair value gains and losses are recognized immediately in income within the profit and loss account. However, where such assets are held within a bank's nontrading portfolio, it would generally be the case that they will be carried at amortized cost, less provision for any credit risk. Following, in part, the principles in FRS 4 in relation to capital repayments dependent upon changes in an index or an underlying instruments, such changes are likely to be recognized immediately, although general practice is far from clear in this area.

Finally, complex financial instruments of this nature may be held by nonfinancial institutions. In relation to corporates, they are likely to follow the treatment above in relation to bank nontrading books and carry the investment at the lower of amortized cost and net realisable value (that is, net of provisions for any credit risk and the effect of any index adjustments). The law (in this case the *Companies Act 1985*) does permit companies to revalue such investments to current cost (if a current asset) or to market value or a director's valuation (if held for continuing use in the business—that is, a fixed asset). However, should such entities record an unrealized gain, then FRS 3: Reporting financial performance requires any such gain to be shown in the Statement of Total Recognized Gains and Losses (Comprehensive income), while the law requires that gain to be reported in a revaluation reserve. By comparison any unrealized loss below amortized historical cost is required to be charged to the profit and loss account: rather a one-sided solution and likely to put off many from investing in exotic instruments that carry down-side risk.

## 4.  Accounting and Taxation for Structured Notes – Germany
*by Georg Klusak*

### 4.1  Accounting

#### 4.1.1  Similar Accounting Rules for All Relevant Corporations

Generally, the German accounting rules apply to all relevant types of corporate investors or issuers. There is only a limited number of specific provisions that deal with the particularities in the area of banks and insurance companies. However, these specific provisions do not have any material impact on the accounting treatment of the financial instruments contemplated.

#### 4.1.2  No Bifurcation of Structured Bonds

Economically, a compound instrument like the structured notes described consists of (i) a bond and (ii) a derivative element. Some authors in literature therefore hold the view that the financial instrument should be bifurcated and every element treated separately for accounting purposes. However, this view does not properly reflect the fact that a compound instrument is still one single asset. Accordingly, the instrument has to be accounted for as a whole.

Therefore, puts, calls, or collars embedded in a bond are not explicitly reflected in the investor's balance sheet. Instead, the structured bond is shown as single asset.

This is different only if the different elements that form part of the financial instrument may be separated from each other as in the case of a bond with a detachable warrant. Where the issue terms of the financial instrument provide for this option to split the instrument, the two elements are accounted for as separate assets in the balance sheet of the investor. In that case, the assets have to be evaluated in accordance with standard methods including derivative valuation models.

#### 4.1.2  Accounting Rules for the Investor

Under the German accounting framework, assets are shown in the balance sheet at the lower of cost or market. As a consequence, any appreciation of the financial instrument is neglected until the instrument is sold or redeemed and thus the increase in value is finally realized. On the other hand, any decrease immediately triggers the depreciation of the financial instrument and is reflected in the profit and loss statement.

In the case where the derivative element is wrapped into a detachable option or warrant, the option or warrant is capitalized. At maturity, the artificially calculated premium paid for the derivative either forms part of the acquisition cost of the underlying if the option or warrant is exercised or qualifies as deductible expense if the option or warrant expires.

Interest income from coupons is accrued proportionally between the coupon dates. If a bond carries no coupons or different, but pre-fixed coupons as in the case of a step-up bond, the interest accrual is based on the average issue yield.

### 4.1.4  Accounting Rules for the Issuer

Parallel to the accounting of assets, liabilities from compound instruments are treated as a whole. Consequently, puts, calls, or collars embedded in a bond are not shown separately in the issuer's balance sheet.

Liabilities are accounted for at the higher of initial liability and market value. Accordingly, any market movement is immediately reflected in the balance sheet and the profit and loss account respectively.

Payments on coupons are accrued between the coupon dates. If the coupons are pre-fixed, the accruals are based on the issue yield.

### 4.2  Taxation

### 4.2.1  Same Tax Rules for all Relevant Types of Corporations

The German tax framework does not provide for different tax rules in respect of specific corporations like banks or insurance companies. Accordingly, the following comments apply to all sorts of taxable corporations.

### 4.2.2  Conjunction between Taxation and Accounting Treatment

The taxation of income emanating from a structured bond is largely based on the accounting treatment of the relevant product. Accordingly, structured bonds are usually treated as one single instrument.

Furthermore, parallel to the accounting any appreciation in the financial instrument is not treated as taxable gain until it is finally realized when the bond is sold or redeemed.

If the value of the bond has decreased, however, the tax treatment may differ from the accounting described above. This is due to the fact that a depreciation will only be accepted for tax purposes if the structured bond is classified as a short-term investment within the balance sheet of the investor.

At the sale or maturity of the bond, any loss on short-term investments and any gain on both long-term and short-term investments is realized for tax purposes and qualifies as a tax-deductible item or taxable profit respectively.

### 4.3.3 Transfer Tax

There is no securities transfer tax in Germany.

## 5.   Tax Treatment of Structured Notes — Japan

*by Sachihiko Fujimoto and Kenneth Shives*

### 5.1   Corporate Tax Treatment

The corporate tax treatment of derivative transactions in Japan is provided by a corporate tax circular (the "Derivatives Circular"), which is intended to clarify and standardize the timing of gain or loss recognition from derivatives including futures, forward contracts, swaps, options, quasi-guarantee derivatives (for example, credit derivatives or disaster derivatives), and hybrid financial instruments.

Structured notes, the combination of a base security and a derivative element, would be categorized as a hybrid financial instrument, which is defined in the Derivatives Circular as (a) securities vehicles packaging derivatives and financial assets or debts, or (b) products combining financial assets or debts and derivatives. Examples of structured notes may include equity-linked notes, collared FRNs, or dual currency bonds, which are synthesized as the combination of (a) base securities—straight bonds or standard floating rate notes, and (b) derivatives elements—equity options, interest caps or floors, or multiple currency forward contracts.

For corporate tax purposes, structured notes will be treated under either the integrated method or the separate method, primarily contingent upon the correlation between the risk of the principal and interest of the base security, and the derivative elements.

### 5.1.1   Integrated Method

When a particular correlation clearly exists between the risk of the principal and interest of the base security and the derivative element (the "correlation test"), the structured note will be treated as a single security for corporate tax purposes.

As an example, because a collared FRN (the combination of interest caps and floors and a standard floating rate note) contains a clear correlation between the interest rate risk of the floating rate note and the interest caps and floors, the corporate tax consequences of the collared FRN would be determined under the integrated method. As such, the incorporated interest caps and floors, as well as the standard floating rate note would be treated as a single security for corporate tax purposes.

### 5.1.1.1 Structured Note Interest

Payments or receipts of interest on structured notes may include interest and currency swap payments, currency swaps, option premiums, settlement amounts and premiums on interest caps and floors, and premiums on quasi-guarantee derivatives.

All payments or receipts of interest on structured notes will be recognized ratably over the interest computation period (the "accrual method"). Although option premiums are generally recognized at the time of exercise or expiration of the option, option premiums incorporated in structured notes by virtue of higher or lower coupon rates will be recognized under the accrual method when the integrated method applies.

If the interest yield of a structured note is not constant (excluding the situation where the interest yield is determined by a publicized market rate, for example, LIBOR or that the exercise or nonexercise of options causes a change in the interest yield), payments or receipts that are adjusted by the use of a reasonable method, for example, the constant yield method or the straight-line method, should be recognized as gains or loss ratably over each interest computation period of the structured note.

### 5.1.1.2 Structured Note Principal

When the redemption or repayment amount of the principal of a structured note changes as a result of the exercise, termination, or expiration of an option incorporated in the structured note, the redemption, or repayment amount of the principal is determined at the time of the exercise, termination, or expiration of the option incorporated in the structured note. As such, the change in the principal amount is recognized as a gain or loss in the taxable year when the option incorporated in the structured note is exercised, terminates, or expires.

When the redemption amount of the principal of a structured note changes as a result of (a) the occurrence of a "payment event" relating to quasi-guarantee derivatives (credit derivatives or disaster derivatives), or (b) a reason other than the exercise of an option, the change of the principal amount is recognized as a gain or loss in the taxable year when the change in the principal amount is determined.

### 5.2.1   Separate Method

When the derivative elements incorporated in structured notes are not regarded as being clearly correlated to the risk of the principal and interest of the base security, such structured notes should be treated under the separate method. Under the separate method, the derivative elements are segregated from the base security for corporate tax purposes, such that the derivative elements and the base security will be treated independently for purposes determining corporate tax consequences.

As an example, because an equity-linked note (the combination of equity options and a standard note) does not have a clear correlation between the risk of the principal and interest of the standard note and the equity options, the corporate tax consequences of the equity-linked notes would be determined under the separate method. As such, the incorporated equity options and the standard note would be treated separately for corporate tax purposes.

As an exception to the rule, the separate method will not be required, irrespective of the correlation test, when (a) option or interest cap/floor premiums, which are embedded in the structured notes, are not disclosed to the counter-party, or (b) the derivative elements embedded in the structured notes are such derivatives, for example, interest rate swaps, the payments or receipts from which are recognized under the accrual method.

#### 5.2.1.1   Special Rule for Financial Institutions

Financial institutions are permitted to use a "special trading account", the derivative transactions or the structured notes recorded under which shall be re-valued at the end of the accounting year on a mark-to-market basis for corporate tax purposes. The Derivatives Circular is not applicable to such derivative transactions or structured notes recorded in a special trading account by a financial institution. The special trading account does not apply to entities other than financial institutions.

### 5.2   Withholding Tax Treatment

Although no specific guidelines for derivatives transactions in Japan exist, the withholding tax treatment of derivatives transactions may follow the corporate tax treatment provided under the Derivatives Circular.

While interest payments on securities are subject to withholding tax, withholding tax is generally not imposed on payments related to derivatives contracts, for example, payments on interests rate swaps, currency swaps, option premiums, settlement amounts and premiums on interest caps and floors, and premiums on quasi-guarantee derivatives.

Under the integrated method whereby the structured security is deemed a single security for Japanese corporate tax purposes, any payments related to the incorporated derivative elements that are construed as interest payments will be subject to withholding tax regardless of whether or not the payments would be subject to withholding tax if the derivative elements were treated independently for tax purposes.

With regard to the withholding tax treatment of redemption gains (the redemption amount that exceeds the face amount of the note) on a structured note, the redemption gain may be regarded by the Japanese tax authorities as "interest income" such that it may be subject to withholding tax, depending on the nature of the structured note.

# 6.   Accounting for Structured Notes — Australia

*by Ian Hammond and Regina Fikkers*

### 6.1   Introduction

There is currently no Australian accounting standard dealing comprehensively with accounting for financial instruments with embedded derivatives, such as structured notes and hybrid securities.

Standards dealing with accounting for structured notes and hybrid securities have been issued in the US and by the International Accounting Standards Committee (IASC). Additionally a joint working group (the JWG) of national standard setters are working together to develop a longer term standard on financial instruments. The JWG includes representatives from the IASC, Australia, Canada, France, Germany, Japan, New Zealand, the nordic countries, the UK and the US.

The Australian Accounting Standards Board (AASB) has begun a project to develop an accounting standard for the measurement and recognition of financial instruments including those with embedded derivatives. The AASB project will be based on the recommendations of the March 1997 IASC Discussion Paper "Accounting for Financial Assets and Financial Liabilities" and the tentative views of the JWG. The AASB has a policy of harmonizing Australian standards with IAS. However, the Board has not announced an intention to adopt IAS 39, "Financial Instruments: Recognition and Measurement" or an interim measure, preferring to await the outcome of the JWG.

Australia has already adopted a disclosure standard developed by the IASC. The disclosure requirements of this standard cover structured notes and hybrid securities.

Until a standard is developed, there are two relevant methods of accounting for financial instruments in Australia, market value accounting and accrual accounting.

## 6.2    Market Value Accounting

Under Australian GAAP, reference must first be made to the accounting standards dealing with particular industries. Market value accounting is prescribed by specific accounting standards, regulatory rules, and/or industry practice on a broad base for the life insurance industry, general insurance industry, investment trust industry, and superannuation funds. This means that any investor in structured notes or hybrid securities from these industries would use market value accounting.

For all other industries, existing Australian practice would require the question of intent to be considered. Where a counterparty uses structured notes or hybrid securities as a trading position, including where they are used as a mechanism to increase risk, market value accounting is appropriate.

Market value accounting requires access to periodic market values or fair values of all the components of the transaction with changes in the values recognized in the profit and loss statement as they occur.

## 6.3    Accural Accounting

When market value accounting is not required, under Australian GAAP accrual accounting is usually used for monetary assets and liabilities. Where derivatives are used to reduce or offset risk on the underlying instrument, accrual accounting is also used; however, it is usually referred to as "hedge accounting." Hedge accounting would allow the transaction to be accounted for as if there was only one instrument. To qualify for hedge accounting there must be designation and a high correlation of price movements between the underlying note and the packaged derivatives.

Accrual accounting allows any premiums paid or received to be deferred and amortized over the life of the transaction. Any additional payments or receipts are incorporated with the returns on the underlying note instrument and included in the same category of income or expense (for example, interest).

If the economic characteristics and risks of an embedded derivative are clearly and closely related to those of the host contract they are not usually bifurcated or separated under Australian GAAP. They are accounted for as one instrument at historical cost with the cumulative income return accounted for on an accruals basis. On the other hand, bifurcation may be more appropriate where the risks of the derivative are different or increase the risks from the underlying instrument.

## 6.4    Structured Notes

Where market value accounting is not required, an Australian-structured note would be accounted for at its historical cost and interest is accrued as determined by the terms of the transaction.

## 6.5   Callable Bonds

Where market value accounting is not required, an Australian callable bond would be accounted for on an accruals basis. This would require the bond to be accounted for at the historical cost of the initial investment. Interest receipts or payments are accounted for on an accruals basis. Generally, the call option is not accounted for separately. If the call option is about to be exercised and notice has been given, any additional receipts/payments above the face value of the bond should be accrued as interest in the profit and loss statement and included in the carrying value of the bond.

## 6.6   Inverse Floating Rate Notes

Unless market value accounting is required, an Australian inverse floating rate note would generally be bifurcated as the interest rate risk is effectively doubled by the use of the derivatives. The individual derivatives would be included on the balance sheet at market value, with changes in the market value included in the profit and loss statement. The fixed-rate bond component would be accounted for on an accruals basis.

## 6.7   Range (Accrual) Notes

Range notes would generally be accounted for on an accruals basis. This would require the note to be accounted for at its historical cost. Any premiums paid/received on the associated derivatives would be deferred and amortized to the profit and loss statement over the life of the transaction. Any other receipts and payments are included in the profit and loss statement on an accruals basis with the interest on the underlying note.

However, where the additional returns are substantially higher than market interest rates, bifurcation, as outlined above for inverse floating rate notes, may be more appropriate.

Where the underlying security is not purchased the derivative structure should use market value accounting. Market value accounting would require the swap structure to be recognized at its cost and any changes in value recognized in the profit and loss statement when they occur.

## 6.8   Dual-currency Bonds

As the coupon is in a different currency to the underlying instrument, dual-currency bonds should be bifurcated into their separate currency components.

Under Australian GAAP, the principal or coupon of the dual-currency bond that is denominated in the local currency will be accounted for either using accrual accounting or market value accounting depending on the intention of the holder or issuer. Where accrual accounting is used for the local currency component, the exposure that is denominated in a foreign currency (either the initial cost of the bond or the accrued coupon) may also be accounted for using accrual accounting. However, the foreign currency component is required to be translated into the local currency at the period end rate, with any currency gains or losses included in the profit and loss statement.

## 6.9 Disclosure

Australian Accounting Standards AASB 1033 "Presentation and Disclosure of financial instruments" was issued in December 1996 and initially applied for years ending on or after December 31, 1997. Compliance with AASB 1033 also ensures conformity with International Accounting Standard IAS 32 "Financial Instruments; Disclosure and Presentation."

For structured notes and hybrid securities the following information would need to be summarized in the notes to the financial statements:

- Accounting policies and methods adopted including the basis for recognition, whether market value accounting or accrual accounting had been applied.
- Significant terms and conditions that may effect the amount, timing, and certainty of future cash flows. This would include disclosure of notional amounts of embedded derivatives, stated interest terms, maturity dates, and any related security.
- The objectives for holding or issuing the financial instruments, including the context needed to understand those objectives and strategies.
- Information about exposure to interest rate risk, including effective interest rates and contractual repricing dates.
- The amount that best represents the maximum credit risk exposure at the reporting date on the basis that the counterparty fails to perform their obligations under the transaction. Any concentrations of credit risk that arise from a single counterparty or group of counterparties must also be disclosed.
- Net fair values, that is, market values must be disclosed at balance date. Separate disclosure is also made of the aggregate of fair values for those financial assets or financial liabilities that are not readily tradeable on organized markets in standardized form.
- The methods adopted in determining market values and any significant assumptions made.
- Where a financial asset has been recognized at an amount in excess of market value, details of this need to be disclosed and the reasons why management expects the carrying amounts to be recovered.

## 6.10 Proposed Guidance

The AASB accounting standard project will be based on the recommendations of March 1997 IASC Discussion Paper "Accounting for Financial Assets and Financial Liabilities" and the tentative views of the JWG. The discussion paper explores the issues of a wider use of market value accounting for all financial instruments.

The measurement proposals included in this discussion paper would require all financial assets and liabilities including those with embedded derivatives to be accounted for on a market value basis with gains and losses included in the profit and loss statement. There are some proposed exceptions for gains and losses arising on market valuing of hedges of anticipated transactions; however, these exceptions are not likely to be relevant to structured notes or hybrid securities.

The significant increase in use of market values or fair values obviously assumes that these values can be either obtained directly from liquid and organized markets or estimated on a reasonable basis.

### 6.11  Conclusion

While Australian Accounting Standards clearly deal with the disclosure requirements arising from the use of structured notes there is only limited guidance available on accounting for such instruments with embedded derivatives. The whole area of market value versus accrual accounting is determined by reference to current market practice adopted for accounting for all financial instruments. The ability of counterparties to observe market values or estimate using appropriate indices and observable interest rates will be a critical factor in the acceptance of an increased use of market value accounting.

## 7.  Tax Treatment of Structured Notes — Australia

*by Bill Testa and Grahame Roach*

### 7.1  Introduction

The Australian tax issues in relation to structured notes are summarized below. It is noted that it is difficult to generalize as to what the tax implications may be, and each transaction should be considered individually. The tax implications may also vary depending on the nature of the taxpayer entity.

In the following we consider the likely tax outcomes for institutional investors in structured notes, as well as issuers of structured notes.

Further, the Australian Government has for some time been considering proposals to reform the taxation treatment of financial arrangements. An outline of relevant proposals is also set out below.

## 7.2    Tax Treatment — Investor

The existing Australian tax regime is generally based upon the "form" rather than the substance of a transaction. Therefore, where the embedded derivative transaction is dealt with under the same contract that gives rise to the fixed income instrument, the tax implications should not have to be considered separately. The derivative component of the structured note will merely enhance or offset the interest or discount return associated with the security; that is, the tax treatment of the overall return will be considered.

However, if the derivative associated with the structured note is entered into as a separate transaction (for example, a swap payment is calculated and paid under another agreement) the taxation implications arising from this transaction would also need to be considered separately. The Australian tax treatment of derivative transactions is complex and is not considered here.

Interest, and returns in the form of a discount, are considered to be income under ordinary concepts. If the recipient is in the business of money lending or is a financial institution, it is likely to be taxed on an accruals basis. All other taxpayers are likely to be taxed on a receipts basis or due and receivable basis. However, there are specific provisions that prescribe the derivation of returns arising from certain long-term deep discount or deferred interest securities ("qualifying securities"). Certain structured notes may constitute "qualifying securities" depending on their terms.

Broadly, a "qualifying security" is a security that has:

- a term exceeding 12 months;
- an "eligible return" (that is, it is reasonably likely that the sum of all payments, other than coupons paid at least yearly, exceeds the issue price); and
- if the eligible return can be precisely ascertained, the eligible return is greater than 1.5% per annum.

The eligible return associated with a qualifying security (that is, typically discount or deferred interest) is required to be brought to account for tax purposes on an accruals basis in accordance with a formula that varies depending upon whether the security has a fixed or variable return. In essence, however, the formula seeks to bring the eligible return to account on a compounding yield to maturity accruals basis. Any periodic interest (that is, paid at least yearly) is brought to account under the general provisions.

Gains and losses on disposal of structured notes would typically be assessable or deductible for tax purposes as if they were ordinary income or on revenue account.

Interest received by a nonresident not carrying on business through a permanent establishment in Australia is subject to withholding tax at a rate of

10%. Withholding tax also applies to payments in the nature of interest (for example, discount) and amounts reasonably regarded as in substitution for interest. In some cases withholding tax may also apply where a nonresident transfers a security to an Australian resident, or to a nonresident carrying on business in Australia, for an amount exceeding the issue price.

Certain exceptions to withholding tax can apply. One exception is where the interest is incurred by the resident in carrying on a business through a permanent establishment outside Australia. Another exception applies where the issue of the securities satisfies a detailed "public offer" test.

## 7.3   Tax Treatment — Issuer

The interest and discount expense incurred by an issuer of a structured note will typically be deductible on a daily accruals basis, assuming that the funds are borrowed for the purpose of deriving assessable income in Australia.

As discussed above, the tax implications arising from any embedded derivative transactions should not have to be considered separately. For most structures, the effect of the embedded derivative will typically be considered either an increase or offset of the interest or discount expense associated with the security, unless there is a capital protection element attached thereto (see below).

In relation to securities issued which fall within the "qualifying security" category discussed above, the issuer is typically entitled to a deduction for the eligible return (that is, the discount or deferred interest) on the same basis as the recipient is required to include it as assessable income (that is, a compounding yield to maturity accruals basis), so long as a deduction would otherwise have been allowable under the general provisions. However, these special rules do not apply to bearer securities, securities issued offshore, or those that are issued directly or indirectly to a nonresident associate.

It is noted that the Australian taxation authorities have recently attacked certain capital protected products on the basis that a component of the interest charged was of a capital nature (that is, to the extent that an excessive interest cost could be seen as a cost of hedging the loan principal). In these cases it was sought to deny a deduction for the cost of the capital protection However, this should not be of concern to most financial institutions (for example, banks and moneylenders) where any hedging costs incurred should be considered on revenue account in any case.

It is noted that the issuer will often hedge or onsell the exposure arising from the embedded derivative transaction. To a large degree the tax treatment of a derivative transaction depends on the nature of the taxpayer's business activities, the part played by the transaction in those business activities, and the purpose for which the taxpayer enters into the transaction; that is, whether the transaction should be characterized as being of a revenue or a capital nature. The treatment of such hedges is outside the scope of this chapter.

## 7.4 Tax Reform

The latest proposals for reform that may impact upon the tax implications arising from the operation of structured notes include:

- The proposed general rule is that all income, expense, gains, and losses under financial arrangements would be taxed on revenue account (that is, as ordinary income/expense).
- A taxpayer would be able to elect to use market value for tax purposes for financial assets and liabilities that are marked-to-market for the purposes of the taxpayer's audited profit and loss statement in its financial accounts.
- Where the mark-to-market election is not exercised, and in situations where the return is "certain," the tax value of financial assets and liabilities, including hybrid and synthetic financial assets and liabilities, would be determined on an accruals basis by applying an appropriate "rate of return" to the asset's or liability's opening tax value.
- A realization basis is proposed for assets and liabilities where mark-to-market is not elected and the future returns or obligations are uncertain.

Given the complexity of the issues and the fact that further public consultation is envisaged, a final outcome and start date for the proposals is extremely difficult to predict.

# 18

# The Market for Structured Notes

## 1. Overview

The market for structured notes is now an established and integral component of the market for capital market investment products and financial derivatives. The market is large and complex.

In examining the dynamics of the market it is essential to understand that the market is not of recent origin. In fact, the market has both a long and clear history. However, it is useful to segment the market development into two distinct major phases: traditional structured notes and modern structured notes.

Traditional structured notes include transactions such as callable bonds or equity-linked bonds (convertible securities, exchangeable securities, and debt with equity warrants). These types of transactions have a long history and have been an established product for investors for some time. Modern structured notes include variations on such traditional structures but include innovative and new security structures that are designed in response to investor demand to create specific exposures to market price movements consistent with the investor's requirements. For example, the step-up and multi-step callable bond structures are predicated on the traditional callable bond. These structures combine a fixed interest bond with a call option on the bond written by the investor in favor of the issuer. However, the newer structures extend the original structures in a number of ways to cater to investor requirements in terms of value created from the option and the risk of exercise or nonexercise of the embedded interest rate options.

The defining elements of the modern structured notes when compared to the more traditional structured note formats include:

- **Insulation of the issuer from the embedded derivative element** — in traditional structured notes, the issuer is at risk for the embedded derivative element. For example, the issuer assumes the liquidity and interest rate risk inherent in purchasing the call embedded in a callable bond or selling the put embedded in a puttable bond. Similarly, a convertible issuer assumes the intrinsic equity price risk embedded in a convertible note. In contrast, in a modern structured note, the issuer is almost always *completely insulated from the embedded market risk*. This protection is engineered by the entry into derivative transactions that are designed to eliminate any such market risk exposure. The issuer therefore is attracted to the transaction on a pure arbitrage or opportunistic funding basis where it is guaranteed a satisfactory financing rate, *irrespective of the performance of the security*. The only risk assumed by the issuer is the risk of counterparty default on the derivative dealer providing the hedge for the structured note.

- **Isolation of credit risk from market risk** — traditional structured notes combine, from the perspective of an investor, credit risk and market risk. This reflects the fact that the issuer was not always one with unimpeachable credit quality. Modern structured notes very markedly seek to isolate and separate the two risks. This is achieved by restricting the acceptable issuer universe to a limited number of very high credit quality (AA rating or equivalent minimum). The isolation of these risk elements represents the desire on the part of the investor population to separate credit default risk from the market risk sought to be assumed. The increased focus on credit derivatives and related instruments as a mechanism for both trading and assuming credit risk specifically in no small way reflects a similar logic.[1]

- **Isolation of credit risk from market risk** — the insulation of the issuer from the market risk elements of a structured note and the emphasis within the note structure on market risk allows investor requirements to emerge as the dominant consideration in the design and creation of these securities. It also vastly broadens the range and volume of transactions that are feasible. The growth of the market for structured notes over the recent past in no small measure reflects the emergence of these considerations.

In this chapter, the principal focus is the modern market for structured notes. The initial focus is on the key dynamics underlying the market. This is followed by sections focused on the evolution of the market, specific market structural considerations, the secondary market for structured notes, and the regulatory framework.

---

[1] It is likely that a logical means for asset allocation within investor portfolios will entail treatment of *credit default risk* as a pure and distinct asset class that will require separate management.

## 2. Market Dimensions

As noted above, the overall market for structured notes is complex. One of the difficulties in relation to analyzing the market is the absence of detailed and accurate statistics that might allow some of the market dynamics to be dissected.

The key dimensions[2] or characteristics of the market requiring analysis include:

- Size of the market.
- Types of transactions and transaction characteristics, including issuer, maturities and transaction size.
- The issuance formats (public issues versus private placements).
- Relationship of structured notes to related markets (both asset and derivative).

### 2.1 Market Size

There are significant difficulties in estimating the size of the global market for structured notes. There are limited sources of data available. The absence of data reflects the fact that the bulk of issuance is not undertaken in the public market. The bulk of issuance is undertaken privately or documented under either medium-term note (MTN) programs or under other continuously offered debt issuance formats. This practice makes it difficult to accurately estimate the size of the market or its characteristics.

The size of the global market for structured note products is estimated at around US$250-300 billion in new issue volume per annum.[3] Annual volume varies from year to year but is estimated to have been rising steadily in recent years. The most important aspect of the data is the growth in both issuance volumes and outstandings in structured note products. This growth underlines the important role of these types of transactions in capital markets.

**Exhibit 18.1** and **18.2** sets out statistics on structured note new issuance estimates.

---

[2]  For a discussion of the structure of the US structured note market see Crabbe, Leland E. and Argilagos, Joseph D. "Anatomy of the Structured Note Market" (Fall 1994) *Journal of Applied Corporate Finance* 85-98.

[3]  This total includes modern and traditional note structures, including callable debt. It does not include traditional equity-based structured notes such as convertible notes.

**Exhibit 18.1**
**Structured Note Volumes – Estimate 1**

**Structured Note Issuance by Currency***

|                        | 1997      | 1998      | 98% Chg  | 1999     | 99% Chg  |
|------------------------|-----------|-----------|----------|----------|----------|
| US$                    | 34.71     | 32.23     | (7.1%)   | 23.23    | (27.9%)  |
| Yen                    | 1,834.90  | 1,140.45  | (37.8%)  | 997.38   | (12.5%)  |
| DM                     | 80.38     | 72.49     | (9.8%)   | 0.67     | (99.1%)  |
| Italian lire           | 30,368.20 | 48,938.70 | 61.2%    | 2,484.64 | (94.9%)  |
| Portuguese escudos     | 529.68    | 1,182.97  | 123.3%   | 49.47    | (95.8%)  |
| Spanish peseta         | 673.68    | 128.45    | (80.9%)  | 22.00    | (82.9%)  |
| British pound sterling | 1.95      | 0.94      | (51.7%)  | 2.50     | 166.5%   |
| Canadian dollars       | 0.98      | 0.54      | (44.9%)  | 0.55     | 2.2%     |
| Swedish krona          | 5.10      | 3.17      | (37.9%)  | 0.95     | (70.0%)  |
| Swiss franc            | 1.18      | 3.73      | 216.4%   | 0.33     | (91.1%)  |
| French franc           | 16.33     | 23.50     | 43.9%    | 0.09     | (99.6%)  |
| Austrian schilling     | 13.37     | 21.04     | 57.4%    | 0.47     | (97.8%)  |
| Norwegian krona        | 5.23      | 2.69      | (48.7%)  | 1.41     | (47.3%)  |
| Euros                  | 0.00      | 0.00      | n/a      | 84.63    | n/a      |
| ECU                    | 0.52      | 2.35      | 350.6%   | 0.00     | n/a      |

*Currency volumes in billions*
*Source:* Bloomberg, LP.

*Notes:*
1. All statistics are based on initial settlement date. Product-type classifications are fixed income or fixed income hybrid structures recognized by Bloomberg, LP as "Structured Notes". Statistics are based on securities released for display on the Bloomberg, and may not be indicative of total market activity.
2. Statistics provided for the period January 1, 1997 through December 31, 1999, as of January 11, 2000. All statistics subject to revision. Statistics include all International, US Corporate, and US Government Agency Structured Notes.

*Source:* Bloomberg. (Contact: Michael Miller, Bloomberg Financial Markets, in the US — 609-279-3459).

**Exhibit 18.2**
**Structured Note Volumes — Estimate 2**

**Total Structured Note Issuance**

| Year | Amount (US$ m) | Number of Issues |
|------|----------------|------------------|
| 1994 | 14,392.33 | 395 |
| 1995 | 27,344.05 | 752 |
| 1996 | 47,922.16 | 1578 |
| 1997 | 70,371.73 | 2166 |
| 1998 | 66,506.86 | 1834 |
| 1999 | 64,555.15 | 1999 |
| **Total** | 291,092.28 | 8724 |

**Issuance by Currency**

| | Japanese yen Amount (US$ m) | Issues | US$ Amount (US$ m) | Issues | Italian lira Amount (US$ m) | Issues | Euro/ECU Amount (US$ m) | Issues | Portuguese escudo Amount (US$ m) | Issues |
|------|------|------|------|------|------|------|------|------|------|------|
| 1994 | 7,631.27 | 236 | 3,973.01 | 95 | 520.79 | 21 | 71.99 | 2 | 0 | 0 |
| 1995 | 20,451.95 | 514 | 3,449.87 | 133 | 754.4 | 29 | 7.48 | 1 | 0 | 0 |
| 1996 | 22,297.39 | 791 | 9,040.02 | 339 | 4,968.40 | 181 | 1,404.76 | 16 | 888.37 | 42 |
| 1997 | 20,235.70 | 899 | 17,013.16 | 497 | 13,359.27 | 330 | 2,077.40 | 17 | 4,313.29 | 164 |
| 1998 | 11,019.85 | 712 | 13,151.27 | 248 | 15,370.59 | 285 | 4,716.02 | 97 | 5,020.32 | 184 |
| 1999 | 11,122.89 | 802 | 7,672.21 | 243 | 1,336.09 | 53 | 36,969.91 | 732 | 44.65 | 3 |
| Total | 92,759.05 | 3954 | 54,299.53 | 1555 | 36,309.55 | 899 | 45,247.57 | 865 | 10,266.62 | 393 |

| | Sterling Amount (US$ m) | Issues | DM Amount (US$ m) | Issues | French franc Amount (US$ m) | Issues | Others Amount (US$ m) | Issues | Total Amount (US$ m) | Issues |
|------|------|------|------|------|------|------|------|------|------|------|
| 1994 | 557.14 | 12 | 417.61 | 9 | 713.11 | 8 | 507.41 | 12 | 14,392.33 | 395 |
| 1995 | 840.38 | 16 | 934.43 | 40 | 385.21 | 3 | 520.34 | 16 | 27,344.05 | 752 |
| 1996 | 3,136.13 | 59 | 1,892.86 | 60 | 1,146.41 | 8 | 3,147.83 | 82 | 47,922.16 | 1578 |
| 1997 | 4,292.79 | 58 | 3,849.37 | 91 | 2,045.65 | 24 | 3,185.10 | 86 | 70,371.73 | 2166 |
| 1998 | 2,245.21 | 67 | 2,858.13 | 67 | 3,368.06 | 48 | 8,757.42 | 126 | 66,506.86 | 1834 |
| 1999 | 5,662.81 | 97 | 161.52 | 3 | 16.37 | 2 | 1,568.71 | 64 | 64,555.15 | 1999 |
| Total | 16,734.47 | 309 | 10,113.91 | 270 | 7,674.80 | 93 | 17,686.80 | 386 | 291,092.28 | 8724 |

*Notes:*
The above statistics are based on listed EMTN issues.

*Source:* Capital NET MTNWare www.capn.com.

## 2.2    Transactions Characteristics

The available data and anecdotal evidence can be utilized to identify the following principal characteristics of the market:

- **Issuers** — the majority of issuers in the structured note market are of high credit quality. The ratings levels of the majority of issuers are, as noted above, AA or better. The major types of issuers are sovereigns, quasi-sovereign issuers (wholly or substantially government owned), financial institutions, and corporations. The ratings threshold applies irrespective of the type of issuer. In the US domestic market, a major group of issuers is the Federal government agencies who are AAA-rated (see detailed discussion below). In international markets, the majority of issuance is by sovereigns, supranationals (such as the multilateral development agencies; for example, the World Bank), financial institutions, and selected corporations. The type of issuer and the concentration of credit quality reflects the investor desire for isolation and separation of credit and market risk in structured notes generally. In recent years, the credit quality of issuers has declined. An important factor in this decline has been the increased participation retail investors who are less credit sensitive than institutional investors. **Exhibit 18.3** sets out the ratings of issuers of structured notes.
- **Transaction size** — the typical transaction size for a structured note is:
  1. US$5-20 million for a private transaction although individual tranches may be as small as US$100,000.
  2. US$10-100 million for a private placement or issue undertaken within the framework of a MTN program.
  3. US$100 million or more for a public transaction.
     The individual transaction size reflects the highly customized nature of the investment and its orientation to the requirements of the individual investor. The predominant activity in the market is for this type of highly focused security design to meet investor specifications. However, the market, from time to time, experiences surges of activity entailing similar transactions that are issued to meet broadly based investor demand for a specific type of exposure. Examples of this type of activity include the market for inverse FRNs, collared FRNs, range FRNs, EMU convergence structures, and reverse convertibles.
- **Maturities** — the majority of structured notes are short in maturity with a significant concentration between 1 to 3 years. However, longer term issuance is not unknown and certain types of structured notes are of very long (up to 10 year) life. This concentration of shorter maturities reflects the shorter time horizons over which the investor seeks to capture the desired market exposure. It also reflects the depth and liquidity of the underlying asset and derivative markets that is required to structure of these types of instruments. **Exhibit 18.4** on page 963 sets out the distribution of maturities of structured notes.

**Exhibit 18.3**
**Structured Notes: Credit Rating of Issuers**

Structured Notes — Issuer Classified by S&P Rating
Issuance Volume (US$ Million) Classified by S&P Rating Category

| | AAA | | AA+/AA/AA− | | A+/A/A− | | BBB+/BBB/BBB− | | Others | | Total | |
|---|---|---|---|---|---|---|---|---|---|---|---|---|
| | Amount (US$m) | Issues | Amount (US$m) | Issues | Amount (US$m) | Issues | Amount (US$m) | Issues | Amount (US$m) | Issues | Amount (US$m) | Issues |
| 1994 | 1,463.44 | 29 | 4,899.52 | 112 | 2,598.81 | 79 | 1,556.47 | 14 | 3,874.09 | 161 | 14,392.33 | 395 |
| 1995 | 4,588.18 | 81 | 4,831.79 | 114 | 4,048.65 | 131 | 5,606.13 | 77 | 8,269.31 | 349 | 27,344.05 | 752 |
| 1996 | 8,669.70 | 166 | 13,280.02 | 323 | 9,520.39 | 315 | 4,403.35 | 256 | 12,048.71 | 518 | 47,922.16 | 1578 |
| 1997 | 14,681.83 | 295 | 18,252.46 | 632 | 11,812.98 | 360 | 6,987.47 | 295 | 18,636.97 | 584 | 70,371.73 | 2166 |
| 1998 | 20,130.46 | 413 | 20,263.43 | 533 | 8,991.69 | 322 | 2,762.66 | 186 | 14,358.62 | 380 | 66,506.86 | 1834 |
| 1999 | 14,508.29 | 405 | 25,577.27 | 714 | 11,279.72 | 395 | 2,114.65 | 126 | 11,075.22 | 359 | 64,555.15 | 1999 |
| Total | 64,041.90 | 1389 | 87,104.50 | 2428 | 48,252.24 | 1602 | 23,430.73 | 954 | 68,262.92 | 2351 | 291,092.28 | 8724 |

## Structured Notes — Issuer Classified by Moody's Rating
## Issuance Volume (US$ Million) Classified by Moody's Rating Category

| | Aaa | | Aa1/Aa2/Aa3 | | A1/A2/A3 | | Baa1/Baa2/Baa3 | | Others | | Total | |
|---|---|---|---|---|---|---|---|---|---|---|---|---|
| | Amount (US$m) | Issues | Amount (US$m) | Issues | Amount (US$m) | Issues | Amount (US$m) | Issues | Amount (US$m) | Issues | Amount (US$m) | Issues |
| 1994 | 1,682.82 | 32 | 5,672.90 | 133 | 2,747.75 | 89 | 1,807.16 | 26 | 2,481.70 | 115 | 14,392.33 | 36.44 |
| 1995 | 4,741.81 | 90 | 5,836.37 | 176 | 5,987.00 | 172 | 4,239.39 | 114 | 6,539.50 | 200 | 27,344.05 | 36.36 |
| 1996 | 9,398.40 | 189 | 17,980.56 | 426 | 9,563.96 | 389 | 3,139.71 | 211 | 7,839.54 | 363 | 47,922.16 | 30.37 |
| 1997 | 17,341.82 | 320 | 25,598.50 | 839 | 12,321.50 | 378 | 4,163.22 | 254 | 10,946.69 | 375 | 70,371.73 | 32.49 |
| 1998 | 21,309.16 | 435 | 26,377.11 | 698 | 8,626.64 | 313 | 2,381.24 | 257 | 7,812.71 | 131 | 66,506.86 | 36.26 |
| 1999 | 13,784.21 | 402 | 34,460.35 | 913 | 9,196.70 | 422 | 1,602.97 | 93 | 5,510.93 | 169 | 64,555.15 | 32.29 |
| Total | 68,258.21 | 1468 | 115,925.80 | 3185 | 48,443.54 | 1763 | 17,333.68 | 955 | 41,131.06 | 1353 | 291,092.28 | 33.37 |

*Notes:*
The above statistics are based on listed EMTN issues.

*Source:* Capital NET MTNWare www.capn.com.

**Exhibit 18.4**
**Structured Notes — Maturities of Structured Notes**

**Issuance Volume (US$ million) Classified by Original Maturity**

| | <1 years | | 1 years to 3 years | | 3 years to 5 years | | 5 years to 7 years | | 7 years to 10 years | | Over 10 years | | Total | |
|---|---|---|---|---|---|---|---|---|---|---|---|---|---|---|
| | Amount (US$m) | Issues | Amount (US$m) | Issues | Amount (US$m) | Issues | Amount (US$m) | Issues | Amount (US$m) | Issues | Amount (US$m) | Issues | Amount (US$m) | Issues |
| 1994 | 454.18 | 23 | 2,722.85 | 86 | 5,002.17 | 144 | 1,868.73 | 87 | 639.89 | 11 | 3,704.52 | 44 | 14,392.33 | 395 |
| 1995 | 433.74 | 29 | 1,926.08 | 64 | 4,350.94 | 121 | 5,414.72 | 243 | 1,144.45 | 33 | 14,074.12 | 262 | 27,344.05 | 752 |
| 1996 | 1,106.35 | 62 | 10,388.93 | 317 | 8,397.31 | 255 | 9,036.30 | 402 | 3,375.86 | 116 | 15,617.42 | 426 | 47,922.16 | 1578 |
| 1997 | 4,935.46 | 186 | 8,098.06 | 291 | 10,679.26 | 288 | 10,197.60 | 405 | 7,719.62 | 243 | 28,741.73 | 753 | 70,371.73 | 2166 |
| 1998 | 6,426.52 | 291 | 9,524.85 | 256 | 6,303.68 | 174 | 9,051.74 | 242 | 5,842.85 | 127 | 29,357.22 | 744 | 66,506.86 | 1834 |
| 1999 | 5,718.91 | 223 | 7,534.22 | 244 | 4,479.10 | 134 | 8,552.55 | 288 | 3,596.00 | 150 | 34,674.37 | 960 | 64,555.15 | 1999 |
| Total | 19,075.15 | 814 | 40,194.98 | 1258 | 39,212.46 | 1116 | 44,121.66 | 1667 | 22,318.67 | 680 | 126,169.38 | 3189 | 291,092.28 | 8724 |

*Notes:*
The above statistics are based on listed EMTN issues.

*Source:* Capital NET MTNWare www.capn.com.

- **Types of transactions** — there are a wide variety of transactions undertaken. **Exhibit 18.5** and **Exhibit 18.6** set out patterns of issuance.

---

**Exhibit 18.5**
**Structured Notes — Types of Issues (Number of Issues)**
**— Estimate 1**

**Structured Note Issuance by Product Type (# of securities sold)**

|                                | 1997  | 1998  | 98% Chg  | 1999  | 99% Chg  |
|--------------------------------|-------|-------|----------|-------|----------|
| Variable Principal Redemption  | 822   | 843   | 2.6%     | 1,041 | 23.5%    |
| Variable Interest Redemption   | 206   | 326   | 58.3%    | 288   | (11.7%)  |
| Inverse FRN                    | 366   | 291   | (20.5%)  | 193   | (33.7%)  |
| Step-up                        | 1,068 | 922   | (13.7%)  | 720   | (21.9%)  |
| Step-down                      | 182   | 236   | 29.7%    | 349   | 47.9%    |
| IAN                            | 111   | 99    | (10.8%)  | 34    | (65.7%)  |
| Range FRN                      | 148   | 181   | 22.3%    | 127   | (29.8%)  |
| Dual-indexed FRN               | 48    | 30    | (37.5%)  | 31    | 3.3%     |
| Deleveraged FRN                | 151   | 77    | (49.0%)  | 236   | 206.5%   |
| Ratchet FRN                    | 23    | 2     | (91.3%)  | 11    | 450.0%   |
| Multi-currency                 | 147   | 123   | (16.3%)  | 150   | 22.0%    |
| Miscellaneous                  | 156   | 81    | (48.1%)  | 100   | 23.5%    |
| Capped FRN                     | 44    | 4     | (90.9%)  | 56    | 1300.0%  |
| Total                          | 3,472 | 3,215 | (7.4%)   | 3,336 | 3.8%     |

*Notes:*
1. Statistics provided for the period January 1, 1997 through December 31, 1999, as of January 11, 2000. All statistics subject to change. All statistics are based on initial settlement date.
2. Statistics include all International, US Corporate, and US Government Agency Structured Notes.
3. Product-type classifications are fixed income structures recognized by Bloomberg, LP as "Structured Notes." Statistics are based on securities released for display on Bloomberg.

*Source:* Bloomberg. (Contact: Michael Miller, Bloomberg Financial Markets, in the US — 609-279-3459).

## Exhibit 18.6
## Structured Notes — Types of Issues (Number of Issues)
## — Estimate 2

| | 1994 Amount (US$ m) | Issues | 1995 Amount (US$ m) | Issues | 1996 Amount (US$ m) | Issues |
|---|---|---|---|---|---|---|
| FX-linked | 448.48 | 5 | 6,407.51 | 143 | 12,689.51 | 350 |
| Credit-linked | 0 | 0 | 0 | 0 | 560.55 | 11 |
| Equity-linked | 256.27 | 4 | 163.94 | 23 | 2,015.53 | 80 |
| Commodity-linked | 75 | 1 | 65 | 2 | 76.67 | 7 |
| Interest Rate-linked | 13,544.69 | 383 | 20,707.60 | 584 | 32,479.90 | 1129 |
| Other | 67.89 | 2 | 0 | 0 | 100 | 1 |
| Total | 14,392.33 | 395 | 27,344.05 | 752 | 47,922.16 | 1578 |

| | 1997 Amount (US$ m) | Issues | 1998 Amount (US$ m) | Issues | 1999 Amount (US$ m) | Issues |
|---|---|---|---|---|---|---|
| FX-linked | 14,723.55 | 508 | 20,561.31 | 766 | 8,673.97 | 539 |
| Credit-linked | 2,317.06 | 38 | 4,397.98 | 111 | 2,523.87 | 101 |
| Equity-Linked | 4,978.08 | 202 | 9,586.28 | 260 | 15,764.78 | 543 |
| Commodity-linked | 45.07 | 4 | 75.14 | 3 | 0 | 0 |
| Interest Rate-linked | 48,204.78 | 1412 | 31,845.81 | 691 | 37,487.86 | 815 |
| Other | 103.19 | 2 | 40.35 | 3 | 104.67 | 1 |
| Total | 70,371.73 | 2166 | 66,506.86 | 1834 | 64,555.15 | 1999 |

*Notes:*
Methodology: the above statistics are based on listed EMTNs for which the structure is known. The classification used is as follows:

***Issue Groups***

*Commodity-linked* — Category that groups notes where interest or redemption is linked to the performance of a specific commodity or commodity index.

*Credit-linked* — Notes where interest and/or redemption payments are dependent on a specific credit event not occurring.

*FX-linked* — Notes where interest or redemption is linked to an exchange rate. Includes the following issue types:

1. Dual currency
2. Currency-linked
3. Redemption: currency-linked
4. FX range factor

5.  Reverse multi-currency
6.  Reverse dual currency

*Equity-linked* — Interest or redemption is linked to the performance of a specific share or index. Includes the following issue types:
1.  Convertible to equity
2.  Convertible preference shares
3.  Equity-linked
4.  Equity index-linked
5.  Redemption: equity index-linked
6.  Reverse convertible to equity

*Interest rate-linked* — Interest/redemption is linked to a specific interest-rate benchmark or bond. Includes the issue types:
1.  Collared FRN
2.  Capped FRN
3.  Convertible to bonds
4.  Constrained dual basis
5.  Optional basis conversion
6.  Yield-linked
7.  LIBOR-linked
8.  Swap rate-linked
9.  Redemption: swap rate-linked
10. Reverse Hybrid
11. FRN/FX
12. FRN/Step-Up
13. Floored FRN
14. FX/FRN
15. FX/Step-up FRN
16. FX/Reverse FRN
17. FX/Reverse step FRN
18. Periodic cap
19. Interest range factor
20. Reverse convertible to bonds
21. Reverse FRN
22. Reverse step-up FRN
23. Step down
24. Step-up
25. Step-up FRN
26. Step-down FRN
27. Step-up/FRN
28. Step-up-down hybrid
29. Triple basis
30. Zero dual basis

| *Issue Types:* | |
|---|---|
| **Capped FRN** | A floating rate note with a maximum rate capping the interest payable. |
| **Collared FRN** | Floating rate note with minimum and maximum rates limiting the interest payable. |
| **Constrained dual basis** | A note that switches from one interest payment type to another during the life of the note with a cap, collar, or floor during the floating rate period. The two interest types can be any combination of a floating-rate period with either a fixed-rate period or zero-coupon period. |
| **Convertible to bonds** | Note that may be converted to one or more different bonds. |
| **Convertible to equity** | Note that may be converted to shares. |
| **Credit-linked** | Note where interest and/or principal payments are dependent on certain credit events not occurring. |
| **Currency-linked** | Note bearing interest at a rate linked to an exchange rate. |
| **Dual currency** | The redemption amount is payable in a currency other than the currency of issue. |
| **Equity index-linked** | A note that pays interest linked to the performance of a specified index. Examples include stock market indices, baskets of stocks, and funds. |
| **Equity range factor** | Accrual notes and knock-in/outs where interest/redemption is linked to the movement of a share or equity index. Examples include accrual notes and knock-ins/outs. |
| **Equity-linked** | Note that pays a rate of interest linked to the performance of a specific share. |
| **Fixed rate** | Issue bearing a fixed rate of interest. |
| **Floored FRN** | A floating-rate note with a floor minimising the interest payable. |
| **FRN** | Issue bearing a floating rate of interest. |
| **FRN/FX** | A floating-rate note that becomes a note bearing a fixed rate of interest after a specified date. |
| **FRN/Step Up** | An issue that initially pays interest on a floating-rate basis and then pays interest at an ascending fixed-rate scale "stepping up" on the dates specified. |
| **FX Range Factor** | Accrual notes and knock-in/outs where interest/redemption is linked to the movement of an exchange rate. |
| **FX/FRN** | A fixed-rate note that converts to a floating-rate note on a specified date. |

| | |
|---|---|
| **FX/Reverse FRN** | A fixed-rate note that converts to a reverse floating rate note on a specified date. |
| **FX/Reverse step-up FRN** | A fixed-rate note that changes to a reverse step-up floating rate after a specified date. |
| **Interest range factor** | Accrual notes and knock-in/outs where interest/ redemption is linked to the movement of an interest-rate benchmark. |
| **Miscellaneous** | Notes that cannot be categorised within another issue type; that is, an issue with both structured interest and redemption amounts. |
| **Optional basis conversion** | A note where the issuer or the noteholders have the option to convert interest payments from one basis to another; for example, fixed to floating. |
| **Periodic cap** | Notes that pay a floating rate of interest subject to a changing cap. |
| **Redemption: Currency-linked** | Notes with a redemption amount linked to an exchange rate. |
| **Redemption: Equity index-linked** | Notes with a redemption amount linked to the performance of a specified equity index. Examples include stock market indices, baskets of stocks, and funds. |
| **Redemption: Swap Rate-linked** | Notes with a redemption amount linked to a swap rate. |
| **Reverse convertible to bonds** | Typically high coupon notes where redemption will be the lesser of the value of a specified bond or basket of bonds, and the par value of the note. |
| **Reverse convertible to equity** | Typically high coupon notes that will be converted to a share, basket, or stock index if the equity price is less than the par value of the note. |
| **Reverse dual currency** | A note that pays interest in a currency different to that of issue. Redemption is in the currency of issue. |
| **Reverse FRN** | A note that pays interest as a given rate minus the floating index; for example, 3% — 3-month JPY LIBOR. |
| **Reverse hybrid** | Any reverse floating rate variation, which cannot be categorised in a separate issue type. |
| **Reverse multi-currency** | A note that pays interest in several different currencies. Redemption is in the currency of issue. |
| **Reverse step-up FRN** | A reverse FRN where the given rate increases on specified dates, increasing the interest payable. |
| **Step-down** | A note bearing interest on a descending scale, "stepping down" on the dates specified. |
| **Step-down FRN** | A floating-rate note where the margin decreases on |

| | the dates specified, causing the interest rate payable to "step down". |
|---|---|
| **Step-up** | A note that pays interest on an ascending fixed-rate scale "stepping up" on the dates specified. |
| **Step-up FRN** | A note bearing interest at increasing floating rates specified by the issuer. |
| **Step-up-down Hybrid** | An irregular step-up/down variation that cannot be categorised under other type. For example, a coupon that increases in some interest periods and decreases in others. |
| **Swap rate-linked** | A note that pays a rate of interest linked to swap rates. |
| **Triple basis** | A note that has three different interest payment types during the life of the note. Examples include FRN/FX/FRN, FX/Collared FRN/FX, or FRN/Reverse FRN/FX. |
| **Unknown** | The nature of the note cannot be determined. |
| **Yield-linked** | A note that pays a rate of interest linked to the yield on a specified security — typically a bond. |
| **Zero-coupon** | A note that pays no interest and is issued at a discount from its principal amount. |
| **Zero dual basis** | A note that switches from one interest payment type to another during the life of the note. The two interest types can be any combination of a zero-coupon period with either a fixed-rate or floating-rate period. |

*Additional Notes:*
- Many notes have interest payments linked to both an exchange rate and an index, for example. In these cases the following priorities will be given (that is, if the interest is linked to an index and an exchange rate, then it will be categorized as index linked):
  1. Index-linked
  2. Equity-linked
  3. Yield-linked
  4. Currency-linked
  5. Swap Rate-linked
  6. Range factor
  7. LIBOR-linked
  8. FRN/Fixed/Zero

For the most part in uncertain cases, the least common issue type is selected.

*Source:* Capital NET MTNWare www.capn.com.

## 2.3 Issuance Formats

The range of issuance format for structured notes is very varied. They range from public registered debt transactions, public eurobond transactions, quasi-public transactions, such as Section 144a issues, MTN issues, and pure private placements. In the US and some European domestic markets, they have also taken the form of bank note, bank deposit note, and bank certificate of deposit issues. The issuance has not been confined to term transactions. There have been structured note transactions involving commercial paper, both in domestic markets (US commercial paper),[4] as well as international markets (primarily, in euro commercial paper form).[5]

The early activity, particularly that in the period 1985 to 1990 (see discussion below in the context of market evolution), was focused on public transactions, both in the eurobond and in key domestic markets, including the US domestic market. However, over time, the issuance format has shifted to the issue of structured notes primarily under the rubric of MTN programs, both euro MTN and US domestic, SEC registered programs, and pure private placements.

The movement away from the public to the private market reflects a variety of factors:

- The move towards a high level of customization to individual investor requirements.
- The lack of concern about the liquidity associated with a public transaction. This reflected a greater level of acceptance of the capacity to obtain liquidity from the dealer community as and when needed (this issue is considered in detail in a later section). It also reflects the shorter maturity profile that to a large extent vitiates the need for the equivalent need for liquidity.[6]
- The desire to avoid public scrutiny of the structures based on a desire to avoid competitors reverse engineering products and to preserve competitive position for as long as possible.

---

[4] For example, see the issue of PIPs (Performance-indexed Paper) undertaken through Salomon Brothers that entailed the issue of US$-denominated interest-bearing commercial paper linked to currency values; see Kimelman, Nancy, Callahan, James, and Demafeliz, Salvador (September 23, 1986) *Performance Indexed Paper: A Foreign Currency Indexed Money Market Instrument*; Salomon Brothers Inc., Bond Market Research, New York.

[5] For example, see the issue of MIRACLES issued by SEK through Nomura Securities entailing the issues of euro commercial paper with embedded derivative components in response to investor requests; see "SEK Faith In MIRACLE Pays Off" (December 1988) *Corporate Finance* 36.

[6] As discussed below, cause and effect are very hard to determine in this regard. A number of investors would argue that the shorter maturity *is the result of the absence of liquidity* and a concession regarding the illiquidity of these securities.

- The speed with which issues can be undertaken under MTN programs or private placements avoiding potential delays in undertaking transactions.
- The overall flexibility in dealing under a MTN or private placement format rather than public market framework.

The MTN issuance framework is ideally suited to the issuance for a wide variety of reasons. The MTN structure is very flexible and while not originally designed for this purpose lends itself to the issue of structured note products.[7]

In a regulated context such as the US domestic market, the MTN format can encompass a Section 415 shelf registration. This enables securities to be issued for a specified period after the effective date of the registration without the requirement for a registration to be undertaken at the time of issue of each security offering. This enhances the speed with which structured notes can be issued without sacrificing the protection offered by and investor requirement for (in terms of investment eligibility) a registered security. In the eurobond market, the MTN program is structured within a format that allows individual security issues undertaken to satisfy the criteria for and achieve listing on a stock exchange that expands the range of investor who can purchase structured notes.

Current practice is to ensure that the documentation for a MTN program allows issuance up to the maximum amount allowed *in a wide variety of security formats*. The typical language in use would encompass the issue of not only traditional forms of fixed income instruments (fixed- and floating-rate bonds with a range of maturities including perpetual securities), but also structured or hybrid securities. The structures allowed would typically include put and call options or interest and/or principal amounts linked and contingent upon financial asset prices. Asset classes permitted would include currencies, interest rates/ prices of debt instruments, commodity prices (including commodity price indexes), equity index values or the price of specific equity stocks, and (increasingly) credit spread or credit default risk. Older MTN programs that do not enable the issuer the requisite flexibility have over recent years progressively been restructured to provide this scope for structure note issuance.

A key component of the flexibility afforded to issuers, investors, and investment bankers by MTN programs is the capacity to issue notes in limited volumes. Most programs allow issues in minimum amounts commencing at

---

[7]  For a discussion of the evolution of MTN issuance frameworks, see Crabbe, Leland E., Payne, Joyce A. and Schoenbeck, Michael "Anatomy of the MTN Market I" (1994) *Capital Market Strategies* Issue 1 13-21; Crabbe, Leland E., Payne, Joyce A., and Schoenbeck, Michael "Anatomy of the MTN Market II" (1994) *Capital Market Strategies* Issue 2 25-31; Fisher, Mark "MTNs Are Dead. Long Live DIPS (Or Is It CONs?)" (March 1993) *Corporate Finance*, 27-33; Irvine, Steven "The Sub-LIBOR Struggles of Minati Misra" (January 1997) *Euromoney* 30-33.

would otherwise make certain types of issues uneconomic because the fixed cost of undertaking a particular issue for a small amount would be greater than the funding cost saving achievable.

The economics of an MTN issue are also generally favourable with the fact that the program expenses can be amortized over a large volume of issuance *under the terms of the program*, which significantly reduces the cost of such activity on a per issue basis. The revolving nature of MTN programs that allows the issue and repayment and further issuance to replace maturing transactions within the program framework is also helpful in reducing the costs of the program.

The role played by MTN programs in facilitating structured note issuance should not be underestimated.[8] Anecdotal evidence suggests that the level of structured note issuance as a percentage of total issuance under MTN programs for sovereign entities and financial institutions is high, averaging around 30-40% of total issuance.

### 2.4    Relationship of Structured Notes to Asset/Derivative Markets

The relationship between the structured note securities and the underlying asset and derivative markets is important. This reflects the primary fact that the structured note design has as its central focus the creation of exposure to the price movements *in the relevant asset market* consistent with the specifications of the investor.

This inherent relationship dictates that the range of instruments available and the depth and liquidity of the underlying assets and derivative components determine the limits of the types of structured note products that can be created. In essence, as structured notes represent a mechanism by which the desired exposure to the asset is created, the security itself reflects the nature of the asset market.

This relationship and its limitations do not derogate from the important role of structured note markets. The availability of a primary and secondary market in structured notes assists in enhancing the liquidity and depth of the market in the underlying product. The fact that structured notes allow the participation of entities who may not be able to or may be otherwise restricted in their participation in these markets assists in improving the depth of the underlying asset and derivative markets. This factor is evidenced by the fact that during various periods demand for derivative and ultimately asset transactions required

---

[8]    In 1993 alone, Federal Reserve statistics indicate that 31% of issuance under *corporate MTN programs in the US* was in the form of structured notes; see Crabbe, Leland E. and Argilagos, Joseph D. "Anatomy of the Structured Note Market" (Fall 1994) *Journal of Applied Corporate Finance* 85-98 at 86.

in the design of structured note products have substantially dominated the level of activity in the relevant asset market. This phenomenon has been experienced for both short and extended periods of time.

# 3.    Key Market Dynamics

## 3.1    Rationale

The rationale of structured notes relates to the flexibility of these instruments and the capacity of these securities to be utilized to achieve a broad range of advantages.[9] These advantages and benefits are primarily investor-oriented, reflecting the underlying dynamics of the market. These factors include the following:

- **Regulatory factors** — these structures can be used to overcome regulatory restrictions on the entry by certain investors into derivative transactions or markets.
- **Credit enhancement** — the notes are typically engineered to provide a degree of credit enhancement to the investor in relation to certain types of transaction, primarily derivative transactions involving market price-based mutual credit exposure, through use of the note principal and cash flows as collateral.
- **Customization** — the ability to design notes to enable capture, with a high degree of precision and accuracy, a market view and position in anticipation of the expectation. This includes the capacity to structure the exposure using both symmetric/linear products (forwards) and asymmetric or nonlinear products (options) to define the risk-reward profile sought.
- **Leverage** — the capacity (if desired) to create leverage (both positive and negative) within the note structure to increase the sensitivity to the anticipated market price fluctuations.
- **Transaction costs** — the ability through the use of structured notes to lower transaction costs provide cost savings for investors.

## 3.2    Market Participants

The market for structured notes includes the following among its major participants:

- Investors
- Issuers
- Investment banks, securities dealers/traders and other financial institutions

---

[9]    See discussion in Chapter 1.

*   Arbitrageurs.

Each group of market participants has different objectives and the dynamics of their market participation is characterized by different motivations.

### 3.2.1  Investors

Structured note investors include a broad and varied range of market participants. Investors include institutional investors, professional funds managers, banks/financial institutions, retail investors, and corporations. There are significant geographic differences in terms of the type of investor and the principal motivations for participation.

The US market is dominated by mutual funds, investment companies, and the trust departments of banks.[10] Other key investors include insurance companies, pension funds, as well as total return or hedge fund investors. The principal motivation for these investors appears to be seeking investments that provide returns and exposures to markets in a manner not readily available from traditional fixed interest investment products. Overcoming regulatory or credit barriers to derivative transactions is also a component of that participation.

The type of transactions entered into varies significantly. A substantial component of the US investor universe is money market investors whose traditional focus is short-term instruments such as certificates of deposits (CDs) or commercial paper. These investors seek structured products in order to achieve incremental returns. This is so particularly during periods when the yield curve is strongly positive in slope and absolute rate levels are low. The search for incremental return is constrained to a large degree by the dominating concern to ensure stability of capital values. These investors will typically seek structured investments with minimal credit risk (AA/AAA credits), short maturities (up to 2 years), and strong liquidity characteristics. The notes structured for these investors will generally not place principal at risk but rather will allow coupon to be risked in the search for additional return. The structures are generally also not highly leveraged and ideally pay some coupon on the funds invested. Examples of structures targeted at these investors are the callable note, IAR structures, as well as the collared and range FRN structures. Linkages to currency, commodity, or equity markets are rare.

An additional group of structured note investors seek return enhancements. These are income-oriented investors who are willing to sell options with the premium being embedded within the income stream to provide the target level

---

[10]  For a discussion of the US market, see Crabbe, Leland E., and Argilagos, Joseph D. "Anatomy of the Structured Note Market" (Fall 1994) *Journal of Applied Corporate Finance* 85-98; Peng, Scott and Dattatreya, Ravi (1994) *The Structured Note Market*; Probus Publications, Chicago at Chapter 1.

of earnings. The term of the investments is typically longer with maturities of up to five to seven years being feasible. The risk tolerance of this group of investors is not substantial and favours principal protection and limited degrees of leverage. Types of instruments that have attractions for these investors include many of the interest rate-linked structures such as CMT products, callable debt products, inverse FRNs, as well as collared or capped FRN structures. Some currency risk may be contemplated but is not likely to be a significant component of the investment strategy in relation to structured products.

The most aggressive group of investors in structured notes encompasses total return investors willing to adopt higher risk-reward profiles. This group includes total return mutual funds and hedge funds. The principal characteristics of this demand are a high tolerance for leverage and willingness to risk principal to generate returns. The asset classes utilized are varied in line with price expectations. Linkage to currencies, commodities, equity, and credit markets are frequently to be found. The maturities of the notes are generally short—up to three years with a strong concentration in the 1-year spectrum. This maturity preference is consistent with the focus on return and is designed to create the *maximum* sensitivity to the relevant market sector over a concentrated time horizon to allow the full value of the anticipated price move to be captured. The nature of the investment strategy also dictates a higher need for liquidity to either lock in the gain or limit exposure to loss through the sale of the investment.

Two other investor groups require special consideration: index funds and retail investors.

A significant level of demand for structured products derives from investors seeking to replicate an index on the relevant assets. In a number of cases, the investor is seeking exposure to an asset class, such as commodities, where it would be difficult to replicate the index. In other cases, the investor may be prevented from entry into derivative transactions or may desire to minimize the tracking or rebalancing risks associated with replicating the index with an investment portfolio of assets or derivatives contracts. Investment in securities with embedded forwards on the relevant index allows these investors to replicate indexes more efficiently.

The second investor group is retail investors who may seek to capture higher returns or enhance yields within moderate risk constraints. This demand is either met through structured notes targeted to individual investor accounts usually entailing the issue of publicly registered offerings or, more efficiently, in the form of bank notes or CDs with embedded derivative elements. The second structure is originated through the purchase by the relevant bank of a structured note in the required form that is then matched with an offsetting issue of bank paper (in the required format) that shifts the structured note exposure to the investor. This pattern of activity is evident in the US domestic market for instruments such as callable bonds where these banks have leveraged their retail distribution into originating and underwriting efforts with major issuers of structured notes such as the major government agencies.

The international investor base for structured notes is similar to those in the US domestic market but with a number of significant differences.

European investor demand is less institutionally focused than the US market.[11] The market exhibits a stronger retail orientation including participation from private banks, principally on behalf of high net worth individuals. The participation from mutual funds is less prominent although in some markets, such as the SICAVs in continental Europe, the demand can, from time to time, be significant.

The investment rationale is different. The need to overcome investment constraints is significantly more important than in the US. Restrictions in entry into derivative transactions, investment regulations that limit investments to *listed securities*, and the credit constraints on some investors are dominant considerations. The investor requirement for total return is also a strong element in using structured notes to create exposures to various market asset and prices in an appropriate form. This encourages a relatively broad range of structured note products to be designed and marketed into these markets.

The retail participation, both direct and indirect through the continental universal banks servicing this market, also favours the use of public issues or listed private placements (within MTN formats) to allow purchase by this group of investors. The nature of the investment base dictates maturities in the medium range (up to three to five years) although shorter terms are favoured for structures designed to have high exposure to market price movements. The need for secondary market liquidity is relatively lower as investors tend to hold the investment to final maturity.

Asian participation can be segmented into Japanese demand and other Asian demand. Both market sectors are interesting segments and include wider participation by banks and financial institutions (as investors in their own right) and corporate investors than in the comparable markets in Europe and North America.

The Japanese market is dominated by the major institutional investors, primarily insurance companies. The bank trust departments and the mutual funds or their equivalents are also significant investors.[12]

The dominant investor requirement is for yield against which capital or

---

[11] For a discussion of the European market, see Dunbar, Nicholas "Medium Term Notes" (January 1998) *Futures & Options World* 50; Mahtani, Arun "European Insurers Shun Structured Notes" (February 13, 1999 *International Financing Review* Issue 1270 85.

[12] For a discussion of the Japanese market, see Rutter, James "SEK's Japanese Dilemma" (June 1997) *Euromoney* 28.

principal risk is traded off. The requirement for return is prompted by a variety of pressures. The relatively low level of Japanese interest rates encourages the assumption of risk to enhance returns from fixed interest portfolios. The activity of Japanese investors in several periods in the 1980s and most recently since 1995 reflects this pressure. The need for return is also based on the structure and competitive demand for high current income (which in the case of the life insurance industry, at least, forms the basis of bonuses paid). This higher return is sought to achieved through assumption of asset price risk (debt, equity, currency, credit, and/or commodity), and/or derivative risk (usually in the form of sold optionality). The willingness to risk capital and also coupon income is high. The tolerance for leverage is also significant resulting in often aggressive design of structured notes. Retail participation has become a significant factor particularly in products that are yield enhanced. For example, dual-currency bonds or FRNs with above market guaranteed returns deriving from sold optionality have retail appeal.

The market is tolerant of medium to longer maturities (up to 10 years), although as with other market segments there is a concentration at the short end of the maturity spectrum. Reasonable levels of secondary market trading in structured notes are evident from time to time. For example, secondary market activity in range FRNs products was very active when increases in interest rates caused the coupon on these notes to set at zero. This reflected investor reluctance to hold nonincome generating investments that were disposed of at a capital loss. Similarly, large scale sales of dual currency structures by both retail and institutional investors were evident when a weaker yen prompted profit taking on these structures.

A significant element of the Japanese market for structured notes is the participation of trading companies and corporate groups. These investors utilize structured notes as a mechanism for enhancing the yield on portfolios of liquid assets. The often large portfolios of cash or near-cash investments maintained by many of these organizations as a means for enhancing their financial flexibility have, historically, seen the adoption of aggressive, return-oriented investment strategies being utilized to increase the yield on this cash. This has been particularly evident during periods of low nominal and positively sloped yield curves. This activity can be viewed as part of the "zaitech" activities of these entities.[13] The structured note demand from corporate groups and trading companies is often shorter in maturity (one to two years) than that from other sectors of this market segment.

An interesting feature of the investment demand from this sector is the

---

[13] See Das, Satyajit "Key Trends in Corporate Treasury Management" *Corporate Finance*, Euromoney Publications (April 1992) 40-43; and (May 1992) 33-39.

appetite for credit risk in the context of structured note products. Unlike other market segments, particularly Europe and North America, the Japanese market exhibits a greater tolerance for higher degrees of credit risk in structured note issuers as a means for boosting investment returns. This tolerance is limited, however, to well-known issuers (typically, household consumer brand names).

The remaining Asian demand is primarily from Korea, Hong Kong, Indonesia, and, to a lower degree, from Malaysia and Thailand. This demand is centred on banks/financial institutions and corporate groups, as well as high net worth individuals/families, either acting in their own right or through private companies. The demand is yield driven seeking return enhancement in return for assuming market risks. The demand has created certain problems as a number of investors have made purchases of structured notes without a full understanding of the market risk profile of such instruments. Losses sustained on some such investments have resulted in litigation.[14] Asian demand has declined significantly following the Asian monetary crisis in July 1997.

### 3.2.2 Issuers

As noted above, there is strong bias towards high-rated issuers in the market for structured notes favoring the required separation of credit and market risk.[15] The major issuers include sovereigns, quasi-sovereigns, supra-nationals, multilateral development agencies, banks/financial institutions, and multi-national corporations.

The issuers, provided they meet the relevant rating quality threshold, only require the capacity to issue the types of instruments sought by investors to participate in the market. Other requirements include the capacity to respond rapidly to investor enquires and the existence of competitive funding targets.

For the issuers, the major incentive is the ability to generate lower funding costs and also diversify the base of investors in their securities. Issuer participation is a competitive process with issuer's competing with other issuers in terms of funding targets and speed and responsiveness to investor requirements to undertake issues of structured notes.

An interesting aspect of the issuance by highly rated opportunistic borrowers is the increased portion of their financing requirements that have been generated from this type of funding. There is increased evidence that structured note issuance has in recent times constituted the major source of their fundraising.

---

[14] See Oliver, Charles "Once Bitten, Twice Shy" (June 1995) *Corporate Finance* 23-26.
[15] For example, Federal Reserve statistics indicate that over 97% of structured notes issued in the US market are by issuer's rated A or above; see Peng, Scott and Dattatreya, Ravi (1994) *The Structured Note Market*; Probus Publications, Chicago 8.

This raises two significant issues:

• The impact of changes in investor attitudes to these types of securities (such as the change in market conditions evidenced in 1995) on capacity to raise finance. These types of market events may have the effect of either increasing the cost of funding for these issuers or increasing the difficulty of accessing the required quantum of funding or both.
• The shorter maturity that characterizes structured notes generally. This factor results in a significant and growing concentration of refinancing risk in the portfolios of these issuers.

There is a distinctive pattern of issuer participation that has a geographic basis. The US market segment is dominated by the government agencies. Issuance by this group makes up around 70% of all structured note issuance in this market. The principal issuers are:

• Federal Home Loan Bank System (FHLB)
• Student Loan Marketing Association (SLMA or Sallie Mae)
• Federal Farm Credit Bank System (FFCB)
• Federal National Mortgage Association (FNMA or Fannie Mae)
• Federal Home Loan Mortgage Corporation (FHLMC or Freddie Mac).

Each of these entities are implicitly or explicitly rated AAA, based on their government ownership and implied guarantee of the US government.[16] Financial institution issuers are the next important group of issuers.

The bias to the government agencies and financial institutions reflects a range of factors:

• The implied government support in the case of the agency issuers expands the range of investors in these products.
• The large financing requirements of these issuers allow these entities to readily meet investor demands on an ongoing basis. In contrast, corporate financing requirements may not be as flexible, making it more difficult for nonfinancial corporations to participate in structured note issuance in a consistent manner.
• The short- to medium-term maturity concentration in structured note securities is more consistent with the requirements of these issuers.
• The high level of expertise (most evident in the case of financial institutions)

---

[16] For a discussion of the role of these government agencies, see Fabozzi, Frank J. and Fabozzi, T. Dessa "Treasury And Agency Securities" in Fabozzi, Frank J. and Fabozzi, T. Dessa (editors) (1995) *The Handbook of Fixed Income Securities—Fourth Edition*; Irwin, Chicago at Chapter 7.

- The high level of expertise (most evident in the case of financial institutions) in derivatives trading required to understand and ensure the absence of market risk to the issuer is not widely available outside dealers and large issuers with sophisticated treasury operations.

The type of issuer in international markets is somewhat different to that in the US. While the credit quality threshold and the key competences are similar, the major issuers are drawn from a relatively small group of opportunistic borrowers encompassing sovereign or quasi-sovereign issuers, supra national, particularly multi-lateral development agencies such as the World Bank, banks, and selected nonfinancial corporations. The US agencies are not in contrast significant issuers of structured notes outside the US domestic segment of the market.

Two trends are evident in term of the international issuer base in structured notes:

- **Increasing issuance by banks/financial institutions** — increasingly, major derivatives dealers (active in arranging structured note issues) have used their *own balance sheet* to issue structured notes.[17] This is often done in the form of MTN issues or private placements. This development is driven by the desire of the dealers to *internalize* all aspects of the structured note process, increase the speed of issuance, maintain confidentiality, and preserve proprietary structures.
- **Increased issuance by special-purpose arbitrage vehicles** — a significant volume of structured note issues is undertaken by special-purpose repackaging vehicle.[18] These special-purpose arbitrage vehicles now actively compete with conventional issuers for structured issuance opportunities. The special-purpose arbitrage vehicles are structures such as Citicorp Alternative Investment Strategies group's Alpha, Beta, and Centauri structures.[19] These structures are all highly (AAA) rated, the issuers quite separate from the parent bank. They issue structured notes to raise the lowest cost available funds. The funds are then reinvested in a variety of assets to lock in a positive funding spread. These issuers because of their ability to respond rapidly to issuance request and flexibility in terms of types of issue structures have become major issuers of structured notes.

---

[17] See Rutter, James "Testing New Ideas In-house" (February 1998) *Euromoney* 28.

[18] See Chapter 1.

[19] See "The Big ESI" (November 24, 1993) IFR Swaps Issue 45 1-2; Clifton, Kieran "Best User Of EMTNS: Beta Finance Corporations" (June 1996) Euromoney 80-81; Lee, Peter "MTNs: Citicorps's New Constellation" (November 1996) *Euromoney* 14-16; Rutter, James "Repackaging Of All Kinds Of Credits" (July 1997) *Euromoney* 29.

### 3.2.3   Investment Banks

Investment banks, securities dealers and traders, and other banks/financial institutions play an important element in facilitating the market in structured notes. These entities provide the following functions:

- Identification of investor demand.
- Design of the security to meet the investor's requirements.
- Identification and eliciting the participation of issuers on acceptable terms.
- Executing the construction of the security and the design and hedging of the derivative elements.
- Documenting the issue.
- Providing secondary market liquidity in the security through market making as required.

A modest number of financial institutions provide the full range of services and can be called active participants in the process. They include the major US investment banks, a number of US money centre banks, principally through their security dealing/merchant banking operations, the UK/European universal banks, and the Japanese securities companies.

The pattern of participation is interesting. It reflects two factors: firstly, an investor or placement/distribution bias, and, secondly, a derivatives trading focus. The participation in structured notes design, trading, and placement reflects one or other emphasis.

For some participants, the structured note product is a natural extension of the process of placing and distributing securities to an established investor client base. The demand for customized product requires these institutions to seek to design and package the security by combining the relevant elements from other market counterparties as and when required. In some cases, this created the incentive to enhance the institution's capabilities in the relevant area, most likely derivatives trading, to support the activity and to capture a larger share of earnings from the transaction. For other participants, their capability in derivatives technology, which facilitated the structuring of these securities, allowed them to market product to potential investors. In a number of cases, this allowed these institutions to develop their placement operations and expand the range of their investment banking/underwriting activities.

The development of the structured note market with its sustained and strong growth made it a profitable component of the capital market activities of these institutions through the early 1990s. The lack of transparency of pricing and the rewards for innovation, trading, and structuring skill allowed these participants to, in effect, command economic rents and returns that were simply not available from traditional distribution and derivatives business that were increasingly commoditized.

opportunistic funding practices to seek to capture the profits of financial institutions actively packaging these complex debt/derivative packages in an effort to further reduce borrowing costs, albeit at the expense of an increased risk profile.

This latter type of approach is exemplified by SEK who in late 1989 entered into arrangements with a specialist risk management consultancy firm, Westminster Equity, to initially, analyze, and subsequently to design and manage suitable risk positions utilizing dynamic hedging and risk management techniques. The focus was to assume the risk either for the term of the transaction or for a bridging period after which the exposure would be hedged with a market counterparty, presumably on terms more favorable than that available when the transaction was initially entered into.

Utilizing this approach, SEK was prepared to enter into transactions whereby the borrower issued debt instruments with embedded derivative elements as required by investors. The major difference was that instead of immediately immunizing itself from the risk of the derivative structure by simultaneous execution of a swap that passed the risks of derivative elements onto a financial institution, SEK, in conjunction with Westminster Equity, assumed the risk of the position and sought to manage it dynamically. The major advantages to SEK was the capacity to generate the funding and significant margins under LIBOR (claimed to be in the range of 200-300bps below LIBOR).

This approach, which essentially seeks to disintermediate the financial institutions from the structuring and risk management role in these types of transaction, has not been adopted by a large number of borrowers, presumably, because of the increased risks involved.[20]

### 3.2.4  Arbitrageurs

The final category of participant is the pure arbitrager, usually an investor or trader, seeking to profit from pricing discrepancies. The major pricing differences sought to be identified and then arbitraged is the pricing of the structured note as the sum of its individual components versus its current market price. Where a price difference is identified the arbitrageur would purchase or sell the structured note and hedge its own exposure by trading in the components to replicate the instrument.

The opportunity for such arbitrage occurs with surprising frequency, particularly in volatile market conditions. Under these conditions, investors seeking to sell or, less frequently, purchase particular notes will incorrectly price the notes, allowing this type of activity. A major by-product of this activity is the

---

[20]  See Das, Satyajit (1994) *Swaps and Financial Derivatives*; LBC Information Services, Sydney, McGraw-Hill, Chicago at Chapter 19.

repackaging and asset swap activity in the secondary market described in detail below. In addition to the repackagers, primarily, investment banks and dealers, there are investors and traders who specialise in trading these instruments to capture the arbitrage margin available as an enhanced return on investment funds for their own account.

These participants play an economically important role in the structured note markets in providing liquidity in secondary market trading and also in ensuring the boundary values for these notes based on their arbitrage based component valuation.

## 4.   Market Phases

The market for structured notes has evolved through a number of distinct phases.[21] The periods identified are somewhat arbitrary and general. However, they allow a useful analysis of broad market trends and patterns.

The market phases identifiable are as follows:[22]

- Development (up to 1985).
- Growth (1986 to 1989).
- Proliferation (1990-1994).
- Market distress (1994-1995).
- Recovery (1995-1997).
- Commoditization (1998+).

As already discussed, the market for structured notes can be divided into a traditional and modern period. The market phases identified relate to modern structured notes. The issue of more traditional structured notes, particularly convertible/equity-linked securities and conventional callable securities, follows a more consistent pattern. This reflects the maturity of the products, the level of market acceptance of the instruments, and the more generic structures involved.

Modern structured notes can be traced to transactions such as dual-currency securities that emerged originally in the Swiss bond market in the middle 1970s. The issues undertaken during the early phase were significantly less custom designed than structured notes available today. The essential element of specific

---

[21] See, generally, Ireland, Louise, "Designer Debt" (January 1990) *Corporate Finance*, Euromoney Publications 22-24; Brady, Simon, "Investors Get Into Embeddos'" (July 1991) *Supplement to Euromoney* 3-20; Burchett, Shannonand Turner, Chris "How To Cut Funding Costs And Please Investors" (September 1994) *Corporate Finance* 46-49.

[22] This evolutionary history owes something to but is not identical to Peng, Scott and Dattatreya, Ravi (1994) *The Structured Note Market*; Probus Publications, Chicago at 13,14.

engineering of the security to introduce the risk exposure is evident. However, the separation of credit and market risk or the isolation of the issuer from the market risk of the structure is not present in these early structures.

The late 1970s and early 1980s also saw experimentation with commodity price-linked structured bonds, both in the public and private bond markets. These issues were primarily by commodity producers seeking to trade off upside price potential in return for lower funding costs. The structures were hedged against underlying commodity production and sales. The purchasers were either speculators seeking to directly capture commodity price rises or investors allocating investment capital to *real* assets and away from monetary or financial assets to preserve purchasing power in a period of high inflation and negative real interest returns.

This particular market phase covers the period up to around 1985. This phase can be termed the development period. The volume of transactions is low and the transactions infrequent. The nascent state of derivatives markets also limited the structuring and design possibilities significantly.

Around 1985, the confluence of a number of factors allowed acceleration in the growth of the market for structured notes. These included:

- The increasing availability of derivative products, initially in interest rates and currencies.
- Emergence of investor interest, primarily from Europe and Japan, for customized investment products.
- A growth in cross-border investment interest and an expansion of the types of investments made by asset managers. This reflected in part the increasing application of finance theory and quantitative investment concepts in the management of portfolios.
- Increase in the role of total return investors in capital markets.
- Focus by derivative dealers on asset side applications of derivatives.

The emergence of these factors saw increased issuance of structured notes with the introduction of instruments such as inverse FRNs, arrears reset structures, capped and floored FRNs, currency-linked notes (ICONs, and so on), and equity index-linked notes.

A notable feature of this period was the strong participation of Japanese investors who were significant investors in these instruments. Constrained by arcane and Byzantine investment restrictions that precluded investment in certain asset classes and entry into derivative transactions, these investors, fueled in no small part by large volumes of funds to invest and an increased focus on international markets, provide the impetus for innovation.

This period witnessed rapid growth in volumes. There was also increased issuer participation by aggressive issuers who were positioned to rapidly supply the range of investment products sought. This financing avenue that offered a new source of cost-effective funding was embraced by a number of astute issuers. These issuers used the growing structured note market to diversify away from traditional bond markets where the new issue arbitrage margins had been reduced through competition.

Most of the elements associated with the current structured note market developed during this phase. A large number of the structured note products available currently were developed during this period in an extraordinary burst of innovation and creativity.[23]

This growth phase in the market lasted from 1986 to 1989. A significant characteristic of this growth phase was the use of public bonds issues (both eurobond and, to a lesser extent, US domestic market issues) as the basic issue format for structured product. The secondary market was poorly developed and liquidity in these instruments was low. Where an investor sought to liquefy an investment, the notes were inevitably repackaged through an asset swap with the derivative elements being neutralized in the course of the repackaging (in a pattern that was to be the essential basis of all secondary market activity in the structured note market).

This process of maturation of the market was affected by the stock market crash in October 1987. However, the effect was minimal except for its impact on equity products. The major effects were in the market for Nikkei-linked instruments, although the relatively moderate effect of the crash on Japan meant that these problems were not significant in the context of the overall market development. The stock market declines in 1987 and again in 1988 in fact ushered in a world recession and an economic environment characterized by low inflation and growth that fueled the proliferation phase of the market for structured notes.

The principal features of this period that gave impetus to the rapid growth in structured note volumes included:

- Falling short-term rates.
- Low returns (in nominal terms) on fixed interest investments.
- A very positive and steeply sloped yield curve.
- Declining credit spreads in bond markets, particularly in the higher echelons of the credit spectrum.

These factors were predominant in the US market from 1990. They were also present to different degrees in a large number of other major global markets.

The prevailing market environment encouraged progressively greater degrees of risk assumption in order to extract higher returns in fixed income

---

[23] This period is documented together with many of hallmark transactions in Das, Satyajit "Option Swaps: Securitizing Options Embedded in Securities Issues" (Summer 1988) *Journal of International Securities Markets* 117-138.

investments. The product proliferation followed distinctive cycles.

The initial impetus was to facilitate trading implied forward interest rates and implied yield curve shapes through the available range of interest rate and CMT/CMS products. The fact that the implied forward yield curve consistently *overestimated* spot rates and the narrowing in the spread between short and long rates during this period allowed investors to capture significantly above-market returns from structured note investments designed to monetize this view. Embedded sales of options, the assumption of prepayment and liquidity risks, and extensions to call structures (step-up and multi-step callable notes) all provided useful boosts to portfolio returns during this phase.

The returns were further enhanced by some structured note investors in a variety of ways including:

- **Increasing credit risk** — increasing the range of acceptable structured note issuer's to cover A/BBB-rated credits.
- **Incorporating leverage** — to increase the derivative component as a multiple of the issue principal to increase the market sensitivity of the instrument.
- **Utilizing exotic optionality** — to enhance returns within specified risk boundaries for institutional investors and allow the creation of lower cost-structured product for retail investors.

The type of market risk incorporated also underwent a rapid process of extension. The initial focus on interest rate products was supplemented by structures incorporating exposure to currency markets, commodities, and equity indexes. The geographic scope of the linkages also broadened to cover not only established markets (US, Germany, UK, Japan, and so on) but smaller markets (Italy, Spain, Portugal, Scandinavian markets, Canada, and Australasia), as well as emerging markets (mainly in Latin America initially, but spreading to Asia and Eastern Europe).

The initial emphasis was on principal-protected structures where all or part of the coupon was placed at risk in order to enhance yield. As this period developed, a larger number of institutional investors became prepared to risk all or a portion of the note principal in the search for yield enhancement. The process placing principal at risk was generally confined to institutional investors with a higher risk tolerance with retail investment products being designed to put only a modest portion of principal (up to a maximum of 20-30%) at risk.

The process of asset class and geographic extension was more important for US investors whose initial focus had been US interest rate-based instruments. For international investors, a broader asset and geographic focus was always a strong component of their investment strategies involving the use of structured products. Similarly, the increasing willingness to embrace principal at-risk structures was a more significant issue for US investors than for international investors. The latter group having embraced the concept far more readily at an earlier date.

The proliferation period saw an extraordinary rate of growth and innovation with a rapid extension of the range of offerings of product. The increased range of derivative products available and the depth and liquidity of these markets placed almost no constraint on the development of structured notes in response to investor demand.

The Gulf crisis in 1991 gave increased impetus to commodity, particularly energy-related, structures. Low nominal returns on fixed interest investments and the volatility of commodity markets also provided an impetus for a large shift of investment flows to commodity investments. The difficulties of commodity investments in direct form favoured the use of structured notes linked to commodity prices and this provided additional impetus to growth. The increased range of option products, particularly exotic options,[24] and the range of cross-market products in combination with increased interest in trading correlations between market variables encouraged whole new categories of structured note instruments to be designed.

This period of activity also coincided with the transfer of issuance activity from the public markets to the private market; in particular, the MTN format of issuance. The secondary market also grew in importance but activity continued to be spasmodic and the overall level of liquidity remained poor, albeit stronger, particularly in certain products and at particular times.

This market phase ended in late 1994/early 1995. The two principal factors that led to the market change were related. A series of aggressive interest rate increases by the Federal Reserve signaled the end of the rally in fixed interest markets. The corresponding rises in international rate levels generally translated this trend to the global financial markets.

The rises lead to significant losses in structured note portfolios as transactions undertaken in expectation of a more benign interest rate environment fell sharply in value. The added leverage and in some cases higher credit risk component further amplified the declines in value. The hostile environment revealed the results of over-aggressive and often imprudent investment strategies involving structured note investments. A number of major losses emerged, culminating in the eventual bankruptcy of Orange County through losses totalling around US$1.5 billion as a result of investments in interest-linked structured notes and excessively leverage.

These losses, which were followed by regulatory scrutiny and litigation, forced a major reassessment of the use of structured notes. The immediate impact was the fall in new issuance activity and a rise in secondary market

---

[24] See Das, Satyajit (1996) *Exotic Options*: London/Sydney; IFR Publishing/Law Book Company.

activity. The latter was the result of the need by major investors in structured notes to sell current holdings. The sales reflected a mixture of loss minimization, regulatory or management policy, as well as a marked change in investment attitudes. The pattern of activity in the secondary market evident during this period is discussed in the following sections.

The phase of market distress covers 1994 and 1995. In reality, this period did not see a total elimination of new issue activity involving structured notes. Even in the US market that bore the brunt of the distress, issuance of callable note structures and other structured notes continued at a strong pace. The structures sought were however less aggressive and placed little more than coupons at risk and generally reflected more modest risk-reward trade-offs than those that had been evident in the past.

The international market, both European and Japanese, were less affected by the distress than the US domestic market. In part, this reflected the fact that the structured note market purchased by these investors were less exposed to purely US interest rates than corresponding US investor portfolios. A number of other Asian investors were adversely affected by investments in structured notes and this period marked a significantly diminution in their activity in this market.

By late 1995/early 1996, the structured note market had begun to recover momentum. The factors driving this recovery included the more benign interest rate environment, declining nominal interest rates, and increased concern about declining returns on fixed-rate investment portfolios.

A major factor was the fall in Japanese interest rates. Short-term interest rates declined to near 0% pa and the slope of the yen yield curve became steeply positive as the Japanese economy experienced deflationary pressures with falling asset (particularly real estate) values and asset quality problems in the banking sector. An additional factor was that major institutional investors needed to increase exposure to yen to avoid currency losses on investments as a result of an appreciating yen, but were concerned about generating adequate levels of current yield on their portfolios. These factors forced increased consideration of structured note products.

The recovery in the structured note market in this period, at least to date, was initially modest. Volumes increased albeit not to the levels of 1993 and 1994. A major aspect of this period was the increased reliance on the secondary market (including the use of trust-based asset-repackaging structures) to acquire structured notes.

The rehabilitation of the market was largely complete by late 1996/early 1997. The next and current phase of the market was the conversion of structured notes into a commodity product. During this period, structured notes became more accepted as a mainstream financial product within capital markets.

The mainstream acceptance of structured products was driven by similar factors to that which had provided the basis for the markets strong growth in the early 1990s. The economic environment characterized by low nominal interest rates was a key driver. Additional factors included the unprecedented returns from the equity markets (in particular, the US market). In this environment, investor demand for products that provided higher returns than available from traditional saving instruments dominated the structured note market.

The commodization phase was characterized by several factors:

- The market saw limited product innovation. Traditional established structures dominated the market. However, structures using exotic optionality and structures linked to *new asset classes* (ranging from emerging market debt and equity securities, credit risk, and insurance risk) were introduced.
- Participation by hedge funds and retail investors became more significant. Hedge funds increasingly used structured notes as a mechanism for monetizing expectations on rates and price efficiently. Retail investors (either directly or through pooled investment vehicles) became as important a market factor as institutional investors. This reflected greater investment expertise and knowledge, as well increased investment in distribution channels to access these investor groups.
- The rapid standardization of the process of issuance of structured notes with issuance processes, hedging, documentation, and operational aspects becoming established.

The market is currently in this commodity phase with steadily increasing volumes. Structured notes are now increasingly viewed as a commodity product available from leading derivative dealers complementing traditional financial products.

## 5.   Structured Notes — The Secondary Market

The role of the secondary market for structured notes and its evolution is evident from the discussion on market development. This role has increasingly become a more central one in the operation of structured note products.

The requirement for secondary market trading is motivated primarily by the need for the investor to sell an investment holding. This requirement may be predicated upon realization of, as a result of anticipated asset price changes, or elimination of the market exposure to limit losses or further exposure to potential losses. Additional demand derives from traders and arbitrage participants who seek to capture value from unbundling and reconstituting the security into or from its components while deriving a value gain. More recently, demand for these structures has been driven by investors seeking customized exposure who are able to achieve their investment objectives through acquisition of the required asset in the secondary market. The motivation in this regard is purely price with the secondary market product offering greater value than a new issue.

Structured notes have traditional been less liquid than conventional fixed income securities reflecting a number of factors:

- **Limited investor base in structured products** — this limitation extends to the purchase of repackaged structured notes that are neutralized as to the derivative components through asset swaps. The latter universe has increased significantly in recent years.
- **Customized nature of instruments** — structured notes to individual specifications creating a lack of product homogeneity that impedes secondary market trading.
- **Transaction costs** — structured notes exhibit higher transaction costs that reflect the lower liquidity of these instruments and the ultimately higher cost in terms of multiple bid-offer spreads that must be sustained in repackaging the security to place it with counterparties as to each relevant component.

However, in recent times, structured notes have increased in liquidity as a result of an increase in the range of investors (both direct and repackaged), and the increased focus on using asset swap mechanics to repackage structured notes for placement as traditional fixed interest securities.

Concern regarding the illiquidity of structured notes extends beyond the investors. A number of issuers have become increasingly sensitive to the impact of investor discord with the lack or price of secondary market liquidity having the potential to damage *the issuer's reputation*. The most interesting response to this challenge has been from the World Bank who implemented an arrangement in early 1994 that was designed to improve secondary market liquidity in its structured notes. The arrangement entailed a liquidity facility made up of a number of dealers who were under an obligation to make markets in structured note products issued by the World Bank. The World Bank also extended its support to the program by agreeing to support the liquidity facility by repurchasing or restructuring existing notes in conjunction with the dealers.

The structure does not eliminate the higher transaction costs and financial incentives required by the issuer and dealers to repackage or trade in these instruments. It does however provide comfort to the investor that the issuer and the obligated dealers will make markets in the security.

The activity level under the liquidity facility is not known. A few other major issuers have instituted similar arrangements to support the secondary market in their structured notes.

The impetus to secondary market trading in structured notes derived from the market distress period of 1994/1995. Prior to that secondary market interest had been spasmodic. The activity that had occurred had been related to investors exiting structured investments with the dealer purchasing the note, engineering the reversal of the derivative component, and distributing the security as a higher yielding fixed- or floating-note security to conventional investors in asset swap products.[25] The latter continues to be the basic mechanism for providing any required secondary market liquidity and establishing benchmark secondary market bid prices for these notes.

However, in the market conditions that prevailed in late 1994 and early 1995, the volume of structured notes that began to appear for sale increased dramatically as investors exited their investments for the reasons previously identified. The market conditions resulted in dealers rapidly repositioning their secondary market trading in these instruments to allow them to be repackaged. This took a number of deliberate repositioning actions:

- The amalgamation or linking of structured note-trading with asset swap desks (a process that was well under way in some respects) was central to the execution of this secondary market trading.
- Investment was made in broadening of the investor base in structured notes to encompass an increased range of institutions:
  1. Other structured note investors who might perceive greater value in the secondary market for certain types of exposure as an alternative to investing in a new issue. This allowed pricing on a straight trading basis.
  2. Issuer demand to repurchase structured notes on issue priced on a buy-back basis.
  3. Asset swap buyers prepared to purchase structured notes that had been asset swapped to reverse engineer the market risk component to create, typically, an FRN priced off LIBOR targeted to bank and, to a lesser extent, the fixed income investor.

The last category of investor dominates the secondary market trading for these structured notes. The incentive to provide this secondary market liquidity for these asset swap buyers reflected the perceived opportunity to purchase short to intermediate maturity assets of high credit quality at attractive yields. Many of the repackagings saw AAA-rated agency paper in the US, for example, placed with investors at rich yields well above LIBOR (anywhere up to 20/25 bps above LIBOR). This was well above the direct new issuance levels for these borrowers. The process saw the successful repackaging of a significant volume of the outstanding structured note products.

One of the first major transactions involved the sale of the Orange County portfolio that was disposed off through an auction process managed by Salomon Brothers on behalf of the County. The auction is estimated to have focused on the disposal of US$4.7 billion of structured notes that were asset swapped for

---

[25] For discussion of asset swap products, see Das, Satyajit (1994) *Swaps and Financial Derivatives*; LBC Information Services, Sydney, McGraw-Hill, Chicago at Chapter 18.

placement with a wide range of investors.

Following on the success of the auction, a number of investment banks, including Salomon Brothers, Lehman Brothers, Deutsche Bank, and Morgan Stanley, announced public bids for up to US$8.1 billion of 59 issues of structured notes issued by the major US agencies. The significant difference in this case was that the investment banks were *not acting on behalf of any investor*. The objective was to provide general liquidity to investors in these instruments seeking to exit their investments.

The process envisaged was that the prices to be paid and the amount of notes to be repurchased would be based on a Dutch auction procedure. Investors would submit offers on two bases. One basis was a noncompetitive tender in which the investor would sell to the dealer on the highest spread accepted relative to a benchmark Treasury security on an asset swap basis accepted in the competitive tender. The alternative was competitive bids whereby the investor offered to sell the securities to the dealer at price spreads above the base price designated by the investor up to a specified maximum price. The procedure, proposed by Salomon Brothers, entails use of a proprietary formula to allow determination and comparison of bids based on the base price of these securities, the price spread established through the auction process and a Treasury adjustment based on the difference between a base yield set by Salomon for each security for the purposes of the tender and the yield on a reference Treasury at a specific date. The adjustment appeared to embody a duration-based formula designed to ensure that the bids on the security moved in line with the reference securities.

The results of the auction are not known. However, subsequently, Lehman Brothers separately made a tender offer to repurchase US$9 billion of collared FRNs (covering some 57 issues) to provide additional liquidity to investors in these notes on an asset swap basis. Unlike the US agency offer that had a domestic US focus, the bid for the collared FRNs was oriented to international investors.

The development of the secondary market in structured notes has seen the introduction of a number of structured note-repackaging vehicles. The central concept of these trust-based structures is their ability to create trust receipts that represent either repackaged structured notes or structured notes created through repackaging that are sold to investors. The trust receipts are rated by one or more of the major rating agencies and the trust receipt is tradeable to facilitate liquidity. In essence, it is the conversion of asset swaps into public and tradeable securities.[26]

In overall terms, the structures significantly enhances the potential of both

---

[26] See Chapter 1.

repackaging of structured notes by effectively allowing securitized and tradeable asset swaps and the creation of new structured notes as an alternative to new issues of such products. Repackaging vehicles of this type exist both in the US domestic market and in the Euromarket, performing similar roles in the structured note market.

The repackaging vehicles compete increasingly with a nascent market in structured note repurchase agreements. These transactions are designed to allow investors to take advantage of attractively priced structured notes in the secondary market. The structured note repurchase agreement operates like a synthetic asset swap in which the investor's net exposure is an effective coupon of Treasuries plus a spread. An example of a structured note repurchase agreement is set out in **Exhibit 18.7**.

---

**Exhibit 18.7**
**Structured Note Repurchase Agreement**

Structured note repurchase agreements are economically equivalent to a synthetic asset swap that is undertaken as a repurchase agreement to avoid the necessity of the investor entering into the derivative contracts. The terms of a typical structured note repurchase agreement are summarized below:

| | |
|---|---|
| Maturity | 3 years |
| Notional Amount | US$10 million |
| Collateral | General Treasury Collateral |
| Repo Margin | 102% |
| Investor Pays | 2-year CMT — 55 bps |
| Payment | Quarterly on an actual/actual basis |
| Reference Security: | 3-year AAA-rated 2-year CMT floater with a coupon of 2-year CMT — 40 bps priced at 98.65% of par |

The reference security in this transaction is a 2-year CMT FRN. The security yields 2-year CMT minus 40 bps priced at 98.65% of face value to yield 2-year CMT minus 55 bps, which is equivalent on an asset swap basis to 3-month LIBOR plus 5 bps.

In the structured note repurchase agreement, the dealer/investment bank lends the investor 98.65% of face value and the investor pledges general treasury collateral. The investor pays 2-year CMT minus 55 bps. Simultaneously, the investor purchases the reference security. The investor thorough this series of transactions receives an effective return of

Treasuries plus 15 bps.

## 6.   Regulatory Considerations

The market for structured notes has evolved under limited regulatory supervision. This lack of oversight reflects the regulatory structure of over-the-counter derivatives markets generally.

The regulatory framework that has governed this market historically was the CFTC rules that were generally applicable only in the US market. Under this framework, structured notes with embedded elements that resemble futures and option contracts may be subject to CFTC regulation. Transactions are exempt from regulation where the commodity element does not predominate. The test of exemption utilized is to decompose the security value into the commodity dependent and independent parts with exemption being granted if the commodity dependent part is lower in value than the commodity independent part.

In practice, the CFTC rules did not represent a major restriction on the structured note market. In particular, the fact that the rules did not apply to structured notes with embedded linkages to interest rates and currency values meant that a major portion of transactions did not need to be tested in the first instance. The international market did not have any comparable regulations.

The problems that emerged in 1994 and 1995 during the market distress phase saw increased scrutiny of structured notes. This scrutiny was part of a general review of over-the-counter derivative markets. The review was led by major regulators concerned about systemic risk elements and the potential impact of a major failure in derivatives markets on the financial system overall.

This regulatory focus, while not confined to the US, was certainly concentrated on the US market. Major factors in this regard included the political desire to avoid systemic problems such as those associated with the Savings & Loans industry and the collapse of the market for junk bonds. An additional factor was the concern regarding the Section 2a-7 money market funds that constituted a significant investment pool and, more importantly, one that had come to be regarded by investors as a near substitute for bank deposits.

The regulatory reviews were almost universally positive on the role played by derivative instruments in financial markets. The risk of derivatives in general and in systemic risk terms was also considered low. However, the use of structured notes, particularly by unsophisticated investors, was the subject of some concern. The major thrust of the reports focused on two major areas:

- Ensuring the adoption of appropriate internal controls and risk management systems by derivative users.
- Development of comprehensive, consistent accounting rules and disclosure

requirements in relation to derivatives activity.[27]

These conclusions emerged from reports from bodies such as the Government Accounting Office, SEC, Office of the Comptroller of the Currency (OCC), Office of Thrift Supervision, Federal Reserve, and the FASB.

More specific regulatory action in respect of structured note investments emanated from certain regulators. This ranged from general concern (OCC and the Federal Reserve) to broad guidelines regarding the evaluation of structured note investments *prior to purchase*, entailing stress testing under different market conditions and consideration of pricing and liquidity (OTS). The major action was from the SEC that detailed certain types of structured notes as being inappropriate for Section 2a-7 money market funds. These instruments included capped FRNs, COFI FRNs, differential index FRNs, CMT FRNs, inverse and leveraged FRNs and multi-step callable notes. These instruments were considered unsuitable for these investors as a result of the interest rate risk of these structures. The increased price volatility of these securities was considered inappropriate for funds that were widely viewed as having very stable net asset values with low risk of the value falling below par.

The reviews in other markets resulted in similar conclusions on structured note investments, but the step of specifically excluding certain types of investments for specific investor groups was not followed.

The major rating agencies undertook their own reviews of structured note issues during this period. The reviews led to both Standard & Poor and Moody's introducing a new rating signature to structured products. Under this scheme, structured notes considered to have high market risk components are assigned a supplementary rating (R). This denoted the risk to coupon or principal from a market risk linkage or maturity or prepayment uncertainty.[28]

## 7.  Future Prospects

The market for structured notes has emerged globally as an integral component of the global capital market. The flexibility, structuring potential, and return-enhancing properties of these instruments make them an essential component of investment management strategies for all asset managers.

The essential power of the structured note derives from the inherent capacity

---

[27] For an overview of US accounting and disclosure requirements in relation to derivatives activity, see Williams, Jan R. (1994) *1994 GAAP Guide*; Harcourt Brace & Co., New York.

[28] See Kriz, John J. "Derivatives Risk and Moody's Counterparty Ratings" (1994) *Capital Market Strategies* 3 17-22; Efrat, Isaac, Gluck, Jeremy, and Powar, David (July 3, 1997) Moody's Refines Its Approach to Rating Structured Notes; Moody's Investor Service — Global Investors Service, New York.

that such instruments provide to expand the investment range of an investor substantially beyond that available directly in the capital markets. The combination of traditional fixed income investments and derivative structures allows the creation of a range of investments exactly matched to the investor's requirements. The substantial return enhancements available reflects not only the capacity to perfectly align portfolios to required parameters but substantial savings in transaction costs and reductions in market frictions such as withholding taxes and restrictions on certain types of investments.

An essential element of such instruments is the capability of these instruments to allow participation in derivative transactions by investors who would be precluded by reason of counterparty credit considerations from entering into transactions designed often *to reduce the risk of the investment.* The credit-enhancement applications of structured notes are not fully appreciated and this feature of itself is a critical component of the growth of the market. The growing trend to disintermediation and the increasing use of mutual or pooled fund investment structures to bypass traditional arrangements for mobilizing investment capital brings with it the problem of engineering the access to credit lines to allow implementation of investment strategies and management of portfolio risk. The inherent structural flaw of these investment vehicles that limits their access to credit necessitates the reliance on structured investment products to allow investment activities to be discharged.

The considerable problems in the market during 1994 and 1995 highlight the problems of excess and the lack of control in the use of these instruments. However, there is no evidence that the problems that were in ample evidence would have been avoided or even reduced in the absence of the availability of structured notes. The failures seem more directly attributable to failures of more basic forms of internal financial control and aggressive and unrestricted risk-taking than the use of derivatives.[29]

This is not to say that improvements in the market could not be effected. Increasing investor, dealer, and regulatory understanding of the instruments, enhancing the capacity and technology of risk evaluation, improving risk management systems, in particular among investors and derivative users, and improving the reporting, disclosure, and accounting for these instruments are all important ongoing concerns.

The pessimistic prognostications of the period of market distress called for the structured note market to disappear. This forecast appears premature with the market showing continued life, albeit in a more conservative framework. The

---

[29] See the detailed discussion in Das, Satyajit "Guideline For Utilization of Derivative Instruments In Risk Management" *ASX Derivatives Perspectives* (2nd Quarter, 1995) 25-32.

prospects for the market continue to be bright. The period of growth and proliferation has established structured notes as an essential and highly integrated segment of the capital market. The fact that these instruments have facilitated investments that have allowed investors to achieve results—both in terms of enhanced returns and risk management—that would not have been possible without the existence of these products is likely to ensure the survival and continued development of these instruments as a permanent feature of international markets.

# Index

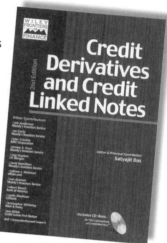